The Oxford Handbook of Prevention in Counseling Psychology

OXFORD LIBRARY OF PSYCHOLOGY

Editor in Chief PETER E. NATHAN

The Oxford Handbook of Prevention in Counseling Psychology

Edited by

Elizabeth M. Vera

OXFORD
UNIVERSITY PRESS

OXFORD
UNIVERSITY PRESS

Oxford University Press is a department of the University of Oxford. It furthers the University's objective of excellence in research, scholarship, and education by publishing worldwide.

Oxford New York
Auckland Cape Town Dar es Salaam Hong Kong Karachi
Kuala Lumpur Madrid Melbourne Mexico City Nairobi
New Delhi Shanghai Taipei Toronto

With offices in
Argentina Austria Brazil Chile Czech Republic France Greece
Guatemala Hungary Italy Japan Poland Portugal Singapore
South Korea Switzerland Thailand Turkey Ukraine Vietnam

Published in the United States of America by
Oxford University Press
198 Madison Avenue, New York, NY 10016

Library of Congress Cataloging-in-Publication Data
The Oxford handbook of prevention in counseling psychology / edited by Elizabeth M. Vera.
p. cm.—(Oxford library of psychology)
ISBN-13: 978–0–19–539642–3
1. Counseling psychology. I. Vera, Elizabeth, 1967–
BF636.6.O944 2012
158.3—dc23
2012015030

9 8 7 6 5 4 3 2
Printed in the United States of America
on acid-free paper

SHORT CONTENTS

OXFORD LIBRARY OF PSYCHOLOGY

The *Oxford Library of Psychology*, a landmark series of handbooks, is published by Oxford University Press, one of the world's oldest and most highly respected publishers, with a tradition of publishing significant books in psychology. The ambitious goal of the *Oxford Library of Psychology* is nothing less than to span a vibrant, wide-ranging field and, in so doing, to fill a clear market need.

Encompassing a comprehensive set of handbooks, organized hierarchically, the *Library* incorporates volumes at different levels, each designed to meet a distinct need. At one level are a set of handbooks designed broadly to survey the major subfields of psychology; at another are numerous handbooks that cover important current focal research and scholarly areas of psychology in depth and detail. Planned as a reflection of the dynamism of psychology, the *Library* will grow and expand as psychology itself develops, thereby highlighting significant new research that will impact on the field. Adding to its accessibility and ease of use, the *Library* will be published in print and, later on, electronically.

The *Library* surveys psychology's principal subfields with a set of handbooks that capture the current status and future prospects of those major subdisciplines. This initial set includes handbooks of social and personality psychology, clinical psychology, counseling psychology, school psychology, educational psychology, industrial and organizational psychology, cognitive psychology, cognitive neuroscience, methods and measurements, history, neuropsychology, personality assessment, developmental psychology, and more. Each handbook undertakes to review one of psychology's major subdisciplines with breadth, comprehensiveness, and exemplary scholarship. In addition to these broadly conceived volumes, the *Library* also includes a large number of handbooks designed to explore in depth more specialized areas of scholarship and research, such as stress, health and coping, anxiety and related disorders, cognitive development, or child and adolescent assessment. In contrast to the broad coverage of the subfield handbooks, each of these latter volumes focuses on an especially productive, more highly focused line of scholarship and research. Whether at the broadest or most specific level, however, all of the *Library* handbooks offer synthetic coverage that reviews and evaluates the relevant past and present research and anticipates research in the future. Each handbook in the *Library* includes introductory and concluding chapters written by its editor to provide a roadmap to the handbook's table of contents and to offer informed anticipations of significant future developments in that field.

An undertaking of this scope calls for handbook editors and chapter authors who are established scholars in the areas about which they write. Many of the nation's and world's most productive and best-respected psychologists have agreed to edit *Library* handbooks or write authoritative chapters in their areas of expertise.

For whom has the *Oxford Library of Psychology* been written? Because of its breadth, depth, and accessibility, the *Library* serves a diverse audience, including graduate students in psychology and their faculty mentors, scholars, researchers, and practitioners in psychology and related fields. Each will find in the *Library* the information they seek on the subfield or focal area of psychology in which they work or are interested.

Befitting its commitment to accessibility, each handbook includes a comprehensive index, as well as extensive references to help guide research. And because the *Library* was designed from its inception as an online as well as a print resource, its structure and contents will be readily and rationally searchable online. Further, once the *Library* is released online, the handbooks will be regularly and thoroughly updated.

In summary, the *Oxford Library of Psychology* will grow organically to provide a thoroughly informed perspective on the field of psychology, one that reflects both psychology's dynamism and its increasing interdisciplinarity. Once published electronically, the *Library* is also destined to become a uniquely valuable interactive tool, with extended search and browsing capabilities. As you begin to consult this handbook, we sincerely hope you will share our enthusiasm for the more than 500-year tradition of Oxford University Press for excellence, innovation, and quality, as exemplified by the *Oxford Library of Psychology.*

Peter E. Nathan
Editor-in-Chief
Oxford Library of Psychology

ABOUT THE EDITOR

Elizabeth M. Vera

Elizabeth M. Vera is a Professor of Counseling Psychology in the School of Education at Loyola University Chicago. Dr. Vera's scholarship focuses on prevention, social justice, and promoting well-being in urban adolescents of color. An author of several books and numerous articles, Dr. Vera is a Fellow of Division 17 of the American Psychological Association.

CONTRIBUTORS

Eve Adams
Department of Counseling and Educational Psychology
New Mexico State University
Las Cruces, NM

Rabiatu Barrie
Counseling Psychology
Loyola University Chicago
Chicago, IL

Kathleen M. Benson
Department of Counseling Psychology
University of Akron
Akron, OH

Steven D. Brown
School of Education
Loyola University Chicago
Chicago, IL

Cindy Buchanan
Trauma, Health, and Hazards Center
University of Colorado at Colorado Springs
Colorado Springs, CO

Lydia P. Buki
Department of Kinesiology and Community Health
University of Illinois at Urbana-Champaign
Champaign, IL

Cynthia M. Bulik
Departments of Psychiatry and Nutrition
University of North Carolina
Chapel Hill, NC

Melissa L. Morgan Consoli
Departments of Counseling, Clinical, and School Psychology
University of California, Santa Barbara
Santa Barbara, CA

Robert K. Conyne
Professor Emeritus, Counseling
University of Cincinnati
Cincinnati, OH

Brian P. Daly
Department of Psychology
Drexel University
Philadelphia, PA

Steven J. Danish
Life Skills Center
Department of Psychology
Virginia Commonwealth University
Richmond, VA

Kimberly Dasch
Department of Psychology
University of Delaware
Newark, DE

M. Meghan Davidson
Department of Educational Psychology
University of Nebraska, Lincoln
Lincoln, NE

Ginger Dickson
Department of Counseling and Educational Psychology
New Mexico State University
Las Cruces, NM

Michael Duffy
Department of Educational Psychology
Texas A&M University
College Station, TX

Lisa M. Edwards
Department of Counselor Education and Counseling Psychology
Marquette University
Milwaukee, WI

Dawn Eichen
Department of Psychology
Temple University
Philadelphia, PA

Dorothy L. Espelage
Child Development Division, Educational Psychology
College of Education
University of Illinois at Urbana-Champaign
Champaign, IL

Marsha Davis
College of Public Health
University of Georgia
Athens, GA

Lisa Y. Flores
College of Education
University of Missouri
Columbia, MO

Michael M. Gale
School of Education
Division of Counseling Psychology
University at Albany, SUNY
Albany, NY

Patton O. Garriott
Counseling Center
University of Missouri
Columbia, MO

Dianna Marisol González
College of Education
New Mexico State University
Las Cruces, NM

Nelly Gonzalez
Department of Counseling, Clinical, and School Psychology
University of California, Santa Barbara
Santa Barbara, CA

Rachel W. Gow
Department of Psychology
Virginia Commonwealth University
Richmond, VA

Jason Hacker
School of Education
Loyola University Chicago
Chicago, IL

Sally M. Hage
School of Education
University at Albany, SUNY
Albany, NY

Melinda Haley
Educational Psychology and Special Services
University of Texas at El Paso
El Paso, TX

Alexa E. Hanus
School of Education
Department of Psychology
University at Albany, SUNY
Albany, NY

Robert D. Hill
Department of Educational Psychology
University of Utah
Salt Lake City, UT

Tracie Hitter
Department of Counseling and Educational Psychology
New Mexico State University
Las Cruces, NM

Arthur M. Horne
College of Education
University of Georgia
Athens, GA

Janice E. Jones
Cardinal Stritch University
Glendale, WI

Mone't A. Kendall
Syracuse University
Syracuse, NY

Maureen E. Kenny
Department of Counseling, Developmental, and Educational Psychology
Boston College
Boston, MA
Lynch School of Education
Chestnut Hill, MA

Kristen Lamp
School of Education
Loyola University Chicago
Chicago, IL

Clare Lenhart
Department of Public Health
Temple University
Philadelphia, PA

Deborah E. Linares
Department of Kinesiology and Community Health
University of Illinois at Urbana-Champaign
Champaign, IL

Larisa Buhin Loncar
American College of Management and Technology
Dubrovnik, Croatia

Susana Ayala Lopez
Department of Counseling, Clinical, and School Psychology
University of California, Santa Barbara
Santa Barbara, CA

Sabina Low
Department of Psychology
Arizona State University
Wichita, KS
Laura Luna
Department of Counseling and Educational Psychology
New Mexico State University
Las Cruces, NM
Pei-Wen Winnie Ma
Department of Psychology
William Paterson University
Wayne, NJ
Connie R. Matthews
New Perspectives, LLC
Suzanne E. Mazzeo
Departments of Psychology and Pediatrics
Virginia Commonwealth University
Richmond, VA
Mary Beth Medvide
Department of Counseling
Boston College
Boston, MA
Lynch School of Education
Chestnut Hill, MA
Yadira Montoya
Department of Kinesiology and Community Health
University of Illinois at Urbana-Champaign
Champaign, IL
Michelle Murray
Counseling Center
University at Albany, SUNY
Albany, NY
Geoffrey Nelson
Department of Psychology
Wilfrid Laurier University
Waterloo, Ontario, Canada
Helen A. Neville
College of Education
University of Illinois at Urbana-Champaign
Champaign, IL
Pamela Orpinas
College of Public Health
University of Georgia
Athens, GA
William D. Parham
Clinical Services Director, Counseling Center
University of California, Irvine
Irvine, CA
Julia C. Phillips
Counseling Center
University of Akron
Akron, OH
Alex L. Pieterse
School of Education
Division of Counseling Psychology
University at Albany, SUNY
Albany, NY
Megan K. Polanin
Loyola University Chicago
Chicago, IL
Paul E. Priester
School of Adult Learning
North Park University
Chicago, IL
Isaac Prilleltensky
School of Education and Human Development
Department of Educational and Psychological Studies
University of Miami
Coral Gables, FL
James R. Rogers
Department of Counseling Psychology
University of Akron
Akron, OH
John L. Romano
Counseling and Student Personnel Psychology Program
Department of Educational Psychology
University of Minnesota
Minneapolis, MN
Jonathan Schwartz
Department of Counseling and Educational Psychology
New Mexico State University
Las Cruces, NM
Munyi Shea
Department of Psychology
California State University, Los Angeles
Los Angeles, CA

Richard Q. Shin
School of Education
Syracuse University
Syracuse, NY

Lisa B. Spanierman
Department of Educational and Counselling Psychology
McGill University
Montreal, Quebec, Canada

Suzette L. Speight
Department of Psychology
University of Akron
Akron, OH

Lucia J. Stubbs
Department of Counselor Education and Counseling Psychology
Marquette University
Milwaukee, WI

Kyle J. Telander
School of Education
Loyola University Chicago
Chicago, IL

Anita Jones Thomas
School of Education
Loyola University Chicago
Chicago, IL

Mindi N. Thompson
Department of Counseling Psychology
University of Wisconsin at Madison
Madison, WI

Laura D. Turner-Essel
Department of Psychology
University of Akron
Akron, OH

Elizabeth M. Vera
School of Education
Loyola University Chicago
Chicago, IL

Christine J. Yeh
Department of Counseling Psychology
University of San Francisco
San Francisco, CA

Michael Waldo
Department of Counseling and Educational Psychology
New Mexico State University
Las Cruces, NM

CONTENTS

Part One • Fundamentals of Prevention

Part Two • Best Practices in the Prevention of Behavioral, Emotional, and Health Problems

PART 1

Fundamentals of Prevention

CHAPTER

1 Prevention and Counseling Psychology: A Simple yet Difficult Commitment

Elizabeth M. Vera *and* Megan K. Polanin

Abstract

In the introductory chapter of this handbook, core aspects of prevention science and practice will be presented. Included in this presentation are definitions of prevention; how prevention has been conceptualized within the field of psychology; why prevention is necessary; why counseling psychologists are particularly well suited to engage in prevention activities; the benefits of including mental health prevention as part of a larger wellness agenda; and how prevention is part of a commitment to social justice and cultural relevance. It is hoped that presenting these ideas will help orient the reader to what is to come in the remaining chapters as well as ground the volume in a common language and philosophical base.

Key Words: prevention, counseling psychology, social justice, cultural diversity

Counseling psychologists have been called to engage in prevention for most of the field's history. Passionate leaders in the field have provided sound rationales and strong empirical evidence of its value. Thus, it is easy to conclude that the field's commitment to prevention should be simply unequivocal. Few would argue that the idea of prevention simply makes sense. An ounce of prevention *is* worth a pound of cure. Cost-benefit analyses support this claim (Conduct Problems Prevention Research Group, 1999; Tolan & Dodge, 2005). However, counseling psychology's commitment to prevention is apparently not so simple, in that its popularity appears to wax and wane (Adams, 2007; Hage & Romano, 2010; Vera, 2000). For example, Goodyear et al. (2008) conducted a job analysis of counseling psychologists and found that only 25% engaged in prevention and outreach work, a figure that was significantly lower than a similar analysis conducted in the mid-1980s (Watkins, Lopez, Campbell, & Himmel, 1986). There seems to be some hesitation to being truly committed to prevention as a core element of our science and practice. A nonwavering commitment to prevention will require something that has not yet happened within our field. What might this missing element be?

Friere (1970) argued that systemic change requires a critical mass of empowered "converts" who can act as agents of change. *The Oxford Handbook of Prevention in Counseling Psychology* is a compilation of the work of prevention experts in the field who arguably constitute the "converts," and the publication of this volume is one piece of evidence that this critical mass now exists. Other pieces of evidence are the several other prevention texts that have been written by counseling psychologists (e.g., Conyne, 2004; Kenny, Horne, Orpinas, & Reese, 2009). The handbook's array of excellent applications of prevention science being conducted by counseling psychologists suggests that prevention in counseling psychology may now be here to stay. Perhaps an even more exciting piece of evidence is the forthcoming publication of the *Best Practice Guidelines for Prevention* by the American

Psychological Association (Hage et al., 2007). This recent accomplishment may reflect a trend in the general field of psychology to embrace prevention once and for all.

In the introductory chapter of this handbook, several core aspects of prevention science and practice will be presented. It is hoped that presenting these ideas will help ground the volume in a common language, conceptual framework, and philosophical base, as well as to orient the reader to the remaining chapters. How the subsequent chapters reflect the conceptual framework will also be discussed. Thus, the following topics will be presented in this introduction:

1. What is prevention?
2. How has prevention been conceptualized within the field of psychology?
3. Why is prevention needed in our field and in society? What is lacking in our field's current remedial, individual treatment perspective that can be corrected with an infusion of prevention?
4. Why are counseling psychologists particularly well situated to engage in this type of work?
5. How would embedding prevention efforts into a larger wellness-promotion framework benefit society and our profession?
6. How is prevention related to our field's commitment to issues of social justice and cultural relevance?

Defining Prevention

Outside the field of psychology, prevention appears to have been accepted by mainstream society. Illustrations of this point come in many forms. Conyne (2004) reminded us that a wide-scale acceptance of prevention is evident in how the concept has found its way into our idioms, such as "an apple a day keeps the doctor away." He also provided examples of "everyday prevention" in activities such as taking vitamins, wearing a seatbelt, and exercising. In very basic terms, prevention is understood to be "doing something now to prevent (or forestall) something unpleasant or undesirable from happening in the future" (Albee & Ryan, 1998, p. 441). What one specifically "does" may be determined by what one is specifically trying to prevent, of course, but the underlying premise remains.

Within the field of psychology, however, a commitment to prevention has been less widespread. Among many prevention pioneers in the field of psychology, George Albee, a clinical psychologist, former APA president, and the author of groundbreaking studies in the 1950s and 1960s, communicated some of the most passionate arguments for the importance of prevention in our society and field. Albee (1986, 2002) championed the belief that large-scale societal factors (e.g., poverty, racism, sexism) were largely responsible for the emergence of mental illness. These societal factors resulted in an unequal distribution of resources and, accordingly, psychological reactions of powerlessness and distress for the majority of people who face them. In the same way that a tainted water source results in disease for those who drink from it, toxic social conditions create pathology for those who are most impacted by these conditions. Thus, the overarching reason we need prevention research and practice, in both society and the field of psychology, is to identify and then eliminate negative social conditions that result in personal dysfunction (Albee, 1986; Kessler & Albee, 1975). This position is in contrast to what is a more common state of affairs within our field, which is to treat those individuals, one by one, who are tainted by the existence of these toxic societal conditions.

Although a remedial approach to mental health service delivery aids those *already individually affected*, in many ways it is an insufficient model, which will be discussed shortly. However, in essence, a preventive approach allows for individuals to be reached at a population-wide level *before* the onset of mental health issues. Emory Cowen, another pivotal figure in the field of prevention, noted that psychologists "have become increasingly aware, indeed alarmingly, of the frustration and pessimism of trying to undo psychological damage once it had passed a certain critical point in addition to the costly, time-consuming, culture-bound nature of mental health's basic approaches and their unavailability to large segments of society in great need" (Cowen, 1980, p. 259). This last point of the quote is worth reiterating. Even if remedial efforts were universally successful in undoing the psychological damage done by unhealthy forces in our society, psychological services are not widely available to the entire population nor are there enough psychologists providing such services to meet the enormous demand (Ringel & Sturm, 2001). This point will be revisited later in this chapter.

Due to the passionate debate about how truly preventing problems requires an arsenal of professional actions, Romano and Hage (2000) broadened the definition of prevention to include the following: (1) stopping a problem behavior from ever occurring; (2) delaying the onset of a problem behavior; (3) reducing the impact of a problem behavior; (4) strengthening knowledge, attitudes, and behaviors that promote emotional and physical well-being; and (5) promoting institutional, community, and government policies that further physical, social, and emotional well-being. This more inclusive definition of prevention emulates the evolution that has occurred within the field in conceptualizing the different facets of prevention.

Conceptualization of Prevention

A core question that continues to engender debate in the field is what falls under the umbrella of prevention work. Caplan (1964) argued that prevention should include interventions that aim to assure adequate physical, psychosocial, and sociocultural resources that subsequently enable individuals to both avoid and withstand future stressors. Wagenfeld (1972) viewed prevention as: (1) interventions in life crises of individuals, and (2) altering the balance of physical, social, cultural, and psychosocial forces in the community. Cumming (1968) stated that there are two main strategies involved in mental health preventive efforts. The first strategy entails discovering what causes mental illness and then removing said cause. The second seeks to characterize populations that are resistant or immune to this disease and subsequently mold other populations to resemble the healthy one. Based on these broad conceptualizations, many activities would constitute prevention.

Historically, the most common conceptualization utilized in the public and mental health fields was a tripartite model that identified three levels of prevention: primary, secondary, and tertiary levels (Caplan, 1964). *Primary prevention* was defined as efforts taken to decrease the number of new cases of a disorder. Levine (1998) compared primary prevention to an inoculation in that a vaccination is intended to fend off the development of a specific disease. Hence, primary prevention strategies are generally aimed at healthy individuals, with an objective to keep them healthy. Cowen (1996) identified the following required components of an intervention to qualify as primary prevention: it must be group-oriented, it must be delivered prior to symptom emergence, and it must aim to strengthen the adjustment of unaffected groups.

Secondary prevention entailed early identification and treatment in order to lower the prevalence of new cases (Caplan, 1964). In other words, secondary prevention would characterize interventions targeted at specific, not general, populations due to their vulnerability to a specific problem. For example, creating a drug/alcohol abuse awareness program for children of substance abusing parents might be classified as secondary prevention. The notion of being "at-risk" is deeply embedded within this type of prevention, and, as a result, it has been met with some controversy. Determining what classifies an individual as being "at-risk" for any type of problem requires an extensive epidemiological database on psychological and behavioral disorders. Furthermore, in an ideal world, these databases would include information taken from a diverse sample that represents the variations of a given population.

While extensive information has been collected on some categories of disorders, in particular diseases that are physical in nature, mental health databases remain relatively incomplete. Thus, it is difficult to determine what truly creates "risk" for certain individuals above and beyond what is known from correlational studies. Longitudinal studies are more effective at collecting information that might point to the causes of particular problems. However, there are few disorders that we know to be truly caused by underlying factors or behaviors, hence confounding an accurate assessment of risk status.

Finally, *tertiary prevention* was the term used to describe programs that aimed to minimize the long-term effects and severity of symptoms in individuals with existing disorders (Caplan, 1964). Relapse prevention is a prototypical example of tertiary prevention in that for substance addiction, for example, the goal of a tertiary prevention program for those who are addicted is to keep them sober, limiting the long-term effects of the disorder. Given that the target population for tertiary prevention is individuals who have already suffered from a disorder and those that are symptomatic, it could be argued that this type of prevention is difficult to differentiate from therapy, or more remedial approaches to intervention. Nonetheless, this tripartite model of conceptualizing prevention has stood the test of time, albeit with some revisions, as will be discussed next.

Decades after Caplan (1964), Gordon (1987) offered a different theoretical framework from which to view prevention efforts that in some ways built on the model offered by his predecessor. Mrazek and Haggerty (1994) utilized Gordon's (1987) paradigm when they created a report for the Institute of Medicine in which they viewed prevention as part of a continuum, including treatment and maintenance, for a variety of mental disorders. As such, the term "prevention" was solely utilized for programming that occurs *before* the onset of a formally recognized disorder. As in Caplan's (1964) approach, prevention was divided into three subcategories: universal, selective, and indicated (Gordon, 1987). *Universal preventive interventions* target an entire population that has not been identified on the basis of risk. In other words, universal prevention targets the general public as a whole. *Selective preventive interventions* are aimed at individuals or populations possessing biological, psychological, or social risk factors, thus making it more likely that they will develop specific mental disorders. *Indicated preventive interventions* target individuals in need of the most support who either bear physical symptoms or biological markers foreboding of mental disorders, although they are not yet symptomatic. These individuals must not meet criteria for a particular mental disorder at the time (Munoz, Mrazek, & Haggerty, 1996). This is what differentiates indicated prevention from remedial intervention (i.e., therapy).

What are the advantages and disadvantages to tripartite conceptualizations of prevention that have been offered by Caplan (1964) and Gordon (1987)? Some scholars have argued that the frameworks are too narrow (Cowen, 2000; Durlak & Wells, 1997) and create false classifications. For example, in targeting the general population, one cannot be certain that some of the participating individuals would not actually be "at risk" and hence, not truly being inoculated in the same way as others who are not at risk. Furthermore, we may inadvertently classify and therefore stigmatize individuals in our secondary (or selected) prevention efforts. Imagine a program aimed at preventing violence in children "at risk" for such behavior. If offered in a school or other public setting, it would be nearly impossible for the participants not to be stigmatized by their selection for the program. It would also be impossible to know for certain whether our selection criteria were truly identifying causal risk factors or merely correlational factors. For example, poverty is often identified as a risk factor for violent behavior (Reese & Vera, 2007), yet we know that not all poor individuals act violently, and it is far more often the case that the vast majority are *not* violent. This is an example of where a risk factor is not a *causal* factor. Thus, it is difficult to know whether the populations being targeted for secondary prevention efforts (or selected/indicated prevention programs) are being accurately identified.

An important reason that one might wish to differentiate primary (or universal) from secondary (or selective/indicated) prevention efforts, however, often has to do with the cost involved in implementing both types of programs. A primary or universal prevention program delivered unilaterally to a large group of individuals, regardless of "risk" status, is likely to be far more costly than a secondary program (or selective and indicated) in which only select individuals are invited to participate, thus requiring fewer resources. In settings where human and monetary resources are often at a premium, such as in public schools, it may be cost prohibitive to implement universal or primary prevention programs, and it may be easier to justify the expenditure of resources for efforts aimed at those at higher risk.

Another reason it may be important to differentiate between primary and secondary prevention efforts has to do with the efficacy of the intervention for specific populations. For example, it is logical to believe that interventions might be designed differently depending on whether the participants had little or vast amounts of experience with a particular situation like exposure to substance abuse. Prevention specialists may appropriately work very differently with youths whose parents are substance abusers than they would with youths whose parents are not. Tailoring the content of prevention efforts to meet the needs of the population is considered to be a best practice in the prevention field today (Hage et al., 2007). Therefore, since prevention is not a "one-size fits all" field (Roosa, Dumka, Gonzales, & Knight, 2002), susceptibility to a particular disorder may be a very important factor to take into account when designing programs.

In addition to these more real world implications of the tripartite models of prevention, there are significant philosophical reasons why scholars have taken issue with this approach. Health promotion has been more recently recognized as an important component of prevention efforts, which would include skill building, fostering resilience, and building a variety of assets that would be related not only to avoiding a host of disorders but also to having a thriving existence where one reaches his or her potential in life (Romano & Hage, 2000). Mzarek and Haggerty (1994) included a discussion of this idea in their differentiation of programs that aim to discourage the development of pathology versus those that focus on the development of personal potential. Obviously, the outcomes associated with these types of program would be different. In the former instance, success is defined by a problem's absence. In the latter, success is defined by the presence of particular phenomena. Weissberg and Greenberg (1998) argued for a broader wellness promotion and skill-building approach to prevention that serves to reduce risk factors while also enhancing protective factors. Prevention efforts for young people would be most effective then, when coordinated with efforts to promote strengths, resilience, and health (Cowen, 1983; Weissberg & Greenberg, 1998). Thus, more recently, Cowen (2000) and Weissberg, Kumpfer, and Seligman (2003) have argued for the synthesis of primary prevention and health promotion programs conceptually in that promoting health also can impact prevention of disease.

Additionally, the aforementioned tripartite frameworks do not sufficiently emphasize a systemic approach to prevention. The tripartite approaches emphasize the target of the intervention as individuals. However, it is also the case that, as Albee (1986) argued, if disease is being caused by toxic social conditions, said conditions should be the target of intervention. That is, preventive interventions should target larger systems and policies surrounding the general population through relevant contextual systems in those individuals' lives such as families, schools, community organizations, health services, and legislation (Black & Krishnakumar, 1998). This argument demonstrates the need for both person-centered and environment-centered prevention efforts.

Person-centered interventions are those that work directly with individuals who may develop disorders and typify the majority of prevention strategies (e.g., skill building, psychoeducation) (Conyne, 2004). Environment-centered interventions work indirectly to benefit individuals by impacting the systems in which those individuals reside. Metaphorically, this process would involve enriching the soil so that plants will thrive. The systems targeted in environment-centered interventions could be familial, community, or organizational in nature. Based on Bronfenbrenner's ecological systems theory (Bronfenbrenner, 1979), such interventions might be aimed at the participants' microsystem, which includes peers, school, family, child care, and neighborhood; or the mesosystem, which contains the relationships among entities in the microsystem; the exosystem, which includes places of business and industry, federal and state governments, social media, health and social services agencies, school organizations, and extended family members; or lastly, the macrosystem, which includes cultural values, attitudes and ideologies, and dominant belief systems.

"Environment-centered approaches seek to reduce or eliminate at a systems level the variety of oppressive societal conditions that serve to marginalize and disenfranchise persons" (Kenny & Hage, 2009, p. 3). Parenting programs that indirectly promote well-being in children are examples of interventions aimed at the microsystem. A campaign to eliminate billboards that advertise alcohol or cigarettes or enacting policy that makes it illegal to have liquor stores within specific distances from schools and parks are examples of environment-centered prevention efforts that focus on the exosystem.

The challenge of environment-centered prevention approaches is that it requires psychologists to intervene with policy makers who contribute to shaping systems (e.g., banning vendors from obtaining liquor licenses for stores that are in close proximity to schools). Frost and Ouellette (2004) argued that this arena may not be a common place where mental health professionals intervene, but it is an appropriate one with historical precedence. They point to several examples where psychology has a history of lending its voice to policy debates on major social issues (e.g., *Brown v. Board of Education*, affirmative action).

While many prevention specialists are comfortable engaging in person-centered efforts, it can be more of a challenge to design and implement environment-centered programs. One reason that such interventions can be challenging is that it is more difficult to document success. Oftentimes, the effects of policy changes occur many years after the change has been implemented. Additionally, it can take years for policies to be proposed and refined, and for the necessary consensus to be built in order for them to be approved. When they are ultimately approved, it may be a significant amount of time before the requested change happens. We have seen how certain policy changes such as health care reform can travel a very contentious road en route to a vote, and then even when the reform has been passed, the changes are phased in over a period of years.

Another reason that environment-centered prevention programs are challenging is that they often require intimate knowledge of the community that one intends to help. However, by partnering with community members, psychologists can be part of efforts that empower citizens to change community conditions. Psychologists can serve as catalysts of change, or social change agents, as opposed to taking on policies individually. Kenny and Hage liken this role for psychologists to that of the "community organizer" (Kenny & Hage, 2009). Kettner, Daley, and Nichols (1985) provide a detailed description of the type of planned community change involved in designing environment-centered prevention efforts. First, they characterize such efforts as limited in scope, directed toward enhancing the quality of life of community members, providing a role for those affected by change (i.e., the community members), and guided by a person who acts as a change agent. Hence, psychologists may act as consultants to such a process that is led and designed by leaders in the community, or they may act as the change agents who help organize the community to directly communicate with policy makers about the change they desire.

In either case, the role of advocate is one that many counseling psychologists may not be used to including in their professional identities. Fortunately, a critical mass of psychologists, led by many counseling psychologists, developed competencies and training guidelines for becoming advocates (Kiselica & Robinson, 2001). As will become clear in many chapters of this handbook, engaging in prevention efforts that are multifaceted will require psychologists to expand their roles beyond direct service and into the realms of advocacy and policy change. This expansion has been described as a necessary aspect of embracing a social justice agenda (Vera & Speight, 2003).

Why Do We Need More Prevention?

Considering our nation's current economic conditions, effective prevention programs are more necessary than ever. Many of the conditions that Albee (1986) noted as influencing the emergence of mental illness are becoming more widespread in the United States. For example, according to the US Bureau of Labor Statistics (2011), the current unemployment rate stands at 9.1%, including 13.9 individuals unable to secure work and a source of income. The poverty rate is at 14.3% (US Census Bureau, 2009). The median wealth of White households is now 20 times that of African American households and 18 times that of Hispanic households, according to an analysis of newly available government data from 2009. The bursting of the housing market bubble in 2006 and the recession that followed from late 2007 to mid-2009 took a far greater toll on the wealth of minorities than Whites (Pew Research Center, 2011). Almost 51 million US citizens are without health insurance coverage—a staggering 16.7% (DeNavas-Walt, Proctor, & Smith, 2010). An average of 195,000 hate crime victimizations occurred each year from 2003 to 2009 in this country. Ninety percent of these hate crimes were suspected to be motivated by racial/ethnic prejudice (US Bureau of Justice Statistics, 2009). Racial and ethnic minorities are vastly overrepresented in these statistics. Based on statistics such as these, one might suspect that the conditions that foster and exacerbate mental health problems are affecting more and more of the population.

Remedial intervention programs, or those that provide intervention and support after symptoms have emerged, do little to curb the emergence of new cases (Albee, 2000). Prevention efforts, alternatively, cast a larger net, impede the emergence or exacerbation of psychological symptoms, and according to the vast majority of empirical literature, appear to be efficacious (Durlak & Wells, 1997; Lipsey & Wilson, 1993; Wilson, Lipsey, & Derzon, 2003). Moreover, the results of quantitative reviews have indicated that preventive interventions positively influence a host of developmental outcomes (Catalano et al., 2002) in addition to preventing specific types of problems.

Though research shows prevention to be effective, the challenge of engaging in such work is not so simple. It requires more than an emotional response to human suffering, but also a worldview that facilitates action. Albee (1986) vehemently contended that human beings are perfectly capable of ending poverty and preventing many of the diseases that devastate hundreds of millions of families throughout the world. Unfortunately, there are personal and systemic reasons that a mainstream conversion to prevention, especially one that prioritizes advocacy and environment-centered interventions, within the field has been so slow in happening. So, what is standing in the way?

There are personal worldviews that influence whether psychologists will adhere to a prevention framework the way Albee (1986) envisioned it. The first factor is a belief in a just world. Supporters of this just world belief contend that people get what they deserve in life, that virtue is rewarded, and that hard work and sacrifice lead to success (Rubin & Peplau, 1973). Believing that hard work alone results in success only serves to perpetuate injustice and powerlessness in that it is one's reaction to toxic social conditions, not the conditions themselves that result in mental illness. Alternatively, those endorsing a humanistic perspective assign equal value and potential to the lives of all human beings. Such a perspective aligns with a focus on prevention in that if all individuals are entitled to the opportunity to live their best lives and no one "deserves" to be given advantages, then prevention may be viewed as empowering the masses (Albee, 1986).

Another contrarian personal belief that may negatively impact a commitment to prevention is a belief in a fixed mechanistic process of societal evolution. Largely advocated by Herbert Spencer (Spencer, 1873–1881), this view asserts that the most "fit" individuals in any society will not only survive, but prosper. It relies heavily on the science of genetics to explain social class position. Thus, those who suffer from greater problems and poorer health, both physical and mental, might be viewed as "inferior" and unworthy of prosperity and well-being. In fact, much of our world's history has been marked by oppression of lower classes of people by "superior" groups (Blum, 1978). Adherents to this belief system would oppose efforts aimed at social change to prevent psychopathology (Albee, 1986).

Albee (1986) outlined an alternative personal ideology that is much more consistent with his view of prevention. This ideology posits that the world is often random and arbitrary in dealing out rewards and punishments. Proponents of this belief support the idea that innocent, hard-working individuals and groups can be victimized, exploited, and hurt through no fault of their own. This perspective places responsibility on human beings to create social structures that support and protect equity and justice for all. This egalitarian position expects society to help its victims, correct injustices, and interfere meaningfully when powerful individuals attempt to exploit others (Albee, 1986).

What would it take to realize social justice or to create a just society in which basic human needs are met, unnecessary stress is reduced, the competence of all individuals is maximized, and psychopathology is minimized? Rawls (1971) concluded that two basic principles must be involved. First, each individual should have access to the same basic rights as others. Next, social and economic inequalities must be set up so that they are to the greatest benefit of the least advantaged and create access and opportunity for all people. Prevention in psychology has as its goal to minimize the existence of psychopathology, at a minimum. Albee (2000) argued that, in order to do so most effectively, prevention efforts must adhere to the view of responsibility for supporting each other and controlling the exorbitant and unreasonable use of power. Thus, those committed to prevention must be willing to develop programs that address the impact of injustice and ultimately lead to ending injustices such as exploitation, racism, and sexism in our society (Kenny & Hage, 2009; Speight & Vera, 2008).

Structurally, there have also been impediments to the field embracing a commitment to prevention. Within the mental health professions, remediation is reinforced and proactive efforts are, at best, constrained by legal and financial barriers. Insurance companies typically do not reimburse preventive mental health services or client advocacy efforts. If the scope of prevention is not individual in nature, questions of who will pay for services rendered become even more unanswerable. There is some complicity on the part of training programs within our field. In the ever-increasingly competitive internship environment, the need for more and more "direct service hours," typically defined by the number of therapy and assessment hours one has amassed during training, has left little time for students to pursue prevention activities as a part of or separate from their field-based training experiences (Romano & Hage, 2000; Vera, 2000). Thus, future generations of counseling psychologists may very much be interested in becoming trained in prevention, yet will find it difficult to fit such experiences into their programs of study. To restate the perspectives of one group of students, prevention is easier said than done (McCrea, Bromley, McNally, O'Byrne, & Wade, 2004). Thus, training will need to be transformed in order for prevention to become a mainstay of the professional activities of future psychologists.

Counseling Psychology and Prevention

Counseling psychologists are particularly well poised, although not exclusively so, to define the cutting edge of prevention research and practice within the field of psychology. In fact, much of the prevention leadership within the larger field of psychology comes from a core group of counseling psychologists (Hage et al., 2007). In order to better understand the synergy between prevention and counseling psychology, the historical roots of counseling psychology must be briefly reviewed. The field of counseling psychology emerged as a result of unique historical, social, political, and professional influences during the first half of the 20th century. Among the most commonly cited influences are: the work of Frank Parsons and subsequent development of the vocational guidance movement; the mental hygiene movement; the rise of psychometrics and the study of individual differences; the emergence of counseling and psychotherapy from nonmedical and nonpsychoanalytic approaches (Rogers, 1942); and social and economic developments as a result of World War II (Hage & Romano, 2010).

Counseling psychology's divisional status within the American Psychological Association, Division 17, was established in 1946, referred to as the Division of Personnel and Guidance Psychologists (Heppner, Casas, Carter, & Stone, 2000). Although the division was established a half decade earlier, it wasn't until the Northwestern Conference in 1951 that the field began to define itself as formally valuing social advocacy (Fouad et al., 2004). It was here where the terms "counseling psychology" and "counseling psychologist" were first introduced (Super, 1955). At this time, conference leaders prepared descriptions of the roles and functions of counseling psychologists as well as recommended training. The field's foci were on facilitating optimal personal development and an understanding of the way that people were influenced by their environments (i.e., person-environment fit).

In 1964, the Division of Counseling Psychology hosted the Greystone Conference, which sought to reexamine relevant issues in the field and formulate recommendations for future training. In their final report, Thompson and Super (1964) suggested that the future of the field was dependent on counseling psychology's ability to "derive strength from variety and to achieve unity in diversity" (p. 26). The 1950s and 1960s social movements including the passage of civil rights, desegregation, voting rights, and employment rights; the Vietnam War; and the women's movement brought attention to societal inequities.

At this same time, attention to prevention was largely dictated by the political context in the United States. Prevention efforts in this country increased during the 1960s and 1970s, when Presidents Kennedy, Johnson, and Carter advocated for growth of community mental health centers, the reduction of desolate living conditions in our country, and major increases in primary prevention funding. In 1963, the US Congress passed the Community Mental Health Centers Act to provide wider scale services, including prevention, in the community (Spaulding & Balch, 1983). It was also at this point in time that the discipline of community psychology emerged as a subspecialty where psychologists who worked in newly formed community mental health arenas converged to share their mutual concerns about the inadequacies of the field and the need for more attention to creating social change. Similar to counseling psychology, community psychology was also committed to shifting away from treatment and more toward prevention, and the inclusion of an ecological perspective in viewing human functioning (i.e., person-environment fit) (Bennett et al., 1966). The Swampscott, Massachusetts, conference in 1965 is the official birthplace of community psychology (Rappaport, 1977). A social action agenda for prevention was especially prominent during federal legislation of the 1960s, when programs such as Head Start and Upward Bound were created to support educational successes and school readiness of children and adolescents (Hage & Romano, 2010).

During the 1980s, however, the political climate in the United States shifted. President Reagan stood at the center of calls for personal responsibility (Hall, 2005). The focus shifted to studying physical and organic causes of mental disorders. The development of formal diagnostic classification, third-party payments, and the efforts of powerful individuals and institutions to align mental health with the field of medicine culminated in the field's deemphasis on preventive interventions. Albee referred to this shift as selling our souls to the devil (Albee, 2000). However, despite the politics of the time, a commitment to prevention and fostering wellness was not dead.

Counseling psychology's third national conference was held in 1987. Despite popular politics, leaders in the field reaffirmed the traditional strengths of the field (i.e., prevention, life-span development, vocational development), and called for more nontraditional functions for counseling psychologists (Rude et al., 1988). This decade solidified the importance of viewing individuals in their unique sociocultural contexts including culture, ethnicity, gender, and diversity. Additionally, professionals named the need for counseling psychologists to consider ways to improve social conditions and intervene on a personal or institutional level when social or organizational variables operate in an oppressive manner (Kagan et al., 1988). This laid the groundwork for counseling psychologists to become major innovators in the multicultural movement. Gelso and Fretz (2001) identified unifying themes that clarified the core identity of counseling psychology, and these themes still remain at the heart of the profession: working within a developmental perspective, focusing on strengths and assets across all levels of human functioning; the utilization of appropriately concise treatment mediums; an adherence to viewing clients within their unique environments; a focus on educational and career development, preventive and psychoeducational methods; a commitment to multiculturalism and diversity; and finally, a concentration on evaluating and improving psychological services via the integration of science and practice.

In 2001, Division leadership used the Houston conference as a forum to reclaim foundational values of justice and equality through the creation of social action groups (McCrae et al., 2004; Meara & Davis, 2004). This conference served as a call to the next generation of counseling psychologists to take political and social action, to move the field beyond the status quo, and to establish a new paradigm for the future. In particular, these calls focused on fighting for justice (Roysircar, 2009; Toporek, Gerstein, Fouad, Roysircar, & Israel, 2006) and for counseling psychologists to focus their research and practice on social justice issues.

Since the Houston conference and more recent Chicago conference in 2008, counseling psychology has become a very diverse field characterized by a wide range of professional roles, work settings, professional interests, and research. The most recent specialty guidelines of the American Psychological Association (APA) defines counseling psychology as a domain focused on the "personal and interpersonal functioning of typically developing individuals across the life span and on emotional, social, vocational, educational, health-related, developmental, and organizational concerns" (APA, 2011a). As a psychological specialty, counseling psychology includes research and applied work in four domains: counseling process and outcome; supervision and training; career development and counseling; and prevention and health. The Society of Counseling Psychology (Division 17) added that the practice of this specialty "encompasses a broad range of practices that help people improve their well-being, alleviate distress and maladjustment, resolve crises, and increase their ability to live more highly functioning lives" (APA, 2011b). Clearly, prevention and wellness promotion are embedded in these definitions and have been so throughout the history of the profession.

The field of prevention outside of psychology has been historically led by other disciplines such as medicine and its subdiscipline public health. The professional field of public health, which originally began as a subspecialty of the field of medicine but is now interdisciplinary, had prevention as its hallmark from its inception (Rosen, 1993). While historically public health had more of a focus on physical disease prevention rather than mental health per se, promoting psychological wellness has become an important focus of the field. Behavior change also became a mainstay of public health research and interventions given that behavioral factors, such as diet and exercise, were found to be causally associated with multiple diseases. Thus, ameliorating adverse behavioral risk factors has become a major function of public health professionals and community-based, public health agencies (Rosen, 1993). Thus, over time, public health's attention to prevention became more psychological in nature while around the same time in history, psychology was becoming more interested in prevention, around the second half of the 20th century.

The role of the US government in validating the field of prevention officially began in 1930, when the Narcotics Division of the Treasury Department changed its name to the Division of Mental Hygiene in recognition of a "mental health approach" (Spaulding & Balch, 1983, p. 66). The change is attributable to the convergence of the mental hygiene and child guidance movements that began to emphasize the identification and elimination of social factors that were linked to the emergence of mental dysfunction (Hage & Romano, 2010). This newly named division was authorized to conduct research that identified the causes, prevalence, and means of prevention and treatment of mental and nervous diseases (Spaulding & Balch, 1983). Shortly after World War II, the US Public Health Service established the Communicable Disease Center (CDC), which at the end of the last century became the Centers for Disease Control and Prevention (Romano & Hage, 2000). The establishment of both the CDC and the Division of Mental Hygiene led to the creation of the National Institute of Mental Health, part of the National Institutes of Health, which have been major sources of both public policy and funding of research activities aimed at prevention since their inception (Spaulding & Balch, 1983).

Fortunately, it appears that the political climate for prevention is still in favor. The most current iterations of the US government's Healthy People Initiative (originally proposed in 1979), continue to provide national goals to reduce premature deaths and enhance the quality of life from infancy through older adulthood (Hage & Romano, 2010; Reese & Vera, 2007). As Hage and Romano note, the 2010 Healthy People Executive Summary stated:

> Full achievement of the goals and objectives of Healthy People, 2010 depends on a health system reaching all Americans and integrating personal health care and population-based public health. The vision of Healthy People in healthy communities

involves broad-based prevention efforts and moves beyond what happens in physicians' offices, clinics, and hospitals—beyond the traditional medical care system—to the neighborhoods, schools, workplaces, and families in which people live their daily lives. These are the environments in which a large portion of prevention occurs. (www.healthypeople.gov/data/midcourse)

In conclusion, counseling psychology has always had at its core fostering wellness, preventing dysfunction, paying attention to environment, and a focus on development across the life span. The field's continued commitment to prevention is one reason that counseling psychology is so well positioned to provide leadership to the larger field on a prevention agenda, and it has done so. It is important to note that community psychology has also been leading psychology's efforts to commit to prevention and that many psychologists have been working in public health, which has always been focused on prevention. Given that prevention and wellness promotion continue to be federal priorities, there are clear opportunities for collaboration among these subspecialties that will provide even stronger prevention leadership into the future.

Wellness Promotion and Skill Building

As can be seen by briefly reviewing the history of prevention and the history of counseling psychology, there has been an evolution toward reaffirming the importance of prevention politically and professionally, not only as a mechanism for protecting human dysfunction but also for enhancing well-being and mental health. Mainstream psychology became more obviously interested in such this approach in the late 1990s, when "positive psychology" became part of the field's lexicon (Seligman, 1999). This approach emphasizes enhancing strengths and building skills that promote wellness, authentic happiness, and a meaningful existence (Conyne, 2004; Seligman, 2002) while importantly maintaining that the absence of pathology is not synonymous with being mentally healthy (Catalano, Berglund, Ryan, Lonczak, & Hawkins, 2002). In other words, it promotes the ideology that "problem free is not fully prepared" (Pittman, Irby, Tolman, Yohalem, & Ferber, 2003, p. 4).

Clearly, mainstream mental health service delivery efforts would be radically transformed if the focus of our efforts shifted to fostering social and emotional competencies in individuals as opposed to relying on remedial approaches to service delivery. One immediate result is that mental health promotion services could be more inextricably part of an overall national health agenda. We have seen that the Healthy People initiative maintains its political popularity. This political commitment to wellness promotion has resulted in part from the impressive amount of research accumulating on the benefits of doing so in children and adolescents in the literature on positive youth development. Such programs have gained prominence as a way to help adolescents become competent, engaged, and responsible adults (Roth, Brooks-Gunn, Murray, & Foster, 1998). Adopting a wellness promotion philosophy would also allow the field to prioritize the goals of its interventions. One example of such a set of priorities is found in the positive youth development literature (Catalano et al., 2002).

Positive youth development activities and programs prioritize the promotion of 15 specific goals based on their empirical relationship to a host of positive developmental outcomes (Catalano et al., 2002). First, they *promote bonding*. This includes finding opportunities for youth to attach to positive adult role models. Next, they *foster resilience* by helping individuals to overcome, adapt, and cope with negative factors they may experience. Additionally, they *promote emotional and social competence*. Social competence focuses on interpersonal skills development (i.e., communication, conflict resolution), which results in healthier participation in relationships with both peers and adults. Emotional competence refers to individuals' abilities to recognize their own and others' feelings, reading nonverbal cues, while also regulating their own emotions and expression. *Cognitive and behavioral competencies* exist as other significant foci. Cognitive competence deals with critical thinking and good decision-making skills as well as strategies to help students learn efficiently, thus promoting academic success. Behavioral competence includes empowering youth to take responsibility for their actions and exercising self-control. Additionally, programs foster *moral development* by encouraging kids to explore ideas of what is right and wrong, practice empathy, and develop respect for the rights of others. The promotion of *self-determination*, another goal, aids youth in goal setting and the practice of self-agency, becoming master of one's own destiny.

Positive youth development programs *foster spirituality* including exploring the meaning and purpose of life and thinking about living a meaningful life. Next is the goal of *fostering self-efficacy*. This goal is met by providing opportunities for both direct and vicarious experiences that build success and self-confidence. These programs also aim to *foster a clear and positive identity* via challenging youth to think more complexly about who they are, their cultural group memberships, which traits they possess, and what they value. Next, they promote *a belief in the future* by helping individuals to construct hope and an optimistic orientation. Practically speaking, such programs should aid students in career and future planning. Finally, these programs should provide recognition for *positive behavior*, and *opportunities for prosocial involvement* such as civic participation or community group activities, which lead to the development of more *prosocial norms*.

These 15 areas of positive youth development are all seen as competencies that foster wellness. Masten (2001) referred to these competencies in her description of resilience promotion as reflecting "everyday magic." Accordingly, she argued that the ability to thrive and be successful in the face of adversity is not a magic trait that only certain individuals possess but rather it can be fostered in everyone by enhancing and building capacities such as the 15 mentioned above. Not only will the outcome be children and adolescents who avoid health-compromising risk, but ultimately ones who engage in prosocial behaviors and become better citizens.

In order for resilience, competencies, and adaptive skills to be developed, necessary resources found in individuals, families, schools, organizations, and communities must be widely available in society (Masten, 2001). In order for programs to teach skills and competencies while providing enriching, growth-promoting opportunities, researchers must obtain an understanding of what developmental assets and experiences youth must realize in order to achieve positive developmental outcomes.

As a related example, the Search Institute characterized 40 developmental assets that should guide the development of wellness promotion efforts in children and youth: 20 external and 20 internal assets. External assets include building contextual networks that provide support, empowerment, boundaries, expectations, and constructive use of time, while internal assets include nurturing a commitment to learning, positive values, social competencies, and a strong, positive identity (Benson, 1997). In a related effort, Roth and her colleagues (1998) put together a comprehensive synthesis of 15 evaluated youth development programs. Programs that were most successful in improving the lives of youth in need of support shared several themes: (1) leaders created "places of hope" through community building, listening to youth, and bringing adults and youth together for clear, constructive purposes; (2) leaders were willing to work outside of the conventional institutional framework and utilize their own creative skills; (3) programs viewed participants as resources to be developed as opposed to issues that needed to be managed; (4) programs provided safe, warm, caring, empowering, flexible, and family-like environments; (5) desired programmatic outcomes were tangible products and performances; and (6) programs were long-term in nature. Each of these analyses revealed that enhancing human potential involves fostering individual competencies and gathering/strengthening environmental resources.

A shift toward promoting human strengths would inform prevention programs and public policy that foster competence, increase human capital, and improve the mental and physical health of communities of people. It would also help to establish a social action agenda that identified the type of resources that must be present to eradicate social injustices in society. Thus, viewing prevention as part of an overall health agenda to promote wellness, both physical and mental in nature, by definition requires prevention specialists to look at the structure of resources that exist in our society and to focus efforts at societal injustices as we attempt to build assets and environments that foster success. This has led many scholars to conclude that prevention, it its current evolution, is part of a commitment to social justice (Kenny & Hage, 2009; Vera & Speight, 2003).

Social Justice and Cultural Relevance in Prevention

Many scholars have written about the inextricable connection between prevention and social justice (Kenny & Hage, 2009; Kenny et al., 2009, Speight & Vera, 2008; Vera & Speight, 2003). By working to ameliorate social conditions that compromise mental health and well-being, prevention is part of a social justice agenda, as originally conceptualized by Albee (1986) among others. One of the implications of using prevention efforts to bring about social justice is creating truly collaborative relationships with community participants and ensuring that our programs reflect the cultural realities they encounter. Vera and Speight (2003) highlighted the importance of preventive intervention goals being socially relevant and valued by those participating. Lerner and his colleagues (2005) added that, in order for efforts to be successful, those involved in the program must be allowed an active voice in all aspects of the project. In other words, community members should be allowed ample opportunities to be involved in program development, implementation, and evaluation (Lerner, 1995; Reiss & Price, 1996; Vera & Reese, 2000). By doing so, preventionists develop their program participants into involved individuals who act as agents of change for their own communities (Stringer, 1999).

The importance of cultural relevance in prevention efforts cannot be understated because each individual is embedded within an entirely unique system of characteristics, norms, values, customs, and belief systems, all of which results in unique worldviews and experiences. Prevention efforts remain most efficacious when efforts are made to design programs that are relevant and meaningful to all participants. The more preventive interventions are consistent with participants' values, beliefs, and desired outcomes, the more culturally relevant they will be (Nation et al., 2003). Given the alleged significant diversity of program participants, this is no easy task. Largely because of their traditional emphasis on prevention and multiculturalism, counseling psychologists have led the way in advocating for the need for culturally relevant prevention programming (Reese & Vera, 2007).

To illustrate how cultural relevance can play a role in the success of prevention efforts, Wilson, Lipsey, and Derzon (2003) conducted a meta-analysis to investigate the impact of altering preventive interventions to meet specific cultural groups' needs. Results indicated meaningful outcomes across populations; however, issues related to participation and attrition, acceptance of the program, and overall satisfaction were not equivalent across groups. Retention and attrition exist as a large issue within the field of prevention (Reese, Vera, Simon, & Ikeda, 2000). Kumpfer, Alvarado, Smith, and Bellamy (2002) argued that focusing on cultural relevance as a key aspect of programming improves recruitment, retention, and outcome effectiveness. Investigators must have knowledge of the community in which they are working in order to develop positive working relationships with community members and produce programming that is valued by the community at large (Reese & Vera, 2007). The importance of attending to and incorporating the cultural realities of participants into prevention efforts has become a best practice of prevention work in the last decade (Hage et al., 2007; Kumpfer & Alvarado, 2003; Wandersman & Florin, 2003).

To achieve cultural relevance, often preventionists must be willing to spend time in the community and engage in efforts that are valued by its members. These initial efforts may indirectly affect the outcomes of prevention programs by demonstrating commitment to the community and a deeper understanding of participants' norms and values (Kenny & Gallagher, 2000), as well as a deeper understanding of the social conditions that contribute to mental health problems. This type of approach to prevention typifies it as an important part of a social justice agenda. To summarize the words of Albee (1986),

> Psychologists must join with persons who reject racism, sexism, colonialism, and exploitation and find ways to redistribute social power and to increase social justice. Primary prevention research inevitably will make clear the relationship between social pathology and psychopathology and then will work to change social and political structures in the interest of social justice. It is as simple and as difficult as that! (p. 897)

Organization of the Handbook

In conceptualizing the presentation of this handbook, the intention is that readers gain knowledge in four main areas. The first area is foundational and philosophical. The chapters contained in the "Foundations of Prevention" section represent seminal background and theoretical and philosophical knowledge about the field of prevention in counseling psychology. Experts in the field have shared their knowledge of the history of prevention within psychology over time (Conyne), best practices and guidelines in prevention science and application (Hage, Schwartz, & Murray), prevention in the 21st century and beyond (Romano), ethical complexities of engaging in prevention work (Schwartz, Hage, & González), prevention's role in a social justice agenda (Kenny & Medvive), advocacy as prevention (Pieterse, Hanus, & Gale), recommendations on teaching and training (Matthews), the connections between prevention and critical psychology (Prilleltensky & Nelson) and fundamentals in evaluating prevention efforts (Davis, Orpinas, & Horne).

The second section of the handbook features contributions that highlight the best practices of preventing specific types of psychological disorders or unhealthy behaviors that can lead to disease and negative social outcomes. Chapters on preventing aggression and violence in children and adolescents (Espelage & Low), substance abuse (Priester & Jones), suicide (Rogers & Benson), school dropout

(Shin & Kendall), eating disorders (Mazzeo, Gow, & Bullock), intimate partner violence (Davidson, Schwartz, & Waldo), behavioral problems (Daly, Buchanan, Dasch, Eichen, & Lenhart), sexual risk taking (Edwards & Stubbs), and health disparities (Buki, Montoya, & Linares) provide overviews of best practices in primary and secondary prevention efforts.

The third section of this handbook features a review of programs that seek to promote wellness and thriving in specific populations such as older adults (Hill & Duffy), first-generation college students (Thompson & Phillips), returning veterans (Danish), Latin American immigrants (Morgan, Gonzales, & Lopez), Asian immigrants (Ma, Shea, & Yeh), African American youth (Thomas, Speight, Turner-Essel, & Barrie), refugees (Buhin Loncar), Mexican American students (Flores & Garriott). Within this section, environment-centered interventions aimed at changing institutional barriers are also reviewed. Specifically, heterosexism (Haley, Adams, Dickson, Hitter, & Luna) and racism (Neville and Spanierman) are featured in this section. Finally, promoting well-being across the life span with career counseling (Brown, Lamp, Telander, & Hacker) and exercise (Parham) are also presented.

In the final section, the future of prevention is presented. This chapter, authored by Vera and Polanin, describes accomplishments that have been made as well as directions for future attention, future directions for the field (Vera and Polanin).

In the chapters, authors were encouraged to highlight their work with an eye toward a culturally relevant framework. Instead of generalizations about how an issue is prevented across populations, a focus on what types of prevention and or mental health promotion would work for specific populations was preferred. Thus, the second section of the handbook demonstrates primary and secondary approaches to prevention with a focus on cultural relevance. The wellness promotion framework is reflected in the chapters contained in the third section. Thus, the second and third sections of the book represent examples of Romano and Hage's (2000) expanded definition of prevention.

As was stated earlier, this handbook represents the critical mass of scholars who are striving to make prevention a permanent, nonwavering aspect of the field of counseling psychology. We are hopeful that the readers of this handbook represent the next generation of prevention specialists within the field of psychology and that they will be inspired by what they read.

References

Adams, E. M. (2007). Moving from contemplation to preparation: Is counseling psychology ready to embrace culturally responsive prevention? *The Counseling Psychologist, 35*(6), 840–849.

Albee, G. W. (1986). Toward a just society: Lessons from observations on the primary prevention of psychopathology. *The American Psychologist, 41*(8), 891–898.

Albee, G. W. (2000). Commentary on prevention and counseling psychology. *The Counseling Psychologist, 28*(6), 845–853.

Albee, G. W. (2002). Just say no to psychotropic drugs! *Journal of Clinical Psychology, 58*(6), 635–648.

Albee, G. W., & Ryan, K. (1998). An overview of primary prevention. *Journal of Mental Health, 7*(5), 441–449.

American Psychological Association (2011a). *Public description of counseling psychology.* Retrieved August 15, 2011, from http://www.apa.org/ed/graduate/specialize/counseling.aspx

American Psychological Association (2011b). *Society of Counseling Psychology.* Retrieved August 15, 2011, from http://www.apa.org/about/division/div17.aspx.

Bennett, C. C., Anderson, L. S., Cooper, S., Hassol, L., Klein, D. C., & Rosenbaum, G. (Eds.). (1966). *Community psychology: A report of the Boston Conference on the Education of Psychologists for Community Mental Health.* Boston, MA: Boston University Press.

Benson, P. L. (1997). *All kids are our kids: What communities must do to raise caring and responsible children and adolescents.* San Francisco: Jossey-Boss.

Black, M. M., & Krishnakumar, A. (1998). Children in low-income, urban settings: Interventions to promote mental health and well-being. *American Psychologist, 53,* 635–646.

Blum, J. M. (1978). *Pseudoscience and mental ability.* New York: Monthly Review Press.

Bronfenbrenner, U. (1979). *The ecology of human development: Experiments by nature and design.* Cambridge, MA: Harvard University Press.

Caplan, G. (1964). *Principles of preventive psychiatry.* New York: Basic Books.

Catalano, R. F., Berglund, M. L., Ryan, J. A. M., Lonczak, H. S., & Hawkins, J. D. (2002). Positive youth development in the United States: Research findings on evaluations of positive youth development programs. *Prevention and Treatment, 5,* 1–111.

Conduct Problems Prevention Research Group. (1999). Initial impact of the Fast Track prevention trial for conduct problems: I. The high risk sample. *Journal of Consulting and Clinical Psychology, 67,* 631–647.

Conyne, R. K. (2004). *Preventive counseling: Helping people to become empowered in systems and settings* (2nd ed.). New York: Brunner-Routledge.

Cowen, E. L. (1980). The wooing of primary prevention. *American Journal of Community Psychology, 8,* 258–284.

Cowen, E. L. (1983). Primary prevention in mental health: Past, present, and future. In R. D. Felner, L. A. Jason, J. N. Moritsugu, & S. S. Farber (Eds.), *Preventive psychology: Theory, research and practice* (pp. 11–25). New York: Pergamon Press.

Cowen, E. L. (1996). The ontogenesis of primary prevention: Lengthy strides and stubbed toes. *American Journal of Community Psychology, 24*(2), 235–249.

Cowen, E. L. (2000). Psychological wellness: Some hopes for the future. In D. Cicchetti, J. Rappaport, I. N. Sandler, & R. P. Weissberg (Eds.), *The promotion of wellness in children and adolescents* (pp. 477–503). Washington, DC: Child Welfare League of America Press.

Cumming, E. (1968). Unsolved problems of prevention. *Canada's Mental Health Supplement, 56,* 12.

DeNavas-Walt, C., Proctor, B. D., & Smith, J. C. (2010). *Income, poverty, and health insurance coverage in the United States: 2009.* Retrieved August 22, 2011, from http://www.census.gov/prod/2010pubs/p60-238.pdf

Durlak, J. A., & Wells, A. M. (1997). Primary prevention mental health programs for children and adolescents: A meta-analytic review. *American Journal of Community Psychology, 25,* 115–152.

Fouad, N. A., McPherson, R. H., Gerstein, L., Blustein, D. L., Elman, N., Helledy, K. I., & Metz, A. J. (2004). Houston, 2001: Context and legacy. *The Counseling Psychologist, 32,* 15–77.

Friere, P. (1970). *Pedagogy of the oppressed* (M. B. Ramos, Trans.). New York: Seabury Press.

Frost, D. M., & Ouellette, S. C. (2004). Meaningful voices: How psychologists, speaking as psychologists, can inform social policy: Comment. *Analyses of Social Issues and Public Policy (ASAP), 4*(1), 219–226.

Gelso, C. J., & Fretz, B. R. (2001). *Counseling psychology* (2nd ed.). Fort Worth, TX: Harcourt College Publishers.

Goodyear, R. K., Murdock, N. L., Lichtenberg, J. W., McPherson, R., Koetting, K., & Petren, S. (2008). Stability and change in counseling psychologists' identities, roles, functions, and career satisfaction across fifteen years. *The Counseling Psychologist, 36,* 220–249.

Gordon, R. (1987). An operational classification of disease prevention. In J. Steinberg & M. Silverman (Eds.), *Preventing mental disorders: A research perspective* (pp. 20–26). Rockville, MD: US Department of Health and Human Services: National Institute of Mental Health.

Hage, S., & Romano, J. (2010). History of prevention and prevention groups: Legacy for the 21st century. *Group Dynamics: Theory, Research, and Practice, 14,* 199–210.

Hage, S. M., Romano, J., Kenny, M. E., Matthews, C. R., Schwartz, J. P., & Waldo, M. (2007). Best practice guidelines on prevention practice, research, training, and social advocacy for psychologists. *The Counseling Psychologist, 35,* 493–566.

Hall, W. C. (2005). The great composer: A behind the scenes look at Ronald Reagan's rhetorical symphony. In P. Kengor & P. Schweizer (Eds.), *The Reagan presidency: Assessing the man and his legacy* (pp. 167–180). Oxford, England: Rowman & Littlefield.

Heppner, P. P., Casas, J. M., Carter, J., & Stone, G. L. (2000). The maturation of counseling psychology: Multifaceted perspectives, 1978–1998. In S. D. Brown & R. W. Lent (Eds.), *Handbook of counseling psychology* (3rd ed., pp. 3–49). New York: Wiley.

Kagan, N., Armsworth, M. W., Altmaier, E. M., Dowd, E. T., Hansen, J. C., Mills, . . . Vasquez, M. J. T. (1988). Professional practice of counseling psychologist in various settings. *The Counseling Psychologist, 16,* 347–365.

Kenny, M., & Gallagher, L. (2000). Service learning as a vehicle in training psychologists for revised professional roles. In F. T. Sherman & W. R. Torbert (Eds.), *Transforming social inquiry, transforming social action* (pp. 189–206). Norwell, MA: Kluwer Academic.

Kenny, M. E., & Hage, S. M. (2009). The next frontier: Prevention as an instrument of social justice. *Journal of Primary Prevention, 30,* 1–10.

Kenny, M. E., Horne, A. E., Orpinas, P., & Reese, L. E. (2009). *Realizing social justice: The challenge of preventive interventions.* Washington, DC: American Psychological Association.

Kessler, M., & Albee, G. W. (1975). Primary prevention. *Annual Review of Psychology, 26,* 557–591.

Kettner, P. M., Daley, J. M., & Nichols, A. W. (1985). *Initiating change in organizations and communities: A macro practice model.* Belmont, CA: Brooks/Cole.

Kiselica, M. S., & Robinson, M. (2001). Bringing advocacy counseling to life: The history, issues, and human dramas of social justice work in counseling. *Journal of Counseling and Development, 79*(4), 387–397.

Kumpfer, K. L., & Alvarado, R. (2003). Family-strengthening approaches for the prevention of youth problem behaviors. *American Psychologist, 58,* 457–465.

Kumpfer, K. L., Alvarado, R., Smith, P., & Bellamy, N. (2002). Cultural sensitivity and adaptation in family based interventions. *Prevention Science, 3,* 241–246.

Lerner, R. M. (1995). *America's youth in crisis: Challenges and options for programs and policies.* Thousand Oaks, CA: Sage.

Lerner, R. M., Lerner, J. V., Almerigi, J., Theokas, C., Naudeau, S., Gestsdottir, S., . . . vonEye, A. (2005). Positive youth development, participation in community youth development programs, and community contributions of fifth grade adolescents: Findings from the first wave of the 4-H study of positive youth development. *Journal of Early Adolescence, 25*(1), 17–71.

Levine, M. (1998). Prevention and community. *American Journal of Community Psychology, 26*(2), 189–206.

Lipsey, M. W., & Wilson, D. B. (1993). The efficacy of psychological, educational, and behavioral treatment: Confirmation from meta-analysis. *American Psychologist, 48,* 1181–1209.

Masten, A. S. (2001). Ordinary magic: Resilience processes in development. *American Psychologist, 56*(3), 227–238.

McCrea, L. G., Bromley, J. L., McNally, C. J., O'Byrne, K. K., & Wade, K. A. (2004). Houston 2001: A student perspective on issues of identity, training, social advocacy, and the future of counseling psychology. *The Counseling Psychologist, 32,* 78–88.

Meara, N. M., & Davis, K. L. (2004). The Houston 2001 National Counseling Psychology Conference: Making a difference for the specialty. *The Counseling Psychologist, 32*(1), 99–108.

Mrazek, P. J., & Haggerty, R. J. (Eds.). (1994). *Reducing risks for mental disorders: Frontiers for preventive intervention research.* Washington, DC: National Academy Press.

Munoz, R. F., Mrazek, P. J., & Haggerty, R. J. (1996). Institute of Medicine report of prevention of mental disorders: Summary and commentary. *American Psychologist, 51*(11), 1116–1122.

Nation, M., Crusto, C, Wandersman, A., Kumpfer, K., Seybolt, D., & Morrissey-Kane, E. (2003). What works in prevention: Principles and effective prevention programs. *American Psychologist, 58,* 449–456.

Pew Research Center (2011). *Wealth gaps rise to record highs between whites, blacks, Hispanics.* Washington, DC: Pew Research Center. Retrieved August 22, 2011, from http://pewsocialtrends.org/2011/07/26/wealth-gaps-rise-to-record-highs-between-whites-blacks-hispanics/

Pittman, K., Irby, M., Tolman, J., Yohalem, N., & Ferber, T. (2003). *Preventing Problems, promoting development, encouraging engagement: Competing priorities or inseparable goals?* Based upon Pittman, K. & Irby, M. (1996). *Preventing problems or promoting development?* Washington, DC: The Forum for Youth Investment, Impact Strategies, Inc. Available online on www.forumfyi.org.

Rappaport, J. (1977). *Community psychology: Values, research and action.* Sydney: Holt, Rinehart, and Winston.

Rawls, J. (1971). *A theory of justice.* Cambridge, MA: Belknap.

Reese, L. E., & Vera, E. M. (2007). Culturally relevant prevention: The scientific and practical considerations of community-based programs. *The Counseling Psychologist, 35,* 763–778.

Reese, L. E., Vera, E. M., Simon, T. R., & Ikeda, R. M. (2000). The role of families and caregivers as risk and protective factors in preventing youth violence. *Clinical Child and Family Psychology Review, 3,* 61–77.

Reiss, D., & Price, R. H. (1996). National research agenda for prevention research: National Institute of Mental Health Report. *American Psychologist, 51,* 1109–1115.

Ringel, J., & Sturm, R. (2001). National estimates of mental health utilization and expenditures for children in 1998. *Journal of Behavioral Health Services and Research, 28,* 319–333.

Rogers, C. R. (1942). *Counseling and psychotherapy: Newer concepts in practice.* Oxford, England: Houghton Mifflin.

Romano, J., & Hage, S. (2000). Prevention and counseling psychology: Revitalizing commitments for the 21st century. *The Counseling Psychologist, 28,* 733–763.

Roosa, M. W., Dumka, L. E., Gonzales, N. A., & Knight, G. P. (2002). Cultural/ethnic issues and the prevention scientist in the 21st century. *Prevention and Treatment, 5*(1), Article 0005a, doi: 10.1037/1522–3736.5.1.55a.

Rosen, G. (1993). *A history of public health* (Exp. ed.). Baltimore, MD: Johns Hopkins University Press.

Roth, J., Brooks-Gunn, J., Murray, L., & Foster, W. (1998). Promoting healthy adolescents: Synthesis of youth development program evaluations. *Journal of Research on Adolescence, 8,* 423–459.

Roysircar, G. (2009). *Therapist, heal society and thyself: Social justice advocacy in disaster response work.* Keynote address at the National Multicultural Summit and Conference, New Orleans, LA.

Rubin, Z., & Peplau, A. (1973). Belief in a just world and reactions to another's lot: A study of participants in the national draft lottery. *Journal of Social Issues, 29*(4), 73–92.

Rude, S. S., Weissberg, M., & Gasza, G. M. (1988). Looking into the future: Themes from the third national conference for counseling psychology. *The Counseling Psychologist, 16,* 423–430.

Seligman, M. E. P. (1999). The president's address. *American Psychologist, 54,* 559–562.

Seligman, M. E. P. (2002). Positive psychology, positive prevention, and positive therapy. In C. R. Snyder & S. J. Lopez (Eds.), *Handbook of positive psychology* (pp. 3–9). New York: Oxford University Press.

Spaulding, J., & Balch, P. (1983). A brief history of primary prevention in the twentieth century: 1908–1980. *American Journal of Community Psychology, 11,* 59–80.

Speight, S. L., & Vera, E. M. (2008). Social justice and counseling psychology. In R. Lent & S. Brown (Eds.), *Handbook of counseling psychology* (pp. 54–67). Hoboken, NJ: Wiley.

Spencer, H. (1873–1881). *Descriptive sociology.* New York: Appleton.

Stringer, E. T. (1999). *Action research: A handbook for practitioners* (2nd ed.). Thousand Oaks, CA: Sage.

Super, D. E. (1955). Transition: From vocational guidance to counseling psychology. *Journal of Counseling Psychology, 2*(1), 3–9.

Thompson, A. S., & Super, D. E. (Eds.). (1964). *The professional preparation of counseling psychologists: Report of the 1964 Greystone Conference.* New York: Bureau of Publications, Teachers College, Columbia University.

Tolan, P. H., & Dodge, K. A. (2005). Children's mental health as a primary care and concern: A system for comprehensive support and service. *American Psychologist, 60,* 601–614.

Toporek, R. L., & Williams, R. A. (2006). Ethics and professional issues related to the practice of social justice in counseling psychology. In R. L. Toporek, L. H. Gerstein, N. A. Fouad, G. Roysircar, & T. Israel, (Eds.), *Handbook for social justice in counseling psychology: Leadership, vision, and action* (pp. 17–34). Thousand Oaks, CA: Sage.

US Bureau of Justice Statistics (2009). *Hate crimes, 2003–2009.* Retrieved August 22, 2011, from http://bjs.ojp.usdoj.gov/index.cfm?ty=pbdetail&iid=1760

US Bureau of Labor Statistics (2011). *Employment situation summary.* Retrieved August 22, 2011, from http://www.bls.gov/news.release/empsit.nr0.htm

US Census Bureau (2009). *Official and National Academy of Sciences (NAS) based poverty rates: 1999 to 2009.* Retrieved August 22, 2011, from http://www.census.gov/hhes/www/poverty/poverty.html

Vera, E. M. (2000). A recommitment to prevention work in counseling psychology. *The Counseling Psychologist, 28*(6), 829–837.

Vera, E. M., & Speight, S. L. (2003). Multicultural competence, social justice, and counseling psychology: Expanding our roles. *The Counseling Psychologist, 31,* 253–272.

Wagenfeld, M. O. (1972). The primary prevention of mental illness: A sociological perspective. *Journal of Health and Social Behavior, 13*(2), 195–203.

Wandersman, A., & Florin, P. (2003). Community interventions and effective prevention. *American Psychologist, 58,* 441–448.

Watkins, C., Lopez, F., Campbell, V., & Himmel, C. (1986). Contemporary counseling psychology: Result of a national survey. *Journal of Counseling Psychology, 33,* 301–309.

Weissberg, R. P., & Greenberg, M. T. (1998). School and community competence-enhancement and prevention programs. In W. Damon (Series Ed.) & I. E. Sigel & K. A. Renninger (Vol. Eds.), *Handbook of child psychology: Vol. 4. Child psychology in practice* (5th ed., pp. 877–954). New York: Wiley.

Weissberg, R. P., Kumpfer, K. L., & Seligman, M. E. P. (2003). Preventions for children and youth that works: An introduction. *American Psychologist, 58,* 425–432.

Wilson, S. J., Lipsey, M. W., & Derzon, J. H. (2003). The effects of school-based intervention programs on aggressive and disruptive behavior. A meta-analysis. *Journal of Consulting and Clinical Psychology, 71,* 136–149.

CHAPTER

2 A History of Prevention in Counseling Psychology

Robert K. Conyne

Abstract

This chapter's two tables present illustrative markers of prevention events that have occurred within counseling psychology and within prevention per se. These markers are addressed selectively in the chapter's narrative, which is organized sequentially as follows: (1) "Early Antecedents"; (2) "A Decade of Fomentation: The 1960s"; (3) "Prevention Emerges in the 1970s"; (4) "Prevention Expands: 1980s–Current," with attention to 1980–1989, 1990–1999, 2000–2010; and (5) "Future Directions." The thesis is that prevention in counseling psychology remains an artifact of *hope*. Although impressive scholarly production has occurred at an increasing pace since around 1985 and the Society of Counseling Psychology has formalized its support of prevention through its Prevention Section, "real world" demonstrations of gains—through training curricula, research, and employment—suggest that prevention remains still on the outside looking in. Yet due largely to the noticeable increase in prevention professional literature and to passage of health care reform legislation, the time for prevention in counseling psychology may finally have come—though we should be mindful that we've heard that refrain sung before.

Key Words: prevention, history, counseling psychology, prevention per se, hope, early antecedents, 1960s, 1970s, 1980–Current, 2010, future, health care reform.

Introduction

This historical review of prevention in counseling psychology begins at the end. A brief summary of its current status is provided through examining two recent relevant and representative quotations. I will then proceed to trace some of the dominant events that have served to bring us to this point.

First, what is the current situation? The next two quotations provide an indication. The editors of the fourth edition of the *Handbook of Counseling Psychology* (Brown & Lent, 2008) state in their introduction (p. xii):

> Although Brent Mallinckrodt's content analysis [note: of research published in the *Journal of Counseling Psychology* and *The Counseling Psychologist* between 2000 and 2006] did not reveal that prevention per se engages the research attention of large numbers of counseling psychologists... we **hope** [bold added for emphasis] the chapters in Part V (Development and Prevention) will stimulate readers to give renewed thought to promoting positive development and resiliency and preventing (rather than only treating) psychological and health-related problems.

Second, in a watershed special issue of *The Counseling Psychologist*, "Prevention in Counseling Psychology" (coedited by Romano & Hage, 2000), the editors concluded their major contribution with these words:

> Our **hope** [again, bold added] is that this major contribution will help create a shared vision aimed at

> addressing the enormous needs of today's children, youth, families, and communities and will revitalize the commitments of counseling psychology toward an enhanced prevention focus in the 21st century. (p. 754)

And so it goes. Note the operant verb, *hope*, used in both quotes. Indeed, hope is a critically important variable that can serve to motivate and sustain the need for action and change. Yet more than hope is needed to yield tangible and sustainable change. I will return to this premise later in this chapter.

Approach Used in This Chapter to Examine the History of Prevention in Counseling Psychology

Prevention has been visited by a continuing series of roller coaster–like rides over the decades, where attention given it rises only to plummet to a trough, then swing back again, up and down. Alarms have been sounded before about prevention's ephemeral status in the profession. As Vera pointed out (2000) when commenting on the Romano and Hage special issue on prevention in counseling psychology, it was not the first "wake-up call given to the field" (p. 836). She observed that others (Conyne, 1987; Goodyear & Shaw, 1984; McNeil & Ingram, 1983; and more) had preceded them. Vera called on counseling psychology to reaffirm its roots in prevention and development and to no longer "pretend to be something we are not" (p. 836). This statement begs the question, "What, then, are we, and how did we arrive at this point?" This question motivates the purpose for this book chapter.

To begin answering this question it is instructive to consider two streams of historical development in prevention, one that has occurred in counseling psychology and the other within prevention "per se" (to borrow Mallinckrodt's designation, cited earlier). It may be helpful to refer periodically to two tables that I've created to capture at least some of the salient markers in each of these areas: Table 2.1, "Some Important Markers for Prevention in Counseling Psychology: 1892–Current," and Table 2.2, "Some Important Markers for Prevention Per Se: 1854–Current."

Events in each table are organized into four parts. Note that selection of the events to include in the tables, as well as how they are organized, results from my idiosyncratic judgment; other experts no doubt would construct their systems differently.

In Table 2.1 the four parts are titled: (1) "Some Antecedent Events: 1892–1966"; (2) "Prevention in Counseling Psychology Emerges: 1968–1982"; (3) "Prevention in Counseling Psychology Gains Some Traction: 1984–1999"; and (4) "Prevention in Counseling Psychology Accelerates (It Seems): 2000–2010."

Events in Table 2.2 are organized sequentially: (1) "Some Antecedent Events: 1854–1959"; (2) "A Fomenting Decade Stimulates Change: 1960–1969"; (3) "Primary Prevention Emerges from the Change Period: 1970–1979"; and (4) "Prevention Scholarship Expands and Focuses: 1980–Current."

These streams of historical events have flowed independently, intersecting periodically but generally maintaining relatively autonomous and separate pathways. Unfortunately, this condition occurs often in academic disciplines and specialized professional practice, where a "silo mentality" is both all-too-prevalent and highly resistant to alteration. This situation is especially pernicious for advancing prevention, whose origins and ongoing activities are multidisciplinary.

What follows is a historical narrative intended to highlight exemplary markers that illustrate the unfolding of prevention in counseling psychology. Signposts included will be presented sequentially (early antecedents, 1960s, 1970s, 1980–2000 [1980–89, 1990–99, 2000–2010], future). You will note that the amount of preventive activity reported increases substantially as time proceeds. Topics discussed will be drawn from items contained in each table, that is, directly from those related to the history of prevention in counseling psychology and those selected from the history of prevention itself. Due to space limitations, no attempt will be made to discuss all events included in the two tables but, for a wider vantage point, it would be worthwhile to refer to the contents contained in each table.

Tracing the Evolution

Examples of Early AntecedentsPrevention in counseling psychology is an outgrowth of developments in the multidisciplinary focus referred to as "prevention" and of an oft-recurring set of themes emphasizing strengths, person-environment fit, and social change that has reverberated through the history of counseling psychology itself. For a reminder of early expressions of these themes, note the following three examples taken from 1953–1961:

> Counseling psychology . . . concerns itself with *hygiology*, with the normalities even of abnormal persons, with locating and developing personal and social resources and adaptive tendencies so that the

Table 2.1 Some Important Markers for Prevention in Counseling Psychology: 1892–Current

A. SOME ANTECEDENT EVENTS: 1892–1966

1892 American Psychological Association (APA) formed

1898 Jesse B. Davis begins career as high school counselor

1899 William Rainey Harper, president of the University of Chicago promotes "scientific study of college students"

1905 Joseph H. Pratt conducts "thought-control classes" for tuberculosis patients, realizing that therapeutic benefits result from bringing them together

1907 Jesse B. Davis started first vocational guidance program in schools (Grand Rapids, Michigan)

1908 Clifford Beers publishes *A Mind That Found Itself: An Autobiography*; beginnings of mental hygiene movement

1908 Frank Parsons, the "Father of Vocational Guidance," begins the Vocation Bureau of Boston, which was engaged in social action

1909 Parson's classic and influential *Choosing a Vocation* is published posthumously

1922 Alfred Adler develops "collective counseling," a new form of group guidance; later, he develops "family councils" to help resolve and improve their interrelationships

1925 C. R. Foster writes *Extra Curricular Activities* to encourage counselors to hold "many group conferences with students on the subject of future educational or vocational plans" (p. 182)

1931 Richard D. Allen writes *A Group Guidance Curriculum in the Senior High School*

1939 E. G. Williamson writes *How to Counsel Students*, in which he sowed seeds for an ecological approach to counseling

1945 APA reorganizes, with Division 17 becoming the Division of Counseling and Guidance

1949 Boulder Conference adopts scientist-practitioner model for doctoral preparation in professional psychology

1951 Northwestern Conference initiates the term, "counseling psychology" and seeks to define itself

1953 Gustad writes about dealing with the "normalities" of life, its "hygiology"

1956 APA definition of counseling psychology was to develop an individual's life, promote harmony with the environment, and influence society...

1960s and beyond Carkhuff and Truax (human relations skill development), Egan (the skilled helper), Ivey (microcounseling), Kagan (interpersonal process recall), Mosher and Sprinthall (deliberate psychological education), and others develop human relations skills training and delivery programs

1961 Leona Tyler conceptualizes counseling psychology as connecting individuals with compatible environments and by accentuating strengths

1962 C. Gilbert Wrenn writes *The Counselor in a Changing World*, connecting counselor involvement with broader societal issues

1964 Greyston Conference seeks to clarify professional identity, status issues, and confidence in the profession of counseling psychology

1964 Joseph Samler authors a definition of counseling psychology emphasizing strengths and environmental coping skills and suggests that counseling psychologists become involved in social action (in Whiteley, 1980, pp. 164–165)

1965 A wave of "newer" therapeutic approaches emerges, and a growing number of psychologists begin to engage in private practice

1966 Donald Blocher publishes *Developmental Counseling*

B. PREVENTION IN COUNSELING PSYCHOLOGY EMERGES: 1968–1982

1968 Jordaan, Myers, Layton, and Morgan (1968) define remedial, developmental, and **preventive** roles for counseling psychologists. "Prevention" enters the counseling psychology lexicon

1970s A small number of college and university counseling/student development centers (notably Colorado State University, Illinois State University) experiment and engage in an array of campus-based preventive interventions, including environmental assessment and change programs

1972 Wes Morrill, Eugene Oetting, and James Hurst publish the seminal "Counseling Intervention Cube," which clearly articulates preventive goals for counseling interventions targeted at individual, group, and institutional levels that could be delivered directly or indirectly

1973 David Drum and Howard Figler publish *Outreach in Counseling: Applying the Growth and Prevention Model in Schools and Colleges*

1975 Haskell defines prevention as being proactive with a focus on skill development and environmental change

1976 Allen Ivey connects prevention to social justice and to social and economic inequities, and calls for use of a psychoeducator approach

Table 2.1 ***(Continued)***

1977 Judith and Michael Lewis publish first edition of *Community Counseling: A Human Services Approach*, with second edition in 1983. Third edition with Judy Daniels and Michael D'Andrea in 2003 is retitled *Community Counseling: Empowerment Strategies for a Diverse Society*
1979 Ivey describes counseling psychology as "the most broadly based applied specialty" (p. 3).
1980 John Whiteley edits a historical development of counseling psychology
1982 Norman Kagan and colleagues conclude a 2-year study of counseling psychology to envision its future decade

---

C. PREVENTION IN COUNSELING PSYCHOLOGY GAINS SOME TRACTION: 1984–1999
1984 Goodyear and Shaw coedit special issues of the *Personnel and Guidance Journal*: " Primary Prevention in Schools" (vol. 62, no 8) and "Primary Prevention on Campus and in the Community" (vol. 62, no. 9)
1987 The Third National Conference, known as the "Georgia Conference" (University of Georgia) meets to define the future of counseling psychology and encourage proactive outreach and working with diverse populations and emerging settings. Still preoccupied with professional identity issues, prevention, life-span development, skill building and other "innovative and nontraditional functions" emerged among the themes
1987 Robert Conyne's *Primary Preventive Counseling* published, perhaps the first text in counseling psychology to specifically focus on prevention
1990's Psychoeducation groups, brief group approaches, prevention groups emerge
1999 Archival definition of counseling psychology suggests a place for prevention

---

D. PREVENTION IN COUNSELING PSYCHOLOGY ACCELERATES (IT SEEMS): 2000–CURRENT
2000 Donald Blocher identifies prevention as an "opportunity missed" by counseling psychology. He asks, "Where are counseling psychologists?"
2000 Prevention Section formally established within the Society of Counseling Psychology
2000 "Prevention in Counseling Psychology," a special issue of *The Counseling Psychologist* organized by John Romano and Sally Hage (vol. 28, no. 6). George Albee is among the respondents. Its publication represents an important milestone in counseling psychology
2000 A focus on prevention groups begins with "Recommendations of the APA Division 49 Task Force for the Use of Groups for Prevention" (Conyne, Chair), followed by "The Use of Groups for Prevention" special issue of the *Journal for Specialists in Group Work, 26,* coedited by Robert Conyne and Andy Horne, and by publications of Conyne (2004b), Conyne and Hage (2009), Conyne and Clanton Harpine (2010, including Hage and Romano's review of prevention groups), and Waldo, Schwartz, Horne, and Cote (2011).
2001 4th National Counseling Psychology Conference in Houston advances social justice, innovative approaches, and advocacy for the profession and for underserved populations
2004 Robert Conyne's *Preventive Counseling,* second edition published, 17 years after the first
2007 Best Practice Guidelines on Prevention by Sally Hage, John Romano, Robert Conyne, Maureen Kenny, Connie Matthews, Jonathon Schwartz, and Michael Waldo published in *The Counseling Psychologist* (vol. 35, no. 4)
2007 "Culturally Relevant Prevention," a major contribution to *The Counseling Psychologist* by Le'Roy Reese and Elizabeth Vera (vol. 35, no. 6)
2008 Process for seeking formal APA approval for Prevention Guidelines is launched
2008 5th National Counseling Psychology Conference in Chicago focuses on global and international initiatives
2008 Fourth edition of *Handbook of Counseling Psychology* is published; prevention tangentially included.
2009 *Realizing Social Justice: The Challenge of Preventive Interventions* published (Maureen Kenny, Andy Horne, Pamela Orpinas, & Le'Roy Reese, Eds.), heralding the integration of prevention interventions to further social justice
2009 *Prevention in Counseling Psychology: Theory, Research, Practice and Training* online journal is first published by Prevention Section of the Society of Counseling Psychology
2010 Robert Conyne adapts Albee's incidence model in *Prevention Program Development and Evaluation*
2010 Allen Ivey e-mail to Prevention Section Listserv (Feb. 2, 2010):
"I'd argue that all prevention efforts are social justice interventions. Prevention changes the way we think about ourselves and systems... THE REAL EFFECTIVENESS OF PSYCHOTHERAPY WILL SHOW UP WHEN WE ARE COMMITTED TO PREVENTION, NOT REMEDIATION!!" (capital letters retained).
2010 "Prevention Groups: Evidence-Based Approaches to Advance the Field," special issue coedited by Robert Conyne and Elaine Clanton Harpine, *Group Dynamics: Theory, Research, and Practice.*

Table 2.2 Some Important Markers for Prevention Per Se: 1854–Current

A. SOME ANTECEDENT EVENTS: 1854–1959

1854 Dr. John Snow removes London's Broad Street pump handle to prevent cholera

1935 Social Security Act

1951 Veterans Administration creates position of counseling psychologist

1952 American Personnel and Guidance Association is formed, changes name to American Association for Counseling and Development (1983) and then to current name, American Counseling Association (1992): self-identified as the association of "professional counselors"

1957 National Defense Education Act is established allowing for training thousands of school counselors and preparing counselors at the doctoral level

B. A FOMENTING DECADE STIMULATES CHANGE: 1960–1969

1960s Decade of accelerated change in areas of civil and women's rights, with antiwar protests and political activism at the forefront. Human potential movement begins to develop

1963 Community Mental Health Centers Act institutionalizes preventive interventions

1964 Gerald Caplan, known as the "Father of Preventive Psychiatry," describes primary, secondary, and tertiary prevention in *Principles of Preventive Psychiatry*, building on public health and epidemiological principles

1965 President Johnson's "Great Society" legislation

1965 Medicare, Medicaid Act

1965 Following the Swampscott Conference, Community Psychology is begun as an APA division with a focus on prevention in community settings

1966 Charles Whitman kills 14 and wounds 32 at the University of Texas, Austin, bringing increased attention and resources to campus mental health

C. PRIMARY PREVENTION EMERGES FROM THE CHANGE PERIOD: 1970–1979

1970 Caplan shows how mental health consultation can have preventive effects in *Theory and Practice of Mental Health Consultation*

1970s Human potential movement flourishes

1970 Julian Rappaport offers the "upstream" metaphor to emphasize prevention's before-the-fact approach

1973 Health Maintenance Organization Act (managed care)

1975 Annual Vermont Conferences on the Primary Prevention of Psychopathology begin

1977 President's Commission on Mental Health

1977 Julian Rappaport publishes *Community Psychology: Values, Research and Action*

1977 Donald Klein and Steven Goldston publish *Primary Prevention: An Idea Whose Time Has Come*

1978 President Carter establishes Commission on Mental Health with Task Force on Prevention

1979 *Healthy People: The Surgeon General's Report on Health Promotion and Disease Prevention* published (followed by updates in 1990, 2000, 2010, with 2020 being prepared)

D. PREVENTION SCHOLARSHIP EXPANDS AND FOCUSES: 1980–CURRENT

1980s and beyond: Epidemics such as AIDS, tuberculosis, hunger and starvation, malaria, and natural disasters (e.g., hurricanes, earthquakes, tornadoes) bring worldwide attention to the role of prevention, as do programs aimed at reducing incidence of such destructive behaviors as cigarette smoking and excessive drinking of alcohol

1980 Mental Health Systems Act

1981 Julian Rappaport publishes "In Praise of Paradox: A Social Policy of Empowerment Over Prevention"

1982 George Albee publishes his conceptualization for reducing incidence through prevention (increase strengths and decrease stressors)

1983 Robert Felner and colleagues coedit *Preventive Psychology: Theory, Research, and Practice*

1985 Emory Cowen defines person-centered approaches to primary prevention in mental health

1986 George Albee describes primary prevention's role in producing a "just society"

1987 Universal, selective, and indicated types of prevention are identified by Gordon, elaborated by Mrazek and Haggerty (1994), and adopted by the Institute of Medicine

1988 Richard Price and colleagues coedit APA edition, *14 Ounces of Prevention: A Casebook for Practitioners*, showing detailed evidence-influenced examples of how to do prevention

1993 Coie et al. publish the "Science of Prevention," containing recommendations to guide a national prevention research agenda

1996 Steven Brown and Robert Lent coedit first edition of the *Handbook of Counseling Psychology*, with the fourth edition published in 2008

Table 2.2 *(Continued)*

1997 Prevention Institute, a national nonprofit organization, was founded to serve as a focal point for primary prevention practice—promoting policies, organizational practices, and collaborative efforts that improve health and quality of life

1997 Joseph Durlak and Wells publish an influential meta-analysis of 177 prevention programs demonstrating that they produced 59% to 82% significantly more positive outcomes than realized by control group participants

1998 APA Presidential Task Force on Prevention: Promoting Strength, Resilience, and Health in Young People

1999 Siegel's work in interpersonal neurobiology initiates a line of promising research for prevention.

2000s Developmental-contextualism, ecological counseling, multicultural psychology, positive psychology, health promotion, health psychology, strength-based psychology, wellness, life skills, resilience, social justice, advocacy, stress, coping, and neuropsychology assume importance and influence prevention (and vice versa)

2003 Elizabeth Vera and Suzette Speight organize a major contribution in *The Counseling Psychologist* "Multicultural Competence, Social Justice, and Counseling Psychology: Expanding Our Roles" (vol. 31, no. 3).

2003 Thomas Gullotta and Martin Bloom from the discipline of social work publish *Encyclopedia of Primary Prevention and Health Promotion*

2004 Robert Conyne and Ellen Cook edit *Ecological Counseling*, a person-environment approach with prevention goals.

2006 Brent Mallinckrodt, newly appointed editor of the *Journal of Counseling Psychology* calls for studies of both prevention and remedial interventions with preference given to qualities related to assets, strengths, and positive adaptation

2006 Elsie Smith organizes "Strength-Based Counseling for Youth," a major contribution in *The Counseling Psychologist* (vol. 34, no. 1).

2006 Shane Lopez and colleagues organize a major contribution "Positive Aspects of Human Functioning: A Cornerstone of Counseling Psychology" in *The Counseling Psychologist* (vol. 34, no 2)

2006 Mental Health Parity Act provides for broader coverage of health, including mental health equivalence

2007 Keith Herman and colleagues provide a major contribution, "Culturally Sensitive Health Care and Counseling Psychology: An Overview," in *The Counseling Psychologist* (vol. 35, no. 5).

2010 Michelle Obama's leadership in "Let's Move," a multifaceted program to reduce childhood obesity, and California Governor Schwarzenegger's 2010 Health, Nutrition and Obesity Summit illustrate recent organized efforts that have heightened attention to prevention

2010 Passage of Patient Protection and Affordable Care Act (P.L. 111–148, March 23, 2010) and the Health Care and Education Reconciliation Act of 2010 (P.L. 111–152, March 30, 2010).

> individual can be assisted in making more effective use of them. (Gustad, 1953, cited in Whiteley, 1980, p. 19)
>
> Counseling psychology involves (a) the development of an individual's inner life…, (b) the individual's achievement of harmony with his [sic] environment…, and (c) the influencing of society to recognize individual differences and to encourage the fullest development of all persons within it. (American Psychological Association [APA], 1956, p. 283)
>
> Counseling psychology includes work with normal people and people having vocational and educational problems…trying to find an environment compatible with a client personality structure rather than to try to change his [sic] personality…the focus is on assets, strengths, possibilities for further development. Personality difficulties are dealt with only when they constitute obstacles to the individual's forward progress. (Tyler, Tiedeman, & Wrenn, 1961, pp. 6–7)

Three decades before counseling psychology became organized as a unique focus in psychology, marked by its designation as the Division of Counseling and Guidance in 1945, its adoption of a "scientist-practitioner" model of doctoral training at the Boulder Conference in 1949, and its adoption of the term "counseling psychology" at the Northwestern Conference in 1951, prevention's seeds were sown through the educational, social organizing, and mental hygiene innovations of Jesse B. Davis and Frank Parsons (1909), and Clifford Beers (1908). Their early contributions set the foundation for a counseling psychology to evolve being guided by attention to themes revolving around prevention, as well as treatment.

Some 60 years earlier (1854) during a raging cholera epidemic in London, Dr. John Snow traced the source of water being consumed by residents and found that those drinking water from one of those lines experienced unusually high rates of cholera. His simple but highly effective experimental intervention was to remove the handle from the Broad Street pump, thus denying polluted drinking water to users along that line, resulting in a noticeable plummeting in the incidence (rate of development of new cases) of cholera. This public health strategy (remove the source of disease) became a bedrock principle of prevention.

Gerald Caplan, revered as the "Father of Preventive Psychiatry," built on environmental change and other principles to initially shape prevention in mental health. His conception of a 3-tiered approach (Caplan, 1964), involving primary (i.e., before the appearance of a disorder), secondary (i.e., early in a disorder's progression), and tertiary prevention (i.e., repairing and restoring positive functioning) significantly altered understandings of mental health practice.

A Decade of Fomentation: The 1960s

The United States during the decade of the 1960s was rocking and reeling, lurching often perilously, through sometimes exciting and generally tumultuous times. The Vietnam War stimulated significant reactions both at home and abroad, including both peaceful and violent protests and demonstrations. Public discourse and demonstrations extended, as well, to civil and women's rights, and to young people's urgings for freedom and discovery. During the decade political assassinations cruelly cut short the lives of President John F. Kennedy, Senator Robert M. Kennedy, and Dr. Martin Luther King Jr. The "Great Society" of President Lyndon B. Johnson was introduced during this decade, as was the Community Mental Health Centers Act (noted for its mandate for preventive services), and Medicare and Medicaid. These initiatives, along with the Social Security Act of 1935, represented political strategies aimed at improving the economic and health status of Americans.

Throughout this decade of fomentation and change (only some of which has been touched on here) the Division of Community Psychology of the American Psychological Association was established at the Swampscott Conference in 1965, to become an association to embrace prevention and social change as primary foci. Also, counseling psychology's Greyston Conference in 1964 convened to clarify issues of professional identity and to project confidence in the profession and the status of counseling psychology.

Prevention Emerges in the 1970s

During the late 1960s and throughout the ensuing decade, prevention in mental health entered the professional practice and research arena, alongside the flourishing human potential movement. Notable accomplishments occurred in scholarly works and in political legislation.

Among the significant scholarly works that appeared were Gerald Caplan's (1964) identification of primary, secondary, and tertiary prevention in his *Principles of Preventive Psychiatry* (mentioned above) and his illustration of how mental health consultation can exert preventive effects in the *Theory and Practice of Mental Health Consultation* (1970); Julian Rappaport's (1977) influential text on community psychology, in which prevention was accorded a central role; and Donald Klein and Steven Goldston's (1977) compilation of papers endorsing primary prevention as an "idea whose time has come." (As it turns out, Klein and Goldston were more optimistic than realistic in their pronouncement.) The Vermont Conference on the Primary Prevention of Psychopathology began a series of meetings in 1975 that proved to be consequential in promoting research and practice in prevention. And the first in a continuing series of national reports on the nation's health, *Healthy People: The Surgeon General's Report on Health Promotion and Disease Prevention* (1979) was published (followed by updates in 1990, 2000, and 2010, with 2020 being prepared).

Mental health and prevention garnered political attention, also, during this time. In 1973 the Health Maintenance Organization Act was produced, giving rise to the appearance of health maintenance organizations (HMOs) and the promise, yet to be realized, of supporting preventive mental health. Toward the end of the decade, President Carter established the President's Commission on Mental Health, which contained a Task Force on Prevention.

Prevention initiatives also were produced by counseling psychologists. The Greyston Conference had spawned a number of attempts to define and refine counseling psychology and the roles and functions of counseling psychologists. At the end of the 1960s, Jordaan, Myers, Layton, and Morgan (1968) addressed the issue of roles for counseling psychologists inclusively. They defined three roles: (1) remedial, (2) developmental, and (3) *preventive* (italics added for emphasis). "Prevention" now had entered the counseling psychology lexicon. Others, such as Clack (1975), Haskell (1975), and Ivey (1976) began to define prevention as being proactive, with a focus on skill development and environmental change.

As if whooshing in to fill a vacuum, during the 1970s a small number of innovative and risk-taking college and university counseling/student development centers (notably the first of these, established at Colorado State University, followed by Illinois State University and a handful of others) experimented and engaged in an array of campus-based preventive interventions, directions that largely went against the grain at the time. In remarks given at the occasion of receiving APA Division 17's 2010 Prevention Section Lifetime Achievement Award (August 14, 2010), Ivey attested to the contrarian response to these early prevention activities, observing "I recall being roundly criticized by other counseling center directors for this prevention orientation—they asked 'Why aren't you in your office doing therapy?'"

These unique college and university counseling centers sought to augment the traditional remedially focused, individual-level delivery of service to students with developmental and preventive ones, aimed at students to be sure, but also at other campus populations and at the campus environment itself. These offerings included environmental assessment and change programs, the use of trained student paraprofessionals, psychoeducation, outreach services to residence halls, an expanded repertoire of groups, institutional research, and preventive consultation with campus administrators and faculty members. Significantly, these ongoing experiments also produced a body of literature supporting and describing them (e.g., Banning & Kaiser, 1974; Blocher, 1974; Conyne, 1975, 1978; Daher, Corazzini, & McKinnon, 1977; Ivey, 1976; Western Interstate Commission for Higher Education, 1972), illustrating a practitioner-scientist approach.

This comprehensive array of services emerged from the zeitgeist of the times emphasizing change and experimentation. One of the seminal scholarly products that emerged was the publication by Weston Morrill, Eugene Oetting, and James Hurst (1974) of the "Counseling Intervention Cube." This conceptual model clearly articulated remedial, developmental, and preventive goals for counseling interventions targeted at individual, group, and institutional levels that could be delivered directly or indirectly. It is my opinion that this document was one of the most momentous publications in the history of counseling psychology because of the comprehensive schema posited for conceptualizing counseling interventions and the prominent place it accorded those interventions intended to be preventive in their goals. Moreover, this document legitimized and gave impetus to the creative exploration of counseling psychology practice over decades. Two of the many sources appearing around this time included David Drum and Howard Figler's (1973) *Outreach in Counseling: Applying the Growth and Development Model in Schools and Colleges* and Judith Lewis and Michael Lewis's (1977, 1983) essential text *Community Counseling: A Human Services Approach* (which later morphed to Lewis, Lewis, Daniels, & D'Andrea's *Community Counseling: Empowerment Strategies for a Diverse Society*, first published in 2003).

Allen Ivey, a prolific contributor and substantive influencer of counseling psychology to this day, participated in the Colorado State University innovations occurring in its Student Development Center, the first one in the nation. As pointed out above, in 1976 Ivey was an early proponent of prevention being connected to social justice and economic inequities and he called for a psychoeducator approach to target these areas. Noting the explosion of practices being engaged in by counseling psychologists during the 1970s, Ivey was moved to identify counseling psychology as the most broadly based applied specialty in psychology.

Fast forward to February 3, 2010. Still feeling the passion, Ivey sent the following message to the Prevention Section Listserve:

> I'd argue that all prevention efforts are social justice interventions.
> Prevention changes the way we think about ourselves and systems ....
> THE REAL EFFECTIVENESS OF
> PSYCHOTHERAPY WILL
> SHOW UP WHEN WE ARE COMMITTED TO
> PREVENTION, NOT REMEDIATION!! (note: capital letters retained)

At the beginning of the next decade, John Whiteley (1980) edited a legacy volume summarizing critical developmental points in the origins and growth of counseling psychology, a source referenced often in the present chapter. In it, he gave considerable attention to the first two counseling psychology conferences (Northwestern, Greyston) and to how the field was being gradually conceptualized and refined. As I've pointed out, suggestive hints for prevention run throughout this period but it was not until the 1970s that prevention in counseling psychology received direct attention and support, however ambivalently.

Prevention Expands: 1980s–Current

1980–1989

Of course, calamities and disasters accompany the passage of time, striking with untold fury often at the most unexpected times—although, of course, there is never a "good" time. The 1980s and beyond seemed especially ripe for such fractious events. World epidemics such as AIDS ran amok. More localized epidemics, such as hunger and starvation, malaria, and tuberculosis scourged Africa and most other "Third World" countries. Natural disasters, such as Hurricane Katrina, the Haiti earthquakes, and tornadoes, cyclones, tsunamis, wildfires, and mudslides ravaged millions of people. Human-made disasters, such as the surprise attack on New York City's World Trade Center on September 11, 2001, and the episodic murders of students occurring at such locations as Columbine in Colorado and at Virginia Tech University shocked and devastated. Two wars, one in Iraq and the other in Afghanistan, ripped asunder not only bodies but also hearts and souls. Climate change debates and strategies captured the world's attention as never before with the realization that the health of our planet may be at stake. Unhealthy lifestyle choices, such as cigarette smoking, excessive alcohol consumption, poor nutrition, and lack of exercise, and thin or nonexistent social support systems contributed to the declining physical and mental health of millions of people in the United States and around the world. Indeed, all levels of Bronfenbrenner's (1979) ecosystem have been and are threatened.

Why mention any of this? Because each disastrous event in its own way, and all collectively, serve to bring attention to prevention. Were we ready? Are we prepared? How can we recover? Can the anguish and death of millions be prevented? How can we improve our lifestyles? Can global warming be averted? Can person-environment transactions become more harmonious?

It is against this backdrop that a number of prevention products appeared over the last 30 years. These publications sought to define, clarify, and strengthen the nascent field. A few representative examples will be discussed below.

The work of George Albee was of central importance. Among other contributions, Albee envisioned preventive interventions in mental health as the only way to reduce the incidence of a disorder (i.e., the number of new cases or the rate of development of any disorder) and that all other approaches, no matter how vitally important, were able to make only "after-the-fact" adjustments. He concretely operationalized incidence reduction in a strengths/stressors ratio, providing the means for prevention program design and evaluation to proceed planfully (Albee, 1982, 1985). A second, especially significant, contribution made by Albee was to closely connect prevention with social justice and system change (Albee, 1986). He believed that social pathogens were at the root of mental health problems and that these unhealthy conditions were located most frequently and intensely in poor communities. Ridding poverty and other forms of social and economic inequity from these communities is a preventive strategy of high priority, he urged.

Julian Rappaport, who had authored an already important text in community psychology (1977) suggested in his presidential address to the Division of Community Psychology (Rappaport, 1981) that empowerment is an essential process for any prevention effort. He insisted preventionists be careful to work *with* people not do things *to* them in projects that should aim toward promoting increased control by program participants over decisions and power in a community.

Through a series of insightful publications, Emory Cowen deepened the understanding of preventive mental health. His 1980, 1983, 1985, and 2000 discussions of person-centered preventive approaches were especially instrumental. Not to be confused with the person-centered counseling of Carl Rogers, Cowen's indicated that person-centered prevention strategies could proceed through two routes by helping people to: (1) anticipate and cope more positively with the stressful life situations they face, such as divorce; and (2) enhance their life competency skills through skill training, being involved in competency-facilitating experiences such as mentoring, and learning how to positively alter the major settings of their lives, such as school, work, and family.

An important prevention publication appearing within counselor education and counseling psychology during this time was the double issue of the *Personnel and Guidance Journal* coedited by Goodyear and Shaw (1984), "Primary Prevention in Schools" (vol. 62, no. 8) and "Primary Prevention on Campus and in the Community" (vol. 62, no. 9). These collections of articles demonstrated that preventive interventions were a reality throughout the educational system of the United States.

Conyne's (1987) text *Primary Preventive Counseling: Empowering People and Systems* followed three years later. It was perhaps the first one in counseling psychology and counselor education to specifically emphasize prevention. Although when I wrote it I thought that prevention within counseling psychology and counselor education was on the cusp of emerging strongly as a force (seemingly falling prey to the same misreading that afflicted Klein and Goldston 10 years earlier when they predicted then that "the time had come" for primary prevention), the fact that it took another 17 years for the second edition of this book to appear was one indication that a longer-range perspective was needed.

Also in 1987, the Third National Conference, known as the "Georgia Conference" (University of Georgia) met to define (if nothing else, counseling psychology, and counseling, are prone to bouts of redefinition) the future of counseling psychology. Along with asserting the importance of traditional approaches, considerable attention was given to proactive outreach, and working with diverse populations and emerging settings. Prevention, life-span development, skill building, and other "innovative and nontraditional functions" emerged among the themes of the conference, giving credence to their future viability.

Developmental counseling had begun to amass a literature base, noticeably starting with Blocher's (1966) first-edition text of that name. Fassinger and Schlossberg (1992), 26 years later, provided a particularly rich description of developmental counseling. Note its large overlap with definitions of prevention in counseling:

> Inherent in our philosophy is a non-pathological focus on normalcy and day-to-day problems of living with an emphasis on strengths in our clients.... We see ourselves as educators, we emphasize the empowerment of individuals, we value preventive as well as ameliorative intervention efforts and we work for enhanced functioning in all people... our scope includes environmental as well as individual intervention... the effective use of community resources and social political advocacy where appropriate .... We emphasize developmental approaches to working with people including attention to their sociocultural context and the influence of gender, race, age, ethnicity, sexual orientation, (dis) ability and socio-history. These characteristics give us the unique opportunity to be in the forefront... of... effective service delivery. (Brown & Lent, 1992, p. 244)

An influential and unique conception of prevention was developed by Gordon (1983), elaborated by Mrazek and Haggerty (1994), and adopted by the prestigious Institute of Medicine. This schema contrasted with the tripartite concept of primary, secondary, and tertiary prevention, yet still envisioned three types: (1) "universal," addressing an entire population, (2) "selective," addressing a subset of a population deemed to be at potential risk, and (3) "indicated," addressing another subset of a population deemed to be at clear risk.

Richard Price, Emory Cowen, Raymond Lorion, and Julia Ramos-McKay (1988) edited an APA-sponsored publication, *14 Ounces of Prevention: A Casebook for Practitioners*. Fourteen exemplary prevention programs occurring across the life span were selected from a thorough review of 300 submitted program proposals. Detailed descriptions of these effective prevention programs were intended to provide concrete guidance to benefit practice, teaching, and research. As a whole, these positively evaluated programs demonstrated that prevention could be delivered through carefully created, delivered, and monitored programs.

1990–1999

Designing and conducting prevention programs systematically and scientifically was addressed by Coie and his associates (1993) in the document, "The Science of Prevention." A national research agenda for prevention was set forth. This document presented a cogent argument for developing an evidence base for prevention, which has become an ongoing initiative in mental health and in preventive mental health.

For instance, Nancy Tobler published a number of studies, including meta-analyses (e.g., 1993) investigating the effectiveness of substance abuse prevention programs. Durlak and Wells (1997) were curious about prevention's evidence base and in 1997 they published a large meta-analysis of 177 prevention programs demonstrating that these programs produced 59% to 82% significantly more positive outcomes than realized by control group participants. In another large study, Nation et al. (2003) used a review-of-reviews approach to identify principles of prevention programs found to be effective. These principles include comprehensiveness, use of varied teaching methods, containing sufficient dosage, being theory driven, being delivered with appropriate timing, being socioculturally relevant, possessing outcome evaluation, and using well-trained staff.

In 1996 the Center for the Study and Prevention of Violence (CAPV; 2002–2004) at the University of Colorado at Boulder launched its "Blueprints for Violence Prevention" project. Employing sets of selection criteria, "model" and "promising" prevention programs—called "Blueprints"—are identified that have demonstrated effectiveness. The resulting online resource (http://www.colorado.edu/cspv/blueprints/) is easily accessible and provides researchers and program developers with useful guidance about prevention programs that work.

While evidence mounts for the effectiveness of prevention, the archival definition of counseling psychology (APA, 1999), which still is currently in place, does little more than hint at a place for prevention: "Psychoeducational/preventive programming" is identified as a procedure and technique for counseling psychology, which the statement indicates can be "preventive, skill enhancing, or remedial."

However, with some too-few positive exceptions, counseling psychology and counselor education curricula generally remain to be penetrated by either specialized courses in prevention or by courses in which prevention is infused (Conyne, Newmeyer, Kenny, Romano, & Matthews, 2008; Matthews, 2003, 2004). Hage and Romano (2010) drew from the 2009 APA Presidential Task Force on the Future of Psychology Practice, which noted that psychologists need expanded models of training to prepare them for "the new world psychology finds itself in" (Martin, 2009, p. 67). Certainly, expanded training in prevention is one such area for future development, which then means that room in already-crowded counseling psychology curricula needs to be made for prevention.

The lack of substantial curricula in counseling psychology devoted to prevention is not the only obstacle to be faced for prevention to be advanced. At this chapter's beginning I noted the conclusion by Mallinckrodt that published research in prevention from the years 2002–2006 (to be separated from the more voluminous amount of general scholarly work on the topic appearing in books and book chapters) was largely missing from the *Journal of Counseling Psychology* and *The Counseling Psychologist*. Indeed, a research review conducted by O'Byrne, Brammer, Davidson, and Poston (2002) supports that contention, showing that 52 of 4,028 articles (1.29%) published in 4 counseling journals during the period from 1985–1999 focused on primary prevention. Demonstrating that prevention works is an outstanding challenge that counseling psychology researchers need to pursue.

Yet a third large gap needs to be closed, in addition to curricula and research, and that is advocating that prevention becomes a core part of roles, functions, tasks, and positions that are assumed by counseling psychologists. As Hage and Romano (2010) observe, work involvement of counseling psychologists in prevention is fragmented, at best, and it seems to be decreasing over time (Fretz & Simon, 1992; Goodyear et al., 2008). For substantiation, they point to a random sample survey of counseling psychologists, reporting that only about one quarter of those responding (n = 167) engage in prevention/outreach activities (Goodyear et al., 2008). This figure can be compared to more than one third (n = 232, 35.9%) of counseling psychologists who participated in primary prevention activities 15 years earlier (Watkins, Lopez, Campbell, & Himmel, 1986). The apparent downward slope of prevention activity contrasts with an increasing level of attention being given to it, as measured by the quantity of scholarly production that has been accelerating since around 1980. Clearly, attention needs to be given to how counseling psychologists can deliver prevention in their work and to get properly paid for it. Health care reform may help spur and focus energies to this end.

2000–2010

Romano and Hage (2000) and Conyne (2000) both have issued "calls for action" to resolve and strengthen the place of prevention in counseling psychology. As Romano and Hage put it with regard to the archival definition of counseling psychology, there is a need to: "Modify the archival definition of counseling psychology... to clearly state prevention as a fundamental activity of the profession. In the current definition, prevention is suggested; it is time for prevention to be unambiguously identified as central to counseling psychology" (2000, p. 855).

During the new millennium, a number of expressions of what might be termed "positive mental health" appeared. These areas include: positive psychology, health promotion, health psychology, strength-based psychology, wellness, life skills, resilience, social justice, advocacy, stress reduction, coping, and aspects of neuropsychology. In addition, a number of publications addressed "system change," noticeably in the areas of social justice, multicultural counseling, and advocacy, as a medium for promoting health. Because both positive mental health and system change are fundamental elements of prevention, it seems ironic that prevention has not been included centrally within discussions of these concepts and approaches (the Kenny et al., 2009, resource on social justice and preventive interventions is a clear exception). One wonders, therefore:

"Where is prevention in these positive mental health and system change approaches?"

Before becoming jaded about the typical absence or limited presence of prevention in counseling psychology training and practice, we must note that all is not lost; it is heartening to note that momentum sped up for prevention in counseling psychology during the 2000s. The latest edition of Brown and Lent's *Handbook of Counseling Psychology* (2008) reached out, however modestly, to include prevention by giving it at least some tangential coverage, a gain not realized in previous editions. Recent summaries of prevention history compiled by Kenny and Romano (2009) and by Hage and Romano (2010) document the increasing pace of prevention activity and its recognition. Another clear marker of this progression was the formal establishment of the Prevention Section in 2000 within the Society of Counseling Psychology, to be discussed next.

In the past, counseling psychologists with strong prevention interests had made at least two other attempts to organize, but these did not prove to be sustainable. In the mid-1970s and for a period of about 5 years, several counseling psychologists and counselors working in college counseling centers established a Prevention Interest Group within Commission VII (College and University Counseling Centers) of the former edition of the American College Personnel Association that was located within the American Personnel and Guidance Association. Some of the participants included Jack Corazzini, Lois Huebner, Bob Conyne, Lynn Rapin, Jim Clack, Lou Ann Keating, Kathy Hamilton, Chuck Meade, and Steve Paul.

Approximately 20 years later within the Society of Counseling Psychology itself a Special Interest Group (SIG) in Prevention was formed, running from 1990 through formal incorporation as a Prevention Section in 2000 (special note: I thank John Romano for providing historical documentation for the SIG and beginning stages of the Section). In 1994 the SIG's name was expanded to become "Prevention and the Public Interest," thus combining two existing groups, the former Prevention SIG and the previous Public Interest Committee.

The objectives of the Prevention and Public Interest SIG were to network, to promote practice and research, to facilitate communication of the SIG within counseling psychology and with other APA groups, and to increase visibility of prevention and public policy initiatives. Early chairs of the SIG included EnaVasquez Nuttall, Stanley Baker, and John Romano; Robert Lent and Jeffrey Prince were active with the Public Interest committee, later to be known for one year (1994) as the Prevention Special Task Group (STG); its particular charge was to serve as liaison function of public interests with APA's Board for the Advancement of Psychology in the Public Interest (BAPPI) committees within the APA Public Interest Directorate.

In 1999, status was granted to the Prevention SIG (which, under John Romano's editorship, had been producing issues of a newsletter from spring 1993) as a Prevention Section-in-Formation. Movement toward Section status was then guided by a Provisional Organizing Committee comprised of Robert Conyne, Sally Hage, Maureen Kenny, John Romano, and Michael Waldo. The current Prevention Section was formally established within Division 17 in 2000. It has functioned effectively over these last 10 years and its future prospects appear to be viable. Its chairs have included John Romano (2000–2002), Michael Waldo (2002–2004), Maureen Kenny (2004–2006), Andy Horne (2006–2008), and Jonathon Schwartz (2008–2010). The Section functions within the Society of Counseling Psychology with approved bylaws, has elected officers, established in 2009 an online journal (*Prevention in Counseling Psychology: Theory, Research, Practice, and Treatment*), manages a Listserv, sponsors student research, and is spearheading the process of obtaining approval from APA for a comprehensive set of Prevention Guidelines. Starting in 2005 the Section annually honors Lifetime Achievement in Prevention winners. So honored to date have been: John Romano (2005), Robert Conyne (2006), Michael Waldo (2007), Steven Danish (2008), Maureen Kenny (2009), and Allen Ivey (2010). In addition, in 2008, special recognition was accorded posthumously to George Albee for his lifetime contributions to prevention. In 2009, Katherine Raczynski from the University of Georgia won the Graduate Student Prevention Research Award.

According to its Bylaws (2006), the purpose of the Prevention Section is to further the theory, research, teaching, and practice of prevention, advocacy, and public interest initiatives among counseling psychologists. The Section describes itself as incorporating a full array of preventive, developmental, policy, advocacy, and community-focused activities. Specific objectives of this Section, which mirror those of the Prevention and Public Interest SIG from which it came, are to: (1) Bring together counseling psychologists who have an interest in prevention through their teaching, practice, and/or research activities. The networking may occur through newsletters, convention programs, and/or individual communications; (2) Promote the practice and research of prevention within counseling psychology; (3) Facilitate communication between counseling psychology and other groups within APA, including APA's Public Interest Directorate and the Board for the Advancement of Psychology in the Public Interest (BAPPI); and (4) Give visibility to the teaching, practice, and research initiatives of counseling psychologists in their prevention, advocacy, and public policy activities.

At about the same time as the Prevention Section was being formed, Romano and Hage's (2000) major contribution in *The Counseling Psychologist*, "Prevention in Counseling Psychology," appeared, representing an important milestone in counseling psychology. Among other notable features, it presented a definition of prevention that included five dimensions (stop, delay, reduce, strengthen, and support) and set forth four major agenda for advancing prevention in counseling psychology: (1) increased use of integrative and systemic models and approaches, (2) greater emphasis on early preventive interventions with children and youth, (3) integrating preventive interventions with diversity, and (4) advancing training through attention to eight domains and sets of related skills that support the science and practice of prevention. That publication deserves much credit for nurturing and stimulating much of the prevention energy and output being witnessed in the Society of Counseling Psychology over the last decade.

The topic of "prevention groups" received considerable attention during this time period, initiated by the document "Recommendations of the APA Division Task Force for the Use of Groups for Prevention" (2000), chaired by Robert Conyne. Two special issues of group-oriented journals (in counseling and in psychology) focused on groups being used to accomplish prevention goals: (1) The *Journal for Specialists in Group Work* (2001) addressed "The Use of Groups for Prevention" (coedited by Robert Conyne and Andy Horne); and (2) *Group Dynamics: Theory, Research, and Practice* is set to publish "Prevention Groups: Evidence-Based Approaches to Advance the Field" (coedited by Robert Conyne and Elaine Clanton Harpine, 2010). Other publications focused on prevention groups included those by Conyne (2004b); Conyne and Hage (2009); Hage and Romano (2010); Waldo, Schwartz, Horne, and Cote (2011); and in the social work discipline a chapter by Nash and Snyder (2004).

In 2001 the 4th National Counseling Psychology Conference in Houston advanced social justice, innovative approaches, and advocacy for the profession and for underserved populations. *The Handbook for Social Justice in Counseling Psychology*, coedited by Rebecca Toporek, Larry Gerstein, Nadya Fouad, Gargi Roysircar, and Tania Israel, was one important example of the generativity spawned by the Houston Conference. Its introductory chapter, "Social Justice and Counseling Psychology in Context," by Fouad, Gerstein, and Toporek, provides a compelling rationale for their interconnection. Rattling around in all this exciting work is prevention—but one has to look fairly hard to find it. The Houston Conference was followed 7 years later by the Chicago Conference, where counseling psychology was asked to consider and advance its work in international and global affairs.

Enough scholarly work in prevention, however, had accumulated to easily support the compilation in 2003 of Thomas Gullotta and Martin Bloom's edited volume, *Encyclopedia of Primary Prevention and Health Promotion*. This extensive work (consuming 1,179 pages), organized from a social work perspective, demonstrates the breadth and depth of prevention practice and research and also serves to remind us that prevention is a multidisciplinary approach that both transcends and derives from several sources.

The Prevention Guidelines (Hage et al., 2007) referred to earlier were published in what was to become an award-winning article in *The Counseling Psychologist*. They contain suggestions for counseling psychologists about prevention practice, education, and research. In 2008 a work group of Prevention Section members, facilitated by Sally Hage and John Romano and including Maureen Kenny, Kris Varjas, Robert Conyne, Connie Matthews, Andy Horne, Anneliese Singh, Jonathon Schwartz, Michael Waldo, Ellen Vaughn, and Joel Wong, as well as interested others not involved in the Section, began reshaping the article's contents into the prescribed pattern for formally approved guidelines that is stipulated by APA Governance. Benefiting from procedural consultation provided by Terry Gock and initial review of its work by relevant APA committees, the final document was submitted by the Prevention Section work group to APA Governance in February, 2010, and is awaiting final results of the review process.

A series of prevention in counseling psychology volumes was published during the last half of the decade, beginning with the second edition of

Conyne's *Preventive Counseling* (2004a). A series of social justice–prevention sources also appeared, attesting to the growing importance of this linkage. Le'Roy Reese and Elizabeth Vera (2007) published a major contribution in *The Counseling Psychologist*, "Culturally Relevant Prevention," as did Keith Herman and associates (2007), "Culturally Sensitive Health Care and Counseling Psychology." Other important social justice and prevention resources include chapters by Vera and Speight (2003), Speight and Vera (2008), and by Vera, Buhim, and Isacco (2009); Rebecca Toporek et al.'s (2006) *Handbook for Social Justice in Counseling Psychology*; and Maureen Kenny, Andy Horne, Pamela Orpinas, and Le'Roy Reese's (2009) edited work *Realizing Social Justice: The Challenge of Preventive Interventions*. The Preface to that book by the coeditors and its initial chapter (Kenny & Romano, 2009) clearly project the positive correlation between social justice and prevention.

Positive psychology, like social justice, represents a scholarly and practice domain connected closely to both counseling psychology and to prevention. A number of publications in the area of positive psychology emerged during this period, as well. Examples include Seligman's *Authentic Happiness* (2002a) and two edited volumes by Snyder and Lopez, their *Handbook of Positive Psychology* (2002), and *Positive Psychology: The Scientific and Practical Explorations of Human Strengths* (2007). Connections of positive psychology with both counseling psychology (Lopez & Edwards, 2008; Lopez et al. 2006; Smith, 2006) and with prevention (e.g., Conyne, 2004a; Seligman, 2002b) have been highlighted, yet await significantly fuller development. Conyne's (2010) book on program development and evaluation processes applied to prevention demonstrates the reliance of prevention programming on planning and evaluation processes.

Future Directions

The most recent report of the US surgeon general, focusing on the prevention of obesity, clearly documents the essential role of broad-scale prevention practices in promoting optimal health. It further provides a stellar instance of how prevention has taken hold at the highest levels of health policy and research as a key goal and set of strategies in health care. The following quotation is illustrative of the surgeon general's report (US Department of Health and Human Services, 2010):

> Interventions to prevent obesity should focus not only on personal behaviors and biological traits, but also on characteristics of the social and physical environments that offer or limit opportunities for positive health outcomes. Critical opportunities for interventions can occur in multiple settings: home, child care, school, work place, health care, and community. (p. 5)

The relationship between personal behaviors, biological traits, and social and physical environments is being deepened and expanded through exciting studies in the area of neuroscience, interpersonal neurobiology, and epigenetics. Siegel's (1999) introduction of research in interpersonal neurobiology (IPNB) holds considerable promise for prevention programs using an interpersonal or group-delivery format. See Gantt and Cox (2010) for some emerging leads. Promising and significant advancements will continue to occur in the broad area of neuroscience as they relate to health research, practice, and training—including prevention.

As one example, Edith Chen and colleagues (Chen, 2010) study how psychosocial and psychobiological pathways contribute to socioeconomic status and to physical health outcomes for children. They have consistently found that poorer health is associated with those who are low, as compared to high, in socioeconomic status (SES). Their findings indicate that this relationship applies whether health is measured as the prevalence rate of illness, the severity of illness, or the likelihood of mortality. Socioeconomic status also is involved with most types of diseases, and for many risk factors for diseases. Chen indicates that this relationship is found in many countries, including those with and those without universal health care, and it has been demonstrated across the life span, from childhood to older adulthood.

In short, research conducted with healthy people and with those suffering from certain diseases, such as asthma, demonstrate that exposure to certain environmental stimuli early in life programs biological systems that affect physical health throughout the lifecourse. One assumes that analogous patterns also may apply to mental and emotional functioning. Thus, this and similar neuroscience research suggest that exposure in early childhood to low SES, when patterns of immune responsivity are being developed and established, can become fixed through epigenetic modifications. Implications for prevention theory, research, practice, and training remain to be unearthed.

Electronic technologies present promising ways through which prevention and promotion activity can be pursued for positive ends (note: as with any technology, adverse uses also can occur; cyber bullying provides a clear example). Wii applications provide users with opportunities to virtually play sports, such as bowling, downhill skiing or baseball, and health promotion exercises, such as yoga and balancing (Lazarus, 2010). Senior citizen centers are just one of many settings where Wii is being used to support the health of its users. Personal health records (PHRs), such as those by Google Health, WebMD Health Manager, and Microsoft Healthvault, allow users to monitor and measure a number of health indices, such as cholesterol (Borzo, 2010). Social networking vehicles, such as Facebook and Twitter, among others, allow users to connect and communicate, thus offering the potential to maintain and enhance relationships virtually. Smartphone applications are available for mental health professionals to monitor and support clients between sessions and to provide users with the ability to chart their mood, energy level, diet, sleep patterns, and stress management activities (Versel, 2010). Further developments in health-oriented electronic vehicles and applications can be expected to occur in the future, along with the possibilities for prevention.

At the macro level national health care reform has been signed into law by the president in the form of the Patient Protection and Affordable Care Act (P.L. 111–148 on March 23, 2010) and the Health Care and Education Reconciliation Act of 2010 (P.L. 111–152 on March 30, 2010). The following discussion underscores the inevitable connection of prevention with political processes; not all readers may agree with the perspective I will take.

The American Psychological Association's CEO, Norman Anderson, noted several gains for psychology in health care reform (2010, April 7) in the following broad categories: (1) integrated health care, (2) mental and behavioral health care, (3) *prevention and wellness* (italics added for emphasis), (4) psychology workforce development, (5) *elimination of health disparities* (again, italics added), (6) support for psychological research, and (7) involvement with consumers, families, and caregivers.

Let's return to the two areas I highlighted of the seven listed. Prevention and wellness indicators include eliminating cost-sharing for eligible health services; expanding prevention and wellness initiatives targeting depression, elder abuse, and postpartum conditions; and directing the Clinical Preventive Services Task Force to consider best practices presented by scientific societies when developing recommendations. In terms of eliminating health disparities, indicators include collecting data and developing quality measures to proceed in eliminating health disparities, and developing a national strategy to improve delivery of health care services and outcomes in patient health.

Of course, in a larger sense, the two health care reform acts are preventive in scope by their very nature, for they are aimed at extending health care coverage to millions of uninsured persons, reducing health care costs for those who do and do not have insurance, and ending discriminatory practices surrounding issues such as preexisting conditions. The parity provision to equate mental and behavioral health care with medical and surgical services also clearly supports a preventive agenda. These prevention initiatives within the health care reform package build on decades of hard work by countless numbers of researchers, practitioners, advocates, politicians, and citizens.

How will counseling psychology mesh with this significant change in the national health care fabric? Momentum is building both within the profession and in health care to support prevention. Counseling psychology has stood rather flat-footed before in its capacity to assertively pursue a prevention agenda. Predictions about "the time for prevention having finally arrived" have fallen far short over the decades. In brief, the history of prevention in counseling psychology is replete with false starts and with assertions of support unmatched by continuous action. As a result, counseling psychology training and practice in prevention still lag, even though publications have been markedly increasing.

This erratic track record led scholars such as Blocher, as I pointed out earlier, to pointedly wonder where counseling psychologists were when advancements occurred within prevention itself and in related areas, such as positive psychology, occupational health and safety, and developmental human ecology. Indeed, as he observed in 2000, many opportunities were missed. Calls and resolutions for action have been sounded to activate a counseling psychology that strongly integrates prevention within it and connects with public issues and policy. Doing so will address Vera's (2000) plea, mentioned at the outset of this chapter, for counseling psychology to become more of what it really is.

At the start of this chapter I brought to your attention the frequent use of the operant verb, "hope," when discussing the future of prevention in counseling psychology. Indeed, prevention itself is a very hopeful concept. Moreover, we know, as I pointed out earlier, that hope and its close cousin, optimism, are critically important factors in promoting growth and change. Yet, hope also must be complemented by intentionality and by concerted action, too, if sustainable change is to be realized.

Two quotations come to mind about hope that I think are pertinent for prevention in counseling psychology. Anne Lamott has written, "Hope begins in the dark, the stubborn hope that if you just show up and try to do the right thing, the dawn will come. You wait and watch and work: You don't give up." And the second, by Barack Obama: "Hope is that thing inside us that insists, despite all the evidence to the contrary, that something better awaits us if we have the courage to reach for it, work for it, and fight for it." It is necessary to buttress hope with purposeful and continuous action.

Although it's been said before, even by me more than once in print, "the time *is* now" for prevention to flourish in counseling psychology and as a national agenda force for change in health care. The conditions seem especially ripe for its full emergence, with a series of impressive scholarly works spurring and reflecting increasing attention to prevention in the profession, and with the passage of the national health care reform acts contributing to a more supportive societal context for it to be applied. The hard work awaits of making room in jam-packed counseling psychology curricula for prevention training and of developing roles and functions—that generate wages—for counseling psychologists to apply prevention.

References

Albee, G. (1982). Preventing psychopathology and promoting human potential. *American Psychologist, 37,* 1043–1050.

Albee, G. (1985). The argument for primary prevention. *Journal of Primary Prevention, 5,* 213–219.

Albee, G. (1986). Toward a just society: Lessons from observations on the primary prevention of psychopathology. *American Psychologist, 41,* 891–898.

American Psychological Association. (1956). Division of Counseling Psychology, Committee on Definition. Counseling psychology as a specialty. *American Psychologist, 11,* 282–285. Cited in J. Whiteley (Ed.), *History of counseling psychology,* 1980, p. 283.

American Psychological Association. (1999). Archival description of counseling psychology. *The Counseling Psychologist, 27,* 589–592.

Anderson, N. (2010, April 7). American Psychological Association Health Care Reform Activities Update. Retrieved April 8, 2010, from http://mail.google.com/mail/?hl=en&tab=wm#search/Norman+Anderson/127da1288f6c018a

Banning, J., & Kaiser, L. (1974). An ecological perspective and model for campus design. *Personnel and Guidance Journal, 52,* 370–375.

Beers, C. W. (1908). A *mind that found itself: An autobiography.* New York: Longmans, Green.

Blocher, D. (1966). *Developmental counseling.* New York: Ronald Press.

Blocher, D. (1974). Toward an ecology of student development. *Personnel and Guidance Journal, 52,* 360–365.

Blocher, D. (2000). *The evolution of counseling psychology.* New York: Springer.

Borzo, J. (2010, October 25). Tracking your health. *The Wall Street Journal,* R-7.

Bronfenbrenner, U. (1979). *The ecology of human development.* Cambridge, MA: Harvard University Press.

Brown, S., & Lent, R. (Eds.). (1992). *Handbook of counseling psychology* (2nd. ed.). New York: Wiley.

Brown, S., & Lent, R. (Eds.). (2008). *Handbook of counseling psychology* (4th ed.). New York: Wiley.

Bylaws. (2006). Prevention: A Section of the Division of Counseling Psychology (17) of the American Psychological Association. Retrieved April 12, 2010, from http://www.div17.org/preventionsection/bylaws.htm

Caplan, G. (1964). *Principles of preventive psychiatry.* New York: Basic Books.

Caplan, G. (1970). *The theory and practice of mental health consultation.* New York: Basic Books.

Center for the Study and Prevention of Violence. (2002–2004). *Blueprints for violence prevention.* Retrieved September 24, 2008, from http://www.colorado.edu/cspv/blueprints/

Chen, E. (2010). Psychological determinants of health laboratory. Retrieved September 9, 2010, from http://www2.psych.ubc.ca/~healthpsych/edith.htm

Clack, R. J. (1975). *Report of the Midwest Subcommittee on Prevention* paper. Counseling Center, Illinois State University, Bloomington-Normal. Cited in J. Whiteley (Ed.), *The history of counseling psychology,* 1980, p. 201. Monterey, CA: Brooks/Cole.

Coie, J., Watt, N., West, S., Hawkins, J., Asarnow, J., Markman, H., . . . Long, B. (1993). The science of prevention: A conceptual framework and some directions for a national research program. *American Psychologist, 48,* 1013–1022.

Conyne, R. (1975). Mapping for counselor action. *Personnel and Guidance Journal, 54,* 150–155.

Conyne, R. (1978). An analysis of student-environment mismatches. *Journal of College Student Personnel, 19,* 461–465.

Conyne, R. (1987). *Primary preventive counseling: Empowering people and systems.* Muncie, IN: Accelerated Development.

Conyne, R. (2000). Prevention in counseling psychology: At long last, has the time now come? *The Counseling Psychologist, 28,* 838–844.

Conyne, R. (2004a). *Preventive counseling: Helping people to become empowered in systems and settings* (2nd ed.). New York: Brunner-Routledge.

Conyne, R. (2004b). Prevention groups. In J. DeLucia-Waack, D. Gerrity, C. Kalodner, & M. Riva (Eds.), *Handbook of group counseling and psychotherapy* (pp. 621–629). Thousand Oaks, CA: Sage.

Conyne, R. (2010). *Prevention program development and evaluation: An incidence reduction, culturally-relevant approach.* Thousand Oaks, CA: Sage.

Conyne, R., & Clanton Harpine, E. (Eds.). (2010). Prevention groups: Evidence-based approaches to advance the field

[Special issue]. *Group Dynamics: Theory, Research, and Practice, 14,* 193–280.

Conyne, R., & Cook, E. P. (Eds.). (2004). *Ecological counseling: An innovative approach to conceptualizing person-environment interaction.* Alexandria, VA: American Counseling Association.

Conyne, R., & Hage, S. (2009). Prevention groups. In B. Erford (Ed.), *The ACA encyclopedia of counseling* (pp. 406–407). Alexandria, VA: American Counseling Association.

Conyne, R., & Horne, A. (Eds.). (2001). The use of groups for prevention [Special issue]. *Journal for Specialists in Group Work, 26,* 205–292.

Conyne, R., Newmeyer, M., Kenny, M., Romano, J., & Matthews, C. (2008). Two key strategies for teaching prevention: Specialized course and infusion. *Journal of Primary Prevention, 29,* 375–401.

Cowen, E. (1980). The wooing of primary prevention. *American Journal of Community Psychology, 8,* 254–284.

Cowen, E. (1983). Primary prevention in mental health: Past, present, and future. In R. Felner, L. Jason, J. Moritsugu, & S. Faber (Eds.), *Preventive psychology: Theory, research, and practice* (pp. 11–25). New York: Pergamon.

Cowen, E. (1985). Person-centered approaches to primary prevention in mental health: Situation-focused and competence-enhancement. *American Journal of Community Psychology, 13,* 31–49.

Cowen, E. (2000). Community psychology and routes to psychological wellness. In J. Rappaport & E. Seidman (Eds.), *Handbook of community psychology* (pp. 79–99). New York: Kluwer.

Daher, D., Corazzini, J., & McKinnon, R. (1977). An environmental redesign program for residence halls. *Journal of College Student Personnel, 18,* 11–15.

Drum, D., & Figler, H. (1973). *Outreach in counseling: Applying the growth and prevention model in schools and colleges.* New York: Intext.

Durlak, J., & Wells, A. (1997). Primary prevention programs for children and adolescents: A meta-analytic review. *American Journal of Community Psychology, 25,* 115–152.

Fassinger, R. E. & Schlossberg, N. K. (1992). Understanding the adult years: Perspectives and implications. In S. Brown & R. Lent (Eds.), *Handbook of counseling psychology* (2nd ed., pp. 217–250). New York: John Wiley.

Felner, R., Jason, L., Moritsugu, J., & Farber, S. (1983). *Preventive psychology: Theory, research, and practice.* New York: Pergamon.

Fretz, B., & Simon, N. (1992). Professional issues in counseling psychology: Continuity, change and challenge. In S. D. Brown & R. W. Lent (Eds.), *Handbook of counseling psychology* (2nd ed., pp. 3–36). New York: Wiley.

Gantt, S., & Cox, P. (Eds.). (2010). Neurobiology and building interpersonal systems: Groups, couples, and beyond [Special issue]. *International Journal of Group Psychotherapy, 60,* 455–604.

Goodyear, R., Murdock, N., Lichtenberg, J., McPherson, R., Koetting, K., & Petren, S. (2008). Stability and change in counseling psychologists' identities, roles, functions, and career satisfaction across 15 years. *The Counseling Psychologist, 36,* 220–249.

Gordon, R. (1983). An operational classification of disease prevention. *Public Health Reports, 98,* 107–109.

Gullotta, T., & Bloom, M. (Eds.). (2003). *Encyclopedia of primary prevention and health promotion.* New York: Kluwer.

Gustad, J. (1953). The definition of counseling. In R. F. Berdie (Ed.), *Minnesota Studies in Student Personnel Work, 3. Roles and relationships in counseling.* Cited in J. Whiteley (Ed.), *The history of counseling psychology,* 1980, p. 19.

Hage, S., & Romano, J. (2010). History of prevention in groups: Legacy for the 21st century. In R. Conyne & E. Clanton Harpine (Eds.), Prevention groups: Evidence-based approaches to advance the field [Special issue], *Group Dynamics: Theory, Research, and Practice, 14,* 199–210.

Hage, S., Romano, J., Conyne, R., Kenny, M., Matthews, C., Schwartz, J., & Waldo, M. (2007). Best practice guidelines on prevention practice, research, training, and social advocacy for psychologists. *The Counseling Psychologist, 35,* 493–566.

Haskell, E. (1975). *Prevention: A program dimension for college and university counselors.* Report of the Western Subcommittee on Prevention. Unpublished paper, Counseling Center, San Francisco State College. Cited in J. Whiteley (Ed.), *The history of counseling psychology,* 1980, pp. 201–202.

Herman, K., Tucker, C., Ferdinand, L., Mirsu-Paun, A., Hansan, N., & Beato, C. (2007). culturally sensitive health care and counseling psychology: An overview. *The Counseling Psychologist, 35,* 633–649.

Ivey, A. (1976). Counseling psychology, the psychoeducator model and the future: A definition in 1976. In J. Whiteley (Ed.), *The history of counseling psychology,* 1980, 196–204.

Ivey, A. (2010, February 3). Communication to Prevention Section listserv. http://mail.google.com/mail/?hl=en&tab=wm#search/Ivey/126950a5ac0f3d15

Jordaan, J., Myers, R., Layton, W., & Morgan, H. (1968). The counseling psychologist: A definition in 1968. In J. Whiteley (Ed.), *The history of counseling psychology,* 1980, 179–195.

Kenny, M., & Romano, J. (2009). Promoting positive development and social justice through prevention: A legacy to the future. In M. Kenny, A. Horne, P. Orpinas, & Reese (Eds.), *Realizing social justice: The challenge of preventive interventions* (pp. 17–36).

Klein, D., & Goldston, S. (Eds.). (1977). *Primary prevention: An idea whose time has come.* Rockville, MD: National Institute of Mental Health.

Lazarus, M. (2010, January 14). The most heart healthy Wii games. Retrieved October 31, 2010, from http://www.healthgamers.com/2010/research-theory/the-most-heart-healthy-wii-games/

Lewis, J., & Lewis, M. (1977, 1983). *Community counseling: A human services approach.* New York: Wiley.

Lewis, J., Lewis, M., Daniels, J., & D'Andrea, M. (2003). *Community counseling: Empowerment strategies for a diverse society.* Pacific Grove, CA: Brooks/Cole.

Lopez, S., & Edwards, L. (2008). The interface of counseling psychology and positive psychology: Assessing and promoting strengths. In S. Brown & R. Lent (Eds.), *Handbook of counseling psychology* (4th ed., pp. 86–102). New York: Wiley.

Lopez, S., Magyar-Moe, J., Petersen, S., Ryder, J., Krieshok, T., O'Byrne, K., Lichtenberg, J., & Fry, N. (2006). Counseling psychology's focus on positive aspects of human functioning. *The Counseling Psychologist, 34,* 205–227.

Martin, S. (2009). Roadmap for change: An APA task force previews its recommendations for transforming psychology practice to meet the demands of a new world. *Monitor on Psychology, 40,* 66–67.

Matthews, C. (2003, August). Training for prevention competency in counseling psychology. In M. Kenny (Chair), *Competencies for prevention training in counseling psychology.* Symposium presented at the 111th Annual Convention of the American Psychological Association, Toronto, Ontario, Canada.

Matthews, C. (2004). *Counseling and prevention: How is the field doing?* Unpublished manuscript.

McNeil, B., & Ingram, J. (1983). Prevention and counseling psychology: A survey of training practices. *The Counseling Psychologist, 11,* 95–96.

Morrill, W., Oetting, E., & Hurst, J. (1974). Dimensions of counselor functioning. *Personnel and Guidance Journal, 52,* 354–359.

Mrazek, P., & Haggerty, R. (Eds.). (1994). *Reducing risks for mental disorders: Frontiers for preventive intervention.* Washington, DC: National Academy Press.

Nash, J. K., & Snyder, S. (2004). Prevention groups. In C. Garvin, L. Gutierrez, & M. Galinky (Eds.) *Handbook of social work with groups* (pp. 176–194). New York: Guilford Press.

Nation, M., Crusto, C., Wandersman, A., Kumpfer, K., Seybolt, Morrissey-Kane, E., & Davino, K. (2003). What works in prevention: Principles of effective prevention programs. *American Psychologist, 58,* 449–456.

O'Byrne, K., Brammer, S., Davidson, M., & Poston, W. (2002). Primary prevention in counseling psychology. *The Counseling Psychologist, 34,* 330–344.

Parsons, F. (1909). *Choosing a vocation.* Boston: Houghton Mifflin.

Price, R., Cowen, E., Lorion, R., & Ramos-McKay, J. (Eds.). (1988). *14 ounces of prevention: A casebook for practitioners.* Washington, DC: American Psychological Association.

Rappaport, J. (1977). *Community psychology: Values, research, and action.* New York: Holt, Rinehart, and Winston.

Rappaport, J. (1981). In praise of paradox: A social policy of empowerment over prevention. *American Journal of Community Psychology, 9,* 1–25.

Recommendations of the Task Force for the Use of Groups for Prevention (R. Conyne, Chair) (2000). Division 49, American Psychological Association.

Reese, L., & Vera, E. (2007). Major contribution: Culturally-relevant prevention: The scientific and practical considerations of community-based programs. *The Counseling Psychologist, 35,* 763–778.

Romano, J., & Hage, S. (2000). Major contribution: Prevention in counseling psychology. *The Counseling Psychologist, 28,* 733–763.

Seligman, M. (2002a). *Authentic happiness: Using the new positive psychology to realize your potential for lasting fulfillment.* New York: Free Press.

Seligman, M. (2002b). Positive psychology, positive prevention, and positive therapy. In C. Snyder & S. Lopez (Eds.), *Handbook of positive psychology* (pp. 3–12). New York: Oxford University Press.

Shaw, M., & Goodyear, R. (Eds.). (1984). Primary prevention in schools; Primary prevention in campus and the community. *Personnel and Guidance Journal,* 62.

Siegel, D. (1999). *The developing mind.* New York: Guilford.

Smith, E. (2006). The strength-based counseling model. *The Counseling Psychologist, 34,* 13–79.

Snyder, C., & Lopez, S. (Eds.). (2002). *Handbook of positive psychology.* New York: Oxford University Press.

Snyder, C., & Lopez, S. (Eds.). (2007). *Positive psychology: The scientific and practical explorations of human strengths.* Thousand Oaks, CA: Sage.

Speight, S., & Vera, E. (2008). Social justice and counseling psychology: A challenge to the profession. In S. Brown, & R. Lent (Eds.), *Handbook of counseling psychology* (4th ed., pp. 54–67). New York: Wiley.

Toporek, R., Gerstein, L., Fouad, N., Roysircar, G. & Israel, T. (Eds.). (2006). *Handbook for social justice in counseling psychology: Leadership, vision, and action.* Thousand Oaks, CA: Sage.

Tyler, L., Tiedeman, D., & Wrenn, C. G. (1961). The current status of counseling psychology. Unpublished paper. Cited in J. Whiteley (Ed.), *The history of counseling psychology*, 1980, p. 8. Monterey, CA: Brooks/Cole.

US Department of Health and Human Service. (2010, January). *The surgeon general's vision for a healthy and fit nation: 2010.* Rockville, MD: US Department of Health and Human Services, Office of the Surgeon General. Retrieved September 9, 2010, from http://www.surgeongeneral.gov

Vera, E. (2000). A recommitment to prevention work in counseling psychology. *The Counseling Psychologist, 28,* 829–837.

Vera, E., Buhim, L., & Isacco, A. (2009). The role of prevention in psychology's social justice agenda. In M. Kenny, A. Horne, P. Orpinas, & L. Reese (Eds.), *Realizing social justice: The challenge of preventive interventions.* (pp. 79–96). Washington, DC: American Psychological Association.

Vera, E., & Speight, S. (2003). Multicultural competence, social justice, and counseling psychology: Expanding our roles. *The Counseling Psychologist, 31,* 253–272.

Versel, N. (2010, June 6). Smartphone apps serve as "electronic therapist" for mental health patients. Retrieved October 31, 2010, from http://www.fiercemobilehealthcare.com/story/smartphone-apps-serve-electronic-therapist-mental-health-patients/2010-06-01

Waldo, M., Schwartz, J., Horne, A., & Cote, L. (2011). Prevention groups. In R. Conyne (Ed.), *Oxford handbook of group counseling* (pp. 452–468). New York: Oxford University Press.

Watkins, C., Lopez, F., Campbell, V., & Himmel, C. (1986). Contemporary counseling psychology: Results of a national survey. *Journal of Counseling Psychology, 33,* 301–309.

Western Interstate Commission for Higher Education (WICHE). (1972). *The ecosystem model: Designing campus environments.* Boulder, CO: Author.

Whiteley, J. (Ed.). (1980). *The history of counseling psychology.* Monterey, CA: Brooks/Cole.

CHAPTER

3 Prevention in the 21st Century

John L. Romano

Abstract

The importance of prevention and the future of prevention research and applications in the 21st century are explored in this chapter. Specifically, eight areas that promise to be important for the future growth and development of prevention science in the years ahead are reviewed. The eight areas are: evidence-supported prevention practices, prevention and neuroscience and genetics, prevention and technology, prevention and elder populations, education and training for prevention, economics of prevention, prevention in health care settings, and multidisciplinary and community partnerships. Each of these areas is reviewed emphasizing prevention psychology generally, and counseling psychology specifically. Examples are provided for roles for psychology, and the potential for prevention research and interventions. The chapter discusses the importance of psychologists collaborating with professionals from other disciplines to understand how advances in new knowledge will affect prevention science in the future, not only in the United States but also internationally.

Key Words: prevention, prevention psychology, counseling psychology, prevention in the 21st century, prevention applications, prevention research

Prevention in the 21st Century

Prevention and its impact promises to expand exponentially throughout the 21st century. This optimistic prediction is based on the increasing recognition of the importance of prevention among the lay public, among scholars from many academic disciplines, and among professionals across different societal institutions and community contexts. The prediction is also based on changing demographics, such as the aging of the US population and an increase of US ethnic minorities. Some of the topics highlighted in this chapter demonstrate how prevention science can increase the quality of life as people age, and how prevention can help to reduce health and educational disparities between White and non-White population groups.

It is very encouraging that recent US national legislation supports prevention. For example, the 2010 Patient Protection and Affordable Care Act (PPACA) (www.healthcare.gov) provides for preventive services such as screening and counseling to prevent physical and mental health problems. PPACA also requires insurers to pay for evidence-based prevention services at no cost to the patient. Counseling services can include interventions to stop smoking, treat depression, and change lifestyle behaviors that negatively affect health (e.g., increase physical activity, develop healthy eating habits, reduce stress, etc.). Examples of other prevention activities provided by PPACA are counseling for healthy pregnancy and well-baby services for infants and children. Other federal legislation supportive of prevention includes the 2008 Mental Health Parity and Addiction Equity Act (www.hhs.gov). This law requires that group health plans provide the same insurance coverage for physical health, mental health, and addiction services. At state and local levels, laws and policies have been enacted to restrict cigarette use in public places, to increase healthy food choices in school buildings, and support anti-bullying policies. Internationally, many similar preventive efforts are taking place to improve the quality of life and to prevent mental and physical health problems across the globe (www.who.int/en/). Thus, while challenges will continue to exist in promoting and implementing a prevention agenda in the academy and society, there are reasons to be optimistic about the future of prevention in psychology and the other health sciences.

This chapter will discuss current and future opportunities for prevention research, teaching, and applications in the 21st century, recognizing that previous barriers will likely give way to new challenges. The chapter will briefly review the history of prevention from the 20th to the 21st century, especially as the history relates to counseling psychology and the future of prevention within psychology. Attention will then turn to recent research and other forms of scholarship and activities in prevention science, showing how population and political changes in the 21st century will demand and support greater attention to prevention. The main body of the chapter will discuss several areas for expansion and opportunity for prevention science during the 21st century.

Prevention will be discussed across multiple contexts and disciplines. In order to clarify definitions, the following terms used in the chapter are defined as follows:

- Health: A state of complete physical, mental, and social well-being and not merely the absence of disease or infirmity. Defined by the World Health Organization (WHO) Constitution (www.who.int/hac/about/definitions/en/index.html).
- Prevention: Stop a problem before it occurs; reduce the risk of a problem occurring; reduce the impact of an existing problem; strengthen knowledge, attitudes, and behaviors that promote physical and emotional well-being (i.e., enhance protective factors); and support institutional, community, and government actions that promote physical and emotional well-being (Romano & Hage, 2000).
- Prevention Psychologist: Psychologist who emphasizes prevention work in her/his research, practice, teaching, and/or community engagement and outreach.
- Prevention Science: Multidisciplinary field that involves the theory, research, and practice related to the prevention of social, physical, and mental health problems (National Research Council and Institute of Medicine, 2009).

Prevention from the 20th to the 21st Century

Prevention has realized much progress during the 20th century, including advances in the health sciences, psychological specialties, social welfare system, and in the political arena. The history of prevention has been detailed by several authors (e.g., Conyne, 2004; Kenny & Romano, 2009; National Research Council and Institute of Medicine, 2009; Romano & Hage, 2000; Spaulding & Balch, 1983), and a chapter in this handbook chronicles the history of prevention specifically within counseling psychology (see Chapter 2, this volume). Therefore, a detailed history will not be repeated here. However, it is important to note that different historical accounts of prevention emphasize different components of the history. Cumulatively, the history shows the number of disciplines, scholars, and events that have shaped and influenced the study and application of prevention during the last 100 years. Prevention pioneers and recent scholars have laid a strong foundation on which prevention science can build in the years ahead.

The human services professions gained momentum during the 20th century through their promotion of social activism. Historians of counseling psychology highlight the early 20th-century social reform movements of vocational guidance (e.g., Frank Parsons), mental hygiene (e.g., Clifford Beers), and the study of individual differences (e.g., Alfred Binet) as major contributions forming the foundation of counseling psychology (Whiteley, 1984). The history of counseling psychology reflects an orientation that emphasizes (1) personal growth and development, (2) attention to life transitions to reduce the negative impact of such changes, and (3) importance of prevention across the life span. While historically counseling psychology has promoted the first two areas of emphasis, the third area, prevention, has not kept pace (Kleist & White, 1997; O'Byrne, Brammer, Davidson, & Poston, 2002).

However, at the turn of the 21st century, prevention gained renewed emphasis within the speciality of counseling psychology. In the early years of the 21st century, major contribution issues of *The Counseling Psychologist* (TCP) focused on prevention (Hage et al., 2007; Reese & Vera, 2007; Romano & Hage, 2000). Prior to the Romano and Hage major contribution, prevention was not clearly articulated in the title of any previous major contribution topics of TCP despite its history as a flagship journal of the profession (Romano & Hage). Other developments that promoted prevention within counseling psychology in recent years include the formation of a Prevention Section within the American Psychological Association's (APA) Society of Counseling Psychology (Division 17), and major volumes on prevention authored by counseling psychologists (e.g., Kenny, Horne, Orpinas, & Reese, 2009). This current handbook on prevention in counseling psychology is another example of the growth of prevention in the 21st century.

Counseling psychologists provided leadership for the development of a set of *Prevention Guidelines* for psychologists (see Chapter 4, this volume). The Guidelines first appeared in TCP as a major contribution (Hage et al., 2007). Since that time, with support of the Society of Counseling Psychology and other APA Divisions, a work group of representatives from several APA divisions has refined the guidelines with guidance from APA Boards, Committees, Divisons, and public comments. Now called *Guidelines for Prevention Practice, Research, and Education*, the Guidelines are currently under review by APA. It is hoped that the Prevention Guidelines will eventually be adopted by the APA Council of Representatives to inform and guide prevention work of psychologists.

Once approved by APA Council, the Prevention Guidelines will be promulgated as aspirational, best practices for psychologists. It is hoped that the Guidelines will promote prevention practice, research, and education as being central to the field of psychology, and that prevention will play a prominent role in the education and activities of psychologists. (For a complete description of the Prevention Guidelines see Chapter 4, this volume.)

Importance of Prevention in the 21st Century

It is nearly impossible to read or listen to media reports about lifestyle behaviors, and psychological and physical health concerns within and outside the United States without being reminded about the importance of prevention. Through medical advances, many countries have eradicated or significantly reduced many physical health problems through the discovery and use of vaccines and improved medical procedures. Medical advances have resulted in an increase of life expectancy at birth in the United States, from approximately 47 years at the turn of the 20th century to approximately 78 years in 2007 (Curry & Fitzgibbon, 2009; Xu, Kochanek, Murphy, & Tejada-Vera, 2010). While medical advances will continue, many of the current problems related to health, disability, and mortality are related to behaviors of lifestyle. In one study, McGinnis and Foege (1993) estimated that 40% of all deaths in the United States can be attributed to tobacco and alcohol use, poor diet, and lack of physical activity, behaviors that are to a large degree under personal control. The three leading causes of death in the United States are heart disease, cancer, and strokes, followed by respiratory diseases, accidents, Alzheimer disease, and diabetes (Xu et al., 2010). With the exception of Alzheimer disease, the other causes of death have strong relationships to lifestyle behaviors, primarily cigarette smoking, poor nutrition, misuse of alcohol, and lack of physical activity. All of these behaviors are amenable to prevention interventions, and, therefore, prevention science will become increasingly relevant and important within the US health care framework. Alzheimer's disease, a recent addition as a top 10 leading cause of death in the United States, has become more prevalent as the US population ages, and research is currently investigating ways to prevent the onset of the disease (Szekely, Breitner, & Zandi, 2007).

While prevention science has not focused as much on prevention in the later years of life compared to younger ages, it is predicted that prevention practices and research with the elder population will increase significantly during the 21st century. Several prevention programs important to elders are programs to strengthen cognitive functioning, programs that encourage social networking and activities to reduce elder isolation, and programs that monitor elder compliance with medical recommendations (Konnert, Gatz, & Hertzspring Meyen, 1999; Murdaugh & Insel, 2009). Prevention with the elderly will be discussed further below and is highlighted in Chapter 20, this volume.

Beyond the borders of the United States and other industrialized nations, prevention is also very relevant. However, in countries with low income economies and weak health infrastructures, the immediacy of crisis health care will continue to take precedence over prevention. Nevertheless, increased attention to the health risks of cigarette smoking, misuse of alcohol, poor nutrition, and lack of attention to medical advice will be necessary. It is critically important that nations, especially those with low income economies, utilize the science and applications of prevention to reduce the 40-year life expectancy gap between richer and poorer nations (World Health Report, 2008). Especially in countries with low income economies, there are large discrepancies among the populations with respect to access to health care and ability to pay for it, as well as cultural stigma associated with psychological care. In the future, all countries must continue to monitor and improve social conditions that breed poor health and that create psychological stress and instability. These social conditions include poverty, discrimination, disenfranchisement, war, weak educational and health care infrastructures with limited access to services, and rapid expansion of urban population centers. It is important to consider prevention beyond the US context because of the increasingly prominent role of counseling psychology internationally (Gerstein, Heppner, Ægisdóttir, Leung, & Norsworthy, 2009).

Prevention Research, Practice, and Education: Areas of Expansion

The future of prevention research, practice, and education are discussed in this section. These areas of expansion will be influenced by many factors including changes in population demographics technological and medical advances, and changes in university structures and knowledge generation.

Evidenced-Supported Prevention

Evidenced-supported prevention interventions will continue to be demanded in the future by stakeholders, policy makers, and funding agencies. Therefore, prevention practitioners are encouraged to utilize research-supported prevention interventions. Similarly, prevention researchers are encouraged to be diligent in developing research programs that adequately assess the effectiveness and efficacy of prevention interventions.

Equally important as evidence-supported interventions are interventions that are theory-based. Prevention initiatives that are coordinated and grounded in theory will strengthen prevention work in the 21st century. Historically many prevention interventions, especially school-based interventions, have been offered in uncoordinated and fragmented ways (Greenberg et al., 2003). The training of prevention psychologists needs to include theories that promote a prevention perspective. Examples of these theories will be discussed below in the section on educating prevention psychologists.

US government agencies have developed registries of evidence-supported prevention programs that can assist prevention practitioners identify appropriate prevention programs for their purposes and target population. For example, the US Health and Human Services Department's Substance Abuse and Mental Health Services Administration (SAMHSA) has compiled a National Registry of Evidence-Based Programs and Practices (NREPP) that includes 196 interventions (at this writing) that support mental health promotion, substance abuse prevention, and mental health and substance abuse treatment (nrepp.samhsa.gov). Prevention interventions and programs apply to be included in the registry and they must meet criteria related to the quality of the research supporting the intervention and the intervention's readiness for dissemination. While SAMSHA encourages policy makers and those searching for an appropriate intervention not to limit their search to this registry, NREPP is one source that provides empirically-supported prevention programs that may meet the needs of an organization, institution, or community. NREPP does not endorse the interventions and programs listed, but they have been independently assessed by two reviewers on criteria based on research quality and readiness for dissemination. One advantage of NREPP is that users can search the registry for prevention programs that target particular demographics of the intended audience as well as behaviors targeted for prevention and/or health promotion.

The National Research Council and Institute of Medicine (2009) volume focuses specifically on the prevention of mental, emotional, and behavioral disorders of young people, and summarizes empirically supported prevention programs. Programs include those that emphasize prevention related to family functioning, such as *The Positive Parenting Program (Triple P)*, which includes five levels of parental guidance and support based on family and parental needs. Triple P, also listed by NREPP, includes universal (applicable to all) prevention components and units to address family difficulties. Triple P is applicable from birth to age 12, with extensions for ages 13–16 years. The program has been implemented in several countries. Triple P components have been evaluated with randomized and controlled studies showing positive effects (Ireland, Sanders, & Markie-Dadds, 2003; Turner & Sanders, 2006).

A school-based prevention program that is highlighted by the National Research Council and Institute of Medicine (2009), and listed by NREPP, called *Promoting Alternative THinking Strategies (PATHS)*, is for preschool and elementary school children to enhance social and emotional development. PATHS has been implemented throughout the United States and in many countries. PATHS has been studied extensively through randomized, controlled studies showing that the program improves children's social and emotional competence (Domitrovich, Cortes, & Greenberg, 2007; Kam, Greenberg, & Kusche, 2004).

These are only two examples of prevention interventions that have been reviewed by independent panels of experts and found to meet specified criteria. The importance of delivering empirically supported prevention programs will increase in the future to help ensure that the best available intervention is used in any given situation. Unfortunately, too often prevention interventions are implemented with little empirical justification for their use with a given population and in a particular setting. Since funding for prevention may be more limited in the immediate future as US federal and state governments grapple with severe budget deficits, schools and communities must use the most effective prevention interventions to maximize their impact on the populations served.

Culturally Competent Prevention

Related to empirically supported prevention interventions is the importance of delivering culturally appropriate interventions (Reese & Vera, 2007). Prevention specialists must demonstrate cultural competence with the communities and institutions where they practice. Cultural competence not only includes competence related to ethnicity and other demographics of the population served, but also prevention specialists must be knowledgeable about the institutional culture where they are working. For example, in school settings, understanding the dynamics of a school calendar, the role of the community, and power dynamics within the school will greatly assist the prevention specialist. Similarly, in other institutions, for example a corporate setting or nursing home, the prevention specialist must become familiar with the institutional culture of the setting and the people who work in it.

To help ensure that a prevention intervention is appropriate for a community or institution it is important that major stakeholders be involved from the very beginning of the process. Involvement includes early discussions with community and institutional leaders about the needs in the community or institution (e.g., school). Development and administration of a needs assessment will help to identify the most important areas of need. In diverse communities, the use of elicitation research (Ajzen, 2006; Fishbein & Ajzen, 2010) to identify variables most salient to the prevention targets of change will help to ensure that the intervention addresses important components of change. Important variables to assess through elicitation research include assessing norms, attitudes, perceived personal control, and intentions of the target group as the variables relate to the prevention intervention. Romano and Netland (2008) provide an example of elicitation research, drawing from the theory of reasoned action and planned behavior (Ajzen, 1991; Fishbein & Ajzen, 1975). The theory emphasizes the importance of elicitation research prior to finalizing the development of a prevention intervention. The main value of elicitation research is appreciating that one size does not fit all, especially for prevention interventions that are applied in communities and institutions that are composed of subgroups different from the majority population. Examples of subgroups may include recent immigrants, gay and lesbian individuals, and ethnic minority group members.

Prevention, Neuroscience, and Genetics

The 21st century will yield major advances in neuroscience, increasing our understanding of brain functioning and the influence of genetics in disease prevention. The mapping of the human genome in 2003, with all of its complexities, offers exceptional promise for the diagnosis, treatment, and prevention of physical and psychological disorders (genomics.energy.gov). For example, Wasserman, Terenius, Wasserman, and Sokolowski (2010) reported at an international 2009 Nobel Conference held in Stockholm, Sweden, on the role of genetics in suicide prevention and mental health. While acknowledging the complexity of the topics presented, and the difficulty translating basic science research into clinical practice, the conference established an important foundation to further the relationship between basic science research and the prevention of mental disorders. Others have also reported on the role of genetics in the prevention of problems such as obesity (Bray, 2008) and schizophrenia (Olgiati et al., 2009).

Basic science research, now in its infancy with respect to understanding psychological processes and behaviors, will have major implications for prevention research and applications during the next 50 years. For example, Ames and McBride (2006) reported on research from neuroscience, cognitive science, and genetics showing how research can help explain why people differ in their susceptibility to engage in risk behaviors, such as initial use of alcohol and drugs. In addition, the National Research Council and Institute of Medicine (2009) have cited the rapid growth of developmental neuroscience with respect to understanding the relationship between genetics, brain development, neural systems, and mental and emotional behavioral problems of young people.

The implications of cutting-edge neuroscience research for prevention science are vast, but not without challenges. In addition to the need to develop a much greater understanding of how basic structures of human physiology interact with psychological processes, there are also ethical challenges, such as the potential for stigma and bias toward those who are identified as at-risk for a disorder as a result of genetic screening. However, denying prevention interventions to those at risk also creates an ethical dilemma. The National Research Council and Institute of Medicine (2009) recommend that the ethics and feasibility of using individual genetic and neurobiological risk factors be studied prior to developing and implementing a prevention intervention with a sample deemed at-risk based on genetic testing. The complexities that will confront prevention psychologists in the future are highlighted by Smerecnik, Mesters, de Vries, and de Vries (2009) in their research with adults. They found that public health messages about genetic risk factors for a disease did not translate into preventive behaviors, and in some cases had adverse effects, perhaps due to the belief that gene make-up is beyond individual control, and therefore, a person has little power to alter the course of disease. In addition, while gene identification and testing have already begun, reliable screening assessments in most cases have not been developed (Ames & McBride, 2006). Despite these types of challenges, Plomin and Davis (2009) predict that genetic research will continue to be conducted at a tremendously rapid pace. As we gain more knowledge about the influence of genes on behavior, there is tremendous potential to achieve a greater understanding of the etiology and trajectories of problems, and when and how best to intervene to prevent them.

Applied psychologists, such as counseling psychologists, do not typically engage in extensive study of genetics, molecular biology, brain functioning, and other areas of basic science research during their training. Therefore, it will be important for prevention psychologists to collaborate with scientists engaged in basic research to better understand how cutting-edge neuroscience research might inform more specialized prevention research andapplications.. Neuroscience research may assist prevention psychologists in different ways. For example, understanding how the brain processes rewards and punishments associated with risk behaviors may result in better methods to identify individuals most likely to engage in risk behaviors. In the future, improved gene assessment and screening will help professionals identify individuals at risk for mental and physical health problems, and offer the potential for early interventions to prevent or lessen the impact of a problem.

Prevention and Technology

The latter part of the 20th century saw profound changes in ways that information is shared and communicated among individuals and groups. There is no reason to expect that electronic communication will abate in the future as technology appliances become smaller and more powerful. Examples of readily available current technology applications include access to the internet, e-mail communication, video-conferencing, and rapidly advancing social networking devices and applications. While it is not known how or to the extent that technology will impact lives in the future, the uses of technology will become more sophisticated, powerful, and more readily available during the 21st century.

Prevention psychologists must examine how technology can enhance their prevention interventions and research. Some current uses of technology applications to strengthen prevention interventions include frequent communication between program leaders and participants about the prevention intervention to give and receive new information, to offer psychological support to program participants, and to collect data about the intervention. Prevention interventions can also be enhanced through electronic chat rooms and online asynchronous and synchronous discussions that offer intervention participants opportunities to receive psychological support and information from each other. Social media allow for regular communication among participants in support of a prevention intervention.

In terms of prevention research, needs assessment measures can be administered electronically with immediate feedback to the researcher as well as major stakeholders. After the prevention intervention has begun, regular assessment of participant variables related to the prevention intervention can also be assessed electronically. For example, in a school-based bully prevention program, researchers can collect weekly information about the number of incidents of harassment and bullying that students experienced during the week. In another example, Chinman, Tremain, Imm, and Wandersman (2009) report on an internet designed system, *Interactive Getting to Outcomes (iGTO)*, that has been used to build large-scale capacity for prevention activities across multiple coalitions in two states. The iGTO is a web application to improve the performance of prevention practices by providing guidance to prevention specialists about how best to achieve positive results from their prevention practices. A formative evaluation of iGTO found that the application improved the performance of prevention practices compared to programs that did not use iGTO.

Technological innovations are appearing with more frequency in the prevention literature. For example, Prochaska, Evers, Prochaska, Van Marten, and Johnson (2007) delivered a multimedia web-based bully prevention program to nearly 2,500 middle and high school students. The program, based on the researchers' Transtheoretical model of behavior change, included components for teachers and parents, and assessed outcomes measuring students' participation in one of three roles associated with bullying (i.e., bully, victim, or passive bystander) compared to control students. The results of the study, referred to as an effectiveness trial (compared to a well-controlled efficacy trial), showed that the intervention was successful in reducing the number of students who participated in the three roles associated with bullying. The researchers concluded that a relatively low intensity web-based prevention intervention is effective in reducing self-report rates of students engaging in bullying behaviors.

In another technology innovation, Marsch, Warren, and Badger (2006) used a computer-based substance abuse prevention program with middle-school students. The program, called *HeadOn: Substance Abuse Prevention for Grades 6–8*, provided self-guided education, information, and refusal skills related to substance use. The study showed that the computer-based program yielded similar results as an in-person life-skills program on variables such as self-reported rates of use, intentions to use, beliefs about prevalence of use among peers and adults, and likelihood of refusing drugs if offered. The researchers comment on the benefits of the computerized prevention program in terms of cost-effectiveness and ensuring fidelity of the program compared to programs that are delivered in person.

The use of technology to enhance prevention research and interventions is very much at an early stage. As technological devices and applications become more sophisticated and powerful, they offer much promise to advance the science and practice of prevention. It is important that prevention specialists remain abreast of technological advances, and seek creative ways to use technology in prevention research and practice.

Prevention and the Elderly

The elder population of the United States is growing rapidly. The Administration on Aging (AoA) (www.aoa.gov), an office of the US Department of Health and Human Services, reports that in 2009 there were 39.6 million adults 65 years and older. This represents about 13% of the US population. By 2030, AoA estimates that the number of seniors 65 years and older will increase to about 72 million Americans or 19% of the population. With the first baby boomers turning 65 years in January 2011, the number of elders living in the United States will double between the years 2000 and 2030. While historically much of prevention science has focused on children, adolescents, and younger adults, it is important that prevention specialists give increased attention to prevention research and applications with senior citizens.

Goetzel et al. (2007) summarize research related to the health benefits of elders engaging in health promotion behaviors and activities, such as maintaining a healthy diet, getting regular physical exercise, and managing stress, targets of prevention also important for younger persons. However, prevention interventions will differ depending on the age of participants. Prevention with elders is supported by the AoA through health and wellness program objectives that help seniors live independently, maintain their health, and reduce chronic disease. In order to help meet these objectives, the AoA offers grant programs that support evidence-based disease and disability prevention programs for the elderly (www.aoa.gov).

There are several ways that prevention science is important to the senior population. Since Americans are living longer and life expectancy will likely increase during the 21st century, prevention psychologists can help people live meaningful and productive lives into old age. Prevention may take the form of preventing initial onset of disorders, reducing risks associated with the aging process, and assisting with management of disease. In addition, prevention interventions can assist with later-life issues such as writing health care directives, and working with elder caregivers to reduce caregiver stress. Prevention psychologists might also serve as consultants to assisted living facilities and nursing homes to educate staff on the relevance of prevention and ways to implement prevention interventions. For example, in one chain of Minnesota nursing homes, behavioral problems of the residents are increasingly being treated with nonpharmaceutical methods, such as massage, aromatherapy, and meaningful interpersonal conversations (Wolfe, 2010). While alternatives to pharmaceuticals for certain conditions of the elderly require additional study to assess their effectiveness compared to treatment with medications, nondrug interventions may enhance elder well-being without incurring the side-effects and limitations of pharmaceutical therapies. Other examples of prevention opportunities with the elderly were discussed by Hill, Thorn, and Packard (2000), writing in the *Handbook of Counseling Psychology*. These authors include examples such as helping to ensure safe living environments of the elderly and assisting with medication management.

Most elders experience significant losses of close interpersonal relationships, and casual social interactions are also reduced. Elders may not know how to replace these losses, and prevention interventions can help elders develop skills and learn about resources to form new social networks and relationships. In addition, after retirement seniors may experience reduced feelings of personal accomplishment and self-efficacy, and less overall life satisfaction. The combination of losses can lead to depressed feelings, low self-esteem, and suicidal ideation. Not surprisingly, suicide is a major risk for elders (Pearson & Brown, 2000). The National Institute of Mental Health reports that the risk of suicide for Americans 65 years and older is higher compared to the general population, and risk increases with age, especially for non-Hispanic White males 85 years and older (www.nimh.nih.gov). Thus, there is a need for suicide prevention interventions with elders.

Elders are also at risk for mistreatment and abuse. Prevention psychologists can be available to consult about the prevention of elder maltreatment and violence by educating elder caregivers about signs of abuse and mistreatment, and by consulting with nursing home staff and administrators and other institutions that care for elders. Consultations may include staff and administrator training about symptoms of elder abuse, and workshops to help personnel and relatives manage psychological stress associated with elder care.

Konnert, Gatz, and Hertzsprung Meyen (1999) suggest additional prevention interventions for elders. These include programs that use intergenerational discussion groups with elders and children. These groups are mutually beneficial, as children learn from elders' sharing their life history and wisdom, while elders learn from youth about issues important to the younger generation. Intergenerational programs have been researched showing benefits to members of both groups (Holmes, 2009; Schwalbach & Kiernan, 2002). These and other types of programs offered through religious, business, and community organizations can help elders develop social networks and reduce isolation and aloneness, while also facilitating feelings of increased self-worth, and personal accomplishment and satisfaction.

Prevention Education and Training

Throughout this chapter, it is argued that prevention will be given greater attention in the 21st century, and psychologists will be increasingly asked to apply their knowledge and skills within a prevention framework. Therefore, it is imperative that future psychologists receive prevention education and training during their education. However, currently, prevention education in the graduate training of psychologists is not given much attention (O'Byrne, Brammer, Davidson, & Poston, 2002). Snyder and Elliott (2005), writing about the training of clinical and counseling psychologists in the 21st century, emphasize the importance of prevention training as a key component of the future education of applied psychologists. They also recommend that prevention education be learned in didactic classroom instruction and through applied field experiences where students have opportunities to apply prevention skills under supervision.

Eddy, Smith, Brown, and Reid (2005) surveyed 262 prevention researchers about their knowledge and training in 13 prevention science content areas (e.g., prevention research, program design, cultural issues, ethics). The sample consisted of trainees, early career professionals, and established prevention researchers. Survey results showed that early career professionals did not have high levels of training and knowledge in any of the content areas, while established prevention researchers showed high levels of knowledge and skills in only six of the 13 content areas. Further, the six content areas of high knowledge and skills for the experienced researchers were the older and more traditional areas of prevention (e.g., program design and prevention research). The newer areas of knowledge and skills (i.e., gender and culture issues and community collaborations) showed lower levels of knowledge and skills for all groups surveyed. The authors emphasize that graduate students need to develop core competencies to work in prevention so that they as the next generation of prevention scientists are adequately prepared in all areas of prevention.

Conyne, Newmeyer, Kenny, Romano, and Matthews (2008) also emphasize the importance of prevention training in graduate psychology education. They report on two strategies: specialized course in prevention and infusion of prevention content and practice into existing courses. The first option has an advantage in that prevention knowledge and skills are taught in one class in a systematic way, similar to other core courses in the curriculum. A major disadvantage is that unless the course is required, not all students will receive the education offered by the course. Even for students who may want to register for an elective prevention course, extensive program course requirements will often discourage them from doing so. A major disadvantage to adding a specific prevention course requirement to the existing curriculum is that prevention is not a core competency required to obtain a psychology license, and prevention is not emphasized in APA academic program and internship accreditation criteria.

Infusing prevention content and skills into existing, required courses offers the advantage that students will receive prevention training throughout several courses in the curriculum. However, for infusion to occur, agreement and cooperation is needed from program faculty, and infusion of prevention content and skills may be limited to courses taught by faculty who are most interested in and knowledgeable about prevention. In addition, some faculty, even those with prevention knowledge and skills, may feel that their existing course structure does not allow for infusion of additional content.

Nevertheless, there are several ways to infuse prevention perspectives and content into existing courses without overly burdening the course. For example, in psychotherapy and counseling theory courses, instructors could develop units or assignments on theories and perspectives that support prevention applications and research such as the Theory of Reasoned Action/Planned Behavior (Ajzen, 1991; Fishbein & Ajzen, 1975; Romano & Netland, 2008), a positive psychology framework (Snyder & Lopez, 2007), Transtheoretical model of change (Prochaska, Johnson, & Lee, 2009), and a social justice perspective (Kenny et al., 2009). In addition, more commonly taught theories, such as Adlerian, behavioral, and cognitive behavioral could be discussed within a prevention framework, using examples from the prevention literature.

Also, in group counseling theory and skills courses, prevention concepts, skills, and applications can be infused throughout, especially group courses that emphasize applications of group work across the remediation to prevention spectrum (Hage & Romano, 2010). Prevention specialists work extensively with groups and use different group skills. Prevention group work may include forming and facilitating community and stakeholder groups when initiating a prevention intervention, leading groups as part of a prevention intervention, and developing psychoeducational groups to deliver universal or primary prevention programs. Graduate students can be exposed to these and other prevention group applications and develop their skills and understanding through class discussions and assignments.

Other core courses in psychology graduate education where prevention concepts and perspectives can be infused include courses on multiculturalism and career development. In these courses applications of prevention science can be demonstrated through examples when discussing career development interventions with diverse client populations (Kenny, Blustein, Chaves, Grossman, & Gallagher, 2003; Reese & Vera, 2007; Rivera-Mosquera Phillips, Castelino, Martin, & Mowry Dobran, 2007; Scheel, Madabhushi, & Backhaus, 2009). Promoting career development and preventing academic failure must begin in early childhood and continue throughout the years of schooling. The promotion of academic success and career enhancement can be achieved by addressing barriers that hinder student academic success, including institutional, familial, and societal challenges that may contribute to poor academic achievement and reduce hopes for career success. Barriers and challenges may include children living in poverty, discrimination, family instability, crime, and insufficient funding for education. These challenges reside beyond the individual student, and they must be identified and attended to in order to improve student success. Therefore, teaching psychology graduate students about the impact of the systems within which children and adolescents live and learn, and how to advocate to correct systemic inequities is extremely important to the work of prevention psychologists.

Finally, practica and internship experiences offer opportunities for graduate students to engage in prevention work. In addition to didactic instruction, prevention specialists of the 21st century must also engage in applied prevention experiences under the guidance of skilled supervisors committed to prevention. While some practice settings may offer more opportunities than others, most practicum and internship placements usually give some attention to prevention. For example, college and university counseling centers usually offer prevention outreach activities to the campus community such as programs to prevent sexual violence, to use alcohol responsibly, and to manage stress. Practicum students and interns may gain experience by participating in national prevention campaigns supported by their placement site such as National Depression Screening Day (October), National Alcohol Screening Day (April), and National Eating Disorders Awareness Week (February). These programs highlight major areas of national concern, and address topics from a preventive perspective. Graduate students could develop prevention programs, specifically tailored for populations served by their practicum or internship site, thus complementing the national campaigns. Other opportunities to develop prevention skills for trainees include designing and implementing workshops on various topics important to practicum site clientele, and of interest to the trainee, for example, effective parenting skills, bully prevention, and developing healthy relationships. Practicum and intern trainees may also be able to participate in prevention research programs, although these opportunities may be limited depending on the training site.

Teaching prevention to graduate psychology students can be accomplished in different ways, and each offers advantages and disadvantages. However, while one strategy or a combination of strategies will give students training in prevention, implementation of prevention training into graduate programs requires the interest and commitment of faculty as well as a systemic commitment across the profession of psychology. Program faculty must value prevention as an important area of study for psychologists, and appreciate the importance of teaching prevention knowledge and skills. Likewise, psychological organizations, accreditation committees, and licensing boards must clearly articulate the importance of prevention in their written documents, policies, and requirements. If the profession of psychology gives prevention research and practice greater attention and priority, psychology graduate training programs will be more inclined to emphasize prevention as an important area of study.

Economics of Prevention

During the 21st century, it will be important for psychologists to show the financial benefits of prevention. Within the specialty of counseling psychology, addressing this issue is especially important, since many counseling psychologists develop careers in educational institutions that have experienced significant budget reductions in recent years, and which likely are to continue in the foreseeable future. Budget constraints may result in fewer allocations for prevention programs and research, since prevention may be viewed as less urgent compared to programs that address crisis and remedial needs. Similar budget issues may affect psychologists employed in other settings, such as community mental health agencies, research centers, and business and industrial settings. Although the 2010 US federal health care legislation, Patient Protection and Affordable Care Act, advocates for and funds prevention interventions, demonstrating the cost-benefits of prevention will be increasingly important for prevention psychologists.

Several studies have addressed the cost-benefit ratios of prevention interventions and programs. These studies have been conducted across different areas of prevention interventions, including alcohol use prevention (Kraemer, 2007; Spoth, Guyll, & Day, 2002), smoking cessation and relapse prevention with pregnant women (Ruger & Emmons, 2008), and teen pregnancy prevention (Rosenthal et al., 2009). All of these studies have concluded that the economic benefits of prevention outweigh the financial costs.

To further demonstrate the financial benefits of prevention, as well as overall benefits to society, a recent longitudinal study followed for over 20 years more than 1,400 individuals who participated as children in an inner-city early childhood education program (Reynolds, Temple, Ou, Arteaga, & White, 2011). The researchers reported that compared to a control group of children who received usual services, individuals who participated in the early childhood program were higher on several indices of well-being, including higher incomes, educational attainment, lower involvement with the justice system, and lower substance abuse. The authors address the important implications of this study for public policy initiatives and developmental science.

Swisher, Scherer, and Yin (2004) conducted a comprehensive review of the literature and found seven studies that reported cost-benefit analyses for prevention programs that met their criteria for inclusion. In order to be included in the analysis, the studies must have reported cost-benefit ratios, focused on primary prevention, included a range of programs and outcomes, and included community and educational partners. These criteria yielded seven studies across the prevention classifications of universal (for the general population), selective (for at risk populations), and indicated (for very at-risk populations) programs. No cost-benefit analyses were found for indicated programs. Included in the analysis were universal programs to prevent alcohol, drug, and cigarette use. The financial benefits for three prevention programs in this category ranged from $2.40 to $19.65 for every dollar spent on the prevention program. Two selective programs for families with children who received special services yielded cost-benefit ratios of $1 to $4 (i.e., $1 spent on prevention yielded $4 in benefits) and $1 to $8.74. Two comprehensive community-wide prevention programs to reduce alcohol and drug use yielded ratios of $1 to $2.88 and $1 to $8.12. Collectively these financial benefits demonstrate the positive economic impact of prevention. The range of economic benefits vary primarily based on the approach to prevention and the cost-benefit analysis (Swisher et al., 2004).

Prevention has been shown to be cost effective when applied at different stages of life, such as the positive economic value of prevention services when implemented in the first decade of life (Reynolds, Rolnick, Englund, & Temple, 2010), and the positive economic impact of preventing depression in elders (Smit, Ederveen, Cuijpers, Deeg, & Beekman, 2006). Psychologists are generally not trained in the economics of their science, and typical training programs emphasize remedial approaches to care. Thus, it is important that prevention scientists and practitioners partner with experts in cost-benefit analyses to demonstrate the value of prevention from economic and human development perspectives.

Prevention and Health Care Settings

Behavioral medicine has an important role to play in the overall health of the population, and prevention science must be a leader in efforts to improve the nation's health. The leading causes of death in the United States, heart disease and cancer, accounted for nearly 50% of all deaths in 2007 (Xu et al., 2010). Three lifestyle behaviors are major contributing factors to these deaths as well as to other health problems. The lifestyle behaviors are tobacco use, unhealthy diet and nutrition, and lack of physical exercise (Curry & Fitzgibbon, 2009). For many years prevention researchers and practitioners have worked to prevent, stop, or reduce these life style behaviors and the negative health consequences associated with them (e.g., Shumaker, Ockene, Riekert, 2009).

However, much more can be accomplished by prevention psychologists in these and other areas of behavioral health, especially in health care settings (Johnson Bennett & Millstein, 2003). While Johnson Bennett and Millstein write that the empirical literature on prevention contributions of psychologists in health care settings is limited, they remind us of the many advantages and opportunities that health care settings offer prevention psychologists. For example, people seek out physicians for medical problems that may be associated with lifestyle behaviors or emotional stress, and medical personnel discuss with patients their risk for future disorders unless changes are made in current behavior, such as increasing physical exercise or stopping cigarette smoking. Unfortunately, medical personnel usually function under severe time constraints and often lack the training to actually assist patients in making needed behavioral changes. Also, medical personnel may underestimate the difficulties and motivations of patients to change harmful behaviors and initiate health enhancing behaviors. Therefore, patients may be given advice to make changes without assistance on how to be successful in changing harmful behaviors or initiating new positive behaviors. A health facility that includes in close proximity psychologists or other mental health professionals would help to facilitate patient referrals to behavioral specialists who can assist them in making lifestyle changes. Alternatively, referrals can be made to health psychologists who have established positive working relationships with medical facilities in the community.

In addition to patient referrals made by medical personnel, psychologists can be instrumental in promoting prevention in health care settings through outreach programs to the community. These programs can take many forms, such as presentations and workshops on reducing risk of childhood obesity and diabetes, managing stress associated with care-giving, communicating with parents about child and adolescent risk behaviors, and teaching job-seeking skills to the unemployed. In addition to in-person presentations, psychologists could also consult with medical personnel about literature that health care facilities distribute to patients, or post on websites. These information sources often discuss health issues associated with prevention, and psychologists can consult on the contents to help ensure that the information addresses important psychological aspects related to the topic. Other areas of potential activity for psychologists in health care settings include in-service training of medical personnel about the latest research in prevention science from the psychological literature and the implications of this research for the practice of medicine.

Counseling psychology has been a leader in psychology and in other mental health professions, advocating for the importance of acknowledging cultural differences in the design and implementation of research, training, and services. Helping to promote and develop cultural competence and expertise within the health care industry is another important consultative role for prevention psychologists (Herman et al., 2007). Consultative roles for prevention psychologists may include providing cultural competency training to health care professionals and support staff, identifying cultural characteristics that may enhance or detract from prevention and health care services, facilitating the involvement of ethnic and low-income persons in the design and implementation of services, and reviewing health care information distributed by the medical facility to ensure that it is presented in a sensitive and culturally appropriate way to different cultures of the community. Attending to issues of culture in health care is not only ethically responsible, but also necessary to reduce heath disparities among low-income and ethnic minority communities (Tucker et al., 2007). It is important that prevention psychologists establish and maintain partnerships and collaborations with ethnic minority and low-income communities, as well as with community organizations that serve these groups to maximize psychology's impact on promoting cultural awareness and cultural competence in health care.

Currently, most of prevention research and interventions occur in settings outside medical institutions, especially prevention research with children (Johnson Bennett & Millstein, 2003). However, health care settings offer important opportunities for prevention psychologists to develop and implement interventions and research programs (DeLeon, Giesting, & Kenkel, 2003). The relationship between physical, behavioral, and emotional health will advance in the 21st century, and our understanding of how they contribute to the overall health and well-being of the population will increase. It behooves psychologists and health care professionals to develop active and strong collaborative partnerships to maximize the health and well-being of patients, families, and communities.

Prevention and Multidisciplinary Partnerships

Prevention is a multidisciplinary specialty, and in the 21st century it will be increasingly important for prevention psychologists to work across disciplinary boundaries to implement and strengthen their prevention interventions and research. The speed of innovations and advances in science and technology require that prevention psychologists collaborate with other disciplines to better understand and prevent major psychological and behavioral disorders. In addition, to implement fully prevention research and intervention programs, interdisciplinary, community, and institutional partnerships must be developed and maintained. An interdisciplinary and collaborative perspective is supported by US government agencies and mandated by agencies that fund prevention research. Agencies such as the National Institute of Mental Health (NIMH), Substance Abuse and Mental Health Services Administration (SAMHSA), and the Graduate Psychology Education (GPE) program (through the US Department of Health and Human Services [HHS]) emphasize the importance of collaboration across scholarly disciplines, community agencies, and institutions. In addition, as discussed in this chapter, collaborations are necessary for prevention psychologists to supplement their knowledge and skills in fields such as neuroscience, technology, and economics, and to work in institutions that typically do not employ prevention psychologists, for example, schools, medical facilities, and nursing homes.

While this chapter has identified prevention topics and groups that will require increased attention in the future, major societal and political issues must also be attended to by prevention psychologists working in partnership with others. These issues include promoting the academic achievement of all children and preventing school failure and school dropout, especially among youth living in poverty and among some ethnic minority group students. Several recent papers have shown how counseling psychologists can collaborate with school personnel to promote a prevention agenda to enhance the academic achievement of all students (Kenny, Waldo, Warter, & Barton, 2002; Romano & Kachgal, 2004; Scheel et al., 2009).

In terms of children's mental health promotion, the Missouri Prevention Center (MPC), founded in 2007, is an example of how the *Guidelines for Prevention Practice, Research, and Education* (cited above; Hage et al., 2007) might be implemented. The MPC, led by counseling psychologists, uses interdisciplinary teams of professionals and students to advance their research, service, and training objectives (Herman, Reinke, Stormont, Puri, & Agarwal, 2010). Collaborations with community organizations are an important and necessary component to help MPC reach its goals. Collaborations include those with schools and Head Start programs.

Systemic changes must be made in order to strengthen and sustain the impact of prevention interventions across the life span. Systemic interventions will require that prevention psychologists partner with community stakeholders, policy makers, and governmental bodies to bring about institutional, community, and legislative actions necessary to infuse prevention practices throughout society. In recent years, institutional and government policies (e.g., antibullying legislation, cigarette-smoking restrictions, health care legislation) to prevent problems and promote health have been enacted. While such policies and legislation are often controversial, as people have different values and beliefs associated with them, they offer important benefits to individuals and communities. Prevention psychologists may also have different opinions about suggested policies and legislation that promote prevention. However, it is important to understand the issues and engage in the debate. Prevention psychologists possess the training and knowledge to advocate for laws and policies that reduce risks and promote health and well-being across the population. Examples of controversial issues, designed to prevent problems and enhance life, being debated in many communities in the United States and abroad include those related to teaching sex education in the schools, providing quality and affordable health care, and limiting unhealthy food and drink choices to children and adolescents in schools. Prevention psychologists must first decide about their own values and beliefs associated with these and other issues, and then take actions as they deem appropriate. Actions may include participating in letter writing campaigns to legislators, writing editorials and letters to local newspapers, joining community advocacy groups, and testifying before government agencies and policy-making bodies deliberating the issue. Social and political issues that are associated with a prevention perspective will be debated throughout the century. It is important that prevention psychologists, in partnership with others, become knowledgeable about and actively involved in the dialogue and use their professional knowledge and skills to inform the discussion.

Summary

This chapter summarized important areas of prevention science that will influence prevention work and demand increased attention in the 21st century. The areas summarized are not meant to exclude other issues, settings, or populations that may require increased attention during the century. Psychology as a profession, and counseling psychology as a specialty, must give more attention to prevention in the training of new psychologists, in the development and implementation of prevention research and applications, and use their expertise to inform policy-makers who are deliberating about issues related to the prevention of physical and psychological disabilities and distress, and the importance of enhancing health promotion behaviors and emotional well-being. The knowledge explosion and technological innovations that will continue in the 21st century require that prevention psychologists collaborate with other disciplines and specialties, and with community and government stakeholders, to implement a comprehensive prevention agenda across the United States and around the world.

Acknowledgment

The author acknowledges the contributions of Mr. Ziqiu Li (Counseling Psychology Ph.D. student, Educational Psychology, University of Minnesota) in the development of this chapter.

References

Ajzen, I. (1991). The theory of planned behavior. *Organizational Behavior and Human Decision Processes, 50,* 179–211.

Ajzen, I. (2006). *Constructing a TpB questionnaire.* Retrieved from http://www.people.umass.edu/aizen/tpb.html

Ames, S. L. & McBride, C. (2006). Translating genetics, cognitive science, and other basic science research findings into applications for prevention. *Evaluation & the Health Professions, 29,* 277–301.

Bray, M. S. (2008). Implications of gene-behavior interactions: Prevention and intervention for obesity. *Obesity, 16*(Supplement 3), S72–S78.

Chinman, M., Tremain, B., Imm, P., & Wandersmann, A. (2009). Strengthening prevention performance using technology: A formative evaluation of Interactive Getting to Outcomes. *American Journal of Orthopsychiatry, 79,* 469–481.

Conyne, R. K. (2004). *Preventive counseling* (2nd ed). New York: Brunner-Routledge.

Conyne, R. K., Newmeyer, M. D., Kenny, M., Romano, J. L., & Matthews, C. R. (2008). Two key strategies for teaching prevention: Specialized course and infusion. *Journal of Primary Prevention, 29,* 375–401.

Curry, S. J., & Fitzgibbon, M. L. (2009). Theories of prevention. In S. A. Shumaker, J. K. Ockene, & K. A. Riekert (Eds.), *The Handbook of Health Behavior Change* (3rd ed, pp. 3–17). New York: Springer.

DeLeon, P. H., Giesting, B., & Kenkel, M. B. (2003). Community health centers: Exciting opportunities for the 21st century. *Professional Psychology: Research and Practice, 34,* 579–585.

Domitrovich, C. E., Cortes, R. C., & Greenberg, M. T. (2007). Improving young children's social and emotional competence: A randomized trial of the preschool "PATHS" curriculum. *Journal of Primary Prevention, 28,* 67–91.

Eddy, J. M., Smith, P., Brown, C. H., & Reid, J. B. (2005). A survey of prevention science training: Implications for educating the next generation. *Prevention Science, 6,* 59–71.

Fishbein, M., & Ajzen, I. (1975). *Belief, attitude, intention, and behavior: An introduction to theory and research.* Reading, MA: Addison-Wesley.

Fishbein, M. & Ajzen, I. (2010). *Predicting and changing behavior: The reasoned action approach.* New York: Psychology Press (Taylor & Francis).

Gerstein, L. H., Heppner, P. P., Ægisdóttir, S., Leung, S. M. A., & Norsworthy, K. L. (Eds.). (2009). *International handbook of cross-cultural counseling.* Thousand Oaks, CA: Sage.

Goetzel, R. Z., Reynolds, K., Breslow, L., Roper, W. L., Shechter, D. C., Stapleton, D. C.,... McGinnis, J. M. (2007). Health promotion in later life: It's never too late. *American Journal of Health Promotion, 21,* 1–5.

Greenberg, M. T., Weissberg, R. P., O'Brien, M. U., Zins, J. E., Fredericks, L., Resnik, H., & Elias, M. J. (2003). Enhancing school-based prevention and youth development through coordinated social, emotional, and academic learning. *American Psychologist, 58,* 466–474.

Hage, S. M., & Romano, J. L. (2010). History of prevention and prevention groups: Legacy for the 21st century. *Group Dynamics: Theory, Research, and Practice, 14,* 199–210.

Hage, S. M., Romano, J. L., Conyne, R. K., Kenny, M., Matthews, C., Schwartz, J. P., & Waldo, M. (2007). Best practices guidelines on prevention practice, research, training, and social advocacy for psychologists. *The Counseling Psychologist, 35,* 493–566.

Herman, K. C., Reinke, W. M., Stormont, M., Puri, R., & Geetika, A. (2010). Using prevention science to promote children's mental health: The founding of the Missouri Prevention Center. *The Counseling Psychologist, 38,* 652–690.

Herman, K. C., Tucker, C. M., Ferdinand, L. A., Mirsu-Paun, A., Hasan, N. T., & Beato, C. (2007). Culturally sensitive health care and counseling psychology: An overview. *The Counseling Psychologist, 35,* 633–649.

Hill, R. D., Thorn, B. J., & Packard, T. (2000). Counseling older adults: Theoretical and empirical issues in prevention and intervention. In S. D. Brown & R. W. Lent (Eds.), *Handbook of counseling psychology* (3rd ed., pp. 499–531). New York: Wiley.

Holmes, C. L. (2009). An intergenerational program with benefits. *Early Childhood Education, 37,* 113–119.

Ireland, J. L., Sanders, M. R., & Markie-Dadds, C. (2003). The impact of parent training on marital functioning: A comparison of two group versions of the Triple P-Positive Parenting Program for parents of children with early onset conduct problems. *Behavioural and Cognitive Psychotherapy, 31,* 127–142.

Johnson Bennett, S., & Millstein, S. G. (2003). Prevention opportunities in health care settings. *American Psychologist, 58,* 475–481.

Kam, C. M., Greenberg, M. T., & Kusche, C. A. (2004). Sustained effects of the PATHS curriculum on social and psychological adjustment of children in special education. *Journal of Emotional and Behavioral Disorders, 12,* 66–78.

Kenny, M. E., Blustein, D. L., Chaves, A., Grossman, J. M., & Gallagher, L. A. (2003). The role of perceived barriers and relational support in the educational and vocational lives of urban high school students. *Journal of Counseling Psychology, 50,* 142–155.

Kenny, M. E., Horne, A. M., Orpinas, P., & Reese, L. E. (Eds.). (2009). *Realizing social justice: The challenge of prevention interventions.* Washington, DC: American Psychological Association.

Kenny, M. E., & Romano, J. L. (2009). Promoting positive development and social justice through prevention: A legacy for the future. In M. E. Kenny, A. M. Horne, P. Orpinas, & L. E. Reese (Eds.), *Realizing social justice: The challenge of prevention interventions* (pp. 17–35). Washington, DC: American Psychological Association.

Kenny, M. E., Waldo, M., Warter, E. H., & Barton, C. (2002). School-linked prevention: Theory, science, and practice for enhancing the lives of children and youth. *The Counseling Psychologist, 30,* 726–748.

Kleist, D. M., & White, L. J. (1997). The values of counseling: A disparity between a philosophy of prevention in counseling and counsellor practice and training. *Counseling and Values, 41,* 128–140.

Konnert, C., Gatz, M., & Hertzsprung Meyen, E. A. (1999). Preventive interventions for older adults. In M. Duffy (Ed.), *Handbook of counseling and psychotherapy with older adults* (pp. 314–334). New York: Wiley.

Kraemer, K. L. (2007). The cost-effectiveness and cost-benefit of screening and brief intervention for unhealthy alcohol use in medical settings. *Substance Abuse, 28,* 67–77.

Marsch, L. A., Warren, B. K., & Badger, G. J. (2006). Applying computer technology to substance abuse prevention science: Results of a preliminary examination. *Journal of Child and Adolescent Substance Abuse, 16,* 69–94.

McGinnis, J. M., & Foege, W. H. (1993). Actual causes of death in the United States. *Journal of the American Medical Association, 270,* 2207–2212.

Murdaugh, C. L., & Insel, K. (2009). Problems with adherence in the elderly. In S. A. Shumaker, J. K. Ockene, & K. A. Riekert (Eds.), *The handbook of health behavior change* (3rd ed, pp. 499–518). New York: Springer.

National Research Council and Institute of Medicine. Committee on the Prevention of Mental Disorders and Substance Abuse Among, Youth, and Young Adults: Research Advances and Promising Interventions. Board on Children, Youth, and Families, Division of Behavioral and Social Sciences and Education. M. E. O'Connell, T. Boat, & K. E. Warner (Eds.). (2009). *Preventing mental, emotional, and behavioural disorders among young people: Progress and possibilities.* Washington, DC: The National Academy Press.

O'Byrne, K. K., Brammer, S. K., Davidson, M. M., & Poston, W. S. C. (2002). Primary prevention in counseling psychology: Back to the future? *The Counseling Psychologist, 30,* 330–344.

Olgiati, P., Mandelli, L., Lorenz, C., Marino, E., Adele, P., Ferrari, B.,... Serretti, A. (2009). Schizophrenia: Genetics, prevention, and rehabilitation. *Acta Neuropsychiatrica, 21,* 109–120.

Pearson, J. L., & Brown, G. K. (2000). Suicide prevention in later life: Directions for science and practice. *Clinical Psychology Review, 20,* 685–705.

Plomin, R., & Davis, O. S. P. (2009). The future of genetics in psychology and psychiatry: Microarrays, genome-wide association, and non-coding RNA. *Journal of Child Psychology and Psychiatry, 50,* 63–71.

Prochaska, J. O., Evers, K. E., Prochaska, J. M., Van Marter, D., & Johnson, J. L. (2007). Efficacy and effectiveness trials: Examples from smoking cessation and bullying prevention. *Journal of Health Psychology, 12,* 170–178.

Prochaska, J. O., Johnson, S., & Lee, P. (2009). The transtheoretical model of behavior change. In S. A. Shumaker, J. K. Ockene, & K. A. Riekert (Eds.). *The handbook of behavior change* (3rd ed., pp. 59–83). New York: Springer.

Reese, L. E., & Vera, E. M. (2007). Culturally relevant prevention: The scientific and practical considerations of community-based programs. *The Counseling Psychologist, 35,* 763–778.

Reynolds, A. J., Rolnick, A. J., Englund, M. E., & Temple, J. A. (Eds.). (2010). *Childhood programs and practices in the first decade of life: A human capital integration.* New York: Cambridge University Press.

Reynolds, A. J., Temple, J. A., Ou, S., Arteaga, I. A., & White, B. A. B. (2011). School-based early childhood education and age-28 well-being: Effects by timing, dosage, and subgroups. *Sciencexpress,* published online June 9, 2011, www.sciencemag.org/content/early/recent

Rivera-Mosquera, E., Phillips, J. C., Castelino, P., Martin, J. K., & Mowry Dobran, E. S. (2007). Design and implementation of a grassroots precollege program for Latino youth. *The Counseling Psychologist, 35,* 821–839.

Romano, J. L., & Hage, S. M. (2000). Prevention and counseling psychology: Revitalizing commitments for the 21st century. *The Counseling Psychologist, 28,* 733–763.

Romano, J. L., & Kachgal, M. M. (2004). Counseling psychology and school counseling: An underutilized partnership. *The Counseling Psychologist, 32,* 184–215.

Romano, J. L., & Netland, J. D. (2008). The application of the theory of reasoned action and planned behavior to prevention science in counseling psychology. *The Counseling Psychologist, 36,* 777–806.

Rosenthal, M. S., Ross, J. S., Bilodeau, R., Richter, R. S., Palley, J. E., & Bradley, E. H. (2009). Economic evaluation of a comprehensive teenage pregnancy prevention program. *American Journal of Preventive Medicine, 37,* S280–S287.

Ruger, J. P., & Emmons, K. M. (2008). Economic evaluations of smoking cessation and relapse prevention programs for pregnant women: A systematic review. *Value in Health, 11,* 180–190.

Scheel, M. J., Madabhushi, S., & Backhaus, A. (2009). The academic motivation of at-risk students in a counseling prevention program. *The Counseling Psychologist, 37,* 1147–1178.

Schwalbach, L. E., & Kiernan, S. (2002). Effects of an intergenerational friendly visit program on the attitudes of fourth graders toward elders. *Educational Gerontology, 28,* 175–187.

Shumaker, S. A. Ockene, J. K., & Riekert, K. A. (Eds.). (2009). *The handbook of health behavior change* (3rd ed.). New York: Springer.

Smerecnik, C. M. R., Mesters, I., de Vries, N. K., & de Vries, H. (2009). Alerting the general population to genetic risks: The value of health messages communicating the existence of genetic risk factors for public health promotion. *Health Psychology, 28,* 734–745.

Smit, F., Ederveen, A., Cuijpers, P., Deeg, D., & Beekman, A. (2006). Opportunities for cost-effective prevention of late-life depression. *Archives of General Psychiatry, 63,* 290–296.

Snyder, C. R., & Elliott, T. R. (2005). Twenty-first century graduate education in clinical psychology: A four level matrix model. *Journal of Clinical Psychology, 61,* 1033–1054.

Snyder, C. R., & Lopez, S. J. (2007). *Positive psychology: The scientific and practical explorations of human strengths.* Thousand Oaks, CA: Sage.

Spaulding, J., & Balch, P. (1983). A brief history of primary prevention in the twentieth century: 1908–1980. *American Journal of Community Psychology, 11,* 59–80.

Spoth, R. L., Guyll, M., & Day, S. X. (2002). Universal family-focused interventions in alcohol-use disorder prevention: Cost-effectiveness and cost-benefit analyses of two interventions. *Journal of Studies on Alcohol and Drugs, 63,* 219–228.

Swisher, J. D., Scherer, J., & Yin, R. K. (2004). Cost-benefit estimates in prevention research. *Journal of Primary Prevention, 25,* 137–148.

Szekely, C. A., Breitner, J. C. S., & Zandi, P. P. (2007). Prevention of Alzheimer's disease. *International Review of Psychiatry, 19,* 693–706.

Tucker, C. M., Ferdinand, L. A., Mirsu-Paun, A., Herman, K. C., Delgado-Romero, E., van den Berg, J. J., & Jones, J. D. (2007). The roles of counseling psychologists in reducing health disparities. *The Counseling Psychologist, 35,* 650–678.

Turner, K. M. T., & Sanders, M. R. (2006). Help when it is needed first: A controlled evaluation of brief, behavioral, family intervention in a primary care setting. *Behavior Therapy, 37,* 131–142.

Wasserman, D., Terenius, L., Wasserman, J., & Sokolowski, M. (2010). The 2009 Nobel conference on the role of genetics in promoting suicide prevention and the mental health of the population. *Molecular Psychiatry, 15,* 12–17.

Whiteley, J. M. (1984). Counseling psychology: A historical perspective. *The Counseling Psychologist, 12,* 3–109.

Wolfe, W. (2010, December 5). Nursing homes seek end to stupor. *Minneapolis Star Tribune.* wolfe@startribune.com

World Health Report 2008. Retrieved October 4, 2010 from http://www.who.int/whr/previous/en/index.html

Xu, J., Kochanek, K. D., Sherry L., Murphy, S. L., & Tejada-Vera, B. (2010, May 20). Deaths: Final data for 2007. *National Vital Statistics Reports, 58* (19). US Department of Health and Human Services, Centers for Disease Control and Prevention, National Center for Health Statistics.

CHAPTER

4 Best Practice Guidelines on Prevention: Improving the Well-Being of Individuals, Families, and Communities

Sally M. Hage, Jonathan Schwartz *and* Michelle Murray

Abstract

The health care system in the United States is shifting toward a focus on prevention. Several reasons account for this shift, including staggering health care costs and research indicating many illnesses are preventable through behavioral interventions. Hence, increasing evidence linking mental and physical health outcomes make the involvement of psychologists crucial in promoting a prevention orientation within the health care system. Counseling psychologists have been leaders in the development and ratification of a set of prevention practice guidelines for psychologists. These guidelines, entitled *Prevention Science and Practice Guidelines for Psychologists*, provide an aspirational model for best practice in the area of prevention. This chapter aims to further psychologists' and other mental health care professionals' understanding and application of the principles of the *Prevention Guidelines* (APA, Under Review) to their work. Specific examples of model programs in areas of psychological practice, research, training, and social advocacy illustrate each of the prevention guidelines.

Key Words: prevention, guidelines, training, research, practice, social action, advocacy

The United States health care system is in the midst of a paradigm shift; namely, the country is moving from a system focused on the treatment of disease to one that also promotes health and wellness. Government leaders along with the American public are voicing the need to place prevention initiatives at the forefront of major health care priorities. For example, a recent poll indicated that 71% of Americans favor increasing our investment in disease prevention and making prevention a top priority in future health reform (Trust for America's Health, 2009b). In addition, legislative reform of the health care system increasingly mandates inclusion of prevention services as an important component of overall health care. For example, the 2010 Affordable Care Act makes wellness and prevention services accessible by requiring health plans to cover prevention services without co-pays. These services include counseling to promote a healthier lifestyle (e.g., proper nutrition, weight management) and to reduce depression, and well-baby prevention services (http://www.healthcare.gov/law/index.html).

At least two factors appear to account for the recent shift to a prevention focus. The first factor is an increased awareness of the staggering cost of the current system, particularly in relation to the recent economic downturn. Health care spending in the United States is approaching $2 trillion a year, and is expected to double in the next 10 years. As noted by President Obama, "In the absence of a radical shift towards prevention and public health, we will not be successful in containing medical costs or improving the health of the American people" (Trust for America's Health, 2009a). The second factor moving the US system toward prevention is increased awareness of research indicating that negative health behaviors (e.g., smoking, poor diet, lack of exercise, and excessive alcohol) account for at least 50% of all chronic health problems and 40% of premature deaths in the United States (Centers for Disease Control and Prevention, 2009). Chronic health conditions are projected to become the leading cause of disability globally by the year 2020; if not successfully prevented, they will become the most expensive problems faced by health care systems worldwide (World Health Organization, 2010).

Furthermore, evidence increasingly suggests that mental illness, such as depression, is inexorably linked with chronic health problems, such as cardiovascular disease and diabetes (Vogelzangs et al., 2008). This link between physical well-being and mental health requires health professionals to work more closely in implementing health promotion strategies. In addition, evidence is growing that mental health symptoms and issues are interrelated with other problems of youths, such as drug use, delinquency, and school failure (Mrazek, Biglan, & Hawkins, 2004). Hence, the input and leadership of psychologists and other mental health professionals is critical in the implementation of a prevention focus in our health care system.

It is also crucial that efforts by psychologists and others to focus the mental health field toward prevention extend across the life span, beginning when children are very young and continuing into older age. For example, it is estimated that from birth, between 9% and 20% of children experience social and emotional problems that negatively affect their functioning and development (Brauner & Stephen, 2006; Costello et al., 1996), whereas studies suggest that current services meet the needs of only 13% of minority group children and 31% of nonminority children (Ringel & Sturm, 2001). Additionally, while people age 65 and older comprise only 12% of the US population, they account for 16% of suicide deaths (Centers for Disease Control and Prevention, National Center for Injury Prevention and Control, 2005). Furthermore, the majority of older adults who die by suicide—up to 75%—reported visiting a physician within a month before death (Conwell, 2001).

Therefore, it is important for psychologists and other health care professionals to gain the knowledge and skills needed to inform individuals, families, and their communities about health promotion and disease prevention strategies (World Health Organization, 2010). For prevention efforts to be effective, intervention and education need to happen across multiple contexts, including, but also beyond, the traditional psychotherapy relationship. Psychologists need to utilize client interactions as opportunities for prevention, but they also need to be involved in prevention programming within the contexts of communities, schools, and governments, and at the policy level. The demand to expand the types of roles that psychologists assume and prepare for requires the development of new models of training, practice, research, and social advocacy. As noted by the 2009 APA Presidential Task Force on the Future of Psychology Practice, a "major overhaul" of graduate psychology's training programs is needed in order to prepare psychologists for "the new world psychology finds itself in" (Martin, 2009, p. 66).

Leaders in Prevention

Within the field of psychology, counseling psychologists are uniquely positioned to provide the leadership necessary to further a movement toward a prevention focus; indeed, they have already begun to do so. Counseling psychology has a long-standing historical commitment to the practice of prevention (Gelso & Fretz, 2001; Romano & Hage, 2000), as well as to multiculturalism and social justice (Kenny, Horne, Orpinas, & Reese, 2009; Vera & Speight, 2003). These unique specialty areas in counseling psychology make the field especially suited for providing leadership in fostering the knowledge, skills, and experience of psychologists in the area of prevention.

In addition, counseling psychologists in the Prevention Section of the Society for Counseling Psychology, Division 17 of the American Psychological Association (APA), have led the development and ratification of the *Prevention Science and Practice Guidelines for Psychologists*, which are near acceptance by APA. These practice guidelines provide psychologist with "a set of recommendations to facilitate continued development of prevention within psychological specialty areas" (APA,Under Review, p. 2). The purpose of the guidelines is aspirational; thus, they are aimed at facilitating the continued systematic development of the profession and to help assure a high level of professional practice in the area of prevention.

Goal of Chapter

The goal of this chapter is threefold: (1) to provide a rationale for the inclusion of prevention across the specialty of Counseling Psychology, (2) to assist counseling psychologists in understanding and applying the principles of the Prevention Guidelines (APA, 20XX) to their work, and (3) to provide specific examples of practice, research, training, and social advocacy by psychologists that serve to illustrate the broad recommendations put forth by the Prevention Guidelines.

What Is Prevention?

One of the most frequently cited definitions of prevention is Caplan's (1964), which includes three dimensions of prevention activities: primary (i.e., stopping the problem before it occurs), secondary (i.e., delaying the onset of a problem), and tertiary (i.e., reducing the impact of a problem). Caplan's definition was originally aimed at the prevention of physical disorders, but fails to capture the complex etiology of social and psychological problems (Albee, 1983; Hage et al., 2007).

Romano and Hage (2000) developed a more expansive definition of prevention that we adopt in this chapter, which includes efforts to enhance personal and collective well-being as well as initiatives that create social and political change aimed at improving environments where people live, learn, and work. Thus, when referring to prevention in this chapter, we mean efforts that result in one or more of the following: (1) stopping a problem behavior from ever occurring; (2) delaying the onset of a problem behavior; (3) reducing the impact of a problem behavior; (4) strengthening knowledge, attitudes, and behaviors that promote emotional and physical well-being; and (5) promoting institutional, community, and government policies that further physical, social, and emotional well-being (Romano & Hage, 2000).

Brief Overview of the Development of the Prevention Guidelines

The original set of 15 prevention best practices guidelines was published in *The Counseling Psychologist* (TCP) as the lead article of a TCP major contribution (Hage et al., 2007). The special issue received the Outstanding Contribution Award from Sage Publishing and Division 17 at the 2008 APA convention. At the 2008 APA convention Council meeting a motion was approved to adopt the proposed Prevention Guidelines as a new business item at the 2008 Convention, and the project was assigned to APA's Committee on Professional Practice and Standards (COPPS) to provide feedback and consultation to Division 17 and the developers of the guidelines.

In 2009, COPPS and APA's Board of Professional Affairs (BPA) reviewed the original TCP published guidelines and provided feedback to the guidelines work group. This group, which had been expanded from the developers of the original set of guidelines to include representatives from several APA divisions, began the process of revising the guidelines into a form appropriate to APA requirements for practice guideline development (APA, 2002). Subsequently, the original set of 15 guidelines underwent multiple revisions, following each step in the APA review feedback process, and was condensed into a set of 10 guidelines (see Table 4.1). A new title was also chosen for the revised guidelines. For the purposes of brevity, these guidelines will hereafter be referred to in this chapter as simply "Prevention Guidelines."

The set of 10 Prevention Guidelines are informally organized into 4 specialty areas within the field of prevention psychology: (1) practice (Guidelines 1–3), (2) research and evaluation (Guidelines 4–7), (3) education and training (Guideline 8), and (4) social, political, and legislative action (Guidelines

Table 4.1 Summary of 10 Prevention Science and Practice Guidelines

1. Psychologists are encouraged to select and implement preventive interventions that are theory- and evidence-based.
2. Psychologists are encouraged to use culturally relevant prevention practices adapted to the specific context in which they are implemented.
3. Psychologists are encouraged to develop and implement interventions that reduce risks and promote human strengths.
4. Psychologists are encouraged to support research and evaluation to promote prevention science.
5. Psychologists are encouraged to conduct prevention research and evaluation studies that incorporate environmental contexts.
6. Psychologists are encouraged to consider ethical issues in prevention research.
7. Psychologists are encouraged to consider social justice implications of prevention research.
8. Psychologists are encouraged to increase their awareness, knowledge, and skills essential to prevention through continuing education, training, supervision, and consultation.
9. Psychologists are encouraged to engage in systemic and institutional change strategies that strengthen the health of individuals, families, and communities, and prevent psychological and physical distress and disability.
10. Psychologists are encouraged to engage in governmental, legislative, and political actions to enhance human functioning.

9–10). Within each of these four specialty areas, a subset of guidelines serves to delineate the aspirational principles in each area. As noted in the conclusion to the guidelines document, the guidelines as a whole "represent a summons to psychology to give greater attention to prevention in practice, research, training, and social action" (APA, Under Review, p. 17).

The remainder of this chapter will provide specific examples of practice, research, training, and social action by psychologists that serve to illustrate the broad recommendations put forth by the Prevention Guidelines. In order to best assist readers in understanding and applying the principles of the Prevention Guidelines, a similar structure will be followed for each of the four sections. In each section, one of the four subsets of the Prevention Guidelines will be briefly described, followed by illustrative applications of programs that reflect the ideals of this specialty area within the field of prevention.

Practice for Prevention

Description

Guidelines 1–3 provide important foundational knowledge and recommendations for psychologists preparing to engage in prevention practice. To begin, psychologists engaging in prevention practice are encouraged to develop programs from a sound theoretical base, as such programs have been shown to be most effective. In addition, ensuring that resources are put to best use requires that prevention practitioners engage in rigorous program evaluation, targeting the specific goals and cultural contexts of the prevention program. Hence, it is essential that prevention programs be designed, selected, and implemented with a specific cultural context in mind, and with the involvement and input of members of the target community. Such programs are more likely to be sustained and to be relevant to the lives of the participants. Finally, psychologists are encouraged to focus their efforts not just at reducing risks, such as school failure or family dysfunction, but also to simultaneously work to build strengths and protective factors, such as social and communication skills, and career readiness. Practice interventions that combine the reduction of risk with the promotion of strengths are more apt to empower participants to successfully gain control of their life course.

Program Illustrations

This section focuses on several programs that implement guidelines for practice. These programs serve as models of preventive practice by utilizing the guidelines as fundamental ingredients for the programs' basis. The three programs chosen to serve as effective examples of the three guidelines in preventive practice are: Advancing Career Counseling and Employment Support for Survivors, Black Parenting Strengths and Strategies program, and Research and Intervention for Sexual Health: Theory to Action.

EXAMPLE 1: ADVANCING CAREER COUNSELING AND EMPLOYMENT SUPPORT FOR SURVIVORS

Advancing Career Counseling and Employment Support for Survivors (ACCESS) is a strength-based intervention program with a foundation utilizing Guideline 3: developing and implementing an intervention that reduces risks and promotes human strengths (APA, 20XX). The ACCESS program provides survivors of intimate partner violence with justice through the restoration of occupational, educational, and economic opportunities (Chronister, 2010; Chronister & Davidson, 2010; Chronister & McWhirter, 2006). It is a 2-hour career counseling program held weekly for 5 sessions that implements group processes and psychoeducational curricula (Chronister, 2006; Chronister, Linville, & Palmer, 2008). Although described as an intervention, ACCESS adheres heavily to a preventive standpoint by empowering survivors through skill-building exercises and increasing awareness of supportive and abusive power dynamics to prevent further revictimization (Chronister, 2010; Chronister, Wettersten, & Brown, 2004).

The ACCESS program adheres to Guideline 1: implementing a program that is theory and evidence-based (APA, 20XX), by explicitly designing and administering a curriculum based on social cognitive career theory (Lent, Brown, & Hackett, 1994) and models of empowerment (Freire, 1970). Social cognitive career theory has been widely researched and implemented in interventions for marginalized populations (Chartrand & Rose, 1996; Morris, Shoffner, & Newsome, 2009). It is supported as an effective method for working with battered women because it works to reduce the barriers that women face, as well as increase their support systems and foster greater self-efficacy and outcome expectations for their career pursuits and goals (Chronister & McWhirter, 2006; Morris et al., 2009).

ACCESS also utilizes the theory of critical consciousness (Freire, 1970) to enhance empowerment by facilitating a change in the victims' thinking (Chronister, 2010; Chronister & McWhirter, 2006).

Critical consciousness is defined as "learning to perceive social, political, and economic contradictions, and to take action against the oppressive elements of reality" (Freire, 1970, p.19). In ACCESS, critical consciousness is enhanced through dialogue, group identification, posing problems, identifying contradictions, power analysis, and critical self-reflection (Chronister, 2010; Chronister & McWhirter, 2006). Finally, the ACCESS curriculum also uses five career components that have been identified as the most critical ingredients to successful career interventions (Brown & Krane, 2000). These interventions include written exercises, individualized career skills assessment, work information, role modeling, and attention to building support (Brown & Krane, 2000).

ACCESS also demonstrates Guideline 2: attending to cultural relevancy through adaptation to a specific context (APA, 20XX) by using previously evaluated evidence-based interventions in career counseling and interpersonal partner violence. In addition, ACCESS adapts the group intervention model as an effective way to create a safe environment that fosters empowerment and facilitates the development, awareness, and use of occupational and life skills (Chronister, 2010). Not only does the theoretical approach support empowerment and work toward reducing barriers for this population, but the program also encourages an open group dialogue in which individuals can share individual experiences, cultural identities, beliefs, values, and so forth (Chronister, 2010; Chronister & McWhirter, 2006). This approach provides a safe space for the survivors of abuse by facilitating group identification and interaction among participants. Postintervention evaluations show that ACCESS has positive effects on survivors' vocational self-efficacy and critical consciousness, as well as self-reported progress on their goals at a 5-week follow-up (Chronister, 2010; Chronister & McWhirter, 2006). It has also been reported that vocational knowledge, self-esteem, and motivation for change increased after the program (Chronister et al., 2008). ACCESS is an exemplary model of a theory-based prevention program that demonstrates effectiveness with the target population of women survivors of abuse. For more information about the ACCESS program, visit the website at: www.access-dv.org.

EXAMPLE 2: BLACK PARENTING STRENGTHS AND STRATEGIES PROGRAM

The Black Parenting Strengths and Strategies program (BPSS) is an intervention program for low-income African American families that targets parenting practices associated with early development of conduct problems in children (Coard, Foy-Watson, Zimmer, & Wallace, 2007). Families in BPSS meet weekly in 2-hour sessions for 12 weeks (Coard et al., 2007). The program follows Guideline 1 (APA, 20XX) in that it pulls from Ogbu's (1981) cultural-ecological model and Ward's (2000) theory on the impact of culture on parenting behavior. Ward (2000) states that it is the role of African American parents to protect their children and teach them how to cope with hostility, prejudice, and discrimination from the dominant culture. BPSS uses the well-established, empirically supported Parenting the Strong-Willed Child (PSWC) program (Forehand & Long, 2002) and actively promotes positive racial socialization, defined as "the process by which messages are transmitted or communicated inter- and intragenerationally regarding the significance and meaning of race and ethnicity" (Coard et al., 2007, p. 801).

Results from program evaluations indicate that PSWC improves the parent-child relationship and increases positive child behaviors by teaching parents universally adaptive child noncompliance management and prevention skills (Coard et al., 2007; McMahon & Forehand, 2003). BPSS utilizes the skills taught in PSWC, such as attending, rewarding, ignoring, giving effective directions, and using time-outs appropriately to prevent behavior problems (Coard et al., 2007). By integrating PSWC with strategies promoting positive racial socialization, BPSS is better able to serve the target population.

BPSS reflects Guideline 2 (APA, 20XX) through the implementation of a culturally relevant prevention program for low-income African American families. In the transition of making PSWC culturally specific, various content and delivery adaptations were made (Coard et al. 2007). For example, language was adapted by using the African American perspective use of *we*; delivery of content was adapted by using African proverbs, poems, symbols, and prayers; and content was adapted by addressing the challenges of advocating for one's child on issues of curriculum bias or low teacher expectations and dealing with overt and subtle incidences of racism, prejudice, and discrimination (Coard et al., 2007).

In addition, BPSS builds on strengths of African American families and teaches parenting skills within a sociocultural and sociopolitical context (Coard et al., 2007). For example, session topics include "social and emotional development in

Black children, increasing children's confidence in school environments, developing positive self-image in Black children, promoting positive and developmentally appropriate parent–child discussions about racial issues, and enhancing children's problem-solving skills" (Coard et al., 2007, p. 805). By increasing children's success through aiding in the development of cultural, social, and emotional health as well as empowering parents by improving parental skills and involvement, BPSS also demonstrates Guideline 3 (APA, 20XX). BPSS is an exceptional example of blending an evidence-based approach with culturally relevant strategies to implement an effective prevention program. To find out more about BPSS, visit http://sites.google.com/site/uncgaafss/home.

EXAMPLE 3: RESEARCH AND INTERVENTION FOR SEXUAL HEALTH: THEORY TO ACTION

Research and Intervention for Sexual Health: Theory to Action (RISHTA) is a culturally relevant intervention that effectively illustrates the three Prevention Guidelines for practice. RISHTA is an HIV/AIDS and STI awareness project working at the community, individual, and medical provider levels in Mumbai, India (Schensul, Verma, & Nastasi, 2004). The RISHTA project reflects Guideline 1 because it is developed from the narrative intervention model (NIM; Schensul et al., 2004), a theory-based ecological approach. NIM connects men's sexual health symptoms with the cultural, relational, and psychological factors that increase HIV/STI risk, and reduces the risks by integrating education and risk reduction with medical treatment (Schensul et al., 2009). The NIM approach utilizes empirically supported cognitive-behavioral change models for risk reduction (Azjen & Fishbein, 1980; Kelly et al., 1992) that build on the epistemology of Indian systems of medicine (Schensul et al., 2006).

RISHTA, an acronym meaning "relationship" in Hindi and Urdu languages, is a project that focuses on lower income areas in Mumbai, India (Nastasi & Hitchcock, 2009; RISHTA, 2007; Schensul et al., 2009). Past research in these areas has shown that married men between the ages of 21 to 40 are at a higher risk for contracting HIV/STI due to this population's involvement in sexually risky activities at or just before the onset of marriage (Schensul et al., 2009; Verma, Rangaiyan, Singh, Sharma, & Pelto, 2001). In an attempt to best reach the program's target population, RISHTA collaborates with community officials, medical providers, and members of the target population to understand how the men conceptualize sexual health and sexual health problems from a cultural perspective (RISHTA, 2007; Schensul et al., 2009). RISHTA's multilevel approach illustrates Guideline 2 by adapting a model that would best serve the target population. For example, RISHTA ensures that the interventions are effective by teaching HIV/STI prevention through the cultural conceptualization of sexual problems as *gupt rog*, or "secret illness" (Kulhara & Avasthi, 1995; Pelto & Verma, 1999). Addressing HIV/STI prevention under the context of *gupt rog* has the result that larger numbers of men are more willing to seek treatment due to the known saliency of the problem, and service providers can more comfortably start a discussion with the men seeking treatment (Schensul et al., 2009). The reframing of HIV/STI prevention as *gupt rog* allows the issues of sexual health to be addressed directly, rather than in a taboo fashion.

Since RISHTA's implementation in 2002, men that visited medical providers trained in the narrative intervention model have shown a significant increase in STI/HIV knowledge, and a decrease in *gupt rog* problems (STIs, such as gonorrhea) and extramarital sex (RISHTA, 2007). The goals of RISHTA reflect Guideline 3 by effectively promoting positive sexual health and reducing the risk of STI/HIV transmission through the reduction of risky sexual behaviors and an increase in STI/HIV awareness. As of 2011, RISHTA has begun a second phase of the project targeting married women in lower income areas of Mumbai.

By using a culturally relevant theoretical approach, and being mindful of culture-specific views toward sexual health on a variety of levels, RISHTA is an excellent model of prevention practice in an international setting. To find out more about RISHTA go to www.popcouncil.org/projects/250_RISHTA.asp.

Research and Evaluation for Prevention

Description

Guidelines 4–7 detail necessary components of effective prevention research and evaluation. Guidelines 4 and 5 recommend that prevention researchers incorporate a social contextual approach to their research. Specifically, researchers need to adopt an evidence-based approach in selecting specific interventions for implementation in a target community. Furthermore, they need to assess the differential impact of service delivery systems at multiple levels in partnership with members of a community. In particular, as noted by Guideline 6, it is critical to evaluate possible negative impacts that prevention interventions may have on individuals, a community, and the larger society. Finally, as Guideline 7 recommends, prevention researchers have an important role in addressing societal issues, such as social inequality, equal rights, oppression, discrimination, and exploitation of members of society. Prevention and social justice are "inextricably linked," and thus the promotion of social justice is important in the planning, implementation, evaluation, and dissemination of prevention research.

Program Illustrations

Three model prevention programs that successfully apply the guidelines for research and evaluation are outlined in this section. The models that demonstrate at least one of the research and evaluation guidelines include: Asian/Pacific Islander Youth Violence Prevention Center, Latinos en Camino al Exito Universitario, and Youth Action Research Prevention.

EXAMPLE 1: ASIAN/PACIFIC ISLANDER YOUTH VIOLENCE PREVENTION CENTER

The Asian/Pacific Islander Youth Violence Prevention Center (APIYVPC) is a comprehensive program that uses a social ecological model and an interdisciplinary, community-based approach to conduct violence prevention research with Asian and Pacific Islander youth (Guideline 5). Housed in the University of Hawai'i at Mānoa, APIYVPC is comprised of a community advisory board, scientific advisory board, executive committee, senior scientists/mentors, and community workgroups. The advisory boards, executive committee, and senior scientists include researchers with backgrounds in psychology, social work, psychiatry, public health, urban and regional planning, and sociology (Umemoto et al., 2009). The community workgroups include a local high school student task force, a women's support group for mothers recovering from substance abuse, and a teacher and counselor workgroup. By partnering with local organizations and schools in the community, APIYVPC is better able to incorporate environmental contexts into its research and evaluation studies (Umemoto et al., 2009).

APIYVPC is providing a foundation in an area where research is lacking by conducting research on prevalence, risk, and protective factors related to youth violence in Hawai'i (Guerrero, Goebert, Alicata, & Bell, 2009; Umemoto et al., 2009). By conducting an assessment of the epidemiology of risk and protective factors at multiple levels, APIYVPC can better understand the historically underrepresented target population. APIYVPC's mission to reduce and prevent interpersonal youth violence among the Asian and Pacific Islander population reflects Guideline 4 in that it is consistent with best practices in prevention science. Collaboration with the community to conduct rigorous and culturally responsive research allows APIYVPC to build a comprehensive program that promotes prevention research and supports the evaluation of their own programs (Guerrero et al., 2009; Umemoto et al., 2009). As stated in the program's mission, APIYVPC aims to create a national prototype by developing an effective, comprehensive, public health and culturally competent model for the API community. By producing and disseminating research about a problem for a specific population that has been previously overlooked and not researched, APIYVPC successfully applies the social justice implications of Guideline 7.

Not only does APIYVPC disseminate their research through scholarly publications and local student presentations, but the program also takes on the ethical responsibility to adequately train all of their employees in how to conduct rigorous science, and analyze and present scientific data. In addition, APIYVPC regularly conducts training seminars on various topics (i.e., grant writing, facilitating career development for the student researchers and API staff). The program also regularly holds community focus groups to conduct a needs assessment for the youth prevention and intervention programs run by APIYVPC. The program's attention to ethical standards in staff training, program evaluation, cultural relevance, and collaborative community partnerships shows APIYVPC's consideration of the unique ethical issues that are part of prevention research.

The APIYVPC's promotion of prevention research and evaluation, as well as collaboration at multiple ecological levels has established a comprehensive and sustainable program. Through constant evaluation, APIYVPC allows for flexibility and innovation, which works to facilitate a community-wide reduction in youth violence (Umemoto et al., 2009). More information on the APIYVPC can be found at: http://apiyvpc.org/.

EXAMPLE 2: LATINOS EN CAMINO AL EXITO UNIVERSITARIO

Latinos en Camino al Exito Universitario (Latinos on a Path to Higher Education) is a culturally and linguistically sensitive grassroots precollege program that aims to reduce dropout and improve college entrance rates for Latino youth (Rivera-Mosquera, Dowd, & Mitchell-Blanks, 2007; Rivera-Mosquera, Phillips, Castelino, Martin, & Mowry Dobran, 2007). Housed in the University of Akron's Counseling, Testing, and Career Center, the program was inspired by other established, federally funded precollege programs such as Educational Talent Search and Upward Bound, and integrates Bandura's theory of self-efficacy to build on the strengths and skills of the students (Rivera-Mosquera, Dowd, et al., 2007). In addition to its cultural relevance, Latinos en Camino al Exito Universitario also uses a formal pre- and posttest evaluation in an attempt to improve on existing pre-college programs (Rivera-Mosquera, Dowd, et al., 2007). For example, the program was evaluated in a pretest posttest design, and the descriptive statistics demonstrated that participants and their parents all felt that the program increased their understanding and confidence in planning for college and career, as well as in improving the participants' study skills (Rivera-Mosquera, Dowd, et al., 2007). By being culturally relevant to their target population and developing and revising the intervention based on empirical evidence and theory, Latinos en Camino al Exito Universitario attends to Guideline 4 in promoting sound prevention science.

Latinos en Camino al Exito Universitario also meets the principles of Guideline 5 by employing a multilevel approach to increase college preparedness, facilitate career exploration, and build academic skills among Latino youth within a community setting (Rivera-Mosquera, Dowd, et al., 2007; Rivera-Mosquera, Phillips, et al., 2007). Rather than publicizing the program in a school setting where the target population may not be attending, Latinos en Camino al Exito Universitario reaches their target population by creating culturally relevant partnerships in community settings (Rivera-Mosquera, Phillips, et al., 2007). For example, Latinos en Camino al Exito Universitario provides outreach in a setting where at-risk Latino youth may be more receptive and accessible by collaborating with a local Catholic church (Rivera-Mosquera, Phillips, et al., 2007).

Latinos en Camino al Exito Universitario's purpose is twofold in that not only does it provide an intervention to increase the completion of high school and continuation onto higher education for Latino youth, but it also creates an opportunity for predoctoral counseling center interns to consult, develop, and implement programs in multicultural settings (Rivera-Mosquera, Dowd, et al., 2007). The program provides training for the next generation of prevention researchers by building a set of prevention research skills and hands-on experience. Not only does the training of predoctoral students in prevention research promote prevention science, but it also attends to the ethical concerns of adequately preparing culturally competent researchers.

The program's integration of social justice implications, as recommended in Guideline 7, is inherent in its purpose. Latinos en Camino al Exito Universitario was created to facilitate systemic change by better executing areas where existing education programs were lacking (Rivera-Mosquera, Phillips, et al., 2007). The program addresses a serious societal issue by serving an underserved population in need of resources and advocacy to increase access to higher education. Latinos en Camino al Exito Universitario provides outreach in Spanish to increase access to higher education through the utilization of community partnerships with Catholic churches, parents and families, and local organizations (Rivera-Mosquera, Phillips, et al., 2007). By implementing more stringent research methods from an established theoretical background, Latinos en Camino al Exito Universitario provides a template in which future programs can model themselves.

EXAMPLE 3: YOUTH ACTION RESEARCH PREVENTION

Youth Action Research Prevention (YARP) is an intervention that aims to reduce drug use and risky sexual behaviors among urban adolescents in public schools (Berg, Coman, & Schensul, 2009). By utilizing participatory action research in which at-risk adolescents are the researchers, the program empowers the community and facilitates social change. YARP builds students' self-efficacy and skills to participate in social action by teaching them how to conduct research within their communities and how to promote a change in public policy (Berg et al., 2009).

YARP reflects Guideline 4 in promoting prevention science implementing an intervention with the goal of preventing drug use and risky sexual behavior (Berg et al., 2009). The program is a 3-year summer and after-school program for students ages 14 to 16, in which participants become Youth Action Researchers. The participants work as a group to create, implement, and evaluate a program that aims at changing societal norms related to drug use and risky sexual behavior while promoting social advocacy for urban youth. YARP operates on the basis of ecological theory, identity theory, learning and instructional theories (i.e., social learning theory), and critical and transformative theories (i.e., participatory action research). The goal of YARP is to prevent drug use and risky sexual behaviors in its' participating researchers, as well as the community. Through effectively implementing a student-designed prevention program, YARP challenges students' drug and sexual behaviors that conflict with research, and help students gain critical consciousness (Berg et al., 2009). As the at-risk adolescents work toward the common goal to reduce drug use and risky sexual behaviors among their peers, they must engage in critical self-reflection about their own decision making. Not only does YARP strive to decrease student drug use and risky sexual behavior as long-term goals, but it also has short-term and intermediate outcome goals. Short-term goals of YARP include improving decision-making skills, self-esteem, assertiveness, and internal locus of control; while intermediate outcomes include a positive assessment of education and career option expectations, improved self-efficacy, and more knowledge about STIs and the effects of drugs (Berg et al., 2009).

Education for Prevention

Description

Guideline 8 recommends that psychologists gain training and supervised experience in prevention approaches and applications. This guideline notes the existing focus on remediation in graduate training programs and urges psychologists to take initiative in expanding their learning options to include prevention. Several knowledge and skills domains have been identified as essential to engaging in prevention work (Hage et al., 2007; O'Neil & Britner, 2009). These domains include understanding the nature of prevention, as well as how to design, implement, and evaluate programs; assess community needs; incorporate cultural and contextual factors into preventive interventions; engage in grant writing; and, finally, engage in policy development. Training in these areas can be obtained through various avenues, including coursework, service learning, respecialization programs, postdoctoral fellowships, continuing education programs, self-study, conferences focused on prevention, and combinations of such alternatives.

Program Illustrations

The two programs chosen as effective demonstrations of Guideline 8, education in preventive practice, are: the Missouri Prevention Center and the First Year Experience training program at Boston College.

EXAMPLE 1: MISSOURI PREVENTION CENTER

The Missouri Prevention Center (MPC), housed in the University of Missouri, works to promote the mental health and well-being of children and their families through developing, implementing, evaluating, and disseminating family- and school-based interventions, particularly aimed at reducing depression and aggression among youth. The MPC is founded on a conceptual model that is influenced by public health, ecological, and multicultural frameworks. In addition, the center's staff includes an interdisciplinary team of counseling psychologists, school psychologists, special educators, graduate students, and community leaders (Herman et al., 2009; Reinke et al., 2009).

Although the MPC strives to utilize all of the prevention practice guidelines, the center is especially reflective of Guideline 8, which emphasizes increasing the awareness, knowledge, and skills essential to prevention through continued education, training, supervision, and consultation. As stated by Herman et al. (2009), the MPC "firmly believe[s] that a primary barrier to effective dissemination of effective practices is the lack of trained personnel (in both practice and research) who can advance the field. Our hope is to train a cadre of practitioners and researchers in many fields (counseling psychology, school psychology, school counseling, special education) who can develop and implement best practices in prevention and also who can train the next generation of prevention scientists" (p. 659). By employing graduate students, the MPC is providing students with the experience and knowledge to become future prevention scientists. The participating graduate students are trained in prevention science research through a weekly, year-round seminar that addresses many critical elements of prevention science research, such as challenges and controversies, ethical and social justice issues, culturally relevant interventions; and sophisticated research designs (Kellam, Koretz, & Mosciski, 1999). The seminar is followed by a 2-hour weekly group supervision that focuses on applying the topics of the seminar to conduct community-based participatory research (Herman et al., 2009; Reinke et al., 2009). For a detailed understanding of the center's model, structure, activities, and research, go to http://education.missouri.edu/orgs/prevention/about/MPC_start.php.

EXAMPLE 2: BOSTON COLLEGE'S FIRST YEAR EXPERIENCE

Boston College's First Year Experience (FYE) is a second example of an educational program that uses a hands-on approach to train counseling psychologists by increasing awareness, knowledge, and skills essential to prevention. FYE is a 4- to 6-hour weekly program for 1st-year doctoral students. The students are placed in a community or school setting under the supervision of faculty to gain professional experience in prevention, collaboration, and advocacy (Kenny & Gallagher, 2000; Kenny, Waldo, Warter, & Barton, 2002). In this nontraditional field experience, students work in settings such as urban public schools, courts, and detention centers (Boston College, 2010). In these settings, students are able to gain a better understanding of the roles of a psychologist with populations typically outside the scope of the counseling profession in order to provide a base in the roles of social justice and advocacy (Boston College, 2010). Students meet in weekly seminars to discuss and reflect on their experiences; at the end of the year, students are required to present a summary of their experiences along with any thoughts about future interventions and research in counseling psychology (Boston College, 2010; Conyne, Newmeyer, Kenny, Romano, & Matthews, 2008). Several programs are developed for the FYE, such as Tools for Tomorrow and City Connects (Conyne et al., 2008), both of which are collaborative efforts among teachers, administrators, counselors, and FYE graduate students to provide students in urban public schools the support needed to ensure readiness for postsecondary work and education (Conyne et al., 2008). Information on outreach projects, such as Tools for Tomorrow can be accessed at: http://www.bc.edu/content/bc/schools/lsoe/research-outreach/faculty-research.html; and information for City Connects can be accessed at: http://www.bc.edu/schools/lsoe/cityconnects/.

Social and Political Action for Prevention

Description

Guidelines 9 and 10, perhaps more than any of the others, describe important new roles for counseling psychologists in making a positive difference in the communities in which they work. Guideline 9 points to the necessity of addressing systemic barriers to social justice when engaging in prevention. Psychologists need to focus on "the causes of the causes" in promoting the health and well-being of individuals, communities, and organizations. When psychologists neglect institutional impediments such as poverty, racism, and sexism, their interventions fall short of contributing to lasting and in-depth change. For example, our prevention efforts need to "impact the structure, role relationships, premises, rules, and assumptions governing systems to better empower communities and promote justice and equity" (APA, 20XX). Furthermore, to carry out such changes, Guideline 10 promotes psychologists' involvement in governmental, legislative, and political actions to further prevention efforts. Examples of such efforts include legislative action to support positive health outcomes and to reduce discrimination based on gender, race, socioeconomic status, religious or spiritual background, and sexual orientation.

Program Illustrations

This section outlines model prevention programs that successfully apply the guidelines for social action and political and legislative advocacy for prevention. The models outlined that demonstrate the guidelines are the: SPEC approach, and the Fraternity Peer Rape Education Program.

EXAMPLE 1: STRENGTHS, PREVENTION, EMPOWERMENT, AND COMMUNITY MODEL

SPEC, an acronym that stands for strengths, prevention, empowerment, and community change, is a model that can be applied to any prevention program or initiative to promote well-being. To promote well-being at the personal, relational, and collective levels, SPEC implements policies and practices in community settings across four domains: temporal, ecological, participation, and capabilities (Prilleltensky, 2005). Temporal refers to the timing of the intervention, reactive versus proactive. Prilleltensky (2005) argues for adopting a preventive approach in order to reduce the financial and human costs that frequently follow the more commonly utilized reaction approach. The ecological domain refers to meeting the goal of enhancing personal wellness through addressing root causes of problems, creating systems that increase community participation, removing barriers to services and supports, and endorsing social policies that enhance well-being (Prilleltensky, 2005), which adheres to Guideline 10. The participation domain refers to involving and empowering the people of the community to have both a "choice and a voice" in making decisions for the programs and social policies (Prilleltensky, 2005). This collective orientation, as opposed to an individual approach, illustrates

Guideline 9 through the focus on engaging in systematic and institutional change. For example, one of the SPEC programs housed in the University of Miami School of Education, Miami SPEC, focuses on systemic change by promoting and educating local organizations that provide health services to families in a strengths-based, prevention approach (Evans, 2007). Lastly, the capabilities domain encourages the building of competencies and utilizing of skills in an engaging and ethical way (Prilleltensky, 2005). The SPEC model engages in systematic and institutional change strategies that strengthen health and utilize prevention and aims to engage in government or legislative advocacy to enhance human functioning.

Evans, Hanlin, and Prilleltensky (2007) illustrate the SPEC model in a case study involving changing the salient values, beliefs and assumptions, and practices of an existing program to be more community oriented and empowerment- and strength-focused by using a preventive approach. Provided with the persistent message of primary prevention, empowerment, participation, and changing community conditions, the program's employees became highly motivated toward change (Evans et al., 2007). Including employee participation in developing new principles and philosophies for the program in a collaborative process was also found to be powerful and rewarding for the program's employees (Evans et al., 2007). However, implementing new structures within the program proved to be more difficult, and SPEC project leaders faced some resistance. Evans et al. noted that they should have instituted clear and detailed collaboration terms of reference for partnership earlier in the process to avoid conflict; and since they were "guests" lacking a formal agreement, they were unable to point out shortcomings in the change process. Although there are many struggles with changing an already existing program's internal framework to become more effective, Evans et al. demonstrates that it is possible if done correctly. To find out more on how to create a program that implements SPEC or change a program to follow the SPEC model, visit: http://www.specway.org/.

EXAMPLE 2: FRATERNITY PEER RAPE EDUCATION PROGRAM

The Fraternity Peer Rape Education Program (FPREP) is a sexual assault education program that trains fraternity members to be peer rape educators for their own chapter. Evidence suggests that members of fraternities are more likely than the general college population to hold sexist attitudes, abuse alcohol, and be perpetrators of sexual aggression (Fritner & Rubinson, 1993; Schwartz & DeKeseredy, 2000). FPREP is a collaborative effort between the University of Illinois at Urbana-Champaign's Greek affairs office, the gender and women's studies department, and the Office of Women's Programs (Wantland, 2005, 2008). The program is a 2-semester course offered through the gender and women's studies department that engages students to understand their attitudes toward rape and the roles they play in rape-supportive environments. Consistent with Guideline 9, students are active participants in their learning through interactive exercises, journaling, guiding discussions, and hands-on assignments. The first semester is focused on sexual violence in the United States and how violence influences the students' lives, and the second semester requires students to develop, implement, and evaluate workshops on sexual violence prevention in their fraternity chapters. At the completion of the class, change in attitudes toward rape and student interactions in rape-supportive fraternity environments are measured through self-reflection papers and journals, interviews, and observations recorded in a field log by researchers (Wantland, 2008).

Although the class is not required, the Greek affairs office strongly encourages chapter representatives to take the course to engage in community change within the prominent culture of fraternities. Not only has the FPREP course helped shift the individual student's views of rape and recognition of rape-supportive behaviors, it has also empowered students to take on a more communal sense of responsibility within the actions of the fraternity and viewing themselves as agents for change (Wantland 2008). Research of the effects of FPREP indicates fraternity members' shift in worldview away from believing that "bad things only happened to bad people" (p. 64), to recognizing the rape-supportive behaviors within their peer groups (Wantland, 2008). Fraternity members who completed the FPREP course also indicated that they were more likely to speak up against rape-supportive actions or behaviors (Wantland, 2008). By promoting a new outlook for fraternity members and encouraging them to become agents for positive change, FPREP strives to implement Guideline 10 by training fraternity men to be peer rape educators for their own fraternity chapters, where they can transform the fraternity culture from within.

Conclusion

In this chapter we have described the changes that are taking place in the health care system, which argue for renewed efforts in the implementation of the recommendations of the Prevention Guidelines for the field of psychology. In addition, we have noted the considerable gains that have been made in identifying and implementing evidence-based, culturally relevant prevention interventions that have been shown to enhance the health and well-being of individuals, families, and communities. Our hope is that increased awareness of these evidence-based approaches will spur policy and legislative changes that will lead to more widespread adoption of these programs.

Further dissemination of evidence-based prevention approaches will, undoubtedly, lead to positive changes and improved health outcomes for our communities. However, as noted by Bumbarger, Perkins, and Greenberg (2010), to accomplish the goal of wide-scale dissemination of evidence-based prevention in our communities, "programs must be carefully selected to fit a specific need and context, implemented with sufficient quality and fidelity, and be sustained long-term" (p. 441). Hence, additional efforts are needed by researchers, practitioners, educators, policy makers, and community leaders to work out the many challenges inherent in "real world" adaption and implementation of evidence-based prevention programs and strategies across culturally and contextually diverse communities.

Future Directions

As the implementation of a prevention focus expands, a number of new questions and/or challenges emerge, including:

1. What is the role of social justice in implementing a prevention focus? Are systemic interventions aimed at changing unjust social systems a necessary part of prevention strategies and programs?
2. When implementing prevention strategies and programs, how will we demonstrate that such interventions truly have a positive impact on the long-term health and well-being of our communities? How do we better form effective partnerships with target communities in this process?
3. When evaluating prevention programs and strategies, what specific criteria will be utilized to evaluate whether advances have been achieved in the "health" or "wellness" of a community? Whose input is needed to make these decisions? How do we avoid imposing our own culturally bound values about what constitutes health and wellness?
4. As psychologists and mental health professionals, how do we better prepare ourselves to take on the multiple roles needed in developing, implementing, evaluating, and disseminating effective prevention programs and strategies? What changes are necessary in our training programs and accreditation committees in order to better prepare leaders in prevention?

References

Albee, G. W. (1983). Political ideology and science: A reply to Eysenck. *American Psychologist, 38*(8), 965–966. doi:10.1037/0003-066X.38.8.965

American Psychological Association (APA). (2002). Criteria for practice guideline development and evaluation. *American Psychologist, 57,* 1048–1051.

American Psychological Association. (Under Review). *Prevention science and practice guidelines for psychology.* Washington, DC: Author.

Azjen, I., & Fishbein, M. (1980). *Understanding attitudes and predicting social behavior.* Englewood Cliffs, NJ: Prentice-Hall.

Berg, M., Coman, E., & Schensul, J. J. (2009). Youth action research for prevention: A multi-level intervention designed to increase efficacy and empowerment among urban youth. *American Journal of Community Psychology, 43,* 345–359.

Boston College, The Carolyn A. and Peter S. Lynch School of Education (2010). *Counseling psychology doctoral student handbook, 2010–2011.* Retrieved April 10, 2011, from http://www.bc.edu/content/bc/schools/lsoe/academics/departments/cdep/graduate/counsel.html.

Brauner, C. B., & Stephen, B. C. (2006). Estimating the prevalence of early childhood serious emotional/behavioral disorder. *Public Health Reports, 121,* 303–310.

Brown, S. D., & Krane, N. E. (2000). Four (or five) sessions and a cloud of dust: Old assumptions and new observations about career counseling. In S. D. Brown & R. W. Lent (Eds.), *Handbook of counseling psychology* (3rd ed., pp. 740–766). New York: Wiley.

Bumbarger, B. K., Perkins, D. F., & Greenberg, M. T. (2010). Taking effective prevention to scale. In *Handbook of youth prevention science* (pp. 433–444). New York: Routledge.

Caplan, G. (1964). *Principles of preventive psychiatry.* Oxford, England: Basic Books.

Centers for Disease Control and Prevention, National Center for Injury Prevention and Control. (2005). *Web-based Injury Statistics Query and Reporting System (WISQARS).* Retrieved March 2, 2011 from http://www.cdc.gov/injury/wisqars/index.html.

Chartrand, J. M., & Rose, M. L. (1996). Career interventions for at-risk populations: Incorporating social cognitive influences. *The Career Development Quarterly, 44*(4), 341–354.

Chronister, K. M. (2006). The intersection of social class and race in community intervention research with women domestic violence survivors. *American Journal of Community Psychology, 37,* 75–182.

Chronister, K. M. (2010, August). Career counseling interventions for survivors of intimate-partner violence. In J. P. Schwartz & S. Chapman (Cochairs), *Social justice research and trauma—Notes from the field.* Symposium conducted at the American Psychological Association 117th Annual Convention, San Diego, CA.

Chronister, K. M., & Davidson, M. M. (2010). Promoting distributive justice for intimate partner violence survivors with group intervention. *The Journal for Specialists in Group Work, 2,* 115–123.

Chronister, K. M., Linville, D., & Palmer, K. (2008). Domestic violence survivors' access of career counseling services: A qualitative investigation. *Journal of Career Development, 34,* 339–361.

Chronister, K. M., & McWhirter, E. H. (2006). An experimental examination of two career interventions for battered women. *Journal of Counseling Psychology, 53,* 151–164.

Chronister, K. M., Wettersten, K. B., & Brown, C. (2004). Vocational psychology research for the liberation of battered women. *The Counseling Psychologist, 32,* 900–922.

Coard, S. I., Foy-Watson, S., Zimmer, C., & Wallace, A. (2007). Considering culturally relevant parenting practices in intervention development and adaptation: A randomized controlled trial of the Black Parenting Strengths and Strategies (BPSS) program. *The Counseling Psychologist, 35,* 797–820.

Conwell, Y. (2001). Suicide in later life: A review and recommendations for prevention [Supplemental material]. *Suicide and Life Threatening Behavior, 31,* 32–47.

Conyne, R. K., Newmeyer, M. D., Kenny, M., Romano, J. L., & Matthews, C. R. (2008). Two key strategies for teaching prevention: Specialized course and infusion. *Journal of Primary Prevention, 29,* 375–401.

Costello, E., Angold, A., Burns, B. J., Erkanli, A., Stangl, D. K., & Tweed, D. L. (1996). The Great Smoky Mountains study of youth: Functional impairment and serious emotional disturbance. *Archives of General Psychiatry, 53*(12), 1137–1143.

Evans, S. D., Hanlin, C. E., & Prilleltensky, I. (2007). Blending ameliorative and transformative approaches in human service organizations: A case study. *Journal of Community Psychology, 35,* 329–346.

Forehand, R. L., & Long, N. (2002). *Parenting the strong willed child: The clinically proven five-week program for parents of two- to six-year-olds.* Chicago: Contemporary Books.

Freire, P. (1970). *Pedagogy of the oppressed.* New York: Continuum.

Fritner, M. P., & Rubinson, L. (1993). Acquaintance rape: The influence of alcohol, fraternity membership, and sports team membership. *Journal of Sex Education and Therapy, 19,* 272–284.

Gelso, C. J., & Fretz, B. R. (2001). *Counseling psychology* (2nd ed.). Fort Worth, TX: Harcourt.

Guerrero, A. P. S., Goebert, D. A., Alicata, D. A., & Bell, C. K. (2009). Striving for a culturally responsive process in training health professionals on Asian American and Pacific Islander youth violence prevention. *Aggression and Violent Behavior, 14,* 499–505.

Hage, S., Romano, J., Conyne, R., Kenny, M. E., Matthews, C., Schwartz, J. P., & Waldo, M. (2007). Best practice guidelines on prevention practice, research, training, and social advocacy for psychologists. *The Counseling Psychologist, 35,* 493–566.

Herman, K. C., Reinke, W. M., Stormont, M., Puri, R., & Agarwal, G. (2009). Using prevention science to promote children's mental health: The founding of the Missouri Prevention Center. *The Counseling Psychologist, 38,* 652–690.

Kellam, S. G., Koretz, D., & Moscicki, E. (1999). Core elements of developmental epidemiologically based prevention research. *American Journal of Community Psychology, 27,* 463–483.

Kelly, J. A., St. Lawrence, J. S., Stevenson, L. Y., Hauth, A. C., Kalichman, S. C., Diaz, Y. E.,... Morgan, M.G. (1992). Community AIDS/HIV risk reduction: The effects of endorsements by popular people in three cities. *American Journal of Public Health, 82,* 1483–1489.

Kenny, M., & Gallagher, L. A. (2000). Service learning as a vehicle in training psychologists for revised professional roles. In F. S. Sherman & W. R. Torbert (Eds.), *Transforming social inquiry, transforming social action: Creating communities of practice at the university and in the community* (pp. 189–205). Norwell, MA: Kluwer.

Kenny, M. E., Horne, A. M., Orpinas, P., & Reese. L. E. (Eds.). (2009). *Realizing social justice: The challenge of prevention interventions.* Washington, DC: APA Books.

Kenny, M. E., Waldo, M., Warter, E. W., & Barton, C. (2002). School-linked prevention: Theory, science, and practice for enhancing the lives of children and youth. *The Counseling Psychologist, 30,* 726–748.

Kulhara, P., & Avasthi, A. (1995). Sexual dysfunction on the Indian subcontinent. *International Review of Psychiatry, 7,* 231–240.

Lent, R. W., Brown, S. D., & Hackett, G. (1994). Toward a unifying social cognitive theory of career and academic interest, choice, and performance [Monograph]. *Journal of Vocational Behavior, 45,* 79–122.

Martin, S. (2009). Roadmap for change: An APA task force previews its recommendations for transforming psychology practice to meet the demands of a new world. *Monitor on Psychology, 40,* 66.

McMahon, R. J., & Forehand, R. L. (2003). *Helping the noncompliant child: A clinician's guide to effective parent training* (2nd ed.). New York: Guilford.

Morris, C. W., Shoffner, M.F., & Newsome, D. W. (2009). Career counseling for women preparing to leave abusive relationships: A social cognitive career theory approach. *Career Development Quarterly, 58,* 44–53.

Mrazek, P., Biglan, A., & Hawkins, J.D. (2004). *Community-monitoring systems: Tracking and improving the well-being of America's children and adolescents.* Falls Church, VA: Society for Prevention Research. Retrieved from http://www.preventionresearch.org

Nastasi, B. K., & Hitchcock, J. (2009). Challenges of evaluating multilevel interventions. *American Journal of Community Psychology, 43,* 360–376.

Ogbu, J. U. (1981). Origins of human competence: A cultural-ecological perspective. *Child Development, 51,* 413–429.

O'Neil, J. M., & Britner, P. A. (2009). Training primary preventionists to make a difference in people's lives. In M. E. Kenny, A. M. Horne, P. Orpinas, & L. E. Reese (Eds.), *Realizing social justice: The challenge of preventive interventions* (pp. 141–162). Washington, DC: American Psychological Association.

Pelto, P. J., Joshi, A., & Verma R. (1999). The development of Indian male sexuality. *Population Council: South and Southeast Asian Regional Office,* p. 54.

Prilleltensky, I. (2005). Promoting well-being: Time for a paradigm shift in health and human services. *Scandinavian Journal of Public Health, 33,* 53–60.

Reinke, W. M., Splett, J., Robeson, E., & Offutt, C. (2009). Combining school and family interventions for the prevention and early intervention of disruptive behavior problems in children: A public health perspective. *Psychology in the Schools, 46,* 33–43.

Ringel, J. S., & Sturm, R. (2001). National estimates of mental health utilization and expenditures for children in 1998. *The Journal of Behavioral Health Services and Research, 28*(3), 319–333. doi:10.1007/BF02287247

RISHTA. (2007). *Addressing Gupt Rog: Narrative prevention counseling for STI/HIV prevention: A guide to AYUSH and allopathic practitioners.* New Delhi, India: Population Council.

Rivera-Mosquera, E., Dowd, E. T., & Mitchell-Blanks, M. (2007). Prevention activities in professional psychology: A reaction to the prevention guidelines. *The Counseling Psychologist, 35,* 586–593.

Rivera-Mosquera, E., Phillips, J. C., Castelino, P., Martin, J. K., & Mowry Dobran, E. S. (2007). Design and implementation of a grassroots precollege program for Latino youth. *The Counseling Psychologist, 35,* 821–839.

Romano, J. L., & Hage, S. M. (2000). Prevention and counseling psychology: Revitalizing commitments for the 21st century. *The Counseling Psychologist, 28,* 733–763.

Schensul, S. L., Mekki-Berrada, A., Nastasi, B. K., Singh, R., Burleson, J. A., & Bojko, M. (2006). Men's extramarital sex, marital relationships and sexual risk in urban poor communities in India. *Journal of Urban Health, 83,* 614–624.

Schensul, S. L., Niranjan, S., Singh, R., Verma, R. K., Nastasi, B. K., & Mazumder, P. G. (2009). Multilevel perspectives on community intervention: An example from an Indo-US HIV prevention project in Mumbai, India. *American Journal of Community Psychology, 43,* 277–291.

Schensul, S. L., Verma, R. K., & Nastasi, B. K. (2004). Responding to men's sexual concerns: Research and intervention in slum communities in Mumbai, India. *International Journal of Men's Health, 3,* 197–220.

Schwartz, M. D., & DeKeseredy, W. S. (2000). Aggregation bias and woman abuse: Variations by male peer support, region, language, and school type. *Journal of Interpersonal Violence, 15,* 555–565.

Trust for America's Health. (2009a). Implementation of America's healthcare reform law. Retrieved November 1, 2010, from http://healthyamericans.org/health-reform/

Trust for America's Health. (2009b). *Poll: American public supports investment in prevention as part of health care reform.* Washington, DC: Author.

Umemoto, K., Baker, C. K., Helm, S., Maio, T., Goebert, D. A., & Hishinuma, E. S. (2009). Moving toward comprehensiveness and sustainability in a social ecological approach to youth violence prevention: Lessons from the Asian/Pacific Islander Youth Violence Prevention Center. *American Journal of Community Psychology, 44,* 221–232.

Vera, E. M., & Speight, S. L. (2003). Multicultural competence, social justice, and counseling psychology: Expanding our roles. *The Counseling Psychologist, 31,* 253–272.

Verma, R. K., Rangaiyan, G., Singh, R., Sharma, S., & Pelto, P. J. (2001). A study of male sexual health problems in a Mumbai slum population. *Culture, Health and Sexuality, 3,* 339–352.

Vogelzangs, N., Kritchevsky, S. B., Beekman, A. T., Newman, A. B., Satterfield, S., Simonsick, E. M., & Penninx, B. W. (2008). Depressive symptoms and change in abdominal obesity in older persons. *Archives of General Psychiatry, 65,* 1386–1393.

Wantland, R. (2005). Feminist frat boys?: Fraternity men in the (women's studies) house. *Feminist Formations, 17,* 156–163.

Wantland, R. (2008). Our brotherhood and your sister: Building anti-rape community in the fraternity. *Journal of Prevention and Intervention in the Community, 36,* 57–73.

Ward, J. V. (2000). *The skin we're in: Teaching our teens to be emotionally strong, socially smart and spiritually connected.* New York: Simon and Schuster.

World Health Organization. (2010). *Integrating prevention into health care, Fact sheet No. 172.* Retrieved from http://www.scribd.com/immaniacs/d/32316439-WHO-Factsheet

CHAPTER

5 Ethical Principles for the Practice of Prevention

Jonathan P. Schwartz, Sally M. Hage *and* Dianna Marisol González

Abstract

The role of prevention in the field of psychology, due to increasing evidence of the utility of prevention, has grown significantly in recent years. Unfortunately, although there has been increasing attention to training competent prevention practitioners, there has been less attention to explicating meaningful guidelines for ethical issues raised in prevention. In this chapter we will discuss the importance of prevention, identify unique ethical issues in prevention, highlight previous guidance provided for addressing these issues, and suggest ideas for starting a new ethical code for prevention practice.

Key Words: prevention, ethics, training, research, practice, social action, advocacy

As evidence supporting the utility of prevention interventions grows (Catalano, Berglund, Ryan, Lonczak, & Hawkins, 2002; Greenberg, Domitrovich, & Bumbarger, 2001; Kumpfer, Alvarado, & Smith, 2004; O'Connell, Boat, & Warner, 2009), increasing attention has been brought to the intrinsic differences between preventive interventions and traditional psychological treatments and the utility of the training of psychologists for these new roles and skills (Bloom, 1993; Pope, 1990; Schwartz & Hage, 2009; Trickett, 1992, 1998). The 2009 American Psychological Association (APA) Presidential Task Force on the Future of Psychology Practice emphasized the need to adjust the training of psychologists to meet the needs of an ever changing society (Martin, 2009). In reaction to the 2009 Summit on the Future of Psychology Practice, Eby, Chin, Rollock, Schwartz, and Worrell (2011) stated the need for training programs to prepare psychologists to competently conduct systemic and prevention work. Unfortunately, there is a lack of guidance from the major mental health organizations on how to navigate the unique ethical issues that arise in prevention work (American Counseling Association [ACA], 2005; American Psychiatric Association, 2001; American Psychological Association [APA], 2002; National Association of Social Workers [NASW], 2008). Thus, the purpose of this chapter is to provide a rationale for a prevention focus in the field of counseling psychology, to explicate the differences between prevention and treatment, and to present unique ethical issues that arise within the field of prevention. In addition, the chapter will review previous guidance for ethical prevention work, and present an outline for an initial framework for a new ethical code for prevention work.

Importance of Prevention

In support of an increased focus on prevention in mental health fields, George Albee (1986) argued that there is a moral imperative to prevent suffering before it happens. Moreover, prevention averts problems before they have become too difficult to ameliorate, thus supporting the need for early prevention interventions (Prilleltensky, 1997). Despite the obvious need for prevention, the money spent on wellness promotion and prevention is almost nonexistent when compared to the funds that are spent on treatment (Institute of Medicine, 2002). Ironically, the flow of funds is contrary to the well-established financial advantage of prevention measures over psychological treatment, such that it is estimated that every one dollar spent on prevention would save seven dollars spent on treatment (Greenwood, 2008). Due to the increasing awareness of the utility of prevention there is growing public support for expanding our investment in prevention (Trust for America's Health, 2009).

For moral, practical, and financial purposes, it is clear that our current understanding of national and international mental health needs strongly supports a mandate for increasing preventive services. Indeed, due to the lack of available mental health treatment, research suggests that only 10%–15% of those with mental illness receive appropriate services (US Public Health Service, 1999; US Department of Health and Human Services [US DHHS], 1999). The efficacy of prevention to address the current national health and mental health needs has been clearly supported in the literature (Crepaz et al., 2006; Durlak & Wells, 1997; Greenberg, Domitrovich, & Bumbarger, 2001). Moreover, there needs to be an increased attention to mental health disparities based on socioeconomic status, racial and ethnic group identification, and geographic location (US DHHS, 2000), as mental health disparities are products of systemic oppression. Hence, prevention requires practitioners to focus on the social institutions and systems that support inequities stemming from oppressive forces such as poverty and discrimination, rather than a singular focus on the individual, which can result in blaming and pathologizing (Kenny & Romano, 2009; Prilleltensky, 1997; Vera & Reese, 2000). Thus, an understanding of mental health disparities naturally leads to a shift of focus from solely individual change to preventive interventions that attempt to create change within multiple systems (Conyne, 2004, 2009; Durlak, 2003; Hage et al., 2007).

Difference Between Prevention and Treatment

The ethical codes of major mental health organizations fail to address the unique ethical issues raised in prevention. For example, the APA (2002) fails to address issues related to the different challenges inherent in conducting prevention interventions that impact multiple systems. Prevention is unique and different from psychologists' other activities (i.e., individual, group, and family therapy, consultation, and assessment) and therefore raises the need to address distinct ethical issues. Before examining the ethical concerns surrounding prevention, however, it is important to first define prevention. There have been different definitions of prevention with sometimes competing foci. Romano and Hage (2000) provided an inclusive definition of prevention that we will use for this chapter. They define prevention as including one or more of the following five dimensions: (1) stopping problem behavior before it occurs (primary prevention); (2) delaying the onset of problem behavior (secondary prevention); (3) reducing the negative impact of current problem behavior (tertiary prevention); (4) promoting strengths to reduce risks; and (5) promoting structural policies that promote well-being.

Understanding the Diversity of Prevention and Implications for Ethics

Limited attention has been paid to the training necessary to prepare psychologists to conduct competent prevention work. The limited literature that discusses prevention training has focused on gaining knowledge and skills in understanding prevention as a field, as well as how to design, implement, and evaluate programs, assess community needs, incorporate cultural and contextual factors into preventive interventions, and engage in grant writing, advocacy, and policy development (Hage et al., 2007; O'Neil & Britner, 2009). There has been less attention and detail on how to identify and address the ethical issues that arise in conducting prevention work. Training on ethics has consistently stressed the need for practitioners to be proactive rather than reactive in their response to ethical issues (de las Fuentes, Willmuth, & Yarrow, 2005; Kitchener, 2000), and this approach often includes studying core fundamental ethical issues and principles relevant to the diverse responsibilities of psychologists (Beauchamp & Childress, 1994; Steinman, Richardson, & McEnroe, 1998). Therefore, it is important to understand the ethical issues involved in prevention works and the diversity of roles psychologists undertake.

There are unique aspects of prevention that can potentially impact the ethical behavior, decision making, and roles of psychologists. Perhaps most importantly, prevention targets groups of people (i.e., communities, high risk populations, schools) and often attempts to create change in not just individuals but also the multiple systems in which people interact (Trickett, 1998). Hence, the impact and implications of prevention are not just for individuals but for all people they come in contact with within their ecological systems. This broad-scale impact leads to challenging ethical issues. The primary ethical issue is protecting and promoting the autonomy of participants. This can be challenging in traditional therapy and further complicated in prevention interventions.

Due to the nature of prevention interventions, ethical practice dictates the need to involve the target population/community in every stage of the prevention process, planning, implementing, monitoring, and evaluating (Bogenschneider, 1996; Nation et al., 2003; Weissberg et al., 2003), which raises unique ethical issues. There is mounting evidence that for prevention interventions to be successful, they must be adapted to the specific context in which they will be implemented (Durlak, 2003; Kumpfer, Alvarado, & Smith, 2004; Lerner, 1995; McIntosh, Jason, Robinson, & Brzezinski, 2004; Nation et al., 2003; Vera & Reese, 2000; Weissberg et al., 2003). The participation of community leaders, members, and service providers (i.e., nurses, teachers) not only protects against the imposition of practitioners' values but also facilitates the fit of the intervention with the specific community context (Kumpfer et al., 2004; Nation et al., 2003; Weissberg et al., 2003). Since it is important that prevention programs are well supported over time (Lerner, 1995; Reiss & Price, 1996; Vera & Reese, 2000), another reason for practitioners to collaborate with the community is to ensure that the prevention programs are sustained.

Creating successful community collaborations necessitates new roles for psychologists and raises unique ethical concerns. In establishing a true partnership ethical issues are created related to power dynamics and privilege as well as ethical issues such as maintaining confidentiality with multiple partners as the intervention is conducted. Models such as participatory action research (Kidd & Kral, 2005; Reason, 1994) and community-based participatory research (Israel, Schultz, Parker, & Becker, 1998) provide a structure and guidance to the ethical issues involved in true community collaboration.

An additional and related issue in conducting prevention interventions is obtaining informed consent. Informed consent is an important and central issue in ethical practice to ensure truly autonomous participation. This process is complicated in prevention work, which typically impacts multiple individuals and systems. For example, informed consent is a different process when it needs to be obtained for a prevention intervention at a school that will impact all the children at the school, their families, and potentially their community. Also, unlike traditional therapeutic interventions, preventive interventions not only involve a large group of participants but typically serve those who are not actively seeking services (Conyne, 2004). Thus the typical ethical guidance for establishing a therapeutic relationship with a client cannot be followed. So the questions of whose consent is necessary and what if someone does not want to consent are paramount (Goodman et al., 2004). For example, unique to work in prevention is often the lack of a clearly defined client (Bloom, 1996; Pope, 1990), which can complicate the design of the informed consent process. So prevention interventions are often provided in a setting (i.e., school) without active consent from the participants. The imposed nature of the intervention has the potential of exacerbating the existing power imbalance between practitioners or researchers and participants, as the prevention practitioner is viewed as acting with expertise and authority to address a problem (Trickett, 1992, 1998).

The use of a group or community as participants in prevention work can also complicate the process of maintaining confidentiality (Bloom, 1996; Pope, 1990). Rather than having one confidentiality agreement between the practitioner and client, prevention denotes multiple individuals receiving the intervention and often multiple individuals involved in service delivery. Potentially exacerbating these confidentiality issues is the fact that prevention topics often involve sensitive issues and material (e.g., substance use and abuse, HIV/AIDS, violence). Hence, some interventions, particularly secondary prevention, that target high-risk groups, may involve stigma related to participation (Offord, Kraemer, Kazdin, Jensen, & Harrington, 1998). Thus, receiving a prevention intervention denotes a risk to confidentiality. For example, a prevention intervention that trains teachers to intervene with children who are at a high risk for dropout because of poor grades poses multiple risks for confidentiality. To identify the children who are at high risk as well as potentially separating those students to intervene connotes risks to confidentiality. It is important to convey potential risks of confidentiality to participants as they make the decision to participate as well as to take feasible steps to protect participant's confidentiality. For example, if possible, meeting after school or at times when other students are meeting for other group activities would provide some level of confidentiality.

Another unique ethical challenge to prevention work is the risk of not respecting multicultural differences (Reese & Vera, 2007). Although there is noted danger in individual therapy for value imposition and ethnocentric interventions (Sue & Sue, 2002), it can be argued that this danger is much greater for prevention interventions. Each stage of prevention intervention (design, implementation, evaluation) involves value-laden decisions (Danish, 1990). In this pursuit, it is imperative that preventionists understand their own culture, values, and biases and those that underlie their prevention work (Sanson-Fisher & Turnbull, 1987; Sparks & Park, 2000), and that they communicate their beliefs clearly to the target population (Watts, 1994). If cultural values and biases are not adequately addressed, there is a danger that prevention practitioners will impose their values in an oppressive way that may be damaging for the target population (Trickett, 1998; Trickett & Levin, 1990). Indeed, it has been suggested that ethical efforts toward prevention should engage in social change and the elimination of injustice (Hage & Kenny, 2009). Thus, ethical prevention practitioners must balance power in their relationship with the target population (Brabeck & Ting, 2000), while addressing systemic oppression.

Unique to typical primary prevention programs is the need to conduct a large-scale needs assessment (Romano & Hage, 2000). A needs assessment often involves competence in methodologies designed to understand individuals and their context. Thus, understanding a target population involves assessment beyond individual problem behavior to an understanding of the multiple contexts informing the target behavior. Such procedures often require the use of both qualitative and quantitative research methods (D'Aunno & Price, 1985). A lack of competence in assessment at the planning stage can lead to additional ethical concerns. These ethical concerns relate to the inherent risk of harm in applying interventions without an understanding of the context of behavior (Sue, Arredondo, & McDavis, 1992).

Unlike individual therapy, understanding potential gains and harm are more complicated in prevention work. Due to the possibility of both direct and indirect harm and the complications inherent in preventive interventions, issues of informed consent are important throughout the process of an intervention. Unforeseen results may become apparent during the course of an intervention (Durlak & Wells, 1997), and unique ethical issues are often raised in evaluating prevention programs. For example, some programs have either not been effective or actually been related to an increase in the target behavior (Lynam et al., 1999). Since preventive interventions impact not only the individual, but the individual's immediate system and larger community (Albee, 1986; Durlak & Wells, 1997), evaluation issues are complicated, and prevention interventions often involve greater potential for negative outcomes (Caplan & Caplan, 1994). For example a change in behavior in an individual could have unforeseen results for that individual's family or community.

For example, an effective prevention program often attempts not only to educate and create awareness and/or behavior change in members of a community, but also to effect environmental and cultural change in the community. Examples of specific approaches to evaluation in prevention include needs assessment, formative and summative evaluation, and long-term follow-up (Romano & Hage, 2000). Additionally, prevention researchers must be competent in methods to evaluate multiple ecological levels. For example, evaluation of a prevention program that only focuses on one ecological level (e.g., individual), may only assess gains in knowledge (not behavior change), leading to an incomplete assessment. Furthermore, conducting an evaluation immediately after the intervention, with no further follow-up, may lead to misleading results. Finally, prevention interventions that focus on social change often do not fit within a traditional research quantitative research design (Prilleltensky & Nelson, 1997). To understand the subjective and contextual experience of the participant necessitates knowledge of qualitative methods.

Methods of evaluation of prevention interventions and research methodology maybe change to have begun to receive attention increasing attention in the prevention literature (Conyne, 2004). The term "prevention science" was introduced in 1991, as part of a National Institute of Mental Health–sponsored conference to emphasize prevention as an empirically informed research discipline. Scholars increasingly emphasize the importance of incorporating both formative and summative evaluation. A lack of formative feedback reduces the replicability of the intervention and ultimately slows down the advancement of prevention science (Durlak & Wells, 1997; Guterman, 2004; Mrazek & Haggerty, 1994; Price,

Cowen, Lorion, & Ramos-McKay, 1989; Waldo & Schwartz, 2003). Similarly, the lack of clear summative evaluation poses multiple ethical dilemmas. Problems in research design, outcome measures, targets for evaluation, and/or a lack of long-term outcome measures could lead to a misinterpretation of results. Specifically, misinterpretation of outcome data could raise ethical issues regarding the potential negative impact on a community and a field (Bloom, 1996).

Mentioned throughout this discussion of the unique aspects of prevention is the need to address systemic barriers. The role of promoting social justice through advocacy is often neglected in the training of psychologists, particularly within the context of prevention (Kenny & Hage, 2009). Social justice and prevention can be viewed as symbiotic, and the majority of prevention work has systemic and societal implications (Kenny & Hage, 2009; Price & Behrens, 2003; Vera, 2000). Thus, prevention practitioners have the responsibility to address societal issues of oppression and exploitation (Perry & Albee, 1994; Schwartz & Lindley, 2009). Therefore in doing prevention work, psychologists must understand and deal ethically with the complex interchange of social forces such as racism and poverty in creating and sustaining socially just prevention interventions. Psychologists engaged in prevention have an ethical responsibility to strive to be agents of social justice in the communities in which they work (Hage, 2005; Vera & Speight, 2003).

In summary, successful prevention programs have been found to have a strong generative base, addressing multiple ecological levels (e.g., individual, family, school, community) and multiple mediating factors (e.g., risk and protective). Moreover, successful prevention programs must be culturally relevant, developmentally appropriate, of sufficient dosage, and include quality formative and summative evaluation (Durlak, 2003; Nation et al., 2003; Rotheram-Borus & Duan, 2003). Effective dissemination of prevention research is necessary to inform the public, government officials, and other professionals about effective practice and create systemic change (Kenny & Hage, 2009; Rotheram-Borus & Duan, 2003). Furthermore, additional research is needed to better understand the effects of developing or adapting prevention and treatment programs for specific cultural and language groups (Weisz et al., 2005). Each component of successful prevention work necessitates dealing with unique ethical issues.

Summaries of Earlier Prevention Ethics Proposals

Prevention work deals with unique ethical dilemmas and should require approaches to address such ethical distinctiveness within prevention work (Pope, 1990; Schwartz & Hage, 2009; Trickett, 1990). Some have suggested that developing ethical guidelines can serve to shape the preventionist role as well as to provide guidance for solving ethical dilemmas (Pope, 1990). Despite the divergence of ethical issues in prevention, it appears that recent developments in prevention work have gained momentum toward the position that ethical guidelines for prevention should be created (Bloom, 1996; Pope, 1990; Schwartz & Hage, 2009). Yet, standards for prevention work remain absent, as there are certain conditions that are necessary before the development of ethical guidelines occurs.

Prerequisite Conditions

Some preventionists have argued that it may be too soon to create ethical guidelines, as preventionists have yet to develop their professional identity (Pope, 1990). Establishing a collective identity could inform the ethical positions that preventionists should take based on a shared reference group. The importance of a professional identity and community can be instrumental in moving toward the creation of guidelines for those conducting prevention work (Pope, 1990). However, Trickett and Levin (1990), who suggested that preventionists may find themselves confused about their identity in this evolving field because they receive little recognition and esteem from colleagues in other fields. Furthermore, a preventionist identity can be challenging to develop as a result of the diversity found in prevention work (Schwartz & Hage, 2009). This diversity includes variance in target populations, settings, methodologies, and goals that encompass the discipline of prevention (Schwartz & Hage, 2009), as well as the different classifications (i.e., primary, secondary, tertiary) of prevention work (Hage & Romano, 2000).

Despite these fundamental barriers to creating ethical guidance for prevention work, some recommendations to assist with forming a more cohesive identity among preventionists have been made. Foremost it is important that those who do prevention work embrace the different aspects of their identity and roles (Pope, 1990). Preventionists might want to consider several roles as they form their professional identity. These roles would include leader, collaborator, ally, community investor, and ecologist (Hage & Kenny, 2009). "Leader" is defined as the role of a social change preventionist agent who actively works at an individual to a societal level to promote social justice (Hage & Kenny, 2009). The role of a collaborator includes establishing and maintaining collaborative partnerships with diverse individuals in the community and organizations, and with colleagues. The role of a preventionist ally is highly important in an effort to recognize and honor community healers as instrumental to the professional identity of a preventionist. Hage and Kenny (2009) also suggest that preventionists should see problems from an ecological perspective and thus include the strengths and competencies from all levels of community systems. Consequently, preventionists will also view themselves from an ecological framework.

The diversity innate in the work conducted by preventionists brings in itself the dilemma of what can and should be considered when reflecting on the collective identity of preventionists. These considerations in professional identity may influence the method in which a preventionist may proceed with ethical dilemmas. Questions that arise include whether prevention ethical guidelines would encompass the approaches and beliefs of all preventionists, or merely those of primary preventionists. For example, would primary prevention, which has received the dominant attention in the field of prevention, be considered the gold standard, thus influencing ethical values?

Once a group identity is established, a second condition that may be prerequisite to forming ethical guidelines for prevention is the consideration of what accounts for behaviors conducted by preventionists. Trickett and Levin (1990) argued that primary prevention work inherently holds three assumptions: primary prevention is value-driven, context-bound, and should include collaborative relationships with communities being served. The first assumption, that prevention is value-driven, also impacts the context-bound nature of prevention as well as the need to form collaborative relationships. Understanding that prevention work can intrinsically involve personal beliefs is important to highlight, as being unaware of one's personal beliefs may result in inappropriately imposing such beliefs on a target community. Pope (1990) argues that one of the general principles of ethical codes is "above all, do no harm." Considering this principal and the recommendations made by the "Guidelines on Multicultural Education, Training, Research, and Organizational Change for Psychologist" (APA, 2003), preventionists are encouraged to examine and disclose values that exist behind their prevention work.

Recent work by Reese and Vera (2007) also supports the importance of examining values and beliefs held by preventionists. This process is of particular importance in understanding the value of making prevention work culturally relevant. Cultural relevance is defined as matching values and beliefs between the intervention and the community it intends to serve (Reese & Vera, 2007). Cultural relevance can have an impact on participant participation, satisfaction, retention, and acceptance of the program (Reese & Vera, 2007). The importance of cultural relevance in prevention is consistent with the recognition that primary prevention is an act of "premeditated intrusion into the lives and settings of individuals and groups" (Trickett & Levin, 1990, p. 9). Further support for the establishment of collaborative partnerships includes that the preventionist become familiar with the culture of the community (Hage & Kenny, 2009). Recommendations to assist this process include (1) developing positive working relationships with community members and (2) developing and implementing programs that are valued by the community (Reese & Vera, 2007).

No standards have been developed to assist with the process of exploring cultural relevance, potential bias, and value imposition; however, some questions have been suggested to assist the preventionist in this area of growth. What images do preventionists have of society? What images does society have of preventionists? What are the possibilities for direct harm to the people being treated and to those indirectly affected by prevention interventions (Pope, 1990; Trickett & Levin, 1990)? This process of examination helps to reduce the cultural biases that inadvertently exist as a result of different cultures and worldviews between the preventionist and the community being served (Hage & Kenny, 2009; Reese & Vera, 2007). Furthermore, it can help develop the professional identity of a preventionist as a multicultural and social change agent that is "strength-based, focuses on prevention, and empowerment, and proactively engages in creating social change by addressing community conditions through education, research, intervention, and political processes" (Hage & Kenny, 2009, p. 85).

Recommendations for an Ethics of Prevention

In an effort to move toward developing ethical guidelines for prevention work, several suggestions have been proposed (Schwartz & Hage, 2009; Trickett, 1998) to assist preventionists with the procedures to resolve ethical dilemmas. Some of the proposals consist of recommendations that can be utilized for individual ethical dilemmas, while others consist of preambles for prevention guidelines.

Schwartz and Hage (2009) offered five recommendations to facilitate and guide the ethics of prevention. These include:

1. Given the number and complexity of variables that impact prevention, preventionists need to incorporate multiple ecological contexts, including families, schools, industry, communities, and government, into their work.
2. The cultures of the communities impacted by a preventive intervention vary enormously; preventionists must understand their cultural values and biases and avoid imposing them on the targeted population.
3. Prevention programs should be developed from a sound theoretical base, be empirically supported, and address issues of replicability as well as long-term outcomes or effects.
4. In all prevention work, dynamics of privilege and power exist between preventionists and community members; prevention research needs to involve the community in determining the research goals and methods so as to ensure that programs are developed to meet the community's specific needs.
5. Prevention interventions should not be limited to a focus on individuals and the more proximal context of the system. Preventionists need to develop and implement transformative preventive interventions that aim at long-term systemic change that empowers both individuals and communities.

The recommendations by Schwartz and Hage (2009) are consistent with recommendations made by Trickett (1998), who suggested that ethical prevention work requires an ecological approach to ethical issues. An ecological approach would include a collaborative approach that takes form when working with the community at every portion of the planning, implementation, evaluation, and feedback phase (Schwartz & Hage, 2009), including working through ethical dilemmas, examining the role of the preventionist and acknowledgment of power dynamics that can impact that work, conducting a needs assessment to understand concerns and its implications on the community, and finally, utilizing prior evidence that would support such prevention work (Trickett, 1998). Moreover, Pope (1990) suggested an approach to implementing ethical standards as a collaborative approach by including as many individuals involved in prevention work as possible in order to tap into their experience and expertise.

Further, several authors have pointed out the importance of recognizing that prevention work is also context bound, which is consistent with the recommendation that prevention work be culturally relevant. Thus, it is important for the preventionist to be educated and understand the worldview of community participants (Reese & Vera, 2007). Having such awareness and understanding is stated to "minimize the occurrence of cultural bias that prevention professionals may inadvertently interject into the development and implementation strategies they employ in their interventions" (Reese & Vera, 2007, p. 771).

Bond and Albee (1990) make a separate but related recommendation that all preventionists need to be trained in a comprehensive and ongoing manner to analyze and respond to the ethical implications of prevention efforts from multiple perspectives as they arise. They argue that it is not necessary to develop all possible ethical dilemmas that may surface from prevention work; however, training must occur in order for preventionists to have the capacity to identify and analyze the challenge at every point in their work. This individual perspective of ethical standards is echoed by Trickett (1992), who states that ethical dilemmas stem from the context of practice. That is, as preventionists engage in their work, ethical dilemmas will surface and be defined by the preventionist. Having an understanding of an ecological perspective, Trickett (1992) argues, will help the preventionist in their resolution of ethical dilemmas.

Start of a New Ethical Code

Establishing a formal system of ethics allows a profession to govern explicit behavioral standards (Pope, 1990). A formal system of ethics would lead to accountability for the field as well as creating an environment that allows for aspirational ethics. In creating an ethical code, it is important to be inclusive of different perspectives and viewpoints of the often disparate field of prevention. The diversity of viewpoints is exemplified in the training background of preventionists (i.e., social work, counseling psychology, community psychology). An inclusive organization for those doing prevention work would facilitate this process. For example, as suggested by Hage and Kenny (2009), collaborative partnerships might be created among counseling psychologists, community psychologists, industrial/organizational psychologists, developmental psychologists, school psychologists, and social psychologists, as well as social workers, mental health counselors, school counselors, and marriage and family counselors.

Start of a Preamble

The preamble to a major mental health code creates a context for the ethical code that follows. There are major components that should be included in the preamble to an ethical code for prevention. Foremost, the responsibility of the prevention practitioner to maintain the autonomy and empowerment of participants at multiple ecological contexts should be emphasized. The axiom to "do no harm" should be the foremost focus of practitioners and researchers as they evaluate the multiple potential impacts of their prevention intervention collaboratively with the participants. Furthermore, adherence to a social justice value set and target should be the underpinning of every ethical decision. An understanding of the impact of oppression and a focus on empowering and advocating for the population/community should drive every stage of the intervention.

Example of Potential Ethical Codes

Examining ethical issues in the unique aspects of prevention work as well as the previous literature on ethical guidance leads to core ethical issues that should be addressed. There is a need for substantial ethical guidance in this area, though a meaningful ethical code for prevention work would take collaboration and additional research ideas to begin this discussion. Although not inclusive of the potential ethical issues that could be addressed in prevention work, an outline of an ethical code will be provided at each stage of prevention work (Conyne, 2004). An effort was made to identify the most salient ethical issues that may arise at each stage.

PLANNING

- *Needs Assessment*:

(a) Psychologists design a needs assessment in collaboration with members of the population/community in which they intend to intervene and have the stated needs of the population/community guide the assessment.

(b) Psychologists use appropriate qualitative/quantitative/mixed methods to assess not only the needs but the unique context of the population/community.

(c) Psychologists design the needs assessment to understand the whole ecological system of the population/community.

(d) Psychologists design the needs assessment to understand not only frequency but adaptability of behavior for the specific context in which it is displayed.

- *Value Imposition*:

(a) Psychologists take the necessary steps to avoid imposing their values, worldview, cultural assumptions, and biases on the target community.

(b) Psychologists understand their values, worldview, cultural assumptions, and biases and state them in collaborating with population/community members in planning the intervention.

(c) Psychologists allow the values, worldview, and cultural assumptions of the population/community to guide their intervention.

INTERVENTION

- *Exploration of Issues of Privilege and Power:*

(a) Psychologists work collaboratively with population/community representatives and leaders to provide an environment that leads to clear, autonomous, and informed participation.

(b) Psychologists provide ongoing discussion of privilege and power with those involved in the prevention intervention.

- *Social Justice*:

(a) Psychologists attend to systemic sociocultural oppressive barriers (i.e., racism, sexism, poverty) in creating socially just and sustainable prevention programs.

(b) Psychologists focus on empowering the community by creating sustainable change and giving voice to community members.

- *Informed Consent:*

(a) Psychologists ensure that all potential participants that may be impacted by the intervention (family, community) understand the possible harm and benefits of their participation.

(b) Psychologists conduct informed consent as an ongoing process that is informed by the developing prevention intervention.

- *Confidentiality:*

(a) Psychologists take special precautions to maintain the confidentiality of those that are targeted in prevention intervention.

(b) Psychologists ensure that each party involved in planning, delivery, and evaluation of prevention interventions agrees to and signs a confidentiality agreement.

EVALUATION

(a) Psychologists conduct both formative and summative data analyses on their prevention interventions.

(b) Psychologists report prevention outcomes in collaboration with the participants and within a socially just context.

Conclusion

The outline of ethical standards listed above demonstrates the potential ethical guidance that could be provided at each stage of prevention interventions. There are core differences between prevention and treatment, such as the systemic focus and large-scale target population, as well as specific differences, such as confidentiality issues in secondary prevention. The ultimate goal of an ethical code is to protect the autonomy and rights of the client. In prevention, an effort needs to be made to protect the autonomy and rights of the community. This effort necessitates an ethical code that directly addresses ecological systems and cultural context and promotes social justice. Ultimately there is a need to address ethical standards for prevention from an organizational, theory, and research-driven approach to provide meaningful guidance for prevention work. An organization that brings the disparate groups that conduct prevention together will provide important and diverse perspectives to the discussion. Theoretical approaches that bring in ecological and social justice approaches will provide a common lexicon and guidance in dealing with ethical issues.. Finally, research is needed that examines the ideal way to address ethical issues in prevention work. For example, what are the best approaches to ensure autonomous participation of all those impacted by prevention interventions? How can a preventionist ensure confidentiality of those trained to provide the interventions? What are the best methods to assess sustainable results at multiple ecological levels? What is the best method to include participants in interpreting results? The ultimate goal is to provide prevention practitioners and researchers who are competent in addressing the ethical issues that are raised in prevention work.

References

Albee, G. W. (1986). Toward a just society: Lessons from observations on the primary prevention of psychopathology. *American Psychologist, 41*, 891–898.

American Counseling Association. (2005). *ACA code of ethics.* Alexandria, VA: Author.

American Psychiatric Association. (2010). *The principles of medical ethics: 2010 edition revised.* Arlington, VA: Author.

American Psychological Association. (2002). Ethical principles of psychologists and code of conduct. *American Psychologist, 57*, 1060–1073.

American Psychological Association. (2003). Guidelines on multicultural education, training, research, practice, and organizational change for psychologists. *American Psychologist, 58*, 377–402.

Beauchamp, T. L., & Childress, J. F. (1994). *Principles of biomedical ethics* (4th ed.). New York: Oxford University Press.

Bogenschneider, K. (1996). An ecological risk/protective theory for building prevention programs, policies, and community capacity to support youth. *Family Relations, 45*, 127–138. doi:10.2307/585283

Bloom, M. (1993). Toward a code of ethics for primary prevention. *Journal of Primary Prevention, 13*, 173–182.

Bloom, M. (1996). *Primary prevention practices.* Thousand Oaks, CA: Sage.

Bond, L. A., & Albee, G. W. (1990). Training preventionists in the ethical implications of their actions. *Prevention in Human Services, 8*, 111–126.

Brabeck, M. A., & Ting, K. (2000). Feminist ethics: Lenses for examining ethical and psychological practice. In M. M. Brabeck (Ed.), *Practicing feminist ethics in psychology* (pp. 17–35). Washington, DC: American Psychological Association.

Caplan, G., & Caplan, R. B. (1994). The need for quality control in primary prevention. *The Journal of Primary Prevention, 15*, 15–29. doi:10.1007/BF02196344

Catalano, R. F., Berglund, M., Ryan, J. M., Lonczak, H. S., & Hawkins, J. (2002). Positive youth development in the United States: Research findings on evaluations of positive youth development programs. *Prevention and Treatment, 5*, 15. doi:10.1037/1522-3736.5.1.515a

Conyne, R. K. (2004). *Preventive counseling* (2nd ed.). New York: Brunner-Routledge.

Crepaz, N., Lyles, C. M., Wolitski, R. G., Passin, W. F., Rama, S. M., Herbst, J. H.,. . . Stall, R. (2006). Do prevention interventions reduce HIV risk behaviours among people living with HIV? A meta-analytic review of controlled trials. *AIDS, 20*, 143–157.

Danish, S. J. (1990). Ethical considerations in the design, implementation, and evaluation of developmental interventions. In C. B. Fisher & W. W. Tryon (Eds.), *Ethics in applied developmental psychology: Emerging issues in an emerging field. Annual advances in applied developmental psychology* (Vol. 4, pp. 93–112). Westport, CT: Greenwood.

D'Aunno, T., & Price, R. H. (1985). Organizational adaptation to changing environments: Community mental health and drug abuse services. *American Behavioral Scientist, 28*, 669–683.

De Las Fuentes, C., Willmuth, M. E., & Yarrow, C. (2005). Competency training in ethics and practice. *Professional Psychology: Research and Practice, 36*, 362–366.

Durlak, J. (2003). Effective prevention and health promotion programming. In T. P. Gullotta & M. Bloom (Eds.), *Encyclopedia of primary prevention and health promotion* (pp. 61–69). New York: Kluwer.

Durlak, J. A., & Wells, A. M. (1997). Primary prevention mental health programs for children and adolescents: A meta-analytic review. *American Journal of Community Psychology, 25,* 115–152.

Eby, M. D., Chin. L. J., Rollock, D., Schwartz, J. P., & Worrell, F. C. (2011). Professional psychology training in the era of a thousand flowers: Dilemmas and challenges for the future. *Training and Education in Professional Psychology, 5,* 57–68.

Greenberg, M. T., Domitrovich, C., & Bumbarger, B. (2001). The prevention of mental disorders in school-aged children: Current state of the field. *Prevention and Treatment, 4,* Article 1.

Greenwood, P. (2008). Prevention and intervention programs for juvenile offenders. *The Future of Children, 18,* 185–210.

Goodman, L. A., Liang, B., Helms, J. E., Latta, R. E., Sparks, E., & Weintraub, S. R. (2004). Training counseling psychologists as social justice agents: Feminist and multicultural principles in action. *The Counseling Psychologist, 32,* 793–837.

Guterman, N. B. (2004). Advancing prevention research on child abuse, youth violence, and domestic violence: Emerging strategies and issues. *Journal of Interpersonal Violence, 19,* 299–321.

Hage, S. M. (2005). Future considerations for fostering multicultural competence in mental health and educational settings: Social justice implications. In M. G. Constantine, & D. Sue (Eds.), *Strategies for building multicultural competence in mental health and educational settings* (pp. 285–302). Hoboken, NJ: Wiley.

Hage, S. M., & Kenny, M. E. (2009). Promoting a social justice approach to prevention: Future directions for training, practice, and research. *Journal of Primary Prevention, 30,* 75–87.

Hage, S., Romano, J., Conyne, R., Kenny, M. E., Matthews, C., Schwartz, J. P., & Waldo, M. (2007). Best practice guidelines on prevention practice, research, training, and social advocacy for psychologists. *The Counseling Psychologist, 35,* 493–566.

Institute of Medicine, Committee on Assuring the Health of the Public in the 21st Century. (2002). *The future of the public's health in the 21st century.* Washington, DC: National Academy Press.

Israel, B., Schultz, A., Parker, E., & Becker, A. (1998). Review of community based research: Assessing partnership approaches to improve public health. *Annual Review of Public Health, 19,* 173–202.

Kenny, M. E., & Romano, J. L. (2009). Promoting positive development and social justice through prevention: A legacy for the future. In M. E. Kenny, A. M. Horne, P. Orpinas, L. E. Reese, M. E. Kenny, A. M. Horne, .L. E. Reese (Eds.), *Realizing social justice: The challenge of preventive interventions* (pp. 17–35). Washington, DC: American Psychological Association. doi:10.1037/11870–001

Kenny, M. E., & Hage, S. M. (2009). The next frontier: Prevention as an instrument of social justice. *Journal of Primary Prevention, 30,* 1–10.

Kidd, S. A., & Kral, M. J. (2005). Practicing participatory action research. *Journal of Counseling Psychology, 52,* 187–195.

Kitchener, K.S. (2000). *Foundations of ethical practice, research and teaching in psychology.* Mahwah, NJ: Erlbaum.

Kumpfer, K. L., Alvarado, R., & Smith, P. (2004). Drug abuse prevention tools and programs. In R. H. Coombs (Ed.), *Addiction counseling review: Preparing for comprehensive, certification, and licensing exams* (pp. 467–486). New York: Lahaska Press, Houghton Mifflin.

Lerner, R. M. (1995). Developing individuals within changing contexts: Implications of developmental contextualism for human development research, policy, and programs. In T. A. Kindermann, J. Valsiner, T. A. Kindermann, J. Valsiner (Eds.), *Development of person–context relations* (pp. 13–37). Hillsdale, NJ: Lawrence Erlbaum Associates, Inc.

Lynam, D. R., Milich, R., Zimmerman, R., Novak, S. P., Logan, T. K., Martin, C.,... Clayton, R. (1999). Project DARE: No effects at 10-year follow-up. *Journal of Consulting and Clinical Psychology, 67*(4), 590–593.

Martin, S. (2009). Roadmap for change: An APA task force previews its recommendations for transforming psychology practice to meet the demands of a new world. *Monitor on Psychology, 40,* 66.

McIntosh, J. M., Jason, L. A., Robinson, W. L., & Brzezinski, L. (2004). Multiculturalism and primary prevention: Toward a new primary prevention culture. *Journal of Primary Prevention, 25,* 1–15.

Mrazek, P., & Haggerty, R. (Eds.). (1994). *Reducing risks for mental disorders: Frontiers for preventive intervention research.* Washington, DC: National Academy Press.

Nation, M., Crusto, C., Wandersman, A., Kumpfer, K., Seybolt, D., Morrissey-Kane, E., & Devino, K. (2003). What works in prevention: Principles of effective prevention programs. *American Psychologist, 58,* 449–456.

National Association of Social Workers. (2008). *Code of ethics of the National Association of Social Workers.* Washington, DC: Author.

O'Connell, M. E., Boat, T., & Warner, K. E. (Eds.). (2009). *Preventing mental, emotional, and behavioral disorders among young people: Progress and possibilities.* Washington, DC: National Academies Press.

Offord, D. R., Kraemer, H., Kazdin, A. E., Jensen, P. S., & Harrington, R. (1998). Lowering the burden of suffering from child psychiatric disorder: Trade-offs among clinical, targeted, and universal interventions. *Journal of the American Academy of Child and Adolescent Psychiatry, 37,* 686–694.

O'Neil, J. M., & Britner, P. A. (2009). Training primary preventionists to make a difference in people's lives. In M. E. Kenny, A. M. Horne, P. Orpinas, & E. Reese (Eds.), *Realizing social justice: The challenge of preventive interventions* (pp. 141–162). Washington, DC: American Psychological Association.

Perry, M., & Albee, G. W. (1994). On "The Science of Prevention." *American Psychologist, 49,* 1087–1088.

Price, R. H., & Behrens, T. (2003). Working Pasteur's quadrant: Harnessing science and action for community change. *American Journal of Community Psychology, 31,* 219–223.

Price, R. H., Cowen, E. L., Lorion, R. P., & Ramos-McKay, J. (1989). The search for effective prevention programs: What we learned along the way. *American Journal of Orthopsychiatry, 59,* 49–58.

Pope, K. S. (1990). Identifying and implementing ethical standards for primary prevention. *Prevention in Human Services, 8,* 43–64.

Prilleltensky, I. (1997). Values, assumptions, and practices: Assessing the moral implications of psychological discourse and action. *American Psychologist, 52,* 517–535.

Prilleltensky, I., & Nelson, G. (1997). Community psychology: Reclaiming social justice. In D. Fox & I. Prilleltensky (Eds.), *Critical psychology: An introduction* (pp. 166–184). Thousand Oaks, CA: Sage.

Reason, P. (1994). Three approaches to participative inquiry. In N. Denzin & Y. Lincoln (Eds.), *Handbook of qualitative research* (pp. 324–339). London: Sage.

Reese, L. E., & Vera, E. M. (2007). Culturally relevant prevention: The scientific and practical considerations of community-based programs. *The Counseling Psychologist, 35,* 763–777.

Reiss, D., & Price, R. H. (1996). National research agenda for prevention research: The National Institute of Mental Health report. *American Psychologist, 51,* 1109–1115.

Romano, J., & Hage, S. (2000). Prevention: A call to action. *The Counseling Psychologist, 28,* 854–856.

Rotheram-Borus, M., & Duan, N. (2003). Next generation of preventive interventions. *Journal of the American Academy of Child and Adolescent Psychiatry, 42,* 518–526. doi:10.1097/01.CHI.0000046836.90931.E9

Sanson-Fisher, R., & Turnbull, D. (1987). "To do or not to do?": Ethical problems for behavioural medicine. In S. Fairbairn, G. Fairbairn (Eds.), *Psychology, ethics and change* (pp. 191–211). New York: Routledge.

Schwartz, J. P., & Hage, S. M. (2009). Prevention: Ethics, responsibility, and commitment to public well-being. In M. E. Kenny, A. M. Horne, P. Orpinas, & L. E. Reese (Eds.), *Realizing social justice: The challenge of preventive interventions* (pp. 123–140). Washington, DC: American Psychological Association.

Schwartz, J. P., & Lindley, L. D. (2009). Impacting sexism through social justice prevention: Implications at the person and environmental levels. *Journal of Primary Prevention, 30,* 27–41.

Schwartz, J. P., & Waldo, M. (2003). Reducing fender role conflict among men attending partner abuse prevention groups. *Journal for Specialists in Group Work, 28,* 355–369. doi:10.1177/01933922030284008

Sparks, E. E., & Park, A. H. (2000). The integration of feminism and multiculturalism: Ethical dilemmas at the border. In M. M. Brabeck (Ed.), *Practicing feminist ethics in psychology* (pp. 203–224). Washington, DC: American Psychological Association. doi:10.1037/10343–010

Steinman, S. O., Richardson, N. F., & McEnroe, T. (1998). *The ethical decision-making manual for helping professionals.* Pacific Grove, CA: Brooks/Cole.

Sue, D. W., Arredondo, P., & McDavis, R. J. (1992). Multicultural counseling competencies and standards: A call to the profession. *Journal of Counseling and Development, 70,* 477–486.

Sue, D. W., & Sue, D. (2002). *Counseling the culturally different: Theory and practice* (4th ed.). Hoboken, NJ: Wiley.

Trickett, E. J. (1992). Prevention ethics: Explicating the context of prevention activities. *Ethics and Behavior, 2,* 91–100.

Trickett, E. J. (1998). Toward a framework for defining and resolving ethical issues in the protection of communities involved in primary prevention projects. *Ethics and Behavior, 8,* 321–337.

Trickett, E. J., & Levin, G. B. (1990). Paradigms for prevention: Providing a context for confronting ethical issues. *Prevention in Human Services, 8,* 3–21.

Trust for America's Health. (2009). *Poll: American public supports investment in prevention as part of health care reform.* Washington, DC: Author.

US Department of Health and Human Services. (2000). *Healthy people 2010.* Washington, DC: Government Printing Office.

US Public Health Service. (1999). Mental health: A report of the Surgeon General. Washington, DC: National Institute of Mental Health.

Vera, E. M. (2000). A recommitment to prevention work in counseling psychology. *The Counseling Psychologist, 28,* 829–837.

Vera, E. M., & Reese, L. E. (2000). Preventive interventions with school-age youth. In S. D. Brown & R. W. Lent (Eds.), *Handbook of counseling psychology* (pp. 411–434). New York: Wiley.

Vera, E. M., & Speight, S. L. (2003). Multicultural competence, social justice and counseling psychology: Expanding our roles. *The Counseling Psychologist, 31,* 253–272.

Watts, R. J. (1994). Graduate training for a diverse world. *American Journal of Community Psychology, 22,* 807–809. doi:10.1007/BF02521562

Weissberg, R. P., Kumpfer, K. L., & Seligman, M. E. P. (2003). Prevention that works for children and youth: An introduction. *American Psychologist, 58,* 425–432.

Weisz, J. R., Sandler, I. N., Durlak, J. A., & Anton, B. S. (2005). Promoting and protecting youth mental health through evidence-based prevention and treatment. *American Psychologist, 60,* 628–648.

CHAPTER

6 Teaching Prevention: Preparing the Next Generation of Psychologists

Connie R. Matthews

Abstract

Despite the importance placed on prevention in the field, most counseling and counseling psychology training programs are not addressing prevention in substantive ways (Matthews, 2003a, 2003b), nor have they in the past (McNeill & Ingram, 1983). There have been periodic calls for increased emphasis on prevention training in professional preparation programs (e.g., Britner & O'Neil, 2008; Conyne, 1997; DeLeon, Dubanoski, & Oliveira-Berry, 2005; Kiselica & Look, 1993; Romano & Hage, 2000a). This chapter will address ways to incorporate prevention material into a graduate psychology or counseling curriculum through either a specialized course or infusion or a combination of the two. It will also address the need to offer more opportunities for continuing professional education in the area of prevention.

Key Words: teaching, training, prevention.

Prevention in Professional Training Curricula

Prevention has consistently been considered integral to counseling psychology (e.g., Chwalisz & Obasi, 2008; Conyne, 1994, 1997; Hage et al., 2007; Kiselica & Look, 1993; McNeill & Ingram, 1983; Romano & Hage, 2000a; Vera & Reese, 2000; Vera & Speight, 2003). Some have suggested that this connection goes back as far as Frank Parsons (Conyne, 1994) and Clifford Beers (Kleist & White, 1997). Yet, despite the importance placed on prevention, most counseling and counseling psychology training programs are not addressing prevention in substantive ways (Matthews, 2003a, 2003b), nor have they in the past (McNeill & Ingram, 1983). There have been periodic calls for increased emphasis on prevention training in professional preparation programs (e.g., Britner & O'Neil, 2008; Conyne, 1997; DeLeon, Dubanoski, & Oliveira-Berry, 2005; Kiselica & Look, 1993; Romano & Hage, 2000a).

A few scholars have offered thoughts on elements that might be included in prevention training. Conyne (1997) identified 10 additional skill sets: primary prevention perspective, personal attributes and behaviors, ethics, marketing, multicultural competency, group facilitation, collaboration, organization, trends and political dynamics, and research and evaluation. Romano and Hage (2000a) suggested eight domains for prevention training: community and multidisciplinary collaboration, social and political history, protective factors and risk-reduction strategies, systemic interventions, political and social environment, psychoeducational groups for prevention, prevention research and evaluation, and prevention ethics. O'Neil and Britner (2009) offered nine skill sets around three theoretical frameworks. They identified a primary prevention definition, multidisciplinary approach, and social justice perspective as the theoretical frameworks, with the skill sets including therapeutic and interpersonal professional skills; ethics; research and evaluation; intervention; program development and marketing; diagnosis and conceptualization; political, organizational, and environmental assessment; group consultation and collaboration; and diversity and multicultural skills.

Even a cursory review of these lists shows that there is some level of agreement on the areas of training important in preparing psychologists and counselors to do work in the area of prevention. This then leads to the question, if we know what training is needed, why aren't we doing it? Two popular arguments are that there is not as much demand for prevention, either from the public or among graduate students, especially since third-party payers are less likely to reimburse for prevention than for treatment (Davidson, Waldo, & Adams, 2006; Kiselica & Look, 1993; Kleist & White, 1997; Romano & Hage, 2000a), and that demands of accrediting boards define graduate training through their curricular requirements (Davidson et al., 2006; Romano & Hage, 2000a). Fortunately, there are signs of change in both of these areas. Health care reform legislation in 2010 included recognition of the importance of prevention and early intervention (O'Brien, 2010). That legislation led to the establishment of a National Prevention Council, which, in June 2011, for the first time ever, published a National Prevention Strategy that included mental and emotional well-being as one of the priorities (National Prevention Council, 2011). Likewise, education and training is receiving more attention in the area of prevention (e.g., Hage et al., 2007), including a recent special issue of *Journal of Primary Prevention* (O'Neil & Britner, 2008). A recent special issue of *Journal of Clinical Psychology* (Snyder & Elliott, 2005), with a focus on training, included numerous calls for greater attention to prevention. Accreditation standards will likely continue to drive graduate curricula and might not evolve as quickly as some would like. Still, it is important to note that there is nothing in current standards that prevents incorporation of prevention and there are areas that invite inclusion of prevention to those who might be so inclined. If there is indeed a climate more open to including prevention training in professional preparation programs, how might this be accomplished?

Conyne, Newmeyer, Kenny, Romano, and Matthews (2008) suggest that there are three primary approaches for teaching prevention: specialized courses or sequences of courses, infusion of prevention material into existing courses within a program or department, and integrating courses from other departments into students' programs of study as required or elective courses. They also suggest that such approaches need not be mutually exclusive. Matthews and Skowron (2004) likewise address teaching prevention through a specialized course and or infusion. O'Neil and Britner (2009) take a broader approach, arguing for a prevention curriculum. This chapter will address ways to incorporate prevention material into a graduate psychology or counseling curriculum through either a specialized course or infusion or a combination of the two. It will also address the need to offer more opportunities for continuing professional education in the area of prevention.

A Multicultural and Social Justice Approach to Training

Prevention has long been associated with social justice. Throughout his career, Albee wrote about the role of social inequities in the development and maintenance of mental illness and the attendant importance of keeping social justice in the forefront of primary prevention (e.g., Albee, 1983; Albee & Gullotta, 1997; Kessler & Albee, 1975). Indeed, his "incidence formula" directly linked oppression to the rate of mental illness and social support as a mediating factor (Albee, 1983; Albee & Ryan-Finn, 1993). Recent research around minority stress has shown support for his arguments (e.g., Lehavot & Simoni, 2011; Meyer, 2003; Sue, 2010) Contemporary prevention efforts have continued to recognize the central role of social justice in prevention work. The *Journal of Primary Prevention* recently published a special issue related to social justice (Kenny & Hage, 2009). The Prevention Section of the Society of Counseling Psychology, a division of the American Psychological Association (APA), published *Realizing Social Justice: The Challenge of Preventive Interventions* (Kenny, Horne, Orpinas, & Reese, 2009). Likewise, social justice advocates are recognizing the centrality of prevention to efforts at creating a more equitable and just society. Five chapters on prevention work in schools made up a major section of the *Handbook for Social Justice in Counseling Psychology: Leadership, Vision, and Action* (Toporek, Gerstein, Fouad, Roysircar, & Israel, 2006). Arguments for increased attention to prevention run throughout a theme issue of *The Counseling Psychologist* devoted to social justice (Carter, 2003). Thus, as we work on this handbook, prevention and social justice seem inextricably connected. Therefore, as we address prevention training, it is likewise important that we do so within a social justice framework.

Ratts (2011, p. 35) argued that "multiculturalism and social justice are two sides of the same coin. They are separate yet interconnecting concepts that have transformed the counseling profession in profound ways." He argued that the Multicultural Counseling Competencies and the Advocacy Competencies should be used as complementary documents. Others have also noted the importance of drawing the connection between multiculturalism and social justice (e.g., D'Andrea & Daniels, 2010; Sue & Sue, 2008; Vera & Speight, 2003). Reese and Vera (2007) brought this discussion to prevention, advocating that prevention must be culturally relevant and must incorporate social justice if it is to be meaningful. It therefore seems fitting that we draw on the tripartite model of awareness, knowledge, and skills established for developing multicultural competence (Sue, Arredondo, & McDavis, 1992) to offer a framework for training psychologists to do "culturally relevant prevention" (Reese & Vera, 2007, p. 763) that promotes social justice.

Awareness

LINKING PREVENTION TO COUNSELING PSYCHOLOGY

Conyne (1997) stresses the importance of helping students to develop a "primary prevention perspective" (p. 262). Just as "awareness" is a critical part of multicultural counseling training (Association for Multicultural Counseling and Development [AMCD], 1992; APA, 2002; Arredondo et al., 1996), so, too, is awareness fundamental to training in prevention. Thus, material that addresses the "primary prevention perspective" is important to include in the training curriculum, either through infusion, a separate course, or both. As with many components of the curriculum, the depth of coverage might vary with respect to the attention paid to the "primary prevention perspective" in a course whose focus is prevention compared to what might occur through infusion.

Infusion of material that expands students' awareness of prevention would most logically fall in professional orientation courses. Such courses typically introduce students to the roles and functions of counseling psychologists and counselors. Thus, adding to students' awareness roles that fall outside of the one professional/one client (or one therapy group) model is critical to helping them to understand how fundamental prevention is to the counseling psychologist's role. Conyne (2004) offers a conceptual model that draws heavily from Morrill, Oetting, and Hurst's cube model of counselor functioning (1974, as cited in Conyne, 2004). Morrill et al.'s model suggests three primary elements of counseling: the target, the purpose, and the method. Each of these primary elements has several elements within it. For example, the model lists three purposes of counseling: remediation, prevention, and development. Thus, prevention is clearly fundamental to counseling. Conyne (2004) then considers how prevention interacts with the several levels of target and method to demonstrate the centrality of prevention to counseling. Conyne's (2004) conceptual model, which is chapter three of his book, *Preventive Counseling: Helping People to Become Empowered in Systems and Settings* (2nd ed.), would be valuable reading in a professional orientation course to define the role of prevention in counseling psychology and counseling. The book would make an excellent text in a dedicated course, as would this handbook.

Prevention has always been a part of counseling and counseling psychology. Still, the focus in the field has moved more toward a medical model with remedial work at the individual level (Hage, 2003). Many students and professionals remain unaware of the centrality of prevention to counseling and counseling psychology or even what it means. Because prevention has fallen away from the standard curriculum, it is important to build awareness of what distinguishes prevention, or, better still, how prevention enhances the field and our ability to make a difference in people's lives. It is appropriate to incorporate this information into professional orientation classes, as well as courses devoted to prevention. As is the case with much specialized material, coverage might be brief, more of an overview, in a professional orientation course and more in-depth in a course that focuses on prevention.

UNDERSTANDING WHAT MAKES PREVENTION DISTINCTIVE

Conyne (1997, 2000, 2004, 2010), Romano and Hage (2000), and O'Neil and Britner (2009) have all offered elements of what they consider to be defining characteristics of prevention. These include the following:

Prevention is proactive rather than reactive; it has a "before-the-fact orientation" (Conyne, 2000, p. 265). This is significant because it runs counter to the reactive remedial approach that has become more commonplace. Rather than wait for people with problems to show up or be referred for services, mental health professionals working in prevention must anticipate where there are likely to be difficulties and intervene prior to the emergence of problems. This involves constant attention to the social landscape in order to understand the nature of struggles facing particular populations in particular settings at particular times.

Prevention aims to reduce the incidence and impact of individual and social problems. This addresses Albee's incidence formula (1983; Albee & Ryan-Finn, 1993) directly through recognition that reducing the incidence and impact of individual social problems can impact rates of mental illness. This expands our understanding beyond primary prevention to include secondary and tertiary prevention as well. Romano and Hage (2000) argue that primary prevention, although important, is too narrow to fully capture the intricacies of mental health and mental illness. Thus, reducing the incidence and impact might include intervening prior to problem behavior occurring, delaying initiation of problem behavior, or limiting the impact of problem behavior once it occurs.

Prevention promotes resilience and health. Although "prevention" suggests keeping something from occurring, this often can best be accomplished through building strength in individuals and systems. Although early approaches to prevention tended to focus on reducing risk factors, there has been increasing understanding that strengthening resiliency factors is also important. Indeed, Albee's incidence formula (1983; Albee & Ryan-Finn, 1993) is expressed as an equation, wherein organic factors, plus stress, plus exploitation are divided by coping skills, plus self-esteem, plus support groups to determine the incidence of mental illness. Thus, while it is important to reduce factors in the numerator, it is also important to enhance the factors in the denominator. Prevention must be involved with both. In addition, Vera (2000) points out that health promotion and resiliency enhancement programs have the potential to improve quality of life, even in the absence of symptomatic indicators.

Prevention targets people and systems that are currently healthy or showing signs of risk. The focus is not on those who are already experiencing dysfunction. This is a departure from remedial approaches that aim to restore healthy functioning to people and systems that are suffering. As such, this frequently represents an area of struggle for those trying to argue in favor of prevention. In an era of limited means, using scarce resources on healthy people can be a hard sell when the needs of people who are suffering are going unmet. Yet, as Conyne (2004) points out, prevention, reducing incidence, represents the most promising way of eventually closing the gap between need and resources. This is an important connection for trainees to make if they are to understand the contribution that prevention makes, not only to the field, but also to human welfare.

Prevention is collaborative and multidisciplinary. It involves working with others within and outside of one's discipline. Comprehensive prevention programs often involve collaborations with professionals from medicine, public health, epidemiology, sociology, marketing, and other disciplines that might be pertinent to a specific project. Prevention also involves working with community stakeholders. Conyne (2010, p. 40) describes a "coexpert model" wherein prevention professionals and community members work together in program development and implementation. Counseling psychologists and other mental health professionals bring theoretical, scientific, and programmatic expertise, while community stakeholders bring knowledge of the community. Together they are able to develop preventive interventions that are theoretically driven, scientifically sound, and relevant to the community.

Prevention is empowering. By working with individuals and communities to strengthen their resilience in the face of challenges, counseling psychologists engaged in prevention work encourage a sense of self-reliance and self-efficacy. Not only do communities have a sense of ownership in programs they have helped to create, they share in the sense of accomplishment when these programs are successful.

ADDRESSING THE CHALLENGES OF PREVENTION

Although time considerations will likely situate this topic in dedicated prevention courses, it is important to help students to understand that there are considerable challenges to doing prevention and aid them in committing themselves to the work despite the challenges. Israelashvili (2008, p. 404) refers to this as "the transition from acquaintance to engagement." Prevention does not always come easily to students. Early in their work, Kessler and Albee (1975, p. 558) described prevention in the following way:

> The field of primary prevention is analogous in many ways to the great Okefenokee Swamp. Attractive

from a distance and especially from the air, it lures the unwary into quagmires, into uncharted and impenetrable byways. There are islands of solid ground, sections of rare beauty, unexpected dangers, and violent inhabitants. If one explores, and survives, the area becomes compelling, even addictive. Meanwhile, the rest of the outside world goes on unconcerned and unaware.

Prevention makes intuitive sense, yet it is complicated. There are challenges.

Israelashvili (2008) suggests that a fundamental challenge lies in the field's positivist approach to science. It is often difficult to substantiate direct line cause and effect arguments that prevention is beneficial. Israelashvili (2008) stresses the importance of familiarizing students with scientifically rigorous research that demonstrates the effectiveness of specific prevention programs in addressing specific problems. Davidson et al. (2006) identify several additional barriers to student engagement in prevention. They suggest that funding is difficult enough for individual and group counseling, even more so for prevention, which is not generally reimbursed through health insurance or other traditional means. They point out that funding for prevention generally comes through grants. Thus, it is important to familiarize students with the various funding streams that typically invite proposals for preventive interventions. Students might also resist giving up the sense of fulfillment that comes with helping individual clients. Providing a social justice framework for prevention can help students to feel a sense of making a difference in the world that might compensate for this (Davidson et al., 2006). Likewise, helping students to understand what they as counseling psychologists can bring to interdisciplinary collaborations might help make such collaborations feel less intimidating (Davidson et al., 2006). Finally, Vera (2000) reminds us to be wary of quick fixes wherein knowledge of risk factors identified through work in prevention might be used to profile people rather than aid them. Students must be helped to understand what prevention research can and cannot tell us.

Knowledge

THEORY

Just as a solid theoretical foundation is important in therapy and research on the therapeutic process, so, too, is it important to provide theoretical grounding for prevention practice and research. It seems unlikely that many programs would offer a full course devoted to theory in prevention. Thus, this material is likely to be infused, either in a general counseling theory course or a course devoted to prevention. Coverage might be a bit more extensive in a prevention specific course; however, in either case coverage would be little more than an introduction, as most theories courses tend to provide for all theories. Still, it is important for students to be introduced to theories associated with prevention so that they are at least familiar enough to understand what they read in the professional literature on prevention. In assigning reading, it can be helpful to assign an article or chapter that explains the theory in some depth, as well as an article that shows the theory being applied to prevention programming. This not only shows the theory in action but also introduces students to what prevention programming looks like. Choosing application articles from a variety of content areas (e.g., substance abuse prevention, bullying prevention, prevention of intimate partner violence, etc.) can further inform students about the breadth of areas in which prevention might occur.

Social learning theory/social cognitive theory (e.g., Bandura, 1977, 1989, 2001) is likely to receive some attention in traditional theory courses, as this is a cornerstone of contemporary behavioral approaches. The focus on human agency, as well as the interaction between internal processes and external processes make this theoretical approach as appropriate for prevention as it is for therapy. Furthermore, recent work on cultural applications of social cognitive theory (e.g., Bandura, 2002) makes it even more appealing in light of recent movement toward "culturally relevant prevention" (Reese & Vera, 2007, p. 763). It is important, however, that students gain an understanding and appreciation of the theory from a prevention perspective and not solely from an individual therapeutic perspective.

Although the work of George Albee is likely to show up in several areas, it is important to include discussion of his social justice theory with respect to enhancing mental health and preventing mental illness (1983, 1986, 1993, 1999). His incidence formula, described earlier, warrants thorough coverage in discussion of prevention theory, as it is at the core of much prevention work that purports to have a social justice focus. This theory has provided a foundation for comprehensive prevention efforts operating at both the personal and environmental levels.

The health belief model (Rosenstock, 1974; Strecher & Rosenstock, 1997) is an early prevention theoretical model that came out of public health, as did many of our early models of prevention. It grew out of a desire to explain why people were not taking advantage of major health initiatives that were readily available, although it came to be used to explain why people do act as well as why they do not act in their own best interests. The health belief model helped us to understand that people tend to act or not act based on perceived vulnerability more than on actual vulnerability. Although it has been criticized as focusing too much on the individual and not enough on environmental factors (Rosenstock, 1990), it can help to explain behavior in areas where individual action is necessary, such as HIV protective efforts and drinking and driving (Strecher & Rosenstock, 1997).

The theory of reasoned action is another theory often associated with prevention, part of a group of theories based on behavioral intention (Fishbein, Middlestadt, & Hitchcock 1994). The theory of reasoned action has been used extensively in prevention research and is well supported (Romano & Netland, 2008). Romano and Netland offer a thorough review of the theory's use in prevention research and its. potential application in counseling psychology training.

ETHICAL ISSUES SPECIFIC TO PREVENTION

Review of the ethical codes of both the APA (2010) and the American Counseling Association (ACA, 2005) suggests that both are written with a focus on traditional individual and group counseling, with some attention paid to supervision and training. Although numerous sections of both codes cut across psychologists' and counselors' roles (e.g., principles or codes pertaining to competence and diversity), neither code offers much specific guidance to psychologists or counselors doing preventive interventions. In some instances, the codes as written might be difficult to follow in some prevention contexts. For example, informed consent is a fundamental aspect of both codes, yet, if one defines "client" narrowly as individuals receiving services, one might be left wondering how to reasonably obtain informed consent for a universal prevention project targeting an entire community. This does not make informed consent irrelevant or less important; the community still needs to be informed, consulted, and provided the opportunity to agree to preventive interventions. Whether in a dedicated prevention course or infused into a general ethics course, students can be taught to use critical thinking to apply the spirit of ethics codes in broader contexts. In this example, "client" might be defined as the community as a whole, with informed consent coming from community leaders (Pope, 1990). Whitbeck (2006) offers a useful model for consulting tribal elders when doing prevention work with Native American communities. It is a model that could usefully have broader application.

There are several resources that warrant closer attention when more extended time is available. At the time of this writing, *Guidelines for Prevention Practice and Research* are working their way through APA governance. They will likely be approved by the time this handbook is published and should be available on the APA website (http://www.apa.org). Hage et al. (2007) published an earlier version of the Guidelines as an article with more extended discussion. These Guidelines, although not an enforceable ethics code, do nonetheless offer direction for psychologists and others in developing and implementing professionally responsible, culturally relevant, and scientifically grounded interventions. Likewise, Pope (1990), Bloom (1993), and Schwartz and Hage (2009) have offered thoughtful articles and chapters regarding important ethical considerations to address when engaged in prevention. Any or all of these resources would provide fodder for thoughtful discussion regarding ethical considerations specific to prevention.

RISK AND PROTECTIVE FACTORS

Because the focus of prevention is to keep things from happening (Romano & Hage, 2000a), attention to the factors that create risk for, as well as those that provide protection from, the things we are trying to prevent has been central to research and scholarship in prevention (Coie et al., 1993). Hage et al. (2007) include incorporation of risk and protective factors as one of 15 best practice guidelines for work in the area of prevention. Thus, any efforts at training prevention professionals must address risk and protective factors. This makes intuitive sense, yet it is more complicated than it might seem at first pass, and the challenge lies in conveying the complexity of risk and protection in what is likely to be a fairly limited amount of time. This is an area that might lend itself well to a multipronged approach. There are many aspects of this topic that could appropriately be covered in developmental psychology courses. Indeed, one might argue that such information belongs in courses on human development whether or not they are linked to a prevention curriculum. Coverage of risk and protective factors could be enhanced by addressing the concept of risk and protective factors in a broad way in a prevention specific course, while addressing specific risk and protective factors related to specific concerns in human development courses. This could help ensure that risk and protective factors are addressed across the life span, as very often such discussions are limited to children and youth.

Focusing on risk and protective factors more generally in a prevention specific course provides the opportunity to examine the complexity of risk and protection. Definitions of risk and protective factors can be rather straightforward. Coie et al. (1993, p. 1013) offer the following: "Risk factors are variables associated with a high probability of onset, greater severity, and longer duration of major mental health problems. Protective factors, in contrast, refer to conditions that improve people's resistance to risk factors and disorder." Operationalizing those definitions is more cumbersome because risk and protective factors are dynamic, operate on multiple levels that interact with each other, and are developmental (Bogenschneider, 1996; Coie et al., 1993; Durlak, 1998). In addition, multiple risk or protective factors can be associated with one problem area, while the same risk or protective factor might be associated with multiple types of problems. Several authors have attempted to identify common or generic risk and protective factors (e.g., Coie, 1993; Durlak, 1998). Bogenschneider (1996) prefers the terms "risk processes" and "protective processes" because they better reflect the dynamic nature of risk and protection. More recently, resilience and vulnerability have been added to the discussion (Arbona & Coleman, 2008). Associated with risk and protective factors, they add another dimension.

A prevention specific course can provide an opportunity to address the complexity of risk and protective factors, and resilience and vulnerability in greater depth than infusion into other courses. It can help students to build a framework for understanding research that they read or conduct or programming that they might develop or implement that targets risk and protective factors associated with specific problem areas. It is important, however, in building that framework, to include caution about how risk and protective factors, and resilience and vulnerability might be misused and used either to profile people (Vera, 2000) or to hold individuals accountable for failure to overcome adversity (Arbona & Coleman, 2008). It is also important to stress the multiple levels on which risk and resiliency, and vulnerability and protection occur, and that the environmental level is at least as important as the individual level. Likewise, cultural considerations must be incorporated into discussion of risk and protective factors, as discrimination, oppression, and other "socially toxic environments" (Vera & Shin, 2006, p.81) have been linked to psychological distress and vulnerability (Arbona & Coleman, 2008; Carter, 2007; Vera & Shin) and a strong sense of cultural identity has been found to be protective (Arbona & Coleman).

CULTURAL COMPETENCE IN THE CONTEXT OF PREVENTION

Over the past two decades, multiculturalism and cultural competence have increasingly been recognized as vitally important aspects of psychological practice. Both the APA and the ACA have produced guidelines for culturally competent practice (APA, 2002; Arredondo et al., 1996; AMCD, 1992). Both APA (2009) and Council for the Accreditation of Counseling and Related Educational Programs (CACREP, 2009) accreditation standards require coursework that addresses cultural diversity. Thus, any accredited program ought to be working toward developing cultural competence in trainees. It is nonetheless important that multicultural training incorporate prevention specific information and that prevention training stress the importance of cultural relevance (Conyne, 2010; O'Neil & Britner, 2009; Reese & Vera, 2007).

As discussed above, the cultural influences on risk and protective factors are crucial to address. This gets at the heart of a social justice framework to prevention training. Reviewing some of the research on minority stress theory in the context of Albee's incidence formula (Albee & Ryan-Finn, 1993) can help bring the formula to life and highlight the intersection of prevention and culture. Providing information on health disparities can also help to provide context (Institute of Medicine, 2011; US Department of Health and Human Services, 2001).

It is also critical to convey the importance of offering programming that is culturally relevant to the communities to which they are targeted (Harthun, Dustman, Reeves, Hecht, & Marsiglia, 2008; Reese & Vera, 2007; Walsh, DePaul, & Park-Taylor, 2009). Thus, general courses in diversity and multicultural counseling must include ways to incorporate culture into prevention programming, just as they address ways to incorporate culture into the therapeutic relationship. Courses specific to prevention must incorporate culture into material on program development. In both instances, it might be helpful to assign reading that provides examples of programs that have been successful in making prevention culturally relevant. A *Counseling Psychologist* theme issue (Carter, 2007) on culturally relevant prevention provides several such examples, as do several chapters in *Handbook for Social Justice in Counseling Psychology* (Toporek et al., 2006). The *Journal of Primary Prevention* is another good source for examples. As with therapeutic counseling, classroom learning must be supplemented with face-to-face interactions. See the sections below on service learning and practicum experiences for more discussion of this.

As with training in remedial counseling, it is also necessary for students to examine their own cultural background, as well as their cultural assumptions, attitudes, and beliefs. This takes on additional meaning in the context of prevention. Psychologists and counselors practicing prevention often go into communities that are different from their own to do programming. How they approach those communities can be critical to the eventual acceptance and success of the program. Whitbeck (2006) discusses the importance of consulting with community elders prior to engaging in any efforts to implement programming. Conyne (2010, p. 90) refers to a "coexpert" approach, wherein the prevention professional can bring expertise in the science of prevention and knowledge of evidence of effectiveness for various approaches, while members of the community can bring expertise regarding the cultural norms of the community. Together they can design a program that is both culturally relevant and scientifically supportable.

EMPOWERING INDIVIDUALS AND SYSTEMS

Consistent with a social justice approach, trainees must learn the process of working in ways that empower rather than disempower the people with whom they are working. Prevention is about working with rather than working for or providing to communities. This means approaching prevention from a collaborative perspective (Conyne, 2004; 2010) rather than a top-down, expert perspective. The clinical skills that trainees are learning throughout their program can be useful here (O'Neil & Britner, 2009), although they will likely need guidance in translating those skills into larger, system level and community level contexts.

The American Counseling Association (Lewis, Arnold, House, & Toporek, 2003) has endorsed Advocacy Competencies to guide counselors and other mental health professionals in effective means of advocating with and on behalf of students, clients, systems, and communities. Empowerment of constituents is a central component of the competencies. The document offers a framework for working in empowering ways and can provide a starting point for helping trainees to position prevention within that framework.

INTERACTION OF INDIVIDUAL AND SOCIAL REALMS

One of the hallmarks of Albee's (1983, Albee and Ryan-Finn 1993) incidence formula is that it brings to the forefront the interaction of personal and environmental factors. Organic factors within the person do play a role in the development of problems, but, so too, do the stressors imposed by the environment. Likewise, responding to those problems, either proactively through prevention or reactively through remediation, also requires addressing concerns at both the personal and environmental levels. Helping students to understand this interaction is fundamental to helping them to understand the need to approach prevention from a holistic, comprehensive perspective if serious inroads are to be made.

Bloom (1996) offers a model that attempts to operationalize Albee's theory by describing the various elements that might be relevant in understanding any given situation. His "configural equation" (p. 5) provides a framework for analyzing the situation and developing a response. He suggests that prevention efforts are geared toward: "increasing individual strengths + increasing social supports + increasing physical environment resources," while "decreasing individual limitations + decreasing social stresses + decreasing physical environmental pressures" (p. 6). The model has two-way arrows showing the interconnections between the various elements on each level and between levels. Although responses might not be needed in each area and any single prevention effort might not address all areas, having an understanding of the interconnections is necessary for prevention efforts to fully address the whole context.

A special issue of *Journal of Primary Prevention* (Kenny & Hage, 2009) focusing on social justice offers a series of articles that describe several areas in which prevention efforts can include complementary action on both personal and environmental levels. Articles address heterosexism (Matthews & Adams, 2009), sexism (Schwartz & Lindley, 2009), and racism (Buhin & Vera, 2009).

POLITICAL RAMIFICATIONS OF PREVENTION

Prevention, especially social justice oriented prevention, is a political act (Albee, 1983, 1986, 1999;

Albee & Ryan-Finn, 1993). By locating human suffering within the environment as well as within the person, perhaps more in the environment than the person, psychologists engaged in prevention are challenging the established practice of treating individual problems at the individual level. In suggesting that the proper response to suffering might be proactive changes in the environment rather than reactive changes in the individual, we not only challenge, we outright attack the status quo. Hence prevention is political, and students embarking on this venture need to understand this so that they are prepared to respond effectively. This is part of the quagmire Kessler and Albee (1975) discuss in the quote above. O'Neil and Britner (2009) suggest that students can use the assessment and diagnostic skills they are learning to assess political environments, as well as conceptualization skills to respond to them. Still, it is unlikely that most trainees will draw these connections on their own. Thus, preparing trainees for the political ramifications of the work they will do and helping them to use the skills they are learning to respond is an important aspect of prevention training that should run throughout a curriculum.

Skills

Assessment and Evaluation Skills. Training in assessment is an integral part of both APA and CACREP accreditation standards (APA, 2009; CACREP, 2009). This is an important aspect of prevention as well and might be an area in which infusion into existing courses would work with or without a prevention specific course, although coverage in both areas could enhance the learning experience. Although individual and family assessment is relevant to prevention, especially secondary prevention (Hage et al., 2007), proactive efforts must be made to include discussion of the ways in which traditional assessment is applicable to prevention as well as remediation. In addition, skills in larger-scale assessment activities are needed as well. Learning to conduct needs assessments is especially important, as this often represents an important early step in prevention program development. Not only does an effective needs assessment help to frame the problem to be addressed, it also lays the groundwork for evaluation (Stringer, 2007; Witkin & Altschuld, 1995). Furthermore, the needs assessment provides an opportunity to engage the community early in the process (Hawkins, Catalona, & Associates, 1992; Stringer, 2007). Conyne (2010) suggests a two-step approach that begins with conducting an assessment of the local environment and follows with a search for evidence-based programs. He stresses the importance of the interaction between programs that are both locally based and scientifically grounded. Witkin and Altschuld (1995; Altschuld & Witkin, 2000) offer a straightforward approach to conducting and using needs assessments; Hawkins et al. (1992) and Stringer (2007) offer more in-depth discussions for involving community stakeholders in the process.

Programmatic evaluation is another essential assessment skill for those doing prevention. Given that much of the funding for prevention comes from federal, state, and local grants (Davidson et al., 2006), program evaluation is often required as a stipulation for funding. Furthermore, evidence of success is generally required for continued funding. Thus, the ability to do a reliable evaluation is a critical element for receiving financial support for prevention. Evaluation is linked closely with the needs assessment and program planning. Careful articulation of needs and goals and objectives early in the project leads to easier and more precise evaluation at the end of the project (Conyne, 2004). It is important to help students to recognize this connection and to understand that it is difficult to pull a sound evaluation from a poorly planned program. Discussion of formative and summative evaluation (Conyne, 2004) is also necessary to distinguish between assessing the process of program development and implementation and determining the outcomes of our interventions. "Did we do what we set out to do?" and "Did we accomplish what we set out to accomplish?" are different questions, requiring different processes of evaluation.

As with assessment of any type, it is helpful if students have the opportunity to practice conducting formative and summative evaluations. This is especially important because programmatic evaluations are likely to be conceptually new to them. In a one semester or term course, it might not be possible to conduct a full evaluation. It might, however, be possible to have them design an evaluation plan for an existing or hypothetical program. Such an assignment might be paired with later experiential learning activities, such as service learning or field experience courses (see below for more information on service learning and field experience).

GROUP FACILITATION SKILLS

Group facilitation skills are important in prevention as they are in remedial therapeutic work. Although many of the concepts and skills are similar, students must learn to apply them in the context of prevention. For example, psychoeducational groups are a common method of service delivery for primary and secondary prevention (Conyne, 1997). Students need to develop skills that ensure that such groups remain psychoeducational and do not become teaching or therapy groups. They must be able to establish and maintain a functioning group that engages in both transmission and processing of information in proper proportions (Conyne).

In addition, group facilitation training should include applying those skills to consultation and collaboration contexts (O'Neil & Britner, 2009). Collaboration is a fundamental part of prevention work, especially that which has a social justice perspective. Approaches that work to actively engage community stakeholders tend to be more successful than hierarchical approaches in which the prevention professional takes on the role of leader, directing the community in proper responses (Lasker & Weiss, 2003). Still, collaborative projects can be complex, so skills in facilitating conversations among diverse stakeholders are an important element in the prevention professional's repertoire.

Coverage of facilitating psychoeducational groups, as well as application of group facilitation skills in consultation and collaboration contexts can easily be incorporated into an existing course in group facilitation. Ideally, there would also be opportunities for students to practice skills in these contexts, as well as in therapeutic contexts.

RESEARCH SKILLS

Although research training is a fundamental part of most graduate programs in psychology and counseling, this does not necessarily mean that such training includes skill development in areas specific to prevention. Incorporating information about prevention research into existing research courses ensures that all students develop some familiarity with prevention science. Although many traditional research methods are used in prevention, it is important to frame them in the context of prevention. In addition, research methods particularly appropriate to prevention activities might need to be added to existing courses. For example, the collaborative approach of participatory action research (e.g., Kidd & Kral, 2005; Stringer, 2007) can be especially appropriate in prevention as groups of people come together to understand and resolve problems in their own community. Functioning as a research facilitator in a collaborative process rather than a research director in a hierarchical process is a skill that students typically do not learn in most general research courses. Other qualitative methods are also used in prevention, along with quantitative methods, so opportunities to engage in both paradigms are important.

Hage et al. (2007) describe several areas to which psychologists should be attentive with respect to research. They encourage psychologists to be familiar with the current state of prevention science and to position their research within that framework in a manner that moves the field forward. Thus, prevention research should be done in the context of a bigger picture and not in isolation as a single project. They also stress the need for competence in the breadth of methods that are used in conducting prevention research, as discussed above. They address the need to be attentive to ethical issues that might arise in prevention research. Although all research should be done in an ethical manner, there are concerns specific to prevention that should be addressed. They encourage research that is attentive to environmental issues as well as individual concerns and that incorporates a social justice perspective. All of these areas should be addressed when training students to engage in prevention research.

As with other skill areas, having opportunities to practice prevention research skills as well as learn about them is a vital part of the learning experience. When possible, students should be invited to be on research teams with faculty conducting research in the area of prevention. When such opportunities are not present or plentiful enough within a department, efforts should be made to facilitate collaborations with faculty members in other departments. At a minimum, faculty who supervise theses and dissertations should develop the competence in prevention research to mentor students wishing to do independent research in prevention.

FIELD EXPERIENCES

Significant hours of practice-based field experience represent core areas of both APA (2009) and CACREP (2009) accreditation standards. Practicum and internship courses are integral elements of any counseling or applied psychology graduate program. Still, definitions of what constitutes clinical experience remain rather narrowly defined and aligned with remedial therapeutic approaches. Romano and Hage (2000b) advocated expanding those definitions to include prevention science and practice. This call needs to be resounded and remain a focus until changes occur that make it easier for students to participate in prevention oriented field experiences without adding to already full course loads or extending the length of their programs. Just as arguments for inclusion of qualitative approaches to research have echoed over the past decade, so, too, do we need to argue for approaches to practice that are more inclusive and allow for community-based interventions that promote institutional and systemic change as well as individual change. We need to expand our field experience parameters to create opportunities for students to engage in supervised practice where they can be engaged in prevention activities that promote social justice at the environmental as well as individual level. Such opportunities can lead to transformative learning (Birkenmaier & Cruce, 2011) from both a social justice and prevention perspective. In addition to APA and CACREP, groups like the Association of Psychology Postdoctoral and Internship Centers (APPIC) that set the standards for end stage training need to move beyond a narrow remedial framework to incorporate prevention and environmental level interventions into their definitions of practice.

Birkenmaier and Cruce (2011) describe a competitive practicum program wherein students write proposals for stipends to engage in social justice work in the community. They must provide clearly articulated goals and describe the outcomes they wish to achieve. They must also link their plan to the overarching goals of the university funding source. Thus, students not only gain experience in the activities involved with the plan they present, they also gain experience in writing a funding proposal. Although it is true that most universities do not have funding to support field experiences of any sort, the process offers promising learning opportunities, even without the funding. For example, rather than simply arrange for a practicum site, students could be asked to write a proposal for the experience they wish to gain in the organization with which they wish to work. They could be asked to link the proposal to specific aspects of prevention program planning, implementation, and or evaluation. Such a process could be part of a two-course sequence that includes a didactic course followed by a practicum experience. The proposal could be a final project in the didactic course, laying the foundation for the field experience they will gain in the course that follows. Depending on the setting, program, and time frame, students might also have the opportunity to carry out the evaluation they designed in the didactic course (described above). In such instances, an evaluation plan need not be hypothetical but could be linked to a real program through a real organization.

When full-time field experience in prevention is not possible or practical, efforts can be made to incorporate prevention activities into traditional field experiences. Conyne et al. (2008) describe a program in which master's students are expected to engage in prevention activities at their practicum site, then write a paper describing the experience and engaging in self-reflection regarding what they learned about prevention. Such an approach represents a reasonable compromise when specific prevention oriented field experiences are not feasible.

SERVICE LEARNING

Another avenue for developing skills in the practice of prevention is service learning. Hage et al. (2007) suggest that service learning experiences often provide opportunities to engage in community based prevention activities in a manner that might be more flexible than formal field experiences. Graduate programs, students, and the community organizations with which they are involved are freer to design activities that meet the needs of the community rather than the demands of accrediting bodies or licensing boards. Conyne et al. (2008, p. 387) describe a program in which doctoral counseling psychology students engage in a "First Year Experience," which includes social justice oriented prevention work in the community, along with a seminar in which students have an opportunity to reflect on the experience. Projects are designed through collaboration between the student, the program, and the community organization with which the student is affiliated. This process itself provides real world experience in the collaborative aspects of prevention. Conyne at el. describe a variety of projects with which students have been involved. They range from relatively small, targeted projects to universal prevention to systemwide efforts. Depending on the stage of any given project, students might also have the opportunity to be involved in formal program evaluation. The appeal of service learning is that education and personal and scholarly reflection can be combined with service activities that make a difference in people's lives, both those being served by the projects and students engaged in the process (Oden & Casey, 2007).

Continuing Professional Development

Given the low rates at which prevention has been integrated into counseling and counseling psychology to date (Matthews, 2003a, 2003b; McNeill & Ingram, 1983), it seems likely that many of those psychologists training the future generation of psychologists have not themselves had formal training in prevention. Some of them have found their way to prevention and are doing cutting edge work in the field. Still, if prevention is to be integrated into psychology training in a significant way, there have to be opportunities for the trainers to develop competence in prevention. Likewise, as with all areas of psychology, there have to be opportunities for continued professional development beyond graduate school, as well as opportunities for networking and exchanges of ideas that move a field forward. In the field of psychology such continuing professional development generally occurs through professional conferences and professional journals.

Content analyses of counseling psychology journals (Matthews, 2003a; O'Byrne, Brammer, Davidson, & Poston, 2002) have found that coverage of prevention related topics has not fared any better in professional journals than in training programs. Perhaps this makes sense. If psychologists are not being trained in prevention, they are probably less likely to engage in prevention science and practice, which means they are less likely to publish prevention related material in professional journals. Still, this does leave a vacuum. It is important for those engaged in prevention science and practice to publish their work in journals typically read by counseling psychologists. It is, of course, likewise important for the editors of those journals to actively solicit and support scholarly work in the area of prevention.

Although this author is not aware of any formal content analyses of APA conferences, quick perusals of recent program books would suggest that prevention oriented programming is probably represented at conferences at about the same rate that prevention is represented in journals and training programs. Again, this could be the logical consequence of few scientist-practitioners receiving formal training in prevention. Nonetheless, it means that the opportunities for ongoing professional development are limited through traditional means. Thus, there is a need to increase the prevention offerings at professional conferences as well as in professional journals.

Conclusion and Future Directions

Despite continued commentary that prevention has been integral to counseling psychology from the beginning, translation of this commitment into practice has been slow. Romano and Hage's (2000a) call for a recommitment to prevention in counseling psychology was much heralded. Yet, even at the time, Conyne (2000) reminded us that this was not the first call for greater focus on prevention. Still, there have been some hopeful signs. The Romano and Hage article was the first time that prevention was the focus of a major contribution in *The Counseling Psychologist* (Vera, 2000). In the decade that followed, prevention has been prominent in several issues, including another major contribution in 2007 (Carter, 2007). This author has had the opportunity to review submissions to the student poster session over the past 2 years and submissions to the Prevention Section have been among the highest of any section. As discussed above, the increasing attention that counseling psychology is giving to social justice has provided opportunities to incorporate prevention more visibly due to the long connection between prevention and social justice. This handbook represents another indication that prevention is gaining ground in the field.

Incorporating prevention more formally and consistently into training seems critical to giving it the push needed to move it into a more central position in the field. Qualitative approaches to research existed on the periphery for years. Once graduate programs began providing opportunities for training in qualitative approaches along with training in traditional quantitative approaches, more qualitative research began being reported in professional journals and at professional conferences. Likewise, multicultural counseling existed on the margins for many years until it became part of the required curriculum. The presence of scholarship on multicultural counseling and diversity in professional journals and conferences has increased exponentially since then. We need to remember that, at the time, the curriculum was also full and there was no room for adding additional material, yet we found ways to do so and the field has been richer for having done so. As this chapter and this handbook have shown, prevention is central to the social justice goals of the profession. As prevention becomes more infused in the scholarly conversation in psychology, current and future generations of psychologists will have the opportunity to see prevention as the integral part of the field to which it has long been held. This will be necessary if the presence of prevention in the field is ever to match the importance it has had in our minds.

Thus, as a field, we must ask ourselves, how do we translate the strength of our rhetoric into practice? How do we facilitate a paradigm shift in definitions of psychological science and practice to make room for proactive interventions at both the personal and environmental levels? How do we prepare the next generation of psychologists to prevent human suffering as well as treat it?

References

Albee, G. W. (1983). Psychopathology, prevention, and the just society. *Journal of Primary Prevention, 4,* 5–40.

Albee, G. W. (1986). Toward a just society. *The American Psychologist, 41,* 891–898.

Albee, G. W. (1999). Prevention, not treatment, is the only hope. *Counselling Psychology Quarterly, 12,* 133–146.

Albee, G. W. & Gullotta, T. (1997). *Primary Prevention Works.* Thousand Oaks, CA: Sage.

Albee, G. W., & Ryan-Finn, K. D. (1993). An overview of primary prevention. *Journal of Counseling and Development, 72,* 115–123.

Altschuld, J. W., & Witkin, B. R. (2000). *From needs assessment to action: Transforming needs into action strategies.* Thousand Oaks, CA: Sage.

American Counseling Association. (2005). *Code of Ethics.* Alexandria, VA: Author.

American Psychological Association (APA). (2002). *Guidelines on multicultural education, training, research, practice, and organizational change for psychologists.* Washington, DC: Author. Retrieved from: http://www.apa.org/pi/oema/resources/policy/multicultural-guidelines.aspx

American Psychological Association. (2009). *Guidelines and principles for accreditation of programs in professional psychology.* Washington, DC: Author. Retrieved from: http://www.apa.org/ed/accreditation/about/policies/guiding-principles.pdf

American Psychological Association (2010). *Ethical principles of psychologists and code of conduct: 2010 amendments.* Washington, DC: Author. Retrieved from: http://www.apa.org/ethics/code/index.aspx

Arbona, C., & Coleman, N. (2008). Risk and resilience. In S. D. Brown & R. W. Lent (Eds.), *Handbook of counseling psychology* (4th ed., pp. 483–499). Hoboken, NJ: Wiley.

Arredondo, P., Toporek, M. S., Brown, S., Jones, J., Locke, D. C., Sanchez, J., & Stadler, H. (1996). *Operationalization of the multicultural counseling competencies.* Alexandria, VA: AMCD. Retrieved from: http://www.counseling.org/Resources/Competencies/Multcultural_Competencies.pdf

Association for Multicultural Counseling and Development (AMCD). (1992). *Cross-cultural competencies and objectives.* Alexandria, VA: Author. Retrieved from: http://www.counseling.org/Resources/Competencies/Cross-Cultural_Competencies_and_Objectives.pdf

Bandura, A. (1977). Self-efficacy: Toward a unifying theory of behavioral change. *Psychological Review, 84,* 191–215.

Bandura, A. (1989). Human agency in social cognitive theory. *American Psychologist, 44,* 1175–1184.

Bandura, A. (2001). Social cognitive theory: An agentic perspective. *Annual Review of Psychology, 52,* 1–26.

Bandura, A. (2002). Social cognitive theory in cultural context. *Applied Psychology: An International Review, 51,* 269–290.

Birkenmaier, J., & Cruce, A. (2011). Reframing field education: Promoting social justice in practicum. In J. Birkenmaier, A. Cruce, E. Burkemper, J. Curley, R. J. Wilson, & J. J. Stretch (Eds.), *Educating for social justice: Transformative experiential learning.* Chicago: Lyceum Books.

Bloom, M. (1993). Toward a code of ethics for primary prevention. *Journal of Primary Prevention, 13,* 173–182.

Bloom, M. (1996). *Primary prevention practices.* Thousand Oaks, CA: Sage.

Bogenschneider, K. (1996). An ecological risk/protective theory for building prevention programs, policies, and community capacity to support youth. *Family Relations, 45,* 127–138.

Britner, P. A., & O'Neil, J. M. (2008). The teaching of primary prevention: Concluding thoughts and a call to action. *Journal of Primary Prevention, 29,* 455–459. doi: 10.1007/s10935-008-0152-x

Buhin, L., & Vera, E. M. (2009). Preventing racism and promoting social justice: Person-centered and environment-centered interventions. *Journal of Primary Prevention, 30,* 43–59. doi: 10.1007/s10935-008-0161-9

Carter, R. T. (2003). Social justice and multicultural competence in counseling psychology [Special section]. *The Counseling Psychologist, 31*(3), 253–313.

Carter, R. T. (2007). Culturally relevant prevention [Theme issue]. *The Counseling Psychologist, 35*(6).

Chwalisz, K., & Obasi, E. (2008). Promoting health and preventing and reducing disease. In S. D. Brown & R. W. Lent (Eds.), *Handbook of counseling psychology* (4th ed., pp. 517–534). Hoboken, NJ: Wiley & Sons.

Coie, J. D., Watt, N. F., West, S. G., Hawkins, J. D., Asarnow, J. R., Markman, H. J.,. . . Long, B. (1993). The science of prevention: A conceptual framework and some directions for a national research program. *American Psychologist, 48,* 1013–1022.

Conyne, R. K. (1994). Preventive counseling. *Counseling and human development, 27,* 2–10.

Conyne, R. K. (1997). Educating students in preventive counseling. *Counselor Education and Supervision, 36,* 259–269.

Conyne, R. K. (2000). Prevention in counseling psychology: At long last, has the time now come? *The Counseling Psychologist, 28,* 838–844.

Conyne, R. K. (2004). *Preventive counseling: Helping people to become empowered in systems and settings* (2nd ed.). New York: Brunner-Routledge.

Conyne, R. K. (2010). *Prevention program development and evaluation: An incidence reduction, culturally relevant approach.* Thousand Oaks, CA: Sage.

Conyne, R. K., Newmeyer, M. D., Kenny, M., Romano, J. L., & Matthews, C. R. (2008). Two key strategies for teaching prevention: Specialized course and infusion. *Journal of Primary Prevention, 29,* 375–401. doi: 10.1007/s10935-008-0146-8

Council for the Accreditation of Counseling and Related Educational Programs (CACREP). (2009). *2009 standards.* Alexandria, VA: Author. Retrieved from: http://www.cacrep.org/doc/2009%20Standards%20with%20cover.pdf

D'Andrea, M., & Daniels, J. (2010). Promoting multiculturalism, democracy, and social justice in organizational settings. In J. G. Ponterotto, J. Manuel Casas, L. A. Suzuki, & C. M. Alexander (Eds.), *Handbook of multicultural counseling* (3rd ed., pp. 591–602). Los Angeles, CA: Sage.

Davidson, M. M., Waldo, M., & Adams, E. M. (2006). Promoting social justice through preventive interventions in schools. In R. L. Toporek, L. H. Gerstein, N. A. Fouad, G. Roysircar, & T. Israel (Eds.), *Handbook for social justice in counseling psychology: Leadership, vision, and action* (pp. 117–129). Thousand Oaks, CA: Sage.

DeLeon, P. H., Dubanoski, R., & Oliveira-Berry, J. M. (2005). An education for the future. *Journal of Clinical Psychology, 61,* 1105–1109. doi: 10.1002/jclp.20146

Durlak, J. A. (1998). Common risk and protective factors in successful prevention programs. *American Journal of Orthopsychiatry, 68,* 512–520.

Fishbein, M., Middlestadt, S. E., & Hitchcock, P. J. (1994). Using information to change sexually transmitted disease-related behaviors: An analysis based on the theory of reasoned action. In R. J. DiClemente & J. L. Peterson (Eds.), *Prevention AIDS: Theories and methods of behavioral interventions* (pp. 61–69). New York: Plenum.

Hage, S. M. (2003). Reaffirming the unique identity of counseling psychology: Opting for the "Road Less Traveled By." *The Counseling Psychologist, 31,* 555–563. doi: 10/1177/0011000003256434

Hage, S. M., Romano, J. L., Conyne, R., Kenny, M., Matthews, C., Schwartz, J. P., & Waldo, M. (2007). Best practice guidelines on prevention practice, research, training, and social advocacy for psychologists. *The Counseling Psychologist, 35,* 493–566. doi: 10.1177/0011000006291411

Harthun, M. L., Dustman, P. A., Reeves, L. J., Hecht, M., & Marsiglia, F. F. (2008). Culture in the classroom: Developing teacher proficiency in delivering a culturally-grounded prevention curriculum. *Journal of Primary Prevention, 29,* 435–454. doi: 10.1007/s10935–008–0150-z

Hawkins, J. D., Catalona, R. F., Jr., & Associates. (1992). *Communities that care: Action for drug abuse prevention.* San Francisco: Jossey-Bass.

Institute of Medicine (IOM). (2011). *The health of lesbian, gay, bisexual, and transgender people: Building a foundation for better understanding.* Washington, DC: National Academies Press.

Israelashvili, M. (2008). From acquaintance to engagement: Support in confronting primary prevention hassles. *Journal of Primary Prevention, 29,* 403–412. doi: 10.1007/s10935–008–0147–7

Kenny, M. E., & Hage, S. M. (Guest Eds.). (2009). The next frontier: Prevention as an instrument of social justice [Special issue]. *Journal of Primary Prevention, 30*(1).

Kenny, M. E., Horne, A. M., Orpinas, P., & Reese, L. E. (Eds.). (2009). *Realizing social justice: The challenge of preventive interventions.* Washington, DC: American Psychological Association.

Kessler, M., & Albee, G. W. (1975). Primary prevention. *Annual Review of Psychology, 26,* 557–591.

Kidd, S. A., & Kral, M. J. (2005). Practicing participatory action research. *Journal of Counseling Psychology, 52,* 187–195. doi: 10.1037/0022–0167.52.2.187

Kiselica, M. S., & Look, C. T. (1993). Mental health counseling and prevention: Disparity between philosophy and practice? *Journal of Mental Health Counseling, 15,* 3–14.

Kleist, D. M., & White, L. J. (1997). The values of counseling: A disparity between a philosophy of prevention in counseling and counselor practice and training. *Counseling and Values, 41,* 128–140.

Lasker, R. D., & Weiss, E. A. (2003). Creating partnership synergy: The critical role of community stakeholders. *Journal of Health and Human Services Administration, 26,* 119–139.

Lehavot, K., & Simoni, J. M. (2011). The impact of minority stress on mental health and substance abuse among sexual minority women. *Journal of Consulting and Clinical Psychology, 79,* 159–170. doi: 10.1037/a0022839

Lewis, J., Arnold, M.S., House, R., & Toporek, R. (2003). *Advocacy competencies* [Electronic version]. Retrieved July 5, 2012, from http://www.counseling.org/Publications Advocacy competencies.

Matthews, C. R. (2003a). *Counseling and prevention: How is the field doing?* Unpublished manuscript: Penn State University.

Matthews, C. R. (2003b). Training for prevention competency in counseling psychology. In M. Kenny (Chair), *Competencies for prevention training in counseling psychology.* Symposium presented at the 111th Annual Convention of the American Psychological Association, Toronto, Ontario, Canada.

Matthews, C. R., & Adams, E. M. (2009). Using a social justice approach to prevent the mental health consequences of heterosexism. *Journal of Primary Prevention, 30,* 11–26. doi: 10.1007/s10935–008–0166–4

Matthews, C. R., & Skowron, E. A. (2004). Incorporating prevention into mental health counselor training. *Journal of Mental Health Counseling, 26,* 349–359.

McNeill, B. W., & Ingram, J. C. (1983). Prevention and counseling psychology: A survey of training practices. *The Counseling Psychologist, 11,* 95–96.

Meyer, I. H. (2003). Prejudice, social stress, and mental health in lesbian, gay, and bisexual populations: Conceptual issues and research evidence. *Psychological Bulletin, 129,* 674–697. doi: 10.1037/0033–2909.129.5.674

National Prevention Council. (2011). *National prevention strategy.* Washington, DC: US Department of Health and Human Services, Office of the Surgeon General.

O'Brien, J. (2010). *Strategic initiative #4: Health care reform.* Retrieved from Substance Abuse and Mental Health Services Administration website: www.samhsa.gov/about/sidocs/SAMHSA_SI_paper.pdf

O'Byrne, K. K., Brammer, S. K., Davidson, M. M., & Poston, W. S. C. (2002). Primary prevention in counseling psychology: Back to the future. *The Counseling Psychologist, 30,* 33–344.

Oden, R. S., & Casey, T. A. (2007). Advancing service learning as a transformative method for social justice work. In J. Z. Calerón (Ed.), *Race, poverty, and social justice: Multidisciplinary perspectives through service learning* (pp. 3–22). Sterling, VA: Stylus.

O'Neil, J. M., & Britner, P. A. (Eds.). (2008). The teaching of primary prevention [Special issue]. *Journal of Primary Prevention, 29*(5). doi: 10.1007/s10935–008–0151-y

O'Neil, J. M., & Britner, P. A. (2009). Training primary preventionists to make a difference in people's lives. In M. E. Kenny, A. M. Horne, P. Orpinas, & L. E. Reese (Eds.), *Realizing social justice: The challenge of preventive interventions* (pp. 141–162). Washington, DC: American Psychological Association.

Pope, K. S. (1990). Identifying and implementing ethical standards for primary prevention. *Prevention in Human Services, 8,* 43–64.

Ratts, M. J. (2011). Multiculturalism and social justice: Two sides of the same coin. *Journal of Multicultural Counseling and Development, 39,* 24–37.

Reese, L. E., & Vera, E. M. (2007). Culturally relevant prevention: The scientific and practical considerations of community-based programs. *The Counseling Psychologist, 35,* 763–778. doi: 10.1177/0011000007304588

Romano, J. L., & Hage, S. M. (2000a). Prevention and counseling psychology: Revitalizing commitments for the 21st century. *The Counseling Psychologist, 28,* 733–763.

Romano, J. L., & Hage, S. M. (2000b). A call to action. *The Counseling Psychologist, 28,* 854–856.

Romano, J. L., & Netland, J. D. (2008). The application of the theory of reasoned action and planned behavior to prevention science in counseling psychology. *The Counseling Psychologist, 36,* 777–806.

Rosenstock, I. M. (1974). Historical origins of the health belief model. In M. H. Becker (Ed.), *The health belief model and personal health behavior* (pp.1–8). Thorofare, NJ: Charles B. Slack.

Rosenstock, I. M. (1990). The health belief model: Explaining health behavior through expectancies. In K. Glanz, F. M. Lewis, & B. K. Rimer (Eds.), *Health behavior and health education: Theory, research, and practice* (pp. 39–62). San Francisco: Jossey-Bass.

Schwartz, J. P., & Hage, S. M. (2009). Prevention: Ethics, responsibility, and commitment to public well-being. In M. E. Kenny, A. M. Horne, P. Orpinas, & L. E. Reese (Eds.), *Realizing social justice: The challenge of preventive interventions* (pp. 123–140). Washington, DC: American Psychological Associations.

Schwartz, J. P., & Lindley, L. D. (2009). Impacting sexism through social justice prevention: Implications at the person and environmental levels. *Journal of Primary Prevention, 30,* 27–41. doi: 10.1007/s10935-008-0162-8

Snyder, C. R., & Elliott, T. R. (2005). Visions of clinical psychology training for the twenty-first century [Special issue]. *Journal of Clinical Psychology, 61*(9).

Strecher, V. J., & Rosenstock, I. M. (1997). The health belief model. In K. Glanz, F. M. Lewis, & B. K. Rimer (Eds.), *Health behavior and health education: Theory, research, and practice* (2nd ed., pp. 41–59). San Francisco: Jossey-Bass.

Stringer, E. T. (2007). *Action research* (3rd ed.). Thousand Oaks, CA: Sage.

Sue, D. W. (2010). *Microaggressions in everyday life: Race, gender, and sexual orientation.* Hoboken, NJ: Wiley.

Sue, D. W., Arredondo, P., & McDavis, R. J. (1992). Multicultural competencies/standards: A call to the profession. *Journal of Counseling and Development, 70,* 477–486.

Sue, D. W., & Sue, D. (2008). *Counseling the culturally diverse: Theory and practice* (5th ed.). Hoboken, NJ: Wiley.

Toporek, R. L., Gerstein, L. H., Fouad, N. A., Roysircar, G., & Israel, T. (Eds.). (2006). *Handbook for social justice in counseling psychology: Leadership, vision, and action.* Thousand Oaks, CA: Sage.

US Department of Health and Human Services. (2001). *Mental health: Culture, race, and ethnicity—A supplement to "Mental health: A report of the surgeon general."* Rockville, MD: US Department of Health and Human Services, Public Health Service, Office of the Surgeon General.

Vera, E. M. (2000). A recommitment to prevention work in counseling psychology. *The Counseling Psychologist, 28,* 839–837.

Vera, E. M., & Reese, L. E. (2000). Preventive interventions with school-age youth. In S. D. Brown & R. W. Lent (Eds.), *Handbook of counseling psychology* (3rd ed., pp. 411–434). Hoboken, NJ: Wiley & Sons

Vera, E. M. & Shin, R. (2006). Promoting strengths in a socially toxic world: Supporting resiliency with systemic interventions. *TThe Counseling Psychologist, 34,* 80–89.

Vera, E. M., & Speight, S. L. (2003). Multicultural competence, social justice, and counseling psychology: Expanding our roles. *The Counseling Psychologist, 31,* 253–272.

Walsh, M., DePaul, J., & Park-Taylor, J. (2009). Prevention as a mechanism for promoting positive development in the context of risk: Principles of best practice. In M. E. Kenny, A. M. Horne, P. Orpinas, & L. E. Reese (Eds.), *Realizing social justice: The challenge of preventive interventions* (pp. 57–78). Washington, DC: American Psychological Association.

Whitbeck, L. B. (2006). Some guiding assumptions and a theoretical model for developing culturally specific preventions with Native American people. *Journal of Community Psychology, 34,* 183–192.

Witkin, B. R., & Altschuld, J. W. (1995). *Planning and conducting needs assessments: A practical guide.* Thousand Oaks, CA: Sage.

CHAPTER

7 Design and Evaluation of Prevention Programs

Marsha Davis, Pamela Orpinas *and* Arthur M. Horne

Abstract

Evaluation is the application of social science methods to determine the effectiveness and efficiency of prevention programs. Evaluation is critical for determining the worth, need, and effectiveness of a program. This chapter presents an overview of the principles, methods, and practices for designing and evaluating prevention programs. The design and evaluation process is outlined in 10 steps: setting up the evaluation team and engaging stakeholders, determining the budget, using a logic model to define the program, determining the evaluation question, determining the outcome variables and measurement, selecting a sample, collecting the data, analyzing and interpreting the data, reporting, and using the data for program improvement. In each step, the authors provide examples of real world applications. Challenges and future directions for evaluation are discussed.

Key Words: program evaluation, program design, logic model, evaluation methods, formative evaluation, process evaluation, outcomes evaluation

Design and Evaluation of Prevention Programs

Beyond individual interventions, health professionals design and implement social programs to promote health and reduce the burden of disease in hospitals, schools, worksites, and communities. The following true story highlights the importance of evaluating these efforts. A few years ago, a doctoral student in counseling psychology implemented a program to reduce violence in a public school. All parties involved loved the program: Administrators bragged that the school had the problem of school aggression under control, teachers were delighted that the most difficult kids were out of their classes, and the participating, highly aggressive students were excited to spend time out of the classroom. In spite of this social success, the program did not reduce violence. Without the proper evaluation, time and resources are wasted implementing programs that do not achieve the desired goals or, even worse, that could have detrimental effects.

Evaluation uses social science research methodology to systematically collect information about program activities, program implementation, and outcomes to examine program effectiveness, improve program efficiency, and inform decisions about future programming. This chapter draws on landmark texts on program evaluation (see Patton, 2008; Rossi, Lipsey, & Freeman, 2004) and the authors' practical evaluation experience to highlight the major concepts in evaluation. The chapter is organized in three sections. Section one introduces program evaluation by explaining the relation between design and evaluation and by defining the different types of program evaluation. Section two details 10 steps that will guide the evaluation process. The final section highlights future directions.

Program Design and Evaluation: The Basics

This section defines program evaluation, discusses its importance, and identifies the questions that program evaluation answers.

Program Evaluation: Definition and Importance

Definitions of program evaluation abound, and this chapter uses a broad definition. Program evaluation is an examination of the worth, merit, or significance of an object (Scriven, 1998). It involves the systematic collection of information about the activities, characteristics, and outcomes of programs to make judgments about the program, improve program effectiveness, and inform decisions about future programming (Patton, 2008).

Evaluation uses concepts, criteria, and methods from multiple fields, such as psychology, public health, philosophy, political science, sociology, anthropology, education, economics, communications, public administration, information technologies, statistics, and psychometrics. It is important for evaluators to recognize and build on the strong relation between evaluation and other fields of study and practice. The more systematic, thorough, and disciplined the evaluation procedures are, the more beneficial and accurate will be the outcomes obtained.

Evaluation uses social research methodologies and draws on scientific tradition. It has to be judged by scientific standards and it should use all the techniques and principles from science. But, science is not the only important characteristic. Evaluation is also a political activity, a function performed within a social system (Rossi et al., 2004). Thus, evaluation can be a vehicle for advocacy and policy change.

Evaluation has important implications for maintaining and improving prevention services and protecting individuals. Evaluation serves society by providing affirmations of worth, value, improvement (and how and when this should happen), accreditation, accountability, and—when necessary—a basis for terminating ineffective programs or policies.

Seasoned evaluators as well as beginning practitioners would benefit from the extensive web-based resources for program evaluation, as shown in Box 7.1.

Box 7.1. Web-Based Resources

American Evaluation Association (AEA):

http://www.eval.org/

The website of this professional organization contains some resources for the general public, but most are for members only. However, check the "AWA365: A Tip-a-day by and for Evaluators."

Free Management Library: Basic Guide to Program Evaluation

http://managementhelp.org/evaluatn/fnl_eval.htm

This website guides the reader through planning and implementing a program evaluation.

CDC: Program Evaluation Resources:

http://www.cdc.gov/healthyYouth/evaluation/resources.htm

This website contains links to useful evaluation resources: evaluation handbooks, tools, newsletters, briefs, and tutorials. Examples of resources from this website are: logic model basics, goals and objectives checklist, preparing an evaluation report, and data collection methods.

University of Kansas, Community Toolbox: A Framework for Program Evaluation:

http://ctb.ku.edu/en/tablecontents/index.htm

Internet-based resource for practical, user-friendly information on community-building, with a section devoted to program evaluation: "Part J, Chapters 36–39: Evaluating Community Programs and Initiatives."

University of Toronto, Online Heath Program Planner:

http://www.thcu.ca/ohpp/index.cfm

Online planning support tool with detailed examples and worksheets for creating logic models, writing outcome objectives, collecting and analyzing situational assessment data and more.

University of Wisconsin-Extension: Program Development and Evaluation:

http://www.uwex.edu/ces/pdande/Evaluation/

This website offers numerous resources for new evaluators, for easy-to-read handouts and PowerPoint slides.

Questions in Program Evaluation

The questions that program evaluation will answer depend on the maturity of the program (e.g., evaluating a recently developed program vs. an established one), information desired (e.g., identifying the components of the program that make a difference, examining community support), and the critical decisions that will result from the evaluation (e.g., changing program staff, allocating more resources). We have organized the evaluation questions into seven distinct types of evaluation, which follow the natural cycle of program development: needs assessment, community assessment, formative evaluation, process evaluation (monitoring), short- and long-term outcome evaluation, and economic evaluation. Table 7.1 details the questions that each type of evaluation answers, the primary audiences, and the purpose.

Design and Evaluation Steps

Program evaluation is an ongoing process in which programs are evaluated and refined to obtain the best results. We have organized this process into the 10 steps described below.

Step 1: Set Up the Evaluation Team and Engage Stakeholders

The evaluation team is generally composed of several members with distinct roles. The evaluators may be external to the program or designated internal staff persons. The lead evaluator is responsible for all evaluation activities, including planning and managing the evaluation, formulating evaluation questions, designing data collection protocols, reporting findings, and communicating with stakeholders. Additional expertise may be needed in a specific prevention area (e.g., violence prevention, alcohol use/abuse, obesity) to help formulate programmatic activities and to identify the appropriate evaluation questions. Box 7.2 provides examples of resources for specific health topics. Technical support for data collection (e.g., telephone survey centers) or data analyses (statistical consultants) may also be warranted.

Stakeholders are the persons or groups that will use the results of the evaluation for some purpose (e.g., program selection, program improvement, or accountability to a sponsor). The stakeholder group encompasses whoever commissioned the evaluation, as well as those who will use the results. Typical stakeholders in prevention programs are program managers and staff; local, state, and regional groups interested in prevention; funders and grantees; universities and educational institutions; local, state, and federal government agencies; and representatives of populations affected by the issue. If the evaluation is to contribute maximally to the provision of meritorious programs, this full range of stakeholders should be involved in the evaluation process. For example, stakeholders in a non–for profit organization dealing with violence against women may include the different funding agencies, policy makers, medical personnel at local hospital who refer women to the agency, staff members who work with battered women, community referral services for placement of women after being in the battered women's shelter, and women who have used the services.

Stakeholders have several roles. First, they provide the time and resources required for the evaluation. They may provide extra funding or change the responsibilities of a staff member to do this work. Second, they frequently formulate the questions to be addressed and the criteria to be employed in interpreting the results. Third, they bear primary responsibility for applying the findings.

Engaging stakeholders throughout the course of an evaluation is critical to its success. Several strategies will increase stakeholder involvement.

1. Identify audiences early in the evaluation planning process.
2. Throughout the entire evaluation process, involve stakeholders actively, continuously, and consistently; create a plan for involving stakeholders and for maintaining regular communication.
3. Communicate results early and clearly.
4. Match communication style to the stakeholder needs.
5. Provide recommendations that are feasible and within the constraints of the organization.

Step 2: Determine the Budget

Evaluation costs should be built into the design and implementation of the program. While evaluation costs may appear to take away from the resources devoted to program operation, evaluation is critical to demonstrate program efficiency and effectiveness. Evaluation is a wise investment in the future funding, improvement, and continuation of a program, as evaluation can help determine the overall efficiency and effectiveness of the invested resources.

The amount of resources available for the conduct of the evaluation will guide important decisions for

Table 7.1. Examples of Program Evaluation Questions Related to Type of Evaluation

Type of Evaluation	Key Evaluation Questions	Primary Audiences	Purpose
Needs assessment	How big and costly is the problem? Where is the problem the greatest? What other programs exist to address the problem? What are the characteristics of the proposed target group for the program? What is the existing level of knowledge about and attitudes toward the problem?	People responsible for allocating programmatic resources People responsible for planning program and related activities	Planning evaluation Developing efficient and effective programs
Community assessment	What are the problems in the community? What are the unmet needs? What resources already exist for addressing problems? What other resources are needed? What are facilitators and barriers for a program?	People responsible for allocating programmatic resources People responsible for planning program and related activities	Planning evaluation Developing efficient and effective programs
Formative evaluation	Are the proposed program materials appropriate to the target audience? Are the program messages understood and well received?	People responsible for planning program and related activities	Planning evaluation Developing efficient and effective programs
Process evaluation (monitoring)	Is the program being delivered as planned? Is the appropriate population being recruited to participate in the program? Are participants continuing to participate in the program? Is the program being delivered to the appropriate audience? What is the context in which the program functions? What is the reach and receipt of program materials by the target audience? What is the level of use of program activities? What are barriers/facilitators to implementing the program?	Program director Program staff Funders	Program improvement Accountability Link to outcome findings
Outcome evaluation: short-term	Are the hypothesized short-term or intermediate changes occurring as a result of the program?	People responsible for allocating program resources Groups concerned with program effectiveness	Accountability Testing scientific hypotheses Continuation decision
Outcome evaluation: long-term (impact evaluation)	Are the major long-term hypothesized differences occurring as a result of the program?	People responsible for allocating program resources Groups concerned with program effectiveness	Accountability Testing scientific hypotheses Continuation decision
Economic Evaluation. Cost-benefit evaluation	Is the cost of the program commensurate with its effects?	People responsible for allocating program resources Groups concerned with program effectiveness	Accountability Continuation decision

Box 7.2. Resources for Health Topics from CDC

Framework for Program Evaluation:

ftp://ftp.cdc.gov/pub/Publications/mmwr/rr/rr4811.pdf
Practical tool designed to summarize and organize essential elements of program evaluation for public health professionals. Includes the six steps of program evaluation practice and standards for effective program evaluation.

Community Health Assessment:

http://www.cdc.gov/healthycommunitiesprogram/tools/change/downloads.htm
Resource to guide program staff and community members in program evaluation of community programs. Provides a step-by-step resources to identify needs and develop an action plan. Includes a list of additional resources, as well as some templates in Spanish.

Tobacco:

http://www.cdc.gov/tobacco/tobacco_control_programs/surveillance_Evaluation/index.htm
This website provides links to several documents for evaluating tobacco prevention and control programs, as well as smoke free policies.

Unintentional Injuries:

http://www.cdc.gov/ncipc/pub-res/demonstr.htm
This document provides clear and simple definitions of evaluation (useful for any topic), and provides examples of how to integrate evaluation activities into injury prevention programs.

Physical Activity:

http://www.cdc.gov/nccdphp/dnpa/physical/handbook/pdf/handbook.pdf
This document describes six steps for evaluating physical activity programs.

the evaluation. For example, an experimental design will be more expensive than a case study, and face-to-face interviews of participants will require more staff resources than a web-based survey. Budget items specific to the evaluation are personnel, meeting space, recruitment material, data collection (training of data collectors, printing of forms, data entry), statistical consultant, and printing and copying the final report.

Step 3: Describe the Program Using a Logic Model

To develop a meaningful evaluation plan, the evaluation team must clarify the components of the program, diagram its theory of change, and construct a program logic model. Only through this process can an evaluator understand how the program works logistically and theoretically. Without this understanding, no meaningful evaluation can be conducted. Box 7.3 provides some resources on developing a logic model.

A logic model is a simple, pictorial view of how the program works, detailing its components and expected outcomes (W. K. Kellogg Foundation, 2004). The systematic review of the program to identify these key components can be a challenging and illuminating process, as frequently program staff has not examined the expected process of change. To develop the logic model, the evaluators together with program staff can identify relevant materials from reviews of written documentation such as grant proposals, minutes of meetings, and program materials. In addition, evaluators can conduct interviews, focus groups, and observations to refine the goals of a program, the characteristics of the implementation, and the relation between activities and outcomes. In grant writing, the logic model could be proposed as an activity for the first year of the grant or could be completed before submitting the grant, to show the funders the breadth and characteristics of the intervention. However, as the grant evolves, the program may change, and these changes should be reflected in the logic model. The logic model has six main components (Figure 7.1):

A. **Resources or Inputs**: Materials, resources, personnel needed to run the program

B. **Program Activities:** Activities, processes, or actions of the program

Box 7.3. Resources for Developing a Logic Model

W. K. Kellogg Foundation

http://www.wkkf.org/knowledge-center/publications-and-resources.aspx

Evaluation Handbook, 1998
Framework for thinking about evaluation, practical step-by-step blueprint for designing and conducting evaluation with the idea that evaluation should be supportive and responsive to projects rather than the end goal. Case studies provided throughout.

***Logic Model Development Guide*, 2004**
Designed as a companion to the Kellogg Foundation Evaluation Handbook, focuses on development and use of the program logic model. Examples and checklists throughout.

Kirby, D. *BDI Logic Models: A Useful Tool for Designing, Strengthening and Evaluating Programs to Reduce Adolescent Sexual Risk-Taking, Pregnancy, HIV and Other STDs*. ETR Associates.

http://www.etr.org/recapp/documents/BDILOGICMODEL20030924.pdf
The BDI (Behavior-Determinant-Intervention) logic model is applied to a program for adolescent sexual and reproductive health.

C. **Outputs:** Scope and size of services provided

D. **Initial outcomes:** Changes in participants that are a direct, immediate result of participation in the program

E. **Intermediate outcomes:** Changes in participants that occur as a result of initial outcomes

F. **Long-term outcomes (Impact):** Changes in participants that occur over time, the larger impact of the program (e.g., reduction in rates of morbidity and mortality)

The logic model should also reflect "if/then" statements relevant to the program and articulate the program impact theory. Such a statement would be: If evaluators have **A** (resources) and do **B** (activities), they will obtain the **C** (outputs), which will result in **D** (initial outcomes), followed by **E** (intermediate outcomes), and finally **F** (long-term health outcomes). Initial and intermediate outcomes are the constructs that will mediate change, and should be selected based on theory, prior research, and experience. After the program is evaluated, the evaluation team may need to revise the logic model to reflect what the program is really doing.

Following this logic model, the program staff and evaluator can assess whether the activities are potent enough to produce the desired change, review whether the theoretical bases of the program are appropriate, and identify the outcome evaluation questions. Table 7.2 and Box 7.4 exemplify a logic model applied to a prevention program for Latino families.

Step 4: Determine the Specific Evaluation Questions

After developing a detailed and accurate logic model of the program, the evaluator must plan the evaluation. We focus on three types of evaluation: formative, process, and outcome.

The purpose of *formative evaluation* is to develop program materials and delivery strategies. Programs have a higher likelihood of success if they are developed with the input of the target population. Formative evaluation, often using qualitative methods, involves assessing the factors influencing the content of the program and its delivery; understanding the causes of an individual behavior and cultural

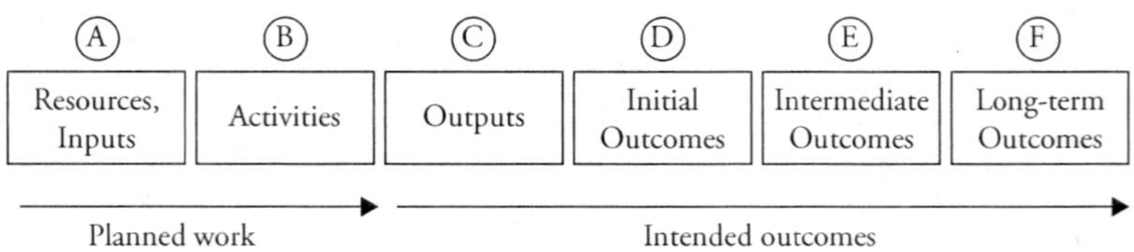

Figure 7.1. Basic components of a logic model (Adapted from W. K. Kellogg Foundation, 2004)

Table 7.2. Familias Fuertes Logic Model

Inputs	Activities	Outputs	Initial Outcomes	Intermediate Outcomes	Long-Term Outcomes
Program manuals, videos, and supplies for the sessions Funding Community liaison, project coordinator, facilitators DVD projector Space for sessions Food Childcare: space, volunteers, childcare materials	Train facilitators Seven weekly sessions (2 hours each) Meal served before each session Childcare	Number of: • Facilitators trained • Sessions implemented • Participants • Meals served • Children in childcare	*Parents*: increased knowledge of parenting skills *Youth*: increased knowledge for managing stress and peer pressure *Family*: increased awareness of importance of family communication and appreciation for each other	*Parents*: improve positive parenting practices • Enhance positive relationship with child • Communicate family values against high-risk behaviors • Increase consistent parental discipline and supervision • Maintain age-appropriate expectations *Youth*: Enhance preventive cognitions • increase negative attitudes toward high-risk behaviors • Enhance goal-oriented decisions *Youth*: Improve decision-making with peers • Increase resistance to peer pressure • Enhance appreciation of good friends *Youth*: improve family relationships • Enhance positive relationship with parent • Understand and accept family values against high-risk behaviors Follow parental rules	Reduced high-risk behaviors among youth • alcohol and drug use • aggression • early sexual activity and teen parenthood school dropout

Box 7.4. Description of the Logic Model: An Example Using the "Familias Fuertes" Program

In 2007, the Pan American Health Organization (PAHO) identified the Strengthening Families Program for Parents and Youth aged 10–14 years (SFP10–14; Molgaard, Spoth, & Redmond, 2000) as the best prevention program for Latin American families. PAHO adapted the program for Latin Americans by modifying some strategies and creating videos with actors who reflected a wide range of Latino racial groups, portrayed different family structures, and used a standardized Spanish language (Pan American Health Organization, 2009). The adapted version, Familias Fuertes (i.e., Strong Families), has been implemented in many Latin American countries and with Latinos in the United States. The long-term goals of Familias Fuertes parallel those of SFP10–14: to prevent the initiation and reduce the prevalence of high-risk behaviors among adolescents (e.g., use of alcohol and other drugs, early sexual intercourse, and school dropout) by strengthening relationships among family members and by promoting self-regulation and positive conflict resolution strategies. Table 7.2 details the logic model for this program; below we describe each component.

A. **Resources or Inputs**: Those who wish to implement the program should think about all the resources needed. Although PAHO provides the facilitator manual and the accompanying videos for free, the implementation has additional costs and logistical problems that should be resolved. Recruitment and retention will be most successful if the program is implemented in the community where the targeted families live (Reidy, Orpinas, & Davis, 2011). Thus, establishing a positive relationship with a community liaison is paramount. After obtaining the community members' approval and securing their interest in the program, implementers should solve practical problems, such as securing space for the sessions and the meal, having the materials for each session ready, locating a DVD projector, providing quality childcare, and handling the logistics of serving the food. Additional costs associated with the program are the 3-day training of facilitators, payment for facilitators' time for planning and implementing the sessions, and payment for a coordinator who will handle the implementation logistics.
B. **Program Activities:** Similar to SFP10–14, Familias Fuertes consists of seven weekly sessions for parents and their children aged 10–14 years. Six to 12 families participate in this group program. Facilitators who have completed the facilitator training workshop lead the sessions, each of which lasts about 2 hours. In the 1st hour, youth and parents participate in separate sections; in the 2nd hour, the whole family works together. The sessions include a combination of films, interactive exercises, and discussions. The intervention includes a family meal shared before the sessions start. To increase participation, childcare for nonparticipating children is provided at each session.
C. **Outputs:** Outputs refers to process evaluation measures that indicate whether the program was delivered as expected. A number of measurable aspects of implementation are relevant to Familias Fuertes: number of facilitators trained, number of sessions implemented, number of participants (parents, youth, and children in childcare), number of meals served
D. **Initial outcomes:** As a result of participating in the program, we expect that parents will increase their knowledge of parenting skills, youth will increase their knowledge for managing stress and handling peer pressure, and all family members will increase their awareness of the importance of communication skills and appreciation for each other. Thus, the initial outcomes are mostly related to changes in knowledge and awareness.
E. **Intermediate outcomes:** Intermediate outcomes are at a deeper level, reflected in expected changes in self-efficacy (e.g., communication, consistent discipline), attitudes, skills, goal orientation, and behaviors (e.g., resist peer pressure, follow parental rules), as detailed in Table 7.2. These changes are expected to lead to an overall positive relationship with the family, a better decision-making process with peers, and a stronger support for schooling.
F. **Long-term outcomes (Impact):** The long-term outcomes are behavioral changes related to improved health (e.g., avoid the use of alcohol, refuse to use drugs, refrain from responding with aggression, postpone sexual activity, and delay parenthood). Closely related to health, another long-term goal of Familias Fuertes is to increase high school completion.

Box 7.5. Resources for Process Evaluation

Saunders, R. P., Evans, M. H., & Joshi, P. (2005). Developing a process-evaluation plan for assessing health promotion program implementation: A how-to guide. *Health Promotion Practice, 6*(2), 134–147. http://hpp.sagepub.com/cgi/content/abstract/6/2/134
Comprehensive, systematic framework for developing a process evaluation plan to assess the implementation of a targeted health promotion intervention. Guided by previous frameworks.

Center for Court Innovations. *Avoiding failures of implementation: Lessons from process evaluations* http://www.courtinnovation.org/_uploads/documents/Failure%20Final.pdf

World Bank. (2004). *Ten steps to a results-based monitoring and evaluation system.* http://www.oecd.org/dataoecd/23/27/35281194.pdf

World Bank. (2004). *Monitoring and Evaluation (M&E): Some Tools, Methods and Approaches. Influential Evaluations: Evaluations That Improved the Performance and Impacts of Development Programs.*
http://www.worldbank.org/oed/ecd/tools/
This provides eight case studies of evaluations and reviews which have had a significant impact.

influences; and pretesting the program materials to determine receptivity.

For example, in a formative evaluation for a program to prevent childhood obesity in preschool children, the evaluator interviewed key informants—daycare staff, food service personnel, and families—to unveil the facilitators and barriers to healthy eating and physical activity. The results showed three primary targets for the program: parents did not have access to affordable produce in their neighborhoods, parents needed healthier options (other than vending machines or fast food) to stave off the child's hunger when picking up the child from daycare, and parents desired support from other parents. As a result of incorporating their needs, this obesity prevention program had four components: a farmer's market at the preschool, healthy snacks for children and parents to "grab and go" as they left daycare at the end of the day, activities for the child and parent to do at home that reinforced the healthy eating and physical activity at school, and a web-based discussion forum for parents to support each other in these changes.

The purpose of *process evaluation* is to document the recruitment of participants and the quality of implementation of program components. This information will be essential to infer about the program effectiveness. Process evaluation provides information by which to judge operational performance of the program, make needed changes in day-to-day activities, report for accountability purposes, interpret outcomes of a program, and aid in creating a model for the pathways to behavior change. Box 7.5 provides resources for conducting process evaluations.

We advocate the use of a comprehensive model for process evaluation, as proposed by Baranowski and Stables (2000), that measures the following components: (1) the recruitment and maintenance of participants, (2) the context within which the program functions, (3) the resources available to the program and the participants, (4) the implementation of the program, (5) the receipt of materials by the target population, (6) the barriers to implementing the program, (7) the initial use of the program activities, (8) the continued use of the program, and (9) the contamination of the treatment and control groups. These components are important for the successful implementation of the program and for its evaluation, including statistical power, internal validity, external validity, dosage, and moderation of effect. Quantitative (surveys of staff or participants, observation checklists) and qualitative measures (interviews, content analysis) can be used to measure these components.

The purpose of *outcome evaluation* is to determine the level of change in the hypothesized constructs. Depending on the stage and the length of the program, the outcome evaluation may focus on short-term outcomes such as changes in attitudes and beliefs, intermediate outcomes such as changes in behavior, or longer-term outcomes in trends of morbidity or mortality.

Three types of design are commonly used in outcome evaluation: experimental, quasi-experimental, and nonexperimental designs. Most research studies use experimental designs, and most program evaluations use nonexperimental designs. However, as the program matures, designs that are more commonly used in research are also used in evaluation. The challenge for evaluators is to choose the most appropriate design for answering the evaluation questions.

Experimental designs use random assignment of individuals or units (schools, churches, clinics) to one or more groups. Because of random assignment, the groups will be similar and the threat of selection bias is minimized. Thus, the evaluator will be more confident to attribute changes to the program. However, experimental designs are not always possible. Randomization is not appropriate when a program is early in its development, resources to conduct the evaluation are limited, and it is ethically unacceptable to randomize and have a true control (no intervention) group.

Quasi-experimental designs allow the evaluator to compare between two or more groups that were formed by means other than random assignment. The types of quasi-experimental designs range from the complex and robust designs to those where causation cannot be shown. Cook and Campbell (1979) and Shadish, Cook, and Campbell (2001) describe these designs in detail. Quasi-experimental designs vary in measurement time points used (pre- and posttest, or posttest only). Quasi-experimental designs also vary the type of control groups: (1) same individuals or groups evaluated at two points in time; (2) different individuals or groups evaluated at two points in time (historical control).

Nonexperimental designs include case studies or one-group designs, with no control group. Usually, measurements are taken pre- and postprogram. While these designs are the weakest for making causal inferences about program effectiveness, they are appropriate for programs in the early stages of development. These designs do not take into account natural changes in behavior (e.g., aggressive behavior tends to increase from fall to spring semester, or unhealthy eating increases during the holiday season) or changes that could be due to an external event unrelated to the intervention (e.g., new school principal). To strengthen this design, it is important to collect contextual data that document conditions before and after program implementation

Sometimes scientific ideas may conflict with the reality of evaluation. The best design may not be possible because of cost, resources, feasibility, or program implementation. Thus, to make the best decisions about design, the evaluator should keep at the forefront what questions need to be answered and what decisions will result from those answers. The evaluator should use appropriate caution in interpretation of the data, communicate results accurately, and note limitations of findings.

Step 5: Determine Outcome Variables and Develop Measures

The logic model should clearly depict all relevant outcomes and clarify the connections between initial, intermediate, and long-term outcomes. Most relevant to Step 5, the evaluator must clearly identify ways to measure those outcomes.

To make the best choice of initial and intermediate outcome variables, the evaluator should consider the questions the stakeholders are asking, the strength of the scientific evidence linking outcomes to activities, the likelihood of being able to demonstrate change for a given outcome, the ability to statistically detect small effects, the costs and logistics of measuring the desired outcome, and the availability of a good instrument to measure the outcomes.

The selection of good measurement instruments is important to accurately evaluate the impact of the program. Measurement experts agree that the scores of an instrument should be reliable and valid in samples similar to the one where the program will be implemented and evaluated. Unfortunately, no instrument measures a construct perfectly, and reliability refers to the amount of error in this measurement. If measures are not reliable (i.e., they have a high degree of measurement error and the scores are inconsistent over time), judgments based on those measures need to be tentative. The lower the reliability, the more tentative the decision must be. Types of reliability are internal consistency of the scores, test-retest reliability, and interrater consistency. The most common measure of *internal consistency* of the items of a scale is Cronbach's alpha, which measures the relation among the items, assuming that the items of a scale are measuring a unique construct. Cronbach's alpha ranges between 0 and 1, and an alpha higher than .70 indicates an acceptable internal consistency. *Test-retest reliability* measures sources of error due to administration (e.g., the teacher was watching students' responses) and temporary states in the individual (e.g., the child was sick). Test-retest reliability is assessed by administrating an instrument twice to a group of people, allowing at least 2 weeks between administrations. To have adequate test-retest reliability, the correlation between scores on the two tests should be greater than .80, indicating consistency of responses over time.

If observers are rating participants, *interrater reliability* should be established. The two raters would observe the same phenomenon (e.g., quality of delivering a lesson of a prevention program or number of times a child acts out in class) and are expected to code the event independently. The degree of agreement (or a Kappa statistic) between the two raters is calculated to indicate the level of reliability. Although the cut-off score of an acceptable Kappa is not universally established, values over .75 are generally considered good.

Validity is the extent to which an instrument measures what it is intended to measure. Types of validity are content, criterion (predictive and concurrent), and construct validity (convergent and divergent). *Content* validity, determined by expert review of the instrument, measures the extent to which the items cover the construct. *Criterion* validity is the degree to which a score predicts a criterion (gold standard) that will happen at some point in the future (predictive validity) or at the same time of the present measurement (concurrent validity). For example, a school counselor could assess whether teacher-rated study skills of ninth graders predict dropout at the end of high school or whether study skills are related to achievement in the biology class that the students are currently enrolled. Predictive and concurrent validity yield quantifiable indices, usually correlation coefficients, ranging from 0 to 1, with higher correlations indicating higher validity. *Construct* validity is whether the items measure the theoretical construct and not other related constructs. For example, a researcher is evaluating a new, shorter version of stress scale for new mothers. Research participants complete this scale along with the original long version, as well as a number of measures for different constructs. The researcher expects that mothers who score high on the abbreviated stress scale will also score high on the well-known longer stress scale (convergent validity), and will score low on scales that measure other unrelated constructs (divergent or discriminate validity). Isolating constructs is difficult. In this example, the evaluator will expect that stress will have some overlap with anxiety and depression, but will not overlap with less related constructs such as anger or intelligence.

In addition to these psychometric properties, the instrument should be culturally sensitive, developmentally appropriate, and at a difficulty level suitable for the sample (reading level, vocabulary, use of mathematical concepts, and length).

Instrument development, done properly, can take a great deal of time and expertise. Thus, it is wise to search for existing instruments and determine whether they are appropriate to evaluate the program. The evaluator should consider content, precision of measurement, availability, expense, and data collection feasibility.

If no instruments are available, the evaluator needs to construct one, following these general guidelines for writing items:

- Identify approximately 20 items for measuring a unified psychosocial construct.
- Identify enough items to cover the complexity and breadth of the construct when developing an index or checklist measure.
- Ask one question at a time.
- Avoid heavy or biased wording.
- Spell out acronyms.
- Use mutually exclusive categories.
- Use exhaustive categories.
- Avoid negatives and, most important, avoid double negatives.
- Write items at the appropriate reading level.
- Highlight terms that can be easily missed.
- For recall items, allow a specific time period that is consistent with the behavior.
- Use ranges rather than precise values for sensitive items.
- Use response options such as "don't know" and "not applicable" sparingly.

Once the items are written, the evaluator should follow these steps prior to using the instrument in the outcome evaluation:

- Check the instrument for clarity, content, and possible technical flaws.
- Assess reading level.
- Ask experts to review the draft; revise if necessary.
- Pretest one-on-one with at least 10 participants; revise if necessary.
- Pilot the revised instruments with at least 30 participants; revise if necessary.
- Administer to group of 50 to 100 participants.
- Examine validity, reliability, response sets, and feasibility of data collection; revise if necessary.

Step 6: Select Sample

The evaluator should have a plan for selecting participants from the program to provide data. The first question is whether all participants or just a sample of them should complete the assessment. This choice depends on the sample size needed and the feasibility of data collection. The evaluator will then design the procedure for selecting respondents from the target population that will allow generalization to the desired population, generate an appropriate number for subgroup analyses, and minimize sampling error. Below are some examples of sampling schemes.

Simple random sampling is used when every person has an equal chance of being chosen. Use simple random sampling in evaluation studies where it is possible to obtain a list of all eligible persons and it is too expensive or unnecessary to get data on the entire sample. Stratified random sampling is used to assure that certain groups of people (e.g., ethnicity, gender, zip code) have an equal chance of being chosen. In this sampling scheme, the sample is sorted by key variables before the sample is selected. This procedure is possible if the evaluator can obtain a list of all eligible participants with the needed stratifying information. The main advantage of all random sampling schemes is that they allow generalizing the results back to the study population.

Convenience sampling, a form of nonrandom sampling, is useful with hard-to-locate populations or when the budget is limited. In this situation, the evaluator takes samples—or assesses whoever is available—from places where the population can easily be reached. For example, a program designed to promote condom use among gay men meeting in bars and sex clubs would require a convenience sample. As a word of caution, this study sample may not be representative of the study population.

Step 7: Gather Data

All methods of data collection have advantages and shortcomings, as Tables 7.3 and 7.4 depict. Thus, using a variety of methods will enhance usefulness and accuracy of the evaluation. Preemptive planning is the best strategy against anticipated problems. General strategies to improve data collection are the following:

- Train data collectors to follow an established protocol, avoid biases in judgment, and maintain a respectful and confidential environment.
- Maintain confidentiality of the participants. For example:

1) Collect surveys in sealed envelopes.
2) Do not ask for demographic information when the sample is small (e.g., there may be only one Asian nurse in the company).

- Develop strategies to remove literacy barriers. For example:

1) Use a computer-assisted survey interview (CASI) technology, so respondents can read the question in a computer while hearing audio clips through headphones. The main drawback of this method is the high cost, mainly of special software, programming, and a computer.
2) For Likert-type scales, use facial icons (e.g., smiley faces, neutral faces, or frowning faces) or other graphic representation of the scale to help respondents understand the response categories.
3) Read the questions from a preprogrammed computer. For Likert-type responses, the interviewer can display a graphic representation of the scale, and participants enter their responses using a remote keypad. This procedure reduces social desirability bias by enabling the participant to disclose information confidentially, creates an easy interview pace, and reduces or eliminates missing data.
4) Read the questions from a paper survey, but make sure that the person feels secure to respond without trying to "impress" the interviewer.

- Provide a clear definition of constructs to be measured. At one elementary school, when we surveyed students about their perception of school safety, many children responded that their school was *very unsafe*. The principal was surprised as she believed that bullying was relatively low at that school. To clarify the situation, teachers asked children to write essays about this why the school was unsafe. Overwhelmingly, students wrote that the construction of their new playground made the school very unsafe, not bullying. Thus, clearly, researchers and students were identifying different constructs.
- Establish clear time frames that will facilitate recollection of event. For example:

1) Ask for behaviors since a specific event such as New Year's.
2) Ask for information during a specific time frame: prior day, week, month, current academic semester, or year. Common events such as food recall require very short time frames; infrequent events require larger time frames. When evaluating a program, measure the events after or during program implementation.

- Understand how reports have been handled in the past at that institution. For example, teachers may feel reluctant to discuss classroom problems, if in the past colleagues who reported management problems received a negative annual evaluation.

• Inform all constituents about how the results will be handled, in particular, who will have access to the data and how the data will be aggregated in report of results.

• Use more than one method to capture the impact of the program. Qualitative data collection can provide interesting quotes and examples that can help bring numbers to life. Interviews of outliers can help understand why they did not conform to the norm. Relying solely on disciplinary referrals or nurses' injury logs to evaluate a bullying prevention intervention has the problem that not all children who bully others are referred to the office or get injured.

• Understand natural variations over time, which may be affecting the results. Many studies have shown that school aggression increases from fall to spring semester. Thus, a violence prevention program that does not have a comparison school will most likely show an increase in aggression.

Data collection strategies are not limited to those listed in Tables 7.3 and 7.4. Writing essays and taking photos can be a useful way to convey a message. In today's world of technology, many new strategies are being evaluated, all with pros and cons, such as blogs, text messaging, or e-mail surveys.

Step 8: Analyze and Interpret Data

After data collection, the tedious and time-consuming phase of entering the data and creating a clean, error-free database starts. If the database has errors, every result will be flawed. Develop a systematic procedure for entering the data and for checking for errors. For example, double enter all the data or at least check 20% for accuracy. If the evaluator finds problems, identify the source and develop strategies to solve them. Systematic problems are easier to solve than random problems. For example, are most of the problems related to one data entry person or to a certain set of questions? A preliminary data analysis can also spot out-of-range scores, missing values, and outliers. The descriptive analyses should include: central tendencies (mean,

Table 7.3. Advantages and Disadvantages of Quantitative Data Collection Methods

Surveys	
Advantages	**Challenges**
• Provide results that are easily quantified and analyzed. • May provide a more accurate prevalence rate because many behaviors and symptoms are not public (e.g., relational aggression, depression symptoms). • Can capture the unique perspective of the participants themselves. • Are relatively inexpensive, in terms of cost per respondent. • Provide more anonymity than other methods; thus, respondents are more likely to tell the truth. • Can use established scales; thus, increasing reliability and validity. • Are useful to reach large numbers of persons. Are not influenced by evaluator biases.	• Are difficult to construct when available scales do not fit the needs or areas of interest. New scales or items may have to be developed locally. • Provide little assurance of the quality of the responses. Thus, it is important to convey the importance of the survey and to assure confidentiality. • Are strongly influenced by the reading level of respondents. Data collectors may need to read the surveys out loud or use computer-assisted technology. • Have very low response rate when they are not completed in a closed environment. • Cannot be linked to other measures, if they are administered anonymously (no names or codes attached). Comparisons of pretest and posttest will be done at a group level, and impact on specific respondents cannot be examined. • May increase participants' fear of telling the truth, if they are administered confidentially (with name or a code attached). • Preclude a more in-depth, qualitative understanding of the problem. • Provide limited information about the context of the problem or the reasons for why the problem exists. Cannot examine whether the meaning of items are the same across groups of participants (e.g., by gender or race).

Table 7.3 *(Continued)*

Behavioral Observations	
Advantages	**Challenges**
• Do not require extra time of participants to be completed. • Can provide information about behaviors in different settings (e.g., community, playground, cafeteria, classroom, hallways). • Provide a firsthand account of the behavior and of the relation among different participants (e.g., bullies, victims, and bystanders) and between participants and contextual factors. • Can provide information about the sequence of events that lead to a behavior. • May provide information about participants who may have difficulty expressing verbally or are afraid to speak. • Can use available behavioral observation systems. Collect the data where the event happens.	• May change the behavior to be observed due to the presence of the observer. • Are difficult or impossible to use when evaluating behaviors that are private. • Require trained interviewers, particularly to distinguish nuances of the behavior and to code more complex behaviors and sequences of behaviors. • Are time consuming and expensive. • Are not useful for very low frequency behaviors. • Require trained observers who can maintain objectivity during the observation process. May not inform about *why* people act in certain ways.
Existing Records	
Advantages	**Challenges**
• Provide a wide coverage of space, allowing for comparisons among different communities or between the local community and national data (e.g., teenage pregnancy, school dropout rate). • Provide a wide coverage of time, allowing for examination of changes over time. • Supply counts of events that are easy to report. Are inexpensive and unobtrusive.	• Are difficult and time consuming to handle when records are not computerized. • May have incomplete, disorganized, inaccurate, or out-of-date information. • May reflect local idiosyncrasies in counting and reporting (e.g., what constitutes a "school fight"). • May not match the needs of the particular program. • Access to the data or records may be challenging, requiring agency cooperation (e.g., school district, health department, police). • May have confidentiality restrictions.

Note. Surveys and Behavioral Observations Measures were adapted from Orpinas, P., & Horne, A. M. (2006). *Bullying prevention: Creating a positive school climate and developing social competence.* Washington, DC: American Psychological Association (p. 154). Reproduced with permission from the authors.

mode, median), dispersions (range, standard deviation, variance), and frequency distributions.

The data analysis starts by reviewing the evaluation questions, as they should guide the analyses. Some general guidelines for analyzing and interpreting the data are detailed next.

- Assess the available evidence.
- Do not oversimplify the data (e.g., presenting only overall frequencies)
- Account for differential effects and conditions (e.g., examine differences between those who completed the program and those who left, examine differences by relevant demographic variables).
- Use multiple techniques (e.g., qualitative and quantitative measures)
- Be aware of statistical assumptions and account for violations in assumption.
- Use methods appropriate for audiences and the purpose of the evaluation.
- Examine multiple and conflicting evidence.
- Look for consistency and confirmation with other sources of information.
- Consider and cite limitations of the evaluation design, data, and analyses.

Table 7.4. Advantages and Disadvantages of Focus Groups and Interviews

Focus Groups	
Advantages	**Challenges**
• Provide opportunities for clarification and probing. • Allow observing nonverbal responses as data collectors are interacting directly with participants. • Provide flexibility to explore the topic in detail. • Offer insights into *why* the behavior occurs and the dynamic interaction of behaviors, cognitions, and environment. • Increase synergistic effect, as participants build on each others' thoughts. • Are inexpensive. Provide information about group dynamics.	• Provide limited generalizability. • Reduce independence of responses, which may result in biased results. • May provide a "halo" of credibility, more than is warranted. • Require specific facilitator knowledge and skills to run the group (e.g., avoid group domination of a few individuals, allow space for all to participate, create a positive group dynamic) • Require specific skills to summarize and interpret results. • Reduce participation due to fear of respondents (e.g., the "boss" or a "bully" is present).
Interviews	
Advantages	**Challenges**
• May provide useful information for program delivery or solutions, particularly when key personnel or community gatekeepers are included. • Develop rapport with interviewees. • Provide in-depth information. • Gather quotes and "stories" useful to exemplify a situation or problem. Provide valuable insight into a topic.	• May reflect personal biases of the interviewee and lack of representation. • Are difficult to generalize. • Require trained interviewers to reduce interviewer bias. • Are limited to small samples. • Are time consuming.

Two analyses are particularly important to improve the program. First, the evaluator should examine whether the program was effective for all participants or only for some subgroups (e.g., only for the girls, only for the highly aggressive students). Second, the evaluator should assess which components of the program were particularly effective.

Table 7.5 provides examples of typical analyses for each time of experimental design.

Step 9: Reporting

The purpose of reporting is to communicate information about the evaluation and to facilitate its use. Reporting is an ongoing process that includes communicating information about purposes, context, activities, results, and implications of an evaluation. The evaluator should consider all the stakeholders for the evaluation and consider who will use the information and why. The following are guidelines for reporting:

- Be comprehensive and include the rationale for the evaluation, the questions to be answered by the evaluation, the methods used, the results, and limitations of the evaluation.
- Differentiate audiences by purposes and develop evaluation reports based on their needs and preferred mode of communication.
- Attend to human rights, ethics, and laws.
- Use multimedia and multiple delivery channels.
- Facilitate discussion and interaction among the stakeholders and provide opportunities for feedback

Reports may take the form of written documents, media releases (press, TV, radio, social media), formal presentations, meetings and small group discussions, panel reviews, direct mail, newsletters, staged interviews of key participants with dissemination provisions, and publications in professional journals. The evaluation report should be accurate, balanced, and fair, including positive and negative results. The language of the report should be direct and focused, with the level of detail matched to the stakeholders' point of view.

Table 7.5. Analysis Strategies for Evaluation Designs

Type of design	Sample question	Typical outcome analysis	Other analytic considerations
Outcome monitoring	Do the participants in the breast cancer screening program get screened?	Frequency of desired outcome (proportion)	Also useful to characterize those who do and do not achieve the desired outcome; compare these groups by other relevant characteristics. Use independent sample t-tests for continuous variables and chi-squares for categorical variables.
Pre-post one group only (same individuals measured in both pre- and posttest)	Do scores on a 20-point test of knowledge about contraception improve after students complete the health education program? (continuous outcome measure)	Paired t-test for continuous outcome measure	Because attrition is often a problem with pre-post designs, compare the baseline characteristics of those lost to follow-up and those retained. Use independent sample t-tests for continuous variables and chi-squares for categorical variables Consider doing the main outcome analysis separately for subgroups of interest (subgroup analysis)
	Does the percentage of kids who have witnessed at least one incident of domestic abuse in the past month decrease after families participate in the program? (dichotomous outcome measure)	McNemar's test is a type of chi-square test used for paired data of this type	
Quasi-experimental, pre-post two group community programs (different people at pre- and posttest)	Does awareness of the dangers of sun exposure increase following a publicity campaign?	For all these types of designs: If outcome measure is continuous, use ANOVA with control for covariates (baseline differences) If outcome measure is dichotomous, the simplest test is chi-square but it does not allow inclusion of interesting differences between the groups (covariates). A more complex analysis is possible with logistic regression, incorporating both baseline measures and the grouping variable (for example, intervention vs. control group) into the model	Begin by examining for pre-existing differences between the groups; comparisons could use independent sample t-tests for continuous variables, chi-square tests for categorical variables. Consider doing the main outcome analysis separately for subgroups of interest (subgroup analyses)
Quasi-experimental, pre-post historical controls	Do more women using the clinic this year have adequate weight gain during their pregnancy than women who came to the clinic in past years?		
Quasi-experimental, two group, posttest only	Following the adolescent pregnancy prevention program, do fewer young women in the intervention group become pregnant as compared to the control group?		

Step 10: Use Data for Program Improvement

The final step of program evaluation is to use the data gathered in the previous steps to identify what works and what needs improvement. This information is crucial to continue forward. For example, a program to improve high school graduation may have reduced dropout rate of girls but not of boys, or maybe the program was successful only when students participated in at least four of the six sessions. This information—who benefits or when the program is successful—is important to identify areas that need to be improved or modified, components of programs that could be deleted, and successes that should be celebrated. Quantifiable information about success can help to garner additional resources and increase staff morale.

Conclusions and Future Directions

This chapter provides an overview of the essential characteristics and processes for evaluating prevention programs. This overview identifies the steps necessary for effective evaluation and provides resources for identifying where to obtain further information. We hope that this chapter has conveyed the importance of evaluation. Too often programs are conceptualized, planned, and implemented with little regard for measurement of impact. When building an adequate evaluation fails, it is impossible to understand whether the program reached the objective and whether expenditure of time and money invested was worth it.

Proficiently developing and executing an evaluation plan may require skills that community members may not have. Practitioners who are planning to evaluate a program should consider contacting universities professors or staff members at research institutions who have experience in program evaluation. They can provide their expertise to help build the logic models and develop a meaningful evaluation plan. In addition, pairing with doctoral students may be mutually beneficial: Students can write a publishable manuscript and community members can receive free services. This process will also build evaluation capacity in the community organization.

Many challenges in the field of program evaluation still remain. A first challenge is the identification of the relevant mediating variables that explain why and how the program works. As behavioral theory becomes more precise, evaluators will know better how to identify initial and intermediate outcomes. In addition to theory, with the development of more sophisticated statistical methods, researchers will better understand the predictability of mediating variables for explaining outcome variables.

A second challenge is to identify the most important moderators that influence program outcomes. Moderators explain under which circumstances the program works (e.g., only when implemented in the community) and for whom it works best (e.g., only for first time offenders, not recidivists). These variables are not possible to control, but understanding their influence can help practitioners streamline the implementation of the program.

A third challenge is that, while operating in an era of accountability, many programs are implemented based on beliefs or convenience rather than science (theoretical models based on empirical evaluations). Frequently, policy makers concentrate on implementing programs they believe in, but that unfortunately have no ongoing or long-term evaluation of impact. For example, evaluations of popular programs, such as boot camps for aggressive youth, have proven not only ineffective but detrimental. Many of our current school models exemplify the preponderance of faith over scholarship. For example, the educational model of "pay for performance," which supports paying teachers based on students' academic performance on standardized tests, assumes that the teacher performance equates to children's learning. As we stated in the introduction, evaluation should be an effective vehicle for advocacy and policy.

A fourth challenge is the economic constraints that many prevention programs are going through, evaluation being the first area to be eliminated. Many government funding agencies expect a minimum of 10% of the value of the project to be devoted to evaluation, which may not be enough to subcontract with an external evaluator. Thus, agencies that lack the expertise and funding to conduct the evaluation will do their best with limited resources, often resulting in less meaningful evaluations. This problem further emphasizes the need to build academic-community partnerships. An additional benefit of that partnership is that academia can learn from practitioners and practitioners from academicians. Researchers and evaluators have much to learn from those working in the field. Even though much as been published on evidence-based practice, there is no ready venue for reporting practice-based evidence.

Questions for Future Directions

1. How can faculty at universities and community partners work together to build evaluation capacity at the local level and learn from each other about best practices?
2. How can evaluation results contribute to translational practice (moving from research to implementation in the field)? What can we learn from evaluation studies to help generalize to other settings?
3. How can we balance the scientific ideal (randomized experiments) with the practicality restraints of conducting evaluation in field settings?
4. What are the best strategies to combine qualitative methods, such as stories of impact, with qualitative methods to communicate the value of a program?

References

Baranowski, T., & Stables, G. (2000). Process evaluations of the 5-a-day projects. *Health Education and Behavior, 27*(2), 157–166.

Cook, T. D., & Campbell, D. T. (1979). *Quasi-experimentation: Design & analysis issues for field settings.* Boston: Houghton Mifflin.

Kusek, J. Z., & Rist, R. C. (2004). *Ten steps to a results-based monitoring and evaluation system: A handbook for development practitioners.* Retrieved from The World Bank website: http://www.oecd.org/dataoecd/23/27/35281194.pdf

Molgaard, V. K., Spoth, R. L., & Redmond, C. (2000). Competency training—The Strengthening Families Program: For parents and youth 10–14 (NCJ 182208; August 2000). *OJJDP Juvenile Justice Bulletin* (NCJ 182208). Retrieved December 27, 2009, from http://www.ncjrs.gov/pdffiles1/ojjdp/182208.pdf

Orpinas, P., & Horne, A. M. (2006). *Bullying prevention: Creating a positive school climate and developing social competence.* Washington, DC: American Psychological Association.

Pan American Health Organization. (2009). *Manual Familias Fuertes—Guía para el facilitador: Programa familiar para prevenir conductas de riesgo en adolescentes. Una intervención para padres y adolescentes entre 10 y 14 años.* Washington, DC: Pan American Health Organization.

Patton, M. Q. (2008). *Utilization-focused evaluation* (4th ed.). Thousand Oaks, CA: Sage.

Reidy, C. H., Orpinas, P., & Davis, M. (2011). Successful recruitment and retention of Latino study participants. *Health Promotion Practice*, doi: 10.1177/1524839911405842.

Rossi, P. H., Lipsey, M. W., & Freeman, H. E. (2004). *Evaluation: A systematic approach* (7th ed.). Thousand Oaks, CA: Sage.

Saunders, R. P., Evans, M. H., & Joshi, P. (2005). Developing a process-evaluation plan for assessing health promotion program implementation: A how-to guide. *Health Promotion Practice, 6*(2), 134–147. doi: 10.1177/1524839904273387

Scriven, M. (1998). Minimalist theory: The least theory that practice requires. *American Journal of Evaluation, 19*(1), 57–70.

Shadish, W. R., Cook, T. D., & Campbell, D. T. (2001). *Experimental and quasi-experimental designs for generalized causal inference.* Boston: Houghton Mifflin.

W. K. Kellogg Foundation. (2004). *Logic model development guide: Using logic models to bring together planning, evaluation, and action.* Retrieved from www.wkkf.org

CHAPTER

8 Advocacy and Prevention: Dismantling Systems of Oppression

Alex L. Pieterse, Alexa E. Hanus *and* Michael M. Gale

Abstract

The impact of environmental factors on psychological functioning has received much attention in the psychological literature and has expanded the scholarship on mental heath beyond individual-level variables and intrapsychic processes. The current chapter therefore reviews the role of societal oppression on the psychological functioning of individuals from historically marginalized groups. In addition the chapter frames prevention as an important social justice tool that can be used in order to facilitate the well-being of individuals and groups who continue to experience oppression based on such factors as race, sexual orientation, and gender. The chapter concludes by providing a case illustration of social justice–based prevention as it applies to antiracism advocacy.

Key Words: prevention, advocacy, societal oppression, antiracism, empowerment

> We argue that educators and human service professionals have an obligation to contribute at least in some modest way to the liberation of the oppressed people they serve. (Watts, Abdul-Adil, & Pratt, 2002)

> Teach our students about social justice and injustice and behavioral consequences. Show how people who are exploited learn emotional distress. Become politically active. Join a radical support group in the struggle against the fictions that hold together the exploitative consumer society in which the upper 1% own more than the lowest 90%. (Albee, 1998)

Prevention as a tool of health promotion has garnered consistent attention in the fields of psychology and counseling. Kessler and Albee (1975), writing in the *Annual Review of Psychology*, succinctly captured the scope of prevention by stating "Our reading for a year leads us to the conclusion that practically every effort aimed at improved child rearing, increasing effective communication, building inner control and self-esteem, reducing stress and pollution etc.—in short everything aimed at improving the human condition, at making life more fulfilling and meaningful—may be considered to be a part of primary prevention of mental or emotional disturbance" (p. 557). From this perspective, prevention is a concept that informs psychological practice at a fundamental level, yet prevention has yet to be centralized in training, research, and practice (Albee, 1969, 1996; Coyne, 2000; Vera, Buhin, & Isacco, 2009). The current chapter therefore aims to outline the central nature of prevention within counseling and psychology, and to place prevention entirely within the context of social justice and advocacy (Coyne, 2000; Kaplan, 2000; Kenny & Hage, 2009; Murphy & Frank, 1979; Vera & Speight, 2007). After reviewing definitions of prevention, we examine the role of oppression in mental health. Next we outline social justice advocacy models and discuss prevention as an integral part of social justice advocacy. In arguing for a more sustained and centralized focus on prevention, we discuss the need for a radical shift in counseling and psychology, and outline what we view as the most critical elements of social justice–driven prevention. Finally, we encourage a rethinking of current training models in counseling psychology and provide a brief case illustration of social justice–driven prevention.

Defining Prevention Within Counseling and Psychology

Within the field of mental health, prevention has been defined as "efforts to enhance personal and collective well-being, as well as initiatives that create social and political change aimed at improving environments where people live, learn and work" (Hage et al., 2007, p. 497). Prevention has commonly been viewed as including three components: primary, secondary, and tertiary. Primary prevention is focused on reducing the incidence of psychological disorders, while secondary and tertiary prevention efforts focus more on reducing the negative impact of psychological disorders (see Caplan, 1964). More recently, prevention has been framed as a tool of social justice and as such, contemporary approaches to prevention emphasize the inclusion of sociopolitical activism that target systems of oppression thought to be influential in the development and maintenance of psychological disorders (Kenny & Hage, 2009; Prilleltensky, 2003; Vera, Buhin, & Isacco, 2009). Typically, psychological intervention tends to fall into the tertiary prevention category in as much as psychotherapy intervention is focused on symptom reduction or rehabilitation of mental health.

The psychological community has had a longstanding interest in primary prevention. (Albee, 1986; Caplan, 1964; McNeill & Ingram, 1983). The 1978 report of the *Task Panel on Prevention* defined prevention as:

> A group of approaches that share the common objective of (1) lowering the incidence of emotional disorders (i.e. the rate at which new cases occur) and (2) promoting conditions that reinforce positive mental health. (p. 1829)

Implicit in this definition is the need to focus on social determinants of, mental health. In this way, approaches to prevention inherently include a sociopolitical agenda and are based on a political ideology of equality and shared resources (Prilleltensky, 2008). Contemporary prevention scholars therefore incorporate an explicit call for psychologists to attend to oppressive structures/systems that impinge on mental health—a call exemplified in guideline #4 from the working group for best practices in prevention research, practice, and training: "Psychologists are encouraged to develop preventive interventions that address both the individual and the contextual/systemic factors that contribute to psychological distress and well-being" (Hage et al., 2007, p. 510).

Within counseling psychology, the focus on prevention has consistently emphasized the need to respond to the harmful psychological effects of oppression, discrimination, and inequality (Ivey, 1976; Kiselica & Robinson, 2001; Lopez & Cheeks, 1977). Accordingly, counseling psychologists have been encouraged to engage in multidisciplinary collaboration, to understand sociopolitical factors associated with mental health, to engage in a significant restructuring of training in order to encourage sociopolitical activism, and to employ research methodologies that are consistent with the needs and cultural contexts of individuals from historically oppressed groups (Ivey, 1976; Kenny & Hage, 2009; Vera & Speight, 2003; Warnath, 1973). In order to facilitate a greater appreciation of the role of prevention in dismantling systems of oppression, a brief review of the psychological correlates of oppression and discrimination is now provided.

Psychological Effects of Societal Oppression and Discrimination

The impact of societal oppression on mental health has received much attention in the social science literature in the past few decades. The resulting literature suggests that experiences of oppression and discrimination are associated with psychological distress and have an adverse influence on mental health (Carter, 2007; Paradies, 2006; Pascoe & Richman, 2009; Williams & Mohammed, 2009). In 1969, psychologist George Albee alerted the mental health community to the notion that the medical-model approach to our training and practice turned a blind eye to the very real consequences of living in an unjust, oppressive society. Albee suggested that this oppression itself likely served as a major source of emotional disturbance, and asserted that some forms of mental illness may be more accurately conceptualized as symptoms of the stresses experienced by being a member of a minority group in the United States. Numerous studies have now established that oppression negatively impacts the mental health of various marginalized groups in the United States, with much of the focus related to the effects of racism, heterosexism, and poverty.

Prior to examining the specific effects of oppression on mental health, it is important to first recognize that the definition of mental health reflects societal patterns of interaction and dominance. The history of psychology and psychiatry includes diagnostic categories that reflect definitions of mental illness shaped by the relationship between dominant and subordinate groups within the social hierarchy (Prilleltensky, 2008). Examples include the 19th-century diagnosis of *drapetomania*—a "psychiatric disorder" defined by attempts to escape the confines of slavery (Thomas & Sillen, 1972), and the classification of homosexuality, childhood masturbation, and lack of vaginal orgasm as mental disorders (Wakefield, 1992). A brief review of the psychological impact of three forms of oppression within the United States is now provided.

Racism

Racism remains a pervasive phenomenon in US society (Bonilla-Silva, 2003), and has been defined by Carter (2007) as

> The transformation of racial prejudice into individual racism through the use of power directed against racial groups and their members, who are defined as inferior by individuals, institutional members, and leaders, which is then reflected in policy and procedures with the intentional and unintentional support and participation of the entire race and dominant culture. (p. 24)

The pervasive nature of this phenomenon is supported in the literature; in an examination of experiences with racist events in a community sample of African Americans, Klonoff, Landrine, and Ullman (1999) found that 96% of their participants reported experiencing racial discrimination in the past year. Confirming this rate, Sellers and Shelton (2003) found that more than 50% of their sample of African American college students reported more than a dozen daily racial hassles with strangers, and similar rates have been reported across different racial groups (Contrada et al., 2001).

Research has provided direct evidence of the psychological and emotional effects of racism, including decreased self-esteem and perceived control, depression, and generalized anxiety disorder (Carter, 2007; Williams, Neighbors, & Jackson, 2003). Increased experiences with race-related stress have been shown to predict higher anxiety and depression scores (Utsey & Payne, 2000), as well as increased levels of somatization and an overall increased endorsement of total psychological symptoms (Klonoff, Landrine, & Ullman, 1999). Additionally, targets of racial discrimination exhibit lower levels of control and problem-solving skills (Broman, Mavaddat, & Hsu, 2000). Experiences of racial discrimination have also been correlated with increased levels of stress responses such as anger, frustration, paranoia, fear, and somatic symptoms (Clark, Anderson, Clark, & Williams, 1999). Scholars now suggest that race-based experiences fall within the domain of traumatic experiences (e.g., Bryant-Davis & Ocampo, 2005; Carter, Forsyth, Mazzula, & Williams, 2005). Indeed, research reveals that among veterans, racial minorities have increased rates of PTSD (post-traumatic stress disorder), even when accounting for premilitary factors such as poverty, prior affective disorders, and substance abuse (Frueh, Brady, & de Arellano, 1998). A more detailed review of the harmful psychological effects of racism as well as strategies and interventions designed to ameliorate and reduce the incidence of racism-related trauma is provided in this volume (see Neville and Spanierman, Chapter 30, this volume).

Heterosexist Oppression

Homophobia and heterosexism are additional forms of oppression that exert negative psychological effects. The term "homophobia" is used to describe an irrational fear of same-sex relationships, while the term "heterosexism" describes an ideological system that denies, derogates, or penalizes any nonheterosexual form of behavior, identity, relationship, or community (Kitzinger, 1997). In this way, homophobia highlights the attitudes of specific individuals, while heterosexism highlights oppression as a social phenomenon incorporated into the systemic workings of society (Aguinaldo, 2008). The frequency of exposure to gay oppression has been demonstrated in the literature; Lesbian, Gay, Bisexual and Transgendered (LGB) individuals are twice as likely as heterosexual people to have experienced a life event related to prejudice (Mays & Cochran, 2001), while a national survey of LGBT (lesbian, gay, bisexual, and transgender) youth revealed that 90% of respondents reported sometimes or frequently hearing homophobic remarks at school, with 37% of these respondents reporting having heard these remarks from faculty or school staff (GLSEN, 1999). While these statistics highlight exposure to homophobia on an individual level, gay oppression or heterosexism on a systemic level denies the rights of gay couples to benefits routinely enjoyed by heterosexual couples (National Gay and Lesbian Task Force, 2010). The consequences of this form of oppression on the mental health of LGBT individuals have also been established through empirical investigation. Evidence from research suggests that compared with their heterosexual counterparts, gay men and lesbians suffer from more mental health problems including affective disorders, substance use disorders, and suicide (Garofalo et al., 1998; Gilman et al., 2001; Meyer, 2003). Overall, the accepted explanation for the cause of these rates is that stigma, prejudice, and discrimination create a toxic environment that can lead to mental health problems for those who belong to stigmatized minority groups (Friedman, 1999). Here we refer readers to Haley, Adams, Dickson, Hitter, and Luna (Chapter 29, this volume) for a more detailed review and discussion of the psychological impacts of heterosexism and strategies and interventions designed to reduce its impact.

Social Class Oppression

Those living under conditions of socioeconomic oppression also experience threats to emotional well-being. Scholars in this area define classism as existing along two dimensions: institutional classism, where social institutions create and sustain the deprivation of those in poverty, and interpersonal classism, characterized by prejudice, stereotyping, and discrimination (Lott & Bullock, 2007). Life in poverty can include experiences in many areas that are destructive to psychological health, including a lack in basic nutritional resources, inadequate or unsafe housing, and increased exposure to threatening events such as physical and sexual assault (Belle & Doucet, 2003). A number of studies document the psychological effects of conditions related to socioeconomic oppression, indicating that the poor are as much as two times more likely to experience psychiatric disorders as their economically secure counterparts (Bruce, Takeuchi, & Leaf, 1991). This finding has been replicated with specific populations, and seems to highlight depression as a primary struggle; homeless and housed low-income mothers experience twice the rate of major depression as middle-class mothers (Bassuk, Buckner, Perloff, & Bassuk, 1998), and Siefert and colleagues (2000) found that one third of their sample of welfare recipient mothers also met diagnostic criteria for major depression.

While oppression has clearly been associated with negative mental health outcomes including depression, anxiety, self-esteem, substance use, and suicide, additional areas of consideration include colonialism and internalized oppression. Colonialism describes the systematic denigration of the humanity of colonized persons, leading to feelings of inferiority, identity confusion, and self-doubt (Fanon, 1967). Internalized oppression is a related condition in which individuals who belong to oppressed groups believe themselves to be inferior to those in the dominant culture (Moane, 2003). In considering how these ideas may impact one's sense of identity with a particular group, Freire (1970) offers that an internalized identity consistent with the stereotypes sustained by those in power can develop into a desire to maintain distance from one's own group, and attempt to assimilate to the norms of the oppressor.

Considering the historical trauma of the United States, including the genocide and displacement of indigenous groups, slavery, Jim Crow segregation, and the internment of Japanese Americans, it is clear that colonialism and internalized oppression may take a tremendous, and *additional* toll on the mental health of those who have been oppressed (Smith, Chambers, & Bratini, 2009). Indeed, internalized oppression is thought to contribute to high rates of suicide, substance abuse, and domestic violence among Native Americans (McBride, 2002), and to the development of self-hatred, self-destructive behavior, and crime among African Americans (Tatum, 1994). It is important to note that internalized oppression extends beyond racial oppression and applies to any marginalized group. In a meta-analysis of 31 studies examining the relationship between internalized homophobia and mental health, higher levels of internalized homophobia were associated with greater levels of mental health problems including depression and anxiety (Newcomb & Mustanski, 2010).

This brief overview clearly demonstrates that oppression is associated with negative mental health outcomes for oppressed individuals, yet this process is not explicitly recognized or incorporated in psychological and psychiatric diagnostic systems (Prilleltensky & Gonick, 1994). While mental health professionals may work with oppressed populations in addressing these matters at the individual level, researchers and practitioners point out that these interventions are not only reactionary, but they also place the responsibility of addressing negative psychological outcomes on the oppressed individual (Aguinaldo, 2008). In addressing this limitation, the social justice advocacy movement represents an approach that works to ameliorate and possibly eliminate the negative health outcomes associated with systemic oppression and discrimination. A brief review of social justice advocacy models is now provided, followed by a more in-depth look at how social justice models inform preventative efforts associated with the psychological impact of oppression.

Models of Social Justice Advocacy

Although social justice advocacy has a long-standing history within mental health fields (see Aldarondo, 2007; Kiselica & Robinson, 2001), current definitions of advocacy reflect varying points of emphasis. Lewis, Lewis, Daniels, and D'Andrea (1998) have defined advocacy as "an indirect service aimed at strengthening socially devalued populations and working toward creating responsive helping networks" (as cited in Toporek & Liu, 2001, p. 387). Toporek and Liu (2001) add to this definition by identifying the location of intervention in stating that advocacy represents "action/s a mental health professional, counselor, or psychologist takes in assisting clients and client groups to achieve therapy goals through participating in clients' environments" (p. 387). Toporek (2000) in turn describes this community participation as "action taken by counseling professionals to facilitate the removal of external and institutional barriers to clients' well-being" (p. 6). Finally, in capturing the varying definitions and broad scope of advocacy, Ratts, Lewis, and Toporek (2010) simply state, "advocacy involves taking social justice ideals and putting them into action" (p. 6).

Given these relatively broad definitions, and considering the complexity of the structures and systems we are called to work within and upon, it follows that the roles we may take as advocates vary widely in terms of the level of involvement and point of intervention. Perhaps the clearest framework for conceptualizing the differences in advocacy models is provided by Lewis and Lewis (1983). In their discussion of advocacy in the context of community psychology, they make a distinction between case-level and class-level advocacy approaches. Specifically, they describe case-level approaches as consisting of actions that attempt to expand access to services or additional assistance on behalf of individuals. In this way, mental health professionals work within a given system to help clients on a case-by-case basis. In contrast, class-level advocacy is described as actions that address the larger social, economic, legal, and governmental policies that oppress members of the population being served. In this way, rather than working within a given structure or system, class-level advocacy calls on mental health professionals to address the policies that govern and legitimize these systems, in attempts to create new services and opportunities in advocating for equality. The essential distinction, then, is whether we work within the structure to expand services on an individual level, or step outside the structure to facilitate policy changes that may impact the larger community.

Numerous advocacy approaches and models have been offered since Lewis and Lewis (1983) defined these ideas, and they reflect the values and specific goals of a range of fields, including feminist psychology, liberation psychology, community psychology, and multicultural counseling. While more recent advocacy approaches come from a range of fields, each model may still be conceptualized within the overall framework of case- or class-level advocacy in different ways. Prior to examining these models and the important differences between them, it is important to also acknowledge the overlapping goals of each approach in the context of our work as therapists. Lerner (1972) articulates this common ground by stating:

> The conflict over individual versus group methods... rests on a false dichotomy because the essential nature of psychotherapy and social action is the same... to promote effective action on one's own behalf, in the former case by removing internal psychological obstacles to such action, and in the latter, by removing external social obstacles to it... The only real dichotomy is between those who work on their clients and those who work for their clients. (p. 11)

While Lerner's statement highlights the common goal of advocacy as the promotion of effective action on a client's behalf, important differences in these advocacy methods remain, and are important to consider further. The following section will examine specific case- and class-level advocacy approaches, and will explore the important differences between these approaches in the context of prevention. We view case-level approaches as intervention and class-level approaches as prevention, and briefly describe each in this context, however note that a more detailed review of social justice approaches to prevention is presented in this volume (see Kenny & Medvide, Chapter 9)

Social Justice Advocacy as Intervention

Advocacy models that take a case-level approach have been further characterized as "service defined" (Davies, Lyon, & Moni-Catania, 1998) in that they often begin with identifying additional services for a given client. Specifically, traditional case-level advocacy offers a client a range of options for assistance based on the availability of the needed service or on the overall mission of the advocacy organization. In this way, traditional, "service defined" advocacy tends to focus on specific, and often narrowly defined, problems (Goodman & Epstein, 2008) and tends to place the advocate in the expert role rather than serving as a collaborator in the process (Miller, 2008). In recognizing these limitations, additional advocacy models that take a more collaborative, flexible approach have been proposed. For example, Toporek and Liu (2001) describe empowerment as a mode of advocacy that focuses on the interactions between the therapist and client, with the goal of providing clients with the knowledge and skills they need to act as independent advocates for themselves. In this role, therapists initially become involved in the client's environment and work to acknowledge the role of power dynamics and oppression, but Toporek and Liu (2001) describe this involvement as remaining within the context of established socioeconomic, sociocultural, and sociopolitical climates. Following this, the empowerment model may be understood as a case-level approach to advocacy in the sense that the therapist is working within the system to assist clients on an individual basis.

Continuing the push for increased collaboration and flexibility, Bowes and Sim (2006) describe their version of citizen advocacy as an approach that attempts to identify the client as the expert, and looks to prioritize the client's perspective in identifying appropriate services for her unique situation. In this process, the authors acknowledge that clients' ideas about advocacy may not conform to dominant ideas and existing systems of advocacy, and in this way, citizen advocacy looks to work outside the realm of traditional social services. While citizen advocacy allows for a more flexible and collaborative approach in identifying necessary services, feminist relational advocacy (Goodman, Glenn, Bohlig, Banyard, & Borges, 2009) expands on this approach to further highlight the importance of the relationship between the client and advocate, and attempts to also acknowledge the oppressive role of larger systems in creating participants' difficulties. In this way, feminist relational advocacy moves beyond the act of targeting clients' specific problems and looks to acknowledge and give voice to the larger web of stress that occurs under an oppressive environment (Miller, 2008).

Overall, though these advocacy approaches include more collaboration and flexibility than traditional, service defined models, and push to explicitly acknowledge the larger systems of oppression at play, these models may still be categorized as case-level approaches. Namely, whether the main task is identifying additional services, empowering the client to serve as a self-advocate or to identify his or her own solution, or helping the client examine and think about the stress they experience as a result of larger oppressive systems, the focus or point of intervention for each of these models is with the individual client. Additionally, and perhaps most importantly, the work with the client remains within the context of a larger oppressive environment, and does nothing in the way of working to change the policies that govern and legitimize this environment. In this way, case-level advocacy models seek to provide direct, individualized services to clients in helping them to navigate or cope with the systems of oppression in place. This advocacy approach becomes particularly limiting and problematic, then, when the larger system is the etiology of a client's distress. That is, these models are largely reactive and call us to work with people in the context of the struggles they already experience, rather than addressing the cause of the struggle by working to change the operating mechanisms of oppression.

In contrast, class-level advocacy approaches directly acknowledge that client distress must be understood in the context of the environment, and that often times the environment is what necessitates intervention or change—not the client. In this way, class-level approaches to advocacy diagnose the pathology of the environment, and take necessary steps to "treat" or intervene at this level. These approaches may be understood as prevention approaches to advocacy, while the former, case-level advocacy approaches remain reactive. Specific examples of class-level advocacy models include Toporek and Liu's (2001) social action approach, as well as Buhin and Vera's (2009) person-centered and environment-centered interventions.

Social Justice Advocacy as Prevention

In their description of social action, Toporek and Liu (2001) call the therapist to be actively engaged in attempts to remove the sociopolitical barriers faced by his or her clients through actions outside of traditional psychotherapy. They explain that these interventions occur on a macrosocial level, and may include engaging in legislative or policy issues that affect clients. In this way, Toporek and Liu view advocacy as a catalyst for legislative and/or institutional change. In advocating effectively in this manner, they call on therapists to gain an understanding of how historical and contemporary laws may structure and reinforce client distress, and further, that they be actively involved within professional organizations, media, and government to educate and mediate issues related to discrimination and prejudice.

Taking a similar, prevention oriented approach to advocacy, Buhin and Vera (2009) describe interventions that may be performed at the person and environment levels in preventing racism. Specifically, they identify racism as enforced at both the interpersonal and institutional levels, and therefore offer advocacy approaches that address both areas. In examining the complexity of these social systems in perpetuating and reinforcing racism, Buhin and Vera (2009) point out that traditional therapy may be an inefficient method in addressing racism, and directly call on White individuals to take a greater load of responsibility in dismantling their own racism. To this end, they describe a number of person-focused primary prevention programs that may be implemented with White children to address the development of racist attitudes and beliefs in working to prevent racism in future generations. Finally, in delineating advocacy methods to address institutional racism, Buhin and Vera call for mental health professionals to perform environment-centered interventions by communicating with policy makers in attempts to change and shape future social policy in favor of equality. In doing so, they provide behavioral strategies that may make communication between social scientists and policy makers more effective by calling social scientists to ask more relevant, meaningful research questions, to provide more direct, "bottom-line" policy implications into scholarly writings, and to foster close relationships with policy makers.

In considering Toporek and Liu's (2001) social action approach, and Buhin and Vera's (2009) person- and environment-centered interventions, it is clear that they may be characterized as class-level approaches to advocacy. Specifically, these models call on mental health professionals not only to acknowledge the structural oppression clients face but also to work toward changing the system. In this way, these approaches take a prevention stance by attempting to address an individual's suffering at its source—by working to change oppressive systems, these advocacy models work to prevent further distress. Thus, in revisiting the essential differences between Lewis and Lewis's (1983) original description of case- and class-level advocacy models, it is clear that these approaches may also be conceptualized in the context of prevention. Namely, we may understand each level of advocacy as the extent to which each approach focuses on prevention of distress versus providing tools to cope or adjust to distress.

Overall, this distinction does not seek to minimize the crucial importance and necessity of advocacy models that operate in a more case-level context. Surely we must acknowledge the very real and debilitating mental health consequences our clients currently suffer as a result of systemic oppression, and continue working to provide them with here-and-now services and coping tools to minimize this distress. Additionally, this distinction does not indicate mutual exclusivity. Instead, the larger picture of advocacy models in the field today reveals some combination of both approaches—this combined approach is perhaps most exemplified in the ACA advocacy competencies (Lewis, Arnold, House, & Toporek, 2002), with the competency domains falling on a continuum moving from microlevel to macrolevel interventions. As such, these competencies involve strategies where a therapist seeks to empower the client through collaboration, or working with the client, and strategies where the therapist seeks to empower the client by advocating on the client's behalf.

While keeping these important points in mind, we offer that as a profession with an ethical obligation to the greater society, and as a profession with the knowledge and skills necessary to make a greater impact, we must focus an equal amount of effort—if not more—on advocacy strategies that target the cause of oppression. As George Albee (1983) points out: "No mass disorder afflicting humankind is ever brought under control or eliminated by attempts at treating the affected individual" (p. 24). It is clear from this brief review of social justice advocacy models that prevention lies at the heart of advocacy. Simply stated, one goal of social justice advocacy is the elimination of oppressive structures that negatively impact psychological health, a goal that is encapsulated in the notion of prevention (Vera & Speight, 2007).

Elements of Prevention as Advocacy in Counseling Psychology

Given the preceding description of social justice advocacy as an approach to preventing psychological dysfunction associated with oppression, we now turn to outlining specific elements of prevention within counseling psychology. An ecological approach to mental health appreciates that mental health is reflective of both individual level and systemic level variables including such factors as individual behavior and personality, sociopolitical history, cultural context, and the larger impact of social institutions (Bronfenbrenner, 1979; Arredondo & Rosen, 2007). As such, elements of prevention within counseling psychology should incorporate both individual and systemic level variables, and should have applicability to therapists, clients, and the environment that impacts the therapeutic work. Specific elements highlighted in our discussion include practitioner dispositions and ideology, education as prevention through the teaching of resistance, action research as both informing and facilitating prevention, centralization of prevention in training, and prevention as an interdisciplinary effort. We will also identify the best practices principals (Hage et al., 2007) that most closely embody those aspects of prevention we are seeking to highlight in the following discussion.

Individual Dispositions and Political Ideology

Critiques of the social advocacy movement have cautioned against hidden agendas and the imposition of ideology within the counseling movement (Smith, Reynolds, & Rovnak, 2009; Weinrach & Thomas, 1998). However, it is clear that that the social justice advocacy/prevention movement is firmly grounded in a political ideology that critiques merit-based and market-driven approaches to the distribution of resources (Prilleltensky, 2003). Furthermore, social justice advocates identify the inequitable distribution of resources as a critical source of psychological distress (Prilleltensky, Dokecki, Frieden, & Wang, 2007). Prevention advocates should therefore be transparent in their goals and methodology, and be clear about the political ideology that undergirds their preventative efforts. As such, a focus on systemic change in order to redistribute the power arrangement in society as a means of ameliorating psychological distress should be explicitly stated. In this context, Moane (2003) describes the larger goal as being one of transformation: "One of the aims of liberation psychology is to develop an understanding of the role of psychology and of the psychologist in social transformation" (p. 92). In attempting to define our role as psychologists in this process, class-level or prevention oriented advocacy approaches often raise concern that counseling and psychology are becoming tools to further political agendas (Toporek & Liu, 2001). Some members of the profession (e.g., Weinrach & Thomas, 1998) challenge social action by stating that science should not be political. While Toporek and Liu (2001) call for guidelines and training to address this issue by ensuring that advocacy actions are for the purpose of the client rather than to satisfy political or personal needs of the therapist, we hope to remind readers that as a profession, we work for the common goal of improving the well-being of our clients, and this goal is without controversy. Where the conflict begins is how we, as a profession, decide to work toward this goal. To state that science should be free of politics is to remove science from the context within which it is created. Particularly with regard to social science, when our well-being occurs within the context of political structures that have direct impact on our social status and mental health (e.g., Carter, 2007; Meyer, 2003; Newcomb & Mustanski, 2010; Smith, Chambers, & Bratini, 2009), to remove politics from the study of social science borders on the realm of impossibility. If we are to engage in prevention-oriented advocacy approaches, we must rid ourselves of the fear to acknowledge politics and come to embrace our roles as social scientists as embedded in political structures. When we have the unique knowledge and skill-set to address political structures in a way that improves the well-being of our clients, we reject the notion that we should refrain from doing so in the name of "scientific integrity," despite our scientific knowledge of the harm these political structures currently create. Furthermore, by embracing the ethic of caring, and the characteristics of integrity and humility (Tervalon & Murray-Garcia, 1998; Trusty & Brown, 2005), social justice prevention advocates strive to uphold the well-being of the client as the primary and overarching goal, while understanding that the furthering of a political agenda is only in service of this goal. Our focus on ideology here fits most closely with prevention practice guideline #15, which states, "Psychologists are encouraged to engage in governmental, legislative, and political advocacy activities that enhance the health and well-being of the broader population served" (Hage et al., 2007, p. 496).

Education as a Tool of Prevention

Education is a fundamental tool in the prevention sciences (Hage et al., 2007). Depending on how education is utilized, it may be thought of as a primary or tertiary prevention strategy. We believe education serves multiple purposes within social justice–driven prevention. First, there is a need to educate those in power about the social, moral, and economic benefits associated with prevention (see Albee, 1983). Indeed, there is a large body of research that clearly documents the efficacy of prevention efforts (Romano & Hage, 2000). To illustrate, systematic and meta-analytic reviews indicate that prevention efforts are efficacious in reducing the rates of suicide (Mann et al., 2005), drug use (Tobler et al., 2000) and depression (Jane-Llopis, Homsan, Jenkins, & Anderson, 2003). It is appropriate, then, to ensure that those in power who make legislative and public policy decisions are aware of these findings so they may incorporate preventative measures in future public planning.

An additional area of education that has been underutilized as a tool of prevention is that of educating the targets of oppression on such areas as resistance, internalized stigma, and the raising of critical consciousness (Ivey, 1995). Following this, social justice–based prevention practitioners can use education as a means of informing oppressed groups about the nature of their oppression, the structural dynamics associated with their oppression, and how to engage in activism. This strategy holds the promise of reducing harmful psychological effects associated with being oppressed through the empowerment of oppressed individuals, groups, and communities (Prilleltensky, 2003). Literature in this area provides empirical evidence to indicate that individuals who engage in sociopolitical activism in response to real or perceived threats to physical and psychological safety, report higher levels of life-satisfaction, self-efficacy, and a sense of empowerment (Boehnke & Wong, 2011; Watts, Abdul-Adil, & Pratt, 2002). In Watts's work with young African American men, the growing sense of empowerment as result of heightened awareness of systemic oppression resulted in less negative attitudes, and greater participation in "liberation behaviors" such as community activism that tend to provide a greater sense of self and self-esteem. Thus, utilizing principles of liberation psychology, counseling psychology may seek to empower, educate, and facilitate strategies in which the oppressed can confront and resist the their oppression.

In recognizing an additional area for educational intervention, a critical aspect of an oppressive system is the manner in which it requires the oppressed group to tolerate and even participate in their own oppression (see Pieterse, Howitt, & Naidoo, 2011). Fanon (1967), in a brilliant analysis of the psychological impact of colonization, outlined a type of mental colonization in which the colonized internalize the negative and destructive stereotypes applied to them by the colonizer (e.g., intellectual inferiority, psychological immaturity, and proclivities to violence). Indeed, Biko (1978), the famed South African freedom fighter, indicated that the "greatest tool in the hand of the oppressor is the mind of the oppressed" (p. 68). We have noted the manner in which internalized oppression is associated with adverse psychological outcomes. Therefore we argue that providing oppressed individuals and communities with new frameworks in which to understand their life experiences, thereby working to resist internalized oppression, is a critical and necessary component of social justice–based prevention.

The notion of resistance to oppression has received little traction within the psychological community (Watts & Serrano-Garcia, 2003), as opposed to the large literature on coping and resilience. Social justice–based prevention, however, incorporates resistance as a central approach to reducing psychological distress associated with oppression. Graham (2005) highlights the need to give voice and recognition to the perspectives and ideas for practice that are located within oppressed communities, and indicates that such efforts both inform competent practice and serve as a source of empowerment for oppressed communities. It should be noted that counseling psychology has a crucial role to play in the facilitation of resistance and empowerment. Moane (2008) describes a "cycle of liberation" in which individuals who are introduced to resisting oppression at personal and interpersonal levels become interested in facilitating change at a political level, which in turn, sets a pattern of change occurring simultaneously. Given that the training of counseling psychologists includes instruction on the facilitation of change at both individual and group levels, and the role of systems in this process, social justice–based prevention seems a natural fit for counseling psychology. The guideline most consistent with this point of emphasis is guideline #5: "Psychologists are encouraged to implement interventions that seek to reduce risks as well as promote strengths and well-being across the life span" (Hage et al., 2007, p. 495).

The Role of Research in Prevention

Research is a fundamental tool that can be used to inform social justice–based preventative practice. The utility of research is twofold; one is to provide a means of evaluating current approaches to prevention-based practice. An illustration of this type of research is to examine the association between policies extending protections to marginalized populations, and the corresponding prevalence of psychological disorders. Some findings in this area of research have revealed that living in states without such protective policies predicted a stronger association between minority group membership and psychiatric disorders, including generalized anxiety disorder, PTSD, and dysthymia (Hatzenbuehler, Keyes, & Hasin, 2009). Research of this nature can be very instrumental in driving policies that are more consistent with prevention-based approaches. The second role of social justice–based research is the utilization of research as an act of liberation, through giving voice and privileging the experiences of oppressed individuals and communities (Sonn & Meredith, 2006). Scholars like Smith (1999) have described more traditional approaches to research among oppressed communities as extending the exploitative and disempowering role of colonialism. She describes Western scientific methods as imposing a paradigm of knowledge construction that is inconsistent with many indigenous communities and, as such, contributes to the sense of powerless that comes from being displaced. Fortunately there are emerging methods and examples of how to utilize research as a preventative and empowerment-based strategy (Fine, 2006).

One such research strategy includes participatory action research (PAR). PAR is a methodology grounded in critical approaches and community-based intervention (Pyrch, 2007; Smith, 2010). As a preventative tool, PAR has been used in such contexts as drug resistance programs with US adolescents (Gosin, Dustman, Drapeau, & Harthun, 2003), and working with individuals living in poverty (Smith & Romero, 2010). Components of PAR that directly inform social justice–based prevention include mutuality and collaboration, sharing of power and resources, facilitation of consciousness raising, and provision of tools for social change (Smith & Romero, 2010). Furthermore, PAR is an inherently strength-based approach. It values and legitimizes the voices of individuals and groups who heretofore have been silenced through the oppressive practices of racism, classism, heterosexism, and other forms of domination and control (Pyrch, 2007).

A final area where research can directly inform prevention in the context of social justice is that of health disparities. There is ample data to indicate that significant differences exist in health outcomes across racial lines. Generally, people of color tend to have worse outcomes and have less access to health care than their White counterparts (see Pieterse & Carter, 2010). Given the availability of culturally relevant approaches, both in relation to intervention and prevention (Reese & Vera, 2007; Griner & Smith, 2006), PAR offers the hope of providing outcome data associated with preventative interventions in the area of health and wellness, as well as data that speaks to the process of empowerment among people of color, and the mechanisms associated with reclaiming one's voice and proactively engaging in activities designed to increase health and well-being. The best practice prevention guideline that reflects the focus on research is practice guideline #7: "Psychologists are encouraged to be competent in a variety of research methods used in prevention research." (Hage et al., 2007, p. 496)

Interdisciplinary Collaboration and Coalition Building

A hallmark of social justice is collaboration, which implies a sharing of resources and ideas, and a commonality of goals, objectives, and ideology (Goodman et al., 2004; Romano & Hage, 2000). Following this, counseling psychology may need to look at the efforts of their community psychology colleagues to fully appreciate the notion of collaboration and coalition building in the service of social justice–driven prevention. Prilleltensky (2001) has identified prevention, collaboration, and coalition building as central aspects of the field of community psychology. Folayemi (2001), in describing the development of the Pro-Youth Coalition (PYC), illustrates the nature of collaboration that is driven by a social-justice agenda. Here, a social justice goal of reducing community violence led to a broad based partnership of community workers, program directors, gang members, policy makers, academics, and practitioners. A key social justice–informed element of the PYC organizational strategy was placing the decision-making power with the grassroots community it was designed to serve, thereby allowing the "final say to rest in the hands of those who are most greatly affected" (pp. 194–195). Although the elements of coalition building offered by Folayemi may sound intuitive, they are worth repeating, as they encapsulate those critical dispositions on which the success of effective coalition building depend: trust, commitment, adaptability, patience, focus, respect, communication, and participation. While counseling psychology can contribute extensively in the areas of social justice–driven research and expertise in building relationships at individual and group levels, for counseling psychology to become a stronger voice of social justice–based prevention, in vivo exposure to grassroots activism and the building of community alliances is critical. Perhaps a point of departure could be building stronger ties with professional associations such as Division 27 of the American Psychological Association, the Society for Community Research and Action, in an effort to exchange expertise, share goals, and build on a common vision of community well-being through the elimination of structural oppression. This focus on interdisciplinary collaboration is best reflected in practice guideline #13: "Psychologists are encouraged to design, promote, and support systemic initiatives that prevent and reduce the incidence of psychological and physical distress and disability" (Hage et al., 2007, p. 496).

Training for Prevention Advocacy

We have already noted the long-standing commitment of counseling psychology to social justice–informed prevention. Indeed, social justice has assumed a more prominent place in the identity of counseling psychology (Fouad et al., 2004), and much of the recent emphasis on prevention in counseling has been within the context of social justice (Kenny & Hage, 2009). Not withstanding these positive developments, reviews of training approaches in counseling and counseling psychology have found consistent evidence of a lack of attention to, or infusion of, prevention in the training models for counseling psychology (Matthews & Skowron, 2004; McNeil & Ingram, 1983; Romano & Hage, 2000). This data is surprising given Mason and Nakkula's (2008) finding on how prevalent prevention-based articles are within counseling related journals.

Matthews and Skowron (2004) describe both a single course, and an infusion approach to centralizing prevention within the training of counselors. One theoretical approach that is missing from their description, however, is that of liberation psychology (Moane, 2003). It is important to emphasize that social justice–based prevention represents a significant philosophical and political shift within the field of psychology and counseling. Even a cursory review of accreditation requirements associated with such professional associations as the APA and the American Counseling Association (ACA) illustrates how central the medical model is within the mental health field. Here, the focus is on remediation largely occurring at the level of the individual. Furthermore, the field of psychotherapy has recently come under attack for it's lack of adherence to the "scientific model" (Baker, McFall, & Shohan, 2008). Yet, before one can critique the lack of focus on systemic forces and oppression, one must acknowledge that the accreditation requirements are firmly rooted in a larger political and economic context that appreciates health care as a commodity driven by forces of the market (Prilleltensky, 2001). Thus, a shift in training to accommodate social justice–based prevention does not merely reflect a change in emphasis, but represents a fundamental shift in ideology. This shift applies at every level of training and practice. To illustrate, Vera and Speight (2003) suggest that social justice approaches to training will include more egalitarian approaches to student-instructor relationships, yet this simple shift occurs within a larger institutional culture that is fundamentally structured on hierarchy. Furthermore, applying an ecological perspective to mental health practice occurs within a larger social culture that diminishes and questions the ongoing nature of societal oppression. Simply stated, this shift represents a challenge to the status quo and therefore includes the risk of backlash. These are the types of realities that require a coalition of social justice allies at every level of training and practice (Albee, 1998). Fortunately, there are models for social justice training that explicitly address prevention in the literature. McWhirter and McWhirter (2007a; 2007b) describe an empowerment-based approach that bears the hallmarks of a social justice–based prevention model. The five "Cs" they describe reflect aspects of prevention described in our discussion: collaboration, community, critical consciousness, competence, and context. Furthermore, the suggestions offered by Vera and Speight, while also in the context of social justice, speak directly to training efforts that hold prevention as central to the work of counseling psychology. These suggestions include increasing faculty commitment to political activism, and teaching students about injustice and the dynamics of power. The practice guideline that mostly reflects our emphasis on training is guideline #12: "Psychologists are encouraged to foster awareness, knowledge, and skills essential to prevention in psychological education and training" (Hage et al., 2007, p. 496).

Applying Social Justice–Based Prevention to Antiracism: A Case Illustration

Social justice–based prevention is a complex, ideologically driven, and active process. Therefore, in order to demonstrate some of the points highlighted in our discussion, a brief illustration of the nature of social justice–based prevention is provided, employing the following hypothetical vignette:

> In an effort to increase the racial diversity of it's student body, a 4-year college has actively reached out

to the urban Black and Latino communities within a mid-sized city. In the preceding 5 years, a steady rise in Black and Latino students has been accompanied by a similar rise in rates of attrition among this student group. Recognizing that rates of college graduation among Blacks and Latinos are significantly lower than their White and Asian counterparts, the President of the college has commissioned the Office of Diversity and Equal Opportunity to review the situation and propose an intervention.

A social justice–informed prevention strategy reflective of the prevention elements we have outlined would include the following steps:

• Examine the problem from an ecological perspective by identifying the individual, institutional, and social variables that are implicated with the attrition of Black and Latino students.

• Complete an analysis of the experience of Black and Latino students within the framework of institutional racism.

• Educate the school administration on how institutional racism impacts students of color.

• Request that other administrative offices beyond the office of diversity and equal opportunity be involved in responding to the concern, including representatives from student life, the registrar, human resources, and academic affairs. Here the goal is for the institution to take responsibility and ownership for attending to the needs of students of color, as opposed to assigning prime responsibility to the office of diversity.

• Educate Black and Latino students on the dynamics of oppression and work with students to identify points of resistance and activism. This may include demanding that the administration focus on improving racial climate, and drawing attention to the lack of racial diversity among faculty.

• Draw public attention to any form of racial harassment and discrimination that Black and Latino students may be experiencing.

• Facilitate the development of student coalitions in order to respond to race-based discrimination and prejudice.

• Identify individuals, groups, and organizations that may play an important role in preparing Black and Latino students for their college experience. In forming a broad-based coalition to this end, sources of support may include family networks, faith-based groups, community centers, sports and athletic organizations, and local community resources.

• Implement research activities that engage the Black and Latino communities in identifying potential barriers to college completion, as well as potential strategies for success.

• Engage Black and Latino students as part of the research effort by including them as paid research assistants.

• Implement a longitudinal study to examine the impact of these prevention strategies. Follow up with Black and Latino students who have graduated to gain their perspective.

• Provide training sessions for faculty on their role in improving racial climate.

• Provide training for resident life staff in prejudice reduction and antiracism advocacy.

• Build a coalition of individuals from the institution who have embraced a needs-based approach as opposed to a merit-based approach to the allocation of resources.

Concluding Thoughts and Summary

A core element of social justice praxis is self-reflection (Fine, 2006). Given the role of consciousness raising in social justice–based prevention, a collective self-reflection in counseling psychology is needed if prevention is to become more centralized. The following questions, therefore, are offered in order to facilitate that process.

1. To what extent is counseling psychology willing to close the gap between rhetoric and reality? Are we willing to commit our energies to the political activism required within our professional organization, in order to secure leadership and resources that would allow us to centralize social justice–based prevention?
2. Are we willing to challenge current curricula requirements for accreditation and confront the oppressive nature of these requirements in relation to limiting the types of courses we can offer?
3. Are we willing to be less guarded about our identity as counseling psychologists and build alliances with other organizations (e.g., community psychology, social work, and public health) that would facilitate a prevention-focused ideology? In other words, are we willing to sacrifice some power so we may help the powerless?

While these questions are philosophical in nature, it is important to remind the reader that a shift toward social justice–based prevention is, at its heart, an ideological shift; a privileging of community versus the individual, and a call to move beyond notions of meritocracy toward notions of sustainability (Bess et al., 2009).

The rights of individuals to enjoy liberty, to pursue happiness, and to be afforded health, education, and safety have been enshrined in documents such as the United States Declaration of Independence (1776) and more recently, the United Nations Declaration of Human Rights (1942). These documents capture an ideology that undergirds the notion that individuals should be afforded basic rights and privileges (e.g., physical safety, food, shelter) based only on their fundamental needs as human beings. Social justice advocacy serves as a tool to restore these basic rights to those individuals and groups who have seen these rights diminished through various forms of discrimination and systemic oppression. Social justice–based prevention attempts to reduce and eliminate adverse health outcomes associated with ongoing discrimination and oppression. This chapter has provided a review of the critical elements associated with social justice–based prevention. We recognize that the dismantling of systems of oppression will require a sustained and collaborative effort. Furthermore, we acknowledge that current social arrangements in which certain groups enjoy unearned advantages while others experience oppression and marginalization is an arrangement that is firmly entrenched. However, we join with Watts et al. (2003) in the belief that mental health professionals are obligated to work toward the liberation of those oppressed individuals and groups we serve, and in meeting this obligation, social justice–based prevention represents one important tool in the ongoing effort to secure well-being for all.

References

Aguinaldo, J. P. (2008). The social construction of gay oppression as a determinant of gay men's health: "Homophobia is killing us," *Critical Public Health, 18,* 87–96. doi: 10.1080/09581590801958255

Albee, G. W. (1969). Who shall be served? *Professional Psychology, 1,* 4–7. doi: 10.1037/h0028786

Albee, G. W. (1983). Psychopathology, prevention, and the just society. *The Journal of Primary Prevention, 4,* 5–40. doi: 10.1007/BF01359083

Albee, G. W. (1986). Toward a just society: Lessons from observations on the primary prevention of psychopathology. *American Psychologist, 41,* 891–898. doi: 10.1037/0003066X.41.8.891

Albee, G. W. (1996). Revolutions and counterrevolutions in prevention. *American Psychologist, 51,* 1130–1133. doi: 10.1037//0003–066X.51.11.1130

Albee, G. W. (1998). Fifty years of clinical psychology: Selling our soul to the devil. *Applied and Preventive Psychology, 7,* 189–194. doi: 10.1016/S0962–1849(05)80021–6

Aldarondo, E. (2007). *Advancing social justice through clinical practice.* Manway, NJ: Lawrence Erlbaum.

Arredondo, P., & Rosen, D. C. (2007). Applying principles of multicultural competencies, social justice and leadership in training and supervision. In E. Aldorondo (Ed.), *Advancing social justice through clinical practice* (pp. 443–458). Mahwah, NJ: Erlbaum.

Baker, T. B., McFall, R. M., & Shoham, V. (2008). Current status and future prospects of clinical psychology toward a scientifically principled approach to mental and behavioral health care. *Psychological Science in the Public Interest, 9,* 67–103.

Bassuk, E. L., Buckner, J. C., Perloff, J. N., & Bassuk, S. S. (1998). Prevalence of mental health and substance use disorders among homeless and low income housed mothers. *American Journal of Psychiatry, 155,* 1561–1564.

Belle, D., & Doucet, J. (2003). Poverty, inequality, and discrimination as sources of depression among U.S. women. *Psychology of Women Quarterly, 27,* 101–113.

Bess, K. D., Prilleltensky, I., Perkins, D. D., & Collins, L. V. (2009). Participatory organizational change in community based health and human services: From tokenism to political engagement. *American Journal of Community Psychology, 43,* 135–148. doi: 10.1007/s10464–008–9222–8

Biko, S. (1978). *I write what I like: Selected writings.* London, UK: Bowerdean Press.

Boehnke, K., & Wong, B. (2011). Adolescent political activism and long-term happiness: A 21-year longitudinal study on the development of micro-and macro-social worries. *Personality and Social Psychology Bulletin, 37,* 435–447. doi: 10.1177/0146167210397553

Bonilla-Silva, E. (2003). *Racism without racists.* Lanham, MD: Rowman & Littlefield.

Bowes, A., & Sim, D. (2006). Advocacy for Black and minority ethnic communities: Understandings and expectations. *British Journal of Social Work, 36,* 1209–1225.

Broman, C. L., Mavaddat, R., & Hsu, S. (2000). The experience and consequences of perceived racial discrimination. *Journal of Black Psychology, 26*(2), 165–180. doi: 10.1177/0095798400026002003

Bronfenbrenner, U. (1979). *The ecology of human development.* Cambridge, MA: Harvard University Press.

Bruce, M. L., Takeuchi, D. T., & Leaf, P. J. (1991). Poverty and psychiatric status: Longitudinal evidence from the New Haven epidemiologic catchment area study. *Archives of General Psychiatry, 48,* 470–474.

Bryant-Davis, T., & Ocampo, C. (2005). Racist-incident-based trauma. *The Counseling Psychologist, 33*(4), 479–500. doi: 10.1177/0011000005276465

Buhin, L., & Vera, E. M. (2009). Preventing racism and promoting social justice: Person centered and environment-centered interventions. *Journal of Primary Prevention, 30,* 43–59. doi: 10.1007/s10935–008–0161–9

Caplan, G. (1964). *Principles of preventive psychiatry.* New York: Basic Books.

Carter, R. T. (2007). Racism and psychological and emotional injury: Recognizing and assessing race-based traumatic stress. *The Counseling Psychologist, 35,* 13–105. doi: 10.1177/0011000006292033

Carter, R. T., Forsyth, J., Mazzula, S., & Williams, B. (2005). Racial discrimination and race based traumatic stress. In R. T. Carter (Ed.), *Handbook of racial–cultural psychology and counseling: Training and practice* (Vol. 2, pp. 447–476). New York: Wiley.

Clark, R., Anderson, N., Clark, V. R., & Williams, D. R. (1999). Racism as a stressor for African Americans: A biopsychosocial model. *American Psychologist, 54,* 805–816. doi: 10.1037//0003–066X.54.10.805

Contrada, R. J., Ashmore, R. D., Gary, M. L., Coups, E., Egeth, J. D., Sewell, A., .. . Chasse, V. (2001). Measures of ethnicity-related stress: Psychometric properties, ethnic group differences, and associations of well-being. *Journal of Applied Psychology, 31,* 1775–1820. doi: 10.1111/j.1559–1816.2001.tb00205.x

Coyne, R. K. (2000). Prevention in counseling psychology: At long last, has the time now come? *The Counseling Psychologist, 28,* 838–844. doi: 10.1177/0011000000286005

Davies, J., Lyon, E., & Monti-Catania, D. (1998). *Safety planning with battered women: Complex lives/difficult choices.* Thousand Oaks, CA: Sage.

Fanon, F. (1967). *Black skins, white masks.* New York: Grove Press.

Fine, M. (2006). Bearing witness: Methods for research oppression and resistance. A textbook for critical research. *Social Justice Research, 19,* 83–108. doi: 10.1007/s11211–006–0001–0

Folayemi, B. (2001). Case story #1: Building the grassroots coalition. *American Journal of Community Psychology, 29,* 193–197. doi: 10.1023/A:1010318427695

Fouad, N.A.,McPherson, R. H., Gerstein, L., Bluestein, D. L., Elman, N., Ihle Helleday, K., et al. (2004). Houston, 2001. *The Counseling Psychologist, 32,* 15–77.

Freire, P. (1970). *The pedagogy of the oppressed.* New York: Continuum.

Friedman, R. C. (1999). Homosexuality, psychopathology, and suicidality. *Archives of General Psychiatry, 56,* 887–888. doi: 10.1001/archpsyc.56.10.887

Frueh, B. C., Brady, K. L., & de Arellano, M. A. (1998). Racial differences in combat-related PTSD: Empirical findings and conceptual issues. *Clinical Psychology Review, 18*(3), 287–330. doi: 10.1016/S0272–7358(97)00087–1

Garofalo, R., Wolf, R. C., Kessel, S., Palfrey, J., & DuRant, R. H. (1998). The association between health risk behaviors and sexual orientation among a school-based sample of adolescents. *Pediatrics, 101,* 895–902. doi: 10.1542/peds.101.5.895

Gay, Lesbian, and Straight Education Network. (1999). *GLSEN's national school climate survey: Lesbian, gay, bisexual and transgender students and their experiences in school.* New York: Author.

Gilman, S. E., Cochran, S. D., Mays, V. M., Hughes, M., Ostrow, D., & Kessler, R. C. (2001). Risks of psychiatric disorders among individuals reporting same-sex sexual partners in the National Comorbidity Survey. *American Journal of Public Health, 91,* 933–939. doi: 10.2105/AJPH.91.6.933

Goodman, L. A., Liang, B., Helms, J. E., Latta, R. E., Sparks, E., & Weintraub, S. R. (2004).Training counseling psychologists as social justice agents: Feminist and multicultural principles in action. *The Counseling Psychologist, 32,* 793–837.

Goodman, L. A., & Epstein, D. (2008). *Listening to battered women: A survivor-centered approach to advocacy, mental health, and justice.* Washington, DC: American Psychological Association.

Goodman, L. A., Glenn, C., Bohlig, A., Banyard, V., & Borges, A. (2009). Feminist relational advocacy: Process and outcomes from the perspective of low-income women with depression. *The Counseling Psychologist, 37,* 848–876. doi: 10.1177/0011000008326325

Gosin, M. N., Dustman, P. A., Drapeau, A. E., & Harthun, M. L. (2003). Participatory action research: Creating and effective prevention curriculum for adolescents in the Southwestern US. *Health Education research, 18,* 363–379. doi: 10.1093/her/cyfo26

Graham, M. (2005). Empowerment revisited – Social work, resistance, and agency in Black communities. *European Journal of Social Work, 7,* 43–46. doi: 10.1080/136919145042000217393

Griner, D., & Smith, T. B. (2006). Culturally adapted mental health interventions: A meta-analytic review. *Psychotherapy: Theory, Research, Practice, Training, 43,* 531–548. doi: 10.1037/0033–3204.43.4.531

Hage, S. M., Romano, J. L., Coyne, R. K., Kenny, M., Matthews, C., Schwartz, J. P., & Waldo, M. (2007). Best practice guidelines on prevention practice, research, training, and social advocacy for psychologists. *The Counseling Psychologist, 35,* 493–566. doi: 10.1177/0011000006291411

Hatzenbuehler, M. L., Keyes, K. M., & Hasin, D. S. (2009). State-level policies and psychiatric morbidity in lesbian, gay, and bisexual populations. *American Journal of Public Health, 99*(12), 2275–2281. doi: 10.2105/AJPH.2008.153510

Ivey, A. E. (1976). An invited response: the counselor as teacher. *Personnel and Guidance Journal, 54,* 431–434. doi: 10.1002/j.2164–4918.1976.tb04283.x

Ivey, A. E. (1995). Psychotherapy as liberation: towards specific skills and strategies in multicultural counseling and psychotherapy. In J. G. Ponterotto; J. M. Casas; L. A. Suzuki., & C. M. Alexander (Eds). *Handbook of multicultural counseling* (pp. 53–72). Thousand Oaks, CA: Sage Publications.

Jane-Llopis, E., Hosman, C., Jenkins, R., & Anderson, P. (2003). Predictors of efficacyin depression prevention programs: meta-analysis. *British Journal of Psychiatry, 183,* 384–397. doi: 10.1192/bjp.183.5.384

Kaplan, R. (2000). Two pathways to prevention. *American Psychologist, 55,* 382–396.

Kenny, M. E., & Hage, S. M. (2009). The next frontier: Prevention as an instrument of social justice. *Journal of Primary Prevention, 30,* 1–10. doi: 10.1007/s10935–008–0163–7

Kessler, M., & Albee, G. W. (1975). Primary prevention. *Annual Review of Psychology, 26,* 557–591. doi: 10.1146/annurev.ps.26.020175.003013

Kiselica, M. S., & Robinson, M. (2001). Bringing advocacy counseling to life: The history, issues, and human dramas of social justice work in counseling. *Journal of Counseling and Development, 79,* 387–397.

Kitzinger, C. (1997). Lesbian and gay psychology: A critical analysis. In D. Fox & I. Prilleltensky (Eds.), *Critical psychology: An introduction* (pp. 202–216). Thousand Oaks, CA: Sage.

Klonoff, E. A., Landrine, H., & Ullman, J. B. (1999). Racial discrimination and psychiatric symptoms among Blacks. *Cultural Diversity and Ethnic Minority Psychology, 5,* 329–339. doi: 10.1037/1099–9809.5.4.329

Lerner, B. (1972). *Therapy in the ghetto: Political impotence and personal disintegration.* Baltimore, MD: Johns Hopkins University Press.

Lewis, J. A., Arnold, M. S., House, R., & Toporek, R. L. (2002). *Advocacy competencies: Task Force on Advocacy Competencies.* Alexandria, VA: American Counseling Association. [Electronic version] available at http://www.counseling.org/Resources/Competencies/Advocacy_Competencies.pdf

Lewis, J. A., & Lewis, M. D. (1983). *Community counseling: A human services approach.* New York: Wiley.

Lewis, J. A., Lewis, M. D., Daniels, J. A., & D'Andrea, M. J. (1998). *Community counseling: Empowerment strategies for a diverse society* (2nd ed.). Pacific Grove, CA: Brooks/Cole.

Lopez, R. E., & Cheek, D. (1977). The prevention of institutional racism: Training counseling psychologies as agents for change. *The Counseling Psychologist, 7*(2), 64–69. doi: 110.1177/001100007700700228

Lott, B., & Bullock, H. E. (2007). *Psychology and economic injustice.* Washington, DC: American Psychological Association.

Mann, J. J., Apter, A., Bertolote, J., Beautrais, A., Currier, D., Haas, A.,... Hendin, H. (2005). Suicide prevention strategies. *Journal of the American Medical Association, 294,* 2064–2074. doi: 10.1001/jama.294.16.2064

Mason, M. J., & Nakkula, M. J. (2008). A risk and prevention counselor training program model: Theory and practice. *Journal of Primary Prevention, 29,* 361–374. doi: 10.1007/s10935-008-0148-6

Matthews, C. R., & Skowron, E. A. (2004). Incorporating prevention into mental health counselor training. *Journal of Mental Health Counseling, 26,* 349–359.

Mays, V. M., & Cochran, S. D. (2001). Mental health correlates of perceived discrimination among lesbian, gay, and bisexual adults in the United States. *American Journal of Public Health, 91,* 1869–1876. doi: 10.2105/AJPH.91.11.1869

McBride, B. A. (2002). Aspects of community healing: Experiences of the Sault Sainte Marie tribe of Chippewa Indians. *American Indian and Alaska Native Mental Health Research, 11,* 67–83.

McNeill, B. W., & Ingram, J. C. (1983). Prevention and counseling psychology: A survey of training practices. *The Counseling Psychologist, 11,* 95–96. doi: 10.1177/0011000083114014

McWhirter, B. T., & McWhirter, E. A. (2007a). Toward an emancipatory communitarian approach to the practice of psychology training. In E. Aldorondo (Ed.). *Advancing social justice through clinical practice* (pp. 391–416). Mahwah, NJ: Erlbaum.

McWhirter, B. T., & McWhirter, E. A. (2007b). Grounding clinical training and supervision in an empowerment model. In E. Aldorondo (Ed.). *Advancing social justice through clinical practice* (pp. 417–442). Mahwah, NJ: Erlbaum.

Meyer, I. H. (2003). Prejudice, social stress, and mental health in lesbian, gay, and bisexual populations: Conceptual issues and research evidence. *Psychological Bulletin, 129*(5), 674–697. doi: 10.1037/0033-2909.129.5.674

Miller, J. (2008). Violence against urban African American girls: Challenges for feminist advocacy. *Journal of Contemporary Criminal Justice, 24*(2), 148–162. doi: 10.1177/1043986208315477

Moane, G. (2003). Bridging the personal and the political: Practices for a liberation psychology. *American Journal of Community Psychology, 31,* 91–101. doi: 10.1023/A:1023026704576

Moane, G. (2008). Applying psychology in contexts of oppression and marginalization: liberation psychology, wellness, and social justice. *The Irish Journal of Psychology, 29,* 89–101.

Murphy, L. B., & Frank, C. (1979). Prevention: The clinical psychologist. *Annual Review of Psychology, 30,* 173–207. doi: 10.1146/annurev.ps.30.020179.001133

National Gay and Lesbian Task Force. (2010). *Relationship recognition for same-sex couples in the U.S.* Retrieved October 20, 2010, from: http://www.thetaskforce.org/

Newcomb, M. E., & Mustanski, B. (2010). Internalized homophobia and internalizing mental health problems: A meta-analytic review. *Clinical Psychology Review, 30,* 1019–1029. doi: 10.1016/j.cpr.2010.07.003

Paradies, Y. C. (2006). Defining, conceptualizing and characterizing racism in health research. *Critical Public Health, 16*(2), 143–157. doi: 10.1080/09581590600828881

Pascoe, E. A., & Richman, L. S. (2009). Perceived discrimination and health: A meta-analytic review. *Psychological Bulletin, 135,* 531–554. doi: 10.1037/a0016059

Pieterse, A. L., & Carter, R. T. (2010). An exploratory investigation of the relationship between racism, racial identity, perceptions of health, and health locus of control among American women of African descent. *Journal of Health Care for the Poor and Underserved, 21,* 334–348.

Pieterse, A. L., Howitt, D., & Naidoo, A. V. (2011). Racial oppression, colonization and self-efficacy: Towards an empowerment model for individuals of African heritage. In E. Mpofu (Ed.), *Counseling people of African ancestry* (pp. 93–108), London: Cambridge University Press.

Prilleltensky, I. (2001). Value-based praxis in community psychology: moving toward social justice and social action. *American Journal of Community Psychology, 29,* 747–778. doi: 10.1023/A:1010417201918

Prilleltensky, I. (2003). Understanding, resisting, and overcoming oppression: Toward psychopolitical validity. *American Journal of Community Psychology, 31,* 195–201. doi: 0091-0562/03/0300-0195/0

Prilleltensky, I. (2008). The role of power in wellness, oppression, and liberation. *Journal of Community Psychology, 36,* 116–136. doi: 10.1002/jcop.20225

Prilleltensky, I., Dokecki, P., Frieden, G., & Wang, V. O. (2007). Counseling for wellness and justice: Foundations and ethical dilemmas. In E. Aldarondo (Ed.), *Advancing social justice through clinical practice* (pp. 19–42). Mahwah, NJ: Erlbaum.

Prilleltensky, I., & Gonick, L. (1994). Politics change, oppression remains: On the psychology and politics of oppression. *Journal of Political Psychology, 17,* 127–148.

Pyrch, T. (2007). Participatory action research and the culture of fear: Resistance, community, hope and courage. *Action Research, 5,* 199–215. doi: 10.1177/1476750307077324

Ratts, M. J., Lewis, J. A., & Toporek, R. L. (2010). Advocacy and social justice: A helping paradigm for the 21st century. In M. J. Ratts, R. L. Toporek, & J. A. Lewis (Eds.), *ACA advocacy competencies: A social justice framework for counselors* (pp. 3–10). Alexandria, VA: American Counseling Association.

Reese, L. E., & Vera, E. M. (2007). Culturally relevant prevention: The scientific and practical considerations of community-based programs. *The Counseling Psychologist, 35,* 763–778. doi: 10.1177/0011000007304588

Romano, J. L., & Hage, S. M. (2000). Prevention and counseling psychology: Revitalizing commitments for the 21st century. *The Counseling Psychologist, 28,* 733–763. doi: 10.1177/0011000000286001

Sellers, R. M., & Shelton, J. N. (2003). The role of racial identity in perceived racial discrimination. *Journal of Personality and Social Psychology, 84,* 1079–1092. doi: 10.1037/0022-3514.84.5.1079

Siefert, K., Bowman, P. J., Heflin, C. M., Danziger, S., & Williams, D. R. (2000). Social and environmental predictors of maternal depression in current and recent welfare recipients. *American Journal of Orthopsychiatry, 70,* 510–522. doi: 10.1037/h0087688

Smith, L. T. (1999). *Decolonizing methodologies: research and indigenous people.* Dunedin, NZ: University of Otago Press.

Smith, L., Chambers, D. A., & Bratini, L. (2009). When oppression is the pathogen: The participatory development of socially just mental health practice. *American Journal of Orthopsychiatry, 79,* 159–168. doi: 10.1037/a0015353

Smith, S. D., Reynolds, C. A., & Rovnak, A. (2009). A critical analysis of the social advocacy movement in counseling. *Journal of Counseling and Development, 87,* 483–491.

Smith, L., & Romero, L. (2010). Psychological interventions in the context of poverty: Participatory action research as practice. *American Journal of Orthopsychiatry, 80,* 12–25. doi: 10.1111/j.1939–0025.2010.01003.x

Sonn, C., & Meredith, M. (2006). Disrupting the dynamics of oppression in intercultural research and practice. *Journal of Community and Applied Psychology, 16,* 337–346. doi: 10.1002/casp.877

Tatum, B. (1994). The colonial model as a theoretical explanation of crime and delinquency. In A. T. Sulton (Ed.), *African American perspectives on crime, causation, criminal justice administration, and crime prevention* (pp. 33–52). Woburn, MA: Butterworth-Heinemann.

Tervalon, M., & Murray-Garcia, J. (1998). Cultural humility versus cultural competence: A critical distinction in defining physician training outcomes in multicultural education. *Journal of Health Care for the Poor and Underserved, 9,* 117–125.

Thomas, A., & Sillen, S. (1972). *Racism and psychiatry.* New York: Brunner/Mazel.

Tobler, N. S., Roona, M. R., Ochshorn, P., Marshall, D. G., Streke, A. V., & Stackpole, K. M. (2000). School based adolescent drug prevention programs: 1998 meta-analysis. *Journal of Primary Prevention, 20,* 275–336. doi: 10.1023/A:1021314704811

Toporek, R. L. (2000). Creating a common language and framework for understanding advocacy in counseling. In J. Lewis & L. Bradley (Eds.), *Advocacy in counseling: Counselors, clients, and community* (pp. 5–14). Greensboro, NC: Caps Publications.

Toporek, R. L., & Liu, W. M. (2001). Advocacy in counseling psychology: Critical issues of race, class, and gender. In D. B. Pope-Davis & H. L. K. Coleman (Eds.), *The intersection of race, class and gender in counseling psychology* (pp. 385–413). Thousand Oaks, CA: Sage.

Trusty, J., & Brown D. (2005). Advocacy competencies for professional school counselors. *Professional School Counselor, 8,* 259–265.

Utsey, S. O., & Payne, Y. A. (2000). Differential psychological and emotional impacts of race related stress. *Journal of African American Men, 5,* 56–72.

Vera, E. M. (2007). Culture, prevention, and the politics of disparities. *The Counseling Psychologist, 35,* 860–867. doi: 10.1177/0011000007306532

Vera, E. M., Buhin, L., & Isacco, A. (2009). The role of prevention in psychology's social justice agenda. In M. E. Kenny., A. M. Horne., P. Orpinas., & L. E. Reese (Eds.), *Realizing social justice: The challenge of preventive interventions* (pp. 79–96). Washington DC: American Psychological Association.

Vera, E. M., & Speight, S. L. (2007). Advocacy, outreach, and prevention: Integrating social action roles in professional training. In E. Aldorondo (Ed.). *Advancing social justice through clinical practice* (pp. 373–390). Mahwah, NJ: Erlbaum.

Vera, E. M., & Speight, S. L. (2003). Multicultural competencies, social justice, and counseling psychology: Expanding our roles. *The Counseling Psychologist, 31,* 253–272. doi: 10.1177/0011000003031003001

Wakefield, J. (1992). The concept of mental disorder: On the boundary between biological facts and social values. *American Psychologist, 47,* 373–388. doi: 10.1037/0003–066X.47.3.373

Warnath, C. F. (1973). *New directions for college counselors.* Oxford, England: Jossey-Bass.

Watts, R. J., Abdul-Adil, J. L., & Pratt, T. (2002). Enhancing critical consciousness in young African American men: A psychoeducational approach. *Psychology and Men and Masculinity, 3,* 41–50. doi: 10.1037//1524–9220.3.1.41

Watts, R., & Serrano-Garcia, I. (2003). The quest for a liberating community psychology: An overview. *American Journal of Community Psychology,* 31, 73–78. doi: 10.1023/A:1023022603667

Watts, R. J., Williams, N. C., & Jagers, R. J. (2003). Sociopolitical development. *American Journal of Community Psychology, 31,* 185–194. doi: 10.1023/A:1023091024140

Weinrach, S. G., & Thomas, K. R. (1998). Diversity-sensitive counseling today: A postmodern clash of values. *Journal of Counseling and Development, 76(2),* 115–122.

Williams, D. R., & Mohammed, S. A. (2009). Discrimination and racial disparities in health: Evidence and needed research. *Journal of Behavioral Medicine, 32,* 20–47. doi:10.1007/s10865–008–9185–0

Williams, D. R., Neighbors, H. W., & Jackson, J. S. (2003). Racial/ethnic discrimination and health: Findings from community studies. *American Journal of Public Health, 93*(2), 200–208. doi: 0.1007/s10464–009–9231–2

CHAPTER

9

Prevention in Pursuit of Social Justice

Maureen E. Kenny *and* Mary Beth Medvide

Abstract

Although prevention is in many ways aligned with social justice goals, it often falls short of accomplishing the level of social change critical for the advancement of social justice. Progress toward social justice requires a careful blend of person-focused ameliorative activity with transformative social change. Professionals must be equipped with multicultural competencies, insight into power dynamics, and skills in outreach, advocacy, collaboration, empowerment, social action, and political literacy, among other skills. Although most prevention activity is not fully transformative, numerous examples can be identified of activities that further social justice. Further strides in the promotion of social justice through prevention will require changes in the training, credentialing, and remuneration of psychologists.

Key Words: prevention, social justice, systemic change, ameliorative, transformative

Introduction

This volume presents an array of research and practice that represents cutting-edge developments in the field of prevention and seeks to outline future directions for the field. Amid that discussion, this chapter focuses on the goals for prevention activity and addresses how prevention efforts can accomplish social change that will benefit society across multiple levels. In this regard, we consider the promotion of social justice to be a key promise of prevention, but a promise that has not yet been widely realized.

Social justice has received increasing attention in professional discourse in the fields of psychology and education. This is an ambitious goal that deserves careful monitoring, so as not to become empty rhetoric devoid of critical social action to impel substantive change. Although both social justice and prevention have gained attention in training and research literature (Toporek, Gerstein, Fouad, Roysircar, & Israel, 2006; Goodman et al., 2004), surveys of training and practice reveal that person-centered remedial approaches that are neither preventive nor social justice-oriented remain the norm. In this chapter, we seek to present models, strategies, and exemplars of practice that will serve, we hope, to stimulate social justice–oriented prevention.

Social justice can be advanced through a variety of political and social activities. We argue that for psychologists, prevention is a key activity for the promotion of social justice. We also argue that many and most prevention activities fall short in efforts to realize social justice. We begin the chapter with a definition of social justice and then consider the unique role prevention can play in promoting social justice. We discuss the kinds of prevention efforts that meet the criteria for social justice prevention. We then consider existing frameworks that can serve as guides in designing, implementing, and evaluating social justice prevention efforts, and the skills, competencies, and strategies integral to effecting prevention in the service of social justice. Finally, we consider the current status of social justice–oriented prevention and issues that need to be addressed for more fully realizing the potential of prevention for promoting social justice.

Social Justice as Goal

Although a variety of definitions of social justice exist, the definition provided by Bell (2007) is often cited in the counseling psychology literature. According to Bell, the goal of social justice entails "full and equal participation of all groups in a society that is mutually shaped to meet their needs. Social justice includes a vision of society in which the distribution of resources is equitable and all members are physically and psychologically safe and secure" (p. 1). This definition speaks to social justice both as outcome and process; both of which are critical to a full realization of social justice.

As outcome, the distribution of resources is not necessarily equal, but it is equitable and provides for physical and psychological safety. This outcome is consistent with what has been described by Prilleltensky (1997) as "distributive justice" or the "fair and equitable allocation of bargaining power, resources, and allocation in society" (p. 522). When access to societal resources is imbalanced, the possibility for making choices that contribute to social and economic success is more prevalent for some persons than for others. Societal resources include, but are not limited to, access to education, health care, shelter, a safe environment, and employment (Adams, Bell, & Griffin, 2007). With regard to process, social justice is "democratic and participatory, inclusive and affirming of human agency and human capacity for working collaboratively to create change" (Bell, 2007, p. 2). Social justice extends beyond a concern for access to resources, and seeks equity in social and political power, which is often curtailed by systemic oppressions, such as racism, classism, heterosexism, sexism, and ableism, among others. These oppressions, which pervade social institutions and individual consciousness, shape interactions among individuals and groups and sustain conditions of social injustice.

Limitations of Psychological Treatment

Although the roots of counseling psychology, and community psychology, emphasize prevention, the field of psychology has focused primarily on psychological treatment. Although psychological treatment in its efforts to reduce human suffering is often aligned with social justice goals, it falls short in adhering to a social justice agenda. The limitations of psychological treatment relate to the impact, access, and fit or congruence of traditional therapy with social and cultural values (Vera, Buhin, & Isacco, 2009).

Because treatment is not offered until after a problem occurs, it is limited in the extent to which human suffering is prevented. Psychological treatment does not reduce the incidence of new mental health problems, but seeks to eliminate the distress and dysfunction of persons who are already diagnosed with mental health difficulties (Albee, 2000). In fact, the presence of a psychiatric diagnosis is typically a prerequisite for payment of mental health services by health insurance providers.

In addition, as noted by many authors (e.g., Albee, 2000; Vera & Speight, 2007), remedial approaches tend to support the status quo or exacerbate conditions associated with social injustice. Treatment is limited in its benefits if it fails to address the underlying social conditions or injustices that contribute to psychological disorders. Furthermore, because social conditions, such as poverty, racism, and other forms of oppression, are associated with psychological and physical disorders, those who are economically and socially disadvantaged suffer most and, under current conditions, are less likely than privileged groups to have access to quality health and mental health care (Agency for Healthcare Research and Quality, 2008). At present, health and mental health disparities on the basis of race and ethnicity, gender, education, and income are prevalent in the United States (US Department of Health and Human Services, 2000). Blacks in the United States, for example, are overrepresented in low-income groups, are less likely to have health insurance, and are more likely to live in unsafe neighborhoods and exhibit more unhealthy behaviors, resulting in lower life expectancies than Whites (Weisfeld & Perlman, 2005). These disparities are unjust, avoidable, and unfair because they are a product of social, rather than genetic conditions (Giles & Liburd, 2007). The root factors contributing to health disparities can be traced back to discrimination, poverty, and other forms of oppression. These root factors in turn affect the community environment (e.g., higher rates of unemployment) and behavioral factors (e.g., diet, exercise, tobacco use), which in combination produce a higher need for medical services (Giles & Liburd, 2007). This injustice is exacerbated by the fact that there is not enough available quality and affordable health and mental health care to meet the needs of all of those suffering from physical and psychological distress.

In recent years mental health professionals have made significant strides in efforts to make psychological treatment more culturally relevant and responsive and to increase the cultural competence and outreach activities of mental health professionals (Crethar, Rivera, & Nash, 2008; Constantine, Hage, Kindaichi, & Bryant, 2007). Nevertheless, those who are in most dire need of mental health services, including the poor, persons of color, recent immigrants (especially those without legal status in the United States), and those residing in rural communities, are often least likely to access services. Research reveals, for example, that Blacks, Asians, and Latinos are half as likely as Whites to receive needed mental health treatment (Weisfeld & Perlman, 2005). Although this in part is related to economic, legal, and systemic health care factors, psychotherapy remains incongruous with the values of many racial and ethnic groups who view mental health treatment as stigmatizing or who may lack trust in mental health professionals (Sue & Sue, 1999). Help may traditionally be sought from family and local community members who share a common language and cultural values (Atkinson, Thompson, & Grant, 1993; Constantine et al., 2007). For others, linguistic barriers may limit participation in traditional psychotherapy when the availability of bilingual mental health professionals is limited (Constantine et al., 2007). As noted by Vera, Daly, Gonzales, Morgan, and Thakral (2006), the numerous barriers that impede access to quality services among underserved groups suggest that alternative helping strategies, including prevention should be considered.

Prevention as a Social Justice Activity

Although we argue that prevention is aligned with social justice goals by limiting suffering, we also acknowledge the limitations of much prevention activity as a mechanism for social justice. Although three types of prevention are noted in the literature, primary prevention offers greatest potential for alleviating suffering and promoting social justice (Kenny & Romano, 2009). Secondary prevention seeks to reduce risk factors among those who demonstrate early stages of dysfunction or whose environments present them with conditions that, based on epidemiological research, heighten risk for psychological dysfunction. Children who have grown up in families where the mother has been battered, for example, could receive an early intervention to foster social-emotional or academic competencies that might otherwise be delayed as a result of stress in the home environment. A risk of this approach is that both the mothers and the children are assumed to be deficient in some manner. Tertiary prevention is most akin to psychological treatment and works toward problem reduction among those already experiencing difficulty (e.g., assisting battered woman in locating physically and psychologically safe environments).

Primary prevention is directed toward individuals with no identified deficits or problems. These efforts are directed toward building strengths and sources of resilience in order to maintain positive development and to prevent the development of any disorders. An approach that affirms strengths is more consistent with a social justice orientation than an approach that defines others in terms of deficits. Since primary prevention is proactive and occurs prior to the onset of any difficulties, it offers the opportunity to prevent suffering and to reduce disparities in the health and mental health care systems. Primary prevention makes maximum use of limited resources, can prove cost effective in comparison with treatment, and can generate equity for the most vulnerable and marginalized members of society. Public health initiatives such as antismoking legislation, routine immunizations, water fluoridation, and motorcycle helmet laws illustrate the powerful and pervasive benefits of primary prevention (Cohen & Chehimi, 2007).

Despite the potential benefits, prevention efforts can share biases of treatment approaches if care is not taken to attend to the cultural relevance and responsiveness of the intervention and the cultural competence of the prevention practitioner. Harper (2007) noted this in his discussion of HIV prevention strategies for gay male adolescents. Specifically, he argued that prevention programs should fuse individual-level influences on sexual identity development with a careful consideration of systemic forms of homophobia and heterosexism. Practitioners who choose to simply modify existing programs based on prevention with heterosexual populations risk creating a prevention strategy that further alienates an already marginalized group. Prevention may be experienced as culturally incongruent when community members and other relevant stakeholders are not involved in all phases of the intervention. Multiculturalism has been identified elsewhere as a critical knowledge base informing a social justice vision of prevention (Kenny & Romano, 2009).

It is thus clear that all prevention activity does not foster social justice. The poverty and oppression that stem from structural inequities related to race, class, gender, sexual orientation, disability, religion, and age, mandate attention to diversity in a social justice agenda. Like other forms of psychological intervention however, prevention can serve to support the status quo if it does not challenge the underlying systemic causes of psychological distress. In order for prevention to foster social justice, sensitivity to and respect for diversity are insufficient. Structural and social changes that recognize and affirm community strengths and empower community members are needed (Kenny & Hage, 2009).

Social Justice Models of Prevention

The late George Albee (e.g., 1983, 1986, 2000; Albee & Ryan-Finn, 1993) was a community psychologist and an early and strong advocate for social justice. Albee embraced prevention as a means for reducing the social conditions that contribute to social dysfunction. Integral to Albee's understanding of prevention as a mechanism for social justice is an emphasis on the role of oppression and social inequality as causal factors in physical and mental illness (Trickett, 2007). In order to illustrate the relationship of social conditions to dysfunction, Albee (Albee & Ryan-Finn, 1993) proposed an incidence formula that also provides a guide for the design of preventive interventions. The formula conceptualizes the incidence of mental health problems as a function of organic factors, stress, and those environmental factors that foster oppression and inequity divided by the strengths of the individual or group to resist the negative effects of oppression. Although Albee did not deny the role of organic conditions within the person in the etiology of mental illness, he highlighted the environmental components of the formula that are most amenable to broad-scale change.

Following from the incidence formula, primary prevention might seek to reduce the toxic environmental conditions that are highlighted in the numerator of the equation. In this regard, prevention would seek to foster essential social change to reduce oppression, racism, and victimization. Albee (1981), for example, described how prevention might be used specifically to reduce sexism. A large body of subsequent research has affirmed Albee's identification of the role of environmental oppressors in psychological distress. See, for example, Buhin and Vera (2009), Schwartz and Lindley (2009), and Matthews and Adams (2009) for reviews of the impact of racism, sexism, and heterosexism on psychological well-being and the implications for social justice prevention. In addition to reducing oppression, social change might also be directed toward enhancing positive environmental conditions, such as access to nutritious food, clean water, and safe settings that support physical activity and healthy lifestyles. For example, Frazier, Cappella, and Atkins (2007) found that an after-school program with children in Chicago helped to foster adaptive social skills and positive peer relationships among the participants and provided practitioners with additional opportunities to identify children in need of mental health services.

Albee's contribution to the conceptualization of social justice prevention has been advanced in recent years by the writings of another community psychologist, Isaac Prilleltensky. Prilleltensky and Nelson (Chapter 10, this volume) further describe the contributions of critical psychology to prevention. We briefly describe how the work of Prilleltensky and colleagues (Nelson & Prilleltensky, 2005; Prilleltensky, 1997; Prilleltensky, Dokecki, Frieden, & Wang, 2007) complements the work of Albee in delineating a model of social justice prevention. Prilleltensky joins Albee and other critics of psychology who critique the role of individual psychotherapy in maintaining the status quo and reinforcing current systems of power and privilege. Like Albee (1986), Prilleltensky extols the benefits of prevention as more effective and humane than an exclusive focus on treatment (Prilleltensky, 1997), but urges prevention practitioners to go beyond ameliorative change (Prilleltensky & Nelson, 1997) by addressing the "causes of the cause" (p. 88) to effect transformative, systemic change (Joffe & Albee, 1988; Prilleltensky & Nelson, 1997). Ameliorative change, which characterizes most prevention work, reduces the pain of clients and helps them to feel better, but does not transform the conditions that create and sustain oppression and inequity (Prilleltensky & Nelson, 1997). Transformative change that eradicates environmental oppressions focuses on the numerator of Albee's incidence formula.

Although both Albee and Prilleltensky maintain that social change is key to effective primary prevention from a social justice perspective, they also recognize that personal strengths (as depicted in the denominator of the equation) buffer the negative impact of organic and environmental stressors and are thus also important to prevention. Albee referred specifically to coping skills and self-esteem as person-centered strengths and support groups as environmental strengths that can foster resilience against societal stress. *Keepin it R.E.A.L*, a school-based prevention program for youth in the Southwest (Gosin, Marsiglia, & Hecht, 2003), is consistent with Albee's recommendations for enhancing resilience and reinforcing personal and cultural strengths. The program was developed to build resistance to the forces that lead to substance abuse by capitalizing on the strengths and cultural practices of youth in that community. Program evaluation suggested that tailoring the curriculum to culturally relevant values helped the students to actively engage in the activities and develop a personal connection to the materials covered in the lesson plans.

Prilleltensky (Prilleltensky, Dokecki, Frieden, & Wang, 2007) describes an interactive relationship among the personal, relational, and collective stressors and resources that comprise the numerator and denominator of Albee's (Albee & Ryan-Finn, 1993) formula. Wellness at a collective or community level, for example, can be fostered when societal stressors or injustices are diminished, but for social justice to be achieved, capacity also needs to be developed at the personal and relational levels (Nelson & Prilleltensky, 2005; Prilleltensky et al., 2007). The power to affect one's future or the future of one's group is derived from both capacity and opportunity (Prilleltensky, 2008). For example, academic, social, and employability skills/capacities need to be developed on personal and relational levels in order that individuals and groups can take advantage of the opportunities afforded to them as a result of transformative systemic change that increases access to good schools and jobs (Kenny & Romano, 2009).

Prilleltensky's (e.g., Evans & Prilleltensky, 2007) writings also add to the work of Albee (1983, 1986, 2000) by attending substantively to both distributive and procedural justice. Embedded across efforts to effect change is an analysis of power dynamics in relation to desired processes and outcomes. Empowerment is a desired outcome at the personal, relational and collective levels, but is also integral to the processes through which wellness and social justice are realized (Prilleltensky, 2008). Psychologists, including those engaged in prevention work, can disempower clients and contribute to societal practices that perpetuate conformity and oppression (Prilleltensky, 2008). Prilleltensky (2008) suggests that understanding and ongoing vigilance concerning the psychological and political bases for power, wellness, liberation, and oppression are needed for social change to be effected. Programs that seek to transmit social capital and promote social cohesion can undermine social justice if they deprive marginalized groups of autonomy and the opportunity to gain social and political power. Conflict and political action are often needed for transformative social change.

In sum, we maintain that for prevention to be a tool for the realization of social justice, it should seek to eliminate forces of oppression through systemic change and also support the development of those individual and community assets that foster self-determination and the attainment of community goals. As we describe further below, community collaboration and empowerment are integral for the reduction of oppression and increase in social justice (Kenny & Romano, 2009).

Principles and Competencies for Social Justice–Based Prevention

A number of authors (e.g., Banyard & Goodman, 2009; Constantine et al., 2007; Crethar, Rivera, & Nash, 2008; Goodman et al., 2004; Hage & Kenny, 2009; Kenny & Romano, 2009; Prilleltensky, 2001; Suárez, Newman, & Reed, 2008) have sought to identify the characteristics of social justice interventions and social justice prevention more specifically. Feminist and multicultural paradigms have informed articulation of these characteristics, along with social justice models. Because these principles have been described fully elsewhere, we review them briefly here as they inform further consideration of prevention strategies and the competencies needed to engage in social justice prevention.

Since the concept of distributive justice is derived from the belief that inequity follows from social and political factors, the social and political contexts are the primary targets of social justice interventions (Kenny & Hage, 2009; Goodman et al., 2004). The psychologist or other prevention practitioner who enters this work must then be equipped with a keen awareness of the ways in which injustice, oppression, power, and sociocultural privilege operate across the personal, community, and societal levels, and engage in ongoing analysis and reflection in collaboration with all stakeholders about the dynamics of these forces in the present environment (Crethar et al., 2008). This ongoing analysis serves to identify the goals and focus of the intervention and the processes for implementation and evaluation. Since the intervention is focused on systemic factors, the preventionist must be knowledgeable about intervention strategies for effecting systemic change at the community, institutional, and societal/political levels and methods for evaluating change across these levels (Constantine et al., 2007).

Procedural justice focuses on the importance of collaborative and participatory processes that affirm human capacity and agency in attaining social justice (Bell, 2007). While procedural justice is mostly about the processes of social justice intervention, it also speaks to the desired outcomes. That is, since social injustice contributes to oppression and feelings of powerlessness, intervention should seek not only to increase equity in access to and distribution of resources, but strive also to enhance the efficacy and power of individual, family, community, and organizational groups (Goodman et al., 2004). Building capacity and strength across all of these levels is thus a goal of intervention (Banyard & Goodman, 2009). The desired outcome is that the community will gain the knowledge and tools that they need so that involvement of outside professionals is no longer needed.

With regard to process, the voices of all stakeholders should be valued and included in decision-making, following from the belief that community members know better than professionals from outside of the community what is best for them (Fondacaro & Weinberg, 2002). For the professional, a respect for diversity coupled with an ability and commitment to ongoing critical reflection on issues of race, oppression, power, and privilege in one's own life are critical (Prilleltensky, 2001). This level of awareness and ongoing reflection are needed in order to share power with all constituent groups and to make sure that privilege and oppression are not manifested in the collaboration. Collaboration across professions in addition to community groups may be needed to include maximal knowledge and voice. For this reason, professionals must be equipped with skills in building democratic, trustful partnerships with community collaborators that minimize power differences; demonstrate culturally relevant practice; and be knowledgeable concerning indigenous models of helping and healing (Constantine et al., 2007). They should also be prepared and committed to an ongoing and daily process of confronting recurring inequities and societal injustices (Crethar et al., 2008).

Strategies for Effecting Social Justice Prevention

Given that psychology has traditionally focused on ameliorative change, a challenge for the field is to transcend traditional boundaries to accomplish transformative change and progress toward social justice goals. The focus of the counseling psychology field on promoting strengths and instituting culturally relevant developmental, social, and vocational interventions, make it congruent with social justice prevention (Hage et al., 2007). Nevertheless, counseling psychologists may not be adequately prepared to engage in social justice prevention because of limited training in strategies that relate to systemic transformation and limited opportunities to practice these skills in the current mental health system. Several roles for professionals have been noted as strategic to these efforts. Cohen and Chehimi (2007), for example, describe public health strategies for putting primary prevention into practice that can be applied by psychologists and others focused on social justice. Promoting community and health care provider education, fostering coalitions and networks through collaboration and community organizing, changing organizational practices from a systems perspective, and influencing policy and legislation through advocacy at the local, state, and federal levels all focus on transformative change. Skills, such as community organizing, building diverse and effective coalitions, framing problems in such a way as to build coalitions of support across constituent groups and decision-makers, and developing effective approaches for media advocacy, are integral to these efforts (Cohen, Chavez, & Chehimi, 2007). These strategies move the preventionist outside of the office and away from traditional person-centered approaches to engagement in outreach, collaboration, advocacy, youth and community organizing, and social action.

Although outreach, advocacy, collaboration, and activism are not exclusive to prevention, these strategies can be applied to advance a social justice prevention framework, can be directed toward social change, and may thus remedy some of the "causes of the cause" (Prilleltensky, 1997). For example, in order to effect systemic change, psychologists can serve as advocates and change agents in interactions with structures and institutions that are perceived as oppressive by marginalized individuals or groups (Constantine et al., 2007). Community organizers may work behind the scenes to support community voice and efforts in planning and coordinating prevention activities (Chávez, Minkler, Wallerstein, & Spencer, 2007). Whereas advocacy usually involves the efforts of professionals working with or on behalf of a community in challenging unjust institutional barriers and policies, social action involves direct efforts to reduce oppression and adverse social conditions (Chávez et al., 2007; Kenny & Hage, 2009). Dissemination of information to the public that increases awareness of systemic factors that foster injustice is another important strategy in social justice advocacy (Toporek, Lewis, & Crether, 2009). These strategies are not discrete and often overlap in practice. We next describe some of these strategies and their application to social justice prevention.

Outreach

A variety of outreach efforts are aligned with social justice prevention. Outreach means that psychologists and other mental health providers leave the confines of their university, hospital, or agency offices to share resources and engage with the community (Vera et al., 2006). Although person-centered outreach efforts can be ameliorative in focus, outreach can also be transformative in scope. For example, whereas providing medical or psychological services through a local church is primarily ameliorative, joining with community members to identify their needs and organize to access desired resources and effect community change is transformative in intent. For example, McCormick et al. (2000) found that the CHAMP (Chicago HIV Prevention and Adolescent Mental Health Project) Family Program was made more effective through the collaboration among university researchers, community practitioners, and parents of children targeted in the prevention effort. When parents were invited to take an active role by working with researchers to develop program components, the result was a prevention program that reflected the specific strengths of the community and barriers to participation, such as access to childcare. McCormick et al. helped families to identify resources and support networks, but Baptiste et al. (2005) noted that the CHAMP intervention did not influence structural change in the community, which limited its effectiveness. At a broader international level, social justice oriented outreach may focus on nation-building activities or resolving ethnopolitical conflicts.

Social justice oriented preventionists may also seek to collaborate with governmental, civic, health, educational, and business organizations, among others, in efforts to seek transformative change on the organizational level. Collaborations and coalition building can be effective in efforts to reach goals and solve complex problems that go beyond the capacity of any single group or organization. Collaborations that include multiple disciplines along with the community can enhance the knowledge and power bases of all participants in understanding and solving complex issues. The development and maintenance of effective collaborations is typically challenging, however, and requires careful analysis and planning (Cohen & Wolfe, 2007). Prothrow-Stith (2007) highlighted this challenge in her discussion of the integration of public health strategies with traditional violence prevention approaches in community-based outreach initiatives for children and adolescents. Although these fields have different foci, underlying commonalities can be harnessed through collaboration to create an effective multidisciplinary approach to youth violence prevention.

Some collaborations entail work between several community agencies or a university and agency. The term "outreach scholarship" (Jensen, Hoagwood, & Trickett, 1999; Lerner & Overton, 2008) refers to collaborations between university researchers and community members that strive to advance knowledge of applied and contextually relevant theory and research and build mutually beneficial and sustainable programs. Community-based participatory action research (PAR) may be carried out as part of a collaboration that gives voice to the community and contributes to desired social change (Arthur & Lalande, 2009; Cohen & Wolfe, 2007). PAR involves an ongoing process of collaborative planning, action, observation, reflection, evaluation, and change among all stakeholders for a practical purpose (Stringer, 2004). Participants should be actively involved in all facets of the evaluation, with the project not reaching its conclusion until social action has been carried out (Arthur & Lalande, 2009). Lykes, Terre Blanche, and Hamber (2003) used PAR in their work with Mayan and South African women to capture the women's experiences with political and military repression. Through ongoing relationships with the researchers, the women engaged in projects that enabled them to make meaning of their experiences in relation to oppressive social structures. Consistent with a PAR approach, the authors discuss how their own perspectives and understandings changed through this collaborative meaning-making process.

Modifications in the culture and climates of schools, health delivery systems, workplace environments, law enforcement, and other government agencies that are affected as a result of outreach activities can have significant ameliorative and transformative effects that can promote further change over time. Prilleltensky and colleagues (Evans, Hanlin, & Prilleltensky, 2007) developed the acronym SPEC (strengths-based, prevention, empowerment, and community-focused) to describe transformational principles at the personal, relational, and collective level that are needed to enhance well-being and social justice. These principles should be applied both to practices within an organization and in relationships with external organizations. Prilleltensky and colleagues (e.g., Evans et al., 2007) have implemented this change process in health, human, and community service agencies through collaborative action research between these agencies and the university. They note the success of their efforts and document some of the challenges inherent in this type of work. Bess, Prilleltensky, Perkins, and Collins (2009), for example, applied the SPEC model highlighted by Evans and associates in action-oriented work with community agencies to increase social justice values and to effect community empowerment and change. Through focus groups, participant observation, and qualitative interviews, Bess et al. captured the experiences of community members and enhanced dialogue among agency staff and marginalized community members.

Social Justice Advocacy

In promoting social justice ideals, the Best Practice Guidelines on Prevention (Hage et al., 2007) encourage psychologists "to engage in governmental, legislative and political advocacy activities that enhance the health and well-being of the broader population served" (p. 550). Psychologists can exercise advocacy through involvement with persons and groups across local, national, and international organizations, including community organizations, policy arms of professional organizations (e.g., American Psychological Association), and legislative entities. Although advocacy is described in greater detail elsewhere in this volume (Pieterse, Hanus, & Gale, Chapter 8), advocacy efforts are central to social justice and warrant attention in a discussion of prevention and social justice. Citing the work of Shore (1994) and Albee (1996), Hage et al. note the historic social justice impact of legislative accomplishments, such as civil rights legislation, social security, and Medicare. Somewhat more recently, political advocacy by psychologists has facilitated passage of the Campus Care Counseling Act (2004) and the reauthorization of the Individuals with Disabilities Act (Hage et al., 2007).

At the local, state, national, and international levels, psychologists can use their professional knowledge to advocate for legal reforms that seek to expand equity and access to quality health care, housing, education, and employment; to extend and fund prevention and health promotion programs; and to reduce discrimination based on race and ethnicity, sex, social class, religion, spiritual background, and sexual orientation. Although such acts may appear more political than psychological, it is well to note Prilleltensky's (2008) analysis of the ways in which power and politics inevitably pervade research and practice in psychology. Psychology is not an objective and value-free field, but rather has shaped public policy over the years in both positive (e.g. *Brown v. Board of Education*, affirmative action; Buhin & Vera, 2009) and negative ways (e.g., using social science knowledge to fight national liberation movements around the world during the 1960s; Prilleltensky, 2008).

With regard to political and legislative advocacy, the research knowledge base of psychology has much to offer in guiding the development of public policy. Buhin and Vera (2009), for example, at the request of the Center for Urban Research and Learning at their university, developed a summary of current research on Latino school dropouts that was presented to their state legislature along with recommendations for policy changes and programs to reduce the dropout rate. Since legislators do not generally take the time to read professional journals, a scholarly, yet readable, synthesis of the literature has the potential to inform legislative debate and decision making beyond the voices of less well informed special interest groups. Although the specific impact of their prepared summary could not be determined, it was one of a number of sources of information that contributed to desired state policy changes that impact Latino education. Current national debate on health care, educational reform, immigration, gay marriage, and international human rights are only a few of the many policy issues that could be informed by high quality research briefs.

In her role as a pediatric psychologist, Maureen Black provides an example of how psychologists may offer direct client service, while also seeking to influence policy makers to effect wise decisions regarding the health and well-being of children and families, especially those living in poverty. For more than three decades, she has been collaborating with dieticians and pediatricians in studying factors associated with malnutrition and poor child development. Beyond the confines of the health clinic, she has worked to connect families with the kinds of public assistance that increase access to healthy food and nutrition education. On a broader advocacy level, she has been involved in writing policy briefs for law makers and wrote an op-ed piece for the Baltimore newspaper, providing evidence from research and practice, in educating and appealing to the public to support the Healthy, Hunger-Free Kids Act of 2010 (Dingfelder, 2010).

Although legislative and political advocacy offer most promise in effecting broad systemic change, social justice advocacy, as depicted in the American Counseling Association framework (Toporek et al., 2009), can vary in terms of the level of client involvement (acting with versus acting on behalf of the client) and level of intervention (focus on individual, school/community, or public arena) in ways that overlap with our discussion of education and outreach. Advocacy at the individual level includes work with clients to develop skills and strategies so they can recognize and challenge sociopolitical barriers to well-being and advocate for themselves. In comparison with this empowerment approach, direct advocacy on behalf of a client may be considered desirable when the professional has critical resources or status that are not available to the client. At the school/community level, advocates can collaborate with school and community initiatives, or advocate on behalf of the community or schools by assuming a leadership role in effecting organizational or systemic change. At the broader public level, the advocate can collaborate with a client or school/community in broadly disseminating information to increase public understanding of societal injustice or can engage directly in social action or political advocacy. With regard to advocacy at the school and community levels, Matthews and Adams (2009) describe their efforts to prevent the negative mental health consequences of heterosexism as board members of the local Parents and Friends of Lesbians and Gays (PFLAG) chapter and their work with local school districts to create more affirming environments for LGB youth. These efforts can positively impact community, school, and family environments and thus address social change at a proximal level.

The American Counseling Association (ACA) has established a set of Advocacy Competencies (Lewis, Arnold, House, & Toporek, 2002) that provide valuable guidance in identifying the skills and processes involved in effective advocacy. Advocacy, systemic change, and social justice are now considered core functions of the school counselor role as an outgrowth of the ACA Advocacy Competencies, the Transforming School Counseling Initiative (TSCI) that began in the 1990s, and the development of the American School Counselor (2003) National Model (Toporek et al., 2009; Ratts, DeKruyf, & Chen-Hayes, 2007; Singh, AUrbano, Haston, & McMahon, 2010). Advocacy is also being integrated into the specialty of school psychology (Rogers & O'Bryon, 2008). The roles of advocate and social change agent require the professional to move beyond the role of the "nice counselor" (Bemak & Chung, 2008) and to engage in advocacy, with and on behalf of the client, that challenges existing systems. Such efforts require political savvy, skill in consciousness raising, the ability to initiate difficult dialogues, and strategies in dealing with probable responses to and resistance to systemic change (Bemak & Chung, 2008; Lopez-Baez & Paylo, 2009; Singh et al., 2010).

Social Justice Education

Access to education and knowledge is a core social justice issue. That is, providing young people with the complex knowledge and analytic skills to ensure full participation in the economic marketplace and in the democratic process can serve to diminish social inequities and foster distributive justice (Cochran-Smith, Gleeson, & Mitchell, 2010). In fostering access to knowledge, it is also important to consider the type of knowledge that is valued and taught and whose perspectives are represented and whose interests are being served (Cochran-Smith et al., 2010). The dissemination of knowledge can be directed toward societal stability or transformative change. One critique of educational reform as a function of No Child Left Behind (NCLB) is that standardized testing has devalued the complex knowledge, questioning, and critical debate of ideas that is central to political participation and is rewarded in higher status occupations, thus undermining movement toward social justice (Cochran-Smith et al., 2010). Some psychologists note that increasing student critical knowledge of how social and political structures contribute to oppression can help low-income students of color to reject negative societal messages about one's race, ethnic group, religion, sex, or sexual orientation that serve to undermine academic engagement and motivation (Nicholas et al., 2008).

Social justice education is designed explicitly to engage persons across all sectors of society in understanding the sources and costs of oppression and in building the desire and capacity to change patterns and behaviors that foster oppression in oneself, and one's communities and institutions (Bell, 2007). In this regard, Prilleltensky and Fox (2008) advocate for the enhancement of psychopolitical literacy. They argue that although the public at large understands the role of individual (e.g., personality traits and biological) and relational (e.g., parenting, domestic abuse) factors in affecting well-being, an understanding of the role of political factors and especially power as it relates to well-being and justice is not fully understood. Individual and relational understandings of justice and well-being, without consideration of systemic factors, contribute to victim blame and maintenance of the status quo. The promotion of psychopolitical literacy among professional helpers, parents, teachers, clergy, journalists, and other media representatives with regard to the relationship of psychological and political factors with wellness and justice might increase the possibility for social change. Training programs in psychology, education, and counseling must foster critical awareness of the ways in which social policies and practices contribute to psychological distress, foster self-awareness and reflection, and develop organizational, collaborative, and leadership skills for promoting social change (Steele, 2008). Clinical supervisors must also attend to social justice issues in the supervision process to further promote skills and sustain awareness to patterns of oppression (Chang, Hays, & Milliken, 2009).

Psychopolitical literacy can be promoted through presentations of social and historical analyses and critical psychology research in the public media. Communicating research findings that demonstrate the relationship between social and political factors and wellness may represent one step in mobilizing social change efforts. Dorfman (2007) provides an analysis of media advocacy strategies, including development of the message, obtaining media access, and overcoming barriers to media access, which may be useful in getting transformative knowledge to the public and advance justice and healthy public policy. Dorfman argues that when media advocacy is successfully undertaken, groups engaging in the process develop new skills and form relationships with journalists whose reporting can help to establish credibility to a cause. These factors ultimately serve to increase awareness of the advocates' cause and strengthen their influence in the community.

In efforts to increase the knowledge base that informs social justice, the Hage et al. (2007) guidelines for best practice encourage psychologists to "consider the social justice implications of prevention research" (p. 533). Research can, for example, be designed to examine sources of oppression, to inform prevention programming, or to evaluate the impacts of prevention efforts or social policy change. Research findings that are read only by other academics are likely to have limited impact in shaping public opinion or government policy. Although publication in highly rated scholarly journals may be most strategic for advancing one's academic career trajectory, social justice is advanced when researchers prepare their findings for dissemination to multiple audiences and in multiple outlets and with care to the accurate interpretation of findings. The three-city studies (Chase-Lansdale et al., 2003; Coley, Bachman, Votruba-Drzal, Lohman, & Li-Grining, 2007) that follow families and children in Boston, Chicago, and San Antonio, to assess the impact of the 1996 Welfare Reform Act are examples of social policy related research. This research program not only yields findings to inform further policy developments, but also informs the design of interventions and programs to meet the needs of children and families who have experienced the effects of welfare reform. As recommended by Hage et al., the study authors were also attentive to the presentation of their findings in the public media. For example, in discussing the results of the 2001 16-month follow-up of early adolescents in the three-cities study (Chase-Lansdale et al., 2003), Coley, a study author, was quick to point out that preliminary findings revealing psychological benefits for 10- to 14-year-olds when their mothers gained employment were tentative, with long-term effects and the impact of any negative change in the job market from its then healthy status being unknown (Estvanik, 2003).

Empowerment and Social Action

A potential limitation of social/political advocacy is that community members can be neglected or marginalized in the process. That is, when advocacy is conducted on behalf of rather than with the client or community, community members may be deprived of opportunities to learn about how to develop and exert power. For that reason, interventions that seek to empower community members by offering skills and support that enable social action and self-advocacy are desirable. Through empowerment and the development of efficacy, critical awareness, and individual and collective skills for social and political action, persons, organizations, and communities gain control over issues they have identified as important for their well-being (Chávez et al., 2007). Helping to cultivate these skills is an example of what Goodman and colleagues (2004) refer to as "leaving clients with the tools for social change" (p. 798).

Community organizing is a long-term process intended to build strengths and the skill of community members to effect change. People define the membership of their community, their goals, and desired methods, implementation strategies, and outcomes. An analysis of power, oppression, and privilege by the community members is critical in assessing the problem and the strategies for change. Increasing community understanding of how institutional barriers and inequities impact individual and group justice and well-being is an initial step in the empowerment process (McWhirter, 1998). Advocacy and organized activism may also be infused as tools in community organizing efforts (Chávez et al., 2007).

Although most person-centered interventions are ameliorative to the extent that they seek to develop personal assets (e.g., social competence, self-esteem) or skills to cope with or express resilience in the face of oppressive conditions, person-centered interventions can also seek to empower clients and develop attitudes and knowledge for increased control over their lives and skills for social action (Crethar et al., 2008). Related to our previous discussion of social justice education and psychopolitical literacy (Prilleltensky & Fox, 2007), critical consciousness entails a heightened awareness of the economic, sociopolitical, and psychological effects of systemic oppression. Critical consciousness is integral to the model of liberation psychology, influenced by the work of Paolo Freire (1972). According to Freire (1972), liberation from oppression, can be initiated through a process of conscientization or ongoing analysis of the sources of oppression and deconstruction of the lives of the oppressed. Conscientization is integral to reducing the psychological oppression that occurs when those who have been marginalized by society internalize a sense of inferiority and self-deprecation. In work with African American youth in the United States, Watts (Watts & Flanagan, 2007; Watts, Williams, & Jagers, 2003) developed a model of sociopolitical development for conceptualizing how critical consciousness can foster empowerment and social action. To the extent that critical awareness can be coupled with a sense of agency or collective efficacy to effect group change and with opportunities to participate in the social and political process, youth may be impelled to engage in sociopolitical activism. Fostering critical awareness in the absence of social action can leave young people with despair or hopelessness about the possibilities for change (Watts et al., 2003). Recognizing the development of critical consciousness as a first step, Watts, Abdul-Adil, and Pratt (2002) developed the Young Warriors Program, a psychoeducational intervention and action research project that works with young African American men ages 11 to 21 to critically analyze the messages about gender, race, social class, and culture communicated through popular culture, such as hip-hop.

Education and outreach programs that strive to promote positive youth development are consistent with a social justice perspective on prevention to the extent that they emphasize strengths, rather than deficits, and seek to provide all youth with the skills needed to participate fully in society (Kenny & Romano, 2009). Such programs may be limited in realizing social justice aims, however, when they neglect attention to and analysis of the structural barriers that limit youth participation (Watts & Flanagan, 2007). Service learning and civic engagement programs are often ameliorative, with a focus on social integration, rather than social change. Approaches that cultivate youth voice and combine social justice education and instruction in social and political analysis with youth organizing and social action, however, have the potential to reach transformative goals (Butin, 2007; Wade, 2001). Consistent with a focus on empowerment and social justice education, the Citizen Scholars Program at the University of Massachusetts, for example, seeks to make explicit connections between service-learning and social justice through a four-semester critical service-learning pedagogy. Evaluation suggests that the program not only develops understanding of oppression, but also increases commitment to social action (Mitchell, 2007).

In Los Angeles, organizations such as Teaching to Change LA, a project of the Institute for Democratic Education and Access at the University of California Los Angles (UCLA) and Just Schools California have sought to empower youth with critical knowledge and tools to effect change by partnering with youth in community-based participatory action research (Rogers, Morrell, & Enyedy, 2007). As part of this initiative, urban youth enroll in a college-level summer seminar that strengthens academic skills, while simultaneously teaching youth about the struggle for educational justice in their communities. After studying a social problem relevant to their community, examining relevant research literature, and using social science methods to learn more about the problem, the students present their findings to the mayor and the broader public. As part of this partnership, high school students also publish a newsletter, *Learning Power News*, through which young people share their experiences, dreams, and social and political analyses. These types of social research and activism projects are a means for developing the type of critical consciousness and collective power described earlier in this chapter (Watts & Flanagan, 2007).

Fine and colleagues (Fine & Torre, 2004; Weis & Fine, 2001) have utilized participatory strategies to work with a diverse group of adolescents in public schools in the Northeast to foster critical consciousness and raise awareness about barriers to academic opportunity. Similarly, Fine (Fine et al., 2003; Sirin & Fine, 2007) has worked outside of the schools to explore the sociopolitical context underlying identity among oppressed groups. Collectively, these projects aim to critique a status quo that perpetuates social injustice by giving voice to these participants and arming them with the knowledge and tools to fight oppression.

Despite these efforts, social justice remains largely an aspirational goal, with much prevention activity with youth and across the life span, directed toward ameliorative change. As part of the Healthy People 2010, the Centers for Disease Control and Prevention, Division of Adolescent and School Health convened a national panel that identified 21 critical health objectives for adolescents and young adults. Evaluation revealed minimal progress toward meeting those objectives, especially among the poor, and concluded that broad systemic change will be needed for progress in adolescent and young adult wellness to be attained (Park, Brindis, Chang, & Irwin, 2008). Although the efforts we describe above that focus on education, empowerment, advocacy, and outreach are advancing social justice, the review of Healthy People 2010 goals reveals that much work remains to be done, including changes in political, legal, economic, and social structures (Park et al., 2008).

Conclusion

The value of social justice has gained attention in discourse among psychologists in recent years (Kenny & Hage, 2009). The goal of increasing social justice can be advanced through a variety of political and psychological activities. We have argued that prevention is an important vehicle for promoting social justice, while also recognizing that much prevention work falls short in such efforts. Traditional prevention activity focuses on the denominator of Albee's (Albee & Ryan-Finn, 1993) incidence formula. Psychoeducational interventions, for example, typically seek to enhance strengths and coping strategies so that individuals and groups can better resist the negative impacts of oppression. While enhancing personal, family, and community strengths and building social capital across society is integral to social justice, it fails to alter the social conditions and structures that create and sustain social injustice. As Prilleltensky (Prilleltensky & Nelson, 1997, p. 88) has noted, it is necessary to alter the "causes of the cause." For this to be accomplished psychologists can no longer focus exclusively on the psychological dimensions of their work, but need to attend to "psychopolitical validity" or the extent to which their work addresses the political and psychological factors related to wellness and social justice (Prilleltensky & Fox, 2008).

With recognition of the limited social change activity in contemporary prevention practice, we have sought to identify some of the skills and practices that can be applied in efforts to foster social justice. Such skills, encompassing outreach, advocacy, collaboration, social justice education, empowerment, and social action, need to become more prevalent in the training of psychologists in order to move from person-centered and remedial approaches to interventions that effect social change. We have noted examples of some of the ways in which these skills have been applied in social justice efforts. As noted by Albee (1986, 2000) and Prilleltensky (2008), however, person-focused ameliorative strategies should not be eliminated, but augmented with activities that increase political awareness, critical consciousness, social action, and systemic change. Such activities, furthermore, need to maintain the power of all stakeholders and recognize that needs, goals, and strategies will be defined differently across cultures (Prilleltensky, 2008). While these multiple goals make sense conceptually, they are often more difficult to realize in prevention research and practice.

Future Directions

Those who are committed to promoting social justice must consider ways to more effectively harness good intention and rhetoric (e.g., Kenny & Hage, 2009; Kenny Horne, Orpinas, & Reese, 2009) to increase the level of social justice action in prevention. As we have noted earlier in this chapter, professional training needs to attend more fully to the range of skills in outreach, advocacy, social justice education, empowerment, and social action, among others that equip psychologists to engage in systemic intervention. These skills, of course, must be taught in conjunction with a critique of theory, models of social justice intervention, the development of multicultural competence, and the unique ethical issues that arise in the course of social justice prevention (see Schwartz & Hage, 2009). Although a number of resources are available to guide professional training in this regard (Conyne, Newmeyer, Kenny, Romano, & Matthews, 2008; O'Neil & Britner, 2009), training programs remain challenged in their efforts to provide opportunities for students to practice these skills. State licensing boards in the United States continue to favor traditional person-centered remedial approaches in approving hours toward licensure. Indeed, this bias is shared by health insurance providers and hence employers who generally provided payment for traditional psychotherapy and not for political and social action (Hage & Kenny, 2009). At present, social justice prevention is carried out pro bono by those committed to this work or is funded through external grants or university projects. Political and social advocacy are needed to alter this reality.

Beyond these practical concerns, the ideal of social justice prevention is vast and complicated. Simultaneous ameliorative and transformative intervention at the personal, relational, and community levels may be meaningful conceptually and offer the most promise for fostering social justice, but may be very challenging to carry out in practice. Future work needs to address specifically and in depth this array of challenges and ways to sustain this work over time, especially when grant funding expires and political priorities that determine funding shift. This work will require extensive collaboration among diverse professionals, who lend different skills to this process, and to collaborations with community members and all stakeholders, who bring different needs and perspectives to the process. Building professional, personal, and financial capacities to carry this out is a critical next step in realizing the promise of social justice prevention.

References

Adams, M., Bell, L. A., & Griffin, P. (Eds.). (2007). *Teaching for diversity and social justice* (2nd ed.). New York: Routledge.

Agency for Healthcare Research and Quality. (2008). *National healthcare disparities report.* Retrieved from http://www.ahrq.gov/qual/nhdr08/nhdr08.pdf

Albee, G. W. (1981). The prevention of sexism. *Professional Psychology, 12,* 20–28. doi: 10.1037/0735-7028.12.1.20

Albee, G. W. (1983). Psychopathology, prevention, and the just society. *Journal of Primary Prevention, 4,* 5–36.

Albee, G. W. (1986). Toward a just society: Lessons from observations on the primary prevention of psychopathology. *American Psychologist, 41,* 891–898. doi: 10.1037/0003-066X.41.8.891

Albee, G. W. (1996). Revolutions and counterrevolutions in prevention. *American Psychologist, 51,* 1130–1133. doi: 10.1037/0003-066X.51.11.1130

Albee, G. W. (2000). Commentary on prevention and counseling psychology. *Counseling Psychologist, 28,* 845–853. doi: 10.1177/0011000000286006

Albee, G. W., & Ryan-Finn, K. D. (1993). An overview of primary prevention. *Journal of Counseling and Development, 72,* 115–123.

American School Counselors Association. (2003). *The ASCA national model: A framework for school counseling programs.* Alexandria, VA: Author.

Arthur, N., & Lalande, V. (2009). Diversity and social justice implications for outcome approaches to evaluation. *International Journal of Advanced Counseling, 31,* 1–16. doi: 10.1007/s10447-008-9063-z

Atkinson, D. R., Thompson, C. E. & Grant, S. K. (1993). A three-dimensional model for counseling racial-ethnic minorities. *The Counseling Psychologist, 21,* 257–277. doi: 10.1177/0011000093212010

Banyard, V. L., & Goodman, L. (2009). Collaboration for building strong communities: Two examples. In M. E. Kenny, A. M. Horne, P. Orpinas, & L. E. Reese (Eds.). *Realizing social justice: The challenge of preventive interventions* (pp. 271–287). Washington, DC: American Psychological Association.

Baptiste, D. R., Paikoff, R. L., McKay, M. M., Madison-Boyd, S., Coleman, D., & Bell, C. (2005). Collaborating with an urban community to develop an HIV and AIDS prevention program for Black youth and families. *Behavior Modification, 29,* 370–416. doi: 10.1177/0145445504272602

Bell, L. A. (2007). Theoretical foundations for social justice education. In M. Adams, L. A. Bell, & P. Griffin (Eds.). *Teaching for diversity and social justice* (2nd ed., pp. 3–16). New York: Routledge.

Bemak, F., & Chung, R. C. (2008). New professional roles and advocacy strategies for school counselors: A multicultural/social justice perspective to move beyond the nice counselor syndrome. *Journal of Counseling and Development, 86,* 372–382.

Bess, K. D., Prilleltensky, I., Perkins, D. D., & Collins, L. V. (2009). Participatory organizational change in community-based health and human services: From tokenism to political engagement. *American Journal of Community Psychology, 43,* 134–148, doi: 10.1007/s10464-008-9222-8

Buhin, L., & Vera, E. M. (2009). Preventing racism and promoting social justice: Person-centered and environment-centered interventions. *Journal of Primary Prevention, 30,* 43–59. doi:10.1007/s10935-008-0161-9

Butin, D. W. (2007). Justice-learning: Service-learning as justice-oriented education. *Equity and Excellence in Education, 40,* 177–183. doi:10.1080/10665680701246492

Chang, C. Y., Hays, D. G., & Milliken, T. F. (2009). Addressing social justice issues in supervision: A call for client and professional advocacy. *The Clinical Supervisor, 28,* 20–35 doi: 10.1080/07325220902855144

Chase-Lansdale, P. L., Moffitt, R. A., Lohman, B. J., Cherlin, A. J., Coley, R. L., Pittman, L. D., & Votruba-Drzal, E. (2003). Mothers' transitions from welfare to work and the well-being of preschoolers and adolescents. *Science, 299*(S612), 1548–1552. doi: 10.1126/science.1076921

Chávez, V., Minkler, M., Wallerstein, N., & Spencer, M. S. (2007). Community organizing for health and social justice. In L. Cohen, V. Chávez, & S. Chehimi (Eds.), *Prevention is primary: Strategies for community well-being* (pp. 95–120). San Francisco, CA: Jossey-Bass.

Cochran-Smith, M., Gleeson, A. M., & Mitchell, K. (2010). Teacher education for social justice: What's pupil learning got to do with it? *Berkeley Review of Education, 1*(1), 35–61. Retrieved from http://escholarship.org/uc/ucbgse_bre

Cohen, L., Chávez, V., & Chehimi, S. (Eds.). (2007). *Prevention is primary: Strategies for community well-being.* San Francisco, CA: Jossey-Bass.

Cohen, L., & Chehimi, S. (2007). Beyond brochures: The imperative for primary prevention. In L. Cohen, V. Chávez, & S. Chehimi (Eds.), *Prevention is primary: Strategies for community well-being* (pp. 3–24). San Francisco, CA: Jossey-Bass.

Cohen, L., & Wolfe, A. (2007). Working collaboratively to advance prevention. In L. Cohen, V. Chávez, & S. Chehimi (Eds.), *Prevention is primary: Strategies for community well-being* (pp. 141–160). San Francisco, CA: Jossey-Bass.

Coley, R. L., Bachman, H. J., Votruba-Drzal, E., Lohman, B., & Li-Grining, C. P. (2007). Maternal welfare and employment experiences and adolescent well-being: Do mothers' human capital characteristics matter? *Child and Youth Service Review, 29,* 193–215. doi: 10.1016/j.childyouth.2006.07.004

Constantine, M. G., Hage, S. M., Kindaichi, M. M., & Bryant, R. M. (2007). Social justice and multicultural issues: Implications for the practice and training of counselors and counseling psychologists. *Journal of Counseling and Development, 85,* 24–29.

Conyne, R. K., Newmeyer, M. D., Kenny, M. E., Romano, J. L., & Matthews, C. R. (2008). Two key strategies for teaching prevention: Specialized course and infusion. *The Journal of Primary Prevention, 29,* 375–401. doi: 10.1007/s10935–008–0146–8

Crethar, H. C., Rivera E. T., & Nash, S. (2008). In search of common threads: Linking multicultural, feminist, and social justice counseling paradigms. *Journal of Counseling and Development, 86,* 269–278.

Dingfelder, S. (2010). Feeding the children. *Monitor on Psychology, 41,* 48–50.

Dorfman, L. (2007). Using media advocacy to influence policy. In L. Cohen, V. Chávez, & S. Chehimi (Eds.), *Prevention is primary: Strategies for community well-being* (pp. 205–230). San Francisco, CA: Jossey-Bass.

Estvanik, N. (2003). New research: Has welfare reform hurt children? *Boston College Magazine.* Retrieved from http://bcm.bc.edu/issues/summer_2003/ll_homework.html

Evans, S. D., Hanlin, C. E., Prilleltensky, I. (2007). Blending ameliorative and transformative approaches in human service organizations: A case study. *Journal of Community Psychology, 35,* 329–346. doi: 10.1002/jcop.20151

Evans, S. D., & Prilleltensky, I. (2007). Youth and democracy: Participation for personal, relational, and collective well-being. *Journal of Community Psychology, 35,* 681. doi: 10.1002/jcop.20172

Fine, M., Freudenberg, N., Payne, Y., Perkins, T., Smith, K., & Wanzer, K. (2003). "Anything can happen with the police around": Urban youth evaluate strategies of surveillance in public places. *Journal of Social Issues, 59,* 141–158. doi: 10.1111/1540–4560.t01-1-00009

Fine, M., & Torre, M. E. (2004). Re-membering exclusions: participatory action research in public institutions. *Qualitative Research in Psychology, 1,* 15–37.

Fondacaro, M. R., & Weinberg, D. (2002). Concepts of social justice in community psychology: Towards a social ecological epistemology. *American Journal of Community Psychology, 30,* 473–492. doi: 10.1023/A:1015803817117

Frazier, S. L., Cappella, E., & Atkins, M. S. (2007). Linking mental health and after school systems for children in urban poverty: Preventing problems, promoting possibilities. *Administration and Policy in Mental Health and Mental Health Services Research, 36*(3), 389–399. doi: 10.1007/s10488–007–0124–0

Freire, P. (1972). *Pedagogy of the oppressed.* New York: Penguin Books.

Giles, W. H., & Liburd, L. C. (2007). Achieving health equity and social justice. In L. Cohen, V. Chávez, & S. Chehimi (Eds.), *Prevention is primary: Strategies for community well-being* (pp. 25–40). San Francisco, CA: Jossey-Bass.

Goodman, L., Liang, B., Helms, J., Latta, R., Sparks, E., & Weintraub, S. R. (2004). Training counseling psychologists as social justice agents: Feminist and multicultural principles in action. *The Counseling Psychologist, 32,* 793–836. doi: 10.1177/0011000004268802

Gosin, M., Marsiglia, F. F., & Hecht, M. L. (2003). Keepin' it R.E.A.L: A drug resistance curriculum tailored to the strengths and needs of pre-adolescents of the southwest. *Journal of Drug Education, 33,* 119–142. doi: 10.2190/DXB9–1V2P -C27J-V69V

Hage, S., Romano, J., Conyne, R., Kenny, M., Matthews, C., Schwartz, J., & Waldo, M. (2007). Best practice guidelines on prevention in practice, research, training, and social advocacy for psychologists. *The Counseling Psychologist, 35,* 493–566. doi: 10.1177/0011000006291411

Harper, G. W. (2007). Sex isn't that simple: Culture and context in HIV prevention interventions for gay and bisexual male adolescents. *American Psychologist, 62*(8), 803–819. doi: 10.1037/0003–066X.62.8.806

Jensen, P., Hoagwood, K., & Trickett, E. (1999). Ivory towers or earthen trenches? Community collaborations to foster "real world" research. *Applied Developmental Science, 3,* 206–212. doi: 10.1207/s1532480xads0304_4

Joffe, J. M., & Albee, G. W. (1988). Powerlessness and psychopathology. In G. W. Albee, J. M. Joffe, & L. A. Dusenbury (Eds.). *Prevention, powerlessness, and politics: Readings on social change* (pp. 53–56). Thousand Oaks, CA: Sage.

Kenny, M. E., & Hage, S. M. (2009). The next frontier: Prevention as an instrument of social justice. *The Journal of Primary Prevention, 30,* 1–10. doi: 10.1007/s10935–008–0163–7

Kenny, M. E., Horne, A. M., Orpinas, P., & Reese, L. E. (Eds.). (2009). *Realizing social justice: The challenge of preventive interventions.* Washington, DC: American Psychological Association.

Kenny, M. E., & Romano, J. (2009). Promoting positive development and social justice through prevention: A legacy for the future. In M. E. Kenny, A. M. Horne, P. Orpinas, & L. E. Reese (Eds.), *Realizing social justice: The challenge of preventive interventions* (pp. 17–35). Washington, DC: American Psychological Association.

Lerner, R. M., & Overton, W. F. (2008). Exemplifying the integrations of the relational developmental system. *Journal of Adolescent Research, 23*(3), 245–255. doi: 10.1177/0743558408314385

Lewis, J., Arnold, M. S., House, R., & Toporek, R. L. (2002). *ACA Advocacy Competencies.* Alexandria, VA: American Counseling Association. Retrieved from http://www.counseling.org/Content/NavigationMenu/RESOURCES/ADVOCACYCOMPETENCIES/advocacy_competencies1.pdfLopez-Baez, S. I., & Paylo, M. J. (2009). Social justice advocacy: Community collaboration and systems advocacy. *Journal of Counseling and Development, 87,* 276–283.

Lykes, M. B., Terre Blanche, M., & Hamber, B. (2003). Narrating survival and change in Guatemala and South Africa: The politics of representation and a liberatory community psychology. *American Journal of Community Psychology, 31*(1/2), 79–90. doi: 10.1023/A:1023074620506

Matthews, C. R., & Adams, E. M. (2009). Using a social justice approach to prevent the mental health consequences of heterosexism. *Journal of Primary Prevention, 30,* 11–26. doi: 10.1007/s10935–008–0166–4

McCormick, A. M., McKay, M. M., Wilson, M., McKinney, L., Paikoff, R., Bell, C., & Scott, R. (2000). Involving families in an urban HIV prevention intervention: How community collaboration addresses barriers to participation. *AIDS Education and Prevention, 12*(4), 299–307.

McWhirter, E. H. (1998). Emancipatory communitarian psychology. *American Psychologist, 53,* 322–323. doi: 10.1037/0003–066X.53.3.322

Mitchell, T. D. (2007). Critical service-learning as social justice education: A case study of the citizen scholars program. *Equity and Excellence in Education, 40,* 101–112. doi:10.1080/10665680701228797

Nelson, G., & Prilleltensky, I. (2005). *Community psychology: In pursuit of liberation and well-being.* New York: Palgrave Macmillan.

Nicholas, G., Helms, J. E., Jernigan, M. M., Sass, T., Skrzypek, A., & DeSilva, A. M. (2008). A conceptual framework for understanding the strengths of Black youths. *Journal of Black Psychology, 34*(3), 261–280. doi: 10.1177/0095798408316794

O'Neil, J. M., & Britner, P. A. (2009). Training primary preventionists to make a difference in people's lives. In M. E. Kenny, A. M. Horne, P. Orpinas, & L. E. Reese (Eds.), *Realizing social justice: The challenge of preventive interventions* (pp. 1141–1162). Washington, DC: American Psychological Association.

Park, J. M., Brindis, C. D., Chang, F., & Irwin, C. E. (2008). A midcourse review of the healthy people 2010: 21 critical health objectives for adolescents and young adults. *Journal of Adolescent Health, 42,* 329–334. doi:10.1016/j.jadohealth.2008.01.008

Prilleltensky, I. (1997). Values, assumptions, and practices: Assessing the moral implications of psychological discourse and action. *American Psychologist, 52,* 517–535. doi: 10.1037/0003–066X.52.5.517

Prilleltensky, I. (2001). Value-based praxis in community psychology: Moving toward social justice and social action. *American Journal of Community Psychology, 29,* 747–778. doi: 10.1023/A:1010417201918

Prilleltensky, I. (2008). The role of power in wellness, oppression, and liberation: The promise of psychopolitical validity. *Journal of Community Psychology, 36,* 116–136. doi: 10.1002/jcop.20225

Prilleltensky, I., Dokecki, P., Frieden, G., & Wang, V. O. (2007). Counseling for wellness and justice: Foundations and ethical dilemmas. In E. Aldarondo (Ed.), *Advancing social justice through clinical practice* (pp. 19–42). Mahwah, NJ: Erlbaum.

Prilleltensky, I., & Fox, D. R. (2007). Psychopolitical literacy for wellness and justice, *Journal of Community Psychology, 35,* 793–805. doi: 10.1002/jcop.20179

Prilleltensky, I., & Nelson, G. (1997). Community psychology: Reclaiming social justice. In D. Fox & I. Prilleltensky (Eds.), *Critical psychology: An introduction* (pp. 166–184). Thousand Oaks, CA: Sage.

Prilleltensky, I., & Prilleltensky, O. (2007). Webs of well-being: The interdependence of personal, relational, organisational and communal well-being. In J. Haworth and G. Hart (Eds.), *Well-being: Individual, community and social perspectives* (pp. 57–74). New York: Palgrave Macmillan.

Prothrow-Stith, D. (2007). Strengthening the collaboration between public health and criminal justice to prevent violence. In L. Cohen, V. Chávez, & S. Chehimi (Eds.), *Prevention is primary: Strategies for community well-being* (pp. 313–328). San Francisco, CA: Jossey-Bass.

Ratts, M., DeKruyf, L. & Chen-Hayes, S. (2007). The ACA Advocacy Competencies: A social justice advocacy framework for professional school counselors. *Professional School Counseling, 11,* 90–97.

Rogers, M. R., Morrell, E., & Enyedy, N. (2007). Studying the struggle: Contexts for learning and identity development for urban youth. *American Behavioral Scientist, 51,* 419–443. doi: 10.1177/0002764207306069

Rogers, M. R., & O'Bryon, E. C. (2008). Advocating for social justice: The context for change in school psychology. *School Psychology Review, 37,* 493–498.

Schwartz, J. P., & Hage, S. M. (2009). Prevention: Ethics, responsibility, and commitment to public well-being. In M. E. Kenny, A. M. Horne, P. Orpinas, & L. E. Reese (Eds.), *Realizing social justice: The challenge of preventive interventions* (pp. 123–140). Washington, DC: American Psychological Association.

Schwartz, J. P., & Lindley, L. D. (2009). Impacting sexism through social justice prevention: Implications at the person and environmental levels. *Journal of Primary Prevention, 30,* 27–41. doi: 10.007/s10935–008–0162–8

Shore, M. (1994, September). Narrowing prevention. *Readings: A Journal of Reviews and Commentary in Mental Health,* 13–17.

Singh, A., Urbano, A., Haston, M., & McMahon, E. (2010). School counselors' strategies for social justice change: A grounded theory of what works in the real world. *Professional School Counseling, 13,* 135–145.

Sirin, S. R., & Fine, M. (2007). Hyphenated selves: Muslim American youth negotiating their identities across the fault lines of global conflict. *Applied Developmental Science, 11*(3), 151–163.

Steele, J. M. (2008). Preparing counselors to advocate for social justice: A liberation model. *Counselor Education and Supervision, 48,* 74–84.

Stringer, E. (2004). *Action research in education.* Upper Saddle River, NJ: Pearson.

Suárez, Z. E., Newman, P. A., & Reed, B. G. (2008). Critical consciousness and cross-cultural/intersectional social work practice: A case analysis. *Families in Society, 89,* 407–417.

Sue, D. W., & Sue, D. (1999). *Counseling the culturally different: Theory and practice* (3rd ed.). Hoboken, NJ: Wiley.

Toporek, R. L., Gerstein, L., Fouad, N., Roysircar, G. S., & Israel, T. (Eds.). (2006). *Handbook for social justice in counseling psychology: Leadership, vision, and action.* Thousand Oaks, CA: Sage.

Toporek, R. L., Lewis, J. A., & Crethar, H. C. (2009). Promoting systemic change through the ACA Advocacy Competencies. *Journal of Counseling and Development, 87,* 260–268.

Trickett, E. J. (2007). George Albee and the nurturing spirit of primary prevention. *Journal of Primary Prevention, 28,* 61–64. doi: 10.1007/s10935–006–0072–6

US Department of Health and Human Services (2000). *Healthy People 2000.* Retrieved from http://www.cdc.gov/nchs/data/hp2000/hp2k01.pdf

Vera, E. M., Buhin, L., & Isacco, A. (2009). The role of prevention in psychology's social justice agenda. In M. E. Kenny, A. M. Horne, P. Orpinas, & L. E. Reese (Eds.), *Realizing social justice: The challenge of preventive interventions* (pp. 79–96). Washington, DC: American Psychological Association.

Vera, E. M., Daly, B., Gonzales, R., Morgan, M., & Thakral, C. (2006). Prevention and outreach with underserved populations. In R. L. Toporek, L. Gerstein, N. Fouad, G. Roysircar, & T. Israel (Eds.), *Handbook for social justice in counseling psychology: Leadership, vision, and action* (pp. 86–99). Thousand Oaks, CA: Sage.

Vera, E. M., & Speight, S. L. (2007). Advocacy, outreach, and prevention: Integrating social action roles in professional training. In E. Aldarondo (Ed.), *Advancing social justice through clinical practice* (pp. 373–389). Mahwah, NJ: Erlbaum

Wade, R. (2001). *"And justice for all" Community service-learning for social justice.* Denver: Education Commission of the States.

Watts, R. J., Abdul-Adil, J., & Pratt, T. (2002). Enhancing critical consciousness in young African American men: A psychoeducational approach. *Psychology of Men and Masculinity, 3,* 41–50.

Watts, R. J., & Flanagan, C. (2007). Pushing the envelope on youth civic engagement: A developmental and liberation psychology perspective. *Journal of Community Psychology, 35*(6), 779–792.

Watts, R. J., Williams, N. C., & Jagers, R. J. (2003). Sociopolitical development. *American Journal of Community Psychology, 31,*(1/2), 185–194. doi: 10.1023/A:1023091024140

Weis, L. & Fine, M. (2001). Extraordinary conversations in public schools. *Qualitative Studies in Education, 14*(4), 497–523. doi: 10.1080/09518390110046355

Weisfeld, A., & Perlman, R. L. (2005). Disparities and discrimination in health care: An introduction. *Perspectives in Biology and Medicine, 48*(1), S1–S9. doi:10.1353/pbm.2005.0046

CHAPTER

10 Critical Psychology, Prevention, and Social Justice

Isaac Prilleltensky *and* Geoffrey Nelson

Abstract

Critical psychology and prevention have a goal in common: the promotion of individual and community well-being. Their ways of achieving it, however, vary. In this chapter we explore similarities and differences between these two disciplines in terms of values, ontology, epistemology, and practices. Whereas prevention has assumed a value-neutral, positivist and largely individualistic approach, critical psychology has endorsed an explicitly value-laden and social action orientation. The value of social justice, very prevalent in critical psychology, assumes a marginal position in prevention. With the notable exception of George Albee and his disciples, prevention professionals have embraced the promotion of health and the reduction of personal risk factors as their main goals. Whereas critical psychologists have done a great deal to show the role of injustice in mental health and psychosocial problems, they have not done as well as preventionists in systematically implementing and evaluating psychosocial interventions. We argue for a synergy between critical psychology and prevention to promote both sustainable well-being and social justice.

Key Words: prevention, critical psychology, social justice, well-being, values, status quo, action research

Introduction

In 1991, three giants of psychology, prevention, and social justice went to a very cold place to talk about child and family well-being. Although it was very chilly outside, they generated a lot of heat inside with provocative notions about the failure of psychology to deal with poverty, its dismal track record preventing childhood problems, and its inability to foster social justice. The audience, Canadian school psychologists, psychiatrists, teachers, and social workers, listened intently. The venue was the Winnipeg Convention Center. The occasion was the first ever prevention conference at the Child Guidance Clinic. The speakers, no longer with us, were George Albee, Emory Cowen, and Seymour Sarason. Isaac, who had long admired these pillars of community psychology, managed to convince them to come to Winnipeg on the promise that they would see not just snow, but each other. They were all good friends and liked the idea of getting together. I, Isaac, liked the idea of spending time with them and exposing my colleagues to their scholarship. I called each one of them and promised them that the other two were coming (it was more of a promissory note than a real promise, really, as I had not yet secured anybody's commitment). That way I piqued their interest in coming to the Child Guidance Clinic of Winnipeg, where both of us, Geoff and Isaac, had worked prior to joining Wilfrid Laurier University in Waterloo, Ontario.

Needless to say, it was a memorable event for me, Isaac, who watched adoringly how my heroes wove connections among psychology, prevention, and social justice. Over the years, I managed to stay connected with George and Seymour more than with Emory, but I always read admiringly his exquisite and elegant writing. Emory Cowen was the first of the three to pass away. He died in 2000. George Albee died in 2006, and Seymour Sarason died in 2010. George Albee was the external examiner of my doctoral dissertation, a request that started a much appreciated friendship. I kept in touch with Seymour Sarason once in a while. Seymour was kind enough to review my first book, *The Morals and Politics of Psychology: Psychological Discourse and the Status Quo*, for *Contemporary Psychology*. While he generally praised the book, he thought I was too optimistic about the future of psychology. He knew best.

With tears in my eyes, I recently addressed tributes for Seymour at the annual convention of the American Educational Research Association in Denver and at the International Conference of Community Psychology in Puebla, Mexico. I recalled the lovely two days that Seymour and I spent together in New Haven when I visited him in 2007. Seymour took a personal interest in my new job as dean of education and called often to find out how I was doing.

The linkages among psychology, prevention, and social justice have roots that extend far beyond the scholarly work of these three men, but for us, it seems fitting to acknowledge their contributions to preventing psychosocial problems by looking at issues of context, power, justice, and privilege. In *Realizing Social Justice: The Challenge of Preventive Interventions*, the authors acknowledge the enduring legacy of George Albee as a champion of prevention and social justice in psychology, but they realize the unfulfilled promises as well.

> The late George Albee was an advocate for social justice and prevention for more than 50 years .... Despite the longevity of Albee's ideas, prevention has not fulfilled its social justice promise. Social injustice remains rampant in health status, educational and occupational attainment, and income levels. These disparities are often most poignant when comparisons across racial/ethnic groups, gender, and ability status are examined. (Kenny, Horne, Orpinas, & Reese, 2009, pp. 3–4)

We concur. Social justice has not yet made significant inroads into prevention. While most prevention advocates acknowledge the role of social determinants in health and well-being, the practice has not caught up with the passion. We believe that prevention and psychology have not fully embraced social justice because mainstream psychological discourse and action support the societal status quo. From traditional victim-blaming discourses (Prilleltensky, 1994) to positive psychology's present apologia for the system (Ehrenreich, 2009), the preeminent behavioral science still engages in context minimization (Shinn & Toohey, 2003): the neglect of context in accounting for behavioral and psychosocial challenges.

Critical psychology grew, in part, as a reaction to the individualistic reductionism of the mother discipline (Teo, 2009). The tendency to place blame for suffering squarely in the shoulder of victims had profound implications for social justice: no need to bother reforming the system, therapy will do (Adler & Stewart, 2009). To challenge these hegemonic notions, critical psychology grew from an intellectual enterprise to a social movement with discursive and practical applications (Chamberlain & Murray, 2009; Durrheim, Hook, & Riggs, 2009; Fox, Prilleltensky, & Austin, 2009; Hepburn, 2003; Prilleltensky & Nelson, 2002).

In light of the role of social justice in both prevention and critical psychology, this paper addresses a three-legged stool consisting of two disciplines (prevention and critical psychology) and one value (social justice). Specifically, the goals of this chapter are to (1) review the status of social justice in critical psychology and prevention, (2) distill divergence and convergence between critical psychology and prevention, and (3) offer recommendations for making critical psychology and prevention more synergistic and attuned to social justice at the same time.

What Is Critical Psychology?

Multiple Roots, Similar AimsIt would be more accurate to talk about critical psychologies than a critical psychology, as there are multiple strands of this scholarly movement. And while roots vary, many critical psychologists share similar aims. We will recognize their commonalities in their original struggles. Today, many critical psychologists acknowledge the contributions of Ignacio Martín Baró (1994) to the emergence of liberation psychology (Watkins & Shulman, 2008; Quiñones Rosado, 2007). Baró was a Spanish Jesuit Priest, killed for his convictions in 1989 in El Salvador, where he had been developing a psychology of liberation. He claimed psychologists should work to develop a psychology of emancipation to assist the poor and the oppressed in overcoming conditions of domination. A second Latin American credited with fostering consciousness-raising and emancipatory pedagogy is Paulo Freire (1970, 1973, 1994), who coined the term "pedagogy of the oppressed," a notion widely used in critical circles in education and psychology (Stevens, 2007). Contemporary proponents of critical and liberation psychology in Latin America include Maritza Montero (2007, 2010) in Venezuela and Ignacio Dobles Oropeza in Costa Rica (Dobles Oropeza, 2009; Oropeza, Arróliga, & Zúñiga, 2007).

In Africa, Frantz Fanon, a psychiatrist originally from Martinique, who later lived in Algeria, developed a psychology of oppression and colonization that became highly influential in postcolonial theory (Bulhan, 1985; Fanon, 1965; Hook, 2004; Parker, 2007). More recent work describing critical psychology in Africa is presented in Hook's book (2004). In Europe, the Frankfurt School of critical theory was very influential in fostering in social science a critique of the status quo (Teo, 2005). In Germany, Klaus Holzkamp advanced a psychology of emancipation and subjectivity that assumed the official label of critical psychology in that country (Teo, 1998; Tolman, 1994). In England, Ian Parker (2007) and Erica Burman (1997) established the discourse unit at Manchester Metropolitan University, which is still active, and in Australia, Valerie Walkerdine (2002) created a critical psychology unit in the University of Western Sydney, which operated in the early part of this century. In Ireland, Geraldine Moane (2011) works at the intersection of feminist, critical, postcolonial, and liberation psychology.

In 1993, Fox and Prilleltensky founded the radical psychology network and later cooperated in editing *Critical Psychology: An Introduction* (Fox & Prilleltensky, 1997). That book helped to disseminate internationally emerging concepts and theories in the field. A decade later, Fox et al. (2009) edited a much revised second version of that book with many new authors (readers are referred to that book and to Teo, 2005, for further historical accounts of critical psychology. For developments in liberation psychology, we recommend Watkins & Shulman, 2008).

What do these authors, in this very brief and incomplete sketch of critical psychology, have in common? Following Teo (2009) and Nelson and Prilleltensky (2010), we might delineate their commonalities in terms of ontology, epistemology, and praxis. Ontology entails the subject matter of a particular discipline. In the case of critical psychology, the person in historical and political context is the appropriate subject matter. Critical psychologists acknowledge that people and their environments are in a state of creative tension whereby each is constituted in its relationship with the other. Rejecting mechanistic models of human beings, critical psychologists grant individuals a sense of agency, but not in disregard of political structures that come to shape their habits and beliefs. Material and cultural configurations of power that shape social experience are the object of study. Power struggles resulting in oppression, resistance, and liberation are very much part of the world explored by critical psychologists. These are social phenomena that result in suffering, striving, and occasional thriving.

Epistemology refers to the study of knowledge, while methodology refers to the tools we use to obtain that knowledge. Critical psychologists employ quantitative and qualitative methods to understand the human and social experience of domination and resistance. "The researcher works in solidarity with oppressed groups and strives to amplify their voices through a process of dialogue and consciousness-raising. The function of deconstruction, reconstruction and construction is to challenge and transform knowledge and society" (Nelson & Prilleltensky, 2010, p. 258). An emancipatory epistemology seeks ways to inform action. As Teo observed, "emancipatory relevance means that research should contribute to overturning oppressive social situations" (2009, p. 45). Part of the process of gathering information for social change is generating doubts in community members about what they take to be immutable and fatalistic realities. This process of problematization (Montero, 2007) is often called consciousness-raising. In critical epistemology, the aim is not just to collect data but to interact with the provider of data in ways that question taken-for-granted assumptions about the way the world is and is supposed to be. "Critical consciousness involves decoding the social lies that naturalize the status quo, while searching for alternative interpretations of one's situation" (Watkins & Shulman, 2008, p. 18). As Nussbaum (2006) explains,

> People adjust their preferences to what they think they can achieve, and also to what their society tells them a suitable achievement is for someone like them. Women and other deprived people frequently exhibit such "adaptive preferences," formed under unjust background conditions. These preferences will typically validate the status quo. (p. 73)

In terms of praxis, critical psychologists self-consciously explicate their values and allow them to inform research and action. Value-neutrality is challenged as an impossible stand, for neutrality always supports the status quo (Prilleltensky, 1994). According to Teo, the Frankfurt School of critical theory "specifically laid out values to guide critical research: an organization of society to meet the needs of the whole community and to end social injustice. Critical social research should be guided by these ethical-political ideas and should generate knowledge that has emancipatory relevance" (2009, p. 49).

As may be readily seen, the ontology, epistemology, and praxis embraced by critical psychologists is shared by feminist, environmental, race, and post-colonial theorists, among other intellectuals and activists who understand the social world is constituted by power differentials (Fox et al., 2009; Hook, 2004; Huygens, 2007; Teo, 2005). These inequities have distinct repercussions for the humans on either side of the power equation. Critical psychologists, together with other critical social scientists and theorists, object to two fundamental things: the way society is organized and the way social science supports the status quo. In psychology's case, there is a long history to upholding the societal status quo by deflecting social problems into deep intrapsychic motivational, emotional, cognitive problems (Hook, 2004; Prilleltensky, 1994). The most recent incarnation of that proclivity is positive psychology, which, while well-meaning, minimizes the role of circumstances (such as social injustice) in people's happiness (see for example Lyubomirsky, 2007, or Seligman, 2002). "The real conservatism of positive psychology" writes Barbara Ehrenreich, "lies in its attachment to the status quo with all its inequalities and abuses of power" (2009, p. 170). She rightly assumes that the benefits of positive psychology may be accessible to middle-class people who are not overly bothered by inequality and injustice.

> Like pop positive thinking, positive psychology attends almost solely to the changes a person can make internally by adjusting his or her own outlook .... Positive psychologists' more important contribution to the defense of the status quo has been to assert or "find" that circumstances play only a minor role in determining a person's happiness .... Why advocate for better jobs and schools, safer neighborhoods, universal health insurance, or any other liberal desideratum if these measures will do little to make people happy? Social reformers, political activists, and change-oriented elected officials can all take a much-needed rest .... In the great centuries-long quest for a better world, the baton has passed to the practitioners of "optimism training," the positive psychologists, and the purveyors of pop positive thinking. (Ehrenreich, 2009, pp. 171–172)

Whereas some critical psychologists prefer discursive methods of social and disciplinary critique, others pursue community action more vigorously (for a variety of approaches, see Fox & Prilleltensky, 1997; Fox et al., 2009; and Henriques, Hollway, Urwin, Venn, & Walkerdine, 1984). While discursive critiques are very much needed, to criticize positive psychology, for instance, we work mostly in the applied camp of critical psychology. As community psychologists, we believe in action research and in promoting people's well-being.

To be more precise about what we seek as critical community psychologists and preventionists, we describe below our conception of well-being along with our values, assumptions, and practices. We distill implications for social justice and social change and end this section with a critique of critical theories.

Well-Being

Well-being is a positive state of affairs, brought about by the simultaneous and balanced satisfaction of personal, interpersonal, organizational, communal, and environmental objective and subjective needs, and by the enactment of just policies and practices in each one of these domains (Prilleltensky, 2008; Prilleltensky & Prilleltensky, 2006). Objective needs refer to material requisites such as housing, clothing, and economic resources, while subjective needs refer to psychological elements of wellness such as self-determination, sense of control, dignity, and emotional support. Objective signs of well-being refer to measurable and material conditions, whereas subjective signs pertain to psychological and perceptual phenomena, such as sense of control, belonging, and safety. Both types of signs, objective and subjective, are related but sufficiently distinct to merit their own categorization. A person may be well physically but not well psychologically.

As may be seen in Table 10.1, the satisfaction of objective and subjective needs depends on the enactment of just policies and practices. In fact, studies on social determinants of health demonstrate that societies with more equal distribution of resources experience fewer psychosocial challenges than those with fewer egalitarian policies (Marmot, 2004; Wilkinson & Pickett, 2009). Comparisons within and across countries demonstrate that inequality is bad for you, and it is especially bad for those with fewer resources (Levy & Sidel, 2006).

Table 10.1 offers an overview of the five sites of well-being, as well as examples of risk and protective objective and subjective factors. Our

Table 10.1 Ecological Model of Well-Being

	Sites of Well-Being				
	Individual	**Relational**	**Organizational**	**Communal**	**Environmental**
Objective Signs	+health +money +shelter -illness -poverty -homelessness	+networks +instrumental support +equality -isolation -violence -domination	+human resources +effective structures +financial resources -lack of human resources -chaos -lack of financial support	+social capital +low rate of trust +marginalization -lack of trust -high crime -policies of inclusion	+clean air +green spaces +conservation -pollution -urban decay -waste
Subjective Signs	+efficacy +control +meaning -lack of competence -lack of control -alienation	+voice +choice +affection -repression -constraints -neglect	+support +affirmation +stimulation -isolation -condemnation -alienation	+belonging +reciprocity +sense of community -rejection -greed -isolation	+safety +respect for nature +concern for sustainability -fear -environmental neglect -consumerism
Values	+autonomy +freedom -lack of power -subjugation	+caring +compassion -neglect -dismissal	+participation +collaboration -marginality -dictatorial	+diversity +inclusion -discrimination -exclusion	+protection of resources +sustainability -depletion of resources -consumerism
Justice	My due/Our due	My due/Your due/Our due	My due/Its due/ Our due	My due/Their due/ Our due	My due/Nature's due/Our due

Adapted from Prilleltensky (2008) with permission from the *American Journal of Community Psychology.*

conceptualization of well-being is ecological in nature. It claims that a favorable state cannot be achieved in solitude in each one of the ecological silos, but rather in concert with the other domains of life. All domains of wellness are interconnected. Studies demonstrate the synergistic linkages among environmental, communal, workplace, interpersonal, and individual levels of wellness (Nelson & Prilleltensky, 2010; Rath & Harter, 2010). In favorable conditions of nurturance, safety, and stimulation, children learn and perform better. Under adverse occupational conditions, workers develop psychological and physical symptoms. The well-being of the private citizen is very much dependent on the state of fairness, equality, and justice prevailing in his or her community (Nussbaum, 2006).

While the various sites of well-being possess intrinsic wellness, they also have instrumental value in the wellness of other sites. Thus, the natural environment deserves to be preserved for its own sake, but also for the sake of the community and its inhabitants. They all work in concert (Prilleltensky & Prilleltensky, 2006). Individual well-being, as seen in Table 10.1, may be enhanced by positive objective signs such as physical health and diminished by negative signs such as illness. We can see instances of positive or negative objective and subjective signs across the various sites of well-being.

Values

To advance the well-being of individuals, relationships, organizations, and the like, we need a set of values that will guide us. In each column in Table 10.1, we present a group of values aimed to foster the well-being of each particular site. These values are intrinsically beneficial to the well-being of a particular entity (e.g., person, organization) and extrinsically beneficial to the holistic well-being of an entire community. These are values that support not only positive outcomes, but also positive processes. They guide us in our aims, but also in our daily actions.

While not very many critical psychologists make a point of explicitly articulating their values, we believe it is essential. Without clarity of convictions we may easily find ourselves in paradoxical situations such as positive psychology, which seeks to promote wellness, a highly desirable value, but does so by focusing solely on individual values and neglecting the environment. Ultimately, you cannot promote personal well-being when people live in highly polluted environments and crime infested neighborhoods. Many wealthy people isolate themselves from social and environmental perils by living in gated communities up in the mountains, far from the pollution, but so far we have not seen any type of psychology, positive or otherwise, that claims to be exclusively for the well to do. Liberation and critical psychology are explicitly aligned with the disadvantaged, those who cannot escape crime or pollution.

But critical psychologists do not just advocate a multiplicity of values to encompass the various sides of wellness. They also claim that these values, as shown in Table 10.1, are subject to reigning conceptions of justice. Justice, in its most basic form, deals with the fair and equitable allocation of resources, obligations, and bargaining powers in society (Miller, 1999). To determine how to allocate resources, obligations, and bargaining powers we require a set of criteria. Without criteria we cannot reasonably argue for one type of distribution or another. An ideal set of criteria would balance what is due me with what is due other people, organizations, or the natural environment, as shown in the last row of Table 10.1.

The criterion used to distribute opportunities in society is contested terrain. In most capitalist societies merit is used. Merit encompasses effort and ability. Students deserve scholarships based on their achievements, and athletes deserve medals due to aptitude and hard work. But what happens when not all students, or athletes for that matter, start life with similar opportunities? What happens when millions of children cannot attend school, or attend schools that are poorly resourced with underpaid teachers? It is entirely possible that many potentially brilliant kids cannot reach their potential due to diminished opportunities in life. Can we then turn back on them and tell them they are not smart enough or did not achieve enough? Could they not have done much better under favorable circumstances, like the kids in the "good" part of town? By using strictly individualistic criteria for justice, we neglect the very conditions that may have given rise to excellence. And yet, individual capacity and effort are almost always used to justify inequality (Ravitch, 2010). Those who work hard achieve more in life: Total disregard for the conditions that lead to achievement. Under conditions of equality, in which all students have access to similar privileges, it would be fair to reward the ones who have worked hard to progress (Facione, Scherer, & Attig, 1978). But under conditions of inequality, it would be unfair to punish those who did not achieve high grades due to environmental, social, organizational, and communal factors outside of their control (Darling-Hammond, 2010; Hargreaves & Shirley, 2009; Payne, 2009). Children do not choose where they are born or where they go to kindergarten.

Faced with this inconvenient truth, many apologists for the status quo blame the parents instead of the children; while many others blame the teachers, and the principals, and the unions (Hargreaves & Shirley, 2009; Ravitch, 2010). Missing from these discussions is the educational "elephant in the room": poorly resourced public schools, a thrust to privatize public education, histories of colonization, exclusion, segregation, red-lining, and policies of legalized discrimination.

As in the case of educational injustice, there is behavioral injustice (Adler & Stewart, 2009). Certain segments of the population have ample access to healthy role models who exercise and eat well while others have only access to 7-Eleven and unsafe communities without sidewalks or bike paths. Furthermore, many poor people live in obesogenic environments that perpetuate the consumption of high fat foods and limit fitness opportunities. As Adler and Stewart observed,

> Although some individuals are able to make and maintain change, the medical model largely ignores the forces contributing to the development and maintenance of obesity. Patients walk out of the health care provider's office only to reenter the same environment that led to their weight gain in the first place. The commercial and structural forces in their environment still are powerful. These people thus may be caught in "vicious cycles" of "accelerators" of the obesity epidemic .... resulting from the interaction of an increasingly obese individual with an "obesogenic environment" that encourages an overconsumption of food and discourages physical activity. (Adler & Stewart, 2009, p. 55)

Critical psychologists challenge the myth that people can improve their health at any time because they have freedom to do so. This would obviate the gross inequities in access to resources that shape, to a large extent, life's opportunities for wellness. This is not to say that people are devoid of agency to struggle for social justice and a more equitable state of affairs. But to ignite that agency, we need to acknowledge first that the environment does not present similar opportunities to all. In the case of obesity, for example, we agree with Adler and Stewart that it is "unjust to hold people accountable for things over which they have little control .... This places the primary responsibility on society to provide equal opportunities for all people to be able to make the healthier choices, and it reframes the discussion as one of justice rather than blame" (2009, p. 61). It is unjust to hold people accountable for things that are beyond their control. Societies that distribute resources more equitably and make access to healthier environments easier attain higher levels of psychosocial health and well-being (Wilkinson & Pickett, 2009). Among problems prevented through equality are teenage pregnancy, mental illness, obesity, infant mortality, and lack of trust.

Practices

Critical psychologists engage in theory, research, and action. Theory and research focus on three main questions: (1) what are the psychological, cultural, and social mechanisms through which privilege and power in society reproduce themselves; (2) how does the discipline of psychology contribute to oppressive policies and practices in government, schools, hospitals, social services, private practice, and discourse; and (3) what are successful ways of partnering with minorities and disadvantaged groups to seek empowerment, inclusion, peace, and social justice.

With respect to the first question, Derek Hook's (2004) *An Introduction to Critical Psychology* offers multiple insights through which Western notions of superiority suffused the psyche of colonizers and colonized alike. Similarly, Kelly Oliver's (2004) *The Colonization of Psychic Space: A Psychoanalytic Theory of Oppression* discerns the role of the unconscious in perpetuating the illusion of justified privilege in the dominant classes. Watkins and Shulman (2008), in turn, describe the many cultural practices of consumerism, environmental degradation, and violence that deny the emergence of authentic relationships with other human beings and with the earth. Through cultural and psychological critique, these authors expose ways in which white supremacy became hegemonic.

The second question, dealing with the complicity of psychology in perpetuating capitalist structures of domination, has received wide attention. Several books have documented ways through which discursive and therapeutic practices have tried to pathologize homosexuality, blame mothers for children's autistic features, and overall project social maladies deep into the caverns of personal maladjustment (Fox & Prilleltensky, 1994; Fox et al., 2009; Parker, 2007; Prilleltensky, 1994; Wilkinson & Pickett, 2009). As noted above, even positive psychology risks sacrificing its healthful attributes by continuing an unfortunate tradition of neglecting the role of context in wellness (Ehrenreich, 2009; Pawelski & Prilleltensky, 2005; Shinn & Toohey, 2003).

The third question deals with the quest for participatory, collaborative, and emancipatory means to seek justice for the poor, colonized, and marginalized. There are inspiring examples of critical and community psychologists partnering with women and minorities in trying to restore hope, honor memories, and change policies and practices at the local, regional, and national levels. Brinton Lykes (Lykes, 1997, 1999; Lykes & Coquillon, 2009) has been working in Guatemala with indigenous women for many years, gaining their trust, and finding ways to empower them to gain control of their lives despite great sadness and trauma occasioned by military and paramilitary troops. Multiple and meaningful projects have sprung from their work together, including photo voice exhibitions and psychosocial recovery efforts. In genuine partnerships of solidarity, the women transform their psychological and social reality, as well as gain recognition of past atrocities and injustice.

While many critical psychologists explore the phenomenology of the oppressed and mount projects to advance their civil rights, Ingrid Huygens (2007) in Aotearoa, New Zealand, studied processes of Pakeha (White inhabitants) change in response to the Treaty of Waitangi. The treaty, signed in 1840 between the British crown and the Maori leadership, conferred on the Maori indigenous population rights and privileges that were never honored by the White colonizers. In her work, Huygens documents the process whereby the dominant group tries to educate itself on the wrongs of the past and engage in constructive action to establish genuine and authentic reciprocal relationships among the two groups. Her illuminating study offers several insights into the cultural transformation of dominant groups. According to her, such change requires a critical and emotional process of openness to the challenges of an oppressed group, the pursuit of counterhegemonic accounts of the relationship between the two groups, and accepting responsibility for the outcomes of domination. Furthermore, the change requires striving toward reciprocal and fair relationships based on recognition of past injustices (Huygens, 2007). Questioning the legitimacy of White privilege is a key part of the process.

In addition to action research, critical psychologists engage in various form of practice, such as therapy, consultation, organizational development, and community change. Prilleltensky and Nelson (2002) describe in detail how the values of self-determination, empowerment, caring, compassion, respect for diversity, and social justice inform practice in educational, clinical, organizational, health, and community settings. In all cases, critical psychologists honor the process of empowerment and justice as much as the outcome. This means giving voice and choice to the partner with whom we work, respecting their dignity by acknowledging their strengths and power differentials, and seeking avenues to gain control of their lives in ways that enhance reciprocal empowerment and not personal aggrandizement.

A critical psychological approach may be conceptualized along four domains of practice: capabilities, participation, ecology, and temporality. The first domain refers to the focus of attention in practice. We can focus on strengths or deficits. A critical psychology approach honors people's assets and dignity in coping with life's challenges and oppressive conditions. The second domain refers to the level of voice and choice in services and community action. At one end there is empowerment and at the other, alienation. The third domain pertains to the level of intervention. The continuum ranges from individual to community and policy level advocacy. Finally, the temporal domain draws attention to prevention versus treatment and rehabilitation. In our view, a critical psychology approach would endorse a strength-based, preventive, empowering, community change orientation. These four principles are the basis of the acronym SPEC, which we have used in our organizational development and community work (Bess, Prilleltensky, Perkins, & Collins, 2009; Evans, Hanlin, & Prilleltensky, 2007; Prilleltensky, 2005). In this book, the major emphasis is on prevention, which, in our view, needs to be complemented by the other three principles, as we will later show.

Limitations of Critical Psychology

Several critiques can be leveled against critical psychology. We concentrate here on three. First, it has not penetrated yet in a meaningful way the discourse of psychology. Psychology continues to individualize problems and neglect the context of psychosocial challenges. Perhaps it is an inevitable outcome of a critical movement to remain at the margins. Second, the level of critique has not yet been matched by practical applications in critical psychology. A systematic study of critical theories and approaches in the social sciences indeed found that critique often remains at the level of theory, without a clear articulation of alternatives for action (Davidson et al., 2006). This may very well reflect the lineage of critical psychology, which was based largely in the Frankfurt School of critical theory. While the Latin American influence of liberation psychology is definitely more applied than the European tradition, its legacy has not been fully embraced yet. Our third reservation has to do with the lack of systematic research on critical psychology applications in community settings. Here lies a potentially useful synergy between critical psychology, a radical but largely theoretical enterprise, and prevention, a less radical but eminently applied venture. To explore zones of congruence among these two approaches, we turn our attention to prevention.

What Is Prevention?

Public Health Roots

Prevention has its roots in public health. In contrast to mainstream health services that treat diseases or health problems of individual patients, public health is concerned with the health of entire populations. Public health uses epidemiological methods to determine the incidence (number of new cases) and prevalence (number of current cases) of a disease in a population and the factors that place people at risk for the disease. Even when the precise causal agent of a disease is unknown, public health approaches can be successfully applied in prevention. The story of John Snow and the Broad Street pump in London, England, as told by George Albee, is a good illustration of this point.

> John Snow figured out that cholera was a water-borne disease long before the noxious agent causing cholera had been identified. He observed that the pattern of cholera infection was related to where drinking water came from; in the most famous act in the history of public health, he removed the handle

from the Broad Street pump and stopped a cholera epidemic. (Albee, 1991, p. 26)

Public health focuses on three components that are relevant to diseases or psychosocial problems: (1) characteristics of the host (i.e., the person who contracts the disease), (2) characteristics of the environment, and (3) the agent (i.e., the mode of disease transmission) (Bloom, 1984). For example, if we look at the epidemiology of motor vehicle accidents or fatalities, we can examine characteristics of the host or driver (e.g., blood alcohol level, reckless or high-speed driving), the environment (e.g., how well lit the road is at night, slipperiness of the road in rain, ice, or snow), and the agent or the car (e.g., safety of the car). Preventive measures to reduce motor vehicle fatalities include changing the host (e.g., driver's education, "Don't Drink and Drive" campaigns), changing the environment (e.g., improvement of road safety), and changing the agent (e.g., improving car safety, installation of air bags). Ralph Nader's famous book, *Unsafe at Any Speed*, provided evidence about the lack of safety of the Corvair and other unsafe features of autos built in the United States and was a significant landmark in improving auto safety through advocacy (Nader, 1965).

Principal Tenets of Prevention

DEFINITION AND TYPOLOGIES

Beginning in the 1960s, some mental health professionals like Albee and Cowen recognized the potential value of preventive approaches to mental health issues. They elaborated the shortcomings of individual clinical interventions, noting that they provided too little too late, that they did not target those in greatest need, that they used a style that was out of touch with how many people view their problems, and that there would never be enough clinicians to treat everyone in need (Cowen, 2000). Even if psychotherapy was 100% effective, they argued, it would still not be effective in reducing rates of mental health problems in a population; only prevention could do that. In an article titled "The Futility of Psychotherapy," Albee (1990) stated, "[A]s the history of public health methods (that emphasize social change) has clearly established, no mass disease or disorder afflicting humankind has ever been eliminated by attempts at treating affected individuals" (p. 370). Early prevention efforts were inspired by the wisdom of preventive intervention as captured in the adages, "An ounce of prevention is worth a pound of cure," and "A stitch in time saves nine."

Community psychiatrist Gerald Caplan (1964) distinguished between primary, secondary, and tertiary prevention in mental health. Primary prevention refers to measures taken to reduce the incidence of mental health problems; secondary prevention refers to early detection and intervention to keep a problem from worsening; and tertiary prevention refers to rehabilitation to reduce disability that could result from a disorder. Noting "definitional slippage" in early prevention efforts, Cowen (1980) asserted that true prevention, or primary prevention, can be defined by its focus on incidence reduction, its focus on a population not individuals, and its intentional focus on preventing mental health issues.

The old typology of primary, secondary, and tertiary prevention has given way to a newer typology created by the US Institute of Medicine (IOM, 1994). The IOM typology distinguishes between universal, selective, and indicated approaches to prevention.

Universal prevention focuses on all members of the population in a geographical area (e.g., a neighborhood) or a setting (e.g., a school).

Selective prevention, which is also known as the high-risk approach, targets participants on the basis of external characteristics (e.g., parental divorce, low family income) and/or on internal characteristics (e.g., low birth-weight, peer rejection). Selective prevention is based on the assumption that there are known risk factors for certain mental health problems, and that prevention can have the greatest impact by targeting individuals at highest risk (Offord, Kraemer, Kazdin, Jensen, & Harrington, 1998).

Finally, indicated prevention is aimed at participants who show mild or early-developing mental health problems (e.g., young children who show marked opposition and defiance). Indicated prevention is what used to be called secondary prevention, while universal and selective prevention are what was previously called primary prevention.

RISK, PROTECTION, AND RESILIENCE: A THEORETICAL FRAMEWORK FOR PREVENTION

The primary theoretical framework that has guided the development of selective preventive interventions is resilience theory, which involves an examination of risk and protection (Luthar & Cicchetti, 2000). Risk factors are those adverse conditions or events that increase the likelihood of negative outcomes, while protective factors are assets or resources that help to offset, or buffer, risk factors. Thus, protective factors serve as moderator variables that interact with risk factors to reduce negative outcomes (Roosa, 2000).

Albee (1982) views the incidence of mental health problems as an equation involving risk and protective factors:

$$\text{Incidence} = \frac{\text{Risk factors}}{\text{Protective factors}}$$

$$= \frac{\text{Organic causes} + \text{Stress} + \text{Exploitation}}{\text{Coping skills} + \text{Self-esteem} + \text{Support systems}}$$

In addition to its focus on risk and protection, resilience theory is ecological in nature and examines the interaction of risk and protective factors within and across multiple ecological contexts: microsystem, exosystem, and macrosystem (Sandler, 2001). Resilience theory focuses on the question of how some people are able to maintain a positive developmental trajectory in the face of adversity, while others suffer and experience negative outcomes.

Understanding the mechanisms of risk, protection, and resilience can have important implications for prevention (Luthar & Cicchetti, 2000; Robinson, 2000). In fact, selective or high-risk prevention programs and the different components that they provide (e.g., social support, coping skills training) can be conceptualized as protective factors for people who are disadvantaged (Robinson, 2000).

Rutter (1987) has postulated four central resilience mechanisms that can help people cope with adversity and prevent problems: (1) reducing risk impact, (2) interrupting unhealthy chain reactions stemming from stressful life events, (3) enhancing self-esteem and self-efficacy, and (4) creating opportunities for personal growth. Each of these mechanisms focuses on processes that moderate the impacts of adverse conditions on negative outcomes. Thus, for example, programs that promote self-esteem (Haney & Durlak, 1998) are believed to help people cope with adverse conditions that threaten their sense of self-worth (Sandler, 2001). Selective prevention programs can also be guided by mediational models. For example, in their long-term, quasi-experimental evaluation of the Child-Parent Centers for low-income children in Chicago, Reynolds, Ou, and Topitzes (2004) found that preschool and early elementary school programs had positive impacts on arrests at age 18 and high school completion by age 20. To explain these findings, Reynolds et al. tested whether or not different factors mediated the impacts of program participation on these outcomes. In support of a mediational model, they found that "the primary mediators of effects for both outcomes were attendance in high-quality elementary schools and lower mobility (school support hypothesis), literacy skills in kindergarten and avoidance of grade retention (cognitive advantage hypothesis), and parent involvement in school and avoidance of child maltreatment (family support hypothesis)" (p. 1299).

THE PROMOTION OF WELL-BEING

Emory Cowen (1991, 1994, 2000) pointed to the need to go beyond prevention to wellness enhancement. The notion of positive mental health can be traced back to the book that Marie Jahoda (1958) prepared for the US Joint Commission on Mental Illness and Health. The emergence of concepts of well-being has arisen in response to the deficit-oriented focus of the *Diagnostic and Statistical Manual* (DSM) in all its various revisions. Positive mental health (Jahoda, 1958), positive psychological and social functioning (Keyes, 2007), quality of life (Nelson & Saegert, 2009), subjective well-being (Diener, 2000), well-being (Prilleltensky & Prilleltensky, 2006), and wellness (Cowen, 1991) are some of the concepts and terms that have been developed to capture how individuals can flourish. Research by Keyes (2007) suggests that mental health and mental health problems can be constructed as two distinct continua, with mental health ranging from languishing to flourishing and mental health problems ranging from the absence of symptoms of mental illness to severe manifestations of mental illness. Thus, preventing mental health problems does not necessarily promote mental health.

How then can mental health and well-being be promoted? Cowen (1994) outlined several key pathways toward the promotion of well-being.

Attachment

It is important for infants and young children to form secure attachments to their parents and caregivers. Thus, programs like home visitation that strive to promote attachments may yield long-term benefits.

Competencies

The development of age-appropriate competencies is also important for well-being. Programs that are designed to develop social competencies (e.g., social problem-solving skills, assertiveness), academic competencies, and other competencies are important for the promotion of well-being.

Social environments

Healthy and socially just environments are important for well-being. Thus, one strategy to promote well-being is to change social systems toward those characteristics and processes that have been shown to be important for well-being. This includes engaging in social action to eliminate degrading social conditions, including poverty, racism, and sexism (Albee, 1986).

Empowerment

Psychological and political empowerment refers to perceived and actual control over one's life (Rappaport, 1981). Empowering interventions are those that enhance citizens' self-determination, democratic participation, and opportunity to have control over the course of their lives.

Resources to cope with stress

Finally, being able to cope effectively with adversity is another key pathway to well-being. Therefore, having the skills and resources to meet the challenges posed by the stressors of life is essential for well-being. Stressors are often seen as presenting an opportunity for growth. Programs that provide people with resources and coping skills can potentially promote well-being.

Like prevention, these strategies to promote well-being focus on populations, and they follow the universal approach so that everyone in the population under study receives the intervention. Unlike selective prevention, which is based on resilience theory, the postulated mechanisms of promotion focus on the direct effects of promotive factors on well-being or on reducing exposure to adverse conditions (Sandler, 2001). For example, promoting competencies, such as social problem-solving skills, is hypothesized to have a direct impact on well-being. Mediational models, described earlier, can also be applied to evaluate the impacts of programs that strive to promote well-being.

Prevention Research

A large body of research has accumulated that has examined the impacts of prevention programs, their cost-benefits, and their implementation.

IMPACTS

There is now quite a bit of evidence attesting to the effectiveness of prevention programs in reducing a variety of psychosocial problems both in the short term and the long term (Durlak & Wells, 1997). Prevention programs have been applied to a wide variety of mental health and psychosocial problems, such as violence against women in youth dating relationships (Wolfe et al., 2003), criminal offending (Farrington & Welsh, 2003), depression and anxiety problems in adults (Dozois & Dobson, 2004), women's postpartum depression (Dennis et al., 2009), and marital distress (Markman, Renick, Floyd, Stanley, & Clements, 1993). However, the bulk of prevention research has focused on children and families, reasoning that it is better to intervene earlier rather than later.

Research has established the preventive impacts of different programs for children. For example, take the problem of child abuse and neglect. David Olds and colleagues used a randomized design to evaluate a nurse home visitation program for women with one or more of the following risk factors: single, teen-aged, or low income. The program, which began during pregnancy and continued until the children were 2 years old, was implemented in an impoverished, rural community in the state of New York, in which rates of child abuse and neglect were quite high. After 2 years, they found a significant impact of the program for those mothers with all three risk factors on rates of child abuse and neglect. A total of 14% of the children in the control group abused or neglected their children compared with 4% of those who participated in the nurse home visitation program (Olds, Henderson, Chamberlin, & Tatelbaum, 1986). What is most remarkable about this study is that the impacts of the program were stronger when the children were older. Using the method of survival analysis, Zielinski, Eckenrode, and Olds (2009) found that 68% of the youth in the control group were not abused or neglected by age 15, compared with 76% of the youth whose mothers participated in the program. The impacts were more pronounced for the group with all three risk factors with 63% of the control group youth not being abused or neglected compared with 81% of the nurse home visitation group.

The previously mentioned study of the Chicago Child-Parent Centers also examined the impacts of the program on child abuse. Unlike the nurse home visitation program, this program started later when the children were 3 years of age and provided preschool education, continuing educational support into elementary school, family support, and a variety of other programs for the parents. At age 17, children in the comparison group had a rate of 11% of court petitions for child maltreatment compared with 5% of children in the intervention group. In contrast to the selective prevention programs of the

Child-Parent Centers and the nurse home visitation program, Prinz, Sanders, Shapiro, Whitaker, and Lutzker (2009) implemented the Triple P, Positive Parenting Program, on a population-wide base in South Carolina. Using a randomized design, 18 counties were randomized into Triple P or a no program control. Triple P is designed to enhance parenting skills using a social learning approach. After the intervention, they found significant differences favoring the counties that were assigned to the Triple P program on rates of substantiated child maltreatment, out-of-home placements, and child maltreatment injuries. In addition to these exemplary studies, systematic and meta-analytic reviews have shown that there is considerable evidence that child abuse and neglect can be prevented (Geeraert, Van de Noortgate, Grietans, & Onghenea, 2004; Lundahl, Nimer, & Parsons, 2006; MacLeod & Nelson, 2000; MacMillan et al., 2009).

Perhaps a most impressive feature of prevention programs for children is their enduring impacts. While many prevention programs begin during preschool, their impacts continue to be observed in middle childhood, adolescence, and adulthood (Karoly, Kilburn, & Cannon, 2005; Manning, Homel, & Smith, 2010; Nelson, Westhues, & MacLeod, 2003). One well-known preschool prevention program that has shown positive long-term impacts is the Perry Preschool program that was implemented in a low-income community in Ypsilanti, Michigan (Schweinhart, 2005). Three- and 4-year-old children, with low IQs and whose families were living in poverty, were randomly assigned to the Perry Preschool or a control group. For 2 years, the children in the Perry Preschool program participated in classroom activities, and the teachers made home visits each week to every mother and child, assisting the mothers with child-rearing skills. The researchers followed up the participants at age 40. Compared with participants in the control group, participants in the Perry Preschool program at age 40 were: less likely to be arrested five or more times (36% vs. 55%) and more likely to be employed (70% vs. 50%), earn $20,000 or more (60% vs. 40%), and have a savings account (76% vs. 50%).

COST-BENEFITS

Economic evaluations of prevention programs have also been undertaken to document the cost-benefits of these programs. Several longitudinal studies have shown that prevention programs for children yield a substantial return on investment (ROI) (Belfield, Nores, Barnett, & Schweinhart, 2006; Reynolds & Temple, 2008). These studies demonstrate that for every $1 invested in the program, that the ROI is $5 for Olds' nurse home visitation program for the high-risk group, $10 for the Chicago Child-Parent Centers, and $13 for the Perry Preschool program. Thus, not only has prevention been shown to be effective, cost-benefits research has also shown that prevention makes economic sense.

IMPLEMENTATION

In view of the evidence that prevention works, prevention research has begun to examine *how* prevention programs work. Thus, there has been increased attention to the qualities of effective prevention programs. Based on their review of effective prevention programs, Nation et al. (2003) concluded that the most effective prevention programs are those that (1) are comprehensive, (2) use varied teaching methods, (3) provide sufficient "dosage" or intensity, (4) are theory-driven, (5) promote positive relationships with adults and peers, (6) are appropriately timed, (7) are socioculturally relevant, (8) use well-trained staff, and (9) use research to evaluate outcomes. Implementation research focuses on whether these different qualities are present in the prevention program. As well, prevention programs are based on a logic model or theory of change that specifies the program activities and intended outcomes. Implementation research also examines the extent to which programs are implemented as planned, thus indicating the fidelity of implementation to the program model. This fidelity research is important to determine if implementation of program components is linked to outcomes. In their review of 59 implementation studies of prevention programs, Durlak and Dupre (2008) found the degree of implementation fidelity was linked to positive outcomes. Prevention programs need to follow a program model, but they also need to be adapted to local contexts and populations to make them relevant. While these two emphases, fidelity and adaptation, might seem to conflict with one another, Hawe (2004) has suggested that both are important and can be reconciled by making a distinction between the form and function of program components. She posits that the particular form the intervention takes can vary from context to context, but that it is important to retain the essential functions of the program components. For example, if the intervention principle is to harness social support from people's social networks, this function can be met through different forms (e.g., a mutual support group in one context, peer-to-peer support in another context).

Critique of Prevention

Several criticisms can be levied against prevention. First, while prevention has proved to be valuable, it is, by and large, ameliorative in that it does not strive to change the social conditions that give rise to the problems it strives to prevent. That is, most of the attention of prevention is focused on enhancing protective factors (the bottom half of Albee's equation), rather than on reducing adversity and exploitation (the top half of Albee's equation). The vast majority of prevention programs are micro-centered in their focus on the individual and the family. In a review of 526 studies, Durlak et al. (2007) found that none of the studies examined changes in community-level outcomes. Two recent universal prevention and promotion programs for young children, Sure Start Local Programmes in the UK (Melhuish, Belsky, Leyland, Barnes, & the National Evaluation of Sure Start Research Team, 2008) and Better Beginnings, Better Futures in Canada (Peters et al., 2010), have targeted and found impacts of these programs on community conditions.

A second criticism of prevention is that the participants in these programs are relegated to the role of service-recipients and data sources. With the exception of the Better Beginnings program in Canada, community members are usually not given the opportunity to be active agents who have a voice in the programs that are designed by professionals for them. Prilleltensky (2005) has argued that prevention programs should be empowering and encourage participation not just in program activities, but in program design and management. Prevention programs and research are largely silent on issues of power and participation.

A third criticism relates to efforts to medicalize prevention and focus on deficits. Reports by the IOM and the National Institute of Mental Health (NIMH) (Heller, 1996) take an overly narrow view of the prevention of specific mental disorders to the neglect of mental health promotion and social action (Albee, 1996). As well, research funding from the NIMH in 2006 included the prevention of comorbidity, disability, and relapse, which are clearly tertiary or treatment interventions. That they are included along with primary prevention hearkens back to Cowen's (1980) warning about definitional slippage. In sum, Isaac has argued for a holistic model of strengths, prevention, empowerment, and community change (SPEC) (Prilleltensky, 2005), but the main points of critique of prevention suggest that prevention is not often accompanied by a focus on strengths, empowerment, or community change.

Points of Divergence and Convergence Between Critical Psychology and Prevention

Points of Divergence

After reading the previous sections on critical psychology and prevention, it should be apparent that these two fields have very different roots and emphases. In Table 10.2, we contrast critical psychology and prevention on three key dimensions.

VALUES

As we noted earlier, critical psychology is an explicitly value-based approach. Its critique of the societal status quo is based on values of power-sharing and social justice (Prilleltensky, 1994). Prevention, in contrast, claims to be a value-neutral, scientific enterprise, and the field has come to be known as "prevention science" (Coie et al., 1993; Heller, 1996). Albee (1996; Perry & Albee, 1994) has critiqued prevention's growing overemphasis on

Table 10.2 Points of Divergence Between Critical Psychology and Prevention

Dimension	Critical Psychology	Prevention
Values	Explicitly value-based approach that emphasizes values of power-sharing and social justice	Claims to be value-neutral, but emphasizes values of health, caring, and compassion
Ontology/Epistemology	Social and institutional structures are rooted in historical reality but can be changed through researchers working in partnership with oppressed people	Single, external reality that can be predicted and controlled through controlled research
Practices	Value-based praxis focused on transformative social change	Research-informed programs focused on amelioration

scientism and its underemphasis on values of social justice and social change.

> Our most serious reservations concern the near total absence of prevention program proposals that strike at the social injustices that play a major role in the appearance of mental and emotional problems. (Perry & Albee, 1994, p. 1088)

While claiming to be value-neutral, prevention implicitly emphasizes the values of health, caring, compassion, and scientific inquiry, which stand in sharp contrast to the explicit social justice values of critical psychology.

ONTOLOGY/EPISTEMOLOGY

Critical psychology is based on a paradigm of social transformation (Nelson & Prilleltensky, 2010). Critical knowledge is needed to uncover institutional interests, power, and values that have historically constrained or supported social change. Moreover, the critical paradigm emphasizes working in solidarity with oppressed people toward their social change goals. In contrast, prevention is based on the natural science paradigm of logical positivism or rational empiricism, which holds that there is one external reality that can be predicted and controlled. The voluminous experimental and quasi-experimental prevention research that we have reviewed shows the emphasis of prevention on traditional scientific methods.

PRACTICES

In terms of intervention, critical psychology is based on a value-based praxis (Nelson & Prilleltensky, 2010; Prilleltensky & Nelson, 2002). Working in solidarity with oppressed people, critical psychologists strive to make fundamental or transformative changes in social systems. The key focus in value-based praxis is to reduce power imbalances and social and economic inequalities. This is done through a cycle of action research that is value-based, participatory, self-reflexive, and oriented toward social change. In contrast, the practice of prevention focuses on the planning, implementation, and evaluation of prevention programs. Typically prevention programs are developed by prevention researchers and are based on an empirically supported theory of change. As was noted earlier, prevention tends to be more ameliorative than transformative in nature, because of its micro-centered focus and its lack of emphasis on participation of and power-sharing with the prevention program participants.

Points of Convergence

Following the same parameters as in the previous section, we will examine parallels between critical psychology and prevention in terms of values, ontology/epistemology, and practices.

VALUES

While the two fields under examination privilege different values, we believe that in the end both seek to promote well-being. Critical psychologists do that through an examination of inequality and injustice, while preventionists do that mainly through the pursuit of health. We believe that the pursuit of justice encompasses the pursuit of health, caring, and compassion. A "just" society without compassion and health is a heartless and uncaring society. At the same time, a "healthy" and "caring" society without just distribution of resources and obligations is a society that cares only about those with sufficient subjective and objective resources.

ONTOLOGY/EPISTEMOLOGY

Critical psychology and prevention share a contextual and ecological view of personal and social problems. Both fields understand, at least etiologically, the role of culture, policies, and risk and protective factors. They appreciate the contextual nature of psychosocial problems and the need to intervene at multiple levels. Even though preventionists have not devised and implemented fully comprehensive community-based programs, they acknowledge the influence of multilevel factors in stress, coping, and thriving (Durlak et al., 2007).

PRACTICES

In our critical view, psychosocial action to promote community well-being should concentrate on furthering strengths, prevention, empowerment, and community change. Preventionists, as noted above, meet only the second criteria of the four. The convergence on proactive action is needed and welcome, as effective prevention can reduce human suffering and save money. However, the absence of a strength-based, empowering, and community change perspective makes the field of prevention vulnerable to lack of sustainability.

Moving Forward

Both of us identify with critical psychology and with prevention. Geoff has been involved in one of the truly comprehensive community-based prevention programs, the Better Beginnings, Better

Futures project (Peters et al., 2010); and both of us have produced for the government of Canada recommendations for preventing child abuse at the local and national levels. In addition, both of us have tried to merge critical psychology into psychological practice in various domains (Prilleltensky & Nelson, 2002; Nelson & Prilleltensky, 2010). As demonstrated in the preceding pages, we believe that both prevention and critical psychology can contribute to the promotion of well-being, but we also believe that both suffer from shortcomings that could, and probably should, be overcome.

Values

It is evident from the preceding discussions that prevention would be more effective if it dealt not just with individual suffering, but also with community wellness. Similarly, prevention would be more sustainable if it fostered transformation and not just amelioration. Critical psychology's emphasis on social justice should be incorporated into prevention. To do that, the field of prevention would have to accept a "both/and" philosophy according to which the alleviation of suffering should not come at the expense of eliminating the roots of suffering. In actual practice, this would mean helping people cope with particular issues, such as vulnerability to school failure, and consciousness-raising about the many educational injustices that beset poor communities. Similarly, helping in the prevention of obesity would entail more than individual skills, such as fitness and nutrition, and include collective action to bring low cost fruits and vegetables to the neighborhood. Bringing attention to nutrition as a social justice issue would empower citizens not just to change their behaviors but also to address power differentials and political interests preventing the community from having access to fresh fruits and vegetables (Adler & Stewart, 2009).

We advocate for values of caring, compassion, health, self-determination, and social justice. The first four values of that list depend greatly on the presence of the last one. Opportunities for self-determination are greatly influenced by distributive justice. Do children in this community have a chance to develop hobbies and expertise in a particular area of life? Do mothers have an opportunity to get an education that is high quality, accessible, and affordable? The answer to both questions must be a resounding yes. For as long as prevention focuses mostly on behavioral change, without environmental change, it is betraying its ecological view of causality and influence.

In a smoking prevention project with immigrant children in Canada, the youngsters not only learned how to resist the temptation, but also went to city hall with a petition to ban smoking from public spaces (Prilleltensky, Nelson, & Sanchez, 2000). In a youth development project in Australia, participants helped prevent discrimination and environmental degradation through the creation of new park and social action projects (Morsillo & Prilleltensky, 2007). Matthews and Adams (2009) described a project to prevent the negative consequences of heterosexism that included civic action and political awareness. Kivnick and Lymburner (2009), in turn, describe a community program to promote social justice consciousness with youth through the arts. Buhin and Vera (2009) discuss interventions to prevent racism at both the individual and policy levels. These are but a few examples of how the value of social justice is promoted through political action to improve community well-being.

Ontology/Epistemology

The action research model of critical psychology and the empirical model of prevention need not be in contradiction. It is possible to merge the values of social action with research designs aimed to demonstrate efficacy. Sticking too closely with an emerging design may obstruct the possibility of showing potent effects of interventions. While strict adherence to positivist approaches may exclude the voice of the community in the investigation, it is possible to have community voice and choice in designing interventions with comparison groups. That was the model used in the Better Beginnings Better Futures project (Peters et al., 2010). That research project merged participation with rigorous research designs, as well as the use of quantitative and qualitative methods. Participant voice was as important as outcome measures.

Practices

In our view, preventive interventions are much more developed than critical psychology interventions. Prevention research has evolved to the point where best practices shape future interventions (Durlak et al., 2007; Nation et al., 2003). Also in our view, the science of collective action has not been as well studied as the science of individual action. As Hage and Kenny (2009) indicate, "further work is needed in developing and evaluating interventions, especially those focused on environmental change" (p. 76). In one of our research projects we are studying how to change organizations so that they could be more effective in changing communities (Bess et al., 2009; Evans et al., 2007). Our work is aimed at fostering well-being through the enactment of four principles: strengths, prevention, empowerment, and community change (SPEC). As discussed previously, it is hard to sustain preventive interventions if they do not address empowerment, strengths, and community change. Our framework for change in organizations is not as well developed and validated as certain prevention programs, such as the work of Olds on child abuse prevention (Olds et al., 1986; Zielinski et al., 2009), or the work of Sanders on parenting (Sanders et al., 2008). Action research critical psychology approaches, such as the SPEC project, have not yet achieved the level of reproducibility and effectiveness as the home visiting programs of Olds, or the Positive Parenting Program of Sanders. At the same time, it may be said that these very successful parenting and home visiting programs are not designed to change radically social circumstances leading to so much child abuse and neglect. That is a potential contribution of critical psychology.

It is difficult to predict how difficult it would be for mainstream prevention programs, such as those by Sanders and Olds, to incorporate a social change aspect to them. Similarly, it is hard to anticipate whether critical psychology approaches would embrace the methodological specificity and rigor of well-established research prevention programs. As far as we are concerned, we should try both. Research should explore the feasibility of incorporating social justice and social transformation elements into already effective universal or selected prevention programs. At the same time, we should study ways of fostering social justice and social change with the same methodological rigor of certain prevention programs. Prevention's allegiance to health sciences may have facilitated the development of systematic and reproducible efforts. Critical psychology's allegiance to social change may have fostered an activist orientation that, while useful and important, may have neglected the need to document effective ways of changing the world. We don't just want to change the world; we want to do it in effective ways.

References

Adler, N., & Stewart, J. (2009). Reducing obesity: Motivating action while not blaming the victim. *The Milbank Quarterly, 87,* 49–70.

Albee, G. W. (1982). Preventing psychopathology and promoting human potential. *American Psychologist, 37,* 1043–1050.

Albee, G. W. (1986). Toward a just society: Lessons from observations on the primary prevention of psychopathology. *American Psychologist, 41,* 891–898.

Albee, G. W. (1990). The futility of psychotherapy. *Journal of Mind and Behavior, 11,* 369–384.

Albee, G. W. (1991). No more rock-scrubbing. *The Scientist Practitioner, 1*(1), 26–27.

Albee, G. W. (1996). Revolutions and counterrevolutions in prevention. *American Psychologist, 51,* 1130–1133.

Belfield, C. R., Nores, M., Barnett, S., & Schweinhart, L. (2006). The HighScope Perry Preschool Program: Cost-benefit analysis from the age 40 follow-up. *Journal of Human Resources, 41,* 162–190.

Bess, K., Prilleltensky, I., Perkins, D., & Collins, L. (2009). Participatory organizational change in community based health and human services: From tokenism to political engagement. *American Journal of Community Psychology, 43,* 134–148.

Bloom, B. L. (1984). *Community mental health: A general introduction.* Monterey, CA: Brooks/Cole.

Buhin, L., & Vera, E. (2009). Preventing racism and promoting social justice: Person-centered and environment-centered interventions. *Journal of Primary Prevention, 30,* 43–59.

Bulhan, H. A. (1985). *Frantz Fanon and the psychology of oppression.* New York: Plenum Press.

Burman, E. (1997). Developmental psychology and its discontents. In D. Fox & I. Prilleltensky (Eds.), *Critical psychology: An introduction* (1st ed., pp. 134–149). London: Sage.

Caplan, G. (1964). *Principles of preventive psychiatry.* New York: Basic Books.

Chamberlain, K., & Murray, M. (2009). Critical health psychology. In D. Fox, I. Prilleltensky, & S. Austin (Eds.), *Critical psychology: An introduction* (2nd ed., pp. 144–158). London: Sage.

Coie, J. D., Watt, N. F., West, S. G., Hawkins, J. D., Asarnow, J. R., Markman, H. J.,... Long, B. (1993). The science of prevention: A conceptual framework and some directions for a national research program. *American Psychologist, 48,* 1013–1022.

Cowen, E. L. (1980). The wooing of primary prevention. *American Journal of Community Psychology, 8,* 258–284.

Cowen, E. L. (1991). In pursuit of wellness. *American Psychologist, 46,* 404–408.

Cowen, E. L. (1994). The enhancement of psychological wellness: Challenges and opportunities. *American Journal of Community Psychology, 22,* 149–179.

Cowen, E. L. (2000). Community psychology and routes to psychological wellness. In J. Rappaport & E. Seidman (Eds.), *Handbook of community psychology* (pp. 79–99). New York: Kluwer Academic.

Darling-Hammond, L. (2010). *The flat world and education: How America's commitment to equity will determine our future.* New York: Teachers College.

Davidson, H., Evans, S., Ganote, C., Henrickson, J., Jacobs-Priebe, L., Jones, D. L.,... Riemer, M. (2006). Power and action in critical theory across disciplines: Implications for critical community psychology. *American Journal of Community Psychology, 38,* 35–49.

Dennis, C.-L., Hodnett, E., Kenton, L., Weston, J., Zupancic, J., Stewart, D. E., & Kiss, A. (2009). Effects of peer support on prevention of postnatal depression among high risk women: Multisite randomized controlled trial. *British Medical Journal, 338,* 1–9.

Diener, E. (2000). Subjective well-being: A science of happiness and a proposal for a national index. *American Psychologist, 55,* 34–43.

Dobles Oropeza, I. (2009). *Memorias del dolor: Consideraciones acerca de las comisiones de la verdad en América Latina*. San José, Costa Rica: Arlekín.

Dobles Oropeza, I., Baltodano Arróliga, S., & Zúñiga, V. (Eds.). (2007). *Psicología de la liberación en el context de la globalización neoliberal*. San José: Universidad de Costa Rica.

Dozois, D. J. A., & Dobson, K. S. (Eds.). (2004). *The prevention of anxiety and depression: Theory, research, and practice*. Washington, DC: American Psychological Association.

Durlak, J. A., & DuPre, E. P. (2008). Implementation matters: A review of research on the influence of implementation on program outcomes and the factors affecting implementation. *American Journal of Community Psychology, 41*, 327–350.

Durlak, J. A., Taylor, R. D., Kawashima, K., Pachan, M. K., DuPre, E. P., Cello, C. I., . . . Weissberg, R. P. (2007). Effects of positive youth development programs on school, family, and community systems. *American Journal of Community Psychology, 39*, 269–286.

Durlak, J., & Wells, A.M. (1997). Primary prevention mental health programs for children and adolescents: A meta-analytic review. *American Journal of Community Psychology, 25*, 115–152.

Durrheim, K., Hook, D., & Riggs, D. (2009). Race and racism. In D. Fox, I. Prilleltensky, & S. Austin (Eds.), *Critical psychology: An introduction* (2nd ed., pp. 197–214). London: Sage.

Ehrenreich, B. (2009). *Bright-sided: How the relentless promotion of positive thinking has undermined America*. New York: Metropolitan Books.

Evans, S., Hanlin, C., & Prilleltensky, I. (2007). Blending ameliorative and transformative approaches in human service organizations: A case study. *Journal of Community Psychology, 35*(3), 329–346.

Facione, P., Scherer, D., & Attig, T. (1978). *Values and society: An introduction to ethics and social philosophy*. Englewood Cliffs, NJ: Prentice Hall.

Fanon, F. (1965). *The wretched of the earth*. New York: Grove Press Inc.

Farrington, D. P., & Welsh, B. C. (2003). Family-based prevention of offending: A meta-analysis. *Australian and New Zealand Journal of Criminology, 36*, 127–151.

Fox, D., & Prilleltensky, I. (Eds.). (1997). *Critical psychology: An introduction* (1st ed.). London: Sage.

Fox, D., Prilleltensky, I., & Austin, S. (Eds.). (2009). *Critical psychology: An introduction* (2nd ed.). London: Sage.

Freire, P. (1970). *Pedagogy of the oppressed*. New York: Seabury Press.

Freire, P. (1973). *Education for critical consciousness*. New York: Seabury Press.

Freire, P. (1994). *Pedagogy of hope: Reliving pedagogy of the oppressed*. New York: Continuum.

Geeraert, L., Van de Noortgate, W., Grietans, H., & Onghenea, P. (2004). The effects of early prevention programs for families with young children at risk for physical child abuse and neglect: A meta-analysis. *Child Maltreatment, 9*, 277–291.

Hage, S., & Kenny, M. (2009). Promoting a social justice approach to prevention: Future directions for training, practice, and research. *Journal of Primary Prevention, 30*, 75–87.

Haney, P., & Durlak, J. A. (1998). Changing self-esteem in children and adolescents: A meta-analytical review. *Journal of Clinical Child and Adolescent Psychology, 27*, 423–433.

Hargreaves, A., & Shirley, D. (2009). *The fourth way: The inspiring future for education change*. Thousand Oaks, CA: Corwin.

Hawe, P., Shiell, A., & Riley, T. (2004). Complex interventions: How "out of control" can a randomized trial be? *British Medical Journal, 328*, 1561–1563.

Heller, K. (1996). Coming of age of prevention science: Comments on the 1994 National Institute of Mental Health-Institute of Medicine prevention reports. *American Psychologist, 51*, 1123–1127.

Henriques, J., Hollway, W., Urwin, C., Venn, C., & Walkerdine, V. (Eds.). (1984). *Changing the subject*. London: Methuen.

Hepburn, A. (2003). *An introduction to critical social psychology*. London: Sage.

Hook, D. (Ed.). (2004). *Introduction to critical psychology*. Cape Town: University of Cape Town Press.

Huygens, I. (2007). *Processes of Pakeha change in response to the Treaty of Waitangi*. Hamilton, New Zealand: University of Waikato.

Jahoda, M. (1958). *Current concepts of positive mental health*. New York: Basic Books.

Karoly, L. A., Kilburn, M. R., & Cannon, J. S. (2005). *Early childhood interventions: Proven results, future promise*. Santa Monica, CA: RAND Corporation.

Kenny, M., Horne, A., Orpinas, P., & Reese, L. (Eds.). (2009). Social justice and the challenge of preventive interventions: An introduction. In. M. Kenny, A. Horne, P. Orpinas, & L. Reese (Eds.), *Realizing social justice: The challenge of preventive interventions* (pp. 3–14). Washington, DC: American Psychological Association.

Keyes, C. L. M. (2007). Promoting and protecting mental health as flourishing: A complementary strategy for improving national mental health. *American Psychologist, 62*, 95–108.

Kivnick, H., & Lymburner, A. (2009). CitySongs: Primary prevention in the field. *Journal of Primary Prevention, 30*, 61–73.

Levy, B., & Sidel, V. (Eds.). (2006). *Social injustice and public health*. New York: Oxford University Press.

Lundahl, B. W., Nimer, J., & Parsons, B. (2006). Preventing child abuse: A meta-analysis of parent training programs. *Research on Social Work Practice, 16*, 251–262.

Luthar, S. S., & Cicchetti, D. (2000). The construct of resilience: Implications for interventions and social policy. *Development and Psychopathology, 12*, 857–885.

Lykes, M. B. (1997). Activist participatory research among the Maya of Guatemala: Constructing meanings from situated knowledge. *Journal of Social Issues, 53*(4), 725–746.

Lykes, M. B. (1999). In collaboration with A. Caba Mateo, J. Chavez Anay, I. A. Laynex Caba, U. Ruiz. Telling stories—rethreading lives: Community education, women's development and social change among the Maya Ixil. *International Journal of Leadership in Education: Theory and Practice, 2*, 207–227.

Lykes, M. B., & Coquillon, E. D. (2009). Psychosocial trauma, poverty, and human rights in communities emerging from war. In D. Fox, I. Prilleltensky, & S. Austin (Eds.), *Critical psychology: An introduction* (2nd ed., pp. 285–299). London: Sage.Lyubomirsky, S. (2007). *The how of happiness*. New York: Penguin.

MacLeod, J., & Nelson, G. (2000). Programs for the promotion of family wellness and the prevention of child maltreatment: A meta-analytic review. *Child Abuse and Neglect, 24*, 1127–1149.

MacMillan, H. L., Wathen, C. D., Barlow, J., Fergusson, D. M., Leventhal, J. M., & Taussig, H. N. (2009). Interventions to prevent child maltreatment and associated impairment. *Lancet, 373*, 250–266.

Manning, M., Homel, R., & Smith, C. (2010). A meta-analysis of the effects of early developmental prevention programs for in at-risk populations on non-health outcomes in adolescence. *Children and Youth Services Review, 32,* 506–519.

Markman, H. J., Renick, M. J., Floyd, F. J., Stanley, S. M., & Clements, M. (1993). Preventing marital distress through communication and conflict management training: A 4- and 5-year follow-up. *Journal of Consulting and Clinical Psychology, 113,* 153–158.

Marmot, M. (2004). *The status syndrome: How social standing affects our health and longevity.* New York: Henry Holt.

Martín-Baró, I. (1994). *Writings for a liberation psychology.* Cambridge, MA: Harvard University Press.

Matthews, C., & Adams, E. (2009). Using a social justice approach to prevent the mental health consequences of heterosexism. *Journal of Primary Prevention, 30,* 11–26.

Melhuish, E., Belsky, J., Leyland, A. H., Barnes, J., & the National Evaluation of Sure Start Research Team. (2008). Effects of fully-established Sure Start Local Programmes on 3-year old children and their families in England: A quasi-experimental observational cross sectional study. *Lancet, 372,* 1641–1647.

Miller, D. (1999). *Principles of social justice.* Cambridge, MA: Harvard University Press.

Moane, G. (2011). *Gender and colonialism: A psychological analysis of oppression and liberation* (2nd ed.). London: Macmillan.

Montero, M. (2007). La problematización como aspecto critic en el proceso de liberación. In I. Dobles Oropeza, S. Baltodano Arróliga, & V. Leandro Zúñiga (Eds.), *Psicología de la liberación en el context de la globalización neoliberal* (pp. 216–229). San José, Costa Rica: Universidad de Costa Rica.

Montero, M. (2010). Community psychology's voyage into complexity: On liberation change and politics. In G. Nelson, & I. Prilleltensky (Eds.), *Community psychology: In pursuit of liberation and well-being* (2nd ed., pp. 519–530). New York: Palgrave.

Morsillo, J., & Prilleltensky, I. (2007). Social Action with Youth: Interventions, Evaluation, and Psychopolitical Validity. *Journal of Community Psychology, 35,* 725–740.

Nader, R. (1965). *Unsafe at any speed: The designed-in dangers of the American automobile.* New York: Grossman.

Nation, M., Crusto, C., Wandersman, A., Kumpfer, K. L., Seybolt, D., Morrissey-Kane, E., & Davino, K. (2003). What works in prevention: Principles of effective prevention programs. *American Psychologist, 58,* 449–456.

Nelson, G., & Prilleltensky, I. (2010). *Community psychology: In pursuit of liberation and well-being* (2nd ed.). New York: Palgrave.

Nelson, G., & Saegert, S. (2009). Housing and quality of life: An ecological perspective. In V. R. Preedy & R. R. Watson (Eds.), *Handbook of disease burdens and quality of life measures* (pp. 3363–3382). Heidelberg, Germany: Springer-Verlag.

Nelson, G., Westhues, A., & MacLeod, J. (2003, December). A meta-analysis of longitudinal research on preschool prevention programs for children. *Prevention and Treatment, 6.* Available at http://journals.apa.org/prevention/volume6/toc-dec18–03.html

Nussbaum, M. (2006). *Frontiers of justice.* Cambridge, MA: Harvard University Press.

Offord, D. R., Kraemer, H. C., Kazdin, A. E., Jensen, P. S., & Harrington, R. (1998). Lowering the burden of suffering from child psychiatric disorder: Trade-offs among clinical, targeted, and universal interventions. *Journal of the American Academy of Child and Adolescent Psychiatry, 37,* 686–694.

Olds, D. Henderson, C. R., Chamberlin, R., & Tatelbaum, R. (1986). Preventing child abuse and neglect: A randomized trail of nurse home visitation. *Pediatrics, 78,* 65–78.

Oliver, K. (2004). *The colonization of psychic space: A psychoanalytic social theory of oppression.* Minneapolis: University of Minnesota Press.

Parker, I. (2007). *Revolution in psychology: Alienation to emancipation.* London: Pluto Press.

Pawelski, J., & Prilleltensky, I. (2005). That at which all things aim: Wellness, happiness, and the ethics of organizational life. In R. Giacalone (Ed.). *Positive psychology in business ethics and corporate social responsibility* (pp. 191–208). Charlotte, NC: InfoAge.

Payne, C. (2009). *So much reform, so little change: The persistence of failure in urban schools.* Cambridge, MA: Harvard University Press.

Perry, M. J., & Albee, G. W. (1994). On the "science of prevention." *American Psychologist, 49,* 1087–1088.

Peters, R. DeV., Bradshaw, A. J., Petrunka, K., Nelson, G., Herry, Y., Craig, W.,... Rossiter, M. (2010). The "Better Beginnings, Better Futures" ecological, community-based early childhood prevention project: Findings from Grade 3 to Grade 9. *Monographs of the Society for Research in Child Development, 75*(3), 1–176.

Prilleltensky, I. (1994). *The morals and politics of psychology: Psychological discourse and the status quo.* Albany: State University of New York Press.

Prilleltensky, I. (2005). Promoting well-being: Time for a paradigm shift in health and human services. *Scandinavian Journal of Public Health, 33,* 53–60.

Prilleltensky, I. (2008). Migrant well-being is a multilevel, dynamic, and value dependent phenomenon. *American Journal of Community Psychology, 42*(3–4), 359–364.

Prilleltensky, I., & Nelson, G. (2002). *Doing psychology critically: Making a difference in diverse settings.* New York: Palgrave.

Prilleltensky, I., Nelson, G., Sanchez, L. A. (2000). Value-based smoking prevention program with Latin American Youth: Program evaluation. *Journal of Ethnic and Cultural Diversity in Social Work, 9*(1–2), 97–117.

Prilleltensky, I., & Prilleltensky, O. (2006). *Promoting well-being: Linking personal, organizational, and community change.* Hoboken, NJ: Wiley.

Prinz, R. J., Sanders, M. R., Shapiro, C. J., Whitaker, D. J., & Lutzker, J. R. (2009). Population-base prevention of child maltreatment: The U.S. Triple P system population trial. *Prevention Science, 10,* 1–12.

Quiñones Rosado, R. (2007). *Consciousness in action: Toward an integral psychology of liberation and transformation.* Caguas, Puerto Rico: ilé Publications.

Rappaport, J. (1981). In praise of paradox: A social policy of empowerment over prevention. *American Journal of Community Psychology, 9,* 1–25.

Rath, T., & Harter, J. (2010). *Well being: The five essential elements.* New York: Gallup Press.Ravitch, D. (2010). *The death and life of the great American school system: How testing and choice are undermining education.* Basic Books.

Reynolds, A. J., Ou, S.-R., & Topitzes, J. W. (2004). Paths of effects of early childhood intervention on educational attainment and delinquency: A confirmatory analysis of the Chicago Child-Parent Centers. *Child Development, 75,* 1299–1328.

Reynolds, A. J., & Temple, J. A. (2008). Cost-effective early childhood development programs from preschool to third grade. *Annual Review of Clinical Psychology, 4,* 109–139.

Robinson, J. L. (2000). Are there implications for prevention research from studies of resilience? *Child Development, 71,* 570–572.

Roosa, M. W. (2000). Some thoughts about resilience vs. positive development, main effects vs. interactions, and the value of resilience. *Child Development, 71,* 567–569.

Rutter, M. (1987). Psychosocial resilience and protective mechanisms. *American Journal of Orthopsychiatry, 57,* 316–331.

Sanders, M., Ralph, A., Sofronoff, K., Gardiner, P., Thompson, R., Dwyer, S., & Bidwell, K. (2008). Every family: A population approach to reducing behavioral and emotional problems in children making the transition to school. *Journal of Primary Prevention, 29,* 197–222.

Sandler, I. (2001). Quality and ecology of diversity as common mechanisms of risk and resilience. *American Journal of Community Psychology, 29,* 19–55.

Seligman, M. E. P. (2002). *Authentic happiness.* New York: Free Press.

Schweinhart, L. J. (2005). *Lifetime effects: The High/Scope Perry Preschool study through age 40.* Ypsilanti, MI: High/Scope Educational Research Foundation.

Shinn, M., & Toohey, S. M. (2003). Community contexts of human welfare. *Annual Review of Psychology, 54,* 427–459.

Stevens, G. (2007). The international emergence and development of community psychology. In N. Duncan, B. Bowman, A. Naidoo, J. Pillay, & V. Roos (Eds.), *Community psychology: Analysis, context and action* (pp. 27–50). Cape Town: University of Cape Town Press.

Teo, T. (1998). Klaus Holzkamp and the rise and decline of German critical psychology. *History of Psychology, 1,* 235–253.

Teo, T. (2005). *The critique of psychology: From Kant to postcolonial theory.* New York: Springer.

Teo, T. (2009). Philosophical concerns in critical psychology. In D. Fox, I. Prilleltensky, & S. Austin (Eds.), *Critical psychology: An introduction* (2nd ed., pp. 36–53). London: Sage.

Tolman, C. W. (1994). *Psychology, society, and subjectivity: An introduction to German critical psychology.* London: Routledge.

US Institute of Medicine (1994). Reducing risk for mental disorders: Frontiers for preventive intervention research. Washington, DC: National Academy Press.

Walkerdine, V. (Ed.). (2002). *Challenging subjects: Critical psychology for a new millennium.* New York: Palgrave.

Watkins, M., & Shulman, H. (2008). *Toward psychologies of liberation.* New York: Palgrave.

Wilkinson, R., & Pickett, K. (2009). *The spirit level: Why more equal societies almost always do better.* New York: Penguin.

Wolfe, D. A., Wekerle, C., Scott, K., Straatman, A., Grasley, C., & Reitzel-Jaffe, D. (2003). Dating violence prevention with at-risk youth: A controlled outcome evaluation. *Journal of Consulting and Clinical Psychology, 71,* 279–291.

Zielinski, D. S., Eckenrode, J., & Olds, D. L. (2009). Nurse home visitation and the prevention of child maltreatment: Impact on the timing of official reports. *Development and Psychopathology, 21,* 441–453.

PART 2

Best Practices in the Prevention of Behavioral, Emotional, and Health Problems

CHAPTER

11 Understanding and Preventing Adolescent Bullying, Sexual Violence, and Dating Violence

Dorothy L. Espelage *and* Sabina Low

Abstract

In this chapter, the social ecological framework was used to identify unique and shared risk and protective factors of bullying experiences (victimization, perpetration), sexual violence, and dating violence perpetration in adolescents. Individual predictors included sex, race, anger, empathy, callousness, and impulsivity. Family violence, parenting style, and parental monitoring are discussed as risk factors. Attitudes and behaviors of friendship also contribute to the onset and continuation of these outcomes. Teacher's attitudes and school climate play a very important role in exacerbating bullying and sexual violence, but can also serve as protective agents. When prevention programs are designed or selected from the many marketed programs, it is important for consumers to consider the extent to which the programs include many of the risk and protective factors.

Key Words: school bullying, dating violence, homophobic teasing, sexual harassment

Bullying, sexual, and dating violence among adolescents are all major public health problems that occur at relatively high rates and demand attention to alleviate the considerable suffering they cause (Foshee & Matthew, 2007; Espelage & Horne, 2008, for reviews). These problems undoubtedly share some developmental correlates, and evidence is emerging that these problems co-occur among early adolescents (Basile, Espelage, Rivers, McMahon, & Simon, 2009; Espelage & Horne, 2008). It is now widely recognized that adolescents' liability for aggression, delinquent acts, risky sexual behavior, substance use, and violence reflect age-dynamic developmental trajectories engendered by multiple, cumulative risk processes operating at psychological, social, and broader ecological levels (e.g., Capaldi, Stoolmiller, Clark, & Owen, 2002; Crouter & Booth, 2006; Dishion & Patterson, 2006; Mayes & Suchman, 2006; Tartar et al., 1999).

Social-Ecological Framework of Bullying, Sexual Violence, and Dating Aggression

A social ecological framework has been used to explore the risk and protective factors of bullying, sexual, and dating violence, whereby child and adolescent behavior is shaped by a range of nested contextual systems, including family, peers, and school environments (Bronfenbrenner, 1977, 1979; Heise, 1998; Centers for Disease Control and Prevention [CDC], 2004). The ecological perspective provides a conceptual framework for investigating the independent and combined impact of these social contexts and dynamic, transactional influences on behavioral development. The microsystem includes structures with which children and adolescents have direct contact, such as families, peers, and schools. The mesosystem, another component of the ecological framework, comprises the interrelations among microsystems. This ecological framework has been applied to the conceptualization of bullying perpetration and victimization, and highlights reciprocal influences on bullying behaviors between individual, family, school, peer group, community, and society (Espelage & Swearer, 2003; Garbarino & deLara, 2002; Swearer & Doll, 2001). In this chapter, the social ecological framework will be used to identify unique and shared risk and protective factors of bullying experiences (victimization, perpetration), sexual violence and dating violence perpetration. When prevention programs are designed or selected from the many marketed programs, it is important for consumers to consider the extent to which the programs include many of the risk and protective factors reviewed in this chapter.

Bullying

Definition

Olweus (1978) first described bullying as "mobbing," where a group or individual teases or harasses another individual. More recently, Frey, Hirschstein, Edstrom, and Snell (2009) described bullying as a social construct that disrupts social connections among students. Further, Ross and Horner (2009) summarized the many definitions that are found in the literature:

> Common definitions of *bullying* involve repeated acts of aggression, intimidations, or coercion against a victim who is weaker in terms of physical size, psychological or social power, or other factors that result in a notable power differential. (p. 748)

This chapter will focus on school-based bullying, however, in a national survey of 1,588 youth between the ages of 10–15 years, Ybarra, Diener-West, and Leaf (2007) report that one third of youth who had been bullied at school were harassed online. This is an important direction for future research in this area.

Prevalence and Negative Impacts

School bullying is not a local problem to the United States; rather it is recognized worldwide (Espelage & Swearer, 2003). Observational studies have shown that as many as 30% of students are involved in bullying as either the bully or victim during their school years (Frey & Hirschstein, 2009). Hymel and Swearer (2010) recently reported that 35% of students indicated being bullied at least once in the last 2 months with as many as 11% of those sampled reporting being bullied more than 2 or 3 times in the last 2 months. Moreover, some research has found that bullying roles remain relatively stable across time. In a sample of 516 middle school students, Espelage, Bosworth, and Simon (2001) found that individuals who perpetrated bullying characteristics continued to do so across multiple time-points. Similarly, Sourander, Helstela, Helenius, and Piha (2000) conducted an 8-year longitudinal study that found bullying at age 8 was associated with bullying at age 16.

Although the pervasiveness of bullying is cause for concern, the negative consequences of bullying are indisputable. Researchers have indicated that bullying has been linked to anger and misconduct (Bosworth et al., 1999) and being criminal and delinquent (Olweus, 2002). Victimization, on the other hand, has been linked to poor physical health (Rigby, 1999), low self-esteem (Rigby & Slee, 1993), depression (Sweeting, Young, West, & Der, 2006), anxiety (Swearer et al., 2001), and school avoidance (Kochenderfer & Ladd, 1996). Indeed the negative impacts of bullying and being bullied are pervasive and dramatic.

Individual Risk Factors

Certain individual characteristics heighten one's risk for being victimized. In demographic terms, boys are more often victimized than girls (Espelage & Holt, 2001; Kumpulainen et al., 1998), although this depends somewhat on the form of victimization; whereas boys are more likely to experience physical bullying victimization (e.g., being hit), girls are more likely to be targets of indirect victimization (e.g., social exclusion) (Jeffrey, Miller, & Linn, 2001). In one of the few studies addressing the influence of race on bullying, Black students reported less victimization than White or Hispanic youth (Nansel et al., 2001). However, Juvonen and colleagues (2003) found that Black middle school youth were more likely to be categorized as bullies and bully-victims than White students. Another study found that Hispanic students reported somewhat more bullying than Black and White youth (Nansel et al., 2001). However, it is likely that race/ethnicity is not directly related to bullying involvement, but rather there is a more nuanced association that is influenced by factors such as the school environment. For instance, in a relatively recent review of the literature, youth report less victimization in classrooms in which there is greater ethnic diversity and no racial/ethnic group is in a numerical minority (Graham, 2006).

Empathy has consistently been found to be negatively associated with aggression and positively associated with prosocial skills (Feshbach & Feshbach, 1982; Kaukiainen et al., 1999; Mehrabian, 1997; Miller & Eisenberg, 1988). The inverse correlation between aggression and empathy was found to be stronger in studies that focused on the emotional component of empathy than in studies in which cognitive empathy was measured (Endresen & Olweus, 2001; Mehrabian, 1997). This might be especially relevant in the case of bullying, in which the aggressors are able to understand others' emotional states without sharing the victims' feelings. Bullies' careful selection of victims who are vulnerable and disliked by their peers reflects good perspective-taking. However, the fact that they use violence to achieve their goals, disregarding the pain that they inflict on their victims, suggests that for some youth, perspective-taking does little to inhibit aggression. More recently, Nickerson, Mele, and Princiotta (2008) evaluated the association among parental attachment, empathy, and gender to predict the behavior of 105 middle school students who reported being either defenders (intervened to stop bullying) or outsiders (not involved or stood by passively). The results indicated that greater empathy was associated with being a defender rather than an outsider, even after controlling for parental attachment.

In a study of 347 Cypriot adolescents (12 to 18 years), significant associations were found among *callous-unemotional* (CU) traits and bullying, victimization, and proactive and reactive aggression (Fanti, Frick, & Georgiou, 2008). Specifically, youth who reported more callous and uncaring traits also reported more bullying perpetration, even after controlling for gender and victimization. In addition, youth were classified as being in one of four groups (low on bully and victim scales group, victim only group, bullying only group, bully/victim group) and their callous and uncaring scores were compared. Higher scores on the callous subscale were associated with a greater likelihood of being in the bully/victim group than the low group, the bully only group, and the victim only group. Greater scores on the uncaring subscale were associated with an increased chance of being in the bully only group than being in the low group or victim only group.

Anger and *hostility* have consistently emerged as important correlates of bullying. In several studies of bullying behavior (e.g., name calling, teasing, threatening), anger was the strongest predictor of bullying cross-sectionally and longitudinally (Bosworth et al., 1999; Espelage et al., 2001). *Impulsivity* also plays an important role in bullying perpetration and victimization. In a prospective study of factors that predicted bullying over a 4-month period, Espelage et al. (2001), found a significant association between impulsivity and a behavioral measure of bullying (e.g., name calling, teasing, threatening other students) among a sample of 214 sixth-grade students.

Finally, bullying is strongly associated with both alcohol and drug use (Berthold & Hoover, 2000; Pepler et al., 2002). In their study of fifth to eighth graders (mean age 12.7 years), Pepler and colleagues (2002) found that for both boys and girls, bullies were almost five times more likely to report alcohol use and seven times more likely to report drug use than nonbullies. In their middle school sample, Berthold and Hoover (2000) found that youth who bullied others were also more likely to smoke, chew tobacco, and drink alcohol than students who did not bully. In addition to these findings, students who bully are not the only students who are at risk for alcohol and drug use. Alcohol consumption appears to be related to victimization as well (Thompson, Sims, Kingree, & Windle, 2008). The relation between substance use and victimization is particularly evident for victims of bullying who are aggressive (i.e., bully-victims). For instance, in one study of 7th- through 11th-grade students, aggressive victims and aggressive nonvictims reported more alcohol and drug use than nonaggressive victims and nonaggressive nonvictims (Brockenbrough, Cornell, & Loper, 2002). Bystanders (i.e., individuals who observe bullying) are also at risk for substance use (Rivers, Poteat, Noret, & Ashurst, 2009). Overall, involvement in bullying is clearly related to substance use.

Contextual Influences

Family, peer, and school contexts can exert positive or negative influences on bullying involvement, and are critical to measure when trying to understand bullying dynamics.

FAMILY CONTEXT

With respect to the *family context*, bullies, as a group, report that their parents are authoritarian, condone "fighting back," use physical punishment, lack warmth, and display indifference to their children (Baldry & Farrington, 2000; Loeber & Dishion, 1984). Quality of parent-child relations may also play a role. Children who had insecure, anxious-avoidant, or anxious-resistant attachments when 18 months old were more likely than children with secure attachments to become involved in bullying at ages 4 and 5 (Troy & Sroufe, 1987). Espelage et al. (2000) examined the bullying behaviors and parental styles of 558 middle school students. They found that parents who use physical discipline in the home are more likely to have children who bully. Other studies have shown that the strategies families use to resolve conflict in the home may influence bullying behavior. Children who perceive fair resolutions to conflicts with their parents are less likely to engage in bullying behaviors (Brubacher, Fondacaro, Brank, Brown, & Miller, 2009), while those who come from families using poor conflict resolution strategies are more likely to engage in bullying behaviors (Duncan, 2004). It seems that the values parents endorse and how they communicate these values affects the likelihood that their children will be involved in bullying and/or victimization.

Child maltreatment is also associated with involvement in the bullying dynamic in general (i.e., role as a bully, victim, or bully-victim), being the victim of maltreatment is closely related to victimization or victimization with aggressive tendencies (Bowes et al., 2009). Fang and Corso's (2008) study lends support for their hypothesis that different types of child abuse (i.e., sexual, physical) and neglect are related to the perpetration of these actions as individuals approach adulthood. The general consensus is that experiencing parental abuse places youth at risk for perpetration of bullying through adolescence and beyond.

Adolescents who report high rates of bullying tend to have problematic relationships with their parents that are typically characterized by conflict (Pepler, Jiang, Craig, & Connolly, 2008) and ambivalent relationships with their family members (Connolly & O'Moore, 2003). Research has found an indirect relationship between mother and father disengagement and bullying in a sample of adolescents (Flouri & Buchanan, 2003). Thus, exposure to parental conflict puts youth at increased risk for bullying at school since parents or caregivers are modeling ways to be aggressive toward others (Bowes et al., 2009). Middle school students receiving less parental supervision have been found to be significantly more likely to bully others (Espelage et al., 2000). Adolescent boys 13–18 years of age involved in indirect bullying either as bullies or bully-victims reported receiving less parental supervision than indirect victims and students uninvolved in bullying (Marini et al., 2006). Thus, low parental supervision appears to put youth at risk for bullying others. Overall, the evidence stresses the importance of considering family relationships in conjunction with the quality of relationships between the parents and youth who are at-risk for bullying involvement.

PEER CONTEXT

Peer affiliation and socialization is an instrumental aspect to explaining involvement in bullying perpetration (Pellegrini & Van Ryzin, 2011; Salmivalli, Lagerspetz, Bjorkqvist, Osterman, & Kaukiainen, 1996). Consequently, it is vital to closely examine peer groups to fully understand the bullying dynamic. Three theories that shed light on the peer group's effect on aggression and bullying are the dominance theory, homophily hypothesis, and attraction theory. The dominance theory posits that bullying can be perceived as an avenue to obtain a higher social status (i.e., dominance) within a group (Pellegrini, 2002). However, bullying may result from an underlying mechanism to assimilate to the behavior of one's friends or those peers who are highly influential in the school setting. This assimilation is captured by the term "homophily," which means that individuals who associate with one another tend to be similar to one another in attitudes and behavior (Kandel, 1978). Results of one study suggest that the homophily hypothesis pertains to less severe aggressive behaviors for adolescents, such as teasing (Espelage, Holt, & Henkel, 2003). Lastly, the attraction theory states that adolescents are likely to pursue relationships with peers who reflect personality traits or behaviors indicative of independence, such as aggression, instead of with peers who represent adult-like values and conformity (Bukowski, Sippola, & Newcomb, 2000). These theories represent the myriad of explanations for how adolescents navigate peer relationships, which undoubtedly influence their involvement in bullying situations.

Within a bullying context, peers play a powerful role by encouraging aggressive behaviors, decreasing the likelihood of victimization, and buffering the adverse psychological effects that are associated with victimization. The literature indicates that peer influences are at least partially to blame for bullying behaviors. Observational studies conducted by Canadian researchers provided rich empirical data of how students participated or did not participate in bullying episodes on the playground (Craig & Pepler, 1995, 1997; O'Connell, Pepler, & Craig, 1999). It was evident that bullying was a group phenomenon because peers were present 85% of the time (Craig & Pepler, 1997), peers reinforced bullies' behaviors 81% of the time (Craig & Pepler, 1995), and intervened to help the victim only 11% of the time (Craig & Pepler, 1997). Salmivalli (2010) developed descriptors for the various roles that students take during bullying episodes, including reinforcers, assisters, and passive bystanders. Furthermore, Salmivalli, Huttunen, and Lagerspetz (1997) found that categories of students who were involved in the perpetration of bullying (i.e., bullies, assistants, and reinforcers) were members of bigger peer groups than those who defended the victims, were uninvolved, or were victimized themselves.

Much more research needs to be conducted on the role of the bystander and the reasons why onlookers do not intervene to assist the victim. Rigby and Johnson (2006) studied the characteristics of youth that are willing to intervene in bullying situations. In this study, four hundred Australian primary and secondary students viewed a videotape of a bullying situation and were subsequently asked what they would do. Multiple regression analysis indicated that greater willingness to intervene was associated with being younger, having rarely or never bullied others, having been victimized, and having a positive attitude toward victims. In addition, students were more likely to intervene if they believed their friends expected them to support victims. These findings suggested that friends' attitudes weighed heavily in a student's decision to intervene, highlighting the need for research that addresses peer influence. This was further supported in a study of seventh and eighth graders in which multilevel analyses indicated that student's willingness to intervene to help a victim was associated with less bullying in one's peer group (Espelage, Green, & Polanin, 2012). These findings suggest that it is important to explore predictors of attitudes and behaviors across multiple levels, including individual and peer groups.

Several studies have investigated the effects of friendships and popularity of students who bully. Bullies tend to have an easier time making friends than victims and bully-victims (Nansel et al., 2001), and spend more time with other bullies than other students (Espelage & Holt, 2001). Interestingly, Espelage and Holt (2001) also found that students who bullied others engaged in this type of aggression at levels that were similar to those of their friends. Furthermore, deviant peers often encourage bullying through their willingness to engage in negative behaviors in general. For instance, Espelage et al. (2000) found that individuals who were more likely to damage property, fight, and interact with gangs were also more likely to perpetrate bullying in early adolescence.

Although peers can have a negative influence on youth who bully by encouraging these behaviors, peers can also serve as positive role models and buffer the negative outcomes associated with bullying. Even perceptions of students' social support are linked to their bully/victim status. For instance, Holt and Espelage (2007) found that bully-victims and victims report lower levels of social support than bullies and uninvolved peers. Additionally, the results of one study demonstrated that having a close friend decreased the likelihood that a student would be victimized and prevented the escalation of victimization for students who were already the targets of peer aggression (Hodges, Boivin, Vitaro, & Bukowski, 1999). Similarly, being liked by peers appears to serve as a protective factor against victimization (Pellegrini, Bartini, & Brooks, 1999).

Even though the quantity of friendships decreases one's likelihood of being victimized, the behaviors and qualities of the victims' friends matter more than the number of friends alone. Supporting this notion, a study by Hodges, Malone, and Perry (1997) found that students who were bullied were less likely to be targeted if their friends exhibited externalizing behaviors instead of behaviors or traits that could be interpreted as "weak." These authors speculated that externalizing peers might be more likely than internalizing peers to stand up to bullies and actively offer protection. Moreover, peers can be excellent sources of emotional and psychological support. For instance, peer support can serve as a protective factor for those who are at risk for experiencing negative psychological outcomes by promoting psychological well-being (McCreary, Slavin, & Berry, 1996). Furthermore, peer support bolsters self-esteem in adolescents (Colarossi & Eccles, 2003) and helps alleviate stress (Hartup, 1996). Thus, peer support and friendships can positively affect the lives of students who are victimized.

SCHOOL CONTEXT

Bullying perpetration and victimization occurs at the highest rate within schools in comparison to other environments (Ybarra, Espelage, & Martin, 2010). Thus, it makes sense that bullying prevention needs to be informed by how schools contribute to bullying perpetration. School climate has long been recognized as an important factor in student outcomes, resulting in the identification of a number of factors that affect and are affected by school climate. Anderson's (1982) comprehensive review of the literature identified several important factors influencing school climate. These factors were categorized into three groups: *milieu* (i.e., characteristics of the individuals and groups in the school); *social system* (i.e., the variables that address the relationships within the school); and *culture* (i.e., variables that include group beliefs and values).

School personnel play a key role in creating a positive or negative school climate. Recent research suggests that teachers may actually tolerate bullying, resulting in increases in bullying behaviors (Yoneyama & Naito, 2003). Teachers have also been found to be inaccurate in estimating the amount of bullying that occurs in their schools (Holt & Keyes, 2004). Additionally, teachers may lack knowledge about how to effectively respond when they observe bullying (Espelage & Swearer, 2003). Teachers' abilities to respond to bullying have implications for student perceptions of effective interventions. Adair, Dixon, Moore, and Sutherland (2000) found that almost half of the students surveyed believed that bullying could not be stopped. When students observe a lack of awareness and responsiveness on the part of teachers, they may feel hopeless and believe that effective solutions are impossible (Dupper & Meyer-Adams, 2002; Houndoumadi & Pateraki, 2001). Unnever and Cornell (2003) also found that the majority of students felt that their peers and their teachers would not stop bullying.

Emerging research lends support to the notion that staff attitudes toward bullying impact their willingness to intervene in bullying episodes. For instance, elementary school teachers who believed that bullying is normative behavior were less likely to intervene than teachers who did not hold this belief and were also less likely to involve parents in dealing with bullying situations (Kochenderfer-Ladd & Pelletier, 2007). Similarly, among elementary through high school staff, staff who endorsed the statement that "bullying is a part of life that everyone has to go through" were more likely to also think that if they intervened it would make the bullying situation worse (Bradshaw, Sawyer, & O'Brennan, 2007). Through developing a better sense of how school personnel's attitudes directly and indirectly influencing bullying, more successful prevention and intervention programs can be developed.

Finally, bullying has a significant impact on perceptions of safety at school. Nansel and colleagues (2003) found that victims and bully-victims in the sixth grade perceived their school climate as more negative than bullies or uninvolved students. Glew and colleagues (2005) found that among third, fourth, and fifth graders, both victims and bully-victims were more likely than bystanders to report feeling that they do not belong at school. They also found that bullies, victims, and bully-victims were more likely than bystanders to report that they felt unsafe at school (Glew et al., 2005).

Research has explored a number of academic factors that may relate to the experience of being involved in bullying, such as connectedness to school. This is an important factor to consider, since school belonging has been found to predict academic competence for students who bully or are victims of bullying (Ma, Phelps, Lerner, & Lerner, 2009). When teachers were asked to rate their students on school engagement, students identified as bullies, victims, or bully-victims were rated as being highly disengaged from school, with bully-victims receiving the highest school disengagement ratings (Juvonen et al., 2003). Within a longitudinal study, fifth- and sixth-grade students identified as bullies self-reported lower rates of school belonging compared to students uninvolved in bullying (Ma et al., 2009). Students identified as victims reported rates of school belonging that were similar to those reported by uninvolved students. Similarly, among children 10–11 years of age, the experience of being victimized was only moderately related to low school belonging (Beran, 2008). However, it was theorized that being victimized leads to stress, which may inhibit some children's ability to concentrate, thus decreasing school engagement. In fact, a study that compared an experimental school, which received an intervention that successfully reduced the number of discipline referrals, to a matched control school found that students' scores on measures of academic achievement increased within the experimental school but not the control school (Twemlow et al., 2001). Furthermore, within the experimental school, teachers reported that victims of bullying became less withdrawn and more verbal within the classroom after the intervention. In summary, being involved in bullying may decrease academic engagement, particularly for bullies and bully-victims, and decreases in bullying and other forms of violence within schools may lead to improved academic outcomes for all students.

Summary of Risk and Protective Factors for Bullying Perpetration

Several risk and protective factors have consistently emerged as predictors of bullying perpetration and victimization across early to late adolescence.

These risk and protective factors are important to consider across the social-ecological domains as we examine the shared and nonshared characteristics with the outcomes of sexual violence and dating violence into late adolescence. That is, individual-level risk factors may not be sufficient in explaining the elaboration of bullying behavior—peer and school contexts may support and amplify these behaviors by normalizing and reinforcing these patterns of social interaction. Risk factors for bullying perpetration include individual characteristics such as being male, family violence, less empathy, anger disposition, positive attitudes toward bullying; in some cases perpetration is also associated with other forms of delinquency. Protective factors include the ability to have secure attachments with parents and teachers and receiving positive social support. Peer group affiliation also plays an important role as members appear to socialize one another to bully others through group norms that support bullying perpetration. Teacher and school characteristics also serve as both risk and protective factors.

Sexual Violence

The problem of sexual violence and harassment in adolescent interpersonal relationships is approaching pandemic proportions in part because the violence and the harassment have been normalized. Sexual harassment in schools is a public event, with witnesses and bystanders, and permission to proceed is granted by the presence of adults who look on and do not intervene (Stein, 1993, 1995, 1999). Moreover, first occurrences of sexual harassment/violence among students seem to be happening at younger and younger ages (Stein, 2005). Sexual violence in schools, which often gets named as something else in an effort to cast it as benign (e.g., the use of the term "bullying"), frequently is not reported to law enforcement or school officials. When it is surveyed, it is not disaggregated from incidents of physical violence, so the incidents of sexual violence are often classified as "physical violence." Moreover, the well-documented rise of teen dating violence (sometimes called "intimate partner violence") as revealed though the Youth Risk Behavior Survey may also lend evidence to an overall increase in teen violence, whether it is restricted to dating partners or not (Brown, Chesney-Lind, & Stein, 2007; Stein, 2005).

Definitions

Sexual violence is defined as "nonconsensual completed or attempted contact between the penis and the vulva or the penis and the anus involving penetration, however slight; nonconsensual contact between the mouth and the penis, vulva, or anus; nonconsensual penetration of the anal or genital opening of another person by a hand, finger, or other object; nonconsensual intentional touching, either directly or through the clothing, of the genitalia, anus, groin, breast, inner thigh, or buttocks; or nonconsensual non-contact acts of a sexual nature such as voyeurism and verbal or behavioral sexual harassment" (CDC, 2004, p. 1). All the above acts also qualify as sexual violence if they are committed against someone who is unable to consent or refuse.

Sexual harassment at school is a form of sex discrimination under federal law Title IX (1972) and is defined as unwelcome sexual advances, requests for sexual favors, and other verbal or physical contact of a sexual nature when the conduct is sufficiently severe, persistent, or pervasive to limit a student's ability to participate in or benefit from the education program, or to create a hostile or abusive educational environment. Sexual harassment in schools is behavior that interferes with the right to receive an equal educational opportunity (Stein, 1999, citing *Davis v. Monroe County Bd of Education*, 1999). After decades of battling for recognition of the problem, the Supreme Court's decision in Davis established that peer-to-peer sexual harassment exists among our youth, that the adults are liable for damages, and it is incumbent on school districts to prevent the illegal conduct.

Prevalence

Research on peer-to-peer sexual harassment in K-12 education has been underway since the late 1970s and more formally undertaken in the 1990s through survey research. Sexual harassment in schools ranges from jokes, comments, graffiti, sexually degrading skits, and attempted sexual assault and rape. These behaviors are often conducted in public, sometimes in front of adults and school personnel who do not intervene. Such reactions from adults give students, be they witnesses, targets or perpetrators, the impression that sexual harassment conduct is considered normal and appropriate. Permission to proceed with harassing, violence, and battering behaviors in private becomes normalized and appropriate in part because it is tolerated in public and thus creates a climate of tolerance for sexual harassment (Stein, 2005).

Tolman and colleagues hypothesize that sexual harassment is a dress rehearsal for heterosexual relationships; that "there is a slippery slope from incidents of sexual harassment, which are normalized, to violence in a simultaneously occurring early teen dating experiences" (Tolman, Spencer, Rosen-Reynoso, & Porche, 2003, p. 162). The lines between flirting and dominance and aggression may be hard to distinguish. Fineran and Bennett's research (1999) links "sexual harassment and beliefs about male power embedded in compulsory heterosexuality, which allows, even encourages, developing boys and girls to be socialized into the established hierarchy of males over females and to learn to grow comfortable with it" (Tolman et al., 2003, p. 162). Victims of sexual harassment have significantly poorer mental and physical health, more trauma symptoms, and greater school avoidance than those not sexually harassed (Fineran & Gruber, 2004; Larkin, 1994). Girl victims fare consistently worse on such measures (American Association of University Women Educational Foundation [AAUW], 2001; Fineran & Gruber, 2004); further, sexual risk behavior, pregnancy, and suicidality also are associated with victimization in girls (Silverman, Raj, Mucci, & Hathaway, 2001; Silverman et al., 2004).

Sexual harassment surveys attest to the pervasive problem facing students. Two national scientific surveys were commissioned by the American Association of University Women (AAUW) in 1993 and 2001, both conducted by Harris Interactive. The earlier survey used a random sample of 1,600 boys and girls (grades 8 through 11) in 79 public schools, while the more recent 2001 survey was comprised of a sample of 2,064 students, again in grades 8–11. Both surveys found sexual harassment to be widespread, with 83% of females and 79% of male students indicating that they were sexually harassed (AAUW, 2001).

Results from the 2001 AAUW study yielded additional information about sexual harassment within secondary schools and supported findings from previous investigations. For instance, 70% of students surveyed had experienced nonphysical sexual harassment (e.g., sexual rumor spreading) and 58% of students had experienced physical sexual harassment (e.g., having clothing pulled off or down) at some point during their lives. As such, consistent with findings from the earlier 1993 AAUW survey, less serious and subtler forms of sexual harassment appear to occur most frequently. Furthermore, adolescents reported that nonphysical and physical sexual harassment occurred most often at the hands of their peers (76% and 82% respectively); in contrast, 7% of students noted harassment by teachers in each of these arenas. However, in the 2001 survey, 38% of students reported being sexually harassed by teachers and other school employees (AAUW, p. 5). Moreover, 2001 survey results showed an increase from 1993 both in awareness about, and incidents of, sexual harassment, yet by 2001, students had come to accept sexual harassment as a fact of school life (AAUW, pp. 4, 32).

Findings from the AAUW study revealed that 38% of girls reported having first been sexually harassed in sixth grade. Further, the few empirical studies of sexual harassment among middle school students have indicated that the rates of sexual harassment increase throughout middle school and into high school (McMaster, Connolly, Pepler, & Craig, 2002; Pellegrini, 2001). Sexual violence and sexual harassment data on middle school students in sixth and seventh grades is sparse. The two main data sources on relationship violence in schools (the YRBS and national surveys on sexual harassment in schools) do not cover students younger than eighth grade. However, other research suggests that adolescents begin to experience sexual harassment and sexual violence as early as age 12 (sixth or seventh grade), suggesting that prevention programs should target younger middle school students (Schewe, 2002).

Sexual violence statistics also comes from the annual reports of nationwide school crime and safety administered by the National Center for Education Statistics and Bureau of Justice Statistics (DeVoe et al., 2004). In a category entitled "violent incidents," which includes items such as rape, sexual battery, and physical attack, 20% of all US schools reported one or more serious violent incidents, with 14% of elementary schools, 29% of middle schools, and 29% of high schools reporting "violent incidents." For the category of rape or attempted rape, a total of 143 incidents in 126 middle schools, representing 1% of all schools, were reported. A total of 650 incidents of sexual battery occurred in 520 elementary schools, representing 1% of all schools. A total of 582 middle schools reported 1,141 incidents of sexual battery, representing 4% of schools nationwide (Miller & Chandler, 2003).

Risk and Protective Factors for Sexual Violence Perpetration

Although sexual harassment/violence is a pervasive problem for middle and high school students, the individual characteristics of some students may put them at increased risk for perpetration. In terms of gender differences, it appears that more boys than girls harass their peers (AAUW, 1993, 2001).

Among girls, more African American students (63%) report harassing peers than did Hispanic or White females (50% each). Conversely, among boys, African American and White students report similar rates of engaging in harassment (67% and 66% respectively), whereas Hispanic boys indicated having engaged in lower levels of harassment (56%). With respect to specific manifestations of sexual harassment, White boys are more likely to call a peer gay or lesbian than boys of other races/ethnicities, and Black boys are more likely to touch, grab, or pinch someone sexually than boys of other races/ethnicities (AAUW, 2001).

Contextual Influences on Sexual Violence Perpetration

Very little is known about contextual influences on sexual harassment/violence in school settings. Studies are needed to explore peer, family, and school influences on sexual violence perpetration. Drawing from what is known about sexual harassment generally, there is reason to believe that these contexts operate in a similar fashion as with bullying. In terms of family context, drawing on the bullying literature and social learning theory, it is probable that children from families that condone any type of aggressive behaviors (and more specifically those of a sexual nature), will be more apt to sexually harass their peers (Baldry, 2003; Jacobsen & Straker, 1982; Shields & Cicchetti, 2001). It also might be that, as is the case with bullying, youth with secure attachments and adequate parental support are less likely to be involved in sexual harassment, potentially protected by personality features derived as from positive parental relationships. With respect to peer context, the AAUW studies (1993, 2001) revealed that perpetrators of sexual harassment felt their behaviors were justified because "all kids do it" and because of pressure from peers to engage in such behaviors. Social network analyses and hierarchical linear modeling were recently used, and results indicated that among students who had friends that were dismissive of sexual harassment (condoning) and held traditional views of masculinity in the sixth grade, individual levels of sexual harassment increased over the middle school years (Birkett & Espelage, 2009). Thus, as with bullying, peers appear to play an important role in modeling, reinforcing, and normalizing harassment. Finally, in regard to school context, existing studies have found that sexual harassment often occurs in public arenas, and that treatment of these incidents witnessed by school staff have a critical impact on how students view the school climate. Finally, there appears to be a general acceptance of sexual harassment in schools that likely influences perpetration rates; as noted by over a third of AAUW (1993, p.12) study participants, "It's [sexual harassment] just part of school life/a lot of people do it/it's no big deal."

Relations Between Bullying and Sexual Harassment/Violence

Figure 11.1 below summarizes the shared and nonshared risk and protective factors for bullying and sexual harassment/violence across different ecological contexts, primarily drawn from independent investigations. Little research has explored associations between bullying and sexual harassment/violence. The few studies that have, however, suggest that students who sexually harass their peers often also bully their peers. For example, Pepler and colleagues (2002) found that sexual harassment perpetration in students in grades 5 through 8 was associated with increased rates of bullying. Similarly, Pellegrini (2001) found that boys who were aggressive were also likely to engage in sexual harassment. Similarly, students who reported experiencing sexual harassment victimization were more likely to report dating violence victimization than those students who had not experienced sexual harassment (McMaster et al., 2002). Pepler and colleagues (2006) found a positive association between sexual harassment perpetration and bullying perpetration among students. In this cross-sectional study of 961 elementary school (grades 6 through 8) and 935 middle school students (grades 9 through 12), sexual harassment perpetration was more prevalent among students who bullied others than those who did not. While these studies are an important first step, leading sexual harassment scholars have questioned the equating of sexual harassment and bullying without adequate empirical support (Rodkin & Fischer, 2003; Stein, 2003). Longitudinal studies spanning into late adolescence are needed in order to validate the temporal sequence of bullying, harassment, and accompanying risk factors (i.e., precursors and concurrent).

Homophobic Teasing as a Pathway to Sexual Violence

Considerable attention has been given to sexual harassment perpetration in schools; more recently homophobic teasing has begun to be recognized as an important form of sexual violence. Both sexual harassment and homophobic teasing have been associated with bullying perpetration. Little effort

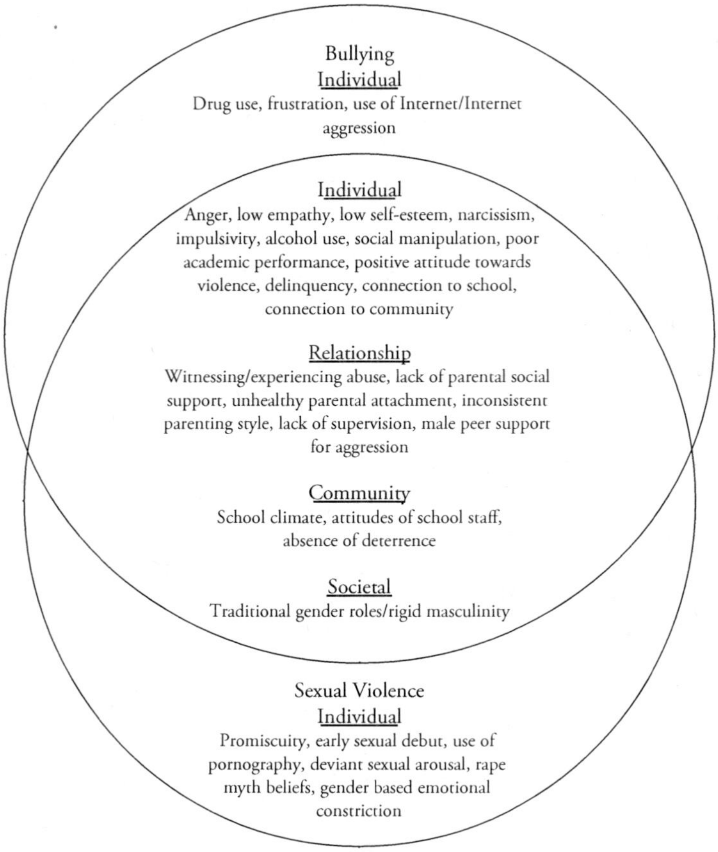

Figure 11.1. Venn diagram of shared and nonshared risk/protective factors

has been made to integrate the areas of bullying and homophobia, despite the shared interest of these two fields in studying prevalent forms of aggression. The often sexualized nature of some forms of homophobic victimization provides a useful framework for making the link between sexual harassment and sexual violence (Kosciw, 2004; Pilkington & D'Augelli, 1995; Rivers, 2001). Furthermore, given the reported high rates of victimization from both bullying and homophobia during this time (Eslea & Rees, 2001; Pilkington & D'Augelli, 1995), this association warrants consideration. Although several qualitative studies have been conducted examining the role of homophobia in aggressive behavior (Kimmel & Mahler, 2003; Phoenix, Frosh, & Pattman, 2003; Plummer, 2001; Rivers, 2001), few quantitative studies have examined the relation between homophobic verbal content and bullying among middle school students.

DEFINITION AND PREVALENCE.

Homophobia includes negative beliefs, attitudes, stereotypes, and behaviors toward gays and lesbians or those perceived to be gay and lesbian (Wright, Adams, & Bernat, 1999). Examples of the behavioral component of homophobia include teasing, threats, harassment, and assault (including sexual assault). Reports of victimization of gays and lesbians are equally extreme. For example, the National Gay and Lesbian Task Force (1984) sampled 2,074 youth from eight cities in the United States, of which 37% indicated that they had been victimized by peers in either junior high school or high school. In their study of antigay/lesbian abuse in schools across the state of Pennsylvania (which consisted of 461 gay men and 260 lesbians), Gross, Aurand, and Adessa (1988) noted that 50% of gay men and 12% of lesbians surveyed had experienced some form of victimization in junior high school (12–14 years), rising to 59% for gay men and 21% for lesbians in high school (14–18 years). According to Berrill (1992), based on evidence collated from various state and national task forces and coalitions at the time, estimates of the prevalence of school-based victimization for gay and lesbian youths resident in the United States ranged from 33% (N = 167; Aurand et al., 1985) to 49% ($N = 721$; Gross et al., 1988). In a UK national postal survey of 4,216 gays, lesbians, and bisexuals, Mason and Palmer (1996) found that, of those respondents under 18 years of age, 40% of all violent attacks had taken place at school, with 50% of those being perpetrated by same- or similar-aged peers.

More recently, Pilkington and D'Augelli (1995) reported that 83% of gay and lesbian youth experienced some form of victimization, which included verbal insults, threats of violence, physical assault, and sexual assault. These forms of victimization clearly parallel those behaviors associated with bullying as identified by bully researchers. Rivers (2001) reported that name-calling, assault, and teasing were frequent forms of bullying experienced by gay and lesbian students (82%, 60%, and 58% respectively), and that a majority of the name-calling was homophobic in nature. Rumor spreading (59%) and social isolation (27%), which could be considered relational forms of aggression, were also reported.

Integrating Bullying, Sexual Harassment/ Violence, and Homophobic Teasing

Homophobic behavior and bullying are not limited exclusively toward gay and lesbian students. Heterosexual students might also be victims of homophobia, not because of their sexual orientation, but because of their perceived differences and departure from traditional masculine/feminine gender role expectations (Kimmel & Mahler, 2003). In many ways, homophobia is linked to traditional masculine and feminine ideologies (Mandel & Shakeshaft, 2000; Phoenix et al., 2003; Skelton, 1996). Similarly, bullying is often used to police masculine and feminine behavior among young males and females (Eder et al., 1995; Epstein, 2001). Additionally, harassing and labeling others as gay or lesbian has been defined as a form of sexual harassment (AAUW, 2001; Fineran, 2002; Stratton & Backes, 1997), and has been shown in one qualitative investigation that in extreme cases could lead to overt sexual assault (Rivers, 2001).

Several US and UK studies began the process of integrating the studies of homophobia and bullying. In the UK, for example, Plummer (2001) interviewed 30 men to retrospectively examine homophobic content from boyhood to young adulthood. These respondents reported that calling others homophobic epithets was not always a direct reference to their sexual orientation, but that it was often used to denote someone as being unmasculine. Phoenix and colleagues (2003) examined the association among masculinity, homophobia, and bullying through interviews with middle school boys. Eighty percent reported that homophobia, in the form of teasing and name-calling, was extremely common. Only 8% stated that they were *not* homophobic. Kimmel and Mahler (2003) retrospectively examined the association among bullying, victimization, and homophobia as experienced by school shooters in the past two decades. Information was collected from local and national news articles mentioning the occurrences. They found that *almost all* school shooters had been bullied, and more specifically, had been repeatedly teased as being gay (although no evidence suggested the shooters were gay). The authors also argued that bullying research has neglected to address the content of bullying. The authors identified this content as relating to local school culture, peer interactions, and gender ideologies.

For gay and lesbian youth, intentional "outing" by peers (often based on perceptions of "difference" rather than disclosure) can lead to extremes of violence including assaults with weapons and, ultimately, sexual assault. According to Pilkington and D'Augelli (1995) almost 1 in 10 of their sample reported having being assaulted with a weapon, and almost 1 in every 5 (18%) disclosed that they had experienced at least one incident of sexual assault as a consequence of their sexual orientation. In the UK, Rivers (2001) found that in addition to physical, verbal, and relational forms of aggression experienced by 190 former victims of school-based homophobic bullying, 11% reported having being sexually assaulted at school either by peers or by teachers. Furthermore, reports of sexual assault were found to be positively and significantly related to bullying, taking place in the locker rooms before or after physical education classes. Kosciw's (2004) study of the school-related experiences of 887 gay, lesbian, bisexual, and transgender youth (ages 13–20), drawn from 48 states and the District of Columbia, shows the interrelationships between sexist remarks, negative remarks relating to individual gender expression and, ultimately, sexual harassment. In this study, 74% of youth reported having heard personally directed sexist remarks from other students at school with the majority of those (70%) reporting them as a frequent occurrence. Fifty-three percent (53%) reported being criticized frequently for not being stereotypically "masculine" or "feminine"; however, almost two thirds of the entire sample (63.5%) reported at least one episode of sexual harassment in the previous year at school.

Recently, a *bully-sexual violence pathway theory* has been proposed in the literature (Espelage, Basile, & Hamburger, 2012) in which bullying perpetration and homophobic teasing are hypothesized to be predictive of sexual violence perpetration during early to late adolescence. More specifically, this theory posits that bullying for some youth falls on the lower continuum of the bully-SV pathway. It stands to reason that the need for control and dominance that underlies bullying is transferred to increasingly escalating forms of aggression and into relationships that are characteristic of the developing adolescent. That is, bullying in the form of name-calling and rumor spreading has been associated with homophobic teasing (Poteat & Espelage, 2005), which creates a climate in which sexual harassment perpetration is likely to develop as boys and girls attempt to counter the homophobic teasing by sexually harassing others. This might manifest itself in different ways. For example, a bully perpetrator who also uses homophobic teasing may turn to sexual harassment perpetration as he or she gets older and becomes more interested in the opposite sex. Alternatively, a male adolescent who is perceived to be gay and targeted with homophobic epithets may sexually harass girls as a way to demonstrate his heterosexuality. Future studies need to explore this theory more completely.

Adolescent Dating Violence

Definition

Violence in dating relationships can take on physical, psychological, and sexual forms. Physical dating violence includes acts such as slapping or punching a partner. Emotional/psychological abuse includes behaviors such as manipulation and verbal battering (e.g., swearing, derogatory comments). Researchers have found that physical aggression within dating relationships is less prevalent than psychological aggression between partners (Espelage, Holt, & Isaia, 2007; Jackson, Cram, & Seymour, 2000). Since interpersonal violence among adults is also discussed in a separate chapter within this volume, the focus of this brief review will be limited to adolescents.

Prevalence

Dating violence is a serious concern and as many as one in four teens report sexual, physical, verbal, or psychological abuse each year (Foshee, 1996). Henton and colleagues (1983) found that the first episode of dating violence typically occurs by age 15 years (Henton, Cate, Koval, Lloyd, & Christopher, 1983), and Burcky and colleagues (1988) noted that 29% of girls reported their first incident of dating violence to have occurred between the ages of 12 and 13—the average age of students in sixth and seventh grades. These studies highlight the critical importance of early prevention efforts. More recent studies have replicated those early findings. A wide range of prevalence rates have been reported for high school students experiencing dating violence (e.g., 9% to 46%; Gray & Foshee, 1997; Katz, Kuffel, & Coblentz, 2002; Roscoe & Callahan, 1985), and at least one study found no significant difference in rates of dating violence from 9th to 12th grade (Howard, Wang, & Yan, 2007). In a recent study of 7,824 female high school students, 9% of the adolescent girls reported experiencing physical dating violence (Howard & Wang, 2003). Higher rates emerged from a study of 526 8th and 9th graders; 36% reported experiencing physical dating violence victimization and 20% reported having perpetrated physical violence at some point in their lives (Arriaga & Foshee, 2004). Rates for nonphysical violence are alarming as well, with estimates that one in five adolescents report experiencing emotional aggression (Halpern et al., 2001). A more recent investigation of 684 African American and Caucasian middle and high school adolescents indicated that 37% experienced physical dating violence and 62% were victimized by emotional abuse in dating relationships (Holt & Espelage, 2005). These figures are especially important given that physical dating violence is often preceded by emotional and psychological abuse (Murphy & O'Leary, 1989; Ronfeldt, Kimerling, & Arias, 1998). The high prevalence of dating violence among early adolescents makes it clear that prevention and intervention efforts should be initiated before ninth grade (Howard et al., 2007). High school students also reported high rates of dating violence, with more than 9% of both boys and girls being hit, slapped, or otherwise physically hurt by a dating partner; and more than 10% of girls and 4% of boys reported being forced to have sexual intercourse.

Adolescent dating violence is associated with multiple negative outcomes. Carlson's (1987) review indicated that victims often report feelings of confusion, anger, sadness, or diminished self-esteem. In a study of 123 high school students, 56% of victims indicated that, although the incident(s) upset them, there were no long-term effects; however, 8% reported more long-standing emotional disturbance (Burcky et al., 1988). In a diverse sample of 684 African American and Caucasian middle and high school adolescents greater physical and emotional dating victimization was associated with more anxiety/depression (Holt & Espelage, 2005). Victims of dating violence are more likely to engage in other health-risk behaviors, such as substance use, physical fighting, and risky sexual activity (Silverman et al., 2001; CDC, 2006). In addition, dating violence is associated with poor academic achievement and reduced school safety (California Attorney General's Office & California Department of Education, 2004); with teen dating violence victims in the ninth grade being twice as likely to have mostly D or F grades as other ninth graders. One of the most disturbing findings from the literature on teen dating violence is that adolescents who are involved in dating violence have an increased likelihood of being involved in violent adult relationships (Magdol, Moffitt, Caspi, & Silva, 1998; Smith, 2003).

The widespread prevalence of dating violence early in adolescence, its negative effect on young people, and the association between adolescent dating violence and serious adult domestic violence all justify and highlight the importance of understanding how risk and protective factors in early adolescence relate to dating violence involvement in later adolescence.

Etiology of Adolescent Dating Violence

The prevention of teen dating violence does not have the depth of rigorous longitudinal etiological research that can be used to inform prevention efforts in other areas such as substance abuse and conduct problems. Some research does suggest that efforts to address dating violence could be informed by the overlap among dating violence, bullying perpetration, and sexual violence. Pepler and colleagues (2002) found that sexual harassment perpetration among students in Grades 5 through 8 was associated with increased rates of bullying. Similarly, students who reported bullying their peers also reported more violence in their dating relationships (both physical and social) than nonbullies (Connolly, Pepler, Craig, & Taradash, 2000). Pepler and colleagues (2006), in a cross-sectional study of 961 middle school (grades 6 through 8) and 935 high school students (grades 9 through 12) found that sexual harassment perpetration was more prevalent among students who bullied others than among those who did not.

Research has demonstrated that youth problem behaviors tend to be interrelated and share common risk and protective factors (Donovan, Jessor, & Costa, 1991; Jessor, 1991). The evidence indicates that this finding appears to hold true for adolescent dating violence as well (Howard et al., 2007). Dating violence has been consistently found to be associated with other forms of aggression and violence (Riggs & O'Leary, 1989). The belief that it is acceptable to use violence is strongly associated with inflicting violence against a dating partner (Malik et al., 1997; O'Keefe, 1997; Tontodonato & Crew, 1992). Involvement in other violent behaviors increases the odds of an adolescent becoming a victim of dating violence (Howard et al., 2007). Boys who are aggressive, involved in fights, or carry guns are more likely to engage in sexual harassment (Pellegrini, 2001; Howard et al., 2007). Violence against peers has been correlated with using sexual and physical violence against dates (Ozer et al., 2004). Early antisocial behavior and aggression have been shown to predict later use of violence against dating partners in three longitudinal studies (Capaldi & Clark, 1998; Lavoie et al., 2002; Simons et al., 1998) and a study by Brendgen et al. (2001) showed aggression perpetrated by young adolescent boys was associated with dating violence perpetration at the age of 16 and 17 years.

Using alcohol and drugs has also been consistently found to be strongly associated with dating violence for both adolescent boys and girls (Burcky et al., 1988; O'Keeffe, Brockopp, & Chew, 1986; O'Keefe, 1997; Silverman et al., 2001). A number of studies have also specifically found an association between substance use and involvement in dating violence for females (Koss & Dinero, 1989). Howard and colleagues (2007) showed that having used a variety of drugs over the past month was associated with increased dating violence among adolescent girls, and Foshee and colleagues (2001) found that alcohol use predicted perpetration of dating abuse by females.

Research also indicates that adolescent dating violence can be understood in part as resulting from deficits in youths' interpersonal skills. Likelihood of involvement in dating violence has been associated with teens' use of threats or violence to solve problems, inability to manage anger or frustration, and poor social skills. In their review of 12 longitudinal studies examining predictors of dating violence perpetration, Foshee and Matthew (2007) highlight the associations of skills and competencies with dating violence perpetration, and argue for evidence that adolescents who have poor conflict management skills are likely to have more discord in their relationships. However, the association of skills—such as anger management and ability to empathize and cope with difficulties with dating partner—with dating violence perpetration have failed to hold in some longitudinal studies (Foshee et al., 2001). Foshee and Matthew conclude that these skills might not be directly linked to the etiology of dating violence, but might be important in the development of other types of youth violence. This conclusion is premature given the methodological limitations of the dating violence literature and does not explain the concordant associations among dating violence perpetration and other forms of youth aggression and violence (Ozer et al., 2004). Thus, it is our contention that these psychological attributes and competencies associated with dating violence perpetration are also consistently associated with perpetration of other forms of violence, including sexual violence and bullying (Basile et al., 2009; Ozer et al., 2004), suggesting that targeting these modifiable risk and protective factors will likely have a positive impact on minimizing multiple forms of violence.

Peer Socialization and Support

Peers have been shown to play an important role in contributing to dating violence perpetration among adolescents. Among males, peers have been long recognized as major socializing agents and supports for violence against women. Male peer support has been defined as "the attachments to male peers and the resources that these men provide which encourage and legitimate woman abuse" (DeKeseredy, 1990, p. 130). Male peer support can take the form of routine activities (e.g., social events, academic assistance), informational support (e.g., sexual, physical, and psychological advice about dating), affiliation with abusive male peers, peer patriarchal attitudes (e.g., justification for use of physical abuse toward dating partner), and finally peer pressure to have sex. Extending this finding to females and specifically to dating aggression, Arriaga and Foshee (2004) conducted a thorough investigation of how having a friend that engaged in dating violence influenced an individual's own dating aggression perpetration and victimization. A sample of eighth- and ninth-grade students (n = 517) completed survey measures on their own dating aggression perpetration and responded to several questions about their male and female friends' dating violence history. As hypothesized, friend dating violence was associated with an individual's level of perpetration of violence concurrently and was associated with an increase in perpetration over a 6-month period.

Advancing Prevention Science Through Social-Developmental Theory

Despite considerable growth in prevention programming, our ability to positively impact bullying, sexual or teen dating violence in North America is negligible and still in infancy (for review Espelage & Horne, 2008). For example, Smith, Schneider, Smith, and Ananiadou (2004) synthesized evaluation studies of whole-school bullying prevention programs and found that, across most studies, outcomes were negligible or negative. Vreeman and Carroll's (2007) review of bullying prevention evaluations found the majority of studies did not show positive effects, but whole-school focused interventions were more effective than interventions delivered through classroom curricula or social skills training alone. Merrell, Gueldner, Ross, and Isava (2008) conducted a meta-analysis of school bullying preventive interventions and found positive effects for roughly one third of the outcomes measured across the selected studies. The most recent meta-analysis by Ttofi and colleagues (2008) concluded that school-based antibullying programs have demonstrated effectiveness for reducing bullying and victimization, but mostly for programs in Europe. These authors also cautioned against drawing any firm conclusions given the paucity of rigorously designed randomized controlled trials. With regard to teen dating violence, Foshee and Matthew (2007) noted that evaluations of only 11 programs can be found in the research literature. Of these evaluations, only three assessed program effects on dating violence perpetration and only two of the three involved an experimental design. In the largest evaluation of a school-based dating violence prevention program, Foshee and colleagues (1998, 2004, 2005) evaluated their Safe Dates program in 14 public schools among 8th and 9th graders. Results indicated that students in the Safe Dates treatment group reported less dating violence perpetration across all time points (except 1 month post), however, effect sizes were negligible to small. Thus, while there is limited evidence that teen dating violence programs can affect attitudes and knowledge (Foshee & Matthew, 2007; Weisz & Black, 2009) there is limited evidence of the durability of effects on knowledge and attitudes (Begun, 2003), and pooled effect sizes across 19 published studies on attitudes and knowledge reveal the meaning of these changes are negligible (Ting, 2009; R^2 = .106 and .115 respectively). These effect sizes are concerning, and point to a larger concern for the field; mainly, the inability to determine what changes are

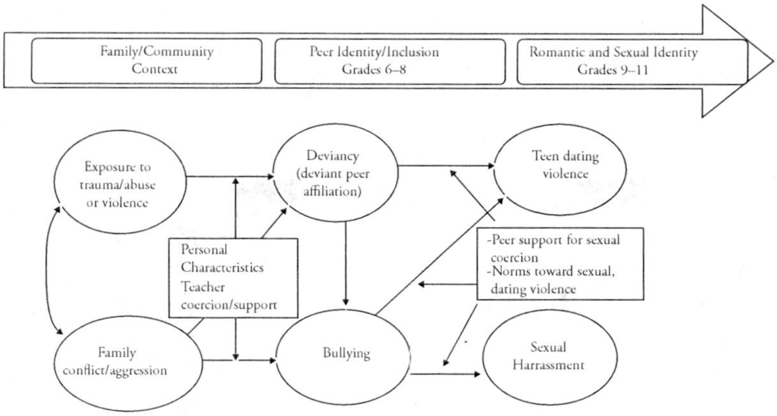

Figure 11.2. Comprehensive theoretical model of bullying, sexual violence, & dating violence

meaningful, and therefore, what programs should be recommended.

However, our ability to mount maximally efficacious, efficient, and optimally timed preventive interventions is limited in several ways, including methodological rigor (Cornelius & Resseguie, 2007; Meyers & Stein, 2004; Weisz & Black, 2009), but perhaps most importantly a lack of theories that both encompass and integrate our understanding of shared risk and protective factors. Social interaction theory and developmental theory, when taken together, hold promise for targeting the mechanisms and optimal timing of intervention. Figure 11.2 below illustrates the additive and interactive relations among individual, familial, teacher, and peer relations in a social-developmental context. The top arrow illustrates the importance of understanding how changing developmental demands may correspond with and influence the respective social relations across nested and interrelated ecologies. For example, peers become an increasing source of companionship and influence during early-to-mid adolescence (Crockett, Losoff, & Peterson, 1984; Rubin, Bukowski, & Parker, 1998), and thus, homophily increases. As a result, shared attitudes and behavioral orientations become solidified, and formation and identification with peer groups becomes paramount (e.g., through rules and exclusion). Because bullying is maintained by peer contingencies, and is an assertion of power to manipulate peer status (see Pellegrini & Bartini, 2001), it is not surprising that bullying, especially social forms of aggression, manifest and are elaborated on during this time. However, as the developmental demands are focused on romantic and sexual identity this model suggests that bullying will become characterized by homophobic teasing and sexual content. Implicit in this model is the assertion that coercion, modeling, and reinforcement of aggression in familial, peer, and teacher relations explain the maintenance and diversification of bullying behavior.

Also implicit in this model are implications for prevention efforts. Interventions or strategies that target the peer context (e.g., Second Step; Committee for Children, 2008) may be optimally effective for bullying prevention, but may be optimized when in the context of teacher training on classroom climate and positive behavior approaches to management. Although families may not be as accessible or receptive to prevention efforts (as opposed to a captured audience in school-based settings), social learning theory suggests they are an important target at either the universal (see Families for Safe Dates, adaptation of Family Matters curriculum, http://www.ojp.usdoj.gov/nij/topics/crime/violence-against-women/workshops/teen-dating-violence-day2.htm#two3), or indicated level. Finally, a social-ecological developmental model suggests the most effective interventions would target one or more nested systems in the micro-system, such as the Green Dot strategy (www.livethegreendot.com).

Summary and Future Directions

Despite the growth in the number of prevention programs for bullying, and to a lesser extent, dating violence, there remain a number of challenges for the field to overcome before it can reach more full maturity. In regard to basic science, there is a need to understand the shared and nonshared features of bullying, harassment, and dating violence trajectories, so that more targeted interventions can be developed. With regard to prevention science, there remains a strong need to enhance the rigor and dissemination of evaluation studies (i.e., focus on behavior change, generalizability, and multireporter and multimethod approaches), and secondly, to map intervention efforts onto our existing knowledge of the underlying processes of bullying, harassment, and dating violence. The lack of rigorous investigations makes it challenging to provide a cogent picture of what programs should be recommended, especially when we consider the limited information on durability of effects, and the consistently small effect sizes. Once we obtain a clear and convincing consensus on effective programs, it will be essential to identify the most salient components of prevention efforts, so that we can maximize the efficiency (and in turn cost effectiveness), potency and adoption of programs.

References

Adair, V. A., Dixon, R. S., Moore, D. W., & Sutherland, C. M. (2000). Ask your mother not to make yummy sandwiches: Bullying in New Zealand secondary schools. *New Zealand Journal of Educational Studies, 35,* 207–221.

American Association of University Women Educational Foundation (AAUW). (1993). *Hostile hallways: The AAUW survey on sexual harassment in America's schools* (No. 923012). Washington, DC: Harris/Scholastic Research.

American Association of University Women Educational Foundation. (2001). *Hostile hallways: Sexual harassment and bullying in schools.* Washington, DC: Harris/Scholastic Research.

Anderson, C. S. (1982). The search for school climate: A review of the research. *Review of Educational Research, 52*(3), 368–420.

Arriaga, X. B., & Foshee, V. A. (2004). Adolescent dating violence: Do adolescents follow in their friends' or their parents' footsteps? *Journal of Interpersonal Violence, 19,* 162–184.

Aurand, S., Adessa, R., & Bush, C. (1985). *Violence and discrimination against Philadelphia lesbian and gay people.* Unpublished Report: Philadelphia Lesbian and Gay Task Force.

Baldry, A. C. (2003). Bullying in schools and exposure to domestic violence. *Child Abuse and Neglect, 27,* 713–732.

Baldry, A. C., & Farrington, D. P. (2000). Bullies and delinquents: Personal characteristics and parental styles. *Journal of Community and Applied Social Psychology, 10,* 17–31.

Basile, K. C., Espelage, D. L., Rivers, I., McMahon, P. M., & Simon, T. R. (2009). The theoretical and empirical links between bullying behavior and sexual violence perpetration. *Aggression and Violent Behavior, 14*(5), 336–347.

Beran, T. (2008). Consequences of being bullied at school. In D. Pepler & W. Craig (Eds.), *Understanding and addressing bullying: An international perspective* (pp. 44–66). Bloomington, IN: Authorhouse.

Berthold, K. A., & Hoover, J. H. (2000). Correlates of bullying and victimization among intermediate students in the midwestern USA. *School Psychology International, 21,* 65–78.

Berrill, K. T. (1992). Anti-gay violence and victimization in antigay hate crimes: Official response and public policy. In G. M. Herek & K. T. Berrill (Eds.), *Hate crimes: Confronting violence against lesbians and gay men* (pp. 289–305). Newbury Park, CA: Sage.

Berthold, K. A., & Hoover, J. H. (2000). Correlates of bullying and victimization among intermediate students in the midwestern USA. *School Psychology International, 21,* 65–78.

Birkett, M., & Espelage, D. L. (2009). *Homophily and sexual harassment perpetration among middle school students.* Paper presented at Annual Conference of the American Psychological Association, Toronto, CA.

Bosworth, K., Espelage, D., & Simon, T. (1999). Factors associated with bullying behavior in middle school students. *The Journal of Early Adolescence, 19,* 341–362.

Bowes, L., Arseneault, L., Maughan, B., Taylor, A., Caspi, A., & Moffitt, T. E. (2009). School, neighborhood, and family factors are associated with children's bullying involvement: A nationally representative longitudinal study. *Journal of the American Academy of Child Adolescent Psychiatry, 48,* 545–553.

Bradshaw, C. P., Sawyer, A. L., & O'Brennan, L. M. (2007). Bullying and peer victimization at school: Perceptual differences between students and school staff. *School Psychology Review, 36,* 361–182.

Brendgen, M., Vitaro, F., Bukowski, W. M., Doyle, A., & Markiewicz, D. (2001). Developmental profiles of peer social preference over the course of elementary school: Associations with trajectories of externalizing and internalizing behavior. *Developmental Psychology, 37,* 308–320.

Brockenbrough, K. K., Cornell, D. G., & Loper, A. B. (2002). Aggressive attitudes among victims of violence at school. *Education and Treatment of Children, 25,* 273–287.

Bronfenbrenner, U. (1977). Toward an experimental ecology of human development. *American Psychologist, 32,* 513–531.

Bronfenbrenner, U. (1979). *The ecology of human development: Experiments by nature and design.* Cambridge, MA: Harvard University Press

Brown, L. M., Chesney-Lind, M., & Stein, N. (2007). Patriarchy matters: Toward a gendered theory of teen violence and victimization. *Violence Against Women, 13,* 1249–1273.

Brubacher, M., Fondacaro, M., Brank, E., Brown, V., & Miller, S. (2009). Procedural justice in resolving family disputes: Implications for childhood bullying. *Psychology, Public Policy, and Law, 15,* 149–167.

Bukowski, W. M., Sippola, L. K., & Newcomb, A. F. (2000). Variations in patterns of attraction to same- and other-sex peers during early adolescence. *Developmental Psychology, 36,* 147–154.

Burcky, W., Reuterman, N., & Kopsky, S. (1988). Dating violence among high school students. *The School Counselor, 35,* 353–358.

California Attorney General's Office & the California Department of Education (2004). *A preventable epidemic: Teen dating violence and its impact on school safety and academic achievement.* Sacramento, CA: Author.

Capaldi, D. M., & Clark, S. (1998). Prospective family predictors of aggression toward female partners for at-risk young men. *Developmental Psychology, 34,* 1175–1188.

Capaldi, D. M., Stoolmiller, M., Clark, S., & Owen, L. D. (2002). Heterosexual risk behaviors in at-risk young men from early adolescence to young adulthood: Prevalence, prediction, and association with STD contraction. *Developmental Psychology, 38,* 394–406.

Carlson, B. E. (1987). Dating violence: A research review and comparison with spouse abuse. *Social Casework, 68*(1), 16–23.

Centers for Disease Control and Prevention (CDC). (2004). *Sexual violence prevention: Beginning the Dialogue.* Atlanta, GA: Centers for Disease Control and Prevention.

Centers for Disease Control and Prevention. (2006). *Youth risk behavior surveillance—United States 2005*. Complete report available as a pdf file at http://www.cdc.gov/mmwr/PDF/SS/SS5505.pdf or in table form at http://www.cdc.gov/HealthyYouth/yrbs/index.htm.

Colarossi, L. G., & Eccles, J. S. (2003). Differential effects of support providers on adolescents' mental health. *Social Work Research, 27,* 19–30.

Committee for Children. (2008). *Second Step: Student success through prevention*. Seattle, WA.

Connolly, I., & O'Moore, M. (2003). Personality and family relations of children who bully. *Personality and Individual Differences, 35,* 559–567.

Connolly, J., Pepler, D., Craig, W., & Taradash, A. (2000). Dating experiences of bullies in early adolescence. *Child Maltreatment, 5,* 299–310.

Craig, W. M., & Pepler, D. J. (1995). Peer process in bullying and victimization: An observational study. *Exceptionality Education Canada, 5,* 81–95.

Craig, W. M., & Pepler, D. J. (1997). Observations of bullying and victimization in the school yard. *Canadian Journal of School Psychology, 13,* 41–59.

Crockett, L., Losoff, M., & Petersen, A. C. (1984). Perceptions of the peer group and friendship in early adolescence. *Journal of Early Adolescence, 4,* 155–181.

Crouter, A. C., & Booth, A. (2006). *Romance and sex in adolescence and emerging adulthood: Risks and opportunities*. The Penn State University family issues symposia series. Mahwah, NJ: Erlbaum.

DeKeseredy, W. S. (1990). Male peer support and woman abuse: The current state of knowledge. *Sociological Focus, 23,* 129–139.

DeVoe, J., Peter, K., Kaufman, P., Miller, A., Noonan, M., Snyder, T., & Baum, K. (2004). *Indicators of school crime and safety: 2004*. (NCES 2005002/NCJ 205290). US Departments of Education and Justice. Washington, DC: US Government Printing Office.

Dishion, T. J., & Patterson, G. R. (2006). The development and ecology of antisocial behavior in children and adolescents. In D. Cicchetti & D. J. Cohen (Eds.), *Developmental psychopathology: Vol. 3. Risk and adaptation* (2nd ed., pp. 503–541). New York: Wiley.

Donovan, J. E., Jessor, R., & Costa, F. (1991). Adolescent health behavior and conventionality-unconventionality: An extension of problem-behavior theory. *Health Psychology, 10,* 2–61.

Duncan, R. D. (2004). The impact of family relationships on school bullies and victims. In D. L. Espelage & S. M. Swearer (Eds.), *Bullying in American schools: A social-ecological perspective on prevention and intervention* (pp. 227–244). Mahwah, NJ: Erlbaum.

Dupper, D. R., & Meyer-Adams, N. (2002). Low-level violence: A neglected aspect of school culture. *Urban Education, 37,* 350–364.

Eder, D., & Kinney, D. (1995). The effect of middle school extracurricular activities on adolescents' popularity and peer status. *Youth and Society, 26,* 298–323.

Endresen, I. M., & Olweus, D. (2001). Self-reported empathy in Norwegian adolescents: Sex differences, age trends, and relationship to bullying. In A. C. Bohart & C. Arthur, & Stipek, D. J. (Eds.), *Constructive and destructive behavior: Implications for family, school, and society* (pp. 147–165). Washington, DC: American Psychological Association.

Epstein, D. (2001). Boyz' own stories: Masculinities and sexualities in schools. In W. Martino, & B. Meyenn (Eds.), *What about the boys? Issues of masculinity in schools* (pp. 96–109). Philadelphia, PA: Open University Press.

Eslea, M., & Rees, J. (2001). At what age are children most likely to be bullied at school? *Aggressive Behavior, 27,* 419–429.

Espelage, D. L., Basile, K. C., & Hamburger, M. E. (2012). Bullying experiences and co-occurring sexual violence perpetration among middle school students: Shared and unique risk factors. *Journal of Adolescent Health, 50,* 60–65.

Espelage, D. L., Bosworth, K., & Simon, T. R. (2000). Examining the social context of bullying behaviors in early adolescence. *Journal of Counseling and Development, 78,* 326–333.

Espelage, D. L., Bosworth, K., & Simon, T. R. (2001). Short-term stability and prospective correlates of bullying in middle-school students: An examination of potential demographic, psychosocial, and environmental influences. *Violence and Victims, 16,* 411–426.

Espelage, D. L., Green, H. D., & Polanin, J. (2012). Willingness to intervene in bullying episodes among middle school students: Individual and peer-group influences. *Journal of Early Adolescence*. Online first.

Espelage, D. L., & Holt, M. K. (2001). Bullying and victimization during early adolescence: Peer influences and psychosocial correlates. In R. Geffner & M. Loring (Eds.), *Bullying behaviors: Current issues, research, and interventions* (pp. 123–142). Binghamton, NY: Haworth Press.

Espelage, D. L., Holt, M. K., & Henkel, R. R. (2003). Examination of peer group contextual effects on aggression during early adolescence. *Child Development, 74,* 205–220.

Espelage, D. L., Holt, M. K., & Isaia, A. (2007). Dating violence among adolescents: Understanding the roles of attachment, self-esteem, dominance, and need for interpersonal control. In K. A. Kendall-Tackett & S. M. Giacomoni (Eds.), *Intimate partner violence* (pp. 14–15). Kingston, NJ: Civic Research Institute.

Espelage, D. L., & Horne, A. M. (2008). School violence and bullying prevention: From research-based explanations to empirically based solutions. In S. D. Brown, & R. W. Lent (Eds.), *Handbook of counseling psychology* (4th ed., pp. 588–598). Hoboken, NJ: Wiley.

Espelage, D. L., & Swearer, S. (2003). Research on school bullying and victimization: What have we learned and where do we go from here? *School Psychology Review, 32*(3), 365–383.

Fang, X., & Corso, P. S. (2008). Gender differences in the connections between violence experienced as a child and perpetration of intimate partner violence in young adulthood. *Journal of Family Violence, 23,* 303–313.

Fanti, K. A., Frick, P. J., & Georgiou, S. (2008). Linking callous-unemotional traits to instrumental and non-instrumental forms of aggression. *Journal of Psychopathology and Behavioral Assessment, 31,* 285–298.

Feshbach, N. D., & Feshbach, S. (1982). Empathy training and the regulation of aggression: Potentialities and limitations. *Academic Psychology Bulletin, 4*(3), 399–413.

Fineran, S. (2002). Sexual harassment between same-sex peers: Intersection of mental health, homophobia, and sexual violence in schools. *Social Work, 47,* 65–74.

Fineran, S., & Bennett, L. (1999). Gender and power issues of peer sexual harassment among teenagers. *Journal of Interpersonal Violence, 14,* 626–641.

Fineran, S., & Gruber, J. (2004). *Research on bullying and sexual harassment in secondary schools: Incidence, interrelationships, and psychological implications*. Paper presented at the Association for Gender Equity Leadership in Education, Washington, DC.

Flouri, E., & Buchanan, A. (2003). The role of mother involvement and father involvement in adolescent bullying behavior. *Journal of Interpersonal Violence, 18*(6), 634–644.

Foshee, V. A. (1996). Gender differences in adolescent dating abuse prevalence, types and injuries. *Health Education Research, 11,* 275–286.

Foshee, V., Linder, F., MacDougall, J., & Bangdiwala, S. (2001). Gender differences in the longitudinal predictors of adolescent dating violence. *Preventive Medicine, 32,* 128–141.

Foshee, V. A., & Matthew, R. A. (2007). Adolescent dating abuse perpetration: A review of findings, methodological limitations and suggestions for future research. In D. Flannery, A. Vazonsyi, & I. Waldman (Eds.), *Cambridge handbook of violent behavior* (pp. 431–449). New York: Cambridge University Press.

Frey, K. S., Hirschstein, M. K., Edstrom, L. V., & Snell, J. L. (2009). Observed reductions in school bullying, nonbullying aggression, and destructive bystander behavior: A longitudinal evaluation. *Journal of Educational Psychology, 101*(2), 466.

Garbarino, J., & deLara, E. (2002). *And words can hurt forever: How to protect adolescents from bullying, harassment, and emotional violence.* New York: The Free Press.

Glew, G. M., Fan, M., Katon, W., Rivara, F. P., & Kernic, M. A. (2005). Bullying, psychosocial adjustment, and academic performance in elementary school. *Archives of Pediatric Adolescent Medicine, 159,* 1026–1031.

Graham, S. (2006). Peer victimization in school: Exploring the ethnic context. *Current Directions in Psychological Science, 15* (6), 317–321.

Gray, H. M., & Foshee, V. A. (1997). Adolescent dating violence: Differences between one-sided and mutually violent profiles. *Journal of Interpersonal Violence, 12,* 126–141.

Gross, L., Aurand, S., & Adessa, R. (1988). *Violence and discrimination against lesbian and gay people in Philadelphia and the Commonwealth of Pennsylvania.* Unpublished report: Philadelphia Lesbian and Gay Task Force.

Groth, A. N. (1979). *Men who rape.* New York: Plenum Press.

Halpern, C. T., Oslak, S. G., Young, M. L., Martin, S. L., & Kupper, L. L. (2001). Partner violence among adolescents in opposite-sex romantic relationships: Findings from the national longitudinal study of adolescent health. *American Journal of Public Health, 91*(10), 1679–1685.

Hartup, W. W. (1996). The company they keep: Friendships and their developmental significance. *Child Development, 67,* 1–13.

Heise, L. (1998). Violence against women: An integrated ecological framework. *Violence Against Women, 4,* 262–290.

Henton, J., Cate, R., Koval, J., Lloyd, S., & Christopher, F. S. (1983). Romance and violence in dating relationships. *Journal of Family Issues, 4,* 134–142.

Hodges, E. V. E., Boivin, M., Vitaro, F., & Bukowski, W. M. (1999). The power of friendship: Protection against an escalating cycle of peer victimization. *Developmental Psychology, 35,* 94–101.

Hodges, E. V. E., Malone, M. J., & Perry, D. G. (1997). Individual risk and social risk as interacting determinants of victimization in the peer group. *Developmental Psychology, 33,* 1032–1039.

Holt, M., & Espelage, D. (2005). Multiple victimization of adolescents. In K. Kendall-Tackett & S. Giacomoni (Eds.), *Victimization of children and youth: Patterns of abuse, response strategies.* Kingston, NJ: Civic Research Institute.

Holt, M. K., & Espelage, D. L. (2007). Perceived social support among bullies, victims, and bully-victims. *Journal of Youth and Adolescence, 26,* 984–994.

Holt, M. K., & Keyes, M. A. (2004). Teachers' attitudes toward bullying. In D. L. Espelage & S. M. Swearer (Eds.), *Bullying in American schools: A social-ecological perspective on prevention and intervention* (pp. 121–139). Mahwah, NJ: Erlbaum.

Houndoumadi, A., & Pateraki, L. (2001). Bullying and bullies in Greek elementary schools: Pupils' attitudes and teachers'/parents' awareness. *Educational Review, 53,* 19–26.

Howard, D. E., & Wang, M. Q. (2003). Risk profiles of U.S. adolescent girls who were victims of dating violence. *Adolescence, 38,* 1–14.

Howard, D. E., Wang, M. Q., & Yan, F. (2007). Psychosocial factors associated with reports of physical dating violence among U.S. adolescent females. *Adolescence, 42,* 311–324.

Hymel, S., & Swearer, S. (2010). Bullying: An age-old problem that needs new solutions. *Education.com.* Retrieved from http://www.education.com/reference/article/bullying-about-power-and-abuse-of-power/

Jackson, S. M., Cram, F., & Seymour, F. W. (2000). Violence and sexual coercion in high school students' dating relationships. *Journal of Family Violence, 15,* 23–36.

Jacobsen, R. S., & Straker, G. (1982). Peer group interaction of physically abused children. *Child Abuse and Neglect, 6,* 321–327.

Jeffrey, L. R., Miller, D., & Linn, M. (2001). Middle school bullying as a context for the development of passive observers to the victimization of others. In R. A. Geffner, M. Loring, & C. Young (Eds.), *Bullying behavior: Current issues, research, and interventions* (pp. 143–156). Binghamton, NY: Haworth Press.

Jessor, R. (1991). Risk behavior in adolescence: A psychosocial framework for understanding and action. *Journal of Adolescent Health, 12,* 597–605.

Juvonen, J., Graham, S., & Schuster, M. A. (2003). Bullying among young adolescents: The strong, the weak, and the troubled. *Pediatrics Springfield, 112*(1), 1231–1237.

Kandel, D. B. (1978). Homophily, selection, and socialization in adolescent friendships. *American Journal of Sociology, 84,* 427–436.

Katz, J., Kuffel, S. W., & Coblentz, A. (2002). Are there gender differences in sustaining domestic violence?: An examination of frequency, severity, and relationship satisfaction. *Journal of Family Violence, 17,* 247–271.

Kaukiainen, A., Bjorkqvist, K., Lagerspetz, K., Osterman, K., Salmivalli, C., Rothberg, S., & Ahlbom, A. (1999). The relationships between social intelligence, empathy, and three types of aggression. *Aggressive Behavior, 25,* 81–89.

Kimmel, M. S., & Mahler, M. (2003). Adolescent masculinity, homophobia, and violence: Random school shootings, 1982–2001. *American Behavioral Scientist, 46,* 1439–1458.

Kochenderfer, B. J., & Ladd, G. W. (1996). Peer victimization: Cause or consequence of school maladjustment? *Child Development, 67,* 1305–1317.

Kochenderfer-Ladd, B., & Pelletier, M. E. (2007). Teachers' views and beliefs about bullying: Influences on classroom management strategies and students' coping with peer victimization. *Journal of School Psychology, 46,* 431–453.

Kosciw, J. G. (2004). *The 2003 National School Climate Survey: The school-related experiences of our nation's lesbian, gay, bisexual and transgender youth.* New York: Gay, Lesbian, and Straight Education Network.

Koss, M. P., & Dinero, T. E. (1989). Discriminant analysis of risk factors for sexual victimization among a national sample of college women. *Journal of Consulting and Clinical Psychology, 57,* 242–250.

Kumpulainen, K., Räsänen, E., Henttonen, I., Almqvist, F., Kresanov, K., Linna, S.-L., . . . Tamminen, T. (1998). Bullying and psychiatric symptoms among elementary school-age children. *Child Abuse and Neglect, 22,* 705–717.

Larkin, J. (1994). Walking through walls: The sexual harassment of high school girls. *Gender and Education, 6,* 263–280.

Lavoie, F., Hébert, M., Tremblay, R., Vitaro, F., Vézina, L., & McDuff, P. (2002). History of family dysfunction and perpetration of dating violence by adolescent boys: A longitudinal study. *Journal of Adolescent Health, 30,* 375–383.

Loeber, R., & Dishion, T. (1984). Boys who fight at home and school: Family conditions influencing cross-setting consistency. *Journal of Consulting and Clinical Psychology, 52*(5), 759–768.

Ma, L., Phelps, E., Lerner, J. V., & Lerner, R. M. (2009). Academic competence for adolescents who bully and who are bullied: Findings from the 4-H study of positive youth development. *The Journal of Early Adolescence, 29,* 862–897.

Magdol, L., Moffitt, T. E., Caspi, A., & Silva, P. A. (1998). Developmental antecedents of partner abuse: A prospective-longitudinal study. *Journal of Abnormal Psychology, 107,* 375–389.

Malik, S., Sorenson, S. B., & Aneshensel, C. S. (1997). Community and dating violence among adolescents: Perpetration and victimization. *Journal of Adolescent Health, 21*(5), 291–302.

Mandel, L., & Shakeshaft, C. (2000). Heterosexism in middle schools. In N. Lesko (Ed.), *Masculinities at school* (pp. 97–130). New York: Plenum.

Marini, Z. A., Dane, A. V., Bosacki, S. L., & YLC-CURA (2006). Direct and indirect bully-victims: Differential psychosocial risk factors associated with adolescents involved in bullying and victimization. *Aggressive Behavior, 32,* 551–569.

Mason, A., & Palmer, A. (1996). *Queer bashing: A national survey of hate crimes against lesbians and gay men.* London: Stonewall.

Mayberry, M. L., & Espelage, D. L. (2007). Associations among empathy, social competence, and reactive/proactive aggression subtypes. *Journal of Youth and Adolescence, 36*(6), 787–798.

Mayes, L. C., & Suchman, N. E. (2006). Developmental pathways to substance use. In D. Cicchetti & D. J. Cohen (Eds.). *Developmental psychopathology: Vol. 3. Risk and adaptation* (2nd ed., pp. 599–619). New York: Wiley.

McCreary, M. L., Slavin, L. A., & Berry, E. J. (1996). Predicting problem behavior and self-esteem among African-American adolescents. *Journal of Adolescent Research, 11,* 216–234.

McMaster, L. E., Connolly, J., Pepler, D. J., & Craig, W. M. (2002). Peer to peer sexual harassment in early adolescence: A developmental perspective. *Development and Psychopathology, 14*(91–105).

Mehrabian, A. (1997). Relations among personality scales of aggression, violence, and empathy: Validational evidence bearing on the risk of eruptive violence scale. *Aggressive Behavior, 23,* 433–445.

Merrell, K. W., Gueldner, B. A., Ross, S. W., & Isava, D. M. (2008). How effective are school bullying intervention program? A meta-analysis of intervention research. *School Psychology Quarterly, 23,* 26–42.

Miller, A., & Chandler, K. (2003). *Violence in U.S. public schools: 2000 school survey on crime and safety. Statistical analysis report October 2003.* NCES 2004314. Washington, DC: US Department of Education, National Center for Education Statistics.

Miller, P. A., & Eisenberg, N. (1988). The relationship of empathy to aggressive and externalizing/antisocial behavior. *Psychological Bulletin, 103,* 324–344.

Murphy, C., & O'Leary K. D. (1989). Psychological aggression predicts physical aggression in early marriage. *Journal of Consulting and Clinical Psychology, 57*(5), 579–582.

Nansel, T. R., Haynie, D. L., & Simons-Morton, B. G. (2003). The association of bullying and victimization with middle school adjustment. *Journal of Applied School Psychology, 19,* 45–61.

Nansel, T. R., Overpeck, M., Pilla, R. S., Ruan, W. J., Simmons-Morton, B., & Scheidt, P. (2001). Bullying behavior among U.S. youth: Prevalence and association with psychosocial adjustment. *Journal of the American Medical Association, 285,* 2094–2100.

National Gay and Lesbian Task Force (1984). *National antigay/lesbian victimization report.* Washington, DC: Author.

Nickerson, A. B., Mele, D., & Princiotta, D. (2008). Attachment and empathy as predictors of roles as defenders or outsiders in bullying interactions. *Journal of School Psychology, 46,* 687–703.

O'Connell, P., Pepler, D., & Craig, W. (1999). Peer involvement in bullying: Insights and challenges for intervention. *Adolescence, 22,* 437–452.

O'Keefe, M. (1997). Adolescents' exposure to community and school violence: Prevalence and behavioral correlates. *Journal of Adolescent Health, 20,* 368–376.

O'Keeffe, N. K., Brockopp, K., & Chew, E. (1986). Teen dating violence. *Social Work, 31,* 465–468.

Olweus, D. (1978). *Aggression in the schools: Bullies and whipping boys.* Oxford, England: Hemisphere.

Olweus, D. (2002). *Bullying at school.* Malden, MA: Blackwell.

Ozer, E., Tschann, J., Pasch, L., & Flores, E. (2004). Violence perpetration across peer and partner relationships: Co-occurrence and longitudinal patterns among adolescents. *Journal of Adolescent Health, 34,* 64–71.

Pellegrini, A. D. (2001). A longitudinal study of heterosexual relationships, aggression, and sexual harassment during the transition from primary school through middle school. *Applied Developmental Psychology, 22,* 119–133.

Pellegrini, A. D. (2002). Affiliative and aggressive dimensions of dominance and possible functions during early adolescence. *Aggression and Violent Behavior, 7*(1), 21–31.

Pellegrini, A. D., & Bartini, M. (2001). Dominance in early adolescent boys: Affiliative and aggressive dimensions and possible functions. *Merrill-Palmer Quarterly, 47,* 142–163.

Pellegrini, A. D., Bartini, M., & Brooks, F. (1999). School bullies, victims, and aggressive victims: Factors relating to group affiliation and victimization in early adolescence. *Journal of Educational Psychology, 91,* 216–224.

Pellegrini, A. D., & Van Ryzin, M. J. (2011). Part of the problem and part of the solution: The role of peers in bullying, dominance, and victimization during the transition from primary school to secondary school. In D. L. Espelage & S. M. Swearer (Eds.), *Bullying in North American schools, 2nd Edition* (pp. 91–100). New York: Routledge.Pepler, D. J., Craig, W. M., Connolly, J., & Henderson, K. (2002). Bullying, sexual harassment, dating violence, and substance use among adolescents. In C. Wekerle & A.-M. Wall (Eds.), *The violence and addiction equation: Theoretical and clinical issues in substance abuse and relationship violence* (pp. 153–168). New York: Brunner-Routledge.

Pepler, D. J., Craig, W. M., Connolly, J. A., Yuile, A., McMaster, L., & Depeng, J. (2006). A developmental perspective on bullying *Aggressive Behavior, 32,* 376–384.

Pepler, D., Jiang, D., Craig, W., & Connolly, J. (2008). Developmental trajectories of bullying and associated factors. *Child Development, 79,* 325–338.

Phoenix, A., Frosh, S., & Pattman, R. (2003). Producing contradictory masculine subject positions: Narratives of threat, homophobia, and bullying in 11–14 year old boys. *Journal of Social Issues, 59,* 179–195.

Pilkington, N. W., & D'Augelli, A. R. (1995). Victimization of lesbian, gay, and bisexual youth in community settings. *Journal of Community Psychology, 23,* 34–56.

Plummer, D. C. (2001). The quest for modern manhood: Masculine stereotypes, peer culture and the social significance of homophobia. *Journal of Adolescence, 24,* 15–23.

Poteat, V. P., & Espelage, D. L. (2005). Exploring the relation between bullying and homophobic verbal content: The Homophobic Content Agent Target (HCAT) Scale. *Violence and Victims, 20,* 513–528.

Rigby, K. (1999). Peer victimisation at school and the health of secondary school students. *The Journal of School Psychology, 69,* 95.

Rigby, K., & Johnson, B. (2006). Expressed readiness of Australian schoolchildren to act as bystanders in support of children who are being bullied. *Educational Psychology, 26,* 425–440.

Rigby, K., & Slee, P. (1993). Dimensions of interpersonal relation among Australian children and implications for psychological well-being. *Journal of School Psychology, 133,* 33–42.

Riggs, D. S., & O'Leary, K. D. (1989). A theoretical model of courtship aggression. In M. A. Pirog-Good (Ed.), Violence in dating relationships: Emerging social issues (pp. 53–71). New York: Praeger.

Rivers, I. (2001). The bullying of sexual minorities at school: Its nature and long-term correlates. *Educational and Child Psychology, 18,* 33–46.

Rivers, I., Poteat, V. P, Noret, N., & Ashurst, N. (2009). Observing bullying at school: The mental health implications of witness status. *School Psychology Quarterly, 24,* 211–223.

Rodkin, P. C., & Fischer, K. (2003). Sexual harassment and the cultures of childhood: Developmental, domestic violence, and legal perspectives. *Journal of Applied School Psychology, 19,* 177–196.

Ronfeldt, H. M., Kimerling, R., & Arias, I. (1998). Satisfaction with relationship power and the perpetration of dating violence. *Journal of Marriage and the Family, 60,* 70–78.

Roscoe, B., & Callahan, J. E. (1985). Adolescents' self-report of violence in families and dating relations. *Adolescence, 20,* 545–553.

Ross, S. W., & Horner, R. H. (2009). Bullying prevention in positive behavior support. *Journal of Applied Behavior Analysis, 42*(4), 747.

Rubin, K. H., Bukowski, W., & Parker, J. G. (1998). Peer interactions, relationships, and groups. In W. Damon (Series Ed.) & N. Eisenberg (Vol. Ed.), Handbook of child psychology: Vol 3. Social, emotional, and personality development (5th ed., pp. 619–700). New York: Wiley.

Salmivalli, C. (2010). Bullying and the peer group: A review. *Aggression & Violent Behavior, 15,* 112–120.

Salmivalli, C., Huttunen, A., & Lagerspetz, K. M. J. (1997). Peer networks and bullying in schools. *Scandinavian Journal of Psychology, 38,* 205–312.

Salmivalli, C., Lagerspetz, K., Bjorkqvist, K., Osterman, K., & Kaukiainen, A. (1996). Bullying as a group process: Participant roles and their relations to social status within the group. *Aggressive Behavior, 22,* 1–15.

Schewe, P. A. (2002). Guidelines for developing rape prevention and risk reduction interventions. In P. A. Schewe (Ed.), Preventing intimate partner violence: Developmentally appropriate interventions across the lifespan (pp. 107–136). Washington, DC: American Psychological Association.

Shields, A., & Cicchetti, D. (2001). Parental maltreatment and emotion dysregulation as risk factors for bullying and victimization in middle childhood. *Journal of Clinical Child Psychology, 30,* 349–363.

Silverman J. G., Pratt C., Reed E., Nagy B. J., Whitaker D. K., Baker C.,... Pavlos C. (2004). The CARE Communities project: An academic, practitioner, and federal public health agency collaboration to improve intimate partner violence services for underserved communities. *Public Health Reports, 119*(6), 590–593.

Silverman, J. G., Raj, A., Mucci, L. A., & Hathaway, J. E. (2001). Dating violence against adolescent girls and associated substance use, unhealthy weight control, sexual risk behavior, pregnancy, and suicidality. *Journal of the American Medical Association, 286,* 572–579.

Simons, R. L., Lin, K., & Gordon, L. C. (1998). Socialization in the family of origin and male dating violence: A prospective study. *Journal of Marriage and Family, 60,* 461–478.

Skelton, C. (1996). Learning to be "tough": The fostering of maleness in one primary school. *Gender and Education, 8,* 185–197.

Smith, P. K. (2003). *Violence in schools: The response in Europe.* London: Routledge.

Smith, J. D., Schneider, B. H., Smith, P. K., & Ananiadou, K. (2004). The effectiveness of whole-school antibullying programs: A synthesis of evaluation research. *School Psychology Review, 33*(4), 547.

Sourander, A., Helstela, L., Helenius, H., & Piha, J. (2000). Persistence of bullying from childhood to adolescence: A longitudinal 8-year follow-up study. *Child Abuse and Neglect, 24,* 873–881.

Stein, N. (1993). Sexual harassment in schools. *School Administrator, 50,* 14–16.

Stein, N. (1995). Sexual harassment in K-12 schools: The public performance of gendered violence. *Harvard Educational Review, 65,* 145–162.

Stein, N. (1999). *Classrooms and courtrooms: Facing sexual harassment in K-12 Schools.* New York: Teachers College Press.

Stein, N (2003). Bullying or sexual harassment? The missing discourse of rights in an era of zero tolerance. *Arizona Law Review, 45,* 783–799.

Stein, N. (2005). A rising pandemic of sexual violence in elementary and secondary schools: Locating a secret problem. *Duke Journal of Gender Law and Policy, 12,* 33–52.

Stratton, S. D., & Backes, J. S. (1997). Sexual harassment in North Dakota public schools: A study of eight high schools. *The High School Journal, 80,* 163–172.

Swearer, S. M., & Doll, B. (2001). Bullying in schools: An ecological framework. *Journal of Emotional Abuse, 2,* 7–23.

Swearer, S. M., Song, S. Y., Cary, P. T., Eagle, J. W., & Mickelson, W. T. (2001). Psychosocial correlates in bullying and victimization: The relationship between depression, anxiety, and bully/victim status. In R. Geffner, M. T. Loring, & C. Young (Eds.), *Bullying behavior: Current issues, research, and interventions* (pp. 95–121). Binghamton, NY: Haworth Maltreatment and Trauma Press/ Haworth Press.

Sweeting, H., Young, R., West, P., & Der, G. (2006). Peer victimization and depression in early-mid adolescence: A longitudinal study. *British Journal of Educational Psychology, 76,* 577–594.

Tartar, R., Vanyukov, M., Giancola, P., Dawes, M., Blackson, T., Mezzich, A., & Clark, D. B. (1999). Etiology of early-age onset substance use disorder: A maturational perspective. *Development and Psychopathology, 11,* 657–684.

Thompson, M. P., Sims, L., Kingree, J. B., & Windle, M. (2008). Longitudinal associations between problem alcohol use and violent victimization in a national sample of adolescents. *Journal of Adolescent Health, 42,* 21–27. doi: 10.1016/j.jadohealth.2007.07.003

Twemlow, S. W., Fonagy, P., Sacco, F. C., Gies, M. L., Evans, R., & Ewbank, R. (2001). Creating a peaceful school learning environment: A controlled study of an elementary school intervention to reduce violence. *American Journal of Psychiatry, 158,* 808–810. doi: 10.1176/appi.ajp.158.5.808

Tolman, D. L., Spencer, R., Rosen-Reynoso, M., & Porche, M. V. (2003). Sowing the seeds of violence in heterosexual relationships: Early adolescents narrate compulsory heterosexuality. *Journal of Social Issues, 59,* 159–178.

Tontodonato, P., & Crew, B. K. (1992). Dating violence, social learning theory and gender: A multivariate analysis. *Violence and Victims, 7*(1), 3–14.

Troy, M., & Sroufe, L. A. (1987). Victimization among preschoolers: Role of attachment relationship history. *Journal of the American Academy of Child and Adolescent Psychiatry, 26,* 166–172.

Ttofi, M. M., Farrington, D. P., & Baldry, A. C. (2008). *Effectiveness of programmes to reduce bullying.* Stockholm: Swedish National Council for Crime Prevention.

Unnever, J. D., & Cornell, D. G. (2003). The culture of bullying in middle school. *Journal of School Violence, 2,* 5–28.

Vreeman, R. C., & Carroll, A. E. (2007). A systematic review of school-based interventions to prevent bullying. *Archives of Pediatric and Adolescent Medicine, 161,* 78–88.

Weisz, A. N., & Black, B. M. (2009). *Programs to reduce teen dating violence and sexual assault: Perspectives on what works.* New York: Columbia University Press.

Wright, L. W., Adams, H. E., & Bernat, J. (1999). Development and validation of the homophobia scale. *Journal of Psychopathology and Behavioral Assessment, 21,* 337–347.

Ybarra, M., Diener-West, M., & Leaf, P. (2007). Examining the overlap in Internet harassment and school bullying: Implications for school Intervention. *Journal of Adolescent Health, 41,* S42–S52.

Ybarra, M., Espelage, D. L., & Martin, S. (2010). Unwanted sexual and harassing experiences: From school to text messaging. In D. L. Espelage & S. M. Swearer (Eds.), *Bullying in North American schools* (pp. 62–72). Routledge: New York.

Yoneyama, S., & Naito, A. (2003). Problems with the paradigm: The school as a factor in understanding bullying (with special reference to Japan). *British Journal of Sociology of Education, 24,* 315–330.

CHAPTER

12 Keeping the Dragons at Bay: Research-Based Approaches to the Prevention of Substance Abuse

Paul E. Priester *and* Janice E. Jones

Abstract

Alcohol, tobacco, and other drug abuse (ATODA) is a critical public health issue. Research suggests that there are some principles that can guide effective prevention activities. This chapter explores not only what content should be included in such prevention activities, but also what processes and which contexts are best suited for optimal results. In general, research supports the use of developmentally appropriate activities that decrease risk factors and increase protective factors. Certain skills such as relationship skills and drug refusal skills are shown to be effective components of prevention work. Components that have not been successful include: affective skills training and the didactic imparting of drug information to elementary school students. Specific culturally responsive techniques are required for students of color, as the drug use profiles and risk/protective factors differ by ethnic/racial groups. A discussion of the political and fiscal contextual variables that impact the delivery of prevention activities is also presented.

Key Words: drug use prevention, alcoholism prevention, protective factors, risk factors, evidence-based preventionIntroduction

The term "chasing the dragon" has dual meanings. The first meaning is a literal one, which describes ingesting heroin through the inhalation of fumes. The second meaning is a metaphorical referral to the obsessive, endless, self-destructive pursuit of the intoxication that is evident in the lives of addicts. Substance abuse, of both illicit and licit drugs is a pernicious, omnipresent public health issue that cuts across cultural, racial, and socioeconomic status lines. Globally, the harmful use of alcohol results in 2.5 million annual deaths and 15.3 million people meet diagnostic criteria for drug use disorders (World Health Organization, 2011).

An integral component of the public health perspective has been that it makes much more sense to intervene and prevent the onset of addiction rather than waiting and treating addiction after it has caused destruction in the individual addict's life. Every dollar spent on prevention is estimated to translate into a savings of $10 in later treatment (Pentz, 1998). This chapter will review some of the concepts, research conclusions, and criticisms related to the activities that are being carried out in this domain. Counseling Psychologists are uniquely qualified to lead activities in the prevention of substance abuse given the profession's emphasis on multicultural issues, maintaining a developmental perspective, emphasizing an individual's strengths, and a high regard for quality research. This chapter will examine attempts to "keep the dragons at bay" by means of prevention activities through the lenses of these particular attributes of the field of counseling psychology.

Political, Fiscal Context of ATODA Prevention

Counseling psychology as a field emphasizes the interaction between an individual and the individual's context. It is appropriate to initiate the discussion of the prevention of alcohol, tobacco, and other drug abuse (ATODA) by examining some of these contextual variables. One of the most significant trends in ATODA prevention has been the emphasis on using evidence-based programs. The language can become confusing here, as the different federal agencies use different terms to describe evidence-based programs. The Substance Abuse and Mental Health Services Administration has three levels to indicate the quality of the programs. The highest level includes programs identified as legacy or model programs. The second tier includes programs described as effective. The third level of ATODA prevention programs is described as promising.

The Department of Education employs two levels of programs. The higher tier programs are called exemplary. The lower tier is called promising. The Collaborative for Academic, Social and Emotional Learning has one distinction that identifies high quality programs: select. Thus, we have two federal agencies and a national nonprofit that each uses its own language and criteria to identify evidence-based ATODA prevention programs. To summarize across these three organizations, the higher level of certification typically requires that researchers provide evidence that the program meets the following conditions, as determined by a panel of experts: it is a manual-based program that has been shown to decrease the identified behavior; the evidence for this change meets a high scientific standard; these results have been published in peer-reviewed formats, preferably by two or more independent researchers; and the program is ready for dissemination. The expert panel then determines whether the program may be certified as an evidence-based program. The lower levels of certification are used for programs that have demonstrated some initial support but do not reach the level of criteria established for the higher certification.

The move to a scientifically based model that emphasizes a change in the identified behavior is critical (Cooney, Huser, Small, & O'Connor, 2007). Much of the past research on the effectiveness of ATODA prevention would focus on knowledge of the drugs or a change in attitudes. For example if I were developing a program to decrease inhalant drug use for fifth graders, it would not be sufficient to show that the fifth graders that attended my workshop showed a statistically significant increase in the stated disapproval of the use of inhalants, or in the knowledge of the negative health impacts of inhalant abuse. Rather in order to be designated as an evidence-based program, it would require that a change in behavior was seen in that the fifth graders who attended my workshop participated in inhalant abuse less than a control group. One meta-analysis found that ATODA prevention programs can frequently lead to a positive effect on knowledge and attitudes about drug use, but that this change in knowledge or attitudinal stance had no impact on drug-using behavior of students (Bangert-Drowns, 1988). Typically, third-party evaluators are used in this evaluation process to determine whether the ATODA prevention program has succeeded in decreasing real world behavior.

Consequences of the Evidence-Based Programs System

Having such a system that identifies specific ATODA prevention programs as being "effective" has several real world consequences. First, the majority of ATODA prevention activities are funded by federal sources. One of the results of this system of maintaining lists of "effective" programs is that these federal funding sources require the use of a program from these lists. This has led to the creation of a new public health industry. In this industry, researchers develop ATODA prevention programs and have these programs evaluated. Once the criteria are met, the programs are submitted to the federal agencies for approval. After being granted the evidence-based certification, they are then marketed, typically at an expensive cost to schools or community agencies that wish to use them. The schools or community agencies use the funds obtained by the grants to purchase these programs, but are only allowed to use these designated programs for the grant-funded activities.

Limitations to Preapproved ATODA Prevention Programs

While the concept of only using effective ATODA prevention programs is commendable, there are certain real world limitations to such a situation. The primary limitation is that of fidelity to the program. Oftentimes, these programs are implemented by school teachers who are not trained mental health professionals and may not understand the importance of fidelity to the manualized approach. In fact, research has demonstrated that teachers adapt or change the ATODA prevention programs more frequently than implementing the programs with fidelity (Dusenbury, Brannigan, Falco, & Lake, 2004). Oftentimes, critically important components, such as interactive role-playing are omitted (Ringwalt et al., 2003). The danger of the omission of an interactive component such as role-playing will be clear in a later section of the chapter.

Another limitation to the use of packaged ATODA prevention programs is that such a use is dependent on continued support in the form of federal grants. Recently, the entire Safe and Drug Free Schools program was eliminated from the public school system. This was the major source of funding for schools to engage in ATODA activities. The elimination of this program demonstrates the often fleeting nature of federal sources of funding and the dangers in becoming overreliant on these programs to purchase expensive ATODA prevention programs.

Research-Based Principles Versus Evidence-Based Programs

A helpful distinction that needs to be made is between research-based principles of effective ATODA prevention and evidence-based programs. The research-based principles of effective ATODA prevention perspective embraces the empirical study of what are the critical components of effective ATODA prevention activities. Much of the debate in the ATODA prevention world regarding evidence-based programs versus research-based principles is similar to the discussion that has been occurring in the world of psychotherapy. In that world, there has been heated debate regarding the effectiveness of specific manualized treatments versus what are the critical components that lead to improvement in psychotherapy (Wampold, 2001).

This is an important distinction, as there may be components of an evidence-based program that are not critical to its effectiveness. Alternatively, there may be critical components of a program that are excluded in its implementation, for example the aforementioned role-playing deletion. Lacking such a research-based principles approach, we are not able to identify what leads to successful prevention (Hensen et al., 2010).

There is considerable controversy regarding what constitutes research-based principles in ATODA prevention. There have been numerous meta-analytic studies examining this issue. These meta-analytic studies have sometimes reached conflicting conclusions. Despite some of these contradictions, it is possible to summarize from this large body of research and suggest some conclusions regarding efficacious approaches to decreasing ATODA use. When answering this question, it is critical to break the analysis down into a finer detailed layer of analysis. One needs to also ask what works for specific populations, what is the content of effective ATODA prevention, what are the best methods of delivering this content, who should be the individual that is delivering the program, and where the ATODA prevention activities should occur.

This discussion will start with some broad generalizations about effective research-based principles of ATODA prevention. The analysis will then turn to look at different developmental levels and suggest how specific prevention techniques can be implemented in a developmentally appropriate manner, starting with preschool and ending with the university setting. The focus of this chapter will not be beyond college students, although undoubtedly ATODA prevention is needed in the adult population and there are specific developmental milestones that are high-risk situations for the development of drug or alcohol problems in adulthood. Two such high-risk situations are the transition into a workplace (Spell & Blum, 2008) and the transition into retirement. The focus of this chapter is primary prevention of ATODA in children, adolescents, and young adults. Although an exploration of ATODA prevention in adults is important and worthy of analysis, it is beyond the scope of this chapter.

What Are Appropriate Goals of ATODA Prevention?

In order to answer the question of what elements of ATODA prevention are effective, it is important to begin the discussion with a definition of what a successful outcome would be. Is it realistic to expect that our prevention activities will result in the students never drinking a single beer or smoking a single cigarette? It is a widely accepted axiom in public health that the later that high-risk behaviors are initiated in an individual's developmental trajectory, the less the consequences to the individual. So, reasonable ATODA prevention goals are to delay the onset of such high-risk behavior as much as possible. An example is alcohol abuse prevention at the university level. In this context, a successful prevention intervention would be delaying the consumption of alcohol until the student reached the age of 21. An alternative acceptable outcome would be decreasing the incidences of binge drinking (defined as five or more alcoholic drinks on one occasion) in the population, as opposed to having the expectation that your intervention will result in college students not drinking alcohol whatsoever.

What Are the Contents of Effective ATODA Prevention Programs?

A good place to start the discussion of research-based principles of ATODA prevention is the contents of the prevention activities. In the popular culture in the United States, drug prevention is often a politically popular activity, with more emphasis placed on the fact that such activities are being carried out, rather than whether the contents of the activities are empirically supported by the related body of research (Stoil & Hill, 1996). Some of the standard domains of content in ATODA prevention include: risk and protective factors, refusal skills, relationship skills, affective skills, and drug information.

Risk/Protective Factors

Research has uncovered certain personality characteristics or behaviors that are correlated (either positively or negatively) with drug use. Elements that are positively associated with drug use are termed risk factors. Alternatively protective factors are those attributes that are negatively correlated with drug use. The focus on ATODA prevention activities is to reduce risk factors while simultaneously enhancing protective factors (Hawkins, Catalano, & Arthur, 2002). Examples of risk factors include: low sense of affiliation with prosocial communities, academic failure, high family conflict, associating with drug-using peers, attitudes favorable to drug use, rebelliousness, impulsiveness, and peer rejection. Examples of protective factors include: opportunities for prosocial community involvement, family attachment, social skills, and religiosity (Arthur, Hawkins, Pollard, Catalano, & Baglioni, 2002).

One of the key perspectives in the risk factors area is that the greatest impact can be made with certain factors at certain developmental stages. For example, it is important to focus on early risk factors in young children such as out-of-control aggressive behavior. The thinking is that by intervening at an early stage, counselors, parents, and teachers can help teach the child positive coping mechanisms. If the child can develop these skills, the risk trajectory is averted. If no coping skills are taught to modify this behavior early on, the child will continue on the path to impulsivity and antisocial behavior that will eventually end in substance abuse.

Researchers also suggest that where to focus the development of protective factors differs with developmental stage. For example, it is considered better to intervene with the family when the child is young, fostering a sense of family attachment, while the peer environment may have the biggest impact in adolescents, which may suggest encouraging the students to associate with nonusing peers (Gerstein & Green, 1993).

Although the embracing of the risk/protective factors approach is universal and endorsed by the National Institute of Drug Abuse (1997), it is not without criticism. The first criticism relates to the research paradigm employed by the researchers. If one is using an epidemiological research strategy, as these researchers often employ, results are limited to a correlational nature. To state that academic failure is associated with later drug use is not the same as saying that academic failure caused the subsequent substance abuse. There could be underlying attributes that are impacting both the academic failure and the later subsequent drug use. Correcting the academic failure does not necessarily impact the underlying construct that leads to the later substance abuse. It is surprising that this criticism of this line of research is not voiced more frequently.

A second criticism of the body of research related to risk/protective factors is one related to psychometrics. According to Corrigan, Loneck, Videka, and Brown (2007), there are no instruments currently available that measure the relative levels of risk/protective factors in a psychometrically sound and acceptable manner. This is problematic indeed and makes one question the quality of the related research in this area.

Refusal Skills

Refusal skill training is an intervention where students are taught skills related to avoiding or rejecting the offer of drugs in an assertive manner. This approach uses a coaching model in which students learn these new skills and then get an opportunity to practice them in an interactive format with peers, often accompanied with feedback from peers on how well they succeeded in avoiding the offered drug opportunity. Typically there are four potential verbal responses that are practiced: simple no, declarative statements, excuse, or alternative (Nichols, Graber, Brooks-Gunn, & Botvin, 2006).

Refusal skill training has shown to be a very effective component of ATODA prevention as long as a few guidelines are followed. First of all, it is critical that students get the opportunity to interactively practice and process these skills as they learn them. The importance of this interactive component will be emphasized in the section addressing how prevention programs should be implemented.

A second critical component of successful refusal skill training is that the skill be able to be used in the near future. A useful concept that can be used to describe this is based on Vygotsky's zone of proximal development. The zone of proximal development from a superficial perspective refers to the difference between what a learner can do on their own and what he or she can do with the assistance of an instructor. There have been attempts to place this developmental process in a much larger developmental context, beyond that of the classroom (Kravtsova, 2009). Using this original concept of the zone of proximal development that relates to all developmental processes, we would suggest that a useful construct to employ in understanding the effectiveness of drug refusal skills training is the zone of proximal experimentation.

The zone of proximal experimentation is the amount of distance between where a student is currently and when this student will have the real world opportunity to use a specific mind-altering substance. Drug refusal techniques are effective when they are trained and practiced when this zone of proximal experimentation is narrow (i.e., when the opportunity to experiment with the drug will appear in the near future in the student's social world). In this way, training fifth-grade students' refusal skills for cocaine will not be effective, given the fact that, hopefully, there are very few fifth graders who are offered the opportunity to use cocaine. However, training fifth graders on refusal skills related to inhalant use may be highly effective, as this is the drug with which typical fourth through sixth graders may first experiment. Matching refusal skills with the type of drug abuse occurring in the student's interpersonal world greatly enhances the effectiveness of such an approach (Hawkins et al., 2002).

Relationship Skills

A powerful component of an effective ATODA prevention program is a focus on the development of interpersonal relationship skills. This could be considered a subset of the risk/protective factors discussion, but merits exploration on its own. It is such a powerful ingredient in ATODA prevention that some scholars recommend that it should be the sole focus in elementary school level prevention activities (Stoil & Hill, 1996). At the elementary school level, the relationship skills that are typically focused on include friendship making skills, communication skills, and leadership skills. In junior and senior high school, the focus also includes such critical components as resolving conflicts with peers and parents. As stated, the development of social skills has been identified as a key protective factor and is a highly trainable set of skills (Corrigan et al., 2007). Including it in ATODA interventions, especially when coupled with an interactive component that allows practice and experimentation can maximize the impact of the prevention activities.

Affective Skills

The training of affective skills is frequently included in ATODA prevention activities, especially for younger children. In this approach, students are taught to identify and express their emotional states. We can clearly see a link here between this skill set and some of the highest risk factors mentioned above, such as aggression and inability to modulate negative affect. There is just one slight problem with using affective skills training in ATODA prevention activities, it does not appear to have any impact on later drug use (Soole, Mazerolle, & Rombouts, 2008).

A good example of this is a focus on increasing student self-esteem in the context of ATODA prevention activities. The thinking is that, since addicts have low levels of self-esteem, if we could increase the self-esteem of children before they are offered drugs, they will not use drugs. The conclusion is that low self-esteem leads to subsequent drug use. This is an excellent example of confusing correlation with causation. Researchers are adamant that focusing on increasing children's self-esteem does not result in decreased subsequent drug use (Stoil & Hill, 1996). In fact, some longitudinal research that measured premorbid baseline level of self-esteem suggests that individuals who later become addicts have average or even above average levels of self-esteem prior to drug use (Kinney, 2011). It is the destructive process of becoming an addict and maintaining an addiction that is devastating to an individual's self-esteem.

Drug Information

Another popular component of ATODA prevention activities is the didactic transmission of information related to the impact of drugs on the human body. Here, the assumption is that if we arm our children with accurate medical information about the dangers of the drugs, they will refrain from using drugs. As a universal technique used across all developmental levels, it has been shown to not be an effective strategy for decreasing drug use (Stoil & Hill, 1996). One of the criticisms of such an approach is that we are assuming a level of cognitive capacity that is not present in younger children. It is critical that prevention professionals use a keen developmental mindset when imparting information.

Specifically, Stoil and Hill (1996) suggest that no drug information be given to elementary school children. At the middle school level, only limited information should be given that emphasizes the negative aspects of the use of the drugs. Middle school is considered a developmental level in which too much drug information can actually pique the interest of the students and drive their curiosity to the point where they may experiment with the drugs. At the high school level, detailed medical information can be given to the students. These students now are considered to have the cognitive complexity to integrate all of the information and arrive at the conclusion that experimenting with drugs can be dangerous.

How Should the ATODA Activities Be Delivered?

There are several points in which the meta-analytic studies on ATODA prevention agree emphatically and one of these is that the process in which prevention activities are implemented is a critical component related to efficacy. One of the most critical process-related components is interactivity. Having students interact with each other in the process of completing the prevention activities is an established active component in deterring ATODA (Soole, 2008, Tobler et al., 2000, White & Pitts, 1998). Examples of interactive components include role playing or group discussions. An example of a noninteractive prevention program component would be the didactic dissemination of drug-related information.

A second component of effective ATODA prevention activities on which different researchers agree is the necessity of time intensity. Prevention programs that are comprised of multiple sessions over an extended period of time result in better outcomes than those that are single events or of a short duration (Botvin & Griffin, 2003). There is some controversy regarding the importance of postintervention booster sessions. Booster sessions are activities that reiterate or build on the skills learned in the prevention activity. These booster sessions occur at a specific time period after the prevention activity implementation (often at a 6-month interval). Some researchers have maintained that booster sessions increase the effectiveness of the prevention activity (Tobler et al., 2000 White & Pitts, 1998). Other researchers have not found support for this contention that booster sessions improve the prevention outcomes (Soole, 2008).

A third component of the process of ATODA prevention delivery has to do with the number of students for whom the program is being delivered. A fascinating finding is that small-scale ATODA prevention activities are more successful than large-scale implementations (Tobler et al., 2000). The exact reason for this is unclear. Is it that large-scale implementations result in lower fidelity to the suggested activities? Or do large-scale projects create a relationally cold environment? For whatever reason, this observation is constant among meta-analytic researchers in this field.

In a national survey of school staff who led ATODA prevention activities, researchers examined the frequency of effective content and effective strategies in delivering this content (Ennett et al., 2003). What they discovered is that 62% taught effective content, but only 17% used effective delivery methods, and a mere 14% used effective content matched with effective delivery strategies. This study demonstrates the importance of paying attention to how the ATODA prevention activities are delivered as well as what is the content of the program.

Who Should Deliver the Program?

An interesting component of effective research-based principles of ATODA prevention is the selection of who should be the individual implementing the intervention. Numerous studies and meta-analyses have established that peer-led programs are more effective than those led by teachers, counselors, or other adults (Cuijpers, 2002). Other studies have suggested a linear order regarding the choice of facilitators, highly trained mental health professionals outperformed both peers and teachers, and peers outperformed teachers (Tobler et al., 2000). Teachers are an especially problematic choice for the individual who is chosen to lead the ATODA prevention activities, given their apparent proclivity to modify and/or delete critical components of the programs (Dusenbury et al., 2004, Ringwalt et al., 2003). Unfortunately in school-based prevention activities, teachers are often employed as the facilitators of such programs. At the university level, there is research supporting the contention that the higher the level of training of the professional facilitator, the better the clinical outcomes of the ATODA prevention efforts (Crozier & Gressard, 2005).

In What Context Should Prevention Occur?

An interesting question related to the efficacy of ATODA prevention activities is in which contexts these activities are successful. Communities often feel a high level of pressure to offer these prevention activities at the elementary school level, even though some researchers are of the opinion that this may be one of the least effective milieus in which to do this work (Stoil & Hill, 1996).

There is a lot of pressure from the federal government to carry out these activities in community-based coalitions. This is particularly evident in the current Drug Free Communities grant program administered by the Office of National Drug Control Policy. This program funds 700 community coalitions across the United States in their efforts to decrease underage drinking and drug use. The irony is that there is some research to suggest that community coalitions are a very ineffective setting in which to do ATODA prevention activities, even resulting in higher uses of certain drugs such as inhalants (Collins, Johnson, & Becker, 2007). A caveat to this suggestion relates to African American students. This exception will be discussed in the next section.

Apparently the most effective arena in which to carry out ATODA prevention activities are the middle school and high school settings. Developmentally appropriate interventions at the middle school level are seen as being particularly effective (Soole, 2008). Prevention activities related to preventing marijuana seem to be the most effective at the high school level (Porath-Waller, 2010).

Does Culture Matter? What Is Culturally-Responsive ATODA Prevention?

It is disturbing to note that there has been so little high quality research carried out on the issue of modifying ATODA prevention activities to be culturally responsive to students of color. Researchers only recently have begun to examine this issue and much of the work in this area has not been rigorously designed or evaluated (Sussman, 2005). There has only been one, unpublished, doctoral dissertation completed on the topic: a meta-analysis on the impact of including cultural variables in outcomes of ATODA prevention for students of color (Bledsoe, 2003). There is strong evidence that ethnic/racial minorities have different drug use patterns, trajectories, and culturally specific risk and protective factors (Resnicow, Soler, Braithwaite, Ahluwalia, & Butler, 2000). Given these culturally based differences, it is baffling why there has been a relatively low emphasis placed on these topics.

One of the main controversies in this area is the question of whether extant models of prevention can be used with ethnic/racial minority students as opposed to creating new culturally specific models for distinct groups. Using current ATODA prevention programs, but adding culture-specific content to the model is a strategy endorsed by many researchers (Castro & Alarcon, 2002). The main argument in favor of this approach is the cost savings and the fact that these programs are ready for dissemination (Dent, Sussman, Ellickson, & Brown, 1996). The one unpublished meta-analysis examines this question and finds that the addition of cultural variables onto existing programs did not result in better prevention outcomes. Others argue that given the unique culture and strikingly different drug use patterns, new models need to be developed that are created specifically for each specific ethnic/racial group (Resnicow et al., 2000).

Clearly, the topic of the impact of culture on ATODA prevention is a critical and vital topic that warrants a higher level of attention than is allowed in this context. Granted this, the following discussion will attempt to summarize some of the differences between the four major ethnic/racial groups regarding: drug use patterns, differential risk/protective factors associated with drug use, and clinical suggestions for engaging in ATODA prevention with members of these groups.

African Americans

There are some fascinating drug use patterns for African American students that differ from the majority European American culture and other ethnic/racial groups in critical aspects. African American students have lower rates of use of all substances when compared to European American students, with the exception of marijuana (Johnston, O'Malley, Bachman, & Schulenberg, 2011a). By adulthood, these differences disappear and African American adults have equivalent or higher rates of drug use when compared to the broader European American cultural norms (Johnston, O'Malley, Bachman, & Schulenberg, 2011b).

Risk factors for African American students include: higher school dropout rates, low socioeconomic status, and more chaotic family life (Catalano et al., 1993). African American students are more likely to have a parent die, to have criminal justice involvement, to have the family income decrease, and to be victims of violence (Fitzpatrick & Boldizar, 1993, Resnicow et al., 2000). Given the markedly higher levels of risk factors and stressors, it is impressive that African American students have lower rates when compared to European American students, who have markedly lower levels of such risk factors. This seems to point to underlying sources of resilience within the African American culture.

These protective factors have a unique profile for African Americans. Parents appear to have a much stronger social influence on African American students, when compared to European American students, who are more influenced by peers (Catalano et al., 1993). Other researchers have suggested that the greater role that religion plays in African American culture may play a prominent role in this differential rate of drug use. Researchers have found that religiosity deterred drug use in African Americans but not in European Americans (Amey, Albrecht, & Miller, 1996).

Many researchers have emphasized the inclusion of culturally specific components into ATODA prevention for African American students. Examples of such culturally relevant content include: the study of African history, Kwanzaa, the Nguzo Saba, and traditions such as unity circles and rites of passage (Resnicow et al., 2000). As stated, the question of whether the inclusion of such content into existing programs, versus the ground-up creation of a culturally specific ATODA prevention model, results in improved outcomes is still unanswered.

It is emphasized that prevention professionals work collaboratively with natural support systems in the African American community. Given the primacy of religious beliefs and practices for many African Americans, the church or mosque seems an ideal context in which to carry out such efforts. Brown et al. (2006) attempted to do exactly this. They found that with support and training, over a 3-year period, one third of the African American churches successfully developed and offered ATODA prevention programming, one third were in the process of developing a program, and one third had not begun to do so. Unfortunately, this study focused on the feasibility of using African-American churches as a context for ATODA prevention, rather than on the outcomes of such efforts. This is an example of how African American–specific ATODA prevention efforts may be differentially implemented when compared to European American communities, where research has shown the school to be the more effective context in which to do ATODA prevention efforts.

Latino/as

The drug use pattern for Latino/as also has a unique profile. In contrast to African American youth, Latino/as have higher rates at an earlier age and then the rates dropped significantly in adulthood, with adult rates being lower than their European American counterparts (Substance Abuse and Mental Health Services Administration, 2006). Latino/a 12th-grade students have the highest rates of drug use for several categories including crack, heroin, heroin use without a needle, ice, and Rohypnol (Johnston et al., 2011a). There are some interesting differences in this drug use. For example, drug use is considerably higher for Latino boys than girls (Amaro & Cortes, 2003).

The critical risk factors associated with the Latino/a students include high school dropout rate, lack of parental monitoring, and association with deviant peer groups. Protective factors that have been shown to decrease Latino/a student drug use include drug resistance skills, personal self-management, social skills, parental involvement, and academic success (Substance Abuse and Mental Health Services Administration, 2007). There is some research that suggests that programs that focused on drug refusal skills training had the greatest impact for Latino/as (Bledsoe, 2003).

There have been some excellent evidence-based programs that have been developed and disseminated specifically for Latino/as. Familias Unidas is an example of such a program. Familias Unidas addresses the culturally specific risk and protective factors in a culturally responsive manner through a parent-centered prevention program for immigrant families. This program seeks to foster a sense of connection to the students' school by linking the parents to the school system. The program also has a strong parent education and skill development component (Pantin et al., 2003).

Native Americans

Substance abuse among Native American youth is much higher than among European American youth and other ethnic/racial minorities (Johnston et al., 2011a). Alcohol abuse is associated with 4 of the top 10 causes of death for Native Americans (Peregoy, 1993). Native American students seem to have a unique trajectory. Such youth use larger amounts of alcohol and marijuana and the pace of increased use as they age is higher than other ethnic/racial minority groups and European Americans as well (Dixon et al., 2007).

Research has identified protective factors that are particularly powerful in warding off future drug use in the Native American population. Self-efficacy and drug refusal skills are two such protective factors that have been identified (Galliher, Evans, & Weiser, 2007). In ATODA prevention work, researchers have emphasized the importance of partnering with community members and that researchers should embrace a community-based participatory research model that has extensive community input (Baldwin, Johnson, & Benally, 2009). It is interesting to note that one study that did attempt to include a large community involvement component did not result in any improved outcomes (Schinke, Tepavac, & Cole, 2000).

The Strengthening Families Program is one of the most commonly used evidence-based programs that focuses on parent education and fostering positive family communication skills and bonding. One version of it has been specifically adapted to be culturally responsive to Native Americans (Kumpfer, Pinyuchon, Castelo, & Whiteside, 2008). It is alarming that ATODA is acknowledged as such a critical public health concern for Native American youth and yet there is such a limited amount of research that has explored the culturally specific factors that can contribute to its prevention.

Asian Americans

Asian American youth have long been neglected in ATODA prevention research, perhaps due to the model minority stereotype that perpetuates the myth that Asian American students are all high achievers who do not suffer from problems like substance abuse (Sue & Sue, 2007). While it is true that Asian American students report a lower rate of drug use when compared to the other ethnic/racial groups, that does not mean that it is not still an important public health concern (Johnston et al., 2011a). In fact, Asian American adolescent substance abuse is a growing concern (Hahm, Wong, Huang, Ozonoff, & Lee, 2008). In particular, binge drinking among Asian American students is a serious problem (Hahm, Lahiff, & Guterman, 2004).

Research suggests that the two key risk factors for Asian American youth are academic failure and associating with using peers. It is interesting to note that Asian American students as a group have the lowest levels of interactions with drug-using peers, when compared to other ethnic/racial groups, but when Asian American students do have interactions with such deviant peers, it has a strong negative effect (Thai, Connell, & Tebes, 2010). There is a surprising paucity of literature suggesting culturally relevant ATODA prevention strategies for Asian American students.

Does ATODA Prevention Work for High-Risk Individuals?

There is a small subset of students who engage in high-risk behavior and show very early signs of problematic drug use. Many of these individuals eventually need addictions treatment. This group has often been the focus of ATODA prevention activities. Unfortunately, research suggests that for this approximate 5% of adolescents, prevention has not been shown to be effective in delaying or preventing alcohol, tobacco, or other drug use (Stoil & Hill, 1996). For whatever reason, this small subset of students seems to be on a "fast track" to full-blown addiction and seems particularly impervious to primary prevention activities. For this group, treatment rather than prevention may be a more appropriate clinical goal.

Research-Based ATODA Prevention Principles Applied at Specific Developmental Levels

Since the developmental abilities and the social, relational world of children, adolescents, and young adults are so distinctly different, it makes sense to provide a brief overview of how these broad research-based principles would be applied in the real world. The following is a brief overview of developmentally appropriate research-based ATODA prevention activities at each developmental level, starting with elementary school and ending at the university setting.

Kindergarten to Fifth Grade

In kindergarten through fifth grade, it is best to focus on protective factors that are amenable to training such as friendship skills and communication skills. Fostering a sense of belonging to prosocial groups (be it school, faith community, or girl/boy scouts) is a powerful prevention activity on which to focus. Research suggests that programs should not discuss drug specific content. Refusal skills training can focus on drugs within the students' narrow zone of proximal experimentation. For fourth through sixth graders this fist opportunity to experiment with drugs is typically inhalants. Nationally, 20% of fourth through sixth graders have experimented with the use of inhalants, so it makes sense to provide refusal skills training related to this. The golden rule is to keep all prevention activities on an interactional level. Using student peers as leaders is an excellent option and has shown to increase the effectiveness of prevention activities. Use teachers only as a last resort, and be sure to provide sufficient supervision if you have to rely on teachers to ensure that critical components are not excluded.

Grades 6–8

At the junior high level, you can maintain the work that was started at the elementary level (training students on social skills and fostering a sense of belonging to prosocial groups). In addition, some limited information about drugs can be presented, but in a superficial manner that strongly emphasizes the negative consequences of such use. Peer educational models begin to reach their highest potency as the primacy and importance of peer relationships looms in the students' emotional development. When engaging in social skills training, it is critical to include a component on conflict management. This conflict management component should address how to successfully manage conflicts with parents as well as with peers. Finally, research suggests that the focus of refusal skill training should be on drugs that are within the narrow zone of proximal experimentation, based on data gathered at the local level.

Grades 9–12

It is ironic that some researchers have suggested that high school is the optimal developmental level at which to provide prevention activities and yet is the most infrequently used school setting for such activities (Stoil & Hill, 1996). Prevention activities at this level can focus on drug refusal skill training based on drugs within the narrow zone of proximal experimentation at the school. It is critical to use student peer facilitators in prevention activities at the high school level. At this level, researchers can also feel free to provide the students with the complete accurate information related to drugs and their impact on health.

Two new approaches can be used to effectively to reduce ATODA. The first is using environmentally based interventions. Environmentally based interventions are ones that attempt to make it difficult for the student to do drugs by modifying the environment around the students, rather than directly educating the student. An example of such an environmental program that research has shown to be highly effective is the "Parents that host, lose the most" program.

"Parents that host, lose the most" is a community-based program that was delivered by community coalitions in Ohio. As stated, this program is an environmental intervention that is designed to modify the environment around the student so as to make it more difficult for the student to obtain alcohol. This is accomplished through a number of activities. First, parents are educated about the dangers of providing alcohol to underage minors. The coalition that developed this program realized that one of the primary sources of alcohol for students was parents. This education component is aimed at discouraging parents from hosting parties in which alcohol is knowingly served to minors. Aspects of this education process include teaching the parents about potential legal and financial consequences of hosting such a party.

The next component of this environmental strategy is a media campaign. In this media campaign, signage is placed throughout the community reminding parents not to host parties at which alcohol is served. Yard signs, stickers and signs at retail stores where alcohol is purchased are employed. The intent of this media campaign is to blanket the community with this message and discourage parents from providing alcohol to minors. The first author of this article was recently at the Ojibwa Reservation in Lac du Flambeau, Wisconsin. As part of this media blitz, the one grocery store on the reservation that sold alcohol agreed to place stickers on every package of alcohol, be it a single bottle of wine, 6 pack of beer, or case of beer, reminding parents not to purchase alcohol for minors. Other aspects of this media blitz include press releases to local media.

The third component of this environmental strategy is the use of police officers to assist in discouraging the provision of alcohol to minors. This is completed in two ways. First, police office complete frequent random checks where they employ an underage student who attempts to purchase alcohol from a retail establishment. Second, the police form "party patrols." The party patrols cruise around a community searching for events where there are a large number of students gathered and make sure that no alcohol is being served. A component of this party patrol is a party hotline, where students or concerned parents can call the police and report a party where they suspect that alcohol is being served to minors.

A fourth component to "Parents that host, lose the most" is considered an optional activity, but research has supported its efficacy in discouraging student alcohol use. This component is the development of an informal parent network. In these networks, parents gather and talk about their disapproval of serving alcohol to minors and contact each other if they suspect that another parent is hosting a party where alcohol is being served. Another component of their parent network is educating parents about locking liquor cabinets, as they may be supplying alcohol to their children without even realizing it, in the form of the children stealing alcohol from them.

This program is designed to make it very difficult for high school students to obtain alcohol, by cutting off the source of the illicit alcohol. Research has shown it to be highly effective. The one difficulty in implementing this program is that it requires mobilization among a large array of community members who will agree to work toward a community in which teenage alcohol use is discouraged. See http://www.drugfreeactionalliance.org for more information on this superb and effective program.

The second novel approach to introduce at the high school level is that of the use of a social norms approach. This model will be fully discussed in the following section, as it is routinely used at the university level. The social norms approach has also shown to be an effective component of high school-based ATODA prevention.

University-Based Prevention

Rather than waiting until the college aged student has had a significant drinking episode or gotten in trouble with law due to drinking, the social norms approach takes a proactive approach to diminishing and eliminating ATODA issues for the college aged student. The social norms approach is not about rehabilitation but rather about stopping problems before they start. Social norms approaches in preventing ATODA issues focus on the environment that the students live in and do not focus on the student or his or her personality as areas for change. Working together with policy constraints with the university or college to reduce or refrain from ATODA, the social norms approach has been shown to effectively reduce the incidences of problem ATODA use (Perkins, 2003a).

The social norms approach should be thought of as an environmental approach in that it is not focused on changing a person's attitudes but rather about sharing accurate information about the context in which the student dwells, through the use of population and group norms that will encourage the growth of protective factors and lessen individual problem behaviors. To begin to understand how the use of social norms might be effective on a college campus one must first understand what exactly the social norms on that particular campus are. Oftentimes students inaccurately report the amount of heavy episodic drinking among their peers (Page, Scanlan, & Gilbert, 1999) and this was a common misperception between both male and female students alike. Students tend to perceive more use of alcohol than really was consumed. So the idea is if a person perceives that people drink a lot, he or she will think that is the social norm of that institution is to drink a lot.

There are several reasons for these misperceptions. First, it is easy to remember a person who is drunk or high due to their exaggerated behavior. Second if one sees someone drunk or high at a certain point in time, one tends to associate that time with the person, completely ignoring the other times that one sees that person when he or she is sober. Third, the media tend to support the idea that college aged students are out to party and have a good time because that is why the student goes away from home to go to school. The media tend to idealize ATODA through movies and music videos that make being drunk or high seem like fun and a good time. When a student hears a story about someone having had too much to drink or use, as the story moves through the social context, the story tends to grow as it is retold. Almost everyone is easily influenced by the expectations and norms of the people around them. So if a college aged student does not have an accurate representation of the ATODA around himself or herself, he or she will not be able to accurately gauge what is an appropriate use of alcohol or other drugs, if any. The message needs to be loud and clear that not everyone on the campus is getting drunk or getting high.

Perkins (2003a) proposes a model of social norms approach to prevention that consists of positive steps to preventing ATODA issues for college aged students. The first step is called "Baseline" and this step consists of identification of misperceived and actual norms that are in place. The second is called "Intervention," which is not the same idea that one might think when one thinks about intervention. In this model, intervention consists of repeated, intense exposure to what the norms actually are. Intervention focuses on accuracy of the norms. The third step is called "Predicted Results" and consists of less exaggerated misperceptions of norms and moves into less risky behavior thereby reducing harm.

To capitalize on the social norms approach and create a positive impact using this approach it is necessary to create messages about the actual norms using clear, positive messages. It is more important for students to know that not everyone on their campus drinks, for example, than to see a horrific photo of an alcohol induced car crash. That is not to say that the dangers of ATODA are not to be used, but rather to focus on the positive message that not everyone is using ATODA on their campus. Using these clear, positive messages over and over rather than a one-time exposure will also help to create permanent messages that are held within the student and will become part of their internal messaging. It is important to target everyone on a college campus, not just the students who have been in trouble. It is important to repeat these messages, not simply focus on beginning students or a one-time-a-year message. It must be continuous and ongoing (Perkins, 2003b). In sum, the social norms approach is a clear way to help prevent the use of ATODA on college campuses. Perhaps used in concert with other approaches such as drug and alcohol free activities for students, brief counseling sessions, and education about the harmful effects of ATODA, the social norms approach will help improve compliance with the policies and procedures in place in the college setting, reducing the problem of substance abuse among the college aged population.

When implementing any prevention strategy it is important to use care and fidelity to the approach to ensure the maximum effectiveness. Perkins (2003b) reports that using the social norms approach as a starting point in a prevention plan for young adults is a successful strategy for prevention professionals as it has been shown to yield a benefit on its own. Perkins (2003b) also cautions that even though the social norms approach is cost-effective when examined in relationship to other approaches, it must be implemented with depth and fidelity. To begin this approach on a college campus it will be easiest to address the attitudinal norms held by the college aged students to make them aware of what the majority of students see as responsible behavior when it comes to ATODA.

Conclusion

ATODA prevention is a critically important public health activity. For too long, activity in this area has not been guided by research-based results. There is a lot of emphasis currently in using evidence-based programs. These programs have established evidence of their efficacy, but are often expensive and not implemented with fidelity.

There are some general research-based principles that can guide ATODA prevention activities. It is important to use developmentally appropriate content that matches up with the social world of the student. The level of interaction present in the prevention program has shown to be a critical and effective component. Prevention activities led by student peers is also an effective approach. There is some concern about school teachers implementing prevention activities without the necessary training, due to problems with fidelity and a research base that suggests either peers or trained professionals are the best implementers of these activities. The prevention field has embraced a perspective that focuses on decreasing risk factors associated with drug use and concurrently enhancing protective factors that can prevent later drug use. The salient risk and protective factors can vary based on the ethnic/racial identity of the students. Drug use and drug use trajectories differ markedly by ethnic/racial groups as well. The field of culturally responsive ATODA prevention is nascent, but there are some approaches that research suggests may be productive.

Future Direction

Practitioners may be well advised to embrace a research-based principles approach to preventing ATODA, as opposed to the popular evidence-based approach that is currently being emphasized. Decoupling prevention activities from the political and commercial market of programmed prevention programs can guarantee that research supported prevention activities can continue regardless of the fiscal climate. It is puzzling that counseling psychology as a field has not been more involved in the ATODA prevention field. It seems like a natural fit, given the strengths of such a professional identity. This is especially true regarding the lack of research relating to developing culturally relevant prevention activities.

References

Amaro, H., & Cortes, D. E. (2003). *National strategic plan on Hispanic drug use research: From the molecule to the community*. Princeton, NJ: Robert Wood Johnson Foundation.

Amey, C. H., Albrecht, S. I., & Miller, M. K. (1996). Racial differences in adolescent drug use: The impact of religion. *Substance Use and Misuse, 31,* 1311–1332.

Arthur, M. W., Hawkins, J. D., Pollard, J. A., Catalano, R. F., & Baglioni, A. J. (2002). Measuring risk and protective factors for substance abuse, delinquency, and other adolescent problem behaviors: The Communities That Care Youth Survey. *Evaluation Review, 26,* 575–601.

Baldwin, J. A., Johnson, J. L., & Benally, C. C. (2009). Building partnerships between indigenous communities and universities: Lessons learned in HIV/AIDS and substance abuse prevention research. *American Journal of Public Health, 99,* S77–S82.

Bangert-Drowns, R. L. (1988). The effects of school-based substance abuse education: A meta-analysis. *Journal of Drug Education, 18,* 243–264.

Bledsoe, K. L. (2003). *Effectiveness of drug prevention programs designed for adolescents of color: A meta-analysis* (Unpublished doctoral dissertation). Claremont Graduate University, Claremont, CA.

Botvin, G. J., & Griffin, K. W. (2003). Drug abuse prevention in schools. In Z. Sloda & W. J. Bukoski (Eds.), *Handbook of drug prevention: Theory, science and practice* (pp. 45–74). New York: Kluwer Academic/Plenum.

Brown, D. R., Scott, W., Lacey, K., Blount, J., Roman, D., & Brown, D. (2006). Black churches in substance use and abuse prevention efforts. *Journal of Alcohol and Drug Education, 50,* 43–65.

Castro, F. G., & Alarcon, E. H. (2002). Integrating cultural variables into drug abuse prevention and treatment with ethnic/racial minorities. *Journal of Drug Issues, 32,* 783–810.

Catalano, R., Hawkins, J., Krenz, C., Gillmore, M., Morrison, D., Wells, E., & Abbott, R. (1993). Using research to guide culturally appropriate drug abuse prevention. *Journal of Consulting and Clinical Psychology, 61,* 804–811.

Collins, D., Johnson, K., & Becker, B. J. (2007). A meta-analysis of direct and mediating effects of community coalitions that implemented science-based substance abuse prevention interventions. *Substance Use and Misuse, 42,* 985–1007.

Cooney, S. M., Huser, M., Small, S., & O'Connor, C. (2007). Evidence-based programs: An overview. *What Works Wisconsin—Research to Practice, 6,* 1–8.

Corrigan, M. J., Loneck, B., Videka, L., & Brown, M. C. (2007). Moving the risk and protective factor framework toward individualized assessment in adolescent substance abuse prevention. *Journal of Child and Adolescent Substance Abuse, 16,* 17–34.

Crozier, M. K., & Gressard, C. F. (2005). A national study of substance abuse prevention professionals in higher education. *Journal of Alcohol and Drug Education, 49,* 43–65.

Cuijpers, P. (2002). Peer-led and adult-led school drug prevention: A meta-analysis. *Journal of Drug Education, 32,* 107–119.

Dent, C. W., Sussman, S., Ellickson, P., & Brown, P. (1996). Is current drug abuse prevention programming generalizable across ethnic groups? *American Behavioral Scientist, 39,* 911–918.

Dixon, A. L., Yabiku, S. T., Okamoto, S. K., Tann, S. S., Marsiglia, F. F., Kulis, S., & Burke, A. M. (2007). The efficacy of a multicultural prevention intervention among urban American Indian youth in the southwest U.S. *Journal of Primary Prevention, 28,* 547–568.

Dusenbury, L., Brannigan, R., Falco, M., & Lake, A. (2004). An exploration of fidelity of implementation in drug abuse prevention among five professional groups. *Journal of Alcohol and Drug Education, 47,* 4–19.

Ennett, S. T., Ringwalt, C. L., Thorne, J., Rohrbach, L. A., Vincus, A., & Jones, S. (2003). A comparison of current practice in school-based substance abuse prevention programs with meta-analysis findings. *Prevention Science, 4,* 1–14.

Fitzpatrick, K., & Boldizar, J. (1993). The prevalence and consequences of exposure to violence among African-American youth. *Journal of the American Academy of Child and Adolescent Psychiatry, 32,* 424–430.

Galliher, R. V., Evans, C. M., & Weiser, D. (2007). Social and individual predictors of substance abuse for Native American youth. *Journal of Child and Adolescent Substance Abuse, 16,* 1–16.

Gerstein, D. R., & Green, L. W. (1993). *Preventing drug abuse: What do we know?* Washington, DC: National Academy Press.

Hahm, H. C., Lahiff, M., & Guterman, N. B. (2004). Asian American adolescents' acculturation, binge drinking and alcohol and tobacco using peers. *Journal of Community Psychology, 32,* 295–308.

Hahm, H. C., Wong, F. Y., Huang, Z. J., Ozonoff, A., & Lee, J. (2008). Substance abuse among Asian American and Pacific Islander sexual minority adolescents: Findings from the National Longitudinal Study of Adolescent Health. *Journal of Adolescent Health, 42,* 275–283.

Hawkins, J. D., Catalano, R. F., & Arthur, M. W. (2002). Promoting science-based prevention in communities. *Addictive Behaviors, 27,* 951–976.

Hensen, W. B., Derzon, J., Dusenbury, L., Bishop, D., Campbell, K., & Alford, A. (2010). Operating characteristics of prevention programs: Connections to drug use etiology. In Scheier (Ed.), *Handbook of drug use etiology: Theory, methods and empirical findings* (pp. 597–616). Washington, DC: American Psychological Association.

Johnston, L. D., O'Malley, P. M., Bachman, J. G., & Schulenberg, J. E. (2011a). *Monitoring the Future national survey results on drug use, 1975–2010. Volume I: Secondary school students.* Ann Arbor: Institute for Social Research, The University of Michigan.

Johnston, L. D., O'Malley, P. M., Bachman, J. G., & Schulenberg, J. E. (2011b). *Monitoring the Future national survey results on drug use, 1975–2010. Volume II: College students and adults ages 19–50.* Ann Arbor: Institute for Social Research, The University of Michigan.

Kinney, J. (2011). *Loosening the grip: A handbook of alcohol information.* Columbus, OH: McGraw Hill.

Kravtsova, E. E. (2009). The cultural-historical foundations of the zone of proximal development. *Journal of Russian and Eastern European Psychology, 47,* 9–24.

Kumpfer, K. L., Pinyuchon, M., Castelo, P., & Whiteside, H. O. (2008). Cultural adaptation process for international dissemination of the Strengthening Families Program. *Evaluation and the Health Professions, 31,* 226–239.

National Institute of Drug Abuse. (1997). *Lessons from prevention research.* Washington, DC: US Government Printing Office.

Nichols, T. R., Graber, J. A., Brooks-Gunn, J., & Botvin, G. J. (2006). Ways to say no: Refusal skill strategies among urban adolescents. *American Journal of Health Behavior, 30,* 227–236.

Page, R., Scanlan, A., & Gilbert, L. (1999). Relationship of the estimation of binge drinking among college students and personal participation in binge drinking: Implications for health education and promotion. *Journal of Health Education, 30,* 98–103.

Pantin, H., Coatsworth, J. D., Feaster, D. J., Newman, F. L., Briones, E., & Prado, G. (2003). Familias Unidas: The efficacy of an intervention to promote parental involvement in Hispanic immigrant families. *Prevention Science, 4,* 189–201.

Pentz, M. A. (1998). Costs, benefits, and cost-effectiveness of comprehensive drug abuse prevention. In: W. J. Bukoski & R. I. Evans (Eds.), *Cost-benefit/cost-effectiveness research of drug abuse prevention: Implications for programming and policy* (pp. 111–129). Washington, DC: U.S. Government Printing Office

Peregoy, J. J. (1993). Transcultural counseling with American Indians and Alaskan Natives: Contemporary issues for consideration. In J. McFadden (Ed.), *Transcultural counseling: Bilateral and international perspectives* (pp. 163–191). Alexandria, VA: American Counseling Association.

Perkins, H. (2003a.). The emergence and evolution of the social norms approach to substance abuse prevention. In H. Perkins (Ed.), *The social norms approach to preventing school and college aged substance abuse: A handbook for educators and clinicians* (pp. 3–17). San Francisco, CA: Jossey-Bass.

Perkins, H. (2003b). The promise and challenge of future work using the social norms model. In H. Perkins (Ed.), *The social norms approach to preventing school and college aged substance abuse: A handbook for educators and clinicians* (pp. 280–296). San Francisco, CA: Jossey-Bass.

Porath-Waller, A. J. (2010). A meta-analytic review of school-based prevention for cannabis use. *Health Education and Behavior, 37,* 709–723.

Resnicow, K., Soler, R., Braithwaite, R. L., Ahluwalia, J. S., & Butler, J. (2000). Cultural sensitivity in substance abuse prevention. *Journal of Community Psychology, 28,* 271–290.

Ringwalt, C. L., Ennett, S., Johnson, R., Rohrbach, L. A., Simons-Rudolph, A., Vincus, A., & Thorne. J. (2003). Factors associated with fidelity to substance abuse prevention curriculum guides in the nation's middle schools. *Health Education and Behavior, 30,* 375–391.

Schinke, S. P., Tepavac, L., & Cole, K. C. (2000). Preventing substance abuse among Native American youth: Three year results. *Addictive Behaviors, 25,* 387–397.

Soole, D. W., Mazerolle, L, & Rombouts, S. (2008). School-based prevention programs: A review of what works. *Australian and New Zealand Journal of Criminology, 41,* 259–286.

Spell, C. S., & Blum, T. C. (2008). Adoption of workplace substance abuse prevention programs: Strategic choice and institutional perspectives. *Academy of Management Journal, 48,* 1125–1142.

Stoil, M. J., & Hill, G. (1996). *Preventing substance abuse: Interventions that work.* New York: Plenum Press.

Substance Abuse and Mental Health Services Administration. (2006). *Results from the 2005 national survey on drug use and health: National findings.* Rockville, MD: Department of Health and Human Services.

Substance Abuse and Mental Health Services Administration. (2007). *Drug abuse among Hispanics.* Rockville, MD: Department of Health and Human Services.

Sue, D. W., & Sue, D. (2007). *Counseling the culturally diverse: Theory and practice.* New York: Wiley.

Sussman, S. (2005). Prevention of adolescent alcohol problems in special populations. In M. Galantar (Ed.), *Recent developments in alcoholism* (pp. 225–253). New York: Kluwer Academic/Plenum.

Thai, N. D., Connell, C. M., & Tebes, J. K. (2010). Substance use among Asian American adolescents: Influence of race, ethnicity and acculturation in the context of key risk and protective factors. *Asian American Journal of Psychology, 1,* 261–274.

Tobler, N. S., Roona, M. R., Ochshorn, P., Marshall, D. G., Streke, A. V., & Stackpole, K. M. (2000). School-based adolescent prevention program: 1998 meta-analysis. *Journal of Primary Prevention, 20,* 275–336.

Wampold, B. E. (2001). *The great psychotherapy debate: Models, methods and findings.* Mahwah, NJ: Erlbaum.

White, D., & Pitts, M. (1998). Educating young people about drugs: A systematic review. *Addiction, 93,* 1475–1487.

World Health Organization (2011). *Management of substance abuse: Facts and figures.* Retrieved August 1, 2011, from http://www.who.int/substance_abuse/facts/en/

CHAPTER

13 Suicide Prevention in Counseling Psychology: Where We Have Been, Where We Need to Go

James R. Rogers *and* Kathleen M. Benson

Abstract

The purpose of this chapter is to provide a critical analysis of the status of suicide prevention in the United States and as an area of attention in counseling psychology. Following our analysis of prevention from universal and selected levels, we identify some of the major obstacles to effective prevention efforts and present an argument for a greater need for involvement from counseling psychologists. Identified areas of counseling psychology expertise that can be brought to bear on suicide prevention activities include theory development, application of diverse methodologies in research, psychometrics, and the field's strength-based philosophy and emerging attention to the importance of fostering resilient communities.

Key Words: suicide, prevention, theory, research methods, psychometrics, strength-based

Introduction

Suicide as a Global and National Phenomenon

According to the World Health Organization (WHO), suicide is a major public health problem throughout the world (Wasserman & Wasserman, 2009). Based on data from 51 countries and extrapolation of those data, the WHO estimated the number of suicides in 2002 to be approximately one million with a projected 20 million suicide attempts. In terms of suicide deaths, this figure translates into one death by suicide every 40 seconds, or over 2,000 suicides every day. Further, the WHO has estimated that, unabated, the number of suicides will increase substantially by the year 2020 (WHO, 2010).

United States data suggest that there are over 30,000 deaths by suicide every year with the most recent report from the American Association of Suicidology (AAS, 2012a) indicating 36,909 suicides in 2009. These data translate into one suicide every 14.2 minutes. Using a 25:1 ratio estimate of suicide attempt to suicides, the AAS suggests that suicide attempts in the United States in 2009 numbered approximately 922,725 and some suggest that this is likely a conservative estimate (Maris, Berman, & Silverman, 2000). The impact of suicide goes well beyond those who die by suicide and those who engage in nonlethal suicidal behaviors, however. Again, according to conservative estimates, at least six people are significantly and negatively affected by the loss of a loved one to suicide and being bereaved by suicide often carries with it a risk for suicide for the bereaved (Maris et al.) Based on this 6:1 figure and the recorded 772,398 suicides in the United States from 1983 through 2007, the number of suicide survivors is estimated to be around 4.6 million (AAS).

Moving beyond overt suicidal behaviors, a recent Substance Abuse and Mental Health Services Administration (SAMHSA) report has focused on identifying the prevalence of less overt suicidal behaviors. Based on the *Results from the 2008 National Survey on Drug Use and Health: National Findings*, SAMHSA (2009) estimates that 8.3 million people in the United States over the age of 18 had "serious" thoughts of suicide in 2008. Of those 8.3 million people seriously considering suicide, 2.3 million had made suicide plans, and 1.1 million of those had made a suicide attempt. Finally, of those who had made suicide attempts, 678,000 received medical attention as a result of their behavior. Although it must be kept in mind that these data are estimates based on the self-report responses of 67,500 people, they do present a troubling picture of suicidal behavior in the United States for those 18 years of age and older.

Similar to the SAMHSA (2009) report focused on surveillance of suicidal behaviors with people age 18 and older, the *National Youth Risk Behavior Survey* (YRBS) monitors suicidal behaviors in 9th- to 12th-grade students in public and private schools in the United States every two years. The most recent report (Centers for Disease Control and Prevention, 2010) of the survey based on data from 2009 indicates that 13.8% of students had seriously considered attempting suicide in the 12 months prior to the survey, with 10.9% reporting that they had made a plan for their attempt. Moreover, 6.3% of those responding indicated that they had made at least one suicide attempt, and 1.9% of those who attempted reported that their attempt resulted in medical attention. The good news with regard to the 9th- to the 12th-grade students is that according to these self-reports, with the exception of suicide attempts, these behaviors have decreased since 1991. Despite this good news, as these global and US data suggest, engagement in suicidal behaviors continues to grow.

Attempts to understand and predict suicidal behavior have historically focused on the identification of factors that empirically differentiate between suicidal and nonsuicidal individuals and between individuals who have died by suicide and those who have made suicide attempts. According to the American Association of Suicidology (2010), risk factors that have been identified can be categorized as chronic risk factors and acute risk factors.

Chronic risk factors are defined as factors that increase the risk of suicidality across the life span when present at any point in an individual's lifetime (AAS, 2012b). Further, chronic risk factors can either be perpetuating or predisposing. Perpetuating chronic risks of suicide are permanent and will not change once an individual is exposed to the risk. Demographic characteristics and personal history are examples of perpetuating risk factors and include:

- Race: increased risk for Caucasians and American Indians;
- Sex: increased risk for males;
- Age: increased risk among older adults;
- Marital status: increased risk for those who are separated, divorced, or early widowed;
- History of suicidality: previous suicide attempts, previous ideation, or a history of self-injurious behavior;
- Family history of suicide or suicidal behaviors;
- History of traumatic experiences or abuse;
- History of psychiatric hospitalization;
- History of impulsive or violent behavior; and
- Parental history of violence, substance abuse, psychiatric hospitalization, and divorce.

Predisposing chronic risks increase susceptibility to suicide, however, these factors have the potential to be modified. Examples include, but are not limited to:

- Psychiatric Disorders: most notably, mood disorders, anxiety disorders, schizophrenia, substance use disorders, and Cluster B personality disorders;
- Presence of comorbid psychiatric disorders, especially depression and substance use;
- Physical illness, especially conditions that involve functional impairment, chronic pain, or brain injury;
- Low self-esteem;
- Identity acceptance related to sexual orientation; and
- Positive attitude toward suicide.

The second category of risk factors, acute, represents factors that increase the likelihood of suicidality in the present or near-future. Acute risk factors heighten the risk of suicide and are generally related to recent experiences, changes in mood and attitude, or self-defeating behaviors. The following list includes notable acute risk factors (for a complete list, visit the American Association of Suicidology's webpage, which provides various fact sheets regarding suicidal risk http://www.suicidology.org/web/guest/stats-and-tools/fact-sheets):

- Hopelessness;
- Current suicidal ideation, self-injurious behaviors, or recent suicide attempt;
- Increased use of substances;
- Psychological pain associated with distress;
- Isolation;
- Decreased interest or pleasure;

- Increased impulsivity and/or aggressive behaviors;
- Loss of meaning in life; and
- Refusal to seek help.

The aforementioned risk factors are most commonly used in the context of individual assessment and intervention for suicide risk. Awareness of suicide risk factors among counseling psychologists is an integral part of effective clinical care and appropriate treatment planning. Moreover, suicide risk factors are often used as outcome criteria in suicide prevention programs. These factors have become targets for prevention and suicide prevention programs often define "success" based on the reduction of risk. However, the use of suicide risk factors as outcome criteria in these programs is not without important limitations. A discussion of suicide risk factors utilized in evidence-based suicide prevention programs and the limitations of these factors as outcome criteria are provided in latter sections of this chapter.

The purpose of this chapter therefore is fourfold. First, we discuss suicide prevention as reflected in the literature in counseling psychology. Second we link that literature to the broader suicide prevention movement by identifying currently accepted approaches to suicide prevention. Third, we discuss some of the major obstacles to developing and evaluating effective suicide prevention programs including the assumed connections between suicidal thoughts, suicide attempts, and suicide, and the lack of consensus regarding the suicide nomenclature on prevention efforts. And fourth, we outline what we see as potentially fruitful approaches to advancing the effectiveness of suicide prevention activities of counseling psychologists in the future including the promotion of methodological diversity in the study of suicide.

Suicide Prevention in Counseling Psychology

As a caveat to our overview of suicide prevention as reflected in the counseling psychology literature, it is likely that counseling psychologists are working and publishing in this area outside of the traditional counseling psychology outlets of *The Counseling Psychologist*, *Journal of Counseling Psychology*, and editions of the *Handbook of Counseling Psychology*. However, as these are discipline-defining outlets, we have limited our review of suicide prevention in counseling psychology to a consideration of those publications. Additionally, the distinction between "prevention" as opposed to "intervention" can be blurry. For our purposes we have adopted Gordon's (1983) prevention model employed by the Institute of Medicine (IOM, 1994) and currently used by the Centers for Disease Control and SAMHSA. This prevention model has three classification levels: universal, selective, and indicated. *Universal* prevention efforts are those focused on the general population to prevent the onset of a disorder or condition. Examples of universal efforts in other areas are smoking cessation programs, nutrition education, and safe driving information. *Selective* prevention efforts are those aimed at subgroups of individuals who have been identified as at risk based on relevant factors such as age, sex, or socioeconomic status. Examples here include annual flu shots for the elderly and teen pregnancy programs. Finally, *indicated* refers to prevention efforts aimed at individuals who have been specifically identified as at risk through medical or psychological examinations, tests, or assessments. Thus, the flow of prevention efforts in Gordon's model is from the population, to subgroups, and finally to individuals. Because of the overlap between the concepts of prevention and intervention when working at the indicated or individual level, we focus our discussion of suicide prevention in counseling psychology at the universal and selected levels and consider prevention at the indicated level as treatment where a number of excellent current resources are available (e.g., Michel & Jobes, 2010; Pompili & Tatarelli, 2010; Wenzel, Brown, & Beck, 2009).

The Counseling Psychologist

In order to gauge the involvement of counseling psychology with the issue of suicide prevention, we conducted an electronic search of *The Counseling Psychologist* from 1969 through 2009 using the terms "prevention" and multiple variations of the term "suicide." This search resulted in the identification of 20 articles specifically mentioning and/or discussing suicide prevention in some form. Of those 20 articles, 18 were published from 2000 on. It is important to note that in 2000 *The Counseling Psychologist* published a major contribution issue entitled *Suicide: An Overview* (vol. 28, no. 4) by Westefeld et al. that included the major contribution plus four additional articles on suicide (Hoffman, 2000; Neimeyer, 2000; Silverman, 2000; Werth & Holdwick, 2000). A substantial portion of the Westefeld et al. major contribution focused on issues of suicide prevention. In addition to containing 5 of the 18 articles published since

2000, this major contribution may have served as the impetus for subsequent suicide focused articles submitted to this journal. Thus, it seems based on the number of publications since 2000, counseling psychologists have been involved in the issue of suicide. However, a specific focus on prevention as opposed to assessment and intervention (e.g., Choi, Rogers, & Werth, 2009) was primarily limited to the major contribution.

Journal of Counseling Psychology

In a similar fashion, we performed an electronic search of the *Journal of Counseling Psychology* from 1954 to 2009. Of the 17 articles we were able to locate in this search, only one specifically focused on suicide prevention (LaFromboise & Howard-Pitney, 1995). The remaining articles focused more broadly on assessment (e.g., Dixon, Heppner, & Anderson, 1991, Gutierrez, Osman, Kooper, Barrios, & Bagge, 2000) and treatment (Jobes, Jacoby, Cimbolic, & Hustead, 1997). Notable in this collection of articles is the fact that the program developed and evaluated by LaFromboise and Howard-Pitney in their 1995 article later became one of the very few suicide prevention programs identified by SAMSHA through the National Registry of Evidence-based Programs and Practices (NREPP) as an empirically supported suicide prevention program.

Handbook of Counseling Psychology

In searching the various editions of the *Handbook of Counseling Psychology* (Brown & Lent, 1984, 1992, 2000, 2008), again we perused the index for the terms "prevention" and variations of the term "suicide." In the 1984 edition of the *Handbook of Counseling Psychology*, there was one reference to suicide focusing on issues related to malpractice (Schmidt & Meara, 1984) and some discussion of prevention in general as a growing topic in counseling psychology (e.g., Danish, D'Augelli, & Ginsberg, 1984). For this edition, there was no specific mention of "suicide prevention." By the 1992 edition (Brown & Lent, 1992), there was increased attention to prevention, albeit focused on the prevention of medical conditions (Altmaier & Johnson, 1992), and although the term "suicide" was not indexed, there was reference to suicide in a chapter focusing on depression (McNamara, 1992). Again, there was no reference to suicide prevention as a focus in counseling psychology.

In the third edition of the *Handbook of Counseling Psychology* (Brown & Lent, 2000), there was a substantial increase in focus on prevention with chapters on prevention with school-aged youth (Vera & Reese, 2000), prevention in the workplace (Hesketh, 2000), prevention with older adults (Hill, Thorn, & Packard, 2000), and disease prevention (Hoffman & Driscoll, 2000), but no specific mention of suicide prevention. References to suicide in this edition were limited to a discussion of ethical issues in confidentiality related to clinical work (Kitchener & Anderson, 2000) with a suicidal client and ethical issues related to "rational suicide" growing out of the work of Werth (1992) and Rogers and Britton (1994) and a mention of suicidality related to gender and sexuality in development (Fassinger, 2000). The latest edition of the handbook (Brown & Lent, 2008) continued the trend with a greater emphasis on prevention work in counseling psychology with prevention focused chapters on resilience (Arbona & Coleman, 2008), substance abuse (Martens, Neighbors, & Lee, 2008), eating disorders (Mintz, Hamilton, Bledman, & Franko, 2008), school violence (Espelage & Horne, 2008), and health and development promotion chapters including disease prevention (Chwlaisz & Obasi, 2008; Danish & Forneris, 2008). In contrast to previous editions of the handbook, however, the 2008 edition included a chapter on suicide prevention (Westefeld, Range, Rogers, & Hill, 2008).

In summary, although there has been some attention in the counseling psychology literature to the issue of suicide prevention, it has been both fairly recent and fairly limited. Most of the counseling psychology scholarly literature related to suicidology has focused on the assessment of risk for suicide or interventions at the individual level. In the next section, we present an overview of suicide prevention activities from a broader perspective. As we have indicated previously, we provide this overview using the prevention framework developed by Gordon (1983) and keep our focus on universal and selected approaches to suicide prevention. Specifically, we identify suicide prevention programs recognized by SAMHSA in the National Registry of Evidence-Based Programs and Practices (NREPP).

Evidence-Based Suicide Prevention Programs

In an effort to publicly disseminate knowledge of empirically supported prevention programs, SAMHSA established the NREPP (http://www.nrepp.samhsa.gov/AdvancedSearch.aspx). The NREPP is an online resource that includes various preventive programs for both mental health and substance use disorders that have been demonstrated to be clinically effective. The purpose is to promote the implementation and application of scientifically supported programs as well as increase public access to such programs.

The programs listed in the NREPP were accumulated based on submissions by their developers and are subsequently reviewed by independent raters. The NREPP warns that the registry is not exhaustive due to the nature of submissions; however, it provides the opportunity for practical application of scientifically based prevention programs. In order for the submission to be considered for review, the following minimum eligibility criteria must be met:

1. The program has shown at least one or more positive behavioral outcomes among participants;
2. Outcomes are substantiated by at least one experimental or quasi-experimental research design;
3. Study results have been published in a peer-reviewed scholarly journal or comprehensive evaluation report; and
4. Appropriate documentation of implementation procedures, materials, and resources are available to the public so the programs can be replicated.

Once a program is selected to be fully reviewed, reviewers evaluate the submission based on the quality of research and readiness for dissemination. The quality of the research rating indicates the strength of evidence that supports the program's outcomes (NREPP, 2010c). This is based on six criteria: reliability of measures, validity of measures, intervention fidelity, missing data and attrition, control of potential confounding variables, and the appropriateness of analysis. Readiness for dissemination is a rating based on the quality and availability of resources to effectively implement the program, which includes the availability of program materials, training and support resources, and quality assurance procedures (NREPP, 2010b). Based on these ratings, programs are either selected to be a part of the NREPP or are rejected. Each program listed in the registry provides readers with information about the program, research outcomes, review ratings (quality of research and readiness for dissemination), studies and materials that were reviewed, and contact information.

According to the current NREPP, eight empirically supported suicide prevention programs are available (NREPP, 2010a). The following provides a brief description of each of these programs categorized by the NREPP as either *universal* or *selected* prevention programs. As a side note, and supporting our previous discussion related to the third category in the prevention model, each of the prevention programs identified as *selected* by the NREPP were jointly identified as *indicated* also, making even less clear the distinction between these two categories. Further, one program, "Signs of Suicide," was not classified by the NREPP, however, we have placed it in the selected category based on our review of the NREPP materials. Readers interested in more information on each of these programs are directed to the NREPP website.

Universal Prevention Programs

AMERICAN INDIAN LIFE SKILLS DEVELOPMENT/ZUNI LIFE SKILLS DEVELOPMENT

This is a school-based prevention program designed to reduce the risk of suicide and promote protective factors among American Indian or Alaska Native adolescents aged 13 to 17 years. The program was designed to be implemented during the school year and incorporates lesson plans such as building self-esteem, improving problem-solving and communication skills, psychoeducation on suicide, and fostering the identification of emotions and stress. Outcome variables assessed in this program were hopelessness and suicide prevention skills. Results of a quasi-experimental study (Lafromboise & Howard-Pitney, 1995) indicated that students who participated in the program reported significantly less feelings of hopelessness as compared to students in a control group. Moreover, students in the experimental group exhibited higher suicide intervention skills as compared to their control group student counterparts.

According to an article published by the program developers, Lafromboise and Howard-Pitney (1995) concluded that students who participated in the Life Skills Development Program were significantly less hopeless (M = 3.53) as compared to students in a control group who did not participate in the program (M = 4.67, $t_{(61)}$ = 1.63, p < .05). Similarly, after participation in the Life Skills Development program, students exhibited lower ratings of suicide potential (M = 54.34) as compared to the control group of students (M = 58.86, $t_{(61)}$ = 1.45, p < .07). Lastly, the authors found that students who participated in the program demonstrated higher suicide intervention skills (i.e., appropriate role-play responses to someone expressing suicidal intent, crisis management of a peer; M = 4.67) as compared to students in the control group (M = 3.86,

$F_{(1, 26)} = 10.09$, $p < .05$). References to replication studies conducted on this program can be found at the NREPP site.

LIFELINES CURRICULUM

Lifelines Curriculum is a school-based prevention program developed by Kalafat, Madden, Haley, and O'Halloran (2007) for middle and high school students that promotes a safe environment to encourage help-seeking and recognition of suicidal behavior. School faculty and staff are trained to identify and respond to signs of suicide among the students and a psychoeducation component is provided to the parents. Moreover, students are educated about suicide and how it can be prevented. Outcomes measured were knowledge about suicide, attitudes about suicide and suicide intervention, attitudes about seeking adult help, and attitudes about keeping a friend's secret.

According to an unpublished manuscript, the program developers (Kalafat, Madden, Haley, & O'Halloran2007) concluded that after a 2-week posttest assessment, students who participated in the intervention demonstrated a greater increase in knowledge about suicide ($p < .001$), greater improvement in attitudes about suicide and help seeking ($p < .001$), and greater improvement in attitudes about keeping a friend's suicide intent secret ($p < .001$) as compared to a control group who received physical education classes instead.

UNITED STATES AIR FORCE SUICIDE PREVENTION PROGRAM

Designed to reduce the risk of suicide among US Air Force personnel, this program focuses on strengthening social support, promoting social skill development, and encouraging help-seeking behaviors (Knox, Litts, Talcott, Feig, & Caine, 2003). Initiatives within this program include enlisting the help of Air Force leaders, psychoeducation and training, policy changes, implementation of stress management skills, and collection of research data.

A trend analysis revealed that as compared to the suicide rate among Air Force personnel prior to program implementation, a linear reduction in the suicide rate in the decades following the start of the program occurred (Knox et al., 2003). Based on risk reduction calculations by the authors, this accounted for a 33% reduction in suicide. In comparison to Air Force personnel who did not participate in the program in the years preceding the implementation, those who did participate showed a 54% risk reduction in severe family violence, a 51% risk reduction for homicide, a 30% risk reduction in moderate family violence, and an 18% risk reduction for accidental death. It is important to note, however, that this reduction in suicides was based on 3-year moving average calculations. These calculations included the year 1994, when the suicide rate was at its highest; 1996, when a downward trend was observed prior to the implementation of the program; and years 1999 to 2002, during an upward trend.

Selected/Indicated

CARE (CARE, ASSESS, RESPOND, EMPOWER)

Targeting high school students, this suicide prevention program is aimed at identifying high-risk youth and providing them with brief counseling services (Eggert, Thompson, Herting, & Nicholas, 1995). Once individuals have been identified as high risk (i.e., youth who drop out or are substance abusers), these students participate in a 2-hour computer suicide assessment following by 2 hours of motivational and supportive counseling. Additionally, a 9-week follow-up assessing suicide risk and protective factors is conducted and additional counseling sessions are offered as needed. The goals of the program are to decrease suicidal behaviors, decrease risk factors, and to increase protective factors. Though originally developed for school adolescents aged 13 to 17, the program has been expanded to include young adults aged 18 to 25. Identified outcome variables of the program are suicide risk factors, depressive symptoms, hopelessness, anxiety, anger, drug use, stress, and sense of control.

Suicide risk factors were assessed using the Brief Suicide Risk Behavior Scale from the *High School Questionnaire: A Profile of Experiences* that measures suicidal thoughts, implicit and explicit suicidal threats, and suicide attempts. Eggert et al. (1995) concluded that CARE participants exhibited a 25% reduction in suicide risk factors from baseline to follow-up at both 5 and 10 months. Moreover, when compared to a group of control students at baseline, CARE participants revealed significantly higher levels of suicide risk factors (Cohen's $d = 1.28$). However, when the groups were again compared at the 10-month follow-up, a noticeable decrease in the effect size was observed (Cohen's $d = 0.57$).

CAST (COPING AND SUPPORT TRAINING)

CAST is a suicide prevention program for high school students aged 14 to 19 who have been identified as being at risk for suicide (Eggert, Thompson, Randell, & Pike, 2002). The program provides 12 group sessions lasting 55 minutes to promote life-skills training and social support. Overall goals of the program include increased mood management, improved academic performance, and decreased drug use as measured by the following outcome variables: depressive symptoms, hopelessness, anxiety, anger, drug use, sense of control, and problem-solving/coping skills.

Eggert et al. (2002) conducted a study in which CAST participants were compared to a group of students who participated in CARE and a control group who received routine school interventions for at-risk youth. Suicide risk was assessed via three questions regarding suicidal ideation, threats, and previous suicide attempts. Baseline assessments revealed no significant group differences in respect to suicide risk factors including, suicide ideation, suicide threats, and previous attempt in last month. Results indicated that across all three groups, suicide risk factors declined from baseline to the 10-week follow-up assessment, however, no significant group differences were observed. Additionally, it was found that as compared to a control group, the CAST participants exhibited a significant decline in suicidal intention and positive attitudes toward suicide after the first 4 weeks of the program.

EMERGENCY DEPARTMENT MEANS RESTRICTION EDUCATION

This intervention was developed for parents of adolescents (aged 6 to 19 years old) who presented to the emergency room and were determined to be at risk for suicide (Kruesi et al., 1999). The purpose of this prevention program is to encourage parents to take appropriate precautions at home to minimize access to means, including proper containment or removal of firearms and medications. Intended to be implemented by a trained health care professional, the program includes notifying parents that their child is at risk for suicide, why and how to reduce this risk by restricting access to means, and encouraging problem-solving behaviors. Results indicate that 2 months following the emergency room visit, parents who participated in the intervention were significantly more likely to limit access to both medications and firearms as compared to parents in a control group (Kruesi et al., 1999). The majority of parents who took action reported that they locked up their medications/firearms as opposed to removal of the means.

RECONNECTING YOUTH: A PEER GROUP APPROACH TO BUILDING LIFE SKILLS

Reconnecting Youth is an early identification and resilience building program designed for students aged 14 to 19 years of age in an effort to prevent substance use and mental health problems. At-risk youth, as identified by poor academic performance and likelihood of dropping out, are eligible for participation. The program encourages positive relationship building and social support among peers, group leaders, and parental involvement. With an emphasis on developing healthy behaviors, the program aims to provide youth with appropriate crisis management skills in order to prevent suicidal behaviors and emotional distress. Outcome measures were based on academic performance, drug use, risk and protective factors of mental health problems, and suicidal behaviors.

Program developers utilized the Brief Suicide Risk Behavior Scale from the *High School Questionnaire: A Profile of Experiences* to assess suicidal thoughts, threats, and attempts at baseline, 5-month follow-up, and 10-month follow-up. Participants were assigned to one of three groups, group 1 received one semester of Reconnecting Youth and a suicide risk assessment, group 2 received two semesters of Reconnecting Youth and a suicide risk assessment, and group 3 received the suicide risk assessment (Eggert, Thompson, Herting, & Nicholas, 1995; Thompson, Eggert, & Herting, 2000). Results indicated that as compared to baseline measures of suicide risk factors, all three groups showed significant reductions in suicide risk behaviors. Groups 1 and 3 exhibited greater reduction in suicide risk factors as compared to group 2.

SOS (SIGNS OF SUICIDE)

A 2-day screening intervention for depression and suicide risk among adolescents, SOS was developed for youth aged 13 to 17 years. Psychoeducation is provided to help participants recognize signs of depression and suicide in others and how to respond to the identification of individuals at risk in an effort to increase knowledge and help-seeking behaviors. Identified outcome variables include suicide attempts, knowledge of depression and suicide, and attitudes toward depression and suicide.

Aseltine and DeMartino (2004) compared high school students who participated in SOS and those in a control group, both at baseline and 3 months after program completion. It was found that participants in SOS were 40% less likely to report a suicide attempt in the 3 months following program completion as compared to students who did not participate. Additionally, a small effect of the intervention on increased knowledge of and positive attitudes about depression and suicide was found.

Although the NREPP did not classify the SOS program using the IOM rubric, based on our reading of the program material, we believe that it is appropriate to consider this program as a selective prevention program. We assume that the focusing on subsequent suicide attempts suggests that the program developers considered adolescents as a high risk group.

In sum, excluding direct individual treatment protocols and focusing on *universal* and *selected* prevention programs reviewed by the NREPP, empirically supported suicide prevention programs are few. Even those that have been evaluated as empirically supported have been judged so based on minimal criteria and outcome criteria that are surrogates for suicide and other suicidal behaviors rather than the behaviors themselves (Wortzel, Gutierrez, Homaifar, Breshears, & Harwood, 2010). Examples of surrogates include hopelessness, depression, attitudes, anxiety and stress, and access to medications and firearms, among others. Additionally, the predominate method of data collection across these program studies has been self-report rather than more objective criteria. As such, an NREPP judgment of empirically supported notwithstanding, the question of whether or not these suicide prevention programs prevent suicide is yet unanswered. Next we discuss some of the obstacles to effective suicide prevention.

Obstacles to Suicide Prevention

Defining Suicide and Suicidal Behaviors

As suggested earlier, on the surface it seems that defining suicide should be a relatively straightforward task, that is, suicide is the intentional killing of oneself. Similarly, defining other suicidal behaviors such as suicide attempts and suicidal thoughts or ideation would appear uncontroversial. However, this is not the case as there is no currently accepted nomenclature or classification system for suicide and suicidal behavior (Silverman, 2006). For example, with reference to defining suicide, Silverman has identified 15 definitions of suicide that are frequently referenced in the literature. These definitions range from one offered by the French sociologist Emile Durkheim in 1897 (1897/1951) to one posited by Diego De Leo and colleagues in 2004 (De Leo, Burgis, Bertolote, Kerkhof, & Bille-Brahu, 2004). Although these definitions differ as a function of the theoretical orientations of the authors, representing the disciplines of philosophy, psychology, sociology, psychiatry and public health, Silverman (2006) identified what he viewed as key aspects to defining suicide. These necessary criteria included (1) the outcome of the behavior is death, (2) the act is self-inflicted, (3) there is an intention to die, and (4) there is an awareness (or expectation) that the outcome will be death. Although the first criterion leaves little room for subjective judgment, there can be some ambiguity regarding the second criterion and the third and fourth aspects, intention and awareness, are often impossible to determine retrospectively. Thus, in using these criteria, a considerable amount of subjective interpretation is often called for.

To further highlight the complexities in defining suicide using these criteria, consider the following examples. Suppose a person intends to die, performs a self-inflicted behavior which he or she believes will result in death, but has mistakenly chosen a method that is not lethal. This behavior would be classified as a suicide attempt, despite the fact that three of the four criteria have been met. By contrast, consider a person who dies from a self-inflicted act where his or her intention is not to die, but rather to communicate distress to a significant other and has mistakenly chosen a lethal method. This behavior would likely be classified as a suicide based on only two criteria in the absence of relatively strong evidence of a lack of intent to die and/or an awareness of the lethality of the method.

As complex as defining "suicide" is, defining "suicide attempt" may be even more challenging. As Silverman (2006) suggested, a definition of *suicide attempt* should include the criteria for defining suicide with the exception of physical death. That being the case, the second scenario above would not meet criteria for either a suicide or suicide attempt because of the absence of an intent to die despite the fact that death resulted from the self-inflicted behavior. Further complicating this issue has been the emergence of a variety of alternative terms such as *nonfatal suicidal behavior*, *parasuicide*, *nonsuicidal self-injury*, and *deliberate self-harm*; often definitions of these terms do not include the presence of intent to die as a criterion. The ambiguity surrounding the phrase *attempted suicide* led Silverman to conclude that "The term is vastly overused and misunderstood, and often is used to describe other forms of self-injury and psychological distress" (p. 523). One outcome of the lack of clarity and specificity of these terms is that there is an assumption that suicidal thoughts, suicide attempts, and suicide represent a continuum of behaviors such that prevention of suicidal thoughts or prevention of suicide attempts will ipso facto result in the prevention of suicide. Current data do not strongly support this assumption.

Although we continue to lack a generally accepted nomenclature and classification system for defining and categorizing suicidal behaviors, it seems that progress is being made in this direction. Case in point is the work of Silverman and his colleagues focused on developing a standardized nomenclature (Silverman, Berman, Sanddal, O'Carroll, Joiner, 2007a, 2007b) and the efforts of Silverman, Brenner, and others (Brenner, Silverman, Betthauser, Breshears & Nagamoto, 2009) related to the development of the Self-Directed Violence Classification System (SDVCS). The SDVCS is a classification system for suicide and other suicide-related behaviors that is linked to the Silverman et al. nomenclature and allows for more fine-grained distinctions between self-directed violent behaviors incorporating the four criteria previously identified. Research regarding the SDVCS is currently in progress in the Veterans' Administration system and early empirical results seem promising (Brenner et al., 2009). Clearly, the end goal of these efforts it to develop a classification system that links directly to targeted prevention activities. Despite these current efforts, however, the development of an agreed on definition for suicide and other suicidal behaviors as well as a clear understanding of the relations between ideation, attempts, and completed suicide remain elusive. Next we discuss the implications of the ambiguity surrounding these issues to the goal of suicide prevention.

Stumbling Blocks to Suicide Prevention

Based on our discussion thus far, there are three major stumbling blocks to effective suicide prevention. These include the lack of clarity related to definitions of suicide and other suicidal behaviors; uncertainty regarding the relations between suicidal ideation, suicide attempts, and suicide; and the overuse of intermediate or surrogate variables in suicide prevention research and programming. These interrelated areas are discussed next.

As indicated previously, there continues to be controversy regarding the conceptual or theoretical definitions of suicide and other suicidal behaviors. To complicate the lack of definitional clarity, most of the research looking at suicide prevention has employed self-report of attitudes, knowledge, risk factors, suicidal ideation, and behaviors as the primary means of assessing program outcomes. Thus, assessing prevention program success based on reductions in death by suicide, objective data on suicide attempts, and without a clear understanding of the link between suicide ideation suicidal behavior, the outcomes we are most interested in, requires a level of definitional specificity that has not yet been achieved in suicidology. Evaluating suicide prevention programs based on a reduction in actual suicide deaths of course would represent the ultimate test of any prevention program. However, in addition to the problems with identifying intent and awareness that the behavior will result in death post mortem as necessary criteria for a classification as suicide, there are two other critical issues that need to be considered.

The first of these is the time frame for following prevention program participants. This time frame needs to be tied to a program expectation regarding the duration of the effectiveness of the program or to a theoretical understanding of suicidality as either a time-limited state or a chronic trait. For example, is the program expected to lead to lifetime prevention of suicide or prevention for a more circumscribed time period? To our knowledge, no suicide prevention programs to date have specified expected parameters in this regard. In fact, this issue of follow-up creates a similar problem in intervention research, where Rudd and his colleagues (Rudd, Joiner, Trotter, Williams, & Cordero, 2009) suggested that follow-up studies of psychotherapeutic interventions with suicidal individuals need to extend beyond their current time frames of 12 to 18 months in order to demonstrate effectiveness with regard to preventing suicide.

The second issue is that of the appropriate comparison group or baseline that program effectiveness is to be evaluated against. In the case of individual treatment of suicidal individuals, clients are suicidal at baseline, so follow-up regarding subsequent death by suicide would seem to provide a relatively straightforward evaluation of effectiveness. Not so in the case of *universal* or *selected* prevention activities, however. In neither of these cases is there a clear baseline or comparison group to be used unambiguously to determine effectiveness. Even in rare cases where random assignment to a prevention program and control group is possible, the expectation that subsequent death by suicide would be equally distributed across the groups would be tenuous.

Similar issues arise when using a reduction in suicide attempts as the effectiveness criterion although maybe to a lesser extent. Still, the issues of follow-up time period and appropriate comparison group are the same as in using suicide as the outcome criterion. An additional issue here that has yet to be resolved empirically is the relation between suicide attempts and death by suicide. Although a previous suicide attempt has been identified as a risk factor for subsequent suicide, the vast majority of people who make suicide attempts do not go on to die by suicide (Maris et al., 2000). Thus the issue of whether or not a suicide attempt is appropriate as an intermediate variable or surrogate for suicide comes into question (Wortzel et al., 2010) as the current use of the term "suicide attempt" covers a broad array of behaviors. More appropriately perhaps, programs using suicide attempts as an outcome might be classified as deliberate self-harm (with or without suicidal intent) prevention programs.

Likewise, prevention programs that might be aimed at reducing the incidence of suicidal ideation suffer from a lack of definitional clarity. In part this is due to the way we have attempted to assess suicidal ideation in the field. For example, the SAMHSA (2009) report on the 2008 *National Survey* suggested that 8.3 million adults had "serious thoughts of suicide" and that 1.2 million of those had made a suicide plan, but did not go on to engage in overt suicidal behavior. The first definitional problem here is that "serious" is not defined in the question so there is no way of knowing what differentiates a "serious thought" of suicide from a "nonserious" thought either from a nomothetic or ideographic perspective. Additionally, if one were to argue that all thoughts of suicide are "serious," then it is likely that 8.3 million is an underestimate of suicidal ideation in the adult population. As a follow-up question to affirmative responses on the serious thoughts question, respondents were asked if they made plans for suicide, and if they responded yes, then they were asked if they attempted suicide. Of the 2.3 million who reported making plans, 1.2 million did not go on to make a suicide attempt perhaps suggesting that their serious thoughts of suicide (i.e., serious thoughts + a suicide plan) were further along on a continuum of suicidal ideation but not so far along as to result in overt suicidal behavior. Alternatively and more likely, there are great differences in the subjective meaning of "serious" in this context that are obscured by the limitations of the questions being asked. In terms of prevention then, the question is whether or not prevention of suicidal ideation is amenable to a one-size fits all approach (Rogers & Soyka, 2004) or do thoughts, serious thoughts, and serious thoughts with a plan require different prevention strategies?

Given the difficulties inherent in using suicide deaths and suicide attempts as outcome variables, programs have been evaluated based on their effect on surrogate variables (Wortzel et al., 2010) or intermediate criteria (Pedhazur & Schmelkin, 1991). Specifically, programs have primarily used self-reported changes in knowledge about suicide, attitudes toward help-seeking, depressive symptoms, hopelessness, drug use, and a myriad of other correlates of suicidal behavior in place of suicidal behaviors. Just as Wortzel et al. have argued against continuing to use suicide attempts as a proxy for death by suicide, the use of variables such as those listed above have limited value in terms of assessing the effectiveness of suicide prevention programs. To date there has been little discussion of these critical issues in the suicide prevention literature.

Conclusion

So what can we conclude about the status of suicide prevention activities in general and the involvement of counseling psychology in this area in particular? Based on our reading of the literature we can conclude that the prevention of suicide in the United States as well as from a global perspective has been and continues to be a high priority. Moreover, as a high priority, considerable effort has been expended in developing programs aimed at reducing risk factors shown to be associated with suicidal behavior. Additionally, extant universal and selected prevention programs focus on providing education related to the identification of those risk factors and on finding ways to help suicidal individuals access appropriate services for intervention and treatment. Unfortunately, clear evidence of success for suicide prevention programs in terms of impacting the suicide rate or reducing suicide attempts is hard to come by. To a large extent, lack of progress in reducing suicidal behaviors is a function of a number of challenges endemic to suicidology in general. These include difficulties in defining and differentiating between various classifications of suicidal behaviors, unsupported assumptions about the relationships between suicidal thoughts, suicide attempts, and death by suicide, a tendency to use intermediate criteria or surrogates as outcome variables, and minimal attention to the importance of theory as a guide, not only of which variables to target in prevention programs, but in determining appropriate time frames for evaluating outcome.

As for counseling psychologists, the literature in the discipline does not suggest that suicide prevention at the universal or selected levels has been a focus in the field. Although the publication of the major contribution on suicide in *The Counseling Psychologist* (2000), and the inclusion of a chapter on suicide prevention in the 2008 *Handbook of Counseling Psychology* may suggest increased attention in this area, there is much to be done and many ways that suicidology in general and suicide prevention in particular could benefit from having more counseling psychologists involved in the field. In the final section, we discuss some of our thoughts in this regard.

Future Directions

Advancing Suicide Prevention: Where Do We Go From Here?

Given the current status of suicide prevention efforts and the challenges to those efforts that we have identified, we believe that there are a number of ways that counseling psychology as a discipline is poised to advance suicide prevention efforts. These include the discipline's focus on the importance of theory and theory development, promotion of methodological diversity in research, training in psychometrics, and the field's strength-based philosophy and emerging attention to the importance of fostering resilient communities.

Theory Development

In terms of theory, although we have indicated that suicide prevention efforts would benefit from well articulated theoretical grounding in terms of identifying relevant variables to target and time periods for outcome evaluation, this concern is not limited solely to the suicide prevention field. In fact, the absence of formal theory in suicidology from which testable hypotheses can be derived has been lamented with more recent attention by Maris et al. (2000), Rogers (2001, 2003), and Rogers and Lester (2010), among others. At issue here is that programs to date have been driven by an empirical, risk-factor approach wherein a select few factors chosen from the multitude of correlates of suicidal behavior are measured pre-post program implementation, and changes in those factors are interpreted as demonstrating program effectiveness. With few exceptions, the rationale for choosing those factors is not articulated from a theoretical perspective and thus, different programs may target different "risk factors" and a systematic approach to suicide prevention has not emerged. Additionally, and beyond the issue of theoretically based selection of variables, is the absence of an articulated conceptualization of suicidality along a state/trait continuum. Thus, the selection of time frames for following up program participants with regard to suicidal behavior is at best arbitrary.

Therefore, we believe that counseling psychologists, by virtue of their scientific training and reliance on theory to drive their research, are well positioned to have a positive impact on the field of suicidology in general and suicide prevention program development and implementation in particular. In this respect we support current efforts within the Society for Counseling Psychology of the American Psychological Association toward the creation of a special interest group related to suicide.

Methodological Diversity

Clearly related to the issue of theory development and theory-driven research, is the issue of methodological diversity. This is another area of interest and expertise in counseling psychology as evidenced by the seminal article by Gelso (1979). Here again, a theme in the suicide literature in the past decade has been a concern that scientific suicidology has stagnated as a function of allegiance to a narrow range of methodological approaches and a lack of innovative thinking (Lester, 2000). This criticism of the field has been reiterated by Rogers (2003), Rogers and Lester (2010), Hjelmeland and Knizek (2010), and Rogers and Apel (2010), all of whom have highlighted the need for methodological diversity as necessary for the advancement of suicidology.

More specifically, Hjelmeland and Knizek (2010) identified that 97% of the empirical articles published in the three major suicide journals (i.e., *Archives of Suicide Research*, *Crisis*, and *Suicide and Life Threatening Behavior*) from 2005 through 2007 were quantitative in nature and argued that advances in understanding suicidal behavior could only accrue with the inclusion of nonreductionistic contextualized research represented by qualitative approaches. Supporting and extending this perspective, Rogers and Apel (2010) suggested that, rather than an either/or perspective on quantitative verses qualitative research, suicidology may be advanced through the application of more mixed-methods designs.

The field of counseling psychology has long ago resolved the issue of methodological diversity in this regard by embracing qualitative research as a viable methodological approach to increasing our understanding of psychological phenomena (Morrow & Smith, 2000). We believe that by adding mixed-methods approaches to that arsenal, counseling psychologists could be a force in revitalizing suicidology and suicide prevention research.

Training in Psychometrics

As we have indicated, there are major issues in the current suicide prevention research related to the operational definitions of suicidal behaviors, the relations between suicidal thoughts, suicide attempts, and death by suicide, and the measurement of suicidal thoughts and behaviors. The expertise of counseling psychologists in terms of developing psychometrically sound measures of thoughts, feelings, attitudes, and behaviors can be brought to bear in this area. The primary example of need in terms of psychometric development can be seen in the SAMSHA report based on asking respondents if they had "seriously" considered suicide in the past 12 months. Of the 8.3 million responding yes to that question, six million did not have a suicide plan, and 7.2 million did not report a subsequent suicide attempt. From these data, it seems that the interpretation of "serious" needs further refinement if it is to become a useful classification of suicidal ideation.

This is but one example of the need for psychometric development and refinement of variables related to suicide and suicide prevention. With a focus on the importance of psychometric theory (Bolt & Rounds, 2000), scale development (Dawis, 1987), and an appreciation of the importance of language usage in item development (Schwartz, 1999), we believe counseling psychologists can make significant contributions to the suicide prevention movement.

Strength-Based Focus

In terms of suicide prevention and prevention in general, counseling psychology's developmental and strength-based focus is ideally suited to contribute in this area as well. Specifically, although attention to protective factors with regard to suicide is relatively new in suicidology, that is not the case in counseling psychology. In fact, three of the four editions of the *Handbook of Counseling Psychology* (Brown & Lent, 1992, 2000, 2008) have included sections with chapters on prevention and development in a variety of contexts.

From both a universal and selected prevention perspective, the promotion of characteristics related to psychological health should play a significant role in suicide prevention program development. For example, the promotion of psychological development around resilience-related constructs such as self-efficacy (Bandura, 1982), sense of coherence (Antonovsky, 1987), hardiness (Kobasa, 1979), and optimism (Scheier & Carver, 1985), constructs with which counseling psychologists are familiar, could provide a strong foundation for the development of suicide prevention programs.

Diversity Considerations

Finally, despite a growing literature identifying racial, ethnic, religious, gender, and sexual orientation characteristics related to suicide and suicidal behavior (e.g., Choi, Rogers, & Werth, 2009; Leach, 2006; Leong & Leach, 2008) only one of the NREPP prevention programs has specifically targeted a reduction in suicidality in a high-risk culturally defined population. Lafromboise and Howard-Pitney's (1995) *American Indian Life Skills Development/Zuni Life Skills Development* program is focused on reducing suicidality in the high-risk Native American population. Whether defined along cultural, racial, or ethnic dimensions, Native Americans have historically had a higher rate of suicide than the general population. For example, in 2007 the suicide rate for Native Americans was 12.1 per 100,000 as compared to the national rate of 11.5, making this group a very important target for prevention programming.

We believe that much more needs to be done in the area of suicide prevention regarding attention to identifying diversity-related risk and protective factors for suicide as there is evidence for an increased risk in other groups as well. Counseling psychologists are positioned to contribute expertise in this area by combining their discipline-focused commitments to diversity and prevention to help address the serious and growing public health problem of suicide.

In summary, the challenges and obstacles to effective suicide prevention at the universal and selected levels are many, and intimately linked to basic research questions that continue to plague suicidology in general. Prevention programs that have been posited as having empirical support do so only at a minimal level, and questions remain as to their impact on actual suicidal behaviors. We believe that the needs of suicidology and the suicide prevention movement would be well served by a greater involvement of counseling psychology as a discipline in promoting the understanding and prevention of suicidal behaviors as an important and appropriate role for counseling psychologists.

References

Altmaier, E. M., & Johnson, B. D. (1992). Health-related applications of counseling psychology: Toward health promotion and disease prevention across the life span. In S. D. Brown & R. W. Lent (Eds.), *Handbook of counseling psychology* (2nd ed., pp. 315–347). New York: Wiley.

American Association of Suicidology. (2012a). *U.S.A. suicide: 2009 official final data.* Retrieved April 26, 2012, from http://www.suicidology.org/c/document_library/get_file?folderId=248&name=DLFE-540.pdf

American Association of Suicidology. (2012b). *Risk factors for suicide and suicidal behaviors.* Retrieved from http://www.suicidology.org/c/document_library/get_file?folderId=262&name=DLFE-535.pdf

Antonovsky, A. (1987). *Unraveling the mystery of health: How people manage stress and stay well.* San Francisco: Jossey-Bass.

Arbona, C., & Coleman, N. (2008). Risk and resilience. In S. D. Brown & R. W. Lent (Eds.), *Handbook of counseling psychology* (4th ed., pp. 483–499). New York: Wiley.

Aseltine, R. H., & DeMartino, R. (2004). An outcome evaluation of the SOS suicide prevention program. *American Journal of Public Health, 94,* 446–451. doi: 10.2105/AJPH.94.3.446

Bandura, A. (1982). Self-efficacy mechanism in human agency. *American Psychologist, 37,* 122–147. doi: 10.1037/0003-066X.37.2.122

Bolt, D. M., & Rounds, J. (2000). Advances in psychometric theory and methods. In S. D. Brown & R. W. Lent (Eds.), *Handbook of counseling psychology* (3rd ed., pp. 140–176). New York: Wiley.

Brenner, L. A., Silverman, M. M., Betthauser, L. M., Breshears, R. E., & Nagamoto, H. T. (2009). *Development of the VA VISN 19 MIRECC suicide and self-harm classification system (SSHCS).* Poster presented at the 117th Convention of the American Psychological Association. Toronto, Canada, August 6–9, 2009.

Brown, S. D., & Lent, R. W. (Eds.). (1984). *Handbook of counseling psychology.* New York: Wiley.

Brown, S. D., & Lent, R. W. (Eds.). (1992). *Handbook of counseling psychology* (2nd ed.). New York: Wiley.

Brown, S. D., & Lent, R. W. (Eds.). (2000). *Handbook of counseling psychology* (3rd ed.). New York: Wiley.

Brown, S. D., & Lent, R. W. (Eds.). (2008). *Handbook of counseling psychology* (4th ed.). New York: Wiley.

Centers for Disease Control and Prevention. (2010). *Suicide: Risk and protective factors.* Retrieved from http://www.cdc.gov/ViolencePrevention/suicide/riskprotectivefactors.html

Centers for Disease Control and Prevention. (2010). Youth risk behavior surveillance—United States, 2009. Surveillance summaries, June 4, 2010. *Morbidity and Mortality Weekly Report, 59*(No. SS-5).

Choi, J. L., Rogers, J. R., & Werth, J. L., Jr. (2009). Suicide risk assessment with Asian American college students: A culturally informed perspective. *The Counseling Psychologist, 37,* 186–218. doi:10.1177/0011000006292256

Chwlaisz, K., & Obasi, E. (2008). Promoting health and preventing and reducing disease. In S. D. Brown & R. W. Lent (Eds.), *Handbook of counseling psychology* (4th ed., pp. 517–534). New York: Wiley.

Danish, S. J., D'Augelli, A. R., & Ginsberg, M. R. (1984). Life development intervention: Promotion of mental health through the development of competence. In S. D. Brown & R. W. Lent (Eds.), *Handbook of counseling psychology* (pp. 520–544). New York: Wiley.

Danish, S. J., & Forneris, T. (2008). Promoting positive development and competency across the life span. In S. D. Brown & R. W. Lent (Eds.), *Handbook of counseling psychology* (4th ed., pp. 500–516). New York: Wiley.

Dawis, R. V. (1987). Scale construction. *Journal of Counseling Psychology, 34,* 481–489. doi: 10.1037/0022-0167.34.4.481

De Leo, D., Burgis, S., Bertolote, J., Kerkhof, A. D. M., & Bille-Brahu, U. (2004). Definitions of suicidal behavior. In D. De Leo, U. Bille-Brahe, A. D. M. Kerkhof, & A. Schmidtke (Eds.), *Suicidal behavior: Theories and research findings* (pp. 17–39). Washington, DC: Hogrefe & Huber.

Dixon, W. A., Heppner, P. P., & Anderson, W. P. (1991). Problem-solving appraisal, stress, hopelessness, and suicide ideation in a college population. *Journal of Counseling Psychology, 38,* 51–56. doi: 10.1037//0022-0167.38.1.51

Durkheim, E. (1951). *Suicide: A study in sociology* (J. A. Spaulding & G. Simpson, Trans.). London: The Free Press. (Original work published in 1897).

Eggert, L. L., Thompson, E. A., Herting, J. R., & Nicholas, L. J. (1995). Reducing suicide potential among high-risk youth: Tests of a school-based prevention program. *Suicide and Life-Threatening Behavior, 25,* 276–296. PMid:7570788

Eggert, L. L., Thompson, E. A., Randell, B. P., & Pike, K. C. (2002). Preliminary effects of brief school-based prevention approaches for reducing youth suicide: Risk behaviors, depression, and drug involvement. *Journal of Child and Adolescent Psychiatric Nursing, 15*(2), 48–64. doi: 10.1111/j.1744-6171.2002.tb00326.x

Espelage, D. L., & Horne, A. M. (2008). School violence and bullying prevention: From research-based explanations to empirically based solutions. In S. D. Brown & R. W. Lent (Eds.), *Handbook of counseling psychology* (4th ed., pp. 588–605). New York: Wiley.

Fassinger, R. E. (2000). Gender and sexuality in human development: Implications for prevention and advocacy in counseling psychology. In S. D. Brown & R. W. Lent (Eds.), *Handbook of counseling psychology* (3rd ed., pp. 346–378). New York: Wiley.

Gelso, C. J. (1979). Research in counseling: Methodological and professional issues. *The Counseling Psychologist, 8*(3), 7–35.

Gordon, R. S. (1983). An operational classification of disease prevention. *Public Health Reports, 98*(2), 107–109.

Gutierrez, P. M., Osman, A., Kooper, B. A., Barrios, F. X., & Bagge, C. L. (2000). Suicide risk assessment in a college student population. *Journal of Counseling Psychology, 47,* 403–413. doi: 10.1037//0022-0167.47.4.403

Hesketh, B. (2000). Prevention and development in the workplace. In S. D. Brown & R. W. Lent (Eds.), *Handbook of counseling psychology* (3rd ed., pp. 471–498). New York: Wiley.

Hill, R. D., Thorn, B. L., & Packard, T. (2000). Counseling older adults: Theoretical and empirical issues in prevention and intervention. In S. D. Brown & R. W. Lent (Eds.), *Handbook of counseling psychology* (3rd ed., pp. 499–531). New York: Wiley.

Hjelmeland, H., & Knizek, B. L. (2010). Why we need qualitative research in suicidology. *Suicide and Life Threatening Behavior, 40,* 74–80. doi: 10.1521/suli.2010.40.1.74

Hoffman, M. A. (2000). Suicide and hastened death: A biopsychosocial perspective. *The Counseling Psychologist, 28,* 561–572. doi: 10.1177/0011000000284006

Hoffman, M. A., & Driscoll, J. M. (2000). Health promotion and disease prevention: A concentric biopsychosocial model of health status. In S. D. Brown & R. W. Lent (Eds.), *Handbook of counseling psychology* (3rd ed., pp. 532–567). New York: Wiley.

Institute of Medicine. (1994). *Reducing risk for mental disorder: Frontiers for preventive intervention research.* Washington, DC: National Academy Press.

Jobes, D. A., Jacoby, A. M., Cimbolic, P., & Hustead, L. T. (1997). Assessment and treatment of suicidal clients in a university counseling center. *Journal of Counseling Psychology, 44,* 368–377. doi: 10.1037//0022–0167.44.4.368

Kalafat, J., Madden, M., Haley, D., & O'Halloran, S. (2007). *Evaluation of Lifelines classes: A component of the school-community based Maine Youth Suicide Prevention Project.* Report for NREPP. Unpublished manuscript.

Kitchener, K. S., & Anderson, S. K. (2000). Ethical issues in counseling psychology: Old themes—new problems. In S. D. Brown & R. W. Lent (Eds.), *Handbook of counseling psychology* (3rd ed., pp. 50–82). New York: Wiley.

Knox, K. L., Litts, D. A., Talcott, G. W., Feig, J. C., & Caine, E. D. (2003). Risk of suicide and related adverse outcomes after exposure to a suicide prevention programme in the U.S. Air Force: Cohort study. *British Medical Journal, 327,* 1376–1381.

Kobasa, S. C. (1979). Stressful life events, personality and health. *Journal of Personality and Social Psychology, 37,* 1–11. doi: 10.1037/0022–3514.37.1.1

Kruesi, M. J., Grossman, J., Pennington, J. M., Woodward, P. J., Duda, D., & Hirsch, J. G. (1999). Suicide and violence prevention: Parent education in the emergency department. *Journal of the American Academy of Child Adolescent Psychiatry, 38,* 250–255. doi:10.1097/00004583–1999030000–00010

LaFromboise, T., & Howard-Pitney, B. (1995). The Zuni Life Skills Development curriculum: Description and evaluation of a suicide prevention program. *Journal of Counseling Psychology, 42,* 479–486. doi: 10.1037//0022–0167.42.4.479

Leach, M. M. (2006). *Cultural diversity and suicide: Ethnic, religious, gender, and sexual orientation perspectives.* Binghamton, NY: Haworth.

Leong, F. T. L., & Leach, M. M. (Eds.). (2008). *Suicide among racial and ethnic minority groups: Theory, research, and practice.* New York: Routledge.

Lester, D. (2000). The end of suicidology. *Crisis, 21,*158–159. doi: 10.1027/0227–5910.21.4.158

Maris, R. W., Berman, A. L., & Silverman, M. M. (2000). *Comprehensive textbook of suicidology.* New York: Guilford.

Martens, M. P., Neighbors, C., & Lee, C. M. (2008). Substance abuse prevention and treatment. In S. D. Brown & R. W. Lent (Eds.), *Handbook of counseling psychology* (4th ed., pp. 552–569). New York: Wiley.

McNamara, K. (1992). Depression assessment and intervention: Current status and future directions. In S. D. Brown & R. W. Lent (Eds.), *Handbook of counseling psychology* (2nd ed., pp. 691–718). New York: Wiley.

Michel, K., & Jobes, D. A. (Eds.). (2010). *Building a therapeutic alliance with the suicidal patient.* Washington, DC: American Psychological Association.

Mintz, L. B., Hamilton, E., Bledman, R. A., & Franko, D. L. (2008). Preventing eating and weight-related disorders: Toward an integrated best practices approach. In S. D. Brown & R. W. Lent (Eds.), *Handbook of counseling psychology* (4th ed., pp. 570–587). New York: Wiley.

Morrow, S. L., & Smith, M. L. (2000). Qualitative research for counseling psychology. In S. D. Brown & R. W. Lent (Eds.), *Handbook of counseling psychology* (3rd ed., pp. 199–230). New York: Wiley.

National Registry of Evidence-Based Programs and Practices. (2010a). *About NREPP.* Retrieved December 27, 2010, from http://nrepp.samhsa.gov/AboutNREPP.aspx

National Registry of Evidence-Based Programs and Practices. (2010b). *Readiness for dissemination.* Retrieved December 27, 2010, from http://nrepp.samhsa.gov/ReviewRFD.aspx

National Registry of Evidence-Based Programs and Practices. (2010c). *Quality of research.* Retrieved December 27, 2010, from http://nrepp.samhsa.gov/ReviewQOR.aspx

Neimeyer, R. A. (2000). Suicide and hastened death: Toward a training agenda for counseling psychology. *The Counseling Psychologist, 28,* 551–560. doi: 10.1177/0011000000284005

Pedhazur, E. J., & Schmelkin, L. P. (1991). *Measurement, design, and analysis: An integrated approach.* Hillsdale, NJ: Erlbaum.

Pompili, M., & Tatarelli, R. (Eds.). (2010). *Evidence-based practice in suicidology.* Cambridge, MA: Hogrefe.

Rogers, J. R. (2001). Theoretical grounding: The "missing link" in suicide research. *Journal of Counseling and Development, 79,* 16–25.

Rogers, J. R. (2003). The anatomy of suicidology: A psychological science perspective on the status of suicide research. *Suicide and Life-Threatening Behavior, 31,* 9–20. doi: 10.1521/suli.33.1.9.22783

Rogers, J. R., & Apel, S. (2010). Revitalizing suicidology: A call for mixed methods designs. *Suicidology Online, 1,* 92–94. PMid:11079638

Rogers, J. R., & Britton, P. J. (1994). AIDS and rational suicide: A counseling psychology perspective or a slide on the slippery slope. *The Counseling Psychologist, 22,* 171–178. doi: 10.1177/0011000094221013

Rogers, J. R., & Lester, D. (2010). *Understanding suicide: Why we don't and how we might.* Cambridge, MA: Hogrefe.

Rogers, J. R., & Soyka, K. M. (2004). "One size fits all": An existential-constructivist perspective on the crisis intervention approach with suicidal individuals. *Journal of Contemporary Psychotherapy, 34,* 7–22. doi:10.1023/B:JOCP,0000010910.74165.3a

Rudd, M. D., Joiner, T. E., Jr., Trotter, D., Williams, B., & Cordero, L. (2009). The psychosocial treatment of suicidal behavior: A critique of what we know (and don't know). In P. M. Kleespies (Ed.), *Behavioral emergencies: An evidence-based resource for evaluating and managing risk of suicide, violence, and victimization* (pp. 339–350). Washington, DC: American Psychological Association.

Scheier, M. F., & Carver, C. S. (1985). Optimism, coping, and health: Assessment and implications of generalized expectancies. *Health Psychology, 4,* 219–247. doi: 10.1037/0278–6133.4.3.219

Schmidt, L. D., & Meara, N. M. (1984). Ethical, professional, and legal issues in counseling psychology. In S. D. Brown & R. W. Lent (Eds.), *Handbook of counseling psychology* (pp. 56–96). New York: Wiley.

Schwartz, N. (1999). Self-reports: How the questions shape the answers. *American Psychologist, 54,* 93–105. doi: 10.1037//0003–066X.54.2.93

Silverman, M. M. (2000). Rational suicide, hastened death, and self-destructive behaviors. *The Counseling Psychologist, 28,* 540–550. doi: 10.1177/0011000000284004

Silverman, M. M. (2006). The language of suicidology. *Suicide and Life Threatening Behavior, 36,* 519–532. doi: 10.1521/suli.2006.36.5.519

Silverman, M. M., Berman, A. L., Sanddal, N. D., O'Carroll, P. W., & Joiner, T. E., Jr. (2007a). Rebuilding the Tower of Babel: A revised nomenclature for the study of suicide and suicidal behaviors: Part 1. Background, rationale, and methodology. *Suicide and Life Threatening Behavior, 37,* 248–263. doi: 10.1521/suli.2007.37.3.248

Silverman, M. M., Berman, A. L., Sanddal, N. D., O'Carroll, P. W., & Joiner, T. E., Jr. (2007b). Rebuilding the Tower of Babel: A revised nomenclature for the study of suicide and suicidal behaviors: Part 2. Suicide-related ideations, communications, and behaviors. *Suicide and Life Threatening Behavior, 37,* 264–277. doi: 10.1521/suli.2007.37.3.26 4

Substance Abuse and Mental Health Services Administration. (2009). *Results from the 2008 National Survey on Drug Use and Health: National findings* (Office of Applied Studies, NSDUH Series H-36, HHS Publication No. SMA 09–4434). Rockville, MD: US Department of Health and Human Services.

Thompson, E. A., Eggert, L. L., & Herting, J. R. (2000). Mediating effects of an indicated prevention program for reducing youth depression and suicide risk behaviors. *Suicide and Life-Threatening Behavior, 30,* 252–271. PMid:14670880

Vera, E. M., & Reese, L. E. (2000). Preventive interventions with school-age youth. In S. D. Brown & R. W. Lent (Eds.), *Handbook of counseling psychology* (3rd ed., pp. 411–434). New York: Wiley.

Wasserman, D., & Wasserman, C. (Eds.). (2009). *Oxford textbook of suicidology and suicide prevention.* Oxford, England: Oxford University Press.

Wenzel, A., Brown, G. K., & Beck, A. T. (2009). *Cognitive therapy for suicidal patients: Scientific and clinical applications.* Washington, DC: American Psychological Association.

Werth, J. L., Jr. (1992). Rational suicide and AIDS: Considerations for the psychotherapist. *The Counseling Psychologist, 20,* 645–659. doi: 10.1177/0011000092204009

Werth, J. L., Jr., & Holdwick, D. J., Jr. (2000). A primer on rational suicide and other forms of hastened death. *The Counseling Psychologist, 28,* 511–539. doi: 10.1177/00110000 00284003

Westefeld, J. S., Range, L. M., Rogers, J. R., & Hill, J. M. (2008). Suicide prevention. In S. D. Brown & R. W. Lent (Eds.), *Handbook of counseling psychology* (4th ed., pp. 535–551). New York: Wiley.

Westefeld, J. S., Werth, J. L., Jr., Range, L. M., Rogers, J. R., Maples, M. R., & Holdwick, D. J. (2000). Contemporary issues in suicidology: A reply to Hoffman, Neimeyer, and Silverman. *The Counseling Psychologist, 28,* 573–578. doi: 10.1177/0011000000 284002

World Health Organization. (2010). *Suicide prevention (SUPRE).* Retrieved December 27, 2010, from http://www.who.int/mental_health/prevention/suicide/suicideprevent/en/

Wortzel, H. S., Gutierrez, P. M., Homaifar, B. Y., Breshears, R. E., & Harwood, J. E. (2010). Surrogate endpoints in suicide research. *Suicide and Life Threatening Behavior, 40,* 500–505. doi: 10.1521/suli.2010.40.5.500

CHAPTER

14 Dropout Prevention: A (Re)Conceptualization Through the Lens of Social Justice

Richard Q. Shin *and* Mone't A. Kendall

Abstract

Despite the intense focus on school dropout over the past 40 years, this pervasive social injustice continues to plague the United States. This chapter will provide a review of the extant literature on school dropout risk factors as well as the research on effective intervention and prevention programs. The chapter will begin with a rationale for focusing specifically on schools that serve students and families of color who reside in high poverty communities. The authors will critique the deficit-oriented framework that has been pervasive in school dropout literature. We hope to interrupt the dominant discourses that position poor students of color as inherently "at risk" for school dropout. The authors will present a case for counseling psychologists to develop social justice dropout prevention programs that focus primarily on institutional and structural changes. The chapter will also include a discussion of future directions for the field of counseling psychology.

Key Words: school dropout, prevention, social justice, students of color, school-to-prison pipeline

Dropout Prevention

Lack of school success is a problem that affects children and adolescents from all demographic groups in the United States. Thousands of youth drop out of school with an estimated one in eight children never graduating from high school (Christenson & Thurlow, 2004). The enormity of the problem can be captured by the alarming statistic that one high school student drops out every 9 seconds in the United States (American Youth Policy Forum, 2006). The negative consequences of dropping out of school have only become more severe over time. For instance, unemployment, jobs that pay less than a living wage without benefits, and lower levels of physical and mental health are all likely outcomes for those who drop out of school (Alliance for Excellent Education, 2003; Bureau of Labor Statistics, 2009, 2010). What makes the issue of school dropout one of the most glaring social injustices of our country is the fact that there continues to be disproportionately higher rates of school dropout among youth from devalued and marginalized groups.

In 2008, the estimated dropout rates were 9.9% for African Americans, 18.3% for Latino/as, and 14.6% for Native American students compared to 4.8% for Whites (dropout rates for Asian/Pacific Islanders was 4.4%; National Center for Education Statistics [NCES], 2010). Students living in homes where the family income is in the lowest quartile are seven times more likely to drop out of school than those living in the highest family income quartile (16.4% vs. 2.2%; NCES). It is estimated that lesbian, gay, bisexual, and transgender (LGBT) students are almost three times more likely to drop out of high school (Bart, 1998). Finally, recent data indicate that high school dropout rates for students with (dis)abilities is 30% (US Department of Education, 2007). Although the focus of this chapter will be on prevention programs for students of color who attend underresourced schools, it is difficult if not impossible to fully disentangle the many intersecting oppressive forces faced by people of color, LGBT individuals, youth and families from lower socioeconomic groups, and those with (dis) abilities. For instance, scholars have asserted that dividing students in schools based on perceived (dis)abilities has become a more socially accepted form of segregation for students of color (Ferri & Conner, 2005).

This chapter will provide a broad overview of the extant literature on school dropout risk factors as well as the research on effective intervention and prevention programs. We will discuss how the disproportionately higher rates of early school withdrawal among youth of color living in high poverty neighborhoods have been framed as social, behavioral, and cultural deficits among students and families. The authors will then provide a rationale for why counseling psychologists should reclaim this body of literature to honor the silenced voices of poor students of color who are pushed out of urban schools due to a systematic process of dehumanization, isolation, and ultimately exclusion. We believe that the dropout prevention literature has not adequately addressed how failed school structures, practices, and policies significantly contribute to the high levels of dropout in many urban schools. A case will be made for counseling psychologists to adopt a social justice prevention framework in order to have the greatest impact on the school dropout crisis. The chapter will close with a summary of future directions for counseling psychologists.

Conceptualizing School Dropout

Understanding school dropout as a multidimensional phenomenon may be the most consistent and tangible conclusion from decades of research on the topic (Lehr, Hansen, Sinclair, & Christenson, 2003). The process of early school withdrawal can best be understood as a complex interaction among individual, family, school, and community factors (Christenson, Sinclair, Lehr, & Godber, 2001; Hawkins, Catalano, & Miller, 1992; Rumberger, 2001). There is no single factor that has been shown to be a primary cause for dropping out of school. Similarly, research has also consistently demonstrated that school dropout is not a discrete event (Lehr et al., 2003). Researchers agree that dropping out of school is the outcome of a long process of disengagement from as early as the elementary years (Christenson & Thurlow, 2004; Doll & Hess, 2001). Conceptualizing school dropout as a cumulative event caused by various individual and contextual factors clearly poses numerous challenges to developing effective prevention programs for addressing this complex issue.

There is currently a fairly sizable body of literature investigating a wide range of risk factors that fall within the individual, family, school, and community domains (Prevatt & Kelly, 2003). However, a criticism of research on school dropout has been the predominant emphasis on fixed demographic or status variables like race/ethnicity, gender, and socioeconomic status (Christenson & Thurlow, 2004; Doll & Hess, 2001). Scholars have asserted that the large body of research focusing on these types of demographic variables has projected the implicit message that the most important factors causing school dropout are "located within immutable characteristics of students that are relatively unavailable to intervention or remediation" (Doll & Hess, p. 353). It is perhaps this criticism that sparked a shift in the school dropout literature toward investigating what researchers have labeled alterable variables, like student's behaviors and attitudes toward school as well as family and school practices that influence school engagement and performance.

Poor academic performance and low levels of school engagement are two of the most consistent predictors of dropout. Both factors have been found to impact dropout starting in the first grade and continuing through elementary, middle, and high school (e.g., Alexander, Entwisle, & Kabbani, 2001; Battin-Pearson et al., 2000; Gleason & Dynarski, 2002; Rumberger, 2001). The influences of poor achievement and engagement on early school withdrawal have also been confirmed by a number of studies examining the reasons provided by students after they have dropped out (Bridgeland, DiIulio, & Morison, 2006; Ekstrom, Goertz, Pollack, & Rock, 1986). Another significant risk factor that is a consistent predictor of school dropout is being retained and having to repeat a grade (Alexander et al., 2001; Cairns, Cairns, & Neckerman, 1989; Rumberger). Starting with first grade, retention at any school level increases the probability of students dropping out before graduation. In a national report on school dropout risk factors, Hammond, Linton, Smink, and Drew (2007) state that what "makes retention so powerful is that its effects are additive, where multiple retentions dramatically increase the odds that a student will drop out" (p. 12).

Perhaps the most daunting task that dropout researchers have grappled with over the years is the question of how to accurately predict which students are most likely to leave school early. Realizing the fact that there is likely not one omnipotent risk factor for dropping out of school, researchers have focused on identifying predictive clusters or composites of factors (e.g., Balfanz, Herzog, & Mac Iver, 2007; Cairns et al., 1989; Gleason & Dynarski, 2002). The findings from these studies demonstrate that the use of groupings of risk factors can increase the probability of accurately identifying students who will drop out of school. However, the relatively low predictive ability reported in most of these studies (typically around 40%) and the lack of a clear-cut group of factors that can be viewed as the "best cluster" do not warrant the design and implementation of prevention programs focused on specific factor groupings (Hammond et al., 2007).

Longitudinal studies of cohorts of students have provided some of the most useful information about the personal and academic events that influence students' decisions to leave school early. Scholars have asserted that these studies provide the best opportunity to untangle the various interrelated factors (Hammond et al., 2007). For instance, Jimerson, Egeland, Sroufe, and Carlson (2000) followed an "at-risk" sample of youth from birth up to age 19 to explore the impact of multiple predictors of high school dropouts across development. Their findings are consistent with the concept that school dropout is a process that begins early in development and continues through the time a student formally withdraws from school. The researchers found that patterns seemed to be set by third grade and that early events like poor quality of caregiving interact with later discipline problems and poor academic performance to establish a pathway toward school dropout.

In another longitudinal research project, Entwisle, Alexander, and Olson (2005) randomly sampled 790 public school children in Baltimore in 1982 when they were starting first grade and followed them to young adulthood (age 22). The researchers examined school dropout from what they called a life-course perspective, which takes into account the process of development and the impact of various environmental factors (Alexander et al., 2001). By investigating the influence of these factors over the life course, the researchers found that decisions made in high school result from events and circumstances that are observed in the first grade. Additionally, factors like race, gender, and socioeconomic status measured in the first grade were found to have substantial effects on age 22 educational attainment (Entwisle et al.). The researchers also found, however, that parental support and children's own intrapersonal resources (e.g., temperament/disposition) affect the first-grade transition in ways that can buffer the influence of social risk factors. In addition to providing further evidence for conceptualizing school dropout as a long process of disengagement, another important outcome of longitudinal research has been the identification of markers or warning signs along the path before dropout occurs.

In a recent longitudinal study, Balfanz, Herzog, and Mac Iver (2007) make a strong case for the creation of early identification and intervention programs for students who live in high poverty contexts that focus on the sixth-grade transition. The researchers argue that youth who live in underresourced communities experience a spike in *push* and *pull* factors during this developmental period. Push factors are aspects of school environments that cause students to withdraw before graduation, whereas, pull factors are events and circumstances outside of school that compel students to dropout (Lehr et al., 2004). Due to poor school conditions in high poverty neighborhoods, students may be pushed out of school during the middle grades because of higher levels of chaos and teacher turnover. Students may also feel pulled to disengage from school by increased demands in the home and/or temptations to participate in wayward activities. To identify the combination of risk factors with the highest predictive power for school dropout, the researchers followed a racially diverse sample of 12,972 sixth graders starting in 1996 until 2004. Their analyses revealed that they could accurately predict 60% of the students who would ultimately not graduate from high school by using the following four factors: failing math, failing English, attending school less than 80% of the time, and receiving a poor final behavior grade. The researchers stress the utility of using this set of risk factors to develop early warning systems to get students back on the graduation path as well as the need for whole-school reform efforts.

Research on Dropout Prevention Programs

A review of the extant literature on dropout prevention programs reveals a mixed picture. During the late 1990s and the beginning of the millennium, a number of scholars expressed grave concerns over the lack of empirical evidence for dropout prevention and intervention programs (e.g., Sinclair, Christenson, Evelo, & Hurley, 1998; Lehr et al., 2003; Prevatt & Kelly, 2003). The Interdivisional Task Force on School Dropout Prevention that was formed shortly after the American Psychological Association (APA) passed its first policy statement on school dropout prevention in 1996 described research on high school dropout as overwhelmingly predictive or descriptive in nature (Hess, 1998). The Task Force also reported a dearth of program evaluation studies with only 20 (16.5%) of the 121 articles providing such information. Considering the significant implications of high school completion on youths, families, and communities, researchers have questioned the paucity of published intervention studies, which are crucial for the implementation of districtwide efforts (Doll & Hess, 2001; Lehr et al.).

Considering the complex, multidimensional nature of school dropout, the lack of empirical investigations of prevention programs is not particularly shocking. Researchers face a number of methodological challenges when embarking on such an investigation. First, the lack of a universally accepted definition of dropout has clearly interfered with the research in this area (Egyed, McIntosh, & Bull, 1998; Lichtenstein & Blackorby, 1995). Some have even asserted that establishing an accurate dropout rate would be impossible because there is such wide variation in the ways that schools assess, tally, and follow dropouts (Hale, 2001). Other methodological difficulties include the lack of a uniform definition for "at-risk students" (Larrivee & Bourque, 1991), the reliance on self-report and retrospective data (Allen, Philliber, Herrling, & Kuperminc, 1997; Franklin & Streeter, 1995), and the evaluation of various predictor variables based on different theoretical models (Prevatt & Kelly, 2003). Finally, the experimental research design continues to be touted as the gold standard for prevention program evaluation and is clearly lacking within the dropout literature (Biglan, Mrazek, Carnine, & Flay, 2003; Hammond et al., 2007), however, scholars have also raised concerns about rigidly applying such a standard to school-based, intervention research (Allen & Philliber, 2001; Reese & Vera, 2007).

Fortunately, scholarship focused on dropout prevention programs has matured to a point where there are now several rigorous reviews of the literature. Lehr and colleagues (2003) conducted an extensive review of intervention and prevention studies published in professional journals dated 1980 to 2001. The initial search produced a list of over 300 publications, which was then condensed to 45 using various inclusion criteria (e.g., published in professional journal, included impact data). The researchers calculated effect sizes for 17 of these studies, and 10 (58%) of them yielded moderate to large effect sizes for at least one dependent variable. After isolating these particular studies, the researchers found that the studies used a "wide range of interventions including the use of early reading intervention, tutoring, counseling, mentoring, an emphasis on creating caring environments and relationships, use of block scheduling, and service learning activities" (p. 350). Another important finding from the review was that almost all of the studies (98%, n = 44) targeted student change (e.g., attendance, attitudes toward school). Overall, the researchers conclude that there is a significant need to increase the quantity and quality of studies focused on dropout intervention and prevention programs. They also stress the importance of developing more programs focused on students' contextual influences (e.g., school climate and policies), as well as the need for more longitudinal studies that test the effectiveness of early intervention programs.

Prevatt and Kelly (2003) conducted a literature review on dropout prevention for school-aged children. In their review, the researchers searched various professional sources (e.g., electronic data bases, published reviews) to identify dropout prevention articles from 1982 to 2002. This initial search produced a base of 217 articles, which were then placed into three separate categories according to several inclusion criteria (e.g., published in peer reviewed journal, included empirical analysis). This process generated 18 studies, which met all the researchers' inclusion criteria. The researchers provide a more detailed description of four studies, which employed control or comparison groups and demonstrated strong or promising evidence of statistically significant outcomes. In summarizing these 4 exceptional programs, the researchers stated that they "used a large number of interventions, including bilingual education, academic skill enrichment in specific content areas, student monitoring, behavioral contracting, parent visits, individual tutoring, social skills groups, student orientations, study skills training, peer support, and teacher advising" (pp. 390–391). Many of the findings were consistent with the Lehr et al. (2003) literature review. Prevatt and Kelly call for significant improvements in the conceptual and methodological rigor of dropout prevention research.

The most recent report published by the National Dropout Prevention Center/Network (NDPC/N) provides a thorough review of 50 exemplary dropout prevention programs from across the United States (Hammond et al., 2007). The report provides a summary of the key components and strategies commonly found among some of the most effective programs addressing problem behaviors and/or risk factors. Although the report strongly encourages the use of multiple interventions and the targeting of factors in multiple domains to achieve success in addressing risk factors, all 50 exemplary programs primarily focus on individual risk factors with only 12 (24%) incorporating family interventions. A group of researchers cited in the report state that "the most effective prevention approaches involve complex and multicomponent programs that address early precursors of problem behaviors in youth. The most effective approaches often are those that change the family, school, or community environment in long-lasting and positive ways" (Kumpfer & Alvarado, 1998, p. 6, as cited in Hammond et al.). In terms of common strategies used by exemplary programs, these include *life skills development* (e.g., communication, conflict resolution, 60%), *family strengthening* (e.g., parenting skills, family management, 46%), *academic support* (26%), and *behavioral interventions* (20%). Once again, one of the strongest recommendations from the report is for practitioners to use evidence-based strategies to evaluate programs to assure effectiveness.

Reifying the Narrative

Much of the extant research on risk factors for urban youth of color has focused on person-centered correlates of dropout (Baker et al., 2001; Brown & Rodriguez, 2009). For instance, a large body of research has documented the statistical relationships between dropout rates and various student attributes, like academic competence, motivation, and behavioral difficulties (e.g., Christenson et al., 2001; Rosenthal, 1998; Rumberger & Palardy, 2005). The identification of person-centered risk factors for dropping out of school among youth of color living in high poverty contexts has likely served to improve individual level prevention efforts. Unfortunately, the overwhelming focus on the problems and deficits of urban youth of color has also reinforced the larger societal narrative that paints these youths as destined to lack interest in academics, be involved in gangs, suffer from depression, or to wind up with some other negative psychological or social condition.

There is also an abundance of explanations for high dropout rates among urban youth of color that focus on family and community dysfunctions. Researchers have focused on problems regarding family management practices (Taylor & Lopez, 2005), parental involvement (Englund, Egeland, & Collins, 2008), family cohesion and parental monitoring (Annunziata, Hogue, Faw, & Liddle, 2006), neighborhood distress (Crowder & South, 2003), and community crime and violence (Rosenfeld, Richman, Bowen, & Wynns, 2006). Research that is intended to identify important contextual factors that correlate with school disengagement among youth of color residing in high poverty neighborhoods is not a problem per se. It is the overproduction of such scholarship within the social sciences that silences and distorts epistemologies of people of color (Valencia & Solórzano, 1997). Deficit-informed research also reifies societal myths like the supposed "culture of poverty," which attributes the inequities experienced by poor and working-class people of color to problematic values and cultural deficiencies (Gorski, 2008).

Conveniently plugged into many school dropout articles, there is often a laundry list of statistics about how these individuals harm society at large. Staggering figures are presented to emphasize how much of a "drain" school dropouts are to the US economy. Articles frequently estimate the costs of dropouts in the "billions of dollars" due to lost revenues, welfare dependence, unemployment, crime prevention, prosecution, and incarceration (Joint Economic Committee, 1991). In a recent publication by the APA (2010), there are even more dreadful figures provided like the estimate that "12 million students will dropout over the next decade or so costing the U.S. about *$3 trillion*" (p. 5). Most likely, the primary intention of providing this information is to create a sense of urgency among professionals, but feelings of anger and resentment may also be triggered, especially when considering how smoothly these statistics fit into dominant discourses about poor communities primarily composed of black and brown bodies.

The predominant theories about the low educational achievement and attainment of students of color have been termed "master narratives" (Montecinos, 1995) and "majoritarian stories" (Solórzano & Yosso, 2002) because they are often bound by the constraints of racism and White privilege. Hence, these stories "provide a very narrow depiction of what it means to be Mexican-American, African-American, White, and so on. . . . A master narrative essentializes and wipes out the complexities and richness of a group's cultural life" (Montecinos, p. 293). "Scientific" explanations for the high rates of school dropout among urban youth of color that emphasize individual, familial, and cultural deficits uphold social hierarchies. In other words, these majoritarian stories serve to privilege "Whites, men, the middle and/or upper class, and heterosexuals by naming these social locations as natural or normative points of reference" (Solórzano & Yosso, p. 28). In this context, it is not surprising then that a higher proportion of dropout prevention programs proposed by psychologists have been focused on individual level interventions instead of efforts to eradicate institutional racism, sexism, classism, heterosexism, and ableism.

The overwhelming focus on the problems and "risk factors" among urban youth of color is a perfect example of how the counseling field has colluded with the existing social, political, and economic status quo. In the summary of the most recent publication by the APA (2010) on school dropout it states,

> Facing the high school dropout dilemma will require commitment and investment in high quality early childhood education, attention to social and emotional learning, continual monitoring of student attendance and academic progress, intensive instruction for those falling behind, using alternatives to school push-out, fostering of a positive school climate, and engagement with parents, families, and communities. (p. 6)

Earlier in this APA article, there is a fairly detailed description of the "dropout factories" that are typically found in high poverty, racially diverse communities. These schools are defined as those that frequently have senior classes with 60% fewer students than their entering freshmen classes (APA). Since this and other social injustices (e.g., dropout disparities due to differences in race/ethnicity, sexual orientation, and (dis)ability) are made so prominent in the article, it is quite disappointing that there is not a single recommendation for psychologists to confront these systemic problems.

(Re)Conceptualizing School Dropout for Urban Youth of Color

The scholarship focused on the crisis of school dropout in urban schools needs to pay more attention to the macro-level, sociohistorical mechanisms that perpetuate systemic racism. A growing number of scholars have articulated the apparent link between the racial disparities present in both the educational and criminal (in)justice systems in the United States (see, e.g., Raible & Irizarry, 2010). The parallel processes that occur in both institutions with regard to the overrepresentation of poor people of color are now known as the school-to-prison pipeline (Fenning & Rose, 2007; Wald & Losen, 2003). The growth of the prison industrial complex alongside the expansion of exclusionary discipline practices in urban schools can both be seen as cogs in the larger machine of White supremacy because "all domination is, in the last instance, maintained through social control strategies" (Bonilla-Silva, 2001, p. 103).

The rapid growth of zero tolerance discipline policies that require the automatic suspension, expulsion, and/or arrest of students in recent years is nothing short of frightening. According to the National Center for Education Statistics (NCES, 2003), US public schools initiated more than 3 million suspensions and nearly 100,000 expulsions during the year 2000 alone. There is now more than 30 years of research demonstrating that African American youth are disproportionately subject to the exclusionary discipline consequences of suspension and expulsion (for a review, see Fenning & Rose, 2007). Latino/a students (Brown, 2007), children from poor backgrounds (Casella, 2003), and those with academic problems (Balfanz, Spirikakis, Neild, & Legters, 2003) are also likely to be pushed out of school through exclusionary discipline policies. The literature on dropout prevention programs remains largely silent on this matter.

We feel it is irresponsible to discuss the process of school dropout among youth of color without acknowledging the mass criminalization and incarceration of African Americans and Latinos in the United States. More than three quarters of a million African American men are now behind bars, and 2 million are under some form of correctional supervision (Brewer & Heitzeg, 2008). One in 10 Latinos between the ages of 20 and 29 are under a form of correctional supervision (Mauer & Chesney-Lind, 2002). Angela Davis (1998) writes that "prisons disappear human beings in order to convey the illusion of solving social problems" (p. 643). Perhaps it is easier to "disappear" the bodies of youth of color in urban schools through exclusionary discipline practices than to commit the time, energy, and resources toward eradicating the systems that perpetuate educational disparities.

The ahistorical, decontextualized approach to conceptualizing school dropout for urban youth of color has led to a primary focus on individual and family factors versus the influence of educational policies and school climate issues (Hammond et al., 2007). There has been less focus on the growing body of literature demonstrating the impact of these larger systems on students' decision to leave school early (e.g., Lehr et al., 2004; Miller, Ross, & Sturgis, 2005). For instance, there is a relatively large body of research examining the influence of school climate on dropout (e.g., Wehlage & Rutter, 1986). However many of these studies are still quite problematic because they are often framed in ways that place the blame on "problem" students. School climate studies have focused on factors like absenteeism (Goldschmidt & Wang, 1999), percentage of the student body misbehaving (Goldschmidt & Wang), and problems with attendance, violence, and abuse of teachers (Kaufman, Bradbury, & Owings, 1992). Fortunately, there have been some studies that have intentionally linked school dropout with students' perspectives on school climate and curriculum. Rumberger (1995) found that schools with a high percentage of students rating discipline as unfair had higher dropout rates. In a recent national survey, the most common reason given by dropouts for leaving school was that their classes were not interesting (Bridgeland et al., 2006).

An issue that seems to be another 800-pound gorilla in the room is the proliferation of standards-based reforms and high-stakes testing, which culminated with the passage of the federal No Child Left Behind Act (NCLB). The widespread criticism of NCLB among educators is no secret (see, e.g., Darling-Hammond, 2006; Sunderman & Orfield, 2006). Unrealistic accountability reforms and high-stakes testing can actually increase attrition (Abrams & Haney, 2004) and retention rates (Miller, Ross, & Sturgis, 2005) across grade levels. In addition to the specific concerns about NCLB, there is mounting evidence that these policies increase dropout rates among the most vulnerable students (Allensworth, 2004). In an investigation of trends in Chicago elementary schools after the implementation of high-stakes testing, researchers found that retention rates significantly increased, especially for already marginalized students—those who were overage for grade, minority students, low achievers, and English-language learners (Allensworth, 2004). NCLB and the general topic of high-stakes testing are often alluded to in the dropout prevention literature, but recommendations for eradicating these harmful policies are rarely if ever provided.

Scholars have expressed caution about overemphasizing the importance of contextual factors when conceptualizing the problems experienced by marginalized and devalued groups (Parham & McDavis, 1987). For instance, proposing that the problem of school dropout is solely the result of a dysfunctional educational system may actually disempower individuals and families by sending a message that nothing meaningful can be accomplished before policies and structures are transformed. Another argument that has been proposed is that contextually focused interventions may not address the problem of students and families who are perpetuating their own oppression through the insidious process of internalized discrimination. Although there is some validity to these concerns, we can also examine them from a social justice perspective.

Social Justice Prevention

The field of counseling psychology has historically been concerned with the relationship between individual psychological functioning and the social contexts in which people live. Counseling psychologists have also promoted healthy functioning over the field of psychology's primary emphasis on human deficits and pathology (Albee, 2000). Recently, scholars who have applied a more critical lens to the field have highlighted a problematic incongruence within the principles and practices of counseling psychologists (Speight & Vera, 2004). These scholars have asserted that the counseling psychology field continues to privilege traditional individual-level interventions like counseling and psychotherapy, which is inconsistent with the increasing awareness of how systemic, institutionalized barriers are the root cause for many of the psychological and social difficulties experienced by members of marginalized groups (Fouad, Gerstein, & Toporek, 2006; Vera & Speight, 2003; Prilleltensky, 1997). A solution to this problem may come from a recommitment to some of the fundamental principles of counseling psychology.

A distinguishing characteristic of the counseling psychology field has been the emphasis on prevention and health. Preventive programs have been defined as those that attempt to thwart the onset of psychological difficulties and other negative health-related outcomes (Vera & Reese, 2000). There is now a large body of empirical studies demonstrating that preventive interventions can reduce the incidence of negative psychological outcomes as well as promote the positive development of children and adults (e.g., Catalano, Berglund, Ryan, Lonczak, & Hawkins, 2004; Durlak & Wells, 1997; Tobler & Stratton, 1997; Wilson, Gottfredson, & Najaka, 2001). The integration of prevention with social justice principles in counseling psychology dates back to the late George Albee's (2000) exclamations to utilize prevention as a means for dismantling the systems of power and domination that sustain high levels of poverty, isolation, and exploitation among marginalized groups. More recently, a number of scholars have sought to explicitly promote prevention as a tool for social justice (Conyne, 2004; Vera, Daly, Gonzales, Morgan, & Thakral, 2006) and have helped to distinguish social justice prevention from more general forms of prevention work (Kenny & Hage, 2009).

The goal of social justice is to achieve a society where there is a more equitable distribution of resources and where its members have adequate opportunities to feel secure and experience well-being (Fouad et al., 2006; Goodman et al., 2004; Vera & Speight, 2003). Drawing from this conceptualization, social justice preventive interventions should be aimed at dismantling systems of power and privilege that perpetuate pervasive societal inequities. Key systems of oppression in the United States include White supremacy, patriarchy, heteronormativity, classism, and ableism. These forms of systemic discrimination serve to isolate, exploit, and dehumanize various target groups, while simultaneously allowing the general population to uphold illusions of equality and meritocracy. Although preventive interventions can and should include targeted change at the individual level, we must acknowledge that the field of psychology has a long history of developing theories and techniques aimed at "fixing" the targets of systemic discrimination versus engaging in efforts to dismantle the oppressive forces themselves (Prilleltensky, 1997).

Feminist scholars and practitioners have long been engaged in transforming traditional psychological theories to place a greater emphasis on oppressive sociopolitical conditions (Evans, Kincade, Marbley, & Seem, 2005; Remer, 2008). Additionally, preventive interventions that are aimed specifically at institutional discrimination (e.g., schools) may best be approached using a critical psychology framework (Prilleltensky, 1997). Preventive efforts using a critical psychology approach would explicitly challenge the status quo and place the active pursuit of social justice and the dismantling of systems of power and privilege at the forefront (Nelson & Prilleltensky, 2005). Counseling psychologists who draw from the principles of feminist and critical psychology may be best suited to confront the persistent problem of school dropout in urban schools.

Future Directions

Due to the historical overemphasis on individual-level interventions in the profession (Brown & Rodriguez, 2009), perhaps counseling psychologists should now focus their energies on designing dropout prevention programs aimed primarily at institutional-, structural-, and policy-level injustices. To "right the ship" so to speak, we believe it may be time for counseling psychologists to adopt a more "radical" approach for ameliorating this pervasive social injustice. This new paradigm would rest on the premise that intervening solely with students of color in urban contexts to prevent early school withdrawal perpetuates larger systemic injustices.

The framework would also require counseling psychologists to have faith in youth and families of color, to trust that those who have experienced the suffocating effects of racial and class oppression are resourceful and resilient. Students and families from devalued groups are not merely passive victims of systems of power and control. Marginalized communities of color have always engaged in forms of resistance and subversion, but these efforts are often either ignored within the social sciences or appropriated to support master narratives. Specific to underresourced urban schools, Fine's (Fine, 1991; Fine et al., 2004) groundbreaking studies have demonstrated how youth of color in these contexts never fully internalize nor fully resist the potentially devastating messages projected by these institutions. She writes that "these students speak through dual registers of yearning and anger, pride and shame, engagement and alienation, fear and desire" (p. 2204). Seeing that students of color in oppressive urban schools are already engaged in countermoves against systemic racism should empower counseling psychologists to commit to dropout prevention efforts that are aimed primarily at the institutional and structural levels.

Let us emphasize that we are not advocating for counseling psychologists to throw the baby out with the bath water. Although not reviewed in this chapter, the resilience and strengths promotion paradigms have had a tremendously positive impact on prevention work with youth (e.g., Rutter, 1987; Masten & Coatsworth, 1998). Drawing from this foundation, researchers have demonstrated the effectiveness of "positive youth development" prevention programs that focus on enhancing skills, attitudes, and competencies (Catalano et al., 2004; Vera at al., 2007). Counseling psychologists are encouraged to draw from this research base when designing dropout prevention programs, while also integrating some of the following recommendations for improving urban schools. Clearly, many of the activities listed are not included in the traditional roles of counseling psychologists, but it is imperative that all professionals committed to reducing dropout among urban communities find ways to intervene at multiple systemic levels.

1. *Engage in efforts to improve teacher quality* by participating in interdisciplinary collaboration and in-service trainings. The surplus of underqualified, unprepared teachers in urban schools is not going anywhere anytime soon, so counseling psychologists must find creative and respectful ways to partner with teachers to develop engaging, stimulating, and relevant curricula. Counseling psychologists can also utilize their training in multicultural/social justice skills to help teachers develop and implement culturally relevant pedagogy (Ladson-Billings, 1995) and an explicit antiracist orientation (Raible & Irizarry, 2007). Counseling and education in urban school settings should also help students develop a broader sociopolitical consciousness based on Freire's notion of *conscientization* (Ladson-Billings; Shin et al., 2010).

2. *Establish strong working relationships with principals* to collaborate in improving school culture and community. Creating warm and welcoming environments has been shown to be a primary tool used by social justice–oriented school principles in high poverty urban schools to significantly increase schoolwide student achievement (Theoharis, 2007). Another critical aspect of these successful urban elementary schools is to eliminate "segregated and pull-out programs that prohibit both emotional and academic success for marginalized children" (p. 252). Eliminating special education classrooms, pull-out programs, and separate instruction for already marginalized students is part of a larger movement to create inclusive schools (see, e.g., Causton-Theoharis & Theoharis, 2008). Facilitating this structural change in urban schools has been shown to increase state test scores for all students including those with (dis)abilities and English language learners (Theoharis).

3. *Assist in transforming school disciplinary policies* that are sustaining the school-to-prison pipeline for youth of color in underresourced communities. We would suggest presenting the excellent framework provided by Rose and Fenning (2007) to school leaders. These scholars provide a detailed description of how to critically analyze a school's approach to disciplining students with the ultimate goal of establishing more proactive policies and practices based on positive behavior support (PBS; Sugai & Horner, 2002). The goal of PBS is to implement a "comprehensive approach to the standardization of discipline policies, the proactive teaching of expected behaviors, and development of positive teacher–student interaction that not only addresses the punitive discipline and alienation often experienced by minority students but also promotes a better school climate for all students" (p. 539).

4. *Be the catalyst for community members* to demand excellence in urban schools. One of the challenges facing students and families of color in high poverty, high stress neighborhoods is the lack of time, resources, and perhaps social capital to collectively confront discriminatory institutions. It is said that many of the things that go on in urban schools would never be allowed to occur in more wealthy districts simply because of the pressure from parents. When parents with surplus social and economic privileges catch wind of a perceived injustice happening in their child's school, parents often mobilize immediately demanding accountability. Although dominant discourses say otherwise, many parents of color in urban communities care a great deal about the education their children are receiving. Counseling psychologists are encouraged to initiate authentic and respectful community-based collaborations (Bond & Carmola Hauf, 2007) that are aimed at helping parents hold urban schools accountable for the many ways in which they produce higher rates of dropout for youth of color.

5. *Get educated and get involved* in educational policy that will replace NCLB with legislation that does not provide incentives for schools to push out low-performing students. Scholars have lamented the fact that educators allowed NCLB legislation and the underlying rationale to rise to power (Gentry, 2006). Unfortunately, counseling psychologists have been complicit in this process as well. Although this may seem like the most inaccessible and abstract realm of intervention for counseling professionals who are interested in reducing school dropout rates, influencing policy has always been an important mechanism for mental health professionals committed to advancing social justice (Ackerson & Korr, 2007). Since policy changes can occur at the local, state, and federal levels, opportunities for action can be uncovered at all levels. Maton and Bishop-Josef (2006) provide a succinct review of the challenges and opportunities for psychologists to influence social policy.

6. *Expand our research methodologies* investigating school dropout among youth of color in underresourced communities to create a counternarrative. It is critical that we continue to move away from producing scholarship that is used to reify master narratives. These dominant stories insist that

marginalized groups are the passive recipients of their oppressed conditions. It is imperative that we increase the acceptance and valuing of research approaches that bear witness to the many forms of resistance that youth and families of color engage in (Brown & Rodriguez, 2009; Fine et al., 2004). Michelle Fine (2006) has written eloquently about how social psychologists can conduct research that is explicitly intended to eradicate societal injustices. Counseling psychologists are encouraged to begin infusing more radical constructionist methods (e.g., ethnography, participatory action research) to paint a more comprehensive picture of the coconstructed process of school dropout in urban schools.

Conclusion

The purpose of this chapter was to provide a review of the literature on school dropout risk factors as well as the research on effective intervention and prevention programs. The chapter focused primarily on the crisis of school dropout among youth of color attending urban schools. The authors made every effort to provide a more contextualized analysis of this societal inequity by intentionally focusing on some of the social, historical, political, and structural forces that sustain it. We are hopeful that the information provokes further thought, dialogue, and most importantly action.

References

Abrams, L., & Haney, W. (2004). Accountability and the grade 9 to 10 transition: The impact on attrition and retention rates. In G. Orfield (Ed.), *Dropouts in America: Confronting the graduation rate crisis* (pp. 181–206). Cambridge, MA: Harvard Education Publishing Group.

Ackerson, B. J., & Korr, W. S. (2007). Mental policy and social justice. In E. Aldarondo (Ed.), *Advancing social justice through clinical practice* (pp. 359–369). Mahwah, NJ: Erlbaum.

Albee, G. W. (2000). The Boulder model's fatal flaw. *American Psychologist, 55,* 247–248.

Alexander, K. L., Entwisle, D. R., & Kabbani, N. S. (2001). The dropout process in life course perspective: Early risk factors at home and school. *Teachers College Record, 103*(5), 760–822.

Allen, J. P., & Philliber, S. (2001). Who benefits from a broadly targeted prevention program? Differential efficacy across populations in the teen outreach program. *Journal of Community Psychology, 29,* 637–655.

Allen, J. P., Philliber, S., Herrling, S., & Kuperminc, G. P. (1997). Preventing teen pregnancy and academic failure: Experimental evaluation of a developmentally based approach. *Child Development, 64,* 729–742.

Allensworth, E. M. (2004). Graduation and dropout rates after implementation of high-stakes testing in Chicago's elementary schools: A closer look at students most vulnerable to dropping out. In G. Orfield (Ed.), *Dropouts in America: Confronting the graduation rate crisis* (pp. 157–180). Cambridge, MA: Harvard Education Press.

Alliance for Excellent Education. (2003). *Fact sheet: The impact of education on health and well-being.* Washington, DC: Author.

American Psychological Association. (2010). *Facing the school dropout dilemma.* Washington, DC: Author. Retrieved from http://www.apa.org/pi/families/resources/school-dropout-prevention.aspx

American Youth Policy Forum. (2006). *Whatever it takes: How twelve communities are reconnecting out of school youth.* Retrieved November 13, 2010, from http://www.aypf.org/publications/WhateverItTakes/WITfull.pdf

Annunziata, D., Hogue, A., Faw, L., & Liddle, H. A. (2006). Family functioning and school success in at-risk, inner-city adolescents. *Journal of Youth and Adolescence, 35*(1), 105–113.

Baker, J. A., Derrer, R. D., Davis, S. M., Dinklage-Travis, H. E., Linder, D. S., & Nicholson, M. D. (2001). The flip side of the coin: Understanding the school's contribution to dropout and completion. *School Psychology Quarterly, 16*(4), 406–426.

Balfanz, R., Spirikakis, K., Neild, R. C., & Legters, N. (2003). High-poverty secondary schools and the juvenile justice system: How neither helps the other and how that could change. In J. Wald & D. J. Losen (Eds.), *New directions for youth development: Deconstructing the school-to-prison pipeline* (pp. 71–89). San Francisco: Jossey-Bass.

Balfanz, R., Herzog, L., & Mac Iver, D. J. (2007). Preventing student disengagement and keeping students on the graduation path in urban middle-grades schools: Early identification and effective interventions. *Educational Psychologist, 42*(4), 223–235.

Bart, M. (1998). Creating a safer school for gay students. *Counseling Today, 26,* 36–39.

Battin-Pearson, S., Newcomb, M. D., Abbott, R. D., Hill, K. G., Catalano, R. F., & Hawkins, J. D. (2000). Predictors of early high school dropout: A test of five theories. *Journal of Educational Psychology, 92*(3), 568–582.

Biglan, A., Mrazek, P. J., Carnine, D., & Flay, B. R. (2003). The integration of research and practice in the prevention of youth problem behaviors. *American Psychologist, 58*(6/7), 433–440.

Bond, L. A., & Carmola Hauf, A. M. (2007). Community-based collaboration: An overarching best practice in prevention. *The Counseling Psychologist, 35*(4), 567–575.

Bonilla-Silva, E. (2001). *White supremacy and racism in the post–civil rights era.* Boulder, CO: Lynne Rienner.

Brewer, R. M., & Heitzeg, N. A. (2008). The racialization of crime and punishment: Criminal justice, color-blind racism, and the political economy of the prison industrial complex. *American Behavioral Scientist, 51*(5), 625–644.

Bridgeland, J. M., DiIulio, J. J., & Morison, K. B. (2006). *The silent epidemic: Perspectives of high school dropouts.* Washington, DC: Civic Enterprises, LLC, in association with Peter D. Hart Research Associates for the Bill & Melinda Gates Foundation.

Brown, T. M. (2007). Lost and turned out: Academic, social, and emotional experiences of students excluded from school. *Urban Education, 42*(5), 432–455.

Brown, T. M., & Rodriguez, L. F. (2009). School and the co-construction of dropout. *International Journal of Qualitative Studies in Education, 22*(2), 221–242.

Bureau of Labor Statistics (2009). *Education pays.* Washington, DC: US Department of Labor. Retrieved November 23, 2010, from http://www.bls.gov/emp/ep_chart_001.htm

Bureau of Labor Statistics (2010). *The employment situation—April 2010.* Washington, DC: US Department of Labor. Retrieved November 23, 2010, from http://bls.gov/news.release/pdf/empsit.pdf

Cairns, R. B., Cairns, B. D., & Neckerman, H. J. (1989). Early school dropout: Configurations and determinants. *Child Development, 60,* 1437–1452.

Casella, R. (2003). Punishing dangerousness through preventive detention: Illustrating the institutional link between school and prison. In J. Wald & D. J. Losen (Eds.), *New directions for youth development: Deconstructing the school-to-prison pipeline* (pp. 55–70). San Francisco: Jossey-Bass.

Catalano, R. F., Berglund, M. L., Ryan, J. A. M., Lonczak, H. S., & Hawkins, J. D. (2004). Positive youth development in the United States: Research findings on evaluations of positive youth development programs. *The Annals of the American Academy of Political and Social Science, 591*(1) 98–124.

Causton-Theoharis, J., & Theoharis, G. (2008). Creating inclusive schools for all students. *The School Administrator, 65,* 24–31.

Christenson, S. L., Sinclair, M. F., Lehr, C. A., & Godber, Y. (2001). Promoting successful school completion: Critical conceptual and methodological guidelines. *School Psychology Quarterly, 16,* 468–484.

Christenson, S. L., & Thurlow, M. L. (2004). School dropouts: Prevention considerations, interventions, and challenges. *Current Directions in Psychological Science, 13,* 36–39.

Conyne, R. K. (2004). *Preventive counseling: Helping people to become empowered in systems and settings.* New York: Brunner-Routledge.

Crowder, K., & South, S. J. (2003). Neighborhood distress and school dropout: The variable significance of community context. *Social Science Research, 32*(4), 659–698.

Darling-Hammond, L. (2006). No Child Left Behind and high school reform. *Harvard Educational Review, 76*(4), 642–667.

Davis, A. (1998). Masked racism: Reflections on the prison industrial complex. In P. S. Rothenberg (Ed.), *Race, class, and gender in the United States* (pp. 643–647). New York: Worth.

Doll, B., & Hess, R. S. (2001). Through a new lens: Contemporary psychological perspectives on school completion and dropping out of high school. *School Psychology Quarterly, 16*(4), 351–356.

Durlak, J. A., & Wells, A. M. (1997). Primary prevention mental health programs for children and adolescents: A meta-analytic review. *American Journal of Community Psychology, 25,*115–152.

Egyed, C. J., McIntosh, D. E., & Bull, K. S. (1998). School psychologists' perceptions of priorities for dealing with the dropout problem. *Psychology in the Schools, 35,* 153–162.

Ekstrom, R. B., Goertz, M. E., Pollack, J. M., & Rock, D. A. (1986). Who drops out of high school and why? Findings of a national study. *Teachers College Record, 87,* 3576–3730.

Englund, M. M., Egeland, B. & Collins, W. A. (2008). Exceptions to high school dropout predictions in a low-income sample: Do adults make a difference? *Journal of Social Issues, 64*(1), 77–93

Entwisle, D. R., Alexander, K. L., & Olson, L. S. (2005). First grade and educational attainment by age 22: A new story. *American Journal of Sociology, 110*(5), 1458–1502.

Evans, K. M., Kincade, E. A., Marbley, A. F., & Seem, S. R. (2005). Feminism and feminist therapy: Lessons from the past and hopes for the future. *Journal of Counseling and Development, 83*(3), 269–277.

Fenning, P., & Rose, J. (2007). Overrepresentation of African American students in exclusionary discipline: The role of school policy. *Urban Education, 42*(6), 536–559.

Ferri, B. A., & Conner, D. J. (2005). Tools of exclusion: Race, disability, and (re)segregated education. *Teachers College Record, 107*(3), 453–474.

Fine, M. (1991). *Framing dropouts.* Albany: State University of New York Press.

Fine, M. (2006). Bearing witness: Methods for researching oppression and resistance—A textbook for critical research. *Social Justice Research, 19*(1), 83–108.

Fine, M., Burns, A., Payne, Y. A., & Torre, M. E. (2004). Civics lessons: The color and class of betrayal. *Teachers College Record, 106*(11), 2193–2223.

Fouad, N. A., Gerstein, L. H., & Toporek, R. L. (2006). Social justice and counseling psychology in context. In R. L. Toporek, L. Gerstein, N. Fouad, G. Roysircar, & T. Israel (Eds.), *Handbook for social justice in counseling psychology: Leadership, vision, and action* (pp. 1–16). Thousand Oaks, CA: Sage.

Franklin, C., & Streeter, C. L. (1995). Assessment of middle class youth at-risk to dropout: School, psychological, and family correlates. *Children and Youth Services Review, 17,* 433–448.

Gentry, M. (2006). No child left behind: Neglecting excellence. *Roeper Review, 29(1),* 24–27.

Gleason, P., & Dynarski, M. (2002). Do we know whom to serve? Issues in using risk factors to identify dropouts. *Journal of Education for Students Placed at Risk, 7*(1), 25–41.

Goldschmidt, P., & Wang, J. (1999). When can schools affect dropout behavior? A longitudinal multilevel analysis. *American Educational Research Journal, 36*(4), 715–738.

Goodman, L. A., Liang, B., Helms, J. E., Latta, R. E., Sparks, E., & Weintraub, S. R. (2004). Training counseling psychologists as social justice agents: Feminist and multicultural principles in action. *The Counseling Psychologist, 25,* 413–427.

Gorski, P. C. (2008). Peddling poverty for profit: Elements of oppression in Ruby Payne's framework. *Equity and Excellence in Education, 41*(1), 130–148.

Hale, L. F. (2001). *School dropout prevention: Information and strategies for parents. Communique* (Vol. 29, pp. 2–3). Bethesda, MD: The National Association of School Psychologists.

Hammond, C., Linton, D., Smink, J., & Drew, S. (2007). *Dropout risk factors and exemplary programs.* Clemson, SC: National Dropout Prevention Center, Communities in Schools, Inc.

Hawkins, J. D., Catalano, R. F., & Miller, J. Y. (1992). Risk and protective factors for alcohol and other drug problems in adolescence and early adulthood: Implications for substance abuse prevention. *Psychological Bulletin, 112,* 64–105.

Hess, R. S. (1998). *Drop out prevention knowledge base.* A report of the Interdivisional Task Force on School Dropout Prevention presented at the annual meeting of the American Psychological Association, Boston, MA.

Jimerson, S., Egeland, B., Sroufe, L. A., & Carlson, B. (2000). A prospective longitudinal study of high school dropouts examining multiple predictors across development. *Journal of School Psychology, 38*(6), 525–549.

Joint Economic Committee. (1991). *Doing drugs and dropping out: A report prepared for the use of the subcommittee on economic growth, trade, and taxes of the joint economic committee (102nd Congress, 1st Session).* Washington, DC: Government Print Office.

Kaufman, P., Bradbury, D., & Owings, J. (1992). *Characteristics of at-risk students in the NELS: 88.* Washington, DC: National Center for Education Statistics, Office of Educational Research and Improvement, US Department of Education.

Kenny, M. E., & Hage, S. M. (2009). The next frontier: Prevention as an instrument of social justice. *The Journal of Primary Prevention, 30*(1), 1–10.

Kumpfer, K. L., & Alvarado, R. (1998). Effective family strengthening interventions, *Juvenile Justice Bulletin.* Washington DC: Office of Juvenile Justice and Delinquency Prevention, U.S. Department of Justice. Available online at http://www.ncjrs.gov/pdffiles/171121.pdf

Ladson-Billings, G. (1995). But that's just good teaching! The case for culturally relevant pedagogy. *Theory into Practice, 34*(3), 159–165.

Larrivee, B. L., & Bourque, M. L. (1991). The impact of several dropout prevention intervention strategies on at risk students. *Education, 112,* 48–63.

Lehr, C. A., Hansen, A., Sinclair, M. F., & Christenson, S. L. (2003). Moving beyond dropout towards school completion: An integrative review of data-based interventions. *School Psychology Review, 32*(3), 342–364.

Lehr, C. A., Johnson, D. R., Bremer, C. D., Cosio, S., & Thompson, M. (2004). *Essential tools: Increasing rates of school completion; Moving from policy and research to practice.* Minneapolis: National Center on Secondary Education and Transition, College of Education and Human Development, University of Minnesota.

Lichtenstein, S., & Blackorby, J. (1995). Who drops out and what happens to them? *Journal of Vocational Special Needs Education, 18*(1), 6–11.

Masten, A. S., & Coatsworth, J. D. (1998). The development of competence in favorable and unfavorable environments: Lessons from research on successful children. *American Psychologist, 53*(2), 205–220.

Maton, K. I., & Bishop-Josef, S. J. (2006). Psychological research, practice, and social policy: Potential pathways of influence. *Professional Psychology: Research and Practice, 37*(2), 140–145.

Mauer, M., & Chesney-Lind, M. (Eds.). (2002). *Invisible punishment. The collateral consequences of mass imprisonment.* New York: New Press.

Miller, J., Ross, T., & Sturgis, C. (2005). *Beyond the tunnel: Addressing cross-cutting issues that impact vulnerable youth.* Briefing Paper #2 Redirecting youth from the school-to-prison pipeline: Addressing cross-cutting issues in youth services. A Briefing Paper Series of Youth Transition Funders Group in partnership with the Annie E. Casey Foundation.

Montecinos, C. (1995). Culture as an ongoing dialogue: Implications for multicultural teacher education. In C. Sleeter & P. McLaren (Eds.), *Multicultural education, critical pedagogy, and the politics of difference* (pp. 269–308). Albany: State University of New York Press.

National Center for Education Statistics. (2003). Suspension and expulsions of public elementary and secondary school students, by state, sex and percent of enrollment: 2000. http://nces.ed.gov/programs/digest/d03/tables/dt147.asp.

Nelson, G., & Prilleltensky, I. (Eds.). (2005). *Community psychology: In pursuit of liberation and well-being.* New York: Palgrave Macmillan.

Parham, T. A., & McDavis, R. J. (1987). Black men, an endangered species: Who's really pulling the trigger? *Journal of Counseling and Development, 66,* 24–27.

Prevatt, F., & Kelly, F. D. (2003). Dropping out of school: A review of intervention programs. *Journal of School Psychology, 41*(5), 377–395.

Prilleltensky, I. (1997). Values, assumptions, and practices: Assessing the moral implications of psychological discourse and action. *American Psychologist, 52,* 517–535.

Raible, J., & Irizarry, J. G. (2007). Transracialized selves and the emergence of post white teacher identities. *Race, Ethnicity and Education, 10*(2), 177–198.

Raible, J., & Irizarry, J. G. (2010). Redirecting the teacher's gaze: Teacher education, youth surveillance and the school-to-prison pipeline. *Teaching and Teacher Education, 26*(5), 1196–1203.

Reese, L. E., & Vera, E. M. (2007). Culturally relevant prevention: The scientific and practical considerations of community-based programs. *The Counseling Psychologist, 35*(6), 763–778.

Remer, P. (2008). Origins and evolution of feminist therapy. In J. Frew & M. D. Spiegler (Eds.), *Contemporary psychotherapies for a diverse world* (pp. 397–441). New York: Lahaska Press.

Rosenfeld, L. B., Richman, J. M., Bowen, G. L., & Wynns, S. L. (2006). In the face of a dangerous community: The effects of social support and neighborhood danger on high school students' school outcomes. *Southern Communication Journal, 71*(3), 273–289.

Rosenthal, B. S. (1998). Non-school correlates of dropout: An integrative review of the literature. *Children and Youth Services Review, 20,* 413–433.

Rumberger, R. W. (1995). Dropping out of middle school: A multilevel analysis of students and schools. *American Educational Research Journal, 32,* 583–625.

Rumberger, R.W. (2001). *Why students drop out of school and what can be done.* Paper prepared for the conference, "Dropouts in America: How Severe Is the Problem? What Do We Know About Intervention and Prevention?" Cambridge, MA: Harvard University. Retrieved November 24, 2010, from http://civilrightsproject.ucla.edu/research/k-12-education/school-dropouts/why-students-drop-out-of-school-and-what-can-be-done/rumberger-why-students-dropout-2001.pdf

Rumberger, R. W., & Palardy, G. J. (2005). Test scores, dropout rates, and transfer rates as alternative indicators of high school performance. *American Educational Research Journal, 42*(1), 3–42.

Rutter, M. (1987). Psychosocial resilience and protective mechanisms. *American Journal of Orthopsychiatry, 57*(3), 316–331.

Shin, R., Rogers, J., Silas, M., Smythe-Brown, C. Stanciu, A., Austin, B. (2010). Advancing social justice in urban schools through the implementation of transformative groups for youth of color. *The Journal for Specialists in Group Work, 35*(3), 230–235.

Sinclair, M. F., Christenson, S. L., Evelo, D. L., & Hurley, C. M. (1998). Dropout prevention for youth with disabilities: Efficacy of a sustained school engagement procedure. *Exceptional Children, 65,* 7–22.

Solórzano, D. G., & Yosso, T. J. (2002). Critical race methodology: Counter-storytelling as an analytical framework for education research. *Qualitative Inquiry, 8*(1), 23–44.

Speight, S., & Vera, E. M. (2004). A social justice agenda: Ready, or not? *The Counseling Psychologist, 32*(1), 109–118.

Sugai, G., & Horner, R. H. (2002). Introduction to the special series on positive behavior support in schools. *Journal of Emotional and Behavioral Disorders, 10,* 130–135.

Sunderman, G. L., & Orfield, G. (2006). Domesticating a revolution: No Child Left Behind reforms and state administrative response. *Harvard Educational Review, 76*(4), 526–556.

Taylor, R. D., & Lopez, E. I. (2005). Family management practice, school achievement, and problem behavior in African American adolescents: Mediating processes. *Journal of Applied Developmental Psychology, 26*(1), 39–49.

Theoharis, G. (2007). Social justice educational leaders and resistance: Toward a theory of social justice leadership. *Education Administration Quarterly, 43(2),* 221–258.

Tobler, N. S., & Stratton, H. H. (1997). Effectiveness of school-based drug prevention programs: A meta-analysis of the research. *Journal of Primary Prevention, 18*(1), 71–128.

US Department of Education (2007). *Dropout prevention for students with disabilities: A critical issue for state education agencies.* Washington, DC: US Department of Education. Retrieved October 11, 2010, from http://betterhighschools.org/docs/NHSC_DropoutPrevention_052507.pdf

US National Center for Education Statistics (2010). *Digest of education statistics: 2009.* Washington, DC: US Department of Education. Retrieved November 13, 2010, from http://nces.ed.gov/pubs2010/2010013.pdf

Valencia, R., & Solórzano, D. (1997). Contemporary deficit thinking. In R. Valencia (Ed.), *The evolution of deficit thinking in educational thought and practice* (pp. 160–210). New York: Falmer.

Vera, E. M., Caldwell, J., Clarke, M., Gonzales, R., Morgan, M., West, M. (2007). The Choices Program: Multisystemic interventions for enhancing the personal and academic effectiveness of urban adolescents of color. *The Counseling Psychologist, 35(6),* 779–796.

Vera, E. M., Daly, B., Gonzales, R., Morgan, M., & Thakral, C. (2006). Prevention and outreach with underserved populations. In R. L. Toporek, L. Gerstein, N. Fouad, G. Roysircar, & T. Israel (Eds.), *Handbook for social justice in counseling psychology: Leadership, vision, and action* (pp. 86–99). Thousand Oaks, CA: Sage.

Vera, E. M. & Reese, L. E. (2000). Preventive interventions with school-age youth. In S. Brown & R. Lent (Eds.), *Handbook of counseling psychology* (pp. 411–434). New York: Wiley.

Vera, E. M., & Speight, S. (2003). Multicultural competence, social justice, and counseling psychology: Expanding our roles. *The Counseling Psychologist, 31,* 253–272.

Wald, J., & Losen, D. (2003). *New directions for youth: Deconstructing the school-to-prison pipeline.* San Francisco, CA: Wiley Periodicals.

Wehlage, G. G., & Rutter, R. A. (1986). Dropping out: How much do schools contribute to the problem? *Teachers College Record, 87*(3), 374–392.

Wilson, D. B., Gottfredson, D. C., & Najaka, S. S. (2001). School-based prevention of problem behaviors: A meta-analysis. *Journal for Quantitative Criminology, 17*(3), 247–272.

CHAPTER

15 Integrative Approaches to the Prevention of Eating Disorders and Obesity in Youth: Progress, Pitfalls, and Possibilities

Suzanne E. Mazzeo, Rachel W. Gow *and* Cynthia M. Bulik

Abstract

Both eating disorders and obesity are serious public health concerns. Given the chronic course of these conditions, there is a major emphasis on their prevention. However, many concerns have been raised about the optimal approach to the prevention of both eating disorders and obesity. This chapter reviews controversies in the prevention of eating disorders and obesity, including potential iatrogenic effects of prevention, and whether programming should be implemented at the level of public policy. Next, we review the debate regarding the integration of prevention efforts for these conditions, including the feasibility and acceptability of these integrated approaches. The chapter continues with a brief review of some of the best practices for the integrated prevention of both obesity and eating disorders identified in previous research. Finally, we discuss newer perspectives in this research, including broadening targets of prevention, integrating technology, and enhancing the cultural sensitivity of eating disorder and obesity prevention.

Key Words: prevention, eating disorders, obesity, children, adolescents

Introduction

Both eating disorders and obesity are serious health concerns with significant physical, psychological, occupational, social, and economic effects (Becker, Grinspoon, Klibanski, & Herzog, 1999; Roehling, Roehling, & Pichler, 2007; Schwimmer, Burwinkle, & Varni, 2003; Simon, Schmidt, & Pilling, 2005). These conditions are typically chronic, and treatment effectiveness is often suboptimal (Becker et al., 1999; Whitaker, Wright, Pepe, Seidel, & Deitz, 1997). Thus, experts in the areas of eating disorders (Levine & Smolak, 2009; Stice & Hoffman, 2004) and obesity (Bauer, Haines, & Neumark-Sztainer, 2009) strongly suggest that research focus on the prevention of these conditions. However, many questions remain about the best approaches to the development and implementation of eating disorder and obesity prevention. This chapter focuses primarily on programs with potential to reduce the risk of both conditions. We first discuss the prevalence and risk factors for obesity and eating disorders. Next we review controversies in the prevention of these conditions and review the debate regarding the integration of prevention efforts. The chapter continues with a brief review of some of the best practices for the integrated prevention of both obesity and eating disorders identified in previous research. Finally, we discuss newer perspectives in this research, including broadening targets of prevention (e.g., parents, teachers), and future directions.

Prevalence and Risk Factors for Obesity and Eating Disorders

PREVALENCE OF PEDIATRIC OBESITY

Despite the controversy regarding prevention approaches, childhood obesity, in particular, has recently gained significant attention in both the popular press and the scientific literature. This focus is related to exponential increases in the prevalence of childhood overweight. For example, within the last 3 decades, the percentage of children and adolescents who are overweight or obese has more than doubled (Hedley et al., 2004; Ogden, Carroll, Curtin, Lamb, & Flegal, 2010; Ogden et al., 2006). According to the most recent National Health and Nutrition Examination Survey (NHANES; Ogden et al., 2010), over a third of children (34.7%) ages 6–19 are obese (body mass index [BMI] for age ≥ 95th percentile) or overweight (BMI for age ≥ 85th percentile). Moreover, ethnic disparities in childhood overweight exist with African American and Latino/a children at greater risk than Whites (Ogden et al., 2010). Specifically, 43.0% of Mexican American children, and 38.7% of African American children (ages 6–19) have BMIs ≥ 85th percentile, compared with 32.5% of non-Hispanic White children. Across all racial and ethnic groups, the prevalence of overweight and obesity appears roughly equivalent in 6- to 19-year-old boys and girls (35.3% and 34.1%, respectively). However, when the total sample was divided into specific ethnic/racial groups, some gender disparities were evident. This gender difference was most pronounced within the African American subsample. Specifically, 43.3% of African American girls were overweight or obese, compared with 34.4% of African American boys. It is also important to note that socioeconomic status (SES) is negatively associated with pediatric obesity (Shrewsbury & Wardle, 2008). Thus, these disparities in the prevalence of obesity are likely attributable, at least in part, to the confounding of SES and ethnic and racial group membership.

PEDIATRIC OBESITY RISK FACTORS

Although genetic factors are known to influence BMI (e.g., Maes, Neale, & Eaves, 1997), the rapid increase in pediatric obesity rates is considered primarily attributable to environmental factors. Indeed, Kelly Brownell, a leader in this field, has argued that obesity in Western society is caused by a "toxic environment" (Brownell, 2002, p. 433). In particular, factors such as the overabundance of calorie-dense foods, increases in sedentary behavior and correspondent decreases in physical activity raise the obesity risk of children from all SES and ethnic/racial groups (Brownell, 2002). Early intervention for pediatric obesity is important to prevent the development of obesity-related health problems, which become more evident as children mature (Wang & Dietz, 2002). Further, risk of *adult obesity* increases as an overweight child ages (Serdula et al., 1993; Whitaker et al., 1997). However, longitudinal research indicates that obese children who do not become obese adults have a mortality risk equivalent to that of their thin peers (Guo & Chumlea, 1999).

PREVALENCE OF EATING DISORDERS

Eating disorders are also a significant health problem for many children and adolescents. The three eating disorders defined in the *Diagnostic and Statistical Manual for Mental Disorders* (DSM-IV), anorexia nervosa (AN), bulimia nervosa (BN), and binge eating disorder (BED, which is officially subsumed under eating disorder not otherwise specified; American Psychiatric Association, 1994), were traditionally thought to affect a much smaller proportion of the population than overweight and obesity. Epidemiological research indicates that the prevalence of cases of threshold AN and BN is relatively small (Hoek & van Hoeken, 2003; Hudson, Hiripi, Pope, & Kessler, 2007). Specifically, according to data from a nationally representative sample, AN affects approximately 1% of women and 0.3% of men in the United States and Western Europe, and BN affects approximately 1.5% of women and 0.5% of men (Hudson et al., 2007). However, the number of subthreshold cases of these disorders is much larger (Hudson et al., 2007), and research suggests that these subthreshold cases are associated with significant impairments in the quality of life of affected individuals (Spoor, Stice, Burton, & Bohon, 2007). Further, BED affects a much larger proportion of the population than AN or BN (3.5% of women and 2.0% of men), and is associated with significant impairments in quality of life, daily functioning, and health (Hudson et al., 2007, 2010).

Eating disorders were long considered a problem that nearly exclusively affected White women (Becker, Franko, Speck, & Herzog, 2003); however, recent research suggests that women of color are vulnerable to these conditions. In particular, African American women appear to have slightly lower rates of AN and BN than their White peers, but seem about equally vulnerable to binge eating (Taylor, Caldwell, Baser, Faison, & Jackson, 2007). Among Latinas, binge eating severity was greater than that reported by Whites and African Americans (Fitzgibbon et al., 1998). Additional research has reported that Latinas manifest more disturbed eating attitudes and behaviors than African American girls (Vander Wal & Thomas, 2004), and greater body dissatisfaction than White girls (Robinson et al., 1996). In sum, this body of research suggests that weight-related concerns and behaviors are prevalent among girls from diverse ethnic and racial groups (Neumark-Sztainer et al., 2002).

EATING DISORDER RISK FACTORS

The etiology of eating disorders is linked to a complex combination of biological, psychological, and sociocultural factors (Striegel-Moore & Bulik, 2007). Biological risk factors include female sex, genetics, and childhood eating and gastrointestinal problems (Jacobi, Hayward, de Zwaan, Kraemer, & Agras, 2004). As noted above, AN and BN disproportionately affect women; further, results of both twin and molecular genetic studies have indicated that eating disorder symptomatology is highly heritable (Striegel-Moore & Bulik, 2007). Psychological risks include perfectionism (Wade et al., 2008), while sociocultural risk factors include internalization of the thin ideal, and shape and weight concerns (Jacobi et al., 2004; Striegel-Moore & Bulik, 2007). These and other risk factors likely overlap and interact, leaving some individuals, such as those with genetic or psychological vulnerabilities, especially susceptible to eating disorders when faced with sociocultural pressures such as the thin ideal. This interactive risk factor perspective also explains why threshold eating disorders remain relatively rare, despite the omnipresence of unrealistic body ideals (Striegel-Moore & Bulik, 2007). It is also important to note that most research on eating disorder risk factors, particularly the more rigorous longitudinal studies, have primarily or exclusively included White women (Jacobi et al., 2004); thus future research should include more demographically representative samples.

Finally, in addition to the specific risk factors for obesity and eating disorders described above, researchers have highlighted several risks that appear to enhance children's and adolescents' vulnerabilities to both conditions including high childhood BMI, media use, and weight-related teasing (Fairburn et al., 1998; Haines & Neumark-Sztainer, 2006; Neumark-Sztainer et al. 2007). These risks are discussed in greater detail in the section describing the rationale for integrative prevention efforts.

A Call to Action

Despite the clinical significance and public health relevance of both eating disorders and obesity, many questions about their prevention remain. In particular, there is significant concern that eating disorder and obesity prevention can have iatrogenic effects, thereby unintentionally exacerbating rather than preventing eating disorders and weight-related problems. The following sections briefly review this controversy.

Are Eating Disorder Prevention Programs Potentially Harmful?

Perhaps the most fundamental principle of the ethical codes of all health care providers, including psychologists and others involved in eating disorders and obesity prevention, is nonmaleficence, or "first do no harm" (American Psychological Association, 2002; O'Dea, 2005a, 2005b). Thus, any possibility that prevention efforts could have iatrogenic effects is a significant cause for concern. This possibility was first raised in the area of eating disorders, as is reviewed in the following section. Further, although less data are available in the area of obesity prevention regarding this issue, we review available studies, as well as arguments some authors have made regarding the potential iatrogenic effects of these programs.

Do Eating Disorder Prevention Programs Cause Eating Disorders?

Traditionally, prevention programs, including those targeting eating disorders, include information about the problem that is the focus of the intervention. The intent of this information provision is to prevent the development of new cases (i.e., primary prevention), or facilitate the identification (and encourage treatment-seeking) of emerging or subthreshold cases (i.e., secondary prevention, Mann et al., 1997). However, there are some concerns regarding potential iatrogenic effects of information provision within eating disorder prevention programming. These concerns were raised in a study conducted by Mann and colleagues (Mann et al., 1997), who evaluated a university-based program aimed at the simultaneous primary and secondary prevention of eating disorders. Participants attended a discussion session led by students with histories of eating disorders (one with AN and one with BN). These student leaders provided information about eating disorders and shared personal stories about their experiences with these conditions.

Results indicated that eating disorder symptomatology was slightly elevated at 4-week follow-up in students who attended the discussion sections, compared with a control group. Of note, these apparent iatrogenic effects disappeared at 12-week follow-up (Mann et al., 1997). These results were based on analyses that included only people who provided data at 4-month follow-up. Thus, these findings might be biased if individuals who had greater eating disorder symptomatology, and were in the intervention group, completed the follow-up assessments (Stice & Hoffman, 2004; Stice & Shaw, 2004).

Nonetheless, Mann and colleagues (Mann et al., 1997) highlight these initial posttesting results as concerning. In particular, they emphasize that any increase in eating disorder symptomatology, even a temporary one, is undesirable. Moreover, as part of this same study, Mann and colleagues also investigated the representativeness of their eating disorder prevention program, compared with those of other universities, and found that most offered very similar programs, which combined elements of primary and secondary prevention, including provision of information and personal stories from recovered peers.

As Mann and colleagues (Mann et al., 1997) note, it is perhaps not surprising that information provision was ineffective in the primary prevention of eating disordered behaviors, and indeed, might have increased their frequency. They hypothesized that the recovered students' descriptions of their experiences with eating disorders might have gone too far in destigmatizing or normalizing these conditions, and inadvertently communicated the message that engaging in these behaviors is not especially problematic. This hypothesis is supported by data the authors collected within this study (after the delivery of the intervention). Specifically, the investigators asked participants in both the intervention and control groups to estimate the prevalence of eating disorder symptoms on their campus. Intervention participants' prevalence estimates were significantly higher than those of the control group. Mann et al. further note that their findings are consistent with research on the primary prevention of other problematic health behaviors, such as substance abuse, which has found that information provision is an ineffective primary prevention tool, and is often associated with increases in the targeted behaviors (e.g., Hanson, 1982; Moskowitz, 1989).

Nearly 15 years after the publication of Mann and colleagues' (1997) study, the roles of psychoeducation and personal testimonies in eating disorder prevention remain controversial. A meta-analysis of 15 studies (Stice, Shaw, & Marti, 2007) found that interactive, nondidactic approaches were most effective. In contrast, results of another meta-analysis (Fingeret, Warren, Cepeda-Benito, & Gleaves, 2006), did not find evidence suggesting that psychoeducational approaches were inferior to more interactive or enhanced intervention methods. Despite the lack of a clear conclusion regarding the role of psychoeducation in eating disorder prevention, there appears to be a general trend toward more interactive and less didactic approaches, such as the cognitive dissonance model of Stice and colleagues (Stice, Marti, Spoor, Presnell, & Shaw, 2008; Stice, Shaw, Burton, & Wade, 2006).

Mann and colleagues' (Mann et al., 1997) findings are also sometimes cited to support the argument that eating disorder prevention should be targeted to high-risk individuals, and that universal prevention is not recommended, given concerns regarding potential iatrogenic effects (O'Dea, 2005b). However, as discussed below, universal prevention is often more appealing, both because it can prevent a problem before it develops, and because it is difficult in many settings, such as schools, to target only a select group of individuals and exclude others. Thus, practical realities often require the use of a universal prevention approach. Stice and colleagues' (Stice et al., 2007) meta-analysis also addressed this concern, and suggested that both universal and targeted programs yielded positive effects for younger and older participants. Specifically, Stice and colleagues found that, at follow-up, targeted prevention programs were more effective than universal programs in reducing dieting. However, reductions in thin-ideal internalization and negative affect were similar for both universal and targeted approaches, indicating that prevention programs aimed at the general population of youth are beneficial, and should especially be considered when a targeted approach is not feasible. Similar results were obtained in Fingeret and colleagues' meta-analysis (2006). These meta-analytic findings have led many authors to conclude that carefully developed universal programs are a safe, viable approach to eating disorder prevention (e.g., Levine & Smolak, 2009).

Additional data regarding the effects of incorporating personal stories of eating disorders within prevention efforts were provided in a study by Schwartz and colleagues (Schwartz, Thomas, Bohan, & Vartanian, 2007). Specifically, high school girls in this study were randomly assigned to watch one of two videos: (1) one in which a woman described as a *clinical psychologist* discussed eating disorders, or (2) one in which a woman described as "*a recovered eating disorder patient*" (p. 189, emphasis added) discussed eating disorders. (The same woman appeared in both videos). At posttesting, there were no group differences regarding eating disorder knowledge. However, participants in the personal vignette condition differed from the clinician condition on several outcomes, and in particular, were more likely to report that the presenter they watched was "a good role model" and "nice to look like" (p. 191). The authors comment, "The fact that even these modest changes emerged after watching a single 12-minute video is remarkable" (p. 191). They conclude that their findings add some support to the hypothesis that media presentations of eating disorders could glamorize these conditions, and recommend that developers of prevention programs pay particular attention to implicit messages that might unintentionally bring positive attention to these symptoms.

Do Obesity Prevention Programs Cause Disordered Eating?

The Scope and Significance of Pediatric Overweight

Like eating disorders, childhood obesity is a health issue about which many researchers and clinicians are very concerned; yet many questions remain regarding optimal prevention approaches. Pediatric overweight is so concerning because it is associated with numerous health concerns, including hypertension, asthma, musculoskeletal problems, and Type II diabetes (Gennuso, Epstein, Paluch, & Cerny, 1998; Kiess et al., 2001; Sorof & Daniels, 2002; Williams et al., 1992). Further, quality of life among severely overweight children is significantly impaired, with some indication that it is worse than that of children with cancer (Schwimmer, Burwinkle, & Varni, 2003). Moreover, overweight children ages 10–17 are over 20 times more likely to be obese in adulthood compared to their non-overweight peers (Whitaker et al., 1997). Pediatric overweight is also a risk factor for chronic health problems, such as cardiovascular disease and diabetes, in adulthood (Li et al., 2003; Raitakari et al., 2003). Further, outcomes of adult obesity interventions are notoriously poor (Cooperberg & Faith, 2004; Whitaker et al., 1997), underscoring the importance of early intervention.

The Controversy Regarding Obesity Prevention and Related Policies

Although there is general agreement that something must be done to address the issue of pediatric obesity, what that "something" should be remains unclear. In short, the relatively slow pace of science has not kept up with the public's demands for immediate action (Schwartz, Novak & Fiore, 2009). As a result, there is controversy about some obesity prevention efforts particularly those legislated by school and/or governmental policy makers. Examples include sending parents body mass index (BMI) notification letters, and changing policies regarding the availability of highly palatable foods of low nutritional value within the school setting (Kubik, Lytle, & Story, 2005; Schwartz, Novak, & Fiore, 2009; Story, Nanney, & Schwartz, 2009).

Specifically, several authors have raised concerns that well-intentioned obesity prevention programs could have iatrogenic effects, most notably increases in restrictive parental feeding practices, and disordered eating symptomatology and weight-based stigmatization among children (Carter & Bulik, 2008; Morgan, 2008; O'Dea, 2005a, 2005b). These potential negative outcomes are concerning because a restrictive parental feeding style is associated with overeating and binge eating in children (Fisher & Birch, 1999, 2002). Further, weight stigmatization is also associated with severe psychosocial consequences in children (Eisenberg, Neumark-Sztainer, & Story, 2003; Young-Hyman, Schlundt, Herman-Wenderoth, & Bozylinski, 2003). Strong associations exist between weight-based teasing and depressive symptoms, suicidal ideation, and body dissatisfaction (Eisenberg et al., 2003; Lunner et al., 2000). However, it should be noted that these studies did not specifically examine *change* in either these parental behaviors (such as criticizing their children's weight) or children's symptomatology *following implementation* of an obesity prevention program. Additional research is needed to determine how obesity prevention and related policies explicitly affect these parental and peer attitudes and behaviors, and the implications of these changes for children's eating, weight, and other psychosocial outcomes.

What Do Extant Data Tell Us About the Effects of Obesity Prevention?

A few recent studies have begun to examine the effects of obesity prevention, although much more work is needed in this area (Carter & Bulik, 2008). The following sections review two policy-based approaches that have received research attention: school-based BMI screening, and changing school policy regarding food availability.

BMI SCREENING POLICIES

School-based BMI screening is recommended by expert committees such as the Institute of Medicine as one important approach to the primary and secondary prevention of pediatric obesity (Institute of Medicine, 2004). BMI screening occurs regularly in many schools in the United States and other Westernized countries (Nihiser et al., 2007) and, indeed, is mandated in several states within the United States. In 2003, Arkansas was the first state to implement a state-wide BMI notification program (Justus, Ryan, Rockenbach, Katterapalli, & Card-Higginson, 2007; Scheier, 2004b). Subsequently, increasing numbers of school districts and states have mandated such programs (including Illinois, Maine, New York, Pennsylvania, Tennessee, and West Virginia; Justus et al., 2007; Scheier, 2004b).

Proponents of school-based BMI screening note that it has several features that are appealing to public health advocates. It is a low-intensity and relatively low-cost approach, which can assess nearly all children and alert parents that their child might have a health concern. In this sense, as some have noted (Morgan, 2008), BMI screening is analogous to routine vision and hearing screenings conducted in school settings. Given the vast numbers of uninsured in the United States, many children might not have the opportunity for routine BMI assessment outside of the school setting (Nihiser et al., 2007; Presswood, 2005). This socioeconomic disparity in accessibility to regular BMI assessment is especially salient because children from lower SES groups are at greater risk of pediatric obesity (Shrewsbury & Wardle, 2008). Advocates of BMI screening have also argued that these notifications increase parents' knowledge of the problem of pediatric obesity. Parents of overweight children typically underestimate their offsprings' BMI status (Killion, Hughes, Wendt, Pease, & Nicklas, 2006; Parry, Netuveli, Parry, & Saxena, 2008). If parents are unaware that their child's weight is a problem, they are obviously unlikely to facilitate behavioral changes that would address this issue. However, opponents of BMI screening have expressed concern that this practice will lead to increases in restrictive parental feeding practices, and disordered eating symptomatology and weight-based stigmatization among children (Joiner, 2009; Scheier, 2004a).

Despite the heated controversy about BMI screening, limited research has assessed its outcomes. A few studies have assessed parents' satisfaction with the process, or asked parents how they would prefer screening be handled (Kubik, Fulkerson, Story, & Rieland, 2006; Kubik, Story, & Rieland, 2007). However, a much smaller number of studies have actually examined positive or negative health outcomes. The current review focuses on those studies that assessed outcomes with direct public health implications.

In Arkansas, the first state to mandate BMI screening in schools, rates of overweight and obesity declined very modestly, from 38.1% in the 1st year of data collection to 37.5% in the 3rd year of data collection (Justus et al., 2007). Surveys of Arkansas parents indicate that parents' awareness of their children's weight status significantly improved from baseline to the end of the 1st year of BMI screening; parents were not more likely to put their children on a diet following initiation of the program. Similarly, students did not report increased dieting behaviors or experiences of teasing following initiation of BMI screening (Nihiser et al., 2007).

Chomitz and colleagues (Chomitz, Collings, Kim, Kramer, & McGowan, 2003) used a quasi-experimental approach to examine the effects of BMI screenings in Boston-area public schools. Participants included families from four elementary schools who were assigned to one of three conditions: (1) a personal information (PI) intervention in which parents received a report of their child's BMI status, personalized fitness results, and general physical activity and nutrition information; (2) a general information (GI) intervention in which parents received only the general nutrition and activity information, and (3) a control group, which did not receive any information. Results indicated that parents in the PI group whose children were overweight were more likely to seek medical treatment for their child compared to parents in the GI group (25% vs. 7%); PI parents were also more likely to make changes in their children's diet and physical activity compared to parents in the GI group. The authors expressed concern about the reported initiation of dieting activities, as the materials they sent reflected an "antidieting" approach, and many parents indicated they were implementing these changes without seeking medical attention. Given the risks associated with restrictive dieting among young children, it is important that future studies more thoroughly assess what parents mean when they report the initiation of dieting behaviors. Further, perhaps a brief additional intervention accompanying BMI notification which emphasizes the rationale behind a nondieting approach, could address this potential problem more directly and in greater detail.

Similar concerns about the association between BMI notification and parental restriction were raised by a study conducted in the United Kingdom. Grimmett and colleagues (Grimmett, Croker, Carnell, & Wardle, 2008) assessed the outcomes of an "opt-in" BMI notification program targeting children between the ages of 6–7 and 10–11 years old in London. A limitation of this study was that only 51% of eligible parents actually elected to participate in the program. Nonetheless, this investigation provides some interesting data regarding outcomes of BMI screening. Specifically, parents of overweight girls were more likely to restrict their daughters' intake following BMI notification. Similar changes were not observed among parents of normal-weight girls or of boys of any BMI status. Parents' perceptions of their children's weight did not change significantly following notification, even within the overweight group. Parents of overweight children did report making more positive dietary and physical activity changes in their families at follow-up compared to parents of normal-weight children. No dietary or activity changes were noted in the normal-weight group. Interestingly, within the sample of normal-weight boys and girls, restrained eating decreased and body esteem increased following BMI notification. The authors note that these outcomes might indicate that normal-weight children felt reassured upon learning that their weight was in a healthy range. However, additional research is needed to investigate this hypothesis. No changes in body esteem or restriction were identified among overweight children. Further, no differences were found from pre- to postnotification in reported experiences of teasing among children of all weight statuses.

In sum, Grimmett and colleagues (2008) referred to these results as "broadly reassuring" (p. e686), and noted that overall, they indicated that the screening intervention did not have iatrogenic effects. However, given previous research (Fisher & Birch, 1999, 2002) highlighting links between parental restriction and eating dysregulation in children, the increase in restriction observed among parents of overweight girls in Grimmett and colleagues' study is a concern. Further, previous studies have indicated that the relation between parental restriction and dysregulated eating is particularly strong among overweight children (Faith et al., 2004). Yet, others have argued that some restriction can actually be beneficial to children, and represents a healthy degree of parental control (Robinson, Kiernan, Matheson, & Haydel, 2001; Wardle, Sanderson, Guthrie, Rapoport, & Plomin, 2002). Clearly, further study, with longer follow-up could help clarify the outcomes of any restriction imposed by parents subsequent to BMI notification.

Finally, Kubik and colleagues (Kubik et al., 2006) evaluated outcomes of BMI notification in four elementary schools in Minneapolis. Two schools were assigned to a notification condition, and two received no notification, although students were assessed as usual. Parents with a concern about their child's weight following BMI notification were more likely to make changes in their children's physical activity (24%–27% of parents) than to seek medical attention or make dietary changes (approximately 8%). Further, over half (55%) of parents reported that they did not discuss the results of the notification with their children. This could suggest that parents were unsure about how to have such a discussion, and might have concerns that the topic would make their children feel uncomfortable. Future studies should further investigate this hypothesis. However, our own work with parents of overweight children (Mazzeo, Gow, Stern, & Gerke, 2008) suggests that they are uncomfortable discussing this topic, and fear that they will shame their sons and daughters or cause them to become overly focused on weight to the detriment of overall physical and mental health. Thus, in sum, these data suggest that prevention efforts should include parents and incorporate information and skills training regarding communicating with one's child about weight, appearance, and health.

CHANGING SCHOOL POLICIES REGARDING FOOD AVAILABILITY

Although data remain relatively sparse, a few studies have examined the impact of school food policies on children's health. For example, in an innovative study involving middle school students, Schwartz and colleagues (Schwartz et al., 2009) investigated outcomes of an intervention targeting the removal of snacks of low nutritional value from schools. Six schools were involved (three intervention, three control), and outcomes assessed included changes in food consumption (both at school and at home), body dissatisfaction, and dieting behavior. Results indicated that students in intervention schools decreased their consumption of sugar-sweetened beverages and salty snacks (of low nutritional values, e.g., chips) over the 1-year study period, while students in the control group increased their consumption of these foods and beverages. Students in intervention schools increased their intake of water, 100% juice, less calorically/fat-dense salty snacks (e.g., pretzels), and healthy sweet snacks (e.g., fruit) but control students' consumption of these foods and beverages was unchanged. However, there were no differences between groups in consumption of sweet snacks, such as ice cream. Further, treatment condition was generally unrelated to dietary intake in the home environment. Finally, there were no differences between groups in dieting behavior.

However, body dissatisfaction and dieting increased over time in both groups. Because there were no differences between groups regarding the degree of these increases over the study period, the intervention is unlikely to have played a causal role in this change. Nonetheless, as these authors note, this finding is somewhat disturbing, as it suggests that body dissatisfaction and dieting are ongoing concerns that appear to increase as students age.

Based on this overall pattern of results, Schwartz and colleagues (2009) concluded that changes in school food options can positively influence students' dietary behavior during the school day. However, some behaviors, particularly intake of sweet snacks of low nutritional value, appear less amenable to change. Further, changes made during the school day, which seem to be a response to alterations in food availability at school, did not carry over to eating behaviors outside of school. This is likely attributable to the broader range of foods (especially less healthy foods) available in the home and other out-of-school environments. Further, these findings indicate that school policies regarding food availability did not have adverse consequences, such as increasing body dissatisfaction and dieting. Thus, targeting school policies appears to be one component of a multilevel approach to obesity prevention. Nonetheless, additional work is needed to determine the optimal way to implement similar interventions in the home and other environments in which children spend significant time.

A related investigation of the effects of school policy on students' weight-related outcomes was conducted by Foster and colleagues (Foster et al., 2008). Specifically, these authors investigated the effects of a multicomponent school nutrition policy intervention (School Nutrition Policy Initiative, SNPI) on 4th- to 6th-grade children from 10 schools with a high proportion of low-income students. As part of the SNPI, intervention schools removed all sodas, sugar-sweetened beverages, and snacks of low nutritional value from vending machines and cafeteria service. Water, low-fat milk, and 100% juice were the only beverage choices available in intervention schools during the course of the project. In addition, school staff (in intervention schools) participated in nutrition education, and students were provided 50 hours of nutrition education annually. Students in intervention schools were also offered incentives (e.g., raffle tickets for larger prizes) for the purchase of healthy foods.

Two years after the initiation of the SNPI, significantly fewer children in the intervention group had become overweight or obese (i.e., had a BMI% ≥ 85th for their age and sex), compared with the control group (Foster et al., 2008). Specifically, 15% of children in control schools became overweight during the study period (i.e., their BMI percentile moved from below the 85th to between the 85th and 95th percentiles), compared with 7.5% of children in the intervention schools. Moreover, the intervention was particularly effective for African American children, who were 41% less likely to be overweight at 2-year follow-up than their African American peers in control schools. Further, sedentary behavior increased in the overall control sample, but decreased among students (of all races) in the intervention. In addition, there was no evidence of iatrogenic effects, such as differential increases in body dissatisfaction, or excessive weight loss. These outcomes, especially those regarding the reduction in the incidence of new cases of overweight in the intervention schools, are impressive. However, the authors note that, despite the relative intensity of the SNPI, perhaps an even more intensive program is needed, as 7.5% of children nonetheless became overweight while enrolled in the intervention. Their recommendations include adding policies that directly affect children outside of the school setting (e.g., food available at after school programs or at retail outlets in close proximity to schools). Further, the SNPI did not have significant positive effects on children who were already obese at the time of the program's initiation, suggesting these children likely require more intensive clinical interventions.

Overall, results of Schwartz et al.'s (2009) and Foster et al.'s (2008) interventions are consistent with prior survey findings regarding the association between food availability in schools and students' dietary behaviors. For example, Kubik and colleagues (Kubik et al., 2005) surveyed eighth-grade students and school administrators regarding school food-related policies, dietary behavior, and students' BMIs. Seven food policies hypothesized to be associated with poorer dietary quality were assessed (e.g., using food as a reward in school, allowing food in the classroom). The more of these practices a school allowed, the higher their students' BMIs. Thus, relatively unrestricted food policies are linked to increased obesity rates; however, the optimal amount of restriction that school policies should implement (to promote healthy eating while also not exacerbating/initiating excessive weight concern) remains unknown.

NEED FOR BETTER ASSESSMENT OF EATING DISORDER OUTCOMES IN OBESITY PREVENTION

A review by Carter and Bulik (2008) highlighted several limitations in research assessing potential iatrogenic effects of obesity prevention programs (especially those related to eating disorders). These authors reviewed 22 randomized control trials (RCTs) or controlled clinical trials identified in a Cochrane Collaboration review of childhood obesity programs (Summerbell et al., 2005). Carter and Bulik's review indicated that none of the studies comprehensively assessed eating disorders as an outcome (nor did they assess for the presence of any other psychiatric disorder, such as major depression). Further, no studies reported whether any children in intervention programs lost excessive amounts of weight or developed extreme exercise behaviors. A small number of studies assessed the presence or absence of specific eating disorder symptoms, such as skipping meals or starving for a day or more (two studies), overconcern with weight and shape (one study), and negative body image (five studies). Only one study assessed binge eating as an outcome. However, this symptom was evaluated via a single item, and did not include any data regarding perceived loss of control over eating, a characteristic essential to the definition of this term, nor was the duration of binge eating assessed.

Carter and Bulik (2008) note that, of those studies that did evaluate eating disorder related outcomes, only one (Story et al., 2003) found that the intervention was associated with eating pathology. Specifically, these authors found that unhealthy weight control practices were more common among individuals in the intervention arm of an obesity prevention trial at posttesting. Further, several studies found that obesity prevention efforts appeared to have positive effects on eating pathology, including reduced concern with weight and shape (two studies), and reduced body dissatisfaction (two studies). In addition, parents of children in one obesity intervention reported reductions in restrictive feeding practices over the study period (Harvey-Berino & Rourke, 2003).

Although these initial results are promising regarding the relative absence of iatrogenic effects of pediatric obesity prevention efforts (and the potential benefits of these interventions for reducing eating pathology), they also highlight some significant limitations of research in this area. Specifically, as noted, no studies comprehensively assessed eating disorders, and very few included any measure of eating pathology. Thus, future research should more rigorously evaluate the presence of the full range of eating disorder symptoms among intervention and control group participants. Further, efforts should be made to identify individuals who might be particularly vulnerable to developing eating disorder symptoms following participation in obesity prevention programming. These data could inform future clinical and research endeavors regarding the appropriateness of various prevention approaches for specific individuals.

Is an Integrative Approach to the Prevention of Eating Disorders and Obesity Feasible?

Rationale for Integrating Prevention Efforts

Both eating disorders and obesity are significant public health concerns, and there is increasing recognition that both issues need to be addressed. Moreover, a recent Australian population-based study of adults (Darby et al., 2009) found that rates of comorbid obesity and eating disorder behaviors increased from 1% to 3.5% between 1995 and 2005. This increase was higher than that reported for either condition alone. Further, 20% of individuals who were obese in 2005 also reported comorbid eating behaviors. In contrast, this comorbidity was reported by only 8.5% of obese participants in 1995.

Increasing awareness of the scope and impact of these conditions has led to calls for prevention efforts that target eating disorders and obesity simultaneously. Such integrative approaches are appealing for many reasons, including increased recognition of the shared risk factors for obesity and eating disorders, including high childhood BMI, media use, and weight-related teasing. These overlapping risk factors are briefly reviewed in the following paragraphs.

HIGH CHILDHOOD BMI

High BMI in childhood is a risk factor for both BN (Fairburn, Welch, Doll, Davies, & O'Connor, 1997) and BED (Fairburn et al., 1998) in adulthood. Further, the prevalence of binge eating is higher among overweight boys and girls (Neumark-Sztainer Story, Hannan, Perry, & Irving, 2002). Thus, some have argued that preventing overweight might simultaneously prevent eating disorders (Brownell et al., 2009; Neumark-Sztainer, 2005). Additional support for this hypothesis is provided in the work of Stice and colleagues (Stice, Trost, & Chase, 2003), who (somewhat unexpectedly) found that a weight loss intervention was effective in reducing bulimic behaviors. These findings were especially surprising because several studies have identified a link between dieting and subsequent weight gain (Field et al., 2003; Neumark-Sztainer et al., 2006; Stice, Cameron, Killen, Hayward, & Taylor, 1999), and dieting and binge eating (Field et al., 2003). However, it is likely that the supervised weight loss promoted in Stice and colleagues' trial was a much less extreme and thus, a healthier, more realistic approach to weight loss than the behaviors reported on the survey measures used in the prospective studies of dieting. Further, analogous results were reported in an obesity prevention program targeting African American girls between the ages of 8 and 10 (Robinson et al., 2003). Specifically, girls in the intervention group manifested not only positive outcomes relevant to weight status (e.g., reduced body mass and waist circumference), but also reduced weight concerns. Taken together, these findings suggest that interventions focused on healthy weight control and health promotion can reduce both obesity and eating disorder risks among individuals of diverse ages and racial backgrounds, although more research is needed to assess the generalizability of specific programs.

MEDIA USE

Another risk factor that appears to increase the likelihood of both disordered eating and obesity is *media use* (Haines & Neumark-Sztainer, 2006). Children ages 11–14 spend approximately 6.5 hours daily using media (Roberts, Foehr, & Rideout, 2005), and this time is likely to increase given the relatively recent ubiquity of texting and Internet use via mobile devices. Media use (particularly television viewing) is implicated in the etiology of obesity (Robinson, Borzekowski, Matheson, & Kraemer, 2007). Specifically, it is hypothesized that television viewing might be causally linked to obesity by both displacing physical activity and promoting intake of unhealthy foods (Haines & Neumark-Sztainer, 2006). The vast majority of advertisements shown during children's programming promote the intake of foods of poor nutritional quality (e.g., candy, fast food; Powell, Szczpka, & Chaloupka, 2007; Story & French, 2004). Data also support an association between television viewing and consumption of foods high in fat and calories (French, Story, Neumark-Sztainer, Fulkerson, & Hannan, 2001). Notably, interventions aimed at reducing television viewing have yielded reductions in BMI and obesity in both middle and elementary school students (Gortmaker, et al., 1999; Robinson, 1999; Robinson et al., 2003).

Media images are also thought to promote weight stigmatization in youth. For example, despite the increasing prevalence of overweight and obesity in Western society, only a small minority (~3%) of the women portrayed on television are obese (Greenberg, Eastin, Hofschire, Lachlan, & Brownell, 2003). Moreover, the few overweight characters presented on television are less likely to engage in romantic relationships, have fewer positive social interactions, and are more likely to be unemployed. More recent research has indicated that obese characters on children's sitcoms are given equitable on-screen time and manifest positive characteristics, such as being smart and outspoken. However, obese characters in children's sitcoms were also more likely to be depicted as socially isolated than average weight characters (Robinson, Callister & Jankoski, 2008). Thus, there remains a pernicious link between overweight and negative characteristics in media, including that aimed specifically at children.

Similarly, sociocultural theories of eating disorders have long emphasized the etiological role of media in promoting the thin-ideal (Levine & Harrison, 2004; Stice & Shaw, 1994). Several experimental studies have indicated that exposure to images of fashion models was associated with adverse consequences in women, including lower self-esteem and greater weight and body dissatisfaction, depression, anxiety, and body self-consciousness (Groesz, Levine, & Murnen, 2002; Heinberg & Thompson, 1995; Irving, 1990; Kalodner, 1997; Stice & Shaw, 1994; Tiggemann & Pickering, 1996). Further, a longitudinal study of adolescent girls found that increases in fashion magazine consumption were associated with increases in disordered eating symptomatology (Vaughn & Fouts, 2003).

However, it is important to note that the overall size of the effects of this media exposure on outcomes relevant to disordered eating was generally moderate. This likely explains why clinical eating disorders remain relatively rare, despite the ubiquity of media images promoting the thin-ideal. Nonetheless, it is important not to minimize the potential impact of thin-ideal media. Research has examined potential moderators of the association between media exposure and disordered eating, and found that the effects of such exposure are significantly greater among individuals with preexisting body dissatisfaction and thin-ideal internalization (Mazzeo, Trace, Mitchell, & Gow, 2007; Stice, Spangler, &

Agras, 2001). From the perspective of eating disorder prevention, such findings suggest that it is especially important to target risk factors for disordered eating, such as thin-ideal internalization and body dissatisfaction. Interventions targeting thin-ideal internalization have yielded promising results. The cognitive dissonance approach developed and evaluated by Stice and colleagues (Stice et al., 2006, 2008) is the most well known and rigorously evaluated intervention in this area.

WEIGHT-RELATED TEASING

Teasing about weight and shape is also linked to both eating disorders and obesity in children (Haines & Neumark-Sztainer, 2006). Weight-related teasing is commonly experienced by overweight children and adolescents of both sexes and all racial and ethnic groups (Neumark-Sztainer, Falkner, et al., 2002; Pearce et al., 2002), and weight-related biases have been documented in children as young as 3 (Cramer & Steinwert, 1998). Teasing not only is associated with numerous negative effects on the well-being of overweight youth (Fulkerson, Strauss, Neumark-Sztainer, Story, & Boutelle, 2007) but also appears to be specifically linked with eating pathology within this group (Libbey, Story, Neumark-Sztainer, & Boutelle, 2008). For example, Fulkerson and colleagues (Fulkerson et al., 2007) found that parental weight-based teasing and encouragement to diet were associated with problematic weight-control behaviors in overweight male and female adolescents.

Several studies have also suggested that weight-related teasing and critical comments about weight are related to higher rates of eating pathology, including binge eating, purging, and restriction (e.g., Fairburn et al., 1998; Haines, Neumark-Sztainer, Eisenberg et al., 2006; Neumark-Sztainer et al. 2007; Pike et al., 2006; Stormer & Thompson, 1996; Wade, Gillespie, & Martin, 2007), although not all studies have identified this association (e.g., Stice & Whitenton, 2002). Reliance on participants' retrospective recall of teasing is a limitation of some of these studies. Nonetheless, this relatively consistent pattern of results suggests that reducing weight stigmatization and related teasing, and teaching youth skills that facilitate effective coping with these experiences should be incorporated into prevention efforts.

Finally, integrating obesity and eating disorder prevention under the umbrella of health promotion might remove some of the stigma associated with participating in these types of programs. Prevention programs labeled as "health promotion" efforts appear to be more successful in reducing eating disorder symptomatology than programs that explicitly emphasized eating disorder prevention, according to a review by Stice and Hoffman (2004).

Potential Controversies Regarding Integration of Prevention Efforts

Despite a strong rationale for integrating eating disorder and obesity prevention, there are some notable areas of disagreement between professionals from each of these fields. For example, one tenet of many eating disorders professionals is the notion that "all foods can fit" or that no particular foods should be completely off-limits. The rationale for this approach has been traced to cognitive-behavioral theory (CBT; Schwartz et al., 2009), which proposes that labeling foods as all good (e.g., fruit) or all bad (e.g., "junk foods"), is a form of dichotomous thinking, or a cognitive distortion hypothesized to lead to an increased occurrence of the undesired behavior (in this case, more bingeing on foods designated as "off-limits"; Fairburn, Marcus, & Wilson, 1993). Research supports the efficacy of CBT for binge eating (Brownley, Berkman, Sedway, Lohr, & Bulik, 2007). Further, anecdotal reports suggest that individuals who alter their beliefs about foods and render previously "forbidden" items acceptable, report far less desire to consume them.

Additional support for the argument that no specific foods should be rendered "off-limits" comes from research addressing parental feeding styles—particularly restriction of children's eating. A significant body of research, primarily conducted by Birch and colleagues (Birch, Fisher & Davison, 2003; Fisher & Birch, 1999, 2002), indicates that parental restriction of highly palatable foods (of low nutritional value), is (paradoxically) associated with increased consumption of these foods, especially in parents' absence, and higher BMIs in children (primarily girls) over time.

However, others have argued that this line of reasoning effectively stonewalls policy interventions that could yield positive changes in children's dietary behaviors without causing harm (Brownell, Schwartz, Puhl, Henderson, & Harris, 2009; Schwartz et al., 2009), such as restrictions on marketing to children or food availability in schools. For example, Schwartz and colleagues, as described above, found that changes in school policy (in which some highly palatable, low-nutrition foods were made unavailable during school), had a positive impact on children's dietary behavior, and were unassociated with iatrogenic effects. These authors argue, "we believe it is reasonable to call a food 'bad' if it predominantly consists of ingredients associated with disease (such as sugar, trans fats, or saturated fats) and contributes nothing of value to the diet. A more acceptable way to categorize foods semantically may be as foods to 'promote' versus foods to 'limit'" (p. 785). Further, Schwartz and colleagues suggest that the term "discretionary calories," which is used by dieticians (and on the USDA's mypyramid.gov website) could facilitate individuals' personal awareness of how much and what types of food are needed to optimize health and how much food of low nutritional value is reasonable from a health promotion perspective.

Further, as was discussed above in the review of research on obesity policies such as BMI notifications, some eating disorder specialists have expressed significant concern that obesity prevention programs and policies will lead to extreme dieting among children (Cogan, Smith, & Maine, 2008). This is especially alarming as research has also indicated that dieting is associated with the onset of eating disorder symptoms (Neumark-Sztainer et al., 2006; Patton et al., 1999). However, to date, research does not generally suggest that existing obesity interventions are associated with the onset of dieting in children or adolescents, at least at the aggregate level (Carter & Bulik, 2008). Nonetheless, some individuals, especially those with other underlying predispositions to develop an eating disorder (e.g., genetics), might be especially vulnerable to potential iatrogenic effects of obesity prevention. Thus, it is important that researchers evaluate the effects of their interventions not only at the aggregate level, but also track individual adverse events, including identifying individuals who develop eating pathology following exposure to obesity-related interventions (Carter & Bulik, 2008). Although current data suggest such adverse outcomes will be relatively rare, rapid identification of such individuals, along with tracking of characteristics that might have made them especially vulnerable to negative effects, will be important to consider as interventions and policies evolve and are more broadly disseminated. Such research could also further bridge the gap between the eating disorders and obesity fields.

Further, Schwartz and colleagues (2009) also suggest that semantic issues are of particular importance when considering the issue of restraining or restricting portions. They recommend that terms such as "diet" be avoided, and replaced with concepts such as "limit[ing] portion size" (p. 785). This advice to attend to portion size will likely feel less restrictive if participants in these interventions are also armed with information regarding hunger and satiety awareness, such as that discussed in the following paragraph.

Areas of Consensus

Despite the controversies that exist between the obesity and eating disorders fields, there are several issues of consensus between the two groups regarding best practices for health promotion. These include emphasizing regular structured meals, especially family meals and breakfast eating, promoting hunger and satiety awareness, providing media literacy education (and pressuring marketers to change the manner in which they promote both food and fashion), and supporting the development of a healthy body image and positive dietary and physical activity behaviors (Brownell et al., 2009; Haines & Neumark-Sztainer, 2006; Irving & Neumark-Sztainer, 2002; Neumark-Sztainer, 2005; O'Dea, 2005b; Schwartz et al., 2009). Further, several researchers suggest that many of the concerns about the potential iatrogenic effects of obesity interventions, such as weight stigmatization or body dissatisfaction, could be mitigated if such interventions were reframed as "health promotion" efforts, and thus, targeted all children, regardless of their weight status (O'Dea, 2005a; Schwartz et al., 2009). As Schwartz and colleagues (2009) note, childhood obesity is merely the symptom of the larger societal problems of poor diet and limited physical activity. Similarly, in the area of eating disorders, Rosenvinge and Børresen (1999) note that prevention programs are more likely to succeed if they focus on increasing health promoting or protective behaviors, rather than on decreasing disordered eating symptomatology.

Practical Realities

Although many questions remain regarding the optimal approach to eating disorder and obesity prevention, there is a strong demand to address both conditions. Schools are an ideal setting in which to implement prevention efforts, as it is where the vast majority of children spend much of their waking hours, and eat at least one meal per day (Foster et al., 2008; Rosenvinge & Børresen, 1999). In addition, within the school setting, multisystem interventions can be implemented. An example of such a multisystem approach could include changes in school policies regarding food availability, intervention efforts targeting teachers (e.g., as role models of healthy eating and activity behaviors), parents, and children. In contrast, within the clinical setting the focus is typically primarily on the individual child and his or her family. Thus, many authors have argued that schools are an important starting point for the promotion of healthy weight regulation (Brownell, 2009; Foster et al., 2008).

However, schools face increasing restrictions regarding the use of the instructional time and financial resources (Irving & Neumark-Sztainer, 2002; Luce et al., 2005). Consequently, they are unlikely to have the ability to implement two distinct programs, especially those addressing themes as strongly related as obesity and eating disorders. Prevention efforts addressing the spectrum of eating and weight issues will ultimately be more efficient, cost-effective, and appealing to school administration and staff (Irving & Neumark-Sztainer, 2002; Neumark-Sztainer, 2005). Further, qualitative reports from overweight youth indicate that they prefer interventions occur within the school day, as transportation and time barriers would interfere with their ability to participate otherwise (Neumark-Sztainer & Story, 1997). Thus, prevention program developers should work carefully with school administrators to determine if program content can effectively be incorporated into the school day, as was done in Planet Health, one of the integrative prevention strategies discussed in the next section (Gortmaker et al., 1999).

Exemplars of Integrated Prevention Programs

This section reviews two noteworthy prevention efforts that focused on the broad spectrum of unhealthy weight management behaviors: Planet Health (Austin, Field, Wiecha, Peterson, & Gortmaker, 2005; Austin et al., 2007; Gortmaker et al. 1999), and New Moves (Neumark-Sztainer et al., 2010; Neumark-Sztainer, Story, Hannan, & Rex, 2003).

Planet Health

Planet Health (Austin et al., 2005, 2007; Gortmaker et al., 1999) was designed as a universal, school-based obesity prevention program targeting middle school students. The intervention was incorporated into existing academic and physical education curricula and focused on improving healthy behaviors, such as fruit and vegetable intake and increasing physical activity.

Planet Health was initially evaluated in a sample of 1,295 6th- and 7th-grade students (69% White, 11% African American, 11% Latino/a, 9% Asian/Pacific Islander, and 7% other). Results indicated that Planet Health was effective in reducing obesity among girls. The intervention was also successful in changing many obesity-related behaviors in both genders, including reducing television use, and increasing fruit and vegetable consumption (Gortmaker et al., 1999). Subsequent analyses of outcome data indicated that girls in the Planet Health intervention who reported disordered eating behaviors (purging or diet pill use) at baseline were much less likely to report these behaviors at posttesting, compared to girls in the control group (Austin et al., 2005). However, the effect of the intervention was modified by girls' baseline dieting status. Specifically, Planet Health did not reduce eating disorder behaviors among girls who reported dieting at baseline. However, the intervention did have a significant effect on girls who did not report dieting at baseline. Based on these data, the authors concluded that 59% of new cases of disordered eating behaviors among girls in the control group could have been prevented had they received the Planet Health intervention. Further, they suggest that girls who have already begun to diet by the sixth or seventh grade might need a different intervention than that offered by Planet Health, which is focused on health promotion, not disordered eating.

Although it was not possible for the authors to determine exactly which specific aspects of the Planet Health curriculum might have been most strongly linked to reductions in disordered eating, they suggested that the program's length (occurring over 2 academic years and involving 32 classroom lessons and 30 physical education lessons) provided an appropriate level of intensity (Austin et al., 2005). Further, they noted that delivering the intervention to both sexes, and incorporating lessons into existing curricula (four major courses and physical education), might have led to systematic changes in the school environment. Such changes, in turn, could have reduced the pressure girls felt to achieve societal body shape ideals. Finally, the authors note that Planet Health was presented as a health promotion intervention, and thus did not explicitly mention eating disorders or obesity. Thus, participation in the intervention was possibly less stigmatizing to anyone affected by these conditions than an explicitly targeted prevention program.

Planet Health was further evaluated in a subsequent randomized effectiveness trial that involved a larger sample (Austin et al., 2007). The intervention was conducted by the Massachusetts Department of

Public Health and combined the Planet Health curriculum with material on physical activity and healthy eating published by the Centers for Disease Control and Prevention. Results were similar to those found in the earlier study (Austin et al., 2005); girls in the intervention were two-thirds less likely to develop disordered eating behaviors over the 2-year course of the study if they were in the intervention arm. However, there were no effects on disordered eating behaviors for boys. Nonetheless, results of this effectiveness trial suggest that this program is feasible in diverse school settings, and yields promising outcomes, especially for girls, regarding both eating disorder and obesity risk reduction. As noted above, it is hypothesized that the inclusion of boys in the program might have influenced changes in the school environment (Austin et al., 2005). Thus, although the program did not directly affect boys' obesity or disordered eating outcomes, it is not clear that they should be excluded from future iterations. However, additional research is needed to identify specific aspects of the program that lead to behavioral changes, and to enhance its effectiveness for boys.

New Moves

New Moves (Bauer et al., 2009; Neumark-Sztainer et al., 2010; Neumark-Sztainer, Story, et al., 2003) was intentionally designed to integrate obesity and eating disorder prevention within the school setting. This program targets adolescent girls exclusively, and is primarily implemented during a girls-only physical education class (which was offered as an alternative to the standard coeducation physical education class). New Moves does not explicitly address weight loss or eating disorders, but rather focuses on behavioral changes, such as increasing physical activity and fruit and vegetable intake and decreasing sedentary time (Bauer et al., 2009; Neumark-Sztainer et al., 2010). Of note, more than three quarters of participants in the randomized control trial of New Moves (Neumark-Sztainer et al., 2010) were members of ethnic or racial minority groups.

The alternative physical education class was about 16 weeks in duration and occurred daily (five times/week) during the first semester of the intervention. This class emphasized being "fit" (i.e., active), being "fueled" (i.e., making good nutritional choices), and being "fab" (i.e., self-empowerment, social support for behavioral change). In addition to this class, girls in New Moves also participated in: (1) between five and seven individual sessions that used a motivational interviewing approach to facilitate behavioral change; (2) "lunch bunches" or get-togethers that occurred weekly during the maintenance period (2nd semester); and (3) parent outreach activities, including postcards reinforcing program lessons and a one-time, informal parent event emphasizing New Moves' content (Neumark-Sztainer et al., 2010).

At follow-up, sedentary activity decreased and portion control behaviors increased among girls in the intervention. Further, girls in New Moves reported decreases in unhealthy weight behaviors, and increases in body satisfaction and perceived athletic competence, and self-worth. However, there were no significant changes in BMI or percent body fat (Neumark-Sztainer et al., 2010). The authors suggest that, while these initial results are promising, more comprehensive school-based approaches (including changes in school food and physical activity policies), and more multisystemic interventions (e.g., targeting parents and community members more intensively) are needed to optimize health promotion and effectively reduce obesity risk. Examples of prevention programs that begin to address some of these more systemic issues are reviewed in the following section.

Expanding the Focus of Prevention: Including Parents and Teachers

Parents

There are many reasons to include parents in prevention efforts aimed at enhancing children's eating and weight-related attitudes and behaviors. In particular, parents serve as powerful models of eating and exercise behaviors for their children (Fisher, Mitchell, Smiciklas-Wright, & Birch, 2002; Kohl & Hobbs, 1998). Further, parental feeding behaviors (e.g., restriction of highly palatable foods, monitoring of children's intake, family mealtime rituals) influence children's eating habits and weight (Fisher & Birch, 1999, 2002; Neumark-Sztainer, Hannan, Story, Croll, & Perry, 2003). Parents also model eating and appearance attitudes (Smolak, Levine, & Schermer, 1999; Striegel-Moore & Kearney-Cooke, 1994). Both obesity and eating disorders appear to run in families, which appears to be related to both genetic and environmental factors (Bulik, 2004; Whitaker et al., 1997). Thus, parents can often benefit directly from interventions. Given all of these factors, it is vital to include parents in interventions aimed at improving children's eating and weight behaviors. The following sections review two eating disorder prevention programs that included parent components.

STUDENT BODIES

Bruning Brown and colleagues (Bruning Brown, Winzelberg, Abascal, & Taylor, 2004) involved parents of high school girls in their evaluation of the online prevention program Student Bodies. This program was unstructured, and parents were able to log onto the website during a specific 4-week period. They also had access to a discussion forum, where they could interact with other parents. The parent component of Student Bodies included material encouraging promotion of body size diversity, recognizing and correcting miscommunication, and recognizing unhealthy eating patterns in their children. Parents in this intervention reported decreases in their critical attitudes about weight and shape at posttesting, compared with a control group. Unfortunately, these positive changes in the parents were not associated with comparable positive outcomes in their daughters. These findings should be considered preliminary, however, only a relatively small number of parents were enrolled in this arm of the study (n = 22 intervention and n = 22 control).

NURTURE

Due to both genetic and environmental risk factors, children of women with eating disorders are at greater risk for developing these conditions themselves (Mazzeo et al., 2005). Yet, few interventions target this high risk group. NURTURE (*N*etworking, *U*niting, and *R*eaching out *T*o *U*pgrade *R*elationships and *E*ating), is one novel prevention approach designed to address this gap in the literature (Mazzeo, Zucker, Pisetsky, Swann, & Bulik, 2008). NURTURE targets mothers with current and past threshold and subthreshold AN, or BN who have children between the ages of 0 and 2. This intervention is currently in progress, and here we briefly review the rationale for this program, as well as its content.

NURTURE session content is based on data from focus groups with mothers with eating disorders and extant research (Mazzeo, Zucker, Gerke, Mitchell, & Bulik, 2005). Specifically, in these focus groups, participants' comments supported the belief that even for women who have recovered from an eating disorder, many concerns remain about how to feed their children and provide positive role models around body image and eating issues. Nearly half of mothers reported viewing mealtimes with children as difficult because of expectations of eating together, fighting, the mother's desire to skip the meal, and stress over meal preparation. The majority of mothers expressed fears that their children were overweight or might become overweight. Most also acknowledged concerns about their children's eating behaviors, and desires to restrict their children's intake. Many participants reported that their children made comments about their own (i.e. the mother's) eating, including observing restriction of foods eaten, eating too much, or eating too little. Other concerns raised included worries about using food as a reward, and confusion about appropriate general discipline. Finally, many participants expressed fears that their children would develop eating disorders and feeling ill-equipped to prevent these problems. In sum, the focus group findings confirmed the difficulties these women have with managing anxieties around feeding their children and interacting with them about food and body image issues, and highlighted the urgent need for targeted prevention efforts.

Based primarily on these focus group data, the NURTURE manual development team created an intervention that is now undergoing empirical evaluation in a randomized clinical trial. The intervention is comprised of 16 sessions, conducted in a group setting, and delivered in weekly 1.5-hour sessions. NURTURE's developers initially planned to conduct all groups in-person, but have added an online video component to make it easier for mothers of young children to participate. Initially scheduling with mothers with infants was extremely challenging. Once the option of video participation was available, participants were much easier to schedule.

Topics covered in NURTURE include: (1) Personality and Parenting, (2) Personality and Eating Disorders, (3) Mastering Emotions, (4) Feeding and Eating, (5) Developing a Healthy Body Image, and (6) the Media Savvy Family. NURTURE is grounded in social cognitive theory (SCT) (Bandura, 2004), which emphasizes the interaction among environmental, personal, and behavioral factors, and is widely used in prevention and health behavior modification interventions (Gortmaker et al., 1999). Throughout the intervention, the influence of social learning on behavioral outcomes (e.g., parent's modeling of healthy behavior, society's modeling of ideal body types) is emphasized. Further, this intervention is not "disease-specific," but rather focuses on a range of factors that are believed to be relevant to eating disorders both directly and indirectly. Several authors have suggested that the effectiveness of disease-specific interventions is limited, because they do not adequately address factors that promote resiliency in individuals at risk for disordered eating (Striegel-Moore & Steiner-Adair, 1998), but, rather, primarily focus on modifying specific unhealthy behaviors (e.g., binge eating). NURTURE aims not only to reduce eating disorder-specific environmental exposures, but also to increase overall resilience factors, as is recommended in the literature (Levine, Piran, & Stoddard, 1999).

Preliminary data from this pilot trial will inform the content and process of a subsequent larger controlled clinical trial. We hypothesized that NURTURE will improve participants' efficacy and confidence in feeding their children, increase modeling of healthy eating behaviors and attitudes, decrease parenting anxiety, and increase general parenting self-efficacy. In the long term, this intervention may assist mothers in developing a buffering environment that minimizes modeling of eating disorder–related behaviors and attitudes.

Teachers

Like parents and others who work closely with youth, teachers report concern and confusion about how best to promote healthy eating, while avoiding iatrogenic effects such as unintentionally increasing body image concerns (McVey, Gusella, Tweed, & Ferrari, 2009). To address these concerns, McVey and colleagues developed an online program called The Student Body: Promoting Health at Any Size. This program was primarily developed to address eating disorder prevention, but the topics covered include healthy eating and active living. Thus, *Student Body* could be considered an integrated program as it addresses topics relevant to both eating disorder and obesity prevention. The feasibility and effectiveness of this program were evaluated in a trial that included 78 elementary school teachers and 89 public health practitioners assigned to either the *Student Body* program or a control group. Intervention material included: (1) background information on eating disorders and their prevention; (2) instructions for relevant classroom activities; and (3) supplementary materials for instructors such as articles and external links. Participants in the intervention were provided access to the program for 60 days, and were asked to conduct Student Body activities with their classes during that time (during the regular academic day). Analyses indicated that approximately 91% of teachers led at least one of the online activities with their classes, and 45.5% used all six of them. Moreover, the intervention appeared to influence teachers' weight-related attitudes: 74.6% reported their participation increased their own body acceptance, and 94.7% indicated that their involvement motivated them to change their school environment. Intervention participants also reported increases in knowledge regarding eating disorder behaviors, peer influences on these behaviors, and weight bias. Finally, participants expressed satisfaction with the online approach. Unfortunately, the impact of this program on students was not assessed. However, the authors suggest that this program is promising, as teachers play a fundamental role in establishing school climate and role modeling health behaviors and attitudes.

Future Directions for Eating Disorder and Pediatric Obesity Prevention

Integrating Technology Into Prevention

INTERNET-BASED INTERVENTIONS

Internet-based interventions present content and allow for communication in various ways. Core intervention material is typically presented on a website with participants directed to access the material within a given time frame. Interventions vary in specificity of pacing intervals (e.g., daily, weekly, etc.). Opportunities to communicate with a clinical moderator or other participants also vary across programs. In some interventions, content is presented without opportunities for communication. However, most intervention communication approaches generally fall into one of two categories: asynchronous or synchronous. Asynchronous interventions allow participants to communicate in a forum (e.g., chatroom) at their convenience. Synchronous communication occurs in "real time" with other participants in a specified forum (e.g., chatroom, Zabinski, Celio, Wilfley, & Taylor, 2003). To date, there have been no randomized controlled trials comparing synchronous and asynchronous interventions in the eating disorder or obesity literature.

Another distinction among Internet-based interventions is the degree of facilitator involvement. Content can be presented in a static format or by a facilitator in real time. Similarly, individual and group discussions can be moderated by a facilitator or unmoderated. Two studies (Low et al., 2006; Manwaring et al., 2008) have evaluated the effect of moderated discussion groups on eating disorder and body image concerns among female college students enrolled in an online version of Student Bodies, a program reviewed in greater detail in the following paragraphs (Winzelberg et al., 1998). These studies suggest that positive outcomes can be achieved with and without moderation of discussion groups.

Student Bodies is one of the earliest and most well known Internet-based eating disorder interventions. It was developed for college students with subthreshold eating disorder symptoms (Winzelberg et al., 1998). This program is 8 weeks in duration and includes three core components: psychoeducational readings, a moderated asynchronous discussion group, and an Internet-based body image journal. Several studies have modified and evaluated Student Bodies programs (e.g., Celio et al., 2000; Low et al., 2006; Winzelberg et al., 1998, 2000; Zabinski et al., 2001). Generally, intervention participants report improved eating attitudes and behavior as well as reduced weight and shape concerns posttreatment; however the overall effect sizes for these interventions are small to moderate. This program appears to be most effective for adolescents at higher risk of developing eating pathology, suggesting it might be best considered a targeted prevention approach (Abascal, Bruning Brown, Winzelberg, Dev, & Taylor, 2004).

Since the development of the initial Student Bodies program, members of this research team have developed the Student Bodies2-BED (SB2) program to address both binge eating and overweight (Doyle et al., 2008; Jones et al., 2008). These studies included only adolescents with BMIs ≥ the 85th percentile for their age and sex, who also reported binge eating at least once per week for at last the last 3 months. Thus, these investigations might fall somewhere in between prevention and treatment approach. Nonetheless, results of these pilot trials are promising. Specifically, participation in *SB2* was associated with reductions in BMI, binge eating, and weight and shape concerns (Jones et al., 2008). However, overall adherence to the *SB2* program was low (an average of 29.9% of Internet material was read by participants). Thus, additional research is needed to investigate methods that might increase participant engagement with online intervention content. The authors also suggest that the self-directed nature of the intervention might be too unstructured for an adolescent age group. A pilot study of another Internet-based obesity prevention program targeting at-risk African American girls (ages 8–10), *Food, Fun, and Fitness*, yielded significant increases in fruit, juice, and vegetable intake (1 serving per day) and physical activity (Thompson et al., 2008). A limitation of this pilot is that it did not include a control group. Nonetheless, results are encouraging as they demonstrate feasibility and preliminary positive outcome data in an at-risk adolescent population.

Gow, Trace, and Mazzeo (2010) evaluated an Internet-based intervention aimed at preventing both obesity and disordered eating obesity among 1st-year college students. Participants (N = 170) were randomly assigned to one of four treatment conditions: (1) no treatment, (2) 6-week Internet intervention, (3) 6-week weight and caloric feedback only (via e-mail), and (4) 6-week combined feedback and Internet intervention. Posttreatment, the combined intervention group had lower BMIs compared to the control and single component groups. This study suggests that multiple component, highly structured Internet interventions are feasible and yield positive outcomes in an at-risk college population.

Some features that make Internet-based interventions appealing in eating disorder and obesity prevention include accessibility, anonymity, convenience, individual tailoring, and reduced stigma associated with treatment-seeking (Zabinski et al., 2003). Research with adults suggests most prefer weight management interventions that are not face-to-face (Sherwood et al., 1998). In addition, Internet-based interventions can be more cost effective than face-to-face interventions because maintenance of the program is relatively low after the initial set-up (Taylor, Winzelberg, & Celio, 2001; Zabinski et al., 2003). Intervention material can be updated easily and with little cost while it reaches a large population (Taylor et al., 2001; Zabinski et al., 2003). Technology also facilitates assessment of participant compliance (Zabinski et al. 2003). Demographic variables such as ethnicity and age, as well as concerns about physical appearance might also be equalized in an Internet-based intervention format (Taylor et al., 2001).

Yet, despite their many advantages, several potential concerns have been identified for Internet interventions. For example, while Internet use has expanded greatly, access is not universal, particularly with lower income groups (Zabinski et al. 2003). Also, while many participants might prefer accessing the intervention when it is convenient for them, clinicians might have greater difficulty responding to crisis situations (Taylor et al., 2001; Zabinski et al., 2003). Similarly, anonymity enhances self-disclosure for many participants and reduces shame associated with eating and weight disorders, but can present a challenge with the lack of facial expressions/visual cues available in face-to-face settings (Taylor et al., 2001; Zabinski et al., 2003). Also, there are potential challenges related to ensuring confidentiality and privacy of participant information, unanticipated technological difficulties, and computer skill levels of participants (Zabinski et al., 2003). Nonetheless, existing data on Internet-based interventions demonstrates their feasibility and acceptability. More research is needed to compare their effectiveness with that of face-to-face prevention programs. However, when provision of prevention and/or treatment in a face-to-face setting is not feasible or widespread dissemination is a greater priority, an online approach is a viable option.

OTHER TECHNOLOGY

Personal data assistants (PDAs), text messaging, and smart phone applications have been used as stand-alone interventions as well as adjuncts in multicomponent interventions. Paxton and Franko (2010) highlight the advantages of using PDAs, e-mail, and text messaging as adjuncts to therapy, noting that these methods can enhance self-monitoring and access to psychoeducational material. However, limited outcome data are available on their inclusion in eating disorder and obesity prevention. Thus, this is an area ripe for future research.

Enhancing the Cultural Sensitivity of Eating Disorder and Obesity Prevention

Future prevention efforts in the areas of both obesity and eating disorders should also focus on the cultural sensitivity of interventions. This is especially important in the area of prevention, because many individuals view eating disorders as a problem affecting only European American women (Becker et al., 2003; Gordon, Perez, & Joiner, 2002). In this section, we focus specifically on African American women, as this group is the focus of much of our own prevention and treatment work in this area (e.g., Mazzeo et al., 2008).

Rates of treatment-seeking for eating disorders are significantly lower among African American women, compared with European Americans (Becker et al., 2003; Cachelin, Veisel, Barzengarnazari, & Striegel-Moore, 2000). Binge eating is a significant problem among African American adolescents (Glasofer et al., 2007; Isnard et al., 2003), and African American youth who engage in binge eating report clinical impairment comparable to that of their White peers, suggesting that ethnicity does not provide any buffering effect against these negative outcomes (Glasofer et al., 2007; Isnard et al., 2003).

There is also a significant ethnic disparity in treatments aimed at improving eating behaviors (Ammerman, Leung, & Cavallo, 2006). Most available programs do not target members of traditionally underserved groups. As noted previously, African American children are at particularly high risk of binge eating and overweight (Glasofer et al., 2007; Ogden et al., 2010). Further, a recent report by the American Psychological Association on resilience and optimal development in adolescents suggests that the Africentric strengths of expressiveness, spirituality, and communalism should be considered in the development of programs targeting African American youth (American Psychological Association, 2008). Studies in other areas of adolescent mental health (e.g., substance abuse, Belgrave, Reed, Plybon, & Corneille, 2004), have found that culturally relevant interventions yield positive outcomes with African American adolescent girls. However, no studies have investigated the efficacy of eating disorder prevention programs designed to be culturally sensitive, in either African American adults or children.

Enhancing the cultural sensitivity of interventions is also important because food selection, preparation, and the eating process itself (including how and with whom food is eaten) are significantly influenced by cultural factors (Airhihenbuwa et al., 1996; James, 2004). For example, qualitative research has found that some African Americans are hesitant to make positive changes in their eating behaviors because they want to maintain their connection to African culture (James, 2004). Thus, prevention efforts need to be sensitive to this concern, and highlight the health-promoting aspects of Africentric values and customs related to food selection and eating behavior. Moreover, research on interventions promoting healthy eating in adult women found that African Americans preferred a group approach in which they could both provide and receive support from other women with problems similar to their own (Blixen, Singh, & Thacker, 2006; Blixen, Singh, Xu, Thacker, & Mascha, 2006). This is consistent with the collectivist orientation of the African American community (Blixen, Singh, & Thacker, 2006). Prevention programs should also acknowledge and incorporate cultural differences in body image ideals and building social support for behavior change (versus using an individual approach; Ammerman et al., 2006).

Conclusion

Despite nearly universal agreement that prevention of childhood obesity and eating disorders is an important public health goal, prevention efforts have been hampered primarily by a dis-integrated approach to developing, testing, and implementing prevention programs. Although isolated programs have shown promise, no coordinated effort yet exists that integrates the many health care and research fields that deal with obesity and eating disorders (e.g., psychology, psychiatry, pediatrics, adolescent medicine, exercise physiology, nutrition) as well as policy makers, schools, and government agencies. Leaders from each of these areas must work in a coordinated fashion to develop effective multisystemic approaches to achieve simultaneous prevention of both childhood obesity and eating disorders.

Future Directions

1. How can we develop and implement effective, multisystemic approaches to prevention that integrate obesity and eating disorder prevention?
2. What is the optimal role of public health policy in these multisystemic prevention efforts?
3. How can technology best be used to facilitate these multisystemic prevention efforts?
4. How can these programs be culturally sensitive and yet be implemented in schools and other diverse settings?

References

Abascal, L., Bruning Brown, J., Winzelberg, A. J., Dev, P., & Taylor, C. B. (2004). Combining universal and targeted prevention for school-based eating disorder programs. *International Journal of Eating Disorders, 35,* 1–9.

Airhihenbuwa, C. O., Kumanyika, S., Agurs, T. D., Lowe, A., Saunders, D., & Morssink, C. B. (1996). Cultural aspects of African American eating patterns. *Ethnicity and Health, 1,* 245–260.

American Psychiatric Association. (1994). *Diagnostic and statistical manual of mental disorders* (4th ed.). Washington, DC: Author.

American Psychological Association. (2002). Ethical principles of psychologists and code of conduct. *American Psychologist, 57,* 1060–1073.

American Psychological Association Task Force on Resilience and Strength in Black Children and Adolescents. (2008). *Resilience in African American children and adolescents: A vision for optimal development.* Washington, DC: Author. Retrieved from http://www.apa.org/pi/families/resources/resiliencerpt.pdf

Ammerman, A., Leung, M. M., & Cavallo, D. (2006). Addressing disparities in the obesity epidemic. *North Carolina Medical Journal, 67,* 301–304.

Austin, S. B., Field, A. E., Wiecha, J., Peterson, K. E., & Gortmaker, S. L. (2005). The impact of a school-based obesity prevention trial on disordered weight-control behaviors in early adolescent girls. *Archives of Pediatric and Adolescent Medicine, 159,* 225–230.

Austin, S. B., Kim, J., Wiecha, J., Troped, P. J., Feldman, H. A., & Peterson, K. E (2007). School-based overweight preventive intervention lowers incidence of disordered weight-control behaviors in early adolescent girls. *Archives of Pediatric and Adolescent Medicine, 161,* 865–869.

Bandura, A. (2004). Health promotion by social cognitive means. *Health Education and Behavior, 31,* 143–164.

Bauer, K. W., Haines, J., & Neumark-Sztainer, D. (2009). Obesity prevention: Strategies to improve effectiveness and reduce harm. In L. Smolak & J. K. Thompson (Eds.), *Body image, eating disorders, and obesity in youth: Assessment, prevention, and treatment.* (pp. 241–260). Washington, DC: American Psychological Association.

Becker, A. E., Franko, D. L. Speck, A., & Herzog, D. B. (2003). Ethnicity and differential access to care for eating disorder symptoms. *International Journal of Eating Disorders, 33,* 205–212.

Becker, A. E., Grinspoon, S. K., Klibanski, A., & Herzog, D. B. (1999). Eating disorders. *New England Journal of Medicine, 340,* 1092–1098.

Belgrave, F. Z., Reed, M. C., Plybon, L. E., & Corneille, M. (2004). The impact of a culturally enhanced drug prevention program on drug and alcohol refusal efficacy among urban African American girls. *Journal of Drug Education, 34,* 267–279.

Birch, L. L., Fisher, J. O., & Davison, K. K. (2003). Learning to overeat: Maternal use of restrictive feeding practices promotes girls' eating in the absence of hunger. *American Journal of Clinical Nutrition, 78,* 215–220.

Blixen, C. E., Singh, A., & Thacker, H. (2006). Values and beliefs about obesity and weight reduction among African American and Caucasian women. *Journal of Transcultural Nursing, 17,* 290–297.

Blixen, C. E., Singh, A., Xu, M., Thacker, H., & Mascha, E. (2006). What women want: Understanding obesity and preferences for primary care weight reduction interventions among African-American and Caucasian women. *Journal of the National Medical Association, 98,* 1160–1170.

Brownell, K. D. (2002). The environment and obesity. In C. G. Fairburn & K. D. Brownell (Eds.), *Eating disorders and obesity* (2nd ed., pp. 433–438). New York: Guilford.

Brownell, K. D., Schwartz, M. B., Puhl, R. M., Henderson, K. E., & Harris, J. L. (2009). The need for bold action to prevent adolescent obesity. *Journal of Adolescent Health, 45,* S8–S17.

Brownley, K. A., Berkman, N. D., Sedway, J. A., Lohr, K. N., & Bulik, C. M. (2007). Binge eating disorder treatment: a systematic review of randomized controlled trials. *International Journal of Eating Disorders, 40,* 337–348.

Bruning Brown, J., Winzelberg, A. J., Abascal, L. B., & Taylor, C. B. (2004). An evaluation of an Internet-delivered eating disorder prevention program for adolescents and their parents. *Journal of Adolescent Health, 35,* 290–296.

Bulik, C. M. (2004). Genetic and biological risk factors. In J. K. Thompson (Ed.), *Handbook of eating disorders and obesity* (pp. 3–16). Hoboken, NJ: Wiley.

Cachelin, F. M., Veisel, C., Barzengarnazari, E., & Striegel-Moore, R. H. (2000). Disordered eating, acculturation, and treatment-seeking in a community sample of Hispanic, Asian, Black and White women. *Psychology of Women Quarterly, 24,* 244–253.

Carter, F. A., & Bulik, C. M. (2008). Childhood obesity prevention programs: How do they affect eating pathology and other psychological measures? *Psychosomatic Medicine, 70,* 363–371.

Celio, A. A., Winzelberg, A. J., Wilfley, D. E., Eppstein, D., Springer, E. A., Dev, P., & Taylor, C. B. (2000). Reducing risk factors for eating disorders: Comparison of an Internet- and a classroom-delivered psychoeducational program. *Journal of Consulting and Clinical Psychology, 68,* 650–657.

Chomitz, V. R., Collings, J., Kim, J., Kramer, E., & McGowan, R. (2003). Promoting healthy weight among elementary school children via a health report card approach. *Archives of Pediatrics and Adolescent Medicine, 157,* 765–772.

Cogan, J. C., Smith, J. P., & Maine, M. D. (2008). The risks of a quick fix: A case against mandatory body mass index reporting laws. *Eating Disorders, 16,* 2–13.

Cooperberg, J., & Faith, M. S. (2004). Treatment of obesity II: Childhood and adolescent obesity. In J. K. Thompson (Ed.), *Handbook of eating disorders and obesity* (pp. 443–460). Hoboken, NJ: Wiley.

Cramer, P., & Steinwert, T. (1998). Thin is good, fat is bad: How early does it begin? *Journal of Applied Developmental Psychology, 19,* 429–451.

Darby, A., Hay, P., Mond, J., Quirk, F., Buttner, P., & Kennedy, L. (2009). The rising prevalence of comorbid obesity and eating disorder behaviors from 1995 to 2005. *International Journal of Eating Disorders, 42,* 104–108.

Doyle, A. C., Goldschmidt, A., Huang, C., Winzelberg, A. J., Taylor, C. B., & Wilfley, D. (2008). Reduction of overweight and eating disorder symptoms via the Internet in adolescents: A randomized controlled trial. *Journal of Adolescent Health, 43,* 172–179.

Eisenberg, M. E., Neumark-Sztainer, D., & Story, M. (2003). Associations of weight-based teasing and emotional well-being among adolescents. *Archives of Pediatrics and Adolescent Medicine, 157,* 733–738.

Fairburn, C. G., Doll, H. A., Welch, S. L., Hay, P. J., Davies, B. A., & O'Connor, M. E. (1998). Risk factors for binge eating disorder: A community-based case-control study. *Archives of General Psychiatry, 55,* 425–432.

Fairburn, C. G., Marcus, M., & Wilson, G. T. (1993). Cognitive-behavioral therapy for binge eating and bulimia nervosa: A comprehensive treatment manual. In C. G. Fairburn, & G. T. Wilson (Eds.), *Binge eating: nature, assessment, and treatment* (pp. 361–404). New York: Guilford Press.

Fairburn, C. G., Welch, S. L., Doll, H. A., Davies, B. A., & O'Connor, M. E. (1997). Risk factors for bulimia nervosa: A community-based case-control study. *Archives of General Psychiatry, 54,* 509–517.

Faith, M. S., Berkowitz, R. I., Stallings, V. A., Kerns, J., Storey, M., & Stunkard, A. J. (2004). Parental feeding attitudes and styles and child body mass index: prospective analysis of a gene-environment interaction. *Pediatrics, 114,* e429–e436.

Field, A. E., Austin, S. B., Taylor, C. B., Malspeis, S., Rosner, B., Rockett, H. R., . . . Colditz, G. A. (2003). Relation between dieting and weight change among preadolescents and adolescents. *Pediatrics, 112,* 900–906.

Fingeret, M. C., Warren, C. S., Cepeda-Benito, A., & Gleaves, D. H. (2006). Eating disorder prevention research: A meta-analysis: *Eating Disorders: The Journal of Treatment and Prevention, 14,* 191–213.

Fisher, J. O., & Birch, L. L. (1999). Restricting access to foods and children's eating. *Appetite, 32,* 405–419.

Fisher, J. O., & Birch, L. L. (2002). Eating in the absence of hunger and overweight in girls from 5 to 7 years of age. *American Journal of Clinical Nutrition, 76,* 226–231.

Fisher, J. O., Mitchell, D. C., Smiciklas-Wright, H., & Birch, L. L. (2002). Parental influences on young girls' fruit and vegetable, micronutrient, and fat intakes. *Journal of the American Dietetic Association, 102,* 58–64.

Fitzgibbon, M. L., Spring, B., Avellone, M. E., Blackman, L. R., Pingitore, R., & Stolley, M. R. (1998). Correlates of binge eating in Hispanic, Black, and White women. *International Journal of Eating Disorders, 24,* 43–52.

Foster, G. D., Sherman, S., Borradaile, K. E., Grundy, K. M., Vander Veur, S. S., Nachmani, J., . . . Shults, J. (2008). A policy-based school intervention to prevent overweight and obesity. *Pediatrics, 121,* e794–e802.

French, S., Story, M., Neumark-Sztainer, D., Fulkerson, J. A., & Hannan, P. (2001). Fast food restaurant use among adolescents: associations with nutrient intake, food choices, behavioral and psychosocial variables. *International Journal of Obesity, 25,* 1823–1833.

Fulkerson J. A., Strauss, J., Neumark-Sztainer, D., Story, M., & Boutelle, K. (2007). Correlates of psychosocial well-being among overweight adolescents: The role of the family. *Journal of Consulting and Clinical Psychology, 75,* 181–186.

Gennuso, J., Epstein, L. H., Paluch, R. A., & Cerny, F. (1998). The relationship between asthma and obesity in urban minority children and adolescents. *Archives of Pediatric and Adolescent Medicine, 152,* 1197–1200.

Glasofer, D. R., Tanofsky-Kraff, M., Eddy, K. T., Yanovski, S. Z., Theim, K. R., Mirch, M. C., . . . Yanovski, J. A. (2007). Binge eating in overweight treatment-seeking adolescents. *Journal of Pediatric Psychology, 32,* 95–105.

Gordon, K. H., Perez, M., & Joiner, T. E., Jr. (2002). The impact of racial stereotypes on eating disorder recognition. *International Journal of Eating Disorders, 32,* 219–224.

Gortmaker, S. L., Peterson, K., Wiecha, J., Sobol, A. M., Dixit, S., Fox, M. K., & Laird, N. (1999). Reducing obesity via a school-based interdisciplinary intervention among youth: Planet Health. *Archives of Pediatric and Adolescent Medicine, 153,* 409–418.

Gow, R. W., Trace, S. E., & Mazzeo, S. E. (2010). Preventing weight gain in first year college students: an online intervention to prevent the "freshman fifteen." *Eating Behaviors, 11,* 33–39.

Greenberg, B. S., Eastin, M., Hofschire, L., Lachlan, K., & Brownell, K. (2003). Portrayals of overweight and obese individuals on commercial television. *American Journal of Public Health, 93,* 1342–1348.

Grimmett, C., Croker, H., Carnell, S., & Wardle, J. (2008). Telling parents their child's weight status: psychological impact of a weight-screening program. *Pediatrics, 122,* e682–e688.

Groesz, L. M., Levine, M. P., & Murnen, S. K. (2002). The effect of experimental presentation of thin media images on body satisfaction: a meta-analytic review. *International Journal of Eating Disorders, 31,* 1–16.

Guo, S. S., & Chumlea, W. C. (1999). Tracking of body mass index in children in relation to overweight in adulthood. *American Journal of Clinical Nutrition, 70,* 145S–148S.

Haines, J., & Neumark-Sztainer, D. (2006). Prevention of obesity and eating disorders: a consideration of shared risk factors. *Health Education Research, 21,* 770–782.

Haines, J., Neumark-Sztainer, D., Eisenberg M. E., & Hannan, P. J. (2006). Weight-teasing and disordered eating behaviors in adolescents: findings from Project EAT (Eating Among Teens). *Pediatrics, 117,* e209–e215.

Hanson, D. (1982). The effectiveness of alcohol and drug education. *Journal of Alcohol and Drug Education, 27,* 1–13.

Harvey-Berino, J., & Rourke, J. (2003). Obesity prevention in preschool native-American children: a pilot study using home visiting. *Obesity Research, 11,* 606–611.

Hedley, A. A., Ogden, C. L., Johnson, C. L., Carroll, M. D., Curtin, L. R., & Flegal, K. M. (2004). Prevalence of overweight and obesity among US children, adolescents, and adults, 1999–2002. *Journal of the American Medical Association, 291,* 2847–2850.

Heinberg, L., & Thompson, J. (1995). Body image and televised images of thinness and attractiveness: A controlled laboratory investigation. *Journal of Social and Clinical Psychology, 14,* 325–338.

Hoek, H., & van Hoeken, D. (2003). Review of the prevalence and incidence of eating disorders. *International Journal of Eating Disorders, 34,* 383–396.

Hudson, J. I., Hiripi, E., Pope, H. G., & Kessler R.C. (2007). The prevalence and correlates of eating disorders in the National Comorbidity Survey Replication. *Biological Psychiatry 61,* 348–358.

Hudson, J. I., Lalonde, J. K., Coit, C. E., Tsuang, M. T., McElroy, S. L., Crow, S. J.,... Pope, H. G., Jr. (2010). Longitudinal study of the diagnosis of components of the metabolic syndrome in individuals with binge-eating disorder. *American Journal of Clinical Nutrition, 91,* 1568–1573.

Institute of Medicine. (2004). *Preventing childhood obesity: Health in the balance.* Washington, DC: National Institutes of Health.

Irving, L. (1990). Mirror images: Effects of the standard of beauty on the self- and body-esteem of women exhibiting varying levels of bulimic symptoms. *Journal of Social and Clinical Psychology, 9,* 230–242.

Irving, L. M., & Neumark-Sztainer, D. (2002). Integrating the prevention of eating disorders and obesity: Feasible or futile? *Preventive Medicine, 34,* 299–309.

Isnard, P., Michel, G., Frelut, M. L., Vila, G., Falissard, B., Naja, W.,... Mouren-Simeoni, M. C. (2003). Binge eating and psychopathology in severely obese adolescents. *International Journal of Eating Disorders, 34,* 235–243.

Jacobi, C., Hayward, C., de Zwaan, M., Kraemer, H. C., & Agras, W. S. (2004). Coming to terms with risk factors for eating disorders: Application of risk terminology and suggestions for a general taxonomy. *Psychological Bulletin, 130,* 19–65. doi: 10.1037/0033-2909.130.1.19

James, D. C. (2004). Factors influencing food choices, dietary intake, and nutrition-related attitudes among African Americans: application of a culturally sensitive model. *Ethnicity and Health, 9,* 349–367.

Joiner, C. I. (2009). Body mass index (BMI) report cards: Should schools be responsible for screening? *MCN, The American Journal of Maternal/Child Nursing, 34,* 208.

Jones, M., Luce, K. H., Osborne, M. I., Taylor, K., Cunning, D., Doyle, A. C.,... Taylor, C. B. (2008). Randomized, controlled trial of an Internet-facilitated intervention for reducing binge eating and overweight in adolescents. *Pediatrics, 121,* 453–462.

Justus, M. B., Ryan, K. W., Rockenbach, J., Katterapalli, C., Card-Higginson, P. (2007). Lessons learned while implementing a legislated school policy: body mass index assessments among Arkansas's public school students. *Journal of School Health, 77,* 706–713.

Kalodner, C. (1997). Media influences on male and female non-eating disordered college students: A significant issue. *Eating Disorders: The Journal of Treatment and Prevention, 1,* 109–114.

Kiess, W., Galler, A., Reich, A., Müller, G., Kapellen, T., Deutscher, J.,... Kratzsch, J. (2001). Clinical aspects of obesity in childhood and adolescence. *Obesity Reviews, 2,* 29–36.

Killion, L., Hughes, S. O., Wendt, J. C., Pease, D., & Nicklas, T. A. (2006). Minority mothers' perceptions of children's body size. *International Journal of Pediatric Obesity, 1,* 96–102.

Kohl, H. W., & Hobbs, K. E. (1998). Development of physical activity behaviors among children and adolescents. *Pediatrics, 101,* 549–554.

Kubik, M. Y., Fulkerson, J. A., Story, M., & Rieland, G. (2006). Parents of elementary school students weigh in on height, weight, and body mass index screening at school. *Journal of School Health, 76,* 496–501.

Kubik, M. Y., & Lytle, L. A., & Story, M. (2005). Schoolwide food practices are associated with body mass index in middle school students. *Archives of Pediatric and Adolescent Medicine, 159,* 1111–1114.

Kubik, M. Y., Story, M., & Rieland, G. (2007). Developing school-based BMI screening and parent notification programs: findings from focus groups with parents of elementary school students. *Health Education and Behavior, 34,* 622–633.

Levine, M. P., & Harrison, K. (2004). Media's role in the perpetuation and prevention of negative body image and disordered eating. In J. K. Thompson (Ed.), *Handbook of eating disorders and obesity* (pp. 695–717). Hoboken, NJ: Wiley.

Levine M. P., Piran, N., & Stoddard, C. (1999). Mission more probable: Media literacy, activism, and advocacy as primary prevention. In N. Piran, M. P. Levine, & C. Steiner-Adair (Eds.), *Preventing eating disorders: A handbook of interventions and special challenges* (pp. 3–25). Philadelphia: Brunner/Mazel.

Levine, M. P., & Smolak, L. (2009). Recent developments and promising directions in the prevention of negative body image and disordered eating in children and adolescents. In L. Smolak & J. K. Thompson (Eds.), *Body image, eating disorders, and obesity in youth* (pp. 215–239). Washington, DC: American Psychological Association.

Li, S., Chen, W., Srinivasan, S. R., Bond, M. G., Tang, R., Urbina, E. M., & Berenson, G. S. (2003). Childhood cardiovascular risk factors and carotid vascular changes in adulthood: The Bogalusa Heart Study. *Journal of the American Medical Association, 290,* 2271–2276.

Libbey, H. P., Story, M. T., Neumark-Sztainer, D. R., & Boutelle, K. N. (2008). Teasing, disordered eating behaviors, and psychological morbidities among overweight adolescents. *Obesity, 16,* S24–S29.

Low, K. G., Charanasomboon, S., Lesser, J., Reinhalter, K., Martin, R., Jones, H.,... Taylor, C. B. (2006). Effectiveness of a computer-based interactive eating disorders prevention program at long-term follow-up. *Eating Disorders, 14,* 17–30.

Luce, K. H., Osborne, M. I., Winzelberg, A. J., Das, S., Abascal, L. B., Celio, A. A.,... Taylor, C. B. (2005). Application of an algorithm-driven protocol to simultaneously provide universal and targeted prevention programs. *International Journal of Eating Disorders, 37,* 220–226.

Lunner, K., Werthem, E. H., Thompson, J. K., Paxton, S. J., McDonald, F., & Halvaarson, K. S. (2000). A cross-cultural examination of weight-related teasing, body image, and eating disturbance in Swedish and Australian samples. *International Journal of Eating Disorders, 28,* 430–435.

Maes, H. H., Neale, M. C., & Eaves, L. J. (1997). Genetic and environmental factors in relative body weight and human adiposity. *Behavior Genetics, 27,* 325–351.

Mann, T., Nolen-Hoeksema, S., Huang, K., Burgard, D. Wright, A. & Hanson, K. (1997). Are two interventions worse than one? Joint primary and secondary prevention of eating disorders in college females. *Health Psychology, 16,* 215–225.

Manwaring, J. L., Bryson, S. W., Goldschmidt, A. B., Winzelberg, A. J., Luce, K. H., Cunning, D.,...Taylor, C. B. (2008). Do adherence variables predict outcome in an online program for the prevention of eating disorders? *Journal of Consulting and Clinical Psychology, 76,* 341–346.

Mazzeo, S. E., Gow, R. W., Stern, M., & Gerke, C. K. (2008). Developing an intervention for parents of overweight children. *International Journal of Child and Adolescent Health, 1,* 355–364.

Mazzeo, S. E., Trace, S. E., Mitchell, K. S., & Gow R. G. (2007). Effects of a reality TV cosmetic surgery makeover program on eating disordered attitudes and behaviors. *Eating Behaviors, 8,* 390–397.

Mazzeo, S. E., Zucker, N. L., Gerke, C. K., Mitchell, K. S., & Bulik, C. M. (2005). Parenting concerns of women with a history of eating disorders: Development of a targeted intervention. *International Journal of Eating Disorders, 37,* S77–S79.

Mazzeo, S. E., Zucker, N., Pisetsky, E., Swann, R., & Bulik, C. M. (2008). *Development of a parenting intervention for mothers with eating disorders.* Poster presentation at the annual meeting of the Eating Disorder Research Society, Montreal, Quebec, Canada.

McVey, G., Gusella, J., Tweed, S., & Ferrari, M. (2009). A controlled evaluation of web-based training for teachers and public health practitioners on the prevention of eating disorders. *Eating Disorders, 17,* 1–26.

Morgan. L. (2008). BMI...a weighty issue. *School Nurse News, 25,* 24–26.

Moskowitz, J. (1989). The primary prevention of alcohol problems: A critical review of the research literature. *Journal of Studies on Alcohol, 50,* 54–88.

Neumark-Sztainer, D. (2005). Can we simultaneously work toward the prevention of obesity and eating disorders in children and adolescents? *International Journal of Eating Disorders, 38,* 220–227.

Neumark-Sztainer, D., Croll, J., Story, M., Hannan, P. J., French, S. A., & Perry, C. (2002). Ethnic/racial differences in weight-related concerns and behaviors among adolescent girls and boys: findings from Project EAT. *Journal of Psychosomatic Research, 53,* 963–974.

Neumark-Sztainer, D., Falkner, N., Story, M., Perry, C., Hannan, P.J., & Mulert, S. (2002). Weight-teasing among adolescents: correlations with weight status and disordered eating behaviors. *International Journal of Obesity, 26,* 123–131.

Neumark-Sztainer, D., Friend, S. E., Flattum, C. F., Hannan, P. J., Story, M. T., Bauer, K. W.,...Petrich, C. A. (2010). New Moves—Preventing weight-related problems in adolescent girls: A group-randomized study. *American Journal of Preventive Medicine, 39,* 421–432.

Neumark-Sztainer, D., Hannan, P. J., Story, M., Croll, J., & Perry, C. (2003). Family meal patterns: Associations with sociodemographic characteristics and improved dietary intake among adolescents. *Journal of the American Dietetic Association, 103,* 317–322.

Neumark-Sztainer, D., & Story, M. (1997). Recommendations from overweight youth regarding school-based weight control programs. *Journal of School Health, 67,* 428–433.

Neumark-Sztainer, D., Story, M., Hannan, P. J., Perry, C. L., & Irving, L. M. (2002). Weight-related concerns and behaviors among overweight and non-overweight adolescents: implications for preventing weight-related disorders. *Archives of Pediatric and Adolescent Medicine, 156,* 171–178.

Neumark-Sztainer, D., Story, M., Hannan, P. J., & Rex, J. (2003). New Moves: a school-based obesity prevention program for adolescent girls. *Preventive Medicine, 37,* 41–51.

Neumark-Sztainer, D., Wall, M., Guo, J., Story, M., Haines, J., & Eisenberg, M. (2006). Obesity, disordered eating, and eating disorders in a longitudinal study of adolescents: How do dieters fare five years later? *Journal of the American Dietetic Association, 106,* 559–568.

Neumark-Sztainer, D., Wall, M. M., Haines, J. I., Story, M. T., Sherwood, N. E., & van den Berg, P. A. (2007). Shared risk and protective factors for overweight and disordered eating in adolescents. *American Journal of Preventive Medicine, 33,* 359–369.

Nihiser, A. J., Lee, S. M., Wechsler, H., McKenna, M., Doom, E., Rienold, C.,...Grummer-Strawn, L. (2007). Body mass index measurement in schools. *Journal of School Health, 77,* 651–671.

O'Dea, J. A. (2005a). Prevention of child obesity: first do no harm. *Health Education Research: Theory and Practice, 20,* 259–265.

O'Dea, J. A. (2005b). School-based health education strategies for the improvement of body image and prevention of eating problems. *Health Education, 105,* 11–33.

Ogden, C. L., Carroll, M. D., Curtin, L. R., Lamb, M. M., & Flegal, K. M. (2010). Prevalence of high body mass index in US children and adolescents, 2007–2008. *Journal of the American Medical Association, 303,* 242–249.

Ogden, C. L., Carroll, M. D., Curtin, L. R., McDowell, M. A., Tabak, C. J., & Flegal, K. M. (2006). Prevalence of overweight and obesity in the United States,1999–2004. *Journal of the American Medical Association, 295,* 1549–1555.

Parry, L. L., Netuveli, G., Parry, J., & Saxena, S. (2008). A systematic review of parental perception of overweight status in children. *The Journal of Ambulatory Care Management, 31,* 253–268.

Patton, G. C., Selzer, R., Doffey, C. Carlin, J. B., & Wolfe, R. (1999). Onset of adolescent eating disorders: population based cohort study over 3 years, *British Medical Journal, 318,* 765–768.

Paxton, S. J., & Franko, D. L. (2010). Body image and eating disorders. In M. A. Cucciare & K. R. Weingardt (Eds.), *Using technology to support evidence-based behavioral health practices* (pp. 151–168). New York: Routledge/Taylor & Francis.

Pearce, M. J., Boergers, J., & Prinstein, M. J. (2002). Adolescent obesity, overt and relational victimization, and romantic relationships. *Obesity Research, 10,* 386–393.

Pike, K. M., Wilfley, D., Hilbert, A, Fairburn, C. G., Dohm, F. A., & Striegel-Moore, R. H. (2006). Antecedent life events of binge-eating disorder. *Psychiatry Research, 142,* 19–29.

Powell, L. M. Szczpka, G., & Chaloupka, F. J. (2007). Adolescent exposure to food advertising. *American Journal of Preventive Medicine, 33,* S251–S256.

Presswood, R. F. (2005). School health report card. *School Nurse News, 22,* 27–32.

Raitakari, O. T., Juonala, M., Kähönen, M., Taittonen, L., Laitinen, T., Mäki-Torkko, N.,...Viikari, J. S. A. (2003). Cardiovascular risk factors in childhood and carotid artery intima-media thickness in adulthood: The cardiovascular risk in young Finns Study. *Journal of the American Medical Association, 290,* 2277–2283.

Roberts, D. F., Foehr, U. G., & Rideout, V. (2005). *Generation M: Media in the lives of 8–12 year olds.* Kaiser Family Foundation. Retrieved from http://www.kff.org/entmedia/upload/Generation-M-Media-in-the-Lives-of-8–18-Year-olds-Report.pdf

Robinson, T. N. (1999). Reducing children's television viewing to prevent obesity: a randomized controlled trial. *Journal of the American Medical Association, 282,* 1561–1567.

Robinson, T. N., Borzekowski, D. L. G., Matheson, D. M., & Kraemer, H., C. (2007). Effects of fast food branding on young children's taste preferences. *Archives of Pediatric and Adolescent Medicine, 161,* 792–797.

Robinson, T., Callister, M., & Jankoski, T. (2008). Portrayal of body weight on children's television sitcoms: A content analysis. *Body Image, 5,* 141–151.

Robinson, T. N., Kiernan, M., Matheson, D. M., & Haydel, K. F. (2001). Is parental control over children's eating associated with childhood obesity? Results from a population-based sample of third graders. *Obesity Research, 9,* 306–312.

Robinson, T. N., Killen, J. D., Kraemer, H. C., Wilson, D. M., Matheson, D. M., Haskell, W. L.,...Varady, A. (2003). Dance and reducing television viewing to prevent weight gain in African-American girls: the Stanford GEMS pilot study. *Ethnicity and Disease, 13,* S65–S77.

Robinson, T. N., Killen, J. D., Litt, I. F., Hammer, L. D., Wilson, D. M., Haydel, K. F.,...Taylor, C. B. (1996). Ethnicity and body dissatisfaction: are Hispanic and Asian girls at increased risk for eating disorders? *Journal of Adolescent Health, 19,* 384–393.

Roehling, M., Roehling, V., & Pichler, S. (2007). The relationship between body weight and perceived weight-related employment discrimination: The role of sex and race. *Journal of Vocational Behavior, 71,* 300–318.

Rosenvinge, J. H., & Børresen, R. (1999). Preventing eating disorders—Time to change programmes or paradigms? Current update and further recommendations. *European Eating Disorders Review, 7,* 5–16.

Scheier, L. M. (2004a). Potential problems with school health report cards. *Journal of the American Dietetic Association, 104,* 525–527.

Scheier L. M. (2004b). School health report cards attempt to address the obesity epidemic. *Journal of the American Dietetic Association, 104,* 341–344.

Schwartz, M. B., Novak, S. A., & Fiore, S. S. (2009). The impact of removing snacks of low nutritional value from middle schools. *Health Education and Behavior, 36,* 999–1011.

Schwartz, M. B., Thomas, J. J., Bohan, K. M., & Vartanian, L. R. (2007). Intended and unintended effects of an eating disorder educational program: Impact of presenter identity. *International Journal of Eating Disorders, 40,* 187–192.

Schwimmer, J. B., Burwinkle, T. M., & Varni, J. W. (2003). Health-related quality of life of severely obese children and adolescents. *Journal of the American Medical Association, 289,* 1813–1819.

Serdula, M. K., Ivery, D., Coates, R. J., Freedman, D. S., Williamson, D. F., & Byers, T. (1993). Do obese children become obese adults? A review of the literature. *American Journal of Preventive Medicine, 22,* 167–177.

Sherwood, N. E., Morton, N., Jeffery, R. W., French, S. A., Neumark-Sztainer, D., & Falkner, N. H. (1998). Consumer preferences in format and type of community-based weight control programs. *American Journal of Health Promotion, 13,* 12–18.

Shrewsbury, V., & Wardle, J. (2008). Socioeconomic status and adiposity in childhood: a systematic review of cross-sectional studies 1990–2005. *Obesity, 16,* 275–294.

Simon, S., Schmidt, U., & Pilling, S. (2005). The health service use and cost of eating disorders. *Psychological Medicine, 35,* 1543–1551.

Smolak, L., Levine, M. P., & Schermer, F. (1999). Parental input and weight concerns among elementary school children. *International Journal of Eating Disorders, 25,* 263–271.

Sorof, J., & Daniels, S. (2002). Obesity hypertension in children: A problem of epidemic proportions. *Hypertension, 40,* 441.

Spoor, S. T. P., Stice, E., Burton, E., & Bohon, C. (2007). Relations of bulimic symptom frequency and intensity to psychosocial impairment and health care utilization: Results from a community-recruited sample. *International Journal of Eating Disorders, 40,* 505–514.

Stice, E., Cameron, R. P., Killen, J. D., Hayward, C., & Taylor, C. B. (1999). Naturalistic weight-reduction efforts prospectively predict growth in relative weight and onset of obesity in female adolescents. *Journal of Consulting and Clinical Psychology, 67,* 967–974.

Stice, E., & Hoffman, E. (2004). Eating disorder prevention programs. In J. K. Thompson (Ed.), *Handbook of eating disorders and obesity* (pp. 33–57). Hoboken, New Jersey: Wiley.

Stice, E., Marti, C. N., Spoor, S., Presnell, K., & Shaw, H. (2008). Dissonance and healthy weight eating disorder prevention programs: Long-term effects from a randomized efficacy trial. *Journal of Consulting and Clinical Psychology, 76,* 329–340.

Stice, E., & Shaw, H. (1994). Adverse effects of the media-portrayed thin-ideal on women and linkages to bulimic symptomatology. *Journal of Social and Clinical Psychology, 13,* 288–308.

Stice, E., & Shaw, H. (2004). Eating disorder prevention programs: a meta-analytic review. *Psychological Bulletin, 130,* 206–227.

Stice, E., Shaw, H., Burton, E., & Wade, E. (2006). Dissonance and healthy weight eating disorder prevention programs: A randomized efficacy trial. *Journal of Consulting and Clinical Psychology, 74,* 263–275.

Stice, E., Shaw, H., & Marti, C. N. (2007). A meta-analytic review of eating disorder prevention programs: Encouraging findings. *Annual Review of Clinical Psychology, 3,* 207–231.

Stice, E., Spangler, D., & Agras, W. S. (2001). Exposure to media-portrayed thin-ideal images adversely affects vulnerable girls: A longitudinal experiment. *Journal of Social and Clinical Psychology, 20*(3), 270–288.

Stice, E., Trost, A., & Chase, A. (2003). Healthy weight control and dissonance-based eating disorder prevention programs: Results from a controlled trial. *International Journal of Eating Disorders, 33,* 10–21.

Stice, E., & Whitenton, K. (2002). Risk factors for body dissatisfaction in adolescent girls: a longitudinal investigation. *Developmental Psychology, 38,* 669–678.

Stormer, S., & Thompson, J. K. (1996). Explanations of body image disturbance: a test of maturational status, negative verbal commentary, social comparison, and sociocultural hypotheses. *International Journal of Eating Disorders, 19,* 193–202.

Story, M., & French, S. (2004). Food advertising and marketing directed at children and adolescents in the U.S. *International Journal of Behavioral Nutrition and Physical Activity, 1*(3). Retrieved from http://www.ijbnpa.org/content/pdf/1479-5868-1-3.pdf

Story, M., Nanney, M. S., & Schwartz, M. B. (2009). Schools and obesity prevention: Creating school environments and policies to promote healthy eating and physical activity. *The Milbank Quarterly, 87,* 71–100.

Story M., Sherwood, N. E., Himes, J. H., Davis, M., Jacobs, D. R. Jr., Cartwright, Y., Smyth, M., & Rochon J. (2003). An after-school obesity prevention program for African-American girls: the Minnesota GEMS pilot study. *Ethnicity & Disease, 13,* S54–S64.

Striegel-Moore, R. H., & Bulik, C. M. (2007). Risk factors for eating disorders. *American Psychologist, 62,* 181–198. DOI: 10.1037/0003-066X.62.3.181

Striegel-Moore, R. H., & Kearney-Cooke, A. (1994). Exploring parents' attitudes and behaviors about their children's physical appearance. *International Journal of Eating Disorders, 15,* 377–385.

Striegel-Moore, R. H., & Steiner-Adair C. (1998). Primary prevention of eating disorders: Further considerations from a feminist perspective. In W. Vandereycken & G. Noordenbos (Eds.), *The prevention of eating disorders* (pp. 1–23). New York: New York University Press.

Summerbell, C., Waters, E., Edmunds, L., Kelly, S., Brown, Z. T., & Campbell, K. (2005). Interventions for preventing obesity in children. *Cochrane Database Systematic Review, 3,* Article No.: CD001871. doi: 10.1002/14651858.CD001871.pub2

Taylor, J. Y., Caldwell, C. H., Baser, R. E., Faison, N., & Jackson, J. S. (2007). Prevalence of eating disorders among Blacks in the National Survey of American Life. *International Journal of Eating Disorders, 40,* 10–14.

Taylor, C. B., Winzelberg, A. J., & Celio, A. A. (2001). The use of interactive media to prevent eating disorders. In R. H. Striegel-Moore & L. Smolak (Eds.), *Eating disorders: innovative directions in research and practice* (pp. 255–269). Washington, DC: American Psychological Association.

Thompson, D., Baranowski, T., Cullen, K., Watson, K., Liu, Y., Canada, A.,... & Zakeri. I. (2008). Food, fun, and fitness Internet program for girls: Pilot evaluation of an e-Health youth obesity prevention program examining predictors of obesity. *Preventive Medicine, 47,* 494–497.

Tiggemann, M., & Pickering, A. S. (1996). Role of television in adolescent women's body dissatisfaction and drive for thinness. *International Journal of Eating Disorders, 20,* 199–203.

Vander Wal, J. S., & Thomas, N. (2004). Predictors of body image dissatisfaction and disturbed eating attitudes and behaviors in African American and Hispanic girls. *Eating Behaviors, 5,* 291–301.

Vaughn, K., & Fouts, G. (2003). Changes in television and magazine exposure and eating disorder symptomatology. *Sex Roles, 49,* 313–320.

Wade, T. D., Gillespie, N., & Martin, N. G. (2007). A comparison of early family life events amongst monozygotic twin women with lifetime anorexia nervosa, bulimia nervosa, or major depression. *International Journal of Eating Disorders, 40,* 679–686.

Wade T. D., Tiggemann, M., Bulik, C. M., Fairburn, C. G., Wray, N. R., & Martin, N. G. (2008). Shared temperament risk factors for anorexia nervosa: a twin study. *Psychosomatic Medicine, 70,* 239–244. doi: 10.1097/PSY.0b013e31815c40f1

Wang, G., & Dietz, W. H. (2002). Economic burden of obesity in youths aged 6 to 17 years: 1979–1999. *Pediatrics, 109,* e81.

Wardle, J., Sanderson, S., Guthrie, C. A., Rapoport, L., & Plomin, R. (2002). Parental feeding style and the inter-generational transmission of obesity risk. *Obesity Research, 10,* 453–462.

Whitaker, R. C., Wright, J. A., Pepe, M. S., Seidel, K. D., & Deitz, W. H. (1997). Predicting obesity in young adulthood from childhood and parental obesity. *New England Journal of Medicine, 337,* 869–873.

Williams, D. P., Going, S. B., Lohman, T. G., Harsha, D. W., Srinivasan, S. R., Webber, L. S., & Berenson, G. S. (1992). Body fatness and risk for elevated blood pressure, total cholesterol, and serum lipoprotein ratios in children and adolescents. *American Journal of Public Health, 82,* 358–363.

Winzelberg, A. J., Eppstein, D., Eldredge, K. L., Wilfley, D., Dasmahapatra, R., Dev, P., & Taylor, C. B. (2000). Effectiveness of an Internet-based program for reducing risk factors for eating disorders. *Journal of Consulting and Clinical Psychology, 68,* 346–350.

Winzelberg, A. J., Taylor, C. B., Sharpe, T., Eldredge, K. L., Dev, P., & Constantinou, P. S. (1998). Evaluation of a computer-mediated eating disorder intervention program. *International Journal of Eating Disorders, 24,* 339–349.

Young-Hyman, D., Schlundt, D. G., Herman-Wenderoth, L., & Bozylinski, K. (2003). Obesity, appearance, and psychosocial adaptation in young African American children. *Journal of Pediatric Psychology, 28,* 463–472.

Zabinski, M. F., Celio, A. A., Wilfley, D. E., & Taylor, C. B. (2003). Prevention of eating disorders and obesity via the Internet. *Cognitive Behaviour Therapy, 32,* 137–150.

Zabinski, M. F., Wilfley, D. E., Pung, M. A., Winzelberg, A. J., Eldredge, K., & Taylor, C. B. (2001). An interactive Internet-based intervention for women at risk of eating disorders: a pilot study. *International Journal of Eating Disorders, 30,* 129–137.

CHAPTER

16 Prevention of Intimate Partner Violence

M. Meghan Davidson, Jonathan Schwartz, *and* Michael Waldo

Abstract

Intimate partner violence (IPV) affects millions of people in the United States each year (Centers for Disease Control and Prevention, 2010; Tjaden & Thoennes, 2000) with devastating consequences. Prevention efforts aimed at IPV are urgently needed. This chapter will delineate critical definitions, theories of IPV etiology, and IPV prevalence. Examples of primary, secondary, and tertiary prevention interventions aimed at IPV will be provided. Suggestions for future directions of IPV prevention efforts are provided.

Key Words: intimate partner violence, primary prevention, secondary prevention, tertiary prevention, person-focused, environmentally focused

Why Prevention Versus Treatment

Violence against women is both a human rights abuse and a critical public health issue, with considerable consequences for women in terms of physical, mental, sexual, and reproductive health (Campbell, 2002; Heise, 1996; Joachim, 2000; Mayhew & Watts, 2002). Violence against women also impacts economic independence and capacity to work (Centers for Disease Control and Prevention [CDC], 2003). The Bureau of Justice reported that in 2005, IPV resulted in 1,510 deaths. Of these deaths, 78% were females and 22% were males (Bureau of Justice Statistics, 2007). Victims of repeated IPV experience more devastating consequences compared to victims of one-time incidents (Johnson & Leone, 2005). More severe physical repercussions of IPV may result depending on the brutality and frequency of abuse (Campbell et al., 2002; Heise & Garcia-Moreno, 2002; Plichta, 2004; Tjaden & Thoennes, 2000). Physical IPV has been connected to a variety of harmful health outcomes (Breiding, Black, & Ryan, 2008), some of which may directly result from the physical violence (e.g., bruises, broken bones, concussions, knife wounds). Research has documented the consequences of IPV on the endocrine and immune systems (Crofford, 2007; Leserman & Drossman, 2007), including fibromyalgia, irritable bowel syndrome, gynecological disorders, pregnancy difficulties (e.g., low birth weight, perinatal deaths), sexually transmitted diseases, central nervous system disorders, gastrointestinal disorders, and heart and/or circulatory conditions.

In the United States, societal costs of IPV against women in 1995 exceeded $5.8 billion; these costs included approximately $4.1 billion in direct medical and mental health care, and more than $1.7 billion in lost productivity (CDC, 2003). It is important to view these dollar amounts as underestimates, because criminal justice system costs were not included. Max and colleagues (2004) considered these costs in the context of 2003 dollars and determined that IPV costs exceeded $8.3 billion, including $6.2 billion for physical assault, $1.2 billion in the value of lost lives, $460 million for rape, and $461 million for stalking. Regarding work productivity, those who experience severe IPV lose approximately 8 million days of paid work, equivalent to more than 32,000 full-time jobs (CDC, 2003). As well, women whose partners exhibit severe levels of control such as disallowing them to go to work or school, and/or threatening their lives or their children's lives, have a greater likelihood of having been unemployed in the past, having health problems, and having received public assistance (Lloyd & Taluc, 1999).

Dating violence affects adolescents' physical and psychological well-being, and is associated with behavioral consequences for this population, including failure in school, substance abuse, disordered eating, sexual risk behavior, and suicidal ideation (Ackard & Neumark-Sztainer, 2002; Callahan, Tolman, & Saunders, 2003; Silverman et al., 2001). Research has demonstrated that "lesser" forms of dating violence that are nonphysical in nature (e.g., emotional abuse) among adolescents can lead to more severe violence and abuse in later intimate relationships (Murphy & O'Leary, 1989; O'Leary, Malone, & Tyree, 1994). Adolescents who have experienced abusive dating relationships may recapitulate such abuse in future intimate relationships (Smith, White, & Holland, 2003). Espelage and Low provide a more detailed picture of adolescent dating violence in their chapter on adolescent bullying and related violent behaviors in this volume (Chapter 13).

These assertions clearly indicate the need for a preventive approach to IPV, particularly one that intervenes early in people's lives. Lending additional credence to the necessity for IPV prevention efforts is the body of research that has consistently demonstrated the limited effectiveness of treating adults who have perpetrated IPV, as indicated by the high recidivism rates among perpetrators who participate in batterer programs (e.g., Gondolf, 1999; Lehmann & Simmons, 2009; Schwartz & Waldo, 2003b). Relatedly, Schwartz and colleagues (2006) asserted that prevention is necessary because once the cycle of dating violence has been set in motion, it is challenging to intervene effectively.

Prevalence and Risk Factors for Intimate Partner Violence

Prevalence refers to the number or proportion of people in the population suffering from a certain illness or condition at a point in time or during a specified time period. *Incidence* refers to the frequency of development of an illness or condition in a population during a certain period of time (e.g., 1 year). Thus, when discussing the prevalence of IPV, we are referring to the number of IPV victims at a point in time. Conversely, the *incidence* of IPV is describing the number of separate victimizations of partner violence. Lipsky and Caetano (2009) caution researchers regarding the potential inappropriateness of using incidence in IPV research, as IPV consists of ongoing and repeated behaviors, making it difficult to discern if an individual is a "new case."

Each year, approximately 4.8 million women experience physical assaults and rapes by an intimate partner, whereas approximately 2.9 million men are victims of physical IPV (Tjaden & Thoennes, 2000). Whitaker et al. (2006) asserted that more research attention is being given to partner violence in the relationships of teens and young adults, and that this work is revealing that dating violence is highly prevalent in adolescent intimate relationships. National prevalence rates of partner violence among adolescents vary widely in the literature, but have been shown to range from 20% to 46% (Hickman, Jaycox, & Aranoff, 2004; Silverman, Raj, Mucci, & Hathaway, 2001).

Risk Factors

Potential risk factors for IPV include stereotypical and sexist attitudes that support abusive dating behavior (Franchina et al., 2001), peer attitudes (Reitzel-Jaffe & Wolfe, 2001), previous experiences of childhood maltreatment (e.g., Gratz, Paulson, Jakupcak, & Tull, 2009; Henderson, Bartholomew, Trinke, & Kwong, 2005; Ornduff, Kelsey, & O'Leary, 2001; Ehrensaft et al., 2003; White & Widom, 2003; Wolfe, Wekerle, Scott, Straatman, & Grasley, 2004), witnessing partner violence in the home (Capaldi & Clark, 1998; Ehrensaft et al., 2003; O'Keefe, 1997; Riggs & O'Leary, 1996), and substance abuse (e.g., Connoly et al., 2000; Gorman-Smith et al., 2001; Wekerle & Wall, 2002).

Definitions

Scholars working in the field of intimate partner violence have used a myriad of terms to describe the same phenomena. This inconsistency in terminology has played a role in the wide-ranging estimates of IPV prevalence and predictors found in the literature (Lipsky & Caetano, 2009). Consistent definitions are necessary to accurately assess the incidence of IPV, investigate trends over time, and compare across regions/geographies. Additionally, maintaining consistency in terminology assists researchers in evaluating risk and protective factors uniformly, which in turn strengthens prevention and intervention (CDC, 2010). To address this issue, the CDC's

National Center for Injury Prevention and Control has made a concerted effort to limit the broad scope of these terms by developing uniform definitions. According to the CDC (2010), *intimate partner violence* (IPV) "describes physical, sexual, or psychological harm by a current or former partner or spouse. This type of violence can occur among heterosexual or same-sex couples and does not require sexual intimacy." Additionally, IPV varies widely in both frequency and severity, as well as occurs on a continuum (e.g., one hit to chronic battering).

Regarding definitions for the people involved in IPV, *victim* refers to the person targeted for violence or abuse, *perpetrator* refers to the person who inflicts or causes the violence or abuse, and *intimate partners* refers to current or former spouses, partners, dates, boyfriends, or girlfriends (Saltzman, Fanslow, McMahon, & Shelley, 2002). It is important to note that the term "intimate partners" does not require the individuals to be cohabitating nor involved in current sexual activities. Relatedly, although the CDC and other researchers use the terms "victim" and "perpetrator," their utility seems to define people by events or behaviors in which they have engaged, rather than recognizing these individuals as whole people with additional characteristics. Thus, phrases including "people who have experienced IPV" or "people who have engaged in IPV" may be more holistic in nature.

Concerning definitions of violence, specific delineations of physical violence, sexual violence, threats of violence, and psychological/emotional abuse are provided. *Physical violence* is the intentional use of physical force with potential for causing harm, injury, or death (Saltzman et al., 2002); this may include pushing, throwing, slapping, hitting, choking, burning, or use of a weapon. *Sexual violence* is comprised of three categories: (1) use of physical force to compel a person to engage in a sexual act against her/his will (attempted or completed); (2) a sex act with someone unable to consent because of illness, disability, or the influence of alcohol or other drugs, or because of intimidation or pressure (attempted or completed); and (3) abusive sexual contact (Saltzman et al., 2002). *Abusive sexual contact* is the intentional touching—directly or through clothing—of genitalia, anus, groin, breast, inner thigh, or buttocks of a person against her/his will or of a person who is unable to consent (Saltzman et al., 2002).

Threat of physical or sexual violence refers to communicating via words, gestures, or weapons, the intent to cause physical violence, sexual violence, or abusive sexual contact (Saltzman et al., 2002). *Psychological/emotional abuse* involves trauma to the victim caused by acts, threats of acts, or coercive tactics on a repeated basis or with prior threat of or actual physical or sexual violence (Saltzman et al., 2002); this may include humiliating the victim, controlling the victim, isolating the victim from family/friends, and denying the victim access to money or other basic resources. Additionally, *stalking* is often included among this type of IPV, and refers to an individual repeatedly engaging in threatening or harassing behavior such as following a person, placing harassing phone calls, leaving written messages or objects, appearing at a person's home/work (uninvited), or vandalizing a person's property (Tjaden & Thoennes, 1998). Finally, not all victims will perceive certain behaviors as emotionally or psychologically abusive, and other behaviors not included here may prove abusive if perceived in that manner by the victim (Lipsky & Caetano, 2009).

Etiology

Over the past 30 years, a variety of theories have been posited for the etiology of intimate partner violence. These theories include sociocultural perspectives, interpersonal models, and multisystemic models, and they vary markedly in their breadth and empirical support.

Sociocultural theories of intimate partner violence focus on gender roles, male privilege, and patriarchy to explain the development and maintenance of violence against women. Stemming from social role theory, gender roles are rooted in the notion that individuals will act in ways deemed socially appropriate for their gender (Eagley, 1987). Related to IPV, men who demonstrate greater adherence to traditionally masculine gender identities have been shown to have higher rates of sexism, hostility, and abusive behavior toward women (Schwartz & Waldo, 2003a; Wade & Brittan-Powell, 2001). For example, a meta-analysis conducted by Murnen, Wright, and Kaluzny (2002) found that components of masculine ideology such as negative and hostile beliefs, acceptance of aggression, and men's dominance over women were strongly associated with sexual aggression. This greater likelihood of engaging in aggressive behaviors is theorized as stemming from such aggression being viewed as normative for men socioculturally (Woodin & O'Leary, 2009). Indeed, theory and research indicates that patriarchal norms supporting hostility toward women and male dominance are associated with high rates of violence toward women (Kaufman, 1992).

There is also evidence that threats to masculinity increase the likelihood of male perpetrated IPV (Franchina, Eisler, & Moore, 2001). Gender role conflict as originally defined by O'Neil and colleagues (1995) is "a psychological state in which socialized gender roles have negative consequences on the person or others" (pp. 165–166). More specifically, research demonstrates that strict adherence to masculine gender roles has been categorized as a risk factor for heterosexual IPV, especially for men experiencing conflict from attempting to uphold such masculine norms (Moore & Stuart, 2005; Schwartz, Waldo, & Daniels, 2005). Previous research has shown that gender role conflict is associated with perpetration of IPV by heterosexual men and attitudes that accept the maltreatment of women (e.g., Moore & Stuart, 2005; Schwartz & Waldo, 2003a; Schwartz, Waldo, & Daniels, 2005).

Similarly, feminist theorists incorporate gender roles into their etiology of IPV, but extend this to include power, control, and more macrosystemically, male privilege. The Duluth Model was conceived in the early 1980s and was one of the first documented IPV models to focus on issues of power and control (Domestic Abuse Intervention Programs, 2008). Their well-known "Power and Control Wheel" depicts the multifaceted ways in which abusers utilize this power and control through: minimizing, denying, and blaming; using intimidation; coercion and threats; economic abuse; male privilege; using children; isolation; and emotional abuse. Some research has found supportive evidence among male batterers for elements of the Power and Control Wheel (Dutton & Starzomski, 1997; Gondolf, 2007; Kernsmith, 2005). Relatedly, there is evidence that IPV may stem from men feeling less powerful in a relationship, perhaps utilizing violence/abuse to regain power (Brooks, 1998; Leonard & Senchak, 1996; Sagrestano, Heavey, & Christensen, 1999)

Male privilege is offered by feminist theorists as a societal mechanism in which men are in primary control of economic, educational, political, and legal resources. In addition to these environmental levels of power ascribed through male privilege, societal norms also bestow power to men at the individual level through interpersonal relationships (Carli, 1999). Case (2007) defined male privilege as the societally granted, unearned advantages and rights for men. This control of resources legitimizes female subordination within institutions and more widely in society (Dobash & Dobash, 1979). Violence, then, is seen as a method to promulgate women's subordination (Stanko, 2003). Research conducted in the United States and internationally lends some support to the patriarchal view of IPV's etiology. Increased reported rates of physical and sexual assaults have been found in US states with less female equality (Baron & Straus, 1989), and higher rates of sexual assaults have been documented in countries where there is less occupational and educational equality across genders (Yodanis, 2004).

Several limitations to sociocultural theories of IPV have been noted. First, there is limited research that has specifically and empirically examined patriarchy and its relation to IPV, particularly at the macro level (Woodin & O'Leary, 2009). Second, some scholars contend that violence and abuse perpetrated by women in intimate relationships has not been adequately included in the IPV research agenda examining patriarchy, male gender roles, power, and control (Graham-Kevan & Archer, 2005). As well, feminist theories do not apply in the same ways to same-sex couples and may complicate the reactions to abuse (Burke & Follingstad, 1999). A third criticism is that feminist sociocultural theories of patriarchal-based violence cannot explain why all (or even most) men are not abusive (Healey & Smith, 1998), as well as fails to incorporate theoretical underpinnings of abuse in same-sex intimate relationships (Lie, Schilit, Bush, Montague, & Reyes, 1991).

Interpersonal models of partner violence include social learning theory and attachment theory. Bandura's (1977) social learning theory proposed that behaviors and beliefs are transmitted across generations via learning that results from observation of others and direct experiences.

Social learning is posited to be reinforced through operant and classical conditioning. Social learning theory has been extended to the etiology of partner violence such that IPV is hypothesized to be caused by exposure to abuse and violence within the family of origin, including maltreatment toward the child (Capaldi & Clark, 1998; Ehrensaft et al., 2003; O'Keefe, 1997; O'Leary, 1988; Riggs & O'Leary, 1996; White & Widom, 2003; Wolfe, Wekerle, Scott, Straatman, & Grasley, 2004). The modeling component of social learning theory has demonstrated the majority of empirical support; however, cognitive processing factors may also be imperative in conceptualizing IPV from a social learning theoretical framework (Woodin & O'Leary, 2009). A limitation to social learning research regarding IPV etiology is that most studies examining violence within the family of origin and adult IPV employ a retrospective design. Additional longitudinal research is needed to more completely examine the role of social learning on IPV.

Attachment theories of IPV etiology stem from Bowlby's (1980) original work focused on relationship formation with early caregivers. Bowlby asserted that a secure connection to one or more primary caregivers established in infancy and early childhood was imperative for a child to form positive perceptions of self, environments, and all other interpersonal relationships. When experiences with primary caregivers are not secure (i.e., neglectful, unpredictable, abusive), then individuals will develop insecure attachment working models and will in turn become dismissing of or preoccupied by close relationships. Bowlby (1988) posited that these models of attachment are fairly stable across the life span, although new interpersonal experiences can assist in modifying an attachment style. Dutton (1998) extended Bowlby's attachment theory to postulate that insecurely attached individuals may be more likely than their secure counterparts to exhibit controlling or violent behavior to an intimate partner in response to perceived abandonment or rejection. Indeed, research has demonstrated that male perpetrators of IPV and female partners of abusive men are more likely to be insecurely attached (Babcock, Jacobson, Gottman, & Yerington, 2000; Bookwala, 2002; Henderson, Bartholomew, Trinke, & Kwong, 2005; Follingstad, Bradley, Helff, & Laughlin, 2002; Kesner & McKenry, 1998; Mansfield, Addis, Cordova, & Dowd, 2009; Mauricio & Gormley, 2001).

Multisystemic models of partner violence include ecological theory and background-situational theory. Based on the original work of Urie Bronfenbrenner (1977, 1979) and his ecological model comprised of five nested systems (i.e., individual, microsystem, mesosystem, exosystem, and macrosystem), Dutton (1985) offered a theory of IPV that describes determinants in the individual, family, community, and wider culture. Macrosystem influences include the broad, sociocultural context that informs societal norms regarding violence and gender inequalities (Dutton, 1985). Exosystem components in this view of IPV etiology include the connections between culture and families (e.g., economic opportunities, contact between genders, and community integration), whereas microsystem influences include both family and individual characteristics that may increase the likelihood of abuse. Finally, individual or ontogenetic influences include behavioral, emotional, cognitive, and/or physiological experiences that influence the possibility of violence or abuse (Dutton, 1985).

The gendered adolescent interpersonal aggression (GAIA) model (Smith, White, & Moracco, 2009; White, 2009) is a gendered, social-ecological perspective of adolescent dating violence. Adolescent dating violence is contextualized within the broader realms of both friendships and romantic relationships, while also considering the influences of peers, family, and institutions. Gender is conceptualized as socially constructed, and utilizing a person-centered social-ecological model, the GAIA incorporates gender at all levels of ecology as a meta-construct while also including various markers of social identities (e.g., race, class).

Riggs and O'Leary (1989) formulated a background-situational model of IPV comprised of two factors that contribute to partner aggression—background factors and situational factors. Background factors are those that affect an individual's tendency to be aggressive in general, and may include aggression that was modeled by parents, parent-child aggression, prior use of aggression, and certain personality variables. Situational factors bring about the manifestation of partner violence and may include relationship conflict, stress, substance use, and partner aggression. Background factors delineate who might perpetrate partner violence, whereas situational factors elucidate when IPV might occur (Riggs & O'Leary, 1989). Riggs and O'Leary (1996) and Luthra and Gidycz (2006) have tested the background-situational model with undergraduate samples; 60% to 83% of the variance in violence perpetration by men and 30% to 32% of the variance in violence perpetration by women was explained by the model. This model has also been replicated in samples of high school students (Cano, Avery-Leaf, Cascardi, & O'Leary, 1998) and naval recruits (White, Merrill, & Koss, 2001). Riggs and O'Leary's background versus situational categorization of IPV etiology can also be used to categorize preventive interventions such that background interventions focus on preventing or overcoming problems in individuals' personal backgrounds (person-focused) that contribute to IPV, and situational interventions focus on changing social environments (environment-focused) that contribute to IPV.

Prevention Interventions

Romano and Hage (2000) discuss prevention as endeavors focused on one or more of the following: (1) stopping the occurrence of a problem behavior; (2) delaying a problem behavior's onset;

(3) reducing a problem behavior's impact; (4) promoting emotional and physical well-being through bolstering knowledge, attitudes, and behaviors; and (5) endorsing policies at institutional, community, and government levels that advance physical, social, and emotional well-being. Weisz and Black (2009) state that prevention programs aimed at IPV have proliferated throughout the United States during the past 20 years. Specific foci and funding targeting the reduction of IPV has come from a number of private foundations and federal agencies including the Centers for Disease Control, National Institute of Justice, Liz Claiborne Foundation, and Robert Wood Johnson Foundation (Weisz & Black, 2009). However, Wolfe and Jaffe (2003) asserted that domestic violence and sexual assault prevention initiatives and subsequent evaluation research are "in their infancy."

Prevention interventions that are aimed at adolescents are typically striving to provide primary intervention strategies, accessing the intended audience prior to any occurrence of dating violence (Wolfe & Jaffe, 2003). Secondary prevention interventions target specific high-risk groups, aiming to reduce the incidence of IPV by decreasing known or suspected risk factors. Tertiary prevention efforts recognize that IPV has already transpired and aim to minimize the harmful consequences of IPV by identifying perpetrators and victims, controlling the behavior and its effect, support for victims, and treatment and/or punishment of the perpetrator (Wolfe & Jaffe, 2003). A social justice oriented view of prevention encompasses interventions aimed at the individual level and the multiple environmental contexts containing individuals (Kenny & Hage, 2009). Person-focused and environment-focused prevention programs will be reviewed.

Primary Prevention

The traditional definition of primary prevention is to prevent a problem before it occurs (Caplan, 1964; Romano & Hage, 2000). Primary prevention with a person-centered focus attempts to prevent problems at the individual level. In contrast, primary prevention with an environmental focus attempts to prevent problems by creating contextual change. For example, person-centered primary prevention might attempt to create awareness of the signs of IPV so individuals can avoid involvement in it. On the other hand, environmentally focused primary prevention might attempt to impact cultural norms that oppress women. It is notable that there is often overlap between person-centered and environmental prevention interventions, as some interventions attempt to impact both the individual and the environment. It is important to note that the major theories of IPV explicated above (e.g., gender socialization, attachment) note the fact that the roots of IPV develop at a young age, supporting the need for early primary prevention. In this section, examples of person-centered and environmentally focused primary prevention intervention will be described.

PERSON-FOCUSED PRIMARY PREVENTION.

The majority of person-focused primary prevention interventions for IPV have targeted teenage and young adult men and women. The rationale for targeting adolescent populations is both the prevalence of dating violence at this age (Hickman, Jaycox, & Aranoff, 2004) and the knowledge that IPV starting at this age can become more severe in adulthood (O'Leary, Malone, & Tyree, 1994). The majority of person-focused primary prevention interventions utilize feminist, cognitive-behavioral, and education/awareness approaches. There are a number of person-focused interventions that do not specify a theoretical model and do not conduct meaningful evaluation (Whitaker et al., 2006). The examples provided did specify a theoretical model and provided evidence of their success.

Foshee and colleagues (1996) created the Safe Dates curriculum to prevent dating violence in the schools. The program has a primary prevention and a secondary prevention component. Similar to many person-focused primary prevention programs, Safe Dates comprises a curriculum that intends to increase individuals' knowledge about dating violence. This curriculum addresses gender roles and norms and teaches conflict resolution skills. In addition, Safe Dates attempts to change the culture of the school by including a theater production performed by students and a poster campaign/contest. Safe Dates has strong evidence indicating it changes attitudes about dating violence and prevents dating violence at 1-year and 4-year follow-ups (Foshee et al., 2004). Safe Dates is limited by that fact that it has been normed on a primarily White population (Whitiker et al., 2006), and although it has been adopted widely, there is a lack of research on its utility by other researchers and practitioners and in different contexts.

Schwartz, Magee, Griffin, and Dupuis (2004) conducted a unique person-focused primary prevention intervention with college students. Participants were selected at random out of a large pool who volunteered for a counseling experience for extra credit. Based on feminist and cognitive-behavioral models, the intervention utilized a group approach to increase awareness of issues that contribute to IPV and to increase skills to avoid involvement in IPV. In a group format, participants were able to explore and challenge traditional gender roles and learn and practice communication and anger management skills. Utilizing a group approach, the curriculum was designed to integrate the stages of change (Prochaska & DiClemente, 1982) and stages of group (Tuckman & Jensen, 1977) to create a group environment that would lead toward change. Overall, as compared to a control group that did not receive any intervention, the experimental group had less acceptance of traditional gender roles, increased ability to express emotions, increased management skills, and an increase in healthy assertiveness. Although the findings of this intervention were promising, it does have limitations. There was no long-term follow-up, so it is unclear if the impact was lasting. The control group was not given an intervention, so the comparison was not as meaningful. Also, as a person-focused intervention, no environmental changes were made. Participants may have learned new skills, but were confronted by the same pressures and attitudes after the intervention.

ENVIRONMENTALLY FOCUSED PRIMARY PREVENTION.

There is a lack of environmentally focused primary prevention programs in general, and with regard to IPV specifically (Kenny & Hage, 2009; Schwartz & Lindley, 2009). Although there has been noted success changing knowledge and attitudes concerning dating violence (Ting, 2009), it is more difficult to impact a culture that perpetuates dating violence (Schwartz et al., 2004). Research suggests that ecologically focused prevention interventions are more successful (Hage et al., 2007), but IPV prevention interventions that attempt to change the environment are still rare (Kenny & Hage). This is particularly true for primary prevention, as advocacy efforts in the community often target groups that have already been impacted by IPV. The following are examples of primary prevention programs that have environmentally focused components.

A few programs that attempt to prevent dating violence also attempt to create change in the culture that perpetuates it (Davis & Liddell, 2002). Safe Dates is an example of a program that, although primarily focused on individual change, attempts to change the school culture through theater performances and posters (Foshee et al., 1996). There are also attempts to impact the cultural messages that oppress women and support IPV. Futures Without Violence (FWV, 2012) attempts to change attitudes about violence against women and increase social involvement in equalizing gender disparities through widespread print and media campaigns. Research into the effectiveness of public education has shown that campaigns are most effective when they focus on achieving social mobilization through the recruitment, training, and empowerment of community leaders, and when energy is directed toward sensitizing the news media to the issues (Wray, 2006). The FVPF worked to achieve increased exposure in their messages by making their publications accessible to local agencies and media directors.

It is also important to note that primary prevention approaches that use a feminist approach (Jaffe et al., 1992) often encourage participants to be activists in their community. Person-focused primary prevention can lead to changes in the environment through creating community members who are change agents. There is a need to increase the development of environmentally focused primary prevention programs that can be empirically tested.

Secondary Prevention

As indicated previously, secondary prevention interventions aim to reduce the incidence of IPV by targeting specific high-risk groups. This section will describe a number of secondary IPV prevention programs.

PERSON-FOCUSED SECONDARY PREVENTION.

Wolfe and colleagues (1996) developed the Youth Relationships Project (YRP), an adolescent-focused program that aims to prevent abusive behavior as well as promote healthy, nonviolent relationships. This secondary prevention program is specifically focused on youth who are at risk for IPV due to their history of maltreatment. This is a person-focused prevention program that utilizes a proactive, health-promotion approach that focuses on enhancing relational competencies, assisting youth in decision making, and teaching nonviolent communication skills to use with current and future intimate partners. The YRP focuses on "positive alternatives to aggression based interpersonal problem-solving and gender-based role expectations" (Wolfe et al., 2003, p. 282). The tripartite curriculum, based in learning approaches as well as feminist theory, emphasizes awareness of power dynamics and abuse in intimate relationships, skill development, and social action (Wolfe et al., 1996). The YRP program is delivered in a group format with approximately 6–10 participants per group. Sessions are 2 hours in length and are cofacilitated by a woman and a man, enabling positive modeling of relationship skills including assertiveness and sharing of power. The program is interactive, utilizing a plethora of learning strategies, including videos, behavioral rehearsal, guest speakers, visits to community agencies, and a community social action project. An intervention manual was created by Wolfe and colleagues (1996) so that YRP can be implemented in a standardized manner.

Research has shown the YRP program to yield beneficial effects. Using an experimental design with random assignment to intervention and control conditions, Wolfe et al. (2003) studied adolescents aged 14–16 years who were considered at risk for IPV due to their history of maltreatment. Groups were facilitated at locations in the community (e.g., youth centers), and repeated follow-up measures were collected. Results of the study showed that YRP intervention participants demonstrated decreasing severity and frequency of abuse trajectories compared with participants in the control condition (Wolfe et al., 2003). Adolescents in both the intervention and control conditions showed decreases in both abuse perpetration and victimization over time; however, the participants in the YRP intervention condition decreased at a faster rate compared to those in the control condition. Finally, symptoms of emotional distress decreased among all participants, yet participants in the YRP program demonstrated a more dramatic reduction. This study conducted by Wolfe and colleagues (2003) utilized a rigorous research design, included longitudinal follow-up, and employed growth modeling to incorporate developmental trajectories rather than pictures at one point in time, thus providing strong evidence for the efficacy of the Youth Relationships Project.

PERSON-FOCUSED AND ENVIRONMENTALLY FOCUSED SECONDARY PREVENTION.

Katz (1995) created a secondary prevention intervention that is both person-focused and environmentally focused in scope. The Mentors in Violence Prevention (MVP) program endeavors to decrease men's violence against women by engaging college athletes to both confront and redefine conventional male norms that associate masculinity with power and authority over women. MVP participants are called on to utilize their status among both their peers on campus and younger adolescents in middle and high school to advance more positive and egalitarian attitudes about and behaviors toward women. As stated by Katz (1995), the most critical characteristic of the MVP program is the creation of "a structured opportunity for men to talk with each other about masculinity—particularly as it relates to violence against women" (p. 165). Additionally, the MVP program is predicated on the notion that through publicly renouncing traditional masculinity based in sexism and dominance, male student-athletes can help to counter rape-supportive and battering-supportive beliefs and attitudes. That is, due to their privileged social location, male athletes have an increased credibility among both male peers and younger males. The attitudes of male athletes regarding gender are believed to be highly influential because these men are viewed as successful examples of traditional masculinity.

MVP is a three-session program provided to individual college athletic teams, typically scheduled once per month either before or after the team's season. Each session is 90 minutes in length, and approximately half of the sessions are held in the team's locker room, a space that is comfortable and familiar for participants. Prior to meeting with individual teams, the college or university's athletic director organizes a meeting for the MVP facilitators to provide presentations to the entire team's coaching staff. These presentations allow the facilitators to describe the MVP program, lead the coaches through a typical session, and get support from the coaching staff. Regarding teams that are selected for the MVP program, it is suggested to work with high-profile men's teams including football, basketball, baseball, lacrosse, and hockey.

The curriculum developed for the program is the MVP Playbook, which is comprised of various scenarios portraying potential and actual assaults in residence halls and parties. The scenarios range from overheard sexist comments to threats of physical harm and date rape. Some of the scenarios depict the participants as potential individuals who participate in IPV and/or sexual assault, whereas the majority of situations utilize participants as bystanders. The MVP program is designed to be highly interactive, and participants are encouraged to share experiences they have had in high school and/or college. Additionally, the "train of thought" model developed by Slaby (1994) provides the participants' with an opportunity to better understand the behaviors of people who have experienced IPV or sexual assault, people who have engaged in IPV or sexual assault, and those who have been bystanders. The predominant message conveyed through the discussions of the scenarios is that men must play a pivotal role in decreasing violence against women. Moreover, the MVP program advocates that violence against women is a *men's* issue, and that men must provide leadership to change behavior. These three sessions of the MVP program highlight the person-focused preventive aims.

The call for these men to take on leadership roles within their campus and wider community regarding IPV and sexual assault related attitudes and behaviors is an effort toward environmentally focused prevention. To that end, a fourth session of the MVP program is available for select student-athletes who have expressed a desire to become mentors and speak with younger adolescents about men's violence against women. A set of guidelines for selecting appropriate mentors has been developed, as has a training program. Accompanied by a staff member from the MVP program, these athlete-mentors then meet with classes and athletic teams at both middle and high schools to talk with them about violence against women. This approach also combines person-focused and environmentally focused prevention efforts as it is aimed at reaching the individual as well as creating sociocultural change.

With some similarities to the MVP program, Luoluo Hong (2000) developed Men Against Violence (MAV), a university-based peer education organization that aims to engage men in activism and social change regarding conceptions of masculinity and gender roles, including violence against women. MAV began at Louisiana State University in 1995 as a service organization devoted to opposing and preventing a variety of violence-related activities including stalking, IPV, sexual assault, hate crimes, and hazing; since this time, many universities have created "brother" chapters of MAV. As described by Hong (2000), the organization utilizes a community action–based peer education model as articulated by Fabiano (1994), and is sponsored by the university health center with a health educator serving as the advisor. An elected executive board of undergraduate and graduate students manages the organization with input from an advisory board comprised of faculty, staff, and alumni. Any student is eligible for membership in MAV, whereas faculty, staff, and graduates are welcome to join as alumni members.

The explicit purpose of MAV is to decrease both the frequency and severity of violence among all members of the campus community, with an express emphasis on men's responsibility in this mission. Four primary activities make up the ACES activities in which MAV members participate: (1) awareness, (2) community action, (3) education, and (4) support. The awareness component encompasses media campaigns to the campus and wider community as well as a campuswide newsletter. Community action activities include various service projects, political activism, and programming for students in the areas of sexism, masculinity, and violence. Education efforts are focused on the campus community including university classes, fraternities, and residence halls, but also engage K-12 schools. Support activities are aimed at both people who have experienced violence and people who have engaged in violence. In terms of preparation for members, MAV organizes and hosts training conferences each semester to teach the relevant skills to conduct peer education and engage in the ACES activities.

Overall, MAV is a secondary prevention program that combines person-focused prevention and environmentally focused prevention. It is person-focused as the individuals involved as members of MAV are impacted by their participation in the organization, as are the individuals who attend their educational programs. However, MAV is also environmentally focused as it is ultimately concerned with influencing group norms, both culturally and among peer-reference groups. MAV works to "generate shared norms of nonviolence and communication" (Hong, 2000, p. 270).

It is important to note that to date, the Mentors in Violence Prevention (MVP) program and Men Against Violence (MAV) have not been adequately evaluated regarding effectiveness.

Tertiary Prevention

As indicated above, tertiary prevention focuses on minimizing the harmful consequences of IPV that has occurred, or is occurring, by identifying/controlling/stopping violent behavior, supporting victims, and treating and/or punishing perpetrators (Wolfe & Jaffe, 2003). Tertiary prevention may be the most prevalent form of IPV prevention. There are over 2,000 community-based programs focused on protecting and supporting victims of IPV in the United States by providing emergency shelter to approximately 300,000 women and children each year (National Coalition Against Domestic Violence, 2010), and at least 1,500 programs focused on treating perpetrators (Adams, 2003). Although tertiary prevention efforts are focused on addressing violence that has already occurred, these endeavors can also be seen as having both secondary and primary prevention effects (Waldo & Schwartz, 2008). For example, the intent of perpetrator treatment programs is to decrease the likelihood that perpetrators will engage in violence in the future. This intent is in line with the goals of secondary prevention, targeting high-risk groups and reducing future incidents of IPV. Also, if perpetrators are helped to stop engaging in IPV, they are less likely to model violent behavior in their future relationships, potentially resulting in primary prevention effects (stopping violence prior to it occurring) for their children.

Like primary and secondary prevention, tertiary IPV prevention interventions may be person-focused or environmentally focused. In almost all cases they impact both the environment and individuals. Also, tertiary prevention interventions may be guided by sociocultural, interpersonal, or multisystemic models. Most interventions incorporate knowledge from each of these models. Examples of sociocultural, interpersonal, and multisystemic tertiary IPV preventive interventions will be offered below, highlighting how they impact both environments and individuals.

Perhaps the clearest and most impactful tertiary IPV prevention intervention focused on the social environment has been the enactment of laws that forbid domestic violence (Bohmer, Brandt, Bronson, & Hartnett, 2002). Arising within the context of a growing women's movement, a history of ignoring (at best) and condoning (at worst) domestic abuse began to be reversed in the 1970s (Dobash & Dobash, 1992). Enactment of laws specifically targeting those who engage in domestic violence changed the social environment from one in which IPV flourished to one in which it is discouraged (Dobash & Dobash, 1992). Enforcement of these laws through the arrest and punishment of offenders has been shown to have a decided impact on IPV incidents (Miller, 2003). Laws enabling IPV victims to place a restraining order on people who have abused them change the social environment from one that promoted victimization to one that empowers people to protect themselves (Roberts & Kurst-Swanger, 2002a). There is evidence that protective orders (i.e., restraining orders) have had a significant impact on the reoccurrence of abuse (Carlson, Harris, & Holden, 1999).

Laws that punish abuse, and in turn empower victims, clearly impact the social environment and represent clear examples of sociocultural-based interventions. The laws seek to correct the social injustice that is inherent in one group having illegitimate power over another. Laws addressing IPV can also be seen having impacts on individuals. Recognizing that committing IPV is a crime can impact the propensity for an individual to engage in abuse. Knowing legal recourses are available for protection can impact individuals who have been abused. Both impacts can be understood through interpersonal models. The laws inhibit the aggressive behavior of those who are inclined to abuse, and reinforce self-protective behavior among those who have been abused.

The establishment of shelters for abuse victims represents another environmentally focused tertiary IPV prevention effort that emerged in the 1970s (Walker, 1984). The availability of shelters allows victims to change their social environments from ones in which they live in danger of abuse, to ones where they are safe and receive emotional support and assistance from other shelter residents and staff (Berk, Newton, & Berk, 1986). The positive impact shelters have on individuals can also be understood from an interpersonal perspective. The protection and support abuse victims experience in shelters has been shown to enhance their physical and emotional health (Tutty, Weaver, & Rothery, 1999). In fact, the positive effects of shelters might best be described as multisystemic (Johnson, & Zlotnick, 2009). Shelters impact individuals, increasing their confidence. They impact families by providing services to parents and children (Johnson & Zlotnick, 2009). They impact communities through the tangible symbol they provide both of the existence of IPV and of a compassionate response to it (Walker, 2004). And, they impact society through their social advocacy and political action that raise awareness and promote response to IPV (Walker, 2004).

Despite their many potential benefits, shelters for victims are seen by some as a short-sighted and misfocused response to IPV. It is considered unjust that the perpetrators of abuse remain in their homes and communities, while their victims must relocate to shelters (Traicoff, 1982). Also, sheltering of victims is seen as not impacting the cause of the problem, the perpetrator (Waldo, 1987). Shelter staffs have noted that many abused people return to relationships that continue to be abusive (Hamberger & Hastings, 1991), and people who have perpetrated abuse in one relationship are likely to do so in others (Babcock et al., 2000).

Incarceration of perpetrators is an environmentally focused tertiary prevention intervention in that it frees the community of at least some potential sources of violence (Roberts & Kurst-Swanger, 2002a; 2002b). Incarceration also can be seen as a person-focused interpersonal intervention, providing those who have engaged in IPV an opportunity to reflect on their abusive behavior and motivation to stop. However, like sheltering victims, incarceration of perpetrators has been criticized as short-sighted and misfocused. Persons who are incarcerated for IPV are released eventually, and are prone to recidivism (Babcock & Steiner, 1999). A multisystemic perspective on punishment suggests a number of potential deficits. At an individual level, use of force to punish perpetrators may reinforce their use of force to punish their partners (Waldo, 1987). At the family level, removal of IPV perpetrating partners who contribute income and child care can pose an additional hardship on their families. In fact, some IPV victims would rather tolerate the abuse than lose contact with and support from the abuser. Incarceration also carries a high financial cost for communities and society as a whole (Gelles, 1977).

Recognition of the limits of sheltering victims and incarcerating perpetrators has led to the development of counseling interventions for tertiary prevention of IPV (Walker, 2009). Counseling interventions for both victims and perpetrators are typically focused on individual change, offered in group formats, and guided by either sociocultural or interpersonal models. The primary sociocultural counseling model for tertiary prevention of IPV is the Duluth Domestic Abuse Intervention Project (DAIP; Feder & Wilson, 2005). The DAIP takes the feminist perspective that IPV is a mechanism for exercising power and control in relationships (Adams, 1989). It views IPV as one extrusion of patriarchal societal values that sanction men's power and control over women (Pence & Paymar, 1993). The DAIP employs psychoeducational techniques in a group format to make both victims and perpetrators aware of power and control dynamics in relationships (Pence & Paymar, 1993). Two critical components of the psychoeducational curriculum are the Power and Control Wheel and Equality Wheel. The Power and Control Wheel describes tactics for dominating a partner in an intimate relationship, including using coercion, threats, intimidation, emotional abuse, isolation, minimizing, denying, blaming, children, male privilege, and economic abuse. The Power and Control Wheel is contrasted with the Equality Wheel, which encourages using negotiation, fairness, nonthreatening behavior, respect, trust, support, honesty, accountability, responsible parenting, shared responsibility, and economic partnerships to develop egalitarian relationships. "The curriculum is designed to challenge a lifelong pattern of thinking, rationalizing, and acting that leads to violence and other forms of abuse" (Pence & Paymar, 1993, p. 8).

The DAIP is frequently used with men who have been court-ordered to participate in treatment for IPV (Feder & Wilson, 2005; Hamel & Nicholls, 2007). However, evaluative research on the DAIP suggests it has a high dropout rate (40% to 60%) for court-mandated participants (Buttell & Carney, 2002), and has a limited effect on the attitudes, behavior (Jackson, Feder, David, Maxwell, & Bruce, 2003), and recidivism of those perpetrators who remain in treatment. Critics of the DAIP suggest it is too confrontational (Dutton, 2006), and narrowly focused (Walker, 2009).

Counseling interventions based on interpersonal models have focused on developing self-esteem, cognitive-behavioral approaches to anger management, and improving communication and conflict resolution skills. They examine historical and immediate antecedents to abuse, and explore alternative responses. Examples of work with perpetrators include the EMERGE Model, which began in Boston (Rosenbaum & Leisring, 2002), and the AMEND Model from Denver (Healey, Smith, & O'Sullivan, 1988). A common feature of these and other similar programs is to help perpetrators recognize their abusive behavior, learn new approaches to managing their emotions, and develop relationships that are not abusive. Like the sociocultural approaches, interpersonally based approaches to tertiary prevention have shown mixed results, including disappointing effects on recidivism rates among male batterers (Lohr, Hamberger, Witte, & Parker, 2006). Criticisms of interpersonal models for tertiary prevention counseling have included their focus on personal development (as opposed to correcting societal inequities), cognition (as opposed to affect), and individual change (as opposed to changing relationships) (Dutton, 1994; Hamel & Nicholls, 2007).

Multisystemic models for tertiary prevention of IPV include family systems counseling approaches. These approaches take into account individual and family unit contributions to dysfunctional interactions that result in IPV (Healey, Smith, & O'Sullivan, 1998). Counseling can involve individuals, couples, and entire families, and focuses on communication and conflict resolution skills (Giles-Sims, 1983). Although there are case study reports suggesting the effectiveness of multisystemic approaches (e.g., couples group counseling) (Guerney, Waldo, & Firstone, 1987), there is no systematic research demonstrating that this approach is more effective than approaches based on the sociocultural or interpersonal models. Criticisms of multisystemic models focus on their alleged failure to place blame solely on perpetrators by including victims in the conceptualization and treatment of IPV, and that they may put victims at risk by encouraging them to address relationship concerns with perpetrators without guaranteeing that victims will be protected from perpetrators' retribution outside the counseling session (Pence & Paymar, 1993).

Although tertiary preventive interventions based on sociocultural, interpersonal, and multisystemic models differ in their assumptions and aims, they share many characteristics and intended effects. All three focus on helping individuals change, and by helping those individuals change put them in a position to begin changing social environments. All three employ group techniques, and are likely to offer participants benefits from therapeutic factors that are inherent in supportive group interaction (Schwartz & Waldo, 2003). And, all three have limited empirical evidence demonstrating their efficacy.

Conclusions and Future Directions

Although IPV prevention demonstrates great promise, a number of limitations exist in the field currently. Weisz and Black (2009) assert that there are few published empirical evaluations of IPV prevention interventions for adolescents, stating that the majority of the literature in this area is focused on the college student population. They also note that college prevention interventions only provide suggestions of strategies that may prove beneficial with younger populations as there exist significant developmental differences between middle or high school students and college students (Weisz & Black, 2009). Another significant obstacle in IPV prevention intervention work is addressing actual abusive behavior. Most prevention programs address knowledge and attitudes regarding IPV, although it is unclear if changes in attitudes and knowledge leads to behavioral changes. This limitation has been duly noted in the literature (Hickman et al., 2004; Schewe & Bennett, 2002; Whitaker et al., 2006; Wolfe & Jaffe, 2003). It is recognized, however, that prevention programs have an inherent difficulty in measuring the extent to which the target group avoided dangerous behaviors as a result of the intervention (Weisz & Black, 2009). Whitaker et al. (2006) conducted an analysis of 11 primary prevention interventions and noted that the quality of the research examining the interventions was low, as they (1) lacked behavioral measures, (2) implemented short follow-up periods, (3) omitted retention rates or had high attrition, and (4) failed to attend to fidelity of the intervention.

An additional limitation in the IPV prevention literature is work focused on same-sex IPV, and this is reflective of the negligible research that exists regarding same-sex IPV in general (Duke & Davidson, 2009; Hassouneh & Glass, 2008; McClennen, 2005; McKenry, Serovich, Mason, & Mosack, 2006; National Coalition of Anti-Violence Programs [NCAVP], 2005; Stark, 2007; West, 2002). Additionally, fewer empirical articles focus on same-sex IPV among homosexual males (Seelau et al., 2003). Intimate partner abuse occurs at a similar and perhaps higher frequency among same-sex couples (Balsam, 2001; Greenwood et al., 2002; McKenry et al., 2006, NCAVP, 2005; Poorman, 2001; Seelau, Seelau, & Poorman, 2003; The Network La Red, 2004); however, there are distinctive factors that need to be considered when working with the lesbian, gay, and bisexual population (e.g., Turner, 2004). Examples of cultural components that need to be considered when working in the area of same-sex IPV include myths such as a lesbian utopia, hegemonic masculinity between male partners, and mutual battering, as well as concerns specific to the lesbian, gay, and bisexual community including outing, homophobia, internalized oppression, community ties, and revictimization (see Duke & Davidson, 2009). Thus, prevention efforts aimed at eradicating and reducing same-sex IPV are critically needed and warrant particular focus that may be similar to, and different from, heterosexual IPV prevention.

In turning our attention to future directions in IPV prevention, an "ideal" program was put forth by Weisz and Black (2009). These scholars conducted 61 interviews of dating violence and sexual assault prevention program providers from across the country, and provided thoughts on an "ideal" youth-focused prevention program gleaned from their analysis of these interviews. Parameters of this ideal program include: (1) combining IPV and sexual assault topics given scarcity of resources; (2) providing information across multiple sessions (rather than a one-shot program); (3) including *both* single—and mixed-gender sessions with careful attention to not blame either gender; (4) utilizing a theoretical framework and articulating causes of IPV/SA; (5) incorporating peer education and/or youth leadership elements; (6) awareness and sensitivity to cultural differences and sexual orientation; (7) interactive components such as discussion, role plays, and/or other experiential exercises; (8) a balance of a manualized guide to the program and addressing adolescent questions and interests; (9) opportunities to talk to presenters privately so that public disclosure is avoided; (10) addressing teachers and parents; (11) sufficient pay for educators/program providers' (particularly to retain experienced providers); and (12) evaluation of the program (Weisz & Black, 2009). Whitaker et al. (2006) provide recommendations following their critical review of IPV primary prevention interventions. These authors found only one program designed with racial and/or cultural specificity. Similar to Weisz and Black's (2009) recommendations, Whitaker et al. urge the development of future prevention interventions that consider, examine, and include specific cultural contexts.

Additionally, Whitaker et al. found a preponderance of universal primary prevention interventions and suggested that greater attention needs to be given to selective interventions (i.e., secondary interventions), that is, those programs targeting specific at-risk populations and/or environments. These authors also note the limitations of providing school-based prevention interventions, particularly emphasizing the ways in which some students may not be accessible by schools, and that some students do not engage in school-based activities. Thus, alternative venues such as community-based organizations, faith-based groups, families, and media outlets may provide greater access to a wide range of adolescents (and older individuals) for prevention interventions (Whitaker et al., 2006). Finally, greater attention to rigorous program evaluation is critical to advancing prevention efforts aimed at reducing and eradicating IPV.

Final Thoughts

Efforts to prevent IPV have seen remarkable progress in the last century (Roberts, 2002). IPV by men against women has moved from being ignored and even condoned, to being condemned. Laws have been passed to protect victims and punish perpetrators, and there is an increasing emphasis on enforcing these laws. The focus on protecting and helping victims has expanded to include helping perpetrators change (Walker, 2009). There has been a trend toward movement beyond tertiary preventive services focused on individual victims and perpetrators, to secondary and primary prevention interventions that impact individuals and social environments.

Yet, there is much left to do. For example, an immediate course of action for prevention of IPV is to refine and expand on previous successes. Culturally specific (e.g., sexual orientation, race, ethnicity) IPV interventions are sorely needed. As well, the passing, publicizing, and enforcing of laws against abuse is likely to further reduce IPV. Also, expanding services to victims and perpetrators could not only help these individuals but also enable them to help reduce IPV in future generations by interrupting the intergenerational transmission of family violence (Doumas, Margolin, & John, 1994). Evaluative research is needed to identify the most effective aspects of sociocultural, interpersonal, and multisystemic approaches to counseling victims and perpetrators.

Perhaps the most exciting opportunities for expanding IPV prevention lie in the domains of primary and secondary prevention, impacting both individuals and social environments. Promoting prevention programs that educate and create awareness, but also impact the culture and institutional factors that perpetuate intimate violence are needed.

References

Ackard, D. M., & Neumark-Sztainer, D. (2002). Date violence and date rape among adolescents: Associations with disordered eating behaviors and psychological health. *Child Abuse and Neglect, 26,* 455–473.

Adams, D. A. (1989). Feminist-based interventions for battering. In L. P. Caesar & L. K. Hamberg (Eds.), *Treating men who batter* (pp. 3–23). New York, NY: Springer.

Adams, D. A. (2003). Certified batterer intervention programs: History, philosophies, techniques, collaborations, innovations and challenges. *Clinics in Family Practice, 5*(1), 159–176

Babcock, J. C., Green, C. E., & Robie, C. (2004). Does batterers' treatment work? A meta-analytic review of domestic violence treatment. *Clinical Psychology Review, 23,* 1023–1053. doi:10.1016/j.cpr.2002.07.001

Babcock, J. C., Jacobson, N. S., Gottman, J. M., & Yerington, T. P. (2000). Attachment, emotional regulation, and the function of marital violence: Differences between secure, preoccupied, and dismissing violent and nonviolent husbands. *Journal of Family Violence, 15,* 391–409.

Babcock, J., & Steiner, R. (1999). The relationship between treatment, incarceration, and recidivism of battering: A program evaluation of Seattle's coordinated community response to domestic violence. *Journal of Family Psychology, 13*(1), 46–59.

Balsam, K. F. (2001). Nowhere to hide: Lesbian battering, homophobia, and minority stress. In E. Kaschak (Ed.) *Intimate betrayal: Intimate partner abuse in lesbian relationships* (pp. 25–37). New York: Haworth Press.

Bandura, A. (1977). *Social learning theory.* New York: General Learning Press.

Baron, L., & Straus, M. A. (1989). *Four theories of rape in American society: A state-level analysis.* New Haven, CT: Yale University Press.

Berk, R. A., Newton, P. J., & Berk, S. F. (1986). What a difference a day makes: An empirical study of the impact of shelters for battered women. *Journal of Marriage and the Family, 48,* 481–490.

Bohmer, C., Brandt, J., Bronson, D., & Hartnett, H. (2002). Domestic violence law reforms: Reactions from the trenches. *Journal of Sociology and Social Welfare, 29*(3), 71–87.

Bookwala, J. (2002). The role of own and perceived partner attachment in relationship aggression. *Journal of Interpersonal Violence, 17,* 84–100.

Bowlby, J. (1980). *Attachment and loss.* New York: Basic Books.

Bowlby, J. (1988). *A secure base: Parent-child attachment and healthy human development.* London: Routledge.

Breiding, M. J., Black, M. C., & Ryan, G. W. (2008). Chronic disease and health risk behaviors associated with intimate partner violence—18 U.S. states/territories, 2005. *Annals of Epidemiology, 18,* 538–544.

Bronfenbrenner, U. (1977). Toward an experimental ecological of human development. *American Psychologist, 32*(7), 513–531. doi:10.1037/0003–066X.32.7.513

Bronfenbrenner, U. (1979). *The ecology of human development: Experiments by nature and design.* Cambridge, MA: Harvard University Press.

Brooks, G. R. (1998). *A new psychotherapy for traditional men.* San Francisco, CA: Jossey-Bass.

Bureau of Justice Statistics (2007). *Homicide trends in the U.S.: Intimate homicide.* Retrieved November 24, 2010, from http://bjs.ojp.usdoj.gov/content/homicide/intimates.cfm

Burke, L. K., & Follingstad, D. R. (1999). Violence in lesbian and gay relationships: Theory, prevalence, and correlational factors. *Clinical Psychology Review, 19,* 487–512.

Buttell, F. P., & Carney, M. M. (2002). Psychological and demographic predictors of attrition among batterers court ordered into treatment. *Social Work Research, 26,* 31–41.

Callahan, M. R., Tolman, R. M., & Saunders, D. G. (2003). Adolescent dating violence victimization and psychological well-being. *Journal of Adolescent Research, 18,* 664–681.

Campbell, J. (2002). The health consequences of intimate partner violence. *Lancet, 359,* 1509–1514.

Campbell, J. C., Jones, A. S., Dienemann, J., Kub, J., Schollenberger, J., O'Campo, P.,... Wynne, C. (2002). Intimate partner violence and physical health consequences. *Archives of Internal Medicine, 162,* 1157–1163.

Cano, A., Avery-Leaf, S., Cascardi, M., & O'Leary, K. D. (1998). Dating violence in two high school samples: Discriminating variables. *Journal of Primary Prevention, 18,* 431–446.

Capaldi, D. M., & Clark, S. (1998). Prospective family predictors of aggression toward female partners for at-risk men. *Developmental Psychology, 34,* 1175–1188.

Caplan, G. (1964). *Principles of preventive psychiatry.* New York: Basic Books.

Carli, L. L. (1999). Gender, interpersonal power, and social influence. *Journal of Social Issues, 55,* 81–99.

Carlson, M. J., Harris, S. D., & Holden, G. W. (1999). Protective orders and domestic violence: Risk factors for re-abuse. *Journal of Family Violence, 4,* 205–226.

Case, K. A. (2007). Raising male privilege awareness and reducing sexism: An evaluation of diversity courses. *Psychology of Women Quarterly, 31,* 426–435.

Centers for Disease Control and Prevention (CDC). (2003). *Costs of intimate partner violence against women in the United States.* Atlanta, GA: CDC, National Center for Injury Prevention and Control.

Centers for Disease Control and Prevention, National Center for Injury Prevention and Control, Division of Violence Prevention. (2010, September). Injury prevention & control: Violence prevention. Retrieved November 3, 2010 from http://www.cdc.gov/violenceprevention/intimatepartnerviolence/definitions.html

Connoly J., Pepler, D., Craig, W., & Taradash, A. (2000). Dating experiences of bullies in early adolescence. *Child Maltreatment, 5,* 299–310.

Crofford, L. J. (2007). Violence, stress, and somatic syndromes. *Trauma, Violence, and Abuse, 8,* 299–313.

Davis, T. L., & Liddell, D. L. (2002). Getting inside the house: The effectiveness of a rape prevention program for college fraternity men. *Journal of College Student Development, 43,* 35–50.

Dobash, R. E., & Dobash, R. (1979). *Violence against wives: A case against the patriarchy.* New York: Free Press.

Dobash, R. E., & Dobash, R. (1992). *Women, violence and social change.* London: Routledge.

Doumas, D., Margolin, G., & John, R. (1994). The intergenerational transmission of aggression across three generations. *Journal of Family Violence, 9,* 157–175.

Domestic Abuse Intervention Programs (2008). History of the Duluth model. Retrieved November 3, 2010, from http://www.theduluthmodel.org/history.php

Duke, A., & Davidson, M. M. (2009). Same-sex intimate partner violence: Lesbian, gay, and bisexual affirmative outreach and advocacy. *Journal of Aggression, Maltreatment, and Trauma, 18,* 795–816.

Dutton, D. G. (1985). An ecologically nested theory of male violence toward intimates. *International Journal of Women's Studies, 8,* 404–413.

Dutton, D. G. (1998). *The abusive personality: Violence and control in intimate relationships.* New York: Guilford Press.

Dutton, D. G. (1994). Patriarchy and wife assault: The ecological fallacy. *Violence and Victims, 9,* 167–182.

Dutton, D. G. (2006). Domestic abuse assessment in child custody disputes: Beware the domestic violence research paradigm. *Journal of Child Custody: Research, Issues, And Practices, 2,* 23–42. doi:10.1300/J190v02n04_02

Dutton, D. G., & Starzomski, A. (1997). Personality predictors of the Minnesota power and control wheel. *Journal of Interpersonal Violence, 12,* 70–82.

Eagley, A. H. (1987). *Sex differences in social behavior: A social role interpretation.* Hillsdale, NJ: Erlbaum.

Ehrensaft, M. K., Cohen, P., Brown, J., Smailes, E., Chen, H., & Johnson, J. G. (2003). Intergenerational transmission of partner violence: A 20-year prospective study. *Journal of Consulting and Clinical Psychology, 71,* 741–753.

Fabiano, P. M. (1994). From personal health into community action: Another step forward in peer health education. *Journal of American College Health, 43,* 115–121.

Futures Without Violence (2012). *Our Work.* Retrieved May 4, 2012, from http://www.futureswithoutviolence.org/

Feder, L., & Wilson, D. (2005). A meta-analytic review of court-mandated batterer intervention programs: Can courts affect abusers' behavior? *Journal of Experimental Criminology, 1,* 239–262.

Franchina, J. J, Eisler, R. M., & Moore, T. M. (2001). Masculine gender role stress and intimate abuse: Effects of masculine gender relevance of dating situations and female threat on men's attributions and affective responses. *Psychology of Men and Masculinity, 2,* 34–41.

Follingstad, D. R., Bradley, R. G., Helff, C. M., & Laughlin, J. E. (2002). A model for predicting dating violence: Anxious attachment, angry temperament and need for relationship control. *Violence and Victims, 17,* 35–48.

Foshee, V., Benefield, T., Ennett, S. T., Bauman, K. E., & Suchindran, C. (2004). Longitudinal predictors of serious physical and sexual dating violence victimization during adolescence. *Preventive Medicine: An International Journal Devoted To Practice And Theory, 39,* 1007–1016. doi:10.1016/j.ypmed.2004.04.014

Foshee, V., Linder, G., Bauman, K., Langwick, S., Arriaga, X., Heath, J., . . . Bangdiwala, S. (1996). The Safe Dates Project: Theoretical basis, evaluation design, and selected baseline findings. *American Journal of Preventive Medicine, 12,* 39–47.

Gelles, R. J. (1977). No place to go: The social dynamic of marital violence. In M. Roy (Ed.), *Battered women: A psycho-sociological study of domestic violence* (pp. 46–63). New York: Van Nostrand Reinhold.

Giles-Sims, J. (1983). *Wife battering: A systems theory approach.* New York, NY: Guilford Press.

Gondolf, E. W. (1999). A comparison of reassault rates in four batterer programs: Do court referral program length and services matter? *Journal of Interpersonal Violence, 12,* 41–66.

Gondolf, E. W. (2007). Theoretical and research support for the Duluth Model: A reply to Dutton and Corvo. *Aggression and Violent Behavior, 12,* 644–657.

Gorman-Smith, D., Tolan, P. H., Sheidow, A. J., & Henry, D. B. (2001). Partner violence and street violence among urban adolescents: Do the same risk factors relate? *Journal of Research on Adolescence, 11,* 273–295.

Graham-Kevan, N., & Archer, J. (2005). Investigating three explanations of women's relationship aggression. *Psychology of Women Quarterly, 29*(3), 270–277.

Gratz, K. L., Paulson, A., Jakupcak, M., & Tull, M. T. (2009). Exploring the relationship between childhood maltreatment and intimate partner abuse: Gender differences in the mediating role of emotion dysregulation. *Violence and Victims, 24,* 68–82.

Greenwood, G. L., Relf, M. V., Huang, B., Pollack, L. M., Canchola, J. A., & Catania, J. A. (2002). Battering victimization among a probability-based sample of men who have sex with men. *American Journal of Public Health, 92,* 1964–1969.

Guerney, B., Waldo, M., & Firestone, L. (1987). Wife-battering: A theoretical construct and case report. *American Journal of Family Therapy, 15*(1), 34–43. doi:10.1080/01926188708251287

Hage, S. M., Romano, J., Conyne, R., Kenny, M., Mathews, C., Schwartz, J. P., & Waldo, M. (2007). Guidelines on prevention practice, research, training, and social advocacy for psychologists. *The Counseling Psychologist, 35,* 493–536.

Hamberger, L., & Hastings, J. (1991). Personality correlates of men who batter and nonviolent men: Some continuities and discontinuities. *Journal of Family Violence, 6*(2), 131–147.

Hamel, J. & Nicholls, T. L. (2007). *Family interventions in domestic violence: A handbook of gender-inclusive theory and treatment.* New York: Springer.

Hassouneh, D., & Glass, N. (2008). The influence of gender role stereotyping on women's experiences of female same-sex intimate partner violence. *Violence Against Women, 14*(3), 310–325.

Healey, K. & Smith, C. (1998). *Batterer programs: What criminal justice agencies need to know.* Washington, DC: National Institute of Justice.

Healey, K. M., Smith, C. & Sullivan, C. S. (1998). *Batterer intervention: Program approaches and criminal justice strategies.* Washington, DC : U.S. Department of Justice.

Heise, L. (1996). Violence against women: Global organizing for change. In J. L. Edleson & Z. C. Eisikovits (Eds.), *Future interventions with battered women and their families* (pp. 7–33). Thousand Oaks, CA: Sage.

Heise, L., & Garcia-Moreno, C. (2002). Violence by intimate partners. In E. Krug, L. L. Dahlberg, J. A. Mercy, et al. (Eds.) *World report on violence and health* (pp. 87–121). Geneva, Switzerland: World Health Organization.

Henderson, A. J. Z., Bartholomew, K., Trinke, S. J., & Kwong, M. J. (2005). When loving means hurting: An exploration of attachment and intimate abuse in a community sample. *Journal of Family Violence, 20,* 219–230.

Hickman, L. J., Jaycox, L. H., & Aranoff, J. (2004). Dating violence among adolescents: Prevalence, gender distribution, and prevention program effectiveness. *Trauma, Violence, and Abuse, 5,* 123–142.

Hong, L. (2000). Toward a transformed approach to prevention: Breaking the link between masculinity and violence. *Journal of American College Health, 48,* 269–279.

Jackson, S., Feder, L., David, R. F., Maxwell, C. D., & Bruce, G.T. (2003). *Batterer intervention programs: Where do we go from here?* Washington, DC: National Institute of Justice.

Jaffe, P., Suderman, M., Reitzel, D., & Killip, S. (1992). An evaluation of a secondary school
primary prevention program on violence in intimate relationships. *Violence and Victims, 7,* 129–146.

Joachim, J. (2000). Shaping the human rights agenda: The case of violence against women. In M. K. Meyer & E. Prugl (Eds.), *Gender politics in global governance* (pp. 142–160). Lanham, MD: Rowman and Littlefield.

Johnson, D., & Zlotnick, C. (2009). HOPE for battered women with PTSD in domestic violence shelters. *Professional Psychology: Research and Practice, 40*(3), 234–241.

Johnson, M. P., & Leone, J. M. (2005). The differential effects of intimate terrorism and situational couple violence. *Journal of Family Issues, 26,* 322–349.

Katz, J. (1995). Reconstructing masculinity in the locker room: The Mentors in Violence Prevention Project. *Harvard Educational Review, 65,* 163–174.

Kaufman, G. (1992). The mysterious disappearance of battered women in family therapists' offices: Male privilege colluding with male violence. *Journal of Marital and Family Therapy, 18,* 233–243.

Kenny, M., & Hage, S. (2009). The next frontier: Prevention as an instrument of social justice. *The Journal of Primary Prevention, 30*(1), 1–10. doi:10.1007/s10935–008–0163–7

Kesner, J. E., & McKenry, P. C. (1998). The role of childhood attachment factors in predicting male violence toward female intimates. *Journal of Family Violence, 13,* 417–432.

Kernsmith, P. (2005). Exerting power or striking back: A gendered comparison of motivations for domestic violence perpetration. *Violence and Victims, 20,* 173–185.

Lehmann, P., & Simmons, C. A. (2009). The state of batterer intervention programs: An analytical discussion. In P. Lehmann & C. A. Simmons (Eds.), *Strengths-based batterer intervention: A new paradigm in ending family violence* (pp. 3–37). New York: Springer.

Leonard, K. E., & Senchak, M. (1996). Prospective prediction of husband marital aggression within newlywed couples. *Journal of Abnormal Psychology, 10,* 369–380.

Leserman, J., & Drossman, D. A. (2007). Relationship of abuse history to functional gastrointestinal disorders and symptoms. *Trauma, Violence, and Abuse, 8,* 331–343.

Lie, G., Schilit, R., Bush, J., Montague, M., & Reyes, L. (1991). Lesbians in currently aggressive relationships: How frequently do they report aggressive past relationships? *Violence and Victims, 6,* 121–135.

Lipsky, S., & Caetano, R. (2009). Definitions, surveillance systems, and the prevalence and incidence of intimate partner violence in the United States. In D. J. Whitaker & J. R. Lutzker (Eds.), *Preventing partner violence: Research and evidence-based intervention strategies* (pp. 17–40). Washington, DC: American Psychological Association.

Lloyd, S., & Taluc, N. (1999). The effects of male violence on female employment. *Violence Against Women, 5,* 370–392. Lohr, J. M., Hamberger, L. K., Witte, T. H., Parker, L. M. (2006). Domestic violence. In J. E. Fisher & W. T. O'Donohue (Eds.), *Practitioner's guide to evidence-based psychotherapy.* New York: Springer Science + Business Media.

Luthra, R., & Gidycz, C. A. (2006). Dating violence among college men and women: Evaluation of a theoretical model. *Journal of Interpersonal Violence, 21,* 717–731.

Mansfield, A. K., Addis, M. E., Cordova, J. V., & Dowd, L. (2009). Emotional skillfulness as a key mediator of aggression. *Journal of Aggression, Maltreatment, and Trauma, 18,* 221–247.

Mauricio, A. M., & Gormley, B. (2001). Male perpetration of physical violence against female partners. *Journal of Interpersonal Violence, 16,* 1066–1081.

Max, W., Rice, D. P., Finkelstein, E., Bardwell, R. A., & Leadbetter, S. (2004). The economic toll of intimate partner violence against women in the United States. *Violence and Victims, 19,* 259–272.

Mayhew, S., & Watts, C. (2002). Global rhetoric and individual realities: Linking violence against women and reproductive health. In K. Lee, K. Buse, & S. Fustukian (Eds.), *Health policy in a globalising world* (pp. 159–180). Cambridge: Cambridge University Press.

McClennen, J. C. (2005). Domestic violence between same-gender partners. *Journal of Interpersonal Violence, 20*(2), 149–154.

McKenry, P. C., Serovich, J. M., Mason, T. L., & Mosack, K. (2006). Perpetration of gay and lesbian partner violence: A disempowerment perspective. *Journal of Family Violence, 21,* 233–243.

Miller, J. (2003). An arresting experiment: Domestic violence victim experiences and perceptions. *Journal of Interpersonal Violence, 18,* 695–716.

Moore, T. M., & Stuart, G. L. (2005). A review of the literature on masculinity and partner violence. *Psychology of Men and Masculinity, 6,* 46–61.

Murnen, S. K., Wright, C., & Kaluzny, G. (2002). If "boys will be boys," then girls will be victims? A meta-analytic review of the research that relates masculine ideology to sexual aggression. *Sex Roles, 46,* 359–375.

Murphy, C. M., & O'Leary, K. D. (1989). Psychological aggression predicts physical aggression in early marriage. *Journal of Consulting and Clinical Psychology, 57,* 579–582.

National Coalition Against Domestic Violence. (2010). *Family Violence Prevention and Services Act: Funding need: $175 million.* Retrieved December 9, 2010, from http://www.ncadv.org/files/statecomparisonFVPSA.pdf

National Coalition of Anti-Violence Programs. (2005). *The prevalence of LGBT domestic violence* [Electronic version]. Retrieved October 16, 2008, from http://ncavp.org/issues/DomesticViolence.aspx

O'Keefe, M. (1997). Predictors of dating violence among high school students. *Journal of Interpersonal Violence, 12,* 546–568.

O'Leary, K. (1988). Physical aggression between spouses: A social learning theory perspective. In V. B. Van Hasselt, R. L. Morrison, A. S. Bellack, M. Hersen, V. B. Van Hasselt, R. L. Morrison, ... M. Hersen (Eds.), *Handbook of family violence* (pp. 31–55). New York, NY: Plenum Press.

O'Leary, K. D., Malone, J., & Tyree, A. (1994). Physical aggression in early marriage: Prerelationship and relationship effects. *Journal of Consulting and Clinical Psychology, 62,* 594–602.

O'Neil, J. M., Good, G. E., & Holmes, S. (1995). Fifteen years of theory and research on men's gender role conflict: New paradigms for empirical research. In R. Levant & W. Pollack (Eds.), *The new psychology of men* (pp. 164–206). New York: Basic Books.

Ornduff, S. R., Kelsey, R. M., & O'Leary, K. D. (2001). Childhood physical abuse, personality and adult relationship violence: A model of vulnerability to victimization. *American Journal of Orthopsychiatry, 71,* 322–331.

Pence, E., & Paymer, M. (1993). *Educational groups for men who batter: The Duluth model.* New York: Springer.

Plichta, S. B. (2004). Intimate partner violence and physical health consequences: Policy and practice implications. *Journal of Interpersonal Violence, 19,* 1296–1323.

Poorman, P. B. (2001). Forging community links to address abuse in lesbian relationships. In E. Kaschak (Ed.) *Intimate betrayal: Intimate partner abuse in lesbian relationships* (pp. 7–24). New York: Haworth Press.

Prochaska, J. O., & DiClemente, C. C. (1982). Transtheoretical therapy: Toward a more integrative model of change. *Psychotherapy: Theory, Research, and Practice, 19,* 276–288.

Reitzel-Jaffe, D., & Wolfe, D. A. (2001). Predictors of relationship abuse among young men. *Journal of Interpersonal Violence, 16,* 99–115.

Riggs, D. S., & O'Leary, K. D. (1989). A theoretical model of courtship aggression. In M. A. Pirog-Good & J. E. Stets (Eds.), *Violence in dating relationships: Emerging social issues* (pp. 53–71). New York: Praeger.

Riggs, D. S., & O'Leary, K. D. (1996). Aggression between heterosexual dating partners: An examination of a causal model of courtship aggression. *Journal of Interpersonal Violence, 11,* 519–540.

Roberts, A. B., & Kurst-Swanger, K. (2002a). Court responses to battered women and their children. In A. Roberts (Ed.), *Handbook of domestic violence intervention strategies: Policies, programs, and legal remedies.* New York: Oxford University Press.

Roberts, A. B., & Kurst-Swanger, K. (2002b). Police responses to battered women: Past, present and future. In A. Roberts (Ed.), *Handbook of domestic violence intervention strategies: Policies, programs, and legal remedies.* New York: Oxford University Press.

Romano, J. L., & Hage, S. M. (2000). Prevention and counseling psychology: Revitalizing commitments for the 21st century. *The Counseling Psychologist, 28,* 733–763.

Rosenbaum, A., & Leisring, P. A. (2002). Group intervention programs for batterers. *Journal Of Aggression, Maltreatment & Trauma, 5,* 57–71. doi:10.1300/J146v05n02_05

Sagrestano, L. M., Heavey, C. L., & Christensen, A. (1999). Perceived power and violence in marital conflict. *Journal of Social Issues, 55,* 65–79.

Saltzman, L. E., Fanslow, J. L., McMahon, P. M., & Shelley, G. A. (2002). *Intimate partner violence surveillance: Uniform definitions and recommended data elements* (Version 1.0). Atlanta, GA: Centers for Disease Control and Prevention, National Center for Injury Prevention and Control. http://www.cdc.gov/ncipc/pub-res/ipv_surveillance/intimate.htm

Schewe, P. A., & Bennett, L. W. (2002). Evaluating prevention programs: The benefits and challenges of measuring outcomes. In P. A. Schewe (Ed), *Preventing violence in relationships: Developmentally appropriate interventions across the life span,* (pp. 247–261). Washington, DC: American Psychological Association Press.

Schwartz, J. P., Griffin, L. D., Russell, M. M., & Frontaura-Duck, S. (2006). Prevention of dating violence on college campuses: An innovative program. *Journal of College Counseling, 9,* 90–96.

Schwartz, J. P., & Lindley, L. D. (2009). Impacting sexism through social justice prevention: Implications at the person and environmental levels. *The Journal of Primary Prevention, 30,* 27–41. doi: 10.1007/s10935-008-0162-8

Schwartz, J. P., Magee, M. M., Griffin, L. D., & Dupuis, C. W. (2004). Effects of a group preventive intervention on risk and protective factors related to dating violence. *Group Dynamics: Theory, Research, And Practice, 8,* 221–231. doi:10.1037/1089-2699.8.3.221

Schwartz, J. P., Russell, M., Griffin, M., & Dupuis, C. (2004). Effects of a group preventive intervention on risk and protective factors related to dating violence. *Group Dynamics, 8,* 221–231.

Schwartz, J. P., & Waldo, M. (2003a). Reducing gender role conflict among men who are attending partner abuse prevention groups. *Journal of Specialists in Group Work, 28,* 355–369.

Schwartz, J. P., & Waldo, M. (2003b). Group work with men who have committed partner abuse. In J. J. DeLucia-Waack, D. A. Gerrity, C. R. Kalodner, & M. T. Riva (Eds.), *Handbook of group counseling and psychotherapy* (pp. 576–592). Thousand Oaks, CA: Sage.

Schwartz, J. P., Waldo, M., & Daniels, D. (2005). Gender role conflict and self-esteem: Predictors of partner abuse in court referred men. *Psychology of Men and Masculinity, 6,* 109–113.

Seelau, E. P., Seelau, S. M., & Poorman, P. B. (2003). Gender and role-based perceptions of domestic abuse: Does sexual orientation matter? *Behavioral Sciences and the Law, 21,* 199–214.

Silverman, J G., Raj, A., Mucci, L. A., & Hathaway, J. E. (2001). Dating violence against adolescent girls and associated substance use, unhealthy weight control, sexual risk behavior, pregnancy, and suicidality. *Journal of the American Medical Association, 286,* 572–579.

Slaby, R. (1994). Development of psychological mediators of violence in urban youth. In J. McCord (Ed.), *Growing up violent: Contributors of inner-city life* (pp. 171–206). New York: Oxford University Press.

Smith, P., White, J., & Holland, L. (2003). A longitudinal perspective on dating violence among adolescent and college-aged women. *American Journal of Public Health, 93,* 1104–1109.

Smith, P. H., White, J. W., & Moracco, B. (2009). Becoming who we are: A theoretical explanation of gendered social structures and social networks that shape adolescent interpersonal aggression. *Psychology of Women Quarterly, 33,* 25–29. doi:10.1111/j.1471-6402.2008.01470.x

Stanko, E. A. (2003). *The meanings of violence.* London: Routledge.

Stark, E. (2007). *Coercive control: How men entrap women in personal life.* New York: Oxford University Press.

The Network/La Red. (2004). *LGBTIQ partner abuse.* Retrieved December 12, 2004, from http://www.thenetworklared.org/

Ting, S. (2009). Meta-analysis on dating violence prevention among middle and high schools. *Journal of School Violence, 8,* 328–337. doi:10.1080/15388220903130197

Tjaden, P., & Thoennes, N. (1998). *Stalking in America: Findings from the National Violence Against Women Survey.* Washington, DC: Department of Justice. http://www.ncjrs.gov/pdffiles/169592.pdf

Tjaden, P., & Thoennes, N (2000). Extent, nature, and consequences of intimate partner violence: Findings from the National Violence Against Women Survey. Washington, DC: US Department of Justice. Publication No. NCJ 181867. Available at: www.ojp.usdoj.gov/nij/pubs-sum/181867.htm

Traicoff, M. E. (1982). Family interventions from women's shelters. In J. C. Hansen & L. R. Barnhill (Eds.), *Clinical approaches to family violence* (pp. 105–115). Rockville, MD: Aspen.

Tuckman, B., & Jensen, M. (1977). Stages of small group development. *Group and Organizational Studies, 2,* 419–427.

Turner, A. (2004). *Providing inclusive services: Working with lesbian, gay, bisexual, and transgender survivors of domestic violence and sexual assault.* Hayward: Wisconsin Coalition Against Domestic Violence.

Tutty, L. M., Weaver, G., & Rothery, M. A. (1999). Residents' view of the efficacy of shelter services for abused women. *Violence Against Women, 5,* 869–925.

Wade, J. C., & Brittan-Powell, C. (2001). Men's attitudes toward race and gender equity: The importance of masculinity ideology, gender-related traits, and reference group identity dependency. *Psychology of Men and Masculinity, 2,* 42–50.

Waldo, M. (1987). Also victims: Understanding and treating men arrested for spouse abuse. *Journal of Counseling and Development, 65,* 385–388.

Waldo, M., & Schwartz, J. P. (2008). Prevention perspective. *Prevention in Counseling Psychology: Theory, Research, Practice, and Training, 2,* 3–5.

Walker, L. E. A. (1984). *The battered woman syndrome* (1st ed.). New York, NY: Springer.

Walker, L. E. A. (2004). *Abused women and survivor therapy: A practical guide for the psychotherapist.* Washington, DC: American Psychological Association.

Walker, L. E. A. (2009). *The battered woman syndrome.* New York, NY: Springer.

Weisz, A. N., & Black, B. M. (2009). *Programs to reduce teen dating violence and sexual*

assault. New York: Columbia University Press.

Wekerle, C., & Wall, A.-M. (2002). *The violence and addiction equation: Theoretical and clinical issues in substance abuse and relationship violence.* New York: Brunner-Routledge.

West, C. M. (2002). Lesbian intimate partner violence: Prevalence and dynamics. *Journal of Lesbian Studies, 6*(1), 121–127.

Whitaker, D. J., Morrison, S., Lindquist, C., Hawkins, S. R., O'Neil, J. A., Nesius, A. M.,... Reese, L. (2006). A critical review of intervention for the primary prevention of perpetration of partner violence. *Aggression and Violent Behavior, 11,* 151–166.

White, H. R., & Widom, C. S. (2003). Intimate partner violence among abused and neglected children in young adulthood: The mediating effects of early aggression, antisocial personality, hostility, and alcohol problems. *Aggressive Behavior, 29,* 332–345.

White, J. W. (2009). A gendered approach to adolescent dating violence: Conceptual and methodological issues. *Psychology of Women Quarterly, 33,* 1–15. doi:10.1111/j.1471–6402.2008.01467.x

White, J. W., Merrill, L. L., & Koss, M. P. (2001). Predictors of premilitary courtship violence in a navy recruit sample. *Journal of Interpersonal Violence, 16,* 910–927.

Wolfe, D. A., & Jaffe, P. G. (2003, January). Prevention of domestic violence and sexual assault. Harrisburg, PA: VAWnet, a project of the National Resource Center on Domestic Violence/Pennsylvania Coalition Against Domestic Violence. Retrieved November 8, 2010, from: http://www.vawnet.org

Wolfe, D. A., Wekerle, C., Gough, B., Reitzel-Jaffe, D., Grasley, C., Pittman, A.,. . . , Stumpf, J. (1996). *The youth relationships manual: A group approach with adolescents for the prevention of woman abuse and the promotion of healthy relationships.* Thousand Oaks, CA: Sage.

Wolfe, D. A., Wekerle, C., Scott, K., Straatman, A.-L., & Grasley, C. (2004). Predicting abuse in adolescent dating relationships over one year: The role of child maltreatment and trauma. *Journal of Abnormal Psychology, 113,* 406–415.

Wolfe, D. A., Wekerle, C., Scott, K., Straatman, A.-L., Grasley, C., & Reitzel-Jaffe, D. (2003). Dating violence prevention with at-risk youth: A controlled outcome evaluation. *Journal of Consulting and Clinical Psychology, 71,* 279–291.

Woodin, E. M., & O'Leary, D. (2009). Theoretical approaches to the etiology of partner violence. In D. J. Whitaker & J. R. Lutzker (Eds.), *Preventing partner violence: Research and evidence-based intervention strategies* (pp. 41–65). Washington, DC: American Psychological Association.

Wray, R. J. (2006). Public health communication theory and strategies for interpersonal violence prevention. *Journal of Aggression, Maltreatment, and Trauma, 13*(3–4), 41–60.

Yodanis, C. (2004). Gender inequality, violence against women, and fear: A cross-national test of the feminist theory of violence against women. *Journal of Interpersonal Violence, 19,* 655–675.

CHAPTER

17 Prevention of Conduct Disorder: Do We Have Reason to Be Hopeful?

Brian P. Daly, Cindy Buchanan, Kimberly Dasch, Dawn Eichen *and* Clare Lenhart

Abstract

The cluster of behavior problems known as the disruptive behavior disorders, including oppositional defiant disorder and conduct disorder, represent the most common reason for referral among all childhood mental health problems. Without early preventive and intervention services, these behaviors may escalate over time, becoming more frequent, severe, and maladaptive in nature, resulting in significant and long-lasting negative consequences that affect individuals, families, schools, communities, and society in general. Historically, disruptive behavior disorders were perceived to be some of the most difficult disorders with which to intervene and ameliorate symptoms. Fortunately, evidence-based preventive and early intervention programs delivered across various settings have been developed that improve outcomes for these children and adolescents and their families.

Key Words: disruptive behavior disorders, oppositional defiant disorder, conduct disorder, prevention, early intervention, children and adolescents, evidence-based treatment

Introduction

Disruptive behavior disorders range from noncompliance and disobedience to more dangerous behavior, including aggressive hostility toward authorities and/or peers. These behaviors constitute a major public health problem and have significant acute and long-term negative effects on the lives of the children and adolescents themselves, their parents, their teachers, and society as a whole. Oppositional Defiant Disorder (ODD), Conduct Disorder (CD), and Disruptive Behavior Disorder, Not Otherwise Specified (DBD-NOS) are the disruptive behavior disorders as specified in the *Diagnostic and Statistical Manual* (DSM-IV) and its revision (DSM-IV-TR; American Psychiatric Association, 2000).

When children and adolescents ages 8–16 years that meet specific DSM-IV criteria for diagnoses of ODD and CD are considered together, population prevalence rates are between 5% and 10% (Angold & Costello, 2001). However, the actual prevalence of behavior disorders in youth may be higher due to the fact that prevalence rates are generated through referrals, and many children and adolescents are never referred for mental health services (Phelps & McClintock, 1994; Scott et al., 2010). When children do receive referrals for disruptive behaviors, ODD and CD are the predominant juvenile disorders referred to mental health clinics, accounting for somewhere between one third to two thirds of all child mental health referrals (Kazdin, 1995). Generally, sex differences in disruptive behavior disorders do not emerge prior to age 6, but as children age into adolescence and young adulthood, males receive the preponderance of referrals for disruptive behavior disorders as compared to females.

Early signs of conduct problems most frequently present during the preschool years. These maladaptive behaviors are believed to be continuously distributed and persist as the child ages unless effective preventive intervention is received (Scott et al., 2010). Indeed, early intervention is the most critical step in preventing the progression of these disorders into more serious and stable problems. For example, findings from a study of young children revealed that more than two thirds of 3-year-old children that exhibited difficult behaviors and did not receive intervention continued to demonstrate significant behavior problems at age 9 (Campbell & Ewing, 1990). The developmental trajectory of youth with behavioral challenges is further complicated by an increased likelihood of comorbid conditions that include attention-deficit/hyperactivity disorder (ADHD), bipolar disorder, depression, and chemical dependency (Thomas, 2006). While not all children demonstrating conduct problems at a young age will eventually receive a clinical diagnosis, the behavioral manifestations of conduct disorder persist into adulthood for many individuals, presenting a serious and lifelong dysfunction that negatively impacts health, social relationships, and employment status while also increasing the risk of legal troubles (Webster-Stratton & Dahl, 1995). As such, from a public health point of view, it is critical that clinicians, researchers, and policy makers engage in collaborative efforts to prevent the development of aggressive and disruptive behaviors in young children, and to intervene early once they have been identified (Hill, 2003).

This chapter first reviews incidence and prevalence data and the symptomatic presentation of the disruptive behavior disorders that include ODD, CD, and DBD-NOS. In the next section, we describe the etiology and correlates of behavior problems in youth with a particular focus on pertinent biological, psychological, and sociological factors. Then, we examine relevant clinical, research, and policy considerations for prevention and treatment. Following the discussion of these considerations, we briefly describe several different modalities associated with evidence-based prevention and intervention programs. Next, we detail the application of these programs at different levels, including the biological, individual and group, parent and family, school and community. Outcome data associated with each of the programs also are presented. Finally, we present future directions for clinical work, research, and policy as they related to the understanding, prevention, and treatment of disruptive behavior disorders.

Externalizing Behavior Disorders in Children and Adolescents

Oppositional Defiant Disorder

Oppositional defiant disorder (ODD) is characterized by a persistent pattern of negative, disobedient, and hostile behavior toward authority figures that continues for at least 6 months, and is observed to a greater extent than that which is typically observed in same-age children (see Table 17.1; APA, 2000). These behaviors must cause clinically

Table 17.1 DSM-IV Criteria A for Oppositional Defiant Disorder and Conduct Disorder

DSM-IV Criteria A Symptoms for Oppositional Defiant Disorder
1) Often loses temper
2) Often argues with adults
3) Often actively defies or refuses to comply with adults' requests or rules
4) Often deliberately annoys people
5) Often blames others for his or her mistakes or misbehavior
6) Is often touchy or easily annoyed by others
7) Is often angry and resentful
8) Is often spiteful or vindictive
DSM-IV Criteria A Symptoms for Conduct Disorder
Aggression to people and animals
1) Often bullies, threatens, or intimidates others
2) Often initiates physical fights
3) Has used a weapon
4) Has been physically cruel to people
5) Has been physically cruel to animals
6) Has stolen while confronting a victim
7) Has forced someone into sexual activity
Destruction of Property
8) Has deliberately engaged in firesetting
9) Has deliberately destroyed others' property
Deceitfulness or theft
10) Has broken into someone else's house, building or car
11) Often lies to con others
12) Has stolen items of non-trivial value without confronting a victim
Serious violations of rules
13) Often stays out late without permission, starting before age 13
14) Has run away from home overnight at least twice
15) Is often truant at school, beginning before age 13

significant functional impairment for diagnosis. Onset of ODD usually occurs in early childhood with a median age of onset between 7 to 15 years of age (Kessler et al., 2007). Rates of ODD across genders are slightly higher among males (11.2% males vs. 9.2% females), with overall lifetime prevalence rates estimated at approximately 10% (Nock, Kazdin, Hiripi, & Kessler, 2007). ODD commonly precedes a diagnosis of CD; however, if an individual meets criteria for CD, a diagnosis of ODD is not given, because a diagnosis of CD subsumes the ODD symptoms (APA, 2000).

Conduct Disorder

Conduct disorder (CD) is characterized by more aggressive, defiant, and antisocial behaviors compared to ODD. The repetitive and persistent pattern of behaviors violates the basic rights of others or age appropriate societal norms or rules. Behaviors may include aggression, vandalism, theft, deceitfulness, and running away from home. To receive a diagnosis, three or more behaviors must be present within the past 12 months with at least one behavior occurring during the past 6 months. These behaviors fall under four categories including: (1) aggression toward people and animals; (2) destruction of property; (3) deceitfulness or theft; and, (4) serious violations of rules (See Table 17.1; APA, 2000). Similar to ODD, these behaviors must cause clinically significant functional impairment for diagnosis. One of the most notable features of individuals diagnosed with CD is the lack of remorse generally accompanying these behaviors. In order to receive a diagnosis of antisocial personality disorder (after age 18), an individual must have been diagnosed with, or met criteria for, a previous diagnosis of CD (APA, 2000). Among all children diagnosed with CD, those who demonstrate the most severe or frequent symptoms have the poorest prognosis and are considered the most likely to exhibit antisocial behaviors in adolescence and early adulthood (Woodward & Fergusson, 1999).

There is a notable difference in the gender ratio for those diagnosed with CD, ranging between 4:1 in favor of males before adolescence and 2:1 after adolescence (Moffitt, Caspi, Rutter, & Silva, 2001). However, there is some evidence that prevalence rates of CD have increased recently among females (Putallaz & Bierman, 2004). General rates in community samples range from 2% to 16%, with the most common estimate being around 5% (APA, 2000). CD is divided into two subtypes: childhood-onset type and adolescent-onset type. childhood-onset type includes the presence of at least one symptom prior to the age of 10, while adolescent-onset type is characterized by the absence of any criteria associated with CD prior to 10 years of age. Individuals that receive the child-onset type diagnosis are more likely to have persistent CD and more likely to develop antisocial personality disorder as compared to those with adolescent-onset type (Babinski, Hartsough, & Lambert, 1999; Loeber & Farrington, 2000).

The median age of onset of CD ranges between 9 and 14 years of age (Kessler et al., 2007). Gender differences in behaviors among individuals diagnosed with CD reveal that males are more likely to exhibit physical violence while females are more likely to use relational and indirect aggression (Angold & Costello, 2001). Males also have a greater tendency to be overtly aggressive toward others while females are more likely to ostracize or defame another person. Finally, male teens with CD are more likely to exhibit fighting or stealing while female teens with CD are more likely to engage in lying and substance abuse (Archer & Côté, 2005).

Disruptive Behavior Disorder, Not Otherwise Specified

The diagnosis of disruptive behavior disorder, not otherwise specified (DBD-NOS) is reserved for individuals who exhibit conduct and or oppositional defiant problems but do not meet criteria for ODD or CD. To receive the diagnosis of DBD-NOS, clinically significant impairment in social or academic functioning must be present. Few studies have empirically examined DBD-NOS separately from ODD and CD; however, the gender ratio of DBD-NOS appears to be similar to that of CD (Messer, Goodman, Rowe, & Meltzer, 2006).

Comorbidity of Externalizing Disorders

Although the relationship between ODD, CD, and other impulse control disorders such as ADHD is not well understood, it has been demonstrated that these disorders frequently co-occur. For example, both ODD and CD are comorbid with ADHD at relatively high rates (35%–48%), resulting in more severe symptoms and poorer outcomes for those children with comorbidities as compared to children diagnosed with only one disorder (Waschbusch, 2002). While the majority of children with CD have received a prior diagnosis of ODD, most children diagnosed with ODD and ADHD do not progress to CD (Biederman et al., 2008). The co-occurrence of conduct problems and anxiety disorders ranges between 19% and 53% depending on community or clinical samples (Nottlemann & Jensen, 1995). A longitudinal study found that the presence of externalizing problems in adolescence significantly increased the likelihood of depression present by early adulthood (Kosterman et al., 2009).

Etiology and Correlates of Behavior Problems in Children

It is important to identify pertinent risk factors for behavior problems associated with CD as early identification offers the possibility of intervention and hence prevention of the development of more serious disorders in adulthood such as antisocial personality disorder. Thus, identifying those individuals at risk for behavior problems allows professionals to target preventive interventions towards those youth most in need of services. While this section reviews some of the biological, psychological, and sociological variables associated with the development of behaviors consistent with a diagnosis of conduct disorder, it is notable that researchers continue to struggle with elucidating all of the possible early indicators that put children at risk for the development of conduct problems (Hill, 2003).

Biological

Well-established biological risk factors for ODD and CD include: autonomic responsiveness, functional and structural neurological abnormalities, genetics, antenatal and perinatal complications, and any brain injuries or disease.

AUTONOMIC RESPONSIVENESS

There is some evidence to suggest that a reduction of autonomic responsiveness is the cause of conduct problems in children and adolescents such that youth with ODD or CD display lower levels of salivary cortisol, lower levels of skin conductance reactivity, lower resting heart rate and heart rate reactivity, and decreased startle response when presented with pictures of victimization (Lorber, 2004; Ortiz & Raine 2004).

NEUROLOGICAL ABNORMALITIES

The evidence is more limited for neurological abnormalities that include decreased volume in the right temporal lobe (Kruesi, Casanova, Mannheim, & Johnson-Bilder, 2004), as well as abnormalities in the frontal lobe (Blair, 2001). Findings from studies that employed neurological imaging reveal that atypical frontal lobe activation may reflect a biological substrate of a negative affective style in children with significant conduct problems (Baving, Laucht, & Schmidt, 2000).

GENETICS

While there is some evidence to suggest a genetic linkage in disruptive behavior disorders, more evidence is needed before firm conclusions can be drawn. In one study, family history of psychopathology was associated with child behavior problems such that parents of 3-year-old children classified as hyperactive/oppositional defiant reported greater family histories of ODD and CD, when compared to parents of children with no behavior problems (Harvey, Friedman-Weieneth, Goldstein, & Sherman, 2007). Baker and colleagues (2007) conducted adoption and twin studies and found that over 50% of the variance in antisocial behavior could be attributed to heredity.

ANTENATAL AND PERINATAL FACTORS

Antenatal and perinatal factors also are associated with increased risk for later behavior problems. In a study that examined maternal physical and emotional health, poor maternal physical health during pregnancy was associated with a diagnosis of a disruptive behavior disorder for female adolescents, while adolescents whose mothers reported experiencing emotional difficulties during pregnancy were 2.4 times more likely to meet criteria for a disruptive behavior disorder, even after adjusting for maternal depressive symptoms and family conflict variables (Allen, Lewinsohn, & Seeley, 1998). Children whose mothers smoked during pregnancy were at increased risk for being diagnosed with CD and more likely to have an earlier onset of behavioral problems and delinquent behavior (Wakschlag et al., 2006).

At the perinatal level, newborns that experienced acute anoxia or hypoxia at birth were more likely to be diagnosed with a disruptive behavior disorder in adolescence as compared to a group of healthy peers (Allen et al., 1998). The evidence is decidedly mixed with regard to whether low birth weight is a risk factor for disruptive behavior disorders. For example, findings from a recent study indicate that low birth weight was associated with teacher-reported attention problems at ages 6, 11, and 17, but no association was found for maternal-reported attention problems or increased reports of ODD and CD (Nigg & Breslau, 2007). Other studies reported that low birth weight was a risk factor for ADHD, but was not significantly associated with increased risk for CD (Szatmari, Saigal, Rosenbaum, Campbell, & King, 1990). In contrast, low birth weight was associated with an earlier age of offending, or having an offense recorded by the police department before the age of 14 (Tibbetts & Piquero, 1999), consistent with behaviors associated with conduct disorder.

BRAIN INJURIES OR DISEASE

Brain injury or disease is considered a strong risk factor for later externalizing symptoms. For example, severe traumatic brain injury was found to be associated with increase externalizing symptoms 18 months after the injury (Chapman et al., 2010). Mild traumatic brain injury is similarly associated with later symptoms of ODD/CD (McKinlay, Grace, Horwood, Ferguson, & MacFarlane, 2009).

Psychological

Psychological factors related to the etiology of ODD and CD include cognitive and academic factors, as well as temperament and personality traits.

COGNITIVE AND ACADEMIC FACTORS

The intelligence quotient (IQ) for most children with conduct problems falls in the normal range; however, scores average 8 points less than their peers without conduct problems (Koenen et al., 2006). Additional neuropsychological and academic deficits associated with disruptive behavior disorders include attentional problems, reading problems, and language impairment (Hinshaw, 1992).

TEMPERAMENT AND PERSONALITY

The evidence is equivocal regarding the association between infant temperament and later conduct problems. Lahey and colleagues (2008) found that infant fearfulness predicted later conduct problems in girls, while infant fussiness predicted later conduct problems in boys. In contrast, other studies that employed observational measures of temperament made in the first year of life failed to predict later conduct problems (Aguilar et al., 2000; Belsky et al., 1998). Personality variables are associated with behavior problems such that youth with CD and substance use disorder scored significantly higher on the personality trait of neuroticism, and lower on agreeableness and conscientiousness, than did their siblings without these comorbid diagnoses (Anderson, Tapert, Moadab, Crowley, & Brown, 2007).

Sociological

The extant literature indicates that family characteristics, socioeconomic status, parental functioning, parenting and discipline styles, physical and sexual abuse, and social and environmental factors are risk factors for the development of conduct disorder.

FAMILY CHARACTERISTICS.

Family characteristics related to number of parents in the home, adoption status, and maternal age at time of delivery is strongly associated with a heightened risk of engaging in problematic behavior among children and adolescents. Findings from one study that looked at single and dual-parent families indicated that 3-year-old children who were classified as hyperactive/oppositional defiant were more likely to have single parents (Goldstein et al., 2007). Results from a study that included adopted children found that these children had higher teacher- and parent-reported levels of aggression and delinquent behavior as compared to nonadopted children (Deater-Deckard & Plomin, 1999). Harden and colleagues (2007) studied behavior problems among children born to teenage mothers and reported that these children demonstrated more behavior problems compared to children born to nonteenage mothers (Harden et al., 2007).

SOCIOECONOMIC STATUS

Lower socioeconomic status has consistently been found to be associated with increased risk for behavior problems. Specifically, CD is more prevalent among youth from families of low socioeconomic status (Loeber, Green, Keenan, & Lahey, 1995).

PARENTAL FUNCTIONING

Variables associated with parental functioning such as marital conflict and parenting stress are associated with child behavior problems. In a recent study, a higher level of conflict between parents was associated with an increased risk of hyperactivity and oppositionality among 3-year-old children (Goldstein et al., 2007). In addition, higher self-reported parenting-specific stress was related to higher levels of externalizing disorders among preschool-aged children (Gutermuth-Anthony et al., 2005).

PARENTING AND DISCIPLINE STYLES

A preponderance of evidence indicates that dysfunctional and rejecting family environments in which parents employ inconsistent and severe discipline are associated with behavior problems. For example, inconsistent use of control by parents was associated with increased conduct problems

(Sameroff, Peck, & Eccles, 2004), while rejecting parenting style was associated with increased aggression and delinquency in adolescents (Barnow, Lucht, & Freyberger, 2005). Mothers of children classified as hyperactive and oppositional defiant reported greater physical and verbal aggression in their family when matched against parents of children without behavioral problems (Goldstein et al., 2007). Retrospective reports of being exposed to harsh discipline ("hit in the face" or "hit with an object") were associated with an increase in conduct disorder and antisocial behavior (Derringer, Krueger, Irons, & Iacono, 2010).

PHYSICAL AND SEXUAL ABUSE

Physical and sexual abuse is associated with increased behavior problems. Adolescent females who had been physically abused, or physically and sexually abused, were more likely to be diagnosed with conduct disorder than were girls who had not been abused (Green, Russo, Navratil, & Loeber, 1999). Further, those with a low activity MAOA genotype who retrospectively reported a history of childhood sexual abuse, also reported more symptoms of conduct disorder and antisocial behavior than those with no reported history of childhood sexual abuse and a high activity MAOA genotype (Derringer et al., 2010).

ENVIRONMENTAL AND SOCIAL FACTORS

Environmental and contextual factors can serve as factors in the development of problem behavior (Snyder, Reid, & Patterson, 2003). For example, living in an impoverished and dangerous neighborhood with a high crime rate is associated with increased antisocial behavior (Trentacosta, Hyde, Shaw, & Cheong, 2009). It is important to note that some evidence exists of overdiagnosis of disruptive behavior disorders in minority children and adolescents (Murphy & Jellinek, 1988); however, research in this area is frequently confounded by multiple factors that include social and contextual factors such as socioeconomic status, parental stress, and family constellation variables (McNeil, Capage, & Bennett, 2001). In one study that attempted to untangle these confounds, Patterson and colleagues (1990) found that income level was a stronger overall predictor of disruptive behavior problems than ethnicity.

Prevention and Treatment Considerations

Methods of addressing conduct disorder can be classified as either preventive or remediation-based interventions. Primary prevention strategies are those designed to prevent development of a clinical disorder or disease, in this case externalizing behaviors in youth, and are typically delivered in a group basis and offered across the population of a given school or community (Scott et al., 2010). Secondary prevention of externalizing disorders typically targets groups of children who are exhibiting early-stage behavior problems that, without formal intervention, may lead to a clinical diagnosis of a disruptive behavior disorder (e.g., ODD or CD). In these cases, early detection methods are used to identify such target groups. Tertiary prevention strategies, which are often difficult to differentiate from treatment, occur after the diagnosis and aim to reduce the duration or consequences of symptoms of the disruptive behavior disorder before the occurrence of significant morbidity. Prevention of CD, including both primary and secondary prevention efforts, is most often targeted at young children and includes programming and training for those adults that interact with children such as parents and teachers.

Why is prevention necessary in addressing conduct problems in youth? The extant literature suggests that many children in need of treatment for ODD and CD do not actually receive these services. For example, Kazdin and Kendall (1998) found that fewer than 10% of the eligible population of behavioral disordered children received care following referral. Moreover, among children who do receive intervention for behavior disorders, the majority of children do not receive evidence-based interventions (Chambless et al., 1998). These disappointing statistics are believed to be a reflection of provider's biases regarding therapies or medications, as well as the dearth of evidence-based preventative interventions that have been employed with diverse, community-based samples (Weisz, Doss, & Hawley, 2005). As such, efficacious preventive and remediation-based treatments for externalizing behaviors either do not reach many youth in need of such services or treatment occurs in later childhood or adolescence when outcomes are likely to be poorer (US Surgeon General, 2001).

Preventive efforts differ from traditional remediation-based strategies in the timing of intervention, associated costs, and approach to intervention. Researchers point to several relative strengths of prevention over remediation as a means of addressing conduct disorder in youth. First, the behavioral manifestations of conduct disorder such as antisocial behaviors, violence, and aggression tend to become more entrenched over time and thus more difficult to effectively remediate (Scott et al., 2010). For this reason, in prevention-based models, early intervention efforts are designed to help young children increase their ability to self-regulate behavior, control impulses, and interact in a prosocial manner with peers (Webster-Stratton & Dahl, 1995). The earlier that intervention for conduct disorder is initiated, the more likely the child will learn behavioral regulation skills that help prevent engagement in future risky behaviors such as substance use (Thomas, 2006). Second, primary prevention programs seek to promote the development of competence before there is evidence of a diagnosable disorder, as competence is highly related to positive behavioral outcomes (Webster-Stratton & Dahl, 1995). Thus, providing and fostering prosocial behavioral strategies as a preventive measure for children at risk of developing conduct disorder enables rehearsal and adoption of the desired behavior at a critical developmental period in ways a treatment-only approach is unable to accomplish.

There is a relatively small, but growing body of literature that provides evidence for the successful prevention of conduct disorder. For example, in a longitudinal study of a preventive early-intervention program for young children displaying noncompliant behavior, Long and colleagues (1994) found significant improvements in children's behaviors immediately following the intervention. Further, the results revealed no difference with respect to measures of delinquency, academic achievement, social relationships, or emotional adjustment when comparing children in the intervention group to matched controls 14 years after initial intervention (Long et al., 1994). Thus, early intervention proved beneficial in both the short and long term for those children and families that participated in the program.

Depending on the period of development during which prevention and remediation efforts are initiated, costs may differ substantially. For example, effective prevention efforts require significant investments in personnel and programming early in a child's life. A recent randomized, controlled trial of a parent-focused intervention to prevent the development of conduct disorder in children involved weekly in-person parenting education sessions to help parents better manage the behavioral challenges demonstrated by their children. The estimated cost per child for this program was nearly $3,800, or approximately three times the cost of referral to an outpatient child mental health clinic (Scott et al., 2010). The disparities in cost between prevention and remediation efforts are not fully accounted for by the personnel costs associated with each approach. As noted above, prevention programming tends to be longer term and multifaceted, such that substantial investment of time on the part of parents, teachers, and young children is needed to improve the possibility of achieving sustained, positive behavioral outcomes. In practice, many parents are either unable or unwilling to invest the necessary time associated with participating in an intensive prevention program. Thus, the barrier posed by costs with respect to parental time is considered one of the primary reasons that some well-designed preventive interventions have demonstrated nonsignificant findings. Barkley and colleagues (2000) conducted a randomized, controlled trial of an early childhood intervention to address disruptive behavior, aggression, hyperactivity and inattentiveness. Findings from the trial indicated a lack of significant effects for parent training, which was primarily attributed to poor parental attendance throughout the study. Therefore, the cost to parent's time for attending prevention efforts must be considered when designing and implementing prevention and early-intervention efforts.

Despite the costs associated with prevention in early life, attempts to remediate CD-related behaviors in adolescence or young adulthood often prove to be both more expensive and less effective. As noted earlier, youth with conduct disorder are more likely to be involved in juvenile crime as compared to their peers without CD(Copeland, Miller-Johnson, Keeler, Angold, & Costello, 2007). Cohen and Piquero (2009) estimate the costs to society associated with saving a high-risk juvenile from a life of crime to be between 2.6 to 5.3 million dollars per child. The staggering costs are inflated due partly to the high rates of recidivism among juvenile offenders. Taken together, despite the initial cost associated with early intervention and preventive services, the overall cost-benefit analysis suggests effective prevention programs can generate significant cost savings in time.

Prevention and remediation strategies also differ in their approach to modifying behavior. Early intervention is necessarily multifaceted and often involves the implementation of behavior management strategies for the child in conjunction with parent and teacher training (Thomas, 2006). Aims of this approach include increasing both the frequency of socially appropriate behaviors and decreasing the frequency of negative behaviors. Specific methods to accomplish these goals vary between early intervention programs, but a hallmark of early-life preventive programming is fostering effective parenting techniques to overcome the frequent reliance on counterproductive techniques associated with parenting behaviorally disordered children (Chronis, Jones & Raggi, 2006). Techniques, including the use of praise, rewards, and increased parental attention, are frequently used in prevention efforts to foster appropriate behaviors by the child (Scott, Spender, Doolan, Jacobs, & Aspland, 2001). In conjunction with these positive reinforcement techniques, use of simple, direct commands and time-outs are also incorporated to diminish the frequency of inappropriate behaviors (Scott et al., 2001). In a recent investigation of a parent-focused primary prevention program designed to improve children's behaviors and literacy outcomes, Scott and colleagues (2010) found significant positive impacts for decreased instances of coercive parenting, increased warmth between parent and child, fewer externalizing behaviors on the part of the child, and improved school performance.

Schools and teachers also play a vital role in the comprehensive prevention of conduct disorder in youth. Using techniques similar to those developed in parent training programs, teachers instructed in the use of behavior management strategies and positive classroom management techniques consistently encounter fewer conduct problems among their students as compared to teachers not trained in these prevention strategies (Webster-Stratton, Reid, & Stoolmiller, 2008). Promisingly, school-based prevention programming with teachers produces positive results among students in diverse, low-income urban areas where the prevalence of CD is higher compared to suburban areas (Phelps & McClintock, 1994).

More than simply avoiding antisocial behavior now or in the future, prevention initiatives typically encompass efforts to foster positive youth development (Lerner, Almerigi, Theokas, & Lerner, 2005). Positive youth development refers to the interaction of human development and developmental assets and is conceptualized as the promotion of a child's competence, confidence, connection to others, character, and caring (Lerner et al., 2005). In this way, prevention-based approaches to addressing conduct disorder in youth go beyond intentions to decrease problem behavior and instead aim to retrain a child's behavioral processes while also fostering personal characteristics believed to promote prosocial behavior.

Evidence-Based Prevention and Intervention Strategies and Programs

A corpus of research findings indicate that psychosocial interventions such as behavior modification, cognitive-behavioral therapy (CBT), behavioral parent training and family-based intervention strategies, and large-scale prevention programs are effective early intervention strategies for children with ODD or CD (Burke, Loeber, & Birhamer, 2002; Christophersen & Mortweet, 2001). These interventions all purport to prevent or help ameliorate many of the problematic and disruptive behaviors associated with ODD and CD. Ideally, these early interventions are employed with children exhibiting a variant of normal behavior to improve problem behaviors in childhood and minimize the potential risk of further development of a clinically significant level of maladaptive functioning. In this section we briefly describe a sample of modalities and programs that meet the criteria for evidence-based programs based on scientific evidence indicating that these prevention and intervention programs have a positive effect in their treatment (Eyberg, Nelson, & Boggs, 2008). In the following section, we detail relevant outcome data of the respective programs as relates to the prevention and treatment of disruptive behavior disorders.

Behavior Modification

The goal of behavior modification approaches is to teach the caregiver and teacher effective antecedent-based (e.g., giving effective commands) and consequent-based (e.g., token reinforcement) behavioral interventions that target child compliance and task completion (APA Working Group on Psychoactive Medications for Children and Adolescents, 2006). The token economy is a specific behavioral strategy that provides an organized system for reinforcing positive behavior while also seeking to diminish the frequency of problem behaviors. Essentially, when children demonstrate common behavioral problems, the token economy creates an exchange system in which conditioned reinforcers are either earned or lost depending entirely on the child's behavior.

Classroom behavior management strategies are based on a functional analysis of the child's problematic behavior. Interventions include specific individual, classroomwide, or schoolwide behavioral interventions such as verbal praise, effective commands, a point or token economy system, daily report cards, or time-outs (Chronis et al., 2006).

Cognitive-Behavioral Therapy

Many interventions for children and adolescents demonstrating oppositional behaviors include some components of cognitive-behavioral therapy (CBT). In contrast to behavioral parent training, the child or adolescent is the identified client in treatment and is primarily responsible for making behavioral changes (Kazdin, Bass, Siegel, & Thomas, 1989). Youth are taught how to engage in effective problem-solving strategies and how to improve their interactions with peers, teachers, parents, and caregivers. These skills are taught using the basic therapeutic techniques of CBT, including practice, modeling, role-playing, and reinforcement strategies.

Problem-solving skills training (PSST; Kazdin, 1996) is a cognitively oriented approach for youth with disruptive behaviors that focuses on modification of cognitions such as attributions of hostile intent, which may precipitate aggressive behavior, and maladaptive self-statements, which may mediate other expressions of antisocial behavior. An additional focus is on helping the child learn and use effective problem-solving skills in dealing with problematic interpersonal situations he/she may encounter.

Behavioral Parent Training (BPT)

Behavioral parent training (BPT) is one of the oldest and most substantiated treatment interventions in child mental health, particularly for those children with significant externalizing behavior problems such as aggression and conduct problems (Brestan & Eyberg, 1998; Brinkmeyer & Eyberg, 2003). In fact, one review suggested that parent training should be considered the primary evidence-based family treatment for ODD (Northey, Wells, Silverman, & Bailey, 2003). At a minimum, most interventions for externalizing behaviors include a parent training component, while some interventions exclusively employ parent training interventions.

Behavioral parent training is typically delivered over a series of between 8 and 12 group and/or individual sessions. Throughout the sessions, parents learn about their child's disorder and become equipped with a variety of skills to proactively manage their behavior. For example, parents learn to differentiate between prosocial behaviors they wish to encourage, minor behavioral infractions that can effectively be reduced simply by ignoring, and more significant problem behaviors that must be overtly addressed and corrected. Inconsistent enforcement of rules is discouraged, and techniques for establishing and enforcing rules are presented as well as procedures for establishing time-outs at home. Additionally, parents receive instruction on how best develop a point system with their children such that there are clear and consistent rewards for positive behaviors, as well as appropriate repercussions for problem behaviors. Finally, behavioral parent training helps parents develop the capacity to enforce behavioral expectations across a variety of social settings, to address unique behavior challenges as they arise, and to prevent behavior relapses in the future. In fact, teaching parents how to change the manner in which they interact with their children who are already at risk for developing an externalizing behavior disorder is considered the primary preventative component of parent training (Forehand & Long, 1996).

The Incredible Years Program Series (IYS; Webster-Stratton, 1989; Webster-Stratton & Hancock, 1998) was specifically designed for children presenting with ODD and CD and is directed at preventing and reducing behavioral, social, and emotional problems as well as promoting healthy emotional development by improving individual and family functioning through specific skill-building strategies. The children's program, known as the "Dinosaur Child-Training" curriculum, includes 12 two-hour weekly sessions and is designed for small groups of children (Webster-Stratton, 2004). The curriculum emphasizes communicating feelings, empathy for others, friendship development, anger management, using effective interpersonal problem-solving strategies (e.g., waiting, taking turns), and obeying classroom and school rules (e.g., raising one's hand to speak, following teachers' instructions). Program content includes the following: (1) new friends and school rules; (2) succeeding in school; (3) understanding feelings; (4) problem solving; (5) anger management; and (6) talking with friends and being friendly. The caregivers program, known as the "BASIC Parent-Training Program—Early Childhood," targets caregivers of young children, and also includes 12 two-hour weekly sessions (Webster-Stratton, 2001). The curriculum emphasizes parenting skills to promote children's social competence and to reduce behavior problems; it teaches caregivers how to engage in positive play interactions, help children to learn, provide positive reinforcement through praise and incentives, use limit-setting, and manage misbehavior with appropriate disciplinary strategies.

The Coping Power Program (Lochman & Wells, 2004) is a multifaceted prevention and intervention program for physically aggressive boys or disruptive children and their parents. This program includes both parent and child skill-building sessions with an overarching goal of promoting social competence, self-regulation, school bonding, and parental involvement. The duration of the program is approximately 15 months and includes both parent and child components. The child component focuses on developing coping skills, improving peer relations, increasing social competence, and learning anger management and general social and academic problem-solving skills. The parent component emphasizes skills that target prosocial and disruptive child behaviors, teaches parents how to use rewards and reinforcements, and instructs parents on how to manage stress and improve family communication.

Family-Based Strategies

Parent-child interaction therapy (PCIT; Eyberg, Boggs, & Algina, 1995; Eyberg, 1988) is an empirically supported intervention for children, ages 2–7 years, already exhibiting problematic behavior. This short-term intervention focuses on parent directed interactions, where behavioral management skills are taught; and, child directed interactions, when parents are live coached and taught to play with their child. Families meet for weekly 1-hour sessions for an average of 12 to 16 sessions, during which parents learn two basic interaction patterns. First, parents learn specific positive attention skills (emphasizing behavioral descriptions, reflections, and labeled praises) and active ignoring skills. In the second phase, parents learn and practice giving clear instructions to their child when needed and following through with praise or time-out during in vivo discipline situations. Therapists coach the parents as they interact with their child during the treatment sessions, teaching them to apply the skills calmly and consistently in the clinic until they achieve competency and are ready to use the procedures on their own.

The Triple P—Positive Parenting Program (Triple P; Sanders, 1999) is a multilevel system of parenting intervention, with five levels of intensity designed to match child and family needs based on problem severity. The five levels are as follows: Level 1: Parenting information; Level 2: One- to two-session intervention for mild behavior problems; Level 3: Four sessions for moderate behavior problems; Level 4: parent training program; and Level 5: behavioral family intervention. Core components of the program include guided participation, behavioral rehearsal, and self-regulation of parenting skills (Kaslow, Broth, Smith, & Collins, 2010).

Brief strategic family therapy (BSFT) is targeted toward children and adolescents with conduct, delinquency, and other behavior-related problems and adopts strategies such as joining, reframing, and boundary shifting to restructure problematic family interactions of externalizing youth and their parents (Szapocznik et al., 2002).

Multisystemic therapy (MST) is an evidence-based, intensive, home-based intervention for families that focuses on improving communication, school performance, parenting skills, and peer relations (Chorpita, 2002; Hoagwood, 2001), and is designed to address the role of multiple, interconnected systems in which the adolescent is embedded (Henggeler & Lee, 2003). The interventions are individualized and goals are defined based on the individual needs of a family. Henggeler (1995) described the effectiveness of the approach as being attributed to the combination of different family therapy and cognitive-behavioral therapy techniques and interventions. In other words, this therapy takes what works from each effective treatment modality for behavior problems and integrates it into one approach.

Large-Scale Prevention Programs

The Fast Track Project is a large-scale, multiyear, multimodal program combining intensive universal and targeted interventions, delivered in home and school-based settings, and targeted at young children at high risk for early-onset conduct problems (Conduct Problems Prevention Research Group, 1999a, 1999b). The goals of the Fast Track Project are multifaceted and include increasing child competencies, improving parenting effectiveness, improving the overall school context, and increasing school-home communication. This longitudinal project sought to prevent antisocial behavior across the period from early childhood through adolescence by delivering developmentally appropriate interventions designed for both the elementary school and adolescent phase of the program. The Fast Track Project includes teacher-led classroom curricula, parent training groups, home visits, child social skill training groups, academic tutoring, mentoring, family problem-solving, and child friendship enhancement groups.

Settings for Prevention Programs

Prevention of ODD and CD at the Biological Level

Prevention of conduct problems at the biological level should start with improving prenatal care, including providing education to mothers who smoke cigarettes and use other dangerous substances about the importance of quitting during pregnancy.

Prevention of ODD and CD on the Individual and Group Level

Relative to more substantiated group-based and parent-training programs, isolated individual treatments for disruptive behavior disorders are not considered the most effective prevention modality (Brestan & Eyberg, 1998; Burke et al., 2002). On the other hand, there is some demonstrated support for group-based, child-focused problem-solving skills training programs (Kazdin, 1996; Webster-Stratton & Hammond, 1997). For example, in a study that delivered PSST, children that participated in the treatment group exhibited greater decreases in aggression, externalizing behaviors, and overall behavior problems, as well as improvements in prosocial behavior at follow-up as compared to the control group (Kazdin et al., 1987). In a similar study, children receiving PSST demonstrated significant improvements in behavior than the control group, with gains maintained at 1-year follow-up (Kazdin et al., 1989). Findings from a child training group (4- to 8-year-olds) that utilized the child treatment component of the Incredible Years program revealed significant improvements in problem-solving and conflict management skills in comparison with controls, with gains maintained over time (Webster-Stratton & Hammond, 1997). Taken together, early intervention (before age 8) programs delivered at the group level have the potential to improve early behavior problems and prevent the problems from developing into more significant maladaptive behaviors.

Prevention of OCD and CD on the Parent and Family Level

Family-based interventions using contingency management strategies have demonstrated efficacy for improving behavior in the home setting for children with ODD/CD that include reduced instances of aggression and disruptive behavior and improved compliance with treatment (Walker, Colvin, & Ramsey, 1995; Webster-Stratton, 1994). Findings from interventions that employed behavioral parent training revealed increases in caregivers' sense of competence in responding to their children, decreases in parental and family stress, and reductions in maladaptive parenting behavior (Chronis et al., 2004). Notably, the effects of behavioral parent training are most effective in specific domains, such as compliance with parental requests, rule-following, defiant/aggressive behavior, and parenting skills (MTA Cooperative Group, 1999). In a recent meta-analysis of parent training programs designed to modify disruptive child behaviors while also improving parental behavior and perceptions, findings indicated that parent training is a robust intervention producing effect sizes in the moderate range immediately following treatment (Lundahl et al., 2006). Although smaller in magnitude, parent training effects remained durable at 1-year follow-up.

Children that complete PCIT have demonstrated significant reductions in conduct problems and noncompliant behaviors, as well as improvements in self-esteem (Eisenstadt, Eyberg, McNeil, Newcomb, & Funderburk, 1993). In another study that employed PCIT, preschoolers' externalizing behaviors decreased postintervention at both the 1- and 2-year follow-up (Nixon, 2001). Findings from multiple studies also reveal that for parents at risk for child maltreatment, completing the PCIT program resulted in decreased parenting stress and parent-reported behavior problems (Bagner & Eyberg, 2007; Chaffin et al., 2004; Nixon et al., 2003, 2004; Timmer et al., 2006). Notably, research has demonstrated generalization of the positive effects of PCIT to daycare, preschool, and elementary school settings (McNeil, Eyberg, Eisenstadt, Newcomb, & Funderburk, 1991). In addition, PCIT has been found to be effective with culturally diverse children that meet criteria for ADHD and for children with behavior problems through a 3-month follow-up period (Matos, Bauermeister, & Bernal, 2009). In a recent meta-analysis, large effect sizes were found for children that received PCIT for oppositional defiant symptoms as compared to control groups (Thomas & Zimmer-Gembeck, 2007).

The Triple P program has been found to be efficacious for behaviors associated with ODD across several randomized controlled trials. For example, in a study of self-directed Triple P for mothers with preschool children, findings revealed reduced oppositional and disruptive behaviors with gains maintained up to 3 years (Markie-Dadds & Sanders, 2006). Parents of preschoolers diagnosed with comorbid ADHD and ODD reported fewer behavior problems following participation in the Triple P intervention (Bor, Sanders, & Markie-Dadds, 2002). Three recent meta-analyses supports these findings, with effect sizes ranging from .35 to .70 for trials that used Triple P to reduce disruptive behaviors among children with behavior problems (de Graaf, Speetjens, Smit, de Wolff, & Tavecchio, 2008; Nowak & Heinrichs, 2008; Thomas & Zimmer-Gembeck, 2007).

Brief strategic family therapy may be the only efficacious treatment designed for Latino youth (primarily Cuban) with conduct and substance abuse problems (Santisteban et al., 2003). In those instances in which conduct problems have advanced to a more serious degree, multisystemic family therapy with juvenile delinquents demonstrated impressive reductions in violent and criminal activity at 4-year follow-up (Borduin et al., 1995). MST has documented efficacy with ethnic minority populations, and is cost-effective in comparison to incarceration. Specifically, four clinical trials support the efficacy of MST with African American juvenile offenders (for review, see Huey & Polo, 2008).

Prevention of ODD and CD at the School and Community Level

Schools are considered one of the most important settings in which preventive interventions are conducted, especially for youth in need of programs that focus on decreasing aggression and promoting competence (Greenberg, Domitrovich, Graczyk, & Zins, 2004). A meta-analysis by Wilson and colleagues (2001) found that programs based on behavioral or cognitive-behavioral principles have consistently demonstrated positive effects for children with problem behaviors, especially in school settings. For example, the positive reinforcers within a token economy show distinctive promise in preventing oppositional behavior problems in both children and adolescents (Barkley & Benton, 1998).

Barrera and colleagues (2002) conducted a randomized early intervention in the school setting directed at reducing conduct problems in at-risk early elementary Hispanic and non-Hispanic children. The unique aspect of this study was that the comprehensive intervention combined several evidence-based treatments for reducing disruptive behaviors. For example, parents in the intervention condition received parent training (Incredible Years parenting program; Webster-Stratton, 1992), while children received interventions focused on developing social and behavioral skills (Contingencies for learning academic and social skills [CLASS]; Hops & Walker, 1988; Dina Dinosaur Social Skills Program; Webster-Stratton, 1990). Findings at the end of the intervention revealed that children in the experimental group demonstrated fewer negative social behaviors when compared to children in the control group. At 1-year follow-up, parents reported fewer coercive and antisocial behaviors in the intervention group as compared to the control group. Overall, combining validated interventions shows promise in preventing the development of more severe conduct problems among early elementary school children.

Findings from trials of the Incredible Years that employed the parent and child-training programs in a clinic setting have revealed moderate to large effect sizes. Specifically, 75% of participating children had returned to adaptive levels of functioning when evaluated at 2-year follow-up according to parent—and teacher-report (Reid, Webster-Stratton, & Hammond, 2003). Independent evaluations of this program have generally replicated these findings. For example, an enhanced version of the Incredible Years Series was employed in both center and home-based settings with preschoolers at high risk for conduct problems (Brotman et al., 2005). When compared to the control group, findings indicated that intervention parents displayed significant improvements in negative parenting and stimulation for learning while children demonstrated improved social competence. These findings are interpreted to suggest that prevention programs can be successful in improving specific indices associated with the prevention of later conduct problems in young children that are considered high-risk (Brotman et al., 2005).

Multiple evaluations of the Coping Power Program reveal improvements in children's social competence and reductions in delinquent behavior. For example, Lochman and Wells (2004) randomly assignment aggressive children and their parents to one of the following groups: coping power with child only (CI); coping power with child and parent (CPI); or, control group (services as usual within the school setting). Findings indicated improvements in school behavior for both of the treatment groups (CP and CPI) when compared to the control condition. Children in the CPI group also demonstrated significant improvements in covert delinquency relative to the control group (Lochman & Wells, 2004).

Findings from the Fast Track program demonstrated small to modest benefits for behavior problems such as aggressive behavior, social cognitions, prosocial behavior, and social skills among high-risk elementary school children (Conduct Problems Prevention Research Group, 2002). Additional findings revealed reduced need for and use of special education, which resulted in substantial cost-effectiveness implications despite the considerable cost of the program (Foster, Jones, & the Conduct Problems Prevention Research Group, 2006).

Conclusion

Historically, psychosocial treatment of children and adolescents displaying disruptive and conduct-disordered behavior problems has been perceived as being both difficult and not very productive, with some clinicians viewing the negative behaviors associated with ODD and CD as intractable in nature. However, in recent years, there is a growing body of evidence, including from randomized clinical research trials, that has identified empirically supported prevention and early intervention programs for youth at risk for, or diagnosed with, ODD and CD. Specifically, the extant literature indicates that prevention programs can effectively reduce behavior problems while also enhancing youth competence, suggesting that the greatest hope for reducing the problem of conduct disorder lies in prevention programs that begin in early childhood. In the absence of early intervention, the prognosis is particularly poor for individuals displaying symptoms of disruptive behavior disorders. However, when these disorders are identified at an early age, it is possible to intervene with efficacious treatments across varied settings in order to help these individuals achieve optimal outcomes.

Future Directions

1. How often, and at what dosage, do booster sessions need to be employed following the delivery of preventive and early intervention programs in order to maintain treatment gains for behaviors such as aggression and social skills?
2. Given the high rate of comorbidity between ODD/CD and learning disabilities (e.g., reading disorders), should most early intervention programs also include a component that focuses on enhancing academic skills?
3. Beyond the already identified biological, psychological, and sociological variables associated with the development of behaviors consistent with a diagnosis of CD, which additional early indicators place children at risk for the development of conduct problems?
4. Future directions for the field should focus on elucidating the specific mechanisms of change involved in successful preventive and early intervention programs.
5. Few treatment programs have been designated as evidence-based for minority populations. Thus, future studies should include ethnically diverse populations as part of the treatment sample.

References

Aguilar, B., Sroufe, L. A., Egeland, B., & Carlson, E. (2000). Distinguishing the early-onset/persistent and adolescence-onset antisocial behaviour types: From birth to sixteen years. *Development and Psychopathology, 12,* 109–132.

Allen, N. B., Lewinsohn, P. M., & Seeley, J. R. (1998). Prenatal and perinatal influences on risk for psychopathology in childhood and adolescence. *Development and Psychopathology, 10,* 513–529.

American Psychiatric Association. (2000). *Diagnostic and statistical manual of mental disorders* (Revised 4th ed.). Washington, DC: Author.

American Psychological Association Working Group on Psychoactive Medications for Children and Adolescents. (2006). *Psychopharmacological, psychosocial, and combined interventions for childhood disorders: Evidence base, contextual factors, and future directions.* Washington, DC: American Psychological Association.

Anderson, K. G., Tapert, S. F., Moadab, I., Crowley, T. J., & Brown, S. A. (2007). Personality risk profile for conduct disorder and substance use disorders in youth. *Addictive Behaviors, 32,* 2377–2382.

Angold, A., & Costello, E. J. (2001). The epidemiology of depression in children and adolescents. In I. M. Goodyer (ed.), *The depressed child and adolescent* (2nd ed., pp. 143–178). Cambridge: Cambridge University Press.

Archer, J, & Côté, S. (2005). Sex differences in aggressive behaviour: A developmental and evolutionary perspective. In R. E. Tremblay, W. W. Hartup, & J. Archer, J. (Eds.), *Developmental origins of aggression* (pp. 425–446). New York: Guilford Press.

Babinski, L. M., Hartsough, C. S., & Lambert, N. M. (1999). Childhood conduct problems, hyperactivity-impulsivity, and inattention as predictors of adult criminal activity. *Journal of Child Psychology and Psychiatry, 40,* 347–355.

Bagner, D. M., & Eyberg, S. M. (2007). Parent-child interaction therapy for disruptive behavior in children with mental retardation: A randomized controlled trial. *Journal of Clinical Child and Adolescent Psychology, 36,* 1–12.

Baker, L. A., Jacobson, K. C., Raine, A., Lozano, D. I., & Bezdjian, S. (2007). Genetic and environmental bases of childhood antisocial behavior: A multi-informant twin study. *Journal of Abnormal Psychology, 116,* 219–235.

Barkley, R. A., & Benton, C. M. (1998). *Your defiant child: Eight steps to better behavior.* New York: Guilford Press.

Barkley, R. A., Shelton, T. L., Crosswait, C., Moorehouse, M., & Fletcher, K., Barrett, S.,... Metevia, L. (2000). Multi-method psycho-educational intervention for preschool children with disruptive behavior: Preliminary results at post-treatment. *Journal of Child Psychology and Psychiatry, 41,* 319–332.

Barnow, S., Lucht, M., & Freyberger, H. J. (2005). Correlates of aggressive and delinquent conduct problems in adolescence. *Aggressive Behavior, 31,* 24–39.

Baving, L., Laucht, M., & Schmidt, M. H. (2000). Oppositional children differ from healthy children in frontal brain activation. *Journal of Abnormal Child Psychology, 28,* 267–275.

Barrera, M., Biglan, A., Taylor, T., Gunn, B., Smolkowski, K., Black, C.,... Fowler, R. (2002). Early elementary school intervention to reduce conduct problems: A randomized trial with Hispanic and non-Hispanic children. *Prevention Science, 3,* 83–94.

Belsky, J., Hsieh, K.-H., & Crnic, K. (1998). Mothering, fathering, and infant negativity as antecedents of boys' externalising problems and inhibition at age 3 years: Differential susceptibility to rearing experience? *Development and Psychopathology, 10,* 301–320.

Biederman, J., Petty, C. R., Dolan, C., Hughes, S., Mick, E., Monuteaux, M. C., & Faraone, S. V. (2008). The long-term longitudinal course of oppositional defiant disorder and conduct disorder in ADHD boys: Findings from a controlled 10-year prospective longitudinal follow-up study. *Psychological Medicine, 38,* 1027–1036.

Blair, R. J. R. (2001). Neurocognitive models of aggression, the antisocial personality disorders, and psychopathy. *Journal of Neurology and Neurosurgery in Psychiatry, 71,* 727–731.

Bor, W., Sanders, M. R., & Markie-Dadds, C. (2002). The effects of the Triple P-Positive Parenting Program on preschool children with co-occurring disruptive behavior and attentional/hyperactive difficulties. *Journal of Abnormal Child Psychology, 30,* 571–587.

Borduin, C. M., Mann, B. J., Cone, L. T., Henggeler, S. W., Fucci, B. R. Blaske, D. M., & Williams, R. A. (1995). Multisystemic treatment of serious juvenile offenders: Long-term prevention of criminality and violence. *Journal of Consulting and Clinical Psychology, 63,* 569–578.

Brestan, E., & Eyberg, S. (1998). Effective psychosocial treatments for children and adolescents with disruptive behavior disorders: 29 years, 82 studies, and 5,275 kids. *Journal of Clinical Child Psychology, 27,* 180–189.

Brinkmeyer, M., & Eyberg, S. M. (2003). Parent-child interaction therapy for oppositional children. In A. E. Kazdin & J. R. Weisz (Eds.), *Evidence-based psychotherapies for children and adolescents* (pp. 204–223). New York: Guilford Press.

Brotman, M. L., Gouley, K. K., Chesir-Teran, D., Dennis, T., Klein, G. R., & Shrout, P. (2005). Prevention for preschoolers at high risk for conduct problems: Immediate outcomes on parenting practices and child social competence. *Journal of Clinical Child and Adolescent Psychology, 34,* 724–734.

Burke, J. D., Loeber, R., & Birhamer, B. (2002). Oppositional defiant disorder and conduct disorder: A review of the past 10 years, part II. *Journal of the American Academy of Child and Adolescent Psychiatry, 41,* 1275–1293.

Campbell, S. B., & Ewing, L. J. (1990). Follow-up of hard-to-manage preschoolers: Adjustment at age 9 and predictors of continuing symptoms. *Journal of Child Psychology and Psychiatry, 31,* 871–889.

Chaffin, M., Silovsky, J., Funderbunk, B., Valle, L. A., Brestan, E. V., Balachova, T.,... Bonner, B. (2004). Parent-child interaction therapy with physically abusive parents: Efficacy for reducing future abuse reports. *Journal of Consulting and Clinical Psychology, 72,* 500–510.

Chambless, D. L., Baker, M. J., Baucom, D. H., Beutler, L. E. Calhoun, K. S., Crits-Christoph, P.,... Woody, S. R. (1998). Update on empirically validated studies II. *The Clinical Psychologist, 51,* 1–14.

Chapman, L. A., Wade, S. L., Walz, N. C., Taylor, H. G., & Stancin, T. (2010). Clinically significant behavior problems during the initial 18 months following early childhood traumatic brain injury. *Rehabilitation Psychology, 55,* 48–57.

Chorpita, B. F. (2002). Treatment manuals in the real world: Where do we build them? *Clinical Psychology: Science and Practice, 9,* 431–433.

Christophersen, E. R., & Mortweet, S. L. (2001). *Treatments that work with children: Empirically supported strategies for managing childhood problems.* Washington, DC: American Psychological Association.

Chronis, A. M., Chacko, A., Fabiano, G. A., Wymbs, B. T., & Pelham, W. E. (2004). Enhancements to the standard behavioral parent training paradigm for families of children with ADHD: Review and future directions. *Clinical Child and Family Psychology Review, 35,* 1–27.

Chronis, A. M., Jones, H. A., & Raggi, V. L. (2006). Evidence-based psychosocial treatments for children and adolescents with attention-deficit/hyperactivity disorder. *Clinical Psychology Review, 26,* 486–502.

Cohen, M. A., & Piquero, A. R. (2009). New evidence on the monetary value of saving a high-risk youth. *Journal of Quantitative Criminology, 25,* 25–49.

Conduct Problems Prevention Research Group. (1999a). Initial impact of the fast track prevention trial for conduct problems: I. The high-risk sample. *Journal of Consulting and Clinical Psychology, 67,* 631–647.

Conduct Problems Prevention Research Group. (1999b). Initial impact of the fast track prevention trial for conduct problems: II. Classroom effects. *Journal of Consulting and Clinical Psychology, 67,* 648–657.

Conduct Problems Prevention Research Group. (2002). Evaluation of the first 3 years of the Fast Track prevention trial with children at high risk for adolescent conduct problems. *Journal of Abnormal Child Psychology, 30,* 19–35.

Copeland, W. E., Miller-Johnson, S., Keeler, G., Angold, A., & Costello, E. J. (2007). Childhood psychiatric disorders and young adult crime: A prospective, population-based study. *American Journal of Psychiatry, 164,* 1668–1675.

Deater-Deckard, K., & Plomin, R. (1999). An adoption study of the etiology of teacher and parent reports of externalizing behavior problems in middle childhood. *Child Development, 70,* 144–154.

de Graaf, I., Speetjens, P., Smit, F., de Wolff, M., & Tavecchio, L. (2008). Effectiveness of the Triple P—Positive Parenting Program on parenting: A meta-analysis. *Family Relations, 57,* 553–566.

Derringer, J., Krueger, R. F., Irons, D. E., & Iacono, W. G. (2010). Harsh discipline, childhood sexual assault, and MAOA genotype: An investigation of main and interactive effects on diverse clinical externalizing outcomes. *Behavioral Genetics, 40,* 639–648.

Eisenstadt, T., Eyberg, S. M., McNeil, C., Newcomb, K., & Funderburk, B. (1993). Parent–child interaction therapy with behavior problem children: Relative effectiveness to two stages and overall treatment outcome. *Journal of Child Clinical Psychology, 22,* 42–51.

Eyberg, S. M. (1988). Parent-child interaction therapy: Integration of traditional and behavioral concerns. *Child and Family Behavior Therapy, 10,* 33–46.

Eyberg, S. M., Boggs, S. R., & Algina, J. (1995). Parent–child interaction therapy: A psychosocial model for the treatment of young children with conduct problem behavior and their families. *Psychopharmacology Bulletin, 31,* 83–91.

Eyberg, S. M., Nelson, M. N., & Boggs, S. R. (2008). Evidence-based psychosocial treatments for children and adolescents with disruptive behavior disorder. *Journal of Clinical Child and Adolescent Psychology, 37,* 215–237.

Forehand, R. L., & Long, N. (1996). *Parenting the strong-willed child.* Chicago: Contemporary Books.

Foster, E. M., Jones, D., & the Conduct Problems Prevention Research Group (2006). Can a costly intervention be cost-effective? *Archives of General Psychiatry, 63,* 1284–1291.

Goldstein, L. H., Harvey, E. A., Friedman-Weieneth, J. L., Pierce, C., Tellert, A., & Sippel, J. C. (2007). Examining subtypes of behavior problems about 3-year-old children: Part II. Investigating differences in parent psychopathology, couple conflict, and other family stressors. *Journal of Abnormal Child Psychology, 35,* 111–123.

Green, S. M., Russo, M. F., Navratil, J. L., & Loeber, R. (1999). Sexual and physical abuse among adolescent girls with disruptive behavior problems. *Journal of Child and Family Studies, 8,* 151–168.

Greenberg, M. T., Domitrovich, C. E., Graczyk, P. A., & Zins, J. E. (2004). *The study of implementation in school-based preventive interventions: Theory, research, and practice.* Washington, DC: US Department of Health and Human Services, Substance Abuse and Mental Health Services Administration, Center for Mental Health Services.

Gutermuth-Anthony, L., Anthony, B. J., Glanville, D. N., Naiman, D. Q., Waanders, C., & Shaffer, S. (2005). The relationships between parenting stress, parenting behaviour and preschoolers' social competence and behavior problems in the classroom. *Infant and Child Development, 14,* 133–154.

Harden, K. P., Lynch, S. K., Turkheimer, E., Emery, R. E., D'Onofrio, B. M., Slutske, W. S., . . . Martin, N. G. (2007). A behavior genetic investigation of adolescent motherhood and offspring mental health problems. *Journal of Abnormal Psychology, 116,* 667–683.

Harvey, E. A., Friedman-Weieneth, J. L., Goldstein, L. H., & Sherman, A. H. (2007). Examining subtypes of behavior problems among 3-year-old children: Part I. Investigating validity of subtypes and biological risk factors. *Journal of Abnormal Child Psychology, 35,* 97–110.

Henggeler, S. W. (1995). Home-based delivery of multisystemic therapy: Removing barriers to treatment access for youth with serious clinical problems and their families. *The Child, Youth, and Family Services Quarterly, 18,* 2–3.

Henggeler, S. W., & Lee, T. (2003). Multisystemic treatment of serious clinical problems. In A. E. Kazdin & J. R. Weisz (Eds.), *Evidence-based psychotherapies for children and adolescents* (pp. 301–322). New York: Guilford Press.

Hill, J. (2003). Early identification of individuals at risk for antisocial personality disorder. *The British Journal of Psychiatry, 182,* s11–s14.

Hinshaw, S. P. (1992). Externalizing behavior problems and academic underachievement in childhood and adolescence: Causal relationships and underlying mechanisms. *Psychological Bulletin, 111,* 127–155.

Hoagwood, K. (2001). Evidence-based practice in children's mental health services: What do we know? Why aren't we putting it to use? *Report on Emotional and Behavioral Disorders in Youth, 1,* 84–88.

Hops, H., & Walker, H. M. (1988). *CLASS: Contingencies for Learning Academic and Social Skills. A classroom behavior management program for children with acting-out behaviors.* Delray Beach, FL: Educational Achievement Systems.

Huey, S. J., & Polo, A. J. (2008). Evidence-based psychosocial treatments for ethnic minority youth. *Journal of Clinical Child and Adolescent Psychology, 37,* 262–301.

Kaslow, N. J., Broth, M. R., Smith, C. O., & Collins, M. H. (2010, September). *Family-based interventions for child and adolescent disorders.* Talk presented at the American Association for Marriage & Family Therapy (AAMFT) Research Conference in Washington, DC.

Kazdin, A. E. (1995). *Conduct disorder in childhood and adolescence* (2nd ed.). Newbury Park, CA: Sage.

Kazdin, A. E. (1996). Problem solving and parent management in treating aggressive and antisocial behavior. In E. D. Hibbs & P. S. Jensen (Eds.), *Psychosocial treatments for child and adolescent disorders: Empirically based strategies for clinical practice* (pp. 377–408). Washington, DC: American Psychological Association.

Kazdin, A. E. Bass, D., Siegel, T., & Thomas, C. (1989). Cognitive-behavioral therapy and relationship therapy in the treatment of children referred for antisocial behavior. *Journal of Consulting and Clinical Psychology, 57,* 522–535.

Kazdin, A. E., Esveldt-Dawson, K., French, N. H., & Unis, A. S. (1987). Effects of parent management training and problem-solving skills training combined in the treatment of antisocial child behavior. *Journal of the American Academy of Child and Adolescent Psychiatry, 26,* 416–424.

Kazdin, A. E., & Kendall, P. C. (1998). Current progress and future plans for developing effective treatments: Comments and perspectives. *Journal of Clinical Child Psychology, 27,* 217–226.

Kessler, R. C., Amminger, G. P., Aguilar-Gaxiola, S., Alonso, J., Lee, S., & Ustun, T. B. (2007). Age of onset of mental disorders: A review of recent literature. *Current Opinions in Psychiatry, 20,* 359–364.

Koenen, K. C., Caspi, A., Moffitt, T. E., Rijsdijk, F., & Taylor, A. (2006). Genetic influence on the overlap between low IQ and antisocial behavior in young children. *Journal of Abnormal Psychology, 115,* 787–797.

Kosterman, R., Hawkins, J. D., Mason, W. A., Herrenkohl, T. I., Lengua, L. J., & McCauley, E. (2009). Assessment of behavior problems in childhood and adolescence as predictors of early adult depression. *Journal of Psychological Behavioral Assessment, 32,* 118–127.

Kruesi, M. J., Casanova, M. F., Mannheim, G., & Johnson-Bilder, A. (2004). Reduced temporal lobe volume in early onset conduct disorder. *Psychiatry Research: Neuroimaging, 132,* 1–11.

Lahey, B. B., Rathouz, P. J., Van Hulle, C., Urbano, R. C., Krueger, R. F., Applegate, B., . . . Waldman, I. D. (2008). Testing structural models of DSM-IV symptoms of common forms of child and adolescent psychopathology. *Journal of Abnormal Child Psychology, 36,* 187–206.

Lerner, R. M., Almerigi, J. B., Theokas, C., & Lerner, J. V. (2005). Positive youth development: A view of the issues. *Journal of Early Adolescence, 25,* 10–16.

Lochman, J. E., & Wells, K. C. (2004). The Coping Power program for preadolescent aggressive boys and their parents: Outcome effects at the one-year follow-up. *Journal of Consulting and Clinical Psychology, 72,* 571–578.

Loeber, R., & Birhamer, B. (2002). Oppositional defiant disorder and conduct disorder: A review of the past 10 years: Part II. *Journal of the American Academy of Child and Adolescent Psychiatry, 41,* 1275–1293.

Loeber, R., & Farrington, D. P. (2000). Young children who commit crime: Epidemiology, developmental origins, risk factors, early interventions, and policy implications. *Development and Psychopathology, 12,* 737–762.

Loeber, R., Green, S. M., Keenan, K., & Lahey, B. B. (1995). Which boys will fare worse? Early predictors of the onset of conduct disorders in a six-year longitudinal study. *Journal of the American Academy of Child and Adolescent Psychiatry, 34,* 499–509.

Long, P., Forehand, R., Wierson, M., & Morgan, A. (1994). Does parent training with young noncompliant children have long term effects? *Behavior Research and Therapy, 32,* 101–107.

Lorber, M. F. (2004). Psychophysiology of aggression, psychopathy, and conduct problems: A meta-analysis. *Psychological Bulletin, 130,* 531–552.

Lundahl, B. W., Risser, H. J., & Lovejoy, M. C. (2006). A meta-analysis of parent training: Moderators and follow-up effects. *Clinical Psychology Review, 26,* 86–104.

Markie-Dadds, C., & Sanders, M. R. (2006). A controlled evaluation of an enhanced self-directed behavioural family intervention for parents of children with conduct problems in rural and remote areas. *Behaviour Change, 23,* 55–72.

Matos, M., Bauermeister, J. J., & Bernal, G. (2009). Parent-child interaction therapy for Puerto Rican preschool children with ADHD and behavior problems: A pilot efficacy study. *Family Process, 48,* 232–252.

McKinlay, A., Grace, R. C., Horwood, L. J., Ferguson, D. M., & MacFarlane, M. R. (2009). Long-term behavioural outcomes of pre-school mild traumatic brain injury. *Child: Care, Health, and Development, 36,* 22–30.

McNeil, C. B., Capage, L. C., & Bennett, G. M. (2001). Cultural issues in the treatment of young African American children diagnosed with disruptive behavior disorders. *Journal of Pediatric Psychology, 27,* 339–350.

McNeil, C. B., Eyberg, S. M., Eisenstadt, T. H., Newcomb, K., & Funderburk, B. (1991). Parent–child interaction therapy with behavior problem children: Generalization of treatment effects to the school setting. *Journal of Child Clinical Psychology, 20,* 140–151.

Messer, J., Goodman, R., Rowe, R., & Meltzer, H. (2006). Preadolescent conduct problems in girls and boys. *Journal of American Child and Adolescent Psychiatry, 45,* 184–191.

Moffitt, T. E., Caspi, A., Rutter, M., & Silva, P. A. (2001). *Sex differences in antisocial behavior.* New York: Cambridge University Press.

MTA Cooperative Group. (1999). A 14-month randomized clinical trial of treatment strategies for attention-deficit hyperactivity disorder (ADHD). *Archives of General Psychiatry, 56,* 1073–1086.

Murphy, J. M., & Jellinek, C. (1988). Screening for psychosocial dysfunction in economically disadvantaged and minority group children. Further validation of the Pediatric Symptom Checklist. *American Journal of Orthopsychiatry, 58,* 450–456.

Nigg, J. T., & Breslau, N. (2007). Prenatal smoking exposure, low birth weight, and disruptive behavior disorders. *Journal of the American Academy of Child and Adolescent Psychiatry, 43,* 362–369.

Nixon, R. D. V. (2001). Changes in hyperactivity and temperament in behaviourally disturbed preschoolers after parent-child interaction therapy (PCIT). *Behaviour Change, 18,* 168–176.

Nixon, R. D. V., Sweeney, L., Erickson, D. B., & Touyz, S. W. (2003). Parent-child interaction therapy: A comparison of standard and abbreviated treatments for oppositional defiant preschoolers. *Journal of Consulting and Clinical Psychology, 71,* 251–260.

Nixon, R. D. V., Sweeny, L., Erickson, D. B., & Touyz, S. W. (2004). Parent-child interaction therapy: One- and two-year follow-up of standard and abbreviated treatments for oppositional preschoolers. *Journal of Abnormal Child Psychology, 32,* 263–271.

Nock, M. K., Kazdin, A. E., Hiripi, E., & Kessler, R. C. (2007). Lifetime prevalence, correlates and persistence of oppositional defiant disorder: Results from the National Comorbidity Survey Replication. *Journal of Child Psychology and Psychiatry, 48,* 703–713.

Northey, W. F., Jr., Wells, K. C., Silverman, W. K., & Bailey, C. E. (2003). Childhood behavioral and emotional disorders. *Journal of Marital and Family Therapy, 29,* 523–545.

Nottlemann, E. D., & Jensen, P. S. (1995). Comorbidity of disorders in children and adolescents: Developmental perspectives. *Advances in Clinical Child Psychology, 17,* 109–155.

Nowak, C., & Heinrichs, N. (2008). A comprehensive meta-analysis of Triple P—Positive Parenting Program using hierarchical linear modeling: Effectiveness and moderating variables. *Clinical Child and Family Psychology Review, 11,* 114–144.

Office of the Surgeon General (2001). *Youth Violence: A Report of the Surgeon General.* Washington, DC: US Department of Health and Human Services.

Ortiz, J., & Raine, A. (2004). Heart rate level and antisocial behavior in children and adolescents: A meta-analysis. *Journal of the American Academy of Child and Adolescent Psychiatry, 43,* 154–162.

Patterson, C. J., Kupersmidt, J., & Vaden, N. (1990). Income level, gender, ethnicity, and household composition as predictors of children's school-based competence. *Child Development, 61,* 485–494.

Phelps, L., & McClintock, K. (1994). Papa and peers: A biosocial approach to conduct disorder. *Journal of Psychopathology and Behavioral Assessment, 16,* 53–67.

Putallaz, M., & Bierman, K. L. (2004) *Aggression, antisocial behavior, and violence among girls: A developmental perspective.* New York: Guilford Press.

Reid, J. M., Webster-Stratton, C., & Hammond, M. (2003). Follow-up of children who received the Incredible Years intervention for oppositional-defiant disorder: Maintenance and prediction of 2-year outcome. *Behavior Therapy, 34,* 471–491.

Sameroff, A. J., Peck, S. C., & Eccles, J. S. (2004). Changing ecological determinants of conduct problems from early adolescence to early adulthood. *Developmental Psychopathology, 16,* 873–896.

Sanders, M. R. (1999). Triple P-Positive Parenting Program: Towards an empirically validated multilevel parenting and family support strategy for the prevention of behavior and emotional problems in children. *Clinical Child and Family Psychology Review, 2,* 71–90.

Santisteban, D. A., Coatsworth, J. D., Douglas, J., Perez-Vidal, A., Kurtines, W. M., Schwartz, S. J., & Szapocznik, J. (2003). Efficacy of brief strategic family therapy in modifying Hispanic adolescent behavior problems and substance use. *Journal of Family Psychology, 17,* 121–133.

Scott, S., Spender, Q., Doolan, M., Jacobs, B., & Aspland, H. (2001). Multicentre controlled trial of parenting groups for childhood antisocial behaviour in clinical practice. *British Journal of Medicine, 323,* 1–7.

Scott, S., Sylva, K., Doolan, M., Price, J., Jacobs, B., Crook, C., & Landau, S. (2010). Randomised controlled trial of parent groups for child antisocial behaviour targeting multiple risk factors: The SPOKES project. *Journal of Child Psychology and Psychiatry, 51,* 48–57.

Snyder, J. J., Reid, J. B., & Patterson, G. R. (2003). A social learning model of child and adolescent antisocial behavior. In B. B. Lahey, T. E. Moffitt, & A. Caspi (Eds.), *The causes of conduct disorder and juvenile delinquency* (pp. 27–48). New York: Guilford Press.

Szapocznik, J., Robbins, M. S., Mitrani, V. B., Santisteban, D., Hervis, O., & Williams, R. A. (2002). Brief strategic family therapy with behavior problem Hispanic youth (pp. 83–109). In J. Lebow (Ed.) *Integrative and eclectic psychotherapies* (Vol. 4). In F. W. Kaslow (Ed.) *Comprehensive handbook of psychotherapy,* New York: Wiley & Sons.

Szatmari, P., Saigal, S., Rosenbaum, P., Campbell, D., & King, S. (1990). Psychiatric disorders at five years among children with birthweights less than 1000g: A regional perspective. *Developmental Medicine and Child Neurology, 32,* 954–962.

Thomas, C. R. (2006). Evidence-based practice for conduct disorder symptoms. *Journal of American Academy of Child and Adolescent Psychiatry, 45,* 109–114.

Thomas, R., & Zimmer-Gembeck, M. J. (2007). Behavioral outcomes of parent-child interaction therapy and Triple P—Positive Parenting Program: A review and meta-analysis. *Journal of Abnormal Child Psychology, 35,* 475–495.

Tibbetts, S. G., & Piquero, A. R. (1999). The influence of gender, low birth rate, and disadvantaged environment in predicting early onset of offending: A test of Moffitt's interactional hypothesis. *Criminology, 37,* 843–878.

Timmer, S. G., Urquiza, A. J., Herschell, A., McGrath, J., Zebell, N., Porter, A., & Vargas, E. (2006). Parent-child interaction therapy: Application of an empirically supported treatment to maltreated children in foster care. *Child Welfare, 85,* 919–940.

Trentacosta, C. J., Hyde, L. W., Shaw, D. S., & Cheong, J. (2009). Adolescent dispositions for antisocial behavior in context: The roles of neighborhood dangerousness and parental knowledge. *Journal of Abnormal Psychology, 118,* 564–575.

Wakschlag, L. S., Pickett, K. E., Kasza, K. E., & Loeber, R. (2006). Is prenatal smoking associated with a developmental pattern of conduct problems in young boys? *Journal of the American Academy of Child and Adolescent Psychiatry, 45,* 461–467.

Walker, H. M., Colvin, G., & Ramsey, E. (1995). *Antisocial behavior in school: Strategies and best practices.* Pacific Grove, CA: Brooks/Cole.

Waschbusch, D. A. (2002). A meta-analytic examination of comorbid hyperactive-attention problems and conduct problems. *Psychological Bulletin, 128,* 118–150.

Webster-Stratton, C. (1989). Systematic comparison of consumer satisfaction of three cost-effective parent training programs for conduct problem children. *Behavior Therapy, 20,* 103–115.

Webster-Stratton, C. (1990). *The teachers and children's videotape series: Dina Dinosaur's social skills and problem-solving curriculum.* Seattle, WA: University of Washington Press.

Webster-Stratton, C. (1992). *The Incredible Years: A troubleshooting guide for parents of children aged 3–8.* Toronto, Canada: Umbrella Press.

Webster-Stratton, C. (1994). Advancing videotape parent training: A comparison study. *Journal of Consulting and Clinical Psychology, 62,* 583–593.

Webster-Stratton, C. (2001). *Incredible Years parent group leader training: Leader's guide.* Seattle, WA: Incredible Years.

Webster-Stratton, C. (2004). *Incredible Years child group leader training: Therapist's guide for Dinosaur school treatment program.* Seattle, WA: Incredible Years.

Webster-Stratton, C., & Dahl, R. W. (1995). Conduct disorder. In M. Hersen & R. T. Ammerman (Eds.), *Advanced abnormal child psychology* (pp. 333–352). Hillsdale, NJ: Erlbaum.

Webster-Stratton, C., & Hammond, M. (1997). Treating children with early-onset conduct problems: A comparison of child and parent training interventions. *Journal of Consulting and Clinical Psychology, 65,* 93–109.

Webster-Stratton, C., & Hancock, C. L. (1998). Training for parents of young children with conduct problems: Content, methods, and therapeutic processes. In J. M. Briesmeister & C. E. Schaefer (Eds.), *Handbook of parent training: Parents as co-therapists for children's behavior problems* (2nd ed., pp. 98–152). Hoboken, NJ.: Wiley.

Webster-Stratton, C., Reid, M. J., & Stoolmiller, M. (2008). Preventing conduct problems and improving school readiness: evaluation of the Incredible Years Teacher and Child Training Programs in high-risk schools. *Journal of Child Psychology and Psychiatry, 49,* 471–488.

Weisz, J. R., Doss, A. J., & Hawley, K. M. (2005). Youth psychotherapy outcome research: A review and critique of the evidence base. *Annual Review of Psychology, 56,* 337–363.

Wilson, D. B., Gottfredson, D. C, & Najaka, S. S. (2001). School-based prevention of problem behaviors: A meta-analysis. *Journal of Quantitative Criminology, 17,* 247–272.

Woodward, L. J., & Fergusson, D. M. (1999) Childhood peer relationship problems and psychosocial adjustment in late adolescence. *Journal of Abnormal Child Psychology, 27,* 87–104.

CHAPTER

18 Toward the Prevention of Risky Sexual Behavior Among Latina Youth

Lisa M. Edwards *and* Lucia J. Stubbs

Abstract

Sexual risk-taking among Latina youth has been noted as a critical health concern within the United States. In this chapter, the importance of prevention of risky sexual behavior among Latina youth will be discussed. Current prevalence rates and consequences associated with sexual behavior among Latino/as will be reviewed, along with factors that are relevant to understanding the prevention of sexual activity. Finally, programs that have been developed to prevent risky sexual behavior among Latinas will be reviewed and suggestions for prevention efforts will be presented.

Key Words: Latino/a youth, adolescent, sexual activity, prevention, teen pregnancy, risky behavior

Introduction

Adolescents today are exposed to risky behavior, such as sexual activity, at a much earlier age than in previous times (LeCroy, 2008). Youth generally begin experimenting with sexual activity during the adolescent years (LeCroy, 2008; Takanishi, 1993), and the consequences of this experimentation can include costs to individuals' health, education, and future outcomes. For females, the added risk of pregnancy in addition to acquiring a sexually transmitted disease (STD) is problematic. Young Latinas in particular are at risk because of their early onset of sexual activity and less consistent contraceptive use (Lescano, Brown, Raffaelli, & Lima 2009). Prevention in the area of sexual risk-taking among Latina youth is critical, as it has the potential to promote health and psychosocial wellness and help combat this significant health concern within the United States. In this chapter, we will describe the importance of prevention of risky sexual behavior among Latina youth. We will discuss current prevalence rates and consequences associated with sexual behavior among Latino/as, as well as factors that are relevant to understanding the prevention of sexual activity. Finally, programs that have been developed to ameliorate this health risk behavior will be reviewed and suggestions for prevention efforts will be presented. Throughout the chapter we utilize the term *Latina* to refer to female individuals in the United States with origins in Latin America, and consider this term inclusive of other related terms such as Hispanic and Chicana, and national origin labels such as Mexican or Dominican.

Cultural Context of Latina Adolescent Sexual Activity

Authors have noted that adolescents, as compared to individuals in other developmental periods, are more open to experiencing and engaging in a wider range of behaviors (Arnett, 2000). Adolescence is a critical developmental period because of youths' emerging sexualities and the fact that they are forming identities and lifetime habits at this time (Buzwell & Rosenthal, 1996; Chapin, 2001; Michels, Kropp, Eyre, & Halpern-Felsher, 2005). Adolescents may therefore be at risk for poor sexual decision making because they are less developmentally and emotionally mature (Driscoll, Biggs, Brindis, & Yankah, 2001).

Early sexual activity puts adolescents at risk for a variety of negative outcomes across physical, psychological, and emotional domains (Driscoll et al., 2001; Kirby, 2007). Teens who are sexually active during early adolescence are more likely to have unprotected sex and more sexual partners, and to participate in other risk behaviors such as using drugs and alcohol and dropping out of school (Anaya, Cantwell, & Roteram-Borus, 2003; Franzetta, Terry-Humen, Manlove, & Ikramullah, 2006; Manlove, Logan, Moore, & Ikramullah, 2008; Manlove, Papillio, & Ikramullah, 2004; National Campaign to Prevent Teen Pregnancy, 2003; Silver & Bauman, 2006). The risk of teenage pregnancy for girls, parenthood, abortion, and sexually transmitted diseases also increases with early sexual activity and may lead to significant health complications (Anaya et al., 2003; CDC, 2007a; CDC, 2008b; Vélez-Pastrana, Gonzalez-Rodriguez, & Borges-Hernandez, 2005; Taylor-Seehafer & Rew, 2000). When teens give birth their future prospects decline (Centers for Disease Control and Prevention [CDC], 2007a), they are less likely to complete high school and receive prenatal care, and more likely to continue to live in poverty (Anaya et al., 2003; Hoffman, 2006). In addition, the effects of childbearing on girls may include mental illness, underperformance in school, sexual violence and abuse, family dysfunction, and poor self-esteem (Contreras, Narang, Ikhlas, & Teichman, 2002).

Data from the 2009 YRBS (CDC, 2009) showed that in general, males and ethnic minorities were more likely to engage in risky sexual behaviors. Across ethnic groups, adolescent males are more likely than females to initiate sex at an early age and report having sex with four or more people. African American males initiate sex before 13 years of age at 6 times the rate of White males, and Latino males initiate at twice the rate compared to White males. Similarly, African American males were most likely to have four or more sexual partners, followed by Latinos and White males. With respect to condom use, Latino males and Latina youth are least likely to use condoms of all ethnic groups, followed by African Americans and Whites.

Early and high rates of sexual activity among Latina youth in particular have been identified as significant public health concerns across the United States (CDC, 2007b; Schuster, 2003). Statistics indicate that by 12th grade, 68% of Latinas report having had sex and 22% report having had four or more sexual partners (CDC, 2009). About 5% of Latinas in high school reported first intercourse before age 13, compared to 3% of White and 7% of African American female students (CDC, 2009). Research has noted that Latina teens are least likely to use condoms or any contraception at first sex as compared to their male and female counterparts of all groups (CDC, 2006, 2009; Eaton et al., 2006), which likely often leads to the high rates of pregnancy and sexually transmitted diseases.

With respect to sexually transmitted diseases, rates of chlamydia, gonorrhea, and syphilis are two and three times as high for Latinos as for Whites, and Latinos accounted for 19% of new AIDS diagnoses in 2006 (CDC, 2008a). Latinas also experience disproportionately high rates of HIV infection. In 2006, the rate of HIV infection in Hispanic females ages 13 to 29 was three times the rate for non-Hispanic White females (Prejean, Song, An, & Hall, 2008). Latinas have the highest birthrates of all racial/ethnic groups, with rates declining over the past 15 years about half as fast as those for Whites and African American teens (Ikramullah, Schelar, Manlove, & Moore, 2007). Statistics indicate that 51% of Latinas become pregnant at least once by the time they are 20 years old (National Campaign to Prevent Teen Pregnancy, 2007).

Taken together, the data regarding risky sexual behavior among Latina youth suggest that there is a great need for prevention work in this area. Understanding factors that influence risky behavior is the first step toward prevention, and there are likely a multitude of complex factors that affect outcomes in this area. Some authors have speculated that disparities across ethnic groups in age of debut of sexual intercourse can be explained by differences in socioeconomic level, community, and opportunity; yet these differences don't entirely account for the increased risk for these youth (Miller, Sage, & Winward, 2005). Clearly the unique cultural context of being Latina in US society also plays a role in this puzzle.

Latina youth are expected to navigate their culture of origin as well as mainstream, White culture. They may experience stressors as a result of their biculturalism, including discrimination, acculturation gaps, family obligations, and pressure to be bilingual (Fennelly, Mulkeen, & Giusti, 1998; Flores, Tschann, Dimas, Pasch, & deGroat, 2010; Romero, Carvajal, Volle, & Orduña, 2007; Romero & Roberts, 2003), as well expectations about gender roles and pressure to conform to gender-specific behavior (McLean Taylor, Veloria, & Verba, 2007;

Romero et al., 2007). Researchers have noted that any prevention efforts must incorporate and consider culture, as culture influences beliefs about health including values and practices (Chwalisz & Obasi, 2008).

In the following section, prominent Latino/a cultural values that have been suggested to relate to sexual activity among youth are described. Specifically, we review relevant theory and research about the role of acculturation, familism, religiosity, and gender roles in Latina sexual risk-taking. For each value, we note the complexity of research that has shown that the construct at times might be protective for youth, and at other times, might serve as a risk factor.

Our goal in discussing these values is not to pathologize any aspect of culture, but rather to move the field toward a more nuanced discussion of the complexity of such constructs and how they might operate in the lives of Latina youth. We acknowledge that values such as these might operate in complex ways in any ethnic group, and that within any given culture there is great heterogeneity in the level to which individuals may or may not adhere to such cultural values.

Acculturation

Acculturation has been defined as the process of change that results from continuous contact between two different cultures (Berry, Trimble, & Olmedo, 1986). Several models of acculturation have been proposed and used to guide measures of this construct. Most initial research about acculturation adopted a unidimensional approach, which situated Latino individuals, for example, on a continuum of acculturation between two opposite poles of European American and Latino culture. As individuals assimilated to mainstream culture, this model suggested that they moved toward the European American end of the continuum and away from their Latino culture. A limitation of this approach, however, was that there was no acknowledgment of the possibility that acculturation toward the dominant culture does not necessarily preclude the simultaneous retention of one's culture of origin (Edwards & Lopez, 2006; Marin, 1992; Zane & Mak, 2003). Because acculturation is a multidimensional construct it is measured by a number of variables including: birth place, length of residency in host country, preference and fluency of language, ethnicity of friends, ethnic identity, and disposition toward family and gender roles (Driscoll et al., 2001).

It has been suggested that researchers attend to acculturation as an important variable that can influence an individual and group's values (Berry, 2003; Chun & Akutsu, 2003; Kim & Abreu, 2001) and as an important factor in sexual health interventions (Lescano et al., 2009).

Research about acculturation and sexual activity has noted that youth with low levels of assimilation initiate sexual activity later than those who are more assimilated (Ford & Norris, 1993) and report fewer lifetime sexual partners (Edwards, Fehring, Jarrett, & Haglund, 2008). In contrast, research also exists that suggests that once sexual activity has been initiated, being less assimilated is associated with decreased condom use among Latinos (Marin et al., 1993; Newcomb et al., 1998). Additionally, US-born Latinas are at a decreased risk for unplanned pregnancy than those who are immigrants (Ford & Norris, 1993), suggesting that less assimilation is not always protective against risky sexual behavior.

More recent research has shown complexities in the relationship between assimilation and sexual activity, suggesting that future research will need to investigate these variables more carefully. For example, Guilamo-Ramos, Jaccard, Peña, and Goldberg (2005) found that immigrant adolescents in English-speaking homes were at less risk for sexual activity than their counterparts in Spanish-speaking homes, while for US-born Latino youth the opposite was true.

Familism

Familism, or *familismo*, has been considered a core value of Latino/a culture (Marin, 1993; Sabogal, Marin, Otero-Sabogal, Marin, & Perez-Stable, 1987) and is generally defined as an individual's attachment to his/her family members and attention given to the family over him/herself. Familism includes strong feelings of reciprocity, loyalty, and solidarity among family members (Triandis, Marin, Betancourt, Lisansky, & Chang, 1982). Additionally, familism refers to the feeling of closeness, getting along with, and contributing to the well-being of the family (Cauce & Domenech-Rodriguez, 2002). While research with Latinos has found that aspects of familism (parental monitoring and communication) are protective against delinquency, adolescent aggression, and substance use (Barrera, Gonzales, Lopez, & Fernandez, 2004; Formoso, Gonzales, & Aiken, 2000; Gil, Wagner, & Vega, 2000; Pabon, 1998; Ramirez, Crano, Quist, Burgoon, Alvaro, & Grandpre, 2004; Romero & Ruiz, 2007; Smokowski & Bacallao, 2006), less is known about how familism may influence decisions regarding early sexual behavior.

Some studies have noted that communication between Latino parents and their teens is related to lower incidence of pregnancy (Adolph, Ramos, Linton, & Grimes, 1995), sexual abstinence (Aspy et al., 2009), and increased condom use (Buzi, Smith, & Weinman, 2009). Bourdeau, Thomas, and Long (2008) note that Latino families play a role in sexual socialization because of the increased emphasis that is placed on respect for elders and parents, who are likely to emphasize the importance of virginity and delaying sexual activity until marriage. In two qualitative studies with Latino/a adolescents, the importance of respect toward family members and engaging in behaviors that bring pride to the family was related to youths' reasons for not having sex (Flores, Eyre, & Millstein, 1998; Villarruel, 1998). In the Flores et al. study, Latinas preferred partners who had familistic orientations and whom they expected would be good providers for the family, and these values were related to more traditional sexual attitudes.

While some studies have emphasized that aspects of familism may serve as protective factors against engaging in sexual behavior among Latina youth, it also has been hypothesized that a greater emphasis on families could increase sexual risk for Latino youth, such that youths that identify with Latino culture may feel more inclined to engage in unprotected sex or give birth if pregnancy does occur (Kirby, 2000; Miller et al., 2005). Understanding the protective role of familism, therefore, is important for prevention work in this area. More research is needed to ascertain the aspects of familism or family behaviors that are protective and those that might serve as risk factors for increased sexual activity.

Religiosity

Religiosity has been noted as an important factor related to sexual activity among Latina youth. Religiosity can be considered the degree of participation in, or adherence to, the beliefs and practices of a religion (Mueller, Plevak, & Rummans, 2001), and religiosity has been consistently noted to hold a prominent position in Latino/a culture (Driscoll et al., 2001). A handful of studies exist that show a positive influence of religiosity on sexual activity among Latino/a youth (DuRant et al., 1990; Edwards et al., 2008; Edwards, Fehring, Haglund, & Pruszynski, in press; Liebowitz, Castellano, & Cuellar, 1999). In a recent study with a nationally representative data set, those Hispanic adolescents who held religion as important, attended religious services at least once a week, and had traditional attitudes on sexuality had fewer sexual partners and an older age of sexual debut (Edwards et al., 2008).

It has been noted that religiosity may be related to sexual activity and contraceptive use in different ways (Manlove, Terry-Humen, Ikramullah, & Moore, 2006); thus it is important to study these dependent variables separately. While religiosity is protective for delay of sexual initiation and number of partners, research is mixed about how it relates to contraceptive use. Among teens of all ethnic backgrounds, some evidence indicates that adolescents with higher religiosity report less contraceptive use than their less religious peers (Jones, Darroch, & Singh, 2005; Nonnemaker, McNeely, & Blum, 2006), while other studies suggest no relationship between religiosity and contraceptive use (Bearman & Bruckner, 2001). Finally, in at least one study, family religiosity was a protective factor in terms of contraceptive use (Manlove et al., 2008).

For Latinas, religiosity has been suggested as a reason why they might be less likely to adhere to, or use, contraception as much as their non-Latina peers (Venkat et al., 2008). However, the relationship between religiosity and contraception use among teens, and among Latinas, is not clear. Previous studies with Latino youth also have provided discrepant findings about the influence of religiosity on contraceptive use. Research with large samples of ethnically diverse adolescents (Rostosky, Wilcox, Wright, & Randall, 2004) and Latino adolescents (Manlove et al., 2006) suggests that religious teens and those who engage in religious activities with family are less likely to use contraception as compared to their less religious counterparts. However, other research with Latino college students (Jemmott, Jemmott, & Villarruel, 2002), and adolescents (Villarruel, Jemmott, Jemmott, & Ronis, 2007) found that personal religiosity was associated with an increased use of condoms.

Gender Roles

Gender roles also have been noted to be important in shaping sexual patterns and influencing youths' sexual behavior (Deardorff et al., 2008; Taylor-Seehafer & Rew, 2000). Gender roles have been shown to operate among Latino/a youth (Marston, 2004) and lead to different expectations about sexuality among Latino boys and girls (Driscoll et al., 2001). For males, the gender role of *machismo* is characterized by honor, protectiveness of the family, and courage (Gloria, Ruiz, & Castillo, 2004). The Latino female gender role, *marianismo*, is based on characteristics of the Virgin Mary from Christian theology. *Marianismo* emphasizes that women should be virginal, self-sacrificing, and pure (Cauce & Domenech-Rodriguez, 2002; Gloria et al., 2004) and yet also acquiescing to men's sexual desires (Peragallo, DeForge, Khoury, Rivero, & Talashek, 2002). Paramount to this cultural value is virginity, including sanctions against engaging in premarital sex. At the same time, marianismo signifies a reverence of motherhood, which requires a loss of virginity (Bordeau et al., 2008; Cauce & Domenech-Rodriguez, 2002). These opposing messages have been proposed to contribute to the complexity of the influence of gender roles on sexual activity for young Latinas (Liebowitz et al., 1999), yet little empirical research has been conducted to further elucidate these processes. In a quantitative study of Latina adolescents, Kaplan, Erickson, and Juarez-Reyes (2002) found that endorsement of traditional gender roles was related to delay of sexual activity. Similarly, a study of Latino boys and girls found that those who endorsed traditional gender roles were more likely to report intentions to use condoms. These studies suggest that marianismo may be protective for young Latinas against risky sexual behavior, but much more work is needed in this area.

The prominent cultural values/topics that have been described (acculturation, *familismo*, religiosity, and gender roles) have been identified as factors that might play a role in sexual activity among Latinas. It is important to note, however, that these variables might not be unique to Latinas, and rather may represent factors that are relevant to youth from all ethnic backgrounds. Indeed, longitudinal research has shown that as a whole, adolescents who report higher religiosity tend to delay sexual activity more than those with lower levels of religiosity (Hardy & Raffaeli, 2003). Similarly, socialization about gender role expectations is something that all adolescents face in society (Denner & Dunbar, 2004; Taylor-Seehafer & Rew, 2000). And while acculturation is an experience unique to racial/ethnic minorities, it is clearly not something that only Latinas undergo (Chun & Akutsu, 2003). We contend, therefore, that the constructs described may be applicable to youth from different backgrounds, but *how* these constructs manifest themselves will likely be very different. Additionally, it is the confluence of multiple identities (as adolescent females of Latino background) that marks the unique experience of young Latinas, and therefore must be understood as something different.

Prevention Programs for Decreasing Sexual Risk-Taking

There are a large number of sexual health programs aimed at preventing negative sexual health outcomes among boys and girls of different ethnic backgrounds. Most commonly, prevention programs are designed for large groups of students or youth with consideration for developmental stage/age and gender, but with less of a focus on cultural background. Indeed, scholars have emphasized the importance of taking culture into account in sexuality interventions with Latino adolescents, yet few culturally tailored interventions have been developed for this population (Lescano et al., 2009).

As previously stated, data shows that there are significant sexual health differences among ethnically diverse youth (CDC, 2007a, 2007b), and Latino adolescents are particularly affected by negative sexual health outcomes in comparison to other youth. Given the negative well-being outcomes associated with these sexual health disparities affecting Latino/a adolescents, it is of particular importance to focus on the sexual programming for these youth.

To gain a better understanding of the prevention efforts aimed at Latina adolescents, a comprehensive search of prevention programs for risky sexual behavior was conducted. Sexual health programs were searched using a number of research databases, including federal organizations such as the Centers for Disease Control (CDC), The National Campaign to Prevent Teen Pregnancy, and the US Census Bureau, as well as social science databases. Keywords used in this search included "Hispanic" and "Latino/a," "adolescent," "youth" and "teenager," "sexual health/behavior/activity," "teen pregnancy" and "prevention."

The search yielded many prevention programs, but only those that were empirically evaluated prevention programs for Latino/a youth were included. The specific criteria for inclusion in the search was: (1) program geared toward adolescents or youth, (2) program was empirically evaluated, and (3) program focused specifically on Latino/a youth rather than just including Latino/a youth in its sample participants. A total of 13 programs that fit these criteria were included and can be found in Table 18.1. There were only two programs located that were developed specifically for Latina youth, and one of these programs focused on a combination of African American females and Latina youth. The remaining programs were evaluated for both Latino boys and girls.

As can be seen in Table 18.1, a majority of the programs primarily focused on HIV/AIDS risk

Table 18.1 Prevention Programs for Addressing Risky Sexual Behavior Among Latina/o Youth

Authors	Program	Overall Purpose	Target Population	Program Elements	Evaluation
Villarruel, Jemmott, and Jemmott (2006)	¡Cuídate! Take Care of Yourself: The Hispanic Youth Health Promotion Program	• HIV risk-reduction curriculum for Latino adolescents	• 553 adolescents • 263 treatment group • 287 control group	• Aspects of Latino culture • Family, gender role expectations, etc. • Abstinence and condom use	• Decreased engaging in sex • Decreased having multiple partners • Decreased having unprotected sex • Spanish-speakers were five times more likely to have used a condom at last time of intercourse
East, Kiernan, and Chavez (2003)	California's Adolescent Sibling Pregnancy Prevention Project	• Teen pregnancy prevention program that emphasizes abstinence and contraception for the adolescent siblings of parenting teens	• Elementary, middle, and high school • Male and female • 11–17 years old	• Delivered to siblings of parenting teenagers in California. • Provides case management and sex education	• Delayed initiation of sex • Decreased number of teen pregnancies
Walker and Kotloff (2000); Retrieved November 17, 2010, from http://www.ppv.org/ppv/publications/assets/63_publication.pdf	Hablando Claro: Plain talk	• Increase adult/teen communication about sex and increase sexually active teens' access to contraceptives to decrease unwanted pregnancies, STDs, and HIV/AIDS	• Not specified (but this adaptation of Plain Talk is used primarily at sites with an abundance of Spanish-speakers)	• "Walker and Talkers" or Promotoras program: they hire community residents; • Residents are trained to be community leaders; and • Discuss sexuality and health parties	• Increased communication between youth and adults and increased access to contraceptives, was positively correlated with teens' sexual knowledge and safer sex behaviors • Reduced percentage of sexually active youth pregnancies from 33% to 27%
Koniak-Griffin et al. (2008)	HIV Prevention for Latina Adolescent Mothers and Their Partners	• To provide couple-focused HIV/AIDS prevention information	• Latina teen mothers and their male partners	• 6-week HIV/AIDS prevention curriculum	• At 6 months chances of unprotected sex is significantly reduced • Condom use intentions increased for participants in the experimental group
Jemmott, Jemmott, Braverman, & Fong (2008)	HIV/STD Risk Reduction for African American and Latina Teenage Women	• Reduce HIV risk behaviors among female youth	• Urban, economically underprivileged females • African American and Latina adolescents	• Clinic-based • Culturally specific • Single 4.25-hour group sessions • Discussions, games, and experiential activities	• Reduced number of sex partners • Reduced incidences of unprotected sexual intercourse • Long-term reduction of incidences of STIs

Table 18.1 ***(Continued)***

Authors	Program	Overall Purpose	Target Population	Program Elements	Evaluation
Jemmott, Jemmott, and Fong (1998)	Making Proud Choices	• Empowering inner-city, Latino youth to use condoms if they choose to have sex	• Urban, elementary, and high school youth (up to 24 years old).	• HIV/AIDS prevention and pregnancy prevention • Abstinence is preferred but contraceptive information is also included • Focus on goals	• Evaluation compared safer-sex intervention group (Making Proud Choices) and the control group (Making a Difference). • Increased knowledge of the protective power of condoms for intervention group
Pathways Senderos, National Campaign to Prevent Teen Pregnancy (2007)	Pathways /Senderos	• Create a sense of hope and future-orientation for the youth and emphasis on responsibility and academics	• 50 youths per year • 10–18 years old, and mostly Latino	• (1) Education; • (2) Career; and • (3) Family life and sexual health.	• Only 2 pregnancies in 11.5 years
Sellers, McGraw, and McKinlay (1994)	Poder Latino: A Community AIDS Prevention Program	• Prevent HIV/AIDS among Latino use by promoting an increased use of condoms	• Urban youth • 14–20 years old	• Media campaigns • Workshops in schools health centers; • Educating parents and community	• Delayed sexual initiation. • Male participants (not females) were 92% less likely to initiate sex.
Villarruel, Jemmott, and Jemmott (2006)	Randomized Controlled Trial Testing an HIV Prevention Intervention for Latino Youth	• Validate the efficacy of a prevention intervention to reduce sexual risk behavior among Latino/a adolescents.	• 249 males and 304 females • 13–18 years old	• Conducted for over 3 years • Six 50-minute modules in English or Spanish.	• Reduced reports of sexual intercourse • Increased consistency of condom use • Spanish-speakers were more likely to have used a condom at last intercourse
Kirby, Baumler, Coyle, et al. (2004)	Safer Choices	• Sex education program for high school students	• Designed specifically for Latino/a youth	• 18 month peer-educator focused • HIV workshops at community settings • Use of media • Safe sex messages canvassing in neighborhood	• Youth were 43% less likely to initiate sex and delayed sexual initiation • Increased effective use of contraceptives, HIV testing, and condom availability • Reduced number of unprotected sex incidences

Harper, Bangi, Sanchez, Doll, and Pedraza (2009)	SHEROs	• To prevent HIV infection among female adolescents	• Mexican American female adolescents • 12–21 years old	• 9 sessions in 3 stages • (1) Identifying risky sexual behaviors • (2) Committing to reducing high risk behaviors • (3) Enacting and maintaining solutions	• Improvements across measures of condom attitudes, beliefs regarding a woman's control of her sexuality • Increased likelihood of carrying and using condoms and abstaining from vaginal sex
de Anda (2002)	The GIG: An Innovative Intervention to Prevent Adolescent Pregnancy and Sexually Transmitted Infection in a Latino Community	• To prevent teen pregnancy and sexually transmitted infection in a Latino community	• 609 adolescents	• 6-hour intervention • Pregnancy and STI education	• Increased knowledge about pregnancy and STIs.
Retrieved from http://www.wiseguysnc.org/jovenes.htm; National Campaign, 2007; http://www.wiseguysnc.org/jovenes.htm. Review at http://www.moappp.org/Documents/curriculum_review/Files/WiseGuys.PDF	Wise Guys/Jóvenes Sabios	• Encourages abstinence, provides contraceptive information, and promotes responsible decision-making.	• Latino boys • 11–17 years old	• 10–12 sessions • Discuss values, future goals, and sexuality.	• Increase in parent and teen communication. • Increase in positive attitudes toward women • Increased knowledge of reproduction and safer sexual behavior

reduction (seven programs) whereas pregnancy prevention in conjunction with STIs prevention was a secondary emphasis (four programs). Of these programs, four explicitly stated abstinence promotion as a program goal (California's Adolescent Sibling Pregnancy Prevention Project; ¡Cuídate!; Making Proud Choices; and Wise Guys/Jovenes Sabios). However, the strong emphasis on reducing the transmission of HIV/AIDS was particularly evident as the very names of several programs included in our evaluation used "HIV/AIDS" in their titles. Approximately 30% of the programs had names that included HIV or AIDS in the title. This indicates that the top priority of prevention efforts aimed at Latino youth seems to have been to decrease the incidences of HIV/AIDS.

Several of these programs (six) included salient aspects of Latino culture. A majority of these programs (four) emphasized gender roles (¡Cuídate!; HIV Prevention for Latino Adolescent Mothers and Their Partners; Randomized Controlled Trial Testing and HIV Prevention Intervention for Latino Youth; Wise Guys). Much of the work around gender roles included traditional *marianismo* and *machismo* expectations (Randomized Controlled Trial Testing; HIV Prevention Intervention for Latino Youth), masculinity, and communication (Wise Guys). Additionally, a couple of the programs emphasized parents' cultural values (Hablando Claro; HIV Prevention for Latino Adolescent Mothers and Their Partners), relationship violence (HIV Prevention for Latino Adolescent Mothers and Their Partners; Wise Guys), and immigrant status and acculturation levels (Poder Latino; Wise Guys). Religiosity was also noted as a cultural factor that was included in one of the programs (Poder Latino). Other programs integrated other significant cultural aspects including marital abstinence, *cariño* and *respeto* (love and respect), *promotoras* (peer educators; Hablando Claro), *espejo*—mirroring through oral stories and reflection, oppression (HIV Prevention for Latino Adolescent Mothers and Their Partners), and shared Latino identity (Poder Latino).

Similarly, several of the programs attended to the culturally specific needs of Latino/a youth through language. Specifically, Spanish as well as English were used in six programs: ¡Cuídate!; Hablando Claro; HIV Prevention for Latino Adolescent Mothers and Their Partners; Poder Latino; Randomized Controlled Trial Testing an HIV Prevention Intervention for Latino Youth; and Wise Guys. These programs accomplished this by providing bilingual services and materials/resources to the participants.

An additional shared component among a majority of these programs included increasing sexual health knowledge as a major component. Of the 13 programs, 10 explicitly stated that increasing sexual health information was a major theme in their program. Included in this were components such as teaching basic sexual information to more specific skills such as condom use and sexual negotiation-refusal techniques for future use with partners. Of these programs, nine focused on increasing condom and contraceptive knowledge.

Other programs such as Wise Guys and Hablando Claro focused on increased communication about sex between adolescents and adults. Wise Guys focused on increasing general communication between adolescents and adults, while Hablando Claro specifically focused on raising the rates of child-to-parent communication about sex. It should be noted that communication accounted for around 11% of the decrease of risky sexual behaviors in the program Hablando Claro.

Only a few programs (eight) included components that directly focused on being inclusive of Latino/a adolescents' support systems. These programs varied in their support system involvement as some were community-based and others included siblings, peer educators, parents, male partners, and community members. Given the emphasis on *familismo* and collectivism among Latino/as, researchers have noted that family-based programs are likely to be well received (Guilamo-Ramos & Buris, 2008; Lescano et al., 2009).

Taken together, the review of published, evaluated prevention programs for risky sexual behavior among Latino/a youth suggests that many different types of programs exist, ranging in duration and delivery mode, as well as focus. A scarce number of sexual health programs were developed specifically for Latina youth; however, several of the programs included salient aspects of Latino culture such as gender roles, familismo, and religiosity. As can be surmised from reading this chapter, we believe that the unique cultural context of Latinas' lives is important to understand when studying the prevention of risky sexual behavior and when developing prevention programs. Furthermore, we acknowledge research suggesting that aligning mental health treatment and prevention interventions with clients' cultural backgrounds will yield superior outcomes (Smith, Domenech Rodriguez, & Bernal, 2011). There are many unanswered questions about the exact role of certain constructs in the prevention of sexual activity among Latina youth, but authors have started to assemble recommendations for how to develop effective programming for this population. Readers are directed to three publications by Advocates for Youth: *Youth of Color: At Disproportionate Risk of Negative Sexual Health Outcomes* (2010), *Adolescent Sexual Health and the Dynamics of Oppression: A Call for Cultural Competency* (2010), and *The Sexual Health of Latina Adolescents—Focus on Assets* (2006), for helpful suggestions about prevention efforts with ethnic minority adolescents. Taking the recommendations from these reports and other existing research about this topic, we provide a brief list of key issues/topics that we believe should be considered when developing prevention programs with young Latinas:

1. Development of programs based on needs assessments of Latina youth in their communities.
   a. Understanding community demographics, accessibility of services, sexual health, religious and health beliefs, and other important knowledge about population.

2. Involvement of youth in designing prevention programs to ensure they are relevant, accessible, and meaningful for consumers.
   a. Depending on the focus of the program, also consider including others in the lives of youth—parents, cousins, uncles/aunts, friends.

3. Implementation of practices that acknowledge and respect culture.
   a. Utilizing materials and communication in language of youth and families.
   b. Employing staff who are committed to cultural competence.
   c. Promotion of positive Latino/a ethnic identity.

4. Exploration of gender role expectations from culture, society, family, and self.
   a. Acknowledgment of the intersection of identities as female and of Latina background.
   b. Discussion of other aspects of identity such as social class, sexual orientation, religiosity, etc.
   c. Acknowledgment of the influence of oppression and discrimination in the lives of young Latinas.

5. Inclusion of information about communication about sexual health topics.
   a. Helping teens improve communication with parents, siblings, and other important extended family members.
   b. Consideration of Latino/a communication styles and gender role expectations.

6. Promotion of discussions about contraceptive use and contraceptive negotiation.
   a. Exploration of factors that detract from and promote use of contraceptives, particularly for Latinas.

7. Evaluation of programs for effectiveness.
   a. Development of an evaluation system prior to implementation.
   b. Utilization of appropriate assessments for Latino/a population.

Conclusion

Latina youth have numerous negative outcomes associated with risky sexual behavior and teen pregnancy. Given these health concerns and considering the unique cultural context of Latina adolescents' lives, researchers have begun to incorporate culture into prevention programs aimed at decreasing risky sexual behavior. To date, several programs have been developed for Latino/a youth and have been empirically evaluated. Their successes with various health outcomes are encouraging, and it is hoped that more research in this area will be conducted in the future.

Future Directions

Many questions remain that need to be addressed in order to continue to develop and implement effective prevention of risky sexual behavior among Latina youth. Some pressing questions to further the field include:

- What is the influence of *marianismo* and *machismo* on sexual risk-taking (initiation of sexual activity and contraceptive use) among Latina youth?
- How do Latina youth negotiate sexual encounters and make decisions regarding sexual activity?
- What are the most effective aspects of prevention programs for decreasing risky sexual behavior among Latina/o youth?
- How effective are programs that directly address aspects of young Latinas' cultural context in comparison to those that are more general?

References

Adolph, C., Ramos, D. E., Linton, K. L. P., & Grimes, D. A. (1995). Pregnancy among Hispanic teenagers: Is good parental communication a deterrent? *Contraception, 51,* 303–306.

Advocates for Youth (2006). *The Sexual Health of Latina Adolescents—Focus on Assets.* Washington, DC.

Advocates for Youth (2010). *Adolescent Sexual Health and the Dynamics of Oppression: A Call for Cultural Competency.* Washington, DC.

Advocates for Youth (2010). *Youth of color: At disproportionate risk of negative sexual health outcomes.* Washington, DC.

Anaya, H. D., Cantwell, S. M., & Roteram-Borus, M. J. (2003). Sexual risk behaviors among adolescents. In A. Biglan, M. C. Wang, & H. J. Walberg (Eds.), *Preventing youth problems* (pp. 113–143). New York: Kluwer Academic/Plenum.

Arnett, J. J. (2000). Emerging adulthood: A theory of development from the late teens through the twenties. *American Psychologist, 55,* 469–480.

Aspy, C. B., Vesely, S. K., Tolma, E. L., Oman, R. F., Fluhr, J., Rodine, S., & Marshall, L. (2009). Youth assets and delayed coitarche across developmental age groups. *Journal of Early Adolescence, 30*(2), 277–304.

Barrera, M., Jr., Gonzales, N. A., Lopez, V., & Fernandez, A. C. (2004). Problem behaviors of Chicana/o and Latina/o adolescents: An analysis of prevalence, risk, and protective factors. In R. J. Velasquez, L. M. Arellano, & B. W. McNeil (Eds.), *The handbook of Chicana/o psychology and mental health.* Mahwah, NJ: Erlbaum.

Bearman, P., & Bruckner, H. (2001). Promising the future: Virginity pledges and first intercourse. *American Journal of Sociology, 106,* 859–912.

Berry, J. W. (2003). Conceptual approaches to acculturation. In K. M. Chun, P. B. Organista, & G. Marin (Eds.), *Acculturation: Advances in theory, measurement, and applied research* (pp. 17–37). Washington, DC: American Psychological Association.

Berry, J. W., Trimble, J. E., & Olmedo, E. L. (1986). Assessment of acculturation. In W. J. Lonner & J. W. Berry (Eds.), *Field methods in cross-cultural research* (pp. 291–345). Beverly Hills, CA: Sage.

Bourdeau, B., Thomas, V. K., & Long, J. K. (2008). Latino sexual styles: Developing a nuanced understanding of risk. *Journal of Sex Research, 45,* 71–81.

Buzi, R. S., Smith, P. B., & Weinman, M. L. (2009). Parental communication as a protective factor in increasing condom use among minority adolescents. *International Journal of Adolescent Medical Health, 21,* 51–59.

Buzwell, S., & Rosenthal, D. (1996). Constructing a sexual self: Adolescents' sexual self-perceptions and sexual risk-taking. *Journal of Research on Adolescence, 6,* 489–513.

Carvajal, S., Volle, F., & Orduña, M. (2007). Adolescent bicultural stress and its impact on mental well-being among Latinos, Asian Americans, and European Americans. *Journal of Community Psychology, 35,* 519–534.

Cauce, A., & Domenech-Rodriguez, M. (2002). Latina/o families: Myths and realities. In J. M. Contreras, K. A. Kerns, & A Neal-Barnett (Eds.), *Latina/o children and families in the United States: Current research and future directions* (pp. 3–25). Westport, CT: Praeger.

Centers for Disease Control and Prevention (CDC). (2006, June 9). Youth Risk Behavior Surveillance—United States, 2005. Surveillance Summaries. *Morbidity and Mortality Weekly Report, 55*(No. SS-5).

Centers for Disease Control and Prevention. (2007a). *Trends in the prevalence of sexual behaviors, National Youth Risk Behavior Survey: 1991–2007.* Retrieved January 3, 2009, from http://www.brhpc.org/files/yrbs07_us_sexual_behaviors_trend.pdf.

Centers for Disease Control and Prevention. (2007b). *2007 Youth Risk Behavior Survey.* Retrieved January 3, 2009, from www.cdc.gov/yrbss

Centers for Disease Control and Prevention. (2008a). *HIV/AIDS among Hispanics/Latinos.* Retrieved January 3, 2009, from http://www.cdc.gov/hiv/hispanics/resources/factsheets/hispanic.htm.

Centers for Disease Control and Prevention. (2008b). *Prevention challenges.* Retrieved January 3, 2009, from http://www.cdc.gov/hiv/hispanics/challenges.htm

Centers for Disease Control and Prevention. (2009). *YRBSS Youth online: Comprehensive results 2009.* Accessed March 15, 2010, from http://apps.nccd.cdc.gov/yrbss/.

Chapin, J. (2001). It won't happen to me: The role of optimistic bias in African American teens' risky sexual practices. *The Howard Journal of Communications, 12,* 49–59.

Chun, K. M., & Akutsu, P. D. (2003). Acculturation among ethnic minority families. In K. M. Chun, P. B. Organista, & G. Marin (Eds.), *Acculturation: Advances in theory, measurement and applied research* (pp. 95–119). Washington, DC: American Psychological Association.

Chwalisz, K., & Obasi, E. (2008). Promoting health and preventing and reducing disease. In S. Brown & R. Lent (Eds.), *Handbook of counseling psychology* (4th ed.). New York: Wiley.

Contreras, J. M., Narang, D., Ikhlas, M., & Teichman, J. (2002). A conceptual model of the determinants of parenting among Latina adolescent mothers. In J. Contreras, K. Kerns, & A. Neal-Barnett (Eds.), *Latino children and families in the United States: Current research and future directions* (pp.155–177). Westport, CT: Praeger.

de Anda, D. (2002). The GIG: An innovative intervention to prevent adolescent pregnancy and sexually transmitted infection in a Latino community. *Journal of Ethnic and Cultural Diversity in Social Work, 11,* 251–277.

Deardorff, J., Tschann, J. M., & Flores, E. (2008). Sexual values among Latina/o youth: Measurement development using a culturally based approach. *Cultural Diversity and Ethnic Minority Psychology, 14,* 138–146.

Denner, J., & Dunbar, N. (2004). Negotiating femininity: Power and strategies of Mexican American girls. *Sex Roles, 50*(5–6), 301–314.

Driscoll, A. K., Biggs, M. A., Brindis, C. D., & Yankah, E. (2001). Adolescent Latino reproductive health: A review of the literature. *Hispanic Journal of Behavioral Sciences, 23,* 255–326.

DuRant, R. H., Pendergrast, R., & Seymore, C. (1990). Sexual behavior among Hispanic female adolescents in the United States. *Pediatrics, 85,* 1051–1058.

East, P., Kiernan, E., & Chavez, G. (2003). An evaluation of California's adolescent sibling pregnancy prevention program. *Perspectives on Sexual and Reproductive Health, 35,* 62–70.

Eaton, D., Kann, L., Kinchen, S., Ross, J., Hawkins, J., Harris, W., et al. (2006).Youth risk behavior surveillance—United States, 2005. *Morbidity and Mortality Weekly Report, 55* (No. SS–5).

Edwards, L. M., Fehring, R., Haglund, K., & Pruszynski, J. (2011). Religiosity and sexual risk behaviors among Latina adolescents: Trends from 1995–2008. *Journal of Women's Health, 20,* 871–877.

Edwards, L. M., Fehring, R., Jarrett, K., & Haglund, K. (2008). The influence of religiosity, gender, and language preference acculturation on sexual activity among Latino/a adolescents. *Hispanic Journal of Behavioral Sciences, 30,* 447–462.

Edwards, L. M., & Lopez, S. J. (2006). Perceived family support, acculturation, and life satisfaction in Mexican American youth: A mixed methods exploration. *Journal of Counseling Psychology, 53,* 279–287.

Fennelly, K., Mulkeen, P., & Giusti, C. (1998). Coping with racism and discrimination: The experience of young Latino adolescents. In H. I. McCubbin, E. A. Thompson, A. I. Thompson, & J. E. Fromer (Eds.), *Resiliency in Native American and immigrant families* (pp. 367–383). Thousand Oaks, CA: Sage.

Flores, E., Eyre, S. L., & Millstein, S. G. (1998). Sociocultural beliefs related to sex among Mexican American adolescents. *Hispanic Journal of Behavioral Sciences, 20,* 60–82.

Flores, E., Tschann, J. M., Dimas, J. M., Pasch, L. A., & deGroat, C. L. (2010). Perceived racial/ethnic discrimination, post-traumatic stress symptoms, and health risk behaviors among Mexican American adolescents. *Journal of Counseling Psychology, 57,* 264–273.

Ford, K., & Norris, A. E. (1993). Urban Hispanic adolescents and young adults: Relationship of acculturation to sexual behavior. *Journal of Sex Research, 30,* 316–323.

Formoso, D., Gonzales, N. A., & Aiken, L. S. (2000). Family conflict and children's internalizing and externalizing behavior: Protective factors. *American Journal of Community Psychology, 28,* 175–199.

Franzetta, K., Terry-Humen, E., Manlove, J., & Ikramullah, E. (2006). *Trends and recent estimates: Contraceptive use among U.S. teens.* Washington, DC: Child Trends Research Brief.

Gil, A., Wagner, E., & Vega, W. (2000). Acculturation, familism, and alcohol use among Latino adolescent males: Longitudinal relations. *Journal of Community Psychology, 28,* 443–458.

Gloria, A. M., Ruiz, E. L., & Castillo, E. M. (2004). Counseling and psychotherapy with Latino and Latina clients. In T. B. Smith (Ed.), *Practicing multiculturalism: Affirming diversity in counseling and psychology* (pp. 167–189). Boston: Pearson Education.

Guilamo-Ramos, V., & Buris, A. (2008). *Parent-adolescent communication about sex in Latino families: A guide for practitioners.* The National Campaign to Prevent Teen and Unplanned Pregnancy. Retrieved November 10, 2010, from http://www.thenationalcampaign.org/resources/pdf/pubs/Parent_AdolFINAL.pdf

Guilamo-Ramos, V., Jaccard, J., Peña, J., & Goldberg, V. (2005). Acculturation-related variables, sexual initiation, and subsequent sexual behavior among Puerto Rican, Mexican, and Cuban youth. *Health Psychology, 24,* 88–95.

Hardy, S. A., & Raffaelli. (2003). Adolescent religiosity and sexuality: An investigation of reciprocal influences. *Journal of Adolescence, 26,* 731–739.

Harper, G. W., Bangi, A. K., Sánchez, B., Doll, M., & Pedraza, A. (2009). A quasi-experimental evaluation of a community-based HIV intervention for Mexican American female adolescents: The SHERO's program. *AIDS Education and Prevention, 21,* 109–123.

Hoffman, S. D. (2006). *By the numbers: The public costs of adolescent childbearing.* Washington, DC: The National Campaign to Prevent Teen Pregnancy.

Ikramullah, E., Schelar, E., Manlove, J., & Moore, K. A. (2007). *Facts at a glance: A fact sheet reporting national, state-level, and city-level trends in teen childbearing.* Washington, DC: Child Trends.

Jemmott, J. B., III, Jemmott, L. S., & Fong, G. T. (1998). Abstinence and safer sex HIV risk-reduction interventions for African American adolescents: A randomized controlled trial. *Journal of the American Medical Association, 279,* 1529–1536.Jemmott, J. B., Jemmott, L. S., Braverman, P. K., & Fong, G. T. (2005). HIV/STD risk reduction interventions for African American and Latino adolescent girls at an adolescent medicine clinic. *Archives of Pediatrics & Adolescent Medicine, 159,* 440–449.

Jemmott, L. S., Jemmott, J. B., III, & Villarruel, A. (2002). Predicting intentions and condom use among Latino college students. *Journal of the Association of Nurses in AIDS Care, 13*(2), 59–69.

Jones, R., Darroch, J., & Singh, S. (2005). Religious differentials in the sexual and reproductive behaviors of young women in the United States. *Journal of Adolescent Health, 36,* 279–288.

Kaplan, C. P., Erickson, P. I., & Juarez-Reyes, M. (2002). Acculturation, gender role orientation, and reproductive risk-taking behavior among Latina adolescent family planning clients. *Journal of Adolescent Research, 17,* 103–121.

Kim, B. S. K., & Abreu, J. M. (2001). Acculturation measurement. In J. G. Ponterotto, J. M. Casas, L. A. Suzuki, & C. M. Alexander (Eds.), *Handbook of multicultural counseling* (pp. 394–424). Thousand Oaks, CA: Sage.

Kirby, D. (2000). School-based interventions to prevent unprotected sex and HIV among adolescents. In J. Peterson, & R. DiClemente (Eds.), *Handbook of HIV prevention.* New York: Kluwer Academic/Plenum.

Kirby, D. (2007). *Emerging answers 2007: Research findings on programs to reduce teen pregnancy and sexually transmitted diseases.* Washington, DC: The National Campaign to Prevent Teen and Unplanned Pregnancy.

Kirby, D. B., Baumler, E., Coyle, K. K., Basen-Engquist, K., Parcel, G. S., Harris, R., & Banspach, S. W. (2004). The "Safer Choices" intervention: Its impact on the sexual behaviors of different subgroups of high school students. *Journal of Adolescent Health, 35,* 442–452.

Koniak-Griffin, D., Lesser, J., Henneman, T., Huang, R., Huang, X., Tello, J., . . . Cumberland, W., G. (2008). HIV prevention for Latino adolescent mothers and their partners. *Western Journal of Nursing Research, 30,* 724–742.

LeCroy, C. W. (2008). Intervention with adolescents. In K. M. Sowers, W. Rowe, & L. A. Rapp-Paglicci (Eds.), *Comprehensive handbook of social work and social welfare* (pp. 288–309). Hoboken, NJ: Wiley.

Lescano, C. M., Brown, L. K., Raffaelli, M., & Lima, L. (2009). Cultural factors and family-based HIV prevention intervention for Latino youth. *Journal of Pediatric Psychology, 34,* 1041–1052.

Liebowitz, S. W., Castellano, D. C., & Cuellar, I. (1999). Factors that predict sexual behavior among young Mexican American adolescents: An exploratory study. *Hispanic Journal of Behavioral Sciences, 21,* 470–479.

Manlove, J., Logan, C., Moore, K. A., & Ikramullah, E. (2008). Pathways from family religiosity to adolescent sexual activity and contraceptive use. *Perspectives on Sexual and Reproductive Health, 40,* 105–117.

Manlove, J., Papillio, A. R., & Ikramullah, E. (2004). *Not yet: Programs to delay first sex among teens.* Washington, DC: National Campaign to Prevent Teen Pregnancy.

Manlove, J. S., Terry-Humen, E., Ikramullah, E. N., & Moore, K. A. (2006). The role of parent religiosity in teen's transitions to sex and contraception. *Journal of Adolescent Health, 39,* 578–587.

Marin, G. (1992). Issues in the measurement of acculturation among Hispanics. In K. F. Geisinger (Ed.), *Psychological testing of Hispanics* (pp. 235–251). Washington, DC: American Psychological Association.

Marin, G. (1993). Influence of acculturation on familialism and self-identification among Hispanics. In M. E. Bernal & G. P. Knight (Eds.), *Ethnic identity* (pp. 181–196). New York: SUNY Press.

Marin, B. V., Tschann, J. M., Gomez, C. A., & Kegeles, S. M. (1993). Acculturation and gender differences in sexual attitudes and behaviors: Hispanic vs. non-Hispanic White unmarried adults. *American Journal of Public Health, 83,* 1759–1761.

Marston, C. (2004). Gendered communication among young people in Mexico: Implications for sexual health interventions. *Social Science and Medicine, 59,* 445–456.

McLean Taylor, J., Veloria, C. N., & Verba, M. C. (2007). Latina girls: We're like sisters—most times! In B. J. Ross Leadbeater & N. Way (Eds.), *Urban girls revisited building strengths* (pp. 218–243). New York: New York University Press.

Michels, T. M., Kropp, R. Y., Eyre, S. L., & Halpern-Felsher, B. L. (2005). Initiating sexual experiences: How do young adolescents make decisions regarding early sexual activity? *Journal of Research on Adolescence, 15,* 583–607.

Miller, B. C., Sage, R., & Winward, B. W. (2005). Adolescent pregnancy. In T. P. Gullotta & G. R. Adams (Eds.), *Handbook on the treatment and prevention of dysfunctional behavior: Theory, practice and prevention* (pp. 567–587). New York: Springer.

Mueller, P. S., Plevak, D. J., & Rummans, T. A. (2001). Religious involvement, spirituality, and medicine: Implications for clinical practice. *Mayo Clinic Proceedings, 76,* 1225–1235.

National Campaign to Prevent Teen Pregnancy. (2003). *Teen sexual activity, pregnancy, and childbearing among Latina/os in the United States: Fact Sheet.* Retrieved June 10, 2008, from http://www.thenationalcampaign.org

National Campaign to Prevent Teen Pregnancy. (2007). *Science says: Effective and promising teen pregnancy prevention programs for Latino youth.* Retrieved November 30, 2010, from http://www.thenationalcampaign.org/resources/pdf/SS/SS43_TPPProgramsLatinos.pdf

Newcomb, M. D., Wyatt, G. E., Romero, G. J., Tucker, M. B., Wayment, H. A., Carmona, J. V., . . . Mitchell-Kernan, C. (1998). Acculturation, sexual risk taking, and HIV health promotion among Latinas. *Journal of Counseling Psychology, 45,* 454–467.

Nonnemaker, J. M., McNeely, C. A., & Blum, R. W. (2006) Public and private domains of religiosity and adolescent smoking transitions. *Social Science and Medicine, 62,* 3084–3095.

Pabon, E. (1998). Hispanic adolescent delinquency and the family: A discussion of sociocultural influences. *Adolescence, 33,* 941–955.

Peragallo, N., DeForge, B. R., Khoury, Z., Rivero, R., & Talashek, M. (2002). Latinas' perspectives on HIV/AIDS: Cultural issues to consider in prevention. *Hispanic Health Care International, 1,* 11–23.

Prejean, J., Song, R., An, Q., & Hall, H. (2008). Subpopulation estimates from the HIV incidence surveillance system—United States, 2006. *Morbidity and Mortality Weekly Report, 57*(36), 985–989.

Ramirez, J. R., Crano, W. D., Quist, R., Burgoon, M., Alvaro, E. M., & Grandpre, J. (2004). Acculturation, familism, parental monitoring, and knowledge as predictors of marijuana and inhalant use in adolescents. *Psychology of Addictive Behaviors, 18,* 3–11.

Romero, A. J., & Roberts, R. E. (2003). Stress within a bicultural context for adolescents of Mexican descent. *Cultural Diversity and Ethnic Minority Psychology, 9,* 171–184.

Romero, A. J., & Ruiz, M. (2007). Does familism lead to increased parental monitoring?: Protective factors for coping with risky behaviors. *Journal of Child and Family Studies, 16,* 143–154.

Rostosky, S., Wilcox, B., Wright M., & Randall, B. (2004). The impact of religiosity on adolescent sexual behavior: A review of the evidence. *Journal of Adolescent Research, 19,* 677–697.

Sabogal, F., Marin, G., Otero-Sabogal, R., Marin, B. V., & Perez-Stable, E. J. (1987). Hispanic familism and acculturation: What changes and what doesn't? *Hispanic Journal of Behavioral Sciences, 9,* 397–412.

Schuster, C. (2003, September). Latina adolescent health. *Issues at a Glance.* www.advocatesforyouth.org

Sellers, D. E., McGraw, S. A., & McKinlay, J. B. (1994). Does the promotion and distribution of condoms increase sexual activity? Evidence from an HIV prevention program for Latino youth. *American Journal of Public Health, 84,* 1952–1959.

Silver, E. J., & Bauman, L. J. (2006). The association of sexual experience with attitudes, beliefs, and risk behaviors of inner-city adolescents. *Journal of Research on Adolescence, 16,* 29–45.

Smith, T. B., Domenech Rodriguez, M., & Bernal, G. (2011). Culture. *Journal of Clinical Psychology: In Session, 67,* 166–175.

Smokowski, P. R., & Bacallao, M. L. (2006). Acculturation and aggression in Latina/o adolescents: A structural model focusing on cultural risk factors and assets. *Journal of Abnormal Child Psychology, 34,* 657–671.

Takanishi, R. (1993). The opportunities of adolescence—research, interventions, and policy: Introduction to special issue. *American Psychologist, 48,* 85–87.

Taylor-Seehafer, M., & Rew, L. (2000). Risky sexual behavior among adolescent women. *Journal of the Society of Pediatric Nurses, 5,* 15–25.

Triandis, H. C., Marin, G., Betancourt, H., Lisansky, J., & Chang, B. (1982). *Dimensions of familism among Hispanic and mainstream Navy recruits.* Technical report No. 14. Champaign: Department of Psychology, University of Illinois, Champaign.

Vélez-Pastrana, M. C., Gonzalez-Rodriguez, R. A., & Borges-Hernandez, A. (2005). Family functioning and early onset of sexual intercourse in Latino adolescents. *Adolescence, 40,* 777–791.

Venkat, P., Masch, R., Ng, E., Cremer, M., Richman, S., & Arslan, A. (2008). Knowledge and beliefs about contraception in urban Latina women. *Journal of Community Health, 3,* 357–362.

Villarruel, A. M. (1998). Cultural influences on the sexual attitudes, beliefs, and norms of young Latina adolescents. *Journal of the Society of Pediatric Nurses, 3,* 69–79.

Villarruel, A. M., Jemmott, J. B., & Jemmott, L. S. (2006). A randomized controlled trial testing an HIV prevention intervention for Latino youth. *Archives of Pediatric and Adolescent Medicine, 160,* 772–777.

Villarruel, A. M., Jemmott, III, J. B., Jemmott, L. S., & Ronis, D. L. (2007). Predicting condom use among sexually experienced Latino adolescents. *Western Journal of Nursing Research, 29,* 724–738.

Walker, K. E., & Kotloff, L. J. (2000). *Plain Talk: Addressing adolescent sexuality through a community initiative.* Philadelphia, PA: Public/Private Ventures.

Zane, N., & Mak, W. (2003). Major approaches to the measurement of acculturation amongethnic minority populations: A content analysis and an alternative empirical strategy. In K. M. Chun, P. B. Organista, & G. Marin (Eds.), *Acculturation: Advances in theory, measurement, and applied research* (pp. 39–60). Washington, DC: American Psychological Association.

CHAPTER

19 Ameliorating Cancer Disparities in Medically Underserved Women: A Community-Based Approach

Lydia P. Buki, Yadira Montoya, *and* Deborah E. Linares

Abstract

There is an increasing awareness of inequities in cancer outcomes for marginalized populations. A great number of these health disparities arise in the context of adverse psychosocial conditions. Thus, there is a need to focus on the psychosocial context in which disparities arise. In this chapter, we first introduce our readers to some key factors that make our work in this area imperative. Second, we present an overview of breast and cervical cancer disparities and the main factors that influence screening in medically underserved populations. Third, given the need to anchor prevention efforts in the communities in which disparities arise, as well as the need to involve community participants in the design and implementation of prevention programs, we describe the community readiness model. Finally, we discuss the use of lay health advisors as a community-based intervention that has been widely used to increase cancer screening rates in medically underserved populations.

Key Words: breast cancer, cervical cancer, community intervention, Latinas, health disparities, community readiness

Health disparities have been broadly defined as significant differences in "the overall rate of disease incidence, prevalence, morbidity, mortality, or survival rates in the population as compared to the health status of the general population" (Minority Health and Health Disparities Research and Education Act, 2000). With regard to cancer specifically, the National Cancer Institute (NCI) has asserted that health disparities are "differences in the incidence, prevalence, mortality, and burden of cancer and related adverse health conditions that exist among specific population groups in the United States" (Center to Reduce Cancer Health Disparities [CRCHD], 2011). Although a small portion of these disparities arise due to genetic factors, a great number of health disparities arise in the context of adverse psychosocial conditions (Commission on Social Determinants of Health [CSDH], 2008; Smedley, Stith, & Nelson, 2003). Thus, there is a need to focus on the psychosocial context in which disparities arise. Some of the social contributors to health disparities include inequitable distribution of power, financial and other resources, levels of formal education, gender, race and ethnicity, as well as living conditions including poverty, family context, neighborhood characteristics, access to health care, the natural environment, and the built environment (CSDH, 2008; Healthy People 2020, 2010). Given that psychosocial factors contribute greatly to the development and sustained effects of health disparities, and these factors are largely amenable to prevention, this phenomenon is of great interest to counseling psychologists.

For the purposes of this chapter, we define prevention as the "arresting of adverse developmental, psychological, educational, health, and other life outcomes," as proposed by Reese and Vera (2007, p. 764). In addition, we focus on two specific cancers, breast and cervical, because they are amenable to prevention through effective intervention approaches. In adopting this definition, however, we must clarify the levels of prevention that are possible with regard to these two cancer types. Currently, we cannot effectively prevent the occurrence of breast cancer at a public health level, therefore prevention through early detection is the best way to fight the disease. For example, the main risk factors for breast cancer cannot be changed (e.g., sex, age, genetic predisposition), and not all women exhibit the few lifestyle factors that have been shown to have a positive effect in lowering risk of disease (e.g., having children before the age of 30, engaging in regular physical activity; American Cancer Society [ACS], 2011a). Therefore, the best weapon we have against breast cancer is early detection. Early detection can be achieved through mammography (an x-ray of the breast that can detect tumors when they are too small to be felt by the woman or medical professionals), clinical breast exams (tactile exams performed by a physician or nurse), and breast self-examinations. Through early detection, tumors are detected at earlier stages when there are more opportunities for treatment and a cure (ACS, 2011a). Medical advances have attained remarkable outcomes. For localized tumors, the 5-year survival rate is 98%, for regional disease it is 84%, and for distant metastases it is 24%, reflecting the lower availability of effective treatments for cancers detected at more advanced stages (Howlader et al., 2012). In contrast with breast cancer, cervical cancer can be prevented through regular Pap smear exams (NCI, 2010). With a Pap smear, medical professionals collect cells from the cervix that may show abnormal cell growth before it becomes cancerous, in addition to having the opportunity to identify cells that may have already become malignant. Abnormal precancerous cells may be treated effectively, preventing the cancer from developing; cancerous cells may be treated as well, with better prognosis when detected in the early stages (NCI, 2010).

Thus, given the opportunity to engage in prevention to ameliorate and possibly eliminate these health disparities, we can conceptualize cancer inequities as a social justice issue that must be addressed (Buki & Selem, 2012). What makes health disparities such a vital issue for counseling psychologists, specifically, is when the causes of these disparities cross beyond biology and into the social realm (Buki & Selem, 2012). In addition, there are several key concerns that render this a timely issue. We highlight three of these factors next.

First, population projections show that ethnic minority populations, who are often most affected by health disparities, will undergo dramatic demographic shifts in the coming decades (US Census Bureau, 2008). Latinos currently make up about 16% of the population, and will grow to 25% in the year 2035. Asian Americans currently make up about 4.7% of the population, and will grow to 6.7% in 2035. Among these two groups, most dramatic gains will occur in the older adult population (US Census Bureau, 2008). With larger populations, existing health disparities are likely to worsen, especially within the current financial climate of diminishing resources (Buki & Selem, 2012). The potential sharper inequities would represent a tragic outcome for our national health overall.

Second, given the wide-ranging evidence of health disparities (Smedley et al., 2003), several key organizations have identified the amelioration or elimination of health disparities as a top priority. As time has gone on, the elimination of health disparities has taken on a more pressing focus. For example, for the past 20 years Healthy People (a national initiative that identifies and prioritizes national health objectives for a 10-year period) has had an overarching goal focused on disparities. However, through the years the language used in crafting the goal has become stronger and more comprehensive. In *Healthy People 2000*, the goal was to reduce health disparities among Americans. By the time *Healthy People 2010* was written, authors felt that the goal should go beyond reducing health disparities and call for their elimination. An even broader goal was crafted for *Healthy People 2020*, which included achieving health equity, eliminating disparities, and improving the health of all groups (Healthy People 2020, 2010).

Other federal initiatives include the creation of nine Centers of Excellence dedicated to eliminating ethnic and racial disparities in health, established in the year 2000 by the Agency for Healthcare Research and Quality (AHRQ; AHRQ, 2001). Also in 2000, Congress founded the National Center on Minority Health and Health Disparities with the specific mission of helping the NIH reduce, and ultimately eliminate, health disparities. Through this initiative, each institute and center designed a plan for eliminating health disparities, and the plans have become part of a larger national strategic plan to reduce and ultimately eliminate health disparities (Institute of Medicine [IOM], 2006). Specifically with regard to cancer disparities, in 2001 the National Cancer Institute established the Center to Reduce Cancer

Health Disparities, which is critical to the Institute's efforts to reduce and eventually eliminate cancer health disparities through research, training, and outreach (CRCHD, 2009). We note, however, that most funding provided by the NIH for health disparities is in the form of time-limited projects that usually last about 3 years. There are several downsides to this. First, it takes time to develop trust and engage the community in a research project. Second, many ethnic minority communities are skeptical of individuals who come in to take information from the community without giving back in the form of a sustainable long-term gain. Finally, although it is possible that through these projects we may have garnered knowledge about the issue and even have ameliorated the health disparity, the fact that the funding is not permanent severely limits sustaining the longevity of the gains. These facts render the development of community-based, sustainable prevention projects even more critical if we are to truly make a difference in ethnic minority communities.

Closer to home, in its first-ever strategic plan (Anderson, 2009), the American Psychological Association (APA) crafted a goal designed to expand psychology's role in advancing health. Specifically, one of the objectives within this goal is to promote psychology's role in the amelioration of health disparities (Clay, 2010). Consistent with this objective, the APA has engaged in several educational and legislative efforts to ameliorate health disparities in recent years (for a review, see Buki & Selem, 2012).

Lastly, the elimination of health disparities is consistent with counseling psychology's social justice mandate (Vera & Speight, 2003). Historical injustices and oppressive conditions such as racism, classism, and sexism, continue today in the form of inequitable social conditions from which many health disparities arise (Buki, 2007; Jones, 2010; Smith, 2005). In the health care arena, injustice results when individuals' negative health outcomes are the result of bias in health promotion efforts, societal conditions, negligence, or incompetence (Buki & Selem, 2012). Taking an expanded view of ethics, as required when viewing issues from a social justice lens (Speight & Vera, 2004), as counseling psychologists we are called to engage in prevention, advocacy, and outreach efforts that are culturally relevant and involve individuals in their communities (Reese & Vera, 2007).

In support of these goals, the purpose of this chapter is threefold. First, we introduce our readers to some key factors that make our work in this area imperative. Second, we present an overview of breast and cervical cancer disparities and the main factors that influence screening in medically underserved populations (i.e., traditional predictors of low screening adherence, cultural explanatory models, and the structure of communities). Third, given the need to anchor prevention efforts in the communities in which disparities arise, as well as the need to involve community participants in the design and implementation of prevention programs (Reese & Vera, 2007), we describe the Community Readiness Model (Plested, Edwards, & Jumper-Thurman, 2006), a community-based model that has been successfully used to assess a community's readiness for intervention regarding cancer screening. Further, we discuss a community-based intervention that has been widely used to increase cancer screening rates in medically underserved populations, namely the use of lay health advisors to inform women and recruit them for cancer screenings.

As we discuss the various topics, we place a particular focus on Latina populations. We selected issues related to Latina women as timely for various reasons: (1) Latinas experience a range of health disparities related to these cancers that are well documented; (2) they are part of the fastest growing ethnic minority group, with demographic projections suggesting that as the number of Latina women increases, so will the number of women diagnosed with cancer, making it an even more pressing concern than it is today; and (3) as an immigrant population, mainstream approaches are unlikely to be effective. Instead, the factors that determine disparities are complex and require a focus on cultural aspects of screening and prevention. Thus, we begin by providing an overview of breast and cervical cancer statistics, including a description of key disparities among medically underserved groups.

Cancer Disparities in Medically Underserved Women

In the United States in 2011, it was estimated that 288,130 women would be diagnosed with breast cancer and 39,520 would die from it. Men can develop breast cancer as well, accounting for 1% of all breast cancer cases (ACS, 2011a). However, given the disproportionate prevalence in women, as well as the fact that prevention approaches are not recommended for men at this time (ACS, 2011a), women will be the focus of this chapter.

With regard to cervical cancer, it was projected that 12,710 new cases of invasive cervical cancer would be diagnosed in 2011, although estimates suggest that noninvasive cervical cancer occurs about four times more often. Approximately 4,290 women were expected to die from cervical cancer in 2011, an unfortunate fact given that cervical cancer can be prevented through regular use of Pap tests (ACS, 2011c).

Ethnic minority, low socioeconomic status, immigrant, and older women suffer a disproportionate burden of breast and cervical cancer (IOM, 1999). For example, in the period 2003–2007, the breast cancer mortality rate for African American women was 39% higher than for non-Latina White women, despite the fact that African American women had a lower incidence rate overall. Similarly, although the number of new cervical cancer cases has declined overall, African American women have an incidence rate that remains 39% higher than that of non-Latina White women. The 5-year relative survival rate is lower for African American women (61%) than non-Latina White women (72%). Overall, African American women are twice as likely to die from cervical cancer as non-Latina White women (ACS, 2011b).

Cancer health disparities are evident in other groups as well. For example, across all regions in the United States, American Indian/Alaskan Native women are less likely to be diagnosed with localized breast or cervical cancer than non-Latina White women. Moreover, despite the fact that across groups, Asian American women have the lowest incidence and mortality rates for cervical cancer, women of Vietnamese descent have the highest rates of all ethnic minority women (ACS, 2008). Extant research reveals that Latina women, in particular, suffer a disproportionate burden of breast and cervical cancer. Breast cancer is the leading cause of cancer death among Latina women (ACS, 2009). Despite having lower breast cancer incidence rates than non-Latina White women (Siegel, Ward, Brawley, & Jemal, 2011), Latinas are at higher risk of being diagnosed at later stages, when there are fewer treatment options and prognosis is more guarded. Conservative estimates show that the 5-year breast cancer survivorship rate for Latinas is 85.8%, which is lower than that for non-Latina Whites, at 88.5%. Overall, Latina women are 20% more likely to die from breast cancer even when accounting for age and stage (ACS, 2009). In addition, there is growing evidence that Latina women are being diagnosed at younger ages and are disproportionately affected by a more aggressive type of cancer (Biffl, Myers, Franciose, Gonzalez, & Darnella, 2001; Miranda et al., 2011). Latina women also have higher cervical cancer incidence rates, 12.5 per 100,000, compared to 7.7 per 100,000 among non-Latina White women (Siegel et al., 2011). Moreover, the cervical cancer mortality rate for Latinas is a third higher, 3.1 per 100,000 compared to 2.2 per 100,000 for non-Latina White women (Siegel et al., 2011). The lower breast cancer survivorship rate and higher cervical cancer incidence and mortality rates among Latina women are primarily attributed to this group's lower mammography and Pap smear screening participation (ACS, 2009).

Latinas have consistently shown lower breast and cervical cancer screening rates than non-Latina White women. Data from the 2005 National Health Interview Survey (NHIS) indicated that only 59.6% of Latinas reported having had a mammography exam within the past two years compared to 68.1% of non-Latina White women (ACS, 2009). Similarly, Latina women are less likely to adhere to Pap smear screening guidelines than non-Latina Whites, with 74.5% of Latinas reporting a Pap smear within the past 3 years compared to 81.4% of non-Latina White women (ACS, 2009). In addition, Latina women are less likely than non-Latina White women to engage in timely follow-up when abnormal cancer findings are present (Press, Carrasquillo, Sciacca, & Giardina, 2008). There are many factors that contribute to medically underserved women's lower rates of screening and follow-up. We take these up next.

Factors Influencing Breast and Cervical Cancer Screening

Multiple structural, cultural, and individual-level barriers contribute to decreased screening participation rates and, consequently, to the wide cancer disparities in incidence, mortality, and survival rates among those who are medically underserved (Akers et al., 2007; Peek & Han, 2004). It is critical to understand the factors that contribute to these disparities if we are to design effective preventive interventions (Reese & Vera, 2007). In the remainder of the section, we address the following barriers to screening: (1) traditional predictors of low mammography and Pap smear screening rates, (2) cultural explanatory models, and (3) the structure of communities in which women reside.

Traditional Predictors of Low Screening Adherence

Among medically underserved women, lack of access to health insurance, not having a usual source of care, low levels of formal education, and low income are consistent markers for mammography and Pap smear underuse (Akers et al., 2007; Buki & Selem, 2009; Peek & Han, 2004). In addition, linguistic issues act as barriers for many immigrant women, who may be overwhelmed by the complexities of the US health care system and may not receive interpretation services, despite the fact that language and culture have been recognized as key issues in health care delivery. In fact, there is a federal mandate to provide linguistically and culturally appropriate services by organizations receiving funds from the federal government (US Department of Health and Human Services, 2001), but unfortunately it is not widely implemented as it is an unfunded mandate. In addition, recent research has yielded some interesting findings suggesting that societal factors may trigger psychological responses that interact with biological factors to foster disease. For example, neighborhoods with unhealthy social environments (e.g., poverty, crowding) engender social isolation and depression (Yen & Kaplan, 1999) which, in turn, alter the stress-hormone response. This response activates biochemical pathways that make it possible for cells in breast cancer tumors to survive for longer periods of time, possibly accounting for high mortality rates in African American women (Gehlert et al., 2008).

Cultural Explanatory Models

In conceptualizing cancer health disparities, it is critical to address issues of culture. Culture is a lens that is used to derive meaning from information, thus culture influences individuals' understanding of their health status and options for diagnosis and treatment (Smedley et al., 2003). Culture has been defined as the values, beliefs, expectations, and group norms that are related to particular behaviors or outcomes (Betancourt & López, 1993). For most individuals, their conceptions of health and illness are filled with emotional meaning that emerges from cultural beliefs and values, personal and idiosyncratic beliefs, popular conceptions of illness, and biomedical explanations of illness (which are subject to change over time; Rajaram & Rashidi, 1998). With regard to cancer screening, most health-decision-making models tend to focus on cognitive processes and overemphasize rationality (Flynn, Betancourt, & Ormseth, 2011; Rajaram & Rashidi, 1998). Oftentimes, these models do not consider affect and the emotional components of help-seeking that are likely to influence women's decisions to obtain screenings. For example, a Latina woman who espouses traditional social values such as *familismo* is likely to prioritize the needs of the family over her own. Consistent with *familismo*, family issues take precedence over individual concerns (Sanchez-Burks, Nisbett, & Ybarra, 2000). If a woman has a busy schedule that includes work and caring for several children, she may readily make a medical appointment for a sick child but may not take the time to schedule a mammogram for herself in the absence of overt symptoms of illness. Thus, this woman may not be influenced by health messages that target only the individual and ignore her sociocultural context (Elder et al., 2009). Most researchers and health professionals fail to recognize CEMs despite the fact that by identifying and addressing them, they are more likely to develop health promotion strategies that effectively target the beliefs of medically underserved women (Baker et al., 1997; Rajaram & Rashidi, 1998). Thus, it is important to conceptualize breast and cervical cancer screening as behaviors that are influenced by a woman's sociocultural realities.

Structure of Communities

A growing number of studies indicate that the communities in which women reside have significant effects on their health promotion behaviors such as mammography and Pap smear screening participation (McElroy, Remington, Gangnon, Hariharan, & Andersen, 2006; Mobley, Kuo, Clayton, & Evans, 2009; Wells & Horm, 1998). Thus, we argue that it is critical to also examine an understudied factor in cancer prevention: the structure of communities in which women reside. That is, the resources and assets, or lack thereof, of a community play a key role in women's health behavior and decision making. These resources and assets include the availability of educational programs and screening exams, accessibility to information and services, and quality of the resources available (Bigby, 2007). Regardless of individual sociodemographic characteristics such as race, ethnicity, or income status, women receive widely varying medical care according to where they live and the health system that provides their care. Community context is particularly important to examine among medically underserved women because they are more likely to live in more segregated and economically disadvantaged areas than non-Latina White women (US Census Bureau, 2011; Williams & Collins, 2001). In economically disadvantaged areas, women not only have poor access to health-care-related resources, but also to education and employment opportunities (Bigby, 2007). Women with lower levels of formal education are less likely to obtain information about the importance of screening exams (Kim & Jang, 2008), and women with limited employment opportunities are less likely to have employer-based health insurance (Carrasquillo & Pati, 2006), which would offer the means to pay for the cost of mammograms and Pap smears.

In fact, data on breast and cervical cancer incidence and mortality rates, as well as screening participation rates, differ by geographical location (Eschbach, Mahnken, & Goodwin, 2005). Moreover, variations in diagnosis stage of breast and cervical cancer based on a woman's place of residence have also been documented (Barry & Breen, 2005; Reyes-Ortiz, Eschbach, Zhang, & Goodwin, 2008). Perhaps most interesting are findings showing that for women of a specific ethnic or racial group, rates differ nationally along several dimensions. For instance, African American women are more likely to have obtained at least one mammogram than their non-Latina White counterparts in 10 regions in the country (Goodman, Brownlee, Chang, & Fisher, 2010). Yet, nationally, African American women ages 67–69 are 13% less likely to have obtained at least one mammogram in a 2-year period than non-Latina White women in the same age group (Goodman et al., 2010). Similarly, another study showed that although Latina women made some gains in screening participation rates, these were not uniformly distributed across various Latino communities (e.g., Kang-Kim et al., 2008; Nelson, Bolen, Marcus, Wells, & Meisser, 2003). A longitudinal study conducted in 10 states found that between 1994 and 2004, mammography participation rates among Latina women increased 16% points in New Jersey and 10% points in Florida, yet decreased in Texas and remained unchanged in several states (Kang-Kim et al., 2008).

Even among women with similar sociodemographic and health care characteristics, differences in screening by region have been identified. In a multistate study of Mexican American women, those living in San Francisco were more likely to report having obtained a mammography screening exam within the past 2 years (60%) than those living in Laredo (45%) or Houston (55%), despite having similar demographic characteristics (Ramirez et al., 2000). Findings also suggest that the income level of the neighborhood affects screening rates: women living in impoverished neighborhoods are 33% less likely to obtain a mammography exam than women living in communities with a lower percentage of older adults in poverty (Mobley et al., 2009). In addition, research suggests that racial and ethnic segregation may act as a facilitative factor or barrier to screening for different groups. For example, Native American women living in areas with greater segregation of Native Americans are 16% more likely to have used mammography than those living in less segregated neighborhoods (Mobley et al., 2009). In contrast, Latina women living in higher segregated Latino neighborhoods are 3% less likely to engage in mammography screening than those living in other areas (Mobley et al., 2009).

Interestingly, several studies have examined screening rates among women in Chicago, allowing for a comparison of rates along various factors. Findings suggest that Chicago has the lowest mammography screening rates for Medicare recipients in the country (50.1%) in comparison with the national rate (63.2%; Goodman et al., 2010). Yet, there is wide variation in screening rates among women overall. A community health survey of six different communities in Chicago found that women residing in South Lawndale, a predominately Mexican immigrant neighborhood, had higher breast and cervical cancer screening rates than women in more affluent and predominately non-Latina White communities (Whitman, Shah, Silva, & Ansell, 2007). Specifically, 87% of the women living in South Lawndale reported having ever had a mammography exam and 90% reported having had a Pap test at some point in their lives (Whitman et al.). A second study, a survey of immigrant Mexican women also in South Lawndale, provided support for these findings. Among women who were at least 40 years of age, 87% reported having had mammogram and 95% reported having had a Pap smear screening exam at least once in their lives. These high rates of screening were reported by women with low incomes, no health insurance, and low levels of formal education (Montoya, 2011).

Several aspects of the community context influence screening participation: the physical environment, health care system factors, the availability of social services and other types of organizational support, and the community's social context. The physical environment includes the health care system infrastructure, social institutions, transportation systems, policies, and regulations that determine access to cancer screenings and non-health-related services (Mobley et al., 2009). In a large, national study of racially and ethnically diverse women living in 35 metropolitan areas, researchers found that among women with low incomes, those living in more affluent communities were less likely to report receiving a mammography exam than those living in less affluent communities (Coughlin, King, Richards, & Ekwueme, 2005). This finding suggests that in the high income community, issues such as limited public transportation, low availability of free or reduced cost screenings, and limited accessibility to health centers and information may have influenced the ability of women with low income to obtain cancer screenings (Coughlin et al., 2005). Similarly, transportation barriers for women living in isolated rural communities effectively hinder women's mammography and Pap smear screening participation (Coronado, Thompson, Koepsell, Schwartz, & McLerran, 2004).

Health care system factors that contribute to health disparities include location, hours of operation, reduced cost screenings, bilingual providers and health professionals, availability of support services (e.g., interpreters, outreach workers, health educators), and quality of care (e.g., patient centeredness, efficiency, appropriateness; Akers et al., 2007; Bigby, 2007; Peek & Han, 2004). Women who have reported regular mammography screening have cited that getting health care when they need it is easy, and also reported having a usual source of health care such as a neighborhood clinic (Otero-Sabogal et al., 2004).

Another characteristic of the physical environment that influences screening is the availability of social services and other types of organizational support for women's health promotion services (Sorensen et al., 2003). Non-health-care community organizations such as advocacy groups and religious organizations have proven to be effective collaborators in interventions oriented toward improving cancer prevention among Latinos (Puschel, Thompson, Coronado, Lopez, & Kimball, 2001). For example, Latina immigrants report receiving information on the importance of cancer screening from community sources such as community organizations and church more often than from their health care providers, clinics, or hospitals (Gany, Herrera, Avallone, & Changrani, 2006). Having access to this information has been positively associated with screening among Latina immigrants (Gany et al., 2006). Consequently, state programs that offer free or reduced cost screening exams must be complemented with local efforts that can inform women about services and the importance of early detection (Otero-Sabogal et al., 2004).

Another key aspect of the community environment that may influence a woman's cancer screening behavior is the social context of her neighborhood (Katapodi, Facione, Miaskowski, Dodd, & Waters, 2002; Kreuter & McClure, 2004). Social interactions have the potential to shape a woman's attitudes, beliefs, knowledge, and emotions about breast and cervical cancer and screening exams (Mobley et al., 2009). Specifically, a woman's social network is a social structure that consists of friends, family, colleagues, and other sources of contact (Katapodi et al., 2002). Typically, women receive various forms of social support through these relationships, which lay the foundation for information acquisition about health (e.g., through discussions within the family and peer education; Campos et al., 2008; McCloskey, 2009). Strong social networks through family, friends, neighbors, community- and faith-based organizations, and culturally distinct social services help support and enable preventive health behaviors in ethnic minority women (Bigby, 2007). In addition to providing health information, social networks have been found to provide other types of support such as financial assistance, transportation, and information about other resources within the community (Suarez et al., 2000; Tejada, Thompson, Coronado, & Martin, 2009). However, a social network may also negatively influence screening behavior. For example, a woman who discusses health issues with others who have limited information as she does, may erroneously conclude that she is not at risk for breast cancer because she does not have a family history of the disease, when in fact the proportion of breast cancers that is genetically determined is only 5% (ACS, 2011a). Thus, in order for effective health behavior change to occur, high quality health information and knowledge must permeate the woman's sociocultural context, facilitating accurate information transfer through close social relationships.

The need to attend, specifically, to Latinas' social context is underscored by results of a recent survey showing that 71% of Latinos reported receiving health information from their doctor, friends, family, church groups, or community groups within the past year (Livingston, Minushkin, & Cohn, 2008). Among Latina immigrants from Mexico, encouragement to obtain this exam from trusted women such as daughters and friends has been found to facilitate screening (Tejada et al., 2009).

In sum, there are several community factors that have the potential to greatly influence prevention efforts. We argue that knowing the condition and characteristics of the communities in which medically underserved women reside is critical to changing the current context and improving cancer screening participation. To understand the community context, there are several empirically derived methodologies that can be used by those intending to increase cancer screening rates in ethnic minority women, such as Action Oriented Community Diagnosis (Eng & Blanchard, 1991), Rapid Assessment (McNall & Foster-Fischman, 2007), and the Community Readiness Assessment (CRA), which is an application of the community readiness model (CRM; Plested et al., 2006). Because the CRM has been used specifically in an effort to conceptualize and uncover community factors affecting cancer screening in medically underserved populations, we focus on the CRM in this chapter. Next, we describe the purpose of the CRM and the methodology associated with the CRA, as well as provide an example of its use with the Latina population. We follow that discussion with an example of a community-based intervention that has been used extensively to increase rates of cancer screening in Latina populations, namely the use of lay health advisors (LHAs) to inform and recruit women for screenings, and to help women navigate our complex health care system.

Community Readiness Model and Assessment

Given the importance of community context on breast and mammography screening participation, effective interventions must take into account community conditions. The CRM assists in the conceptualization of the economic, physical, and social environments of a community (Oetting et al., 1995), thus facilitating the identification and development of effective preventive strategies (Jumper-Thurman, Plested, Edwards, Helm, & Oetting, 2001). The CRM adopts a strength-based perspective by taking note of current and potential resources including time, people, money, and space available for prevention efforts (Plested et al., 2006). It emphasizes that all communities are different and that the specific social climate, resources, and leadership characterizing each community determine its ability to address the issue. The CRM proposes that there are six elements that need to be examined to determine a community's readiness to change. The following are the CRM's six elements, adapted specifically as they pertain to the issue of breast and cervical cancer screening in a particular community:

1. Current efforts, programs, or policies on breast and cervical cancer screening targeting women;
2. Level of knowledge about breast and cervical cancer efforts, programs, or policies among women in the community;
3. Extent of support from appointed leaders and influential community members toward programs and services related to breast and cervical cancer screening efforts;
4. The prevailing attitude among women in the community toward breast and cervical cancer screening;
5. Community knowledge about breast and cervical cancer, including the importance of cancer screening and how screening services influence women in the community, and
6. Availability of local resources (e.g., people, time, money, space) to support breast and cervical cancer screening efforts (Plested et al., 2006).

According to the CRM, a community's readiness to address an issue can be classified into 1 of 9 stages, starting from the *No Awareness* stage, in which the community and its leaders do not recognize the issue as a problem, to the *Professionalization* stage, in which a community and its leaders are knowledgeable about the prevalence, risk factors, and causes associated with the issue, and effective programs are in place (Plested et al., 2006). Importantly, the CRM provides guidelines about how to develop interventions tailored to a community's readiness stage, optimizing resources to change the health behavior. Thus, by using the CRA (Plested et al., 2006), which was developed to assess the various aspects of the CRM, researchers can assess the "readiness" of a community to increase screening rates by interviewing leaders of the community who can speak about their professional, social, and community experiences and observations regarding this health behavior.

The CRM has been useful in examining the role of community on breast and cervical cancer screening among Latina women (Borrayo, 2007; Montoya, 2011). For example, Borrayo (2007) applied the CRM to understand the perceived factors Latina women hold toward participating in breast cancer control (screening procedures) and prevention (e.g., risk factor modification, lifestyle changes, and chemoprevention) activities. The information gathered was used to develop breast health education materials that incorporate how "the cultural and psychosocial factors, in the context of important systematic factors, influence women's views about BC [breast cancer] and their decision to participate in BC prevention and control activities" (p. 613).

The CRM model was also adopted to uncover the factors that accounted for the disproportionately high mammography and Pap smear screening participation rates among Mexican immigrant women living in South Lawndale (Montoya, 2011). The CRA revealed that medical, faith-based, and community institutions in South Lawndale mitigate barriers related to language access and awareness of resources, which enhances accessibility to screening exams and services (Montoya, 2011). Specifically, several health facilities and community- and faith-based organizations in the community work on reducing and eliminating place-based factors to increase women's access to information and screening services. Organizational and institutional practices effectively reduced or eliminated known barriers to screening such as language access, transportation, and difficulty navigating the health care system. For example, community organizations played a crucial role in helping women navigate the health care system and become aware of screening resources available in the community (Montoya, 2011). This supports the notion that community members "are in a unique position to formulate priorities for addressing neighborhood level factors that influence health outcomes, to mobilize and advocate for improved healthcare and other services, are effective agents of change and information, and enhance the effectiveness of initiatives to address health problems" (Bigby, 2007, p. 234).

Community-Based Intervention: Using Lay Health Advisors

Several approaches have been employed to improve mammography screening rates among community-dwelling Latinas (Martínez-Donate, 2009). Most interventions have been designed around existing community structures such as a local church or community center. These centers house extant peer networks and infrastructures that can be utilized to transmit health knowledge or information across a community. To realize this potential, health promotion programs have drawn on lay health advisors (LHAs). LHAs are individuals who work within the local community to inform their peers, mobilize community resources, and connect consumers with health care providers to promote healthy behaviors (Rhodes, Foley, Zometa, & Bloom, 2007). Within the literature, there are many similar terms used for LHAs such as "community health advisors and workers, health aides, natural helpers, navigators, paraprofessionals, peer educators, *promotores/as*, and outreach workers (Eng, Parker, & Harlan, 1997). Their roles may vary from one project to another and range on a continuum from natural helping (informal) to the paraprofessional (formal), reflecting the different strategies used in public health interventions (Eng et al., 1997; Rhodes et al., 2007). In a qualitative study of LHAs working on a breast cancer screening promotion project, researchers found that LHAs varied in regard to levels of activity, participation, and proactivity over time, which may explain why the research is equivocal in regard to formulating a clear definition of LHAs (Altpeter, Earp, Bishop, & Eng, 1999).

For the purposes of this chapter, we define an LHA as a community-dwelling individual who takes a proactive, multimodal role within the community and possesses a high degree of initiative (Earp & Flax, 1999; Rhodes et al., 2007). In addition, because LHAs work across various levels of the social and physical environment to enact health behavior change (Ayala et al., 2010), we conceptualize LHA interventions from a socioecologic framework, as tailored to the health promotion arena by Stokols (1996). In accordance with social ecological theory (Bronfenbrenner, 1979), health is influenced by multiple aspects of the physical and social environment, and health behaviors are shaped by the interdependence of environment and social connections; therefore, health promotion is enhanced when multiple levels of the framework are targeted (Grzywacz & Fuqua, 2000; Stokols, 1996, 2000). These systems or levels are adapted from Bronfenbrenner's ecological systems theory (1979) and consist of the following: (1) the microsystem, which includes basic individual or psychosocial components (e.g., emotional processes, genes, gender); (2) the mesosystem, which refers to the institutional factors that shape or structure the environment (e.g., family, religion); (3) the exosystem, which includes the social settings that affect the environment of the individual (e.g., community, culture); and (4) the macrosystem, which refers to external values, policies, and resources that create a context for society to function (e.g., societal values, governmental health policies; Grzywacz & Fuqua, 2000).

Because LHAs share program participants' language, attitudes, norms, beliefs, and ethnic backgrounds, they have the potential to address several systems at once (Earp et al., 1997). Their roles span across several systems including the exosystem (e.g., cultural mediators), and the macrosystem (e.g., informal counselors, health educators, advocates, and community organizers; Earp et al., 1997;

University of Arizona, 1998). For example, in a study among Latinas in Colorado, participants were exposed to a *promotora* intervention at a church or culturally tailored print intervention to increase breast cancer screening rates (Sauaia et al., 2007). Participants in the *promotora* intervention had a significantly higher increase in biennial mammograms than women who were exposed to the print materials alone. The *promotora* intervention was more successful because it addressed several systems, namely the microsystem, mesosystem, and exosystem, when compared to the print intervention, which focused only on the microsystem. Thus, using LHAs is advantageous because the intervention can target various systems at once (Brownstein et al., 2007).

The use of LHAs is also consistent with several elements that have been identified as key in the design of culturally responsive interventions (see Reese & Vera, 2007). First, in using LHAs there is an understanding of how culture influences behavior change, and the intervention is tailored to program participants' culture. Second, there is an understanding that researchers must have knowledge of the community to tailor an invention; this takes place by garnering knowledge from participants and community-dwelling LHAs. Third, there is an understanding that participants should partake in the intervention, and they are involved in the intervention (Reese & Vera, 2007). These elements highlight fundamental aspects of culturally responsive intervention.

Despite the interventions' potential cultural relevance, research has been equivocal in supporting their effectiveness (Elder et al., 2009). Some authors have suggested that the mixed findings arise from the need to have a stronger empirical basis (Rhodes et al., 2007). Also, most studies lack a comparison group or fail to collect pre- and posttest data (Martínez-Donate, 2009; Rhodes et al., 2007). Consistent with Reese and Vera (2007), we note that community-based research is complex and challenging to document. Moreover, preventive interventions of this nature are often difficult to replicate or evaluate because each community has different needs, histories, and barriers, and LHAs may take on different roles depending on need. For example, in a national project using LHAs to increase Latina women's rates of breast and cervical cancer screening, an intervention that was most successful in the Dallas Metroplex area was to hold day-long health fairs at local churches, whereas the most successful intervention in the Hartford, Connecticut, area was to go door to door to identify women in need of screenings (Buki, 1999). Although randomized clinical trials are considered the prototype of scientific evidence, these designs are difficult to achieve in community research because it is not always possible to randomize communities and populations (Meissner et al., 1998; Sauaia et al., 2007). Given the pressing need to reach all women in need of screenings, it is ethically questionable to have a control group in a context of limited resources to assist women with an exam that is potentially lifesaving.

Conclusion

Counseling psychologists have much to contribute to the promotion of healthy behaviors in medically underserved communities. Viewed from a social justice lens, health disparities are a form of oppression that is not inevitable. We have reviewed cancer disparities that are amenable to intervention, where women can successfully increase their adherence to screening behaviors. In this chapter, we proposed that it is imperative that researchers take into account women's community context. In fact, there are multiple, complex factors that influence women's mammography and Pap smear screening. However, we argue that anchoring interventions in the community is critical, given that known predictors of screening participation, such as access to care, access to information about breast and cervical cancer, and knowledge about screening services available varies across different regions, states, and communities. In addition, we argue that researchers must understand sociocultural aspects of health for their interventions to be effective. Traditional frameworks based on the biomedical model fail to recognize that decision making is not always individualistic and linear. Therefore, conceptualizing women's screening decisions drawing from these frameworks may limit our ability to effect behavior change among medically underserved women. We hope through this chapter to inspire counseling psychologists who wish to widen their reach and contribute in a purposeful manner to the amelioration of health disparities in society.

References

Agency for Healthcare Research and Quality. (2001). *Excellence centers to eliminate ethnic/racial disparities (EXCEED): Program brief* (AHRQ Publication No. 01-P021). Retrieved from http://www. ahrq.gov/research/exceed.htm

Akers, A. Y., Newmann, S. J., & Smith, J. S. (2007). Factors underlying disparities in cervical cancer incidence, screening, and treatment in the United States. *Current Problems in Cancer, 31*(3), 157–181.

Altpeter, M., Earp, J. A. L., Bishop, C., & Eng, E. (1999). Lay health advisor activity levels: Definitions from the field. *Health Education & Behavior, 26*(4), 495–512. doi:10.1177/109019819902600408

American Cancer Society. (2008). Cancer disparities: Key statistics. Retrieved from http://www.cancer.org/Cancer/news/Features/cancer-disparities-key-statistics

American Cancer Society. (2009). *Cancer facts & figures for Hispanics/Latinos: 2009–2011*. Atlanta, GA: American Cancer Society, Inc.

American Cancer Society. (2011a). *Breast cancer*. Retrieved from http://www.cancer.org/acs/groups/cid/documents/webcontent/003090-pdf.pdf

American Cancer Society. (2011b). *Cancer facts and figures for African Americans: 2011–2012*. Atlanta: Author.

American Cancer Society. (2011c). *Cervical cancer*. Retrieved from http://www.cancer.org/acs/groups/cid/documents/webcontent/003094-pdf.pdf

Anderson, N. B. (2009). Our first strategic plan. *APA Monitor on Psychology, 40*(10), 9.

Ayala, G. X., Vaz, L., Earp, J. A., Elder, J. P., & Cherrington, A. (2010). Outcome effectiveness of the lay health advisor model among Latinos in the United States: An examination by role. *Health Education Research, 25*(5), 815–840. doi:10.1093/her/cyq035

Baker, E. A., Bouldin, N., Durham, M., Lowell, M. E., Gonzalez, M., Jodaitis, N.,... Adams, S. T. (1997). The Latino health advocacy program: A collaborative lay health advisor approach. *Health Education & Behavior, 24*(4), 495–509.

Barry, J., & Breen, N. (2005). The importance of place of residence in predicting late stage diagnosis of breast or cervical cancer. *Health & Place, 11*, 15–29.

Betancourt, H., & López, S. R. (1993). The study of culture, ethnicity, and race in American psychology. *American Psychologist, 48*(6), 629–637.

Biffl, W. L., Myers, A., Franciose, R. J., Gonzalez, R. J., & Darnella, D. (2001). Is breast cancer in young Latinas a different disease? *The American Journal of Surgery, 182*(6), 596–600.

Bigby, J. A. (2007). The role of communities in eliminating healthcare disparities: Getting down to the grassroots. In R. A. Williams (Ed.), *Eliminating healthcare disparities in America: Beyond the IOM report*. Totowa, NJ: Humana Press.

Borrayo, E. A. (2007). Using a community readiness model to help overcome breast health disparities among U.S. Latinas. *Substance Use & Misuse, 42*, 603–619.

Bronfenbrenner, U. (1979). *The ecology of human development*. Cambridge, MA: Harvard University Press.

Brownstein, J. N., Chowdhury, F. M., Norris, S. L., Horsley, T., & Jack, L. (2007). Effectiveness of community health workers in the care of people with hypertension. *American Journal of Preventive Medicine, 32*(5), 435–447.

Buki, L. P. (1999). Early detection of breast and cervical cancer among medically underserved Latinas. In M. Sotomayor & A. García (Eds.), *La familia: Traditions and realities* (pp. 67–85). Washington, DC: National Hispanic Council on Aging.

Buki, L. P. (2007). Reducing health disparities: The perfect fit for counseling psychology. *The Counseling Psychologist, 35*, 706–715.

Buki, L. P., & Selem, M. (2009). Cancer screening and survivorship in Latino populations: A primer for psychologists. In F. A. Villarruel, G. Carlo, J. M. Grau, M. Azmitia, N. Cabrera, & T. J. Chahin (Eds.), *U.S. handbook of Latina/o psychology* (pp. 363–378). Thousand Oaks, CA: Sage.

Buki, L. P., & Selem, M. (2012). Health disparities: Issues and opportunities for counseling psychologists. In N. Fouad (Ed.), J. Carter, & L. Subich (Assoc. Eds.), *APA handbook of counseling psychology: Vol. 2. Practice, interventions, and applications* (pp. 233–249). Washington, DC: American Psychological Association.

Campos, B., Dunkel-Schetter, C., Abdou, C. M., Hobel, C. J., Glynn, L. M., & Sandman, C. A. (2008). Familialism, social support, and stress: Positive implications for pregnant Latinas. *Cultural Diversity and Ethnic Minority Psychology, 14*(2), 155–162.

Carrasquillo, O., & Pati, S. (2006). The role of health insurance on Pap smear and mammography utilization by immigrants living in United Sates. *Preventive Medicine, 39*, 943–950.

Center to Reduce Cancer Health Disparities. (2009). *Health disparities and CRCHD*. Retrieved from National Cancer Institute website: http://crchd.cancer.gov/disparities/disparities-index.html

Center to Reduce Cancer Health Disparities. (2011). *Health disparities defined*. Retrieved from National Cancer Institute website: http://crchd.cancer.gov/disparities/defined.html

Clay, R. A. (2010). A pivotal year. *Monitor on Psychology, 41*(1), 28.

Commission on Social Determinants of Health. (2008). *Closing the gap in a generation: Health equity through action on the social determinants of health*. Retrieved from World Health Organization website: http://whqlibdoc.who.int/publications/2008/9789241563703_Eng.pdf

Coronado, G. D., Thompson, B., Koepsell, T. D., Schwartz, S. M., & McLerran, D. (2004). Use of Pap tests among Hispanic and non-Hispanic Whites in a rural setting. *Preventive Medicine, 38*(6), 713–722.

Coughlin, S. S., King, J., Richards, T. B., & Ekwueme, D. U. (2005). Breast cancer screening and socioeconomic status—35 metropolitan areas, 2000 and 2002. *Morbidity and Mortality Weekly Report, 54*(39), 981–985. Retrieved from Centers for Disease Control and Prevention website: http://www.cdc.gov/mmwr/preview/mmwrhtml/mm5439a2.htm

Earp, J. A. L., & Flax, V. L. (1999). What lay health advisors do—An evaluation of advisors' activities. *Cancer Practice, 7*(1), 16–21.

Earp, J. A. L., Viadro, C. I., Vincus, A. A., Altpeter, M., Flax, V., Mayne, L., & Eng, E. (1997). Lay health advisors: A strategy for getting the word out about breast cancer. *Health Education & Behavior, 24*(4), 432–451.

Elder, J. P., Ayala, G. X., Parra-Medina, D., & Talavera, G. A. (2009). Health communication in the Latino community: Issues and approaches. *Annual Review of Public Health, 30*, 227–251.

Eng, E., & Blanchard, L. (1991). Action-oriented community diagnosis: A health education tool. *International Journal of Community Health Education, 11*, 93–110.

Eng, E., Parker, E., & Harlan, C. (1997). Lay health advisor intervention strategies: A continuum from natural helping to paraprofessional helping. *Health Education & Behavior, 4*(24), 413–417.

Eschbach, K., Mahnken, D. J., & Goodwin, S. J. (2005). Neighborhood composition and incidence of cancer among Hispanics in the United States. *Cancer, 103*(5), 1036–1044.

Flynn, P. M., Betancourt, H., & Ormseth, S. R. (2011). Culture, emotion, and cancer screening: An integrative framework for investigating health behavior. *Annals of Behavioral Medicine, 42*(1), 79–90.

Gany, F. M., Herrera, A. P., Avallone, M., & Changrani, J. (2006). Attitudes, knowledge, and health-seeking behaviors of five immigrant minority communities in the prevention and cancer screening: A focus group approach. *Ethnicity & Health, 11*(1), 19–39.

Gehlert, S., Sohmer, D., Sacks, T., Mininger, C., McClintock, M., & Olopade, O. (2008). Targeting health disparities: A model linking upstream determinants to downstream interventions. *Health Affairs, 27,* 339–349.

Goodman, D. C., Brownlee, S., Chang, C. H., & Fisher, E. S. (2010). Regional and racial variation in primary care and the quality of care among Medicare beneficiaries. The Dartmouth Atlas: Dartmouth Institute for Health Policy and Clinical Practice. Retrieved from http://www.dartmouthatlas.org/downloads/reports/Primary_care_report_090910.pdf

Grzywacz, J. G., & Fuqua, J. (2000). The social ecology of health: Leverage points and linkages. *Behavioral Medicine, 26*(3), 101–116.

Healthy People 2020. (2010). *Disparities.* Retrieved from http://www.healthypeople.gov/2020/about/disparitiesAbout.aspx

Howlader, N., Noone, A. M., Krapcho, M., Neyman, N., Aminou, R., Waldron, W..... Cronin, K. A. (Eds). (2012). SEER Cancer Statistics Review, 1975–2009. Retrieved from http://seer.cancer.gov/csr/1975_2009_pops09/

Institute of Medicine. (1999). *The unequal burden of cancer: An assessment of NIH research and programs for ethnic minorities and the medically underserved.* Washington, DC: National Academy Press.

Institute of Medicine. (2006). *Examining the health disparities research plan of the National Institutes of Health: Unfinished business.* Washington, DC: National Academies Press.

Jones, C. M. (2010). The moral problem of health disparities. *American Journal of Public Health, 100*(S1), S47–S51.

Jumper-Thurman, P., Plested, B. A., Edwards, R. W., Helm, H. M., & Oetting, E. R. (2001). Using the community readiness model in Native communities. In J. E. Trimble & F. Beauvais (Eds.), *Health promotion and substance abuse prevention among American Indian and Alaska Native Communities: Issues in cultural competence* (pp. 129–158). Rockville, MD: US Department of Health and Human Services.

Kang-Kim, M., Betancourt, J. R., Ayanian, J., Zaslavsky, A. M., Yucel, R., & Weissman, J. S. (2008). Access to care and use of preventive services by Hispanics: State-based variations From 1991 to 2004. *Medical Care, 46*(5), 507–514.

Katapodi, M. C., Facione, N. C., Miaskowski, C., Dodd, M. J., & Waters, C. (2002). The influence of social support on breast cancer screening in a multicultural community sample. *Oncology Nursing Society, 29*(5), 845–852.

Kim, J., & Jang, S. N. (2008). Socioeconomic disparities in breast cancer screening among U.S. women: Trends from 2000 to 2005. *Journal of Preventive Medicine & Public Health, 41*(3), 186–194.

Kreuter, M. W., & McClure, S. M. (2004). The role of culture in health communication. *Annual Review of Public Health, 25,* 439–455.

Livingston, G., Minushkin, S., & Cohn, D. (2008). *Hispanics and health care in the United States: Access, information, and knowledge.* Washington, DC: Pew Hispanic Center.

Martínez-Donate, A. P. (2009). Using lay health advisors to promote breast and cervical cancer screening among Latinas: A review. *Wisconsin Medical Journal, 108*(5), 259–262.

McCloskey, J. (2009). Promotores as partners in a community-based diabetes intervention program targeting Hispanics. *Family & Community Health, 32*(1), 48–57.

McElroy, J. A., Remington, P. L., Gangnon, R. E., Hariharan, L., & Andersen, L. D. (2006). Identifying geographic disparities in the early detection of breast cancer using a geographic information system. *Preventing Chronic Disease 3*(1), A10.

McNall, M., & Foster-Fischman, P. G. (2007). Methods of rapid evaluation, assessment, and appraisal. *American Journal of Evaluation, 28,* 151–168.

Meissner, H. I., Breen, N., Coyne, C., Legler, J. M., Green, D. T., & Edwards, B. K. (1998). Breast and cervical cancer screening interventions: An assessment of the literature. *Cancer Epidemiology Biomarkers & Prevention, 7*(10), 951–961.

Minority Health and Health Disparities Research and Education Act of 2000, Public Law 106–525. Retrieved from Government Printing Office website: http://frwebgate.access.gpo.gov/cgi-bin/getdoc.cgi?dbname=106_cong_public_laws&docid=f:publ525.106.pdf

Miranda, P. Y., Wilkinson, A. V., Etzel, C. J., Zhou, R., Jones, L. A., Thompson, P., & Bondy, M. L. (2011). Policy implications of early onset breast cancer among Mexican-origin women. *Cancer, 117*(2), 390–397. doi:10.1002/cncr.25397

Mobley, L R., Kuo, T., Clayton, L. J., & Evans, W. D. (2009). Mammography facilities are accessible, so why is utilization so low? *Cancer Causes & Control, 20*(6), 1017–1028.

Montoya, Y. (2011). *Community influences on cancer screening behaviors among Mexican immigrant women* (Master's thesis). University of Illinois, Urbana-Champaign, Illinois. Retrieved from http://www.ideals.illinois.edu/handle/2142/24385

National Cancer Institute (2010). *Fact sheet: Pap test.* Retrieved from http://www.cancer.gov/cancertopics/factsheet/detection/Pap-test

Nelson, D. E., Bolen, J., Marcus, S., Wells, H. E., & Meisser, H. (2003). Cancer screening estimates for U.S. metropolitan areas. *American Journal of Preventive Medicine, 24*(4), 301–309.

Oetting, E. R., Donnermeyer, J. F., Plested, B. A., Edwards, R. W., Kelly, K., & Beauvais, F. (1995). Assessing community readiness for prevention. *The International Journal of Addictions, 30*(6), 659–683.

Otero-Sabogal, R., Owens, D., Canchola, J., Golding, J. M., Tabnak, F., & Fox, P. (2004). Mammography rescreening among women of diverse ethnicities: Patient, provider, and health care factors. *Journal of Care for the Poor and Underserved, 15,* 390–412.

Peek, M. E., & Han, J. H. (2004). Disparities in screening mammography: Current status, interventions, and implications. *Journal of General Internal Medicine, 19,* 184–194.

Plested, B. A., Edwards, R. W., & Jumper-Thurman, P. (2006). *Community readiness: A handbook for successful change.* Fort Collins, CO: Tri-Ethnic Center for Prevention Research.

Press, R., Carrasquillo, O., Sciacca, R. R., & Giardina, E.G. V. (2008). Racial/ethnic disparities in time to follow-up after an abnormal mammogram. *Journal of Women's Health, 17*(6), 923–930. doi:10.1089/jwh.2007.0402

Puschel, K., Thompson, B., Coronado, G., Lopez, L., & Kimball, A. (2001). Factors related to cancer screening in Hispanics: A comparison of the perceptions of Hispanic community members, health care providers, and representatives of organizations that serve Hispanics. *Health Education Behavior, 28*(5), 573–590.

Rajaram, S. S., & Rashidi, A. (1998). Minority women and breast cancer screening: The role of cultural explanatory models. *Preventive Medicine, 27*(5), 757–764.

Ramirez, A. G., Talavera, G. A., Villarreal, R., Suarez, L., McAlister, A., Trapido, E.... Marti, J. (2000). Breast cancer screening in regional Hispanic populations. *Health Education Research: Theory & Practice, 15,* 559–568.

Reese, L. E., & Vera, E. M. (2007). Culturally relevant prevention: The scientific and practical considerations of community-based programs. *The Counseling Psychologist, 35,* 763–778. doi: 10.1177/0011000007304588

Reyes-Ortiz, C. A., Eschbach, K., Zhang, D. D., & Goodwin, J. S. (2008). Neighborhood composition and cancer among Hispanics: Tumor stage and size at time of diagnosis. *Cancer Epidemiology, Biomarkers & Prevention, 17*(11), 2931–2936.

Rhodes, S. D., Foley, K. L., Zometa, C. S., & Bloom, F. R. (2007). Lay health advisor interventions among Hispanics/Latinos: A qualitative systematic review. *American Journal of Preventive Medicine, 33*(5), 418–427.

Sanchez-Burks, J., Nisbett, R. E., & Ybarra, O. (2000). Cultural styles, relationship schemas, and prejudice against out-groups. *Journal of Personality and Social Psychology, 79*(2), 174–189.

Sauaia, A., Min, S., Lack, D., Apodaca, C., Osuna, D., Stowe, A.,... Byers, T. (2007). Church-based breast cancer screening education: Impact of two approaches on Latinas enrolled in public and private health insurance plans. *Preventing Chronic Disease, 4*(4), 1–10.

Siegel, R., Ward, E., Brawley, O., & Jemal, A. (2011). Cancer statistics, 2011: The impact of eliminating socioeconomic and racial disparities on premature cancer deaths. *CA: A Cancer Journal for Clinicians, 61*(4), 212–236.

Smedley, B. D., Stith, A. Y., & Nelson, A. R. (Eds.) (2003). *Unequal treatment: Confronting racial and ethnic disparities in healthcare.* Washington, DC: National Academies Press.

Smith, D. B. (2005). *Eliminating disparities in treatment and the struggle to end segregation.* New York: The Commonwealth Fund.

Sorensen, G., Emmons, K., Hunt, M. K., Barbeau, E., Goldman, R., Peterson, K.,... Berkman, L. (2003). Model for incorporating social context in health behavior interventions: Applications for cancer prevention for working class, multiethnic population. *Preventive Medicine, 37,* 188–197.

Speight, S. L., & Vera, E. M. (2004). A social justice agenda: Ready, or not? *The Counseling Psychologist, 32,* 109–118.

Stokols, D. (1996). Translating social ecological theory into guidelines for community health promotion. *American Journal of Health Promotion, 10*(4), 282–298.

Stokols, D. (2000). The social ecological paradigm of wellness promotion. In M. S. Jamner & D. Stokols (Eds.), *Promoting human wellness: New frontiers for research, practice, and policy* (pp. 21–37). Berkeley: University of California.

Suarez, L., Ramirez, A. G., Villarreal, R., Marti, J., McAlister, A., Talavera, G. A.,... Pérez-Stable, E. J. (2000). Social networks and cancer screenings in four U.S. Hispanic groups. *American Journal of Preventive Medicine, 19*(1), 47–52.

Tejada, S., Thompson, B., Coronado, G. D., & Martin, D. P. (2009). Barriers and facilitators related to mammography use among lower educated Mexican women in the USA. *Social Science & Medicine, 68*(5), 832–839.

University of Arizona. (1998). *A summary of the National Community Health Advisor Study.* Baltimore, MD: Annie E. Casey Foundation.

US Census Bureau. (2008). *Percent Distribution of the Projected Population by Sex, Race and Hispanic Origin for the United States: 2010 to 2050.* Retrieved from http://www.census.gov/population/www/projections/summarytables.html

US Census Bureau. (2011). *Housing patterns: Racial and ethnic residential segregation in the United States: 1980–2000.* Retrieved from http://www.census.gov/hhes/www/housing/housing_patterns/papertoc.html

US Department of Health and Human Services. (2001). *National standards for culturally and linguistically appropriate services in health care: Final report.* Retrieved from http://minorityhealth.hhs.gov/assets/pdf/checked/finalreport.pdf

Vera, E. M., & Speight, S. L. (2003). Multicultural competence, social justice, and counseling psychology: Expanding our roles. *The Counseling Psychologist, 31,* 253–272.

Wells, B. L., & Horm, J. W. (1998). Targeting the underserved for breast and cervical cancer screening: The utility of ecological analysis using the National Health Interview Survey. *American Journal of Public Health, 88*(10), 1484–1489.

Williams, R. D., & Collins, C. (2001). Racial residential segregation: A fundamental cause of racial disparities in health. *Public Health Reports, 16,* 404–416.

Whitman, S., Shah, A. M, Silva, A., & Ansell, D. (2007). Mammography screening in six diverse communities in Chicago—A population study. *Cancer Detection and Prevention, 31,* 166–172.

Yen, I. H., & Kaplan, G. A. (1999). Poverty area residence and changes in depression and perceived health status: Evidence from the Alameda County Study. *International Journal of Epidemiology, 28,* 90–94.

PART 3

Promoting Wellness and Adaptation

CHAPTER

20 Promoting Healthy Aging in Counseling Psychology

Robert D. Hill *and* Michael Duffy

Abstract

"Healthy aging" has appeared in the scientific literature as a descriptor of the underlying processes in human aging. It has also been used to promote social policies for health care delivery to older adults. In recent years, "healthy aging" has been expanded through the biopsychosocial model to geriatric care. Counseling psychology espouses ideals of inclusion through a strength-based positive aging paradigm. This affirmative value links counseling psychology and "healthy aging" in health care provision to older persons. At present, the discipline of counseling psychology does not have a strong presence in the science or practice domains of gerontology, geropsychology, or geriatrics. Most mental healthservices delivered to older clientele comes through the scientific and professional discipline of clinical geropsychology, which operates from within a traditional disease-based medical model of care. This chapter describes the added benefits of a healthy aging strength-based approach in geriatric care that could be championed by the discipline of counseling psychology.

Key Words: healthy aging, positive aging, health promotion, older adults, biopsychosocial model, strength-based counseling, geropsychology

Promoting Healthy Aging in Counseling Psychology

The term "healthy aging" has influenced perceptions of health in later life for at least 5 decades. The purpose of this chapter is to: (1) elucidate the term "healthy aging" as it appears in the scientific literature; (2) highlight a healthy aging ideology that has catalyzed social and public policies affirming the health care needs of older adults both within and outside of the United States; (3) describe how the healthy aging concept has been expanded to incorporate demographically driven sociocontextual diversity in the 21st century, and (4) discuss how counseling psychology is uniquely positioned to promote healthy aging through its strength-based framework.

Healthy Aging: A Scientific Construct

At its inception, the term "healthy aging" characterized those older persons who possessed substantial resistance to physical and cognitive decline even near the end of life. Thus, in its earliest use the "healthy aging" label was not distinguishable from other gerontological terms including "optimal aging" or "exceptional aging" that have also described these subsets of very long lived persons (see Bäckman et al., 1998; Canetto, Kaminiski, & Felicio, 1995; Hill et al., 1995; Hill, Stigsdotter, & Bäckman, 1997). Lövdén et al., 2004; Robine, 2006).

More recently, Ryff and Singer (2009) distinguished between healthy aging and other advanced longevity terms by arguing that healthy aging describes elemental physiological processes that undergird systemic adaptation. For example, in cellular metabolism the healthy aging hypothesis could be used to explain how adaptive function at a cellular level works to prevent (or delay) age-related deterioration. The term "healthy aging," in this case, guides basic research investigating microbiological interactions and cellular mechanisms underlying age-related decline. For example, researchers at Johns Hopkins University in the United States and Keio University in Tokyo (Lou et al., 2003) established a link between a protein known as Akt (or protein kinase B) and the diminishment of naturally occurring enzymatic inducers of cell death. At a systemic level, inhibition of the Akt pathway could impact even cell death in brain structures such as the hippocampus and thus preserve general memory functioning in later life. Healthy aging defined in this way elucidates the biological processes that prevent or delay the systemic breakdown of organ function (e.g., the brain) that, as a consequence, prevents deterioration of general cognitive capacities (short-term memory) in later life.

Separate from the biologically driven healthy aging definition, a second domain where the term "healthy aging" has proliferated has been in population studies of health promotion. In this case, "healthy aging" has been employed as an epidemiological term to describe functioning across larger groups. This focus is best characterized by large-scale prospective longitudinal studies of human aging that emphasize nondiseased longevity processes in older adult cohort groups. Guralnik and Kaplan (1989) in their report of predictors of healthy aging from the Alameda County Study noted:

> While it is certainly desirable to age with no chronic diseases, it can be problematic to characterize Healthy Aging according to diagnosed diseases. How important or severe must a disease be to remove someone from the Healthy Aging group? (p. 705)

The Honolulu Heart Study used the term "healthy aging" to describe older persons who were disease-free at study baseline and over the 12-year follow-up period (Benfante, Reed, & Brody, 1985). The impetus of healthy aging in this line of research has been to produce a risk factor model for optimal late-life function. An example of this risk factor model is described by Burke et al. (2003), who enumerated multiple behavioral (physical activity, diet, and abstinence from cigarette smoking), demographic (education, waist circumference), and subclinical disease markers (blood pressure) as risk factors that could derail a healthy aging trajectory.

Whether from the micro (cellular) or macro (population) view, the term "healthy aging" has characterized preventative processes in delaying age-related decline. It is for this reason that intense efforts to study new and emergent issues through the healthy aging label are needed. For example, preclinical symptoms identified at the very early stages of Alzheimer's disease might be, in the future, best placed within the purview of healthy aging versus diseased or pathological aging per se.

Healthy Aging: A Social Policy Catalyst

In the public policy arena, the term "healthy aging" has generated social initiatives to promote quality of life in old age. In this regard, the healthy aging concept has had worldwide appeal. Peel, Bartlett, and McClure (2004; see also Peel et al., 2005) in their review of the term "healthy aging" noted that among the many labels descriptive of growing old, "healthy aging" has received substantial international attention in multiple countries including Canada, Australia, and parts of the European Union. Each country, within in its own cultural context, has endorsed initiatives under the umbrella of healthy aging (or as termed in the United Kingdom, Canada, New Zealand, and Australia "healthy ageing") to promote social policies for better health care access among older citizens. For example, one Canadian healthy aging initiative is based on the concept of age-friendly communities. The healthy aging framework in this policy is supported by three values: (1) the celebration of diversity, (2) a refutation of ageism in all of its forms including economic inequities, and (3) the active creation of opportunities within the community for independence and quality of life (Menec, Button, Blandford, & Morris-Oswald, 2007).

Although interest in healthy aging and its promotion began in the United States, the appeal of this ideology in the larger Western world has been strong, especially as average life expectancy has increased in the past 2 decades for almost every nation in the first world. A hallmark of the American healthy aging approach has been grassroots movements organized through local community efforts, spurred, in part, by national organizations such as the American Association of Retired Persons. From these community enterprises have emerged compelling business models of the 21st-century American healthy aging zeitgeist that over the past decade has garnered fiscal resources in many regions within the United States (see Minnesota Department of Health, 2006).

Since 2000, the Centers for Disease Control (CDC) have spearheaded visible public healthy aging initiatives within the United States. These have been designed to: (1) provide leadership in healthy aging through promoting positive aging lifestyle practices and disease prevention across local community networks, (2) gauge how disease prevention can preserve healthy aging, and (3) develop specific programs that employ behavioral strategies including exercise, diet, and the avoidance of health-damaging behaviors (cigarette smoking, excessive alcohol use, getting regular preventive medical check-ups) to preserve functional independence in later life. In many respects, the CDC has been the institutional champion of American healthy aging catalyzing, at least for disease prevention, the proliferation of knowledge about health issues in old age. One of the more comprehensive definitions of healthy aging can be found on the Minnesota Department of Health's website:

> **Healthy Aging** is the development and maintenance of optimal physical, mental and social well-being and function in older adults. It is most likely to be achieved when physical environments and communities are safe, and support the adoption and maintenance by individuals of attitudes and behaviors known to promote health and well-being; and by the effective use of health services and community programs to prevent or minimize the impact of acute and chronic disease on function. (http://www.health.state.mn.us/divs/orhpc/pubs/healthyaging/dimensions.pdf)

From the basic and applied scientific research, it is well understood that there are multiple limiting contextual or social factors in maintaining healthy aging. Beyond one's lifestyle choices and the biological conditions that undergird health in later life, an affirmative social environment is essential to healthy aging. This is also the case for the intrapersonal or psychology factors associated with growing old that are captured in the term "positive aging" (Hill, 2005, 2008, 2011; Hill & Mansour, 2008). These three factors; the biological, social, and psychological processes of growing old, interact to create an actuarial algorithm that would epitomize the healthy aging phenomenon. One ubiquitous manifestation of this fact can be found in the proliferation of healthy aging calculators such as the one published by Thomas Perls (1999) from the New England Centenarian Study. These calculators operationalize biological, personal, and social determinants of well-being in later life (see http://www.livingto100.com/).

Healthy Aging in the 21st Century

The Maintenance of Healthy Aging

The maintenance of one's personal health status across the adult life span and into old age is one defining feature of healthy aging (Hansen-Kyle, 2005). Construed in this way, healthy aging is the process of chronic disease prevention as it involves, among other things, actualizing "protective" biological, social, and psychological forces that protect us from chronic disease. Like the commonly understood disease risk factor model from epidemiology described earlier in this chapter, behaviors and/or lifestyle choices that postpone disease and disability in old age would fit within the healthy aging label. Specifically, a family history that includes a high percentage of relatives who have lived beyond the average life span, being raised in an environment that has good access to education and health resources, personal engagement in a life-long program of physical fitness, eating a balanced and fat-reduced diet, and fostering a positive attitude toward one's self and others are all prominent features of a healthy aging lifestyle.

This risk/protective factor paradigm is receiving increased empirical attention in relation to the role of specific behaviors and disease processes and how these interact to influence change in one's personal health status over time (Bienias et al., 2003). The most well-known of these are favorable genetics (biological), years of education (social), and a range of personal lifestyle variables including the avoidance of cigarette smoking, excessive alcohol use, a stressful life routine.

In one large-scale longitudinal investigation that attempted to quantify these variables and then examine their main effects and interaction on healthy longevity (Wilcox et al., 2006), the Honolulu Asia Aging Study researchers followed a cohort of nearly 6,000 US-born adult men across a 40-year time frame. These men were assessed initially between 1965 and 1968. They were predominantly of Japanese ancestry and were residing at the time of baseline assessment in the state of Hawaii. Nondisease risk (or protective) factors for healthy survival were identified in these older men from among a battery of 29 measures that included a range of anthropometric and physiological indicators (BMI, FEV1, blood pressure), health habits (cigarette smoking, alcohol consumption, and physical activity), and sociodemographic variables (marital status, income). From these, a survival risk factor score (SRS) was computed for each participant. SRS values were then grouped according to two "survival" phenotypes; exceptional survivors and usual survivors. Distinguishing these groups was the presence of chronic disease; that is, the usual survivors were defined as experiencing various types and stages of disease diagnoses. Of interest in this study was the impact of these risk factor variables (and their combined effects) on nondisease longevity.

In this case, nondisease longevity was defined as healthy aging. The principal finding from this study was that as study participants grew older the influence of SRS variables increased almost exponentially with respect to predicting the emergence of disease; that is, in middle age, disease was detected much earlier in those persons whose SRS scores indicated low adherence to risk factor behaviors (high BMI scores, ongoing cigarette smoking, and divorced marital status). The impact of combined variables was even more remarkable for predicting at earlier ages the detection of disease; that is, the probability was nearly zero that a chronic overweight smoker who was sedentary and recently divorced would be disease free at age 80 years.

Like the Honolulu Asia Aging study, evidence from multiple sources has confirmed that poor health habits, a negative mental attitude and/or chronic mental illness, as well as deprived social conditions all work against healthy aging. These findings open the door to further refinement of explanatory features of health and health behavior including biological, social, and psychological variables (and their interaction) as these relate to intervention planning for an older adult clientele. The next section describes the biopsychosocial model as a conceptual framework for guiding health care provision to older adults.

The Biopsychosocial Model Applied to Healthy Aging

The biopsychosocial model of health has its origins in the late 1970s, when George Engel (1977), in a highly cited article in the journal *Science*, asserted that a new model of medicine was needed to guide health care delivery. A critical feature of this "new" model was a framework that encouraged the practicing physician to address more comprehensively the patient's physical, psychological, and social needs. Engel's assertion was a reaction to what he viewed as a predominantly disease-focused view of medical care. Engel, therefore, articulated what he believed to be a new paradigm of care that was inclusive of growing evidence of the importance of psychological and social factors in the treatment of disease processes. Following introduction of the biopsychosocial model, Engel went further to show how this model of medical care could be incorporated within high-profile medical subspecialties including, for example, cardiology (Engel, 1981). Engel's arguments stimulated broader thinking in the scientific community about disease processes, the role of psychosocial factors, and the benefits of prevention strategies in health care delivery. The introduction of the biopsychosocial model of health care was accompanied by a dramatic shift in public health initiatives that moved from disease intervention (e.g., to cure those who are sick) to disease prevention (e.g., the promotion of health). This shift also opened the door to an expanded national health care prioritization agenda that more comprehensively captures the full spectrum of concerns facing adults from ages 35 years and older in the United States.

The biopsychosocial model, as the name implies, is an approach to health care that considers the interrelationship between biological, psychological, and social processes (and their interaction) on the maintenance of health, the emergence of disease, and the role that these play in recovery from illness and disease. If it is assumed that the concept of healthy aging is captured in this model, then, the mind-set extended from the biopsychosocial framework would emphasize the promotion of health through dimensional efforts that recognize the impact that these domains play on the aging process. Figure 20.1 below is a general diagram of the biopsychosocial model using labels within each of these respective domains. In Figure 20.1, the center focus or the point of intersection would be healthy aging. In this case, each of the component terms of the biopsychosocial model would encompass health care initiatives targeting older adults who are experiencing issues or problems falling within each of these domains. For example, the treatment of osteoporosis in old age would benefit from interventions that also target social isolation as well as grief and bereavement. Thus, a biopsychosocial healthy aging intervention would capitalize on the synergy of multiple treatment strategies that focus on these three problem issues. Treating presenting issues in this way, therefore, might involve pain management medication (for pain associated with inflammation in osteoporosis), the creation of web-based social networks where older adults who share this illness could discuss their needs (social support), and dealing with issues of loss from lack of mobility as a predictable consequence of this medical disorder (e.g., grief counseling). It is clear from the research literature that these types of multidimensional treatments are superior to the single-pronged intervention approach such as the singular delivery of a drug to address a physical pain issue or ameliorate a psychological concern (Crankshaw, Rabiner, & O'Keeffe, 2003; Dahlin-Ivanoff, 2010; Dapp et al., 2005). The biopsychosocial impetus in

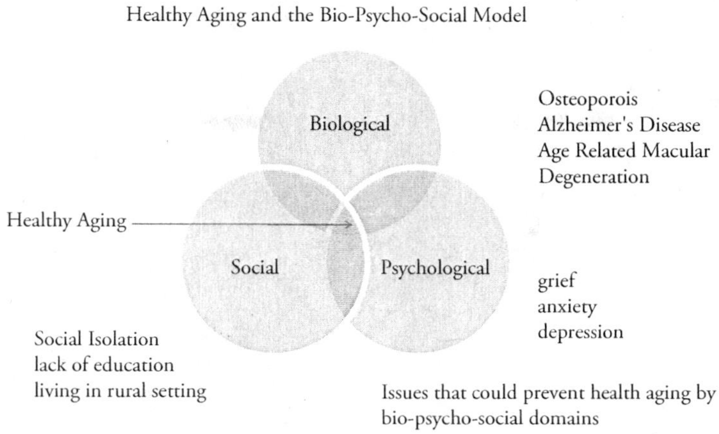

Figure 20.1. Healthy aging and the biopsychosocial model

healthy aging intervention planning is highlighted by several examples of treatment strategies where this intersection occurs to help older adults maintain themselves in contexts where they are the most comfortable and have the greatest access to their own personal resources for sustaining well-being (Bryant et al., 2001; Hansen-Kyle, 2005)

Healthy Aging and Counseling Psychology

Counseling psychology does not have strong traditions in medicine, health promotion, or in health prevention for older adults. Further, broad-based models of health prevention targeting older adults have not been widely studied by the discipline of counseling psychology. To underscore this contention, the January 1999 issue of *The Counseling Psychologist* published a review article where scholarly themes germane to the discipline of counseling psychology were summarized. In this article Heppner (1999) listed 106 *Counseling Psychologist* major contribution articles from 1969 through 1998. Of these, only two were tied to aging; namely, "Counseling Psychology and Aging" (Smyer, 1984) and "Major Social Theories of Aging" (Fry, 1992); this is in contrast to 11 major contribution articles on issues of ethnic diversity. Expanding on this, Werth et al. (2003), in their review of this literature noted a compelling reason for the absence of scholarship or professional writing from the discipline of Counseling Psychology on late-life issues:

> A third [reason] is that counseling psychologists truly are not interested in aging issues, which may be the case, given that Norcross's (1998) team found that only 11% of APA-accredited counseling psychology program training directors listed aging/gerontology as an area of interest for the program faculties.... Thus, there may be a very small proportion of counseling psychologists doing ageing-related work. (p. 804)

Werth et al. (2003) also point out that the discipline of counseling psychology lacks a model of intervention and prevention that could be directly applied to an aging clientele. This has clearly been the case for other topics in the larger public health arena for counseling psychology such as smoking cessation, exercise promotion, and nutrition counseling. In general, issues of health care and health prevention and promotion, which are central identity domains of other divisions within the American Psychological Association (e.g., Division 38; Health Psychology; Division 12; Clinical Psychology), are underrepresented in counseling psychology. Therefore, the supposition that there is a lack of interest within counseling psychology to address the demand for mental health services among older adults is a poignant criticism of this specialty of professional psychology.

Understandably and in defense of the profession of counseling psychology, it is simply not possible for any scientific discipline and/or practice specialty to focus on every topic of human functioning; therefore, organizational decisions must be made about points of focus for Division 17 (Counseling Psychology). And, since its early historical roots in the vocational guidance movement and its ongoing impetus to promote principles of social justice through affirmation of historically marginalized groups in the United States including women, as well as diverse cultural, ethnic, and international groups, older adult issues as an area of focus have received a secondary priority. This would, of course, explain why geropsychology receives very little training emphasis in APA-accredited counseling psychology programs nationally. It could also be the case that this is why a model for addressing the needs of older adults has yet to emerge from within the discipline of counseling psychology. Sadly, this neglect of aging in counseling psychology is in the face of well-developed counseling psychology principles that would favor a rich emphasis on healthy aging. Historically, counseling psychology prided itself on championing a paradigm shift away from the traditional disease-model integral in clinical psychology. Even though counseling psychology places strong emphasis on positive and strength-based psychology, it has yet to apply these principles to older adult concerns.

Thus, having noted its absence in the larger field of counseling psychology, within the extant counseling psychology literature there do exist models of prevention and intervention that could be adapted for older adult concerns. For example, in suicide prevention, Hoffman (2000) has cogently argued for the necessity of conceptualizing suicide behaviors from a multidimensional perspective and has even proposed the biopsychosocial model as a foundational paradigm for understanding and intervening to prevent suicide. The rationale for the biopsychosocial model in suicide prevention is germane because suicide is not only a complex social issue but it is also impacted by multiple forces including intrapsychic processes and biological vulnerabilities. To capture this complexity, Hoffman and Driscoll (2000) employed Engle's 1970 version (Engle, 1977) of the biopsychosocial model with several additional caveats. One of these was based on Hoffman's (2000) critique of Engle's original viewpoint that the biopsychosocial model is implicitly hierarchical in nature; that is, Engle asserted that biological factors were the most salient factor that influences physical health followed by social and psychological factors. Hoffman (2000) argued that the three factors—bio-psycho-social—should not be ranked in terms of importance, but rather, their impact is more aligned with the context in which a phenomenon occurs. Therefore, Hoffman (2000) proposed in her revisionist view of the biopsychosocial model, applied to suicide and its prevention, what she labeled an intergenerational biopsychosocial framework. She states:

> our view that health outcomes result from an ongoing, developmental biopsychosocial process that can yield a range of positive or negative outcomes... health status is a dynamic process that requires ongoing adaptation to biological, psychological, and social challenges that emerge throughout life. (p. 568)

The idea of adaptation which is central to the Hoffman (2000) revisionist view of the biopsychosocial model is also highly relevant to the aging process. The importance of adaptation is acknowledged in the term "healthy aging," as was noted earlier, for favorable late life living. A healthy aging counseling psychology framework employing this paradigm would focus on the idea that human aging is dynamic across the life span; that is, the process of healthy aging means active engagement in change in response to predicable processes inherent in growing old (e.g., as one ages one becomes more frail; therefore, access to health and social resources becomes more difficult and may ultimately require help from others).

The nature of adaptation in later life as a biopsychosocial process would occur in three ways: (1) the recruiting of existing resources, skills, or knowledge to address an emergent and progressive need (the diminishment of eyesight produces the need to seek out strategies such as corrective glasses to temporarily remedy the problem); or (2) the acquiring of new resources, skills, or knowledge skills (when glasses or corrective lenses no longer work, getting assistance from others for transportation and other everyday functions becomes necessary); and (3) the combining of new learning and existing skills to produce an outcome that allows for a shift in focus (e.g., letting go of the need for vision to feel healthy in old age). Later in the chapter a model of adaptation known as SOC (selectivity, optimization, and compensation) will be described in detail. SOC was developed by researchers at the Max Planck Institute in Germany as a foundational concept in successful aging (Baltes & Baltes, 1990).

Although the SOC process of adaptation may seem intuitively obvious, where complexity emerges is in the degree to which nondiseased or healthy aging creates an awareness of a need; that is, when this awareness is created by sources beyond one's own intrapersonal awareness as is the case in pervasive social messages that warn individuals about the impending problems of aging. This also occurs in healthy aging when the individual is required to combine existing skill- or knowledge sets with new learning due to physical change (e.g., loss of aerobic capacity) that produces an emerging need (e.g., diminished stamina). This is not an easy task for an older person who has prided him or herself on being in complete health and fully functional, but due to progressive age-related decline particularly in very old age, every person is faced with the prospect of progressive functional deficits due to aging even to the point where help from others may be needed to meet one's everyday needs.

Hoffman's (2000) view is an excellent starting point for creating a counseling psychology approach to healthy aging. In fact, the term "healthy aging," as noted in previous sections of this chapter, has been expanded in the larger fields of geropsychology and geriatrics through the biopsychosocial model. Thus, a contemporary counseling psychology framework of intervention for older adults could employ the biopsychosocial approach to address adaptation issues in healthy aging. The next section describes an application of the biopsychosocial model in understanding a complex condition in old age that afflicts a small subgroup of older adults and is associated with marginalization of these otherwise healthy older persons; namely, age related macular degeneration or ARMD.

Healthy Aging and ARMD

Age related macular degeneration (ARMD) is a disease of the eye that is associated with progressive diminishment of central vision. ARMD vision decline occurs because of damage to the macula, which is a small area at the back of the eye that plays a critical role in central vision processing. The macula is an oval-shaped highly pigmented yellow spot near the middle of the retina and it contains the largest single concentration of cone cells in the eye, thus it is the primary structure for high resolution vision and it controls focal or centralized vision orientation. There are two types of macular degeneration; a wet and a dry form. The dry form is the most common and is characterized by progressive atrophy of the central retinal region. The wet form is less common and is associated with abnormal blood vessel growth that results as a consequence excessive bleeding and protein leakage around the retina that causes substantial damage to the macula. A risk factor for ARMD is chronological age; that is, ARMD occurs more often in later life and frequently appears in otherwise healthy eyes. Approximately 10% of persons in the United States who are between 66 to 74 years of age will experience symptoms of macular degeneration, and this prevalence increases to 30% among persons 75 years and older (Jager, Mieler, & Miller, 2008). It is without question that ARMD is the leading cause of irreversible vision loss in Americans age 60 and over. Thus, ARMD is a large public health concern for late-life adults.

There is no reliable or effective medical treatment for ARMD, although lifestyle behaviors such as cigarette smoking have been shown to markedly increase its rate of progression. Further, older adults with ARMD report an increased incidence of mental health issues including chronic depression and; in fact, evidence points to stress, depression, and anxiety exacerbating the disease and working to diminish functional independence in ARMD patients (Tolman, Hill, Kleinschmidt, & Gregg, 2005).

The biopsychosocial model is well suited to address issues in ARMD because the medical (or biological) condition is clearly influenced by psychological processes (including depression and stress) as well as maladaptive health behaviors (cigarette smoking). Interventions effective in ameliorating ARMD symptoms emphasize biopsychosocial strategies. Such strategies frequently include helping the patient recruit his or her social support network to assist in everyday function, training of older persons to use assistive devices (e.g., a white cane) to maintain mobility in the presence of progressive visual deficits. Thus, a healthy aging intervention for ARMD means employing the biopsychosocial model of care delivery to facilitate optimal adaptation. Indeed, one of the more promising interventions reported in the literature (see Birk et al., 2004) incorporates clearly delineated components of the biopsychosocial approach: (1) progressive muscle relaxation (psychological treatment); (2) exchange of disease-related experiences (social support); (3) understanding the connections among thought, emotion, and behavior (psychological intervention); (4) engaging general problem-solving skills that emphasize existing personal resources (psychological intervention); and (5) application of pharmacological agents to mediate disease-progression and activate latent biological resources through enriched nutritional diets (biological treatment). Principles embedded in counseling psychology for integrating these various treatment components in an overall treatment plan would fit well within the existing knowledge and skill set of the counseling psychologist.

This example underscores how the biopsychosocial model could be applied to an issue that represents a major public health concern for older adults. A point of importance at this juncture is the construal of individuals who are experiencing ARMD as belonging to a healthy aging group. In other words, "healthy aging," as a classification term, is inclusive of older persons who are experiencing not only ARMD, but other chronic medical conditions that an individual will predictably encounter in later life. The next section highlights several chronic medical conditions that could be addressed through the healthy aging approach.

Healthy Aging and Chronic Medical Conditions

A presumptive threat to the promotion of healthy aging especially as more persons live into very late life is the ever present development of chronic health problems, which impose an unwelcome pressure on well-being and personal comfort in old age. The human body manifests predictable difficulties in physical mobility and, as noted in the biopsychosocial model, this then impacts mental health and the maintenance of meaningful social relationships. Thus, for example, depression is a common accompaniment to chronic medical problems, especially for those older adults who live in nursing homes (Kessler et al., 1994). Even for the most psychologically healthy of us it is hard to be cheerful when the body is beset with constant discomfort or pain, and a question that may be in the mind of many older persons who are living through advanced age is: Does this form of growing old represent healthy aging?

The premise of this chapter is that in very old age and for multiple reasons the answer to this question is "Yes." The healthy aging concept includes older disabled persons and, therefore, older persons who experience disability deserve health prevention efforts that optimize their healthy aging. At the outset, there are two provisos that must be employed, however, to modify the healthy aging construct for this group of individuals. First, very old (85+ years of age and older) adults, in general, (the very stressful context of nursing homes excepted) are not more depressed than their younger age-cohort counterparts (65 years of age or less). After many years of debate, the prevalence of depression among very old adults, in particular, is now thought to be essentially equivalent to the general population (Duffy & Karlin, 2006). This leads to a second proviso: it is doubtless a testimony to the resilience and adaptability of older adults that they remain as psychologically healthy as they do given the medical and environmental stressors they face. Here again we note the positive, strength-based perspective of counseling psychology. Interestingly, the field of community psychology also made a similar paradigm shift in distancing itself from traditional clinical psychology with its similar focus of prevention and positive psychology, with the additional valuable attention to systemic forms of intervention (Murrell, 1984; Gesten & Jason, 1987).

Because there are so many chronic diseases that afflict older persons, there can be a mistaken belief that such disorders are inevitable, "just part of growing old" and nothing can be done about them. In fact most of these diseases are at least treatable, if not curable, and their onset can also be avoided through preventive measures. At the basic research level much headway is being made in the alleviation of aging related health problems. As an example, a recent study of prematurely aged mice finds that telomerase reactivation reactivated brain cells resulting, for example, in restored fertility and an enhanced sense of smell (Jaselioff et al, 2011). As humans age, low levels of telomerase are linked to the erosion of DNA units (telomeres), and the hope is that such basic research will have human application.

At this point it is helpful to elaborate on the definition, extent, and types of chronic disorders affecting older adults. A chronic disease is one that persists for a long time. The US National Center for Health Statistics defines this as lasting for 3 months or more. They are generally not preventable by vaccines or curable through medications. Eighty-eight percent of Americans over 65 years of age have at least one chronic condition. And health-damaging behaviors—particularly tobacco use, lack of physical activity, and poor eating habits—are leading contributors, thus the needed emphasis on prevention.

Happiness, of course, is a challenge when one's body is hurting. Therefore, self-reported depression is a frequent companion of chronic medical disease. The proportion of general medical patients with an affective disorder is 13% for men and 17% for women (Mayou et al., 1991). The proportion in cases with arthritis and diabetes ranges from 20% to 25%. Among patients admitted to hospital or who have been diagnosed with cancer the proportion rises above 30% (McDaniel et al., 1995). Because of this likelihood, forward-thinking doctor's offices often include routine depression screening for older patients, and indeed we see this practice growing in general community settings, in shopping malls, and so forth.

However, a difficulty is that depression in the elderly (as with adolescents) is often "masked." Depression presents as behavioral disturbance or as "gastrointestinal equivalents"; for patients with certain "reclusive" personality styles the internal depression becomes "expressed" in body systems that are especially sensitive to mood disorders. Gastrointestinal tract disorders are for many persons a signal of possible internal stresses (Beliles & Stoudemire, 1998). To add to the problem, the relationship between depression and a chronic medical condition is reciprocal; the medical condition can trigger a depression and in turn the depression exacerbates the medical problem. Understandably, psychoactive drug usage is very common in management of not only chronic conditions, but the emotional consequences that often results from the condition itself or the secondary symptoms associated with the condition (pain, fatigue, disability). This underscores the clear toll that medical problems can take on mental health and well-being in old age. Among the drugs with the highest utilization, drugs for arthritis and heart conditions, antidepressants next represent two of the five most common drugs prescribed.

Figure 20.2 is a listing of common conditions provided by the American Society of Consultant Pharmacists. Next to each condition is a description of aspects of each condition across the biological, psychological, and social domains. Figure 20.2 provides some sense of the range of not only the medical vulnerability experienced by any given older individual, but also the impact that such conditions have on physical, psychological, and social functioning. It should be noted that many older adults have multiple and interacting problems, which places a heavy burden on mental health and wellness.

The prevalence of these chronic medical issues in Figure 20.2 is notable and outstrips prevalence rates and costs for acute medical conditions among the elderly. Chronic conditions for seniors are at a 70.4% prevalence rate, and expenses for chronic conditions are 92.7% of total health expenses for seniors. The three most common conditions are hypertension (31.6%), Chronic Obstructive Pulmonary Disease (23.7%), and cataracts (16.1%). There are also numerous chronic conditions that are very expensive to treat in older adults including cardiovascular disease, urinary problems, and diabetes. Ongoing yearly treatment for these conditions range from $4,300 to $3,400, respectively (Mei-iu, Cheng-vi, & Shwu-chong, 2011). Researchers have underscored the magnitude of these costs as exerting a considerable impact on public health funding for medical care (Angrisano, 2007; Fuchs & Emanuel, 2008).

The Role of Pharmacology

The demography of chronic illness portrayed above for the United States is certainly matched in many other countries. In an Irish study, for example, it was found that 86% of elderly patients had at least one medical condition, 27% had two conditions, and 19% had three chronic conditions (Naughton, Bennett, & Feely, 2010). Interestingly, these data were tracked via a national pharmacy

Medical Problem	Implications for Biological, Psychological, and Social Domains		
	Biological	*Psychological*	*Social*
Arthritis	Immune system	Pain, immobility	Help moving around the house, in-home physical assistance
Bladder Issues	Urinary system	Incontinence, embarrassment	Help toileting
Alzheimer's Disease	Neurological system	Cognitive problems, depression	24-hour care, family caregiving
Glaucoma	Sensory system	Agoraphobia, fear of getting lost	Help to get to appointments, assistance with grocery shopping
Hypertension	Cardiovascular system	Fatigue	Help with heavy lifting
Sleep Apnea	Pulmonary system	Tiredness, cognitive problems	Help with complex medical devices (CPAP)
Diabetes	Endocrine system	Numbness, mood problems	Dietary restrictions, group support for mood issues

Figure 20.2. Medical issues in biopsychosocial domains

utilization database. This is a critical aspect of medical illness; studies like this one have routinely found that older adults use a number of medications ranging variously from three to six daily. Many professionals working in long-term care settings find that it is not uncommon to see people using 10 to 12 medications daily.

These data on medication usage also have profound public health and economic policy implications. The American Association of Retired Persons Public Policy Institute routinely tracks such data. The 2010 First Quarter Report (AARP, 2010) finds that brand name drug prices continue to climb despite low general inflation rate. The report found that "price increases for brand name and specialty prescription drugs widely used by Medicare beneficiaries continued to far outstrip the price increases for other goods and services." In contrast, the report noted that "... the price of widely used generic drugs fell during the same period." In this study, overall the trends showed an overall increase of 5.3% for manufacturers drug prices despite an extremely low rate of general inflation for all consumer goods and services for the same period"

True to the contrariwise pressures of market forces, many citizens will recognize an opposing force leveled by the insurance industry; while drug manufacturers encourage using the brand name, health insurers are often refusing the brand name, being willing only to pay for the much less expensive generic drug. Neither industry pressure is designed to enhance health care for the sufferers of chronic medical problems.

Healthy Aging Treatments

A Developmental Framework

The biopsychosocial model that undergirds much of health care delivery in counseling psychology construes human behavior and pathology through the prism of a more developmental, process-oriented perspective on disorder. This perspective has been characteristic of general developmental psychology, with a renewed use of the concept of developmental psychopathology. This developmental perspective has also been central to the theme of counseling psychology (Drum & Lawler, 1988) as well as to community psychology (Nelson & Prilletensky, 2005) with counseling psychology explicitly espousing a positive mental health view emphasizing a person's strengths rather than a sole focus on deficits. It is only more recently that clinical psychology has also embraced a "positive psychology" approach (Seligman & Csikszentmihalyi, 2000) akin to that developed in community and counseling psychology. The clinical psychology paradigm, however, has not extended this model to issues and problems facing older persons, and this represents a substantial opportunity for counseling psychology to contribute to the healthy aging ideal through building on its traditional foci to promote health and well-being among older persons.

Interestingly, the growing field of clinical geropsychology (now accepted at the American Psychology 2010 Annual Convention by the Council of Representatives as the new specialty of professional geropsychology) offers a developmental perspective that embraces human growth unfolding and adapting throughout the process of adult life. As was noted earlier in this chapter for selectivity and optimization with compensation (SOC), strategies from the ideology of successful aging (Baltes & Baltes, 1990) have been applied to healthy aging. In SOC there is a realistic acceptance of a gradual change from acquisition of skills and capabilities to a focus on employing strategies to deal with progressive loss in both physical and cognitive capacity, which results in a diminishing upper limit on functionality. This is highly relevant to our current discussion about the effects of chronic illness in healthy aging. While accepting these progressive limitations, the SOC framework emphasizes both cognitive and physical plasticity and therefore personal adaptability.

The SOC acronym for the maintenance of healthy aging in late adulthood may be further elucidated as follows: the aging individual must *select* from among available resources and skills. This then allows the person (or the assisting therapist) to *optimize* existing potential and capitalize on the adaptive and plastic nature of the human organism. Thus a person is able to *compensate* for age-related losses and therefore maximize the relative upper limits of function even in the presence of a deteriorating state such as a chronic illness (Hill, Thorn, & Packard, 2000). Thus, a given individual, by applying SOC, can create for him or herself a healthy aging lifestyle even when full functionality is no longer possible (Duffy & Karlin, 2006).

An example of SOC applied to an issue of concern in old age was described by Cignac, Cott, and Badley (2002), who examined whether SOC behaviors could facilitate adaptation to osteoarthritis in 248 older community-dwelling adults with this diagnosis. They defined selection as strategic restriction of activities (withdrawing from field trips that involved extended walking). Optimization was defined as enhancing access to one's reserve capacity by engaging in a program of regular physical exercise to remain fit and minimize pain. Compensation was defined as the propensity to discover alternative means to sustain mobility when impairment was present (using an assistive device such as a walking aid).

The study involved extensive interviews of the participants with respect to how well they employed these SOC principles across 24 activities that would be influenced by their disease (e.g., getting out of bed, preparing meals). These researchers found that almost every older participant engaged in at least one SOC behavior. Compensation was the most frequently reported strategy; however, the ability to engage in one or more SOC behaviors was positively associated with better coping and enhanced quality of life. The more people engaged in SOC behaviors the better they coped with their chronic disease and the more well-being they experienced. In a sense, those who were better at employing SOC experienced a higher level of well-being even though they were challenged with a progressive chronic deteriorative disease. Hill, Thorn, and Packard (2000) provide multiple examples of how SOC can be applied in counseling older clients.

Systemic Interventions

What follows is a selection of brief descriptions of systemic healthy aging interventions that have relevance to maintaining and enhancing positive and healthy aging even in the face of severe physical limitations. However, to preface this section, a word about the concept of "systemic" as it is used in this context is needed. Human behavior is a complex interaction of forces or influences, which cannot be fully understood or manipulated except in unison. Expressed another way, because of the reciprocal and interactive cognitive and physical dimensions of the human organism, an intervention in one domain (e.g., body) can bring change in another domain (e.g. mind). We credit biology for the original concepts of systems theory, and this work was later applied to psychology in such fields as organizational psychology and community psychology, which looked to have larger societal impact than traditional clinical psychology, and in the family systems theories of family therapy.

INDIVIDUAL COUNSELING AND PSYCHOTHERAPY

It may seem counterintuitive to suggest that individual counseling or psychotherapy would be characterized as a systemic approach, but such is the case. In addition to various behavioral and cognitive interventions that may be used, the influence of the therapeutic relationship itself during recuperation from stroke, for example, can measurably improve recovery (Turner & Kelly, 2000). The interpersonal therapeutic effect is often covert and subvocal, as in the case of therapy with older adults with dementia (Duffy, 1999a). Indeed, in addition to formal psychotherapy by a mental health professional, Turner and Kelly (2000) suggest that physicians "can play an important part in helping their patients to maintain healthy coping skills" (p. 124). Counseling and psychotherapy with older adults has developed alongside the general field of psychotherapy research and the effectiveness of behavioral, cognitive, interpersonal and dynamic therapies is now well established (Duffy, 1999b).

COGNITIVE FITNESS/STIMULATION

"Use it or lose it" has become the clarion call for cognitive rehabilitation in late life. Crossword puzzles, chess, bridge, and a variety of new commercial computer games are thought to enhance, repair, or maintain cognitive acuity. There is an active debate regarding the effectiveness of these approaches, with the possibility that genetic endowment might be the best predictor of cognitive fitness. However, while the nomothetic jury is still out in establishing the efficacy of such methods, individual ideographic testimony of elders and therapists would suggest that mental exercising is important. Cameron Camp's fascinating work in adapting Montessori methods for cognitive enhancement with dementia patients is quite convincing (2006). We look forward to an important summary volume on this topic by Paula Hartman-Stein and Asenath LaRue (2011). This provides an excellent review of this complex topic with research findings and community program descriptions.

ENVIRONMENTAL MANIPULATION

A systemic approach derived from environmental and community psychology involves recognition of the psychological impact of the physical environments of older adults. Especially when an older person is a resident in a long-term care facility, the negative or positive influences of their surroundings are ever present. Architects and designers are increasingly employing user surveys and behavior mapping to detect optimal building and room design and not relying on aesthetic or functional assumptions: thus residents may prefer privacy to interpersonal association (Duffy et al., 1986). Attention is given to optimal kitchen design in independent and assisted living settings (Duffy et al., 1984) and corridor design that allows for walking as exercise (Lu et al., 2010).

EXERCISE FOR THE VERY OLD AND CHRONICALLY ILL

This topic has been discussed earlier in this chapter. As an example of systemic interaction between physical, cognitive, and psychological domains, physical wellness has been convincingly shown to positively affect mental health. Duffy and Karlin (2006) traced 12 studies that showed that physical exercise had diminished symptoms of depression. Obviously, exercise regimes for the very old and debilitated need to be attuned to real limitations and pain thresholds, as is done effectively in many nursing homes and assisted living environments (Morris et al., 1999).

CRISIS INTERVENTION

An important intervention emphasized by community psychology and the related field of community mental health has been the concept and intervention in psychological.. While the concept of crisis has a popular meaning that usually refers to a "stressful event" or "emergency," this approach is more specific and refers to the individual's being faced with an experience that challenges previous coping repertoire and leaves the person feeling internally immobilized and "out of control." The admission to a nursing home, for example, confronts the person with sudden multiple and interacting stressful events that challenge the self-perceived capacity to cope (Duffy & Iscoe, 1990). Learning new coping behaviors will not only assist in dealing with the current challenge, but also transfer as new learning to later equivalent situations.

FAMILY INTERVENTIONS

The stress of chronic illness of older parents, the economic and psychological costs of caregiving, the guilt over impatience and outright anger at parents, however justified, the hidden pain of anticipatory grieving, and unfinished family relationship issues, place great stress on multigenerational families (Honn Qualls, 1999). These stresses on adult children are the "great untold story" in society today (Davenport, 1999). The cost, psychological and familial, to adult children is immense and scarcely recognized in public awareness or in public health or economic policies. Working with families of older adults is essential in dealing with their mental health problems. When dealing with a depressed nursing home resident it may be more important to arrange a telephone contact with an absent and neglectful daughter than pursue several weeks of cognitive-behavioral therapy with a depressed older adult (Duffy, 1987).

Conclusions and Future Directions

This chapter has examined the issue of "healthy aging" as a term that not only characterizes the normal aging process but has a specific focus on features of the health and functioning impacted by age-related decline. As a scientific term, "healthy aging" has guided basic research as well as epidemiological studies to uncover processes underlying the fundamental nature of age-related decline and the impact of age-related decline on the human population. Healthy aging research has been a catalyst for broad-based health promotion efforts in the United States and internationally to improve access to social services for adults who, due to their own aging, are marginalized.

Strategies that have supported continuing education of senior citizens, as well as increased social awareness to alter negative stereotypes about older adults are enhanced through the biopsychosocial model of health. This model was briefly summarized in the chapter as it applies to healthy aging. The final section of this chapter focused on how counseling psychology could employ the biospsychosocial model as a framework for building a practice agenda to address the needs of this large and diverse group of adults who will increase in numbers in the 21st century. Counseling psychology has strong traditions in strength-based approaches to care, the application of strategic interventions in rehabilitation espoused through models like SOC, and a strong history in wellness education including stress reduction, exercise promotion, and the avoidance of health-harming behaviors. These approaches could be directly applied to the needs of older adults, and this chapter has provided several examples of how this might be done.

The question arises as to whether outreach to older adults will be viewed in the future as an area that is worthwhile for the discipline of counseling psychology to invest resources and energy to foster. To be sure, there are many worthy causes and it is not possible for any organization to address all of the worthwhile issues or meet the needs of all groups who experience health or marginalization issues. The professional practice specialty of counseling psychology has made substantial inroads in affirming and understanding social justice, diversity, and empowerment issues for multiple underrepresented groups including women and ethnic minorities; therefore, whether older adults as a target group merit the attention of counseling psychology remains unanswered for the future. Interestingly, however, very early in its history, one of the principal leaders of the newly emerging field of counseling psychology, Sidney Pressey, addressed as part of a two-article series in the *Journal of Counseling Psychology* (see Pressey, 1973; Pressey & Pressey, 1972), what he believed was a central concern to the well-being of all persons living in the United States at that time. At the time of the writing of these articles, Sidney Pressey, himself, was residing in an assisted living or, as Pressey labeled it, "an institution for old people," with his wife Alice. The article from the *Journal of Counseling Psychology* from which this final quote is taken is entitled, "Major Neglected Need Opportunity: Old-Age Counseling."

> We are 83 and 81. Sidney, an educational and developmental psychologist and a diplomate in counseling, Alice, a home economist... both associated with a large state university [The Ohio State University].... We have lived over 3 years on one wing of a six-wing one-story residency for the active old. In our wing (currently housing 20 oldsters)... constrictions of life-space are common, so what we found helpful, might be so for other oldsters.... In the three years we have been here, 10 corridor neighbors have died, most have been at least once in the nursing facility on the grounds, and Alice is there at this writing [note: Alice died of a heart attack the following year]. We think such phenomena... finding social contacts in institutions for the old... is in much need of study and that some such person as a resident counselor might greatly aid in developing helpful neighborhoods within such facilities. With increasing infirmities there can be social isolation and health hazards; a counselor should be aware of these problems.... Emerging from all this has been our conviction of the great need of the old for counseling... It has been argued that the old have various and many needs for counseling.... Where then are counselors for older persons to be found and how are they to be prepared? (Pressey, 1972, pp. 362–366)

Pressey's foresight in the 20th century raises a 21st-century question of whether the discipline of counseling psychology should invest resources in training and in scholarship on the normative developmental needs of the old and the very old. If the answer to these questions is in the affirmative, then Pressey's admonition is as germane today as it was in 1972. The authors of this chapter assert that it is time for the field of counseling psychology to consider, once again, its early history and evaluate the importance of geropsychology and its centrality to the long-term vision of the discipline. Certainly, counseling psychology has much to offer older Americans, and the "healthy aging" label represents at least one vehicle for further influence of a counseling psychology strength-based biopsychosocial model of intervention on the provision of health care to older adults.

Questions to Consider

1. How can the biopsychosocial model of health care be adapted for strength-based counseling interventions with older persons?
2. What are the unique needs facing older persons who are from historically marginalized groups (e.g., older women, older persons from ethnic minority groups, older persons with lifelong disabilities)?
3. What kinds of strength-based counseling approaches would be effective for older adults with cognitive impairment?
4. What role could counseling psychology play in addressing the needs of a patient with Alzheimer's disease?
5. What evidence-based intervention approaches incorporate the biopsychosocial model?
6. What innovative ideas will help counseling psychologists better market their specialty to an older clientele?

References

AARP Public Policy Institute. (2010). *2010 first quarter update.* AARP, Publication ID: 43, May.

Angrisano, C., Farrell, D., Kocher, B., Laboissiere, M., & Parker, S. (2007). Accounting for the Cost of Health Care in the U.S. http://www.mckinsey.com/mgi/rp/healthcare/accounting_cost_healthcare.asp

Bäckman, L., Hill, R. D., Herlitz, A., Wahlin, T.-B. R., Wahlin, Å., & Winblad, B. (1998). Verbal and nonverbal episodic memory performance in a 2-year longitudinal study of optimally healthy very old adults. *Journal of Mental Health and Aging, 4,* 139–154.

Baltes, M. M., & Baltes P. B. (Eds.). (1986). *The psychology of control and aging.* New Jersey: Erlbaum.

Baltes, M. M., & Baltes P. B. (1990). *Successful aging: Perspectives from the behavioral sciences.* New York: Cambridge University Press.

Beliles, K., & Stoudemire, A. (1998). Psychopharmacologic treatment of depression in the medically ill. *Psychosomatics, 39*(Suppl.), 2S–19S.

Benfante, R., Reed, D., & Brody, J. (1985). Biological and social predictors of health in an aging cohort. *Journal of Chronic Disease, 38,* 385–395.

Bienias, J. L., Beckett, L. A., Bennett, D. A., Wilson, R. S., & Evans, D. A. (2003). Design of the Chicago Health and Aging Project (CHAP). *Journal of Alzheimer's Disease, 5,* 349–355.

Birk, T., Hickl, S., Wahl, H.-W., Miller, D., Kämmerer, A., Holz, F., . . . Völcker H. E. (2004). Development and pilot evaluation of a psychosocial intervention program for patients with age-related macular degeneration. *The Gerontologist, 44,* 836–843.

Bryant, L. L., Corbett, K. K., & Kutner, J. S. (2001). In their own words: A model of healthy aging. *Social Science and Medicine, 53,* 927–941.

Burke, G. L., Arnold, A. M., Bild, D. E., Cushman, M., Fried, L. P., Newman, A., . . . Robbins, J., for the CHS Collaborative Research Group. (2003). Factors associated with Healthy Aging: The Cardiovascular Health Study. *American Geriatrics Society, 49,* 254–262.

Camp, C. J. (2006). Montessori-Based Dementia Programming™ in long-term care: A case study of disseminating an intervention for persons with dementia. In R. C. Intrieri & L Hyer (Eds). Clinical applied gerontological interventions in long-term care (pp. 295–314). New York: Springer.

Canetto, S. S., Kaminiski, P. L., & Felicio, D. M. (1995). Typical and optimal aging in women and men: Is there a double standard? *International Journal of Aging and Human Development, 40,* 187–207.

Cignac, M. A. M., Cott, C., & Badley, E. M. (2002). Applying selective optimization with compensation to the behaviors of older adults with osteoarthritis. *Psychology and Aging, 17,* 520–524.

Crankshaw, E., Rabiner, D. J., & O'Keeffe, J. (2003). *An overview of programs and initiatives sponsored by DHHS to promote healthy aging: A background paper for the Blueprint on Aging for the 21st Century Technical Advisory Group (TAG) Meeting.* Washington, DC: Office of Disability, Aging and Long-Term Care Policy, US Department of Health and Human Services.

Dahlin-Ivanoff, S., Gosman-Hedström, G., Edberg, A.-K., Wilhelmson, K., Eklund, K., Duner, . . . Landahl S. (2010). Elderly persons in the risk zone: Design of a multidimensional, health-promoting, randomized three-armed controlled trial for "prefrail" people of 80+ years living at home. *BMC Geriatrics, 10,* 27–37.

Dapp U., Anders, J., von Renteln-Druse, W., & Meier-Baumgartner, H. P. (2005). Active health promotion in old age: Methodology of a preventive intervention programme provided by an interdisciplinary health advisory team for independent older people. *Journal of Public Health, 13,* 122–127.

Davenport, D. (1999). Dynamics and treatment of middle generation women: Heroines and victims of multigenerational families. In M. Duffy (Ed.), *Handbook of counseling and psychotherapy with older adults* (pp. 267–280). New York: Wiley.

Drum, D. J., & Lawler, A. C. (1988). *Developmental interventions: Theories, principles and practice.* Columbus: Merrill.

Duffy, M. (1987). The techniques and contexts of multigenerational therapy. *Clinical Gerontologist, 5*(3/4), 347–362.

Duffy, M. (1999a). Reaching the person behind the dementia: Treating comorbid affective disorders through subvocal and nonverbal strategies. In M. Duffy (Ed.), *Handbook of counseling and psychotherapy with older adults* (pp. 562–577). New York: Wiley.

Duffy, M. (Ed.). (1999b). *Handbook of counseling and psychotherapy with older adults.* New York: Wiley.

Duffy, M., Bailey, S., Beck, B., & Barker, D. G. (1986). Preferences in nursing home design: A comparison of residents, administrators and designers. *Environment and Behavior, 18(2),* 246–257.

Duffy, M., & Iscoe, I. (1990). Crisis theory and management: The case of the older adult. *Journal of Mental Health Counseling, 12*(3), 303–313.

Duffy, M., & Karlin, B. E. (2006). Treating depression in nursing homes: Beyond the medical model. In L. Hyer & R. C. Intrieri (Eds.), *Long-term care: Psychological and psychosocial assessment and treatment* (pp. 109–135). New York: Springer.

Duffy, M., Yates, W. S., Stone, R., Rabinowitz, D., Resendiz, J., Congleton, J., . . . Owens, P. (1984). *Consumer preferences for kitchen design in congregate housing facilities: A survey of elderly residents.* Technical Report No. I. College Station: Center for Health Systems and Technology, College of Medicine, Texas A&M University.

Engel, G. L. (1977). The need for a new medical model: A challenge for biomedicine. *Science, 196,* 129–136.

Engel, G. L. (1981). The clinical application of the biopsychosocial model. *Journal of Medicine and Philosophy, 6,* 101–124.

Fry, P. S. (1992). Major social theories of aging and their implications for counseling concepts and practice. *The Counseling Psychologist, 20,* 246–329.

Fuchs, V. R., & Emanuel, E. J. (2008). The perfect storm of overutilization. *Journal of the American Medical Association, 299,* 2789–2791.

Gesten, E. L., & Jason, L. A. (1987). Social and community interventions. *Annual Review of Psychology, 38,* 427–460.

Guralnik, J. M., & Kaplan, G. A. (1989). Predictors of healthy aging: Prospective evidence from the Alameda County Study. *American Journal of Public Health, 79,* 703–708.

Hansen-Kyle L. (2005) A concept analysis of healthy aging. *Nursing Forum, 40*(2), 45–57. Hartman-Stein, P., & LaRue, A. (2011). *Enhancing cognitive fitness in older adults: A handbook for the use and development of community-based programs.* New York: Springer.

Heppner, P. P. (1999). Thirty years of the *Counseling Psychologist*: 1969 to 1999. *The Counseling Psychologist, 27,* 5–13.

Hill, R. D. (2005). *Positive aging: A guide for mental health professionals and consumers.* New York: Norton.

Hill, R. D. (2008). *Seven strategies for positive aging.* New York: Norton.

Hill, R. D. (2011). A positive aging framework for guiding geropsychology interventions.

Behavior Therapy, 42, 66–77.

Hill, R. D., & Mansour, E. (2008). Positive aging and evidence-based psychotherapy. In D. Gallagher-Thompson, A. M. Steffen, &, L. Thompson (Eds.), *Handbook of behavioral and cognitive therapies with older adults.* New York: Springer.

Hill, R. D., Stigsdotter Neely, A., & Bäckman, L. (1997). Predictors of change on the Fuld object memory evaluation in a two-year longitudinal study of optimally healthy very old age. *Aging and Mental Health, 1,* 140–148.

Hill, R. D., Thorn, B. L., & Packard, T. (2000). Counseling older adults: Theoretical and empirical issues in prevention and intervention. In S. D. Brown & R. W. Lent (Eds.),

Handbook of counseling psychology (3rd ed., pp. 499–531). New York: Wiley.

Hill, R. D., Wahlin, Å., Herlitz, A, Winblad, B., & Bäckman, L. (1995). Predicting memory performance in optimally healthy very old adults. *Aging and Mental Health, 1,* 57–67.

Hoffman, M. A. (2000). Suicide and hastened death: A biopsychosocial perspective. *The Counseling Psychologist, 28,* 561–572.Hoffman, M. A., & Driscoll, J. M. (2000). Health promotion and disease prevention: A concentric biopsychosocial model of health status. In S. D. Brown & R. W. Lent (Eds.), Handbook of counseling psychology (pp. 532–567). New York: John Wiley

Honn Qualls, S. (1999). Realizing power in intergenerational power hierarchies: Family reorganization when older adults decline. In M. Duffy (Ed.), *Handbook of counseling and psychotherapy with older adults.* New York: Wiley.

Iscoe, I., & Duffy, M. (2003). The crises of aging. In *The encyclopedia of prevention and health promotion.* New York: Plenum.

Jager, R. D., Mieler, W. F., & Miller, J. W. (2008). Age-related macular degeneration. *New England Journal of Medicine, 358,* 2606–2617.

Jaskelioff, M., Muller, F. L., Paik, J. H., Thomas, E., Jiang, S., Adams, A. C., Sahin, E., Kost-Alimova, M., Protopopov, A., Cadinanos, J., Horner, J. W., Maratos-Flier, E., & Depinho, R. A. (2011) Telomerase reactivation reverses tissue degeneration in aged telomerase-deficient mice. *Nature, 469,* 102–106..

Kessler, R. C., McGonagle, K. A., Zhao, S., Nelson, C. B., Hughes, M., Eshleman, S.,... Kendler, K. S. (1994). Lifetime and 12-month prevalence of DSM-III-R psychiatric disorders in the United States. *Archives of General Psychiatry, 51,* 8–19.

Luo, R. H., Hattori, H., Hossain, M. A., Hester, L., Huange, Y., Lee-Kwon, W., Donowitz, M., Nagata, E., & Snyder, S. H. (2003). Akt as a mediator of cell death, *Proceedings of the National Academy of Sciences, 100,* 11712–11717.

Lövdén, M., Rönnlund, M., Wahlin, Å., Bäckman, L., Nyberg, L., & Nilsson, L.-G. (2004). Stability and change in episodic and semantic memory in old age. *Journal of Gerontology: Psychological Sciences, 59B,* 130–134.

Lu, Z., Rodiek, S., Shepley, M., & Duffy, M. (2010). Influences of physical environment on corridor walking among assisted living residents: Findings from focus group discussions. *Journal of Applied Gerontology, 30,* 463–484.

Mayou, R., Hawton, K., & Feldman, E. (1991). Psychiatric problems among medical admissions. *International Journal Psychiatry Medicine, 21,* 71–84.

Menec, V. H., Button, C. M., Blandford, A. A., & Morris-Oswald, T. (2007). Age-friendly cities project: Portage la Prairie, Manitoba, Canada. Retrieved from the Centre on Aging: http://www.umanitoba.ca/centres/aging/media/Portage_la_Prairie_A-F_report.pdf

McDaniel, J. S., Musselman, D. L., & Porter, M. R. (1995). Depression in patients with cancer: Diagnosis, biology and treatment. *Archives of General Psychiatry, 52,* 89–99.

Mei-iu, C., Cheng-vi, L.,& Shwu-chong, W. (2011). The prevalence of chronic medical conditions and medical expenditures of the elderly by chronic condition indicator (CCI). *Archives of gerontology and Geriatrics, 52*(3), 284–289.

Minnesota Department of Health. (2006). *Creating healthy communities for an aging population: A report of a joint rural health advisory committee and state community health services advisory committee work group.* Office of Rural Health and Primary Care and Office of Public Health Practice, May. http://www.health.state.mn.us/divs/orhpc/pubs/healthyaging/hareportnofs.pdf

Morris, J. N., Fiatarone, M., Keily, D. K., Belleville-Taylor, P., Murphy, K., Lifflehale, S.,... Doyle, N. (1999). Nursing rehabilitation and exercise strategies in the nursing home. *Journals of Gerontology: Medical Sciences, 54,* 494–500.

Murrell, S. A. (1984). Community psychology and older adults: An introduction to the special issue. *Journal of Community Psychology, 12,* 299–300.

Naughton, C., Bennett, K., & Feely, J. (2010). Prevalence of chronic disease in the elderly based on a national pharmacy claims data base. *Age and Ageing, 35*(6), 633–636.

Nelson, G., & Prilletensky, I. (2005). *Community psychology: In pursuit of liberation and well-being.* New York: Palgrave Macmillan.

Norcross, J. C., Sayette, M. A., Mayne, T. J., Karg, R. S., & Turkson, M. A. (1998). Selecting a doctoral program in professional psychology: Some comparisons among PhD counseling, PhD clinical, and PsyD clinical psychology programs. *Professional Psychology: Research and Practice, 29,* 609–614.

Peel, N., Bartlett, H., & McClure, R. (2004). Healthy ageing: How is it defined and measured? *Australasian Journal on Ageing, 23,* 115–119.

Peel, N. M., McClure, R. J., & Bartlett, H. P. (2005). Behavioral determinants of healthy aging, *American Journal of Preventive Medicine, 28,* 298–304.

Perls, T. T., & Silver, M. H. (1999). *Living to 100: Lessons in living to your maximum potential at any age.* New York: Basic Books.

Pressey, S. L. (1973). Old age counseling: Crises, services, potentials. *Journal of Counseling Psychology, 20,* 356–360.

Pressey, S. L., & Pressey, A. D. (1972). Major neglected need opportunity: Old-age counseling. *Journal of Counseling Psychology, 19,* 362–366.

Robine, J. M. (2006). Research issues on human longevity. In J. M. Robine, E. M. Crimmins, S. Horiuchi, & Z. Yi (Eds.). *Human longevity, individual life duration and the growth of the oldest-old population* (pp. 7–42). Dordrecht, Netherlands: Springer, International Studies in Population.

Ryff, C., & Singer, B. (2009). Understanding healthy aging: Key concepts and their integration. In V. L. Bengston, D. Gans, N. M. Putney, & M. Silverstein (Eds.), *Handbook of theories of aging.* New York: Springer.

Seligman, M., & Csikszentmihalyi, M. (2000). Positive psychology: An introduction. *American Psychologist, 55,* 5–14.

Smyer, M. A. (1984). Life Transitions and Aging: Implications for Counseling Older Adults.

Counseling Psychologist, 12, 17–28.

Tolman, J., Hill, R. D., Kleinschmidt, J., & Gregg, C. H. (2005). Psychosocial adaptation to visual impairment and its relationship to depressive affect in older adults with age-related macular degeneration. *The Gerontologist, 45,* 747–753.

Turner, J., & Kelly, B. (2000). Emotional dimensions of chronic disease. *Western Journal of Medicine, 172*(2), 124–128.

http://umanitoba.ca/centres/aging/media/Portage_la_Prairie_A-F_report.pdf

Werth, J. L., Jr., Kopera-Frye, K., Blevins, D., & Bossick, B. (2003). Older adult representation in the counseling psychology literature, *The Counseling Psychologist, 31,* 789–814.

CHAPTER

21 Promoting College Retention in First-Generation College Students

Mindi N. Thompson *and* Julia C. Phillips

Abstract

First-generation college students (FGCS) are those students whose parents did not attend or graduate from college. They are at greater risk for not graduating from college in comparison to students whose parents are college graduates. Counseling psychologists working in higher education are well situated to aid in retention of FGCS through various prevention efforts given our values and expertise. This chapter reviews the literature on characteristics of FGCS. First, we summarize existing empirical research relevant to the experiences of FGCS in institutions of higher education. Second, we offer a brief overview of relevant theories that provide explanatory context for understanding the success of FGCS. Third, we highlight strategic points of intervention for FGCS in order to prevent negative outcomes and overview avenues by which counseling psychologists have been involved in prevention efforts with FGCS. Finally, we explore approaches by which counseling psychologists can contribute to these prevention efforts. Directions for research, theory, and practice will be suggested for current and future generations of counseling psychologists.

Key Words: retention, first-generation college students, prevention

First-generation college students (FGCS) are those students whose parents did not attend and/or graduate from college. As a group, FGCS are at risk for negative educational outcomes, including leaving college without a degree. Counseling psychology as a field is well situated to promote retention for FGCS for two major reasons. First, counseling psychology's history is rooted in addressing the vocational, educational, and social needs of the veterans who were coming home from World War II (Whiteley, 1984). The vast majority of these veterans who went to college were likely the first in their families to do so given that, according to analyses of US Census data, only 5.5% of the US population had a bachelor's degree in 1940 (Chronicle of Higher Education, 2011). In response, college and university counseling centers emerged on campuses to serve this population. Second, counseling psychology's social justice values embody attention toward addressing the needs of those who occupy less privileged positions in society (e.g., Speight & Vera, 2008), consistent with persons whose families are not college educated.

This chapter presents an overview of the literature on FGCS and higher education, including relevant background information, results from empirical studies, and theoretical perspectives that inform our understanding of this group of students. Efforts to prevent negative outcomes such as dropping out of college and to increase the likelihood of positive outcomes such as retention and graduation are described, along with attendant data on evaluations of these prevention efforts. Finally, counseling psychology's role in promoting retention among FGCS is discussed with several key questions highlighted for future counseling psychologists in their roles as scholars, practitioners, and advocates.

First-Generation College Students and Higher Education

First-generation college students (college students who are the first generation in their families to attend college), students from families of low socioeconomic status (SES), and students from families who have recently immigrated to the United States have been documented to have the most difficulty accessing higher education (e.g., Choy, 2001; Martinez & Klopott, 2005). Despite these difficulties, as a group, FGCS have become increasingly prevalent in institutions of higher education. For example, data from the National Center for Education Statistics' Beginning Postsecondary Longitudinal Study demonstrated that FGCS comprised 34% of all students entering 4-year institutions and 53% of all students entering 2-year institutions in 1995 (Choy, 2002). Not surprisingly, attention to better understanding the college experiences of FGCS has increased in recent years. Indeed, a body of literature from several disciplines (e.g., higher education, sociology, psychology) has developed; the focus of this literature has revolved around five primary domains, including: understanding differences between FGCS and their continuing generation college student (CGCS) counterparts (e.g., Ceja, 2006), exploring the educational and vocational aspirations and expectations of FGCS (e.g., Horn & Nunez, 2000), focusing on the transition from high school to college (e.g., Choy, 2001), examining the college experience and development of FGCS (e.g., Pascarella, Pierson, Wolniak, & Terenzini, 2004; Terenzini, Springer, Yaeger, Pascarella, & Nora, 1996), and assessing FGCS' persistence in college and subsequent labor market outcomes (e.g., Nunez & Cuccaro-Alamin, 1998).

FGCS and CGCS: Similarities and Differences

The first body of literature highlights the differences between FGCS and their CGCS peers in terms of demographic characteristics, preparation for college, and decision-making processes regarding which higher education institution to attend. For example, research (e.g., Ceja, 2006; Pascarella et al., 2004) has focused on the relation of family knowledge about higher education to college attendance and completion. Findings have documented the limited knowledge that lower income and FGCS possess pertaining to postsecondary education as compared with their higher income and CGCS peers (Pascarella et al., 2004). More specifically, FGCS cite limited involvement in making choices related to college, less knowledge regarding the admissions process, limited financial support, and less emotional support related to academic success from their parents and families than their CGCS peers (e.g., Billson & Terry, 1982; Cabrera & LaNasa, 2001; Ceja, 2006; Choy, 2001).

FGCS are also more likely to have limited access to role models (Barry, Hudley, Cho, & Kelly, 2009) or supportive adults who can offer insider information regarding the college experience or the culture of institutions of higher education (Lohfink & Paulsen, 2005; London, 1996). The parents of FGCS may also not be aware of the importance of academic preparation for their children. As such, these parents may be less likely to encourage their children to pursue more rigorous courses or become involved in extracurricular activities to enhance their academic experiences; this may, in turn, lead to the student being less prepared academically when they arrive at college (e.g., Martinez & Klopott, 2005; Warburton, Bugarin, & Nunez, 2001).

FGCS also differ from their CGCS peers with regard to the factors that students cite as valuing and looking for in their college experience (e.g., Berger, 2000; Paulsen & St. John, 1997). Indeed, FGCS have been demonstrated to be more concerned with their ability to live at home and be a part of an institution that is known for its high "faculty reputation" whereas CGCS tend to be more focused on whether the institution has a "good reputation" or a "lower tuition" (Lohfink & Paulsen, 2005, p. 419). Based on their finding, these authors concluded that "continuing generation students may have a broader understanding of the range of college choices available to them and take a more cosmopolitan comparison-shopping approach to their college-going decision-making" (Lohfink & Paulsen, p. 419). Limited family knowledge regarding the college admissions process may also contribute to students' decisions to choose to attend institutions of higher education based on certain characteristics (e.g., closer to home, allow the opportunity to continue to work in a particular job, seemingly less costly) rather than those that may be a better fit for their career pursuits (Choy, 2001; Horn & Nevill, 2006).

The demographic characteristics of FGCS (i.e., disproportionately non-European American, female, and from low-income backgrounds; Smedley, Myers, & Harrel, 1993) also contribute to the complexities faced by these students as they occupy multiple oppressed groups (e.g., Choy, 2001; Horn & Nunez, 2000; Lohfink & Paulsen, 2005). Indeed, in their study of the determinants of persistence for FGCS and CGCS, Lohfink and Paulsen demonstrated that the intersection of certain demographic variables (e.g., being low-income, female, or Hispanic) and being a FGCS contributed to greater problems in persistence from the 1st to 2nd year than FGCS with different demographic characteristics (e.g., higher-income, male, non-Hispanic) or who were non-FGCS. Based on these findings, Lohfink and Paulsen concluded that lack of information about college, in addition to limited access to social and economic resources, contributes to difficulties with persistence.

Vocational Development

Second, researchers have begun to attend to the vocational development of FGCS. Findings from research with FGCS have generally supported the notion that FGCS have lower levels of expectations and aspirations regarding their future educational and vocational plans than their CGCS peers (e.g., Horn & Nunez, 2000; Terenzini et al., 1996). Relatedly, findings from vocational research with underrepresented racial/ethnic group members and lower-SES individuals have demonstrated that being a member of an underrepresented racial/ethnic group or being from a lower social class background relates to vocational outcomes. For example, race/ethnicity has been documented to relate to decreased career aspirations and perceptions of opportunities (Fouad & Byars-Winston, 2005), access to positive role models (Zirkel, 2002), and access to career development resources (Diemer, 2002). Social class–related constructs have been demonstrated to be related to career aspirations (Aries & Seider, 2007), perceived career barriers (Metz, Fouad, & Ihle-Helledy, 2009), and motivating factors in career choice (Blustein et al., 2002). Although these relations have not been directly tested using samples comprised solely of FGCS to date, it would appear that many are likely to be applicable to this group. Indeed, a recent investigation (Gibbons & Borders, 2010) examined two groups of seventh graders: prospective FGCS and prospective CGCS. Findings indicated that the prospective FGCS exhibited lower self-efficacy, higher negative outcome expectations, and more perceived barriers to success in college than their prospective CGCS peers. Additionally, within-group differences by gender and ethnicity were noted, with males and students of color demonstrating less self-efficacy, more negative outcome expectations, more barriers, and fewer supports (Gibbons & Borders). Similarly, a study by Wang and Castaneda-Sound (2008) suggested that FGCS had lower levels of academic self-efficacy than their CGCS counterparts; academic self-efficacy, in turn, has been demonstrated to relate to later academic success (i.e., GPA) in a community college sample of FGCS (Majer, 2009).

Transition from High School to College

A third body of research has focused on understanding the transition from high school to college for FGCS (e.g., Choy, 2001; Nunez & Cuccaro-Alamin, 1998; Terenzini & Rendon, 1994). Findings from this body of literature have generally corroborated our knowledge regarding the struggles of college students in general in the transition to college (e.g., being away from home for the first time, being surrounded by peers who are different from themselves and the neighborhoods in which they grew up, time management, personal independence; Dennis, Phinney, & Chuateco, 2005; Hey, Calderon, & Seabert, 2003; Ting, 2003). Although the transition to college may be difficult for all students, scholars propose that the struggles may be particularly pronounced for FGCS. Given the combination of demographic characteristics, familial knowledge, and access to resources reviewed previously, researchers (Choy, 2001; Pascarella et al., 2004) have noted that FGCS are often faced with substantial cultural, social, and academic transitions. Indeed, in her qualitative investigation, Ceja (2006) highlighted the strain that her low-SES, first-generation, Chicana participants cited related to educating their families about the college process while simultaneously transitioning into their role as undergraduate students.

Experience During College

Another body of research has begun to examine the psychosocial and cognitive development of FGCS (e.g., Pascarella et al., 2004; Terenzini et al., 1996). In particular, this work has demonstrated differences in the college experience among FGCS and CGCS during their 1st year in college. For example, in comparison to their CGCS peers, FGCS completed fewer credit hours, took fewer humanities and fine arts classes, studied fewer hours, were more likely to work off campus and less likely to participate in honors programs, and made smaller gains on tests of reading comprehension after their 1st year in college (Terenzini et al.). These differences were noted even after controlling for precollege characteristics such as SES, ability, and aspirations (Terenzini et al.).

Financial literacy and concerns related to finances have also been highlighted as areas of need for FGCS. Specifically, FGCS have been demonstrated to have greater financial literacy needs than their CGCS counterparts, with female FGCS of color exhibiting greater financial literacy needs than white female FGCS (Eitel & Martin, 2009). Not surprisingly, financial concerns have been demonstrated to be related to intentions toward terminating college (Baum & O'Malley, 2003) and self-reported lack of funds for education (a common experience for FGCS; Bui, 2002) has been demonstrated to relate positively to attrition (Tinto, 1993). First-generation students also are more likely to drop out of college because of accumulated debt than their CGCS peers (Somers, Woodhouse, & Gofer, 2000), which in turn has been linked to a decreased likelihood to pursue graduate school (e.g., Haycock & Huang, 2001).

Working off-campus (a common experience for many FGCS) has also received attention in the literature and has been demonstrated to relate to a variety of negative educational outcomes. Working off-campus is associated with increased rates of attrition among FGCS given the difficulties of managing both full-time employment and the necessary demands of college (Billson & Terry, 1982), Indeed, in a recent investigation of mediators of attrition for FGCS, Martinez, Sher, Krull, and Wood (2009) demonstrated that full-time work mediates the relation between low parental education level and attrition among FGCS such that FGCS who do not work off-campus have lower rates of attrition than FGCS who work off-campus. In addition, working off-campus has been demonstrated to relate to other negative educational and vocational outcomes, including: decreased ability to gain relevant paid or unpaid work experience within a chosen area of study (Moreau & Leathwood, 2006), lowered aspirations for graduate school (Pascarella et al., 2004), less time available to study and become involved on campus, lower GPAs (Walpole, 2003, 2008), and less contact with faculty (Walpole, 2008).

FGCS may lack the social networks needed in order to share their experiences and stressors related to college with individuals that they perceive will understand those experiences (e.g., Barry, Hudley, Kelly, & Cho, 2009; Phinney & Haas, 2003). Specifically, among FGCS, Phinney and Haas (2003) documented the common occurrence of feeling overwhelmed by college courses, feeling uncertain regarding how to succeed, isolating oneself socially from others, and experiencing a lack of supportive friends and a lack of understanding from parents. Findings from a recent investigation (Barry et al.) that sought to explore the differences in self-disclosure among 1st-year students indicated that FGCS demonstrated significantly less disclosure of college experiences with family and friends (at home and at college) than their CGCS counterparts. These authors concluded that FGCS may be lacking social networks in which to share their college experiences and gain support.

Persistence, Graduation Rates, and Labor Market Outcomes

Finally, research has focused on the outcomes of persistence rates, graduation rates, graduate school enrollment rates, and labor market outcomes for FGCS. Not surprisingly, FGCS attend disproportionately fewer selective colleges (Carnevale & Rose, 2003; Massey, Charles, Lundy, Fischer, & Bryant, 2003; Terenzini et al., 1996; Walpole, 2008) and are more likely to attend 2-year than 4-year colleges (Choy, 2002). Enrollment in less selective colleges, public, and 2-year colleges has been documented to have long-term impacts on students. For example, students enrolled at these institutions have lower persistence, graduation, and graduate school enrollment rates (Bradford & Farris, 1991; Carnevale & Rose; Ishitani, 2003, 2006; Lohfink & Paulsen, 2005; Nunez & Cuccaro-Alamin, 1998; Terenzini et al.; Walpole). These lowered rates, in turn, have been demonstrated to relate to individuals' abilities to find and maintain stable postcollege employment (Haycock & Huang, 2001; Valadez, 1998).

The negative association between entering and leaving college without a degree for FGCS also has been well documented (e.g., Choy, 2001; Martinez et al., 2009), and college attrition, in general, has been demonstrated to impede social mobility and economic success (Horn, Berger, & Carroll, 2004). Indeed, comparing the annual income of college graduates ($45,221) to individuals of similar ages with some college ($31,936) highlights the importance of completing a college degree, particularly given that 19.5% of the US population under the age of 25 enrolled in college but did not complete a degree (US Census Bureau, 2006a, 2006b). Despite discrepancies in the rates of students withdrawing from college in the 1st year, with FGCS withdrawing at higher rates (Horn & Carroll, 1998), few differences in the salaries, occupations, and positions attained by FGCS and CGCS who earned degrees exist (e.g., Nunez & Cuccaro-Alamin, 1998).

Summary

In combination, this body of literature highlights the need for continued efforts to support FGCS. Indeed, these investigations highlighted some of the ways in which one's college student generation status (including family knowledge and support for education, access to resources, and experience in college) may shape an individual's postsecondary decision-making processes and relate to retention rates. The completion of a college degree, in turn, has been demonstrated to relate to future attainment of occupations.

Theoretical Perspectives for Understanding FGCS

Several theoretical frameworks have been explicated in the higher education literature regarding FGCS (e.g., Bourdieu's [1990] theory of social reproduction; Gloria & Rodriguez's [2000] psychosociocultural theory; Tinto's [1993] theory of student departure; status attainment theory [Blau & Duncan, 1967]; critical social theory [Agger, 1998]). Although a thorough description of all of these theoretical perspectives is beyond the scope of this chapter, we provide a brief overview of the theoretical perspectives most relevant to existing and future prevention programming efforts targeted toward FGCS.

Tinto's (1987) theory of student departure is the most comprehensive and widely cited theory related to persistence and retention rates among FGCS. Tinto's theory emphasizes the influence of precollege characteristics with which students enter college (e.g., gender, race, skills, parental education level, educational achievements) on the students' level of commitment, intention, expectation, and motivation toward the goal of graduation. Academic and social integration, or the degree to which a student's norms, values, and behaviors align with the culture of the institution, is considered to be a critical factor in a student's willingness to remain enrolled in college. Specifically, he proposed that students who are integrated socially (e.g., interactions with peers, involvement in student organizations) and academically (e.g., interactions with faculty, academic performance) into the culture of their institution are less likely to make a decision to leave that institution (Tinto, 1987). Not surprisingly, Tinto's theory has been critiqued by multicultural scholars for its lack of attention to cultural factors and its assumption that students (regardless of cultural identity and background) must assimilate to the university environment (e.g., Guiffrida, 2006; Tierney, 1992). In response, Tinto revised his theory in 1993 and changed the concept of integration to "membership" in recognition of the notion that students' multiple memberships and affiliations assist them through their navigation of higher education.

Bourdieu's theory of social reproduction (1990, 1994) is another commonly cited framework by which scholars have sought to understand persistence decisions among FGCS (e.g., Lohfink & Paulsen, 2005). Bourdieu's theory focuses on conceptualizing the interactions among individuals and social structures. This theoretical perspective emphasizes the reproduction of social class differences through social institutions that perpetuate existing societal structures. As such, it has been applied to the understanding of persistence decisions of FGCS and CGCS.

The theory of social reproduction centralizes three types of capital (economic, cultural, and social) relevant to institutions of higher education (Bourdieu, 1986). Economic capital refers to access to financial resources and material wealth. Cultural capital refers to a set of internalized attitudes, behaviors, knowledge, and practices acquired via socialization that assists in one's advancement or maintenance of social standing. Bourdieu's concept of *habitus* is similar to cultural capital and is conceptualized as the perceptions of opportunities and the appropriate actions and responses needed in a given situation in order to achieve a particular goal; habitus is therefore inherently shaped by an individual's cultural background and values (Bourdieu, 1977). Finally, social capital refers to the personal and social networks and connections an individual possesses that allow the intergenerational transfer of resources, viewpoints, information, and values about education (Bourdieu, 1977). It provides the transmission of opportunities, privileged information, and resources and has an accumulative effect (i.e., the earlier capital is accrued, the easier to expand that capital; Bourdieu, 1986; Coleman, 1988; DiMaggio & Mohr, 1985).

Bourdieu's theory of social reproduction offers a lens through which to understand how differential access to capital directly affects students' interactions with the university and relates to educational outcomes. Accordingly, FGCS are likely to have limited amounts of capital available to them in comparison to CGCS. A lack of access to cultural and social capital from family and friends impacts students' understanding of the context of higher education (e.g., knowledge of the application process, the benefits of completing a degree, making decisions about behaviors and attitudes toward college) and limited economic capital relates to financial difficulties (and its consequences) for FGCS (Wells, 2008). Indeed, Wells demonstrated that those students who had greater access to capital remained in college from the 1st to 2nd year as compared to their counterparts with less access to capital across all racial/ethnic groups.

Psychosociocultural (PSC) theory (Gloria & Rodriguez, 2000) was conceptualized from a psychological perspective and, as such, highlights the noncognitive factors and underlying mechanisms that impact the relationships between the student, the institution, and the interaction between the two. It accounts for self-beliefs, social support, and comfort in the university cultural environment as related to academic persistence (Gloria & Rodriguez). The first dimension, *self-beliefs*, highlights the role of internal beliefs (i.e., self-efficacy beliefs, imposter phenomenon, motivational orientation, coping strategies). The second dimension, *social support*, highlights the perceived social support that students receive while attending college from friends, family, and mentors. *Comfort in the university environment* is the third dimension and describes the process by which campus climates (i.e., the university environment) facilitate an inclusive environment for students from diverse backgrounds; the more inclusive the campus environment, the more culturally congruent they are and the greater likelihood that students' needs will be met (Gloria & Rodriguez).

To date, PSC theory has mainly been applied to understanding the college experience and persistence rates for racial and ethnic minority samples (e.g., Gloria, Castellanos, Lopez, & Rosales, 2005; Gloria & Robinson Kurpius, 2001; Gloria, Robinson-Kurpius, Hamilton, & Willson, 1999; Gloria & Ho, 2003) and White undergraduate students (Rayle, Robinson Kurpius, & Arredondo, 2006), yet the central tenets of this theory have been proposed to be easily adapted to describe the college process for first FGCS (Lin, 2011). The PSC perspective expands Bourdieu's social reproduction theory by focusing on capital that students enter the university environment with (e.g., access or lack of access to family support, material wealth) as well as capital that FGS are able to accrue via their experiences in institutions of higher education (Lin, 2011). Specifically, through their experiences on campus, students may gain access to social and cultural capital.

Prevention Programs for FGCS

The aforementioned theoretical frameworks have guided the development of several prevention programs for FGCS within institutions of higher education. Indeed, several efforts for increasing the retention rates of FGCS have been described in the literature, including: large-scale, federally funded, multiyear programming; initiatives specific to particular institutions of higher education; smaller scale culturally relevant prevention programs within communities; and workshops aimed at enhancing the college experience for FGCS. Although a full description of each of these efforts is beyond the scope of this chapter, we provide an overview of large- and small-scale interventions that have been used to promote the retention of FGCS in higher education.

Large-Scale Interventions

The federally funded TRIO programs (US Department of Education, 2008) represent one large-scale effort designed to help students "overcome the social and cultural barriers to higher education" (Balz & Esten, 1998, p. 334). As profiled in a report from the US Department of Education (DoE; 2008), the TRIO programs were born out of legislation in the 1960s designed to increase economic and educational opportunities for low-income young people in middle school, high school, or college. Being a FGCS is one of the major criteria for participant eligibility in TRIO programs.

The TRIO programs currently encompass a range of initiatives on college campuses that have evolved since their inception. Upward Bound and Talent Search were the original two TRIO programs, followed by others that targeted specific underrepresented groups (e.g., Veterans Upward Bound) for various purposes (e.g., Upward Bound Math and Science to increase representation within the STEM sciences, Ronald E. McNair Postbaccalaureate Achievement Program for mentoring underrepresented students into doctoral programs; DoE, 2008). Other initiatives include the Centers for Educational Opportunities (CeO) program, which targets adults as potential college students and provides assistance with the college admissions process and financial aid literacy; the Student Support Services program for adults, which provides support for participants while they are attending college; and the Child Care Access Means Parents in School, which provides childcare on campus (DoE). In brief, TRIO programs are designed to offer FGCS the social and cultural capital regarding the college experience that their CGCS counterparts receive from their families and socioeconomic milieus (Bourdieu, 1986).

A variety of TRIO precollege programs (e.g., Upward Bound, Talent Search) exist as a mechanism to prepare students for success in institutions of higher education. These programs typically begin with middle and high school students who are involved in regularly scheduled programming and activities on the weekends, after school, and during the summer (Engle, Bermeo, & O'Brien, 2006). Students and their parents are provided information, guidance, and counseling about topics including: the college admissions process, academic requirements for a college-bound student, study skills needed to perform effectively in college, informational material regarding financing college, and career exploration (Engle et al.). These programs are designed to enhance students' academic self-efficacy (e.g., via tutoring) and to increase their sense of belongingness on campus (e.g., via spending time on campus, being familiarized with prospective fellow students, and learning about available campus resources).

Evidence for the programmatic effectiveness of various TRIO programs has been garnered from both experimental and quasi-experimental research. For example, results of two longitudinal and randomized national evaluations of the same sample (Seftor, Mamun, & Shirm, 2009; Myers, Olsen, Seftor, Young, & Tuttle, 2004) suggested that Upward Bound programs were effective in promoting student engagement, college retention, and graduation for certain at-risk populations (including low-income FGCS). Findings also indicated that effectiveness increased with duration in the program such that those students who were enrolled in the programs for longer periods of time received the most benefits (Myers et al.). Results of a quasi-experimental study demonstrated that participation in Talent Search programs in three states resulted in increased financial aid applications and enrollment in postsecondary institutions (Constantine, Seftor, Martin, Silva, & Myers, 2006). Similarly, qualitative data from 135 FGCS who had participated in the Talent Search or Upward Bound Programs in Texas shed insight into the effectiveness and perceived usefulness of the programs (Engle et al., 2006). These authors summarized their findings by noting "three crucial steps along the pipeline to college where support was most helpful in making a successful transition from high school: raising awareness for college; navigating the college admissions process; and easing the initial transition to college" (Engle et al., p. 5). More specifically, the following were identified as elements of the programs' effectiveness: relationships with precollege programming staff members, involving and educating their parents, gaining the knowledge needed for understanding the admissions and financial aid process, learning necessary study skills and gaining curriculum content knowledge for college, and acclimating to college life once at school (Engle et al.).

Another large-scale effort designed for precollege students is the Early College Experience available to future FGCS and other at-risk students. In a recent description of these programs, Hoffman and Webb (2010) noted that 24 states have some variation of early college programs and enroll approximately 42,000 students; the 208 programs associated with the Early College High School Initiative are funded by private foundations and nonprofit associations. These programs start in either sixth, eighth, or ninth grade and run through high school graduation. Upon graduating from high school, students enrolled in the program have had the opportunity to earn 2 years of college credit and/or an associate's degree. The programs vary with respect to how and where college credit is earned, with programs occurring on college campuses, in high schools, or via distance learning. Similar to the TRIO programs, all involve individualized academic, vocational, and personal support for building students' academic skills, self-confidence, and identities as college students.

These Early College Experience programs have been demonstrated to correlate with higher high school GPAs and increased levels of academic self-confidence; in addition, students enrolled in the programs graduate from high school with an average of 17 college credits (Hoffman & Webb, 2010). These authors presented preliminary effectiveness data regarding involvement in Early College Programs in Ohio and California for young Latino and African-American men. Results highlighted the importance of FGCS spending time on college campuses (with professors, student support services personnel, and other college students) in order to increase their awareness of factors and available resources that contribute to student success in college (Hoffman & Webb). In other words, FGCS receive cultural capital regarding the college experience while still in high school (Bourdieu, 1986). Complementing this cultural capital, individualized support such as tutoring and participation in courses that develop study skills and critical thinking help students to be successful. These experiences subsequently lead to increased levels of self-efficacy and more comfort with their identity as a college student, consistent with PSC theory (Gloria & Rodriguez, 2000).

Taken together, precollege programming for potential FGCS has been demonstrated to be an effective mechanism to facilitate success in the transition to college (Bergerson, 2007; Trippi & Cheatham, 1989). For example, involvement in these programs relates to increased graduation rates, greater levels of self-reported academic self-efficacy, and student's increased awareness surrounding the college admissions and financial aid process (e.g., Engle et al., 2006; Hoffman & Webb, 2010).

Whereas the aforementioned TRIO and early college programs are geared toward children and adolescents, other programs and efforts (including some TRIO programs) focus on adults and/or current college students. The TRIO Student Support Services program is available to extend similar types of services provided to younger participants in the TRIO programs to adult students enrolled in college. For example, one model of efficient use of such resources is the University of Wisconsin at Madison's Center for Educational Opportunity (CeO), which combines state, federal, and university resources. Through CeO, structured 1st- and 2nd-year experiences are provided to FGCS, including a weeklong orientation and study skills development and career development courses taught by (in part) counseling psychologists and counseling psychology graduate students (retrieved January 17, 2011, from http://ceo.wisc.edu/). Additionally, tutoring, peer mentoring, and professional advising are offered to students throughout their tenure at the university. Boston College's Learning to Learn (LTL) is another example of a federally funded intervention program for FGCS (retrieved January 17, 2011, from http://www.bc.edu/offices/ltl/about/history.html). Among other services, LTL supports students with an intensive 3-week transitional program, a psychology course focused on critical thinking, academic advising, financial aid counseling, mentoring, and personal counseling services. This program's website reports that LTL participants graduate at rates between 95% and 98% compared with other BC students whose graduation rates are closer to 83%.

It appears, therefore, that offering systemic support to assist FGCS in their transition to college and in their adjustment to the culture of academia is critical. Indeed, in a recent examination of community college factors that contribute to success in transferring students to 4-year institutions, Smith, Miller, and Bermeo (2009) conducted a qualitative analysis of six community colleges in Texas with the highest transfer rates of low income and FGCS to 4-year institutions. Results indicated that the climate of these campuses was particularly inclusive of FGCS. Specifically, these campuses were described as having the expectation of successful transfer of students, which included leaders who were cross-culturally competent with respect to low-income and first-generation issues, and which had structures built into the institution that supported student success and transfer (e.g., the possibility for high school students in these communities to earn college credits at a community college at no cost to the students). These high performing institutions often housed federally funded TRIO Student Support Services (SSS) programs or offered similar services despite not having a TRIO SSS grant. That is, these community college campuses offered students individualized academic, career, and personal assistance. This support included similar elements to those described previously, including: study skills development and learning centers, innovative developmental courses, personalized advising, and efforts to engage students in campus life in innovative and flexible ways such as through learning communities.

Taken together, this body of literature supports the effectiveness of large-scale interventions and student support services for precollege students and FGCS. In particular, participation in these programs has been documented to relate to retention and graduation rates for FGCS (e.g., Chaney, 2010), increased self-efficacy, student engagement (e.g., Seftor et al., 2009; Myers et al., 2004), and greater success in navigating the transition to college (e.g., Bergerson, 2007). These programs have also served as models for the development of some smaller scale and institution-specific interventions.

Smaller Scale and Institution-Specific Interventions

A variety of smaller scale and institution-specific programs have also been developed and integrated into campuses and communities in an effort to meet the needs of FGCS. Although a comprehensive review of all programming is beyond the scope of this chapter, we overview programming efforts focused on cultural relevance, faculty engagement and support, learning communities, and peer support and mentoring.

Some smaller scale programming efforts for college students have focused on increasing faculty support and engagement given that findings from qualitative research (e.g., Cox, 2009; Longwell-Grice & Longwell-Grice, 2007) have indicated that FGCS are fearful of faculty contact and will often avoid such contact as a result. For example, in a qualitative study of FGCS in six English composition classes at a community college, a common theme among the FGCS was anxiety regarding their ability to succeed and fears of failing in college (Cox, 2009). Students in this investigation identified several defensive strategies that they engaged in to cope with the anxiety, including avoidance of academic tasks and activities, postponement of current or future enrollment in classes, avoidance or withdrawal from instructors and support personnel, and redefinitions of success. Two instructors with higher completion rates in their classes were noted to have been attuned to students' potential fears and anxieties and to have addressed them via a supportive and encouraging stance toward students, which included high expectations, explicit instructions for assignments, validation of positive behaviors/academic achievement, and built-in expectations for participation (Cox). These pedagogical strategies were deemed by Cox to have addressed and minimized students' fears and increased their access to faculty members. Relatedly, McKay and Estrella (2008) demonstrated the importance of student-faculty contact in their evaluation of the ability of 12 service learning courses to engage FGCS. Results suggested that quality communication between the faculty members and students involved in service learning projects was especially important in engaging students and integrating them in the college campus experience.

These findings (e.g., Cox, 2009; McKay & Estrella, 2008) highlight the usefulness of interventions designed to increase student-faculty engagement for FGCS. Indeed, efforts toward engagement and integration are proposed to result in increased retention of FGCS (e.g., Martinez et al., 2009; Tinto, 1993). More sophisticated efforts to understand the benefits of engagement are needed, particularly given findings that have indicated that African American FGCS and African American CGCS emphasized the importance of personal mentoring relationships with faculty members more than did European American FGCS (Ishiyama, 2007).

Another smaller scale intervention strategy employed by some colleges and universities to increase college engagement and retention of various groups of students involves the use of learning and living-learning communities. These communities are comprised of groups of students with similar interests and/or identities, which are organized and supervised by college/university personnel. Students involved in the communities take classes together, engage in extracurricular activities together, and (in the case of living-learning communities) live together. Although limited data exist regarding the effectiveness of these communities, initial data appear promising. For example, in a comparison of four groups of students (three of the groups included students in three different living-learning communities and the fourth group of students was not involved in these communities) at one institution, Inkelas and Weisman (2003) reported that students in living-learning communities reported smoother transitions, were more engaged with the college environment, and felt more supported socially and academically than students not involved in these communities. The development of living-learning or learning communities on campuses specifically designed for FGCS seems a promising direction for future endeavors, particularly given that participants in the living-learning programs that focused on 1st-year transitions reported smoother transitions to college than participants in other types of living-learning communities.

Not surprisingly, community colleges have utilized variants of the learning community model to improve educational outcomes, college engagement, and retention rates for low-income, first-generation, ethnic minority, and immigrant students (Engstrom & Tinto, 2008). In a large, mixed-methods investigation of 13 community college campuses with learning communities, results from the quantitative data indicated that students generally perceived the program as effective. Engstrom and Tinto's examination of the qualitative data associated with this finding indicated that students who perceived the program to be effective cited a sense of safety provided by professors whom students felt personally connected to and supported by as the reason for their positive evaluation of the programs. Indeed, participants reported that anxieties and fears were reduced in these supportive relationships such that their academic self-efficacy flourished and their academic engagement and learning was deepened. Further, students identified cross-curricular connections (e.g., linking basic writing with a content course such as history) as enhancing their learning and the integration of information about student services as laying the groundwork for their success.

A smaller scale effort for students at the precollege level was designed and implemented by a group of counseling psychologists with the specific intent to provide culturally relevant prevention programming; the Latinos En Camino Program was developed and implemented by a predoctoral intern and university counseling center staff for Latino adolescents, the majority of whom were FGCS (Rivera-Mosquera, Phillips, Castelino, Martin, & Dobran, 2007). This programming used local connections and was modeled from TRIO programs (e.g., the program offered guidance regarding the college admissions process and academic requirements for college-bound students, study skills enhancement, financial aid issues, career exploration, and tutoring). These services were offered from a multicultural perspective and included special emphasis on providing culturally relevant interventions (e.g., providing information in Spanish and English, integrating Latino values in career exploration exercises, addressing immigration issues, bringing in Latino/a role models) but without the resources and support offered by federal funding. As such, it provides an example of the ways that counseling psychologists may use our specific skills to extend programming efforts for FGCS. In summary, prevention programming focused on improving the experiences of FGCS include both large- and smaller-scale efforts for individuals from sixth grade through college. Large-scale efforts, such as the TRIO programs, have existed for several decades and are often funded by the federal government (Engle et al., 2006; DoE, 2008). More recent large-scale programming has combined the use of federal, state, and private funds (see Hoffman & Webb, 2010, for a review). These large-scale efforts have increased our understanding of the elements that are most effective in working with FGCS and allowed for the development of several smaller scale and institution-specific programming efforts that can be used as models for future intervention efforts (e.g., McKay & Estrella, 2008; Rivera-Mosquera et al., 2007). Counseling psychologists are well equipped to extend these efforts in their roles within institutions of higher education, schools, and communities.

Counseling Psychology's Role in Retention

Counseling psychology, as a profession, can contribute to retention efforts related to FGCS. Counseling psychologists are well trained to assist with the implementation of such programming efforts within the community given our emphasis on multiculturalism, social justice, vocational development, and prevention. In this section, we will overview traditional and nontraditional roles across various settings from which counseling psychologists can impact the matriculation of FGCS.

Roles in Institutions of Higher Education

Counseling psychologists have traditionally been employed in a number of roles within institutions of higher education, and therefore are in prime positions from which to address the needs of FGCS. Specifically, counseling psychologists work as undergraduate and graduate faculty, as staff psychologists within college and university counseling centers, as student affairs professionals, and as administrators. Indeed, we believe that our review of the empirical research and intervention efforts targeted toward this group highlight the many ways in which counseling psychologists may easily transfer our skills and expertise to advocacy and intervention efforts for FGCS. While the possibilities for impacting FGCS are endless, this section provides a preliminary exploration of some specific examples within college and university settings.

Whereas some of the roles fulfilled by counseling psychologists with regard to FGCS may be specific to their occupations (i.e., serving as a students' psychotherapist versus overseeing an on-campus program), other mechanisms of intervention are shared among counseling psychologists on campus regardless of their specific occupation. For example, the creation of safe spaces for FGCS within institutions of higher education is essential (e.g., Smyth & Helm, 2003). Indeed, research has demonstrated the benefits of feelings of belongingness and connections with similar others who can share experiences and offer support to one another (e.g., Ostrove & Long, 2007). Given the documented findings that FGCS report significantly less disclosure of college experiences with friends and family (Barry, Hudley, Kelly, & Cho, 2009) and findings demonstrating that having a space to disclose such events can lead to stress reduction (Smyth & Helm, 2003), interventions that focus on providing opportunities and spaces for students to share their college experiences warrant further attention.

Relatedly, scholars (e.g., Orbe, 2004) have urged professionals to attend to decreasing stigma associated with being FGCS within the entire context of higher education. As such, some (e.g., Martinez et al., 2009) have encouraged campus staff and faculty to exercise care in relation to the terms used when referring to FGCS. Specifically, these authors suggested that we associate labels such as "first-generation college students" with positive connotations that foster a sense of pride, accomplishment, and expansion of skills for these students rather than a sense that they are deficient in some way; Martinez and colleagues argued that such an approach would alter the environment of higher education and further promote values consistent with a positive psychology approach. Relatedly, these authors recommended that faculty, staff, and administrators be mindful of their reactions to students who lack knowledge to complete or navigate particular activities related to being enrolled as a student in an institution of higher education (e.g., learning online databases, using technology to complete course assignments, registering for classes). Indeed, Martinez and colleagues suggested that "Showing surprise or disdain might inadvertently suggest to a first-generation student that he or she is quite academically and financially different from his or her peers and, given the negative reaction, possibly not as deserving of a college education" (p. 100).

In combination, these practices are intended to promote a sense of "validation" for FGCS on college campuses (Lohfink & Paulsen, 2005). Terenzini and Rendon (1994) argued that "validation" is a key concept relevant to the lives for FGCS (p. 70) in that staff, faculty, and administrators can validate students' ability to be successful in college and reinforce the valuable ideas and opinions that they bring with them to campus. Given our traditional roots in strength-based and developmental perspectives (e.g., Howard, 1992; Speight & Vera, 2008), counseling psychologists are particularly well suited to become leaders of such initiatives and equipped with the skills and expertise to begin to alter the environment of higher education to be more inclusive of FGCS.

Counseling Center Staff

Staff psychologists and administrators housed within college and university counseling centers are particularly suited to meet the needs of FGCS and the campus community via one-to-one contact with students, outreach programming, and trainings offered to faculty and staff across campus. Indeed, college counseling centers can play a critical role in helping to assist FGCS in their navigation of the college experience.

First, counseling centers can act as an information hub and liaison for students who are transitioning to college. Counseling centers can disseminate information regarding campus support services (e.g., math lab, writing lab, career centers) to students via new technologies, including social networking sites. Second, several counseling centers across the United States work with student affairs staff to offer precollege programming (i.e., Summer Bridge Programs) to incoming college freshmen. Through such collaborative programming, counseling center psychologists are able to offer their expertise on topics such as stress, mental health, and wellness. This contact will also increase students' awareness of counseling center services prior to the beginning of their tenure as a student. Relatedly, counseling center staff often participate in the training of graduate assistants and peer mentors in the TRIO programs housed on college/university campuses.

Counseling centers are often called on to provide outreach programming to the campus community. In addition to workshops such as those offered during precollege programming, counseling psychologists can offer workshops on managing financial stressors specific to FGCS, exploring intersections of identities for FGCS, and facilitating difficult dialogues with their CGCS peers. Additionally, counseling center psychologists often serve as liaisons to staff, faculty, and administrators across campus. In this role, psychologists may be called on to act as consultants to various departments or organizations on campus. As professionals with knowledge about FGCS, opportunities exist for training faculty, staff, and other administrators on issues relevant to FGCS.

Finally, counseling center psychologists fulfill a critical role by providing individual counseling to students, including FGCS. As such, they foster the development of a safe space on campus for the student by offering a unique service to FGCS who present with difficulties related to their identity, transition to college, and navigation of the campus environment. Relatedly, counseling center psychologists can offer individual career counseling services for students to engage in career exploration and decision-making. This opportunity may be particularly useful for FGCS whose exposure to career-related learning experiences and knowledge of available career areas may be limited (e.g., Gibbons & Borders, 2010). Although a thorough review of the literature on individual interventions with FGCS is beyond the scope of this chapter on prevention, counseling center psychologists are encouraged to draw useful topics for psychotherapy interventions with FGCS from the psychotherapy literature relative to social class (e.g., Liu, 2002; Liu & Ali, 2008).

Faculty

Faculty members are similarly in a position to serve FGCS through a variety of mechanisms, including their teaching, service, and scholarship roles. First, given the high proportion of FGCS who work off campus in order to support themselves in college, faculty might use class time as a space to help facilitate students making connections between their off campus work and college experiences (Bergerson, 2007). In particular, Bergerson advised faculty to encourage students to talk about their work in classes and suggested that university staff and faculty make efforts to connect students to work opportunities relevant to their academic pursuits. Second, faculty in undergraduate and graduate school departments can be role models themselves and/or can assist FGCS in developing mentoring relationships with upper class FGCS. As noted by Smith, Miller, and Bermeo (2009), faculty and staff who openly identify themselves as having been FGCS serve as strong, motivating forces for FGCS. The identification of mentors who are upperclassmen and upperclasswomen who were themselves FGCS may be especially useful for students who are experiencing a lack of self-confidence regarding their abilities or for students who express other reactions related to the imposter syndrome (see Terrion & Leonard, 2007, for review). Third, faculty (particularly those involved with decisions regarding admission into undergraduate or graduate programs) are encouraged to be cognizant of assumptions regarding specific elements of a student's application. For example, a perceived lack of involvement in extracurricular activities among FGCS may be related to the environmental circumstances surrounding that individual (e.g., the need to work in order to support oneself or one's family, the need to work as caregivers with family members) rather than to a lack of effort or commitment to their education. Similarly, lower GPAs or standardized test scores may be more reflective of a FGCS' limited access to educational opportunities available to their CGCS peers (e.g., standardized testing preparatory classes, hiring of admissions coordinators/advisors, tutoring).

Faculty who are involved in the training of counseling psychology graduate students in particular have a unique opportunity to increase awareness of FGCS as a culturally diverse and underrepresented group in higher education. As such, graduate faculty are encouraged to integrate findings regarding the mental health, experiences in psychotherapy, educational and vocational development, and cultural identity of FGCS into graduate courses and clinical practicum discussions. On campuses with TRIO programs, faculty can encourage graduate students to pursue voluntary or paid positions within the TRIO program as a means of increasing multicultural competence (e.g., counseling psychology graduate students are well trained to work as advisors to TRIO or CeO students). Involvement in these positions will provide counseling psychology graduate students with exposure to administrative positions to which they might later aspire. Finally, counseling psychology faculty can contribute to the existing scholarship on FGCS in order to improve desired outcomes for FGCS. Specifically, scholars could integrate a psychological perspective into the literature on FGCS by exploring such topics as identity development, career development, and mental health among FGCS. Research efforts aimed at developing, implementing, and evaluating effective prevention programs for the retention of FGCS is also warranted.

Administration

Counseling psychologists can serve the interests of FGCS in a more systemic manner in a variety of roles on college and university campuses as administrators. Indeed, counseling psychologists work as administrators within student affairs, academic affairs, and diversity offices. As well, counseling psychologists employed within policy positions by nonprofit or government organizations are particularly well situated to work to meet the needs of FGCS by advancing policy initiatives, accruing resources, and large-scale data analysis. Being in positions of leadership and power can offer counseling psychologists the opportunity to implement initiatives to meet the needs of FGCS and to change the overall climate of institutions of higher education in a more systemic manner.

First, administrators can impact change in a variety of capacities, including increased access to financial assistance and financial education resources for FGCS. Lohfink and Paulsen (2005) argued that need-based aid and work-study aid are essential to retain FGCS, as these students are far more likely to drop out of school as a result of accumulated debt than their CGCS peers. As such, Lohfink and Paulsen encouraged administrators to prioritize work-study opportunities that provide FGCS with monetary incentives as well as other benefits (e.g., developing connections with professionals working on campus, opportunities for job shadowing, expanding career exploratory behaviors). Administrators can also work with institutions' development offices to create or augment existing scholarships specifically for FGCS. Administrators at higher levels of power within a specific institution will have access to the greatest amount of capital to develop such funding initiatives on campus as a result of their position on campus and in the surrounding community.

Administrators working within student affairs, academic affairs, and diversity offices on campus can also support initiatives designed to improve college students' financial literacy. Specifically, offering financial responsibility classes to FGCS may help to address the documented deleterious consequences of high financial stress for college students (e.g., Eitel & Martin, 2009; Somers, Woodhouse, & Gofer, 2000). Some authors (e.g., Northern, O'Brien, & Goetz, 2010) recommended that students with high levels of financial stress attend educational sessions focused on topics such as budgeting, student loan processes, and credit card spending. Relatedly, administrators can facilitate students' awareness of, and access to, resources to defray some of the costs associated with attending college, *despite it being in the institution's best financial interests not to do so.* For example, disseminating information regarding low-cost sources for used textbooks and lower-cost housing and meal plan alternatives may be especially of interest to FGCS.

Further, administrators can attend to the needs of FGCS by understanding more specifically their needs and interests regarding involvement in extracurricular activities and organizations on campus. Based on their findings that CGCS benefited more from clubs than their FGCS counterparts, Lohfink and Paulsen (2005) discouraged administrators and student affairs staff from assuming that merely being involved in campus clubs will contribute to increased retention among FGCS. Instead, these authors suggested that campus organizations and activities be structured in ways that prioritize the values of FGCS by scheduling events during times that the students are likely to be available to attend and by developing campus activities that are likely to most benefit FGCS. Specifically, results demonstrated that FGCS may benefit more from academic activities (which include faculty involvement) than those that are strictly social in nature (Lohfink & Paulsen).

Finally, administrators can support the efforts of school districts by encouraging them to include college exploration and planning programs (Noeth & Wimberly, 2002). Collaboration between school districts and postsecondary education institutions is important in order to facilitate this process (Adelman, 1999). Indeed, based on the results of their qualitative investigation with first-generation urban college students, Reid and Moore (2008) highlighted the need for a community approach to ensuring that students are prepared to succeed in college, with colleges and universities playing a role. Specifically, these authors argued that high expectations are critical, role models must be accessible, and academic rigor must be increased in high school courses. As such, administrators are encouraged to work with local schools and community organizations to develop rigorous courses, to work with parents of FGCS to understand the importance of encouraging such coursework, to facilitate the expansion of community services that will meet the specific needs of FGCS, and to work with school counselors who were identified as disseminators of critical information to students.

Summary and Future Directions

Our hope is that this chapter will alert counseling psychologists and counseling psychology trainees to the importance of attending to FGCS as an underrepresented cultural group within institutions of higher education. We believe that counseling psychology's emphases on a developmental perspective, multiculturalism, social justice, prevention, and career development make us well situated to contribute to addressing the needs of this group of individuals. In addition to the suggestions offered throughout this chapter, we provide some additional, broad-based directions for our profession to consider with regard to FGCS.

First, further research is needed in order to inform the development and continued refinement of approaches to intervention with FGCS. For example, Ishitani (2006) urged scholars to pay attention to individual difference characteristics relevant to FGCS. Specifically, results of his longitudinal research demonstrated that attrition rates differed within FGCS and highlighted the need to consider factors such as family income, high school class rank, grant and work study funding, and high school academic intensity when determining the risk for dropout. He concluded that interventions need to be more refined in their scope given that some subsets of FGCS are at greater risk for dropout during their 1st year while others are at greater risk in their 3rd year (Ishitani). Thus, is seems prudent for future research efforts to focus on increasing our knowledge regarding which interventions work with which individuals at which point in time.

Relatedly, further exploration of intersecting identities among FGCS is warranted and will enhance efforts in research, practice, and advocacy.

Where addressed, much of the attention on intersecting identities in this literature attends to ethnicity and focuses on African Americans and Latino/as. Some attention has been paid to rural populations, including preliminary qualitative research on Appalachian FGCS (e.g., Hand & Payne, 2008), but more research in this and other areas of intersecting identities is clearly needed. No research was identified, for example, on intersecting identities for FGCS who are sexual minorities, and issues of sexuality in general are rarely mentioned. Relatedly, attention to gender and gender identity, age, ability/disability status, religion/spirituality, and immigration status as identities relevant to FGCS is needed. Increasing our knowledge of the intersection of identities among FGCS will aid in efforts to better serve this group. For example, administrators will have more specific data to guide intervention efforts and psychotherapists will have a better understanding of the complexities inherent in their clients as the clients navigate their interrelated identities.

Finally, for the field of counseling psychology, research is warranted to specifically determine our own levels of cross-cultural competency with issues related to FGCS. An assumption of this chapter has been that counseling psychologists are competent in this area, but such an assumption may be premature. Within our profession, FGCS have been relatively neglected in the empirical literature as we have traditionally relied on scholarship from other professions (e.g., educational leadership, sociology). Counseling psychologists may, therefore, need to pursue continuing education in this area in order to increase our own competency and contribute to the training of future counseling psychologists. Indeed, as the number of FGCS on campuses continues to rise (Choy, 2002), it is increasingly likely that trainees and professionals will encounter clients who identify as FGCS themselves or present to counseling with issues relevant to FGCS (e.g., a parent of a FGCS who is experiencing distress related with a daughter attending college, a college graduate who is struggling in his first job after graduation because he has limited support regarding the transition into a white-collar occupation). Furthermore, as attention to FGCS becomes more widespread, it is likely that students and early career psychologists who are focused on social justice and advocacy work will want to contribute to shaping public policy in areas such as the retention of FGCS. As a profession, therefore, counseling psychologists may need to develop continuing education for those midcareer and later career professionals who need to build their advocacy and lobbying skills in order to train the next generation of counseling psychologists.

In conclusion, promoting retention and graduation of FGCS and training future counseling psychologists to meet the needs of FGCS is vitally important for many reasons. Most notably, it is important for the sake of furthering the educational, vocational, psychological, economic, and well-being of individuals from this group of people. Additionally, these efforts will positively impact our society given the benefits that we will reap from tapping into the resources, skills, and ability that FGCS have to offer. Finally, working to meet the needs of FGCS offers counseling psychology as a field some new vocational opportunities to capitalize on. As the field changes and counseling psychologists must increasingly consider occupations that utilize a wider skill set, working to promote retention in FGCS in positions in college and university administration, in precollege programming in schools, or in public policy can be considered as additional career paths for graduate students and early career professionals.

References

Adelman, C. (1999). *Answers in the tool box: Academic intensity, attendance patterns, and bachelor's degree attainment* (ED 431 363). Washington, DC: US Department of Education, Office of Education Research and Improvement.

Agger, B. (1998). *Critical social theories: An introduction.* Boulder, CO: Westview Press.

Aries, E., & Seider, M. (2007). The role of social class in the formation of identity: A study of public and elite private college students. *The Journal of Social Psychology, 147,* 137–157.

Balz, F. J., & Esten, M. R. (1998). Fulfilling private dreams, serving public priorities: An analysis of TRIO students' success at independent colleges and universities. *Journal of Negro Education, 67,* 333–345.

Barry, L. M., Hudley, C., Kelly, M., & Cho, S. (2009). Differences in self-reported disclosure of college experiences by first-generation college student status. *Adolescence, 44,* 55–68.

Baum, S., & O'Malley, M. (2003). *College on credit: How borrowers perceive their education debt.* Braintree, MA: Nellie Mae. Retrieved November 21, 2010, from http://www.nelliemae.com/library/nasls_2002.pdf

Berger, J. B. (2000). Optimizing capital, social reproduction, and undergraduate persistence: A sociological perspective. In J. M. Braxton (Ed.), *Reworking the student departure puzzle* (pp. 95–126). Nashville, TN: Vanderbilt University Press.

Bergerson, A. A. (2007). Exploring the impact of social class on adjustment to college: Anna's story. *International Journal of Qualitative Studies in Education 20,* 99–119.

Billson, J. M., & Terry, M. B. (1982). In search of the silken purse: Factors in attrition among first-generation students. *College and University, 58,* 57–75.

Blau, P. M., & Duncan, O. D. (1967). *The American occupational structure.* New York: Wiley.

Blustein, D. L., Chaves, A. P., Diemer, M. A., Gallagher, L. A., Marshall, K. G., Sirin, S., & Bhati, K. S. (2002). Voices of the forgotten half: The role of social class in the school-to-work transition. *Journal of Counseling Psychology, 49,* 311–323.

Bourdieu, P. (1977). Cultural reproduction and social reproduction. In J. Karabel & A. H. Halsey (Eds.), *Power and ideology in education* (pp. 487–511). New York: Oxford University Press.

Bourdieu, P. (1986). The forms of capital. In J. G. Richardson (Ed.), *Handbook of theory and research for the sociology of education* (pp. 241–258). New York: Greenwood.

Bourdieu, P. (1990). Artistic taste and cultural capital. In J. Alexander & S. Seidman (Eds.), *Culture and society: Contemporary debates* (pp. 205–215). Cambridge: Cambridge University Press.

Bourdieu, P. (1994). Distinction: A social critique. In D. B. Grusky (Ed.), *Social stratification: Class, race, and gender in sociological perspective* (pp. 404–429). New York: Westview Press.

Bradford, C., & Farris, E. (1991). *Survey on retention at higher education institutions: Higher education survey report.* Rockville, MD: Westat.

Bui, K. V. T. (2002). First-generation college students at a four-year university: Background characteristics, reasons for pursuing higher education, and first-year experiences. *College Student Journal, 36,* 3–11.

Cabrera, A. F., & La Nasa, S. M. (2001). On the path to college: Three critical tasks facing America's disadvantaged. *Research in Higher Education, 42,* 119–149.

Carnevale, A. P., & Rose, S. J. (2003). *Socioeconomic status, race/ethnicity, and selective college admissions.* The Century Foundation, Retrieved March 1, 2009, from http://www. tcf. org/Publications/Education/carnevale_rose.pdf

Ceja, M. (2006). Understanding the role of parents and siblings as information sources in the college choice process of Chicana students. *Journal of College Student Development, 47,* 87–104.

Chaney, B. W. (2010). *National evaluation of student support services: Examination of student outcomes after six years.* Washington, DC: US Department of Education, Office of Planning, Evaluation and Policy Development, Policy and Program Studies Service. Retrieved January 2, 2011, from http://www2.ed.gov/about/offices/list/opepd/ppss/reports. html#higher

Choy, S. (2001). *Students whose parents did not go to college: Postsecondary access, persistence, and attainment* (NCES 2001–126). Washington, DC: US Department of Education, National Center for Education Statistics, US Government Printing Office.

Choy, S. P. (2002). *Access and persistence: Findings from 10 years of longitudinal research on students.* Washington, DC: American Council on Education.

Chronicle of Higher Education. (2011). *Adults with college degrees in the United States, by county.* Retrieved January 25, 2011, from http://chronicle.com/article/Adults-With-Colleg e-Degrees-in/125995/

Coleman, J. (1988). Social capital in the creation of human capital. *American Journal of Sociology, 94,* S95–S120.

Constantine, J. M., Seftor, N. S., Martin, E. S., Silva, T., & Myers, D. (2006). *A study of the effect of the Talent Search Program on secondary and postsecondary outcomes in Florida, Indiana, and Texas: Final report from phase II of the national evaluation.* Washington, DC: US Department of Education, Office of Planning, Evaluation and Policy Development, Policy and Program Studies Service, Retrieved January 2, 2011, from http://www2.ed.gov/rschstat/eval/highered/ talentsearch-outcomes/index.html

Cox, R. D. (2009). It was just that I was afraid: Promoting success by addressing students' fear of failure. *Community College Review, 37,* 52–80.

Dennis, J. M., Phinney, J. S., & Chuateco, L. I. (2005). The role of motivation, parental support, and peer support in the academic success of ethnic minority first-generation college students. *Journal of College Student Development, 46,* 223–236.

Diemer, M. A. (2002). Constructions of provider role identity among African American men: An exploratory study. *Cultural Diversity and Ethnic Minority Psychology, 8,* 30–40.

DiMaggio, P., & Mohr, J. (1985). Cultural capital, educational attainment, and marital selection. *American Journal of Sociology, 90,* 1231–1261.

Eitel, S. J., & Martin, J. (2009). First generation female college students' financial literacy: Real and perceived barriers to degree completion. *College Student Journal, 43,* 616–630.

Engle, J., Bermeo, A., & O'Brien, C. (2006). *Straight from the source: What works for first-generation college students.* Washington, DC: The Pell Institute for the Study of Higher Education. Retrieved January 28, 2011, from http://www. diversityweb.org/diversity_innovations/student_development/recruitment_retention_mentoring/documents/ StraightfromtheSource.pdf

Engstrom, C. M., & Tinto, V. (2008). Learning better together: The impact of learning communities on the persistence of low income students. *Opportunity Matters, 1,* 5–21.

Fouad, N. A., & Byars-Winston, A. M. (2005). Cultural context of career choice: Meta-analysis of race/ethnicity differences. *Career Development Quarterly, 53,* 223–233.

Gibbons, M. M., & Borders, L. D. (2010). Prospective first-generation college students: A social-cognitive analysis. *The Career Development Quarterly, 58,* 194–208.

Gloria, A. M., Castellanos, J., Lopez, A. G., & Rosales, R. (2005). An examination of academic nonpersistence decisions of Latino undergraduates. *Hispanic Journal of Behavioral Sciences, 27,* 202–223.

Gloria, A. M., & Ho, T. A. (2003). Environmental, social, and psychological experiences of Asian American undergraduates: Examining issues of academic persistence. *Journal of Counseling and Development, 81,* 93–105.

Gloria, A. M., & Robinson Kurpius, S. E. (2001). Influences of self-beliefs, social support, and comfort in the university environment on the academic nonpersistence decisions of American Indian undergraduates. *Cultural Diversity and Ethnic Minority Psychology, 7,* 88–102.

Gloria, A. M., Robinson-Kurpius, S. E., Hamilton, K. D., & Willson, M. S. (1999). African American students' persistence at a predominantly White university: Influence of social support, university comfort, and self-beliefs. *Journal of College Student Development, 40,* 257–268.

Gloria, A. M., & Rodriguez, E. R. (2000). Counseling Latino university students: Psychosociocultural issues for consideration. *Journal of Counseling and Development, 78,* 145–154.

Guiffrida, D. A. (2006). Toward a cultural advancement of Tinto's theory. *Review of Higher Education: Journal of the Association for the Study of Higher Education, 29,* 451–472.

Hand, C., & Payne, E.M. (2008). First-generation college students: A study of Appalachian student success. *Journal of Developmental Education, 32,* 4–15.

Haycock, K., & Huang, S. (2001, Winter). Are today's high school graduates ready? *Thinking K-16*(5), 3–17.

Hey, W., Calderon, K. S., & Seabert, D. (2003). Student work issues: Implications for college transition and retention. *Journal of College Orientation and Transition, 10,* 35–41.

Horn, L., Berger, R., & Carroll, C. D. (2004). *College persistence on the rise? Changes in 5-year degree completion and postsecondary persistence rates between 1994 and 2000* (NCES 2005–156). Washington, DC: US Department of Education, National Center for Education Statistics.

Horn, L. J., & Carroll, C. D. (1998). *Stopouts or stayouts? Undergraduates who leave college in their first year* (NCES 1999–087). Washington, DC: US Department of Education, National Center for Education Statistics.

Horn, L., & Nevill, S. (2006). *Profile of undergraduates in U.S. postsecondary education institutions: 2003–04, with a special analysis of community college students* (No. 2006–184). Washington, DC: US Department of Education, National Center for Education Statistics.

Horn, L., & Nunez, A. (2000). *Mapping the road to college: First-generation students' math track, planning strategies, and context of support* (NCES 2000–153). Washington, DC: National Center for Education Statistics, US Government Printing Office.

Hoffman, N., & Webb, M. (2010). From hope to belief. *Educational Leadership, 67*(7), 54–58.

Howard, G. S. (1992). Behold our creation: What counseling psychology has become and might yet become. *Journal of Counseling Psychology, 39,* 419–442.

Inkelas, K. K., & Weisman, J. L. (2003). Different by design: An examination of student outcomes among participants in three types of living-learning programs. *Journal of College Student Development, 44,* 335–368.

Ishitani, T. T. (2003). A longitudinal approach to assessing attrition behavior among first-generation students: Time-varying effects of pre-college characteristics. *Research in Higher Education, 44,* 433–449.

Ishitani, T. T. (2006). Studying attrition and degree completion behavior among first-generation college students in the United States. *Journal of Higher Education, 77*(5), 861–885.

Ishiyama, J. (2007). Expectations and perceptions of undergraduate research mentoring: Comparing first generation, low income White/Caucasian and African American students. *College Student Journal, 41,* 540–549.

Longwell-Grice, R., & Longwell-Grice, H. (2007). Testing Tinto: How do retention theories work for first-generation working-class students? *Journal of College Student Retention: Research, Theory and Practice, 9,* 407–420.

Lin, M. M. (2011). *Intersections of race, SES, and first-generation college student status in understanding the factors affecting undergraduate academic persistence: A psychosociocultural approach.* The University of Wisconsin – Madison). *ProQuest Dissertations and Theses.*

Liu, W. M. (2002). The social class-related experiences of men: Integrating theory and practice. *Professional Psychology: Research and Practice, 33,* 355–360.

Lohfink, M. M., & Paulsen, M. B. (2005). Comparing the determinants of persistence for first-generation and continuing-generation students. *Journal of College Student Development, 46,* 409–428.

London, H. (1996). How college affects first-generation students. *About Campus, 7*(5), 9–13, 23.

Liu, W. M., & Ali, S. R. (2008). Social class and classism: Understanding the psychological impact of poverty and inequality. In S. D. Brown & R. W. Lent (Eds.), *Handbook of counseling psychology* (4th ed., pp. 159–175). Hoboken, NJ: Wiley.

Majer, J. M. (2009). Self-efficacy and academic success among ethnically diverse first-generation community college students. *Journal of Diversity in Higher Education, 2,* 243–250.

Martinez, M., & Klopott, S. (2005). *The link between high school reform and college access and success for low-income and minority youth.* Washington, DC: American Youth Policy Forum and Pathways to College Network. Retrieved January 21, 2011, from http://www.aypf.org/publications/index.htm

Martinez, J. A., Sher, K. J., Krull, J. L., & Wood P. K. (2009). Blue-collar scholars: Mediators and moderators of university attrition in first-generation college students. *Journal of College Student Development, 50,* 87–103.

Massey, D. S., Charles, C. Z., Lundy, G. F., Fischer, M. J., & Bryant, R. M. (2003). *The Source of the River: The Social Origins of Freshmen at America's Selective Colleges and Universities.*

McKay, V. C., & Estrella, J. (2008). First-generation student success: The role of faculty interaction in service learning courses. *Communication Education, 57,* 356–372.

Metz, A. J., Fouad, N., & Ihle-Helledy, K. (2009). Career aspirations and expectations of college students: Demographic and labor market comparisons. *Journal of Career Assessment, 17,* 155–171.

Moreau, M. P., & Leathwood, C. (2006). Balancing paid work and studies: Working (-class) students in higher education. *Studies in Higher Education, 31,* 23–42.

Myers, D., Olsen, R., Seftor, N., Young, J., & Tuttle, C. (2004). *The impacts of regular Upward Bound: Results from the third follow-up data collection.* Washington, DC: US Department of Education, Office of the Under Secretary, Policy and Program Studies Service. Retrieved January 2, 2011, from http://www2.ed.gov/rschstat/eval/highered/upward/upward-3rd-report.html

Noeth, R. J., & Wimberly, G. L. (2002). *Creating seamless educational transitions for urban African American and Hispanic students.* ACT Policy Report. Iowa City, IA: ACT.

Northern, J. J., O'Brien, W. H., & Goetz, P. W. (2010). The development, evaluation, and validation of a financial stress scale for undergraduate students. *Research in Brief, 51,* 79–92.

Nunez, A., & Cuccaro-Alamin, S. (1998). *First-generation students: Undergraduates whose parents never enrolled in postsecondary education* (NCES 98–082). Washington, DC: National Center for Education Statistics, US Government Printing Office.

Orbe, M. P. (2004). Negotiating multiple identities within multiple frames: An analysis of first-generation college students. *Communication Education, 53*(2), 131–149.

Ostrove, J. M., & Long, S. M. (2007). Social class and belonging: Implications for college adjustment. *Review of Higher Education: Journal of the Association for the Study of Higher Education, 30,* 363–389.

Pascarella, E. T., Pierson, C. T., Wolniak, G. C., & Terenzini, P. T. (2004). First-generation college students. *Journal of Higher Education, 75,* 249–284.

Paulsen, M. B., & St. John, E. P. (1997). The financial nexus between college choice and persistence. In R. A. Voorhees (Ed.), *Researching student aid: Creating an action agenda*

(New Directions for Institutional Research No. 95, pp. 65–82). San Francisco, CA: Jossey-Bass.

Phinney, J. S., & Haas, K. (2003). The process of coping among ethnic minority first-generation college freshmen: A narrative approach. *Journal of Social Psychology, 143*(6), 707–726.

Rayle, A. D., Robinson-Kurpius, S., & Arredondo, P. (2006). Relationship of self-beliefs, social support, and university comfort with academic success of freshman college women. *Journal of College Student Retention: Research, Theory, and Practice, 8,* 325–343.

Reid, M. J., & Moore, J. L. (2008). College readiness and academic preparation for postsecondary education: Oral histories of first-generation urban college students. *Urban Education, 43,* 240–261.

Rivera-Mosquera, E., Phillips, J. C., Castelino, P., Martin, J. K., & Dobran, E. M. (2007). Design and implementation of a grassroots pre-college program for Latino youth. *The Counseling Psychologist, 35,* 821–839.

Seftor, N. S., Mamun, A., & Shirm, A. (2009). *The impacts of regular Upward Bound on postsecondary outcomes seven to nine years after scheduled high school graduation.* Washington, DC: US Department of Education, Office of Planning, Evaluation and Policy Development, Policy and Program Studies Service. Retrieved January 2, 2011, from http://www2.ed.gov/about/offices/list/ope/trio/index.html#news

Smedley, B. D., Myers, H. F., & Harrel, S. P. (1993). Minority-status stresses and the college adjustment of ethnic minority freshmen. *Journal of Higher Education, 64*(4), 434–452.

Smith, C. T., Miller, A., & Bermeo, C. A. (2009). *Bridging the gaps to success: Promising practices for promoting transfer among low-income and first generation students.* Washington, DC: The Pell Institute for the Study of Opportunity in Higher Education. Retrieved January 28, 2011, from http://www.pellinstitute.org/publications.html

Smyth, J. M., & Helm, R. (2003). Focused expressive writing as self-help for stress and trauma. *Journal of Clinical Psychology, 59,* 227–235.

Somers, P., Woodhouse, S., & Gofer, J. (2000, November). *Persistence of first-generation college students.* Paper presented at the annual conference of the Association for the Study of Higher Education, Sacramento, CA.

Speight, S. L, & Vera, E. M. (2008). Social justice and counseling psychology: A challenge to the profession. In S. D. Brown & R. W. Lent (Eds.), *Handbook of counseling psychology* (4th ed., pp. 54–67). Hoboken, NJ: Wiley.

Terenzini, P., & Rendon, L. (1994). The transition to college: Diverse students, diverse stories. *Research in Higher Education, 30,* 301–315.

Terenzini, P., Springer, L., Yaeger, P., Pascarella, E., & Nora, A. (1996). First-generation college students: Characteristics, experiences, and cognitive development. *Research in Higher Education, 37,* 1–22.

Terrion, J. L, & Leonard, D. (2007). A taxonomy of the characteristics of student peer mentors in higher education: Findings from a literature review. *Mentoring and Tutoring: Partnership in Learning, 15,* 149–164.

Tierney, W. G. (1992). An anthropological analysis of student participation in college. *Journal of Higher Education, 63,* 603–618.

Ting, S. (2003). A longitudinal study of non-cognitive variables in predicting academic success. *College and University, 78,* 27–31.

Tinto, V. (1987). *Leaving college: Rethinking the causes and cures of student attrition* (1st ed.). Chicago, IL: University of Chicago Press.

Tinto, V. (1993). *Leaving college: Rethinking the causes and cures of student attrition* (2nd ed.). Chicago, IL: University of Chicago Press.

Trippi, & Cheatham, (1989). Effects of special counseling programs on Black freshman on a predominately White campus. *Journal of College Student Development, 30,* 35–40.

US Census Bureau. (2006a). *2006 American community survey: Median earnings in the past 12 months.* Retrieved November 18, 2010, from http://factfinder.census.gov/servlet/DTTable?_bm=y&-geo_id=01000US&-ds_name=ACS_2006_EST_G00_&-mt_name=ACS_2006_EST_G2000_B20004

US Census Bureau. (2006b). *2006 American community survey: Educational attainment.* Retrieved November 18, 2010, from http://factfinder.census.gov/servlet/STTable?_bm=y&-geo_id=01000US&-qr_name=ACS_2006_EST_G00_S1501&-ds_name=ACS_2006_EST_G00_

US Department of Education, Office of Postsecondary Education. (2008). *A Profile of the federal TRIO programs and Child Care Access Means Parents in School Program.* Washington, DC: Author. Retrieved November 28, 2010, from http://www2.ed.gov/about/offices/list/ope/trio/index.html

Valadez, J. R. (1998). Applying to college: Race, class and gender differences. *Professional School Counseling, 1*(5), 14–20.

Walpole, M. (2003). Socioeconomic status and college: How SES affects college experiences and outcomes. *Review of Higher Education, 27*(1), 45–73.

Walpole, M. (2008). Emerging from the pipeline: African American students, socioeconomic status, and college experiences and outcomes. *Research in Higher Education, 49,* 237–255.

Wang, C. D. C., & Castaneda-Sound, C. (2008). The role of generational status, self-esteem, academic self-efficacy, and perceived social support in college students' psychological well-being. *Journal of College Counseling, 11*(2), 101–118.

Warburton, E. C., Bugarin, R., & Nunez, A. (2001). *Bridging the gap: Academic preparation and postsecondary success of first-generation students* (NCES 2001–153). Washington, DC: US Government Printing Office.

Wells, R. (2008). Social and cultural capital, race and ethnicity, and college student retention. *Journal of College Student Retention: Research, Theory and Practice, 10,* 103–128.

Whiteley, J. M. (1984). A historical perspective on the development of counseling psychology as a profession. In S. D. Brown & R. W. Lent (Eds.), *Handbook of counseling psychology* (pp. 3–55). New York: Wiley.

Zirkel, S. (2002). Is there a place for me? Role models and academic identity among white students and students of color. *Teachers College Record, 104*(2), 357–376. doi:10.1111/1467-9620.00166

CHAPTER

22 Promoting Resilience in Immigrants: Understanding Latino/a Adaptation and Strengths

Melissa L. Morgan Consoli, Nelly Gonzalez, *and* Susana Ayala Lopez

Abstract

This chapter outlines adversities faced by immigrants as well as factors associated with their resilience. The Latino/a immigrant population is highlighted as the largest immigrant population in the United States. Factors contributing to resilience in this population, as well as programs and approaches used to foster well-being and resilience are discussed. Recommendations for factors to consider in promoting resilience in the Latino/a immigrant population are given, and future directions are highlighted and discussed.

Key Words: immigration, Latino/a population, resilience, adversities, Latino/a-focused prevention programs

Introduction

Immigration in the United States has been a consistent trait of US society, and, throughout history, has involved hundreds of different groups and individuals. Currently, the United States has more immigrants arriving than any other nation in the world (Segal, Elliott, & Mayadas, 2010). In 2008, an estimated 11.9 million undocumented immigrants lived in the United States and over a million people received US citizenship, the highest number in US history (Lynn & Rytina, 2009). The overall population of US immigrants (documented or undocumented) has recently been estimated at 12 or 13 million. Of this population, approximately 76% of the undocumented immigrant population is of Latin American descent, thereby making the Latino/a population, whether documented or not, the largest group of immigrants in the nation (Pew Hispanic Center, 2009a).

Immigrants face many types of adversity, including discrimination, racism, economic hardships, employment difficulties, and interruption of family ties. The impact of such adversities is quite significant, and can affect the mental and physical health of immigrants (McEwen, 2002). Despite these hardships, immigrants have been found to be quite resilient overall (Markovitzky & Mosek, 2005; Padilla, 2006; Reiboldt & Goldstein, 2000; Um & Dancy, 1999), and to utilize various strategies for surviving or even thriving in the face of adversity; including relying on significant relationships for support (e.g., a positive relationship with a camp counselor), external and internal resources, and problem-solving (Flores, Cicchetti, & Rogosch, 2005; Morgan, 2007; Gonzales, 2007). Paradoxical findings indicate that in many cases, recent immigrants have significant health and mental health advantages as compared to native-born US individuals (Bender & Castro, 2000), in particular in Latino/a populations. While programs have been developed to foster resilience in the general population, very little has been developed to facilitate these capacities in immigrant individuals. In conceptualizing such preventive efforts, various factors from the resilience research must be taken into account.

The current chapter addresses resilience in immigrants in the United States; including adversities faced, and means of overcoming these adversities. Research in these areas is discussed, and exemplary programs for facilitating resilience are described. While it is impossible to cover in detail every group of immigrants to the United States in a single book chapter, examples from multiple groups are given in the first part of the chapter. In the last part of the chapter, particular attention is paid to the largest group of US immigrants: Latino/a immigrants.

Brief History of Immigration

Immigration has been a cornerstone of the history of the United States. Other than Native American and Alaskan Native populations, all people in the United States have their roots in immigration. Throughout time, different immigrating groups have been subjected to varying policies, limitations, and discrimination. For example, the first Naturalization Act allowed "free white persons of good character" to become citizens after being residents of the country for a set time period (Daniels, 2002, p. 113); the Bracero Program of 1942 to 1964 gave Mexican workers temporary legal residence in the United States to help meet agricultural needs (later revoked, leaving those program members still in the United States as "illegal") (Hoefer, Rytina, & Baker, 2010), and the recently proposed anti-immigration bill in Arizona allows police officers to search, identify, and detain any undocumented immigrant at any time (Archibold, 2010). Throughout history, immigration legislation has been controversial and intense, and has varied with the political climate. Research shows that in difficult economic times, seeing immigrants as a threat to the nation's economy is more common (Mayda, 2004; Stephan, Renfro, Esses, Stephan, & Martin, 2005; Yakushko, 2009).

Definitions of Immigration

Immigration is a complex process that includes many factors. One person's immigration can look very different from another person's depending on legal and social circumstances (Portes & Rumbaut, 2006; Segal, Mayadas, & Elliott, 2010). The US government uses the terms "immigrant" and "foreign-born" to designate individuals coming from another country who reside in the United States (US Census, 2009). "Foreign-born" may distinguish first-generation immigrants from those who have lived in this country for more than one generation, and may also include people here temporarily, such as international students or temporary workers. Technically, all people migrating to the United States from another land are "immigrants, " although they may have had different experiences depending on how they came to the United States (Yakushko & Morgan, in press).

Differences Among Types of Immigrants

Immigrants have come from many different countries and have experienced various degrees of acculturation, resilience, and overall well-being. Within this group of people who have left their homeland are those who leave voluntarily, those who leave in times of political turmoil and strife, and those who leave without documentation in hopes of bettering their families' economic situation.

LEGAL IMMIGRATION

"Legal immigration" is the term used for individuals who immigrate to the United States with the required documentation and who therefore have permission from the US government to live and work in the United States (i.e., a "green card") (US Department of State, 2010). This status gives individuals the right to live in the United States indefinitely and to seek naturalization (Mulder et al., 2001).

REFUGEES

Each year, the United States allows a certain number of individuals to relocate to the United States from certain countries to escape political strife and turmoil. Since the 1960s, people from the following groups have been admitted to the United States as refugees: Hmong, Kurds, Vietnamese, Cubans, Bosnians, Kosovo Albanians, Iraqis, Iranians, Sudanese, Ukrainians, and Russians (Bemak & Chung, 2002).

UNDOCUMENTED IMMIGRATION

Undocumented immigrants are those who enter the country without legal documentation, including those who cross the Southwestern border, and those who came to the country with legal documentation, but remained when their visas expired (Passel, 2005).

The Pew Hispanic center estimates that there were approximately 11 million undocumented immigrants in the United States as of 2005, with 6.3 million being of Mexican origin. Of the total undocumented population, 24%, or 2.4 million, live in California (these estimates were reached by subtracting the *legal* foreign-born residents from the *total* foreign-born population). It is estimated that 7.2 million undocumented immigrants were employed as of 2005. The most concentrated populations work in farming, cleaning, construction, food preparation, and production. Most of these occupations are low-wage, low-skill jobs. Children constitute approximately one in six of the undocumented immigrant population (Passel, 2005).

Adversities Faced by Immigrants

Multiple adversities are faced by immigrant populations, including the process of immigration itself, discrimination, acculturation difficulties, language barriers, cultural obstacles, economic insecurity, and other systemic oppression (Cervantes, Padilla, & Salgado de Snyder, 1991). These additional stressors in the United States are likely new and unfamiliar to the immigrant, as they are often not the same as those faced in the immigrant's native country. Attempting to cope with these additional stressors while simultaneously dealing with everyday life challenges may create a very high level of stress, which has been associated with mental health problems such as depression, anxiety disorders, and suicide (Selye, 1956; Lazarus, 1966; Lefcourt, 1989). Therefore it would be beneficial for psychologists to understand and lessen these additional stressors for immigrants preventively, *before* they lead to psychological problems.

Immigration Process

The literature on mental health and immigration suggests that the immigration process itself is very stressful for immigrants (Diaz-Guerrero, 1995; Hovey et al., 2001; Ruiz & Padilla, 1977; Salgado de Snyder, 1987). As mentioned above, what the exact process looks like depends on the country of origin and political situation of the immigrant, but in any immigration journey there are potential stresses in all stages. For example, in the premigration stage, there is possible trauma and economic hardship; in the migration stage, difficult losses, traumatic journeys, and difficulty entering the country; and in the postmigration stage, immigrants often find overcrowded and unsafe living conditions, higher crime, and a cycle of poverty (Pumariega, Rothe, & Pumariega, 2005). Recently, migratory grief has emerged as an area of study. This construct entails the sense of loss and yearning for the immigrant's homeland, culture, people, and things left behind (Henry et al., 2005; Keyes & Kane, 2004).

Acculturative Stress

Acculturative stress is potentially another source of adversity for immigrants. Defined as "[stress]in which the stressors are identified as having their source in the process of acculturation" (Williams & Berry, 1991, p.634), acculturative stress is another phenomenon that may underlie a reduction in mental and physical health status. This construct was first noted by Redfield, Linton, and Herskovits (1936), who described it as a "psychic conflict that may arise from conflicting cultural norms" (p. 152). More recently, Berry (1980) has theorized that acculturative stress is a fundamental psychological force in the acculturative process, which every immigrant experiences when changing cultures. The new immigrant must face the challenges of acclimating and adapting to the new country's society and culture and may do so in a variety of ways (acculturation will be discussed in further detail in a subsequent section of the chapter).

Varying amounts of time are needed for the immigrant to adapt to the new host country's language and customs and some individuals never adapt, even after decades. Acculturative stressors can include stress in adjusting to schools, neighborhoods, religious communities, and/or work places, as well as conflicts at home (Suarez-Orozco & Suarez-Orozco, 1995a; Rumbaut & Portes, 2006). These conflicts may concern issues such as intergenerational difficulties, school performance, and/or difficulties in identity formulation in light of the new culture (Al-Johr, 2005; Ross-Sheriff & Husain, 2001).

The process of adjusting successfully (i.e., experiencing less acculturative stress) to a new society depends on a number of factors. Specifically, less acculturative stress has been linked to greater financial opportunity (Short & Johnston, 1997), higher family cohesion (Lueck & Wilson, 2009; Kang, 1996), higher overall well-being (Gore & Aseltine, 1995; Kang, 1996), and bilingualism (speaking and thinking in both English and the native language) (Lueck & Wilson, 2009) in immigrant populations. Maintaining a strong sense of one's ethnic identity has also been found to buffer the effects of acculturative stress (Ryder et al., 2000; Thompson et al., 2000) as has maintaining a bicultural sense of identity through establishing contacts with the majority culture while maintaining one's original ethnic identity (Huang, 1994).

It should be noted that while acculturation is a significant stressor for most people, some may not experience distress and may even thrive in this situation (Rudmin, 2006; Berry, 1980). The impact of acculturative stress and adaptation has been shown to vary by generational status. Studies of first-generation immigrant children have shown them to have better overall mental and physical health than their second- and third-generation counterparts (Sam, Vedder, Ward, & Horenczyk, 2006). This phenomenon has been found with many outcome variables (for example, violence, homelessness, and birth weight) and has been referred to by health professionals as the "immigrant paradox" (Baker, 1996, Bender & Castro, 2000) and will be further described in the "Resilience in Latino/a Immigrants" section below.

Language Barriers

A common barrier faced by many immigrants in this country is the linguistic barrier of not speaking English or not speaking it well. Not speaking the host country's native language is not just a linguistic problem for the immigrant, but also affects access to healthcare services, communication with children's schools, availability of job opportunities or limited advancement possibilities on the job, and access to education. When non-English-speaking immigrants enter schools, hospitals, or courts, they often find there is no interpreter, thus severely limiting the possibilities of communicating with a teacher, doctor, or even a judge. This shortage of trained bilingual service providers, specifically in the mental health field, makes it very difficult for limited-English-proficient immigrants to obtain appropriate services since their goals and concerns cannot be communicated adequately (Partida, 2007; Riddick, 1998).

Discrimination and Racism

Discrimination in the immigrant population ranges from "daily hassles, such as negative stereotypes or prejudiced comments, " to blatant "negative actions based on ethnic group membership" (Sellers & Shelton, 2003, p.25). Often perceived as different from the dominant US culture, immigrants frequently receive differential, and often more negative, treatment than if these perceived variations were nonexistent. Discrimination is most often studied through self-report and not literal evidence of differential treatment, therefore it is called perceived discrimination. Perceived discrimination has been found to be a salient occurrence for many different immigrant groups, including Arab Americans (Ajrouch, 2005), Japanese immigrant youth (Yeh, Arora, Inose, Okubo, Li, & Greene, 2003), Latino/a immigrant youth (Espino & Franz, 2002) and Muslim immigrants (Pew Hispanic Center, 2009). Immigrant individuals in all of these groups reported experiences such as discrimination at work, from friends or neighbors, and in public settings such as restaurants and shopping centers. Purported reasons for discrimination varied from physical appearance to accent (Ajrouch, 2005) to low English proficiency, skin color, or negative stereotypes attached to their nationality (Yeh et al., 2003).

In studies of perceived discrimination containing several different ethnic groups, stereotypes seem to play a big role in determining the level and type of discrimination. For example, in a survey of Asian and Latino/a students, both groups experienced similar exposure to discrimination and greater perceived discrimination, but Latino/as were more often accused of negative behaviors like cheating or breaking the law (Hwang & Goto, 2008). Therefore, ethnic groups who are most often characterized by negative stereotypes (e.g., Latino/as are usually gang members) might report more perceived discrimination than other groups who have less negative stereotypes (e.g., Asians are dedicated to school) (Cordova & Cervantes, 2010; Kao, 2000). In the case of Muslim immigrants, they are more likely to be stereotyped as terrorists due to the 9/11 attacks. As recently as 2009, 58% of surveyed Americans reported that they believed that Muslims (in the United States) are the group most vulnerable to discrimination (Pew Hispanic Center, 2009).

In a qualitative study on perceived discrimination among Latino/a youth, analysis showed a difference between immigrants and US-born Latino/as in the type of discrimination they experienced. US-born Latino/as felt they were most commonly stereotyped as gang members or discriminated against because of their appearance, while Latino/a immigrants' felt discriminated against due to impressions of low acculturation such as being placed in English as a Second Language (ESL) classes, speaking Spanish, and appearance or clothing. In this study, youth perceived discrimination when others criticized them, made offensive comments, made fun of them, or held negative expectations or stereotypes. The study also reported that many of the youth, both immigrants and US-born, perceived discrimination in school from students, staff, and teachers (Cordova & Cervantes, 2010).

The above examples of perceived discrimination are descriptive of between-group discrimination, or discrimination between different ethnic groups.

Nonetheless, within-group discrimination is just as concerning. While ethnic minorities who speak a similar language or have similar phenotypes are often recognized by the dominant society as a big, cohesive group, there are large cultural differences based on nationality and generational status. For example, a Latino/a from Argentina has a very different cultural background (and language dialect) than a Latino/a from Mexico. Individuals from the same ethnic group may focus on these differences, discriminating against other individuals from their broad ethnic group who have a different nationality. Within-group discrimination may also occur due to acculturated individuals not wanting to be stereotyped as an immigrant (Cordova & Cervantes, 2010). For example an Asian American treating an Asian immigrant differently because he/she is an immigrant and not "American, " and not wanting to be considered to be in the same "category." In a recent survey of 2, 929 Latino/as, 84.4% responded that they perceive within-group discrimination as problematic, and recent immigrants who were Spanish-language dominant (as opposed to other languages) were more likely to perceive within-group discrimination (Monforti, 2010).

These encounters with discrimination have been found to be emotionally, psychologically, and physically harmful in multiple studies (Alamilla, Kim, & Lam, 2010; Finch, Kolody, & Vega, 2000; Ornelas, Perreira, Beeber, & Maxwell, 2009; Parra-Cardona, Cordova, Holtrop, Villaruel, & Wieleng, 2008), affecting daily life in multiple ways. For example, individuals might avoid certain activities or situations that place them at risk for being discriminated against, such as going to a mall or a place where security is involved (Ornelas et al., 2009; Parra-Cardona et al., 2008). In more extreme cases, adults may not want to go to work, or children may not want to go to school because of fear of discrimination.

Several variables have been found to moderate the effects of perceived discrimination on health and well-being in ethnic minorities in the United States. Although these studies have not focused on immigrants specifically, their findings can give some insight into possible moderators or mediators within immigrant populations. For example, in a study by Moradi and Risco (2006), sense of control was found to be a partial mediator between perceived discrimination and distress among a sample of self-identified Latino/as. Similarly, a meta-analysis including studies with various ethnic minority populations in the United States concluded that social support positively affects the impact of perceived discrimination on mental health (Pascoe & Richman, 2009, p.23) as well as active or problem-focused coping (Pascoe & Richman, 2009). Parental support has also been found to moderate the relationship between experiences of discrimination and higher academic well-being in Latino/a youth (DeGarmo & Martinez, 2006), while academic motivation appears to mediate the relationship between perceived discrimination and academic success in Latino boys (Alfaro et al., 2009). More research is needed to discern possible moderators or mediators between perceived discrimination and well-being or health in immigrant populations.

Poverty

Poverty is an important factor that places immigrants' mental and physical health at risk (Dohrenwend, 2000). In 2007, 18.6% of immigrants were living at the poverty level, as compared to 12.5% among US natives (US Census, 2009). Living at the poverty level not only entails financial stress, but impoverished individuals are also more likely to experience other stressors linked to their low income. These stressors can include living with other families, having less time to spend with their own family or attending to personal needs, lacking insurance, and living in communities with high crime rates.

The Latin American immigrant population is the largest group of individuals in the United States living below the poverty level (22.9%) (US Census, 2009), followed by individuals from "other areas" such as Africa and Oceania (15.7%), Asians (12.2%), and finally European Americans (9%). This disparity in socioeconomic status among immigrants can be partially attributed to the highest educational level received, legal status, political or economic climates of their native country, and reasons for immigration. For instance, in a study looking at Eastern European immigrants, researchers found that immigrants living below the poverty level were likely to be from countries that experienced war recently, such as Bosnia or Albania (Robila, 2007). Another study on Filipino immigrants highlights the fact that, compared to other immigrant groups, Filipino immigrants arrive to the United States with higher SES and educational levels, which makes it easier for them to obtain employment in the United States (Mossakowski, 2007).

Living in poverty limits immigrants' access to resources and in many cases, forces immigrants to live in more dangerous neighborhoods or communities. Latino/as living in such conditions often report more stressors related to their environment or issues that are highly affected by their SES. For example, Latino/as with lower SES or who live in poverty report higher perceived discrimination compared to other Latino/as with higher SES (Araujo & Borell, 2006).

Living in poverty conditions not only affects the environment in which immigrants find themselves and their access to resources, but it can affect social and family interactions as well. Many Latinas are forced to choose between work and taking care of their families, either limiting the time spent with their children, or seriously impacting their financial resources (Ornelas et al., 2009), parenting styles (Leidy, Guera, & Toro, 2010), and time to seek out other social support networks.

Despite poverty and the many other adversities faced by immigrants, many immigrants show resilience or even thrive despite these hardships. The following section discusses how many immigrants are able to overcome adversity.

Resilience in Immigrants

Resilience has been defined as the ability to make normal, developmental achievements despite obvious adverse social and environmental barriers (Rutter, 1987; Garmezy, 1993). The concept of normal, developmental achievement can be defined as outwardly evidenced competence or age-appropriate stage development (Luthar & Zigler, 1991), while adverse social and environmental barriers involve risk, or exposure to difficulties that can interfere with development (Luthar & Cicchetti, 2000).

Research on the construct of resilience has linked it with such phenomena as increased school achievement, decreased gang involvement (Li, Stanton, Pack, Harris, Cottrell, & Burns, 2002), higher future expectations (Wyman, Cowen, Work, & Kerley, 1993), an internal locus of control (Luthar, 1993), life satisfaction, and decreased depression (Wagnild & Young, 1993).

Resilience has most often been researched within the context of protective factors. The protective factor model of resilience highlights protective processes specific to an individual (for example, high parental involvement or high socioeconomic status) that interact with risk factors to increase or decrease certain outcome variables associated with resilience. Another, less frequently cited model of resilience is the challenge model (Rutter, 1987). This model highlights the individual successfully dealing with moderate levels of stress, thereby increasing the chances of that individual successfully dealing with future stressful situations. Finally, the compensatory model of resilience looks at compensatory factors (e.g., a strong reliance on faith) that help individuals to develop despite adversity (Garmezy, Masten, & Tellegen, 1984). Werner and Smith (1992), in their landmark study of 700 children from the island of Kauai, conceptualized resilience in this way. Because the children were able to view difficult situations positively, they overcame adversities in their lives (O'Leary, 1998).

The terms "resilience" and "protective factors" are often used interchangeably in the psychological literature, but it is important to note that they are separate concepts (Morrison, Robertson, Laurie, & Kelly, 2002). *Resilience* refers to a process where individuals or communities are able to normally develop despite barriers, while *protective factors* are characteristics either associated with or responsible for this developmental process (Morrison et al., 2002).

In addition to protective factors, resilience is mediated by the adversity faced by the individual. Adversity includes risk factors thought to threaten positive adaptation outcomes. It is important to recognize that risk and protective factors impacting resilience may be viewed differently across cultural contexts (Holleran & Waller, 2003). The right combination of protective factors can outweigh the negative impact of the risk factors (Werner & Smith, 1992).

Resilience is a construct that clearly underlies a strength-focused view of adaptation to risk. Strength-focused interpretations of immigrant cultures have been very limited in the professional literature; instead deficit-focused interpretations have dominated (Aguirre & Baker, 2000). As such, resilience literature directly related to immigrants is limited. However, the themes of acculturation, family and social support, spirituality, and self-concept are all protective factors present in the immigrant literature that have been shown to help support or be associated with factors of resilience.

Acculturation

Acculturation refers to the process whereby immigrants adapt to the values and behaviors of the host (US) country (Wang & Gordon, 1994). Acculturation was traditionally looked at linearly, but more recent models have been developed which look at it as a more complex process (Bourhis, Moise, Perreaul, & Senecal, 1997). Specifically, the domains of values, behaviors, and attitudes within acculturation have been recognized, and an individual may have different preferences for each of these with regard to the native culture and the new, dominant culture. Based on the person's preferences, s/he will fall into one of four categories: assimilated, bicultural (integrated), separated (rejection), or marginalized (deculturation) (Berry, 1980; Berry, 2003). Even more recent conceptualizations posit acculturation as a multidimensional process, including social cognition, cultural competence, social identity, social dominance, and social stigma, and as encompassing the two constructs of cultural awareness and ethnic loyalty (Padilla & Perez, 2003). Multiple studies have indicated that the integrated (bicultural) identity is associated with the best mental health outcomes (Bautista de Domanico, Crawford, & Wolfe, 1994), best cognitive abilities (Tadmor & Tetlock, 2006), and better academic outcomes (Padillaet al., 1991).

Several external factors may also influence what acculturation looks like in the case of immigrants. Socioeconomic variables, which influence standard of living and quality of life, may have a huge bearing on what an immigrant is exposed to upon arriving in the United States (Moyerman & Forman, 1992). Those immigrants who stay in ethnic enclaves, because it is more affordable, or because there are easily accessible support networks, for example, may experience acculturation differently than those immigrants who live in the broader society. This type of ethnic social support has been shown to affect which acculturative path is taken (Moyerman & Forman, 1992). In fact, the importance of "place" in which everyday activities are carried out has been tied to well-being. The importance of public parks, streets, and ethnic markets has been demonstrated to be crucial to maintaining a sense of ethnic heritage and has even been the impetus for fighting urbanization and gentrification of traditionally "ethnic" neighborhoods where immigrants reside (Chakrabarti, 2010). Additionally, time of life at immigration has bearing on which acculturative path is taken, with those migrating later in life a bit less likely to integrate cultures (Hovey, 2000). Social support is particularly important in the acculturation experience of Latino/as (Kaniasty & Norris, 2000; Padilla, 2006) and other immigrants for whom relationships are a big source of support.

Family and Community Support

In the broader resilience literature, familial support has been found positively correlated to psychological well-being (Rodriguez, Mira, Paez, & Myers, 2007), to be of great importance in overcoming traumatic experiences (Walsh, 2007), to serve as a protective factor against suicidal ideation (Cho & Hadam, 2010), to help prevent negative mental health outcomes (Ayon, Marsiglia, & Bermudez-Parsai, 2010), and to promote better academic outcomes (Esparza & Sanchez, 2008; Gamble & Modry-Mandell, 2008). As noted above, it also plays an important role in acculturation processes.

With regard to immigrant populations, familial support seems particularly integral to well-being, particularly given the frequent lack of other available support (Dominguez & Lubitow, 2008). For example, in the Latino/a population, *familismo*, or the values placed on "attitudes, behaviors, and family structures operating within an extended family system" (Coohey, 2001, p.130) has been found to be an important factor in promoting resilience.

Support from communities is also an important factor in promoting resilience in immigrants, particularly in the absence of familial support. Communities can encompass the immigrants' religious community (e.g., religious groups and clergy) and educational institutions (e.g., teachers and peers), as well as other entities. For example, immigrants might begin attending a religious congregation and find support from neighbors or other religious members (Ramirez, Lumadue, & Wooten, 2007). In school, children and youth perform better academically when they perceive support from their academic institution (Gonzalez & Padilla, 1997).

Culture-specific support seems to play a specific role in helping immigrant individuals adjust to their new culture while still maintaining ties to their native culture. Links between loss of ties to culture and decreased mental health have been discovered (Birman, 1998; Kaplan & Marks, 1990). In children and youth, academic achievement and school attachment can be affected by lack of connection with their native culture (Feliciano, 2002). Some research suggests that the influence of culture specific social connectedness for an immigrant is dependent on the value which that immigrant places on that type of support (Yoon & Lee, 2010).

Religious Faith/Spirituality

Historically, many immigrant groups (e.g., Irish, Italian, and other Europeans) have turned to religion and spirituality as a means for facing difficulties in their new land (Herberg, 1955; Miller, 1977). This has not changed with more recent immigrant groups, and researchers from many disciplines have highlighted the role that religion plays in the lives of immigrant individuals from Latin and

Central America, Asia, Africa, and the Middle East (Mazumdar & Mazumdar, 2008b). For many, "religion plays a critical role in identity construction, meaning making, and value formation" and can help to form "alternative allegiances and places of belonging" (Levitt, 2003, p.851) in the new land.

While such religious or spiritual beliefs can be manifested in a plethora of ways, their presence has been found to be a factor of resilience (Morgan, 2007; Gonzales, 2007) and to be positively correlated to good mental health. Most people identify with a religion or consider themselves to be spiritual (Schlosser, Foley, Stein, & Holmwood, 2010), therefore, it is not uncommon for individuals to utilize religious or spiritual comfort during difficult times (Walsh, 2007). Termed *positive religious coping*, this phenomenon focuses on the fact that when individuals turn to religion they find themselves better able to deal with the idea of loss of control, might view negative experiences from a "growth" point of view, and find comfort in a higher being or life plan (Pargament, Smith, Koenig, & Perez, 1998). For example, female Bengali immigrants to New York City were found to utilize the social support networks and coping methods from religious communities in their new neighborhoods to better deal with pregnancy (Chakrabarti, 2010). In another study, Afghan immigrant women expressed that their religious beliefs helped them to deal with the wartime situations they had experienced, through providing supportive activities at the mosque, prayer that helped give a sense of hope and control, and support from the religious community (Welsh & Brodsky, 2010). For other immigrant populations, such as Latino/a Catholics, Eastern European Catholics, African Catholics, and Asian Catholics, attachment to particular religious figures, such as the Virgin Mary, is a source of empowerment enabling them to successfully cope with adversities (Kane, 2010). In fact, some immigrant populations are immigrants specifically for religious reasons, searching for a land to freely practice their religion.

Internal Factors

Several more internal or intrapersonal attributes have been found that are present in most resilient people to some degree. As resilience is a process and not completely tied to particular traits, these are not absolutely necessary ingredients for a resilient person, however they have been related at least indirectly to resilience. For example, studies have shown that when social competence, problem-solving skills, autonomy, and sense of purpose and future are present, individuals cope better with adversity (Abelev, 2009; Beltman & MacCallum, 2006; Withers & Russell, 2001). It is important to remember that such characteristics can be mediated by other factors such as the presence of protective factors during childhood (Chavkin & Gonzalez, 2000). Highly resilient people have also been more likely to notice positive meanings within the problems they faced, endure fewer depressive symptoms, and experience more positive emotions than less resilient people (Ong, Bergeman, Bisconti, & Wallace, 2006).

Although there is comparatively little research in this area among immigrants specifically, several internal factors have been highlighted as contributing to successfully dealing with the multiple adversities that they face. For example, a "dual frame of reference" is an internal factor that seems to contribute to resilience for immigrants (Suarez-Orozco & Suarez-Orozco, 1995b). Specifically, it was found that immigrant youth in middleschool frequently used their families' low social and economic condition in their country of origin as reference points in assessing their lives in the United States. Therefore, they might experience less distress in handling the stressors of their daily lives in the United States than those who lack such a basis of comparison. Comparing themselves to their poorer relatives in their native country might help them to feel more successful. In another study, Afghan immigrant women who were able to maintain hopeful perceptions of difficult situations, and to shift the focus of their thinking to the future when things might be different, identified themselves as more resilient (Welsh & Brodsky, 2010). Similarly, Latino/a youth who migrated to the United States and experienced multiple adversities upon arriving were able to keep going through maintaining hopeful and optimistic attitudes (Ko & Perreira, 2010).

Resilience in Latino/a Immigrants

As stated in the introduction, Latino/as are currently the largest group of immigrants in the United States and come from countries ranging from Mexico to Central America, the Caribbean (Cuba, Dominican Republic), and South America. Quite a bit of variation exists between the cultures, languages, and sociocultural and socioeconomic conditions of these countries and their nationals. Among immigrants from these countries to the United States, Mexicans are the fastest growing immigration group (currently making up 30% of all immigrants; Passel & Cohn, 2009), followed by Puerto

Ricans and Cubans (Rumbaut, 2006). By world region, the US Census reports the largest percentage of Latino/a immigrants as being from Central America, followed by the Caribbean, and then South America (US Census, 2010).

The term "Latino/a" has been indicated as the preferred term over "Hispanic" (the term used by the US Census) as it is more reflective of the origins of people from these areas. In the last decade, hundreds of thousands of individuals from these countries obtained legal residence status in the United States It is difficult to assess the number of undocumented individuals residing in the United States, but overall it is estimated that the US Latino/a population makes up about 15% of the total population (whether documented or undocumented. Furthermore, it is estimated that these immigrants and their children will account for approximately 30% of the increase in population in the next several decades (Passel & Cohn, 2009). As the term "Latino/a" represents individuals from a wide variety of backgrounds, countries, and cultures, in this section findings will be discussed in relation to specific ethnic identities whenever possible. It should be noted that examples given are meant to highlight, and not to discuss comprehensively or generalize, information within different subgroups of the Latino/a population.

As with other immigrants, adversities for the Latino/a immigrant population in the United States are often related to immigration status and acculturation and include difficulties with immigration, language barriers, and discrimination (Parra-Cardona, Bullock, Imig, Villaruel, & Gold, 2006). Stressors for some Latino/a immigrants may specifically include not having legal documents to be in the United States, and, as a result, not being able to obtain a driver's license, a long-term job, health care, or an education. In addition, there is the fear of being deported back to their country of origin (Farley, Galves, Dickinson, & Perez, 2005; Parra-Cardona et al., 2006).

Such adversities have been shown to negatively impact health (McEwen, 2002), and it has been noted that certain groups of Latino/a children may be at risk for negative outcomes resulting from adversities more than children in other minority groups, given health and developmental indicators (Arcia, Keyes, & Gallagher, 1994). This is even more likely for undocumented children, given difficulty with access to healthcare and other resources.

A phenomenon termed the "Latino Health Paradox" has been noted in the literature, and refers to the tendency for recent Latino/a immigrants to the United States to have less incidence of low birth weight than US-born people from the same country in subsequent generations (Bender & Castro, 2000). Mexican immigrants have also been found to have significantly fewer mental health disorders than US-born Mexican Americans (Escobar, 2000). This term has been generalized as the "Latino paradox." It has been posited, for example, that Mexicans come to this country with some type of natural protection against mental disorder that breaks down very quickly in US society. It is thought that this protection lies in the strength of Mexican families and the emotional support and security individuals receive from being embedded in a family group (Vega, Kolody, Valle, & Hough, 1986). Some research indicates that this finding may also interact with acculturation processes, as first-generation Latino/as with high acculturation levels also may have lower levels of mental health (Ruiz, 1981). Similarly, Holleran and Waller (2003) report that "instead of equating assimilation with positive adaptation, some researchers suggest that Mexican Americans who try to assimilate actually experience more psychological distress than those who maintain strong cultural ties" (p. 337).

Latino/a immigrants, like other immigrant groups, may migrate to the United States for many reasons, however, the vast majority migrate due to factors and conditions that are out of their control in their home country, such as economics, or political instability. Many times, the hope of escaping these hardships and creating a better life fuels the migration (Noguera, 2006). A survey conducted in Mexico by the Pew Hispanic Center (2009) demonstrated that 1 of every 10 adults say they would migrate to the United States if they had the means and opportunity to do so and 2 out of 10 are inclined to work and live in the United States without legal documentation.

The literature surrounding resilience in Latino/a populations is fairly limited. Many studies look at the Mexican American population specifically, with a few studying other Latino/a populations. The literature on Latino/a immigrants specifically is even more limited. When looking at such studies, it is important to remember that immigrants are a select (often self-selected) group, who may be more ambitious and possibly productive than their native-country-residing counterparts (Salgado de Snyder, 1987). For the purposes of this review, all studies are discussed as referring to "Latino/a resilience" and "Latino/a immigrant resilience, " however it is acknowledged that more research is needed in this area to tease out any complexities, differences, and similarities in resilience between different Latino/a cultures.

Studies on Latino/a resilience to date have consisted largely of the evaluation of prevention programs, which focus on outcome variables. Some of these studies include: exploring resilience with regard to education in the children of immigrants in Southern California (primarily Mexican, Filipino, Vietnamese, Laotian, and Cambodian) (Rumbaut, 2000), resilience with regard to acculturation in Cuban Americans (Portes, 1984; Heilemann, Lee, & Kury, 2002), resilience as related to familial interaction (Holleran & Waller, 2003), resilience related to social support (Abraido-Lanza, Guier, & Colon, 1998; Rew, Thomas, Horner, Resnnick, & Beuhring, 2001), and linking resilience to culture (Gallo, Pinedo, Espinosa de los Monteros, & Arguelles, 2009).

"Protective" resources for Latino/as highlighted in the literature include both positive attitudes and certain personal patterns in responding to and understanding life experiences. Such resources have been shown to utilize personal qualities such as adaptability, ambition, self-esteem, self-efficacy, well-being, a sense of competence, integrity, and perseverance as means to manage and overcome stressful life barriers (Massinga & Pecora, 2004; Morgan, 2007; Gonzales, 2007). Other sources of resilience are functional in nature and include monetary resource acquisition, use of interpersonal relationships, and environmental resources to solve problems (Flores, Ciccheti, & Rogosch, 2005; Morgan, 2007). Such functional resources generally include support systems and community connections (Castro et al., 2007). Very importantly, cultural practices and societal phenomena often impact resilience. These include, among other factors, acculturation and cultural values, role of community, and familial influence (*familismo*).

Acculturation and Cultural Values

As noted, research has shown that resilience is highest in recent Latino/a immigrants, and decreases markedly with acculturation in subsequent generations. Portesand Rumbaut (2006) found that resilience correlates, such as family cohesiveness, academic achievement, and decreased parent conflict, were higher in Mexican-born youth, than in US-born Mexican youth. The somewhat less resilient experiences of second-generation Latino/a immigrants have been attributed to the idea that these individuals are forced to live in two worlds; thus having to navigate the social and cultural expectations of their families' countries of origin, as well as meet the needs of living in US culture (Jenkins & Cofresi, 1998). One notable finding is that when acculturation is accompanied by effective support systems, the impact of adversities is lessened (Finch & Vega, 2003). More research is needed to look at experiences of third- and fourth-generation Latino/as. Clearly, there are strengths that immigrants carry with them to their new country which lend to their initial resilience. Statistics show that those who immigrate are typically skilled workers or middle-class professionals, as the extremely poor do not have adequate resources to even consider leaving their native land. Immigrants often leave their native country due to "relative" not "absolute" deprivation (Portes & Rumbaut, 1990, p. 12).

Past literature has depicted traditional Mexican values as "cultural deficits" that interfere with assimilation into the American culture (Aguirre & Baker, 2000). Some traditional values are *familismo* (family closeness and loyalty), *respeto* (consideration for the sensibilities and needs of others), *dignidad* (dignity, honor), *fidelidad* (loyalty), *orgullo cultural* (ethnic pride), *machismo* (qualities of bravery, courage, generosity, respect for others, protection of and provision for loved ones), and *marianismo* (the centrality of the strong, virtuous mother in the family; Atkinson, 2004). However, over the last 20 years the cultural deficiency perspective has been reexamined by researchers and scholars (Vega, Kolody, Valle, & Hough, 1986). Culture is now often seen as a protector, a basis for identity, and a reservoir of valuable resources for coping and adaptation, even beyond the first generation (Holleran & Waller, 2003).

Among the top protective aspects of culture for Latino/as are "values and beliefs related to collectivism and religiosity" (Holleran & Waller, 2003, p. 346). As in the discussion of spirituality and religion above for immigrants in general, such beliefs and worldviews may be a source of comfort, hope, and guidance in times of adversity (see "Religion and Spirituality" section in "Resilience in Immigrants"). Many studies have highlighted the importance of religious beliefs in the Latino/a population (*religiosidad*) in coping with adversities such as loneliness and depression (Rivera-Ledesma & Montero, 2005), and in facilitating greater well-being, purpose in life (Gallego-Pérez, Garcia-Alandete, & Pérez Delgado, 2007) and resilience (Cook, 2000; Morgan, 2007; Gonzales, 2007; Rivera-Ledesma & Montero, 2005).

Role of Community

The role of community is vital to Latino/a resilience. Immigration patterns show that most immigrants intentionally move to places with other immigrants like themselves, and in many cases, to geographic enclaves that have similar customs and practices to their homeland despite the overarching US culture (Portes & Rumbaut, 1990). Social networks in these areas help to create systems of *confianza.* This is literally translated as "trust, " but contains the idea that personal relationships are more important and meaningful than larger social obligations to legal, religious, or educational institutions that may not have the best interests of the individual at heart. Personal relationships happen within the contexts of these institutions and the building of this *confianza* over time helps to create a system where people establish trust and caring for each other (Lafayette de Mente, 1996). A breakdown of these social systems can result in negative consequences such as higher rates of depression and other mental illnesses, increased susceptibility to or longer recuperation from physical illness, less overall satisfaction with life, and a decreased sense of well-being (Jenkins & Cofresi, 1998). As Holleran and Waller (2003) note, "Mexican-American culture has long embraced the idea that individual and community well-being are inextricably intertwined" (p.347). It now remains for researchers to gain more information about this construct as a factor of resilience, particularly in how the protective factors of ethnic enclaves balance with the advantages of being bicultural in acculturation processes.

Familial Influence (Familismo)

The specific concept of "familismo, " or the attitudes and beliefs that individuals have about the role of extended family in their lives, is considered one of the most important influences on Latino/as (Cuellar, Arnold, & González, 1995) and has been found to be related to resilience in many ways, particularly for the children within that family. For example, families high in *familismo* have been found to have less child abuse or neglect, substance abuse (Gil, Wagner, & Vega, 2000), and difficulties with US culture in general (Santisteban, Dillon, Mena, Estrada, & Vaughan, 2005). It has also been related to positive outcomes such as children's academic achievement and psychological functioning, including their ability to deal with day-to-day problems, and cope with stressors (Kenny, Gallagher, Alvarez-Salvat, & Silsby, 2002). Older Latino/a children have been found to attribute their college and other educational aspirations to the encouragement of their parents, either through direct or indirect messages, even when the parents themselves had little formal education (Klonen, 1996). The literature on resilience with Latino/a youth identifies five key protective factors, central to which are family factors such as parental support/concern and school involvement (Chavkin & Gonzalez, 2000; Wang & Gordon, 1994).

In sum, Latino/as, the largest group of immigrants in the United States, face similar adversities as other immigrants, and have many similarities to other immigrant groups in factors that aid in resilience. However, they also have many specific cultural values and practices that seem to aid in coping with adversity. Much more research is needed to understand and learn from this phenomenon as well as develop adequate programs to meet the needs of this quickly growing sector of our population.

Prevention and Resilience Building Programs

Thus far in this chapter, we have reviewed adversities faced by immigrant populations and factors associated with resilience, and profiled the largest group of immigrants in the nation. The question that remains is: "What can we do with this information?" or, "How can resilience be fostered?" and "What are the resources out there?" These questions are just beginning to be addressed by the research community. The American Psychological Association (APA) began a public campaign called "The Road to Resilience" in 2002, in the aftermath of the 9/11 terrorist attacks. The campaign includes information, handouts, and pamphlets that are available at APA's website. The information is available in both English and Spanish. As one example of this initiative, the APA has published a document promoting resilience called "10 Ways to Build Resilience, " which includes recommendations for fostering resilience in children and adults. Some of the recommendations are: to maintain good relationships with close family members, friends, and others to avoid seeing problems or stressful events as unbearable problems; to accept circumstances that cannot be changed; to develop realistic goals and move toward them; to take decisive actions in adverse situations; to look for opportunities of self-discovery after a struggle with loss; to develop self-confidence; to keep a long-term perspective and consider the stressful event in a broader context; to maintain a hopeful outlook, to expect good things and visualize what is wished for; and to take care of one's mind and body (American Psychological Association, 2010).

Programs that foster resilience are also surfacing. Even though many developers of such programs do not describe their programs as "programs fostering resilience, " many in fact promote positive coping, prevention, strengthening of family, and other factors that have been associated with resilience. In other words, such programs focus on increasing protective factors, without labeling the desired outcome as "resilience" specifically (Kumpfer, 1999).

Some of these social programs serving the Latino/a immigrant population include *Head Start* and the *Big Brothers and Big Sisters Program*. Another exemplary program is the AVANCE program, which is a program with the mission to "unlock America's potential by strengthening families in at-risk communities through effective parent education and support programs" (AVANCE online, 2010). This program began in 1972 in San Antonio, Texas, serving 35 families. The program's goals include assisting children and parents to advance to their full potential, promoting health and well-being in families (the majority of which are Latino/a), and transforming the communities in which they live by participation in different programs. This program is family- and children-centered which, as noted, is a very important value to Latino/a immigrants, and offers a variety of resources for children and their families such as parent education, English classes, home visitations, transportation services, food education and assistance, and advocacy in addressing the particular needs of the family.

Currently, AVANCE is recognized as a national model and best practice in early childhood education and has over 100 program sites across the United States. It is a nonprofit, community-based organization originally conceptualized at Cornell University by graduate students of Uri Bronfenbrenner, and has empirically based evidence demonstrating its comprehensiveness and effectiveness (AVANCE online, 2010).

A few lesser-known programs also appear to be developing throughout the nation with the express purpose of fostering well-being in immigrants. A recent literature review (December, 2010) yielded articles and dissertations outlining *Jovenes Fuertes*, a program fostering social emotional functioning in Latino/a immigrant teens in Oregon (Olivo, 2007), and the Choices Program in Illinois, which works with seventh and eighth graders in a predominantly Latino/a school (many of whom are first-generation immigrants) to foster greater well-being through collaborative programming with teachers, parents, and students (Vera et al., 2007). Undoubtedly, many other programs exist than what have been highlighted here, and program facilitators are encouraged to share their endeavors through publication so that others may learn from them.

Conclusion

In this chapter, we have presented information about the US immigrant population, outlining adversities faced in the process of immigration, with the acculturation process, through language barriers, and with poverty. We have highlighted factors and correlates of resilience pertaining to the immigrant population, including bicultural integration, family and other support, religion and spirituality, and internal factors. In addition, we have spotlighted the largest group of immigrants in our nation, Latino/a immigrants, and discussed factors of resilience specific to them, such as acculturation and cultural values, role of community, and *familismo*, among others. Finally, we have highlighted some programs in the nation which are actively fostering resilience or resilience-like outcomes in children and adults.

It should be clear from the material presented that the area of resilience in immigrant populations is still a relatively new field of study, and that much more needs to be learned to effectively help these newest members of our society to adjust effectively and healthfully. What we do know is that immigrants seem to benefit from cultural values that they bring with them to the United States, from support of all kinds, and from integration of cultures/identities if possible. But we still don't know a lot. What *has* been identified is a start to this body of literature, but many details need to be rounded out before we can most effectively use this body of research to inform policy and develop further prevention and resilience-fostering programs. For this reason it seems crucial that psychologists and other mental health professionals not only share the results of their studies in these areas, but also the challenges, success, and outcomes of prevention programming efforts with immigrant populations. In this way we will progress toward better programming at a much faster rate.

Summary of Factors Promoting Resilience

The main factors that we have identified in the chapter as promoting resilience, and which should be considered in an evidence-based approach to promoting resilience in Latino/a immigrants, include the following:

• Social Support: Resilience is promoted by reliance on significant relationships including parents and individuals outside of the family, such as a camp counselor. Additionally, feeling a sense of support from institutions such as a religious community or, in the case of children or youth, feeling support from the educational institution or the teachers, and from parental involvement facilitates resilience.

• Internal factors: Other factors that increase resilience are social competence, having problem-solving skills, autonomy, having a sense of purpose, having a positive perception (e.g., being more likely to notice positive meaning of problems), having optimistic attitudes, a high self-concept, high adaptability, ambition, self-esteem, sense of control over situation, self-efficacy, integrity, and perseverance.

• Culture: Maintaining close ties to one's culture can also promote resilience. Culture can imply retaining spiritual or religious beliefs, having a strong ethnic identity, having a bicultural identity, preserving cultural heritage, and experiencing lower acculturative stress through engaging in cultural support.

Future Directions

In thinking about what we don't yet know, but need to know about resilience in immigrant populations that might point to future directions, three questions come to mind:

1. What are more specific similarities and differences among resilience processes in different immigrant populations?
2. Can cultural values that benefit one group of immigrants be fostered in other individuals with similar effect, that is, can we take the "best" (i.e., strengths) of a culture and apply them cross-culturally with effectiveness?
3. Now that we are in the process of identifying aspects of resilience, how can these best be fostered, with immigrant populations and with others?

References

Abelev, M. S. (2009). Advancing out of poverty: Social class worldview and its relation to resilience. *Journal of Adolescent Research, 24*(1), 114–141.

Abraido-Lanza, A. F., Guier, C., & Colon, R. M. (1998). Psychological thriving among Latinas with chronic illness. *Journal of Social Issues, 54*, 405–424.

Aguirre, A., & Baker, D. V. (2000). *Structured inequality in the United States: Critical discussions and the continuing significance of race, ethnicity, and gender.* Upper Saddle River, NJ: Prentice Hall.

Ajrouch, K. J. (2005). Arab American elders: Network structure, perceptions of relationship quality, and discrimination. *Research in Human Development, 2*(4), 213–228.

Alamilla, S. G., Kim, B. S. K., & Lam, N. A. (2010). Acculturation, enculturation, perceived racism, minority status stressors, and psychological symptomatology among Latino/as. *Hispanic Journal of Behavioral Sciences, 32*(1), 55–76.

Alfaro, E. C., Umaña-Taylor, A. J., Gonzales-Backen, M., Bámaca, M. Y., & Zieders, K. H. (2009). Latino adolescents' academic success: The role of discrimination, academic motivation, and gender. *Journal of Adolescence, 32*, 941–962.

Al-Johar, D. (2005). Muslim marriages in America: Reflecting new identities. *The Muslim World, 95*, 557–574. doi: 10.1111/j.1478–1913.2005.00111.x.

American Psychological Association.(2010). *The road to resilience: 10 ways to build resilience.* Retrieved December 3, 2010, from http://www.apa.org/helpcenter/road-resilience.aspx

Araujo, B. Y., & Borell, L. N. (2006). Understanding the link between discrimination, mental health outcomes, and life chances among Latinos. *Hispanic Journal of Behavioral Sciences, 28*(2), 245–266.

Archibold, R. C. (2010, April 23). Arizona enacts stringent laws on immigration. *New York Times.* http://www.nytimes.com/2010/04/24/us/politics/24immig.html

Arcia, E., Keyes, L., & Gallagher, J. J. (1994). Indicators of developmental and functional status of Mexican-American and Puerto Rican children. *Journal of Developmental and Behavioral Pediatrics, 15*(1), 27–33.

Atkinson, D. R. (2004). *Counseling American minorities* (6th ed.). New York: McGraw-Hill.

AVANCE online. (2010). AVANCE: Unlocking America's potential. Retrieved on November 25, 2010, from http://www.avance.org

Ayon, C., Marsiglia, F. F., & Bermudez-Parsai, M. (2010). Latino family mental health: Exploring the role of discrimination and familismo. *Journal of Community Psychology, 38*(6), 742–756.

Baker, S. G. (1996). Homelessness and the Latino paradox. In J. Baumohl (Ed.), *Homelessness in America* (pp. 132–140). Phoenix, AR: Oryx.

Bautista de Domanico, Y. B., Crawford, I., & Wolfe, A. S. (1994). Ethnic identity and self-concept in Mexican-American adolescents: Is bicultural identity related to stress or better adjustment? *Child and Youth Care Forum, 23*, 197–206.

Beltman, S., & MacCallum, J. (2006). Mentoring and the development of resilience: An Australian perspective. *International Journal of Mental Health Promotion, 8*, 17–28.

Bemak, F., & Chung, R. C. (2002). Counseling and psychotherapy with refugees . In P. B. Pedersen, J. G. Draguns, W. J. Lonner, & J. E. Trimble (Eds.), Counseling across cultures (2nd ed., pp. 209–232). Thousand Oaks, CA: Sage .

Bender, D., & Castro, D. (2000). Explaining the birth weight paradox: Latina immigrants' perceptions of resilience and risk. *Journal of Immigrant Health, 2*(3), 155–173.

Berry, J. W. (1980a). Acculturation as varieties of adaptation. In A. M. Padilla (Ed.), *Acculturation: Theory, models and some new findings* (pp. 9–25). Boulder, CO: Westview.

Berry, J. W. (1980b). Social and cultural change. In H. C. Triandis & R. W. Brislin (Eds.), *Handbook of cross-cultural psychology: Vol. 5. Social psychology* (pp. 211–279). Boston, MA: Allyn & Bacon.

Berry, J. W. (2003). Conceptual approaches to acculturation. In K. Chun, P. B. Organista, & G. Marin (Eds.), *Acculturation: Advances in theory, measurement, and applied research* (27, pp. 17–37). Washington, DC: American Psychological Association.

Birman, D. (1998). Biculturalism and perceived competence of Latino immigrant adolescents. *American Journal of Community Psychology, 26*(3), 335–354.

Bourhis, R. Y., Moise, L. C., Perreault, S., & Senecal, S.(1997). Towards an interactive acculturation model: A social psychological approach. *International Journal of Psychology, 32,* 369–386.

Castro, F. G., Garfinkle, J., Naranjo, D., Rollincs, M., Brook, J. S., & Brook, D. W. (2007). Cultural traditions as "protective factors" among Latino children of illicit drug users. *Substance Use and Misuse, 42,* 621–642.

Cervantes, R. C., Padilla, A. M., & Salgado de Snyder, V. M. (1991). The Hispanic Stress Inventory: A culturally relevant approach to psychosocial assessment. *Psychological Assessment, 3,* 438–447.

Chakrabarti, R. (2010). Therapeutic networks of pregnancy care: Bengali immigrant women in New York City. *Social Science and Medicine, 71,* 362–369.

Chavkin, N., & Gonzalez, J. (2000). *Mexican immigrant youth and resiliency: Research and promising programs.* Charleston, WV: Educational Resources Information Center.

Cho, Y., & Hadam, N. (2010). Suicidal ideation and distress among immigrant adolescents: The role of acculturation, life stress, and social support. *Journal of Youth and Adolescence, 39,* 370–379.

Coohey, C. (2001). The relationship between familism and child maltreatment in Latino and Anglo families. *Child Maltreatment, 6*(2), 130–142.

Cook, K. (2000). You have to have somebody watching your back, and if that's God, then that's mighty big. *Adolescence, 35,* 717–730.

Cordova, D., Jr., & Cervantes, R. C. (2010). Intergroup and within-group perceived discrimination among U.S.-born and foreign-born Latino youth. *Hispanic Journal of Behavioral Sciences 32,* 259–274.

Cuellar, I., Arnold, B., & González, G. (1995). Cognitive referents of acculturation: Assessment of cultural constructs in Mexican Americans. *Journal of Community Psychology, 23,* 339–356.

Daniels, R. (2002). *Coming to America: A history of immigration and ethnicity in American life* (2nd ed.). New York: HarperCollins.

DeGarmo, D. S., & Martinez, C. R., Jr. (2006). A culturally informed model of academic well-being for Latino youth: The importance of discriminatory experiences and social support. *Family Relations, 55,* 267–278.

Diaz-Guerrero, R. (1995). *Psychology of the Mexican: Culture and personality.* Austin, TX: University of Texas.

Dohrenwend, B. P. (2000). The role of adversity and stress in psychopathology: Some evidence and its implications for theory and research. *Journal of Health and Social Behavior, 41,* 1–19.

Dominguez, S., & Lubitow, A. (2008). Transnational ties, poverty and identity: Latin American Immigrant women in public housing. *Family Relations, 57,* 419–430.

Escobar, J. (2000). Immigration and mental health: Mexican Americans in the United States. *Harvard Review of Psychiatry, 8*(2), 64–72.

Esparza, P., & Sanchez, B. (2008). The role of attitudinal familism in academic outcomes: A study of Urban, Latino high school seniors. *Cultural Diversity and Ethnic Minority Psychology, 14*(3), 193–200.

Espino, R., & Franz, M. M. (2002). Latino phenotypic discrimination revisited: The impact of skin color on occupational status. *Social Science Quarterly, 83*(2), 612–623.

Farley, T., Galves, A., Dickinson, L. M., & Perez, M. J. D. (2005). Stress coping and health: A comparison of Mexican-Americans, and non-Hispanic Whites. *Journal of Immigrant Health, 7,* 213–220.

Feliciano, C. (2002). The benefits of biculturalism: Exposure to immigrant culture and dropping out of school among Asian and Latino youths. *Social Science Quarterly, 82*(4), 865–879.

Finch, B. K., Kolody, B., & Vega, W. A. (2000). Perceived discrimination and depression among Mexican-origin adults in California. *Journal of Health and Social Behavior, 41,* 295–313.

Finch, B. K., & Vega, W. A. (2003). Acculturation stress, social support, and self-rated health among Latinos in California. *Journal of Immigrant Health, 5,* 109–117.

Flores E., Cicchetti, D., & Rogosch, F. A. (2005). Predictors of resilience in maltreated and nonmaltreated Latino children. *Developmental Psychology, 42*(2), 338–351.

Gallego-Pérez, J. F., Garcia-Alandete, J. G., & Pérez-Delgado, E. (2007). Purpose in life test factors and religiosity. *Universities Psychologies, 6,* 213–229.

Gallo, L. C., Penned, F. J., Espinosa de los Monteros, K. E., & Arguelles, W. (2009). Resiliency in the face of disadvantage: Do Hispanic cultural characteristics protect health outcomes? *Journal of Personality, 77,* 1707–1746.

Gamble, W. C., & Modry-Mandell, K. (2008). Family relations and the adjustment of young children of Mexican descent: Do family cultural values moderate these associations? *Social Development, 17,* 358–379.

Garmezy, N. (1993). Children in poverty: Resiliency despite Risk. *Psychiatry, 56,* 127–136.

Gil, A. G., Wagner, E. F., & Vega, W. A. (2000). Acculturation, familism, and alcohol use among Latino adolescent males: Longitudinal relations. *Journal of Community Psychology, 28,* 443–458.

Gonzales, R. R. (2007).(Doctoral dissertation). *Dissertation Abstracts International, 67,* 9-B.

Gonzalez, R., & Padilla, A. P. (1997). The academic resilience of Mexican American high school students. *Hispanic Journal of Behavioral Sciences, 19*(3), 301–317.

Gore, S., & Aseltine, R. H. (1995). Protective processes in adolescence: Matching stressors with social resources. *American Journal of Community Psychology, 23*(3), 301–327.

Heilemann, M. V., Lee, K. A. & Kury, F. S. (2003). Psychometric properties of the Spanish version of the resilience Scale. *Journal of Nursing Measurement, 11*(1), 61–72.

Henry, H. M., Stiles, W. B., & Boron, M. W. (2005). Loss and mourning in immigration: Using the assimilation model to assess continuing bonds with native culture. *Counseling Psychology Quarterly, 18,* 109–119.

Herberg, W. (1955). *Protestant, Catholic, Jew: An essay in American religious sociology.* New York: Doubleday.

Hoefer, M., Rytina, N., & Baker, B. C. (2010). *Estimates of the Unauthorized Immigrant Population Residing in the United States: January 2009.* Office of Immigration Statistics, Policy Directorate, US Department of Homeland Security, http://www.dhs.gov/xlibrary/assets/statistics/publications/ois_ill_pe_2009.pdf.

Holleran, L., & Waller, M. (2003). Sources of resilience among Chicano/a youth: Forging identities in the borderlands. *Child and Adolescent Social Work Journal, 20,* 335–350.

Hovey, J. (2000). Psychosocial predictors of acculturative stress in Mexican immigrants. *Journal of Psychology, 134,* 490–503.

Hovey, J. D., & Magana, C. G. (2002). Exploring the mental health of Mexican migrant farm workers in the Midwest: Psychosocial predictors of psychological distress and suggestions for prevention and treatment. *Journal of Psychology: Interdisciplinary and Applied, 136*(5), 493–513.

Huang, L. N. (1994). An integrative approach to clinical assessment and intervention with Asian-American adolescents. *Journal of Clinical Child and Adolescent Psychology, 23*(1), 21–31.

Hwang, W., & Goto, S. (2008). The impact of perceived racial discrimination on the mental health of Asian American and Latino college students. *Cultural Diversity and Ethnic Minority Psychology, 14*(4), 326–335.

Jenkins, J. H., & Cofresi, N. (1998). The sociosomatic course of depression and trauma: A cultural analysis of suffering and resilience in the life of a Puerto Rican woman. *Psychosomatic Medicine, 60,* 439–447.

Kane, M. (2010). Empowerment in the religious stories and art of the Virgin Mary. *Social Work and Christianity, 37,* 45–64.

Kaniasty, K., & Norris, F. H. (2000). Help-seeking comfort and receiving social support: The role of ethnicity and context of need. *American Journal of Community Psychology*, *28*(4), 545–581.

Kang, C. (1996). Acculturative stress, family environment, and psychological adjustment of Korean American adolescents (Doctoral dissertation). *Dissertation Abstracts International, 57,* B-10.

Kao, G. (2000). Group images and possible selves among adolescents: Linking stereotypes to expectations by race and ethnicity. *Sociological Forum, 15,* 407–430.

Kaplan, M. S., & Marks, G. (1990). Adverse effects of acculturation: Psychological distress among Mexican American young adults. *Social Science and Medicine, 31*(12), 1313–1319.

Kenny, M., Gallagher, L. A., Alvarez-Salvat, R., & Silsby, J. (2002). Sources of support and psychological distress among academically successful inner-city youth. *Adolescence, 37*(145), 161–182.

Keyes, E. F., & Kane, C. F. (2004). Belonging and adapting: Mental health of Bosnian refugees living in the United States. *Mental Health Nursing, 25,* 809–831.

Klonen, E. C. (1996). Conceptual analysis and measurement of the construct of ego-resiliency. *Journal of Personality and Social Psychology, 70,* 1067–1079.

Ko, L. K., & Perreira, K. M. (2010). "It turned my world upside down": Latino youth perspectives on immigration. *Journal of Adolescent Research, 25,* 465–493.

Kumpfer, K. L. (1999). Factors and processes contributing to resilience: The resilience framework. In M. D. Glantz & J. Johnson (Eds.), *Resilience and development: Positive life adaptations* (pp. 179–224). New York: Kluwer Academic/Plenum.

Lafayette De Mente, B. (1996). *NTC's dictionary of Mexican cultural code words.* Lincolnwood, IL: NTC Publishing Group.

Lazarus, R. S. (1966). *Psychological stress and the coping process.* New York: McGraw-Hill.

Lee, J., & Rytina, N. (2009) . Naturalization in the United States: 2008. Washington, DC : U.S. Department of Homeland Security.

Leidy, M. S., Guera, N. G., & Toro, R. I. (2010). Positive parenting, family cohesion, and child social competence among immigrant Latino families. *Journal of Family Psychology, 24*(3), 252–260.

Lefcourt, H. M. (1989). *Personal and social characteristics that alter the impact of stressors.* New York: AMS Press.

Levitt, P. (2003). "You know, Abraham was really the first immigrant": Religion and transnational migration. *International Migration Review, 37,* 847–873.

Li, X., Stanton, B., Pack, R., Harris, C., Cottrell, L., & Burns, J. (2002). Risk and protective factors associated with gang involvement among urban African American adolescents. *Youth & Society, 34*(2), 172–194.

Lueck, K., & Wilson, M. (2009). Acculturative stress in Asian immigrants: The impact of social and linguistic factors. *International Journal of Intercultural Relations, 34*(1), 47–57.

Luthar, S. S. (1993). Annotation: Methodological and conceptual issues on research on childhood resilience, *Journal of Child Psychology and Psychiatry, 34*, 441–453.

Luthar, S. S. & Ziglar E. (1991). Vulnerability and competence: A review of research on resilience in childhood. *American Journal of Orthopsychiatry, 61*, 6–22.

Markovitzky, G., & Mosek, A. (2005). The role of symbolic resources in coping with immigration. *Journal of Ethnic and Cultural Diversity in Social Work: Innovation in Theory, Research, and Practice, 14,* 145–158.

Massinga, R., & Pecora, P. J. (2004). Providing better opportunities for older children in the child welfare system. *The Future of Children, 14*(1), 151–173.

Mayda, A. M. (2004). *Who is against immigration? A cross-country investigation of individual attitudes towards immigrants.* Working Papers, Gueconwpa 05–05–10. Washington, DC: Georgetown University Department of Economics.

Mazumdar, S., & Mazumdar, S. (2008a). Hinduism in America. In D. Cush, C. Robinson, & M. York (Eds.), *Encyclopedia of Hinduism*(pp. 23–33). New York: Routledge.

Mazumdar, S., & Mazumdar, S. (2008b). Religion, immigration, and home-making in diaspora: Hindu space in southern California. *Journal of Environmental Psychology, 29,* 256–266.

McEwen, B. (2002). *The end of stress as we know it.* Washington, DC: Joseph Henry.

Miller, R. M. (1977). Introduction. In R. M. Miller & T. D. Manzik (Eds.), *Immigrants and religion in urban America.* Philadelphia, PA: Temple University Press.

Monforti, J. L., & Sanchez, G. R. (2010). The politics of perception: An investigation of the presence and sources of perceptions of internal discrimination among Latinos. *Social Science Quarterly, 91*(1), 245–265.

Moradi, B., & Risco, C. (2006). Perceived discrimination experiences and mental health of Latina/o American persons. *Journal of Counseling Psychology, 53,* 411–421.

Morgan M. L., (2007). International comparisons of resilience in Mexican national and Mexican immigrant populations

(Doctoral dissertation). *Dissertation Abstracts International, 67,* 9-B.

Morrison, G. M., Robertson, L., Laurie, B., & Kelly, J. (2002). Protective factors related to antisocial behavior trajectories. *Journal of Clinical Psychology, 58*(3), 277–290.

Mossakowski, K. N. (2007). Are immigrants healthier?: The case of depression among Filipino Americans. *Social Psychology Quarterly, 70*(3), 290–304.

Moyerman, D. R., & Forman, B. D. (1992). Acculturation and adjustment: A meta-analytic study. *Hispanic Journal of Behavioral Science, 14*(2), 163–200.

Mulder, T. J., Hollmann, F. W., Lollock, L. R., Cassidy, R. C., Costanzo, J. M., & Baker, J. D. (2001). U.S. Census Bureau measurement of net international migration to the United States: 1990–2000. Washington, DC : Population Division U.S. Census Bureau . http://www.census.gov/population .

Noguera, P. (2006). Latino youth: Immigration, education, and the future. *Latino Studies, 4,* 313–320.

O'Leary, V. E. (1998). Strength in the face of adversity: Individual and social thriving. *Journal of Social Issues, 54,* 425–446.

Olivo, S. M. C. (2007). The effects of a culturally-adapted social-emotional learning curriculum on social emotional and academic outcomes of Latino immigrant high school students (Doctoral dissertation). *Dissertation Abstracts International Section A: Humanities and Social Sciences, 68*(8-A)

Ong, A. D., Bergeman, C. S., Bisconti, T. L., & Wallace, K. A. (2006). Psychological resilience, positive emotions, and successful adaptation to stress in later life. *Journal of Personality and Social Psychology, 91*(4), 730–749.

Ornelas, I. J., Perreira, K. M., Beeber, L., & Maxwell, L. (2009). Qualitative perspectives of Mexican immigrant mothers. *Journal of Family Issues, 30*(11), 1556–1575.

Padilla, A. M. (2006). Bicultural social development. *Hispanic Journal of Behavioral Sciences, 28*(4), 467.

Padilla, A. M., Lindholm, K., Chen, A., Duran, R., Hakuta, K., Lambert, W., & Tucker, G. R. (1991). The English-only movement: Myth, reality, and implications for psychology. *American Psychologist, 46,* 120–130.

Padilla, A. M., & Perez, W. (2003). Acculturation, social identity and social cognition: A new perspective. *Hispanic Journal of Behavioral Sciences, 25,* 35–55.

Pargament, K. I., Smith, B. W., Koenig, H. G., & Perez, L. (1998). Patterns of positive and negative religious coping with major life stressors. *Journal for the Scientific Study of Religion, 37,* 710–724.

Parra-Cardona, J. R., Bullock, L. A., Imig, D. R., Villaruel, F. A., & Gold, S. G. (2006). "Trabajando duro todos los dias": Learning from the life experiences of Mexican-Origin Migrant Families. *Family Relations, 55,* 361–375.

Parra-Cardona, J. R., Cordova, D., Holtrop, K., Villaruel, F. A., & Wieleng, E. (2008). Shared ancestry, evolving stories: Similar and contrasting life experiences described by foreign born and U.S. born Latino parents. *Family Process, 47*(2), 157–172.

Partida, Y. (2007). Addressing language barriers: Building response capacity for a changing nation; Hablamos Juntos II—Language policy and practice in healthcare. *Society of General Internal Medicine, 22,* 347–349.

Pascoe, E. A., & Richman, L. S. (2009). Perceived discrimination and health: A meta-analytic review. *Psychological Bulletin, 135*(4), 531–554.

Passel, J. (2005). *Estimates of the size and characteristics of the undocumented population. A Pew Research Center report.* Washington, DC: Pew Hispanic Center.

Passel, J., & Cohn, D. (2009). *Mexican immigrants: How many come? How many leave?*A Pew Research Center Report. Washington, DC: Pew Hispanic Center.

Pew Hispanic Center. (2009a). *Modes of entry for the unauthorized migrant population.* Retrieved from http://pewhispanic.org/files/factsheets/pdf

Pew Hispanic Center. (2009b). *Muslims widely seen as facing discrimination.* Retrieved from http://www.people-press.org/2009/09/09/muslims-widely-seen-as-facing-discrimination/

Portes, A. (1984). The rise of ethnicity: Determinants of ethnic perceptions among Cuban exiles in Miami. *American Sociological Review, 49,* 383–397.

Portes, A., & Rumbaut, R., (1990). *Immigrant America: A portrait.* Berkeley: University of California Press.

Portes, A., & Rumbaut, R. (2006). *Immigrant America: A portrait*(3rd. ed.). Berkeley: University of California Press.

Pumariega, A. J, Rothe, E. & Pumariega, J. B. (2005). Mental health of immigrants and refugees. *Community Mental Health Journal, 41,* 581–597.

Ramirez, A., Lumadue, C., & Wooten, H. (2007). Spiritual well-being and psychological well-being in Mexican-American Catholics. *Journal of Professional Counseling: Practice, Theory, and Research, 35*(2), 46–61.

Redfield, R., Linton, R., & Herskovits, M. J. (1936). Memorandum for the study of acculturation: Committee report to the Social Science Council. *American Anthropologist, 38,* 149–152.

Reiboldt, W., & Goldstein, A. E. (2000). Positive coping strategies among immigrant Cambodian families: An ethnographic case study. *Family and Consumer Sciences Research Journal, 28,* 489–513.

Rew, L., Thomas, N., Horner, S. D., Resnick, M. D., & Beuhring, T. (2001). Correlates of recent suicide attempts in a Triethnic Group of adolescents. *Journal of Nursing Scholarship, 33*(4), 361–367.

Riddick, S. (1998). Improving access for limited English-speaking consumers: A review of strategies in health care settings. *Journal of Health Care for the Poor and Underserved, 9,* 40–61.

Rivera-Ledesma A. & Montero M. (2005). Espiritulalidad y religiosidad en adultos mayors mexicanos. *Salud Mental, 28,* 51–58.

Robila, M. (2007). Eastern European immigrants in the United States: A socio-demographic profile. *The Social Science Journal, 44,* 113–125.

Rodriguez, N., Mira, B. C., Paez, N. D., & Myers, H. F. (2007). Exploring the complexities of familism and acculturation: Central constructs for people of Mexican origin. *American Journal of Community Psychology, 39,* 61–77.

Ross-Sheriff, F. & Husain, A. (2004). South Asian Muslim children and families. In R. Fong. (Ed.), *Culturally competent practice with immigrant and refugee children and families* (pp. 163–182). New York: Guilford.

Rudmin, F. W. (2006). Debate in science: The case of acculturation. In *AnthroGlobe Journal.* Retrieved from http://malinowski.kent.ac.uk/docs/rudminf_acculturation_061204.pdf

Ruiz, R. (1981). Cultural and historical perspective in counseling Hispanics. In D. Sue (Ed.), *Counseling the culturally different* (pp. 186–215). New York: Wiley.

Ruiz, R., & Padilla, A. (1977). Counseling Latinos. *Personnel and Guidance Journal, 55,* 401–108.

Rumbaut, R. (2000). Profiles in resilience: Educational achievement and ambition among children of immigrants in Southern California. In Taylor, R. & Wang, M. (Eds.) *Resilience Across Contexts: Family, Work, Culture and Community*. New Jersey: Lawrence Erlbaum and Associates.

Rutter, M. (1987). Psychosocial resilience and protective mechanisms. In J. Rolf, A. Masten, D. Cichetti, K. Nuechterlein, & S. Weintraub (Eds.), *Risk and protective factors in the development of psychopathology* (pp. 181–214). New York: Cambridge University Press.

Ryder, A. G., Alden, L., & Paulhus, D. L. (2000). Is acculturation unidimensional or bidimensional? A head-to-head comparison in the prediction of personality, self-identity, and adjustment. *Journal of Personality and Social Psychology, 79*, 49–65.

Salgado de Snyder, V. (1987). Mexican immigrant women: The relationship of ethnic royalty and social support of acculturative stress and depressive symptomatology. *Spanish Speaking Mental Health Research Center, 22*, 73.

Sam, D. L., Vedder, P., Ward, C., & Hoarenczyk, G. (2006). Psychological and sociocultural adaptation of immigrant youth. In J. W. Berry, J. S. Phinney, D. L. Sam, & P. Vedder. (Eds.), *Immigrant youth in cultural transition: Acculturation, identity and adaptation across national contexts* (pp. 117–141). London: Erlbaum.

Santisteban, D. A., Dillon, F., Mena, M. P., Estrada, Y., & Vaughan, E. L., (2005). Psychiatric, family, and ethnicity-related factors that can impact treatment utilization among Hispanic substance-abusing adolescents. *Journal of Social Work Practice in the Addictions, 5*(1–2), 133–155.

Schlosser, L., Foley, P., Stein, E. P., & Holmwood, J. R. (2010). Why does counseling psychology exclude religion? A content analysis and methodological critique. In J. Ponterotto, M. Casas, L. Suzuki, & C. M. Alexander(Eds.), (pp. 453–466). *Handbook of multicultural counseling* (3rd ed). Thousand Oaks, CA: Sage.

Segal, U., Mayadas, N., & Elliott, D. (Eds.). (2010). *Immigration worldwide: Policies, practices, and trends*. New York: Oxford University Press.

Sellers, R. M & Shelton, J. N. (2003) The role of racial identity in perceived racial discrimination. *Journal of Personality and Social Psychology, 8*, 1079–1092.

Selye, H. (1956). *The stress of life*. New York: McGraw-Hill.

Short, K. H., & Johnston, C. (1997). Stress, maternal distress, and children's adjustment following immigration: The buffering role of social support. *Journal of Consulting and Clinical Psychology, 65*, 494–503.

Stephan, W. G., Renfro, C. L., Esses, V. M., Stephan, C. W., & Martin, T. (2005). The effects of feeling threatened on attitudes toward immigrants. *International Journal of Intercultural Relations, 29*, 1–19.

Suárez-Orozco, C., & Suarez-Orozco, M. (1995a). *Transformations: Immigration, family life, and achievement motivation among Latino adolescents*. Palo Alto, CA: Stanford University Press.

Suárez-Orozco, C., & Suarez-Orozco, M. (1995b). Migration: Generational discontinuities and the making of Latino identities. In L. Romanucci-Ross & G. A. DeVos (Eds.), *Ethnic identity: Creation, conflict, and accommodation* (3rd ed., pp. 321–347). Walnut Creek, CA: AltaMira Press.

Tadmor, C. T., & Tetlock, P. E. (2006). Biculturalism: A model of the effects of second-culture exposure on acculturation and integrative complexity. *Journal of Cross-Cultural Psychology, 37*(2), 173.

Thompson, C. P., Anderson, L. P & Bakeman, R. A. (2000). Effects of racial socialization and racial identity on acculturative stress in African American college students. *Cultural Diversity and Ethnic Minority Psychology, 6*, 196–210.

Um, C. C., & Dancy, B. L.(1999). Relationship between coping strategies and depression among employed Korean immigrant wives. *Issues in Mental Health Nursing, 20*, 485–494.

US Census. (2009). *Annual social and economic supplement: Current population survey*. Washington, DC: US Census.

US Census. (2010). *Race and Hispanic origin of the foreign-born population in the United States: 2007*. American Community Surveys, ACS-11. Washington, DC: US Census.

U.S. Department of State. (2010). Types of immigration. Retrieved from http://travel.state.gov/visa/immigrants/types/types_1323.html

Vega, W.A., Kolody, B., Valle, R., & Hough, R. (1986). Depressive symptoms and their correlates among immigrant Mexican women in the United States. *Social Science and Medicine, 22*, 645–652.

Vera, E., Caldwell, J., Clarke, M., Gonzales, R., Morgan, M., & West, M. (2007). The Choices Program: Multisystemic interventions for enhancing personal and academic effectiveness of urban adolescents of color. *The Counseling Psychologist, 35*, 779–796.

Wagnild, G. M., & Young, H. M. (1993). Development and psychometric evaluation of the resilience scale. *Journal of Nursing Measurement, 1*, 165–173.

Walsh, F. (2007). Traumatic loss and major disasters: Strengthening family and community resilience. *Family Process, 46*, 207–227.

Wang, M., & Gordon, E. (Eds.). (1994). *Risk and resilience in inner-city America: Challenges and prospects*. Hillsdale, NJ: Erlbaum.

Welsh, E. A., & Brodsky, A. E. (2010). After every darknessis light: Resilient Afghan women coping with violence and immigration. *Asian American Journal of Psychology, 1*, 163–174.

Werner, E., & Smith, R. (1992). *Overcoming the odds*. Ithaca, NY: Cornell University.

Williams, C. L., & Berry, J. W. (1991). Primary prevention of acculturative stress among refugees: Application of psychological theory and practice. *American Psychologist, 46*, 632–641.

Withers, G., & Russell, J. (2001). *Educating for resilience: Prevention and intervention strategies for young people at risk*. Melbourne, Victoria: Australian Council for Educational Research.

Wyman, P.A., Cowen, E. L., Work, W. C. & Kerley, J. H. (1993). The role of children's future expectations in self-system functioning and adjustment to life stress: A prospective study of urban at-risk children, *Development and Psychopathology, 5*, 649–661.

Yakushko, O. (2009). Xenophobia: Understanding the roots and consequences of negative attitudes towards immigrants. *The Counseling Psychologist, 37*, 36–66.

Yakushko, O., & Morgan, M. L. (in press). Immigration. In N. Fouad & J. Carter (Eds.), *Handbook of counseling psychology*. Washington, DC: American Psychological Association.

Yeh, C. J., Arora, A. K., Inose, M., Okubo, Y., Li, R. H., & Greene, P. (2003). The cultural adjustment and mental health of Japanese immigrant youth. *Adolescence, 38*(151), 481–500.

Yoon, E., & Lee, R. M. (2010). Importance of social connectedness as a moderator in Korean immigrants' subjective well-being. *Asian American Journal of Psychology, 1*, 93–105.

CHAPTER

23 Promoting Positive Identity of African American Girls

Anita Jones Thomas, Suzette L. Speight, Laura D. Turner-Essel, *and* Rabiatu Barrie

Abstract

African American girls face significant barriers to the development and maintenance of a positive, healthy, and affirming identity. They are often placed at risk due to psychosocial factors, as well as their devalued status as both ethnic minorities and women. While psychologists have explored the influence of racial and gender identity development as separate processes, less attention has been placed on gendered racial identity development or the promotion of resilience of African American girls. This chapter describes the developmental process of girls, focusing on the role of oppression and stereotypical images. Factors that influence identity development including racial socialization and Africultural values are presented. The chapter includes an overview of prevention programs that foster a positive sense of self for girls, and ends with directions for research and clinical practice.

Key Words: African American girls, identity development, racial identity, gender identity, rites of passages programs, critical consciousness

I am a Black girl. My life is important. I am the continuation of a history, legacy and tradition of powerful people. The lives of my fore mothers now have meaning through me. I stand today because of who they were .... I am a black girl. I know my worth. I hold myself in high esteem because I value who I am. I treat myself with loving care, respect and honor. I honor and hold sacred my mind, my body and my heart .... I am a Black girl. I have a vision for myself and a vision for my life. It is a vision anchored in love, propelled by integrity and advanced by faith. I am committed to learning how I can improve all aspects of myself so that I will be the best me I can be .... I am a Black girl, I say it, therefore, I am it!... I AM confidence in action!... I AM fearless and free!... I AM inspiration unfolding! I AM Pure Love! I am a Black girl and I Rock!

From The Black Girls Rock! Pledge (Vanzant, 2010).

Whether suburban, rural, inner city, athletic, academic, thin, overweight, dark skinned, light skinned, with braids, straightened hair, or dreadlocks, raised with two parents, one parent, or a grandmother, poor, middle-class, or wealthy, girls of African descent in the United States face significant barriers to the development and maintenance of a positive, healthy and affirming identity. The Black Girls Rock! Pledge (Vanzant, 2010) encourages girls to unleash their full potential which is so often obscured, muffled, trampled, and squashed by forces both internal and external. Growing up in a society characterized by racism and sexism as an African American girl presents both challenges and opportunities.

Generally, psychology has portrayed African American youth as "at risk" due to their devalued racial status. African American girls do face a variety of psychosocial risks, including poverty, single parent status, poor academic expectations, and negative stereotypes (Christian & Barbarin, 2001). About 38% of African American children were living in poverty in 2010 (National Poverty Center, n.d.). Approximately 64% of African American homes are headed by a single parent (United States Census Bureau, 2009), making it more likely for girls to lack a significant male figure in their lives. In 2009, four in five African American teen girls were overweight or obese (Centers for Disease Control [CDC], 2010). African American adolescents account for 23% of teen births (CDC, 2010). African American girls are also frequently thought of as being in "double jeopardy" due to the intersection of gender and race. Yet for every portrait of a young African American girl "at risk" stands an African American girl who has been able to be resilient, withstanding and overcoming obstacles, quietly succeeding in her own world, without much fanfare.

On the other hand, with the presidency of Barack Obama, we are witnessing two African American girls growing up in the White House. The January 2009 *Essence* featured an article by Gwen Ifil entitled "The Malia and Sasha Effect," which was a reflection of not only how the future for Malia and Sasha Obama will be changed as they grow up in the White House, but how the future of all African American girls will change based on two new role models living in an idyllic nuclear family. The girls contradict popular media images of African American women and girls; they are not victims or "hoochie mamas, like the Black girls who shake their rumps in music videos" (p. 81). Gwen Ifil commented that her role model as a child had been a "cocoa colored doll" that she treasured. And indeed, in the 1960s and 1970s in this country, the introduction of Black dolls seemed to help girls to begin to feel more positively about themselves. But the lack of prominent media images on television, movies, and magazines left young girls feeling confused and insecure about their physical appearance and their status in this country. Kiri Davis (2005), in her award-winning video *A Girl Like Me*, replicated the famous Clark studies in which young children were given two dolls (one White, one Black) and asked a series of questions including which doll is prettier, which doll is nicer, which doll they would like to play with, and which doll was the most similar to them. The girls in the video study easily chose the White dolls as the ones who were pretty, nice, and attractive, but painstakingly chose the Black dolls as the one that looked like them. The reactions to the video suggested that although many things have changed, the pervasiveness of racism still has an influence on children. So the fact that Michelle Obama serves as an eloquent, intelligent, strong, and beautiful First Lady, raising two beautiful African American girls has stirred rejuvenation regarding identity development and the portrait of success for African American girls.

Counseling psychologists are in a unique position to use their emphasis on normative developmental processes, an ecosystemic framework, and understanding of cultural identity processes to promote optimal identity development of African American girls. This chapter will discuss the unique identity development of African American girls and adolescents, the influence of oppression on identity development, self-concept, and psychological functioning, and the role of socialization experiences (armoring) in helping girls cope with oppression and fostering positive identity development. Prevention programs that focus on Africentric principles or critical consciousness development will be summarized. The chapter will conclude with suggestions for researchers and service providers.

Positive Identity of African American Girls

What is critical in understanding identity development of African American girls is a comprehension of the intersection of cultural factors as they relate to emerging ideas of the self. Erikson (1968) suggested that identity needs to be examined in light of contexts or societal demands. Bronfenbrenner (1979) had a similar focus on the influence of contextual factors, including larger macrosystem and societal images of various social groups. For Bronfenbrenner, individual development needs to be examined within the context of proximal influences, the microsystem, which includes family, peers, neighborhoods, and schools. More distal factors (i.e., the macrosystem) influence both the individual and the immediate systems surrounding the individual, and include mass media, cultural ideology, and economic and sociopolitical systems. Yet, developmental research and theories continued to focus on universal characteristics and traits, using European standards as comparisons when race or culture was included in the analysis. The 1960s brought more of an emphasis or focus on race as central to identity development and self-concept, and the 1970s with the feminist movement brought attention to gender. It has not been until recently that people have begun to argue the importance of understanding the intersection of identities (Anderson & Collins, 2004; Cole, 2009).

Identity development is a complex process commencing during late school-age in which individuals begin to solidify their sense of self, ideals, values, and belief systems. Identity includes the integration of self-concept and self-esteem with the individual's perceptions of future development. It includes an awareness of group membership, expectations, social responsibilities, and privileges according to group membership (Spencer, 1988). For African American girls, positive identity should include an acceptance of personal traits and characteristics, positive racial and gender identity, and the intersection of other cultural variables, including class and sexual orientation.

Racial Identity Development

African Americans must explore the question "Who am I as an African American?" as part of the process of developing racial identity (Tatum, 1997). Racial identity has been defined as the part of an individual's self-concept or sense of self that is tied to group membership status. Early models of racial identity for African Americans postulated that individuals move from a preawareness of race and its importance, to an internalization of cultural values and norms following a significant racial encounter and intellectual and psychological exploration of race (Cross, 1995). Later models were developed that focused on contextual factors related to racial identity. For example, the multidimensional model of Black identity holds that race as a component of identity is both a situationally influenced and stable property of the individual (Sellers, Smith, Shelton, Rowley, & Chavous, 1998). From this perspective, racial identity is dependent not just on the individual's perception of Blackness, but also on perceptions of the group as a whole and knowledge of how other's perceive Blacks as a group (private and public regard). Racial identity also is influenced by the importance of race at a particular time (centrality). Racial ideology in the model is associated with values and beliefs on norms for the group (Sellers et al., 1998).

Research has been conducted using both models. Despite some criticism of the psychometric properties of scales associated with racial identity measures, research has consistently found a relationship with racial identity and youth outcomes. Research on racial identity in African American youth suggests that positive racial identity serves as a protective factor for positive youth outcomes. Positive racial identity is related to positive self-esteem (Buckley & Carter, 2005; Greene, Way, & Pahl, 2006; Phinney, Chavira, & Williamson, 1992; Rowley, Sellers, Chavous, & Smith, 1998), and promotes psychological well-being and reduces psychological symptoms, particularly depression and anxiety (Sellers, Copeland-Linder, Martin, & Lewis, 2006). Positive racial identity serves as a protective factor for experiences of oppression (Greene et al., 2006). Racial identity has also been studied in its relationship to academic performance. Children who adopt Africentric values have more competitive academic attitudes than children who do not endorse such values (Jagers, Smith, Mock, & Dill, 1997). When examining children who report experiences of discrimination, those who have a more positive racial identity and feel more connected to their culture have better academic achievement.

Gender Identity Development

African American girls similarly need to develop a positive gender identity or sense of womanhood. Gender refers to psychological, social, and cultural features and characteristics associated with "male" or "female" (Gilbert & Scher, 1999). Gender, like race, is socially constructed, based on interactive social processes. Gender socialization occurs in a cultural context shaped in part by race and socioeconomic status, so African American girls need to deconstruct experiences of sexism and gendered oppression in forming their self-concept.

Models of gender identity are similar to racial/ethnic identity models, suggesting that children and adolescents move from having superficial or naive beliefs regarding gender, gender role expectations, and gender identity, to developing more sophisticated comprehension of the sociopolitical connotations of gender.

Downing and Roush (1985) developed a model of feminist identity development based on the Cross (1971) model of racial identity development. The first stage, passive acceptance, is characterized by a lack of awareness of inequalities and gender-based oppression. In the second stage, revelation, the person becomes aware of gender based oppression. In the third stage, embeddedness-emanation, the person begins to reflect on gendered identity status and immerses herself in gender-based activities, followed by the fourth stage, synthesis, which includes a more sophisticated exploration and integration of gender identity status and the achievement of balance. The fifth and final stage, active commitment, includes the attempts to remove oppression through activities. Helms (1990) developed a four-stage model of womanist identity to describe the experiences of women of color. In the first stage, preencounter, individuals have traditional gender roles and behave in ways that seem to devalue women. The second stage, encounter, occurs when individuals have experiences that cause them to question previously held beliefs or gender role expectations. It is in this stage that women begin to question gender as a social construction. In the third stage, immersion/emersion, idealization of women occurs, as well as rejection of traditional or dominant definitions of women, and later is characterized by an exploration of positive values of womanhood. Finally, in internalization, the new definition of womanhood is incorporated into self-concept. Research in adults finds relationships between womanist identity and self-esteem, perceptions of environmental bias, and gender role expectations (Carter & Parks, 1996; Ossana, Helms, & Leonard, 1992).

Hoffman (2006) expanded the notion of gender identity to also include the concepts of gender self-confidence and gender self-concept. Gender self-confidence is the extent to which an individual believes that he/she has met personal standards for masculinity or femininity. Gender self-confidence is grounded in gender identity, and also includes gender self-definition, the level of salience of gender within identity, and gender self-acceptance, comfort level with gender. Gender self-concept is defined by Hoffman as the broad notion of oneself as a man or woman. Research suggests that these concepts are related to feminist and womanist identity development (Hoffman, 2006).

Research on gender concerns in adolescents tends to center on gender role expectations and the effect of gender and biological components on a variety of outcomes. Research on gender identity does suggest that boys and girls have different experiences that influence outcomes. Gender identity and gender role seem to be related to self-esteem and peer acceptance (Egan & Perry, 2001). For example, gender and racial status influences achievement and academic performance and academic efficacy and stereotypes of academic performance (i.e., Davis, 2006; Shih, Pittinsky, & Ambady, 1999; Steele & Ambady, 2006). Davis speculates that as identity changes and develops, African American boys' connection to school and achievement changes. Asian American women score differently on tests in which stereotype threat is stimulated when the target is race versus gender (Shih, Pittinsky, & Ambady, 1999).

Gendered Racial Identity

There is a growing recognition that the constructs of gender and race are intertwined and influence psychological functioning in differing ways (Thomas & King, 2007). As African American girls develop their identity and gender-role perspectives, they must determine how to reconcile negative images and stereotypes and experiences of oppression into their identities and self-concepts. Being African American and female in a society that devalues both of these social identities subjects African American women and girls to a unique, often hostile social context within which one must develop and maintain a positive sense of self. One of the key features of any system of oppression is its internalization by the targets. "The dominant group's stereotyped images of the target group become internalized by target group members as they search for an identity" (Speight, 2007, p. 129). Historically, social and media images of African American women have had a profound effect on the manner in which they are perceived and perceive themselves, shaping their expected roles in society (Stephens & Phillips, 2003).

There are three stereotypes of African American women stemming from slavery: Mammy, Sapphire, and Jezebel (Mitchell & Herring, 1998). Mammy, historically a house slave, is depicted as an obese, dark-skinned woman with broad features who worked in the master's house, typically serving as nanny, housekeeper, and cook. She was expected to take care of the needs of others, often to the neglect of her own needs. Mammy was never seen by Whites as threatening; instead she was perceived of as nurturing, and displaying selfless devotion to others. Sapphire, the second image, references a slave legend of a slave who poisoned her master, and is strongly associated with the character from the *Amos and Andy* radio and television show of the 1940s and 1950s. She is perceived of as nagging, manipulative and controlling of men, harsh, loud, and argumentative. The perceptions of African American women from this character include being arrogant, controlling, loud, hostile, obnoxious, and never satisfied. The stereotype of Jezebel is a consequence of the sexual exploitation and victimization of African American women during slavery. Jezebel is seen as seductive, manipulative and unable to control sex drives (Mitchell & Herring, 1998). African American women are often viewed as promiscuous, loose, immoral, sexually aggressive, and lacking sexual restraint (Jones & Shorter-Gooden, 2003).

Research suggests that the positive functioning of African American women, particularly self-esteem, is negatively influenced by the endorsement of such images (Thomas, Witherspoon, & Speight, 2004). According to Stephens and Phillips (2003,

2005), these images have transformed into the current Jezebel permutations depicted in music videos by freaks, gold diggers, divas, and baby mamas. Although the historical images continue to exploit the sexuality of African American women (Stephens & Phillips, 2005), more modern media images may be interpreted by young women as empowering, as the women manipulate men through sexuality. Research suggests that while young women are aware of and can name the historical images, they are more likely to endorse the stereotypes of the sexualized depictions in hip-hop and rap music videos (Thomas, Hacker, & Hoxha, 2011; Townsend, Thomas, Jackson, & Nielands, 2010), thus supporting the notion of the modern Jezebel image. The modern Jezebel image is positively associated with risky sexual behaviors, and colorism (Townsend et al., 2010).

Macrosystem influences of African American girls, particularly media images, present girls a limited perspective on identity development. Girls are left with confronting and challenging stereotypical roles or succumbing to them. Many African American women and girls cope by adopting the Strong Black Woman image (Beauboeuf-Lafontant, 2009). In fact, African American women are socialized to appear strong, tough, resilient, and self-sufficient (Shorter-Gooden & Jackson, 2000). Research has suggested that African American girls have been socialized to be independent, with an emphasis on self-determination, and the importance of education (Bowman & Howard, 1985; Thomas & King, 2007) in order to promote resilience over negative stereotypes. Counseling psychologists need to include a contextual view of identity development when working with African American girls. Promoting positive racial identity has to be considered in the backdrop of oppression and negative images.

Promoting Positive Identity

There are many factors that contribute to the promotion of positive identity development of African American girls, which may be integrated into prevention programs. Positive identity development should help girls to embrace traditional Africentric values. Constantine, Alleyne, Wallace, and Franklin-Jackson (2006) found that girls who endorsed Africentric beliefs also had higher levels of self-esteem. Gendered racial socialization is an effective tool to encourage identity development. Research has suggested that African American girls have been socialized to be independent, with an emphasis on self-determination, and education (Bowman & Howard, 1985; Thomas & King, 2007) as a way to promote resilience over the oppression of the negative stereotypes and images.

Africultural Values

It is important to understand the legacy of African culture on the functioning of African American girls. Boykin and Toms (1985) outlined nine African cultural values: harmony, spirituality, communalism, movement, verve, expressive individualism, affect, oral tradition, and the social time perspective. Harmony includes a sense of connection and attachment of all living beings, and is linked to spirituality and religion. African spirituality purports that all beings have dignity and worth, and honors the connections between all things, both animate and inanimate. Communalism is the importance of links between people, families, and groups, stressing the well-being of the group in individual functioning such that behaviors and choices are seen as a reflection of the group. Movement and verve refer to spontaneity of movement and the importance of rhythm. Expressive individualism and affect refer to the significance of self-expression. The oral tradition includes the importance of storytelling and passing down oral histories. Social time perspective focuses on the importance of interpersonal relationships within dimensions of time and space.

Racial Socialization

Racial socialization is the process of raising children to have a healthy and positive self-concept within an oppressive society. Research has shown that racial socialization enables African American youth to cope with discrimination (Stevenson, 1997), making it important to understand the role of racial socialization. Racial socialization processes have been linked to outcomes in children and adolescents (Hughes et al., 2006), and research has suggested that practices and messages were related to racial identity attitudes (McHale et al., 2006), self-esteem, depression and anxiety, and anger management, along with school efficacy and achievement in children and adolescents (Constantine & Blackmon, 2002; Marshall, 1995). More implicit forms of racial socialization were linked to positive outcomes for African American children and adolescents. Caughy, Nettles, O'Campo, and Lohrfink (2006) have found that children had greater cognitive competence with parents whose home included African American culture in the form of magazines, artwork, toys, and clothing. Research on racial socialization has suggested that parental socialization can reduce negative affective experiences including depression and anger. Specifically, children socialized in an environment of cultural pride were less likely to be depressed, regardless of gender (Davis & Stevenson, 2006). Stevenson, Herrero-Taylor, Cameron, and Davis (2002) have discussed how cultural socialization can minimize anger and violence in African American youth.

Research has shown that while African American teenagers receive racial socialization messages from their parents, those messages are different for boys and for girls. For example, boys tend to receive more messages on overcoming racism whereas girls receive more messages pertaining to the pursuit of education, premarital sex and relationships with men, independence, and physical beauty (Thomas & Speight, 1999). Girls are socialized to be strong, and are provided with "armoring," the ability to withstand the "double jeopardy" status of being African American and female (Edmondson Bell & Nkomoa, 1998). The emphasis placed on self-determination and assertiveness reflects the image of the strength of Black women. Shorter-Gooden and Washington (1996) propose girls with the sense of strength are psychologically healthier than girls who do not have the sense of strength. Counseling psychologists must address contextual factors when providing services to promote positive identity development and foster resilience of African American girls. Africentric messages that affirm and promote resilience need to be incorporated into preventive services. Counseling psychologists should also consider themselves as agents of change and incorporate positive racial socialization messages into their work.

Prevention Programs

Successful programs need to incorporate Africentric values as a way to ground girls in an affirming context for growth. Programs that confront negative societal images and encourage girls to embrace cultural heritage and engage in self-determination are particularly useful. Programs also need to help girls to engage in "armoring" to buffer against damaging messages, or engage in critical consciousness to critically reflect on their experiences. We will summarize prevention programs for African American girls in what is by no means an exhaustive list of services.

Rites of Passage Programs

In addition to racial socialization from parents, African American girls can be strengthened through supportive programs located within the community. One type of program that appears especially helpful is the "rite of passage." Rites of passage programs involve ritual events that mark individuals' progress from one status to another (Lewis, 1988) reflecting values and beliefs emphasized within a specific culture. Thus, within the African American communities, these programs often serve to foster self-knowledge; encourage appreciation of family, cultural background, and community; increase practical work and study habits; encourage creative self-expression; and foster appropriate understanding of sexuality and issues of sexual health (Lewis, 1988). For African American girls, they also facilitate the navigation of obstacles to positive development through the rejection of racial and gender stereotypes (Rasbury, 2004).

Descriptions of several rites of passage programs for African American girls suggest common characteristics rooted in Africultural values. Many draw from the African tradition of simultaneous and more holistic attention to the mind, body, and spirit. For example, the Sisters in Sisterhood Program in Brooklyn, New York, conducts a rites of passage program for girls ages 8 to 19, which involves performing ritual dances, researching family roots, and practicing meditation (Rasbury, 2004). Other programs (e.g., Candace Rites of Passage Program and the Nehanda Rites of Passage Program) explicitly base their curriculum on the Nguzo Saba, the seven principles (e.g., *Umoja* meaning unity, *Nia* meaning purpose, *Kuumba* meaning creativity) derived from ancient African civilizations (Karenga, 1998). Thus the social, emotional, and cultural development of African American girls form the foundation of these community-based efforts. As such, these programs are thought to be universally beneficial to African American girls as they develop and review their identities throughout childhood and adolescence (Lewis, 1988). Exposure to the concepts embedded in rites of passage serves to anchor girls in the positive values of their culture, an important benefit for all girls in the earlier developmental stages of life. Beyond the fact that many rites programs target specific age groups, they are generally available to support the developmental processes of all girls of African descent.

Rites programs also tend to emphasize same-gender mentorship and the importance of bonding with one another as a female support network. "Sisterhood" is very important, and the prominence of Black female leadership models is thought to have a liberating quality for young girls. In the Candace

Rites of Passage Program for African American girls and women, based in Chico, California, facilitators discussed African female leaders during various segments with participants in order to foster a sense of personal empowerment and identification with cultural history (Monges, 1999).

An emphasis on interpersonal relationships, including mother-daughter and male-female relationships, is a recurring theme in such programs. The Sisterhood Agenda, based in North Carolina, brings same-age groups of girls together under the mentorship of an older member of the community in order to explore the meaning of healthy relationships, sexual health, and peer pressure. The Nehanda Rites of Passage Program in New Jersey uses an African dance and arts–based program to prepare girls for their teenage and adult years, in large part by encouraging them to view themselves in ways than run counter to oversexualized media images of Black women (Rasbury, 2004).

Though several rites of passage programs exist for African American girls and women around the country, there is little empirical data found in the literature regarding the efficacy of these programs. Some empirical research, but still very little, can be found regarding rites of passage programs for African American boys and men (Brookins, 1996; Gavazzi, Alford, & McKenry, 1996; Harvey & Hill, 2004). However, the data that do exist suggest that such programs have a positive effect. Participants in culturally relevant rites of passage programs have been reported to be less sexually active (Rasbury, 2004) and to have reduced numbers of school absences, tardiness, and suspensions (We-Win Institute, 2007). Despite these encouraging findings, it is critical that more empirical studies be conducted on these programs in order to establish their efficacy as promoting positive identity development of interventions for African-American girls.

In addition to rites of passage programs, several school-based programs targeting Black girls have emerged in recent years. Like the rites of passages programs, these interventions emphasize Africultural values, same-gender mentorship, and interpersonal relationships. Fortunately, there has been slightly more empirical attention paid to such programs in the psychological literature. One example is the Sisters of the Nia program, which focuses specifically on enhancing ethnic identity, androgynous gender roles, and mutually positive peer relationships among adolescent Black girls (Belgrave et al., 2004). The 10-week Virginia-based after-school program features a curriculum encompassing African culture, relationship issues, personal hygiene, and critical consciousness. The role of *mzees* (respected elders) is highlighted, with Black female staff members serving as models of female power. Rituals rooted in African traditions, such as the pouring of libations and the recitation of African proverbs, are practiced in order to increase participants' connection to their African heritage. Each group of participants is oriented to the sister-like culture of the program before exploring other topics so that trusting relationships are developing throughout the experience. A between-subjects, pretest/posttest evaluation of Sisters of the Nia conducted with 59 Black girls (age range 11–13) demonstrated significant increases in ethnic identity among participants, but only a marginally significant increase in androgynous gender roles and a marginally significant decrease in relational aggression (Belgrave et al., 2004). Future research with this and similar programs may need to rely on larger sample sizes in order to accurately assess the effectiveness of such interventions.

The Young Empowered Sisters (YES!) Program is another school-based intervention that utilizes African-based principles (Nguzo Saba) and rituals in order to instill a healthy cultural identity and promote particular African values, such as a collectivist orientation. A unique aspect of this program, which targets Midwestern high school girls of African descent, is its more overt focus on raising critical consciousness, increasing awareness of racism, and encouraging participation in liberatory activism. Paulo Freire's concept of *conscientization* serves as one of the pillars of the program's overarching philosophy (Thomas, Davidson, & McAdoo, 2008). Over 70 girls (average age of 14) participated in a between-groups experimental evaluation of the program, with intervention and control group members matched on grade level, age, GPA, and income. Intervention group members participated in the YES! program for 10 weeks during the school day, while control group members underwent their usual daily school routine. Results of pre- and posttests indicated that participants scored significantly higher on Black ethnic identity, racism awareness, collectivist orientation, and Africentric values than did nonparticipants. Also of interest were their significantly higher scores on measures of both *intent* to engage in activism, and their actual participation in liberatory activism efforts (Thomas et al., 2008).

While more empirical data is needed regarding the efficacy of school-based interventions for Black girls, these two programs serve as exemplars for administrators hoping to incorporate more identity-based interventions for their African American female students. Future research is needed to determine the ultimate impact of such interventions on other important outcomes such as school attendance, academic performance, and interpersonal functioning.

Future Directions

The devalued status, poverty rates, teen pregnancy, and other environmental factors that African Americans girls face warrant their designation as an at-risk group. Yet despite the environmental stressors and barriers, many African American girls are resilient, become successful adult members of society, and maintain positive identity from adolescence through adulthood. Positive identity development that is fostered by socialization processes is essential to the resilience of African American girls. Prevention services are needed to promote positive identity development. Counseling psychologists have begun to address the needs with prevention programming centered on Africentric principles and critical consciousness. While empirical evidence supporting these programs' efficacy is sparse, the existing outcome research indicates the promise of such programs. We have summarized prevention programs that incorporate Africentric values and critical consciousness as a way of fostering positive identity development and resilience in girls.

New theoretical arguments on the importance of intersectionality in identity development will need to drive prevention services in the future. The intersectional perspective provides a holistic framework for conceptualizing social identity processes (Cole, 2009; Settles, 2006). Anderson and Collins (2004) contend that social identity categories (i.e., race, gender, class) simultaneously shape the experience of individuals. The levels of salience, importance, or meaning of one identity aspect may become more prominent at times, but generally they contribute in an overlapping and cumulative fashion to shape identity. Intersectional models help to promote salience, the level of awareness of, and the meaning or significance of multiple identity factors. While we have a better understanding of racial and gender/womanist identity development, counseling psychologists will need to lead research efforts on the role of intersectionality on identity. A better understanding of the gendered racial identity and stereotypical roles and negative images is needed, along with the relationship between identity development and psychological functioning. We clearly need more research on social class, race, and gender, along with sexual orientation. There are intragroup differences among African Americans based on social class that have implications for identity development and mental health functioning. African American lesbians may have additional layers for identity development.

The counseling psychology literature on prevention services for African American girls is limited. Counseling psychologists will need to continue to develop prevention services that are culturally relevant. Unfortunately, funding sources are often not willing to fund projects based on culture because it seems intangible. However, the limited research we have presented in this area seems promising and should be continued. We need to know more about the influence of culturally specific prevention programs on positive youth outcomes. Future research in this area should include how these interventions and prevention programs affect other outcomes such as academic achievement attitudes, interpersonal functioning, overall well-being, and life satisfaction. Also, further attention should be paid to the role that critical consciousness plays in the identity development of African American girls and if programming that focuses on the development of critical consciousness can achieve similar results as those centered on Africentric values.

There are many facets to the development of identity. Because of this it is difficult to pinpoint all areas of development that should be tackled to promote optimal development. The current work has provided a promising start, but the efforts to provide African American girls with effective programming to buffer environmental stressors must continue as this work is essential to the state of the African American community at large.

Questions for Theorists, Clinicians, and Researchers

1. What is the process of gendered racial identity development for African American girls?
2. What factors influence or hinder this process?
3. How can optimal development be promoted or fostered?
4. How is gendered racial identity related to youth outcomes, including academic performance and psychological functioning?
5. What is the role of critical consciousness or the ability to critically evaluate or deconstruct negative images on identity development?
6. How do Africentric values positively influence positive identity development?

7. What type of prevention programs are most effective in promoting positive identity development?

8. What types of community-oriented interventions will be effective in promoting positive identity development?

References

Anderson, M. L., & Collins, P. H. (2004). *Race, class, and gender: An anthology* (5th ed.). Belmont, CA: Wadsworth/Thompson.

Beauboeuf-Lafontant, T. (2009). *Behind the mask of the strong Black woman: Voice and the embodiment of a costly performance.* Philadelphia: Temple University Press.

Belgrave, F. Z., Reed, M. C., Plybon, L. C., Butler, S. C., Allison, K. W., & Davis, T. (2004). An evaluation of Sisters of Nia: A cultural program for African American girls. *Journal of Black Psychology, 30,* 329–343.

Bowman, P. J., & Howard, C. (1985). Race-related socialization, motivation, and academic achievement: A study of Black youths in three-generation families. *Journal of the American Academy of Child Psychiatry, 24,* 131–141.

Boykin, A. W., & Toms, F. D. (1985). Black child socialization: A conceptual framework. In H. McAdoo, H. Pipes, & J. L. McAdoo (Eds.), *Black children: Social, educational, and parental environments* (pp. 33–51). Thousand Oaks, CA: Sage.

Bronfenbrenner, U. (1979). *The ecology of human development.* Cambridge, MA: Harvard University Press.

Brookins, C. (1996). Promoting ethnic identity development in African American youth: The roles of rites of passage. *Journal of Black Psychology, 22*(3), 388–417.

Buckley, T. R., & Carter, R. T. (2005). Black adolescent girls: Do gender role and racial identity impact their self-esteem? *Sex Roles, 53,* 647–661.

Carter, R. T., & Parks, E. E. (1996). Womanist identity and mental health. *Journal of Counseling and Development, 74,* 484–489.

Caughy, M. O., Nettles, S. M., O'Campo, P. J., & Lohrfink, K. F. (2006) Neighborhood matters: Racial socialization of African American children. *Child Development, 77,* 1220–1236.

Centers for Disease Control (CDC). (2010). Prevalence of Obesity Among Children and Adolescents: United States, Trends 1963–1965 Through 2007–2008. Retrieved November 16, 2010 from http://www.cdc.gov/

Christian, M. D., & Barbarin, O. A. (2001). Cultural resources and psychological adjustment of African American children: Effects of spirituality and racial attribution. *Journal of Black Psychology, 27,* 43–63.

Cole, E. R. (2009). Intersectionality and research in psychology. *American Psychologist, 64,* 170–180.

Constantine, M. G., Alleyne, V. L., Wallace, B. C., & Franklin-Jackson, D. C. (2006). Africentric cultural values: Their relation to positive mental health in African American adolescent girls. *Journal of Black Psychology, 32,* 141–154.

Constantine, M. G., & Blackmon, S. M. (2002). Black adolescents' racial socialization experiences: Their relations to home, school, and peer self-esteem. *Journal of Black Studies, 32,* 322–335.

Cross, W. E., Jr. (1971). Toward a psychology of Black liberation: The Negro-to-Black conversion experience. *Black World, 20,* 13–27.

Cross, W. E. (1995). The psychology of nigrescence: Revising the Cross model. In J. G. Ponterotto, J. M. Casas, L. A. Suzuki, & C. M. Alexander (Eds.), *Handbook of multicultural counseling* (pp. 93–122). Thousand Oaks, CA: Sage.

Davis, G., & Stevenson, H. C. (2006). Racial socialization experiences and symptoms of depression among Black youth. *Journal of Child and Family Studies, 15,* 303–317.

Davis, J. E. (2006). Research at the margin: Mapping masculinity and mobility of African-American high school dropouts. *International Journal of Qualitative Studies in Education, 19,* 289–304.

Davis, K. (2005). *A girl like me.* Retrieved November 22, 2010, from http://www.mediathatmattersfest.org/watch/6/a_girl_like_me

Downing, N. E., & Roush, K. L. (1985). From passive-acceptance to active commitment: A model for feminist identity development for women. *The Counseling Psychologist, 13,* 695–709.

Edmondson Bell, E. L., & Nkomoa, S. M. (1998). Armoring: Learning to withstand racial oppression. *Journal of Comparative Family Studies, 29*(2), 285–295.

Egan, S. K., & Perry, D. G. (2001). Gender identity: A multidimensional analysis with implications for psychosocial adjustment. *Developmental Psychology, 37,* 451–463.

Erikson, E. (1968). *Identity, youth, and crisis.* New York: Norton.

Gavazzi, S. M., Alford, K. A., & McKenry, P. C. (1996). Culturally specific programs for foster care youth: The sample case of an African American rites of passage program. *Family Relations, 45*(2), 166–174.

Gilbert, L. A., & Scher, M. (1999). *Gender and sex in counseling and psychotherapy.* Boston: Allyn and Bacon.

Greene, M. L., Way, N., & Pahl, K. (2006). Trajectories of perceived adult and peer discrimination among Black, Latino, and Asian American adolescents: Patterns and psychological correlates. *Developmental Psychology, 42,* 218–238.

Harvey, A. R. & Hill, R. B. (2004). Africentric youth and family rites of passage program: Promoting resilience among at-risk African American youths. *Social Work, 49*(1), 65–74.

Helms, J. E. (1990). *"Womanist" identity attitudes: An alternative to feminism in counseling theory and research* (Unpublished manuscript). University of Maryland, College Park, MD.

Hoffman, R. M. (2006). Gender self-definition and gender self-acceptance in women: Intersections with feminist, womanist, and ethnic identities. *Journal of Counseling and Development, 84,* 358–372.

Hughes, D., Rodriguez, J., Smith, E. P., Johnson, D. J., Stevenson, H. C., & Spicer, P. (2006). Parents' ethnic-racial socialization practices: A review of research and directions for future study. *Developmental Psychology, 42,* 747–770.

Ifil, G. (2009, January). The Sasha and Malia effect. *Essence,* 81–82.

Jagers, R. J., Smith, P., Mock, L. O., & Dill, E. (1997). An Afrocultural social ethos: Component orientations and some social implications. *Journal of Black Psychology, 23,* 328–343.

Jones, C., & Shorter-Gooden, K. (2003). *Shifting: The double lives of Black women in America.* New York: Harper Collins.

Karenga, M. (1998). *The African American holiday of Kwanzaa: A celebration of family, community, and culture.* Los Angeles: University of Sankkore Press.

Lewis, M. (1988). *Herstory: Black female rites of passage.* Chicago: African American Images.

Marshall, S. (1995). Ethnic socialization of African American children: Implications for parenting, identity development, and academic achievement. *Journal of Youth and Adolescence, 24,* 377–396.

McHale, S. M., Crouter, A. C., Kim, J., Burton, L. M., Davis, K. D., Dotterer, A. M., & Swanson, D. P. (2006). Mothers' and fathers' racial socialization in African American families: Implications for youth. *Child Development, 77,* 1387–1402.

Mitchell, A., & Herring, K. (1998). *What the blues is: Black women overcoming stress and depression.* New York: Perigee.

Monges, M. M. (1999). Candace rites of passage program: The cultural context as an empowerment tool. *Journal of Black Studies, 29*(6), 827–840.

National Poverty Center (n.d.). Poverty facts. Retrieved from http://npc.umich.edu/poverty/, April 26, 2012.

Ossana, S. M., Helms, J. E., & Leonard, M. M. (1992). Do "womanist" identity attitudes influence college women's self-esteem and perceptions of environmental bias? *Journal of Counseling and Development, 70,* 402–408.

Phinney, J. S., Chavira, V., & Williamson, L. (1992). Acculturation attitudes and self-esteem among high school and college students. *Youth and Society, 23,* 299–312.

Rasbury, A. R. (2004, February 22). Africa-inspired rites lead U.S. preteens to safety. *Women's E News.* Retrieved September 14, 2010, from www.womensenews.org.

Rowley, S. J., Sellers, R. M., Chavous, T. M., & Smith, M. A. (1998). The relationship between racial identity and self-esteem in African American college and high school students. *Journal of Personality and Social Psychology, 74,* 715–724.

Sellers, R. M., Copeland-Linder, N., Martin, P. P., & Lewis, R. L. (2006). Racial identity matters: The relationship between racial discrimination and psychological functioning in African American adolescents. *Journal of Research on Adolescence, 16,* 187–216.

Sellers, R. M., Smith, M. A., Shelton, J. N., Rowley, S. A. J., & Chavous, T. M. (1998). Multidimensional model of racial identity: A reconceptualization of African American racial identity. *Personality and Social Psychology Review, 2,* 18–39.

Settles, I. H. (2006). Use of an intersectional framework to understand Black women's racial and gender identities. *Sex Roles, 54,* 589–601.

Shih, M., Pittinsky, T. L., & Ambady, N. (1999). Stereotype susceptibility: Identity salience and shifts in quantitative performance. *Psychological Science, 10,* 80–83.

Shorter-Gooden, K., & Jackson, L. C. (2000). The interweaving of cultural and intrapsychic issues in the therapeutic relationship. In L. C. Jackson & B. Greene (Eds.), *Psychotherapy with African American women: Innovations in psychodynamic perspectives* (pp. 15–32). New York: Guilford.

Shorter-Gooden, K., & Washington, N. C. (1996). Young, Black, and female: The challenge of weaving an identity. *Journal of Adolescence, 19,* 465–475.

Speight, S. L. (2007). Internalized racism: One more piece of the puzzle. *The Counseling Psychologist, 35*(1), 126–134.

Spencer, M. B. (1988). Self-concept development. In D. T. Slaughter (Ed.), *Perspectives in Black child development: New directions for child development* (pp. 59–72). San Francisco: Jossey-Bass.

Steele, J. R., & Ambady, N. (2006). "Math is Hard!" The effect of gender priming on women's attitudes. *Journal of Experimental Social Psychology, 42,* 428–436.

Stephens, D. P., & Phillips, L. D. (2003). Freaks, gold diggers, divas, and dykes: The sociohistorical development of adolescent African American women's sexual scripts. *Sexuality and Culture, 7,* 3–47.

Stephens, D. P., & Phillips, L. D. (2005). Integrating Black feminist thought into conceptual frameworks of African American adolescent women's sexual scripting processes. *Sexualities, Evolution, and Gender, 7,* 37–55.

Stevenson, H. C. (1997). Managing anger: Protective, proactive, or adaptive racial socialization identity profiles and African American manhood development. *Journal of Prevention and Intervention in the Community, 16,* 35–61.

Stevenson, H. C., Herrero-Taylor, T., Cameron, R., & Davis, G. Y. (2002). "Mitigating instigation": Cultural phenomenological influences of anger and fighting among "big-boned" and "baby-faced" African American youth. *Journal of Youth and Adolescence, 31,* 473–485.

Tatum, B. D. (1997). *Why are all the black kids sitting together in the cafeteria?* New York: Basic Books.

Thomas, A. J., Hoxha, D., & Hacker, J. (2011). Gendered racial identity development of African American girls. *Sex Roles, , 64,* 530–542.

Thomas, A. J., & King, C. T. (2007). Gendered racial socialization of African American mothers and daughters. *The Family Journal: Counseling and Therapy for Couples and Families, 15,* 137–142.

Thomas, A. J., & Speight, S. L. (1999). Racial identity and racial socialization attitudes of African American parents. *Journal of Black Psychology, 25,* 152–170.

Thomas, A. J., Witherspoon, K. M., & Speight, S. L. (2004). Toward the development of the stereotypic roles for Black women scale. *Journal of Black Psychology, 30*(3), 426–442. doi: 10.1177/0095798404266061

Thomas, O., Davidson, W., & McAdoo, H. (2008). An evaluation study of the Young Empowered Sisters (YES!) program: Promoting cultural assets among African American adolescent girls through a culturally relevant school-based intervention. *Journal of Black Psychology, 34*(3), 281–308.

Townsend, T. G., Thomas, A. J., Jackson, T. R., &. Neilands, T. B. (2010). I'm no Jezebel; I am young, gifted and Black: Identity, sexuality and Black girls. *Psychology of Women Quarterly, 34,* 273–285.

US Census Bureau. (2009). Retrieved April 25, 2012, from American Community Survey 2009, http://www.census.gov/newsroom/releases/archives/facts_for_features_special_Editions/cb11ff_01.html

Vanzant, I. (2010). The Black Girls Rock! Pledge. Retrieved April 26, 2012, fromhttp://blackgirlsrockinc.com/live/take-pledge.

We-Win Institute (2007). *Sisters of the Ankh statistics for Open Anderson School.* Retrieved from http://www.we-win.org/ritesofpassage.php

CHAPTER

24 Career Development as Prevention: Toward a Social Cognitive Model of Vocational Hope

Steven D. Brown, Kristen Lamp, Kyle J. Telander, *and* Jason Hacker

Abstract

The purpose of this chapter is to discuss the potential preventive implications of career development interventions, focusing primarily on how school dropout might be prevented and school performance might be promoted. We first use social cognitive career theory (SCCT) as a template by summarizing SCCT's models of interest development, choice, performance, and satisfaction and outlining how these models can be used to design preventively oriented career interventions. We then introduce a social cognitive model of vocational hope that integrates SCCT with other relevant literatures (e.g., causes and consequences of school dropout, multicultural psychology). We define vocational hope, present hypotheses about how it might be promoted, and outline the types of short and long-range outcomes that might be associated with changes in vocational hope.

Key Words: social cognitive career theory, SCCT, school dropout prevention, career development, vocational hope

Evidence from a variety of disciplines has converged over the past two decades on two consistent findings. First, it has become clear that adolescents with positive future outlooks are more stress resistant and resilient, engage in fewer risky antisocial behaviors, have higher educational aspirations, and complete secondary school at higher rates than do students whose futures look bleaker to them. Second, it has also become increasingly clear that having a future expectation in which completing school is necessary for later occupational attainment and life satisfaction is one of the strongest predictors of school engagement and completion rates among children and adolescents. Both findings have also found their way into the best practices literatures on positive social emotional development and school dropout prevention. Greenberg et al. (2003), for example, classified promoting positive beliefs in the future as one of the 15 core competencies in social emotional learning (SEL) interventions. Christenson and Thurlow (2004) labeled school engagement as one of several alterable variables that are critical components of school dropout prevention programs. Career development theories have also identified acquiring a future orientation as a central task of career development (Marko & Savickas, 1998: Savickas, 1991; Savickas, Silling, & Schwartz, 1984; Super, 1980).

Unfortunately, the mechanisms by which positive future expectations might be promoted and school engagement achieved are not as well articulated, especially for the poor, underresourced, and otherwise marginalized children and adolescents in today's society. The difficulties that poor children and adolescents have in creating a positive future for themselves and connecting school to future happiness and success has been well described in the vocational psychology literature by Blustein and his colleagues (e.g., Blustein, 2006; Diemer & Blustein, 2007). Diemer and Blustein (2007), for example, argued that structural barriers that limit access to opportunities (e.g., socioeconomic status, racism, sexism, classicism), reduced teacher expectations, negative family work experiences, and the disappearance of work from many urban communities can make it difficult for poor youth to see a positive future for themselves. In turn, these youth struggle to believe that completing school has real world meaning to their lives.

We suggest in this chapter that career development interventions, if well designed and implemented, may provide mechanisms for helping poor and marginalized youth develop a more positive outlook on their futures and for connecting school achievement to later occupational attainment and life satisfaction (see also Arbona, 2005; Lapan, 2004). Such interventions may also be necessary in today's bleak economic world to help all children and adolescents develop and maintain a hopeful future orientation, although our focus will be primarily on how career interventions might promote future expectations among the disadvantaged.

There is some nascent support in the literature for these hypotheses. For example, several investigators have reported positive relations between diverse students' level of involvement in career planning activities and school engagement (Kenny, Blustein, Haase, Jackson, & Perry, 2006; Kenny, Walsh-Blair, Blustein, Bempechat, & Seltzer, 2010). Others have shown that students enrolled in career and educational guidance programs or who otherwise organized their studies around career goals showed academic achievement gains during high school (Evans & Burck, 1992) and greater life satisfaction 3 years after high school (Lapan, Gysbers, & Petroski, 2001) than those who did not participate in career and educational guidance programs. Finally, Perry, Liu, and Pabian (2010) in a structural equation modeling study with a racially and ethnically diverse sample (10% Caucasian and 90% of minority backgrounds) of urban high school students found that career preparation (defined by career planning behaviors and career decision-making self-efficacy beliefs) accounted for about 32% of the variance in students' school engagement. School engagement, in turn, accounted for about 14% of the variance in school grades, and the relation between career planning and grades was fully mediated by school engagement. Although the direction of causality cannot be determined in this study, the data do suggest that promoting career planning activities and facilitating the development of career decision-making self-efficacy beliefs may have rather substantial relationships (perhaps reciprocal) with students' levels of engagement in school. However, several questions remain about how career planning might best be promoted in order to have a maximum impact on students' school engagement, school interest, school performance, school completion, and their later work and life satisfaction.

There are a variety of models and theories that can be used to design career interventions. We offer in this chapter social cognitive career theory (SCCT) as a viable possibility for several reasons. First, the theory was specifically designed to be integrative, that is, to integrate other empirically supported career theories (e.g., Holland, 1997; Dawis, 2005; Dawis & Lofquist, 1984; Vondracek, Lerner, & Schulenberg, 1986) in an attempt to explain how educational and vocational interests are developed, choices are made, and performance and satisfaction are attained. Thus, SCCT might be able to provide more comprehensive suggestions for career guidance interventions than other, less integrative theories. Second, SCCT was also explicitly developed to explain the career behavior of diverse persons and incorporates hypotheses about the roles of gender, ethnicity, socioeconomic status, and contextual supports and barriers in interest development, choice making, and educational and work adjustment (i.e., satisfaction and performance). Third, SCCT has generated a large amount of both primary and meta-analytic research with diverse samples of children, adolescents, and adults that have largely supported its major hypotheses.

This chapter has two main purposes. First, we will provide an integrative description of SCCT's models of interest development, choice, performance, and satisfaction and discuss their preventive implications, focusing specifically on how they might be used to promote academic success, school engagement and satisfaction, school completion, and positive future orientations of children and adolescents. Second, we will propose a social cognitive model of vocational hope—a construct that is beginning to receive attention in the vocational psychology and career development literatures (Diemer & Blustein, 2007; Juntunen & Wettersten, 2006; Kenny et al., 2010) as potentially important to the future expectations, academic success, and school engagement of students at risk for academic failure and school dropout.

We present the new model of vocational hope for two reasons. First, we believe that the development and maintenance of vocational hope may be a critical variable in career interventions for underresourced and marginalized youth. On the one hand, the SCCT-based career interventions that we describe in this chapter may be effective at helping students to identify talents and build talent-congruent self-efficacy beliefs, explore the occupational world, and plan and make value-congruent work choices. On the other hand, they might not be enough in today's world (and maybe too little too late), especially among those who live in environments where choices are perceived to be limited or even nonexistent. These interventions may, in fact, be seen as irrelevant unless students can be helped to see a positive future for themselves—that attaining a sense of vocational hope may be prerequisite to, or at least a central component of, career interventions.

Our second reason for presenting a social cognitive model of vocational hope is to provide a theoretical scaffolding on which hope-promoting interventions can be designed and research conducted. Such a theoretical scaffolding requires that vocational hope be clearly defined (so that it can be accurately operationalized), its antecedents clearly specified (so that interventions can be developed), and its likely short- and long-term consequences outlined (so interventions can be evaluated).

We will start by providing an overview of SCCT and deriving some suggestions for how preventive interventions might be designed from an SCCT perspective. We will then present our social cognitive model of vocational hope by incorporating key SCCT constructs with constructs from other literatures, including school dropout prevention, school engagement, and multicultural psychology. In the process, we will outline future research needs on our model and provide additional suggestions for preventive interventions that derive from our model of vocational hope.

Social Cognitive Career Theory

Social cognitive career theory (Lent, 2004, 2005; Lent & Brown, 2006a, 2008; Lent, Brown, and Hackett, 1994) has emerged over the past 20 years as a useful and empirically supported framework for understanding academic and career development in diverse children, adolescents, and adults. The theory initially was composed of three interrelated models of interest development, choice making, and work and academic performance (Lent et al., 1994). An additional SCCT model developed to explain and predict educational and work satisfaction (Lent & Brown, 2006a, 2008) was more recently introduced. All four models incorporate an overlapping set of person (e.g., self-efficacy and outcome expectations, knowledge, skills, personality dispositions), contextual (e.g., environmental supports and barriers, learning opportunities and experiences), and behavioral (e.g., goal setting and goal progress) variables that are assumed to help direct the types of interests people develop, the educational and occupational goals that they set for themselves, and the levels of success and satisfaction that they attain in their educational and occupational pursuits.

The interest, choice, and performance models have all generated large bodies of research and several recent, large-scale meta-analyses have provided support for many of SCCT's hypotheses (e.g., Brown et al., 2008; Brown, Lent, Telander, & Tramayne, 2011; Sheu, Lent, Brown, Miller, Hennessy, & Duffy, 2010). Aspects of the more recent satisfaction model have also found support in predicting the domain and life satisfaction of teachers in Italy (Lent et al., 2011) and the United States (Duffy & Lent, 2009), college students from Portugal (Lent, Taveira, Sheu, & Singley, 2009) and the United States (Lent et al., 2005), US engineering students (Lent, Singley, Sheu, Schmidt, & Schmidt, 2007), and Flemish career counseling clients (Verbruggen & Sels, 2010).

Key Social Cognitive Constructs

All SCCT models emphasize three key person variables: Self-efficacy beliefs, outcome expectations, and personal goals. *Self-efficacy* refers to people's beliefs about their abilities to perform specific academic-, occupational-, or work-relevant tasks or courses of actions. Self-efficacy helps people determine the types of academic and occupational environments, and educational and work goals they will approach versus avoid; how much effort they will expend; and how persistent they will be in the face of obstacles. Simply put, students and workers tend to select academic and occupational environments, and take on and persist at tasks, of which they believe they are capable. By the same token, they avoid environments and easily give up on tasks that they believe they are not competent to perform, regardless of actual level of abilities or skills.

Three additional characteristics of self-efficacy beliefs are important. First, self-efficacy beliefs do not represent unitary or global traits, like self-esteem (or even so-called generalized self-efficacy beliefs). They are rather dynamic (i.e., malleable), context-specific beliefs that are linked to specific performance domains. An individual might, for example, hold strong self-efficacy beliefs about his or her ability to master writing tasks, but feel much less competent at math tasks. Similarly, a student might feel less efficacious in his or her ability to master school-related tasks than more socially related tasks. In both cases, the student will be more likely to avoid environments (math classes, school) and be less likely to persist in these environments than a person with higher self-efficacy beliefs in these domains.

Second, self-efficacy beliefs in different performance domains are changeable and responsive to environmental conditions. They are primarily influenced by (1) personal performance accomplishments (receiving *A*s in school will raise academic self-efficacy while receiving failing grades will lower it), (2) vicarious experiences (seeing someone of a similar background succeed in school will boost self-efficacy while having no academically successful role models will lower it), (3) social persuasion and support (having encouraging teachers will boost self-efficacy, while having belittling or nonencouraging teachers will lower it), and (4) physiological or affective states (e.g., experiencing heightened anxiety while attending—or anticipating attending—school will lower self-efficacy, while experiencing a calmer emotional state will raise it). Although the impacts of these four sources of efficacy information depend on a variety of different factors, performance accomplishments are typically the most influential of the four sources.

Third, self-efficacy beliefs are essentially ability perceptions that may or may not correspond well to actual task competencies. Self-efficacy beliefs, however, are the more potent in interest development, choice-making, and persistence (but not performance). Simply put, a girl with high math aptitudes who underestimates her talents is less likely to express an interest in math courses and careers and persist in them than a person with equal math talent, but more talent-congruent self-efficacy beliefs.

Outcome expectations are personal beliefs about the consequences of a given action, along with the value that one places on these consequences. Self-efficacy is concerned with "Can I do this?" Outcome expectations, by contrast, ask, "If I do this, what will happen?" That is, what outcomes will follow my behavior? People's interests and choices are based both on their beliefs in what they can do well (self-efficacy beliefs) and about what their actions will produce (outcome expectations). Outcome expectations are also perceived and, therefore, may or may not match the actual outcomes that may accrue from a given course of action, but are again the more potent of the two on interest development, choice making, and persistence. A child may, for example, see few positive personal outcomes associated with school success despite strong evidence that school success is associated with better life outcomes. This student will be less likely to express interest in doing well in school and persist with school-related tasks than a student who links school success to positive outcomes.

Goals refer to people's determination to engage in a particular activity or to produce a particular future outcome. By setting goals, people help to organize and guide their own behavior, sustain it over long periods even in the absence of external reinforcement, and increase the likelihood that they will attain their desired outcomes. Goals are central to nearly all theories of career development. When we speak of plans, aspirations, or dreams, we are essentially referring to goals, but in much less explicit terms.

SCCT Models

Figure 24.1 presents SCCT's interest and choice models, while Figures 24.2 and 24.3 present its performance and satisfaction models, respectively. SCCT's interest and choice models suggest that self-efficacy beliefs and outcome expectations concerning academic and occupationally relevant tasks give rise to interests. As described by Lent et al. (1994), both early in life, and later on, people develop interest in activities at which they view themselves as competent and that will produce desirable outcomes. Interests, self-efficacy beliefs, and outcome expectations then give rise to goals for pursuing specific activities. And goals make it more likely that people will, in turn, pursue activities that are consistent with their goals. Once people choose, or are required to, engage in a particular activity, they produce a certain pattern of success and failures that enable them to revise or stabilize their self-efficacy beliefs and outcome expectations.

When it comes time to choose a specific college major or occupation, or otherwise engage in the workforce, people will prefer majors, occupations, or jobs on the bases of their interests, which have been developed from their perceptions of competency and expectations of outcomes as long as there are no insurmountable barriers to entering their preferred types of occupations or jobs. In the latter cases, the types of jobs people take may be influenced more by self-efficacy beliefs (i.e., people will still want to pursue work that they think they can do) and outcome expectations (e.g., job availability, pay, family wishes in collectivist cultures) than by interests.

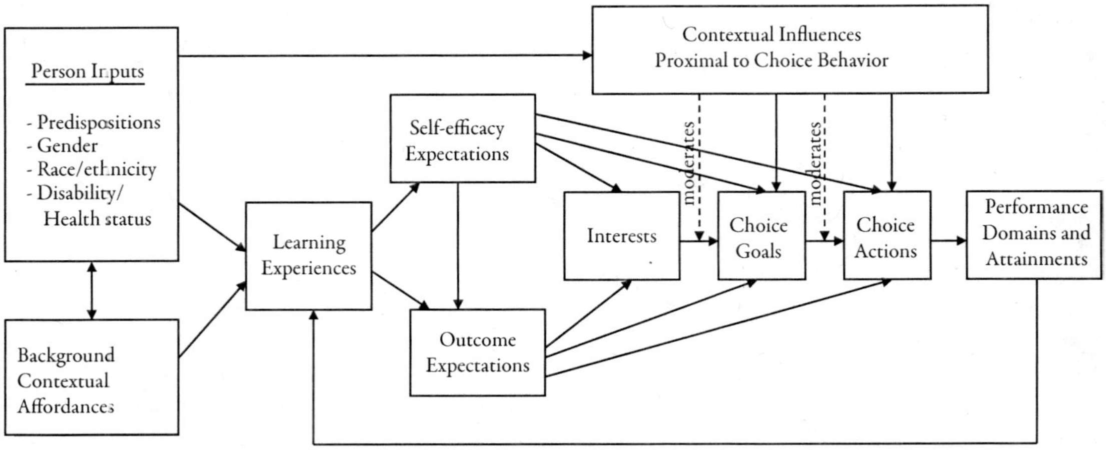

Figure 24.1. SCCT interest and choice model (Lent, Brown, & Hackett, 1994). Reproduced by permission of authors

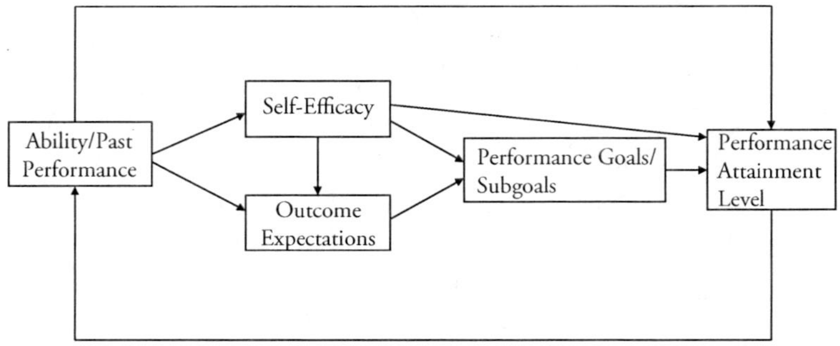

Figure 24.2. SCCT performance model (Lent, Brown, & Hackett, 1994). Reproduced by permission of authors

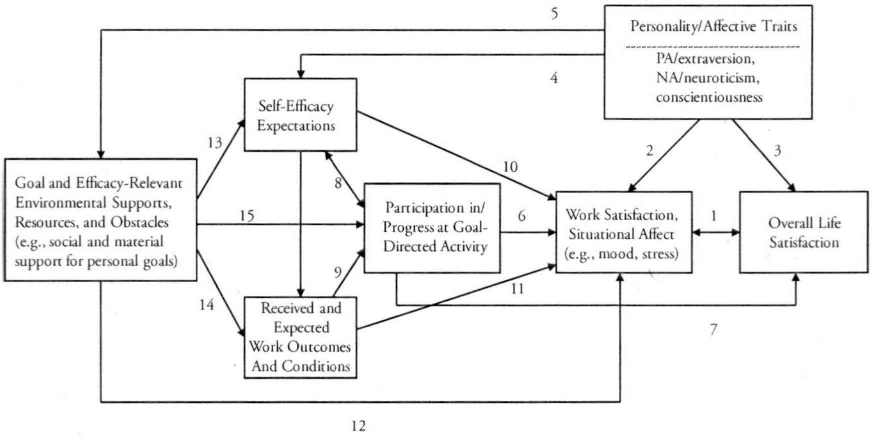

Figure 24.3. SCCT satisfaction model (Lent & Brown, 2008). Reproduced by permission of authors

In the performance model, self-efficacy beliefs and outcome expectations are seen (along with abilities and past experiences) to relate to performance both directly and indirectly via the goals that students or employees develop. In other words, both abilities and indexes of past performance (e.g., school grades) give rise to self-efficacy beliefs (those who have performed well in the past will develop higher self-efficacy beliefs than those whose performance has been more deficient); self-efficacy beliefs in concert with attained abilities and skills lead persons to set more challenging goals for themselves. More challenging goals along with abilities and self-efficacy beliefs are associated with increased academic and work performance.

In the satisfaction model, self-efficacy beliefs and outcome expectations are seen as giving rise to goals. Progress at personally and culturally relevant goals is then seen as central to achieving work or educational satisfaction (and concomitant and subsequent life satisfaction). Although each of the SCCT models posit that self-efficacy beliefs and outcome expectations are key determinants of affect (e.g., interest and satisfaction) and behavior (goal setting, goal progress, performance, and persistence), it must be remembered that in SCCT, both self-efficacy beliefs and outcome expectations are context specific (see Lent & Brown, 2006b). Thus, the content of self-efficacy beliefs and outcome expectations is somewhat different in these models.

In the interest model, self-efficacy beliefs refer to work-related activities (e.g., conduct scientific experiments) or academic tasks (e.g., successfully complete science courses), while in the satisfaction model self-efficacy beliefs focus additionally on behaviors necessary to achieve valued work goals (i.e., to perform tasks requisite to success in one's work or school context). Thus, it is hypothesized in the interest model that people will develop interests in academic majors and occupations in which they feel efficacious. In the performance and satisfaction models, it is hypothesized that workers will set specific goals for themselves if they feel efficacious about their abilities to reach these goals; it is also posited that goal progress is a partial determinant of both performance and satisfaction.

Similarly, outcome expectations are context-specific. Outcome expectations in the interest model focus on the likely positive and negative consequences for engaging in school and pursuing certain college majors or occupations; in the performance and satisfaction models, outcome expectations focus on the likely consequences of goal attainment and reinforcers perceived to be obtainable in the school or work environment.

Other Person Factors

In addition to the core social cognitive variables, SCCT acknowledges that there are other person variables that affect the interests that people develop, the types of choices they make, and the level of satisfaction and success they attain at work and in life. In particular, SCCT highlights personality dispositions and affective tendencies, race/ethnicity, gender, and socioeconomic status. As can be seen in Figures 24.1 and 24.3, these additional person variables are hypothesized in SCCT as having two primary paths of influence. First, they are seen as influencing interests, choices, and satisfaction indirectly via their influences on self-efficacy beliefs and outcome expectations. Thus, for example, persons disposed to high positive affectivity versus those disposed to high negative affectivity will probably benefit more from efficacy-enhancing experiences and see more positive than negative outcomes associated with goal pursuit. One's ethnicity, socioeconomic status, or gender may also influence interests indirectly via self-efficacy beliefs and outcome expectations by the nature of the learning experiences to which the people of color, the poor and underresourced, and women (and men) are exposed (e.g., educational access, discrimination, availability of role models, gender role socialization).

Personality and affective dispositions may, according to SCCT's satisfaction model, also act directly to influence an individual's levels of work and life satisfaction. The influence of race, ethnicity, socioeconomic status, and gender may also affect the types of choices that people make via their influence on the opportunity structures (resources, supports, and barriers) present when choices are formed and implemented. Thus, for example, a child growing up in an impoverished environment may not develop ability-congruent occupational interests due to a relative dearth of learning experiences necessary for self-efficacy beliefs to blossom. He or she might also experience limits on the types of occupations and jobs he/she can implement when the time to enter the work force arrives.

Contextual Factors

SCCT also posits that contextual or environmental features play a critical role in interest development, choice making, and satisfaction. As can be seen in Figure 24.1, environmental influences can moderate choice behavior. For example, environmental barriers can weaken people's ability to translate interests into goals and goals into actions (i.e., choices). For example, children growing up in socially disadvantaged neighborhoods may conclude that they will be unable to attain the means to enter occupations of interest. They may choose instead to pursue more immediately attainable occupations that may be less interest-congruent. On the other hand, environmental supports can facilitate the translation of interests into choices. Thus, although SCCT hypothesizes that people will generally enter fields of work that are congruent with their interests, this can only happen if they have the resources and supports to do so and if there are no insurmountable barriers to translating their interests into real occupational possibilities.

Recent research (e.g., Sheu et al., 2010) has also suggested that contextual supports, barriers, and resources that are more distal to occupational entry have their effect on later choice behavior indirectly via their influences on self-efficacy beliefs (and perhaps outcome expectations). As noted in the discussion of other person inputs, children living in poverty may not be exposed vicariously or directly to the types of experiences that give rise to robust efficacy beliefs in areas of talent and to positive expectations about work.

In addition to negative contextual influences (lack of resources, barriers associated with poverty, race/ethnicity, and gender), SCCT also highlights the role of family, peer, teacher, supervisor, school, and community support in interest development, choice making, and satisfaction. These supportive conditions are hypothesized to operate in the opposite way as negative environmental influences—they facilitate one's abilities to translate interests into choices, attain work- and school-related goals, and facilitate the development of talent-congruent self-efficacy beliefs and positive outcome expectations. Indeed, a variety of individual studies (e.g., Restubog, Florentino, & Garcia, 2010) have highlighted the importance of support to a variety of important career and educational outcomes (e.g., self-efficacy belief development, work and school satisfaction, school engagement). Recent meta-analytic evidence (Brown, Abrams, et al., 2011) suggests that in some cases the positive correlations of supports with career and educational outcomes are statistically larger than the negative correlations between barriers and these same outcomes (e.g., .28 for supports versus –.16 for barriers on self-efficacy beliefs and .23 for supports versus –.08 for barriers on academic performance).

In summary, SCCT's interest and choice models hypothesize that people will develop interests in areas in which they feel efficacious and foresee positive outcomes. They will then choose to enter occupations that are congruent with their interests as long as they have the resources and supports to do so and do not encounter insurmountable barriers to the implementation of their interests. Children growing up in poverty may not, however, encounter the types of experience that would foster talent congruent self-efficacy beliefs (and outcome expectations) unless efficacy-building support is present or can be marshaled for them. They may also encounter substantial barriers to, and less than adequate support for, implementing their primary vocational interests.

SCCT's satisfaction model suggests that people will be satisfied at school and at work if they are "(a) actively involved in pursuing, and making progress at, personally valued goals, (b) feel competent at the tasks required for successful goal pursuit and believe that such pursuit will have favorable outcomes, and (c) see their environments as supportive of their goals and as offering accessible resources to help them pursue their goals" (Lent, 2004, p. 499).

Implications for Career Development Interventions

Social cognitive career theory's interest, choice, satisfaction, and performance models can, we think, inform and provide suggestions for school-based career interventions (see also Brown & Lent, 1996; Fouad & Byars-Winston, 2005; Lent, 2005; Lent, Hackett, & Brown, 1997, 1999). According to SCCT, several key processes occur during childhood and adolescence that set the stage for later choice-making and adjustment. Most centrally, self-efficacy beliefs and outcome expectations are keys to cultivating students' academic and career interests and motivations. They determine the types of occupations and school subjects toward which students will gravitate (or even if they will gravitate toward school), the range of options they see as available to them, and their motivation in pursuing these options. Thus, one major focus for career interventions should be to help children and adolescents identify their talents and skills and develop robust and challenging self-efficacy beliefs in their areas of talent.

Recent research (Rojewski & Yang, 1997) and theory (Gottfredson, 1981, 2005) further suggest that these activities should occur as early as the elementary and junior high school years before educational and occupational aspirations become somewhat ingrained. Rojewski and Yang (1997), for example, found that the educational aspirations that children had developed in 8th grade were the strongest single predictor of 12th-grade aspirations (8th-grade aspirations were most strongly related to academic performance in elementary and junior high years). Similarly, Gottfredson (1981, 2005) has hypothesized that students circumscribe their occupational aspirations, and develop notions of options that are beyond their talents and efforts, between the ages of 9 and 14—prior to entering high school. Thus, early skill- *and* efficacy-building interventions, especially those focused on academic success, seem to be particularly important before students prematurely eliminate from consideration types of work that may be talent-congruent and before they develop less than robust educational and occupational aspirations.

The four sources of efficacy information can be used for organizing such interventions. Helping students acquire incrementally graded success experiences would be a potent source of efficacy information as long as the students are aided cognitively to process their experiences in a way that would facilitate self-efficacy belief development. For example, attributing success to luck, task ease, and (even) effort is likely to have substantially weaker effects on self-efficacy belief development than attributing success to developing capabilities. SCCT, therefore, suggests that attributions to developing abilities and skills are the most efficacy-enhancing, and it advocates challenging less efficacy-adaptive attributions, while promoting talent-based self-explanations (see Brown & Lent, 2006).

The other three sources of efficacy information can also be used to fashion interventions. For example, exposing students to coping models who are similar to them in race and gender can assist students to explore career and academic domains that they might not have otherwise considered. Social support, encouragement, and persuasion can be useful in helping students initiate and persist at new, efficacy-enhancing tasks, as can anxiety management and attributional training activities (e.g., Luzzo, Funk, & Strang, 1996; Luzzo, James, & Luna, 1996).

Students, more than ever in today's world, need also to acquire general workplace and career planning/adaptability skills and develop a strong sense of efficacy over their abilities to execute them (see Turner & Lapan, 2005). General workplace skills would include communication, teamwork, conflict management, and leadership skills as well as multicultural sensitivity and positive work habits and attitudes (Blustein, 2006; Blustein, Kenna, Gill, & Devoy, 2008; Turner & Lapan, 2005). Career planning and adaptability skills would involve career decision-making, job search, and problem-solving skills and self-efficacy beliefs. The four sources of efficacy information can again be used to build necessary skills and efficacy beliefs.

Outcome expectations are as important to interest development and choice-making as are self-efficacy beliefs. SCCT would also, therefore, suggest that interventions expose students to the world of work and to career information sources so that accurate outcome expectations about the working conditions, educational requirements, and reinforcers available in different occupations will be attained. Since many children and adolescents, especially the socioeconomically disadvantaged, have a limited view of the occupational world and limited experiences in it, we would suggest that a broad exploration of the occupational world precede any effort to narrow a child's focus on a particular set of occupations. For example, an interesting intervention in which academically at-risk children explored, via a computer-assisted guidance system, world of work modules associated with each of Roe's (1956) six primary occupational types yielded remarkably large effect sizes on participants' knowledge about occupations and preparation requirements (Maola & Kane, 1976). Children who had participated in this intervention achieved 1.12 and 2.83 standard deviations more occupational knowledge than individually counseled and no-treatment control students, respectively. Similarly large effect sizes were obtained for knowledge of preparation requirements (*d*'s of .89 versus individual counseling and 2.44 versus no treatment). Children in this intervention explored occupations associated with one of Roe's occupational clusters each session over six weekly sessions. This type of intervention may be an effective and efficient way to facilitate children's exploration of, and knowledge about, the occupational world. It certainly deserves replication and further study as a way to build realistic outcome expectations.

Helping children and adolescents set career and educational goals for themselves and providing the necessary support and encouragement so that goal progress is likely will, according to data relevant to SCCT's performance and satisfaction models, be associated with increased academic performance and satisfaction.

SCCT's contextual influences also merit attention in any effort to foster increased career development and planning in children and adolescents. Thus, attention should be given to possible barriers to school achievement, goal progress, and occupational preferences and to developing realistic strategies to overcome or cope with these barriers. The importance of support in the development of self-efficacy beliefs and the ability to translate interests into real occupational choices merits as much attention as overcoming educational and career barriers (see also Brown & Ryan Krane, 2000). Thus, students should also be helped to marshal support for their educational and career plans. Although family support and expectations seem to be important, support provided by caring teachers, counselors, and other adults is also important (Brown et al., 2011; Kenny et al, 2007) and may compensate in instances where parental support may be lacking (Arbona, 2005). The outcome of a dual focus on overcoming or coping with barriers and building supports may represent the type of resilience and resistance strategies suggested by Blustein et al. (2008) as necessary elements of career interventions for poor urban youth. These are also central, as we will discuss later in this chapter, to fostering a sense of vocational hope.

In summary, career interventions designed to promote career development and school performance and satisfaction should, according to SCCT, include the following elements:

- Help children, beginning in elementary school, to identify areas of talent and build strong and robust efficacy beliefs in these areas using all four major sources of efficacy information.
- Help children, beginning in elementary school, to acquire a broad knowledge of the occupational world so that later decisions will be informed by broader occupational knowledge and more accurate outcome expectations.
- Help children and adolescents to develop goals for educational attainment and career exploration and provide support for their goal progress.
- Help adolescents begin to identify occupational possibilities that are congruent with their interests and correspondent with their abilities and values. In addition, help adolescents, early in high school, to reconsider options that they might have prematurely eliminated because of restricted sex-role views (Gottfredson, 2005), underestimated self-efficacy beliefs, or inaccurate occupational knowledge (Brown & Lent, 1996; 2006).
- Explore with adolescents barriers to their tentatively preferred occupational possibilities and help them to develop and implement strategies to cope with or overcome the identified barriers.
- Explore with equal intensity supports that adolescents have or could marshal for their occupational preferences, help them to develop and implement strategies to gain needed supports, and provide support and encouragement.
- Help children and adolescents to learn workplace and career adaptability skills and develop robust efficacy beliefs in their abilities to execute these skills.

Although we think that career development interventions built around the SCCT-derived activities listed above can do much to facilitate future career and life outcomes (e.g., work and life satisfaction), we also agree with others (e.g., Blustein, 2006; Blustein et al., 2008; Diemer & Blustein, 2007) that the motivation to engage in such activities may be severely undermined by a less than positive future orientation in many poor, marginalized, and underresourced youth. We also think that SCCT-derived interventions, with their explicit focus on identifying and overcoming barriers, finding and building support for career plans, identifying talents and building robust efficacy beliefs, and exploring occupations and building positive outcome expectations, can do much to foster a more positive future orientation. However, their impact might be improved by attending explicitly to factors that can generate a more hopeful future orientation, especially during the years before educational and occupational aspirations become somewhat ingrained and occupational possibilities are circumscribed (i.e., during the elementary and junior high years).

We next offer our social cognitive model of vocational hope. We hope it can begin to direct future research and serve as a template for designing interventions to foster increased motivation to undertake career planning, engage and achieve in school, and persist educationally and occupationally in an increasingly tenuous world of work. It is a model that is intended to show how the effects of career interventions based on SCCT and other career theories can be facilitated and their preventive impacts improved by explicitly focusing on building vocational hope.

A Social Cognitive Model of Vocational Hope

Our social cognitive model of vocational hope is presented in Figure 24.4. We will start by defining the key theoretical construct in the model—vocational hope. We will then move to the left side of the model and discuss its key antecedents so that intervention components might be identified. We will then move to the right side of the model and outline the types of consequences that might be associated with increased feelings of vocational hope in order to suggest the short- and long-term preventive outcomes that might be facilitated with hope-producing vocational interventions.

Vocational Hope

We define vocational hope as a *positive motivational state associated with envisioning a future in which meaningful work is attainable.* It has several key theoretical characteristics. First, it is a *state.* That is, vocational hope is malleable, subject to contextual and personal influences, and can be changed (for better or worse) on the basis of personal direct and vicarious experiences and the individual's interpretation of them. Such trait-like characteristics as dispositional hope (Snyder, 2000) and dispositional optimism (Carver & Scheier, 1998) may be related to levels of state vocational hope—more optimistic students may feel greater vocational hope than will less optimistic students. However, they are not the same constructs—vocational hope is influenced by additional personal and contextual factors that may, in some cases, account for more variance in state feelings of hope than do personal dispositions.

Second, vocational hope is *motivational* and will be positively associated with approach versus avoidance behaviors, goal-setting, effort expenditure, and persistence. Thus, students with more vocational hope will be more likely to engage in educational and career development activities, put more effort into them, and persist in the face of obstacles longer than will students with less hope. And since vocational hope is a malleable state, changes in vocational hope will be associated positively with changes in educational and career goal-setting, effort, and persistence.

Third, vocational hope is oriented to the *future.* It does not involve how individuals construe their present life or think about the past, but rather how they envision their future. Although past experiences and current life circumstances can (and do) influence future views, they do not automatically stamp in a specific future. Rather, individuals have the potential to offset their pasts and presents by developing, on their own or with the help of caring others, a positive view of their futures.

Fourth, for vocational hope to prosper, the envisioned future must include *meaningful* work. However, work's meaningfulness is determined by the individual in his or her cultural context. Thus, what might not seem like meaningful work to a university professor in the ivory tower, might be

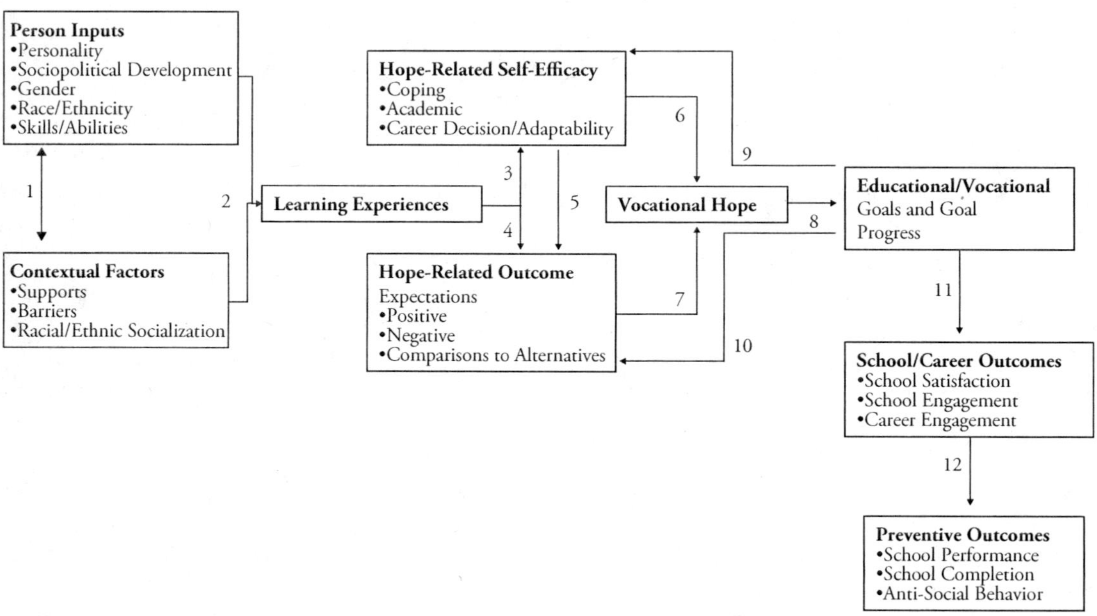

Figure 24.4. Social cognitive vocational hope model

quite meaningful, esteem-enhancing, and meaning-defining to the student envisioning his or her future or the worker living it. And work that might not seem so meaningful to a person in one cultural context might be quite meaningful to a person in another culture. Nonetheless, vocational hope does require the possibility of personally (as defined by the person in his or her cultural context) meaningful work in the future. We would hypothesize that a central component of work's personal meaningfulness reflects the degree to which it is value-correspondent, with values including those that are personally as well as culturally defined. However, we need to know much more about what makes work meaningful to individuals.

Fifth, meaningful work must be viewed as *attainable.* Meaningful work that is seen as attainable by others, but is not regarded as attainable by oneself does not engender great feelings of vocational hope. Thus, both meaningfulness and attainability are both critical requirements for vocational hope to thrive.

Antecedents of Vocational Hope

As can be seen in Figure 24.4 (paths 6 and 7), our social cognitive model of vocational hope hypothesizes that perceptions of self-efficacy and outcome expectations figure prominently in the development of vocational hope. More specifically, it is likely that students will develop the positive future orientation and motivational state associated with vocational hope if they view themselves as able to complete tasks necessary to attain meaningful work in the future and see more positive than negative outcomes associated with their efforts. The current model is, therefore, similar to SCCT models in that self-efficacy beliefs and outcome expectations are featured as predominant causal mechanisms. However, the current model differs from the prior models in the content of self-efficacy beliefs and outcome expectations. For example, in SCCT's interest model self-efficacy beliefs refer to persons' confidence in their abilities to execute tasks associated with various academic majors and occupational fields. Outcome expectations in SCCT's interest model refer to the perceived consequences of pursuing a specific academic major or occupation. In other words, people will generally develop interests in college majors or occupations in which they view themselves as efficacious and foresee positive outcomes associated with pursuit of these majors or occupations.

On the other hand, self-efficacy beliefs in the hope model focus on tasks associated with finding and attaining meaningful work in the face of challenges associated with one's current life circumstances. These hope-related self-efficacy beliefs are complex and need further study, but should include persons' feelings of competency about their abilities to overcome structural, financial, discriminatory, and other forms of barriers as well as their abilities to marshal support for educational and career plans (coping efficacy). Hope-related self-efficacy beliefs would also involve (1) feelings of efficacy to accomplish educational tasks necessary to attain meaningful work (academic/educational self-efficacy) and (2) tasks associated with finding and attaining meaningful work, even when an initial choice might be blocked (career decision making/adaptability efficacy).

While coping efficacy plays an important role in the SCCT interest and choice models, it is seen as central in the hope model. In the interest model, coping efficacy refers to persons' feelings of competence in being able to cope with and overcome barriers to the pursuit of a specific occupation or area of study. Persons who feel competent to perform successfully the work or educational tasks associated with a specific occupation *as well as* to overcome obstacles to success in that type of occupation will express more interest in the occupation than those who feel less able to cope. They will also develop stronger feelings of vocational hope than those who feel competent to perform necessary occupational tasks, but feel less able to cope with the challenges of occupational entry or attainment. Thus, an important part of adolescent career guidance, according to our model of vocational hope, is not only to help adolescents identify efficacy-congruent occupations, but also to help them develop strategies to cope with barriers to entry and success in these occupations and to marshal support for their plans. The latter is critical to increasing an adolescent's sense that meaningful future work possibilities may be attainable.

Similarly, although career decision-making self-efficacy beliefs have received wide-spread study in the vocational psychology literature, their roles have not been clearly explicated in any of the SCCT models. They are critical types of efficacy beliefs in our hope model and particularly come into play when a preferred educational or occupational path is blocked. Persons with robust career decision-making self-efficacy beliefs are confident that they can find and implement new possibilities in these circumstances. Thus, we labeled these in Figure 24.4 as career decision-making/adaptability beliefs to highlight their major influence on the development of vocational hope.

In essence then, our model of vocational hope largely elaborates on SCCT's interest and choice models by suggesting how both interests *and* hope can be fostered. However, hope-related self-efficacy beliefs can also be promoted before an adolescent begins to crystallize his or her interests (e.g., during the preexploration growth period of childhood and early adolescence). Coping, academic, and career decision-making efficacy in our model of vocational hope include those beliefs specific to a particular academic or occupational pursuit (e.g., perceived abilities to overcome barriers to pursuit of a math major) as well as beliefs that structural, financial, discriminatory, and other forms of barriers can be overcome, adequate levels of education can be attained, and work-related decisions made generally. The latter, hope-related efficacy beliefs may, as we indicated above, be excellent intervention targets for early school interventions, while the former, more specific beliefs become excellent targets for later intervention efforts during the high school years and may be facilitated by early attention to hope-related efficacy beliefs.

Finally, the current model recognizes that hope-related self-efficacy beliefs need not be totally individualistic. Rather, persons might feel that they can overcome barriers to attaining meaningful work by a variety of seemingly nonagentic means, including via collective efficacy (i.e., efficacy beliefs at the small group or community level; Bandura, 1998, 2000).

Outcome expectations, in the social cognitive model of vocational hope, refer (in part) to the perceptions of positive outcomes associated with specific educational and occupational pursuits (as in the SCCT interest and choice models) and also include outcomes associated with doing what is necessary to find meaningful work. The distinction between outcome expectations focused on specific pursuits and on engaging in tasks to attain meaningful work is important to understand. Using the SCCT interest model again as an example, outcome expectations refer to the outcomes that are perceived to be associated with the pursuit of a specific major or occupation, whereas the hope model adds to these expectations of outcomes associated with working to attain satisfying work. They essentially ask not only "What will happen if I attain a specific occupation or engage in school?" but also "Is the effort worth it?"

Hope-related positive outcome expectations can include material, social/relational, and self-evaluative consequences (Bandura, 1997) such as an anticipated improved standard of living for self and loved ones (material), respect from others (relational/social), and increased feelings of self-esteem (self-evaluative).

Interestingly, much recent research has shown that financially disadvantaged youth and youth of color have many of the same types of positive outcome expectations about school success and work as do their more privileged counterparts, including seeing the material gains associated with working and the importance of school to later occupational attainment (Kenny et al., 2007; Perry, Przybysz, & Al-Sheikh, 2009; Perry & Vance, 2010; Steinberg, Dornbusch, & Brown, 1992). One may wonder then how to explain the higher school dropout rates of poor youth. Although less than robust hope-related self-efficacy beliefs may provide some explanation, the balance of positive to negative outcome expectations for the effort required of them is also a possibility (e.g., the increased possibility of failure, the loss of friends who do not value educational or occupational attainment), especially if the positive outcomes for alternative paths outweigh in the short run those associated with attaining meaningful work. Gibbons and Borders (2010), for example, found that perceptions of negative outcomes explained more variance in college persistence rates of first-generation college students than did positive outcome expectations for college going.

Thus, given the effort that will be required by many in contemporary society to find meaningful work, our model of vocational hope also emphasizes that two additional types of outcome expectations require consideration. The first is the potential negative outcomes that might be anticipated for putting in the effort to find meaningful work, including financial strain (material), loss of friends with different values (social/relational), or failure and its resultant effect on feelings of self-worth (self-evaluative). The second is the perceived outcomes for often less socially acceptable and easier to attain alternatives (e.g., gang involvement or dropping out of school). Thus, our model of vocational hope suggests that an exploration of hope-related outcome expectations should include not just the positive outcomes associated with attaining meaningful work, but also potential negative consequences associated with necessary effort expenditure and the potential positive consequences of pursuing alternative paths, many of which may be easier to attain.

In summary, our nascent model of vocational hope hypothesizes that vocational hope (envisioning a future in which meaningful work is attainable) is largely a function of hope-related self-efficacy beliefs and outcome expectations. The former refers to confidence in one's ability to (1) overcome obstacles to finding satisfying work and marshal support from others, (2) do as well as one can in school, (3) search for and identify meaningful work alternatives, and (4) adapt to changing circumstances, when necessary. However, thinking "I can do it" is not enough to engender strong feelings of vocational hope. Rather, one must also feel that the effort "is worth it." Outcome expectations refer to the positive and negative material, social, and self-evaluative consequences associated with doing what is required to achieve meaningful work in one's future versus pursuing different alternatives. Finally, consistent with SCCT models, we also hypothesize a positive relation between hope-related self-efficacy beliefs and outcome expectations (path 5) such that increasing feelings of efficacy should result in more positive and fewer negative outcome expectations (i.e., thinking "I can do it" will influence whether I think it is worth it).

Other Person Factors

Similar to SCCT models, the current model places central emphasis on the role of self-efficacy beliefs and outcome expectations in the formation of vocational hope. However, as with all the SCCT models, our model of vocational hope also emphasizes other person variables that may influence the development of vocational hope and specifies their pathways of influence. As can be seen in Figure 24.4, there are a variety of individual difference variables that are important to consider, including personality dispositions (e.g., optimism, neuroticism, extraversion), gender, ethnicity, social class, sexual orientation, and skills and abilities. All of these variables are seen as influencing vocational hope indirectly via their influences on hope-related self-efficacy beliefs and outcome expectations (paths 2, 3, and 4). Thus, for example, persons, regardless of background, who are generally optimistic will feel more vocationally hopeful than those who are less dispositionally optimistic largely because they feel more efficacious in their abilities to do what is necessary to find satisfying work. They also see more positive than negative outcomes as associated with their efforts.

Gender, ethnicity, and social class as socially conferred statuses will also influence feelings of hope via their influence on the socially mediated learning experiences that inform self-efficacy beliefs and outcome expectations. Finally, persons must also possess the skills and abilities (or be helped to acquire them) associated with hope-related self-efficacy beliefs (e.g., coping, academic, career decision-making) for self-efficacy beliefs to prosper. Self-efficacy beliefs that are somewhat higher than talents and skills facilitate performance, while massively overoptimistic beliefs often lead to failure (Bandura, 1997).

Another potential individual difference variable that has begun to receive attention in the vocational psychology and career development literatures is critical consciousness (Freire, 1973, 1993) or sociopolitical development (SPD; Diemer, 2009). SPD, according to Diemer (2009), involves developing a greater awareness of sociopolitical oppression and becoming motivated to reduce sociopolitical inequity via social change. SPD has been found to relate positively to occupational expectations and aspirations (Diemer & Blustein, 2006; Diemer & Hsieh, 2008; Diemer, Hsieh, & Pan, 2009) in poor adolescents of color and to their later occupational attainment (Diemer, 2009). Our model highlights SPD or critical consciousness as important to fostering vocational hope and suggests its mechanism of operation—via its influence on hope-related self-efficacy beliefs and outcome expectations. Efforts to raise SPD may, according to our model, promote school engagement and career aspirations (via vocational hope) by strengthening students' hope-related self-efficacy beliefs (perhaps via collective efficacy) and positive outcome expectations.

Contextual Variables

The environment in which an individual resides also, according to all SCCT models, plays a large role in the development of interests, the making of choices, and achieving various levels of educational and occupational satisfaction and success. The environment and the individual's perception of it also have major roles in the current model of vocational hope. There are environmental factors that can impede the development of vocational hope (environmental barriers) and contextual factors that can foster it (environmental supports). The former include, to name a few, local, national, and international economic conditions; poverty; limited educational and occupational options in the community; lack of educationally and occupationally successful role models; gender or racial discrimination; substandard schools; and peers who do not value educational and occupational success. The latter (supportive conditions) include family educational involvement and expectations, peers who are supportive of educational and occupational attainment, and caring and challenging teachers. The racial socialization provided to children by their parents and other community members (Hughes et al., 2006) may also be a contextual factor with important implications for the development of vocational hope.

There has been much written about the career-limiting influences of environmental barriers experienced by poor and underresourced children and adolescents (e.g., Blustein, 2006; Diemer, 2009; Diemer & Blustein, 2006). There has also been a growing literature on the facilitating effects of environmental supports on the educational and career attainment of disadvantaged youth (Kenny et al., 2007). The social cognitive model of vocational hope not only acknowledges the hindering influences of barriers and facilitating effects of supports, but also hypothesizes the mechanisms by which they hinder or facilitate educational and career behavior. Specifically, as shown in Figure 24.4 (paths 2, 3, and 4), we hypothesize that contextual supports and barriers, like person inputs to which they are related (path 1), influence feelings of vocational hope largely indirectly via their influences on hope-related self-efficacy beliefs and outcome expectations. Thus, for example, poor children who receive helpful racial socialization messages (e.g., preparation for bias; see Phinney & Chavira, 1995; Quintana & Vera, 1999; Scott, 2003) from their parents may feel more efficacious about their abilities to cope with barriers to educational and occupational attainment and see that their efforts are worth it. Similarly, conditions of poverty and nonexistent role models will be associated with low levels of vocational hope via their influences on hope-related efficacy beliefs and outcome expectations. Finally, the presence of supportive and involved families, peers, teachers, and/or counselors can foster a sense of vocational hope by facilitating coping, academic, and decision-making skills and self-efficacy belief development. Such support may also help give rise to more positive than negative outcome expectations associated with trying to attain a meaningful vocational future.

Consequences of Vocational Hope

One immediate consequence of vocational hope, according to our current model, is to motivate approach versus avoidance behavior and persistence via educational and career goal setting (see path 8). More vocationally hopeful students will be more likely to set educational (doing well and engaging in school) and occupational (undertaking career exploration activities) goals for themselves and will be more open to goal setting interventions than will less hopeful students. Much recent research has shown that working toward personally meaningful and valued goals is particularly motivating and is associated with a variety of positive outcomes (Ryan & Deci, 2000). We would hypothesize that the goals that more hopeful students set for themselves will be more personally meaningful than the goals (if they have them) of less hopeful students. Thus, interventions to promote academic and educational goal setting will be more successful for more than for less hopeful students via the influence of vocational hope on the personal meaningfulness of goals.

Students' perceptions of goal progress are then seen as feeding forward to a variety of different affective and behavioral outcomes (path 11) and backward via hope-related self-efficacy beliefs (path 9) and outcome expectations (path 10) to influence further feelings of vocational hope. Progress at goal pursuit will be associated with greater levels of school satisfaction and engagement and satisfaction and engagement in career development activities. It will also further strengthen feelings of vocational hope. On the other hand, failure at goal pursuit will be associated with lower levels of school satisfaction and engagement and will also be associated with reduced feelings of vocational hope via the influence of failure experiences on hope-related self-efficacy beliefs and outcome expectations.

Finally, our model of vocational hope suggests a number of preventive outcomes associated with vocational hope (path 12), including increased graduation rates; reduced teen pregnancy, delinquency, and substance abuse rates; and increased occupational attainment. These outcomes are seen as flowing from vocational hope, largely indirectly, via goal setting/goal progress and school satisfaction and engagement. That is, students who are helped to develop greater feelings of vocational hope (via interventions targeted at hope-related self-efficacy beliefs and outcome expectations) will commit themselves more to school, graduate at higher rates, and engage in fewer antisocial behaviors than will less hopeful students via progress at attaining personally meaningful educational and career development goals and the concomitant feelings of satisfaction that goal progress engenders. The latter hypotheses linking vocational hope to academic and prosocial outcomes via school engagement and satisfaction were derived largely from recent research on the positive relations between school engagement and satisfaction with these outcomes (e.g., Christenson & Thurlow, 2004).

Future Research Needs

We have attempted in developing our social cognitive model of vocational hope to derive our hypotheses from the empirical literature. Most paths in our model, therefore, have sustained some degree of research support. There is for example, meta-analytic evidence to support the hypothesized links between contextual supports and barriers and self-efficacy beliefs and outcome expectations (Sheu et al., 2010). The path from goal progress to satisfaction outcomes has also been supported in several studies (e.g., Lent et al., 2007) as has the link between school engagement and school performance (e.g., Perry et al., 2010) and school completion (Christenson & Thurlow, 2004). The fit of social cognitive hypotheses across gender and race/ethnicity has also received attention (e.g., Betz & Hackett, 1981; Fouad & Smith, 1996; Gainor & Lent, 1998; Tang, Fouad, & Smith, 1999).

However, one hypothesis in our model, while reasonable, is clearly speculative at this point; namely, the hypothesized central mediating role of vocational hope. We have hypothesized that the relations of self-efficacy beliefs and outcome expectations (and by extension personal and contextual variables) on goal progress and other educational and career outcomes are mediated by vocational hope. Thus, future research on our model must test whether vocational hope is as central and critical as we have presented. It could be hypothesized, for example, that self-efficacy beliefs and outcome expectations are sufficient alone to predict goal progress (e.g., Lent et al., 2007). Such a hypothesis would suggest that vocational hope is superfluous and adds unnecessary complexity to a more parsimonious SCCT model. Thus, future tests of our model must not only test how well it fits the data, but also compare its fit to more parsimonious alternatives.

Tests of the model will also require a measure of vocational hope that is faithful to our theory. This, however, may present a challenge. Other attempts to measure hope (albeit from other theoretical perspectives) appear to have encountered difficulties in creating a measure of hope that is not confounded with related constructs. For example, it has been noted that scores obtained from a widely used hope measure (Snyder et al., 1991) frequently correlate so substantially with scores on measures of mastery and various forms of self-regulatory behaviors to suggest that the hope scale may measure mastery beliefs better than it does hope (see Aspinwall & Leaf, 2002; Carver & Scheier, 2002). Similar patterns of relationships have recently been found for a scale developed specifically to measure work hope (Juntunen & Wettersten, 2006), suggesting that scores on this measure may also covary highly with mastery beliefs (e.g., canonical roots of .87 and .80 for work hope and mastery orientation; Kenny et al., 2010). Thus, in the case of the social cognitive model of vocational hope, measures need to disentangle hope from its correlates (self-efficacy beliefs and outcome expectations) and consequences (e.g., goal progress). We hope to have developed such a measure by the time this chapter appears in print.

Tentative Implications for Preventive Interventions

We have briefly summarized SCCT models of interest development, choice-making, satisfaction, and performance and suggested how these can be used to fashion career development interventions for children and adolescents. We have also presented a beginning model of vocational hope that highlights particular aspects of SCCT models (e.g., the role of coping and educational efficacy beliefs), but also adds a beginning conceptual scaffolding to explain how vocational hope may be fostered in the lives of poor and marginalized youth and may be used to direct intervention efforts. We summarize here the implications that we derived from the extant SCCT models and tentatively offer additional implications provided by our model of vocational hope.

We advocated in our earlier discussions of SCCT models of interest, choice, satisfaction, and performance that elementary and junior high counseling efforts be oriented to helping children develop talent-congruent self-efficacy beliefs and gain an expanded view of the occupational world. The former (developing talent-congruent self-efficacy beliefs) requires that students be helped to identify their talents (we do not advocate blindly trying to build self-efficacy beliefs), while the latter (acquiring an expanded view of the occupational world) requires that students be exposed to occupations outside of their immediate environments and media experiences and to the educational requirements of various possibilities. Talent-congruent self-efficacy beliefs can be fostered by exposing students to gender-similar and ethnically similar models, helping them acquire graded success experiences in their areas of talent and attributing the successes to growing talent, and providing support, encouragement, and reinforcement as they engage in talent developing activities. In addition, we advocated that elementary and junior high students need to acquire work readiness skills and robust efficacy beliefs in these areas. The goals of elementary and junior-high school career counseling interventions are to help students gain a greater understanding of the occupational world and of their own unique and shared talents.

Our model of vocational hope adds to these the development of coping, educational, and career decision-making self-efficacy beliefs. Early intervention efforts need to acknowledge the many barriers that poor and marginalized children have to future occupational attainment, help them develop strategies to prevent or otherwise overcome these barriers, and assist them in developing strong and robust coping efficacy beliefs (including marshaling support from others for their coping efforts). Strong and robust coping skills and efficacy beliefs and real support from others may be especially critical to sustain hope in the face of adversity.

Our vocational hope model also suggests that a focus on hope-related outcome expectations is important; that is, helping children develop a sense that doing well in school and achieving occupationally is worth the effort. Exposing them to gender-similar and ethnically similar models is one avenue by which this goal can be approached. We also suggested that critical consciousness or social political development (SPD) may relate to vocational hope and its consequences (i.e., school engagement and success) via its influence on hope-related self-efficacy beliefs and outcome expectations.

The ultimate goals of elementary and junior-high guidance interventions from our perspective are to prevent the premature elimination of viable occupational possibilities and to foster educational engagement and performance via building a positive future outlook (vocational hope). Vocational hope during the high school years can then be further developed and maintained by engaging in more focused exploration of occupational possibilities with particular attention given to fostering efficacy beliefs that barriers can be overcome, supports can be built for future career and educational plans, and adequate levels of educational attainment can be achieved. We would also suggest that the development and maintenance of vocational hope during adolescence would be facilitated with specific occupational possibilities in mind. Although this assumption requires future research (as do all of our hypotheses), we think that helping poor and marginalized students generate (psychometrically and otherwise) specific occupational options that are value-correspondent and efficacy-congruent would show that meaningful work might be available in their future lives. This would then allow them to more readily identify the level of education that they will need to attain these options and allow counselors to work with them on developing targeted coping strategies and efficacy beliefs.

Additional targets for intervention efforts are on the balance of positive versus negative outcomes for educational and occupational involvement and helping make potential positive outcomes (e.g., ability to implement values, sustain oneself financially, and attain respect among family and peers) more salient than negative consequences (e.g., possibility of failure, loss of friends with different values). Also, the positive outcomes of such involvement must outweigh the positive outcomes associated with alternatives (e.g., dropping out of school, gang membership). Although we are not sure at this time how to accomplish the latter (except for fostering hope-related self-efficacy beliefs), programs that immerse students, as early as the junior high school years, in different career fields via field work and hands-on experiences (see Ali et al., 2011) may be a possibility. In the end, visions of the future must not only include work that is viewed as attainable, but it also must be meaningful and worth the effort. We need to learn much more, especially in the current economic climate, about how to foster "it's worth it" beliefs.

Summary and Conclusions

We have described how extant SCCT models can be used to fashion elementary, junior high, and high school career counseling efforts. The goals for elementary and junior high efforts are to prevent the premature elimination of viable educational and occupational options, help students see the connection between school performance and later occupational attainment, and develop a sense that current barriers to educational and occupational attainment can be overcome (i.e., build vocational hope). We advocated for a broad exploration of the occupational world, the identification of talents, and the building of talent-congruent self-efficacy beliefs. We also added, on the basis of our model of vocational hope, a need to acknowledge the real world in which many disadvantaged children live, but also to help them develop the skills, self-efficacy beliefs, and outcome expectations necessary to persevere toward a positive vocational future. Waiting until children make the transition to high school to initiate these efforts may, however, be too little and too late. As we indicated earlier, research has indicated fairly consistently that junior high school educational aspirations seem to be remarkably stable and set the stage for many for educational attainment, completion, and aspirations in high school and beyond.

We highlighted how SCCT models could be used to fashion high school career counseling efforts. We also suggested, via our model of vocational hope, that helping students generate efficacy-congruent and value-correspondent educational and occupational options, although necessary, may be incomplete. Rather, high school counseling efforts need also to acknowledge the real world in which students live while helping them to develop strategies to cope with and overcome obstacles. Further, high school counselors must help students to build the self-beliefs that the obstacles can be overcome on one's own or via collective efforts. Also important is continued effort to help students make more salient the positive outcomes associated with persistence as they compare to the negative outcomes of persistence, and the outcomes associated with giving up or reverting to other means of self-enhancement and sustenance (e.g., dropping out of school, gang involvement).

In the end, we think that having a positive outlook about one's vocational future (that meaningful work is attainable) may be an important source of resilience for many disadvantaged youth and has important preventive implications. We hope that the ideas presented in this chapter can direct future research efforts. Such efforts may allow us to understand vocational hope better and eventually provide a conceptual scaffolding for building hope-producing career interventions and evaluating their short and long-term outcomes.

Acknowledgment

We thank Dr. Robert W. Lent, Andrea Carr, Anneliese Kranz, and Meaghan Rowe-Johnson for reading and commenting on an earlier draft of this chapter.

References

Ali, S. R., Lee, S., Gibbons, S. J., Hoffman, T., Dean, A., & Williams, J. (2011, August). Health science career education programming: A collaborative/preventive approach. In E. H. McWhirter & S. Hage (Chairs), *Using career interventions as a preventive strategy: Implications for policy.* Symposium presented at the 119th Annual Convention of the American Psychological Association, Washington, DC.

Arbona, C. (2005). Promoting the career development and academic achievement of at-risk youth: College access programs. In S. D. Brown & R. W. Lent (Eds.), *Career development and counseling: Putting theory and research to work* (pp. 525–550). New York: Wiley.

Aspinwall, L. G., & Leaf, S. A. (2002). In search of the unique aspects of hope: Pinning our hopes on positive emotions, future-oriented thinking, hard times, and other people. *Psychological Inquiry, 13,* 276–231.

Bandura, A. (1997). *Self-efficacy: The exercise of control.* New York: Freeman.

Bandura, A. (1998). Personal and collective efficacy in human adaptation and change. In J. G. Adair, D. Belanger, & K. L. Dion (Eds.), *Advances in psychological sciences: Vol. 1. Personal, social, and cultural aspects* (pp. 51–71). Hove, UK: Psychology Press.

Bandura, A. (2000). Exercise in human agency through collective efficacy. *Current Directions in Psychological Science, 9,* 75–78.

Betz, N. E. & Hackett, G. (1981). The relationship of career-related self-efficacy expectations to perceived career options in college women and men. *Journal of Counseling Psychology, 28,* 399–410.

Blustein, D. L. (2006). *The psychology of working.* Mahwah, NJ: Erlbaum.

Blustein, D. L., Kenna, A. C., Gill, N., & DeVoy, J. E. (2008). The psychology of working: A new framework for counseling practice and public policy. *Career Development Quarterly, 56,* 294–308.

Brown, S. D., Abrams, M., Lamp, K., Hacker, J., Johnson, M., Siena, A.,…Carr, A. (2011). *The relations of barriers and supports to career and educational outcomes: A meta-analytic investigation.* Manuscript in preparation, Loyola University Chicago.

Brown, S. D., & Lent, R. W. (1996). A social cognitive framework for career choice counseling. *Career Development Quarterly, 44,* 354–366.

Brown, S. D., & Lent, R. W. (2006). Preparing adolescents to make career decisions: A social cognitive perspective. In F. Pajares & T. Urdan (Eds.), *Self-efficacy beliefs of adolescents* (pp. 201–223). Greenwich, CT: Information Age Publishing.

Brown, S. D., Lent, R. W., Telander, K., & Tramayne, S. (2011). Social cognitive career theory, conscientiousness, and work performance: A meta-analytic path analysis. *Journal of Vocational Behavior, 79,* 81–90.

Brown, S. D., & Ryan Krane, N. E.(2000). Four (or five) sessions and a cloud of dust: Old assumptions and new observations about career counseling. In S. D. Brown & R. W. Lent (Eds.), *Handbook of counseling psychology* (3rd ed., pp. 740–766). New York: Wiley.

Brown, S. D., Tramayne, S., Hoxha, D., Telander, K., Fan, X., & Lent, R. W. (2008). Social cognitive predictors of college students' academic performance and persistence: A meta-analytic path analysis. *Journal of Vocational Behavior, 72,* 298–308.

Carver, C. S., & Scheier, M. F. (1998). *On the self-regulation of behavior.* New York: Cambridge University Press.

Carver, C. S., & Scheier, M. F. (2002). The hopeful optimist. *Psychological Inquiry, 13,* 288–290.

Christenson, S. L., & Thurlow, M. L. (2004). School drop-outs: Prevention considerations, interventions, and challenges. *Current Directions in Psychological Science, 13,* 36–39.

Dawis, R. V. (2005). The Minnesota theory of work adjustment. In S. D. Brown & R. W. Lent (Eds.), *Career development and counseling: Putting theory and research to work* (pp. 3–23). New York: Wiley.

Dawis, R. V., & Lofquist, L. H. (1984). *A psychological theory of work adjustment.* Minneapolis: University of Minnesota Press.

Diemer, M. A. (2009). Pathways to occupational attainment among poor youth of color: The role of sociopolitical development. *The Counseling Psychologist, 37,* 6–35.

Diemer, M. A., & Blustein, D. L. (2006). Critical consciousness and career development among urban youth. *Journal of Vocational Behavior, 68,* 220–232.

Diemer, M. A., & Blustein, D. L. (2007). Vocational hope and vocational identity: Urban adolescents' career development. *Journal of Career Assessment, 15,* 98–118.

Diemer, M. A., & Hsieh, C. (2008). Sociopolitical development and vocational expectations among lower-SES adolescents of color. *Career Development Quarterly, 56,* 257–267.

Diemer, M. A., Hsieh, C., & Pan, T. (2009). School and parental influences on sociopolitical development among poor adolescents of color. *The Counseling Psychologist, 37,* 317–344.

Duffy, R. D., & Lent, R. W. (2009). Test of a social cognitive model of work satisfaction in teachers. *Journal of Vocational Behavior, 75,* 212–223.

Evans, J. H. J., & Burck, H. D. (1992). The effects of career education interventions on academic achievement: A meta-analysis. *Journal of Counseling and Development, 71,* 63–68.

Fouad, N. A., & Byars-Winston, A. M. (2005). Work: Cultural perspective on career choices and decision-making. In R. T. Carter (Ed.), *Handbook of racial-cultural psychology: Vol. 1. Theory and research* (pp. 232–255). Hoboken, NJ: Wiley.

Fouad, N. A., & Smith, P. L. (1996). A test of a social cognitive model for middle school students: Math and science. *Journal of Counseling Psychology, 43,* 338–346.

Freire, P. (1973). *Education for critical consciousness.* New York: Continuum.

Freire, P. (1993). *Pedagogy of the oppressed.* New York: Continuum.

Gainor, K. A., & Lent, R. W. (1998). Social cognitive expectations and racial identity attitudes in predicting math and science intentions of Black college students. *Journal of Counseling Psychology, 45,* 403–413.

Gibbons, M. M., & Borders, L. D. (2010). Prospective first-generation college students: A social-cognitive perspective. *Career Development Quarterly, 58,* 194–208.

Gottfredson, L. S. (1981). Circumscription and compromise: A developmental theory of occupational aspirations [Monograph]. *Journal of Counseling Psychology, 28,* 545–579.

Gottfredson, L. S. (2005). Applying Gottfredson's theory of circumscription and compromise in career guidance and counseling. In S. D. Brown & R. W. Lent (Eds.), *Career development and counseling: Putting theory and research to work* (pp. 71–100). New York: Wiley.

Greenberg, M. T., Weissberg, R. P., O'Brien, M. U., Zins, J. E., Fredericks, L., Resnik, H., & Elias, M. J. (2003). Enhancing school-based prevention and youth development through coordinated social, emotional, and academic learning. *American Psychologist, 58,* 466–474.

Holland, J. L. (1997). *Making vocational choices: A theory of vocational personalities and work environments* (3rd ed.). Odessa, FL: Psychological Assessment Resources.

Hughes, D., Smith, E. P., Stevenson, H. C., Rodriguez, J., Johnson, D. J., & Spicer, P. (2006). Parents' ethnic-racial socialization practices: A review of the literature and directions for future study. *Developmental Psychology, 42,* 747–770.

Juntunen, C. L., & Wettersten, K. B. (2006). Work hope: Development and initial validation of a measure. *Journal of Counseling Psychology, 53,* 94–106.

Kenny, M. E., Blustein, D. L., Haase, R. F., Jackson, J., & Perry, J. C. (2006). Setting the stage: Career development and the student engagement process. *Journal of Counseling Psychology, 53,* 272–279.

Kenny, M. E., Gualdron, L., Scanlon, D., Sparks, E., Bluestein, D. L., & Jernigan, M. (2007). Urban adolescents' constructions of supports and barriers to educational and career attainment. *Journal of Counseling Psychology, 54,* 336–343.

Kenny, M. E., Walsh-Blair, L. Y., Blustein, D. L., Bempechat, J., & Seltzer, J. (2010). Achievement motivation among adolescents: Work hope, autonomy support, and achievement-related beliefs. *Journal of Vocational Behavior, 77,* 205–212.

Lapan, R. T. (2004). *Career development across the K-16 years: Bridging the present to satisfying and successful futures.* Alexandria, VA: American Counseling Association.

Lapan, R. T., Gysbers, N. C., & Petroski, G. F. (2001). Helping seventh graders be safe and successful: A statewide study of the impact of comprehensive guidance and counseling programs. *Journal of Counseling and Development, 79,* 320–330.

Lent, R. W. (2004). Toward a unifying theoretical and practical perspective on well-being and psychological adjustment. *Journal of Counseling Psychology, 51,* 482–509.

Lent, R. W. (2005). A social cognitive view of career development and counseling. In S. D. Brown & R. W. Lent (Eds.), *Career development and counseling: Putting theory and research to work* (pp. 101–127). New York: Wiley.

Lent, R. W., & Brown, S. D. (2006a). Integrating person and situation perspectives on work satisfaction: A social-cognitive view. *Journal of Vocational Behavior, 69,* 236–247.

Lent, R. W., & Brown, S. D. (2006b). On conceptualizing and assessing social cognitive constructs in career research: A measurement guide. *Journal of Career Assessment, 14,* 12–35.

Lent, R. W., & Brown, S. D. (2008). Social cognitive career theory and subjective well-being in the context of work. *Journal of Career Assessment, 16,* 6–21.

Lent, R. W., Brown, S. D., & Hackett, G. (1994). Toward a unifying social cognitive theory of career and academic interest, choice, and performance [Monograph]. *Journal of Vocational Behavior, 45,* 79–122.

Lent, R. W., Hackett, G., & Brown, S. D. (1997). A social cognitive framework for studying career choice and transition to work. *Journal of Vocational Education Research, 21,* 3–32.

Lent, R. W., Hackett, G., & Brown, S. D. (1999). A social cognitive view of school-to-work transition. *Career Development Quarterly, 47,* 297–311.

Lent, R. W., Nota, L., Soresi, S., Ginevra, M. C., Duffy, R., & Brown, S. D. (2011). Predicting the job and life satisfaction of Italian teachers: Test of a social cognitive model. *Journal of Vocational Behavior, 79,* 91–97.

Lent, R. W., Singley, D., Sheu, H. B., Gainor, K. A., Brenner, B. R., Treistman, D., & Ades, L. (2005). Social cognitive predictors of domain and life satisfaction: Exploring the theoretical precursors of subjective well-being. *Journal of Counseling Psychology, 52,* 429–442.

Lent, R. W., Singley, D., Sheu, H. B., Schmidt, J. A., & Schmidt, L. C. (2007). Relation of social-cognitive factors to academic satisfaction in engineering students. *Journal of Career Assessment, 15,* 87–97.

Lent, R. W., Taveira, M. d. C., Sheu, H. B., & Singley, D. (2009). Social cognitive predictors of academic adjustment and life satisfaction in Portuguese college students: A longitudinal analysis. *Journal of Vocational Behavior, 74,* 190–198.

Luzzo, D. A., Funk, D. P., & Strang, J. (1996). Attributional retraining increases career decision-making self-efficacy. *Career Development Quarterly, 44,* 378–386.

Luzzo, D. A., James, T., & Luna, M. (1996). Effects of attributional retraining on the career beliefs and career exploration behavior of college students. *Journal of Counseling Psychology, 43,* 415–422.

Maola, J., & Kane, G. (1976). Comparison of computer-based versus counselor-based occupational information systems with disadvantaged vocational students. *Journal of Counseling Psychology, 23,* 163–165.

Marko, K. W., & Savickas, M. L. (1998). Effectiveness of a career time perspective intervention. *Journal of Vocational Behavior, 52,* 106–119.

Perry, J. C., Liu, X., & Pabian, Y. (2010). School engagement as a mediator of academic performance among urban youth: The role of career preparation, parental career support, and teacher support. *The Counseling Psychologist, 38,* 257–268.

Perry, J. C., Przybysz, J., & Al-Sheikh, M. (2009). Reconsidering the "aspiration-expectation gap" and assumed gender differences among urban youth. *Journal of Vocational Behavior, 74,* 349–354.

Perry, J. C., & Vance, K. S. (2010). Possible selves among urban youth of color: An exploration of peer beliefs and gender differences. *Career Development Quarterly, 58,* 257–269.

Phinney, J. S., & Chavira, V. (1995). Parental ethnic socialization and adolescent coping with problems related to ethnicity. *Journal of Research on Adolescence, 5,* 31–54.

Quintana, S. M., & Vera, E. M. (1999). Mexican American children's ethnic identity, understanding of ethnic prejudice, and parental ethnic socialization. *Hispanic Journal of Behavioral Sciences, 21,* 387–404.

Restubog, S. L. D., Florentino, A. R., & Garcia, P. R. J. M. (2010). The mediating role of career self-efficacy and career decidedness in the relationship between contextual support and persistence. *Journal of Vocational Behavior, 77,* 186–195.

Roe, A. A. (1956). *The psychology of occupations.* New York: Wiley.

Rojewski, J. W., & Yang, B. (1997). Longitudinal analysis of select influences on adolescent occupational aspirations. *Journal of Vocational Behavior, 51,* 375–410.

Ryan, R. M., & Deci, E. L. (2000). Self-determination theory and the facilitation of intrinsic motivation, self-development, and well being. *American Psychologist, 55,* 68–78.

Savickas, M. L. (1991). Improving career time perspective. In D. Brown & L. Brooks (Eds.), *Techniques of career counseling* (pp. 236–249). Boston: Allyn & Bacon.

Savickas, M. L., Silling, S. M., & Schwartz, S. (1984). Time perspective in vocational maturity and career decision-making. *Journal of Vocational Behavior, 25,* 258–269.

Scott, L. D. (2003). The relation of racial identity and racial socialization to coping with discrimination among African Americans. *Journal of Black Studies, 33,* 520–538.

Sheu, H. B., Lent, R. W., Brown, S. D., Miller, M. J., Hennessy, K. D., & Duffy, R. D. (2010). Testing the choice model of social cognitive career theory across Holland themes: A meta analytic path analysis. *Journal of Vocational Behavior, 76,* 252–264.

Snyder, C. R. (2000). Hypothesis: There is hope. In C. R. Snyder (Ed.), *Handbook of hope* (pp. 3–21). New York: Academic Press.

Snyder, C. R., Harris, C., Anderson, J. R., Holleran, S. A., Irving, L. M., Sigmon, S. T., et al. (1991). The will and the ways: Development and validation of an individual differences measure of hope. *Journal of Personality and Social Psychology, 60,* 570–585.

Steinberg, L., Dornbusch, S. M., & Brown, B. B. (1992). Ethnic differences in adolescent achievement: An ecological perspective. *American Psychologist, 47,* 723–729.

Super, D. E. (1980). A life-span, life-space approach to career development. *Journal of Vocational Behavior, 16,* 262–289.

Tang, M., Fouad, N. A., & Smith, P. L. (1999). Asian Americans' career choices: A path model to examine factors influencing career choices. *Journal of Vocational Behavior, 54,* 142–157.

Turner, S. L., & Lapan, R. T. (2005). Promoting career development and aspirations in school-aged youth. In S. D. Brown & R. W. Lent (Eds.), *Career development and counseling: Putting theory and research to work* (pp. 417–440). New York: Wiley.

Verbruggen, M., & Sels, L. (2010). Social-cognitive factors affecting clients' career and life satisfaction after counseling. *Journal of Career Assessment, 18,* 3–15.

Vondracek, F. W., Lerner, R. M., & Schulenberg, J. E. (1986). *Career development: A life-span developmental approach.* Hillsdale, NJ: Erlbaum.

CHAPTER

25 A Life Skills, Community-Based Approach for Helping Returning Service Members and Their Families

Steven J. Danish

Abstract

Veterans who experience a variety of stressors without accompanying psychopathology generally feel misunderstood and separate from both their families and communities, as well as from the VA system of care. The purpose of this chapter is fourfold. First, I will describe the development of a strength-based framework that serves as the basis for our approach to communities and people. Second, I will explain how this framework came to be used with service members and their families. Third, I will provide an example of how an individual without military experience is able to involve himself in military issues using a community-based approach. Fourth, I will detail several community-based programs that employ the strength-based framework I have adopted with the military. My hope is that counseling psychologists will realize how their training and philosophy can have a positive impact with a population that can benefit from our perspective.

Key Words: Military Veterans, Wellness Promotion, Community Resources.

The Problem and the Policy Significance

Approximately 2 million service members have served in either Afghanistan (OEF-Operation Enduring Freedom) and/or Iraq (OIF-Operation Iraqi Freedom), with 800,000 having served more than once (Tan, 2009). In contrast to previous wars, all OEF and OIF service members are volunteers.

With the enactment of the FY2010 Supplemental Appropriations Act, Congress has approved a total of $1.121 trillion for military operations, base security, reconstruction, foreign aid, embassy costs, and veterans' health care for the three operations initiated since the 9/11 attacks: OEF (Afghanistan and other counterterror operations); providing enhanced security at military bases; and OIF (Belasco, 2011). Health care costs are considerably higher than in previous wars, in part because in contrast to Vietnam, where the ratio was 2.6 wounded service members per fatality, in Iraq, seven out of eight wounded service members survive (Department of Veterans Affairs [VA], 2006). Health care costs include more than physical injuries. Although the actual numbers vary across studies, as many as 20% of returning Veterans have a diagnosable psychological condition according to a recent Institute of Medicine report (IOM, 2010).

The greatly reduced mortality rates, combined with the multiple deployments, created new, unprecedented problems for the health care system for veterans. First, the Veterans Administration Medical Centers (VAMC) were unprepared for the number of service members needing psychological (behavioral) health services and had to increase the hiring of psychologists (De Angelis, 2008; American Psychological Association (APA), 2010). Second, the VA needed to increase new returning service members' access to care, which meant expanding the hours they are open and adding additional providers and sites to serve those returning veterans who needed services. Third, according to the RAND report (Tanielian & Jaycox, 2008), as of May 2008, over 850,000 OIF and OEF service members were eligible for VA services, yet only about 40% of those eligible sought care. For example, only about half of returning service members reporting symptoms of post-traumatic stress disorder (PTSD) or major depression sought treatment. It has not been clear why so few in need of services have sought help.

One possible explanation has been proposed in the RAND report—the fear of being stigmatized for seeking help for their injuries. Tanielian and Jaycox (2008) identified five reported barriers to care that prevented service members from voluntarily accessing mental health services. Four of the five reported barriers to care—medication aversion, fear of career harm, security clearance denial, higher confidence in family member support, and coworker appraisals—relate to stigma.

More recently, Warner et al. (2011) most recently conducted a study of 3500 Army soldiers in an infantry brigade combat team going through their mandatory Post Deployment Health Assessment (PDHA). Of the total being assessed, 2500 were invited to complete an additional anonymous survey, and 1712 participated (response rate was 68.5%). Reports of depression, PTSD, suicidal ideation, and interest in receiving care were twofold to fourfold higher on the anonymous survey compared with the traditional PDHA. Overall, 20.3% of soldiers who screened positive for depression or PTSD reported that they were uncomfortable reporting their answers honestly on the routine post-deployment screening.

Whereas stigma is likely to be one of the major reasons for the decision not to seek services, there are other possible explanations. Veterans without a diagnosable psychological illness may need help but refuse to accept that their problems are psychopathological in nature. Consequently, the substantial number of service members who have difficulty readjusting to being home and reintegrating into their families, workplaces, and/or communities and do not meet the criteria for having a diagnosable psychological illness—and the number who experience such problems is substantial—may represent the unattended casualties of the longest US war in history. The number of these unattended casualties may actually be as many as 50% of those who have served (Henderson, 2006). Some may have difficulty adapting to their physical injuries; others may have experienced combat stress during their deployment. Nash (2007) has identified a number of these stressors, including: dealing with the physical elements such as heat, cold, and blasts; cognitive stresses such as the ambiguous and changing rules of engagement, fear, and helplessness; social stressors such as isolation from social supports; and spiritual stressors such as the inability to forgive or feel forgiven. Furthermore, when these veterans come home, the need to adjust to a changed environment adds another set of stressors, especially if their time at home is limited because they will be redeployed in less than a year. Veterans who are experiencing these stressors without accompanying psychopathology generally feel misunderstood and separate from both their families and communities as well as from the VA system of care.

Here are several questions that must be addressed when we consider how to best care for these service members and their families:

1. What resources currently exist to aid returning service members who do not need psychological treatment in the traditional, medical model? Seeking any mental health services already carries a stigma (Greene-Shortridge, Britt, & Castro, 2007); service members who face problems in readjustment face essentially a double stigma.
2. What new resources are needed for these returning service members, their families, and their employers?
3. How can we help reintegrating service members and their families achieve a state that is not simply the absence of disease, but the presence of wellness? This generation of returning service members will be parents, employees, and community builders for the next 20–50 years. Enabling them to successfully reintegrate and flourish has tremendous and far-reaching implications for policy and for the overall health of our country, now and many years into the future.

To address these questions is the focus of this chapter. First, I will describe the development of a strength-based framework that serves as the basis for our approach to communities and people. Second, I will explain how this framework came to be used with service members and their families. Third, I will provide an example of how an individual without military experience is able to involve himself in military issues using a community-based approach. Fourth, I will detail several community-based programs that employ the strength-based framework I have adopted with the military.

The Development of a Strength-Based Framework

In 1992, I developed the Life Skills Center at Virginia Commonwealth University (VCU). The

Center's mission is to develop, implement, and evaluate life skills programs for the purpose of promoting health and enhancing personal development. In deciding on the Center's orientation, I decided to emphasize positive developmental approaches to promoting human development as opposed to focusing on facilitating adjustment (a remediation orientation) or forestalling the occurrence of negative outcomes (a prevention orientation). We defined life skills as "those skills that enable individuals to succeed in the different environments in which they live such as school, home, and in their neighborhoods. Life skills can be behavioral (communicating effectively with peers and adults) or cognitive (making effective decisions); interpersonal (being assertive) or intrapersonal (setting goals)" (Danish, Petitpas, & Hale, 1993).

In deciding what populations were appropriate for our life skills programs, we used a prevention research report written by Mrazek and Haggerty (1994) for the IOM. They expanded on a prevention framework developed by Gordon (1987) that was based on a risk-benefit point of view; that is, the risk of getting a disease must be weighed against the cost, risk, and discomfort of the intervention. However, instead of focusing on prevention, we adopted a more strength-based focus. The three categories of interventions that Mrazek and Haggerty identified were universal, selective, and indicated.

As is clear from the names of the three categories, *universal* interventions are ones that are desirable for everybody in an eligible population. These interventions can be advocated confidently for the general public and applied without professional advice or assistance for everyone when the benefits outweigh the costs and risks. *Selective* preventive interventions are most appropriate when the risk of developing a disorder is above average, as these interventions are targeted to individuals or subgroups of a population. Subgroups may be distinguished by age, gender, occupation, family history, or other evident characteristics. The balance of benefits against risk and cost must be assessed in selective interventions because of the increased risk of illness. *Indicated* preventive interventions apply to persons who are at high risk for developing the disorder in the future, especially if they show early symptoms of the disorder. Screening programs are used to identify persons for whom indicated interventions are advisable because such measures are usually not totally benign or minimal in cost.

Universal interventions fit well with counseling psychology's emphasis on recognizing and promoting strengths in all individuals (Watkins, 1983; Fretz, 1982). It enables us to assess individuals in terms of their potential, not their problems, or lack of problems. Being problem-free is not the same as being competent or successful. Therefore, an important focus for interventions should be on defining and teaching individuals the skills, values, attitudes, and knowledge necessary to succeed in life (Danish, Forneris, & Wallace, 2005).

Initially the Life Skills Center's target was on youth. We developed programs and trained others to deliver the programs worldwide, including in Australia, Canada, England, Greece, New Zealand, Portugal, and Scotland, as well as in a number of cities and states in the United States. We received both federal and private grants to conduct our programs. One of the major programs we developed is a sport-based life skills program, SUPER (Sports United to Promote Education and Recreation; Danish, 2002). We found that the skills generally taught as sport psychology skills were really life skills when applied in domains other than sport, such as in school, home, and the workplace.

The initial purpose for the development of our life skills programs was to help youth develop the desired adolescent development outcomes identified by Carnegie Council on Adolescent Development in 1989 and 1995 (Carnegie Council, 1989, 1995). These outcomes are: (1) the ability to process information from multiple sources and communicate clearly; (2) to be en route to a lifetime of meaningful work by learning how to learn and therefore being able to adapt to different educational and working environments; (3) to be a good citizen by participating in community activities and feeling concern for, and connection to, the well-being of others; (4) to be a caring and ethical individual by acting on one's convictions about right and wrong; (5) to be a healthy person; (6) to find a valued place in a constructive group; (7) to learn how to form close and lasting relationships; (8) to feel a sense of worth; (9) to achieve a reliable basis for informed decision-making, especially on matters of large consequence; (10) to be able to use available support systems; (11) to have a positive future orientation; and (12) to learn respect.

As my colleagues and I thought more about these competencies, we came up with a more parsimonious list of competencies needed to be successful in life: the ability to *work well, play well, love well, think well, serve well,* and *be well* (Bloom, 2000; Danish, 2000). We also realized that attaining these competencies was not just important for adolescents, but was equally important for adults. These competencies then became the basis for our intervention goals.

Two conceptual frameworks serve as the basis for a life skills perspective. The first is life development intervention (LDI), a model developed by Danish and D'Augelli (1980; Danish, D'Augelli, & Ginsberg, 1984; Danish & Forneris, 2008); the second is self-determination theory (SDT; Deci & Ryan, 1985, 2000, 2008). We believe that these frameworks are consistent with counseling psychology's unique and traditional approach with its emphasis on self-directed change, being goal-directed, and focusing on the future, with an understanding of what needs to be done in the present to reach one's best possible future.

Life development intervention (LDI) is based on a life-span human development perspective (Danish et al., 1984). The goal of LDI is to help develop capacity and competence in life planning so as to enable individuals to encounter and successfully manage both routine and unexpected life events. Individuals hope that their lives will have continuity so that they do not have to confront change. Change can disrupt routines and relationships with others and may result in stress. The stress caused may have biological, psychological, and social components. For example, service members returning from deployment in Iraq or Afghanistan experience a biological change from hyperarousal (probably the result of some combination of epinephrine, serotonin, and dopamine) to a more relaxed state; a reference change from a warrior to a spouse, parent, son or daughter, and/or community member; a relocation change from a combat zone to a community; and a social change from being part of a military family to a civilian family (Danish & Antonides, 2009). In instances of change, one often experiences a sense of loss related to the end of the status quo.

Returning home may elicit a sense of boredom, ambiguity, isolation, powerlessness, and lack of meaning in service members' lives. The California National Guard kept track of the total number of mental health contacts from 2006 through May 2010 in four separate categories: self-initiated, provider-initiated, requested by the commander, and suggested by a peer. Of the almost 14,000 contacts, less than 25% were for PTSD symptoms, a little over 10% were for substance abuse issues, almost 40% were for marriage and family issues, and about 20% were for job or finance issues (California National Guard, 2010). So it is possible that as many as 60% of these Guard members' difficulties were related to the reintegration process.

If service members feel misunderstood, they may become isolated from those around them, including from friends and family members who observe the changes in them, see the struggles they are experiencing, but do not know how to help or what to do. As a result, service members may become angry about being ignored or misunderstood, and family and

Table 25.1 Potential Postdeployment Changes

Social/Interpersonal	Personal	Emotional Cognitive	Physical	Spirituality
Changes in relationships with family and friends from home (e.g., being misunderstood by them)	Changes in career-related goals	Changes in self-esteem and self-efficacy	Changes in risk-taking behavior (e.g., aggressive driving)	Having difficulty making sense of what you did in combat
Changes in job-related relationships and responsibilities	Changes in sense of purpose and meaning	Changes in locus of control	Changes in substance use (e.g., unlimited access to alcohol)	Feeling guilty
Changes in service-related relationships	Changes in belief system	Changes in emotional control	Changes in physical activity levels	Having conflicting values
Feeling abandoned by the military	Changes in sense of belonging	Changes in cognitive processing	Changes in sleep behavior	Questioning your religious beliefs
		Feeling unsafe and helpless	Changes in diet and nutrition habits	

friends may feel helpless to respond. The changes that take place during reintegration can be increasingly stressful if they continue over an extended period of time and can ultimately have a pervasive and unpredictable effect on an individual. The ultimate outcome may be the beginning of the downward slide of the service member toward substance abuse, homelessness, and even suicide.

Perry and Jessor (1985) referred to the result of stressors that occur during transitions such as these as *health-compromising behaviors* (behaviors that threaten the well-being of an individual such as inappropriate use of substances and physical risk-taking behavior such as speeding and reckless driving). See Table 25.1 for a description of the changes that may take place upon returning home from a deployment that may lead to health-compromising behaviors.

It is important to understand that returning home may mean more to service members than simply not being deployed. Many service members come home with a changed sense of self—a new sense of confidence and self-efficacy that result from the way they have responded to the challenges they have faced. They may return home having found their service experience to be meaningful and valuable (see Greene, 2009, and Kim, 2010, for example). As Bartone (2005) noted in his presidential address to Division 19 (Military Psychology) of the American Psychological Association, that more than anything, "Soldiers have a tremendous need to see their work as meaningful and important" (2005, p. 319). This need likely does not dissipate once they return, but for most, the context that supported this meaning (combat) has vanished. To many of their family and friends at home, they are heroes, and although they may not use the same word, these service members are also proud of their accomplishments. For a more extended discussion of LDI, the reader is referred to Danish (2000), and Danish and Forneris (2008).

The second conceptual framework is SDT and its sub-theory, Basic Needs Theory (BNT) (Deci & Ryan, 2000; Vansteenkiste, Niemiec, & Soenens, 2010). SDT and BNT consider the three psychological needs of competence, autonomy, and relatedness to be essential for ongoing psychological growth, integrity, and well-being for all individuals regardless of age, gender, or culture (Ryan & Deci, 2000). Autonomy is being the source of one's own behavior and having an authentic sense of self-direction and volition. Competence refers to a feeling of being effective in interactions and having the opportunity to demonstrate their capacities (Ryan & Deci, 2000). Relatedness refers to having a sense of belonging and feeling connected to others (Ryan & Deci, 2000). SDT is one of the most commonly used models of motivation. According to Deci and Ryan (2000; Ryan & Deci, 2000, 2008), when these three needs are satisfied, individuals experience positive psychological development and optimal psychological well-being. We believe that the overall goal of life skills programs is to help individuals satisfy these three basic psychological needs. For a more extended discussion of the connection between life development intervention and self-determination theory and how they serve as the conceptual framework for our life skills programs, the reader is referred to Hodge, Danish, and Martin (in preparation).

Transitioning From Youth and Sports to Issues Facing Veterans

In 2004, one of my doctoral students, a West Point graduate, was deployed to Iraq. She had come to VCU following graduation and after completing her 5-year service commitment and had entered the doctoral program in counseling psychology. She was interested in studying life skills and how they could be applied to sport and was actively involved in our programs prior to her deployment. Her experiences in Iraq during deployment and her e-mails to me about what many of her fellow soldiers were facing both during and after deployment led me to realize that the life skills programs we had developed, with some adaptations, might have utility in helping deployed service members and their families before, during, and after deployment.

Our interactions about the needs of service members changed my professional life. I decided to focus my intervention research on service members and their families. I quickly learned of the health care crisis returning service members and their families faced and the need to understand and attack the problem at a scale larger than helping one person at a time. I became committed to dedicating a significant portion of both my time and the Center's to confronting this problem. However, wanting to help and being allowed to help are two different issues.

Taking the First Steps Toward the Transition

Sometimes we forget that when we graduate the ceremony is not called "Graduation," but "Commencement," which means beginning. I have always taken this distinction seriously and have had a number of "beginnings" in my career. The experience of learning about what service members and families go though was just the latest "beginning."

Some people can learn all they want by themselves; I cannot. I need teachers. Two graduate students who are veterans—Lisa Harmon, the West Point graduate who initially motivated me to get involved and is presently a psychologist at a Veterans Administration Medical Center in Vermont, and now Brad Antonides, a student with whom I have written extensively—have been wonderful teachers, as have been a retired Navy psychiatrist, Bill Nash, and a colonel in the Virginia National Guard, Thomas Morgan.

I started the transition by taking three steps. First, I wanted to understand service members, their motivations for volunteering, their experiences in the war, the issues they faced coming home, and how their families were affected by deployment. I did this both by reading and meeting with service members and their families. For example, a student arranged for me to interview five wives of deployed Marines for 2 hours and have them discuss how multiple deployments had affected them and their marriages. When friends found out about my interest, they introduced me to their friends, family members, and acquaintances who had been or were preparing to be deployed; and I had several informative discussions with service members I met in airports. My strategy was to think of these interactions as informational interviews, similar to the method it is recommended that one go through as part of the career decision process.

I also started reading everything I could about the veterans and the reintegration process they go through. I immersed myself in the literature. I attended conferences. One of the most important books I read was *The Sandbox: Dispatches from Troops in Iraq and Afghanistan* by Garry Trudeau (2007). The book is a compilation from a blog that is still available and updated almost daily that provides a forum for service members in Afghanistan and Iraq to share their stories with readers here at home. What I like about it is that it describes the daily experiences of war, not just the fights or the drama. I also enrolled in a course on military culture online (see Course 116 [Online]: Military Cultural Competence at http://deploymentpsych.org/training/training-catalog/military-cultural-competence).

The second step was to take my life development intervention approach and adapt it to facilitate service member reintegration. However, after understanding the health care crisis that I discussed earlier, I realized that both a new *conceptual framework* for the type of services and *a new service delivery model* for service members and their families experiencing reintegration difficulties were needed. As opposed to treating reintegration difficulties as a problem requiring a "medical model" intervention framework, such as psychotherapy, which is the framework most prevalent in the VA, I used the LDI framework, previously mentioned. The two models are contrasted in Figure 25.1.

The two models differ in several ways, but the primary distinction is that in the LDI framework there is no assumption that problems are a result of psychopathology or psychological problems. It is assumed that any difficulties are the result of not being able to reach the dreams and goals service members have for their present and future. In fact, some service members are adamant that they have no need to see a mental health professional, and they may not. However, it may be useful to ascertain whether they are reaching the postdeployment goals they have for themselves and their family, and if they are not, to help them understand that not reaching their goals can be seen as a problem to be overcome.

However, the LDI approach I implemented was more than a different conceptual framework; it was also a different delivery system, closely related to a public health model. One critical characteristic of this model is that psychologists and other providers adopt a seeking rather than a waiting mode (Rappaport, 1977). In other words, instead of waiting for service members to come seeking services, providers reach out to service members where they are and provide whatever services are needed. For such a system to work, psychologists must act as indirect service providers as opposed to being direct

Medical Intervention Framework (illness -> diagnosis -> prescription -> therapy -> cure)

Life Development Intervention (LDI) Framework (dissatisfaction -> goal setting -> life skill enhancement -> goal achievement -> well being or success)

Figure 25.1. The difference between a medical and life development intervention framework

service providers (Danish, 1974). By indirect service providers, I am referring to such actions as developing programs, consulting, training, and supervising others who can help. For example, teachers and school counselors need to understand what effect deployment has on children. Programs and training can be provided to schools and school personnel to help them respond to the needs of these children. Health care providers must understand how IEDs (improvised explosive devices) and other blasts may result in more than polytrauma injuries. Law enforcement personnel such as police and judges must understand the impact reintegration has on service members and their families and consider establishing Veteran's Courts as they have in Buffalo, New York, and several other cities.

Another issue related to the delivery of services is that we recognize that the service member is at the center of the circle surrounded by a community, perhaps an employer, friends, and most of all, a family. The family, be it the family of origin or a spouse and their children or even the service member's "girlfriends/boyfriends," is really the key to reintegration. Therefore, it is essential that the family be part of any reintegration efforts with the service member. Readers wanting to know more about the needs of military families are encouraged to visit the Military Family Research Institute website, www.mfri.purdue.edu, at Purdue University.

An effective delivery system should involve the use of technology. Nearly 40% of service members live in rural areas, and more creative ways must be found to provide them with services. One approach is through telehealth, using technology such as the telephone, skype, or videoconferencing. A variety of services are being delivered in these ways, especially through the VA.

The third step I took involved me doing some soul searching. Several years ago I developed for myself and my graduate class in community psychology a document to understand whether and when to intervene. I knew I wanted to make a difference, as we all do. But what was my motivation? And how much of it was professional and how much was personal? My first step, upon deciding to focus on military issues, was to review this document to better understand my motivations for wanting to work with service members and their families, how feasible it was, and to consider how I might gain entry into this system. See Table 25.2 for a list of questions I asked myself.

One of the areas in Table 25.2 that stood out for me was to ascertain whether my goals and the goals of service members and their families were compatible. For example, most service members were ready to serve the country and go to combat. If I held a belief that going to war was a mistake, and openly communicated this belief, any help I might offer would be summarily rejected. My views about whether going to war was appropriate were irrelevant to wanting to help; my purpose was to develop programs that would help these service members and their families reintegrate successfully following deployment. My immediate task was to understand their plight well enough so that I could work *with* them to develop programs that would optimize their reintegration, not just help them return to the way they were prior to deployment. Working *with* them differed significantly from developing an intervention *for* them. The commitment of the target group to an intervention and the likely success differs considerably when there is a collaborative relationship.

An obvious critical component, then, for undertaking a successful intervention is an understanding of the target group's needs and goals; and for this understanding to take place, open communication is necessary. The military culture makes this understanding extremely difficult. Service members and their families are a unique subculture within the larger society in which they serve. It is a closed community with unique customs, cultural norms, diverse membership, and defining rank structure (Harmon, 2007). The military even has its own shorthand lexicon. The closed community typically includes those who have served and their dependent family members (spouses and children). Sometimes nondependent parents and siblings of military personnel are included. Being part of this community often means that family members will refrain from speaking to outsiders about military and family issues. What is communicated to outsiders both directly and indirectly is that if you had not served, you don't know "what it was like over there and we are not going to tell you." You are an outsider and there is a basic mistrust (Danish & Antonides, 2009). This attitude is directed at all civilians, not just helping professionals.

Sometimes the mistrust and sense of exclusivity goes beyond whether or not you have served in the military. Within the military, there are differences between the branches (Marine, Army, Navy, Air Force, Coast Guard, National Guard, and Reserves), the jobs service members have or had in the military, and whether or not they were in combat. The uniform and the type and location of the patches service members wear on their uniform identify

Table 25.2 Framework for Considering Whether and How to Intervene

1. Can you make a difference?
2. Why do you want to make a difference? Do you understand your needs and values for wanting to make a difference?
   - o Is it for professional reasons? What are they?
   - o Is it for personal reasons? What are they?
   - o Is it for both reasons? What are they?
3. What is the difference you want to make?
4. Are your goals for the difference you want to make and the goals of the target group the same?
   - o Are you doing things "with," "to," or "for" the target group? (You may want to consider a needs assessment to help you answer this).
5. At what levels do you want to make a difference (You may also want to consider a needs assessment to help you answer this as well)?
   - o Individual
   - o Family
   - o Group
   - o Institution
   - o Community
   - o Society
6. What is the focus of your efforts to make a difference?
   - o Leonardo da Vinci described the difference between painting and sculpture. His description, in essence, is that in painting something added, whereas in sculpture something is taken away. Are your plans to be painting or sculpting?
   - o *Promote* development at the intended level
     - ▪ If so, make sure you understand the dreams of the target group
   - o *Prevent* problems from occurring at the intended level
     - ▪ Keep in mind Ryan's (1971) concept of "blaming the victim" in choosing the target group.
   - o *Remediate* or *rectify* problems that have already occurred at the intended level.
     - ▪ Again, keep in mind whether you are blaming the victim (Ryan, 1971).
7. What methods will you use to make a difference and assess whether you have been effective?
   - o Make sure the processes are consistent with your goals.
   - o Have you considered the setting for what you want to do and whether the setting will be appropriate for the methods chosen?
8. What knowledge must you have or acquire to make a difference and assess whether you have been effective?
9. What skills must you have or acquire to make a difference and assess whether you have been effective?
10. What are the ethical implications of what you want to do and how will you assess whether the target of your intervention has been protected?
11. How will you know whether you have made a difference?
    - o What are your intended consequences?
    - o What are the potential unintended consequences?
12. How effective have you been in making a difference?
    - o Why or why not?
      - ▪ Did you differentiate your goals (what you control) from outcomes (what you want someone else to do whom you do not control)?
      - ▪ Was the implementation process done as designed (fidelity)?
      - ▪ Were there different outcomes for different subgroups (gender, ethnicity, etc.)? Why?
13. Can you improve your effectiveness in making a difference?
    - o How?
14. How can you disseminate more broadly what you have done?
    - o Do you need additional knowledge and/or skills?

where and how they have served. Even families of service members who return from combat may feel a sense of being excluded. The family of origin may be replaced by those the service member has served with (his or her military family).

These obstacles were initially serious roadblocks in my effort to work with the returning service members and their families and they remain hurdles that often must be overcome each day. However, the obstacles I faced, and face, differ little from those encountered by all of us when we are trying to understand and work with individuals from a different culture. In fact, I had encountered similar issues when I had started working with another group—professional and elite athletes. Despite my efforts to develop relationships with several veterans' organizations and veterans' service organizations, my first efforts were unsuccessful in establishing the kind of relationships that would provide me an entrée to the culture of the military.

Connecting With the Army National Guard

The Army National Guard (ARNG) is one component of the Army (which consists of the Active Army, the Army National Guard and the Army Reserve.) The Army National Guard is composed primarily of traditional Guardsmen—civilians who serve their country, state, and community on a part-time basis (usually one weekend each month and two weeks during the summer.) Each state, most territories, and the District of Columbia has its own National Guard, as provided for by the Constitution of the United States. The Guard has a unique dual mission that consists of both federal and state roles. For state missions, the governor, through the state adjutant general, commands Guard forces. The governor can call the National Guard into action during local or statewide emergencies, such as storms, fires, earthquakes, or civil disturbances. In addition, the President of the United States can activate the National Guard for participation in federal missions such as the wars in Iraq and Afghanistan. When federalized, Guard units are commanded by the combatant commander of the theater in which they are operating (usa.gov, 2011).

As of July 31, 2011, a total of 350,071 National Guard members had been deployed, and 48,024 were presently deployed. In Virginia, the numbers were 8,823 and 1,672 (Defense Manpower Data Center [DMDC], 2011). These numbers do not include Air National Guard members or any Army, Marine, Navy, or Coast Guard Reservists. One program developed to help the National Guard component of the Armed Forces and their families is the Yellow Ribbon Reintegration Program (YRRP; Joint Services Support, 2011). YRRP consists of information and activities to facilitate access to services supporting the health and well-being of service members and their families through the four phases of the deployment cycle: (1) Predeployment, (2) Deployment, (3) Demobilization, and (4) Postdeployment.

YRRP was started by a mandate from the Secretary of Defense to establish a national combat veteran reintegration program to provide National Guard members and their families with sufficient information, services, referrals, and proactive outreach opportunities through the entire deployment cycle. The assistance and services included some of the following: marriage counseling, services for children, suicide prevention, substance abuse awareness and treatment, mental health awareness and treatment, financial counseling, anger management counseling, domestic violence awareness and prevention, employment assistance, preparing and updating family care plans, development of strategies for living with a member of the Armed Forces with post-traumatic stress disorder or traumatic brain injury, and other services that may be appropriate to address the unique needs these members of the Armed Forces and their families who live in rural or remote areas with respect to family readiness and Service Member reintegration. It is evident that this mandate was meant to be comprehensive and inclusive and was developed because returning National Guard members were experiencing problems throughout the deployment cycle, but especially as they tried to reintegrate upon returning home.

Part of the difficulties was that this was the first time National Guard soldiers had been mobilized to fight in combat. The decision to mobilize the Reserve Components to fight was a surprise to many National Guard soldiers. Many were well established in their communities and had joined the Guard to assist in state emergencies and use the support provided to go to school. They were "citizen-soldiers" and never anticipated going to war. For many, leaving their jobs and careers and their families was a shock. Another problem more specific to the National Guard, was that in contrast to Active Duty forces and many Reserve components, when National Guard soldiers were activated they were often sent far from their homes to Army bases out of state to train and prepare for deployment, many times without colleagues from their state unit. The result of this displacement was that they were away from their homes and family even longer than those on Active Duty because in addition to their deployment period they were away for the training period, often with no source of support. Furthermore, when they returned home, they returned to the base from which they deployed, making it a greater hardship on their families to meet them. Finally, upon returning to their communities and families, they often no longer had the soldiers who had been in combat with them and had become their new "family" to rely on.

Whereas the Yellow Ribbon mandate was clear, the procedure(s) used to reach the objective were not, and it was left up to individual state units to determine how to meet the objectives. One unique aspect of the Virginia National Guard's response to the Yellow Ribbon mandate was to propose that service members and their families would *be better off after completion of their deployment* than they were when the service members were alerted for deployment.

The Virginia National Guard's Director of Manpower and Personnel (the J-1) invited state and federal agencies as well as Veteran Service Organizations in Virginia to serve as partners in helping returning veterans. These partners worked with the Guard to identify available services and then with the help of the Guard's coordination to develop a plan for providing mental health assessments, assistance, and education during the reintegration period. These partners included Virginia's three Veterans Administration Medical Centers; Veteran's Outreach Centers; Virginia Department of Veteran Services and its Wounded Warrior Program that had received $4 million over 2 years to service injured returning veterans; the Virginia Department of Mental Health, Mental Retardation and Substance Abuse Services; the Virginia Community Services Boards, which are the mental health, mental retardation and substance abuse delivery service system in Virginia; several units of Virginia Commonwealth University, a state university, working with returning veterans; and the Brain Injury Association of Virginia. The partners met monthly with the Virginia National Guard for 5 months to develop the Virginia Yellow Ribbon Program.

The first steps were to develop a series of facts and assumptions related to the Virginia Yellow Ribbon Program. Among the facts were: (1) All returning service members would be enrolled in the Veterans Affairs Medical Health Care System; (2) All service members would receive a postdeployment health assessment (PDHA) at the demobilization site; (3) All service members would receive a postdeployment health reassessment (PDHRA) 90 days after demobilization at the 30-day event; (4) Family members would be included at the 30- and 60-day events of the reintegration program; (5) All Virginia National Guard units had Family Readiness groups; (6) The Virginia National Guard had the resources of the Military One Source, a 24-hour-a-day telephone service established by the Defense Department as a "*one stop*" place to go whenever service members or family members needed assistance with any kind of problem; (7) All service members could seek treatment at a VA facility for up to 5 years after demobilization; (8) During deployment there was assistance for families, but following deployment there were no services at the VA for families unless the Service Member was involved and it was a family issue; and (9) Community Service Boards, one of the partners, had limited funding, and their available personnel were not sufficient in numbers nor adequately trained to provide services to all returning service members and their families.

The assumptions that were considered as the implementation of the Yellow Ribbon was being planned included that: (1) the Virginia Wounded Warrior Program would enhance access to capabilities; (2) *not* all family Members knew where to go to seek help; (3) *not* all service members and Commanders knew where to seek help for specific situations; (4) education and work opportunities affect mental health; (5) there was still a negative stigma attached to mental health services; (6) Many units commanders did not feel there was a need for reintegration events and therefore the need for these programs was often challenged; (7) Many service members discouraged family members from seeking treatment; (8) the population needing support would continue to grow as the effects of the wars would be long-term and require long-term treatment and that government sometimes would serve as a barrier; and (9) there was a reluctance among providers to accept TRICARE because of problem with coverage and programs.

There were five meetings, one per month. I was one of two individuals to attend all the meetings. As a result, I became acquainted with the leader of the meetings, the J-1 officer, Colonel Thom Morgan. The J-1 is responsible for manpower and personnel; specifically, he/she has the primary responsibility to provide overall human resource strategic planning, integration, analysis, manpower, and personnel policy, and oversight of the personnel readiness, operational capabilities, and sustainment of the National Guard community. Not being a shy person, I offered a number of suggestions during the meetings and followed through on them. When their YRRP plan was developed, I was invited to participate in several of the events. As an outsider, I mostly observed, but was asked by Colonel Morgan to share my reactions after each event, especially the one he was not able to attend. As it turned out, several suggestions I made were accepted and through my participation I became friendly with many of the J-1 staff. I came away impressed with their dedication to their mission of facilitating the reintegration from deployment of the soldiers and families and preparing other soldiers and families for deployment. It is a tremendous task. I also found that someone with the kind of skills we have, *if we are able to step out of our identity as psychologists and become careful observers*, can have a positive effect on the process. Someone I know suggested that the role is similar to the role Peter Falk played on the old television series *Columbo*. Soldiers consider psychologists "shrinks," and do their best to stay away from them, so it is best if we leave our psychological attire and terminology at home.

As a result of this experience I was invited by Colonel Morgan to accompany him to meetings at the National Guard Bureau. At these meetings a number of states were considering and sharing their ideas about their Yellow Ribbon Reintegration Programs. Programs were directed at a number of critical areas related to reintegration: physical, personal, social/interpersonal, emotional, family, and spiritual. Army researchers and psychologists also presented what they thought were helpful additions to a YRRP. Some were quite interesting in their use of technology. Others were well beyond what could be feasibly done in a National Guard setting. Two reoccurring issues seemed to come up during these meeting—the problem of stigma and how to evaluate the effectiveness of these programs. Because of some work I was doing on both topics, I volunteered to present some information. One of my doctoral students was just completing her dissertation on the applicability of a social norms approach to help seeking with college students (Conley, 2011), and I had been teaching about the RE-AIM evaluation method (Glasgow, et al, 1999) in my community psychology class. As a consequence of these presentations, I was able to meet a number of individuals in decision-making roles for all the National Guard. These connections led me to being able to propose life skills–based intervention programs.

Collaborating With the National Guard on Life Skills Intervention

I also met Colonel Gregg Bliss, the Chief, Soldier and Family Support Division, for the National Guard. He was concerned about the increasing suicide rates among National Guard Army soldiers. Prior to 2008, military rates of suicides were lower than civilian rates. However, in 2008, that pattern was reversed, with the suicide rate in the Army exceeding the age-adjusted rate in the civilian population (20.2 out of 100,000 vs. 19.2) (Defense Centers of Excellence [DCoE], 2011; NIMH, 2009).

In 2009, there were 162 active duty suicides and 80 suicides among members of the Army Reserves and National Guard; in 2010, the number of active duty suicides went down slightly to 156, but the number of Reserve and Army National Guard suicides increased dramatically from 80 to 145, and more than half of these Guard and Reserve soldiers who committed suicide had never been deployed (DCoE, 2011; NIMH, 2009). Since 2010, more soldiers died from suicide than from combat. Despite efforts to better understand the behavioral health issues related to suicide, definite answers were, and are, still lacking. Soldiers who needed help the most were the least likely to seek help. Although the Army has made a concerted effort to reduce the stigma associated with help-seeking, 51% still believed that seeking help would negatively affect their careers (Chiarelli, 2010; Hoge et al., 2008).

In 2009, the Army unveiled their approved model for a peer-oriented prevention approach (Department of the Army, Pamphlet 600–24, 2009). The model involved three steps: having peers *Ask, Care, Escort* (ACE). Colonel Bliss and one of his deputies, Lieutenant Colonel Ashleah Bechtel, explained that the ACE approach was not as appropriate for the Guard because of the limited contact Guard members have with each other and the minimal understanding that their soldiers and leaders have about any changes that take place in soldiers' lives and the causes of these changes. Colonel Bliss was interested in a more preventative approach and one that focused on providing "psychological first aid" and asked us to consider developing a different intervention model.

The result was the development of the APFA (Assessing Psychological First Aid). The goals of APFA are to enable soldiers to report the need for help in a safe environment and to train squad leaders how to identify soldiers in need and then help them seek help. The idea was to turn psychological first aid into a battle drill. The APFA has three objectives to: (1) use the Army leadership model of providing purpose, direction, and motivation to achieve higher unit cohesion; (2) avoid the stigma of identifying human problems as weaknesses; and (3) bring the domain of human concerns into the squad leader's sphere of self-efficacy, influence, and responsibility.

The APFA instrument that Brad Antonides, Ashleah Bechtel, and I developed has two parts: a soldier self-assessment and the squad leader assessment of the soldier. Three questions make up the assessment: The soldier is asked on a 9-point scale from *Not At All* to *A Great Extent* to rate: (1) *To what extent have I decided where I am headed with my life;* (2) *To what extent do I feel as if I am achieving the things I want to accomplish;* and (3) *To what extent do I have the support of family and friends that I need in my life?* Squad leaders are asked on the same 9-point scale to rate each of their soldiers on two of the same questions and a third question which is similar to the third soldier question without the benefit of knowing the soldier's self-ratings: (1) *To what extent does the soldier have a direction for his/her life;* (2) *To what extent does the soldier seem to be achieving the things he/she wants to accomplish*; and (3) *To what extent does the soldier relate well with others?* These questions are all based on self-determination theory (Deci & Ryan, 2000).

Soldiers are also asked if they are satisfied with the way their life is going and if not, would they like some help. If they say yes to help, they are asked if they want help immediately. If they are interested in receiving help either immediately or in the near future, they are given a number of options for help-seeking ranging from friends to military mental health professionals or chaplains to civilian mental health professionals or civilian chaplains. Squad leaders are also asked to rate how confident they are that they can accurately rate the soldier on the three questions, and if they have rated the soldier as having problems, what signs of distress have they noticed such as discipline problems, being late, changes in appearance, and loss of military bearing.

Soldiers complete their ratings at the beginning of drill; squad leaders complete their ratings at the end of drill. We believe that if administered monthly for 6 to 8 months, the process will be normalized for both the soldier and squad leader. Among our hypotheses, we expect that soldiers will increasingly indicate when they are having problems, will increasingly ask for help, and will identify whom they would be willing to talk to. As a result, there will be an increase in soldier self-referrals. Additionally, squad leaders will become increasingly confident that they are able to accurately evaluate their soldiers and become more aware when soldiers are experiencing distress and take steps to intervene at appropriate levels of care. We are presently conducting this study.

The second project, a collaborative effort with Virginia National Guard, is entitled the Virginia National Guard Yellow Ribbon Reintegration G.R.I.P. Program (Goals Reached through Improved Planning). It was developed to meet the Guard leader's intent that their participants would be better off following deployment. The Guard leadership believed that goal setting materials and training proposed by the Life Skills Center team to facilitate GRIP validated what the Guard leadership believed was intuitively the best solution to the issues they sought to address through YRRP.

The intent of the project is to teach soldiers and their families how to dream and set reachable goals using a manualized 1-hour skills-based presentation during predeployment and then to keep in contact with both of them during the rest of the predeployment and the deployment period. Participants will choose goals in an area in which they wish to improve from among the following: *Relationships (family and friends), Health, Employment, Finances, Education, Spirituality*, and *Other.*

The intervention will begin up to six months prior to deployment. Soldiers and families (if the soldier is single, parents may participate) will both set an individual goal and together choose and set a joint third goal. Once they learn the intervention and have identified their dreams and goals, trained monitors will keep in contact with both to help them work toward their goals throughout the remaining predeployment period as well as during deployment. Contact will be maintained by their monitors either by phone or e-mail on average every 8 weeks. The focus of the contact will be to assess progress toward reaching their individual and joint goals, review with them the goal-setting progress if they are having trouble, focus on helping the soldier or family member to put into context the relationship between the goals they have set and the dreams they want, and to help them set additional goals that will enable them to get closer to their dreams as each goal is achieved. The contact will be maintained for up to 6 months following deployment. Therefore, the total time for the project is 2 years.

We hypothesize that those soldiers and family members who attain their goals will reintegrate more successfully than participants who do not achieve their goals and participants who do not receive the full intervention. Funding was allocated for this project last year but because of a series of inexplicable errors, the funds were never made available to either Virginia Commonwealth University or the Virginia National Guard. Funding is presently being sought to implement the project this year.

Piloting a University-Based Life Skills Program

Ruud and his colleagues (2011) conducted a study at the University of Utah comparing the mental health status of veteran and civilian college students. They found suicidal ideation, anxiety, and depression levels significantly higher among students who were veterans than among nonveteran students. This is not surprising. Chiarelli (2010) describes the average soldier as 24 years old. On average, he or she moved from home, family, and friends; has resided in two other states; traveled the world as a result of deployment; was promoted four times; bought a car and wrecked it; been married and had children; has had relationship and financial problems; has seen death; has been responsible for dozens of soldiers; has maintained millions of dollars worth of equipment; and got paid less than $40,000 a year. The average civilian college student has done few of these things but often feels superior to the veteran. Faculty do not understand what student veterans have experienced either, often assuming the veteran is less educated, experienced, worldly, and polished. Veterans tend to have their antennae up looking for situations where they are being shunned and put down and are very good at finding them. It is why student veteran's organizations are important and fairly common. But veterans cannot stay in that cocoon permanently. When they venture out, they often experience an existential loneliness—not feeling valued or wanted by faculty and fellow students alike. This leads to feelings of hurt and anger, but because people who want to appear strong find it difficult to allow themselves to experience hurt, the feelings generally all manifest as anger. Anger can be turned outward toward others or inward toward themselves. When anger turns inward, depression and suicide can follow. Gould (2001) has written about suicide contagion or suicide clusters and has noted that such behavior is more common among young adults. In part, she believes that the media sometimes portrays suicides in an attractive or sensational way, encouraging imitation. Gould notes that clusters may be more pronounced when individuals share common environmental stressors. The military and colleges are such settings. That is why we developed a modest intervention to pilot entitled Movement to Contact (MTC).

The purpose of Movement to Contact Project is fourfold: (1) to understand what perceptions student veterans and their families have of the services offered to them at our university and the barriers they anticipate encountering to access these services; (2) to work with agencies at the university so that they may provide services and resources that are identified by the student veterans and their families as needed; (3) to disseminate widely, throughout the university, accurate information about the services and resources available and provide an opportunity for these student veterans and their families to meet with a well-trained peer familiar with veteran issues who can directly help them and/or help them access the services and resources they need; and (4) in a second phase of the project, provide the general student population with a better understanding of student veterans and their family's strengths and contributions to the university and the country.

The first step is to identify student veterans and/or family members on campus. An email will be sent to them explaining the program and soliciting their feedback. Once the data are collected, we will be able to meet with agencies involved in serving veterans and provide them with feedback from the survey to see if they can add the services identified by the student veterans as needed and if we can provide any training for them about issues such as military culture. We will then disseminate information about the services and resources available including the possibility of meeting anonymously with a well-trained MTC peer familiar with veteran issues. Dissemination of the information will be done through the use of Stall Seat Journals. The concept of the Stall Seat Journal has won awards from the US Department of Education for their novel and effective manner in which they clarify misperceptions about tobacco and alcohol use among college students. Distribution of the Stall Seat Journals occurs through placements primarily in dorm bathrooms (with gender-specific information), and at other select locations such as Student Commons bathrooms and academic classroom building bathrooms. We will evaluate this first phase by assessing whether contact with the veteran-serving agency and the MTC peer increases and whether student veterans and their families feel more satisfied with the services they receive. Finally, in a second phase of the project, the use of "clickers" and Stall Seat Journals will again be used to determine whether we can change the attitudes students have toward student veterans.

With the "GI Bill" authorized in 1944, some 8 million World War II veterans received assistance to attend college. The result was monumental advances in science, literature, art, industry, and economic prosperity (Brokaw, 2004). As those WWII veterans reach the twilight of their lives, we are in need of a new "greatest generation" to move us forward. Today's student veterans may be the next greatest generation.

A Personal Retrospective

As I review my experiences over the last 5 plus years, I come back to Table 25.2. I remain very passionate about my work. I am humbled by some of the opportunities I have had, the people who have provided these opportunities for me, and by some of the veterans I have met. I think we are making somewhat of a difference. I also see all that needs to be done and accept that what I have chosen to work on is a slice of what is needed, not an insignificant slice, but a slice nonetheless.

As we move forward, we must recognize that nearly 20% of over 2,000,000 service members are experiencing PTSD, depression, traumatic brain injuries (TBI), and other injuries that are sufficiently debilitating that they need extensive physical and psychological help. The long-term financial costs according to Bilmes and Stiglitz (2011) could top $2 trillion. The cost to families is incalculable. These costs put into perspective what a small slice my part is. However, instead of overwhelming me, it makes me want to redouble my efforts. I guess it is a function of my innate optimism.

The life skills intervention model and a community-based delivery model we have developed is in many ways a radical departure from how veterans have received services to date. It is not my intention to suggest that what has been done previously is ineffective. We do know that service members have been concerned about the stigma associated with going to the VA and admitting to having a psychological problem. Therefore, it makes sense to see if there are alternative ways to help returning service members who are experiencing reintegration problems. When faced with a new approach, it is often easier to assume it will not work, especially with some service members experiencing serious behavioral or mental health problems. Instead of starting the discussion by identifying whom this new model won't work for, I propose that we start at the other end. Who will benefit by this framework and approach? When we come upon service members or their families who do not benefit from this framework and approach, we can then return to the more traditional approaches or seek other new approaches. The potential benefits of adopting this perspective are several: (1) More service members and their families can be reached this way with less fear of stigma; (2) If this approach proves effective, more resources can be directed toward those services members who can benefit from more intensive interventions; (3) The cost of caring for those who have served may be reduced which is especially important when there are numerous calls to reduce the military budget; and (4) This system may have utility for civilian health care as well.

I am already at work at some additional programs—stay tuned.

Acknowledgment

I would especially like to thank Brad Antonides, whose contributions to this chapter including helping to write some of these sections are immeasurable; to Colonel Thomas Morgan, who has been a friend and willing partner to some of my strange ideas; and to Katherine Lang, for her excellent editing and reference work.

References

American Psychological Association (APA). (2010). Big growth in the number of VA psychologists. *Monitor on Psychology, 41*(6), 11.

Bartone, P. L. (2005). The need for positive meaning in military operations: Reflections on Abu Ghraib. *Military Psychology, 17*(4), 315–324. doi: 10.1207/s15327876mp1704_5

Belasco, A. (2011, March 29). The cost of Iraq, Afghanistan, and other global war on terror operations since 9/11. *Congressional Research Service.* Retrieved from http://www.fas.org/sgp/crs/natsec/RL33110.pdf

Bilmes, L. J., & Stiglitz, J. E. (2011). The long-term costs of conflict: The case of the Iraq War. In D. L. Braddon & K. Hartley (Eds.), *Handbook on the economics of conflict* (pp. 293–311). Cheltenham, UK: Edward Elgar.

Bloom, M. (2000). The uses of theory in primary prevention practice: Evolving thoughts on sports and after-school activities as influences of social competence. In S. J. Danish & T. P. Gullotta (Eds.), *Developing competent youth and strong communities through after-school programming* (pp. 275–302). Washington, DC: CWLA Press.

Brokaw, T. (2004). *The greatest generation.* New York: Random House.

California National Guard. (2010). CANG Pilot Program 2006-May 2010. Unpublished.

Carnegie Council on Adolescent Development. (1989). *Turning points: Preparing American youth for the 21st century.* New York: Carnegie Corporation.

Carnegie Council on Adolescent Development. (1995). *Great transitions: Preparing adolescents for a new century.* New York: Carnegie Council of New York.

Chiarelli, P. (2010). *Army health promotion, risk reduction, suicide prevention report.* Washington, DC: Department of Defense.

Conley, K. (2011). The influence of perception on willingness to seek help among college freshmen (Unpublished dissertation). Virginia Commonwealth University, Richmond.

Danish, S. (1974). Counseling psychology and the Vail Conference: An invited comment on training settings and patterns. *The Counseling Psychologist, 4,* 68. http://tcp.sagepub.com/

Danish, S. J. (2000). Youth and community development: How after-school programming can make a difference. In S. J. Danish & T. P. Gullotta (Eds.), *Developing competent youth and strong communities through after-school programming* (pp. 275–302). Washington, DC: CWLA Press.

Danish, S. J. (2002). *SUPER (Sports United to Promote Education and Recreation) program: Leader manual and student activity book* (3rd ed.). Richmond: Life Skills Center, Virginia Commonwealth University.

Danish, S. J., & Antonides, B. J. (2009). What counseling psychologists can do to help returning veterans. *The Counseling Psychologist, 37*(8), 1076–1089. doi: 10.1177/0011000009338303

Danish, S. J., & D'Augelli, A. R. (1980). Promoting competence and enhancing development through life development intervention. In L. A. Bond & J. C. Rosen (Eds.), *Competence and coping during adulthood* (pp. 105–129). Hanover, NH: University Press of New England.

Danish, S. J., D'Augelli, A. R., & Ginsberg, M. R. (1984). Life development intervention: Promotion of mental health through the development of competence. In S. D. Brown & R. W. Lent (Eds.), *Handbook of counseling psychology* (pp. 520–544). New York: Wiley.

Danish, S. J., & Forneris, T. (2008). Promoting positive development and competency across the lifespan. In S. Brown & R. Lent (Eds.), *Handbook of counseling psychology* (4th ed., pp. 500–516). Thousand Oaks, CA: Sage.

Danish, S. J., Forneris, T., & Wallace I. (2005). Sport-based life skills programming in the schools. *Journal of Applied School Psychology, 21*(2), 41–62.

Danish, S. J., Petitpas, A. L., & Hale, B. D. (1993). Life development intervention for athletes: Life skills through sports. *The Counseling Psychologist, 21*(3), 352–385.

DeAngelis, T. (2008). PTSD treatments grow in evidence, effectiveness. *Monitor on Psychology, 39*(1), 40. http://www.apa.org/monitor/jan08/ptsd.aspx

Deci, E. L., & Ryan, R. M. (1985). *Intrinsic motivation and self-determination in human behavior.* New York: Plenum.

Deci, E. L., & Ryan, R. M. (2000). The "what" and "why" of goal pursuits: Human needs and the self-determination of behavior. *Psychological Inquiry, 11,* 227–268.

Deci, E. L., & Ryan, R. M. (2008). Facilitating motivation and psychological well-being across life's domains, *Canadian Psychology, 49*(1), 14–23.

Defense Centers of Excellence (DCoE). (2011, August 28). *Largest study of suicide and mental health in military to be led by Dr. Ursano.* Retrieved from http://www.dcoe.health.mil/DCoENews/LargestStudyofSuicideandMentalHealthinMilitarytobeLedbyDrUrsano.aspx

Defense Manpower Data Center (DMDC). *Contingency tracking system. From Oct 7, 2001–31 July, 2011.*

Department of the Army, Pamphlet 600–24. (2009). *Health promotion, risk reduction, and suicide prevention.* Washington, DC: Department of the Army.

Department of Veterans Affairs. (2006, June 14). *Audit of veterans health administration's acquisition of medical transcription services.* Washington, DC: VA Office of Inspector General. Retrieved from http://www.va.gov/oig/52/reports/2006/VAOIG-04-00018-155.pdf

Fretz, B. R. (1982). Perspective and definitions. *The Counseling Psychologist, 10*(2), 15–19.

Glasgow, R. E., Vogt, T. M., & Boles, S. M. (1999). Evaluating the public health impact of health promotion interventions: The RE-AIM framework. *American Journal of Public Health, 89*(9), 1322–1327.

Gordon, R. S. (1987). An operational classification of disease prevention. In J. A. Sternbert & M. M. Silverman (Eds.), *Preventing mental disorders: A research perspective*(DHHS Publication No. ADM 87–1492, pp. 20–26). Washington, DC: US Government Printing Office.

Gould, M. S. (2001). Suicide and the media. *Annals of the New York Academy of Sciences, 932,* 200–224. doi:10.1111/j.1749-6632.2001.tb05807.x

Greene, C. H. (2009). *The sky is not falling! Building on force strength.* Personal communication with USSOCOM Service Component Psychology leaders.

Greene-Shortridge, T. M., Britt, T. W., & Castro, T. A. (2007). The stigma of psychological problems in the military. *Military Medicine, 172,* 157–161.

Harmon, L. (2007). A descriptive study of military family needs following a polytrauma (Unpublished dissertation). Virginia Commonwealth University, Richmond.

Henderson, K. (2006). *While they're at war: The true story of American families on the homefront.* Boston: Houghton Mifflin Company.

Hodge, K., Danish, S. J., & Martin, J. (2011). *Developing a conceptual framework for life skills interventions.* Manuscript submitted for publication.

Hoge, C. W., McGurk, D., Thomas, J. L., Cox, A. L., Engel, C. C., & Castro, C. A. (2008). Mild traumatic brain injury in U.S. soldiers returning from Iraq. *New England Journal of Medicine, 358,* 453–463.

Institute of Medicine (IOM). (2010). *Returning home from Iraq and Afghanistan: Preliminary assessment of readjustment needs of veterans, service members, and their families.* Washington, DC: National Academies Press.

Joint Services Support. (2011). *Yellow Ribbon Reintegration Program.* http://www.jointservicessupport.org/yrrp/Default.aspx

Kim, E. (2010). Are you going to be different? *American Journal of Psychiatry, 167*(6), 628–629.

LaBrie, J. W., Earleywine, M., Lamb, T., & Shelesky, K. (2006). Comparing electronic keypad responses to paper-and-pencil questionnaires in group assessments of alcohol consumption and related attitudes. *Addictive Behaviors, 31,* 2334–2338.

Mrazek P. J., & Haggerty R. J. (Eds.). (1994). *Reducing risks for mental disorders: Frontiers for preventive intervention research.* Washington, DC: National Academy Press.

Nash, W. P. (2007). The stressor of war. In C. R. Figley & W. P. Nash (Eds.), *Combat stress injury: Theory, research, and management* (pp. 11–32). New York: Routledge.

NIMH. (2009, July 19). *Evidence-based prevention is the goal of the largest ever study of suicide in the military* [press release]. Rockville, MD: National Institute of Mental Health. Retrieved from http://www.nimh.nih.gov/science-news/2009/evidence-based-prevention-is-goal-of-largest-ever-study-of-suicide-in-the-military.shtml

Perry, C., & Jessor, R. (1985). The concept of health promotion and the prevention of adolescent drug abuse. *Health Education Quarterly, 12*(2), 169–184.

Rappaport, J. (1977). *Community psychology: Values, research, and action.* New York: Holt, Rinehart, and Winston.

Ruud, D. M., Goulding, J., & Bryan, C. J. (2011). Student veterans: A national survey exploring psychological symptoms and suicide risk. *Professional Psychology: Research and Practice, 42*(5), 354–360. doi: 10.1037/a0025164

Ryan, R. M., & Deci, E. L. (2000). Self-determination theory and the facilitation of intrinsic motivation, social development, and well-being. *American Psychologist, 51*(1), 68–78. doi: 10.1037110003-066X.55.1.68

Tan, M. (2009, December 20). A million soldiers deployed since 9/11. *Army Times,* 12. Retrieved from http://www.armytimes.com/news/2009/12/army_deployment121809w/

Tanielian, T., & Jaycox, L. (Eds.). (2008). *Invisible wounds of war: Psychological and cognitive injuries, their consequences, and services to assist recovery.* Santa Monica, CA: RAND.

Trudeau, G. B. (2007). *Doonesbury.com's* The Sandbox*: Dispatches from troops in Iraq and Afghanistan.* Kansas City, MO: Andrews McMeel Publishing.

usa.gov. (2011, September 26). *Department of Defense.* http://www.usa.gov/Agencies/Federal/Executive/Defense.shtml

Vansteenkiste, M., Niemiec, C. P., & Soenens, B. (2010). The development of the five mini-theories of self-determination theory: A historical overview, emerging trends and future directions. In T. Urdan & S. Karabenick (Eds.), *Advances in Motivation and Achievement* (Vol. 16, pp. 105–166). Bingley, UK: Emerald

Watkins, C. E., Jr. (1983). Counseling psychology versus clinical psychology: Further explorations on a theme or once more around the "identity" maypole with gusto. *The Counseling Psychologist, 11*(4), 76–92.

Warner, C. H., Appenzeller, G. N., Grieger, T., Belenkiy, S., Breitbach, J., Parker, J., et al. (2011). Importance of anonymity to encourage honest reporting in mental health screening after combat deployment. *Archives of General Psychiatry, 68*(10), 1065–1071.

CHAPTER

26 Promoting Well-Being and Mental Health in Refugees

Larisa Buhin Loncar

Abstract

The chapter primarily focuses on interventions that have the potential to promote well-being by facilitating and fostering successful acculturation through acquisition of new life skills in refugees and by increasing multicultural competencies of individuals and changing public policies in receiving cultures. Berry's (1997) work on the acculturation process is utilized in considering possible interventions aimed not exclusively at refugee populations but also at increasing the readiness of receiving cultures to promote well-being of refugees. Prilleltensky and Nelson's (2002) theory of well-being, particularly with regard to relational and collective well-being, also provides a theoretical framework for proposed interventions.

Key Words: refugees, well-being, mental health, prevention, multicultural competency, acculturation

Introduction

The term "refugee" is a political designation that indicates a person or group of people who are "outside their country of origin and unable or unwilling to return there or to avail themselves of its protection, on account of a well-founded fear of persecution for reasons of race, religion, nationality, membership of a particular group, or political opinion" (Goodwin-Gill, 2008).

The United Nations High Commission for Refugees (UNHCR) reports close to 10 million refugees worldwide at the end of 2010 (not counting internally displaced persons). Women and children make up 47% of the world refugee populations. The total number of people who successfully return to their homes following a period of time as refugees is negligible, standing at about one sixth of the total population. Half of the world's total refugee population is from African nations and nations in Asia and the Pacific. The United States received over 50,000 new applications for asylum in 2010 (UNHCR, 2011). These statistics illustrate well the size of involuntary movement of multicultural groups of people across the globe in search of safety and in need of multiculturally competent mental health services.

This chapter seeks to address the needs of refugees following their settlement in the host or receiving culture rather than speak about the immediate care that should be provided in refugee camps. The assumption of the author is that the formal immigration status of refugee in the host country has been resolved and the person or persons in this status are now faced with the task of establishing a safe daily routine free of conditions that led to becoming a refugee and ultimately thriving in the new country.

Interventions and approaches discussed in this chapter are oriented toward assisting refugees in acculturating successfully, and achieving general well-being and mental health. Congruent with Berry's theory of acculturation (1980), the author will discuss possible interventions focused on refugees as well as interventions focused on the host or receiving culture. As the topic of this handbook is prevention, the author addresses the use of outreach and prevention in the practice of promoting mental health. Simply decreasing symptoms is only the immediate goal and one that is perhaps best approached through multiculturally competent psychotherapy. Long-term goals of helping professionals working with refugees have to include resiliency, empowerment, and thriving. The author further proposes that working with refugees requires a coordinated, multidisciplinary, multiculturally and globally aware approach because the needs of refugees span the human experience: from basic biological needs like access to food and medical care through existential psychological needs like safety and connectedness, spiritual needs, and finally up to and including sociopolitical needs like active participation in society's decision-making processes that can influence individual well-being (Prilleltensky & Nelson, 2002).

Acculturation, Well-Being, and Mental Health

Berry (1980, 1997) proposed a model of acculturation and adaptation that applies to people who move from one culture to another. Berry suggests that individuals can exhibit several different attitudes toward their own culture (culture of origin) and toward the receiving or host culture. A person could be open to the new culture and choose to engage in exploring new values, norms, and worldviews or he or she could choose to reject most or all that is identified as belonging to or originating in the new culture or receiving culture.

Among the most relevant points in Berry's (1980) work is the idea that the process is not unidirectional. In other words, the refugee who has to adjust to the receiving culture is not the sole actor in the process. The receiving culture plays a significant role in the acculturation process, according to Berry. The receiving culture can be receptive toward incoming persons, curious and engaging with their culture of origin, and willing to add customs, values, and worldviews of other cultures as equal to its own. Berry further hypothesizes that the receiving culture could be disinterested, disengaged, rejecting, and even hostile, or could demand complete loyalty to its own worldview and abdication of any other worldviews that may belong to the culture of origin.

Depending on the combination of influences from these two sources, several outcomes in social identity are possible. Individuals who primarily accept the cultural values, norms, and worldviews of the receiving culture and only minimally maintain contact with their culture of origin are considered to belong to the *assimilation* category (Berry, 1997). Those who reject most of the receiving or host culture and primarily maintain the worldview of and identification with their culture of origin belong to the *separation* category. *Marginalized* individuals are conceptualized as having rejected both identifications and withdrawing from society. Finally, those individuals or groups that achieve a balance between the culture of origin and the receiving culture having incorporated into their way of life values, norms, and worldviews of both to some extent and having developed an internal identification with both, Berry places in the *integration* category. In other words, those people are considered acculturated, integrated, or bicultural—an identity orientation or position that is typically associated with the most positive mental health outcomes for those who have to undergo the process of acculturation.

Yoon, Lee, and Goh (2008) found that acculturation had "a substantial and direct effect" on the subjective well-being of Korean immigrants (p. 252). Yoon and colleagues also found a positive relationship between aculturation and community connectedness. Berry's theory in which the receiving culture is a significant actor has important implications for working with refugees insomuch that it indicates the necessity for interventions that assist refugees in acculturation as well as interventions aimed at making the receiving culture more receptive and multiculturally aware so to make the acculturation process easier and subsequent biculturalism more likely. This "dual emphasis approach" is consistent with writings of other authors on working with multicultural populations for social justice and preventing racism (e.g., Buhin & Vera, 2009; Vera & Speight, 2003)

Refugees face the process of acculturation once they physically settle in the receiving culture (Roytburd & Friedlander, 2008), and the process itself can be stressful (acculturative stress; Rodriguez, Myers, Mira, Flores, & Garcia-Hernandez, 2002) due to pressures to adjust to life in the receiving culture, which may include learning the language and adopting different social norms, values, and behaviors, while simultaneously maintaining strong ties to the culture of origin. Other stressful factors may be due to lack of language skills, perceived differences between the culture of origin and host culture, and racism and discrimination (Berry, Kim, Minde, & Mok, 1987).

Well-being is a broader concept than mental health. Prilleltensky (2005) defines well-being as a successful fulfillment of self-defined personal, relational, and collective needs. In other words, a person who successfully satisfies those needs experiences a sense of personal, relational, and collective well-being (Prilleltensky & Nelson, 2002). According to Prilleltensky and Nelson, personal well-being is influenced by a sense of self-determination, continued personal growth, experiences of control over one's life and self-efficacy, as well as physical and mental health. The same authors propose that relational well-being is achieved through satisfying interpersonal relationships, successfully collaborating with others, and having an opportunity to participate in democratic processes. Finally, collective well-being is influenced by the level of development of structures required for proper community functioning, a sense of community (in the case of refugees, a sense of connection with both the community of origin and a new community in the receiving culture), access to high quality health and education, and a possibility to have an active voice in political processes (Prilleltensky, 2002). Again, for refugees it may be particularly important to be able to participate in processes that strive to contribute to restoration of order, peace, and justice in their country of origin (e.g., Staub, Perlman, Gubin, & Hagengimana, 2005).

Mental health more narrowly describes an absence of symptoms that would indicate mental illness. In the specific case of refugees, mental illness may be related to trauma resulting from the disaster that caused one to become a refugee or it may precede refugee status altogether.

We should expand our definition of mental health to mean more than just absence of mental illness, however, and to include resiliency and thriving. Newman (2005) defines resilience as, "the human ability to adapt in the face of tragedy, trauma, adversity, hardship, and ongoing significant life stressors" (p. 227). Bonnano (2008) further refines the point by claiming that recovery and resilience are not the same constructs. Whereas recovery is the process of returning to a state of functioning prior to developing symptoms of emotional distress or mental illness, "resilience reflects the ability to maintain a stable equilibrium" (Bonnano, p. 102) presumably because of the existence of protective factors in the individual and/or his environment.

To meet these connected yet far-reaching goals, the author proposes and considers psychological, educational, outreach, and advocacy activities that (1) focus on individuals' and groups' existing strengths (Lerner, 1995), (2) place individuals in their biopsychosocial and cultural context in the tradition of counseling psychology (Gelso & Fretz, 1992) and Bronfenbrenner's ecological model of development (1977); (3) restore well-being broadly defined by Prilleltensky and Nelson (2002), and (4) rely on principles of multicultural counseling, social justice, and prevention science to empower refugee clients to thrive and strive toward self-defined psychological, social, and political well-being (Vera & Speight, 2003).

The Scope of Working with Refugees

This section will serve as a brief overview of major issues that refugees frequently present in therapy as well as those that are a part of the acculturation process, but that are more suitably addressed with interventions such as prevention, psychoeducation, and outreach. An in-depth discussion of treatment approaches for particular mental health issues is beyond the scope of this paper. This section therefore is limited to briefly listing most commonly reported mental health concerns among clients who are refugees.

The existing literature on refugees typically either addresses a group of refugees from a particular country or geographic region (e.g., Hmong refugees; Westermeyer & Uecker, 1997) or attempts to summarize commonly encountered issues in refugee populations such as mental health (Pernice & Brook, 1996). Each of these approaches offers certain advantages and has some limitations. By addressing a specific group of refugees (i.e., refugees from Afghanistan; Bemak, Chung, & Pederson, 2003) we create an opportunity for cultural specificities to be adequately addressed and to advocate culturally appropriate interventions. However, the downside of this approach is our limited ability to generalize lessons or draw out guidelines that should be helpful starting points when working with refugees from any part of the world. Also, literature that describes successful interventions with a specific group of refugees naturally lags behind the human and political disaster that created the refugee situation in the first place. In this sense, our knowledge is retrograde and may not be of most use to practitioners who have either already done the work with that population or are now already working with another group of refugees from a different part of the world since it seems that our ability to prevent large-scale human-made catastrophes has not advanced. On the other hand, focusing on a particular problem or concern for refugees as a large group often sacrifices the cultural specificity for universal commonality such as academic adjustment of school-age refugee children or adult language acquisition.

A significant issue with available research literature on refugees is that it often combines voluntary (immigrant labor force) and involuntary (i.e., refugees) immigrants in the same sample and draws conclusions that presumably apply equally to members of both populations (e.g., Pernice & Brook, 1996). It would be important to keep these two groups of migrating individuals conceptually and methodologically separate, as their migration experiences are likely to be quite different and may require different interventions. While it is reasonable to expect that some of the adjustment issues might be the same or similar, future research should attempt to maintain a clear boundary between voluntary and involuntary migrants in order to provide a more valid and reliable picture of needs of both groups and solid information to clinicians working with both.

Working with refugees, mental health professionals can expect to encounter the range of human emotions, clinical diagnoses, and culture-bound syndromes (DMS-IV-TR; American Psychological Association [APA], 2000). Refugee clients can present with difficulties resulting from their preimmigration experiences such as post-traumatic stress disorder (PTSD), anxiety, and depression. PTSD is likely to be the mental health issue most frequently associated with refugees. Fazel, Wheeler, and Danesh (as cited in Vasilevska & Simich, 2010, p. 34) determined the rate of prevalence to be around 10% for refugees resettled in Western countries. Even in refugees who do not present with a typical clinical picture, we can expect some themes related to the loss of their existential grounding: their homes and familiar surroundings, even family members, have been lost. Grieving for all that has been lost may be a common process in refugee clients.

Refugee clients can also present issues relating to difficulties in the acculturation process, like culture shock, homesickness, discrimination, and so forth. Physical complaints are "particularly common among refugees both as part of the socially acceptable mode of seeking treatment for emotional distress but also as a result battle, torture, deprivation, or disease associated with the various phases of the refugee experience" (Westermeyer, as cited in Gong-Guy, Cravens, & Patterson, 1991, p. 645). In her meta-analysis of refugee research, Keyes (2000) discovered that in one fourth of the studies she analyzed, all subjects reported being depressed, "with distress being displayed most often through physical symptoms such as headache, backache, and fatigue" (p. 401).

Of course, clients who have survived torture, including sexual victimization, cannot be overlooked. Gorman (2001) warns that psychologists are more likely to encounter victims of torture in their practice than in the past. Treating victims of torture requires specialized training, and appropriate and prompt referrals are best if one has no experience in the area (Gorman).

If there is a single unifying characteristic of refugee populations then, it could easily be the profound severing of roots to one's prior life (Tribe, 2002) and the resulting disorientation that cannot be overlooked. The manifestation of this disorientation in physical, psychological, or social realms should not be underestimated. Simultaneously, helping professionals should keep in mind Bonanno's (2008) assertion that the human capacity for resilience in the most difficult and potentially traumatizing conditions may have been underestimated. Therefore, and adding the significant body of knowledge about experiences of racial, ethnic, and linguistic minority clients with discrimination and overdiagnosing in mental health services (Department of Health and Human Services (DHHS), 2006), while helping professionals should apply the highest standards of practice in formally and informally assessing for possible presence of trauma, immediately assuming that all refugees will develop PTSD or exhibit some symptoms of trauma would not be advised.

Major obstacles to successful treatment of clients who are refugees are inaccessible services in the clients' language, stigma surrounding mental illness, overall lack of appropriate services, and lack of knowledge about existing services (Gong-Guy, Cravens, & Patterson, 1991). These are structural barriers that require our mental health fields to train linguistically and culturally diverse service providers.

Multicultural Competency in Working With Refugees

While the available literature on refugees is not insignificant, the reality of the current body of knowledge in psychology in general is that it is overwhelmingly based on knowledge produced in the United States by people working in the United States, gathering data on people living in the United States (Arnett, 2008). What this leaves us with is an excessively narrow view of the rest of the world with limited generalizability of our knowledge. For example, Keyes (2000) conducted a meta-analysis of 12 articles dealing with mental health of refugees and found that only four of the studies used assessment instruments that were culturally appropriate. How do we bridge this gap in knowledge and practice, then? How do we ensure that our interventions are multiculturally competent, rooted in social justice, and promoting self-defined well-being at their core?

Reaching beyond traditional training in psychology and psychotherapy to other helping traditions and becoming engaged citizens of the world ourselves by investing some of our energy in gathering information about current events throughout the world with particular attention to emerging and ongoing conflicts seem like reasonable tactics. The extensive body of literature in the fields of counseling psychology and social justice (e.g., Vera & Speight, 2003), multicultural psychology (e.g., Atkinson, Thompson, & Grant, 1993; Sue, 2001; Sue, Arredondo, & McDavis, 1992), critical psychology (Prilleltensky & Fox, 1997), and prevention (e.g., Vera & Reese, 2000) will provide general or global multicultural competencies, while reading the literature on refugees from specific conflicts (e.g., Bemak, Chung, & Pedersen, 2003) will serve as resources for domain-specific multicultural competencies (Buhin, 2006). A comprehensive framework for delivering culturally sensitive prevention programming to diverse groups of clients is offered by Lopez, Edwards, Pedrotti, Ito, and Rasmussen (2002). Their recommendations include developing culturally relevant programs, conducting culturally sensitive evaluations, and sharing relevant findings among shareholders. Lopez and his colleagues even developed a "Rubric for Examining Cultural Appropriateness of Prevention Programming" (p. 9) that should facilitate the work of helping professionals who strive to engage in multiculturally competent prevention with refugee populations.

In multicultural encounters, we first must consider differences and similarities in identities and worldviews between the psychologist, therapist or counselor, and the client (Sue, 2001). Persons who apply for asylum, whose asylum applications are subsequently positively reviewed, and who eventually settle in the United States as refugees are a culturally heterogeneous group with varied preimmigration stories. Attention should be paid to varied sociopolitical and cultural identities of the individual: age, gender, level of education, race, socioeconomic status, sexual orientation, religion, and presence of disabilities, to name a few. The same sociocultural identities that are relevant in the experiences of our clients are relevant for the helping professionals in their work with refugees. Each helping professional should have a solid grasp on the meaning of her or his identity for the working relationship (Lopez et al., 2002). In addition, we propose that it is important for the helping professionals working with refugees to devote time to continuous exploration of definition and meaning of well-being and the role of prevention science and practice in promoting mental health from a global rather than a Eurocentric or a US-centric perspective.

Each aspect of one's sociopolitical identity is likely to offer unique variability in what was experienced, how the experience is being interpreted by the individual him or herself as well as one's family and community, and what the lasting meaning of that experience is (Arredondo, 1999; Constantine, 2002). For example, sexual victimization is a common fear and frequent experience for women and girl refugees, while being forced into paramilitary service or being taken to prisoner camps are more common for boys and men who are refugees. People of higher social status and with higher educational and career attainment typically enjoy better social connectedness and more stability in their societies of origin even at times of unrest and may therefore be better able to escape the worst of humanitarian disasters that develop around them. However, they seem to evidence poorer mental health postimmigration, presumably due to greater social and financial losses (Porter & Haslam, 2005). On the other side are traditionally vulnerable populations: women, the poor, persons living in rural settings (Porter & Haslam), undereducated, mentally ill, or physically challenged individuals with poor mobility and social connectedness who may experience very little ability to remove themselves from the fronts of war and have limited personal power to influence their situations in the receiving countries.

Finally, we must consider differences in interpretation and meaning of the aforementioned sociocultural identities for the helping professional and the client. Experiences in discussing identities can span the entire human emotional range from confusion about necessity to discuss a particular identity, to mistrust of why someone would ask about an identity, particularly if that aspect of one's identity has been used to victimize the client, to anger that someone would pry into another's personal life. Being informed about the nature of conflict and the general background of our clients may help us in predicting client's reactions and preparing in advance to deal with difficult conversations in a productive and healing manner. For example, if the conflict from which our current client has escaped has mainly stemmed from religious differences, questions about religious affiliation may be perceived as threatening even when appearing in what may seem to an institution as an innocuous routine manner such as an intake form.

In delivering multiculturally appropriate prevention interventions with refugees, helping professionals should have clearly stated goals with a solid rationale for how those goals have been chosen and the sensitivity to change those goals when necessary again with a solid rationale for why the change is being made. In the words of Prilleltensky and Nelson (2002), helping professionals need to engage in continuous critical examination of values and assumptions that ground the practices of their professions in order to ensure that their clients' well-being is supported in a socially just way. Possibly more so than with any other population, issues of self-determination and personal power will be prominent with recently traumatized and refugee populations. Research in positive psychology, social cognitive theory, and community psychology claims that, "having a sense of control over our lives is highly correlated with subjective well-being" (Prilleltensky & Prilleltensky, 2006, p. 108). The process of becoming a refugee results in gradual or sudden but always pervasive loss of control over one's own life and having the frightening experience of someone else wielding unchecked power over it. Helping professionals working with refugees hence ought to be particularly sensitive to the power differential inherent in helping relationships and should strive to minimize it while also offering their actual expertise in the area of mental health and well-being.

Promoting Successful Acculturation, Mental Health, and Well-Being

This section of the chapter covers those acculturation needs that would fall into Prilleltensky and Nelson's (2002) personal well-being category but are outside of the realm of traditional therapy and counseling as well as those acculturation needs from the collective well-being category. In Bronfenbrenner's (1994) terms these interventions address refugees' exo- and macrosystems. The section is distributed between person-centered interventions and interventions for the receiving culture. The overall goal is to support positive acculturation (through the development of new life skills) and to prevent or minimize acculturative stress and development of symptoms of emotional distress. Porter and Haslam (2005) found that refugees who were able to secure more stable and higher quality housing and obtain better paying jobs had "significantly better mental health" (p. 608). It can be seen that economic and housing factors do not fall within the purview of traditional psychology. However, interventions that increase clients' skills to exert positive control over their own lives in the segments that Porter and Haslam mention, are congruent with the work of social justice–oriented psychologists and other mental health professionals. Williams and Berry (1991) spoke in favor of a prevention approach that takes place at the local community, national, and international levels (p. 636). Placing a focus on prevention and outreach activities also addresses what Gong-Guy, Cravens, and Patterson (1991) named as the main obstacles to using mental health services among refugees: lack of knowledge about services available in the United States, stigmatization of mental illness, and fear that being diagnosed with having a mental illness could result in deportation (p. 644).

Person-Centered Interventions for Refugee Populations

Levels of intensity and breadth of outreach and prevention interventions will depend on individual and group characteristics as well as the length of time in the receiving culture. Helping professionals could expect intervention needs to flow over time from very concrete (having to do with issues of daily existence, for example) to more ambiguous adjustment and mental well-being questions. In the early days of arriving in the receiving culture, refugees are most likely to need assistance with life's basics: shopping for food, mastering public transportation systems, getting oriented to the community, and adjusting to their new physical surroundings. It is important for helping professionals to maintain a high level of cultural empathy at this time. Basic issues to consider include: administrative procedures and written documentation, meaning of refugee status, life basics (housing, food, schooling, medical assistance), and language courses. Level of need should be addressed separately for each issue and interventions designed accordingly.

Many of the basic concerns mentioned above are perfectly suited for community-based psychoeducational outreach with members of the same community who have lived in the United States for a longer time. This approach accomplishes several things: it deinstitutionalizes assistance, provides an opportunity for community gathering and organizing, and builds a bridge between the refugee community and the helping profession (Tribe, 2002). Caution has to be taken that groups which were and perhaps continue to be in conflict in the country of origin are not placed in the same treatment or outreach context (Tribe). Prevention science advises that the most effective prevention programs are "intensive, multicomponent, and multilevel" (Durlak, 1995, p. 84) and that culturally irrelevant programs will most likely not be successful (Vera & Reese, 2000).

I treat each of the concerns mentioned above briefly, more for clarification than for in-depth exploration because of space and scope limitations. Regarding administration and paperwork or written documentation, regardless of language proficiency, encountering unknown forms and procedures for the first time can be stressful and overwhelming. For refugees who have been systematically persecuted by governmental officials, providing written information without a clear understanding of its purpose could be particularly threatening as one of the worries may be that the information will be used against them. Taking extra time to explain the purpose of a procedure in general and of each particular segment or question may require more effort, but it is a worthwhile investment in an ongoing working relationship based on trust (Tribe, 2002).

As was mentioned at the very beginning of the chapter, the underlying assumption is that the individual or group with whom we are working has achieved the formal immigration designation of *refugee*. Each nation will have its own procedures, rules, and laws framing this designation. In the United States, this designation entitles individuals and families to housing and financial assistance for a period of time. This is the crucial point—one does not maintain the status of refugee indefinitely. Refugees may not be aware of this or they may be worried about being arbitrarily denied this status after it has been granted. It is important that a multiculturally competent person who is also knowledgeable about the legal issues take time to explain what exactly it means to be a refugee; how long that status lasts; what benefits and limitations it brings; what obligations are attached to it, and, possibly most importantly, what will happen after the refugee status expires. It is not difficult to imagine that refugees' response will run the full range of reactions to this last question. Some will yearn to return to their homes, some will dread that very possibility, and many will be ambivalent. A report on experiences of refugees from Kosovo presented jointly by the Centre for Refugee Studies and Joint Centre of Excellence for Research on Immigration and Settlement (2001) recommends periodic information sessions for refugees to introduce new services and remind them of existing community services.

As a way of introducing the need to discuss the next issue, let us revisit the demographics of the world refugee population. The largest numbers of refugees come from African, Asian, and Pacific nations. Nations that have in recent history experienced the kind of political unrest are typically developing or nations in transition (e.g., Rwanda, former Yugoslavia, Afghanistan) and/or are nations with repressive political regimes (for example, the case of the former Soviet Union and its oppressive politics toward Jewish citizens, who sought asylum and became refugees throughout the world). Furthermore, most of the world's refugee population is made up of women and children who are typically of lower socioeconomic and educational level (UNHCR, 2010). Given this background, it is easy to hypothesize that there will be significant differences in the way of life between the country of origin and the receiving country, particularly if the receiving country is a Western European or North American nation that has enjoyed a long period of peaceful political, economic, and industrial development. Familiar surroundings (both geographic and social), familiar food items, and other factors small and large that provide a sense of continuity, predictability, control, and safety, which are hypothesized to be important to one's well-being (Prilleltensky & Prilleltensky, 2006), may be gone in the lives of refugees. In order to promote positive adjustment and a sense of connectedness and belonging to one's immediate physical and social systems (Bronfenbrenner, 1994), multiculturally appropriate psychoeducational outreach interventions could be organized (Williams & Berry, 1991). These interventions can range from trips to the local supermarket to familiarize new refugees with US-style stores and products, assisting to enroll children in schools, explaining access to health care, to providing workshops for the development of job-seeking skills.

A hugely important factor that has implications for all levels of well-being (Prilleltensky & Nelson, 2002) is language fluency. Without being able to speak the language of the receiving country, refugees' ability to effectively interact with the environment outside of their immediate social network is severely limited. This can lead to feelings of reduced self-efficacy and lowered self-esteem. Inadequate language skills restrict employability. Being underemployed or unemployed could have its own negative snowball effect: reduced self-esteem, lowered financial stability, decreased social status in the community, emotional distress, and development of more serious psychological issues (Beiser, Johnson, & Turner, 1993; Williams & Berry, 1991). Obviously, psychologists are not in a position to offer English language classes, but they are in a position to encourage their clients to enroll in them and to advocate at local, state, and federal government levels for the provision of such classes.

Official educational and family services, and health practices that are unfamiliar to refugees may be anxiety-provoking or could be perceived as threatening. When those practices are deemed necessary by the receiving culture, as in the case of childhood vaccinations, regular school attendance, noncorporal child discipline, and the consequences of not adhering to those practices potentially carries negative consequences, the issue becomes particularly sensitive. Special care should be taken to explain these procedures before they are in place as well as the rationale for them and consequences of noncompliance to individuals and groups of refugees for whom these issues are relevant. Addressing these issues can be done individually, but once again this is an excellent opportunity for community-level outreach.

Connecting refugees with existing communities for additional support and empowering them to create their own communities is an important step in acculturation (Yoon, Lee, & Goh, 2008) and achieving well-being (Prilleltensky & Nelson, 2002). This is an appropriate time to consider making alliances with religious and community organizations and involving their resources in assisting refugees (Tribe, 2002). This kind of an outreach process is considered particularly relevant when we are working with people who are linguistic, racial, and ethnic minorities and who come from traditionally more collectivist cultures. Furthermore, as was discussed earlier, the needs of refugees may be too broad for a single mental health professional to manage successfully. However, due attention must be paid so that groups of refugees who were in conflict in their home countries only come in contact under carefully designed conditions (Tribe).

Outreach Interventions for the Receiving Culture

Adaptation is the result of person-environment fit (Caplan & Van Harrison, 1993). Thus far in the chapter, focus has been on interventions geared toward refugees themselves. However, successful acculturation of refugees (including mental health and thriving defined in the broadest sense) will depend partially on the characteristics of the receiving or host culture and its ability to interact positively with incoming groups of people (Berry, 1997). The larger the cultural discrepancy between refugees' culture of origin and the receiving culture the more potential for misunderstanding, anxiety, mistrust, discrimination, and acculturative stress there may be (Berry). In other words, as is stated in the mental health supplement to the 2001 US surgeon general report, the culture of both the provider and the recipient of mental health services matters (DHHS, 2001). From basic ability to speak the language of the refugee group to understanding cultural norms and worldviews, there are multiple opportunities to make a positive impact in refugees' new life. Takeuchi, Sue, and Yeh (1995) concluded that culturally congruent mental health interventions positively affect length and outcome of treatment. However, there is also a possibility of negative interactions that will impede refugees' recovery, adjustment, and thriving. The 2001 report of the Surgeon General discusses the issues of accumulated mistrust toward mental health services based on "historical persecution . . . and present-day struggles with racism and discrimination" (DHHS, 2001, p. 29). One could hypothesize that this early period refugees spend adjusting to the receiving culture is a critical period in terms of formation of attitudes toward the receiving culture, willingness to seek help, and continued recovery and thriving. It is very important then that helping and other professionals who will be in contact with refugee groups make best use of this critical period by utilizing multiculturally competent skills and interventions (Sue, Arredondo, & McDavis, 1992).

Interventions that will be discussed next are systemic in their nature because they will address systems of care, however in some, professionals delivering particular services are targets of interventions whereas in others policies and procedures are targets. Limited access to mental health services, low rates of usage of mental health services, and low return rates following initial sessions by racial minority clients has long been attributed, at least partially, to the culturally incongruent approach to mental health (DHHS, 2001). Factors such as lack of cultural competency of the mental health professional and culturally inappropriate modes of intervening are among the most significant examples of cultural incongruence and failure of the mental health community to adequately address the needs of racial, ethnic, and linguistic minority clients, among which new refugees may now find themselves (Gong-Guy, Cravens, & Patterson, 1991). Multicultural counseling and psychology advise that mental health professionals should design culturally sensitive and relevant interventions and then also implement them in a culturally sensitive way (APA, 2002). In addition, the argument that I propose here is in line with other counseling psychologists' recommendations that effective work with multicultural populations should be expanded beyond psychotherapy (Vera, Buhin, Shin, & Montgomery, 2004) and that prevention of negative interactions, such as racism and discrimination, can also benefit from systemic interventions or interventions that are directed at the public policy level (Buhin & Vera, 2009). Therefore, possible ways in which to prepare the receiving culture for successful interactions with incoming refugee groups must be examined. Although the task may seem overwhelming, we should be reminded that the process of relocating refugees is unfortunately a slow one but in that sense one that allows sufficient time for systemic preparation. The importance of adequate coordination among various government and health services sectors cannot be underestimated.

In the early stages of arriving in the receiving culture, refugees will mainly be concerned with basic life needs: housing, transportation, financial assistance, medical assistance, social services, and schooling, which will require frequent contact at the immediate community level, and county, state, and federal government and service offices. This indicates the possibility of communicating with a large number of professionals with varied levels of multicultural competencies. Even though the process of becoming multiculturally competent is a life-long task (Buhin, 2006), much can be accomplished with even the most basic lessons in effective cross-cultural communication (Jain & Krieger, 2011). Having identified the most likely points of interaction between refugee populations and professionals in the receiving culture, planning outreach interventions becomes an easier task.

Person-Centered Outreach for the Receiving Culture

The literature on multicultural competence in various helping professions has blossomed in recent decades (see, e.g., a review of current literature, which also proposes a model of organizational cultural competence to be used in mental health settings, by Hernandez and his colleagues [2009]). Admittedly, not all of that literature addresses the needs of refugees specifically; rather, this writing draws on findings from research with immigrants, linguistic, ethnic, and racial minorities. Furthermore, there are multiple models of multicultural competencies and approaches to multicultural training (e.g., Hernandez et al.; Sue, 2001; Vontress, 1988; Atkinson, Thompson, & Grant, 1993). Rather than recommend a specific model or approach, areas of work or interactions with refugees in which helping professionals and personnel in health and public services should receive training are reviewed.

Training of personnel in health and public service sectors can be designed as psychoeducational outreach or continued education programs and should address:

- basic communication including the use of qualified interpreters in medical and social service settings (e.g., Jain & Krieger, 2011);
- conducting information-gathering or intake interviews including detecting culturally sensitive and inappropriate questions;
- awareness of culture-bound syndromes (DSM IV-TR; APA, 2000);
- basic information about refugee needs in general and basic cultural information about the particular incoming refugee group.

One of the goals of such training is to increase the capacity of helping professionals to establish culturally appropriate contact and provide multiculturally competent services. Research in multicultural counseling and therapy indicates that such interactions have a positive effect on client satisfaction and willingness to continue treatment (e.g., Takeuchi, Sue, & Yeh, 1995; Vera & Reese, 2000).

Policy-Centered Outreach

Policy-centered outreach could also be conceptualized as dealing with micro-, exo-, and macrosystems in which the refugees have to exist (Bronfenbrenner, 1994) wherein policies and procedures of hospitals, schools, and mental health centers are microsystems or microlevels. Local, county, and state government policies and procedures would be considered exosystems or levels. Finally, federal government (in the case of the United States) and international bodies (such as the Red Cross, Amnesty International, or the UNHCR) form the macrosystem or macrolevel. Critical evaluation and change can and should happen at each of these levels (Prilleltensky & Nelson, 2002; Vera & Speight, 2003).

To reiterate, in the early days of adjusting to their new life, refugees will most frequently interact with immigration officials, housing authorities, institutions that will provide financial support, health care providers, social services, and educational institutions. Once again we are discussing improving person-environment fit (Caplan & Harris, 1993) in order to maximize the utility and success of existing support systems for refugees and reduce perceived cultural differences that are hypothesized to increase acculturative stress (Berry, 1997). One important factor to consider when working with refugees is that it may have been governmental officials themselves in refugees' original country that persecuted them and that, in response, refugees have developed an adaptive mistrust of governmental institutions and institutions that are perceived to be affiliated with the government (Tribe, 2002). Additionally, there may be no equivalent in refugees' culture of origin for certain social services that are now offered or even imposed on them. Encountering these services and unknown professionals who provide them may cause feelings of anxiety and mistrust in refugees.

On the other side of the person-environment interaction are offices, institutions, procedures and policies. Due to institutional and cultural worldviews (macrolevel; Bronfenbrenner, 1994) that are likely different in the receiving culture than the culture of origin of the refugee group, as well as the frequent lack of understanding of cultural differences on behalf of government officials, educators, and social service providers, a break in communication or cooperation may result. A family of refugees may find themselves overwhelmed by requests to fill out forms and give out private information to people with whom they are unfamiliar. The family may start to withdraw from the process, withhold information, miss appointments, and so forth. Several negative outcomes could result: failure to receive necessary financial assistance that can lead to financial difficulties including poor nourishment, emotional stress, and even eviction and homelessness. Or, in case that these self-protective withdrawing behaviors occur in mental health or education settings, they could be misinterpreted as noncompliance or even as signs of family dysfunction and mental illness (recall that the surgeon general report found that members of minority populations are frequently overdiagnosed; DHHS, 2001).

To avoid problems such as these, schools, mental health centers, hospitals, local and state government offices, and offices that provide social and financial assistance, should regularly review and evaluate their institutional policies and procedures for practices that are possibly culturally insensitive, overly burdensome or incomprehensible to people with limited language ability or limited educational background, and even discriminatory. Professionals and institutions with higher levels of multicultural competence can spearhead these efforts and help other professionals and institutions in reaching higher levels of competence by encouraging professional development through continuing education.

All psychologists are guided by the Ethical Principles of Psychologists and Code of Conduct (APA, 2010), which in its five principles includes the principles of Nonmaleficence and Beneficence that states, "Psychologists strive to benefit those with whom they work and take care to do no harm" (p. 3; http://www.apa.org/ethics/code/index.aspx?item=3). It is likely that most helping professions hold similar aspirations and charges. Minimizing harm is the first level of intervention. Striving to improve the well-being of refugees is the next level. This principle can be applied to policy-centered interventions as well: Policies and procedures implemented for work with refugees should not only not cause harm to refugees, but they should contribute to the overall improvement of global functioning or well-being.

Periodic reviews of policies and procedures should include verifying that the language of written materials is accessible or if there is a need for translation or interpretation. Furthermore, cultural appropriateness and necessity of procedures should be critically examined to determine if those are culturally congruent and necessary for refugees' well-being. Professionals are socialized into certain standardized ways of conducting routine procedures, like intake interviews, often without questioning their structure and/or purpose. While this writing by no means advocates arbitrary changes of standard procedures, it does encourage critical and culturally focused examination of alternatives that may provide equal or better results with fewer emotional costs to the refugees involved. Both process and content should be examined in this way. Items whose main function is statistic gathering appear on forms with sufficient frequency. If such an item is potentially culturally threatening, helping professionals should use their multiculturally competent clinical skills to find a different way of obtaining the same information and even consider advocating for procedural changes to have the item removed altogether.

At the macrolevel of policy-oriented interventions we consider advocacy for changes in national and international treatment of refugees. A thorough review of this level of intervention is beyond the scope of this chapter, so only a few ideas will be briefly examined at this time. The UNHCR estimates that approximately 260,000 refugees have been settled in the United States at the end of 2010. Compared to the global number of close to 10 million refugees and the relative place of United States in light of its GDP (the United States is surpassed by Pakistan, Iran, Syria, Germany, Jordan, Kenya, Chad, and China in the total number of refugees given asylum yearly), this picture looks less then glowing. Added to this is the chronic backlog of refugees who have applied for asylum but who wait in temporary placements for the resolution of their immigration/refugee status. Taking these factors into account, the need for a critical examination of procedures required of refugees in order to receive a positive resolution of their status is even more pronounced at the macrolevel. This issue is hugely complex since it involves striking a delicate balance of humanitarian concerns. Capacities of existing social services, the financial and economic state of the nation, and national security are just a few important issues. A large body of scientific literature has been establishing the financial merits and effectiveness of prevention in mental health (Weisz, Sandler, Durlak, & Anton, 2005). If one extrapolates from this line of research and applies it at a global level, it stands to reason that the most successful strategy overall would be in prevention of national and international conflicts that lead to humanitarian disasters and creation of internally displaced persons and refugees. Global political and economic stabilization is a worthwhile goal in this respect so that we can say that reviews of national policies as they pertain to US international relations should also be conducted to ascertain the extent to which they contribute to global stabilization and prevention of future refugee crises.

Conclusion

Working with refugees requires a separate set of knowledge and skills that are globally oriented and span across disciplines. To frame the discussion, Berry's (1997) model of acculturation as well as Prilleltensky and Nelson's (2002) conceptualization of well-being were used. Additionally, the discussion was conducted from a perspective of multiculturally competent practice (Sue, 2001). Besides the success of traditional therapy, there are reasons to believe that preventive interventions designed to improve well-being and foster acculturation or bicultural identity could be useful, effective, and efficient tools in helping this numerous group of clients. It is important to keep in mind demographic heterogeneity of refugees when creating culturally relevant interventions so that we maximize probability of success. It was proposed that the self-knowledge of the helping professionals' sociopolitical identities is equally as important in building a trusting working relationship. As the acculturation process is a question of person-environment fit, it stands to reason that interventions for both parts of this process are necessary. To this end, outreach and advocacy focused on institutional, national, and international policies were considered as potentially valuable tools in assisting current and future refugees.

Future Directions

Research literature on working with refugees is growing. Whether it is organized by refugees' nationality or ethnicity or by a presenting problem, the body of knowledge is significant. It also presents certain challenges particularly when we want to recommend promoting well-being through prevention and outreach. Hardly any research exists on effectiveness of such interventions with refugees. There is even less research available on the issue of prevention and outreach in receiving communities and cultures with the goal of improving mutual understanding and facilitating refugees' acculturation. Acculturation itself is a controversial issue (Schwartz & Zamboanga, 2008). The recommendations proposed here are rooted in solid evidence of prevention science, multicultural counseling, and community-based interventions. However, there is limited evidence of their effectiveness with refugees. Additionally, we need to consider the issue of multiple levels of intervention. There is no knowledge available to psychologists that could help them determine whether person-centered, culture-centered, or policy-level interventions are most effective. In the era of limited funding and growing need, that would be an important answer to have. Psychologists have not yet made good use of their knowledge to advocate for prevention of conflicts that create refugees and training programs that assist psychologists in becoming globally engaged citizens in such a manner might be helpful.

References

American Psychiatric Association (APA). (2000). *The diagnostic and statistical manual of mental disorders: DSM-IV-TR.* (4th ed., text revision). Washington, DC: Author.

American Psychological Association. (2002). *Guidelines on multicultural education, training, research, practice, and organizational change for psychologists.* Washington, DC: Author.

American Psychological Association. (2010). *Ethical principles of psychologists and code of conduct.* Washington, DC: Author. Retrieved from http://www.apa.org/ethics/code/index.aspx

Arnett, J. J. (2008). The neglected 95%: Why American psychology needs to become less American. *American Psychologist, 63*(7), 602–614. doi:10.1037/0003-066X.63.7.602

Arredondo, P. (1999). Multicultural counseling competencies as tools to address oppression and racism. *Journal of Counseling and Development, 77,* 102–108.

Atkinson, D. R., Thompson, C. E., & Grant, S. K. (1993). A three-dimensional model for counseling racial/ethnic minorities. *The Counseling Psychologist, 21,* 257–277.

Beiser, M., Johnson, P. J., & Turner, R. J. (1993). Unemployment, underemployment, and depressive affect among Southeast Asian refugees. *Psychological Medicine, 23*(3), 731–743.

Bemak, F., Chung, R. C.-Y., & Pedersen, P. B. (2003). *Counseling refugees: A psychosocial approach to innovative multicultural interventions.* Westport, CT: Greenwood.

Berry, J. W. (1980). Acculturation as varieties of adaptation. In A. M. Padilla (Ed.), *Acculturation: Theory, models, and some new findings* (pp. 9–25). Boulder, CO: Westview.

Berry, J. W. (1997). Immigration, acculturation, and adaptation. *Applied Psychology: An International Review, 46,* 5–34.

Berry, J. W., Kim, U., Minde, T., & Mok, D. (1987). Comparative studies of acculturative stress. *International Migration Review, 21,* 491–511.

Bronfenbrenner, U. (1977). Toward an experimental ecology of human development. *American Psychologist,* 32, 513—531.

Buhin, L. (2006). Multicultural counseling competencies. In Y. Jackson (Ed.), *Encyclopedia of multicultural psychology* (pp. 318–324). Thousand Oaks, CA: Sage.

Buhin, L., & Vera, E. M. (2009). Preventing racism and promoting social justice: Person-centered and environment-centered interventions. *Journal of Primary Prevention, 30,* 43–59.

Caplan, R. D., & Van Harrison, R. (1993). Person-environment fit theory: Some history, recent developments, and future directions. *Journal of Social Issues, 49,* 253–275. doi: 10.1111/j.1540-4560.1993.tb01192.x

Centre for Refugee Studies. (2001). *A report on the settlement experiences of Kosovar refugees in Ontario.* Toronto: Centre for Refugee Studies and Joint Centre of Excellence for Research on Immigration and Settlement, York University.

Constantine, M. G. (2002). The intersection of race, ethnicity, gender, and social class in counseling: Examining selves in cultural contexts. *Journal of Multicultural Counseling and Development, 30*(4), 210.

Department of Health and Human Services (DHHS). (2001). *Mental health: Culture, race, and ethnicity; A supplement to mental health.* Retrieved from http://www.surgeongeneral.gov/library/mentalhealth/cre/execsummary-1.html

Durlak, J. A. (1995). *School-based prevention programs for children and adolescents.* Thousand Oaks, CA: Sage.

Fazel, M., Wheeler, J., & Danesh, J. (2005). Prevalence of serious mental disorder in 7000 refugees resettled in western countries: A systematic review. *Lancet, 365,* 1309–1314.

Gelso, C. J., & Fretz, B. R. (1992). *Counseling psychology.* San Diego, CA: Harcourt Brace Jovanovich.

Gong-Guy, E., Cravens, R. B., & Patterson, T. E. (1991). Clinical issues in mental health service delivery to refugees. *American Psychologist, 46*(6), 642–648.

Goodwin-Gill, G. S. (2008). *Convention relating to the status of refugees: Protocol relating to the status of refugees.* New York: United Nations. Retrieved from http://untreaty.un.org/cod/avl/ha/prsr/prsr.html

Gorman, W. (2001). Refugee survivors of torture: Trauma and treatment. *Professional Psychology: Research and Practice, 32*(5), 443–451. doi:10.1037//0735-7028.32.5.443

Hernandez, M., Nesman, T., Mowery, D., Acevedo-Polakovich, I. D., & Callejas, L. M. (2009). Cultural competence: A literature review and conceptual model for mental health services. *Psychiatric Services, 60,* 1046–1050.

Jain, P., & Krieger, J. (2011). Moving beyond the language barrier: The communication strategies used by international medical graduates in intercultural medical encounters. *Patient Education and Counseling, 84*(1), 98–104.

Keyes, E. F. (2000). Mental health status in refugees: An integrative review of current research. *Issues in Mental Health Nursing, 21*(4), 397–410. doi:10.1080/016128400248013

Lerner, R. (1995). *America's youth in crisis: Challenges and options for programs and policies.* Thousand Oaks, CA: Sage.

Lopez, S. J., Edwards, L. M., Teramoto Pedrotti, J., Ito, A., & Rasmussen, H. N. (2002). Culture Counts: Examinations of Recent Applications of the Penn Resiliency Program or, Toward a Rubric for Examining Cultural Appropriateness of Prevention Programming. *Prevention & Treatment,* 5, Article 12. No pagination specified. doi: 10.1037/1522-3736.5.1.512c

Newman, R. (2005). APA's resilience initiative. *Professional Psychology: Research and Practice, 36*(3), 227–229. doi:10.1037/0735-7028.36.3.227

Pernice, R., & Brook, J. (1996). Refugees' and immigrants mental health: Association of demographic and post-immigration factors. *Journal of Social Psychology, 136*(4), 511–519.

Porter, M., & Haslam, N. (2005). Predisplacement and postdisplacement factors associated with mental health of refugees and internally displaced persons: A meta-analysis. *Journal of the American Medical Association, 294*(5), 602–612. doi:10.1001/jama.294.5.602

Prilleltensky, I. (2005). Promoting well-being: Time for a paradigm shift in health and human services. *Scandinavian Journal of Public Health, 33*(5), 53–60. doi:10.1080/14034950510033381

Prilleltensky, I., & Fox, D. (1997). *Critical psychology: An introduction.* London: Sage.

Prilleltensky, I., & Nelson, G. B. (2002). *Doing psychology critically: Making a difference in diverse settings.* New York: Palgrave Macmillan.

Prilleltensky, I., & Prilleltensky, O. (2006). *Promoting well-being: Linking personal, organizational, and community change.* Hoboken, NJ: Wiley.

Rodriguez, N., Myers, H. F., Mira, C. B., Flores, T., & Garcia-Hernandez, L. (2002). Development of the Multidimensional Acculturative Stress Inventory for adults of Mexican origin. *Psychological Assessment, 14,* 451–461.

Roytburd, L., & Friedlander, M. L. (2008). Predictors of Soviet Jewish refugees' acculturation: Differentiation of self and acculturative stress. *Cultural Diversity and Ethnic Minority Psychology, 14*(1), 67–74. doi:10.1037/1099-9809.14.1.67

Schwartz, S. J., & Zamboanga, B. L. (2008). Testing Berry's model of acculturation: A confirmatory latent class approach. *Cultural Diversity and Ethnic Minority Psychology, 14*(4), 275–285. doi:10.1037/a0012818

Staub, E., Perlman, L. A., Gubin, A., & Hagengimana, A. (2005). Healing, reconciliation, forgiving, and the prevention of violence after genocide or mass killing: An intervention and its experimental evaluation in Rwanda. *Journal of Social and Clinical Psychology, 24*(3), 297–334.

Sue, D. W. (2001). Multidimensional facets of cultural competence. *The Counseling Psychologist, 29*(6), 790–821. doi:10.1177/0011000001296002

Sue, D. W., Arredondo, P., & McDavis, R. J. (1992). Multicultural counseling competencies and standards: A call to the profession. *Journal of Counseling and Development, 70,* 477–488.

Takeuchi, D. T., Sue, S., & Yeh, M. (1995). Return rates and outcomes from ethnicity-specific mental health programs in Los Angeles. *American Journal of Public Health, 85*(5), 638–643.

Tribe, M. (2002). Mental health of refugees and asylum seekers. *Advances in Psychiatric Treatment, 8,* 240–248.

United Nations High Commission for Refugees (UNHCR). (2010). *Global trends report.* New York: United Nations. Retrieved from http://www.unhcr.org/pages/49c3646c4d6.html

United Nations High Commission for Refugees. (2011). *Asylum levels and trends in industrialized countries: 2010.* New York: United Nations. Retrieved from http://www.unhcr.org/pages 49c3646c4d6.html

Vasilevska, B., & Simich, L. (2010). A review of the international literature on refugee mental health practices. *Canadian Issues/Themes Canadiens,* Summer, 33–38. Available on World Wide Web: http://www.acs-aec.ca/en/publications/canadian-issues

Vera, E. M., Buhin, L., Shin, R. Q., & Montgomery, G. (2004). Enhancing therapeutic practice with racial and ethnic minority clients: Integrating prevention, advocacy, and outreach. In R. T. Carter (Ed.), *Handbook of racial and ethnic minority psychology.* Hoboken, NJ: Wiley.

Vera, E. M., & Reese, L. E. (2000). Preventive interventions with school-age youth. In S. D. Brown & R. W. Lent (Eds.), *Handbook of counseling psychology.* New York: Wiley.

Vera, E. M., & Speight, S. L. (2003). Multicultural competence, social justice, and counseling psychology: Expanding our roles. *The Counseling Psychologist, 31,* 253–272.

Vontress, C. E. (1988). An existential approach to cross-cultural counseling. *Journal of Multicultural Counseling and Development, 16,* 73–83.

Weisz, J. R., Sandler, I. N., Durlak, J. A., & Anton, B. S. (2005). Promoting and protecting youth mental health through evidence-based prevention and treatment. *American Psychologist, 60*(6), 628–648.

Westermeyer, J., & Uecker, J. (1997). Predictors of hostility in a group of relocated refugees. *Cultural Diversity and Mental Health, 3*(1), 53–60.

Williams, C. L., & Berry, J. W. (1991). Primary prevention of acculturative stress among refugees: Application of psychological theory and practice. *American Psychologist, 46*(6), 632–641.

Yoon, E., Lee, R.M., & Goh, M. (2008). Acculturation, social connectedness, and subjective well-being. *Cultural Diversity and Ethnic Minority Psychology, 14*(3), 246–255. doi: 10.1037/1099-9809.14.3.246

CHAPTER

27 ¡Si Podemos! (Yes We Can!): Promoting Academic Success in Mexican American Girls

Lisa Y. Flores *and* Patton O. Garriott

Abstract

A significant educational achievement gap exists between Latinas and their White, African American, and Asian American women counterparts (US Census Bureau, 2009). Sixty-three percent of Latinas over 25 years of age have graduated from high school, and only 14% have completed college. Mexican Americans are less likely than members of other Latino subgroups to graduate from high school and college, making Mexican American girls a student group that is at risk of failing to achieve their educational aspirations . In this chapter, we identify nine critical factors in promoting the educational attainment of Mexican American girls based on our review of the literature. In addition, we highlight prevention programs that were designed to improve students' academic achievement. These programs are evaluated for their focus on the nine critical ingredients. Finally, we provide recommendations for future intervention efforts in research and practice to advance Mexican American girls' educational attainment.

Key Words: Mexican American girls, educational attainment, academic achievement, intervention programs, academic programs

Theoretical and empirical research related to the educational and career development of women and girls has grown significantly over the past 50 years (Farmer, 2006). During this time, a variety of major social forces have opened new opportunities for girls and women in schools and the workplace that were not available to earlier generations and have had a strong influence on women's labor force participation. Parallel initiatives in psychology have raised awareness about issues faced by girls and women in schools and work settings, improved women's participation in psychology, and subsequently, increased psychological research on issues unique to girls and women, such as women's career development.

Promoting Girls' Academic Success

Educational attainment is closely tied to occupational status and is considered an important pathway toward improving social mobility. Thus, promoting girls' educational achievement has direct implications to their lives as well as to society. At an individual level, educational success can improve girls' quality of life as adults by increasing their career options and economic capital. At the same time, utilizing girls' talents is important to the vitality, growth, and competitiveness of our society and economy. Researchers have identified salient issues that influence women and girls' career decision-making, such as gender role socialization, multiple role management, and sexism. In addition to these unique issues, women of color share some common experiences in educational and work settings, such as racial oppression.

Intervention programs that educate girls about issues related to their educational and career planning and prepare them for dealing with any obstacles that they might encounter in the process of reaching their educational and career goals can prevent the underachievement and underutilization of girls' talents and help girls to achieve personal and professional success. In the remainder of this chapter, we focus on educational prevention programs with Mexican American girls. To fully appreciate the need for prevention efforts aimed at enhancing the educational success of Mexican American girls, we first provide a snapshot of this group's educational patterns. Next, we review of the extant literature on Mexican American girls' academic achievement and identify critical ingredients for future prevention efforts geared toward increasing Mexican American girls' academic attainment and achievement. Following this, we highlight prevention programs that aim to promote the educational success of Mexican American girls. We conclude with recommendations for future directions in clinical work and research that can build on our existing knowledge in advancing the educational attainment of Mexican American girls.

Mexican American Girls' Educational Achievement and Aspirations

National statistics indicate that Latinas have higher levels of educational attainment than their Latino counterparts, but lower levels of attainment than their White and Black female counterparts. In 2009, 16.7% of Latinas between the ages of 16 and 24 dropped out of high school (US Census Bureau, 2009). Of Latinas over the age of 25 years, 63% graduated from high school and 14% received a bachelor's degree (US Census Bureau, 2009). In contrast, 91.9%, 84.2%, and 59.4% of White women, Black women, and Latino men completed high school, and 31.9%, 20.6%, and 11.6% completed college, respectively.

Among women in college, patterns begin to emerge that are reflected in the career fields. Women college students overall, and specifically Latinas, are underrepresented in academic majors that lead to prestigious and high-paying careers, such as science, technology, engineering, and mathematics (Gándara, 2006; National Center for Educational Statistics, 2007). As an example, some improvements in the representation of women with undergraduate engineering degrees have occurred over the past decade (National Science Foundation, 2007), however, these changes have been relatively small, and the field continues to be dominated by White men. Latinas received 1.3% of bachelor's degrees in engineering in 2006. These statistics suggest that more work is needed to guard against the future underutilization of talented women in fields that are underrepresented by women, particularly Latinas.

R. Valencia and Black (2002) trace the etiology of myths related to Latino/as' educational struggles to deficit models and misconceptions of Latino culture, and provide evidence that refutes the belief that Latino/as' low educational attainment is a result of not valuing education. A review of the literature reveals that Mexican American adolescent girls have high educational aspirations (Flores, Navarro, & DeWitz, 2008; Flores & O'Brien, 2002), and no differences were found in educational aspirations or expectations between Mexican American and European American high school students (Hurtado & Gauvin, 1997) nor between Mexican American boys and girls or across generational levels (Flores et al., 2008; Ojeda & Flores, 2008). Mexican American adolescent girls aspire to nontraditional careers for women (Flores & O'Brien, 2002; Reyes, Kobus, & Gillock, 1999) and indicate hopes of obtaining a postsecondary or graduate degree (Flores & O'Brien, 2002; Hernandez, Vargas-Lew, & Martinez 1994; Valenzuela, 1993; Wycoff, 1996). Furthermore, Mexican American families highly value education (Okagaki, Frensch, & Gordon, 1995; Tapia, 2000), and parents have high aspirations for their child's educational attainment (Moreno & Lopez, 1999; Moreno & Valencia, 2002), regardless of their own educational background (Garza, 1998).

Living in a racial and gendered society differentially affects Mexican American girls' educational development in comparison to Mexican American boys and girls from other racial/ethnic groups, respectively. Prior research suggests gender differences among Mexican American girls and boys in educational experiences and outcomes. Overall, although Mexican American girls report more positive experiences in secondary school than boys (Gillock & Reyes, 1999), they also indicate lower levels of efficacy in math and science and nontraditional careers for women (Flores & Obasi, 2005; Navarro, Flores, & Worthington, 2007). These girls may not be receiving encouragement in school or at home or other environmental supports (i.e., role modeling) to develop interests and skills in nontraditional career areas. Research indicates that Mexican American women who pursue nontraditional majors in college do just as well academically as their male counterparts, but they report less encouragement from faculty than their male peers and lower academic and occupational self-efficacy than their European American counterparts

(Hackett, Betz, Casas, & Rocha-Singh, 1992). The environments in which these girls' educational and career paths develop operate differently from their peers from other cultural groups to create unique factors in their educational pursuits, and these environmental differences may be more pronounced in educational and career areas in which Mexican Americans and/or women are underrepresented.

To fully maximize intervention effects, programs need to take into account the unique issues that Mexican American girls' encounter that may limit their career options and success in educational settings. Further, the achievement data we presented earlier suggests that these girls may not be achieving their educational dreams or realizing their potential in academic majors and careers that are underrepresented by women. Prior research indicates significant differences between Mexican American high school students' educational aspirations and expectations. Specifically, these students hope for high levels of education, but expect to attain levels lower than what they hope (Flores et al., 2008), suggesting that actual barriers or the perception of barriers may prevent them from realizing their educational goals. Understanding the factors that facilitate Mexican American girls' educational goals and pursuit of a broad range of majors and careers is needed for prevention programs to be most effective at ensuring that their aspirations are realized. In the next section, we identify the most salient factors that we gleaned from the literature that are related to Mexican American girls' educational persistence and achievement.

Critical Ingredients for Educational Interventions With Mexican American Girls

The majority of research that has explored the effects of personal, family, and contextual factors on Mexican American students' educational success has been produced in the past 20 years. Any prevention interventions that aim to promote Mexican American girls' academic achievement must tailor activities toward those empirically based factors that are related to these girls' college enrollment and graduation. In the following section, the empirical literature on Latina girls' educational achievement will be reviewed. This literature is organized around the main predictors of Latinas' educational and career success so that prevention efforts can infuse these elements into interventions to increase girls' access to these supports. We categorized the main intervention and program components in the following areas: (1) personal factors; (2) cultural and familial factors; (3) contextual factors; and (4) sociopolitical issues, based on Gomez et al.'s (2001) model of Latina's career development. Within this model, Latina's educational and career development is conceptualized as an interaction of the person's identity, values, and life goals; her cultural and gender role socialization; her family's aspirations for her; the opportunities, barriers, and resources within her immediate environment; and the historical context in which her career is taking shape.

All of the articles reviewed below included samples of Latino or Mexican American students. We use "Latino" for those studies in which Mexican American students were the largest ethnic subgroup represented in the sample. When samples are comprised exclusively of Mexican American girls, women, or students in general, we also make these specifications.

Personal Factors

PERSONAL DEVELOPMENT

Prevention activities that attend to girls' character development can focus on shaping specific personality characteristics that can help them in their academic pursuits. Prior research on academically successful Mexican American students suggests that maintaining an optimistic outlook was critical to their academic achievements (Arellano & Padilla, 1996). In addition, responsibility and persistence (Alva, 1991; Arellano & Padilla; Gándara, 1995; Hernandez, 2000; A. Valencia, 1994; Wycoff, 1996), openness to experiences (Cornelius-White, Garza, & Hoey, 2004), perceptions of being a hard worker (Gándara, 1995), having high expectations for receiving a college degree (Arbona & Nora, 2007), and endorsing positive affect (Ojeda, Flores, & Navarro, 2011) have been identified as important personal attributes related to Latino students' educational attainment. Mexican American women in college indicated that they were motivated to do well academically because they wanted a good paying job and were interested in furthering their studies (A. Valencia).

Gender role attitudes also play an important role in the academic pursuits of Mexican American girls. Liberal gender role attitudes were associated with academic achievement (Valenzuela, 1993), likelihood of college enrollment and persistence (Cardoza, 1991), and career decision-making self-efficacy (Gushue & Whitson, 2006). The presence of more liberal gender role attitudes seem to placate the negative effects of perceived barriers on Mexican American girls' educational plans (McWhirter,

Hackett, & Bandalos, 1998). Further, feminist attitudes were related to higher career aspirations among a sample of Mexican American high school girls (Flores & O'Brien, 2002).

The development of girls' academic self-concepts also deserves attention in prevention efforts. Academic motivation (Hernandez, 2000; Waxman, Huang, & Padron, 1997), high self-efficacy (Fouad & Smith, 1996; Navarro et al., 2007; O'Brien, Kopala, & Martinez-Pons, 1999; Torres & Solberg, 2001), and a positive view of one's intellectual skills (McWhirter, 1997; Wycoff, 1996) were related to Latino students' academic performance, interests, and intentions. Educational self-concept was predictive of Mexican American college students' 1st-year grade point average (Rodriguez, 1996). Holding a positive image of one's academic abilities may serve as a protective factor from the barriers these students encounter in pursuing their educational goals. Thus, prevention interventions should be designed to promote the academic-related self-esteem, self-confidence, and self-efficacy of Mexican American girls in the hopes of producing positive educational outcomes.

ENCOURAGE GIRLS TO WORK HARD IN SCHOOL AND TAKE RIGOROUS COURSEWORK

Prior academic achievement has been linked to Mexican Americans' educational self-efficacy beliefs (Chin & Kameoka, 2002), college attendance (Ramos & Sanchez, 1995), and college grade point average (Rodriguez, 1996). While some Mexican American youth are aware of the link between current academic performance and future academic and occupational achievement (Bullington & Arbona, 2001), all students may not readily see how current behaviors influence future opportunities. Practitioners can encourage Mexican American girls to gauge whether they are putting their best efforts toward their studies and, if they are not, may want to discuss what is preventing them from doing so.

Findings from a large national dataset indicate that Latino students who complete rigorous coursework in high school increase their likelihood of enrolling in a 4-year college or university (Arbona & Nora, 2007). Practitioners would be wise to introduce this fact to Mexican American girls in elementary school and to encourage these girls to develop good study habits early, to strive to earn good grades, and to take the most challenging classes. These efforts should be reinforced throughout Mexican American girls' academic years.

Cultural and Familial Factors

REINFORCE MEXICAN CULTURAL STRENGTHS

Mexican American students can draw on strengths within their culture to further their educational training. For example, prevention programs can help students develop positive associations with their culture by addressing the benefits of speaking multiple languages in a society that is becoming increasingly diverse. Furthermore, interventions can address the ways in which these girls' educational achievements can help to advance their communities as well as their family's socioeconomic status.

Research found that Anglo oriented acculturation was related to Mexican American students' educational aspirations (Flores et al., 2008; McWhirter et al., 1998; Ramos & Sanchez, 1995), educational expectations (Flores, Ojeda, Huang, Gee, & Lee, 2006; Flores et al., 2008), and higher levels of college self-efficacy and outcome expectations (Ojeda et al., 2011). Other researchers also documented that acculturation was positively related to Mexican American high school students college attendance, but unrelated to their college aspirations or college planning behaviors (Hurtado & Gauvin, 1997). On the other hand, research has found that Mexican acculturation has no effects on educational goals (Flores, Ojeda et al., 2006; Flores et al., 2008) among samples of Mexican American high school students. Although the findings regarding acculturation effects are preliminary, they suggest that maintaining behaviors representative of their culture of origin does not have a negative impact on Mexican American students' educational behaviors. Indeed, Rumberger and Larson (1998) found that Mexican American students who were bilingual in English and Spanish had better grades and completed more credits their counterparts who were Spanish- or English-only speakers. Interventions can promote bicultural acculturation strategies, because the development of skills necessary to navigate the dominant culture can help these students in their academic pursuits. At the same time, practitioners working with Mexican American adolescent girls who are at risk of failing to achieve their academic aspirations should be aware of the challenges that bicultural individuals experience in negotiating the conflicting values and expectations of two cultures (Wycoff, 1996) and help girls' develop coping skills that they can use when these stressors become overwhelming and obstruct their educational goals.

Research suggests that cultural identity can benefit students in their academic endeavors. Case studies revealed that the high school students strongly identified with their Mexican American ethnicity and were aware of ways in which their ethnic background could both facilitate and hinder their educational and career plans (Bullington & Arbona, 2001). Ethnic identity was positively related to self-esteem (Brouillard & Hartlaub, 2005), academic resilience (Gonzalez & Padilla, 1997), and career decision-making self-efficacy (Gushue, 2006; Gushue & Whitson, 2006) among samples of Mexican American and Latino students. Another study found that ethnic loyalty was associated with Mexican American women college students' beliefs that education would be a barrier to marrying (Niemann, Romero, & Arbona, 2000).

In sum, prevention efforts need to (1) promote girls' appreciation of and connection with their cultural background while also providing the tools that they need to navigate the dominant, mainstream society; (2) reinforce the positive aspects of their culture; and (3) address the benefits of their educational success to the family and Latino community. It is also critical that programs address potential cultural conflicts that these girls might experience in their pursuits (i.e., school/work interfering with family) and discuss ways that they might handle mixed messages that they receive.

INVOLVE PARENTS

Mexican American parents can play an important role in supporting their daughters' academic success. In a culture that places a high value on the family, parental involvement should be a central component of any program that is promoting the educational achievement of Mexican American girls. Research indicates that Mexican American parents are an important influence on their children's educational aspirations, achievements, and persistence (Arellano & Padilla, 1996; Bullington & Arbona, 2001; Caldera, Robitschek, Frame, & Pannell, 2003; Gonzalez & Padilla, 1997; Hernandez, 2000; Hernandez et al., 1994; Hurtado & Gauvin, 1997; Lango, 1995; Morales, 1996; Okagaki et al., 1995; Perez, Espinoza, Ramos, Coronado, & Cortez, 2009; Ramos & Sanchez, 1995; Wycoff, 1996) and career aspirations (Flores & O'Brien, 2002). Strong parental support can make a difference when Mexican American girls are making decisions about their education. High parental expectations for earning a college degree were related to college graduation among Latino students (Arbona & Nora, 2007). Mexican American women across all academic levels indicated that their mothers were most supportive in their academic endeavors (Flores & Obasi, 2005; Gillock & Reyes, 1999; Hernandez et al., 1994; Lango, 1995; Wycoff, 1996). Without this support, Mexican American women are more likely to choose to attend a college close to home (Wycoff, 1996) and to not persist in college (Gloria, 1997).

Mexican American parents who want to be supportive of their children's goals may not possess the cultural capital to advise and guide their daughters through the process (Gándara, 1995). This may be especially true of parents who are immigrants, have little formal education, or lack knowledge of the educational system in the United States. The high incidence of poverty and households with low educational levels among Latino households (US Census Bureau, 2009) may explain in part why Mexican American high school girls are more likely than their White counterparts to experience negative family attitudes about attending college (McWhirter, 1997), and why Mexican American girls from lower class backgrounds perceived less parental support for their education (McWhirter et al., 1998). Mexican American girls from low socioeconomic backgrounds and those whose parents have low levels of educational attainment may be at risk for failing to achieve their educational goals because their parents may be unable to provide the type of tangible support that other parents provide to help their daughters navigate the system (Keith & Lichtman, 1994). Prevention programs can design activities to equip these parents with the requisite knowledge and tools to support their daughter's educational goals.

Because educational, cultural, linguistic, and social capitals will vary across Mexican American parents, practitioners need to broaden their conceptions of how parental involvement is defined to take into account the variety of ways that parents can help (Auerbach, 2007). Support can range from providing emotional support and communicating high expectations for success to providing instrumental support and participating in school activities with their child. Latino parents also encourage their children's educational achievement by telling "dichos" or stories that convey strong messages about resilience and success and by instilling positive attitudes about education in their children (Bettie, 2002; R. Valencia & Black, 2002). The lack of involvement of Mexican American parents attending parent-teacher meetings should not be mistaken as a lack of interest, support, or investment in their daughter's education. Practitioners can advocate on behalf of these parents by encouraging schools to hire bilingual faculty and staff or employ a liaison who works specifically with Spanish-speaking Mexican American parents.

In a study of Mexican American high school students, Rodriguez (2002) found generational differences in the styles of parental involvement in children's education. First- and second-generation students reported higher monitoring from parents in how they spent their time and whom they were with than third-generation students. On the other hand, third-generation students reported higher levels of parental participation than first- and second-generation students. Importantly, both types of parental involvement—monitoring and participating in activities—were significantly related to Mexican American students' grades across all generations (Rodriguez). Another study found that Mexican American parents of high- and low-achieving fourth- and fifth-grade students did not differ in their beliefs about the value education or helping with homework (Okagaki et al., 1995). However, parents of high achievers had higher efficacy for helping children do well academically and modeled reading skills more than parents of low-achieving students (Okagaki et al.). Effective educational programs for Mexican American girls would increase parental behaviors that have been linked to students' educational achievement.

Good models for intervention are available for involving Mexican American parents in their child's education planning. One college access program created an outreach component for Latino parents to educate parents about the college application process, strengthen social networks among the parents, and challenge the educational inequities in our society (Auerbach, 2004). Other programs like this can benefit parents with little knowledge of how the higher educational system operates so that they can provide instrumental knowledge and support to their daughters. Parents seemed to be strongly influenced by panel presentations that included other Latino parents with children in college and Latino college students. Auerbach advocates for early interventions with parents, providing bilingual services, ensuring that activities are accessible, and including small group activities to provide opportunities for personal contact. In addition, she recommends that activities include personal narratives and guest speakers from the community, opportunities to connect parents with school personnel, and that interventions attend to the unique concerns of Latino parents (e.g., financial aid, daughters leaving home).

INVOLVE OTHER FAMILY MEMBERS

Having siblings and extended family members who have graduated from high school or college may assist Mexican American girls in achieving their academic goals. These individuals may be in a position to advise these girls on preparing for college because of their prior experiences. Indeed, a study of Mexican American children in elementary school reported that those with older siblings who were making satisfactory academic progress had higher expectations for completing high school than children with older siblings who had dropped out of school (Hess & D'Amato, 1996). An ethnographic study of two academically successful Mexican American high school girls found that they attributed their educational strivings, in part, to having an older sibling in college (Bettie, 2002). Family support was significantly related to higher college self-efficacy and lower stress among a sample of predominantly female Latino students (Torres & Solberg, 2001). Further, family support had an indirect effect on college persistence intentions and stress through its effects on college self-efficacy (Torres & Solberg). At the same time, practitioners should consider the effects on Mexican American girls' educational planning if family members with high levels of educational attainment have had negative experiences in the educational system.

DEVELOP STRONG SOCIAL NETWORKS

Mexican American girls' social support networks extend beyond their family. These girls can benefit from the guidance and support of peers, mentors, and teachers in their educational intentions, and the absence of this support can have deleterious effects on students' educational goals. For example, research findings indicated that Latino college students who lacked social support exhibited higher levels of maladjustment to college (Solberg, Valdez, & Villarreal, 1994) and academic stress (Solberg et al., 1994; Solberg & Villarreal, 1997). On the other hand, perceived support from teachers was related to higher grade point averages among a sample of Mexican American high school (Lopez, Ehly, & Garcia-Vasquez, 2002) and college students' academic invulnerability (Alva, 1991).

Mexican American students identified mentors and role models (Arellano & Padilla, 1996; Flores & Obasi, 2005; Zalaquett & Lopez, 2006), friends and peer support (Gonzalez & Padilla, 1997; Hernandez, 2000; Perez et al., 2009; Tapia, 2000), and faculty and staff relationships (Gonzalez & Padilla, 1997; Hernandez, 2000; Hurtado &

Gauvin, 1997) as important sources of social support in their academic performance, pursuits, and persistence. Mexican American high school students reported that mentors were most helpful in their academic and career decision-making by role modeling behaviors they wanted to emulate, providing verbal encouragement, providing support in their life in general, and providing information or assistance with education-related tasks (Flores & Obasi, 2005). This study found no gender differences in students' descriptions of mentors' support. However, gender differences were found in mentors' effects across several educational and career variables. For instance, Mexican American girls who had a mentor reported higher self-efficacy for attending a 4-year university than boys who had a mentor.

Academically successful Mexican American high school girls perceived higher levels of peer support and teacher feedback than their less successful counterparts (Gonzalez & Padilla, 1997), and Latino students were more likely to attend a 4-year institution when the majority of their peers shared similar plans (Arbona & Nora, 2007). Researchers suggest that relationships with other Latinas in their academic environment (Barajas & Pierce, 2001; Capello, 1994) and teacher support (McWhirter et al., 1998) can serve as protective factors in Latina's educational plans (Barajas & Pierce, 2001; Capello, 1994).

Intervention programs can advance Mexican American girls' educational goals by connecting these girls with mentors who can serve as role models, provide a wide range of images of women in different roles, and provide supplemental support in achieving their educational goals. Based on Flores and Obasi's (2005) findings about mentors' roles in Mexican American students' educational planning, educational programs can encourage peer and adult mentors to share personal academic successes and struggles, to verbally encourage girls' academic progress, and to provide direct guidance on educational pursuits and life in general. Because many Mexican American girls may be first-generation college students, they may have limited opportunities to develop the types of networks that can assist them in preparing for college within their families or communities. Connecting Mexican American girls with other students and adults from similar cultural backgrounds who may be dealing with comparable issues in pursuing their academic goals can provide the support some students need to overcome barriers to their education. Prevention efforts should aim to help girls to seek out and cultivate relationships with others outside of the family who will support their academic goals.

EDUCATE GIRLS ABOUT FINANCIAL SUPPORT OPTIONS FOR EDUCATION

Financial concerns for education are cited as a significant challenge to education for Mexican American girls (Auerbach, 2004; Lopez, 1995; McWhirter, Torres, Salgado, & Valdez, 2007). Financial hardship is related to Latino college students' perception of barriers to their career goals (Perrone, Sedlacek, & Alexander, 2001). The family of Latinas who are first-generation college students may not have the resources to support their education or to adequately inform them of financial aid opportunities. Additionally, Latina college students who must work to financially support their education might experience stress in learning to balance work and school. Effective prevention programs with Mexican American high school girls must educate students about financial aid options and provide guidance on how to complete financial aid applications.

Contextual Factors

ADDRESS EDUCATIONAL CONTEXT

The environmental context in which students are being educated can include the educational climate, course offerings and educational tracks, and student composition, and these may also play a role in students' academic outcomes. Mexican American students experience racial and gender discrimination (Lopez, 1995) and anticipate that they will encounter educational barriers associated with their academic preparation (McWhirter et al., 2007). Research indicates that lack of school engagement (Ream & Rumberger, 2008) and negative perceptions of the educational climate (Castillo et al., 2006; Gloria, 1997; Gloria, Castellanos, Lopez, & Rosales, 2005; Hurtado & Ponjuan, 2005) can make it challenging for Mexican American girls to succeed academically and may lead to nonpersistence decisions. Resilient students reported stronger feelings of belonging in school and a more supportive academic environment than nonresilient students, and a sense of belonging was a significant predictor of Mexican American students' academic resilience (Gonzalez & Padilla, 1997). In addition, Mexican American women in college indicated that living in an environment that they perceived to be uncaring and culturally different was a significant stressor that they encountered in their 1st year of college (Wycoff, 1996). Finally, taking college prep courses and years of bilingual education were significant predictors of grade point average for US-born Mexican-descent students, while college tracking and years of schooling in Mexico were significant predictors of grade point average for foreign-born Mexican students (Padilla & Gonzalez, 2001).

The ethnic and gender composition of students in an academic environment or academic major may also serve as an important factor in Mexican American girls' educational decision-making. Attending a university or enrolling in a major area of study with a small percentage of Latina students may contribute to feelings of isolation and alienation (Hackett et al., 1992). Research suggests that Latinas who attended a predominantly Mexican American university received social support from extended relatives and immediate family, had fewer negative academic experiences, and were more involved on campus, and those who attended a predominantly White university received most of their familial support from mothers and were more likely to express feelings of alienation and isolation on campus (Garza, 1998).

Sociopolitical Factors

CONSCIOUSNESS-RAISING

Researchers point to the significant impact of institutional racism, educational policies, and systemic problems on the academic achievement gap across racial/ethnic groups. Specifically, an overproportionate number of racial/ethnic minorities live in poverty, and students from low socioeconomic backgrounds are more likely to attend poorly funded and underresourced schools, to be taught by teachers who are not certified, to have teachers with low expectations for their success, to attend racially segregated schools, and to attend schools that lack programs that meet students' linguistic and cultural needs (R. Valencia, 2000). In addition, these students may attend schools with school counselors who are not culturally competent. Interventions should focus on raising Mexican American girls' awareness of how sociopolitical factors are linked to educational and social inequalities that are present in the United States. Prevention efforts can help Mexican American girls' advocate for policies that will support their educational advancement and learn how to identify modern-day acts of discrimination (see Sue et al., 2007).

Academic Intervention Programs

The design, implementation, and evaluation of programs that promote the academic retention and educational achievement of Mexican American girls are an important step toward reducing the educational gap. More research is needed to understand the components of prevention programs that are most effective in increasing Mexican American girls' academic achievement and educational attainment. In this section, we provide an overview of intervention programs that promote the academic achievement of Mexican American girls, and we map the critical ingredients that were reviewed in the previous section across each program (see Table 27.1).

Table 27.1 Critical Ingredients by Intervention Program

	ALAS	Career Academies	Cuento Therapy	IHAD	Puente Program	SSS	UB	UBMS
1. Personal Development	X	X	X			X	X	X
2. Academic Encouragement	X	X		X	X	X	X	X
3. Reinforce Cultural Strengths			X	X	X			
4. Parents	X		X*	X				
5. Other Family	X			X				
6. Social Networks	X			X	X		X	X
7. Financial Support Education				X	X			
8. Educational Context	X							
9. Consciousness Raising					X			

Note: ALAS = Achievement for Latinos Through Academic Success; IHAD = I Have a Dream; SSS = Student Success Skills; UB = Upward Bound; UBMS = Upward Bound Math-Science; *Mothers were involved in a variation of Cuento therapy described in Constantino et al. (1984).

Following a description of each program, we provide available evidence of program effectiveness and discuss potential programmatic strengths and limitations. When possible, we have included information on both general effectiveness and effectiveness with Mexican American or Latino students specifically. Intervention programs selected for inclusion met the following criteria: (1) the program was aimed at increasing academic achievement in middle childhood or adolescence; (2) the program had been replicated or had described in enough detail that it could be replicated; (3) data on program effectiveness included random assignment or matched comparison groups, a control group, and measurement of achievement-related outcomes; and (4) the program was either targeted to serve Mexican American girls, Latino youth, or had documented participation of a substantial number of Latino youth.

So that readers may also evaluate the practical significance of research findings presented in this section, when possible we have estimated and reported Cohen's *d* for interventions that have produced significant differences between treatment and control groups. Specifically, effect sizes were calculated where $d = M_1 - M_2/s_{pooled}$ and s_{pooled} = Ö$[(s_1^2 + s_2^2)/2]$. The magnitudes of effect sizes were deemed small = .20, medium = .50, and large = .80 (Cohen, 1988).

Achievement for Latinos Through Academic Success

The Achievement for Latinos through Academic Success (ALAS; Larson & Rumberger, 1995) program was designed to address individual and ecological factors that influence academic nonpersistence decisions among Latino youth. The intervention is designed for "at risk" youth who evidence low academic performance and behavioral problems. The ALAS program addresses student factors related to academic nonpersistence by monitoring student school attendance, providing counseling on adaptive problem-solving strategies, encouraging participation in programmatic social activities, and connecting students to community services (e.g., mental health and drug and alcohol counseling). Family factors are addressed through teacher and counselor reports to family members regarding students' school attendance and performance, training parents in parent-child problem-solving skills and school engagement skills, and providing information regarding community resources. School factors are addressed through the promotion of greater communication and collaboration between teachers, counselors, students, and parents.

Larson and Rumberger (1995) conducted a randomized controlled trial of ALAS among 94 (*n* = 46 treatment group, *n* = 48 control group) Latino seventh- to ninth-grade students in the Los Angeles area. All participants had been identified as "high risk" by their teachers using a rating criteria developed by the researchers. Results of the study showed that the treatment group was more likely to be on course to graduate by the end of ninth grade (72% of students in the treatment group; *d* = .49) and was more likely to be enrolled in school (98% of students in the treatment group; *d* = 1.39) than control group participants. Participants in the treatment group were also more likely than their peers to graduate from high school (32% of students in the treatment group; *d* = .14), but this difference was not statistically significant (Gándara, Larson, Mehan, & Rumberger, 1998).

Career Academies

The Career Academies program was developed over 35 years ago in the interest of facilitating students' completion of high school, entrance into higher education, and successful matriculation into the workforce. Since its inception, Career Academies interventions have been implemented in over 2,500 high schools serving large numbers of students of color (Kemple & Willner, 2008). Career Academies function as "schools-within-schools," and aim to enhance students' interest and competency within a specific career domain through career-related academic coursework, workshops, and internships in the community.

Kemple and Snipes (2000) conducted a randomized controlled trial of the effectiveness of Career Academies in a sample of 1,764 high school students (*n* = 959 treatment group, *n* = 805 control group). Approximately 56% of students in the study identified as "Hispanic." Effects of the intervention were evaluated by subgroups of "High Risk," "Medium Risk," and "Low Risk" students. These groups were determined through indicators (e.g., attendance rates, grade point averages, progression through school) of academic progress by the researchers. Within the High Risk subgroup, results showed that the intervention significantly reduced dropout rates and increased credits earned toward graduation (*d* = .34). Within the Low Risk subgroup, results showed that the intervention increased the likelihood that students were prepared to graduate on time (*d* = .43). In contrast, within the Medium Risk subgroup, the intervention did not appear to have any significant effects on student outcomes. Similarly, aggregated effects of the intervention for the full sample indicated small, nonsignificant outcomes related to academic persistence and achievement. Data were not analyzed to determine differential effects by ethnicity.

Cuento Therapy

Cuento therapy was developed by Constantino, Malgady, and Rogler (1984) as an intervention for Puerto Rican children exhibiting emotional and behavioral problems. Spanish folktales are used in conjunction with role-playing, discussion, and reflection to promote children's cognitive and emotional adjustment. Stories are related to children's personal lives, who are encouraged to be active participants during storytelling sessions (Constantino et al., 1984). Cuento therapy reinforces traditional Latino cultural values and ethnic pride, as it is assumed that acculturative stress plays a role in children's emotional and behavioral problems. Variations in Cuento therapy have included mothers as group facilitators during storytelling sessions, use of Puerto Rican heroines/heroes and biographies as a role-modeling technique, and discussion of coping strategies specific to Puerto Rican children's life experiences in New York City (Constantino et al., 1984; Malgady, Rogler, & Constantino, 1990).

Early studies showed that this intervention improved Puerto Rican children's anxiety, social judgment, and ethnic identity (Constantino et al., 1984; Malgady et al., 1990). Researchers conducted a randomized controlled trial of Cuento therapy with 58 third-grade Mexican American students to examine effects on academic and psychological outcomes. Of treatment group participants, 46% were female, and participants for the study were selected due to failing grades on a high-stakes achievement test. Treatment and control groups received regular reading instruction in traditional classroom settings with the treatment group receiving Cuento therapy as an adjunctive treatment (Ramirez, Jain, Flores-Torres, Perez, & Carlson, 2009).

Cuento therapy participants received 12 one-hour group sessions with a trained therapist involving storytelling in Spanish and English followed by role-playing, discussion, and interaction. Pre-post test scores revealed that the treatment group exhibited lower scores on physiological anxiety (d = .24) and that, while no group differences were observed, both groups experienced mean increases on high-stakes reading test scores (d = .61 for treatment group, d = 1.78 for control group). Finally, the treatment group exhibited higher levels of global (d = .65) and academic (d = .73) self-esteem (Ramirez et al., 2009) than the control group.

IHave a Dream

I Have a Dream (IHAD; Kahne & Bailey, 1999) was established to assist disadvantaged sixth-grade students to complete secondary school and successfully matriculate into postsecondary education. The onset of the IHAD program commenced with Lang, a New York philanthropist, offering to "adopt" 61 sixth-grade students in East Harlem, New York, and pay for their college tuition should they graduate high school. Following its initial success (90% of the original students did receive diplomas), IHAD has since expanded nationally. Recent figures estimate that approximately 200 IHAD programs in 27 different states exist and have served over 15,000 students (I Have a Dream Foundation, 2008).

Although IHAD may differ somewhat in its implementation at different sites, several common elements of the intervention exist. Typical ingredients of the program aim to provide necessary forms of social capital to low-income students through academic, social, and financial supports (Kahne & Bailey, 1999). Specifically, IHAD aims to promote *social trust* between students and program stakeholders through project coordinator and financial sponsors' relationships and bonds with students and their families. *Access to information* is also provided to students and their families regarding career, health, and social services. *Norms and effective sanctions* is another form of social capital provided through the inclusion of high academic expectations and facilitation of prosocial behavior (e.g., coordinated social events). *Direct services* are also provided to students in the form of academic tutoring and counseling while *monetary resources* in the form of a financial sponsor for students to attend college is the final form of social capital provided (I Have a Dream Foundation, 2008; Kahne & Bailey, 1999).

Kahne and Bailey (1999) conducted a randomized controlled trial of two case study IHAD programs in Chicago. One program, La Familia, consisted of predominantly Latino students (31 Mexican American, 14 Puerto Rican, 5 multiracial, 1 European American, 1 African American) while another program, Project Success, comprised 40 African American students. With regard to gender, 56% of participants in the La Familia program and 58% of the participants in the Project Success program were female. Students completing sixth grade

1 year prior to IHAD participants (n = 43 students, n = 46 students) served as a control group in the study. Results of the study showed that graduation rates for IHAD participants in both programs were higher than those of the control group. Participants in the La Familia intervention graduated at a rate of 71% compared to 37% in the control group while participants in the Project Success intervention graduated at a rate of 69% compared to 34% for the control group. College enrollment rates for both groups were also relatively high, at 88% and 96%, respectively. Although the authors of the study did not have available comparison group data with which to contrast these findings, they did note that the rates of college enrollment achieved by IHAD participants exceeded enrollment rates of Latino (54%) and African American (53%) high school graduates in Chicago.

Puente Program

The Puente Program was developed in 1993 and aims to increase the rates of postsecondary attendance among educationally disadvantaged, and specifically Latino, students in California. Puente consists of three essential components: writing, counseling, and mentoring. The writing component includes a 9th- and 10th-grade English sequence in which students are exposed to Mexican American, Latino, and other multicultural literature within college preparatory classes. The counseling component includes assistance with educational and career planning with assigned Puente counselors as well as organized visits to college campuses. The mentoring component includes structured activities with adult role models aimed at increasing students' leadership skills and community involvement (Gándara & Moreno, 2002).

Gándara (2002) used a quasi-experimental, matched between-groups design to evaluate the effectiveness of the Puente program among a sample of Latino Puente (n = 75) and non-Puente (n = 75) students from the same cohort (1994–1998) across three schools in California. Outcome measures included grade point averages (GPA), access to college preparatory classes and tests, and college matriculation. Findings revealed no significant differences between groups with regard to GPA. However, significant differences were observed between treatment and control groups with regard to rates of taking college entrance examinations and rates of 4-year college attendance (43% compared to 24%). In both cases, Puente students significantly outperformed non-Puente students.

Student Success Skills Program

The Student Success Skills (SSS; Brigman, Campbell, & Webb, 2004; Brigman & Webb, 2004) program was conceptually and practically designed to address cognitive, social, and self-management skills of students. *Cognitive* aims include increasing effective study habits, enhancing memory of classroom material, and establishing and adhering to academic performance goals. *Social* aims include improving students' listening and attending skills, promoting peer encouragement, enhancing the capacity to engage in group problem solving, and encouraging healthy optimism regarding students' capacity to achieve their stated goals. *Self-management* skills learned in the program include management of test-performance anxiety, ability to maintain classroom attention, and anger management.

Studies evaluating the effectiveness of the SSS program have demonstrated positive outcomes. In a series of studies using randomized controlled pretest-posttest between-group designs with 1,123 middle and secondary school students in two Florida school districts, researchers found that treatment groups outperformed control groups on a standardized test of academic achievement and evidenced enhanced behavioral control. Specifically, students' receiving the SSS program significantly improved their math (d = .36 to .51) and reading (d = .11 to .25) test scores from pre- to posttest and were also rated by teachers (aware of the purpose of the research) to have made gains in self-management skills related to academic and social behaviors (Brigman & Campbell, 2003; Brigman, Webb, & Campbell, 2007; Campbell & Brigman, 2005; Webb, Brigman, & Campbell, 2005).

Miranda, Webb, Brigman, and Peluso (2007) investigated the effectiveness of the SSS program in a sample of African American and Latino students using data from the original SSS studies (e.g., Brigman & Campbell, 2003). Latino students made up approximately 10% (n = 126) of the total sample. Examination of pretest to posttest score change on a statewide achievement test revealed significant differences between treatment and control groups. When compared to the control group, Latino students receiving the SSS intervention significantly improved math (d = .26) and reading (d = .20) test scores. When tests to determine effects by ethnicity were conducted, no significant differences emerged. The authors interpreted these results as indicating that the SSS intervention was effective in improving students' academic achievement regardless of ethnicity.

TRIO

Federal TRIO programs were initiated by the US Department of Education in 1965 in the interest of increasing postsecondary access and degree attainment among low-income first-generation college students. Currently, six different programs—each designed to meet the broader aims of TRIO—exist and in 2008 served 884,889 participants through 2,853 federally funded programs (US Department of Education, 2008). Two of the six programs offered through TRIO—Upward Bound and Upward Bound Math-Science—are designed to facilitate postsecondary attainment among disadvantaged students enrolled in secondary schools. Students meeting eligibility standards for these two programs have families with taxable incomes that are 150% of the family income levels for determining poverty status and/or parents who did not attend a 4-year college. Between the years of 2000 and 2001, Latino students comprised approximately 19% of students enrolled in Upward Bound and Upward Bound Math-Science programs (National TRIO Clearinghouse, 2003).

The Upward Bound program includes a number of academic services and interventions geared at facilitating secondary school completion and entrance into postsecondary education. These include: instruction in reading and writing, academic and financial counseling, study skills instruction, academic tutoring, mentorship programs with college faculty, information related to postsecondary education, college entrance exam preparation, and work-study positions to facilitate career exploration. These activities typically occur over the course of the academic year as well as for several weeks during the summer (US Department of Education, 2008).

The most recent data available on the effectiveness of traditional Upward Bound programs reveals mixed findings. In 2004 the Department of Education released evaluation data from a randomized controlled trial conducted with students who participated in Upward Bound. Students randomly assigned to receive Upward Bound services (n = 1,500) were compared to students eligible for Upward Bound who did not participate in the program (n = 1,300) on outcomes related to secondary school completion and postsecondary school entrance. Results suggested that: (1) Upward Bound had a very small to negligible effect on total high school class credits earned and grades; (2) Upward Bound increased high school credits earned among students with low academic expectations; (3) Upward Bound had no effect on the treatment group's postsecondary enrollment or postsecondary credits earned; (4) Upward Bound had a large effect on enrollment and credits earned at 4-year colleges among students with low educational expectations; and (5) length of time spent in Upward Bound was positively associated with increased rates of postsecondary enrollment and credits earned. In sum, Upward Bound appears to be effective among students with lower educational expectations and seems to have greater influence on positive educational outcomes at greater doses or length of participation in the program. This latter finding may be particularly relevant for Latino students, who tend to remain in Upward Bound for less time than their African American, Asian American, and White peers (US Department of Education, 2004a).

Additional data specific to outcomes of Upward Bound among Latino participants indicate that the program increased Latino students' enrollment in 4-year colleges from 38% to 50% and credits earned at postsecondary colleges from 13 to 28. These effects led researchers to conclude that, "the effects of Upward Bound on persistence at postsecondary institutions may be particularly large for Hispanic students" (US Department of Education, 2004a, p. 43). Taken together, Upward Bound evaluation data specific to Latino students is both promising and discouraging. Specifically, while Latino students appear to benefit from Upward Bound more so than other student racial/ethnic groups, they are also more likely than their peers to leave the program prematurely. Future research is needed to determine why the effects of Upward Bound are greater for Latino students as well as why Latino participants tend to discontinue their participation in Upward Bound at relatively earlier time points.

Upward Bound Math-Science, similar to traditional Upward Bound programs, seeks to facilitate secondary school success and postsecondary participation among low-income first-generation students. However, students participating in Upward Bound Math-Science programs receive specific guidance related to excelling in math and science-oriented classes while in high school and are encouraged to pursue math-science degrees at institutions of higher education. Latino students made up approximately 20% of participants in Upward Bound Math-Science in the most recent data released on the program from the years 2000–2001.

Using 2000–2001 data, the Department of Education (2004b) reported that participants in Upward Bound Math-Science exhibited modest increases in GPA from the beginning to the end of the program. Specifically, an increase in average standardized GPA from 3.1 to 3.2 was observed, with 35% of participants experiencing GPA increases, 37% experiencing unchanged GPAs, and 28% experiencing a decrease in GPA by the end of the program. Analysis of college entrance exam scores for Upward Bound Math-Science participants revealed that participants' average scores were comparable to national average scores of students reporting middle incomes and higher than averages obtained from students participating in traditional Upward Bound. In terms of postsecondary enrollment, approximately 43% of Upward Bound Math-Science participants attended an institution of higher education following the program. However, this statistic should be interpreted with caution, as data at this reporting period were deemed incomplete (US Department of Education, 2004b). Data in this report were not analyzed to determine outcomes of Upward Bound Math-Science by race/ethnicity.

Other Promising Programs

There were several programs that did not meet criteria for this review, but show promise for future intervention research. These include the Choices Program (Vera et al., 2007), Latinos en Camino al Exito Universitario (Rivera-Mosquera, Phillips, Castelino, Martin, & Dobran, 2007), and the Bridges to High School Program (Gonzales, Dumka, Deardorff, Jacobs-Carter, & McCray, 2004). Preliminary evaluation data for these programs indicate positive effects for socioemotional skills and social self-efficacy (Vera et al., 2007), increased knowledge and confidence about college (Rivera-Mosquera et al., 2007), as well as increased coping and parenting skills (Gonzales et al., 2004).

Conclusion

To summarize, the literature on Latinos' educational development identifies a range of variables that play an important role in Mexican American girls' academic pursuits, and several intervention programs have been developed that have demonstrated positive effects on their educational achievement and attainment. Based on our review of the literature, interventions aimed at youth who are at risk of failing to achieve their academic goals generally tend to (1) provide encouragement and support for students' academic activities, (2) highlight personal qualities that will help them to develop into strong student learners, (3) address perceived educational barriers, and (4) assist students in developing social support networks, including mentoring relationships with peers and professionals. Additional components of academic intervention programs geared exclusively for Latinas focus on aspects of their individual and cultural development that are unique to their life experiences and that research has shown to be an influence on their educational goals. In particular, distinctive features of interventions that are especially relevant to Latinas include a critical social analysis of the combined effects of racial and gender role socialization on their aspirations and the perceptions of others within the educational systems about their abilities. Prevention educational programs for Latinas also highlight the unique influence of the Latino family members and involve family in programs and concentrate on the strengths that these girls' derive from their cultural heritage that can benefit them in their academic pursuits (e.g., bilingual, bicultural abilities). Practitioners should develop awareness of the effects of individual, cultural and familial, environmental, and sociopolitical factors on these girls' educational achievement and seek ways to strengthen these supports within Mexican American girls' and their families through individual- and group-level educational interventions.

Future Directions

Although Latinos are the largest and fastest growing racial ethnic minority group in the United States today, a recent analysis indicated that they have received slight consideration in the vocational literature (Flores, Berkel, et al., 2006). Without sufficient research (1) the educational and vocational literature will likely promote a biased understanding of Mexican American girls' educational and career development (Blustein, 2001), and (2) interventions designed to recruit and retain Mexican American girls and women in educational settings may fail if they do not take into account unique factors related to this group's educational decision-making. A challenge for researchers is to focus on developing rigorous, high quality research programs that build on our current foundation of knowledge to inform the development and refinement of prevention programs. More research on the predictors of Mexican American girls' academic success across all educational levels (elementary, secondary, post-secondary, and professional/graduate) is needed, and these studies can advance knowledge by examining the interaction of other demographic characteristics (social class, generation status) on these girls' educational outcomes. Prevention programs can also benefit from longitudinal studies to better understand which factors can be targeted in early interventions to enhance girls' persistence at higher levels of the educational pipeline.

A challenge for prevention specialists is to ensure that research findings are translated into practice. Educational programs seem to include interventions that focus on components linked to academic success at the individual level at the expense of addressing educational institution and social factors that may limit their success (see Table 27.1). To be most effective, prevention programs should aim to touch on individual, familial, cultural, environment, and social factors that affect Mexican American girls' educational achievement. In addition, more prevention programs can be designed exclusively for teachers (including teachers in training) and parents to enhance their awareness of the educational gap between Mexican American girls' and girls from other racial/ethnic groups and to develop strategies that they can use to encourage and reinforce girls' educational aspirations. More evidence-based studies are needed to test the effectiveness of these intervention programs with large samples of Mexican American girls across the United States, and efforts can be made to implement empirically supported programs in schools and communities across the country. Finally, we need prevention scholars and practitioners to join together to lobby for funding to support the development, assessment, and application of new programs. ¡Si podemos!—We can develop educational interventions that will make a difference in helping Mexican American girls achieve their educational dreams.

References

Alva, S. A. (1991). Academic invulnerability among Mexican-American students: The importance of protective resources and appraisals. *Hispanic Journal of Behavioral Sciences, 13,* 18–34.

Arbona, C., & Nora, A. (2007). The influence of academic and environmental factors on Hispanic college degree attainment. *Review of Higher Education, 30,* 247–269.

Arellano, A. R., & Padilla, A. M. (1996). Academic invulnerability among a select group of Latino university students. *Hispanic Journal of Behavioral Sciences, 18,* 485–507.

Auerbach, S. (2004). Engaging Latino parents in supporting college pathways: Lessons from a college access program. *Journal of Hispanic Higher Education, 3,* 125–145.

Auerbach, S. (2007). From moral supporters to struggling advocates: Reconceptualizing parent roles in education through the experiences of working-class families of color. *Urban Education, 42,* 250–283.

Barajas, H. L., & Pierce, J. L. (2001). The significance of race and gender in school success among Latinas and Latinos in college. *Gender and Society, 15,* 859–878.

Bettie, J. (2002). Exceptions to the rule: Upwardly mobile White and Mexican American high school girls. *Girls and Society, 16,* 403–422.

Blustein, D. L. (2001). Extending the reach of vocational psychology: Toward an inclusive and integrative psychology of working. *Journal of Vocational Behavior, 59,* 171–182.

Brigman, G., & Campbell, C. (2003). Helping students improve academic achievement and school success behavior. *Professional School Counseling, 7,* 91–98.

Brigman, G., Campbell, C., & Webb, L. G. (2004). *Student Success Skills: Group counseling manual.* Boca Raton, FL: Atlantic Education Consultants.

Brigman, G., & Webb, L. G. (2004). *Student Success Skills: Classroom manual.* Boca Raton, FL: Atlantic Education Consultants.

Brigman, G., Webb, L. G., & Campbell, C. (2007). Building skills for school success: Improving the academic and social competence of students. *Professional School Counseling, 10,* 279–288.

Brouillard, P., & Hartlaub, M. G. (2005). Ethnic identity, academic achievement, and self-esteem among Mexican-American university students. *Review of Psychology, 12,* 155–160.

Bullington, R. L., & Arbona, C. (2001). Career development tasks of Mexican-American adolescents: An exploratory study. *Journal of Career Development, 28,* 139–153.

Caldera, Y. M., Robitschek, C., Frame, M., & Pannell, M. (2003). Intrapersonal, familial, and cultural factors in the commitment to a career choice of Mexican American and non-Hispanic White college women. *Journal of Counseling Psychology, 50,* 309–323.

Campbell, C., & Brigman, G. (2005). Closing the achievement gap: A structured approach to group counseling. *Journal for Specialists in Group Work, 30,* 67–82.

Capello, D. C. (1994). Beyond financial aid: Counseling Latina students. *Journal of Multicultural Counseling and Development, 22,* 28–36.

Cardoza, D. (1991). College attendance and persistence among Hispanic women: An examination of some contributing factors. *Sex Roles, 24,* 133–147.

Castillo, L. G., Conoley, C. W., Choi-Pearson, C., Archuleta, D. J., Phoummarath, M. J., & Van Landingham, A. (2006). University environment as a mediator of Latino ethnic identity and persistence attitudes. *Journal of Counseling Psychology, 53,* 267–271.

Chin, D., & Kameoka, V. A. (2002). Psychosocial and contextual predictors of educational and occupational self-efficacy among Hispanic inner-city adolescents. *Hispanic Journal of Behavioral Sciences, 24,* 448–464.

Cohen, J. (1988). *Statistical power analysis for the behavioral sciences* (2nd ed.). Hillsdale, NJ: Erlbaum.

Constantino, G., Malgady, R. G., & Rogler, L. H. (1984). Cuentos folkloricos as a therapeutic modality with Puerto Rican children. *Hispanic Journal of Behavioral Sciences, 6,* 169–178.

Cornelius-White, J. H. D., Garza, A. C., & Hoey, A. T. (2004). Personality, family satisfaction, and demographic factors that help Mexican American students succeed academically. *Journal of Hispanic Higher Education, 3,* 270–283.

Farmer, H. S. (2006). History of career counseling for women. In W. B. Walsh & M. J. Heppner (Eds.), *Handbook of career counseling for women* (pp. 1–44). Mahwah, NJ: Erlbaum.

Flores, L. Y., Berkel, L. A., Nilsson, J. E., Ojeda, L., Jordan, S. E., Lynn, G. L., & Leal, V. M. (2006). Racial/ethnic minority vocational research: A content and trend analysis across thirty-five years. *Career Development Quarterly, 55,* 2–21.

Flores, L. Y., Navarro, R. L., & Dewitz, J. (2008). Mexican American high school students' post-secondary educational goals: Applying social cognitive career theory. *Journal of Career Assessment, 16,* 489–501.

Flores, L. Y., & Obasi, E. M. (2005). Mentors' influence on Mexican American students' career and educational development. *Journal of Multicultural Counseling and Development, 33,* 146–164.

Flores, L. Y., & O'Brien, K. M. (2002). The career development of Mexican American adolescent women: A test of social cognitive career theory. *Journal of Counseling Psychology, 49,* 14–27.

Flores, L. Y., Ojeda, L., Huang, Y., Gee, D., & Lee, S. (2006). The relation of acculturation, problem solving appraisal, and career decision-making self-efficacy to Mexican American high school students' educational goals. *Journal of Counseling Psychology, 53,* 260–266.

Fouad, N. A., & Smith, P. L. (1996). A test of a social cognitive model for middle school students: Math and science. *Journal of Counseling Psychology, 43,* 338–346.

Gándara, P. C. (1995). *Over the ivory walls: The educational mobility of low-income Chicanos.* Albany: State University of New York Press.

Gándara, P. (2002). School Puente: What we have learned about preparing Latino youth for education. *Educational Policy, 16,* 474–495.

Gándara, P. (2006). Strengthening the academic pipeline leading to careers in math, science, and technology for Latino students. *Journal of Hispanic Higher Education, 5,* 222–237.

Gándara, P., Larson, K. A., Mehan, H., & Rumberger, R. W. (1998). *Capturing Latino students in the educational pipeline.* Berkley, CA: Chicano/Latino Policy Project.

Gándara, P., & Moreno, J. F. (2002). The Puente project: Issues and perspectives on preparing Latino youth for higher education. *Educational Policy, 16,* 463–473.

Garza, L. (1998). The influence of pre-college factors on the university experiences of Mexican American women. *Aztlán, 23,* 119–135.

Gillock, K. L., & Reyes, O. (1999). Stress, support, and academic performance of urban, low-income, Mexican-American adolescents. *Journal of Youth and Adolescence, 28,* 259–282.

Gloria, A. M. (1997). Chicana academic persistence. *Education and Urban Society, 30,* 107–122.

Gloria, A. M., Castellanos, J., Lopez, A. G., & Rosales, R. (2005). An examination of academic nonpersistence decisions of Latino undergraduates. *Hispanic Journal of Behavioral Sciences, 27,* 202–223.

Gomez, M. J., Fassinger, R. E., Prosser, J., Cooke, K., Mejia, B., & Luna, J. (2001). Voces abriendo caminos (Voices forging paths): A qualitative study of the career development of notable Latinas. *Journal of Counseling Psychology, 48,* 286–300.

Gonzales, N. A., Dumka, L., Deardorff, J., Jacobs-Carter, S., & McCray, A. (2004). Preventing poor mental health and school dropout of Mexican American adolescents following the transition to junior high school. *Journal of Adolescent Research, 19,* 113–131.

Gonzalez, R., & Padilla, A. M. (1997). The academic resilience of Mexican American high school students. *Hispanic Journal of Behavioral Sciences, 19,* 301–317.

Gushue, G. V. (2006). The relationship of ethnic identity, career decision-making self-efficacy and outcome expectations among Latino/a high school students. *Journal of Vocational Behavior, 68,* 85–95.

Gushue, G. V., & Whitson, M. L. (2006). The relationship of ethnic identity and gender role attitudes to the development of career choice goals among Black and Latina girls. *Journal of Counseling Psychology, 53,* 379–385.

Hackett, G., Betz, N. E., Casas, J. M., & Rocha-Singh, I. A. (1992). Gender, ethnicity, and social cognitive factors predicting the academic achievement of students in engineering. *Journal of Counseling Psychology, 39,* 527–538.

Hernandez, J. C. (2000). Understanding the retention of Latino college students. *Journal of College Student Development, 41,* 575–588.

Hernandez, A., Vargas-Lew, L., & Martinez, C. L. (1994). Intergenerational academic aspirations of Mexican-American females: An examination of mother, daughter, and grandmother triads. *Hispanic Journal of Behavioral Sciences, 16,* 195–204.

Hess, R. S., & D'Amato, R. C. (1996). High school completion among Mexican American children: Individual and family background variables. *School Psychology Quarterly, 11,* 353–368.

Hurtado, M. T., & Gauvin, M. (1997). Acculturation and planning for college among youth of Mexican descent. *Hispanic Journal of Behavioral Sciences, 19,* 506–516.

Hurtado, S., & Ponjuan, L. (2005). Latino educational outcomes and the campus climate. *Journal of Higher Education, 4,* 235–251.

I Have a Dream Foundation. (2008). Retrieved from http://www.ihaveadreamfoundation.org/html/program_Elements.htm

Kahne, J., & Bailey, K. (1999). Role of social capital in youth development: The case of "I Have a Dream" programs. *Educational Evaluation and Policy Analysis, 21,* 321–343.

Keith, P. B., & Lichtman, M. V. (1994). Does parental involvement influence the academic achievement of Mexican-American eighth graders? Results from the National Education Longitudinal Study. *School Psychology Quarterly, 9,* 256–272.

Kemple, J. J., & Snipes, J. C. (2000). *Career Academies: Impacts on students' engagement and performance in high school.* New York: MDRC (Manpower Demonstration Research Corporation).

Kemple, J. J., & Willner, C. J. (2008). *Career Academies: Long-term impacts on labor market outcomes, educational attainment, and transitions to adulthood.* New York: MDRC (Manpower Demonstration Research Coorporation).

Lango, D. R. (1995). Mexican American female enrollment in graduate programs: A study of characteristics that may predict success. *Hispanic Journal of Behavioral Sciences, 17,* 33–48.

Larson, K. A., & Rumberger, R. W. (1995). Doubling school success in highest-risk Latino youth: Results from a middle school intervention study. In R. F. Macias & R. G. Garcia Ramos (Eds.), *Changing schools for changing students.* Santa Barbara: University of California Linguistic Minority Research Institute.

Lopez, E. J., Ehly, S., & Garcia-Vasquez, E. (2002). Acculturation, social support, and academic achievement of Mexican and Mexican American high school students: An exploratory study. *Psychology in the Schools, 39,* 245–257.

Lopez, E. M. (1995). Challenges and resources of Mexican American students within the family, peer group, and university: Age and gender patterns. *Hispanic Journal of Behavioral Sciences, 17,* 499–508.

Malgady, R. G., Rogler, L. H., & Constantino, G. (1990). Hero/heroine modeling for Puerto Rican adolescents: A preventive mental health intervention. *Journal of Consulting and Clinical Psychology, 58,* 469–474.

McWhirter, E. H. (1997). Perceived barriers to education and career: Ethnic and gender differences. *Journal of Vocational Behavior, 50,* 124–140.

McWhirter, E. H., Hackett, G., & Bandalos, D. L. (1998). A causal model of the educational plans and career expectations of Mexican American high school girls. *Journal of Counseling Psychology, 45,* 166–181.

McWhirter, E. H., Torres, D. M., Salgado, S., & Valdez, M. (2007). Perceived barriers and postsecondary plans in Mexican American and White adolescents. *Journal of Career Assessment, 15,* 119–139.

Miranda, A., Webb, L., Brigman, G., & Peluso, P. (2007). Student Success Skills: A promising program to close the academic achievement gap for African American and Latino students. *Professional School Counseling, 10,* 490–497.

Morales, P. C. (1996, August). *Acculturation and vocational identity: The influence of Hispanic familialism.* Paper presented at the annual meeting of the American Psychological Association, Toronto, Canada.

Moreno, R. P., & Lopez, J. A. (1999). Latino parent involvement: The role of maternal acculturation and education. *School Community Quarterly, 9,* 83–101.

Moreno, R. P., & Valencia, R. R. (2002). Chicano families and schools: Myths, knowledge, and future directions for understanding. In R. R. Valencia (Ed.), *Chicano school failure and success: Past, present, and future* (2nd ed). London: Routledge/Falmer.

National Center for Educational Statistics. (2007). *Digest of educational statistics: Postsecondary education.* Retrieved from http://nces.ed.gov/programs/digest/d07/tables/dt07_275.asp

National Science Foundation. (2007). *Moving forward to improve engineering education* (NSB 07–122). Arlington, VA: Author.

National TRIO Clearinghouse. (2003, May). *Racial and ethnic diversity in the federal TRIO programs.* Washington, DC: Council for Opportunity in Education.

Navarro, R. L., Flores, L. Y., & Worthington, R. L. (2007). Mexican American middle school students' goal intentions in mathematics and science: A test of social cognitive career theory. *Journal of Counseling Psychology, 54,* 320–335.

Niemann, Y. F., Romero, A., & Arbona, C. (2000). Effects of cultural orientation on the perception of conflict between relationship and educational goals for Mexican American college students. *Hispanic Journal of Behavioral Sciences, 22,* 46–63.

O'Brien, V., Kopala, M., & Martinez-Pons, M. (1999). Mathematics self-efficacy, ethnic identity, gender, and career interests related to mathematics and science. *Journal of Educational Research, 92,* 231–235.

Ojeda, L., & Flores, L. Y. (2008). The influence of generation level, parents' education level, and perceived barriers on the educational aspirations and expectations of Mexican heritage high school students. *Career Development Quarterly, 57,* 84–95.

Ojeda, L., Flores, L. Y., & Navarro, R. L. (2011). Social cognitive predictors of Mexican American college students' academic and life satisfaction. *Journal of Counseling Psychology, 58*(1), 61–71.

Okagaki, L., Frensch, P. A., & Gordon, E. W. (1995). Encouraging school achievement in Mexican American children. *Hispanic Journal of Behavioral Sciences, 17,* 160–179.

Padilla, A. M., & Gonzalez, R. (2001). Academic performance of immigrant and U.S.-born Mexican heritage students: Effects of schooling in Mexico and bilingual/English language instruction. *American Education Research Journal, 38,* 727–742.

Perez, W., Ezpinoza, R., Ramos, K., Coronado, H. M., & Cortes, R. (2009). Academic resilience among undocumented Latino students. *Hispanic Journal of Behavioral Sciences, 31,* 149–181.

Perrone, K. M., Sedlacek, W. E., & Alexander, C. M. (2001). Gender and ethnic differences in career goal attainment. *Career Development Quarterly, 50,* 168–178.

Ramirez, S. Z., Jain, S., Flores-Torres, L. L., Perez, R., & Carlson, R. (2009). The effects of Cuento therapy on reading achievement and psychological outcomes of Mexican-American students. *Professional School Counseling, 12,* 253–262.

Ramos, L., & Sanchez, A. R. (1995). Mexican-American high school students: Educational aspirations. *Journal of Multicultural Counseling and Development, 23,* 212–221.

Ream, R. K., & Rumberger, R. W. (2008). School engagement, peer social capital, and school dropout among Mexican American and non-Latino White students. *Sociology of Education, 81,* 109–139.

Reyes, O., Kobus, K., & Gillock, K. (1999). Career aspirations of urban, Mexican American adolescent females. *Hispanic Journal of Behavioral Sciences, 21,* 366–382.

Rivera-Mosquera, E., Phillips, J. C., Castelino, P., Martin, J. K., & Dobran, E. S. M. (2007). Design and implementation of a grassroots precollege program for Latino youth. *The Counseling Psychologist, 35,* 821–839.

Rodriguez, J. L. (2002). Family environment and achievement among three generations of Mexican American high school students. *Applied Developmental Science, 6,* 88–94.

Rodriguez, N. (1996). Predicting the academic success of Mexican American and White college students. *Hispanic Journal of Behavioral Sciences, 18,* 329–342.

Rumberger, R. W., & Larson, K. A. (1998). Toward explaining differences in educational achievement among Mexican American language-minority students. *Sociology of Education, 71,* 68–92.

Solberg, V. S., Valdez, J., & Villarreal, P. (1994). Social support, stress, and Hispanic college adjustment: Test of a diathesis-stress model. *Hispanic Journal of Behavioral Sciences, 16,* 230–239.

Solberg, V. S., & Villarreal, P. (1997). Examination of self-efficacy, social support, and stress as predictors of psychological and physical distress among Hispanic college students. *Hispanic Journal of Behavioral Sciences, 19,* 182–201.

Sue, D. W., Capodilupo, C. M., Torino, G. C., Bucceri, J. M., Holder, A. M. B., Nadal, K. L., & Esquilin, M. (2007). Microaggressions in everyday life: Implications for clinical practice. *American Psychologist, 62,* 271–286.

Tapia, J. (2000). Schooling and learning in U.S.-Mexican families: A case study of households. *Urban Review, 32,* 25–44.

Torres, J. B., & Solberg, V. S. (2001). Role of self-efficacy, stress, social integration, and family support in Latino college student persistence and health. *Journal of Vocational Behavior, 59,* 53–63.

US Census Bureau. (2009). *American Community Survey.* Retrieved from http://factfinder.census.gov/servlet/DatasetMainPageServlet?_lang=en&_ts=309196002217&_ds_name=ACS_2009_1YR_G00_&_program=

US Department of Education. (2004a). *The impacts of regular Upward Bound: Results from the third follow-up data collection.* Washington, DC: Education Publications Center.

US Department of Education. (2004b). *A profile of the Upward Bound Math-Science program 2000–2001.* Washington, DC: Education Publications Center.

US Department of Education. (2008). *A profile of the federal TRIO programs and child care access means parents in school program.* Washington, DC: Office of Postsecondary Education.

Valencia, A. A. (1994). The attributes of academically successful Mexican-American university male and female students. *Journal of Multicultural Counseling and Development, 22,* 227–238.

Valencia, R. R. (2000). Inequalities and the schooling of minority students in Texas: Historical and contemporary conditions. *Hispanic Journal of Behavioral Sciences, 22,* 445–459.

Valencia, R. R., & Black, M. S. (2002). "Mexican Americans Don't Value Education!": On the basis of the myth, mythmaking, and debunking. *Journal of Latinos and Education, 1,* 81–103.

Valenzuela, A. (1993). Liberal gender role attitudes and academic achievement among Mexican-origin adolescents in two Houston inner-city Catholic Schools. *Hispanic Journal of Behavioral Sciences, 15,* 310–323.

Vera, E. M., Caldwell, J., Clarke, M., Gonzales, R., Morgan, M., & West, M. (2007). The Choices Program: Multisystemic interventions for enhancing the personal and academic effectiveness of urban adolescents of color. *The Counseling Psychologist, 35,* 779–796.

Waxman, H. C., Huang, S. L., & Padron, Y. N. (1997). Motivation and learning environment differences between resilient and nonresilient Latino middle school students. *Hispanic Journal of Behavioral Sciences, 19,* 137–155.

Webb, L., Brigman, G., & Campbell, C. (2005). Linking school counselors and student success: Replication of the Student Success Skills approach targeting the academic and social competence of students. *Professional School Counseling, 8,* 407–413.

Wycoff, S. E. (1996). Academic performance of Mexican American women: Sources of support that serve as motivating variables. *Journal of Multicultural Counseling and Development, 24,* 146–155.

Zalaquett, C. P., & Lopez, A. D. (2006). Learning from the stories of successful undergraduate Latina/Latino students: The importance of mentoring. *Mentoring and Tutoring, 14,* 337–353.

CHAPTER

28 Promoting Mental Health in Asian Immigrants

Pei-Wen Winnie Ma, Munyi Shea, *and* Christine J. Yeh

Abstract

This chapter focuses on promoting mental health among Asian immigrants. First, we provide background information about this growing and diverse community. Next, we discuss cultural adjustment, underuse of mental health services, and why it is important to develop services for Asian immigrants. We then describe the major factors that contribute to Asian immigrants' mental health, including acculturation, social support, and spirituality, as well as Asian immigrants' use of collectivistic coping strategies. Finally, implications for prevention programs, research, and education are discussed.

Key Words: Asian immigrant mental health, Asian immigrant prevention, Asian immigrant mental health promotion, Asian immigrant adjustment and mental health

Introduction and Overview

In 2005, the foreign-born population comprised 12.5% of the US population (Portes & Rumbaut, 2006). In other words, at least one in 10 people in the United States came from an immigrant or refugee background (Chung & Bemak, 2007). Among the many immigrant groups, Asian immigrants constitute 26% of the foreign-born population (Capps & Passel, 2004). In 2008, nearly 88% of Asian American children grew up in immigrant households (Urban Institute, 2010).

With the increasing diversification of the United States, especially in urban areas, it is imperative for mental health professionals to understand the experience of Asian immigrants. In this chapter, we explore mental health concerns faced by Asian immigrants in the United States, summarize research on the major factors contributing to their psychological well-being, discuss culturally-specific coping strategies, and emphasize strategies to promote mental health for this community. The terms "Asian immigrants" and "Asian Americans" generally refer to people who immigrated from Asia and descendents of immigrants from Asia. In this chapter, we will use these terms interchangeably to describe both immigrants and children of immigrants moving to the United States from East Asia (e.g., China, Japan, and Korea), Southeast Asia (e.g., Vietnam, Thailand, and Malaysia) and South Asia (e.g., India and Bangladesh) (Liu, Murakami, Eap, & Nagayama Hall, 2009).

The Asian immigrants in the United States represent a vast diversity in terms of country of origin (over 30 countries), languages, education level, and socioeconomic status before and after migration (Chung & Bemak, 2007). Since the passing of the Immigration and Naturalization Act in 1965, more Asian immigrants came to the United States for employment, education, and family reunification (Liu et al., 2009). Refugees also came from Southeast Asia due to the Vietnam War and associated fighting in Cambodia and Laos (Chung & Bemak, 2007). There are also a growing number of Asian immigrants who migrate without legal documentation (Portes & Rumbaut, 2006). To effectively provide services to this group, we must understand their mental health concerns within the context of immigration.

Cultural Adjustment and Mental Health Concerns

The transition and adaptation to a new country brings about many emerging challenges. Many Asian immigrants face cultural adjustment difficulties in multiple domains (e.g., personal, familial, academic, vocational, and social) of their lives. For example, since language is a fundamental means for communication, immigrants with limited English language fluency often find it difficult to integrate to the dominant culture (Yeh & Inose, 2002; Yeh, Okubo, et al., 2008). Language barriers also impact Asian immigrants' peer relationships, academic performance, and employment opportunities (Yeh, Kim, Pituc, & Atkins 2008; P.-W. Ma & Yeh, 2010). Change in language use from immigrants' native language to English also signifies a loss of cultural identity. It can also create shame and fear in their interaction with the dominant group (Yeh, Kim, et al., 2008). Other types of cultural adjustment difficulties include loss of familiar social networks (Fung & Wong, 2007); unfamiliarity with social norms, rules, and laws in the United States (Organista, Marin, & Chun, 2010); and racism and discrimination (Alvarez, 2009; Alvarez, Juang, & Liang, 2006; Chung & Bemak, 2007, Yeh, Okubo, et al., 2008).

The challenges and difficulties experienced by people in the process of acculturating to the dominant culture are termed *acculturative stress*, which refers to a feeling of tension and anxiety caused by the demands of adaptation (Berry & Kim, 1988). Immigrants may experience substantial acculturative stress associated with changes on individual (e.g., attitudinal and behavioral adjustment), structural (e.g., changing family dynamics and social network), and cultural (e.g., different cultural norms and expectations) levels. Acculturative stress has been found to be associated with mental health symptoms such as depression, anxiety, and psychosomatic symptoms (B. S. K. Kim, Ahn, & Lam, 2009; Yeh, 2003).

Research has also found other acculturation factors, such as length of time in the United States and English-language fluency, are associated with psychological disorders. Hwang, Chun, Takeuchi, Myers, and Siddarth (2005) reported that as the length of time in the United States increases, the risk of developing depression decreases for Chinese immigrants. They also found that when Chinese Americans initially immigrate (versus after they have been in the United States for a period of time), they are more likely to be depressed as they confront migration stress. In a study based on data from the National Latino and Asian American Study, Takeuchi and colleagues (2007) found that Asian American men who were more fluent in English were less likely to have any lifetime depressive, anxiety, or psychiatric disorder than those who were less fluent in English. However, the same factor is not associated with mental disorders for Asian American women (Takeuchi et al., 2007). The authors hypothesized that Asian immigrant men who are able to speak English well are able to seek a wider range of employment and utilize other types of services and resources, which leads to higher socioeconomic positions in the United States.

When examining the occurrence and prevalence rate of mental health symptoms among Asian immigrants, one must also consider the context of their socioeconomic status. Some Asian immigrant groups have higher educational attainment and tend to be professionals from middle-class backgrounds. These groups are likely to have more resources and access to healthcare. Refugees and Asian immigrants from low-income backgrounds tend to be less educated, working in low-paying jobs, and struggling with economic hardship and day-to-day survival (Rhee, 2009). Poverty, along with acculturative stress, increases the risk for mental health symptoms (Shen & Takeuchi, 2001).

Immigration history is another major factor to take into account. It has been documented that Southeast Asian refugees are at a higher risk for depression and post-traumatic stress disorder (PTSD) in comparison to other Asian groups due to their multiple traumas and stressors before, during, and post migration (Abueg & Chun, 1996; Organista et al., 2010). Many of these refugees escaped their war-torn homeland during the Vietnam War era. Some witness the death of loved ones or nearly escape death during the migration process. In addition, the loss of family members and personal possessions, living in undesirable conditions in refugee camps, and dealing with stressors associated with establishing a new life in the United States all exacerbate the symptoms of PTSD (Abueg & Chun, 1996; Organista, et al., 2010).

The Asian immigrant elderly population, in particular, has been identified as being at high risk for mental health problems. It has been reported that depression and anxiety occur frequently in this group because they have limited resources in dealing with acculturative stressors, such as language barriers and adjustment difficulties (Mui, 1996). It was found that Asian immigrant elders' perceptions of a cultural gap between themselves and their adult children was associated with high levels of depression (Mui & Kang, 2006). In addition, it was noted that Asian American elderly females are vulnerable to higher rates of suicide due to cultural conflicts between generations (Leong, Leach, Yeh, & Chou, 2007).

Despite the evidence of high risks of mental health problems among Asian immigrants, previous literature has consistently documented that they tend to underutilize professional help in comparison to other racial/ethnic groups (e.g., Uba, 1994; Rhee, 2009). Abe-Kim et al. (2007) found that Asian immigrants tend to utilize mental health services at a lower rate in comparison to those who were born in the United States, possibly due to varying levels of enculturation and acculturation, and perceptions of and attitudes toward seeking professional help (Shea & Yeh, 2008). Those who come into contact with mental health professionals often display more severe and chronic symptoms and are likely to prematurely terminate psychotherapy treatment (Sue & Sue, 2008). Literature has identified multiple barriers that contribute to the underutilization of mental health services among Asian Americans. We would like to highlight a few that underscore the need for conceptualizing prevention work for this population.

First, there are limited culturally and linguistically responsive services available in the community (Sue & Sue, 2008). Many mental health agencies are not equipped with bilingual staff and providers. Having to rely on formal or informal interpreters (e.g., younger family members or family friends) during the counseling process can deter immigrants from seeking professional help. Those clients who have difficulty communicating in English may have to rely on using simple words to explain their complex thoughts and feelings (Sue & Sue , 2008). In contrast, if they were able to use their native language, they can easily explain themselves without the loss of emotional complexity during the counseling process. Second, Western psychotherapy tends to focus on verbalizing problems and encourages emotional expression, which contradicts traditional Asian values of keeping personal problems within and restraining one's emotions (Shea & Yeh, 2008; Uba, 1994; Yeh & Hwang, 2000). Disclosing personal problems to a stranger (e.g., a therapist) is also considered to bring shame and disgrace on one's family (Atkinson & Gim, 1989; Shea & Yeh, 2008).

Major Factors Contributing to Asian Immigrants' Mental Health

In this section, we will summarize research on some of the risk and protective factors associated with Asian immigrants' mental health, such as acculturation, social support, and spirituality and religion. These factors can serves as either risk or protective factors, depending how these factors interact with the individual and the situations (Rho & Rho, 2009).

Acculturation

Acculturation refers to changes and the psychosocial adjustment that occurs as a result of people coming in contact with and living in a new cultural environment, and their subsequent negotiation of two or more cultures (Berry, 1995; LaFromboise, Coleman, & Gerton, 1993). The changes could be reflected in behaviors (e.g., language proficiency, activities), attitudes (e.g., openness toward the new culture), and values (e.g., adherence to or rejection of mainstream cultural values). The underlying assumption holds that one culture (typically the majority culture, also referred as the *dominant, mainstream*, or *host* culture) is considered as having more cultural value than the other culture (typically the culture of origin, also referred as the *ethnic, indigenous, home* culture) (Berry, 1995; LaFromboise et al., 1993).

Earlier models tend to view acculturation as a linear, unidirectional process that places people's integration with and differentiation from the dominant culture on a continuum (e.g., Gordon, 1964). Put in another way, this approach assesses acculturation level by examining the extent to which a person adopt the behaviors and values of the dominant culture—with the assumption that one's ethnic identity or culture is inevitably weakened as a function of acculturation (Kim, 2009). Recent models tend to emphasize a multidimensional approach, which regards acculturation as both an orientation toward one's culture of origin and toward the dominant culture (Kim & Abreu, 2001; Zea, Asner-Self, Birman, & Buki, 2003).

Acculturation is recognized as an important factor in Asian American psychological well-being. However, empirical research on acculturation and mental health outcomes has revealed conflicting results. On the one hand, many studies have suggested that lower acculturation levels are related to increased mental health concerns across different age groups, such as stress (Padilla, Wagatsuma, & Lindholm, 1985), family conflicts (Min, 1998; Sodowsky, Lai, & Plake, 1991), cultural adjustment difficulties (Sodowsky & Lai, 1997), depression (Choi, 1997; Chung, Bemak, & Wong, 2000; Jha, 2001; Shin, 1994), and suicidal ideation and behavior (Davis, 1995; Lau, Jernewall, Zane, & Myers, 2002). Further, higher levels of acculturation predicted subjective well-being in a community sample of Korean immigrants (Yoon, Lee, & Goh, 2008) and more positive help-seeking attitudes (Atkinson & Gim 1989; Tata & Leong, 1994; Zhang & Dixon, 2003) among Asian international and Asian American college students. On the other hand, some studies reported a positive relationship or no relationship between acculturation and mental health outcomes. For instance, G. X. Ma and colleagues (2004) found that acculturation to the dominant culture was predictive of increased substance use. Nguyen and Peterson (1993) found that higher levels of acculturation were associated with depression among Vietnamese American college students. Lastly, M. S. Lee, Crittenden, and Yu (1996), in their sample of elderly Korean immigrants, failed to find any relationship between acculturation and depressive symptoms.

Different perspectives have been offered to understand the contradictory findings regarding acculturation and mental health outcomes (Rogler, Cortes, & Malgady, 1991). The first perspective suggests that acculturation is instrumental to immigrants' survival and successful adjustment. For instance, Shen and Takeuchi (2001), in their study of a large Chinese American community sample, reported a link among acculturation, socioeconomic class, and mental health outcomes—suggesting that English proficiency might lead to increased job availability and job mobility, higher income, and enhanced psychological well-being. Research has also found that improved communication skills are likely to enhance positive social interactions among Asian immigrant youths and facilitate cultural adjustment (e.g., Yeh, 2003; Yeh & Inose, 2002). In contrast, immigrant youth with lower English proficiency reported greater intercultural competence concerns (Yeh, Okubo, et al., 2008). Moreover, acculturation of the older Asian immigrant generation may help narrow the generational gap with the younger generation, easing potential intergenerational conflicts due to different acculturation rates (R. M. Lee, Su, & Yoshida, 2005). In sum, acculturation is likely to promote competence in social and occupational functioning and facilitate interpersonal relationships.

The second perspective argues that when a person becomes more assimilated, s/he may also become more aware of the racial and other types of discrimination that occur in the mainstream society as well as experiencing conflict and dissonance when attempting to negotiate competing demands of two different cultures. Consequently, the person may experience increased stress, psychological distress, and intercultural competence concerns (Nguyen & Peterson, 1993; Shen & Takeuchi, 2001; Yeh, A. B. Kim, et al., 2008).

These opposing views, nevertheless, do not address how a person acculturates to the dominant culture while simultaneously retaining her/his own culture of origin. Scholars have critiqued that most acculturation studies assume the unidimensionality of acculturation, that is, the more a person is assimilated, the less the person retains his/her culture of origin (B. S. K. Kim, 2009). This assumption, however, neglects the importance of biculturalism. Enculturation is a concept that refers to the retention or acquisition of values, beliefs, attitudes, and behaviors of one's culture of origin (B. S. K. Kim & Abreu, 2001). Recent support for the notion of bilinear acculturation/enculturationsuggests that a person could develop a cultural orientation toward both the dominant culture and her/his own culture of origin (B. S. K. Kim & Abreu; Zea et al., 2003).

Berry (2006) posited that psychosocial adjustment may depend on the acculturation strategies immigrants employ in relating to both cultures. He proposed four possible acculturation styles or strategies (Berry, 2003; Berry, Kim, & Boski, 1988). *Assimilation* refers to identification with the dominant culture and rejection of one's own ethnic culture; *separation* refers to identification with one's ethnic culture and rejection of the dominant culture; *integration* refers to the synthesis of both cultures—maintaining characteristics of one's ethnic culture while interacting with and learning from the dominant culture; lastly, *marginalization* refers to alienation from both cultures.

Research has generally supported that integration as an acculturation strategy predicts the best psychosocial functioning, followed by either assimilation or separation, with marginalization associated with the highest levels of psychological distress (Berry, 2006; Sam & Berry, 1995; Sayegh & Lasry, 1993). Immigrants who synthesize both cultures tend to experience lower levels of anxiety and fewer psychological problems than those with strictly assimilation, separation, and marginalization strategies (Sam & Berry 1995; Sayegh & Lasry, 1993). Asian adolescents with an integrated acculturation strategy are more likely to report higher grades, higher perceived social competence, and more positive self-esteem than adolescents who employ separation or marginalization strategies (Farver, Narang, & Bhadha, 2002; Ghuman, 1997). By connecting with one's culture of origin and ethnic community, Asian immigrants have more accessible support and resources, which may enhance their subjective well-being and reduce their risk of psychological distress (Yoon, Lee, & Goh, 2008). In addition, interaction with the dominant culture may help promote immigrants' operation in the larger sociocultural context, thereby contributing to their sense of connectedness and feelings of acceptance by the mainstream society (Mehta, 1998).

Assessing the relationship between acculturation and psychological health is complex. Researchers have called for efforts to extend beyond the investigation of a simple, direct relationship between acculturation and mental health outcomes. Acculturation may affect psychological health directly or indirectly via socioeconomic status (Shen & Takeuchi, 2001), stress and acculturative stress (Oh, Koeske, & Sales, 2002; Shen & Takeuchi, 2001), religiosity and spirituality (Farver et al., 2002), social support (Choi, 1997), and social connectedness (Yoon et al., 2008). Two of these—social support and religiosity/spirituality—are discussed in the following sections.

Social Support

Social support has been defined as social resources that are available or provided to individuals by nonprofessionals. It could take the forms of emotional support (e.g., expressing care, sympathy, understanding), companionship (e.g., doing activities together) tangible support (e.g., providing financial resources, assistance with chores), and information or advice (Cohen, Gottlieb, & Underwood, 2000).

Research has suggested that social support is an important factor affecting Asian immigrants' psychological well-being and acculturative stress, as well as ameliorating the effect of acculturative stress (Yeh, Kim, et al. 2008). The disruption of family integration as well as social and emotional support systems could lead to increased family conflicts, social alienation, adjustment difficulties, and profound mental health problems among the individuals and their families (Leong et al., 2007; Shea, Yang, & Leong, 2010).

On the other hand, availability of social support has been associated with lower rate of family conflict among Korean immigrant youth (Moon, 2008), decreased risk for delinquent behavior and serious violence among Vietnamese immigrant youth (Ngo & Le, 2007), and enhanced sense of belonging and life satisfaction among Chinese immigrant youth (Chow, 2007). Parental support, in particular, might be crucial for immigrant youths' positive adjustment. Thomas and Choi (2006) suggested that parental support could serve as a buffer against acculturative stress among Korean and Indian immigrant youths. Similarly, Guerrero and colleagues (2006) found that Filipino immigrant youth in Hawaii who had parental support were less likely to report depression, anxiety, substance use, and poor school performance. In contrast, Cho and Haslam (2010) reported that Korean sojourner youths who lived in the United States without their parents—in comparison to Korean immigrant youths who lived with both parents—were more likely to perceive a lack of parental support and endorse depressive symptoms. These results highlight the importance of parent coresidence and family support.

Other social ecological contexts such as school, teachers, and peers may also play a significant role in immigrant youths' adjustment. Yeh, Okubo, and colleagues (2008) reported that bonding to school and receipt of prosocial acts from peers were associated with lower levels of depression and anxiety among urban Asian immigrant youths, whereas peer victimization was related to higher levels of anxiety in this group. One intriguing finding of their study was that the majority of the immigrant youths preferred coping by connecting with important others (e.g., parents, peers); less than 2% of the students had sought professional psychological help. In a career intervention group study, Chinese immigrant youths overwhelmingly reported that the most helpful aspect of the intervention was the group format and the opportunity to connect and receive support from their peers on critical career and developmental issues (Shea, Ma, Yeh, Lee, & Pituc, 2009). Both studies suggest the importance of peer support and Chinese immigrant youths' preferences for seeking help from close others.

Social support also influences the mental health of older Asian adults. Researchers found that Asian immigrant elders who experienced loss and grief, physical illness, and poverty were more vulnerable to developing depression (Mui, 1996; Mui & Kang, 2006). As stated earlier in the chapter, Asian immigrant elders' psychological distress could be compounded by their language barriers, adjustment difficulties, intergenerational cultural gap, and weakening family support (Mui, 1996; Mui & Kang, 2006). On the other hand, social connectedness and emotional support/companionship have been associated with better psychological well-being and lower levels of depression among older Chinese, Japanese, and Korean immigrants (Gellis & Taguchi, 2004; Wong, Yoo, & Stewart, 2007).

The functions of social support—such as how social support is perceived and utilized—should be understood in the context of Asian cultural values. Family cohesion is highly valued in Asian cultures. Many Asian immigrants lose the network of support including their extended family members and friends in their native countries when they move to the United States (E. Lee, 1996; Min, 1998). The disruption of family integration as well as social and emotional support systems could lead to increased family conflicts, social alienation, adjustment difficulties, and profound mental health problems among individuals and their families (Leong et al., 2007; Shea et al., 2010).

Religion and Spirituality

Although there are no standard definitions for these two terms, "religion" generally refers to an organized system of beliefs, rituals, practices, and community oriented toward a particular faith tradition or doctrine about a sacred other (Dew et al., 2008; Walsh, 2008), whereas "spirituality" is primarily concerned with "meaning-making" and the internal and personal construction of a higher power with or without an organized religion (Walsh, 2008).

Spiritual beliefs and practices are salient in the conceptualization of well-being among Asian American ethnic groups. The central importance of faith and spiritual practice (e.g., prayer, spiritual counseling) among Filipinos (among whom 85% are Catholic) may promote their self-esteem and psychological well-being during times of suffering and adversity (Sanchez & Gaw, 2007). In studying South Asian families' coping responses following the 9/11 terrorist attacks, Inman, Yeh, Madan-Bahel, and Nath (2007) reported that spiritually was endorsed by the families as a source of strength and resilience for dealing with their loss of a love one.

Religious faiths are generally viewed as a protective factor against suicide. However, it should be noted that most empirical studies examining religion and suicide tend to focus on the Western, Christian perspective and neglect the influences of other religious or spiritual beliefs in Asian culture. Leong et al. (2007) provided a summary of the influences of various religious faiths, such as Buddhism and Hinduism, on suicide among Asian Americans. Although suicide is not specifically deterred in Buddhism and Hinduism, the act may be considered selfish and negative within the Asian social context due to its disruption to the family integrity and the community harmony.

Asian Immigrants' Coping Strategies

Indigenous Healing

In addition to religious and spiritual ways of promoting positive well-being among Asian immigrants, research and theory has also discussed how indigenous healing approaches are culturally relevant perspectives of mental health (Burnhill, Park, & Yeh, 2008; Yeh, Hunter, Madan-Bahel, Chiang, & Arora, 2004; Yeh & Kwong, 2009). In fact, a possible explanation for mental health counseling underuse among Asian immigrants may be their preference for indigenous forms of healing, which differ considerably from Western notions of talk therapy (Sue & Sue, 2008; Yeh, Hunter, et al., 2004). Hence, in order to understand how to promote positive health among Asian immigrants, we must explore specific Asian indigenous practices and how they are consonant with interdependent views of health and healing.

Indigenous healers are believed to have special insight, skills, and talents (C. C. Lee & Armstrong, 1995) that are used to help individuals with spiritual, emotional, and physical issues. In Asian cultures, indigenous healers often share the client's cultural values and beliefs and are therefore identified for support and guidance (Helms & Cook, 1999; Sue & Sue, 2008). Indigenous healers have specific explanations for abnormal behavior and mental health and particular methods for dealing with human problems and distress (Harner, 1990; C. C. Lee & Armstrong, 1995). These ideas do not rely on direct verbal communication in order to cope with psychological concerns.

For Asian immigrants, indigenous healing is related to holistic perspectives of well-being (Singh, 1999; Sue & Sue, 2008), which interconnects mind, body, spirit, and nature (Yeh, Hunter, et al., 2004). To promote positive mental health, Asian indigenous healers must conceptualize physical and psychological health as being inextricably linked. Moreover, there is no single cause for mental health problems. Rather, human behavior is interconnected at multiple levels: the individual and the family, nature, spirits, and the ancestral world (Burnhill et al., 2008). Therefore, indigenous healers might view human relationships to be multidimensional (Yeh, Hunter, et al., 2004).

The interdependent perspective provides an important context for understanding how indigenous healers are especially relevant for promoting Asian immigrant mental health. Western forms of counseling tend to center on the intrapsychic realm of cognitive, affective, and behavioral aspects of the individual, whereas spiritual and holistic aspects of the self and healing may be neglected (Highlen, 1996; Sue & Sue, 2008). Many Asian immigrants are uncomfortable speaking to a counselor due to cultural stigmas, cultural incongruities, and language differences and may rather prefer seeing a healer who understands his/her perception of health.

For Asian immigrants, indigenous healing includes acupuncture, traditional Chinese medicine, and *Pranic*, *Qigong*, and *Reiki healing*, to name a few. These approaches are similar in their focus on the interdependence of energies in the body. In contrast to many Western perspectives, psychological problems are resolved by addressing conflicts within the individual (such as energy imbalances) or between the individual and the larger world. An Asian healer may factor in one's relationship with the universe, the acts of previous ancestors, or other considerations as informing the present concerns.

For example, an Indian *Pranic healer* is an individual who uses energy-based techniques that channel the life-force or "prana" to balance and transform the body's energy. This type of healer connects the energy of one's physical and emotional existence with a higher consciousness until they are all harmonized. A Japanese *Reiki healer* is someone who uses a universal life energy to stimulate the body's natural healing process. Finally, a Chinese *Qigong healer* is an individual who can channel or emit external life energy or "Qi" for the purpose of healing others (Yeh & Kwong, 2009).

Traditional Western approaches to counseling and psychotherapy have generally approached physical, mental, and spiritual health as distinct entities (Sue & Sue, 2008) and cognitive, affective, and behavioral functioning as a part of intrapsychic forces. This perspective may be foreign and inappropriate to many Asian immigrants, who see these parts of self and the world as interrelated (Yeh, Hunter, et al., 2004). Many Asian immigrants may have also seen an indigenous healer in their home country. Hence, it is important for mental health counselors to learn about, and collaborate with, indigenous healers, to best serve their Asian immigrant clients (Sue & Sue, 2008; C. C. Lee & Armstrong, 1995).

Collectivistic Coping

Recent theory and research have discussed how individualistic and collectivistic cultural orientations and self-perceptions influence coping styles (e.g., Heppner, 2008; H. S. Kim, Sherman, & Taylor, 2008; Kuo, Roysircar, & Newby-Clark, 2006; Yeh, Borrero, & Kwong, in press; Yeh & Kwong, 2009). Yeh, Arora, and Wu (2006) proposed a model of collectivistic coping that outlined the coping styles of individuals from different collectivistic ethnic/racial groups (e.g., African American, Asian and Asian American, Latino/a). Consistent with literature on collectivistic strategies of coping (Yeh, Arora, et al., 2006; Yeh & Kwong, 2009), Asian immigrants who tend to be more collectivistic may prioritize coping strategies that use family support, intracultural coping, fatalism, forbearance, religion and spirituality, and relational universality.

FAMILY SUPPORT

The meanings and functions of family support are salient in the Asian community: Asian immigrants tend to perceive family as an integral aspect of self-identity and as a source of support and care (Yeh & Wang, 2000). For Asian immigrants who are more relationally oriented, they may prefer to seek help from family. Research has also found that an interdependent identity is a significant predictor of help-seeking from family members among Japanese youth (Yeh, Inose, Kobori, & Chang, 2001).

In addition, the notion of filial piety is based on Confucianism, a belief system that dictates family hierarchies based on age and generation. Because parents and elders are viewed as wiser and more knowledgeable, Asian immigrants often turn to them first in times of trouble (Yeh, Inman, Kim, & Okubo, 2006). Seeking support from the family versus strangers also helps to "save face" because it guarantees that problems are kept within the bounds of the family network. If the concerns are family related, it can bring shame and guilt to the entire family (Hayashino & Chopra, 2009). Research has consistently shown that Asian Americans and immigrants tend to use coping strategies that prioritize talking with family (Conrad & Pacquiao, 2005; Homma-True, 1997; Yeh, Okubo, et al., 2008; Yeh & Wang, 2000), especially when coping with the loss of a loved one (Yeh, Inman, et al., 2006). Reiboldt and Goldstein (2000) researched Cambodian refugee children and their families and found a preference for family and community support versus seeking help from mental health professionals.

Nevertheless, differential acculturation rates within the immigrant family may change the landscape of family dynamics and support systems. For instance, Asian immigrant adults may expect their children to fulfill their filial piety responsibilities in certain ways (e.g., financial assistance, coresidence) (Yeh, Okubo, et al., 2008). Yet their children—who tend to acculturate to the US culture at a faster rate and endorse more individualistic values (Lan, 2002)—may prefer living away from their parents, expressing their care through verbal and affection rather than obligation (Sung, 2000), or transferring some of the duty of care to nonfamily members such as senior home employees (Lan, 2002). The changes in the expectations and responsibilities of filial piety could engender disappointments and intergenerational conflicts in the immigrant family.

INTRACULTURAL COPING

Intracultural coping is defined as the use of support from one's own ethnic or racial group (Yeh, Arora, et al. 2006; Yeh & Kwong, 2009). This type of coping may be influenced by language spoken, proximity to other coethnics, and similarity in mental health perspectives. Collectivistic cultures, and Asian immigrants in particular, may also reside in close-knit communities that are less permeable and more protective than individualistic cultures (Triandis, 1989). In their ethnographic study, Reiboldt and Goldstein (2000) found that Cambodian families tended to rely on ethnically-similar community networks for support. Research on a sample of South Asians (Inman et al., 2007) and East Asians (Yeh, Inman, et al., 2006) also found a strong preference for intracultural coping when dealing with loss and a traumatic event (the World Trade Center attacks). In both of these studies, a large number of Asian immigrants were included, providing further justification for understanding how positive mental health may be promoted within ethnic communities.

FATALISM

Fatalism is a collectivistic coping strategy that entails accepting one's problem as part of fate, or an act of a higher being. Fatalism may involve adapting one's role in the dilemma to fit the environment or situation (Yeh & Kwong, 2009). This type of coping, sometimes referred to as *harmony control*, is distinguished from *secondary control*, which includes denial, avoidance, and reinterpretation of events as ways of coping (Morling & Fiske, 1999). Rather, harmony control is "an active, intentional endeavor in which people recognize the agency in contextual, social, or spiritual forces and attempt to merge with these forces" (Morling & Fiske, 1999, p. 382).

For Asian immigrant communities, fatalism is interconnected to religion and spirituality. For example, in Buddhism and Taoism, there is a tendency to accept problems as they come as a part of the Buddhist notion of suffering as inevitable, or the Taoist idea of adapting to the environment (Tweed, White, & Lehman, 2004). It follows that East Asian versus Western cultures may be more likely to respond to stressful events by adapting to, rather than changing, the environment. This research underscores previous research that found that Asian Americans and immigrants used fatalism to explain the tragic loss of a family member (Yeh, Inman, et al., 2006).

FORBEARANCE

Forbearance is a value in collectivistic cultures that refers to the withholding of one's emotions in order to maintain social harmony. Forbearance is often achieved through self-sacrificeby keeping problems and negative emotions to oneself (Marsella & Dash-Scheuer, 1988). Forbearance is a sign of maturity and honor among Asian immigrants (Yeh & Kwong, 2009) and it is related to the collectivistic value of focusing on significant relationships and maintaining balance versus disrupting relational harmony (Markus & Kitayama, 1991). In fact, Cambodian refugee families living in poverty used forbearance to deal with neighborhood decline (Reiboldt & Goldstein, 2000). Research has also indicated that Asian Americans and immigrants (Fukuhara, 1989; Inman et al., 2007; Yeh, Inman, et al. 2006; Yeh & Inose, 2002) tend to keep their problems to themselves to avoid worrying or burdening important others.

RELATIONAL UNIVERSALITY

Relational universality is a collectivistic coping strategy that relies on a sense of interconnectedness from individuals facing similar struggles (Yeh, Inman, et al., 2006; Yeh & Kwong, 2009). Asian immigrants may prefer to use relational universality when connecting with in-group members around common issues such as racism, identity, language barriers, acculturation, and so forth. Yeh, Inman, et al. (2006) found that Asian Americans and immigrants used relational universality when dealing with their own loss of a family member. This form of coping allows one to validate the self and build closer bonds with similar others. This coping strategy may also be related with intracultural coping and social support seeking, since shared experiences are frequently ethnically or racially embedded for Asian immigrants.

Strategies to Promote Mental Health Among Asian Immigrants

Translating research findings into services that will benefit the Asian immigrant community has been a major goal for many Asian American mental health researchers. As noted earlier in the chapter, Asian immigrants have traditionally been underserved for their mental health needs, and culturally-specific and culturallysensitive prevention services remain limited (Sue & Sue, 2008; Le & Stockdale, 2008; Ying, 2009). In the following section, we will summarize several programs that promote mental health though family, school, and community context.

Strengthen Family Ties

Strengthening Intergenerational/Intercultural Ties in Immigrant Families (SITIF) is a prevention and intervention program that aims to promote intergenerational relationships between immigrant parent and their Chinese American children (Ying, 1999a). Studies have found that first- and second-generation Chinese American adolescents with immigrant parents report more intergenerational conflict than their European American peers from nonimmigrant families (Ho, 1993; R. M. Lee & Liu, 2001). These conflicts are often a result of differential acculturation rates between immigrant parents and their children. Asian immigrant adolescents are likely to adopt Western values, such as independence and self-determination, which contradicttraditional Asian values of interdependence and respect for authority figures (Ma & Yeh, 2005; Ying, 2009).

The SITIF is an 8-week, 2-hour-long sessions, parenting class designed for Chinese immigrant parents with school-age children, but Ying (1999b) suggested that the contents can be easily adapted for the use of other immigrant groups. The program was held at a Chinese language school, where the immigrant children attend Chinese classes on the weekend. This program focuses on increasing parents' awareness to the differences in cultural values between the two generations, teaching parents to effectively empathize with their child's perspective, to cognitively understand the variation of ethnic and American cultures and its impact on child development, and to help parents to cope with stress and develop effective parenting skills, especially communication skills with their children (Ying, 1999a, 1999b, 2009).

A key component of this program is that it promotes cross-cultural understanding and awareness. Through these weekly classes, discussion, and homework, parents learn information on acculturation and ethnic identity formation, and understand their children's behavior in a cultural context. This program also actively teaches parenting skills that will enhance intergenerational relationship and stress-reduction techniques to help cope with distress associated with parenting (Ying, 2009).

Evaluation of the effectiveness of the SITIF program demonstrated improved intergenerational relationships, and an increase in participants' sense of parenting responsibility and control of child. The quality of intergenerational relationship was found to be positively related to child's self-esteem (Ying, 1999a). In a later study (Ying, 2009), parents that participated in the program reported greater mastery in coping with stress and increased awareness and knowledge.

Enhance Social Support in the School Context

Immigrant students that arrive in the United States during their adolescent years often face adjustment challenges on multiple fronts. Some of the issues include lack of English proficiency (Yeh & Inose, 2002), loneliness and alienation (Yeh, Ma, et al., 2004), intergenerational conflict with parents (Ying, 1999b), and negotiation of the different cultural values and norms between the United States and their home country (Yeh et al., 2005).

Prevention and intervention programs for Asian immigrant youth need to consider indigenous methods of coping that align with cultural orientation. Collectivistic cultures, such as many Asian cultures, tend to focus on interpersonal harmony and connectedness (Inman & Yeh, 2007). When faced with distress associated with acculturation process, utilizing social support, especially support from one's own ethnic or racial group (intercultural coping), takes on particular significance (Yeh, Ching, Okubo, & Luthar, 2007; Yeh, Inman, et al., 2006). Building on this idea, Yeh et al. (2007) designed and implemented a school-based peer mentoring program to assist Chinese immigrant youth cope with cultural adjustment issues.

This program emphasizes the utilization of peer support from culturally similar others. Four high school students served as peer mentors, and 23 students were their mentees. Each mentor was assigned to five to six students based on linguistic and cultural match, and the mentee's personal preference (e.g., mentee prefers a mentor of the same gender). These peer mentors were Chinese immigrant students who have had more experience navigating the school and cultural environment. In particular, they were more familiar with the school resources and how to seek help for personal, social, and academic needs.

The length of the program was approximately three months. Through structured weekly individual and group meetings during school hours and after school, peer mentors worked on building a relationship and providing support for their mentees. The peer mentors shared their personal stories of the acculturation process and discussed various topics of interest (e.g., college application, family, school resources). They also meet with mentees for after-school social activities (Yeh et al., 2007). The process of peer-mentors sharing their experience helped normalize the process of cultural adjustment for these recent Chinese immigrant mentees. It also allowed the students to establish a sense of interdependence and connectedness, which are congruent with traditional Asian cultural values (Yeh et al., 2007).

Evaluation of this program revealed that student participants had significantly higher feelings of trust/attachment and closeness to their peers at posttest in comparison to pretest. In other words, participants were able to increase trust in their peers and felt a stronger need for closeness with their peers after a short period of time. This program is a demonstration of how to utilize peer support as a culturally appropriate intervention for cultural adjustment for Asian immigrant youths.

Incorporating Indigenous Healers in Mental Health Treatment

Bemak and Chung (2008) developed a multi-level model (MLM) to effectively work with Asian immigrants and refugees. MLM is a five-level intervention approach that incorporates mental health education (level 1), Western psychotherapy (level 2), cultural empowerment (level 3), indigenous healing (level 4), and social justice and human rights (level 5). The distinguishing characteristic of this culturally responsive program is the collaboration between the Western healing practice and traditional healer. For example, a psychotherapist would refer a Vietnamese adolescent with anger issues to a Buddhist monk to supplement for traditional counseling. The therapist would form a partnership with the Buddhist monk to help the adolescent. Bemak and Chung (2008) described that by engaging in this cultural collaboration, the psychotherapist gains credibility by demonstrating awareness and understanding of the client's cultural belief system and tradition. At present, evaluation of this intervention approach is not yet available.

Conclusion and Summary

In this chapter, we provided background information about the growing and diverse Asian immigrant community. We then discussed the factors contributing to the mental health of Asian immigrants including acculturation level, social support, religion and spirituality, as well as Asian immigrants' coping strategies such as indigenous healing practices and collectivistic coping. We described previous community- and school-based prevention and intervention programs that promote psychological well-being and adjustment among Asian immigrant children, youths, and families. In the following sections, we explore strategies for future research, practice, and prevention work with this vibrant community.

Implications for Research

Past studies on Asian immigrants' mental health have largely focused on psychopathology (e.g., depression, anxiety, substance use) and mental health concerns relative to cultural adjustment and immigration. Recent research has shifted toward a strength-based perspective and begun to address Asian immigrants' resilience and resources such as social connectedness, indigenous practices, collectivistic coping, religiosity, and spirituality. Future research should continue to explore other variables that may enhance Asian immigrants' psychological well-being and protect them against negative affect and behaviors. It should also be noted that some of the cultural and contextual factors reviewed in this chapter can serve as both risk and protective factors. For instance, a higher acculturation level may promote an Asian immigrant's occupational and social functioning in the mainstream society and contribute to her/his positive mental health outcomes. However, it may also lead to increased awareness of the conflicts and dissonance between two cultures as well as experiences of racism and discriminations, rendering the person more susceptible to negative feelings and thoughts.

Second, research on Asian immigrants should capitalize on the strengths of qualitative research methodology in capturing the rich and vast experiences of Asian immigrants, Instead of asking the participants to respond to a set of predetermined questions in a questionnaire survey, qualitative research allows for insights into the subjective experience and multiple dimensions of worldviews embraced by Asian immigrants. Research could also use multi-informant approach (Yeh, Kim, et al., 2008) to engage reciprocal views and enrich the participants' narratives.

Implications for Prevention Work

When conceptualizing prevention work for the Asian immigrant population, it is essential to establish programs around strengthening protective resources and reducing risk factors (Gonzales, Dumka, Mauricio, & German, 2007). Earlier in this chapter, we highlighted prevention and intervention programs that incorporated factors that have been extensively discussed in the literature, such as family support, peer support, encouraging collectivistic coping strategies, and collaborating with indigenous healers. Future prevention work should continue to utilize the strengths and preexisting resources within the Asian immigrant community. Practitioners should also continue to draw from the ever growing scientific knowledge of immigrant mental health to develop culturally responsive prevention programs.

It is also important to take into account the heterogeneity of Asian immigrants as a group and consider within-group cultural differences such as ethnicity, religion, and socioeconomic status. While many of the existing prevention programs can be easily modified to accommodate various racial/ethnic groups, there have been limited empirical studies examining the applicability and effectiveness of a program across various Asian immigrant groups. We suggest incorporating culturally specific components in program development. For example, a program designed to promote sexual health and domestic violence awareness for South Asian teenage girls can integrate Bollywood films as an educational tool (Madan-Bahel, 2008). Similarly, a career intervention program for Asian immigrant youth from low-income backgrounds can designate a session for participants to discuss barriers they perceive in their career and education planning (Shea et al., 2007; P.-W. Ma & Yeh, 2010).

The literature on Asian immigrant mental health underscores the need for developing direct and specific information and materials that can empower and educate this growing community about their concerns, coping strategies, and various intervention options. In particular, many Asian immigrants may not be familiar with psychological problems that emerge as a result of immigration. Further, they may not be aware of available resources that may help them in this new cultural setting. For example, many immigrants do not know that their experiences with racism and discrimination are quite common and they may feel validated as they learn that they are not alone in their new lives. To educate Asian immigrants about mental health, it is important to provide them with specific information about acculturative stress, depression, anxiety, PTSD, substance use, loss, and intergenerational family conflict (among other concerns). This may include lists of symptoms as well as risk factors to help individuals help themselves, as well as those around them who are suffering. It is also critical that psychoeducational information incorporate Asian perspectives of health, which may emphasize the integration of mind, body, and spirit (Yeh, 2000). Such perspectives will align with Asian collectivistic and indigenous approaches to healing and will assist individuals in connecting their concerns with possible coping strategies.

In particular, a psychoeducational format is consistent with the goals of building a sense of empowerment and validation among a group that is often marginalized and invisible (Yeh, Kim, et al., 2008). Psychoeducational information has the potential to be delivered in a way that is nonthreatening and user-friendly. Asian immigrants may also appreciate learning about their mental health issues in a way that is formal and direct and normalizes their experiences.

Asian immigrants also need to have access to information related to collectivistic coping strategies, and various intervention options related to their mental health. This may include resources such as community agencies, local churches, indigenous healers (such as traditional Chinese medicine doctors, acupuncturists), and bilingual counselors. While many Asian immigrants believe in the notion of fatalism, a deeper understanding of their acculturative experiences, related risk factors, and available interventions may also help empower them.

The onus of responsibility should not lie solely with Asian immigrants to promote their own mental health. As the number of Asian immigrants in the United States continues to increase, service providers in various settings need to share this responsibility and learn more about Asian immigrant perspectives of mental health, acculturative experiences, and coping strategies. Schools, clinics, hospitals, churches, and other social service agencies may find ways to prevent psychological problems associated with the immigrant experiences and collaborate with communities to promote positive mental health.

In particular, therapists need to balance clinical utility and cultural sensitivity by understanding their multiple roles for Asian immigrants (Shea et al., 2010). For example, counselors for Asian immigrants need to be adaptive and flexible in attending to various indigenous healing practices and collectivistic coping strategies. Hence, Gallardo, Parham, Trimble, and Yeh (2012) describe how counselors also serve as cultural brokers (Stone, 2005), social advocates (Parham, White, Ajamu, 1999), social justice advocates (Goodman et al., 2004; Sue & Sue, 2008), healers (Parham, 2002; Yeh, Hunter, et al., 2004), cultural bridges (Amatea & West-Olatunji, 2007), mentors, teachers, role models, consultants, and advisors. This role of advocacy and collaborator can also help Asian immigrant clients feel empowered and validated.

Future Directions

The following are a few questions on topics remain to be addressed:

1. Researchers have asserted that there are limited rigorous experimental trials examining psychosocial intervention for immigrants, which can be a standard for evidence-based practice (Gonzales et al., 2007). How do we integrate cultural sensitivity to evidence-based treatment? For example, adherence to a treatment manual will provide validity of a particular type of intervention. But how do we balance scientific evidence with cultural sensitivity of being open and flexible with our treatment approach when working with Asian immigrants from diverse backgrounds?

2. How do we ensure that the goals of a prevention and intervention program align with participants' worldviews? For example, a cultural adjustment workshop may promote acculturation by introducing Western cultural norms and values, but would this conflict with what the participants' existing worldview and compete with their desire to retain their home culture?

References

Abe-Kim, J., Takeuchi, D. T., Hong, S., Zane, N., Sue, S., Spencer, M. S., . . . Alegria, M. (2007). Use of mental health-related services among immigrant and US-born Asian Americans: Results from the National Latino and Asian American Study. *American Journal of Public Health, 97*(1), 91–98. doi: 10.2105/AJPH.2006.098541

Abueg, F. R., & Chun, K. M. (1996). Traumatization stress among Asians and Asian Americans. In A. Marsella, M. Friedman, E. T. Gerrity, & R. M. Scurfield (Eds.), *Ethnocultural aspects of posttraumatic stress disorder: Issues, research, and clinical applications* (pp. 285–299). Washington, DC: American Psychological Association

Alvarez, A. (2009). Racism: "It isn't fair." In N. Tewari & A. Alvarez (Eds.), *Asian American psychology: Current perspectives* (pp. 399–420). New York: Taylor & Francis.

Alvarez, A. N., Juang, L., & Liang, C. T. H. (2006). Asian Americans and racism: When bad things happen to "model minorities." *Cultural Diversity and Ethnic Minority Psychology, 12,* 477–492.

Amatea, E., & West-Olatunji, C. (2007). Joining the conversation about educating our poorest children: Emerging leadership roles for school counselors in high-poverty schools. *Professional School Counseling, 11*(2), 81–89.

Atkinson, D. R., & Gim, R. H. (1989). Asian-American cultural identity and attitudes toward mental health services. *Journal of Counseling Psychology, 36,* 209–212.

Bemak, F., & Chung, R. C.-Y. (2008). Counseling refugees and migrants. In P. B. Pedersen, J. G. Draguns, W. J. Lonner, & J. E. Trimble (Eds.), *Counseling across cultures* (6th ed., pp. 307–324). Westport, CT: Greenwood Press.

Berry, J. W. (1995). Psychology of acculturation. In N. R. Goldberger & J. B. Veroff (Eds.), *The culture and psychology reader* (pp. 457–488). New York: New York University Press.

Berry, J. W. (2003). Conceptual approaches to acculturation. In K. M. Chun, P. B. Organista, & G. Marin (Eds.), *Acculturation: Advances in theory, measurement, and applied research* (pp. 17–37). Washington, DC: American Psychological Association.

Berry, J. W. (2006). Mutual attitudes among immigrants and ethnocultural groups in Canada. *International Journal of Intercultural Relations, 30,* 719–734.

Berry, J. W., & Kim, U. (1988). Acculturation and mental health. In P. R. Dasen, J. W. Berry, & N. Sartorius (Eds.), *Health and cross-cultural psychology: Towards applications* (pp. 207–236). Thousand Oaks, CA: Sage. Burnhill, D. A., Park, J., & Yeh, C. J. (2008). Indigenous models of healing: Implications for counseling. In C. C. Lee, D. A. Burnhill, A. L. Butler, C. P. Hipolito-Delgado, & M. Humphrey (Eds.), *Elements of culture in counseling* (pp. 105–126). Boston: Allyn & Bacon/Longman.

Capps, R., & Passel, J. S. (2004). *Describing Asian immigrant communities.* Washington, DC: Urban Institute, Immigrant Studies Program.

Cho, Y.-B., & Haslam, E. N. (2010). Suicidal ideation and distress among immigrant adolescents: The role of acculturation, life stress, and social support. *Journal of Youth Adolescence, 39,* 370–379. doi: 10.1007/s10964-009-9415-y

Choi, G. (1997). Acculturative stress, social support, and depression in Korean-American families. In P. W. Brown & J. S. Shalett (Eds.), *Cross-cultural practice with couples and families* (pp. 81–97). New York: Haworth Press.

Chow, H. P. H. (2007). Sense of belonging and life satisfaction among Hong Kong adolescent immigrants in Canada. *Journal of Ethnic and Migration Studies, 33,* 511–520. doi: 10.1080/13691830701234830

Chung, R. C., & Bemak, F. (2007). Asian immigrants and refugees. In F. T. L. Leong, A. G. Inman, A. Ebreo, L. H. Yang, L. Kinoshita, & M. Fu (Eds.), *Handbook of Asian American psychology* (2nd ed., pp. 227–244). Thousand Oaks, CA: Sage.

Chung, R. C., Bemak, F., & Wong, S. (2000). Vietnamese refugees' levels of distress, social support, and acculturation: Implications for mental health counseling. *Journal of Mental Health Counseling, 22,* 150–161.

Cohen, S., Gottlieb, B., & Underwood, L. (2000). Social relationships and health. In S. Cohen, L. Underwood, & B. Gottlieb (Eds.), *Social support measurement and intervention* (pp. 328). New York: Oxford University Press.

Conrad, M. M., & Pacquiao, D. F. (2005). Manifestation, attribution, and coping with depression among Asian Indians from the perspectives of health care practitioners. *Journal of Transcultural Nursing, 16,* 32–40.

Davis, W. G. (1995). Level of acculturation of Asian American adolescents as a predictor of depression and suicidal ideation. *Dissertation Abstracts International: Section B: The Sciences and Engineering, 56*(5-B), 2859.

Dew, R. E., Daniel, S. S., Armstrong, T. D., Goldston, D. B., Triplett, M. F., & Koenig, H. G. (2008). Religion/spirituality and adolescent psychiatric symptoms: A review. *Child Psychiatry and Human Development, 39,* 381–398.

Farver, J. A. M., Narang, S. K., & Bhadha, B. R. (2002). East meets West: Ethnic identity, acculturation, and conflict in Asian Indian families. *Journal of Family Psychology, 16,* 338–350.

Fukuhara, M. (1989). Counseling psychology in Japan. *Applied Psychology: An International Review, 38,* 409–422.

Fung, K., & Wong, Y. R. (2007). Factors influencing attitudes towards seeking professional help among East and Southeast Asian immigrant and refugee women. *International Journal of Social Psychiatry, 53,* 216–231.

Gallardo, M. E., Parham, T. A., Trimble, J. E., & Yeh, C. J. (2012). Understanding the skills identification model in context. In M. E. Gallardo, C. J. Yeh, J. E. Trimble, & T. A. Parham (Eds.), *Culturally adaptive counseling skills: Demonstration of evidence based practices* (pp. 1–20). Thousand Oaks, CA; Sage.

Gellis, Z. D., & Taguchi, A. (2004). Depression and health status among community-dwelling Japanese American elderly. *Clinical Gerontologist, 27*(3), 23–38.

Ghuman, P. A. S. (1997). Assimilation or integration? A study of Asian adolescents. *Educational Research, 39,* 23–35.

Gonzales, N. A., Dumka, L. E., Mauricio, A. M., & German, M. (2007). Building bridges: Strategies to promote academic and psychological resilience for adolescents of Mexican origin. In J. E. Lansford, K. Deater-Deckard, M. H. Bornstein (Eds.), *Immigrant families in contemporary society* (pp. 268–286). New York: Guilford Press.

Goodman, L. A., Liang, B., Helms, J. E., Latta, R. E., Sparks, E., & Weintraub, S. R. (2004). Training counseling psychologists as social justice agents: Feminist and multicultural principles in action. *The Counseling Psychologist, 32*(6), 793–836.

Gordon, M. M. (1964). *Assimilation in American life.* New York: Oxford University Press.

Guerrero, A. P. S., Hishinuma, E. S., Andrade, N. N., Nishimura, S. T., & Cunanan, V. L. (2006). Correlations among socioeconomic and family factors and academic, behavioral, and emotional difficulties in Filipino adolescents in Hawaii. *International Journal of Social Psychiatry, 52*(4), 343–359. doi: 10.1177/0020764006065146

Harner, M. (1990). *The way of the shaman.* San Francisco: Harper and Row.

Hayashino, D. S., & Chopra, S. B. (2009). Parenting and raising families. In N. Tewari & A. Alvarez (Eds.), *Asian American psychology: Current perspectives* (pp. 317–336). New York: Taylor & Francis.

Helms, J. E., & Cook, D. A. (1999). *Using race and culture in counseling and psychotherapy: Theory and process.* Needham Heights, MA: Allyn & Bacon.

Heppner, P. P. (2008). Expanding the conceptualization and measurement of applied problem solving and coping: From stages to dimensions to the almost forgotten cultural context. *American Psychologist, 63,* 805–816.

Highlen, P. S. (1996). MCT theory and implications for organizations/systems. In D. W. Sue, A. E. Ivey, & P. B. Pedersen (Eds.), *A theory of multicultural counseling and therapy* (pp. 65–85). Pacific Grove, CA: Brooks/Cole.

Ho, D. Y. (1993). Relational orientation in Asian social psychology. In U. Kim & J. W. Berry (Eds.), *Indigenous psychologies: Research and experience in cultural context* (pp. 240–259). Newbury Park, CA: Sage.

Homma-True, R. (1997). Japanese American families. In E. Lee (Ed.), *Working with Asian Americans: A guide for clinicians* (pp. 114–124). New York: Guilford.

Hwang, W., Chun, C., Takeuchi, D. T., Myers, H. F., & Siddarth, P. (2005). Age of first-onset major depression in Chinese Americans. *Cultural Diversity and Ethnic Minority Psychology, 11*(1), 16–27.

Inman, A. G., & Yeh, C. (2007). Stress and coping. In F. T. L. Leong, A. G. Inman, A. Ebreo, L. Yang, L. Kinoshita, & M. Fu (Eds.), *Handbook of Asian American psychology* (pp. 323–340). Thousand Oaks, CA: Sage.

Inman, A. G., Yeh, C. J., Madan-Bahel, A., & Nath, S. (2007). Bereavement and coping of South Asian families post 9/11. *Journal of Multicultural Counseling and Development, 35,* 101–115.

Jha, A. (2001). Depression and suicidality in Asian Indian students. *Dissertation Abstracts International: Section B: The Sciences and Engineering, 62*(3-B), 1311.

Kim, B. S. K. (2009). Acculturation and enculturation of Asian Americans: A primer. In N. Tewari & A. Alvarez (Eds.), *Asian American psychology: Current perspectives* (pp. 97–112). New York: Taylor & Francis.

Kim, B. S. K., & Abreu, J. M. (2001). Acculturation measurement: Theory, current instruments, and future directions. In J. Ponterotto, J. M. Casa, L. A. Suzuki, & C. M. Alexander (Eds.), *Handbook of multicultural counseling* (2nd ed.). Thousand Oaks, CA: Sage.

Kim, B. S. K., Ahn, A. J., & Lam, N. (2009). Theories and research on acculturation and enculturation experiences among Asian American families. In N.-H. Trinh, Y. Rho, F. Lu, & K. M. Sanders (Eds.), *Handbook of mental health and acculturation in Asian American families* (pp. 25–43). New York: Humana Press.

Kim, H. S., Sherman, D. K., & Taylor, S. E. (2008). Culture and social support. *American Psychologist, 63,* 518–526.

Kuo, B. C. H., Roysircar, G., & Newby-Clark, I. R. (2006). Development of the cultural coping scale: Collective, avoidance, and engagement coping. *Measurement and*

Evaluation in Counseling and Development, 39(3), 161–182.

LaFromboise, T., Coleman, H., & Gerton, J. (1993). Psychological impact of biculturalism: Evidence and theory. *Psychological Bulletin, 114,* 395–412.

Lan, P.-C. (2002). Subcontracting filial piety: Elders care in ethnic Chinese immigrant families. *Journal of Family Issues, 23,* 812–835.

Lau, A. S., Jernewall, N. M., Zane, N., & Myers, H. F. (2002). Correlates of suicidal behaviors among Asian American outpatient youths. *Cultural Diversity and Ethnic Minority Psychology, 8,* 199–213.

Le, T. N., & Stockdale, G. (2008). Acculturative dissonance, ethnic identity, and youth violence. *Cultural Diversity and Ethnic Minority Psychology, 14*(1), 1–9.

Lee, C. C., & Armstrong, K. L. (1995). Indigenous models of mental health interventions: Lessons from traditional healers. In J. G. Ponterottos, J. M. Casas, L. A. Suzuki, & C. M. Alexander (Eds.), *Handbook of multicultural counseling* (pp. 441–456). Thousand Oaks, CA: Sage.

Lee, E. (1996). Asian American families: An overview. In M. McGoldrick, J. Giordano, & J. Pearce (Eds.), *Ethnicity and family therapy* (2nd ed., pp. 227–248). New York: Guilford Press.

Lee, M. S., Crittenden, K. S., & Yu, E. (1996). Social support and depression among elderly Korean immigrants in the United States. *International Journal of Aging and Human Development, 42,* 313–327.

Lee, R. M., & Liu, H. T. (2001). Coping with intergenerational family conflict: Comparison of Asian American, Hispanic, and European American college students. *Journal of Counseling Psychology, 48,* 410–419.

Lee, R. M., Su, J., & Yoshida, E. (2005). Coping with intergenerational family conflict among Asian American college students. *Journal of Counseling Psychology, 52,* 389–399.

Leong, F. T. L., Leach, M., Yeh, C. J., & Chou, E. (2007). Suicide among Asian Americans: What do we know? What do we need to know? *Death Studies, 31*(5), 417–434. doi: 10.1080/07481180701244561

Liu, C. H., Murakami, J., Eap, S., & Nagayama Hall, G. (2009). Who are Asian Americans? An overview of history, immigration, and communities. In N. Tewari & A. Alvarez (Eds.), *Asian American psychology* (pp. 1–29). New York: Taylor & Francis.

Ma, G. X., Tan, Y., Toubbeh, J. I., Su, X., Shive, S. E., & Lan, Y. (2004). Acculturation and smoking behavior in Asian-American populations. *Health Education Research, 19,* 615–625.

Ma, P.-W., & Yeh, C. J. (2005). Factors influencing the career decision status of Chinese American youth. *Career Development Quarterly, 53,* 337–347.

Ma, P.-W. & Yeh, C. J. (2010). Individual and familial factors influencing the educational and career plans of Chinese immigrant youths. *Career Development Quarterly, 58,* 230–245.

Madan-Bahel, A. (2008). *Sexual health and Bollywood films: A culturally based program for South Asian teenage girls.* Youngstown, NY: Cambria Press.

Markus, H. R., & Kitayama, S. (1991). Culture and the self: Implications for cognition, emotion, and motivation. *Psychological Review, 98,* 224–253.

Marsella, A. J., & Dash-Scheuer, A. (1988). Coping, culture, and healthy human development: A research and conceptual overview. In P. R. Dasen, J. W. Berry, & N. Sartorius (Eds.), *Health and cross-cultural psychology: Toward applications* (pp. 162–178). Newbury Park, CA: Sage.

Mehta, S. (1998). Relationship between acculturation and mental health for Asian Indian immigrants in the United States. *Genetic, Social, and General Psychology Monographs, 124,* 61–78.

Min, P. G. (1998). *Changes and conflicts: Korean immigrant families in New York.* Boston: Allyn & Bacon.

Moon, S. S. (2008). Acculturation, social support, and family conflict: Korean-American adolescents' perceptions. *Child Adolescent Social Work, 25,* 227–240. doi: 10.1007/s10560–008–0123-3

Morling, B., & Fiske, S. T. (1999). Defining and measuring harmony control. *Journal of Research in Personality, 33,* 379–414.

Mui, A. C. (1996). Depression among elderly Chinese immigrants: An exploratory study. *Social Work, 41,* 633–645.

Mui, A. C., & Kang, S. Y. (2006). Acculturation stress and depression among Asian immigrant elders. *Social Work, 51,* 243–255.

Ngo, H. M., & Le, T. N. (2007). Stressful life events, culture, and violence. *Journal of Immigrant Health, 9,* 75–84.doi: 10.1007/s10903–006–9018-6

Nguyen, L., & Peterson, C. (1993). Depressive symptoms among Vietnamese-American college students. *Journal of Social Psychology, 133*(1), 65–71.

Oh, Y., Koeske, G. F., & Sales, E. (2002). Acculturation, stress, and depressive symptoms among Korean immigrants in the United States. *Journal of Social Psychology, 142*(4), 511–526.

Organista, P. B., Marin, G., & Chun, K. M. (2010). *The psychology of ethnic groups in the United States.* Thousand Oaks, CA: Sage.

Padilla, A. M., Wagatsuma, U., & Lindholm, K. J. (1985). Acculturation and personality as predictors of stress in Japanese and Japanese-Americans. *Journal of Social Psychology, 125,* 295–305.

Parham, T. A. (2002). Counseling models for African Americans: The what and how of counseling. In T. A. Parham (Ed.), *Counseling persons of African descent: Raising the bar of practitioner competence* (pp. 100–118). Thousand Oaks, CA: Sage.

Parham, T. A., White, J. L., & Ajamu, A. (1999). *The psychology of Blacks: An African centered perspective* (3rd ed.). Englewood, Cliffs, NJ: Prentice Hall.

Portes, A., & Rumbaut, R. G. (2006). *Immigrant America: A portrait* (3rd ed.). Berkeley: University of California Press.

Reiboldt, W., & Goldstein, A. E. (2000). Positive coping strategies among immigrant Cambodian families: An ethnographic case study. *Family and Consumer Sciences Research Journal, 28*(4), *489–513.*

Rhee, S. (2009). The impact of immigration and acculturation on the mental health of Asian Americans: Overview of epidemiology and clinical implications. In N.-H. Trinh, Y. Rho, F. Lu, & K. M. Sanders (Eds.), *Handbook of mental health and acculturation in Asian American families* (pp. 81–98). New York: Humana Press.

Rho, Y., & Rho, K. (2009). Clinical considerations when working with Asian American children and adolescents. In N.-H. Trinh, Y. Rho, F. Lu, & K. M. Sanders (Eds.), *Handbook of mental health and acculturation in Asian American families* (pp. 143–166). New York: Humana Press.

Rogler, L. H., Cortes, D. E., & Malgady, R. G. (1991). Acculturation and mental health status among Hispanics: Convergence and new directions for research. *American Psychologist, 46,* 585–597.

Sam, D. L., & Berry, J. W. (1995). Acculturative stress among young immigrants in Norway. *Scandinavian Journal of Psychology, 36,* 10–24.

Sanchez, F., & Gaw, A. (2007). Mental health care of Filipino Americans. *Psychiatric Services, 58,* 810–815.

Sayegh, L., & Lasry, J. (1993). Immigrants' adaption in Canada: Assimilation, acculturation, and orthogonal cultural identification. *Canadian Psychology, 34,* 98–109.

Shea, M., Ma, P-W., & Yeh, C. J. (2007). Development of a culturally specific career exploraton group for urban Chinese immigrant youth. *The Career Development Quarterly, 56,* 62–73.

Shea, M., Ma, P.-W., Yeh, C. J., Lee, S., & Pituc, S. T. (2009). Exploratory studies on the effects of a career explorationgroup for urban Chinese immigrant youth. *Journal of Career Assessment, 17,* 457–477.doi: 10.1177/1069072709334246

Shea, M., Yang, L. H., & Leong, F. T. L. (2010). Loss, psychosis, and chronic suicidality in a Korean American immigrant man: Integration of cultural formulation model and multicultural case conceptualization. *Asian American Journal of Psychology, 1*(3), 212–223.

Shea, M., & Yeh, C. J. (2008). Cultural values, perceived stigma, relational interdependent self-construal and attitudes towards help-seeking. *Journal of Mental Health Counseling, 30*(2), 157–172.

Shen, B. J., & Takeuchi, D. T. (2001). A structural model of acculturation and mental health status among Chinese Americans. *American Journal of Community Psychology, 29,* 387–418.

Shin, K. R. (1994). Psychosocial predictors of depressive symptoms in Korean-American women in New York City. *Women and Health, 21*(1), 73–82.

Singh, A. N. (1999). Shamans, healing, and mental health. *Journal of Child and Family Studies, 8,* 131–134.

Sodowsky, G. R., & Lai, E. W. M. (1997). Asian immigrant variables and structural models of cross-cultural distress. In A. Booth (Ed.), *International migration and family change: The experience of U.S. immigrants* (pp. 211–234). Mahwah, NJ: Erlbaum.

Sodowsky, G. R., Lai, E. W. M., & Plake, B. S. (1991). Moderating effects of sociocultural variables on acculturation attitudes of Hispanics and Asian Americans. *Journal of Counseling and Development, 70,* 194–204.

Stone, J. H. (2005). *Culture and disability.* Thousand Oaks, CA: Sage.

Sue, D. W., & Sue, D. (2008). *Counseling the culturally diverse: Theory and practice* (5th ed.). Hoboken, NJ: Wiley.

Sung, K. (2000). An Asian perspective on aging East and West: Filial piety and changing families. In V. Bengston, K. Kim, G. Myers, & K. Eun (Eds.), *Aging in East and West: Families, states, and the elderly.* New York: Springer.

Takeuchi, D., Zane, N., Hong, S., Chae, D. H., Gong, F., Gee, G. C.,...Alegria, M. (2007). Immigration-related factors and mental disorders among Asian Americans. *American Journal of Public Health, 97*(1), 84–90.

Tata, S. P., & Leong, F. T. L. (1994). Individualism-collectivism, social-network orientation, and acculturation as predictors of attitudes toward seeking professional psychological help among Chinese Americans. *Journal of Counseling Psychology, 41,* 280–287.

Thomas, M., & Choi, J. B. (2006). Acculturative stress and social support among Korean and Indian immigrant adolescents in the United States. *Journal of Sociology and Social Welfare, 33,* 123–143.

Triandis, H. C. (1989). The self and social behavior in differing cultural contexts. *Psychological Review, 96,* 506–520.

Tweed, R. G., White, K., & Lehman, D. R. (2004). Internally-and externally-targeted control strategies of European Canadians, East Asian Canadians, and Japanese. *Journal of Cross-Cultural Psychology, 35,* 652–668.

Uba, L. (1994). *Asian Americans: Personality patterns, identity, and mental health.* New York: Guilford Press.

Urban Institute. (2010). *Children of immigrants data tool.* Retrieved from http://datatool.urban.org/charts/datatool/pages.cfm

Walsh, F. (2008). Spirituality, healing, and resilience. In M. McGoldrick & K. V. Hardy (Eds.), *Re-Visioning family therapy: Race, culture, and gender in clinical practice* (pp. 61–75). New York: Guilford.

Wong, S. T., Yoo, G. J., & Stewart, A. L. (2007). An empirical evaluation of social support and psychological well-being in older Chinese and Korean immigrants. *Ethnicity and Health, 12,* 43–67.

Yeh, C. J. (2000). Depathologizing Asian-American perspectives of health and healing. *Asian American and Pacific Islander Journal of Health, 8,* 138–149.

Yeh, C. J. (2003). Age, acculturation, cultural adjustment, and mental health symptoms of Chinese, Korean, and Japanese immigrant youth. *Cultural Diversity and Ethnic Minority Psychology Journal, 9,* 34–48.

Yeh, C. J., Arora, A. K., & Wu, K. (2006). A new theoretical model of collectivistic coping. In P. T. P. Wong & C. J. Wong (Eds.), *Handbook of multicultural perspectives on stress and coping* (pp. 55–72). New York: Springer.

Yeh, C. J., Borrero, N. E., & Kwong, A. (2011). Stress and coping among Asian American Pacific Islanderand Native Hawaiian children and youth: An asset approach. In F. Leong, L. Juang, D. Qin, & H. Fitzgerald (Eds.), *Asian American child psychology and mental health, Vol 2: Treatment and prevention* (pp. 101–124). *Child psychology and mental health: Cultural and racial perspectives,* H. E. Fitzgerald (Series Ed.). Westport, CT: Praeger Press.

Yeh, C. J., Ching, A. M., Okubo, Y., & Luthar, S. (2007). Description of a mentoring program for Chinese immigrant adolescents' cultural adjustment. *Adolescence, 42,* 734–747.

Yeh, C. J., Hunter, C. D., Madan-Bahel, A., Chiang, L., & Arora, A. K. (2004). Indigenous and interdependent perspectives of healing: Implications for counseling and research. *Journal of Counseling and Development, 82,* 410–419.

Yeh, C. J., & Hwang, M. (2000). Interdependence in ethnic identity and self: Implications for theory and practice. *Journal of Counseling and Development, 78,* 420–429.

Yeh, C. J., Inman, A., Kim, A. B., & Okubo, Y. (2006). Asian American collectivistic coping in response to 9/11. *Cultural Diversity and Ethnic Minority Psychology, 12,* 134–148.

Yeh, C. J., & Inose, M. (2002). Difficulties and coping strategies of Chinese, Japanese, and Korean immigrant students. *Adolescence, 37*(145), 69–82.

Yeh, C. J., Inose, M., Kobori, A., & Chang, T. (2001). Self and coping among college students in Japan. *Journal of College Student Development, 42,* 242–256.

Yeh, C. J., Kim, A. B., Pituc, S. T., & Atkins, M. (2008). Poverty, loss, and resilience: The story of Asian immigrant youth. *Journal of Counseling Psychology, 55,* 34–48.

Yeh, C. J., & Kwong, A. K. (2009). Asian American indigenous healing. In N. Tewari & A. Alvarez (Eds.), *Asian American psychology: Current perspectives* (pp. 561–575). New York: Taylor & Francis.

Yeh, C. J., Ma, P.-W., Madan, A., Hunter, C. D., Jung, S., Kim, A., . . . Sasaki, K. (2005). The cultural negotiations of Korean immigrant youth. *Journal of Counseling and Development, 83,* 172–181.

Yeh, C. J., Ma, P.-W., Okubo, Y., Maden-Bahel, A., Cort, K. A., Shea, M., . . . Zhang, X. L. (2004, August). *The cultural adjustment of low-income, urban, Asian immigrant high school students.* Poster presented at the annual meeting of the American Psychological Association, Honolulu, HI.

Yeh, C. J., Okubo, Y., Ma, P.-W., Shea, M., Ou, D., & Pituc, S. T. (2008). Chinese immigrant high school students' cultural interactions, acculturation, family obligations, language use, and social support. *Adolescence, 43,* 775–790.

Yeh, C. J., & Wang, Y. W. (2000). Asian American coping attitudes, sources, and practices: Implications for indigenous counseling strategies. *Journal of College Student Development, 41,* 94–103.

Ying, Y. (1999a). Strengthening international/intercultural ties in migrant families: A new intervention for parents. *Journal of Community Psychology, 27,* 89–96.

Ying, Y. (1999b). An educational program for families on intergenerational conflict. In E. Kramer, S. Ivey, & Y. Ying (Eds.), *Immigrant women's health: Problems and solutions* (pp. 282–294). San Francisco: Jossey-Bass.

Ying, Y. (2009). Strengthening intergenerational/intercultural ties in immigrant families (SITIF): A parenting intervention to bridge the Chinese American intergenerational acculturation gap. In N.-H. Trinh, Y. Rho, F. Lu, & K. M. Sanders (Eds.), *Handbook of mental health and acculturation in Asian American families* (pp. 45–64). New York: Humana Press.

Yoon, E., Lee, R. M., & Goh, M. (2008). Acculturation, social connectedness, and subjective well-being. *Cultural Diversity and Ethnic Minority Psychology, 14,* 246–255.

Zea, M. C., Asner-Self, K. K., Birman, D., & Buki, L. P. (2003). The abbreviated multidimensional acculturation scale: Empirical validation with two Latino/Latina samples. *Cultural Diversity and Ethnic Minority Psychology, 9,* 107–126.

Zhang, N., & Dixon, D. N. (2003). Acculturation and attitudes of Asian International students toward seeking psychological help. *Journal of Multicultural Counseling and Development, 31,* 205–222.

CHAPTER

29

Dismantling the Bird Cage: How Counseling Psychologists Can Prevent Heterosexism

Melinda Haley, Eve Adams, Ginger Dickson, Tracie Hitter, *and* Laura Luna

Abstract

This chapter explores the pervasiveness of heterosexism and its impact on the lesbian, gay, bisexual, and transgendered (LGBT) population. In particular, we discuss the negative impact heterosexist beliefs and behaviors have on LGBT individuals at the societal, institutional, and individual levels in order to help counseling psychologists examine their own heterosexism, and/or complacency with the heterosexist discourse in our society and profession. After assessing the psychological, physical, and behavioral consequences that are associated with heterosexism and reviewing the scant literature on prevention efforts, we make suggestions regarding the steps counseling psychologists can take to enhance prevention efforts at these various levels. Finally, we highlight several areas in which empirical knowledge or action is lacking and provide stimulating questions to help focus future research and practice efforts in the prevention of heterosexism.

Key Words: heterosexism, LGBT, lesbian, gay, bisexual, transgender, prevention

The title's reference to the birdcage comes from an essay on oppression, by Marilyn Frye (1983). Frye's analogy of a cage is an apt description of the experience of oppression, where one has limited options. The bars on the cage are "systematically related to each other" (p. 4) so as to immobilize the occupant of the cage. In order to adequately address the oppression of lesbian, gay, bisexual, and transgendered (LGBT) individuals, we must understand and minimize the environmental barriers created to marginalize and devalue the LGBT population. According to the Human Rights Campaign (HRC) data, there are over 10 million gay and lesbian people living within the United States (as cited in Lind, 2004). This figure would be considerably larger if bisexual or transsexual individuals were included.

Within this chapter we felt it was important to acknowledge and include all four groups in this discourse (e.g., gays, lesbians, bisexual, and transgendered individuals), even though it is acknowledged that all four of these groups, while lumped into one acronym LGBT, have different needs, issues, strengths, and complexities. Where commonalities exist we use the LGBT acronym, or the term "sexual or gender minority," and where differences need to be noted, we use the individual terms "lesbian," "gay," "bisexual," and "transgendered." In order to model more inclusive language we have also chosen to use the gender *neutral* singular pronoun of "ze" rather than "he" and "she" and "hir" rather than "him" or "her" to be transgender affirmative as recommended by Counselors for Social Justice (CSJ) and the Association for Lesbian, Gay, Bisexual, and Transgender Issues in Counseling (ALGBTIC).

This chapter will discuss the construct of heterosexism and its impact on the LGBT population, how heterosexism is perpetuated and erroneously accepted as "normal," and how heterosexism is sustained at the societal, institutional, and individual level. Most importantly, this chapter provides suggestions regarding how counseling psychologists can aid in the prevention and intervention of heterosexism at all of these levels.

What Is Heterosexism and How Does It Impact LGBT Individuals?

Heterosexism is an institutionalized manifestation of sexual stigma and is described as a cultural ideology that assumes heterosexuality to be the societal norm and distinctively superior to homosexuality; effectively marginalizing and categorizing non-heterosexual individuals as deviant and abnormal (Herek, 2007). Heterosexism pervades every level of civilization and perpetuates societal and political privileges for heterosexual individuals and serves as a rationale for prejudicial, discriminatory, and oppressive acts toward lesbian and gay individuals (Herek & Berrill, 1992). At the societal level, heterosexism operates to deny equal civil rights and liberties to LGBT individuals and prevents the passage of legislation, laws, and policies that are LGBT affirming (i.e., gay marriage). At the institutional level, heterosexism maintains institutional policies and procedures that are anti-LGBT and allow discriminatory practices against LGBT individuals (i.e., employment benefits have no provision for gay/lesbian couples). At the individual level heterosexism operates to justify disregard and hatred toward individuals who do not conform to heterosexual roles and expectations. Heterosexism is not limited to heterosexuals. *Internalized heterosexism* occurs when gay, lesbian, bisexual, or transgendered individuals accept or internalize society's negative attitudes about homosexuality (Weinberg, 1972).

The manifestations of heterosexism are believed to change over time, while the social stratification of power and resources is continually perpetuated (Walls, 2008). Walls (2008) cited the coexistence of continued violence and discriminatory acts against LGBT individuals alongside research that indicates trends of more positive attitudes toward LGBT persons and growing support for LGBT civil liberties as evidence of the evolution of heterosexist attitudes or *modern heterosexism*. The multidimensional construct of modern heterosexism is comprised of five dimensions that all function by "denying, denigrating, stigmatizing and/or segregating any non-heterosexual form of behavior, identity, relationship, or community" (Walls, p. 27) even while some of the attitudes are positive. For example, *paternalistic heterosexism* expresses, "subjectively neutral or positive attitudes, myths and beliefs that express concern for the physical, emotional or cognitive well-being of non-heterosexual persons while concurrently denying, denigrating, stigmatizing and/or segregating any non-heterosexual form of behavior, identity, relationship, or community" (Walls, p. 28). Similarly, *positive stereotypic heterosexism*, expresses "appreciation of stereotypic characteristics often attributed to lesbians and gay men" (Walls, p. 28). More problematic is *amnestic heterosexism* which denies the "impact of sexual orientation on life chances" (Walls, p. 46). Such attitudes allow heterosexuals to be supportive of LGBT individuals while also voting for antigay politicians or policies. The more blatant discrimination is perpetuated by those espousing *hostile heterosexism*, which holds consistently "negative attitudes, myths and beliefs" (Walls, p. 27), and *aversive heterosexism*, which will "dismiss, belittle, or disregard the impact of sexual orientation on life chances" (Walls, p. 46).

It is our recommendation that counseling psychologists become familiar with, and utilize these more precise terms, rather than use the antiquated term, *homophobia*, which has been defined as, "the dread of being in close quarters with homosexuals" (Weinberg, 1972, p. 4). It is much easier for heterosexuals to dismiss their oppressive attitudes if they are only confronted with the most extreme form of heterosexism, homophobia. The first step in preventing heterosexism is for each of us to assess which type of heterosexist attitudes we hold. Similarly, *biphobia* and *transphobia* are terms used to describe negative attitudes, beliefs, and actions toward bisexual, and transgendered individuals, and we recommend using the modern heterosexism dimensions for assessing one's attitudes about these two populations as well.

Impact of Heterosexism

Worldwide, LGBT individuals are often subjected to insidious violence, discrimination, and oppression due to heterosexist prejudice (Harper & Scheider, 2003; Horn, Szalacha, & Drill, 2008; Land & Kitzinger, 2005; Smith, Foley, & Chaney, 2008). An individual's experience with heterosexism can vary based on the level of openness about hir sexual orientation. The more open one is, the more potential one has to experience heterosexism (Smith & Ingram, 2004). The remainder of this section will review some of the manifestations of heterosexism and counseling psychologists' potential role in addressing these issues.

HATE CRIMES

Hate crimes are bias motivated crimes that occur when someone targets an individual based on their race, ethnicity, disability, religion, sexual orientation, or gender expression. These crimes can encompass many acts, some of which include name calling, hate mail, damage to property, bullying, and bodily harm (Stotzer, 2007; National Archives, 2010). In the United States, hate crimes toward LGBT individuals are the fourth highest reported after crimes against race, ethnicity/national origin, and religion (Smith & Ingram, 2004). When surveyed, 94% of LGBT individuals stated they were victims of at least one hate crime (Smith et al., 2008), and White teenage males were found to perpetrate a staggering 97% of these crimes (Hirschfeld, 2001; Stotzer, 2009). In addition, gay males were the most likely to report victimization 38% (vs. 11%–13% of lesbians or bisexual individuals) (Herek, 2007).

BULLYING AND SCHOOL CLIMATE

Hate crimes in school-age children are often referred to as bullying, which can include a variety of behaviors aimed at LGBT individuals or their families such as antigay epithets, verbal harassment, spreading rumors, physical assault, teasing, and discrimination (Fish, 2008; Goodenow, Szalacha, & Westheimer, 2006; Graybill, Varjas, Meyers, & Watson, 2009). LGBT students were more likely to be bullied (e.g., verbally and sexually harassed, threatened, or injured with a weapon) while at school than students who didn't identify as such (Goodenow et al., 2006; Graybill et al., 2009). Data from the gay, lesbian, and straight education network (GLSEN) 2009 National School Climate Survey indicated that bullying and harassment are frequent among LGBT students between the ages of 13 and 20. The data showed that 84.6% of students reported verbal harassment, 40.1% were physically harassed, and 18.8% were physically assaulted. In addition, 72.4% of students reported hearing derogatory remarks made toward them such as "faggot" or "dyke," while 61.1% stated they felt unsafe at their school due to harassment over their sexual orientation, and 39.9% felt unsafe due to their gender expression (GLSEN, 2009). Hate crimes result in more psychological distress for the victim than nonbiased crimes (Swim, Johnston, & Pearson, 2009).

Goodenow and colleagues (2006) reported school characteristics that were related to harassment, discrimination, and violence against sexual minority youth. These youth were more likely to have experienced violence if they "attended smaller schools, suburban schools, schools with few ethnic minority or low income students, and, paradoxically, schools generally perceived as safe" (p. 580). In addition, other research indicated that school faculty and counselors may contribute to heterosexism at their institutions. For example, in a survey reported by Graybill and colleagues (2009), 74% of surveyed preservice teachers admitted to heterosexist beliefs and negative attitudes toward LGBT youth, while many school counselors and psychologists admitted ignorance in dealing with LGBT youth and the issues impacting them. In addition, due to fear of community backlash, some school professionals censor themselves from talking about LGBT individuals (or issues) in a positive manner (Hanlon, 2009). Van Wormer and McKinney (2003) stated that when instructors do not take a proactive stance in helping students with sexual and gender identity issues, it can lead to major psychological problems for the student.

WORKPLACE HARASSMENT

Harassment in the workplace can take many forms and may range from coworker avoidance behaviors toward LGBT individuals due to heterosexist phobias to actual violence toward a LGBT worker (Obear, 2000). There may be an uncomfortable stigma placed on an LGBT worker that creates hostility in the workplace for that worker. Herek (2007) defines sexual stigma in the workplace as a cultural ideology within institutional practices that create disadvantage to sexual minority groups. Within the workplace there are different types of harassment or discrimination that an LGBT employee might face. For example there is *access discrimination*, which keeps members of minority groups from entering a particular workplace, organization, or industry. Then there is *treatment discrimination*, which happens when individuals are targeted and are not given equal treatment (e.g., fewer rewards, access to resources, or job opportunities) (Button, 2001). Both of these forms of discrimination can cause stress, negative health outcomes, and job dissatisfaction for LGBT workers (Levitt et al., 2009).

ANTIGAY LEGISLATION

Heterosexism is perpetuated at all levels of society and one outcome of heterosexist beliefs is anti-LGBT legislation (Land & Kitzinger, 2005). This legislation has historically denied the LGBT population the same legal status and civil rights as other segments of the population (Cornell, 2007; Hodges & Parkes, 2005), including lack of equal treatment, recognition of same sex relationships, and lack of equal protection in the workplace (Fish,

2008). Legislation aimed at denying LGBT people equal civil and human rights includes the following: Defense of Marriage Act (DOMA), Don't Ask Don't Tell, Anti-Lesbian and Gay Adoption Law, denial of visitation rights, and immigration laws.

Defense of Marriage Act (DOMA).

In 1996 President Clinton signed DOMA into law, which provided a federal definition of marriage as only occurring between "one man and one woman as husband and wife" (Knauer, 2009, p. 5). This federal definition ensures that LGBT individuals, even if living in a state that recognizes same sex marriage, will not be eligible for federal provisions if marital status is a factor in determining these benefits, rights, and privileges (Knauer, 2009; Kitzinger & Wilkinson, 2004; Levitt et al., 2009). Examples of such federal programs that provide benefits to married partners include social security, Medicare/Medicaid, tax benefits, military and veteran's benefits, immigration, and employee benefits (Knauer, 2009; Levitt et al., 2009). Subsequently, 26 states have also passed constitutional amendments that restrict marriage to one man and one woman (Levitt et al., 2009).

The right to legally marry affects other rights non-LGBT individuals take for granted such as visitation rights in hospitals, hospice care, prisons, and other such facilities (Callahan, Mann, & Ruddick, 2007). In some states LGBT individuals can legally lose custody rights to their own biological children because of their sexual orientation or gender identity (Knauer, 2009). In addition, without benefit of legal marriage, an LGBT individual cannot sponsor a partner for citizenship (Balsam, Beauchaine, Rothblum, & Solomon, 2008; Levitt et al., 2009).

Don't Ask, Don't Tell (DADT).

In 1993 President Clinton also signed the DADT military ruling (Lind, 2004) which only in 2010 was repealed (although has yet to be enacted). DADT maintained that for the military "sexual orientation is considered a personal and private matter, and homosexual orientation is not a bar to continued service unless manifested by homosexual conduct" (Knauer, 2009, p. 6). In order to be in compliance, an LGB soldier had to hide hir sexuality whereas this was not a requirement for heterosexual soldiers. If an LGB soldier disobeyed this mandate, ze could have been thrown out of the military and lose all benefits associated with successful service. This penalty would be exacted even if the person simply stated "I'm gay," and was not caught in any sexual act. While many thought DADT would afford protection to LGB military service individuals, this policy has actually led to the expulsion of more LGB soldiers from active service than ever before in US history (Lind, 2004). In addition, it has ramifications for many LGB veterans who feel pressured and stressed while interacting with the Veteran's Administration lest an accidental admission cost them the benefits of service (Knauer, 2009). It is unknown how LGB soldiers will be treated by their comrades and systemically with repeal of DADT.

Adoption law.

Historically, the laws of most states have forbidden gays and lesbians from adopting or had legal rulings stating gay and lesbian individuals were "unfit" to be parents (Blackwell, Dziegielewski, & Jacinto, 2006; Keck, 2009). A few states have passed laws permitting adoption for gay and lesbian *individuals*, while 40 states and the District of Columbia have no restrictions either for or against LGB adoption. However, even within states supportive of LGB adoption, LGB couples often have to transverse adoption agencies with heterosexist biases. There are only 11 states that have what is called "second-parent" adoptions which allow two people who are not related to both be parents of a child (HRC, 2010c).

IMPACT ON HEALTH

There is a plethora of research that supports that individuals who are subjected to heterosexism experience stress that can negatively impact health and wellness. The stress associated with being a sexual or gender minority in a heterosexist society can lead to a two- to threefold increase in risk for psychological distress (Levitt et al., 2009; Smith et al., 2008), which can manifest as depression, anxiety, guilt, shame, sadness, anger; feelings of rejection, hopelessness, or worthlessness; low self-esteem; insomnia; suicidality; self-destructive behaviors; avoidance behaviors; fear of being assaulted; somatic symptoms; substance abuse; chronic homelessness; feelings of social isolation; and dropping out of school (Frost & Meyer, 2009; Glassgold & Drescher, 2007; Goodenow et al., 2006; Hanlon, 2009; Harper & Scheider, 2003; Johnson, Carrico, Chesney, & Morin, 2008; Kertzner, Meyer, Frost, & Stirratt, 2009; Lewis, Derlega, Brown, Rose, & Henson, 2009; McDermott, Roen, & Scourfield, 2008; Moradi, Van den Berg, & Epting, 2009; Smith & Ingram, 2004; Swim et al., 2009).

One insidious consequence of heterosexism for LGBT individuals is internalized heterosexism, which essentially entails the internalization of negative societal messages and rejection of LGBT individuals (Harper & Scheider, 2003; Levitt et al., 2009). In extreme forms, this internalization can lead to rejection of one's own sexual orientation and create problems with identity and self-concept (Frost & Meyer, 2009; Moradi et al., 2009). Szymanski and Carr (2008) discussed the vulnerabilities of individuals who experienced a high amount of gender role conflict. They found these individuals may be more likely to "internalize negative attitudes and feelings about homosexuality" (p. 50) due to heterosexism and are more likely to experience psychological distress, low self-esteem, and poor mental health outcomes. They posit that gender role conflict may be a root cause of psychological distress for sexual and gender minority males.

As reported by McDermott and colleagues (2008), in response to heterosexism and the stress it entails, 19% of LGB individuals had attempted self-destructive behaviors at least once, while 8% attempted more than once. These figures rose dramatically, to 30%, when individuals were subjected to heterosexist bullying and victimization. One form of self-destructive behavior is suicide. Sexual and gender minorities have higher rates of suicidal ideation and attempts than other populations. Personal victimization, especially interpersonal violence, is significantly related to recent suicide attempts (Goodenow et al., 2006) while general social stigma and prejudice is linked to increased suicidality (Levitt et al., 2009). Gay and lesbian youth have two to four times the rate of suicide as other youth with 30% of attempts and completions being related to the stigma society places on LGB sexual identity (Hanlon, 2009; Hirschfeld, 2001; McDermott et al., 2008).

Without productive methods of coping, many LGBT individuals turn to alcohol and other drugs and subsequently have higher substance abuse rates as compared to the general population (Hirschfeld, 2001; Johnson et al., 2008). Substance use may function as a maladaptive coping mechanism for LGBT individuals in various ways. For example, substances can be used to self-medicate in order to avoid the painful reality of living in a heterosexist world. Substances can lower inhibitions related to internalized heterosexism and allow for freedom of sexual expression. Finally, substances can help an individual deal with internalized negative thoughts and feelings related to their sexual orientation or gender expression (Johnson et al., 2008).

The Role of Counseling Psychology in Addressing Heterosexism

D'Augelli (1993, 1996) suggested four systemic strategies to reduce the negative mental health impact of heterosexism, particularly for LGBT youth and young adults: (1) affirmative mental health service delivery, (2) creating safe spaces for identity development, (3) integrating LGBT issues into the curriculum, and (4) changing educational institutional policy to minimally ensure protection and ultimately inclusion. We will utilize this framework more broadly by creating the categories of affirmative services, affirmative training/curriculum, and affirmative institutions to optimize positive LGBT identity development in order to examine prevention interventions and the degree to which counseling psychologists have facilitated, or can facilitate, these interventions.

Affirmative Institutions

Heterosexism impacts LGBT individuals at all levels of society. This section will look specifically at the media's portrayal of LGBT individuals, the efforts of advocacy groups, and issues of heterosexism within the schools and workplace. We will also explore the role of counseling psychologists in working with these institutions to help prevent heterosexism and affirm LGBT individuals.

MEDIA

Positive mass media representations of LGBT individuals have increased in recent decades and include (1) television shows such as *Ellen*, *Will & Grace*, *Queer as Folk*, *Queer Eye for a Straight Guy*, *The "L" Word*, and *Glee*; (2) popular films such as *My Best Friend's Wedding*, *Jeffery*, *Different for Girls*, *Hannah Free*, and *TransAmerica*; and (3) inclusion of LGBT individuals in print media. Fisher, Hill, Grube, and Gruber (2007) researched programming from 2001–2002 and 2002–2003 and found that sexual content associated with sexual minorities was present in 15% of programs overall. However, discussions of sexual situations involving LGBT individuals was found to be relatively infrequent, providing relatively few examples of nonheterosexual characters and models of healthy LGBT sexual relationships for LGBT youth (Fisher et al., 2007).

Few studies have looked at the impact such media portrayals have on attitudes toward homosexuality. Researchers found that viewing a documentary about Harvey Milk had a significant and positive effect on attitudes toward gay men (Riggle, Ellis, & Crawford, 1996). Another study demonstrated that having participants evaluate a positive portrayal of a gay character caused participants to express more positive attitudes toward gay men than participants primed to evaluate a negative portrayal (Bonds-Raacke, Cady, Schlegel, Harris, & Firebaugh, 2007). Schiappa, Gregg, and Hewes (2006) found that increased viewing of the television show *Will & Grace* was correlated with lowered rates of sexual prejudice. This correlation was most pronounced for participants with the least amount of contact with lesbians and gay men. Calzo and Ward (2009) explored the connections between media use and college students' attitudes of acceptance toward homosexuality. Overall their findings indicated that women held more accepting attitudes than men. However for men, greater media consumption was associated with greater attitudes of acceptance. This suggests that media exposure had a positive effect on attitudes for men. Their findings also suggested that it was the consumption of certain media genres that were associated with attitudes toward homosexuality and not all were related to greater acceptance of homosexuality (Calzo & Ward, 2009).

Music videos were found to be associated with more positive attitudes of homosexuality, but results regarding print media were mixed, suggesting to researchers the importance of considering the effects of media genre by type (Calzo & Ward, 2009). Interventions targeted at increasing acceptance of homosexuality using the media may need to consider the type of media genre and viewer characteristics. Future research efforts aimed at such interventions would be helpful as would research that seeks to understand the process by which media has a positive or negative impact on attitudes. Counseling psychologists can advocate for heterosexism prevention by e-mailing television executives regarding more accurate portrayal of LGBT characters in television shows. They can also use more positive portrayals of LGBT characters when working with LGBT youth to help them envision a positive future.

ADVOCACY GROUPS

While there are many advocacy groups such as the Human Rights Campaign (HRC); the Safe Schools Coalition (SSC); the National Center for Lesbian Rights (NCLR); Parents and Friends of Lesbians and Gays (PFLAG); the Gay, Lesbian, and Straight Education Network (GLSEN); the Committee on Lesbian, Gay, Bisexual, and Transgender Concerns (CLGBTC) of the American Psychological Association (APA); the National Gay and Lesbian Task Force; and Lambda Legal; this section will focus on the HRC, GLSEN, and the CLGBTC. Summarized below are some of advocacy efforts and suggestions on how psychologists can contribute to or expand on these efforts.

The Human Rights Campaign (HRC).

The HRC Foundation is a nonprofit organization that supports LGBT individuals through research, education, and advocacy. There are a number of programs funded through the foundation. Below are a few of their initiatives that are particularly relevant to counseling psychologists.

The HRC Foundation Family Project (Human Rights Campaign, 2010b) provides information on adoption, civil unions, donor insemination, family law, marriage, parenting, schools, senior health and housing, state laws and legislation, straight spouses, and transgender issues. Such information can be empowering for those LGBT people wanting to expand and/or solidify their family status in a society that has created many barriers to doing so. The project also provides guidance to those that are working with LGBT families in various settings, such as adoption agencies, social work, and health care institutions. The HRC plans to develop a searchable database of LGBT-friendly adoption agencies that will be accessible through their website. One of their projects, All Children-All Families, works to enhance LGBT competence among child welfare professionals. Psychologists working in adoption agencies, community agencies, or health care institutions can contact the HRC to seek out resources in order to help increase their competence in working with LGBT families. Researchers who focus on any of the topics covered by the Foundation Family Project should consider the implications of their findings and make sure that the HRC is aware of the results. The HRC website also includes resources such as an agency self-assessment and training curriculum. Psychologists working with these agencies can use these resources to implement trainings and suggested institutional changes, or connect with others who can provide such support.

The HRC's Healthcare Quality Index (HQI) is a joint project of HRC's Family Project and the Gay and Lesbian Medical Association (Human Rights Campaign, 2010a). This index rates 178 health care facilities on their policies related to LGBT health care equality and focuses on hospital policies covering patient nondiscrimination, hospital visitation, decision making, cultural competency, and employment policies. The goal is to expand this project to include issues related to long-term care, assisted living, hospice, community health clinics, and other branches of the health care industry. Training programs with practica or internships in hospitals should utilize this website to engage in advocacy for LGBT patients, as well as use these settings as an opportunity to engage in research to reduce health disparities for LGBT patients. The HRC provides a resource guide, *Breaking Down Barriers: An Administrator's Guide to State Law and Best Policy Practice for LGBT Healthcare Access* (Stiff, 2010). Psychologists working in administrative roles can use this guide to help advocate for change within their organization.

In a review of LGBT empirical research, Maher and colleagues (2009) recommended that researchers focused on LGBT topics should collaborate with researchers in other fields of study. This would provide a better picture of the complex factors influencing the experiences of LGBT individuals. For example, psychologists can partner with those doing research in health care or public health to further research on effective interventions aimed at reducing health disparities. Psychologists can also become members of the Gay and Lesbian Medical Association to network with other professionals interested in addressing these health disparities.

The HRC Workplace Project promotes equality in the workplace through advocating for nondiscrimination policies and equal employment benefits, as well as diversity training and encouragement of appropriate marketing. Muñoz and Thomas (2006) highlight some of the research done on best practices for sexual minorities in the workplace, which has demonstrated that there is a positive relationship between affirming organizational climates for sexual minorities and an increase in organizational commitment, lower job stress, and increased perception of top-level management support. Research that focuses on employee satisfaction, productivity, and organizational practices can further demonstrate the benefits of fostering an affirmative working environment (see section entitled "In the Workplace" for more information on this topic).

The Gay, Lesbian, Straight Education Network (GLSEN).

GLSEN is an organization that seeks to educate teachers, students, and the public about the damaging effects of homophobia and heterosexism on both youth and adults. The organization works with policy makers, community leaders, and students to address anti-LGBT bias in educational settings. They provide resources to assist schools in starting up Gay/Straight Alliances and provide training to assist schools in creating a safer climate for LGBT students. GLSEN publishes a national climate survey documenting the experience of LGBT youth in school settings.

GLSEN also conducts research that documents anti-LGBT bias in K-12 education as well as examines the utility of GLSEN's recommended resources and interventions in the creation of safer school environments. GLSEN welcomes the opportunity to partner with researchers and can be contacted directly at research@glsen.org. Research that would support GLSEN's efforts could focus on best practices in providing a safe, supportive, and affirming school environment and how these practices are related to lower levels of substance use and suicidal behavior, as well as higher levels of self-esteem, school involvement, and life satisfaction.

The skills needed by psychologists to assist in the prevention of heterosexism at the institutional level require that these advocacy skills be taught in their graduate programs. APA's Public Interest Directorate has resources and publications for psychologists interested in the public policies impacting LGBT individuals and families, and includes information on effectively communicating with legislators. They have published fact sheets and briefing statements that may be of interest to those engaged in advocacy or research on LGBT concerns that should be a part of counseling psychology curriculum. For example, one publication that could be used in a counseling psychology research course includes (1) recommendations for federal policies to improve health outcomes for sexual and gender minorities, (2) a call for federal-level surveys to include data indicators that adequately address sexual orientation and gender identity, (3) a call for an increase in empirical research related to LGBT persons, and (4) provision of strategies to ensure cultural competency within health care systems (APA, 2010). Counseling psychologists can use this information to design studies that shape policy by (1) distributing empirical findings of their research on LGBT issues to legislators and the leaders of other social institutions such as schools, religious organizations, and hospitals; (2) helping to dispel social myths about LGBT people; and (3) testifying as experts in legal and legislative issues (Kuehl, 2000).

Counseling psychologists should be familiar with the Committee on Lesbian, Gay, Bisexual, and Transgender Concerns (CLGBTC) of the

APA, which advocates for the civil and legal rights of LGBT individuals. This committee conducts and encourages objective and unbiased research on topics relevant for the LGBT community and evaluates the social impact of this research. In addition, the CLGBTC develops educational materials for distribution to clinicians and the public in order to reduce the inaccurate information and stereotypes that are perpetuated about LGBT individuals in counseling practice. The committee has contributed to the report from APA's Task Force on the Appropriate Therapeutic Response to Sexual Orientation and has also worked with Division 44 of APA, the Society for the Psychological Study of Lesbian, Gay and Bisexual Issues, to address concerns regarding the interpretation of Footnote 4 in the APA Commission on Accreditation Guidelines.

Footnote 4

The American Psychological Association (APA) is the accrediting body for counseling psychology doctoral programs. While APA has adapted policies that affirm same-sex sexual attractions and behaviors as "normal and positive variations of human sexuality" (APA Council of Representatives, August 5, 2009), APA continues to allow one policy that is the epitome of institutional heterosexism, "Footnote 4."

Footnote 4 is an exception within Domain D in the accreditation standards, the domain that focuses on cultural issues and diversity (American Psychological Association Committee on Accreditation, 2008). Footnote 4 can be invoked by doctoral programs housed in religious institutions in order to "exercise admissions preferences for trainees who share the values of the religion" (Vera, 2009, p. 747). APA has attempted to walk a tightrope by also stating that Footnote 4 cannot "supersede accreditation guidelines and principles" or "preclude the hiring or admissions of individuals because of personal and demographic characteristics" (Bieschke & Mintz, 2009, p. 777). However as Vera (2009) points out, if such institutions can exercise preferences, then by extension, the converse is that these programs can also reject students who do not share these values. In fact, students can be dismissed for not abiding to religiously based code of conduct or lifestyle statements. For example, Brigham Young University, which has both APA-accredited Counseling and Clinical Psychology Programs, has an Honor Code that states the following:

> Homosexual behavior and/or advocacy of homosexual behavior are inappropriate and violate the Honor Code. Homosexual behavior includes not only sexual relations between members of the same sex, but all forms of physical intimacy that give expression to homosexual feelings. Advocacy includes seeking to influence others to engage in homosexual behavior or promoting homosexual relations as being morally acceptable. (Brigham Young University Honor Code, 2009–2010)

There has been a call from Division 44 of APA to clarify the implementing regulations for Domain D, as all programs are required to adequately address issues of diversity. APA adopted Implementing Regulation C-22(a): Review of Programs Invoking Footnote 4 (APA Commission on Accreditation, 2010), yet much confusion remains. While such programs may teach their students to be supportive and nonjudgmental with their LGBT clients, they are obvious limited in the degree to which they can teach advocacy skills and affirmative therapy. As the previous section on counseling psychology training has shown, actively addressing heterosexist assumptions in training programs is a complex and challenging act. For universities that clearly state heterosexist bias, the flexibility in training provided by the APA accreditation standards may provide room for some of these biases to go unchallenged.

This form of institutional heterosexism can have many ripple effects. Graduates of doctoral programs that evoke Footnote 4 would appear to be more likely to reinforce heterosexism and internalized heterosexism in their clients, their supervisees, and the institutions in which they work. It seems imperative that counseling psychologists advocate for either a complete removal of Footnote 4 or at least greater clarification of what such programs must demonstrate in order to determine that they are truly meeting the accreditation guidelines and principles. As Vera (2009) states, "when we allow trainees to use cultural affiliations as grounds to refuse to examine injustices embedded in some of their beliefs, we are complicit in creating conditions for malfeasance" (p. 748).

It is not public knowledge which doctoral programs invoke Footnote 4 when they are seeking APA-accreditation. However, in our search of the websites of APA-accredited programs at religious institutions the following universities have official statements characterizing homosexuality as immoral or unnatural and/or expressly forbidden: Azusa Pacific University, Baylor University, Biola University, Brigham Young University, Fuller Theological Seminary, Loma Linda University,

Regent University, and Seattle Pacific University. Other universities that offer APA-accredited programs have lifestyle statements that more indirectly reflect heterosexist beliefs and policies by prohibiting sexual behavior outside of marriage (e.g., Catholic University of America). Whether these statements directly claim that marriage is reserved for the holy union between a man and a woman, or omit this general reality, they are reinforcing the heteronormative policies of the country and their religion and are in direct contradiction to the APA policy statement given at the beginning of this section.

We highlight the issue of Footnote 4 as an act of resistance to APA-sanctioned heterosexism (Ladany, Kaduvettoor, & Soheilian, 2008). We find the current compromise to be unacceptable in truly requiring APA-accredited programs to meet the principles of Domain D. We believe at this time that the most effective way to advocate for this change is to make a third-party comment to the Commission on Accreditation when these programs are seeking reaccreditation, or by filing a complaint against the accredited program. Complaints must present evidence for how a program's curriculum is not consistent with the accreditation guidelines and can be submitted at any time. Third-party comments are filed within five working days after the program's self-study is due. Further information about self-study due dates and more recent attempts by APA to clarify the use of Footnote 4 can be found at www.apa.org/ed/accreditation. If anyone has examples of how an APA accredited program used their religiously based policies to deny admittance, employment, or retention of a student or staff member because of their advocacy of LGBT issues and/or their identity as an LGBT person, then it would be an act of advocacy to file a complaint or third-party comment against this program.

PRIMARY AND SECONDARY SCHOOLS

Emerging research supports that school climate and the actions of school personnel make a difference in the perception or actuality of negative experiences for LGBT youth in school (Graybill et al., 2009). Goodenow and colleagues (2006) examined school factors that mitigate the risk experiences documented by sexual minority youth and found that the presence of school support groups for LGB students was significantly associated with lowered victimization and suicidality for sexual minority youth. Perceived staff support was identified as being a protective factor against suicide attempts, even after researchers took into account rates of victimization (Goodenow et al., 2006). This highlights the importance of educating school personnel about LGBT issues faced by youth and providing strategies to help school staff address these issues. The authors pointed out that although there has been an increase in research focused on the experiences of sexual minority adolescents, it is mostly focused on the heightened risk experiences of this population. This led the authors to conclude that a more ecological approach to primary prevention is the key to achieving a safer school environment and that researchers should focus on environmental and contextual factors for sexual minority youth (Goodenow et al., 2006).

An important trend is "safe school," inclusive, nondiscrimination, and antiharassment policies that attempt to reduce the discrimination and violence aimed at LGBT youth by setting clear standards for behavior and consequences (Hirschfeld, 2001). However Hirschfeld (2001) admonishes that "safe school" policies, while a necessary first step, are not enough. He infers that these policies can be somewhat superficial and that more meaningful reforms are necessary such as curricular inclusion of LGBT issues, supporting student's rights to attend prom with a same-sex partner, and efforts to include LGBT themed books or literature in schools and guidance offices. Hirschfeld (2001) stated it is important to emphasize that change is a process, it must be reflective not reactive or reflexive, it must encompass everyone who comes into contact with students, and it must challenge preconceived notions and perceptions.

Szalacha (2003) evaluated the impact of Gay/Straight Alliances (GSAs), school policies, and staff development interventions on student outcomes. Results of this study indicated that GSAs were the most potent forces for institutional change. Hansen (2007) reviewed a variety of school-based support efforts for LGBT youth. She cited research indicating the effectiveness of GSAs in creating a more inclusive environment, but pointed out that the research has focused mainly on reports of participants with no experimental control. In addition, she reviewed research focused on the implementation of staff development efforts to improve the school climate but indicated that no research exists investigating the outcome of staff training on students in the school setting (Hansen, 2007). Pollard (2010) reported that when schools enforce antiharassment policies, these policies can serve as protective factors from victimization and risk behaviors for LGBT students. There are many current interventions noted to demonstrate reduction in victimization and suicidality among LGBT students. Among them are speaker panels, GSAs, and antiheterosexist education. All have been found to increase acceptance and affirmation of LGBT youth (DePaul, Walsh, & Dam, 2009).

Speaker panels

Speaker panels are often used in schools to help educate people about LGBT issues and dispel myths. These panels are often composed of LGBT individuals (and sometimes heterosexual allies) who discuss their own personal stories. These panels can inform and change attitudes and behaviors toward the LGBT population although research evidence of its effectiveness is mixed (Chonody, Siebert, & Rutledge, 2009; Evans & Broido, 2005). Chng and Moore (1991) studied the effectiveness of gay and lesbian panels, and their results indicated no significant change in attitudes as a result of the panel. The panel used was didactic and included members from the local community, not from the peer groups of the students included in the study. Nelson and Krieger (1997) evaluated the effectiveness of implementing a panel composed of gay men and lesbian peers in changing homophobic attitudes among college students. Results showed there was a significant difference between pre- and posttest scores on a modified version of the Attitudes Toward Homosexuality Scale. Researchers determined that the panel was more effective at changing heterosexual students' attitudes about certain aspects of homosexuality, such as stereotypes about lesbians being masculine and gay men being feminine. However, it was less effective at changing more deeply ingrained attitudes such as the morality of homosexuality (Nelson & Krieger, 1997). Researchers concluded that speaker panels of lesbian and gay men could help to foster a positive attitude change toward homosexuality, but emphasized that the delivery and format of the panel is pivotal, leading the authors to make several recommendations. First, panel members should be peers of the audience to accentuate the commonalities between panel members and the audience. Second, the delivery should be interactive rather than didactic, and third, audience participation is critical to fostering this interactive change. Finally, taking the time to elicit feedback following the panel is critical (Nelson & Krieger, 1997).

Gay/straight alliances (GSAs).

As mentioned above, GSAs have been an important strategy for allowing LGBT students to live open lives and counteract heterosexism and homophobia. These alliances can serve as a protective factor, be LGBT affirming, and provide important social support for LGBT youth in schools. These alliances are student-led and incorporate not only LGBT students, but also those students who have LGBT family members, those who are questioning, those who are misidentified as LGBT, and heterosexual individuals who wish to be allies. There are over 3,000 such alliances worldwide and these have been empirically supported in helping to mitigate the stressors and negative impact of heterosexism (DePaul et al., 2009; Valenti & Campbell, 2009). Research supports that LGBT students who go to schools that have GSAs report greater feelings of safety and experience less dating violence and other negative consequences than those in schools that do not (O'Shaughnessy, Russell, Heck, Calhoun, & Laub, 2004). Goodenow and colleagues (2006) proposed that longitudinal studies that follow the changes in school cultures as GSAs are implemented and mature would help in the identification of key factors for successful school change. Counseling psychologists can be guest speakers for these student groups and provide trainings for the faculty sponsors of these groups.

Antiheterosexist education

Antiheterosexist education is defined by Hanlon (2009) as "that which works toward both preventing homophobic attitudes through a LGBT-inclusive curriculum, and responding to anti-LGBT attitudes in meaningful ways" (p. 32). Proponents of such education stress that it is important to engage students in "meaningful discussions" so that students can learn tolerance of differences so that we can "deconstruct biases and stereotypes and encourage critical thought" (Hanlon, 2009, p. 34). It is also important to affirm the identities of LGBT students and create safe spaces in which LGBT and non-LGBT individuals can share and reflect on their experiences (Hirschfeld, 2001).

One type of antiheterosexist education is conducting a workshop addressed to students. Rye and Meaney (2009) reported success in addressing negative attitudes toward homosexuality utilizing a homonegativity awareness workshop with undergraduate students. The attitudes of workshop participants were compared with a control group. Findings indicated that participants in the experimental group held significantly less homophobic attitudes after participation in the workshop when compared with the control group. Individual differences were included in the analysis, with the following differences predictive of higher posttest homonegativity: participant gender, irrational contagion fears about HIV/AIDS, authoritarianism, number of LGB acquaintances, and pretest homonegativity. The findings related to individual difference variables highlight the importance of addressing specific issues that may be problematic for participants, such as providing information on HIV/AIDS to address the participants who may have fear of contagion regarding HIV/AIDS (Rye & Meaney, 2009).

Perhaps the most underutilized resource we have for providing psychoeducational information for the prevention of heterosexism is the Internet (Halkitis, 2010). Specifically, we are recommending that college counseling centers provide podcasts and written information that addresses issues such as safe sex and the coming out process. Counseling psychology programs could help produce these and evaluate their effectiveness.

School counselors and psychologists need to be at the forefront in (1) challenging stereotypes and assumptions, (2) providing positive images of LGBT individuals via speaker panels and using the media, (3) providing counseling to help LGBT youth with issues related to their sexual or gender identity, (4) creating safe zones for students within hostile schools, (5) using inclusive language that does not marginalize LGBT students and families, (6) providing workshops to educate faculty and staff and create more awareness and an affirming environment for LGBT youth, and (7) making sure the school library has current, positive, literature on LGBT characters (DePaul et al., 2009; Hanlon, 2009; Ratts & Hutchins, 2009; Van Wormer & McKinney, 2003). School counselor and psychologist activists are crucial for schools and districts where school board members, teachers, counselors, and school administrators are part of the perpetration of discrimination, intolerance, or ignorance of LGBT issues (Clark, 2010; Goodenow et al., 2006; Hanlon, 2009; Horn et al., 2008).

COUNSELING CURRICULUM

The importance of effective LGBT training in counseling psychology is made clear in the research of Bowers, Plummer, and Minichielo (2005), who demonstrated how homophobia continues to intrude, in subtle and complex ways, on counselor-client relationships due to counselors' limited knowledge, assumptions, and biases. Discussing the harmful effects of heterosexism, Phillips and Fischer (1998) identified graduate psychology programs as "one of the most promising agents for change" (p. 714). Indeed, professional counseling and psychological organizations and accrediting bodies require that LGBT issues be addressed in the training of counselors and psychologists (APA Committee on Accreditation, 2008). The Association for Lesbian Gay, Bisexual and Transgender Issues in Counseling (ALGBTIC) has adopted standards for LGBT counseling competencies to guide the preparation of counselors with the knowledge, awareness, and skills necessary to work affirmatively with LGBT clients (Logan & Barrett, 2005).

Various topics have been suggested as essential in preparing students for affirmative work with LGBT individuals. Duhigg, Rostosky, Gray, and Wimsatt (2010) suggested that training programs should increase awareness about homophobia and sexual minority oppression, provide exposure to and interaction with sexual minorities, and facilitate exploration of values, attitudes, and actions in order to assist heterosexuals in becoming sexual minority allies. Others have recommended that training include the dissemination of information regarding topics such as historical perspectives of homosexuality; homophobia/heterosexism; heterosexual privilege; the impact of discrimination, oppression, and prejudice; anti-LGBT policies and legislation; LGBT identity development; LGBT health and wellness; spirituality/religion; and diversity within the LGBT population (Callahan, 2001; Levitt et al., 2009; Lidderdale, 2002; Pearson, 2003; Phillips, 2000; Reynolds & Hanjorgiris, 2000; Watt et al., 2009). In addition, training should address specific issues relevant to the provision of therapy with LGBT clients such as creating an affirmative environment, bias in assessment and diagnosis, conversion therapy, and affirmative counseling techniques (Lidderdale, 2002). Training should also incorporate opportunities for students to gain experience and skills in understanding and building relationships with administrators and policy makers to prepare future psychologists to function as social justice change agents, (Goodman et al., 2004; Toporek & Vaughn, 2010).

Dillon and colleagues (2004) emphasized the importance of self-reflection in the process of developing affirmative views of LGBT individuals. In particular, self-reflection regarding the student's own sexual identity development, related beliefs, and attitudes about LGBT individuals is a critical first step toward the deconstruction of heterosexist bias. Training programs need to encourage a thorough examination of a trainee's personal values, attitudes, and beliefs regarding religion and spirituality in order to best meet the ethical guidelines of the profession and serve the client (Bartoli, 2007, Winterowd, Adams, Miville, & Mintz, 2009). In addition, the Counseling Psychology Model Training Values Statement Addressing Diversity issues a challenge to counseling psychologists, and students within training programs, to identify personally biased attitudes (Mintz & Bieschke, 2009). Through this reflective process, future psychologists may be able to integrate accurate knowledge about LGBT individuals with their religious beliefs and become Christian-allies. A qualitative study by Borgman (2009), explored how 11 doctoral level Christian psychologists who self-identified as LGB allies resolved any values conflicts. She found that the shift to the role of a Christian-ally is an ongoing process characterized by the motivation to attain a more cohesive sense of self. Participants were described as possessing the qualities of having a questioning mind, and placing value in integrity and spirituality. Factors that facilitated the integration of the Christian-ally identity included relationships, education and training, cultural factors, and specific emotional experiences.

Russell (2010) studied heterosexual allies involved in public efforts to advocate for LGBT individuals and has found that allies are motivated to engage in activism by two distinct trajectories: fundamental values of justice or personal relationships with LGBT individuals. The implications of this difference may seem small, but Russell (2010) pointed out that those that are motivated to action by personal relationships may miss the larger societal and structural inequalities that create heterosexist practices in our society. On the other hand, allies who are concerned due to their fundamental values of justice have a focus on the larger social context and the power distribution within it, making them committed regardless of their personal connections (Russell, 2010). Levitt and colleagues (2009) pointed out that it is important to educate students about anti-LGBT policies and restrictions that exist within local communities, as well as nationally, as many students hold inaccurate assumptions about LGBT rights. Such an intervention could also trigger students' fundamental values of justice and help to develop stronger allies.

The scant research that has examined the efficacy of formal training focused on LGBT issues indicates that such training may indeed be effective in working toward the elimination and prevention of heterosexism. Students have reported specific benefits gained from participating in training and seminars designed to increase their knowledge, positive attitudes, and skills in work with LGBT clients (Foreman & Quinlan, 2008; Pearson, 2003). For example, Phillips and Fischer (1998) found that formal training experiences that required students to explore their own biases toward LGBT individuals and provided contact experience with gay men predicted greater feelings of preparedness in working with lesbians and gay men. Providing accurate information about the issues unique to LGBT individuals appears to be beneficial in moving the profession toward more affirmative therapy for sexual minority clients. However, additional research examining the effectiveness of LGBT training is necessary to inform the design of coursework that effectively deconstructs heterosexism within the profession and society.

Israel and Hackett (2004) examined the effect of information-based interventions versus attitude-based interventions on counselor trainees' knowledge and attitudes toward LGB clients. Posttest results indicated that the participants who received the information condition were more knowledgeable than the other participants who did not receive the information, suggesting that even one class session covering LGB topics may have a significant impact on students' knowledge. An interesting result was that the attitude-exploration-only group reported more negative attitudes toward LGB individuals *following* participation in the workshop (Israel & Hackett, 2004). Given the heterosexist nature of US society, Israel and Hackett (2004) wondered if perhaps after reflecting on their attitudes, participants realized that initial reports of feelings about LGB individuals were not as positive as they thought. As a result of not being challenged to reflect on their views, the participants in the other groups may have remained in a more positive mindset. A more extensive intervention may be necessary to induce a positive attitude change, but additional research is needed to understand this process further.

Biaggio, Orchard, Larson, Petrino, and Mihara (2003) recommended several ways in which training programs can prevent practices that perpetuate heterosexism and create an environment that welcomes diversity. First, a commitment to affirming sexual minorities should be evident in the program mission statement and in procedures for dealing with prejudicial and discriminatory behaviors. Second, programs should engage in the ongoing examination of policies, procedures, and publications to identify and challenge heterosexist structures that may discriminate against sexual minorities (Buhrke & Douce, 1991). For instance, programs that exclude sexual orientation in equal employment opportunity statements, recruiting, and admission publications may discourage openly gay, lesbian, and bisexual persons from applying for positions within programs (Biaggio et al., 2003). Third, training programs should commit to recruiting, hiring, and retaining diverse faculty members and faculty members with expertise in LGBT issues. Fourth, sources of support should be available for LGBT faculty, staff, and students through university organizations and mentoring activities within the program. Although suggestions have not been empirically examined, the extent to which training programs convey a culturally sensitive training environment has been shown to enhance the development of multicultural competencies and improve the affective racial attitudes of students (Dickson & Jepsen, 2007; Dickson, Jepsen, & Barbee, 2008). This provides confidence that creating an environment in which LGBT faculty, staff, and students feel included, valued, and safe can serve to prevent heterosexism within training programs and ultimately within the profession of counseling psychology and the public that we serve.

IN THE WORKPLACE

Many LGBT individuals have to make a decision regarding how to manage their sexual identity in the workplace and whether or not they will come out to colleagues (Button, 2001; Frost & Meyer, 2009). Historically, human rights legislation did not pertain to LGBT people, and this lack of protection left them vulnerable to discrimination in the workplace. This discrimination allowed employers to make hiring and firing decisions based on sexual orientation. As of July 2010, 12 states and the District of Columbia prohibit discrimination based on sexual orientation and gender identity, while 21 states prohibit discrimination based on sexual orientation alone (Human Rights Campaign, 2010d). In addition, LGB rights advocates have won statutory protections in 20 states against discrimination in the workplace (Keck, 2009).

Increasingly, employers are implementing inclusive policies and practices each year as they related to sexual minorities (Hornsby, 2006). However, the type of industry an LGBT individual works in does make a difference. Many Fortune 500 companies, colleges and universities, and city and state governments are including sexual and gender orientation in their nondiscrimination policies, while a few provide domestic partner benefits (Hornsby, 2006). However, not all corporations or work environments strive to reduce prejudice, discrimination, and heterosexism (Chung, Williams, & Dispenza, 2009).

Counseling psychology's roots in vocational psychology positions us to be the leaders in prevention of workplace heterosexism. Chung and colleagues (2009) mandated it as imperative for psychologists and career counselors to educate themselves on the many forms of LGBT discrimination in the workplace, the impact of discrimination on LGBT workers, and the various coping strategies needed for these workers to mitigate hostile environments. Career counseling classes should expose students to the HRC Workplace Project, which has resources for employers and employees and a Corporate Equality Index, which rates US workplaces on their level of LGBT equality (Human Rights Campaign, 2010a). This index allows potential employees, business partners, and the general public to assess each workplace prior to seeking employment, partnership, goods, or services.

Students should also be trained to use Chung's coping framework for heterosexist work environments that includes (1) the *vocational choice model*, which aids LGBT workers in identifying career choices based on potential discrimination; (2) the *identity management model*, which helps individuals strategize about how to manage their LGBT identity in different work settings; and (c) the *discrimination management model*, which helps an individual strategize how to respond to discrimination in the workplace (Chung et al., 2009). It is clear that career counseling interventions must include helping LGBT individuals mitigate heterosexist work environments, but we must also advocate for organizational change itself (Counselors for Social Justice, 2008; Ratts & Hutchins, 2009).

Counseling psychologists, especially those working in Employee Assistance Programs (EAPs) and as organizational consultants, can help LGBT workers in many ways. Obear (2000) discussed an intervention used by workers at AT&T, whereby employees put together a photo album containing pictures of LGBT workers with their partners, families, and loved ones to help normalize and humanize themselves to corporate leaders. Counseling psychologists can help reduce heterosexism in the workplace by (1) providing facts versus myths, (2) leading awareness training and team building exercises that emphasize inclusion of all diverse groups, (3) helping form and develop LGBT resource groups, (4) educating corporate leaders about the impact of heterosexism and discrimination on worker productivity and health, and (5) helping to develop company policies that are inclusive of LGBT people (Hodges & Parkes, 2005; Hornsby, 2006). Counseling psychologists also need to engage in more research on the implications of corporate policies (positive and negative) and how they affect LGBT workers. The little research that has been done showed that affirming corporate policies was positively correlated with reduced discrimination faced by LGBT workers (Button, 2001).

Individual and Remediative Level

There is much that counseling psychologists can do to help prevent heterosexism at the individual level. Perhaps the most important of these efforts is aimed at helping LGBT individuals develop a healthy sexual orientation, gender identity, and gender expression. One important aspect of this work is to provide affirming direct service to LGBT clients, which entails the practice and belief that LGBT individuals are just as normal, healthy, and deserving as their heterosexual counterparts.

PROVIDE AFFIRMING DIRECT SERVICE

Crisp and McCave (2007) suggested guidelines for providing LGBT affirming services to clients. They espouse that practitioners should (1) view LGBT people within their many environments and within their many identities (e.g., other cultural identities, role identities, etc.), (2) work within a strength-based perspective to help develop positive self-esteem and coping skills, (3) work within the client's self-determination and pacing, (4) focus on health and do not pathologize, (5) challenge heterosexist messages, and (6) do not stop with an absence of heterosexism, but actively "affirm, celebrate, advocate, and validate the identities of GLB individuals" (p. 405). In addition, counseling psychologists need to be knowledgeable in many areas such as preferred terminology, LGBT history and leaders, understanding how oppression and policies that have impacted the LGBT community, knowledge of affirming community resources, and knowledge of culturally sensitive practice models such as the LGBT coming out and identity models (Crisp & McCave, 2007).

THE COMING OUT PROCESS

Helping LGBT clients through their coming out process can be an important aspect of providing direct affirming services to LGBT clients. When an LGBT individual feels safe enough to come out to important loved ones and others, it indicates positive development and that one has successfully explored hir sexuality and gender expression. This is often the first step toward forming a positive identity and self-acceptance (Frost & Meyer, 2009). There are many risks for individuals during the coming out process, which may include rejection, ridicule, stigma, hostility, and violence (Herek, Gillis, & Cogan, 2009; Hodges & Parkes, 2005). Rees-Turyn (2007) noted that heterosexist assumptions make the coming out process necessary and perpetual.

The coming out process is very individualized and its success depends on many factors such as the sociopolitical environment (e.g., gay affirming vs. heterosexist environment), ethnic identity, perceived or anticipated support, access to the LGBT community, religion, and so forth (Rees-Turyn, 2007). Whether one chooses to be out in any given situation, or with any given group, is a "function of situational and environmental circumstances that are unrelated to internal conflict" (Frost & Meyer, 2009, p. 98). Some individuals choose not to come out, or do not fully come out, but this option can also lead to consequences such as increased psychological distress and the pressure of leading a "double life" and identity. Individuals lead double lives when they are out in some areas, but not in others (Harper & Scheider, 2003; Levitt et al., 2009). These decisions can lead to self-stigma and self-loathing, which also cause an individual a great deal of stress (Herek et al., 2009).

While coming out can be a difficult process for any LGBT individual, research supports that bisexual individuals have more difficulty than their gay or lesbian counterparts due to the multiple effects of stigmatization and socially isolating impact of biphobia (Herek et al., 2009; Kertzner et al., 2009). Lewis and colleagues (2009) reported that "bisexual women were significantly less 'out' than their lesbian counterparts with 49% of the bisexual women reporting being out to more than 50% of their family, friends, and coworkers compared to 71% of lesbians" (p. 976).

While not sharing one's sexual orientation in dangerous situations can be protective and adaptive (Frost & Meyer, 2009; Herek et al., 2009) research supports that being open with one's sexual orientation leads to healthier outcomes than for those who are not (Lewis et al., 2009; McDermott et al., 2008). Being open allows one to build social support networks that can facilitate growth, positive identity, and positive coping and minimize negative features such as stigma, rejection, prejudice, and hostility (Harper & Scheider, 2003; Rees-Turyn, 2007).

Thus coming out is also a potentially empowering act that can ultimately change heterosexual people's attitudes about LGBT individuals. Coming out as a strategy for change is based on Allport's contact hypothesis (Allport, 1954 as cited in Cogan, 1996). Having interpersonal contact where more than one LGBT individual directly comes out to a heterosexual person who is more than an acquaintance seems to produce positive attitudes about LGBT people (Herek & Capitanio, 1996). While research supports that there is a negative relationship between contact and sexual prejudice, this relationship is moderated by the type of sexual prejudice measure used, the target group being assessed, and where the study was conducted (Smith, Axelton, & Saucier, 2009). Recent research on the contact hypothesis and impact on racial relations in South Africa suggest that a negative effect of contact can result in an oppressed group being less mobilized for social change (Dixon et al., 2010). Counseling psychologists can research the contact hypothesis as it relates to LGBT individuals and families (Patterson, 1996). In addition, further research is needed on the contact hypothesis and how it impacts the impetus for social change.

The following are suggestions from the literature regarding strategies for counseling psychologists to help LGBT individuals through the coming out process: (1) facilitate the development of a healthy and cohesive identity, (2) help the LGBT individual identify positive role models, (3) encourage the development of high self-esteem and differentiation, (4) help LGBT individuals achieve internalized positive affirmations and help clients understand their experiences and work through internalized heterosexism, (5) help the LGBT individual link to needed resources (e.g., GSAs), and (6) work with the community and family members (if given permission by the LGBT individual) to dispel myths, provide facts, and help build acceptance. These interventions can help mitigate the adverse affects of heterosexism such as (1) helping LGBT individuals recover more quickly from attacks and threats, (2) helping them view challenges as opportunities for growth and development, (3) helping them to be more active in their own development, (4) helping them create support networks, and (5) helping them deal with the justified fear and danger of living in a heterosexist society (Bernal & Coolhart, 2005; Crisp & McCave, 2007).

ADVOCATING FOR CLIENTS AND THE ROLE OF ALLIES IN PREVENTION.

There is a paucity of research on the impact of client advocacy as part of best clinical practices for LGBT individuals. While there is limited research on the specific strategies for advocacy there is support for the positive impact of creating social support networks for LGBT youth and their families. Counseling psychologists should become familiar with the resources available in their particular community and be able to connect LGBT individuals and their families to the appropriate organizations to facilitate this support (Matthews & Adams, 2009). The previous research on social support systems indicates the importance of community organizations and LGBT nongay allies in preventing heterosexism in a variety of settings (e.g. schools, clinics, hospitals, government) (Hansen, 2007). For example, advocacy groups such as PFLAG and GLSEN have long been aware of how effective it is to have heterosexual allies in advocating for LGBT civil rights (Russell, 2010). Often such advocacy is based on the ally's relationship with a LGBT family member or friend, but there is some evidence to suggest that contact is not enough to produce allied behaviors that are supportive in addressing systemic inequities for LGB individuals (Riggle & Rostosky, 2010; Russell, 2010). Additional research is needed that seeks to understand the motives of heterosexual allies and how to foster support that is effective at addressing policy change. Such research would likely benefit GLSEN and other advocacy groups' efforts in creating alliances.

Additionally as with other minority status groups, parental and peer support is an important factor in supporting LGBT youth in their development of a healthy identity (Baptist & Allen, 2008). Often however, LGBT youth are forced to seek out "families of choice" (Sanders & Kroll, 2000) through PFLAG and other community organizations to gain the necessary support. Therefore, it is important for counseling psychologists to become social justice advocates and help form supportive LGBT alliances in their communities, particularly by encouraging the development of heterosexual allies. Encouraging clients to engage in social activism is something that Rostosky, Riggle, Horne, and Miller (2009) suggested should be done with caution. Research on LGB individuals during the time of the 2006 marriage amendments concluded that LGB individuals who increased participation in LGB advocacy efforts during this time also reported higher levels of psychological distress. It is particularly important that LGBT community members, allies, and mental health professionals support LGBT individuals in balancing healthy activism with healthy replenishment (Levitt et al., 2009).

Theories of liberation psychology have been applied to LGBT individuals suggesting that "community development, prevention and intervention with LGBT communities cannot be separated from social activism" (Harper & Schneider, 2003, p. 243). For example, counseling psychology students need to be trained to provide relevant literature to school districts or partner with local PFLAG chapters to develop safe schools. We have attempted to identify other such advocacy efforts throughout the chapter.

It is suggested that awareness of the process by which one develops a heterosexual identity can help create affirmative attitudes toward LGBT individuals (Evans & Broido, 2005). One model that can help develop such awareness is the multidimensional model of heterosexual identity development. Worthington, Savoy, Dillon, and Vernaglia (2002) proposed five developmental statuses an individual may experience in developing a heterosexual identity. The five statuses are (1) unexplored commitment, (2) active exploration, (3) diffusion, (4) deepening and commitment, and (5) synthesis. This model and others like it can provide a framework from which to begin to deconstruct heterosexual privilege in practice.

Eliason (1995) conducted a qualitative study exploring the development of a heterosexual identity and found that many students were unaware of their sexual identity, unaware of what it means to be heterosexual in this society, and held stereotypes about LGBT people until they began exploring their identity. This notion has been substantiated by Simoni and Walters (2001) who found an association between evolving identity stages and less heterosexist attitudes. In terms of clinical practice, it is important for counseling psychologists to develop a sexual identity with an awareness of heterosexual privilege, and increase the awareness of their clients (Worthington et al., 2002). Mohr, Weiner, Chopp, and Wong (2009) found that client bisexuality does not influence therapists' judgments regarding psychosocial functioning or client attractiveness. However, it did have a strong effect on the relevance of clinical issues that were related to bisexual stereotypes. This finding remained consistent even after controlling for social desirability, self-efficacy beliefs for avoiding bias, and tendency to pathologize clients, suggesting to researchers the possibility that therapists' beliefs about ability to avoid bias may not reflect the actual risk of developing biased views of clients (Mohr et al., 2009). Counseling psychology programs should include some element of sexuality counseling as part of their curriculum. Doing so might increase counseling psychologist's ability to aid in the development of more heterosexual allies in their communities.

Conclusion

This chapter focused on dismantling the bird cage of heterosexism by identifying the multiple barriers of heterosexism and showing how these impact the LGBT community. This chapter also focused on the myriad of ways that counseling psychologists can be active participants in changing and preventing heterosexism at the societal, institutional, and individual levels. There is still much work needed to be done in order to break down the ingrained heterosexist ideology and practices of society regarding sexual and gender minorities. The success of prevention activities can be measured by the reduction in attitudes, behaviors, and practices that are detrimental to LGBT individuals and the increase of those that are positive and affirming. Specific changes we'd like to see include, but are not limited to a decrease in (1) the practice and philosophy of conversion therapy and conversion groups, and doctoral programs that invoke Footnote 4; (2) hate crimes, violence, and bullying; (3) affirmative action statements that exclude LGBT individuals; (4) the number of states outlawing same sex marriage; and (5) the negative experiences LGBT individuals suffer within religious institutions, schools, military, workplace settings, and from parental reactions resulting in mental consequences such as substance use, mood disorders, and unsafe sexual behavior.

In addition, as a measure of successful heterosexist prevention practices we would like to see an increase in (1) gay affirmative attitudes from all aspects of society, (2) the number of states that allow equal rights for the LGBT population on all levels and for all issues, (3) the espoused knowledge of professionals and laypersons regarding the dynamics of "healthy" families versus anchoring our discussions in the pronounced dichotomy of "LGBT families" versus "heterosexual families," (4) the number of people who are out and the degree of being out in geographically diverse areas, (5) more positive examples in the media of LGBT people with greater variation and less stereotyping in the characters, and, (6) inclusion of LGBT individuals and issues in nondiscrimination and affirmative action statements.

A prevailing theme throughout this discussion of preventing heterosexism in counseling psychology training is the lack of research. Training programs that are LGBT affirming are well positioned to encourage the production of research on LGBT issues. Although LGBT issues are becoming more visible in current research, the scarcity of empirical information regarding the effectiveness of various interventions in preventing heterosexism is a concern that must be addressed by counseling psychologists. The historic lack of research in the area of LGBT issues has been blamed, in part, on people's fear, "of overt and covert stigmatization" as a result of conducting research in this area (Croteau & Talbot, 2000, p. 22). Currently, training program directors can work to ensure that faculty members and students feel secure that their research of LGBT issues will be valued. Bieschke, Eberz, Bard, and Croteau (1998) provide a number of suggestions for establishing a climate wherein LGBT research is promoted and encouraged. According to Matthews and Adams (2009), heterosexism can be challenged through any research that is affirming of the lives of LGBT individuals. We need to inspire students as to the power of research in addressing issues of social injustice. For example, the decision to remove homosexuality from the list of mental disorders was due in part to Evelyn Hooker's research where she compared the MMPI's of "normal" heterosexual man to homosexual men and found minimal differences (Hooker, 1957).

For the first time, the US Department of Health and Human Services' *Healthy People 2010* website has included a webpage on LGBT health. In addition to some of the topics already mention in this chapter, this website suggests the following research is necessary to improve LGBT health: (1) determining what interventions are effective in reducing HIV and other STDs, (2) educating medical personnel on culturally competent care for LGBT patients (including an understanding of transgender health as medically necessary), (3) gathering national data on LGBT Americans, (4) LGBT elder health and well-being, (5) evaluating examples of resiliency in LGBT communities, and (6) developing an LGBT wellness model. All of these topics are well within the purview of counseling psychology research and practice; and in order to be effective in our research advocacy efforts we need to be familiar with the Healthy People website, as well as the Centers for Prevention and Disease Control website on LGBT Health (CDC, 2010).

Future Directions

We also would like to provide the following questions and statements to direct future research and discussion of prevention efforts. Gaps that we found in the research literature included, but are not limited to, the following issues:

1. What is most effective in training counseling psychology students in LGBT issues and the prevention or reduction of heterosexist attitudes in the practice of psychology? For example, does using social media in counseling psychology programs to inform students, help develop positive images of LGBT individuals, and prevent heterosexism?
2. How do we promote and teach advocacy skills at the community level in our students? Which advocacy skills would be most useful or effective? For example, where in the curriculum should we focus on efforts on teaching students to write letters to their state legislature to reduce heterosexism at the societal and institutional level? Will such attitudes increase advocacy skills as professionals?
3. What is the developmental process by which allies develop? What activities help motivate and empower heterosexual allies to move from paternalistic or stereotypic heterosexist attitudes to LGBT affirming attitudes?
4. Two ongoing societal prevention efforts that counseling psychologists can engage in is advocating for gay marriage legislation and the federal Employment Non-Discrimination Act (ENDA), designed to prohibit workplace discrimination based on a person's sexual orientation (Knauer, 2009).
5. We need more qualitative research on the unique experiences of LGB individuals and how to help support their psychological well-being via advocacy.

References

American Psychological Association. (2010). *Advancing psychology: A psychologist's guide to federal advocacy.* Washington, DC: American Psychological Association. Retrieved from http://www.apa.org/about/gr/advocacy/guide.aspx

American Psychological Association, Committee on Accreditation. (2008). *Guidelines and principles for accreditation of professional programs in psychology.* Washington, DC: American Psychological Association.

American Psychological Association, Commission on Accreditation. (2010). *Policy statements and implementing regulations.* Washington, DC: American Psychological Association.

American Psychological Association, Council of Representatives. (2009, August 5). *Resolution on appropriate affirmative responses to sexual orientation distress and change efforts.* Washington, DC: American Psychological Association.

Balsam, K. F., Beauchaine, T. P., Rothblum, E. D., & Solomon, S. E. (2008). Three-year follow-up of same-sex couples who had civil unions in Vermont, same-sex couples not in civil unions, and heterosexual married couples. *Developmental Psychology, 44*(1), 102–116. doi:10.1037/0012-1649.44.1.102

Baptist, J. A., & Allen, K. R. (2008). A family's coming out process: Systemic change and multiple realities. *Contemporary Family Therapy, 30,* 92–110.

Bartoli, E. (2007). Religious and spiritual issues in psychotherapy practice: Training the trainer. *Psychotherapy: Theory, Research, Practice, Training, 44*(1), 54–65.

Bernal, A. T., & Coolhart, D. (2005). Learning from sexual minorities: Adolescents and the coming out process. *Guidance and Counseling, 20*(3/4), 128–138.

Biaggio, M., Orchard, S., Larson, J., Petrino, K., & Mihara, R. (2003). Guidelines for gay/lesbian/bisexual-affirmative educational practices in psychology programs. *Professional Psychology: Research and Practice, 34,* 548–554.

Bieschke, K. J., Eberz, A. B., Bard, C. C., & Croteau, J. M. (1998). Career counselor attitudes and behaviors toward gay, lesbian, and bisexual clients. *Journal of Vocational Behavior, 48*(2), 243–255.

Bieschke, K. J., & Mintz, L. B. (2009). Rejoinder: Addressing concerns and taking on the third rail. *The Counseling Psychologist, 37*(5), 772–779.

Blackwell, C. W., Dziegielewski, S. F., & Jacinto, G. A. (2006). The use of a strength-based approach in addressing discrimination against gays and lesbians. *Journal of Human Behavior in the Social Environment, 14*(3), 1–17.

Bonds-Raacke, J., Cady, E., Schlegel, R., Harris, R., & Firebaugh, L. (2007). Remembering gay/lesbian media characters: Can Ellen and Will improve attitudes toward homosexuals? *Journal of Homosexuality, 53*(3), 19–34.

Borgman, A. L. (2009). LGB allies and Christian identity: A qualitative exploration of resolving conflicts and integrating identities. *Journal of Counseling Psychology, 56*(4), 508–520.

Bowers, R., Plummer, D., & Minichiello, V. (2005). Homophobia in counselling practice. *International Journal for the Advancement of Counselling, 27*(3), 471–489. doi:10.1007/s10447-005-8207-7

Brigham Young University Honor Code. (2009–2010). Retrieved from saas.byu.edu/catalog/2009–2010ucat/GeneralInfo/HonorCode.php#HCOfficeInvolvement

Buhrke, R., & Douce, L. (1991). Training issues for counseling psychologists in working with lesbian and gay men. *The Counseling Psychologist, 19*(2), 216–234.

Button, S. B. (2001). Organizational efforts to affirm sexual diversity: A cross-level examination. *Journal of Applied Psychology, 86*(1), 17–28. doi:10.1037//0021-9010.86.1.17

Callahan, C. J. (2001). Protecting and counseling gay and lesbian students. *Journal of Humanistic Counseling, Education, and Development, 40,* 5–10.

Callahan, J., Mann, B., & Ruddick, S. (2007). Editors' introduction to writing against heterosexism. *Hypatia, 22*(1), 8–15.

Calzo, J., & Ward, L. (2009). Media exposure and viewers' attitudes toward homosexuality: Evidence for mainstreaming or resonance? *Journal of Broadcasting and Electronic Media, 53*(2), 280–299.

Centers for Disease Control and Prevention. (2010). Lesbian, gay, bisexual, and transgendered health. Retrieved from http://www.cdc.gov/lgbthealth/

Chng, C. L., & Moore, A. (1991). Can attitudes of college students toward AIDS and homosexuality by changed in six weeks? The effects of a gay panel. *Health Values, 15*(2), 41–49.

Chonody, J. M., Siebert, D. C., & Rutledge, S. E. (2009). College students' attitudes toward gays and lesbians. *Journal of Social Work Education, 45*(3), 499–512.

Chung, Y. B., Williams, W., & Dispenza, F. (2009). Validating work discrimination and coping strategy models for sexual minorities. *Career Development Quarterly, 58,* 162–170.

Clark, C. T. (2010). Preparing LGBTQ-allies and combating homophobia in a U.S. teacher education program. *Teaching and Teacher Education, 26,* 704–713.

Cogan, J. C. (1996). The prevention of anti-lesbian/gay hate crimes through social change and empowerment. In E. D. Rothblum & L. A. Bond (Eds.), *Preventing heterosexism and homophobia* (pp. 219–238). Thousand Oaks, CA: Sage.

Cornell, D. (2007). The shadow of heterosexuality. *Hypatia, 22*(1), 229–242.

Counselors for Social Justice. (2008). *CSJ position statement on sexism and heterosexism.* Retrieved from http://counselorsforsocialjustice.com/CSJ_Position_-_Sexism_and_Heterosexism.pdf

Crisp, C., & McCave, E. L. (2007). Gay affirmative practice: A model for social work practice with gay, lesbian, and bisexual youth. *Child Adolescence Social Work Journal, 24,* 403–421.

Croteau, J. M., & Talbot, D. M. (2000). Understanding the landscape: An empirical view of lesbian, gay, and bisexual issues in the student affairs profession. In V. A. Wall & N. J. Evans (Eds.), *Toward acceptance: Sexual orientation and today's college campus* (pp. 3–28). Lanham, MD: University Press of America.

D'Augelli, A. R. (1993). Preventing mental health problems among lesbian and gay college students. *Journal of Primary Prevention, 13,* 245–261.

D'Augelli, A. R. (1996). Enhancing the development of lesbian, gay, and bisexual youths. In E. D. Rothblum & L. A. Bond (Eds.), *Preventing heterosexism and homophobia* (pp. 124–150). Thousand Oaks, CA: Sage.

DePaul, J., Walsh, M. E., & Dam, U. (2009). The role of school counselors in addressing sexual orientation in schools. *Professional School Counseling.* Retrieved from http://www.thefreelibrary.com/The+role+of+school+counselors+in+addressing+sexual+orientation+in . . . -a0198412429

Dickson, G., & Jepsen, D. (2007). Multicultural training experiences as predictors of multicultural competencies: Students' perspectives. *Counselor Education and Supervision, 47*(2), 76–95.

Dickson, G., Jepsen, D., & Barbee, P. (2008). Exploring the relationships among multicultural training experiences and attitudes toward diversity among counseling students. *Journal of Multicultural Counseling and Development, 36*(2), 113–126.

Dillion, F. R., Worthington, R. L, Bielstein Savoy, H., Rooney, S. C., Becker-Schutte, A., & Guerra, R. M. (2004). On becoming allies: A qualitative study on lesbian-, gay-, and bisexual-affirmative counselor training. *Counselor Education and Supervision, 43,* 162–178.

Dixon, J. A., Durrheim, K., Tredoux, C. G., Tropp, L., Clack, B., & Eaton, L. (2010). A paradox of integration? Interracial contact, prejudice reduction and perceptions of racial discrimination. *Journal of Social Issues, 66,* 403–418.

Duhigg, J., Rostosky, S., Gray, B., & Wimsatt, M. (2010). Development of heterosexuals into sexual-minority allies: A qualitative exploration. *Sexuality Research and Social Policy: Journal of NSRC, 7*(1), 2–14. doi:10.1007/s13178-010-0005-2

Eliason, M. J. (1995). Accounts of sexual identity formation in heterosexual students. *Sex Roles, 32*(11/12), 821–833.

Evans, N. J., & Broido, E. M. (2005). Encouraging the development of social justice attitudes and actions in heterosexual students. *New Directions for Student Services, 110,* 43–54.

Fish, J. (2008). Far from mundane: Theorizing heterosexism for social work education. *Social Work Education, 27*(2), 182–193.

Fisher, D., Hill, D., Grube, J., & Gruber, E. (2007). Gay, lesbian, and bisexual content on television: A quantitative analysis across two seasons. *Journal of Homosexuality, 52*(3/4), 167–188.

Foreman, M., & Quinlan, M. (2008). Increasing social work students' awareness of heterosexism and homophobia: A partnership between a community gay health project and a school of social work. *Social Work Education, 27*(2), 152–158. doi:10.1080/02615470701709485

Frost, D. M., & Meyer, I. H. (2009). Internalized homophobia and relationship quality among lesbians, gay men, and bisexuals. *Journal of Counseling Psychology, 56*(1), 97–109. doi:10.1037/a0012844

Frye, M. (1983). *The politics of reality: Essays in feminist theory.* Freedom, CA: Crossing Press.

Glassgold, J. M., & Drescher, J. (2007). *Activism and LGBT psychology: An introduction.* Binghamton, NY: Haworth Medical Press. doi:10.1300/J236v11n03-01

GLSEN. (2009). *National school climate survey.* Retrieved from http://www.glsen.org/cgi-bin/iowa/all/library/record/2624.html?state=research&type=research

Goodenow, C., Szalacha, L., & Westheimer, K. (2006). School support groups, other school factors, and the safety of sexual minority adolescents. *Psychology in the Schools, 45*(5), 573–589. doi:10.1002/pits.20173

Goodman, L., Liang, B., Helms, J., Latta, R., Sparks, E., & Weintraub, S. (2004). Training counseling psychologists as social justice agents: Feminist and multicultural principles in action. *The Counseling Psychologist, 32*(6), 793–837. doi:10.1177/0011000004268802

Graybill, E. C., Varjas, K., Meyers, J., & Watson, L. B. (2009). Content-specific strategies to advocate for lesbian, gay, bisexual, and transgender youth: An exploratory study. *School Psychology Review, 38*(4), 570–584.

Halkitis, P. N. (2010). Reframing HIV prevention for gay men in the United States. *American Psychologist, 65*(8), 752–763.

Hanlon, J. (2009). How educators can address homophobia in elementary schools. *Encounter: Education for Meaning and Social Justice, 22*(1), 32–45.

Hansen, A. L. (2007). School based support for GLBT students: A review of three levels of research. *Psychology in the Schools, 44*(8), 839–850.

Harper, G. H., & Schneider, M. (2003). Oppression and discrimination among lesbian, gay, bisexual, and transgendered people and communities: A challenge for community psychology. *American Journal of Community Psychology, 31*(3/4), 243–252. doi:10.1023/A:1023906620085

Healthy People 2020. (2010). *Lesbian, gay, bisexual and transgendered health.* Retrieved from http://healthypeople.gov/2020/topicsobjectives2020/overview.aspx?topicid=25

Herek, G. M. (2007). Confronting sexual stigma and prejudice: Theory and practice. *Journal of Social Issues, 63*(4), 905–925.

Herek, G. M., & Berrill, K. (Eds.). (1992). *Hate crimes: Confronting violence against lesbians and gay men.* Thousand Oaks, CA: Sage.

Herek, G. M., & Capitanio, J. P. (1996). "Some of my best friends": Intergroup contact, concealable stigma, and heterosexuals' attitudes toward gay men and lesbians. *Personality and Social Psychology Bulletin, 22*(4), 412–424.

Herek, G. M., Gillis, J. R., & Cogan, J. C. (2009). Internalized stigma among sexual minority adults: Insights from a social psychological perspective. *Journal of Counseling Psychology, 56*(1), 32–43. doi:10.1037/a0014672

Hirschfeld, S. (2001). Moving beyond the safety zone: A staff development approach to anti-heterosexist education. *Fordham University School of Law, 29*(2), 1–30.

Hodges, N., & Parkes, N. (2005). Tackling homophobia and heterosexism. *Learning Disabilities Practice, 8*(3), 10–16.

Hooker, E. (1957). The adjustment of the male overt homosexual. *Journal of Projective Techniques, 21,* 18–31.

Horn, S. S., Szalacha, L. A., & Drill, K. (2008). Schooling, sexuality, and rights: An investigation of heterosexual students' social cognition regarding sexual orientation and the rights of gay and lesbian peers in school. *Journal of Social Issues, 64*(4), 791–813.

Hornsby, E. E. (2006). Using policy to drive organizational change. *New Directions for Adult and Continuing Education, 112,* 73–83. doi:10.1002/ace.283

Human Rights Campaign. (2010a). *Corporate equality index: Rating American workplaces on lesbian, gay, bisexual, and transgender equality.* Retrieved from http://www.hrc.org/documents/HRC-CEI-2011-Final.pdf

Human Rights Campaign. (2010b). *HRC Foundation.* Retrieved from http://www.hrc.org/about_us/hrc-foundation.asp

Human Rights Campaign. (2010c). *Parenting laws: Joint adoption.* Retrieved from http://www.hrc.org/documents/parenting_laws_maps.pdf

Human Rights Campaign. (2010d). *Statewide employment laws and policies.* Retrieved from http://www.hrc.org/documents/Employment_Laws_and_Policies.pdf

Israel, T., & Hackett, G. (2004). Counselor education on lesbian, gay, and bisexual issues: Comparing information and attitude exploration. *Counselor Education and Supervision, 43,* 179.

Johnson, M. O., Carrico, A. W., Chesney, M. A., & Morin, S. F. (2008). Internalized heterosexism among HIV-positive, gay-identified men: Implications for HIV prevention and care. *Journal of Counseling and Clinical Psychology, 76*(5), 829–839. doi:10.1037/0022-006X.76.5.829

Keck, T. (2009). Beyond backlash: Assessing the impact of judicial decisions on LGBT rights. *Law and Society Association, 43*(1), 151–186.

Kertzner, R. M., Meyer, I. H., Frost, D. M., & Stirratt, M. J. (2009) Social and psychological well-being in lesbians, gay men, and bisexuals: The effects of race, gender, age, and sexual identity. *American Journal of Orthopsychiatry, 79*(4), 500–510. doi:10.1037/a0016848

Kitzinger, C. T., & Wilkinson, S. (2004). Social advocacy for equal marriage: The politics of "rights" and the psychology of "mental health." *Analyses of Social Issues and Public Policy, 4*(1), 173–194.

Knauer, N. J. (2009). LGBT elder law: Toward equity in aging. *Harvard Journal of Law and Gender, 32,* 1–59.

Kuehl, S. J. (2000). Seeing is believing: Research on women's sexual orientation and public policy. *Journal of Social Issues, 56*(2), 351–359.

Ladany, N., Kaduvettoor, A., & Soheilian, S. (2008). *Footnote 4: APA sanctioned homophobia in psychology training.* Roundtable discussion at the Annual APA Convention Boston.

Land, V., & Kitzinger, C. (2005). Speaking as a lesbian: Correcting the heterosexism presumption. *Research on Language and Social interaction, 38*(4), 371–416.

Levitt, H. M., Ovrebo, E., Anderson-Cleveland, M. B., Leone, C., Jeong, J. Y., Arm, J. R.,... Horne, S. G. (2009). Balancing dangers: GLBT experience in a time of anti-GLBT legislation. *Journal of Counseling Psychology, 56*(1), 67–81. doi:10.1037/a0012988

Lewis, R. J., Derlega, V. J., Brown, D., Rose, S., & Henson, J. M. (2009). Sexual minority stress, depressive symptoms, and sexual orientation conflict: Focus on the experiences of bisexuals. *Journal of Social and Clinical Psychology, 28*(8), 971–992.

Lidderdale, M. A. (2002). Practitioner training for counseling lesbian, gay, and bisexual clients. *Journal of Lesbian Studies, 6*(3/4), 111–120.

Lind, A. (2004). Legislating the family: Heterosexism bias in social welfare policy frameworks. *Journal of Sociology and Social Welfare, 31*(4), 21–35.

Logan, C. R., & Barret, R. (2005). Counseling competencies for sexual minority clients. *Journal of LGBT Issues in Counseling, 1*(1), 3–22.

Maher, M. J., Landini, K., Emano, D. M., Knight, A. M., Lantz, G. D., Parrie, M.,... Sever, L. M. (2009). Hirschfeld to Hooker to Herek to high schools: A study of the history and development of GLBT empirical research, institutional policies, and the relationship between the two. *Journal of Homosexuality, 56,* 921–958.

Matthews, C., & Adams, E. (2009). Using a social justice approach to prevent the mental health consequences of heterosexism. *Journal of Primary Prevention, 30*(1), 11–26. doi:10.1007/s10935-008-0166-4

McDermott, E., Roen, K., & Scourfield, J. (2008). Avoiding shame: Young LGBT people, homophobia, and self-destructive behaviors. *Culture, Health, and Sexuality, 10*(8), 815–829.

Mintz, L., & Bieschke, K. (2009). Counseling psychology model training values statement addressing diversity: Development and introduction to the major contribution. *The Counseling Psychologist, 37*(5), 634–640. doi:10.1177/0011000009331923

Mohr, J. J., Weiner, J. L., Chopp, R. M., & Wong, S. J. (2009). Effects of client bisexuality on clinical judgment: When is bias most likely to occur? *Journal of Counseling Psychology, 56*(1), 164–175.

Moradi, B., Van den Berg, J. J., & Epting, F. R. (2009). Threat and guilt aspects of internalized anti-lesbian and gay prejudice: An application of personal construct theory. *Journal of Counseling Psychology, 56*(1), 119–131. doi:10.1037/a0014571

Muñoz, C., & Thomas, K. (2006). LGBTQ issues in organizational settings: What HRD professionals need to know and do. *New Directions for Adult and Continuing Education, 112,* 85–95.

National Archives. (2010, August 4). *Crimes and victims: Hate crimes.* Retrieved from http://webarchive.nationalarchives.gov.uk/+/http://www.homeoffice.gov.uk/crime-victims/reducing-crime/hate-crime/

Nelson, E. S., & Krieger, S. L. (1997). Changes in attitudes toward homosexuality in college students: Implementation of a gay men and lesbian peer panel. *Journal of Homosexuality, 33*(2), 63–81.

Obear, K. (2000). Best practices that address homophobia and heterosexism in corporations. *Diversity Factor, 9*(1), 26–30.

O'Shaughnessy, M., Russell, S., Heck, K., Calhoun, C., & Laub, C. (2004). *Safe place to learn: Consequences of harassment based on actual or perceived sexual orientation and gender nonconformity and steps for making schools safer.* San Francisco: California Safe Schools.

Patterson, C. J. (1996). Contributions of lesbian and gay parents and their children to the prevention of heterosexism. In E. D. Rothblum & L. A. Bond (Eds.), *Preventing heterosexism and homophobia* (pp. 184–202). Thousand Oaks, CA: Sage.

Pearson, Q. M. (2003). Breaking the silence in the counselor education classroom: A training seminar on counseling sexual minority clients. *Journal of Counseling and Development, 81*(2), 292–300.

Phillips, J. C. (2000). Training issues and considerations. In R. M. Perez, K. A. DeBord, & K. J. Bieschke (Eds.), *Handbook of counseling and psychotherapy with lesbian, gay, and bisexual clients* (pp. 337–358). Washington, DC: American Psychological Association.

Phillips, J. C., & Fischer, A. R. (1998). Graduate students' training experiences with lesbian, gay, and bisexual issues. *The Counseling Psychologist, 26*(5), 712–734.

Poland, S. (2010, January). LGB students need support at school. *District Administration, 46*(1), 44.

Ratts, M. J., & Hutchins, A. M. (2009). ACA advocacy competencies: Social justice advocacy at the client/student level. *Journal of Counseling and Development, 87,* 269–275.

Rees-Turyn, A. (2007). Coming out and being out as activism: Challenges and opportunities for mental health professionals in red and blue states. *Journal of Gay and Lesbian Psychotherapy, 11*(3–4), 155–172. doi:10.1300/J23v11n03_09

Reynolds, A. L., & Hanjorgiris, W. E. (2000). Coming out: Lesbian, gay, and bisexual identity development. In R. M. Perez, K. A. DeBord, & K. J. Bieschke (Eds.), *Handbook of counseling and psychotherapy with lesbian, gay, and bisexual clients* (pp. 35–55). Washington, DC: American Psychological Association.

Riggle, E., Ellis, A., & Crawford, A. (1996). The impact of "media contact" on attitudes toward gay men. *Journal of Homosexuality, 31*(3), 55–69.

Riggle, E. D., & Rostosky, S. S. (2010). Psychological distress, well-being, and legal recognition in same-sex couple relationships. *Journal of Family Psychology, 24*(1), 82–86. doi:10.1037/a0017942

Rostosky, S. S., Riggle, E. D. B., Horne, S. G., & Miller, A. D. (2009). Marriage amendments and psychological distress. *Journal of Counseling Psychology, 56*(1), 56–66.

Russell, G. M. (2010). Outgroup activism: Heterosexual allies in the movement for marriage equality. Paper presented in G. M. Russell (Chair), *Same-sex marriage: Impacts, strategies, and new directions.* Panel at the annual convention of the American Psychological Association, San Diego, CA, August 2010.

Rye, B. J., & Meaney, G. J. (2009). Impact of a homonegativity awareness workshop on attitudes toward homosexuality. *Journal of Homosexuality, 56,* 31–55.

Sanders, G. L., & Kroll, I. T. (2000). Generating stories of resilience: Helping gay and lesbian youth and their families. *Journal of Marriage and Family Therapy, 26*(4), 433–442.

Schiappa, E., Gregg, P., & Hewes, D. (2006). Can one TV show make a difference? *Will & Grace* and the parasocial contact hypothesis. *Journal of Homosexuality, 51*(4), 15–37.

Simoni, J. M., & Walters, K. L. (2001). Heterosexual identity and heterosexism: Recognizing privilege to reduce prejudice. *Journal of Homosexuality, 41*(1), 157–172.

Smith, L., Foley, P. F., & Chaney, M. P. (2008). Addressing classism, ableism, and heterosexism in counselor education. *Journal of Counseling and Development, 86,* 303–309.

Smith, N. G., & Ingram, K, M. (2004). Workplace heterosexism and adjustment among lesbian, gay, and bisexual individuals: The role of unsupportive social interactions. *Journal of Counseling Psychology, 51*(1), 57–67. doi:1037/0022-0167.51.1.57

Smith, S. J., Axelton, A. M., & Saucier, D. A. (2009). The effects of contact on sexual prejudice: A meta-analysis. *Sex Roles, 61,* 178–191.

Stiff, M. (2010, June). *Breaking down barriers: An administrator's guide to state law and best policy practice for LGBT healthcare access.* Retrieved from http://www.hrc.org/documents/HRC_Foundation_-_Breaking_Down_Barriers_-_An_Administrators_Guide.pdf

Stotzer, R. (2007). *Comparison of hate crime rates across protected and unprotected groups.* Retrieved from http://www.policyarchive.org/handle/10207/bitstreams/18080.pdfhttps://www.law.ucla.edu/williamsinstitute/publications/Comparison%20of%20Hate%20Crime%20Formatted.pdf

Stotzer, R. L. (2009). Straight allies: Supportive attitudes toward lesbians, gay men, and bisexual in a college sample. *Sex Roles, 60,* 67–80. doi:10.1007/s11199-008-9508-1

Swim, J. K., Johnston, K., & Pearson, N. B. (2009). Daily experiences with heterosexism: Relations between heterosexist hassles and psychological well-being. *Journal of Social and Clinical Psychology, 28*(5), 597–629.

Szalacha, L. A. (2003). Safer sexual diversity climates: Lesson learned from an evaluation of Massachusetts Safe Schools Program for gay and lesbian students. *American Journal of Education, 110,* 58–88.

Szymanski, D. M., & Carr, E. R. (2008). The roles of gender role conflict and internalized heterosexism in gay and bisexual men's psychological distress: Testing two mediation models. *Psychology of Men and Masculinity, 9*(1), 40–54. doi:10.1037/1524-9220.9.1.40

Toporek, R., & Vaughn, S. (2010). Social justice in the training of professional psychologists: Moving forward. *Training and Education in Professional Psychology, 4*(3), 177–182. doi:10.1037/a0019874

Valenti, M., & Campbell, R. (2009). Working with youth on LGBT issues: Why gay-straight alliance advisors become involved. *Journal of Community Psychology, 37*(22), 228–248. doi:10.1002/jcop.20290

Van Wormer, K., & McKinney, R. (2003). What schools can do to help gay/lesbian/bisexual youth: A harm reduction approach. *Adolescence, 38*(151), 409–420.

Vera, E. M., (2009). When human rights and cultural values collide: What do we value? *The Counseling Psychologist, 37*(5), 744–751.

Walls, N. E. (2008). Toward a multidimensional understanding of heterosexism: The changing nature of prejudice. *Journal of Homosexuality, 55*(1), 20–70.

Watt, S., Curtis, G., Drummond, J., Kellogg, A., Lozano, A., Nicoli, G., et al. (2009). Privileged identity exploration: Examining counselor trainees' reactions to difficult dialogues. *Counselor Education and Supervision, 49*(2), 86–105.

Weinberg, G. (1972). *Society and the healthy homosexual.* New York: St. Martin's.

Winterowd, C., Adams, E., Miville, M., & Mintz, L. (2009). Operationalizing, instilling, and assessing counseling psychology training values related to diversity in academic programs. *The Counseling Psychologist, 37*(5), 676–704.

Worthington, R. L., Savoy, H. B., Dillon, F. R., & Vernaglia, E. R. (2002). Heterosexual identity development: A multidimensional model of individual and social identity. *The Counseling Psychologist, 30,* 496–531.

CHAPTER

30 Preventing Racial Injuries, Promoting Racial Justice

Helen A. Neville *and* Lisa B. Spanierman

Abstract

Although most people publicly abhor individual, interpersonal, and institutional forms of racism, racial oppression persists in the United States. This oppression manifests itself in a host of racial inequalities. In this chapter, we define racism and its corollary White privilege and we outline their contemporary expressions. We present the disrupting racism ecological model to describe the multiple and interlocking systems that create and perpetuate racial oppression. We discuss tertiary and social justice prevention-interventions on college campuses that are designed to increase students' critical consciousness and antiracism action. Next, we review the empirical literature on the influence of diversity courses in general, dialogue courses more specifically, and particular pedagogical practices on developing students' critical consciousness. Additionally, we review the research supporting the effects of cocurricular diversity experiences such as interracial friendships. We conclude with a discussion of the limitations of the extant research and provide future directions for prevention-intervention researchers.

Key Words: racism, white privilege, prevention, social justice, critical consciousness

Preventing Racial Injuries, Promoting Racial Justice

On July 12, 2008, 25-year-old Luis Ramirez suffered a brutal beating at the hands of a group of White teenage males in Shenandoah, Pennsylvania; two days later he died as a result of the injuries that he sustained during the attack. This is one of the many individual acts of racism in the United States against immigrants from Mexico and Central America. At least six witnesses observed the group of White teenagers hurling racial slurs while beating Mr. Ramirez. The two teens charged with the beating were acquitted by an all-White jury on charges of murder and ethnic intimidation. Instead, they were found guilty of simple assault, a much lesser offense that implies no intent to injure. The assailants served no jail time. Questions surfaced about how the jury arrived at its verdict, especially given the eyewitness testimony and the fact that the assailants admitted to yelling something to the effect of "Go home you Mexican!" It seems that the jury relied heavily on the defense attorney's characterization of the beating as a street fight in which Ramirez was the aggressor.

We argue that the portrayal of Mr. Ramirez as the aggressor in a mutual brawl among consenting parties is based, in part, on dominant racist ideologies (i.e., set of racist beliefs that make White supremacy appear natural). Such ideologies are based on anti-immigrant sentiments and practices, stereotypes of Latino males as hot-tempered, and a sense of superior group position where Whites are perceived as better than people of color. These racist ideologies in turn justify the continued subjugation of people of color. In this particular case, anti-Mexican sentiments and racist stereotypes of Latino men served to dehumanize the victim as someone whose undocumented status symbolized a drain on the local economy. At the same time, White supremacist attitudes humanized the assailants as upstanding citizens deserving of a second chance.

Racist ideologies and practices thus played a role in all aspects of the criminal case from the initial police investigation of the murder to the jury decision and subsequent sentencing. People committed to antiracism were outraged by the verdict and pushed for justice. As a result of their efforts, a federal grand jury was formed in December 2009. The federal grand jury charged two of the assailants and three police offers at the federal level for a variety of crimes including a hate crime, extortion, and obstruction of justice. In the federal case, the work of individuals, civil rights organizations, the Federal Bureau of Investigation, and the Department of Justice's Civil Rights Division highlight the ways in which people, communities, and even institutions challenge racial injustice. Success in these sorts of legal endeavors can serve as a disincentive for future crimes and miscarriages of justice. Moreover, these coordinated efforts illustrate that people can work collectively to challenge and disrupt racism. This latter point is critical as it allows us to move beyond the victim-perpetrator paradigm to gain insight into the multiple ways in which people resist oppression and struggle for justice and humanity.

Although people resist injustice, racism persists. We wish we could say that the brutal killing of Mr. Ramirez is an isolated incident and that these types of racist attacks are a thing of the past in the United States. Unfortunately, racially motivated hate crimes have not significantly decreased over the years. All race-based hate crimes do not end in murder, but some do. Recently, James Craig Anderson, a 49-year-old African American family man, was beaten and run over with a truck in Mississippi; his murder by a group of White teenage males was ruled a hate crime. At the time of this writing, only one of the seven defendants was charged with capital murder.

We began the chapter with the tragic and senseless murders of Mr. Ramirez and Mr. Anderson to provide examples of the persistence of (1) racism and racial hatred in the United States, (2) dominant racial beliefs that dehumanize people of color; and (3) the ways in which White supremacy legitimizes individual and collective racist behaviors. The aftermath of the Ramirez trial also provides a counternarrative in which people challenge racial injustice. We titled the chapter "Preventing Racial Injuries, Promoting Racial Justice" because we believe racism is ingrained in the fabric of society and cannot be rooted out without a complete transformation of race relationships in society; thus, short of a revolution, we are unable to prevent racism. The pervasiveness and insidiousness of racism is evident in all aspects of US society, which include dominant core values, political and racial ideologies, and socialization (e.g., media, schools, and families). White supremacy shapes policies that promote and perpetuate racial inequalities.

As such, psychologists are unable to *prevent* racism; what we can do as a profession is work with others to decrease racially motivated hate crimes and disrupt subtle forms of everyday or interpersonal racism that people experience in their interactions with others, such as receiving poor service at a restaurant. We can identify overt, racial hatred in youths and emerging adults and hopefully prevent senseless race-based killings. We also can promote greater awareness about the existence of racism, dominant racial ideologies in society, and the injurious impact of racism on people and communities. This awareness could, in turn, lead to greater empathy for targets of racism, decreased subtle forms of racist actions, and increased antiracism activity. Through education and psychological interventions on micro- and macrolevels, we thus are able to disrupt racism and promote racial justice.

In this chapter, we first define racism and its corollary White privilege to provide the context for disrupting racism, preventing racial injuries, and promoting racial justice. Similar to other scholars (Buhin & Vera, 2009), we adopt an ecological framework to guide our prevention recommendations. We describe our ecological model and outline the key prevention-intervention tasks for disrupting racism and promoting racial justice. Drawing on our earlier work, we adopt the position that everyone is affected by racism, albeit in varying ways (Neville, Spanierman, & Lewis, in press). This assertion is different from the claim that all people are responsible for racism or that all people can be racist. Although we argue that White individuals, too, experience costs of being dominant groups members in a White supremacist system (Neville, Worthington, & Spanierman, 2001), we acknowledge the more egregious consequences of racism for people of color. In addition to racial inequalities in health, income, and education (e.g., Brown, Carnoy, Currie, Duster, & Oppenheimer, 2003), everyday and interpersonal racism experiences have deleterious effects on people of color. For example, findings from three recent meta-analyses documented the link between experiences with perceived racism and lower mental health among Asian and Asian Americans (Lee & Ahn, 2011), Latino/a Americans (Lee & Ahn, 2012), and Black Americans (Pieterse, Todd, Neville, & Carter, 2012).

Beyond individual and interpersonal racism, in this chapter we address the structures and institutions of racism. Moreover, we discuss the ways that people of color and White people interface within these structures; that is, how they collude with or resist racial injustices. Although we provide a broad overview of the literature, we focus on how psychologists can intervene within one system—higher education. Many of counseling psychologists are involved with teaching and training the leaders of tomorrow. We thus have an opportunity to help students unlearn racist beliefs, cultivate empathic understanding of the toll of racism on people of color, and develop critical awareness about the existence of racism.

Defining Racism and White Privilege

Racism is a word used in everyday language; yet, there is little agreement on its definition. In our research and teaching, we have observed a range of responses to the query: "What is racism?" Some students cling to the idea that racism is prejudice against any group of people based on a social identity such as race, gender, and religion and that anyone can be a victim or perpetrator of racism. In these types of definitions, it is difficult to overlook the fact that the person adopting the definition has equated race to other social categories such as gender. Embedded in this perspective is the belief that anyone can be racist. We refer this as the *Crash* approach to racism. The Academy Award–winning Hollywood motion picture *Crash* portrays a series of interracial interactions in which each of the characters regardless of their racial group membership displays racial prejudice. In addition to the *Crash* approach, other students assert that racism may have been a problem in the past, but it is not a major problem today. It is not uncommon for such students to support their beliefs with the observation that the president of the United States is Black, and Oprah, a Black woman, is one of the richest women in America. This second perspective captures a color-blind approach to racism, which we describe in greater detail later in the chapter. These popular conceptualizations of racism represent a restricted definition of racism; the definitions focus on individual level prejudice and fail to consider structural or power issues. We reject this limited analysis. Consistent with most racism scholars we assert that racism involves a system of power relations, in which racial groups are designated as superior (i.e., Whites) or inferior (i.e., people of color).

Our definition of racism draws on the early work of Stokely Carmichael (a.k.a. Kwame Ture) and Charles Hamilton (1967/1992), who proposed a radical conceptualization of racism at the height of the Black power movement. In their book *Black Power: The Politics of Liberation*, they argued that racism was "the predication of decisions and policies on considerations of race for the purpose of *subordinating* a racial group and maintaining control over that group" (original emphasis; p. 3). Carmichael and Hamilton described the essential role of power in creating and maintaining unequal social relationships. They explained that racial inequalities are reproduced through institutional processes. According to these activist-scholars, the term "institutional racism" describes the covert ways in which "respected forces in society," such as law enforcement agencies and school systems, undermine the political, economic, and educational progress of subjugated groups (p. 4). Examples of institutional racism include policies and practices that systematically advantage White people at the expense of people of color, such as unequal educational opportunities. The concept of institutional racism allows for an analysis of the ways in which racism is maintained even when societal norms condemn overt, individual expressions of racial hatred.

In addition to power relations that support and perpetuate a racially stratified society with Whites in positions of power and people of color in subordinate positions, Carmichael and Hamilton (1967/1972) identified outward individual and interpersonal expressions of racism in people's day-to-day lives, including blatant discriminatory acts (e.g., uttering racial slurs and committing racial hate crimes). More recently, scholars have uncovered additional types of interpersonal racism to capture the changing nature of the race relations over the past three decades. The new interpersonal types include more subtle expressions, sometimes making it difficult to discern. For example contemporary forms of interpersonal racism might include demeaning comments such as telling Asian Americans that they speak English well, crossing the street when a Black man is walking in the person's direction, and clinging to a racialized university mascot. These subtle expressions of racism also have been referred to as racial microaggressions (Sue et al., 2007) or everyday racism (Essed, 1991).

Building on Carmichael and Hamilton's initial conceptualization, in this chapter we use Thompson and Neville's (1999) definition of racism, which incorporates contemporary interdisciplinary research. According to Thompson and Neville:

> Racism consists of two interlocking dimensions: (a) an institutional mechanism of domination and (b) a corresponding ideological belief that justifies the oppression of people whose physical features and cultural patterns differ from those of the politically and socially dominant group—Whites. (p. 163)

We thus assert that racism is grounded in power relationships in society in which people of color experience myriad disadvantages on the basis of race, including being the targets of interpersonal racism and enduring racial inequalities in terms of wealth, health, and education.

But what of those who are advantaged in US society? In order to understand disadvantage, it is essential to understand the dimensions of advantage. Oftentimes, discussions of racism fail to consider the ways in which the dominant racial group—Whites—experience systematic advantages in society. Researchers and activists refer to these systematic advantages on the basis of race as White privilege. Critical race theory scholar, Sylvia Lazos Vargas (1998) succinctly described White privilege as the:

> Means [of] having entry to structure and institutions that mete out important economic opportunities, having access to neighborhoods, jobs, credit, and tax benefits that by and large are off limits or available in limited fashion to minorities; it means being presumed competent, intelligent, and hardworking; it means not being discriminated against daily by anyone ranging from a restaurant attendant to a car salesperson. (p. 1527)

Thus, White privilege consists of greater access to resources, normative assumption of self-worth, and escaping penalties such as being discriminated on the basis of race.

Disrupting Racism by Preventing Racial Injuries: An Ecological Model

We propose the *disrupting racism ecological model* to contextualize racism and its many systems as well to highlight the various entry points in which to focus prevention-intervention efforts. The proposed model is grounded in the work of ecological theorist Bronfenbrenner (1979) and psychology scholars who have adapted his framework to describe the process of racism (e.g., Buhin & Vera, 2009; Neville et al., in press). It exemplifies how racism is produced and reproduced over time. As illustrated in Figure 30.1, racism exists in multiple nested systems: chrono-, macro-, exo-, meso-, and microsystems. The chronosystem refers to the time dimension of racism; the conditions and expressions of racism change over time. So, while racial inequalities may exist in wealth, education, and health, the specific expressions of racism may change given the particular era. For example, racism during Jim Crow (i.e., state and local laws that mandated racial segregation) manifested itself differently than racism in the age of Obama (i.e., adoption of a "postracial" perspective that denies the cumulative effects of long-standing structural inequities in education, health care, employment, and wealth). The macrosystem provides the context for the expressions of racism at the individual and interpersonal levels. This consists of the dominant ideologies or worldviews that shape beliefs about race and racism, as well as larger cultural values about what is beautiful, intelligent, and valued.

The articulation of the larger values, norms, and racial formations in the macrosystem are represented in the specific contexts or the exosystem. The exosystem consists of external environments or systems that indirectly affect (and are affected by) individuals and their immediate environments. Examples of the exosystem include the educational system, media, and race-related legislation (e.g., the antiaffirmative action bill Proposition 209 in California and the education bill Arizona HB 2281 that bans ethnic studies in K-12 public schools).

At the center of the model, the microsystem consists of the immediate environments in which an individual functions, including family, peer networks, school, work, and neighborhood. Sometimes, these environments interact and reinforce beliefs and actions that may influence a person's experience; the interaction among immediate environments is referred to as the mesosystem. Individual dynamics and interpersonal relationships exist within these multiple systems. As psychologists, we can work with others to disrupt individual and interpersonal dimensions of racism. That is, we can target troublesome cognitions (i.e., beliefs about race and racism), affect (i.e., emotional responses to racial stimuli), and behaviors (i.e., individual or collective actions taken on the basis of one's cognitions and affect). These prevention-intervention efforts can exist within

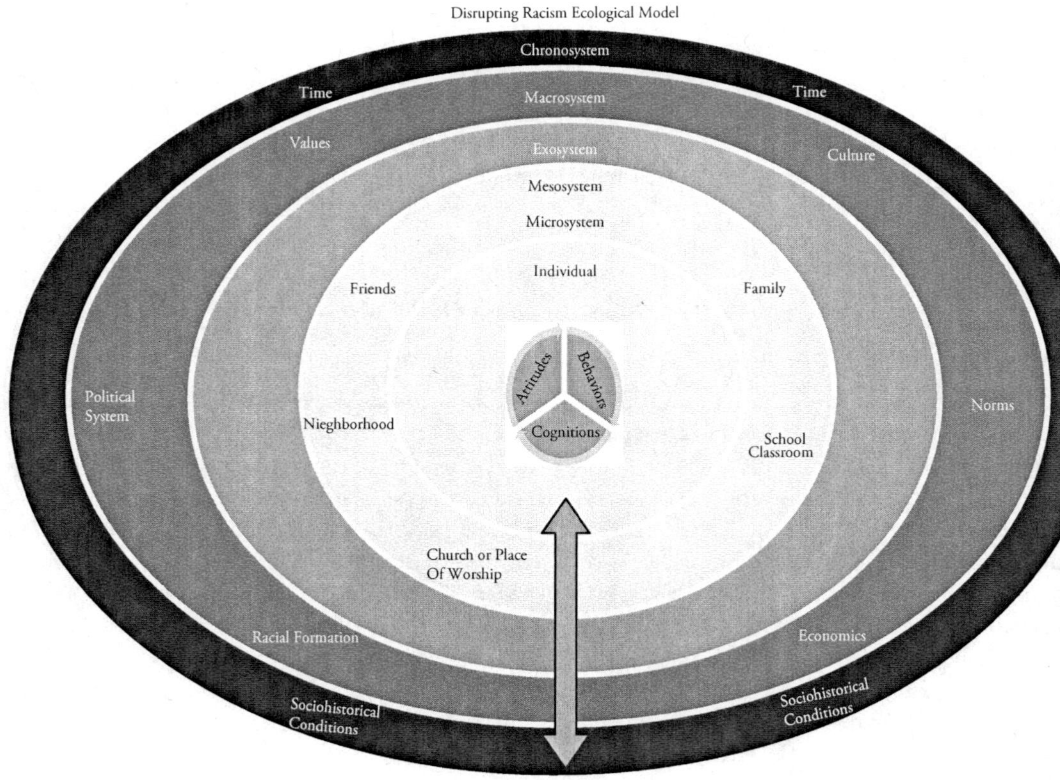

Figure 30.1. Disrupting racism ecological model

one or more contexts such as schools or religious congregations.

Working with others, psychologists can intervene to change racist policies and practices that exist in both proximal (e.g., local high school) and distal (e.g., state and federal educational systems that set school policies) environments. An example of a distal effort is the work of the American Psychological Association (APA) in calling for an end to the use of racist, stereotyped mascots and images. In 2005, the APA passed a resolution calling for the immediate removal of American Indian mascots and symbols that are associated with athletic teams and educational institutions. Drawing on the social science literature (e.g., Fryberg, Markus, Oyserman, & Stone, 2008), the resolution highlights the role of these mascots in perpetuating negative stereotypes, creating racially hostile environments, and serving as a form of racial discrimination. The resolution has supported policy changes in schools and other institutions. Moreover, in May 2011 social psychologist Stephanie Fryberg served as an expert witness for the Senate Committee on Indian Affairs oversight hearing on "Stolen Identities: The Impact of Racist Stereotypes on Indigenous People." In sum, disrupting racism requires action on multiple levels. It extends beyond solely working with people to challenge their individual beliefs and behaviors to transforming immediate environments (e.g., family, peers, and school) and policies and practices that maintain and perpetuate racist practices in society. Disrupting racism also requires an awareness of the particular manifestation of racism at a given historical moment.

What Does Preventing Racial Injuries and Promoting Racial Justice Involve?

Prevention research and practice is varied and involves intervention at several levels. Current conceptualizations of prevention build on Caplan's (1964) original approach to prevent the occurrence, effects, and prevalence of physical diseases. He proposed three prevention levels. Primary prevention involves intervening before a problem even begins with the goal of avoiding the development of unwanted behavior or symptoms. Secondary prevention refers to targeting people at risk for developing a problem before it develops with the goal of delaying the development of the problem. Tertiary prevention, most relevant to our discussion of preventing racial injuries and promoting racial justice, pertains to reducing the negative effects of a problem once it has developed. Because Caplan's health-related notions of prevention do not fully incorporate the role of psychologists in preventing or disrupting social problems such as racism, we augment this conceptualization with Hage et al.'s (2007) idea of prevention. In their conceptualization, prevention extends beyond the traditional primary, secondary, and tertiary paradigm and includes: "strengthening knowledge, attitudes, and behaviors that promote emotional and physical well-being; and . . . promoting institutional, community and government policies that further physical, social, and emotional well-being" (p. 497). Taking into consideration the person-environment context, we assert that increasing people's critical awareness of racism is an aspect of strengthening knowledge that promotes well-being in oneself and in others. Pushing for the adoption of antiracism policies within one's immediate environment also promotes the well-being for all of those operating within the environment. Consistent with the language of Hage and her colleagues, we refer to these prevention efforts as social justice prevention-interventions.

Because racism is deeply embedded in the culture and institutions of the United States, primary prevention efforts (i.e., preventing a problem before it begins) are unrealistic. Children receive messages about the superiority and inferiority of racial groups at a very young age. They receive these messages from watching television programs, engaging with peers, and observing social interactions. If these messages remain unchallenged, they can have a devastating impact on children. For example, children as young as 3 years old begin to develop preferences for White people as being good, beautiful, and smart (Katz, 2003). Unless taught otherwise, many children in the United States adopt these preferences for White. Accordingly, White children may hold negative beliefs about racial minorities, thus subscribing to White superiority beliefs at an early age. These attitudes may in turn influence their social relations as they begin to mature. For racial and ethnic minority children, if these negative and stereotyped messages are not challenged, the children may internalize the negative messages.

A parent shared a painful story with the first author in a project examining Black racial identities that illustrates the internalization of negative racial messages among a young child. At the dinner table, his preschool age son asked: "If I finish my dinner can I become White like Tommy?" The father was surprised and saddened. He had no idea that his son was able to process racial cues and internalize racist messages. In response to this incident, he and his wife made a conscious effort to discuss pride in being Black. This example highlights an underlying premise: as psychologists we are unable to end or stop racism, but instead we can intervene to disrupt racism and its damaging effects among individuals and in systems (e.g., families). We can educate parents and teachers about developmentally appropriate ways to work with youth and emerging adults to challenge beliefs about White superiority. Additionally, we can create prevention-intervention programs to promote racial counternarratives and actions. Educational researcher Lee Ann Bell (2003) and other critical race theorists have explained that people, especially people of color, develop counternarratives that uncover and challenge racism in everyday life. From this perspective, to prevent racial injuries psychologists must be engaged in tertiary intervention efforts (i.e., reducing the negative effects once a problem has developed) to disrupt racism as it manifests within individuals and systems. This can include challenging racist attitudes, beliefs, and actions among White individuals and systems, as well as challenging internalized racism among people (or systems) of color.

Tertiary Racism Prevention: Critical Goals and Efforts That Work in Higher Education

We now shift our attention to feature tertiary and social justice prevention-intervention efforts in one microsystem—higher education. College is a time when students are exposed to new ideas and might challenge previously held assumptions. For many students, especially White students, college represents the first time that they engage in meaningful interactions in heterogeneous spaces in terms of race, ethnicity, religion, international issues, and so forth. During this developmental period, traditionally aged students might explore new identities and redefine themselves. Because there is an opportunity to develop an antiracist identity, it is critical to challenge racist beliefs among White students and internalized racism among students of color. These individuals are the teachers, doctors, lawyers, managers, engineers, and inventors of tomorrow. These future leaders have the opportunity to continue the status quo and perpetuate racial injuries through racial microaggressions, discriminatory practices based on unintended biases (e.g., hiring practices), and supporting policies that unfairly discriminate against and exclude people of color. They also have the opportunity to promote racial justice by engaging in practices and supporting policies that foster the well-being of all people. Psychologists and educators can thus intervene with students during this important developmental period.

Central Goal of Intervention Efforts

On the basis of our conceptualizations of racism and prevention, we assert that the central task of racism prevention-intervention efforts among college students is to promote critical consciousness. Popularized by education theorist Paulo Freire (1971, 1973), critical consciousness or *conscientizacao* refers to awareness of oppression that is embedded within social, economic, and political institutions and action to disrupt oppression. Thus, racial critical consciousness involves two processes: (1) awareness of power and privilege in society with respect to race relations and racial inequality and (2) purposeful action against racial injustice. Both of these processes are consistent with Hage et al.'s (2007) social justice dimension of prevention. Consistent with a Freireian perspective, critical awareness involves engaging questions that explore power in the formation and maintenance of racial inequality such as: "Why do racial disparities exist?" "Why are the high school graduation rates for American Indian, Black, and Latino/a youth significantly lower than their White counterparts?" "Why is the unemployment rate among Black Americans consistently double that of Whites, even when controlling for education level?" "Why are American Indian, Black, and Latino/a individuals underrepresented in the academy, as CEOs of influential companies, and on boards of financial institutions?"

Increasing critical awareness about race and racism involves understanding that racism exists beyond individual prejudice, as does its corollary White privilege. Earlier we provided examples of lay definitions of racism that restrict the concept to individual beliefs that most people can adopt. This limited definition of racism reflects a racial color-blind perspective. As the dominant racial ideology in the United States at this historic moment, color-blind racial ideology (CBRI) refers to a commonly held set of interrelated beliefs that deny or minimize racism (e.g., "Racism may have been a thing of the past, but it is no long a major issue today") or distort racism through adhering to beliefs that people of color have advantages over White people because of their race (Bonilla-Silva, 2003; Neville et al., 2000). People who subscribe to CBRI thus obfuscate racism and evade a power analysis of racism (Frankenberg, 1993).

CBRI pushes for a society in which race(ism) is not considered in understanding one's lived conditions. This is an ideal belief system for a racial utopia. Because the United States is riddled with inequalities based on race(ism), ignoring race only exacerbates the problems and more deeply entrenches the status quo. For example, the "color-blind" educational policy Proposition 209 in California in which race and gender cannot be considered in admission into institutions of higher education has created even greater disparities in enrollment in the University of California system. After the passage of the legislation, the enrollment among Black and Latino/a students in the elite UC schools dropped considerably and has not returned to its pre–Proposition 209 level (Grodsky & Kurlaender, 2010).

CBRI exists in multiple systems as illustrated in the above example. So-called color-blind legislation has harmful effects on its target populations (e.g., students and employees). CBRI also manifests on individual and interpersonal levels. It can be hurtful when a person of color hears someone deny or explain away his or her experiences with racism. For example, we have heard students of color talk about being harassed by campus police as individuals or as groups to illustrate a pattern of racial discrimination on campus. White students often dismiss these stories by explaining these experiences happen to everyone. The denial of racism also manifests itself behaviorally. At the University of Illinois, for example, students wear to class t-shirts with the discontinued racialized mascot, "Chief Illiniwek," even after being told that the shirt represents a racist stereotype that is harmful to students and faculty of color, particularly American Indians. Supporters of the discontinued mascot claim that they are honoring American Indians (see Clark, Spanierman, Reed, Soble, & Cabana, 2011 and Neville et al., 2011). In and of themselves, these images on campus represent racial microaggressions and create hostile learning environments (Clark et al., 2011; Sue et al., 2007).

CBRI is related to a range of negative racial stereotypes, affect, and behaviors. White students who hold higher levels of CBRI endorse greater racial stereotypes and gender intolerance (Neville et al., 2000), racial fear (Spanierman & Heppner, 2004; Spanierman, Poteat, Beer, & Armstrong, 2006), and lower levels of ethnocultural empathy (Burkard & Knox, 2004), social justice beliefs (e.g., Lewis, Neville, & Spanierman, 2012), and awareness of White privilege (e.g., Pinterits, Poteat, & Spanierman, 2009). Among people of color, greater CBRI is related to increased internalized racism (Chen, LePhuoc, Guzman, Rude, & Dodd, 2006; Neville et al., 2005) and lower engagement with social justice issues (e.g., Lewis et al., 2012). One of the central goals of tertiary racism prevention-intervention efforts is thus to challenge CBRI as it manifests in students, faculty, administrators, and campus policies and practices.

Closely linked to challenging CBRI is raising awareness of the existence of White privilege in society and how one has either benefited from or has been disadvantaged by White privilege. Journalism professor and political activist, Robert Jensen (2008) argued, "The ultimate white privilege is to ignore both the statistics and the stories, to hold onto a belief in the fiction of a level playing field, a fair and equitable economy, a color-blind world" (p. 149). In addition to being conceptually and empirically linked to CBRI, lower levels of understanding White privilege are linked to a range of attitudes and behaviors, including increased modern racism attitudes, social dominance orientation or the belief in social hierarchies, and racial fear among Whites (Pinterits et al., 2009).

The next task of social justice prevention-intervention efforts is to promote antiracism action. It is not enough to change attitudes; increased awareness of racism and White privilege are needed to motivate students to take action against racism. There is considerably less research on students' antidiscriminatory behaviors than on prejudice and discrimination. The research in the area highlights the link between racial beliefs and antiracism action. For example, in an innovative study, Stewart, Latu, Branscombe, and Denney (2010) examined antiracism action among a sample of White students attending a predominantly White institution in the southern United States. Drawing on Barack Obama's successful presidential bid and his campaign slogan, "Yes, we can," Stewart and her colleagues solicited help from the student participants to address one discrimination issue on campus—the significant underrepresentation of African American faculty. Participants read a passage explaining the issue on campus and linked the disparity in representation of African American faculty to White privilege. Students were assigned to one of three efficacy conditions; they were told that their efforts to address this problem (via writing a letter to a university administrator and distributing flyers about the issue) had either high, medium, or low efficacy in creating institutional change. Findings suggested that the efficacy condition was related to the students' personal sense of efficacy to create change, which in turn was related to antiracism action. The link between personal effectiveness and antiracism action was mediated by White collective guilt, such that students who endorsed greater perceived personal efficacy in being able to make a difference (or who adopted a "yes, I can" perspective), reported higher levels of race-based guilt, which in turn was related to increased antiracism action.

Promoting Critical Consciousness Through Coursework

Another way that psychologists can intervene in promoting critical consciousness is through fostering positive formal (i.e., courses and workshops) and informal (i.e., social interactions) diversity experiences for students at colleges and universities. Professors and student affairs personnel can join forces to work collectively in these areas to enhance campus climate and create the next generation of leaders who are dedicated to promoting racial justice.

THE INFLUENCE OF DIVERSITY COURSES IN GENERAL ON CRITICAL CONSCIOUSNESS

Consistently, data suggest that college courses, especially those focusing on diversity issues such as racial or ethnic studies or gender and women's studies courses, increase racism awareness and reduce racial prejudice (Denson, 2009; Engberg, 2004; Engberg & Mayhew, 2007). Findings from a recent meta-analysis suggest moderate effects of diversity courses on reduction of racial bias (Denson, 2009). The effect of diversity courses on student beliefs holds true for both required and elective diversity courses (e.g., Cole, Case, Rios, & Curtin, 2011). For example, Chang (2002) investigated the influence of required diversity courses on student racial beliefs. Even after controlling for dispositional factors, students who completed a required diversity course, on average, reported lower levels of racial biases compared to a control group of students who were not enrolled in a diversity course. In terms of support for diversity course experiences in general, Gottfredson and colleagues (2008) examined the complex relations between diversity experiences (e.g., classroom diversity and exposure to multicultural topics in coursework) and outcomes among two samples of law school students. Using hierarchical linear modeling, they found that after controlling for covariates (e.g., age, gender, and LSAT scores), exposure to multicultural course material was associated with both increased attitudes favoring equal opportunity and cognitive openness to cultural diversity; interactions with racially diverse peers was related only to openness to cultural diversity, but not views on equal opportunity.

Denson's (2009) meta-analysis indicates that all students benefit from diversity activities on campus, but that White students benefit to a larger degree. Diversity courses thus may have a different impact on White students compared to students of color. Although a few studies suggest that formal diversity experiences for the most part have a similar influence on students' racial beliefs (e.g., Spanierman, Neville, Liao, Hammer, & Wang, 2008), some studies suggest that diversity courses promote positive racial outcomes for White students only. Lopez (2004), for example, found that after controlling for the influence of racial attitudes at college entrance, participation in diversity-related courses and activities was related to greater levels of social justice attitudes (i.e., awareness of racial inequality and support for educational equity) for White students, but not for Asian American or African American students. Other studies suggest that the impact of diversity courses on students of color depends on the outcome measured. For example, Lewis and her colleagues (2012) examined the link between diversity courses and university-sponsored activities and students' interests in social issues and support for affirmative action. They found that for White students, increased participation in diversity experiences was related to an increase in both outcomes; however, for Black and Latino/a students this association was true for increased interest in social issues, but not increased support for affirmative action. Future research using experimental designs is needed to further explore the potential differential outcomes. Studies also should include racially relevant outcomes, such as White privilege attitudes for White students and racial identity and internalized oppression for students of color.

There is some initial research on the influence of diversity courses on White privilege and racial guilt among White students. For example, among a mostly White sample of undergraduate students (n = 146) enrolled in a general education psychology race and gender course, Case (2007) found that students increased their awareness of racism and White privilege from the beginning to end of the semester. Additionally, she found that White guilt increased among White students as they enhanced their White privilege awareness. Given that increased racial guilt has been linked to greater antiracism action among Whites, this latter finding is particularly important. Methodological limitations temper the findings, however, as a control group was not used.

Emerging qualitative studies in this area help to describe the change process among students enrolled in diversity related courses. In a small sample (n = 5) of students attending a women's liberal arts college, Lawrence and Bunche (1996) found that a multicultural education course about race and racism enhanced White teacher education students' understanding of institutional racism and White privilege. Furthermore, student participants revealed myriad emotions that accompanied this new knowledge (e.g., guilt, anger, and discomfort). Although two of the five students did not abandon their racist socialization by the end of the course, three developed "new white identities" (p. 540). The researchers concluded:

> It seems that race-focused multicultural education can help white students on their journey to unlearn misinformation and provide some guidelines for relearning; it can help white students become more reflective about the effects of racism, and it can influence the development of their racial identities to some degree. (p. 541)

Specific to graduate trainees in applied psychology, Sammons and Speight (2008) examined the changes that students experienced as a result of completing a multicultural counseling course. Using an open-ended critical incidents technique, the researchers found that many students increased their knowledge of multicultural issues (e.g., racial privilege) and self-awareness, but few experienced behavioral changes. Although trainees attributed their changes to a number of course elements (e.g., readings, videos, and instructor influence), most often they mentioned class discussions. Importantly, authors of the above-mentioned studies cautioned against the one-course, one-semester model noting its "limited (albeit important) effect" (Sammons & Speight, 2008, p. 834).

Emerging data also support the influence of diversity courses on beliefs about antiracism action. Among social work undergraduate majors, Nagda and colleagues (2004) found that students who reported greater engagement in diversity related courses and lectures indicated increased confidence in engaging in antiracism action such as challenging someone who makes a racially derogatory joke. Similarly, Kernahan and Davis (2009) found that students who completed a racism course reported greater willingness to take action against racism at the end of the semester compared to students who completed a statistics course.

THE INFLUENCE OF DIALOGUE COURSES ON CRITICAL CONSCIOUSNESS

In addition to typical didactic courses, emerging research has focused on intergroup dialogue courses. Difficult dialogues about race and racism fall within the broad rubric of intergroup dialogues, which are designed to promote critical discussions about prejudice and intergroup conflict with the ultimate goal of working toward social change. Dessel and Rogge (2008) reviewed 23 difficult dialogue studies on a range of topics; 11 of these studies were implemented on college campuses, with the majority centering on race relations. Most of the knowledge in this area is based on nonexperimental designs. Two interrelated longitudinal quasi-experimental designs stand out, both conducted by University of Michigan Professor Patricia Gurin and her colleagues (Gurin, Nagda, & Lopez, 2004; Gurin, Peng, Lopez, & Nagda, 1999); both studies employed a matched comparison control group and both supported the effectiveness of intergroup dialogue activities. Gurin et al. (2004) examined the impact of participation in an intergroup dialogue course on students' democratic sentiments such as perspective taking, self-reported civic activities during college, and anticipated civic activities after graduation. Findings suggested that college seniors who completed an intergroup dialogue course during their undergraduate years reported greater levels of social justice–related outcomes, including participation in campus politics and planning to help promote racial and ethnic understanding after college. Findings lend some support for the role of intergroup dialogue courses in promoting both racial awareness (such as perspective taking) and political action. However, we do not know if these activities were designed to challenge and disrupt racism.

Several qualitative studies highlight the process of change among students enrolled in intergroup dialogue courses. With a particular focus on whiteness, Yeung, Spanierman, and Landrum-Brown (2011) examined undergraduate students (n = 6) enrolled in dialogue course titled "Being White in a Multicultural Society." Reflecting on their experiences during the semester, students reported that they gained knowledge about the existence of institutional racism and White privilege, beyond individual levels. In addition to gaining knowledge about these critical constructs, students reported learning more about themselves as racial beings. For instance, several students reported that they had never thought about their own racial group membership prior to participating in the intergroup dialogue. They also claimed to be better in touch with their emotions around race-related issues as a result of their participation. For example, most experienced White guilt and hopelessness as a result of learning about White privilege. Others spoke of feeling angry upon learning about White domination. Linked to increased knowledge and self-awareness, students reported a number of sociobehavioral outcomes such as disrupting racist jokes, discussing White privilege with their peers outside of class, and pursuing further education about diversity and equity.

SPECIFIC EDUCATIONAL TECHNIQUES THAT WORK

Researchers have investigated the effects of specific educational techniques on increasing critical racial awareness, particularly among White students. Many of these techniques involve the use of some form of print or video media. The ABC Primetime Live Video Segment titled "True Colors" (Pearce & Ross, 1991), for example, is an oft-used pedagogical tool in multicultural courses (see for example Carter, 2003). The 19-minute investigative journalism segment features two discrimination testers—one Black and one White—who were good friends and similar in many respects (e.g., age, dress, mannerisms, and so forth). The discrimination testers interacted with employees in various settings in St. Louis such as a retail store, car dealership, and apartment rental office. In each context, the men were treated differently, in ways that reflected institutional racism and White privilege.

At least one empirical investigation provides data supporting the short-term effectiveness of watching the video among college students. Using an experimental design, Soble, Spanierman, and Liao (2011) randomly assigned White undergraduates to one of two conditions: *True Colors* or a neutral video control condition. They found that students who watched *True Colors* reported an increased awareness of White privilege, institutional racism (i.e., decreased in dimensions of racial color-blindness), empathy about the existence of societal racism, and White guilt immediately after watching the video compared to students in the control condition. In another innovative study, after viewing the film in an undergraduate applied sociology class, students simulated *True Colors* in their own community (see Pence & Fields, 1999). The student discrimination testers reported astonishingly similar results to the original video (e.g., the White tester was offered the apartment for rent while the Black tester was told to call back at a later time). Describing the effects of the experiment, Pence and Fields (1999) explained that the project had an immediate effect on the two student discrimination testers such that they became "disturbed," "confused," and "shocked" (p. 155). When students in the course connected with the material in a personally relevant way, they became outraged and mobilized to conduct racial justice presentations on campus and in the local community.

Discussing Peggy McIntosh's (1988) groundbreaking article on White privilege is another widely used pedagogical tool in diversity education. Lawrence (1996), for instance, asked students to read one of McIntosh's White privileges aloud to their peers during class. White students read the privilege verbatim (e.g., "I can be pretty sure that if I ask to talk to the person in charge, I will be facing a person of my race"), whereas students of color placed a "not" in front of the privilege (e.g., "I can *not* choose blemish cover or bandages in 'flesh' color and have them more or less match my skin"). Students wrote a reflection paper following the experience. Lawrence gleaned the following from White students' responses: (1) several reported a new understanding of racism and White privilege, (2) a range of emotions accompanied this new understanding, and (3) some students developed hope for change (see also Lawrence & Bunche, 1996). In another study among Master's level counseling trainees (n = 34), Ancis and Szymanski (2001) found that White students responded in one of three ways after reading McIntosh's article. The first group of students (almost one third of the sample) reported lack of awareness or denial of White privilege; moreover, they expressed various forms of resistance to or irritation with McIntosh's account. The second group (almost one third of the sample) related a basic awareness of White privilege. These students conveyed sadness and disgust about the existence of racial privilege coupled with an unwillingness to relinquish such privilege. The third group (approximately 40% of the sample) expressed a more comprehensive and complex understanding of White privilege beyond that of the previous group, which also included notions of structural levels of racism and privilege. Notably, among students who achieved this nuanced awareness of White privilege they also reported a commitment to action to disrupt racial privilege.

PROMOTING INTERGROUP FRIENDSHIP AS A STRATEGY TO INCREASE CRITICAL CONSCIOUSNESS

For those campuses that actively recruit a diverse student body, college can provide students opportunities to interact with peers from a variety of racial and ethnic backgrounds. There is mounting empirical evidence documenting the benefits of developing interracial friendships on students in terms of promoting racial awareness, especially among White students (see Neville et al., 2010). There is less written, however, on the ways in which college environments promote these types of interactions. In his influential work on prejudice, psychologist Gordon Allport (1954) observed that increased meaningful intergroup interaction or contact reduced racial and ethnic prejudicial attitudes and behaviors. In Allport's conceptualization, superficial interactions are not strong enough to stimulate change. Instead, interracial interactions must occur in situations in which people interact on equal footing working toward a common collaborative goal. A certain level of trust and social intimacy in the relationship is required for such change to occur. Recent findings, however, indicate that increased intergroup contact can decrease prejudice even when all of these conditions have not been met (see Pettigrew & Tropp, 2008).

There is overwhelming evidence supporting Allport's contact hypothesis, or what scholars have since termed intergroup contact theory. For example, Pettigrew and Tropp (2008) conducted a comprehensive meta-analysis on the link between intergroup contact and prejudice reduction. Across more than 500 studies, they found a small but significant effect supporting the association between increased intergroup contact and decreased prejudice. The studies represent a range of target groups with regard to race, physical ability, sexual orientation, and so forth from around the globe. Although the initial contact hypothesis was designed to capture racial and ethnic prejudice, there were no statistically significant different effects for studies in which racial and ethnic groups were the target compared to those studies in which other social identity groups were targets.

There is growing documentation of the contact-decreased prejudice link specifically in the context of higher education. For example, Antonio (2001) examined the influence of friendship group contact on diversity-related outcomes among students attending a multiracial university. Greater racial diversity in friendship circles and racial diversity in interacting with people outside of this network were both related to increased change in students' perception of cultural awareness and appreciation and a willingness to promote racial understanding. Similarly, Hurtado (2005) found that the quality of interracial interactions resulted in significant increases in educational outcomes consistent with critical consciousness even after controlling for the effects of precollege variables. More specifically, frequent and positive interracial interactions were related to decreased color-blind racial ideology and increased support for institutional racial diversity and civic engagement (e.g., interest in social issues, helping others to vote). Some findings, however, suggest that greater interracial contact promotes more favorable intergroup attitudes for White students but has a negligible effect on racial and ethnic minority students (e.g., Lopez, 2004; Spanierman et al., 2008).

Given the significant number of investigations testing the contact hypothesis, it is surprising that there are few studies examining specific ways courses or universities can promote interracial friendships. There are emerging data on the role of structured learning environments such as living-learning communities in providing students an opportunity to develop such interactions. Using data from the National Study of Living-Learning Programs Residence Environment Survey, Longerbeam (2010) found that perceived supportiveness of one's residence hall in respecting various racial and ethnic groups and in discussing sociocultural issues was related to increased critical thinking skills and civic engagement.

Conclusions and Future Directions

Racism and its corollary White privilege have negative effects on all of those who live in racially oppressive systems. Racism is embedded in every system of the United States, thus making it impossible to eradicate through individual or micro-intervention efforts. Psychologists can however intervene to disrupt racism in most of the interlocking systems within an ecological model and prevent future physical, psychological, economic, and educational injuries. In this chapter, we proposed the disrupting racism ecological model to identify possible entries to prevention efforts. The focus of the chapter was on identifying tertiary, social justice prevention-intervention activities to promote critical consciousness on college campuses. Findings from primarily nonexperimental studies suggest that diversity courses and pedagogical techniques have the potential to enhance students' understanding of race and racism. Furthermore, particular pedagogical techniques such as reading McIntosh's (1988) list of privileges aloud, viewing a video that highlights institutional racism, and testing discrimination in their own communities, seem promising in heightening student outcomes. While courses tend to enhance knowledge of institutional racism and White privilege, as well as students' self-awareness, they do not necessarily decrease racial prejudice or move students to take action against racism.

With notable exceptions, the racism prevention research on college campuses is in early stages of development. Most of the empirical studies do not adopt a prevention framework. As a result, many of the studies employ correlational and nonexperimental designs. The conclusions we are able to draw about the effectiveness of interventions thus are limited. Several quasi-experimental studies have found support for antiracism interventions; however, most of these studies evaluate the effectiveness of a very brief intervention in which only immediate outcomes were assessed. Some researchers have used longitudinal designs and results are promising. Kernahan and Davis (2009), for example, found that students who completed a diversity course increased their awareness of racism (i.e., lower levels of CBRI) and this change was stable over a 1-year period.

Now that empirical foundations for the utility of college level prevention-interventions has been established, future researchers should employ increased methodological rigor by using quasi- and true-experimental longitudinal designs. Findings from these investigations will provide important evidence for the longer-term effectiveness of social justice prevention-intervention efforts. In designing such studies, we encourage researchers to include comprehensive outcome assessments that include both self-report racism indicators and antiracism behavioral indicators. Outcomes also should attend to the specific prevention-intervention goals of the student samples. For example, among White students, researchers should assess awareness of White privilege and experience of White guilt. Among students of color, researchers should examine racial identity development, experiences with racial microaggressions, internalized racism, and resistance to oppression (see Pieterse, Hanus, & Gale, this volume).

Future researchers also must develop more comprehensive theoretical models to describe the development of antiracism action. We know very little about the processes related to the development of antiracism dispositions and behaviors. It appears that increasing White guilt and having meaningful interracial interactions promote critical consciousness among White students. We know less about the factors that may promote critical consciousness among students of color. Thus, theories that capture the complex change process for specific populations are needed to guide prevention-intervention efforts.

Psychologists also can engage in efforts to move beyond single-dose interventions such as one lecture or even one course in which only a select number of students are exposed to the intervention. Instead, they can work collaboratively with other university personnel to completely transform campus environments. Every level of the system (e.g., students, staff, faculty, administrators, policies and procedures) presents a possible entry point for social justice prevention-intervention. Networks of racial justice allies can form collectives by which to promote racial counternarratives, heighten critical awareness of racial issues, and facilitate racial justice behavior. Working together, we can create future generations that think more critically about the effects of racial color-blindness and work actively to disrupt racism.

References

Allport, G. (1954). *The nature of prejudice.* Cambridge, MA: Addison Wesley.

Ancis, J. R., & Szymanski, D. M. (2001). Awareness of white privilege among white counseling trainees. *The Counseling Psychologist, 29*(4), 548.

Antonio, A. L. (2001). Diversity and the influence of friendship groups in college. *Review of Higher Education, 25,* 63–89. doi: 10.1353/rhe.2001.0013

Bell, L. A. (2003). Telling tales: What stories can teach us about racism. *Race Ethnicity and Education, 6,* 3–28.

Bonilla-Silva, E. (2003). *Racism without racists: Color-blind racism and the persistence of racial inequality in the United States.* Lanham, MD: Rowman & Littlefield.

Bronfenbrenner, U. (1979). *The ecology of human development: Experiments by nature and design.* Cambridge, MA: Harvard University Press.

Brown, M. K., Carnoy, M., Currie, E., Duster, T., & Oppenheimer, D. B. (2003). *Whitewashing race: The myth of a color-blind society.* Berkeley: University of California Press.

Buhin, L., & Vera, E. M. (2009). Preventing racism and promoting social justice: Person-centered and environment-centered interventions. *Journal of Primary Prevention, 30,* 43–59.

Burkard, A. W., & Knox, S. (2004). Effect of therapist color-blindness on empathy and attributions in cross-cultural counseling. *Journal of Counseling Psychology, 51,* 387–397. doi:10.1037/0022-0167.51.4.387

Caplan, G. (1964). *Principles of preventive psychiatry.* New York: Basic Books.

Carmichael, S., & Hamilton, C. (1967/1992). *Black power: The politics of liberation.* New York: Vintage.

Carter, R. T. (2003). Becoming racially and culturally competent: The racial-cultural counseling laboratory. *Journal of Multicultural Counseling and Development, 31,* 20–30.

Case, K. A. (2007). Raising white privilege awareness and reducing racial prejudice: Assessing diversity course effectiveness. *Teaching of Psychology, 34*(4), 231–235.

Chang, M. J. (2002). The impact of an undergraduate diversity course requirement on students' racial views and attitudes. *Journal of General Education, 25,* 125–140.

Chen, G. A., LePhuoc, P., Guzmán, M. R., Rude, S. S., & Dodd, B. G. (2006). Exploring Asian American racial identity. *Cultural Diversity and Ethnic Minority Psychology, 12*(3), 461–476. doi:10.1037/1099-9809.12.3.461

Clark, D. A., Spanierman, L. B., Reed, T. D., Soble, J. R., & Cabana, S. (2011). Documenting weblog expressions of racial microaggressions that target American Indians. *Journal of Diversity in Higher Education, 4,* 39–50.

Cole, E. R., Case, K. A., Rios, D., & Curtin, N. (2011). Understanding what students bring to the classroom: Moderators of the effects of diversity courses on student attitudes. *Cultural Diversity and Ethnic Minority Psychology, 17,* 397–405. doi:10.1037/a0025433

Denson, N. (2009). Do curricular and cocurricular diversity activities influence racial bias? A meta-analysis. *Review of Educational Research, 79,* 805–838. doi: 10.3102/00346 54309331551

Dessel, A., & Rogge, M. E. (2008). Evaluation of intergroup dialogue: A review of the empirical literature. *Conflict Resolution Quarterly, 26,* 199–238. doi: 10.1002/crq.230

Engberg, M. E. (2004). Improving intergroup relations in higher education: A critical examination of the influence of educational interventions on racial bias. *Review of Educational Research, 74,* 473–524.

Engberg, M. E., & Mayhew, M. J. (2007). The influence of first-year "success" courses on student learning and democratic outcomes. *Journal of College Student Development, 48,* 241–258.

Essed, P. (1991). *Understanding everyday racism: An interdisciplinary theory.* Thousand Oaks, CA: Sage.

Frankenberg, R. (1993). *White women, race matters: The social construction of whiteness.* Minneapolis: University of Minnesota Press.

Freire, P. (1971). *Pedagogy of the oppressed.* New York: Seabury Press.

Freire, P. (1973). *Education for critical consciousness.* (1st American ed.). New York: Seabury Press.

Fryberg, S. A., Markus, H. R., Oyserman, D., & Stone, J. M. (2008). Of warrior chiefs and Indian princesses: The psychological consequences of American Indian mascots. *Basic and Applied Social Psychology, 30,* 208–218. doi:10.1080/01973530802375003

Gottfredson, N. C., Panter, A. T., Daye, C. E., Allen, W. A., Wightman, L. F., & Deo, M. E. (2008). Does diversity at undergraduate institutions influence student outcomes? *Journal of Diversity in Higher Education, 1,* 80–94.

Grodsky, E., & Kurlaender, M. (2010). *Equal opportunity in higher education: The past and future of California's Proposition 209.* Cambridge, MA: Harvard University Press.

Gurin, P., Nagda, B., & Lopez, G. (2004). The benefits of diversity in education for democratic citizenship. *Journal of Social Issues, 60,* 17–34.

Gurin, P., Peng, T., Lopez, G., & Nagda, B. (1999). Context, identity, and intergroup relations. In D. Prentice & D. Miller (Eds.), *Cultural divides: Understanding and overcoming group conflict* (pp. 133–170). New York: Russell Sage Foundation.

Hage, S. M., Romano, J. L., Conyne, R. K., Kenny, M., Matthews, C., Schwartz, J. P., & Waldo, M. (2007). Best practice guidelines on prevention practice, research, training, and social advocacy for psychologists. *The Counseling Psychologist, 35*(4), 493–566. doi:10.1177/0011000006291411

Hurtado, S. (2005). The next generation of diversity and intergroup relations research. *Journal of Social Issues, 61,* 595–610.

Jensen, R. (2008). Black and white. In B. Singley (Ed.), *When race becomes real: Black and white writers confront their personal histories* (pp. 143–158). Carbondale: Southern Illinois University Press.

Katz, P. A. (2003). Racist or tolerant multiculturalist? How do they begin? *American Psychologist, 58,* 897–909.

Kernahan, C., & Davis, T. (2007). Changing perspective: How learning about racism influences student awareness and emotion. *Teaching of Psychology, 37,* 41–45.

Kernahan, C., & Davis, T. (2010). What are the long-term effects of learning about racism? *Teaching of Psychology, 37,* 41–45. doi:10.1080/00986280903425748

Lawrence, S. M. (1996, Spring). Bringing white privilege into consciousness. *Multicultural Education, 3,* 46–48.

Lawrence, S. M., & Bunche, T. (1996). Feeling and dealing: Teaching white students about racial privilege. *Teaching and Teacher Education, 12*(5), 531–542.

Lazos Vargas, S. L. (1998). Deconstructing homo[generous] Americanus: The White ethnic immigrant narrative and its exclusionary effect. *Tulane Law Review, 72,* 1493–1596.

Lee, D. L., & Ahn, S. (2011). Racial discrimination and Asian mental health: A meta-analysis. *The Counseling Psychologist, 39,* 463–489. doi:10.1177/0011000010381791

Lee, D. L., & Ahn, S. (2012). Discrimination against Latinas/os: A meta-analysis of individual-level resources and outcomes. *The Counseling Psychologist, 40,* 28–65. doi:10.1177/0011000011403326

Lewis, J. A., Neville, H. A., & Spanierman, L. B. (2012). Examining the influence of campus diversity experiences and color-blind racial ideology on students' social justice attitudes. *Journal of Student Affairs Research and Practice, 49*(2), 1–18. doi: 10.2202/1949-6605.6291

Longerbeam, S. D. (2010). Developing openness to diversity in living-learning program participants. *Journal of Diversity in Higher Education, 3*(4), 201–217. doi:10.1037/a0021277

Lopez, G. (2004). Interethnic contact, curriculum, and attitudes in the first year of college. *Journal of Social Issues, 60,* 75–94.

McIntosh, P. (1988). White privilege and male privilege: A personal account of coming to see correspondences through work in women's studies (Working Papers Series No. 189). Wellesley, MA: Wellesley College, Center for Research on Women.

Nagda, B., Kim, C., & Truelove, Y. (2004). Learning about difference, learning with others, learning to transgress. *Journal of Social Issues, 60,* 195–214. doi:10.1111/j.0022-4537.2004.00106.x

Neville, H. A., Coleman, M. N., Falconer, J. W., & Holmes, D. (2005). Color-blind racial ideology and psychological false consciousness among African Americans. *Journal of Black Psychology, 31,* 27–45. doi:10.1177/0095798404268287

Neville, H. A., Lilly, R. L., Duran, G., Lee, R. M., & Brown, L. (2000). Construction and initial validation of the color-blind racial attitudes scale (CoBRAS). *Journal of Counseling Psychology, 47,* 59–70. doi:10.1037//0022-0167.47.1.59

Neville, H. A., Spanierman, L. B., Khuri, L., De La Rosa, B., & Aber, M. S. (2010). Promoting multiracial democratic attitudes among students: Interracial friendships and diversity educational experiences matter. In H. A. Neville, M. B. Huntt, & J. Chapa (Eds.), *Implementing diversity: Contemporary challenges and best practices at predominantly white universities* (pp. 21–41). Urbana: University of Illinois, Center on Democracy in a Multiracial Society.

Neville, H. A., Spanierman, L. B., & Lewis, J. A. (in press). The expanded psychosocial model of racism: A new model for understanding and disrupting racism and white privilege. In N. Fouad & J. Carter (Eds.), *Handbook of counseling psychology.* Washington, DC: American Psychological Association.

Neville, H. A., Worthington, R. L., & Spanierman, L. B. (2001). Race, power, and multicultural counseling psychology: Understanding white privilege and color-blind racial attitudes. In J. G., Ponterotto, J. M. Casas, L. A. Suzuki, & C. M. Alexander (Eds.), *Handbook of multicultural counseling* (2nd ed., pp. 257–288). Newbury Park, CA: Sage.

Neville, H. A., Yeung, J. G., Todd, N. R., Spanierman, L. B., & Reed, T. D. (2011). Color-blind racial ideology and beliefs about a racialized university mascot. *Journal of Diversity in Higher Education, 4*(4), 236–249. doi:10.1037/a0024334

Pearce, K., & Ross, S. (Producers). (1991, September 26). *Primetime Live* [Television broadcast]. New York: ABC News.

Pence, D. J., & Fields, J. A. (1999). Teaching about race and ethnicity: Trying to uncover white privilege for a white audience. *Teaching Sociology, 27*(2), 150–158.

Pettigrew, T. F., & Tropp, L. R. (2008). How does intergroup contact reduce prejudice? Meta-analytic tests of three mediators. *European Journal of Social Psychology, 38*(6), 922–934. doi:10.1002/ejsp.504

Pieterse, A. L., Todd, N. R., Neville, H. A., & Carter, R. (2012). Perceived racism and mental health among Black American adults: A meta-analytic review. *Journal of Counseling Psychology, 59*(1), 1–9.

Pinterits, E. J., Poteat, V. P., & Spanierman, L. B. (2009). The white privilege attitudes scale: Development and initial validation. *Journal of Counseling Psychology, 56*(3), 417–429. doi:10.1037/a0016274

Sammons, C. C., & Speight, S. L. (2008). A qualitative investigation of graduate-student changes associated with multicultural counseling courses. *The Counseling Psychologist, 36*(6), 814.

Soble, J. R., Spanierman, L. B., & Liao, H.-Y. (2011). Effects of a brief video intervention on White university students' racial attitudes. *Journal of Counseling Psychology, 58,* 151–157.

Spanierman, L. B., & Heppner, M. J. (2004). Psychosocial Costs of Racism to Whites scale (PCRW): Development and initial validation. *Journal of Counseling Psychology, 51,* 249–262.

Spanierman, L. B., Neville, H., Liao, H.-Y., Hammer, J. H., & Wang, Y.-F. (2008). Participation in formal and informal campus diversity experiences: Effects on students' racial democratic beliefs. *Journal of Diversity in Higher Education, 1,* 108–125. doi:10.1037/1938-8926.1.2.108

Spanierman, L. B., Poteat, V. P., Beer, A. M., & Armstrong, P. I. (2006). Psychosocial costs of racism to Whites: Exploring patterns through cluster analysis. *Journal of Counseling Psychology, 53,* 434–441.

Stewart, T. L., Latu, I. M., Branscombe, N. R., & Denney, H. T. (2010). Yes we can! Prejudice through seeing (inequality) and believing (in social change). *Psychological Science, 21,* 1557–1562. doi:10.1177/095679761038535

Sue, D. W., Capodilupo, C. M., Torino, G. C., Bucceri, J. M., Holder, A. M. B., Nadal, K. L., & Esquilin, M. E. (2007). Racial microaggressions in everyday life: Implications for clinical practice. *American Psychologist, 62,* 271–286.

Thompson, C. E., & Neville, H. A. (1999). Racism, mental health, and mental health practice. *The Counseling Psychologist, 27,* 155–223.

Yeung, J. G., Spanierman, L. B., & Landrum-Brown, J. (2011). *"Being White in a multicultural society": Understanding whiteness in an intergroup dialogue.* Manuscript submitted for publication.

CHAPTER

31 Cents and Sensibilities: Promoting Mental Health With Sport and Exercise

William D. Parham

Abstract

The focus on prevention is heralded as an area of investigative inquiry and further study of the applications of prevention science and practice across populations, the developmental spectrum, mental health challenges, and social justice domains is encouraged. The observations and comments herein relative to the application of a prevention mindset to sport and exercise will be articulated with a goal of illuminating current views and emerging perspectives. This chapter also doubles as an invitation to counseling psychologists to continue to promote sport and exercise as health and wellness lifestyle activities in which national and international communities can easily, readily, and straightforwardly engage and from which tremendous benefits are virtually guaranteed.

Key Words: mental health, health promotion, sports, athletics, health and wellness

As I begin this narrative I am reminded about recent conversations with collegiate and professional athletic teams as well as with individual athletes with whom I consulted wherein I posed to them the following question: When using MapQuest, if you specify details (address, city, state, zip code) of your current location and enter "East Coast" as your destination, how will MapQuest respond? I'll return later to this question and the responses I receive routinely from these respective audiences. For now, permit me to assert a commonly accepted belief that exercise improves physical health! Investigative reports, both domestic (Bauman, 2004; Beunen, Lefevre, & Philippaerts, 2004; Byberg, Melhus, Gedeborg, et al., 2009; CDC, 2000; Hallal, Victora, Azevedo, & Wells, 2006;) and international (Beunen, Philippaerts, & Delvaux, 2001; Boreham, Robson, & Gallagher, 2004; Hasselstrom, Hansen, Froberg, et al., 2002) extol the health and wellness benefits and virtues of engaging regularly in physical activity. Physical activities that range from simple daily 20-minute walks to rigorous 2- to 3-hour-per-day aerobic workouts have been shown to have positive physical and physiological effects, across the developmental spectrum, relative to reducing risks of several diseases, a nonexhaustive list of which includes cardiovascular diseases (Boreman, Twisk, Neville, et al., 2002; Fletcher, Balady, Amsterdam, et al., 2001; Lefevre, Philippaerts, Delvaux, et al., 2002; Myers, Prakash, Froelicher, et al., 2002; US Public Health Service [USPHS], 1996; Williams, Haskell, Ades, et al., 2007), strokes (Pearson, Blair, Daniels, et al., 2002; Goldstein, Adams, Becker, et al., 2001; Gordon, Contractor, & Leighton, 2001; Macko, Smith, Dobrovolny, et al., 2001; Pearson, Blair, Daniels, et al., 2002; Smith, Blair, Bonow, et al., 2001), hypertension (Bacon, Sherwood, Hinderliter, & Blumenthal, 2004; Cornelissen & Fagard, 2005a; Dickson et al., 2006; Hagberg, Park & Brown, 2000; Hamer, 2006; Park, Song, Cho, et al., 2011; Whelton, Chin, Xin, & He, 2002), some cancers (Calton, Lacey, Schatzkin, Schairer, et al., 2006;

Meyerhardt, Heseltine, Niedzwiecki, et al., 2006; Perkins, Baum, Taylor, & Basen-Engquist, 2009; Tehard, Friedenreich, Oppert, et al., 2006), asthma (National Asthma Education and Prevention Program [NAEPP], 2007; Ram, Robinson, & Black, 2000; Rosimini, 2003), and type 2 diabetes and metabolic syndromes (Anderson, Friedland, Clouse, & Lustman, 2001; DiLoreto, Fanelli, Lucidi, et al., 2005; DPP Research Group, 2002; Hu, Rico-Sans, Lakka, & Tuomilehto, 2006; Morris, 2001). Engaging in regular physical activity has also been shown to strengthen bones, muscles, and joints (Eliakim & Beyth, 2003; Khan, McKay, & Haapasalo, 2000; MacKelvie, Khan, & Petit, 2003) and help in the management of obesity (Alfano, Klesges, Murray, et. al., 2002; Anderson, Wadden, Bartlett, et al., 1999; Bray, 2011; Jakicic, Marcus, Gallagher, et al., 2003; Lee, Djousse, Sesso, et al., 2010; Parsons, Power, Logan, et al., 1999), and back pain (Fuchs, Larson, & Zaichkowsky, 2001; Mikkelsson, Nupponen, Kaprio, et al., 2006). Related, regular physical activity helps promote better sleep (American Academy of Sleep Medicine [AASM], 2008; Brassington, 2001; Horne & Staff, 1983; Jacobs, 2010; Kubitz, Landers, Petruzzello, & Han, 1996; O'Connor, & Youndstedt, 1995; Youndstedt, O'Connor, & Dishman, 1997), reduces susceptibility to the common cold (Cohen, Tyrell, & Smith, 1991), and positively influences sexual activity (Penhollow & Young, 2004; White, Case, McWhirter, & Mattison, 1990). Thus, research supports what intuitively seems reasonable: that exercise positively influences physical health.

These aforementioned observations represent what Brannon and Feist (2010) articulate as examples of a third revolution in health care, namely the revolution characterized by terms such as well-being and wellness as key foci of health care research, education, and interventions. The focus of the second revolution was on eliminating degenerative diseases. The first health revolution, according to these authors, was characterized by a national push to improve sanitation and develop, market, and promote immunizations and vaccinations across the developmental life span, all with the goal of eliminating infectious diseases. Medical advances and related scholarship in these aforementioned areas continue to be evident.

Mental Health and Mental Illness

It is within the context of the third revolution that national and international science- and practice-based conversations about mental health sprang forth in significant volume and continue to command a leading presence in the discourse about holistic health care. Published reports (US Department of Health and Human Services [US DHHS], 1996, 1999, 2008; US Surgeon General, 1999, 2001; WHO, 2005; CDC 2000) and abundant scholarship (Deslandes, Moraes, Ferreirs, Veiga, et. al, 2009; Keyes, 2005; Patel & Prince, 2010; Power, 2010; Shephard, 2001) illuminate mental health as a must-be-included factor in thinking about the overall longevity and quality of individual and community health and well-being. This conclusion, however, has not always been stated strongly as seems to be the case currently.

Contextual Parameters

Investigations of the relationship between exercise and mental health prior to 1970 (Cureton, 1963; Layman, 1960), including the often not cited even earlier work of Franz and Hamilton (1905), advanced conclusions that can be described variously as less than definitive, more timid, less sure, more speculative, and clearly hesitant in their proclamation. The largely only inferential conclusions drawn during those early years about the relationship between exercise and mental health were rooted in at least four observations including definitional challenges, poor research designs, reliance on correlation analyses, and skewed population samples (Cureton, 1963; Layman, 1960; Leith, 1994; Morgan, 1988).

For example, attempts to identify the mechanisms that trigger the mental health benefits of exercise resulted early and progressively in the advancement of three explanations. Scholars argued in favor of advancing physiological explanations. Represented under this umbrella of explanations is the thermogenic hypothesis (a rise in the core body temperature from exercise leads to improved mood) (deVries, 1968; Horne & Staff, 1983) the endorphin hypothesis (increased beta-endorphins post exercise bring on mental health benefits (Christie & Chester, 1982; Christie & Chester, 1982; Steinberg & Sykes, 1985; Colt, Wardlaw & Frantz, 1981), and the monamine hypothesis (psychological benefits arise from an increase in neurotransmitters) (Dishman, 1997; Ebert, Post, & Goodwin, 1972; Post, Kotin, & Goodwin, 1973). Numerous definitional and measurement challenges preclude common agreements about these aforementioned hypotheses. Martinsen (1990) and Farrel (1989) further recognize that the difficulty in studying the physiological mechanisms presumed to be associated with mental health benefits is due in large measure to the need for research subjects to succumb to invasive procedures.

Psychological mechanisms were advanced under the second umbrella of explanations regarding the alleged connection between exercise and mental health benefits. The distraction hypothesis (exercising distracts persons from worrying and feeling distressed) (Bahrke & Morgan, 1978) and the self-efficacy hypothesis (confidence in personal abilities to accomplish tasks) (Bandura, 1997; Gleser & Mendelberg, 1990; Sonstroem, 1978) characterized this set of explanations.

Social mechanisms were advanced as the third umbrella of explanations regarding the exercise–mental health benefits relationship. The social interaction hypothesis (participating in regular physical exercise leads to increased social interactions, which then leads to improved mood and decreased levels of anxiety and depression) represents the main explanatory thesis associated here.

Prompted by the definitional and measurement challenges characteristic of early exercise–mental health benefit investigations and capitalizing on the aforementioned hypotheses regarding the alleged exercise–mental health connection, scholars engaged in more rigorous investigative approaches including using more complex research designs (Leith, 1994; Leith & Taylor, 1990; Morgan, 1988), shifting from more amorphous constructs such as self-esteem and personality to constructs that were more specific and targeted such as depression and anxiety. In at least the last 20 years, as Landers (1997) comments, there has been a noticeable increase in meta-analyses of research designed to illuminate the exercise–mental health relationship. These well critiqued analyses allowed for stronger proclamations to be asserted. As a result of the aforementioned more detailed attention to this area of scholarship, the association between exercise and mental health has been stated more strongly. Several summative analyses (Biddle, Fox, Boutcher, et al., 2000; Coon, Boddy, Stein, et al., 2011; Craft & Landers, 1998; Edwards, 2000, 2001; Faulkner & Sparkes, 1999; Faulkner & Taylor, 2005a; Hendrick & Van der Ouderaa, 2010; Kennard & Lopez, 2003; Leith, 2010; Long & Van Stavel, 1995; Peluso & Guerra de Andrade, 2005; Lutz, 2007; Petruzzelo, Landers, Hatfield, Kubitz, & Salazar, 1991) by Landers (1997), who proclaimed, "there is now ample evidence that a definite relationship exists between exercise and improved mental health" that "is particularly evident in the case of a reduction of anxiety and depression" (p. 5).

Nonetheless, from a scientific point of view, understanding and appreciating the complexities of the exercise–mental health benefits relationship remains formidable. For myriad context-based reasons including but not limited to cultural, sociological, religious/spiritual, and scientific measurement, "official" universally accepted definitions of and precise ways of measuring mental health continue to feel elusive (World Health Report, 2001). In addition, interspersed throughout conversations regarding exercise and mental health are terms such as "quality of life," "enjoyment," "life satisfaction," "longevity," "wellness," "well-being," "fitness," "physical activity" "sport," "competition," and "leisure," to name a few, all of which also lack commonly accepted definitions and multiple measurement challenges. These aforementioned health-related terms, similar to the challenges of defining and measuring "mental health" are relative and require some appreciation of the contexts within which they occur and are expressed and measured.

Relative to expression, for example, quality of life can be expressed as and defined by an individual's subjective appraisal of their overall life experience. Alternatively, quality of life also can be viewed by an individual comparatively, wherein current experiences and opportunities, when compared to how life used to be, are now felt appreciably quite different. What's more, quality of life can be defined by areas of a person's current life experiences where some areas (e.g., work, financial stability) are perceived concurrently to be better than other areas such as interpersonal relationships, family functioning, and pursuit of leisure activities. In addition to an individual context, quality of life can be defined within the contexts of family, team, or organization. Arguably, middle and higher socioeconomic status families enjoy a different quality of life than families struggling below the poverty line. Relative to athletic teams, the quality of life on a team enjoying the fruits of longtime winning and earned status as a champion can be experienced quite differently than teams that struggle with longtime shame of losing. Quality of life within a longtime financially profitable organization can differ appreciably than the quality of life within a small financially troubled organization. Terms such as, "Life satisfaction," "enjoyment," "longevity," "wellness," and "well-being" are equally personal and subjective experiences that can, and usually do, vary across dimensions of time, situations, socialization, economics, politics, culture, race, ethnicity, gender, sexual orientation, religion, and other indices of individual and group identity.

Relative to measurement, quality of life, for example, can be expressed and measured by individual subjective experiences and/or measured using alleged-to-be-objective instruments (e.g., questionnaires, paper-pencil, symptom profiles, structured interviews, etc.) deemed normative on relevant populations. Methodological factors (e.g., population, sample size, control groups, response bias, data collection mechanisms, generalizability of the data, etc.) coupled with person-in-environment factors (e.g., culture, race, ethnicity, gender, sexual identity, religion, age, family, community, traditions, to name a few), impact a researcher's ability to capture close to true "wellness," "well-being" or "quality of life" experiences. Related, given the aforementioned methodological and person-in-environment factors, generalizing a true picture of "wellness," "well-being," and "quality of life" seems formidable. Capturing these aforementioned terms within the context of age-related levels of appreciation also is important to consider. The younger generation is often less concerned about the longer term consequences of their current exercise and health practices compared to senior citizens, whose awareness of health-related consequences of a life lived having employed varying degrees of exercise may be experienced more acutely (Fitzpatrick, Fletcher et. al, 1992). Conversations about "longevity" (Shephard et al., 1981) spawn numerous other questions of context relative to defining and measuring quality of life and related experiences.

Terms such as "exercise." "physical activity." "competition." and "sport" bait definitional and measurement questions about type and kind of activities. These activities also raise questions about level of play ranging from youth, high school, collegiate, professional, elite, to Olympic level competition. And, what about the activities (e.g., pick-up games, organized neighborhood or fitness club leagues) and level of play in which "weekend warriors" engage? How do researchers identify representative samples and capture exercise/mental health benefit profiles that can be generalized? These aforementioned areas also raise questions regarding frequency (e.g., Does participation in sport, exercise, physical activity and competition occur, daily, weekly, monthly?), duration (For what length of time do individuals participate in sport, competition, physical activity, and exercise?), and intensity (With what level of vigor, force, and power do individuals engage in sport, competition, exercise, or physical activity?).

The purpose and scope of this chapter is not to identify a complete list of methodological challenges inherent in defining terms, measuring exercise experiences, or proclaiming what constitutes true resultant mental health benefits. Nor is the purpose and scope of this chapter to provide solutions to these challenges. Several scholars (Biddle, 1995; Craft & Landers, 1998; Cureton, 1963; Glenister, 1996; Gleser & Mendelberg, 1990; Landers, 1997; Layman, 1972; Long & vanStavel, 1995; Mostofsky & Zaichkowsky, 2001; Morgan, 1982, Morgan & Goldston, 1987; Petruzzello, 1995) have commented extensively across time regarding these concerns. Rather, the purpose and scope of this narrative is to illuminate some of the contexts that are needed in order to frame, understand, and appreciate ongoing conversations regarding the relationship between mental health and exercise.

Baseline Core Agreements: Mental Health, Mental Illness

That said, and despite the methodological challenges and related person-in-environment influences identified above, there appear to be commonly held beliefs that mental health/mental illness includes the presence of certain core features. Further, scientific confirmation isn't always needed to confirm what feels intuitively obvious. For example, few would argue against the belief that mental health/mental illness are experiences shared universally irrespective of a person's gender, race, creed, color, nationality, country of origin, ancestral heritage, religious/spiritual beliefs or social, political, or economic status.

Equally agreed on with an intuitively correct feel is the belief that mental health/mental illness experiences can be represented as continuous variables the appreciation of which comes about by using high and low descriptive markers on continuums of values such as quality and functionality. Related, mental health/mental illness are viewed as experiences that are dynamic, fluid and fluctuating to some degree across time and situations. Mental health is not a dichotomous variable, where you either have it or you don't and it is not a static, one-point-in-time experience.

Further, mental health/mental illness are commonly seen as dispositional attributes. Mental health appears to spawn positive intrapersonal, interpersonal, and community benefits. Mental health is also associated with prosocial behaviors

(Richards, Campenni & Muse-Burke, 2010), feelings of personal confidence and competence, positive self-esteem, personal control (Strine, Chapman, Balluz, & Mokdad, 2008), flexibility to respond to life's expected and unexpected challenges, stability, and feeling grounded (Richards, Campania, & Muse-Burke, 2010; Strine, Chapman, Balluz, & Mikdad, 2008). Conversely, mental illness is perceived to be a negative attribute and interferes with intrapersonal satisfaction and self-care, interpersonal relationships, and decision making relative to taking charge of one's life. Mental illness is associated with felt and measurable decreases in self-esteem, confidence, competence, personal control and mastery, and personal and cultural identity (Myers, Sweeny, & Witmer, 2000).

Lastly, mental health–mental illness and physical health–physical illness go hand in hand. One can't be fully understood or appreciated without the other. Contrary to a belief of 17th-century philosopher Rene Descartes, the mind and body are one. *Mental Health: A Report of the Surgeon General* (US DHHS, 1999) is clear in this regard.

Baseline Core Agreements: Exercise

Similar to the assertions in the aforementioned narrative about mental health/mental illness, and irrespective of inherent definitional and measurement challenges, there also appear to be common intuitively obvious core agreements about exercise. One intuitively obvious core agreement centers on the notion that exercise, at a basic level, represents myriad physical movement activities in which (with varying degrees of age and health-related cautions and/or physical limitations) the global citizenry can freely, easily, readily and instantly engage. Deciding to walk for 20 minutes, perform calisthenics, push-ups, sit-ups, leg raises, lunges, squats; perform core strengthening and stability exercises; and practice deep breathing represent movement activities that can all be done now, notwithstanding location and equipment and needing only to decide how much time to spend and energy to express.

Equally agreed on and obvious is the belief that deciding to engage in physical movement, irrespective of the kind, type, duration and intensity, ushers in opportunities to set and accomplish goals. Thus, success is readily built in. Lastly, and building on these first two agreements, movement activities can be measured relative to the frequency, duration and intensity in which the activity is engaged. Thus, progress along multiple dimensions can be charted.

Moving Forward

These juxtaposed common agreements about mental health and exercise respectively when aligned with the voluminous research and scholarship that sprung forth and evolved over the last five decades resulted in a body of work, relative to the exercise–mental health relationship, that feels especially timely today. Consistent with this assertion, investigative reports, both domestic (Landers & Arent, 2001; Biddle, Fox, Boutcher, & Faulkner, 2000; Callaghan, 2004; Daley, 2002; Dishman & Jackson, 2000; Edwards, 2002; Faulkner & Taylor, 2005; Gleser & Mendelberg, 1990; Hendricks & van der Ouderaa, 2010; Jensen, Decker, & Anderson, 2007; Jones & O'Beney, 2004; Kennard & Lopez, 2003; Landers & Arent, 2007; Paluska & Schwenk, 2000; Pate, Pratt, Blair, et al., 1995; Peluso & Guerra de Andrade, 2005; Rendi, Szabo, Szabo, Velenczei, & Kovacs, 2008; US HHS, 1999, 1996; Walsh, 2011; Wand & Murray, 2008) and international (Fox, 2000; Glenister, 1996; Martinsen, 1995; Mental Health Foundation UK, 2005; Ruastorp, Mattsson, Svensson & Stahle, 2006; Utter & Denny, 2006, Utter, Denny, Robinson, Ameratunga, & Watson, 2006; Warburton, Nicol, & Bredin, 2006; World Federation for Mental Health, 2004; Xu, Anderson, & Courtney, 2010) wax lyrical about the mental health and wellness benefits and virtues of engaging regularly in exercise. Further, these benefits are heralded to be seen across the developmental spectrum. Relative to the potential for improving mental and psychological wellness, variously defined, scholars have canvassed and written about a wide area of mental health topics, a nonexhaustive list of which includes depression (Babyak, Blumenthal, Herman, et al., 2000; Balkin, Tietjen-Smith, Caldwell, & Shen, 2007; Blake, 2009; Craft & Landers, 1998; Craft & Perna, 2004; Dunn, Trivedi, Kampert, Clark, & Chambliss, 2005; Faulkner & Taylor, 2009; Lawlor & Hopker, 2001; Martinsen, 1987, 1994, 1990; Mutrie, 2000; North, McCullagh, Tran, et al., 2010; Slawson, 2005; Yoo, Tackett, Crabbe, Bunnell, & Dishman, 2000), anxiety (Edenfield & Blumenthal, 2011; Landers & Petruzzello, 1994; Long & van-Stavel, 1995; Mayo Clinic Staff, 2005b; Petruzzello, 1995; Salmon, 2001; Schlicht, 1994; Taylor, 2000), serious mental illness (Carless & Douglas, 2008; Connolly & Kelly, 2005; McDevitt & Wilbur, 2006; Pelham, & Campagna, 1991; Richardson, Faulkner, McDevitt, et al., 2005), self-esteem (Boyd & Hrycaiko, 1997; Driver & O'Connor, 2003; Edwards, Edwards, & Basson, 2004; Fox, 2000; Schmalz, Deane, Birch, & Davison, 2007;

Sonstroem, 1984; Spence, McGannon, & Poon, 2005; Spence, Poon, & Dyck, 1997), confidence (Perkins, Baum, Taylor, Carmac, & Basen-Engquist, 2009; Stein, Fisher, Berkey, & Colditz, 2007), and panic disorder (Broocks, Bandelow, Pekrun, et al., 1998; Meyer, Broocks, Hillmer-Vogel, & Ruther, 1997).

A nonexhaustive list of investigations studying exercise and its relationship to mental health includes gender (Janney, Richardson, Holleman, et al., 2010) and domestic populations such as children (Ekeland, Heian, & Hagen, 2005; Ekeland, Heian, Hagen, Abbott, & Nordheim, 2004; Gruber, 1986; Larun, Nordheim, Ekeland, Hagen, & Heian, 2006; Sibley & Etnier, 2003), adolescents (Baumeister, Campbell, Krueger, & Vohs, 2003; Kirkcaldy, Shephard, & Siefen, 2002; Rees & Sabia, 2010), the elderly (Arent, Landers, & Etnier, 2000; Blake, Mo, Malik, & Thomas, 2009; Blumenthal, Babyak, Moore, et al., 1999; Churchhill, Galvez, Colcombe, et al., 2002; Colombe & Kramer, 2003; Elavsky, McAuley, Motl, et al., 2005; Fratiglioni, Paillard-Borg, & Winblad, 2004; Hein, Abreu, & Ottenbacher, 2004; Kritz-Silverstein, Barrett-Connor, & Corbeau, 2001; Mayo Clinic Staff, 2005; Motl, Konopack, McAuley, et al., 2005; Pargman, 2011; Poon, Chodzko-Zajko, & Tomporowski, 2006; Singh, Clemens, & Fiatarone, 2001; Tomporowski, 2006; Windle, Hughes, Linck, Russell, & Woods, 2010), teachers (Nishida & Otomo, 2010), the military (Perlman, Cohen, Altiere, et al., 2010), persons going through rehabilitation (Hutchinson, Skrinar, & Cross, 1999), persons with chronic illness and disability (Graham, 2008), and students (Bass, Enochs, & DiBrezzo, 2002; Castelli, 2005; Kantomaa, Tammelin, Demakakos, Ebeling, & Taanila, 2010; Peden, Rayens, Hall, & Beebe, 2001; Tremblay, Inman, & Wilms, 2000; Warner, 2004). Collectively, these and other scholars (Cox, Thomas, Hinton, & Donahue, 2004; Lochbaum, Karoly, & Landers, 2004; Mostofsky & Zaichkowsky, 2001) also have shared observations that suggest that feeling mentally healthy positively influences participation in exercise and that exercise participation aimed at feeling physically healthy and fit positively influences self-perception and confidence.

The Bad News/Good News

Why is the foregoing important? The aforesaid narrative about mental health is offered for consideration based on two "bad news" observations. One primary "bad news" observation fueled the narrative about exercise.

Regarding the first "bad news" observation about mental health, according to the World Health Organization (2001) and the US surgeon general's reports mental illness is a significant problem that adversely impacts close to half of the global population, a reality heretofore "profoundly underestimated" (US DHHS, 1999). What's more, according to the same source, "mental illness, including suicide, ranks second in the burden of disease in established market economies." Specific to depression, from age 15 to 44 depression is a leading cause of disability in the United States. Related, depression ranks second to heart disease in the magnitude of disease burden (a measure of premature life lost and years lived with a disability of specified severity and duration), the top five of which include (1) Ischemic heart disease, (2) Unipolar major depression, (3) Cardiovascular disease, (4) Alcohol use, and (5) Road traffic accidents. During adulthood, one in five Americans have their lives interrupted by mental illness. Mental health problems manifest in families irrespective of social class and background. Anxiety, depression, and schizophrenia are especially present during adulthood. Predictions suggest that mental illness among the elderly will become a significant public health as well as economic problem.

When viewed through the lens of culture, race, and ethnicity, African Americans are more likely to struggle with mental illness than their Anglo counterparts. Native Americans are represented disproportionately with depression and substance use. Asian Americans when seeking mental health services are disproportionately misdiagnosed as problem-free. Hispanic women tend to struggle more than Hispanic men with depression. These and numerous other mental health/mental illness profiles when observed within the context of culture, race and ethnicity are not surprising. The *US Surgeon General Report on Culture, Race, and Ethnicity* (2001), a supplement to the 1999 report, affirms that culture, race, and ethnicity importantly influence the expression of mental health–mental illness in and among American ethnic communities. The Office of Minority Health and Health Disparities has also been vocal on this subject. Despite the very significant presence of mental illness nationally, Regier et al. (1993) and Kessler et al. (1999) remind us that almost two thirds of all persons with diagnosable mental disorders do not seek treatment. Wang, Berglund, Olfson, et al. (2005) add an important dimension when they proclaim that people struggling with mental illness do not access care, on average, until 10 years post development of their illness.

A second "bad news" observation relative to mental health is that treating mental illness is a costly endeavor. According to the US surgeon general's report (US DHHS, 1999) the direct costs for treating mental illness including substance use and Alzheimer disease cost 99 billion dollars. Alarmingly, 69 billion of the total went alone toward the treatment of mental disorders. Indirect costs for mental disorders totaled 79 billion dollars. Lost productivity at work, disruptive interpersonal relationships, and adversely impacted family systems are just a few of the by-products of this very concerning public health problem.

Relative to exercise, there is one "bad news" observation offered for consideration. Despite the recorded immediate and sustained benefits of regular exercise and irrespective of the proliferation of health and fitness programs and state of the art facilities and equipment, the vast majority of US citizens do not engage in regular physical activity. Weinberg and Gould (2011) captured a snapshot of rates of engagement in regular physical activity across industrialized countries and shared these nonexhaustive "narrative photos" for consideration. According to the authors, physical activity levels across industrialized countries begin to decline at about age 6 and continue to decline throughout life. Obesity across industrialized countries in men grew from 12% in 1991 to 19.8% in 2000. Among American adults, in 2000, 56.4% were obese compared to 45% in 1991. Among youth ages 12–21 years approximately half do not engage regularly in physical activity. Fifty percent (50%) of persons who begin a program of regular exercise will cease doing their program in 6 months. The list goes on!

According to the *President's Council on Physical Fitness and Sports Research Digest* (2008) physical inactivity is consistently higher for minority children than their Anglo counterparts. Further, physical inactivity in childhood influences physical inactivity in adolescence, which especially for African American and Hispanic girls becomes a public health challenge as they age given that hyperactivity, obesity, and type 2 diabetes are associated with inactivity. Space does not permit listing and detailing factors that contribute contextually to this rather bleak physical activity profile. Suffice it to say that the aforementioned volume of physical activity is a huge problem that begs aggressive, creative, and strategic attention.

Promising Trends

The belief that physical fitness is important to an overall healthy lifestyle is not new. President Dwight D. Eisenhower, in 1956, and in response to growing concerns regarding the overall physical health of American citizens, created the Council of Youth Fitness and declared this new Council as a cabinet level position. Every American president since then has added their touch to this ongoing program and strengthened their respective resolves to find solutions to a very troubling epidemic. Still going strong, this program now known as the President's Council on Physical Fitness and Sports is, in essence, an advisory committee of volunteers advising the president through the secretary of health and human services. The voices of the various President's Council on Physical Fitness and Sports committees throughout the years have continued to be heard through their primary publication, *President's Council on Physical Fitness and Sports Research Digest*. A nonexhaustive list of topics covered include physical activity guidelines for Americans, promoting physical activity communities for people with disabilities, physical activity in minority communities, and physical activities for children.

No doubt, the President's Council on Physical Fitness and Sports influenced the emergence of an exciting nationwide undertaking, known as the US National Physical Activity Plan (http://www.physicalactivityplan.org/NationalPhysicalActivityPlan.pdf).

The US National Physical Activity Plan represents a large and full-scale set of initiatives, programs, and policies targeting the increase in physical activity across populations (children, youth, adults, elders) in America. This public and private sector collaborative project boast a simple North Star vision: "One day, all Americans will be physically active and they will live, work and play in environments that facilitate regular physical activity." The long-term goal of this very sustainable project is to influence eight societal sectors, namely: (1) business and industry; (2) education; (3) health care; (4) mass media; (5) parks, recreation, fitness, and sports; (6) public health; (7) transportation, land use, and community design; and (8) volunteer and nonprofit. This plan was released initially in 2010. Both of these aforementioned physical fitness movements evidence promises for positive changes in the overall physical and mental health and wellness of individuals and communities.

Future Directions

Despite increased and more definitive clarity from decades of research about the mental health and wellness benefits gleaned from exercise and physical activity, efforts to close the definitional and measurement gaps are still ongoing. Similar conclusions can be drawn about definitions and measurement of experiences like quality of life, wellness, life satisfaction, exercise, and physical activity. In essence, the study of the interactive complexity between exercise and mental health, though encouraging, suggests strongly that much work needs to be done! The multiple contexts (e.g., cultural, social class, political, individual, group, community, domestic, international) within which these interactively complex experiences can be viewed adds a measure of complication to this challenge.

As a way of solving definitional and measurement challenges relative to the exercise–mental health relationship, researchers may want to consider employing more sophisticated research designs, increasing the utilization of qualitative research methods (Crone & Guy, 2008) and generating new investigative strategies. Regarding research designs, advancing the study of the relationship between exercise and mental health in meaningful ways requires increased use of randomized control trials (RCT). The random assignment of participants (thus reducing threats to external validity and increasing attributional quality of the intervention), reduction in systematic errors (increasing the likelihood of pure or true findings), and blind assessment of measures (reducing bias in selected treatment and outcome measures) collectively elevates RCT as the high-bar standard of choice in research designs. Despite the challenges and limits inherent in employing a randomized control trial design in some settings such as community-based environments (Sanson-Fisher, Bonevski, Green, & D'Este, 2007) scientists have seen fit to consider RCT as such a gold standard that they established guidelines, also known as the CONSORT statement (Begg, Cho, Eastwood, et al., 1996; Moher, Schultz, & Altman, 2001), the significance of which is represented in the reality that peer-reviewed health-related and medical journals now require authors to follow the CONSORT guidelines.

The opportunity to discover individual and environmentally based nuanced mediators of behaviors within and across groups ushers in for consideration the increased use of qualitative approaches when conducting research on the relationship between exercise and mental health (Kaptchuk, 2001; Kazdin, 2003). Using structured interviews and focus group formats as tools for capturing realities of urban living, for example, might result in discovering that personal safety or too much cement and not enough grass are factors contributing to less frequent implementation of a runner's outdoor-based fitness regimen. Lack of availability of workout facilities might hamper the efforts of persons living in rural communities from employing their physical fitness program. Irrespective of culture, race, ethnicity, gender, sexual orientation, social class, or religious affiliation, qualitative research strategies hold promise for uncovering barriers to and illuminating facilitators of exercise and physical activities across populations and across the developmental spectrum.

Regarding generating other research strategies, consideration might be directed to involving global research partners concurrently studying populations using technology (live streaming video, face time, etc.) that captures real-time profiles and performances of persons participating actively in exercise and physical activities. What discoveries will be made, across investigators, using side-by-side comparisons of like behavioral and attitudinal expressions of exercise and physical activity and relating said expressions to perceived or real mental health benefits?

Relative specifically to exercise and physical fitness, motivational readiness of individuals and communities to commence and then follow through with regular exercise and physical activities represents ripe areas of investigative inquiry. Related, ways of making engagement in regular exercise and physical activities fashionable, versus simply a response to threats of adverse health consequences for failure to do so, also merits exploration. In this regard, the President's Council on Physical Fitness and Sports and the US National Physical Activity Plan has identified potentially useful strategies. An added pursuit baits the question: Does motivational readiness to commence and follow through with regular exercise and physical activities vary by domestic and global expressions of culture, race, ethnicity, social class, and religion across gender and across the developmental spectrum?

With respect to scholarly outlets, editors of sport and exercise science journals may want to consider increasing the number of "special issues" wherein each issue represents one major contribution to which invited scholars from around the world share their respective person-in-environment contextually nuanced responses. The authors of the major contribution then prepare a rejoinder to the collective responses from the invited authors. Translating research into sustained and user-friendly health and wellness interventions and programs for the consumer rounds out this set of challenges.

Concluding Remarks—Personal and Otherwise

As I bring this discussion to a close allow me to return to the question posed at the beginning of this chapter. The question is: When using MapQuest, if you specify details (address, city, state, zip code) of your current location and enter "East Coast" as your destination, how will MapQuest respond? Invariably, respondents to these questions share that they would immediately receive directions to their desired location. When told that their answer is incorrect they appear momentarily puzzled. When given additional specifications relative to their destination (in stead of "East Coast" the destination is now "New York") they are again asked how will MapQuest respond. Feeling more assured given the increased specificity of their new destination audiences usually reply to the question as they did earlier that is, believing that they will receive directions to their desired destination. When they are told, again, that their answer is incorrect, their puzzled faces turn into ah ha!-moments of satisfaction when they learn that they will receive the directions to their targeted destination when even more specific information (e.g., address, city, state, zip code) is provided. Further, audiences are reminded that their specific longitude/latitude coordinates relative to their current location and desired destination will yield three bits of information. The MapQuest information that will be received includes: (1) a picture showing starting and termination points, (2) narrative text detailing turn right/turn left/go straight directions, and (3) the approximate time it will take to complete the journey. As an added bonus, and because the longitude and latitude coordinates of the current location and destination are known, should the route selected for travel become impassable the global position satellite (GPS) unit, undeterred by the challenge, will immediately recalculate route and generate an alternative road on which to travel.

This recollection of conversations with athletes with whom I have worked is offered as segue into some final comments. The evolution of the study of the relationship between exercise and mental health and wellness, though impressive, continues to bait solutions for the conceptual and methodological challenges that come with the territory. The investigative work that will provide increased understanding and appreciation of the complexities of the exercise-mental health and wellness relationship is ongoing and promising!

Also ongoing but alarming is the increased awareness of national and global, across populations and across the developmental spectrum, levels of exercise and physical inactivity coupled with the growing burdens of mental illness and the seemingly endless costly tolls, financial and otherwise, imposed by these present-day realities. In essence, the scientific quest for an understanding and appreciation of the exercise–mental health relationship is not keeping pace with the ever growing and costly mental illness concerns with which individuals, families, and communities must daily and increasingly contend. Interventions aimed at responding proactively to this urgent situation need to be asserted sooner than later! From an applied perspective, The President's Council of Physical Fitness and Sport and the US National Physical Activity Plan remain leaders in this regard.

From an academic perspective the scholarship of Bronfenbrenner (2005) and Bronfenbrenner and Morris (2006) holds tremendous promise for the study of the relationship between exercise and mental health. Models of behavior change, of which there are many, vary to some degree mostly relative to variables believed to affect change. Irrespective of these differences, however, all models of behavior change promote a commonly agreed on belief that behavior is best understood by studying the complex interaction across time of individuals and the environment within which they function.

Bronfenbrenner's bioecological model (2005) represents a macroparadigmatic attempt to illuminate developmental aspects or characteristics of the individual (e.g., biological, psychological, emotional, social) as these characteristics interface with multilevel subsystems in the environment. The subsystems identified by Bronfenbrenner include microsystemic factors (e.g., families, institutions), mesosystemic factors (e.g., interactions between families and institutions), exosystemic factors (communities, policies, laws), and macrosystemic factors (e.g., all of the above systems within the context of cultures.). This model that highlights the complex interplay within and between individuals and the surrounding ecological systems serves as a conceptual template for investigating phenomena (in the case of this chapter, exercise and mental health) across the developmental spectrum thus allowing for a closer examination of age appropriate responses to myriad intrapersonal, interpersonal, and systemic realities. Related, this model offers a way of looking simultaneously at an individual's motivational readiness to engage tasks and activities and the environmental opportunities and prohibitions that may preclude an individual's participation in individual, family, school, or community activities (Bouffard, Wimer, Caronongan, et al., 2006; Mahoney, Larson, & Eccles (2005).

Staying with the academic perspective, the scholarship of Eccles (1983), who introduced the Eccles expectancy-value model has a tremendous upside. Like the Bronfenbrenner (2005) model that is rooted within a developmental framework, the developmental underpinnings of the Eccles model serve as a backdrop to a premise that choices to engage in activities such as fitness activities are influenced strongly by the importance (value) an individuals assigns to the activity and the individual's beliefs about their ability to succeed and have future successes in the targeted activity (expectancy). The myriad contexts including culture, race, ethnicity, social class, gender, sexual orientation, and religious affiliation within which the value-expectancy concept is operative remain fertile territory to examine.

Moving forward, the study of the relationship between exercise and mental health is a complex undertaking and the urgent need to pursue with due haste an aggressive research agenda aimed at shifting inactivity to increased activity, across groups, domestic and international, is warranted (Dixon, 2010; Dzewaltowski, Estabrooks & Glasgow, 2004). In parallel, thinking creatively and perhaps in the avant-garde about developing and marketing fashionable and hip exercise and physical activity programs also seems essential. Three considerations stimulate these next steps. First, the need to approach investigations that address the exercise-mental health relationship within theoretical frameworks that are rooted in development across the life span can't be underscored enough. Physical activity versus inactivity varies by many factors, and age represents a key context within which this reported variability is understood and appreciated.

Second, research strategies that employ randomized control trials and qualitative approaches using structured focus group formats aimed at capturing nuanced appreciation of personal and environmental mediator variable are essential (deVreede, van Meeteren, Samson, Wittnik, Duursma & Verhaar, 2007; Donnelly, Hill Jacobsen, et. al, 2003). This strategy is especially important in national and global communities challenged by the confines and constrictions of urban blight, social class, environmental corruption, and political strife.

Third, the positions advanced in this conversation call attention to the need to return to the basics. Identical to a functioning GPS system with specific current location and destination longitude and latitude coordinates, 21st century exercise–mental health relationship researchers and practitioners might consider employing the intuitively obvious core agreements about exercise and mental health as origination coordinates.

To recap, intuitively obvious core agreements about exercise suggest that irrespective of time and location and within the context of personal limitations, exercise and physical activity are free, readily accessible, able to be implemented now and able to be measured and charted. Relative to mental health, the intuitively obvious core agreements suggest that mental health/mental illness are not either/or experiences. Rather, they represent experiences using high and low descriptive markers on continuums of values such as quality and functionality. From these starting points, exercise-mental health researchers and practitioners might consider establishing clear, specific, able-to-be-seen 5–10 years down the road, North Star destination images of landmark research and state-of-the-art exercise and physical activity programs. The clarity of one's current location relative to the locked-on coordinates of their desired destination increases appreciations of the journey, reduces frustration getting from one point to another and fosters anticipatory excitement about achieving a targeted goal.

The cents (e.g., decreased costs, financial and otherwise) and sensibilities (the ability to perceive and appreciate surrounding influences) associated with achieving increased exercise and physical activity while simultaneously improving quality and function of mental health and wellness, across populations and across the developmental spectrum seem apparent. The journey to produce gold-star standard research and state-of-the-art exercise and physical activity programs is sure to be wrought with expected and unexpected twists and turns and possible roadblocks. However, anticipatory excitement comes in knowing that irrespective of the research and applied challenges experienced along the way the North Star journey to improve overall quality of living will be achieved, even if it comes along a recalculated route.

References

Alfano, C. M., Klesges, R. C., Murray, D. M., Beech, B. M. & McClanahan, B. S. (2002) History of sport participation in relation to obesity: and related health behaviors in women. *Preventive Medicine, 34*, 1, 82–89.

American Academy of Sleep Medicine (AASM). (2008). Moderate exercise can improve sleep quality of insomnia patients.

ScienceDaily. Retrieved October 21, 2010, from http://www.sciencedaily.com/releases/2008/06/080611071129.htm

Anderson, R. J., Freedland, K. E., Clouse, R. E., & Lustman, P. J. (2001). The precalence of comorbid depression in adults with diabetes: A meta-analysis. *Diabetes Care, 24,* 1069–1078.

Andersen, R. E., Wadden, T. A., Bartlett, S. J., Zemel, B., Verde. T. J., & Franckowiak, S. C. (1999). Effects of lifestyle activity vs. structured aerobic exercise in obese women: A randomized trial. *Journal of the American Medical Association, 281,* 335–339.

Arent, S. M., Landers, D., & Etnier, J. L. (2000). The effects of exercise on mood in older adults: A meta-analytic review. *Journal of Aging and Physical Activity, 8,* 407–430.

Arent, S. M., Rogers, T. J., & Landers, D. (2001). Mental health and physical activity. *Sportwissenschaft, 31,* 239–254.

Babyak, M., Blumenthal, J., & Herman, S. (2000) Exercise treatment for major depression: Maintenance of therapeutic benefit at 10 months. *Psychosomatic Medicine, 62*(5), 633–638.

Bacon, S. L., Sherwood, A., Hinderliter, A., & Blumenthal, J. A. (2004). Effects of exercise, diet, and weight loss on high blood pressure. *Sports Medicine, 35,* 307–316.

Bahrke, M. S., & Morgan, W. P. (1978). Anxiety reduction following exercise and meditation. *Cognitive Therapy and Research, 2,* 323–333.

Balkin, R. S., Tietjen-Smith, T., Caldwell, C., & Shen, Y.-P. (2007). The utilization of exercise to decrease depressive symptoms in young adult women. *Adultspan Journal, 6*(1), 30–35.

Bandura, A. (1997). *Self-efficacy: The exercise of control.* New York: Freeman.

Bauman, A. E. (2004). Updating the evidence that physical activity is good for health: An epidemiological review 2000–2003. *Journal of Science and Medicine in Sport, 7,* 6–19.

Baumeister, R. F., Campbell, J. D., Krueger, J. I., & Vohs, K. D. (2003). Does high self-esteem cause better performance, interpersonal success, happiness or healthier lifestyles? *Psychological Science in the Public Interest, 4*(1), 1–44.

Begg, C., Cho, M., Eastwood, S., Horton, R., Moher, D., Olkin, I., et al. (1996). Improving the quality of reporting of randomized controlled trials. The CONSORT statement. *Journal of the American Medical Association, 276*(8), 637–639.

Beunen, G. P., Lefevre, J., & Philippaerts, R. M. (2004). Adolescent correlates of adult physical activity: A 26-year follow-up. *Medicine and Science in Sports and Exercise, 36,* 1930–1936.

Beunen, G. P., Philippaerts, R. M., & Delvaux, K. (2001). Adolescent physical performance and adult physical activity in Flemish males. *American Journal of Human Biology, 13,* 173–179.

Biddle, S. J. H., Fox, K., Boutcher, S. H., et al. (2000) The way forward for physical activity and the promotion of psychological well-being. In S. J. H. Biddle, K. Fox, & S. H. Boutcher (Eds.), *Physical activity and psychological well-being* (pp. 154–168). London: Routledge.

Blake, H., Mo, P., Malik, S., & Thomas, S. (2009). How effective are physical activity interventions for alleviating depressive symptoms in older people? A systematic review. *Clinical Rehabilitation, 23*(10), 873–887.

Blumenthal, J. A., Babyak, M. A., Moore, K. A., et al. (1999). Effects of exercise training on older patients with major depression. *Archives of Internal Medicine, 159,* 2349–2356.

Boreham, C., Robson, P. J., & Gallagher, A. M. (2004). Tracking the physical activity, fitness, body composition and diet from adolescence to young adulthood: The Young Hearts project, Northern, Ireland. *International Journal of Behavioral Nutrition and Physical Activity, 1*(1), 14.

Boreham, C., Twisk, J., Neville, C., et al. (2002). Associations between physical fitness and activity patterns during adolescence and cardiovascular risk factors in young adulthood: The Northern Ireland Young Hearts Project. *International Journal of Sports Medicine, 23*(1), 22–26.

Bouffard, S., Wimer, C., Caronongan, P., Little, P., Dearing, E., & Simokins, S. D. (2006). Demographic differences in patterns of youth out-of-school time activity participation. *Journal of Youth Development, 1*(1), 24–39.

Brannon, L. & Feist, J (2010) *Health Psychology: An Introduction to Behavior and Health.* Belmont, CA.: Wadsworth.

Brassington, G. S. (2001). Sleep problems. In D. L. Mostofsky & L. D. Zaichkowsky (Eds.), *Medical and psychological aspects of sport and exercise* (pp. 193–204). Morgantown, WV: Fitness Information Technology.

Bray, G. A. (2011). Role of physical activity and exercise in obesity. Retrieved July 12, 2011, from http://www.uptodate.com/contents/role-of-physical-activity-and-exercise-in-obesity

Bronfenbrenner, U. (2005). *Making human beings human: Bioecological perspectives on human development.* Thousand Oaks, CA: Sage.

Bronfenbrenner, U., & Morris, P. (2006). The bioecological model of human development. In W. Damen & R. M. Lerner (Eds.-in-Chief) & R. M. Lerner (Vol. Ed.), *Handbook of child psychology: Vol. 1. Theoretical models of human development* (pp. 793–828). Hoboken, NJ: Wiley.

Broocks, A., Bandelow, D., Pekrun, G., et al. (1998). Comparison of aerobic exercise, clomipramine, and placebo in the treatment of panic disorder. *American Journal of Psychiatry, 155,* 603–609.

Brown, W. J., Burton, N. W., & Rowan, P. J. (2007). Updating the evidence on physical activity and health in women. *American Journal of Preventive Medicine, 33*(5), 404–411.

Byberg, L., Melhus, H., Gedeborg, R., et al. (2009). Total mortality after changes in leisure time physical activity in 50 year old men: 35 year follow-up of population based cohort. *British Medical Journal, 338,* b688.

Callaghan, P. (2004). Exercise: A neglected intervention in mental health care. *Journal of Psychiatric and Mental Health Nursing, 11*(4), 476–483.

Calton, B. A., Lacey, J. V., Schatzkin, A., Schairer, C., et al. (2006). Physical activity and the risk of colon cancer among women: A prospective cohort study. *International Journal of Cancer, 116*(2), 386–391.

Carless, D., & Douglas, K. (2008). The role of sport and exercise in recovering from serious mental illness: Two case studies. *International Journal of Men's Health, 7*(2), 137–156.

Carr, D., & Friedman, M. A. (2005). Is obesity stigmatizing? Body weight, perceived discrimination, and psychological well-being in the United States. *Journal of Health and Social Behavior, 46,* 244–259.

Castelli, D. M. (2005). Academic achievement and physical fitness in third-, fourth- and fifth-grade students. *Research Quarterly for Exercise and Sport, 76*(1), A-15.

Centers for Disease Control and Prevention. (2000). *Physical activity and good nutrition: Essential elements for good health.* Atlanta, GA: Author. Retrieved from http://www.cdc.gov/nccdphp/dnpa/dnpaaag.htm

Christie, M. J., & Chester, G. B. (1982). Physical dependence on physiologically released endogenous opiates. *Life Science, 30,* 1173–1177.

Churchhill, J. D., Galvez, R., Colcombe, S., Swain, R. A., et al. (2002). Exercise, experience, and the aging brain. *Neurobiology of Aging, 23,* 941–955.

Cohen, S., Tyrell, D. A. J. & Smith, A. P. (1991) Psychological stress and susceptibility to common cold. *New England Journal of Medicine, 325,* 606–612

Colcombe, S., & Kramer, A. F. (2003). Fitness effects on cognitive function of older adults: A meta-analytic study. *Psychological Science, 14,* 125–130.

Colt, E. W. D., Wardlaw, S. L. & Frantz, A. G. (1981) The effects of running on plasma B-endorphin. *Life Sciences,* 28, 14, 1637–1640.

Connolly, M., & Kelly, C. (2005). Lifestyle and physical health in schizophrenia. *Advances in Psychiatry Treatment, 11,* 125–132.

Coon, J. T., Boddy, K., Stein, R., et al. (2011). Does participating in physical activity in outdoor natural environments have a greater effect on physical and mental well-being than physical activity indoors? A systematic review. *Environmental Science and Technology, 45*(5), 1761–1772. doi: 10.1021/es102947t

Cornelissen, V., & Fagard, R. (2005a). Effects of resistance training on resting blood pressure: A meta-analysis of randomized controlled trials. *Journal of Hypertension, 23,* 251–259.

Cornelissen, V., & Fagard, R. (2005b). Effects of endurance training on blood pressure, blood pressure-regulating mechanisms, and cardiovascular risk factors. *Hypertension, 46,* 667–675.

Cotman, C. W., Berchtold, N. C., & Christie, L. A. (2007). Exercise builds brain health: Key roles of growth factor cascades and inflammation. *Trends in Neuroscience, 30*(9), 464–472.

Craft, L. L., & Landers, D. (1998). The effects of exercise on clinical depression and depression resulting from mental illness: A meta-analysis. *Journal of Sport and Exercise Psychology, 20,* 339–357.

Craft, L. L., & Perna, F. M. (2004). The benefits of exercise for the clinically depressed. *Primary Care Companion Journal of Clinical Psychiatry, 6*(3), 104–111.

Crone, D., & Guy, H. (2008). I know it is only exercise, but to me it is something that keeps me going: A qualitative approach to understanding mental health service users' experiences of sports therapy. *International Journal of Mental Health Nursing, 17*(3), 197–207.

Cureton, T. K. (193) Improvement of psychological states by measures of physical fitness programs. *IJournal of the Association for Physical and Mental Rehabilitation, 17,* 14–25.

Daley, A. J. (2002). Exercise therapy and mental health in clinical populations: Is exercise therapy a worthwhile intervention? *Advances in Psychiatric Treatment, 8,* 262–270.

Deslandes, A., Moraes, A., Ferreira, C., Veiga, H., et al. (2009). Exercise and mental health: Many reasons to move. *Neuropsychobiology, 59*(4), 191–198.

deVreede, P. L., vanMeeteren, N. L., Samson, M. M., Wittnik, H. M., Duursma, S. A., & Verhaar, H. J. (2007). The effects of functional tasks exercise and resistance exercise on health-related quality of life and physical activity: A randomized control trial. *Gerontology, 53,* 12–20.

deVries, H. A., Beckman, P., Hubner, H., et al. (1968). Electromyographic evaluation of the effects of sauna on the neuromuscular system. *Journal of Sport Medicine and Physical Fitness, 8,* 1–11.

Dickinson, H. O., Mason, J. M., Nicolson, D. J., et al. (2006). Lifestyles interventions to reduce raised blood pressure: A systematic review of randomized controlled trials. *Journal of Hypertension, 24,* 215–233.

DiLoreto, C., Fanelli, C., Lucidi, P., et al. (2005). Make your diabetes patients walk: Long-term impact of different amounts of physical activity on type 2 diabetes. *Diabetes Care, 28*(6), 295–302.

Dishman, R. K. (1997). The norepinephrine hypothesis. In W. P. Morgan (Ed.), *Physical activity and mental health.* Washington, DC: Taylor & Francis.

Dishman, R. K., & Jackson, E. M. (2000). Exercise, fitness, and stress. *International Journal of Sport Psychology, 31,* 175–203.

Dixon, D. (2010). Exercise psychotherapy. In R. A. Carlstedt (Ed.), *Handbook of integrative clinical psychology, psychiatry, and behavioral medicine: Perspectives, practices, and research* (pp. 737–754). New York: Springer.

Donnelly, J. E., Hill, J. O., Jacobsen, D. J., et al. (2003). Effects of a 16-month randomized controlled exercise trial on body weight and composition in young, overweight men and women: The Midwest Exercise Trial. *Archives of Internal Medicine, 163,* 1343–1348.

DPP Research Group. (2002). Reduction in the incidence of type 2 diabetes with lifestyle intervention or metformin. *New England Journal of Medicine, 346,* 393–402.

Driver, S., & O'Connor, J. (2003). Exercise participation, self-esteem, and affective experiences of people with brain injury. *Journal of Cognitive Rehabilitation, 21,* 26–33.

Dzewaltowski, D. A., Estabrooks, P. A., & Glasgow, R. E. (2004). The future of physical activity behavior change research: What is needed to improve translation of research into health promotion practice. *Exercise and Sport Science Review, 32*(2), 57–63.

Ebert, M. H., Post, R. M., & Goodwin, F. K. (1972). Effects of physical activity on urinary MHPG excretion in depressed patients. *Lancet, 2,* 766–769.

Eccles, J. S. (1983). Expectancies, values, and academic behaviors. In J. Spence (Ed.), *Achievement and achievement motivation* (pp. 75–146). San Francisco: Freeman.

Eccles, J. S., & Gootman, J. A. (Eds.). (2002). *Community programs to promote youth development.* Washington, DC: National Academy Press.

Eccles, J. S. & Wigfield, A. (2002) Motivational beliefs, values and goals. *Annual Review of Psychology, 53,* 109–132.

Edenfield, T., & Blumenthal, J. (2011). Exercise and stress reduction. In R. Contrada & A. Baum (Eds.), *The handbook of stress science: Biology, psychology, and health* (pp. 301–319). New York: Springer.

Edwards, S. (2000). Exercise and mental health promotion: The natural partnership. *International Journal of Mental Health Promotion, 2*(1), 17–18.

Edwards, S. (2001). Promoting mental health: Community effects of the exercise experience. *International Journal of Mental Health Promotion, 3*(4), 7–15.

Edwards, S. (2002). Physical exercise and psychological wellness. *International Journal of Mental Health Promotion, 4*(2), 40–46.

Edwards, D. J., Edwards, S. D., & Basson, C. J. (2004). Psychological well-being and physical self-esteem in sport and exercise. *International Journal of Mental Health Promotion, 6*(1), 25–32.

Ekeland, E., Heian, F., & Hagen, K. B. (2005). Can exercise improve self-esteem in children and young people? A systematic review of randomized controlled trials. *British Journal of Sport Medicine, 39,* 792–798.

Ekeland, E., Heian, F., Hagen, K. B., Abbott, J., & Nordheim, L. (2004). Exercise to improve self-esteem in children and young people. *Cochrane Database of Systematic Reviews, 1,* CD003683.

Elavsky, S., McAuley, E., Motl, R. W., et al. (2005). Physical activity enhances long-term quality of life in older adults: Efficacy, esteem, and affective influences. *Annals of Behavioral Medicine, 30,* 138–145.

Eliakim, A., & Beyth, Y. (2003). Exercise training, menstrual irregularities, and bone development in children and adolescents. *Journal of Pediatric Adolescent Gynecology, 16,* 201–206.

Farrel, P. A. (1989). Lack of exercise on peripheral enkephalin entry into whole brain of rats [abstract]. *Medicine and Science in Sport and Exercise, 21,* 525.

Faulkner, G., & Biddle, S. J. H. (2001). Exercise and mental health: It's not just psychology! *Journal of Sport Science, 19,* 433–444.

Faulkner, G., & Sparkes, A. (1999). Exercise as therapy for schizophrenia. *Journal of Sport and Exercise Psychology, 21,* 52–69.

Faulkner, G. E., & Taylor, A. H. (Eds.). (2005a). *Exercise, health, and mental health: Emerging relationships.* London: Routledge.

Faulkner, G. E., & Taylor, A. H. (2005b). From emerging relationships to the future of exercise in mental health promotion. In G. E. Faulkner & A. H. Taylor (Eds.), *Exercise, health, and mental health: Emerging relationships* (pp. 210–228). London: Routledge.

Faulkner, G., & Taylor, A. (2009). Promoting physical activity for mental health: A complex intervention? *Mental Health and Physical Activity, 2*(1), 1–3.

Fitzpatrick, A., Fletcher, S. Gore, D., Jones, D. & Spiegelhalter, S. ((1992). Quality of life measures in health care: Applications and issues of assessment, *British Medical Journal, 305* (6862), 1145–1148.

Fletcher, G. F., Balady, G. J., Amsterdam, E. A., et al. (2001). Exercise standards for testing and training: A statement for healthcare professionals from the American Heart Association. *Circulation, 104,* 1694–1740.

Fox, K. R. (2000a). The effects of exercise on self-perception and self-esteem. In S. J. S. Biddle, K. R. Fox, & S. H. Boutcher (Eds.), *Physical activity and psychological well-being* (pp. 88–117). London: Routledge.

Fox, K. R. (2000b). Physical activity and mental health promotion: The natural partnership. *International Journal of Mental Health Promotion, 2*(1), 4–12.

Fox, K. R., Boutcher, S. H., Faulkner, G. E., et al. (2000). The case for exercise in the promotion of mental health and psychological well-being. In S. J. H. Biddle, K. R. Fox, & S. H. Boutcher (Eds.), *Physical activity and psychological well-being* (pp. 1–9). London: Routledge.

Franz, S. I., & Hamilton, G. V. (1905). The effects of exercise on retardation in conditions of depression. *American Journal of Insanity, 62,* 239–256.

Fuchs, C. Z., Larson, K., & Zaichkowsky, L. D. (2001). Physical exercise in pain management. In D. L. Mostofsky & L. D. Zaichkowsky (Eds.), *Medical and psychological aspects of sport and exercise.* Morgantown, WV: Fitness Information Technology.

Glenister, D. (1996). Exercise and mental health: A review. *Journal of the Royal Society of the Promotion of Health, 116,* 7–13.

Gleser, J., & Mendelberg, H. (1990). Exercise and sport in mental health: A review of the literature. *Israel Journal of Psychiatry Related to Science, 27,* 99–112.

Goldstein, L. B., Adams, R., Becker, K., et al. (2001). Primary prevention of ischemic stroke: A statement for healthcare professionals from the Stroke Council of the American Heart Association. *Circulation, 103,* 163–182.

Gordon, N. F., Contractor, A., & Leighton, R. F. (2001). Resistance training for hypertension and stroke patients. In J. E. Graves & B. A. Franklin (Eds.), *Resistance training for health and rehabilitation* (pp. 237–251). Champaign, IL: Human Kinetics.

Graham, R., Kremer, J., & Wheeler, G. (2008). Physical exercise and psychological well-being among people with chronic illness and disability: A grounded approach. *Journal of Health Psychology, 3*(4), 447–458.

Gruber, J. J. (1986). Physical activity and self-esteem development in children: A meta-analysis. *American Academy of Physical Education Papers, 19,* 30–48.

Hagberg, J., Park, J. J., & Brown, M. D. (2000). The role of exercise training in the treatment of hypertension: An update. *Sports Medicine, 30*(3), 193–206.

Hallal, P. C., Victora, C. G., Azevedo, M. R., & Wells, J. C. K. (2006). Adolescent physical activity and health: A systematic review. *Sports Medicine, 36*(12), 1019–1030.

Hamer, M. (2006). The anti-hypertensive effects of exercise. *Sports Medicine, 36*(2), 109–116.

Haskell, W. L., Lee, I. M., Pate, R. R., et al. (2007). Physical activity and public health: Updated recommendation for adults from the American College of Sports Medicine and the American Heart Association. *Medicine and Science in Sports and Exercise, 39,* 1423–1434.

Hasselstrom, H., Hansen, S. E., Froberg, K., et al. (2002). Physical fitness and physical activity during adolescence as predictors of cardiovascular disease risk in young adulthood: Danish Youth and Sports Study—An eight year follow-up study. *International Journal of Sports Medicine, 23*(1), 27–31.

Hendricks, H., & van der Ouderaa, F. (2010). The effects of physical activity on mental capital and well-being. In L. C. Cooper, J. Field, U. Goswami, R. Jenkins, & B. Sahakian (Eds.), *Mental capital and well-being* (pp. 261–267). Hoboken, NJ: Wiley-Blackwell.

Heyn, P., Abreu, B. C., & Ottenbacher, K. J. (2004). The effects of exercise training on elderly persons with cognitive impairment and dementia: A meta-analysis. *Archives of Physical Medicine and Rehabilitation, 85,* 1694–1704.

Horne, J. A., & Staff, C. H. (1983). Exercise and sleep: Body heating effects. *Sleep, 6,* 36–46.

Howley, E. (2008) 2008 physical activity guidelines for Americans. *President's Council on Physical Fitness and Sports Research Digest.* Washington, D. C.: PCPFSRD

Hu, G., Rico-Sanz, J., Lakka, T. A., & Tuomilehto, J. (2006). Exercise, genetics, and prevention of type 2 diabetes. *Essays in Biochemistry, 42,* 177–192.

Hutchinson, D., Skriner, G., & Cross, C. (1999). The role of improved physical fitness in rehabilitation and recovery. *Psychiatric Rehabilitation Journal, 22*(4), 355–358.

Jacobs, G. (2010). Lifestyle practices that can improve sleep. *talk about sleep: all sleep all the time.* Retrieved October 17,

2010, from http://www.talkaboutsleep.com/sleep-disorders/archives/insomnia_drjacobs_lifestyle_part1.htm

Jakicic, J. M., Marcus, B. H., Gallagher, K. I., et al. (2003). Effects of exercise duration and intensity on weight loss in overweight, sedentary women: A randomized trial. *Journal of the American Medical Association, 290,* 1323–1345.

Jakicic, J. M., Marcus, B. H., Lang, W., & Janney, C. (2008). Effects of exercise on 24-month weight loss maintenance in overweight women. *Archives of Internal Medicine, 168,* 1550–1559.

Janney, C. A., Richardson, C., Holleman, R., et al. (2010). Gender, mental health service use, and objectively measured activity: Data from the national health and nutrition examination survey. *Mental Health and Physical Activity, 3*(2), 104–109.

Jensen, L. W., Decker, L., & Anderson, M. M. (2007). Depression and health promotion lifestyles of persons with mental illnesses. *Issues in Mental Health Nursing, 27*(6), 617–634.

Jones, M., & O'Beney, C. (2004). Promoting mental health through physical activity: Examples from practice. *Journal of Mental Health Promotion, 3*(4), 39–47.

Kantoma, M. T., Tammelin, T. H., Demakakos, P., et al. (2010). Physical activity, emotional and behavioral problems, maternal education, and self-reported educational performance of adolescents. *Health Education Research, 25*(2), 368–379.

Kaptchuk, T. J. (2001). The double-blind, randomized, placebo-controlled trial: Gold standard or golden calf? *Journal of Clinical Epidemiology, 54*(6), 541–549.

Kazdin, A. E. (2003). *Research design in clinical psychology* (4th ed.). Boston: Allyn & Bacon.

Kelly, G. A., Kelly, K. A., Hootman, J. M., & Jones, D. L. (2009). Exercise and health-related quality of life in older community-dwelling adults: A meta-analysis of randomized controlled trials. *Journal of Applied Gerontology, 28*(3), 369–394.

Kemper, H. C., de Vente, W., & van Mechelen, W. (2001). Adolescent motor skill and performance: Is physical activity in adolescence related to adult physical fitness? *American Journal of Human Biology, 13,* 180–189.

Kemper, H. C., Twisk, J. W., & Koppes, L. L. (2001). A 15-year physical activity pattern is positively related to aerobic fitness in young males and females 13–27 years. *European Journal of Applied Physiology, 84,* 395–402.

Kennard, J., & Lopez, B. (2003). Section 3: The relationship between physical exercise and mental health. In J. Kennard & B. Lopes (Eds.), *Mental health and healthy living: A review of literature.* North Yorkshire, UK: Social Exclusion Unit.

Kessler, R. C., McGonagle, K., Zhao, S., et al. (1994). Lifetime and 12-month prevalence of DSM-III-R psychiatric disorders in the United States: Result from a national comorbidity survey. *Archives of General Psychiatry, 51,* 8–19.

Kessler, R. C., Mickelson, K. D. & Williams, D. R. (1999) the prevalence, distribution and mental health correlates of perceived discrimination in the United States. *Journal of Health and Social Behaviors, 40,* 3, 208–230.

Keyes, C. L. M. (2005) Mental illness and/or mental health? Investigating axioms of the complete state model of health. *Journal of Counseling & Clinical Psychology, 73,* (3), 539–548.

Khan, K., McKay, H. A., & Haapasalo, H. (2000). Does childhood and adolescence provide a unique opportunity for exercise to strengthen the skeleton? *Journal of Science and Medicine in Sport, 3,* 150–164.

Kirkcaldy, B. D., Shephard, R. J., & Siefen, R. G. (2002). The relationship between physical activity and self-image and problem behavior among adolescents. *Social Psychiatry and Psychiatric Epidemiology, 37,* 544–550.

Kritz-Silverstein, D., Barrett-Connor, E., & Corbeau, C. (2001). Cross-sectional and prospective study of exercise and depressed mood in the elderly: The Rancho Bernardo Study. *American Journal of Epidemiology, 153,* 596–603.

Kubitz, K. K., Landers, D. M., Petruzzello, S. J., & Han, M. W. (1996). The effects of acute and chronic exercise on sleep. *Sports Medicine, 21,* 277–291.

Landers, D. M. (1997). The influence of exercise on mental health. *President's Council on Physical Fitness and Sports, 2*(12), 1–8.

Landers, D. M., & Arent, S. M. (2001). Exercise and mental health. In R. N. Singer, H. A. Hausenblas, & C. M. Janelle (Eds.), *Handbook of sport psychology* (2nd ed., pp. 740–765). New York: Wiley.

Landers, D. M., & Arent, S. (2007). Physical activity and mental health. In G. Tenenbaum & R. Eklund (Eds.), *Handbook of sport psychology* (3rd ed., pp. 469–491). Hoboken, NJ: Wiley.

Landers, D. M., & Petruzzello, S. J. (1994). Physical activity, fitness, and anxiety. In C. Bouchard, R. J. Shepherd, & T. Stevens (Eds.), *Physical activity, fitness, and health* (pp. 868–882). Champaign, IL: Human Kinetics.

Larun, L., Nordheim, L. V., Ekeland, E., et al. (2006). Exercise in prevention and treatment of anxiety and depression among children and young people. *Cochrane Database of Systematic Reviews, 4.*

Lawlor, D. A., & Hopker, S. W. (2001). The effectiveness of exercise as an intervention in the management of depression: Systemic review and meta-regression analysis of randomized controlled trials. *British Medical Journal, 322,* 763–767.

Layman, E. M. (1960) Contribution of exercise and sport to mental health and social adjustment. In W. R. Johnson (Ed.) *Science and Medicine of Exercise and Sport.* New York: Harper

Lee, I. M., Djousse, L., Sesso, H. D., et al. (2010). Physical activity and weight gain prevention. *Journal of the American Medical Association, 303,* 1173.

Lefevre, J., Philippaerts, R., Delvaux, K., et al. (2002). Relation between cardiovascular risk factors at adult age and physical activity during youth and adulthood: The Leuven longitudinal study on lifestyle, fitness, and health. *International Journal of Sports Medicine, 23,* 32–38.

Leith, L. M. (2010). *Foundations of exercise and mental health* (2nd ed.). Morgantown, WV: Fitness Information Technology.

Leith, L. M., (1994) *Foundations of Exercise and Mental Health.* Morgantown, WV: Fitness Information Technology.

Leith, L. M. & Taylor, A. H. (1990) Psychological aspects of exercise: A decade literature review. *JJournal of Sport Behavior 13,* (4) 219–239.

Lochbaum, M. R., Karoly, P. & Landers, D. M. (2004) Affect response to acute bouts of aerobic exercise: A test of opponent-process theory. *Journal of Sport Behavior, 27,* 330–348.

Long, B. C., & van Stavel, R. (1995). Effects of exercise training on anxiety: A meta-analysis. *Journal of Applied Sport Psychology, 7,* 167–189.

Lutz, R. B. (2007). Physical activity, exercise, and mental health. In J. H. Lake & D. Spiegel (Eds.), *Complementary and alternative treatments in mental health care* (pp. 301–320). Arlington, VA: American Psychiatric.

MacKelvie, K. J., Khan, K. M., & Petit, M. A. (2003). A school-based exercise intervention elicits substantial bone health benefits: A 2-year randomized controlled trial in girls. *Pediatrics, 112*(6), e447.

Macko, R. F., Smith, G. V., Dobrovolny, C. L., et al., (2001). Treadmill training improves fitness reserve in chronic stroke patients. *Archives of Physical Medicine and Rehabilitation, 82,* 879–884.

Mahoney, J., Larson, R., & Eccles, J. (Eds.). (2005). *Organized activities as context of development: Extracurricular activities, after school, and community programs.* Hillsdale, NJ: Erlbaum.

Martinsen, E. W. (1987). The role of aerobic exercise in the treatment of depression. *Stress Medicine, 3,* 93–100.

Martinsen, E. W. (1990). Benefits of exercise for the treatment of depression. *Sports Medicine, 9,* 380–389.

Martinsen, E. W. (1994) Physical activity and depression: Clinical experience. *Acta Psychiatrica Scandinavica, 89,* 23–27.

Martinsen, E. W. (1995). The effects of exercise on mental health in clinical populations. In S. J. Biddle (Ed.), *European perspectives on exercise and sport psychology* (pp. 71–84). Champaign, IL: Human Kinetics Press.

Martinsen, E. W., Hoffart, A., & Solberg, O. (1989). Comparing aerobic with nonaerobic forms of exercise in the treatment of clinical depression: A randomized trial. *Comparative Psychiatry, 30,* 324–331.

Martinsen, E. W., Medhus, A., & Sandvik, L. (1985). Effects of aerobic exercise on depression: A controlled study. *British Medical Journal, 291,* 109–113.

Martinsen, E. W., Strand, J., Paulsson, G., et al. (1989). Physical fitness levels in patients with anxiety and depressive disorders. *International Journal of Sports Medicine, 10,* 58–61.

McDevitt, J., & Wilbur, J. (2006). Exercise and people with serious, persistent mental illness. *American Journal of Nursing, 106*(4), 50–54.

Meyerhardt, J. A., Heseltine, D., Niedzwiecki, D., et al. (2006). Impact of physical activity on cancer recurrence and survival in patients with stage III colon cancer findings from CALGB 89803. *Journal of Clinical Oncology, 24*(22), 535–541.

Mikkelsson, L. O., Nupponen, H., Kaprio, J., et al. (2006). Adolescent flexibility, endurance strength, and physical activity as predictors of adult tension neck, low back pain, and knee injury: A 25 year follow-up study. *British Journal of Sport Medicine, 40*(2), 107–113.

Moher, D., Schulz, K., & Altman, D. (2001). The CONSORT statement: Revised recommendations for improving the quality of reports of parallel-group randomized trials. *Lancet, 357*(9263), 1191.

Morgan, W. P. (1969). A pilot investigation of physical working capacity in depressed and non-depressed males. *Research Quarterly, 40,* 859–861.

Morgan, W. P. (1985). Affective beneficence of vigorous physical activity. *Medical Science of Sport and Exercise, 17,* 94–100.

Morgan, W. P. (1988). Exercise and mental health. In R. K. Dishman (Ed.), *Exercise adherence: It's impact on public health.* Champaign, IL: Human Kinetics.

Morgan, W/ P. (1997) *Physical Activity and Mental Health.* Washington, D. C.: Taylor and Francis

Morgan, W. P. (1982) Psychological effects of exercise. *Behavioral Medicine Update, 4* (1) 25–30.

Morgan, W. P. & Goldston, S. E. (1987) *Exercise and mental health.* Washington, D. C.: Hemishere.

Morgan, W. P. & O'Connor, P. J. (1988) Exercise and mental health. In R. K. Dishman (Ed.) Exercise Adherence: It's Impact on Public Health. Champaign, Il.: Human Kinetics.

Morris, T. (2001). Diabetes in sport and exercise. In D. L. Mostofsky & L. D. Zaichkowsky (Eds.), *Medical and psychological aspects of sport and exercise.* Morgantown, WV: Fitness Information Technology.

Mostofsky, D. L., & Zaichkowsky, L. D. (2001). *Medical and psychological aspects of sport and exercise.* Morgantown, WV: Fitness Information Technology.

Mustelin, L., Silventoinen, K., Pietilaine, K., et al. (2009). Physical activity reduces the influence of genetics effects on BMI and waist circumference: A study in young adult twins. *International Journal of Obesity, 33*(1), 29–36.

Mutrie, N. (2000). The relationship between physical activity and clinically defined depression. In S. J. H. Biddle, K. R. Fox, & S. H. Boutcher (Eds.), *Physical activity and psychological well-being* (pp. 46–62). London: Routledge.

Myers, J., Prakash, M., Froelicher, V., et al., (2000). Exercise capacity and mortality among men referred for exercise testing. *New England Journal of Medicine, 346,* 793–801.

Myers, J. E., Sweeny, T. J., & Witmer, J. M. (2000). The wheel of wellness counseling: A holistic model for treatment planning. *Journal of Counseling and Development, 78,* 251–266.

National Asthma Education and Prevention Program (NAEPP). (2007). Expert Panel Report 3 (EPR-3): Guidelines for the diagnosis and management of asthma-summary report 2007. *Journal of Allergy and Clinical Immunology, 120,* 94–138.

National Physical Activity Plan. (2010). from http://www.physicalactivityplan.org/NationalPhysicalActivityPlan.pdf.

Nishida, J., & Otomo, S. (2010). Influence of exercise and physical activity on the mental health of elementary and junior high school teachers: Individual characteristics and experiences with stress. *Japanese Journal of Educational Psychology, 58*(3), 285–297.

North, T. C., McCullagh, P. & Tran, Z. (1990) Effect of exercise on depression. *Exercise and Sport Science Review, 18,* 1, 379–416.

O'Connor, P. J. & Youngstedt, S. D. (1995) Influence of exercise on human sleep. *Exercise and Sport Science Review, 23,* 105–134.

Paillard-Borg, P. Wang, X. U., Winblad, B. & Fratiglioni, L (2009) Pattern of participation in leisure activities among older people in relation to their health conditions and contextual factors: A survey in a Swedish urban area. *Ageing and Society, 29,* 803–821.

Paluskaka, S. A., & Schwenk, T. L. (2000). Physical activity and mental health: Current concepts. *Sports Medicine, 29,* 167–180.

Pardman, D. (2011). *Boomercise: Exercise as you age.* Morgantown, WV: Fitness Information Technology.

Park, Y.-H., Song, M., Cho, B.-L., et al. (2011). The effects of an integrated health education and exercise program in community dwelling older adults with hypertension: A randomized controlled trial. *Patient Education and Counseling, 82*(1), 133–137.

Parsons, T. J., Power, C., Logan, S. & Summerbell, C. D. (1999) Childhood predictions of adult obesity: A systematic review. *International Journal of Obesity and Related Metabolic Disorders, 23,* (8), 1–107.

Pate, R. R., Pratt, M. S., Blair, S. N., et al. (1995). Physical activity and public health: A recommendation from the Centers for Disease Control and Prevention and the American College of

Sport Medicine. *Journal of the American Medical Association, 273,* 402–407.

Patel, V., & Prince, M. (2010). Global mental health: A new global health field comes of age. *Journal of the American Medical Association, 303,* 1976–1977.

Pearson, T. A., Blair, S. N., Daniels, S. R., et al., (2002). AHA guidelines for primary prevention of cardiovascular disease and stroke: 2002 update consensus panel guide to comprehensive risk reduction for adult patients without coronary or other atherosclerotic vascular diseases. *Circulation, 106,* 388–391.

Peden, A. R., Rayens, M. K., Hall, L. A., & Beebe, L. H. (2001). Preventing depression in high risk college women: A report of an 18-month follow-up. *Journal of American College Health, 49,* 299–306.

Pelham, T., & Campagna, P. (1991). Benefits of exercise in psychiatric rehabilitation of persons with schizophrenia. *Canadian Journal of Rehabilitation, 4,* 159–168.

Peluso, M. A., & Guerra de Andrade, L. H. (2005). Physical activity and mental health: The association between exercise and mood. *Clinics, 60*(1), 61–70.

Penhollow, T. M., & Young, M. (2004). Sexual desirability and sexual performance: Does exercise and fitness really matter? *Electronic Journal of Human Sexuality, 7.* Retrieved from http://www.ejhs.org/tocv7.html

Perlman, L. M., Cohen, J., Altiere, M., et al. (2010). A multidimensional wellness group therapy program for veterans with comorbid psychiatric and medical conditions. *Professional Psychology: Research and Practice, 41*(2), 120–127.

Perkins, H., Baum, G., Taylor, C., et al. (2009). Effects of treatment factors, comorbidities, and health-related quality of life on self-efficacy for physical activity in cancer survivors. *Psycho-Oncology, 18*(4), 405–411.

Petruzzello, S. J. (1995). Anxiety reduction following exercise: Methodological artifacts or "real" phenomenon? *Journal of Sport and Exercise Psychology, 17,* 105–111.

Petruzzelo, S. J., Landers, D. M., Hatfield, B. D., Kubitz, K. A. & Salazar, W. A. (1991) A meta-analysis on the anxiety-reducing effects of acute and chronic exercise. *Journal of Sport Medicine, 11,* 143–182.

Polonsky, W. H. (2002). Emotional and quality of life aspects of diabetes management. *Current Diabetes Report, 2,* 153–159.

Post, R. M., Kotin, J., Goodwin, F. K., et al. (1973). Psychomotor activity and cerebro-spinal fluid amine metabolites in affective illness. *American Journal of Psychiatry, 130,* 67–72.

Power, A. (2010). Transforming the nation's health: Next steps in mental health promotion. *American Journal of Public Health, 100*(12), 2343–2347.

Ram, F. S., Robinson, S. M., & Black, P. N. (2000). Physical training for asthma. *Cochrane Database Systems Review, 2000,* CD001116.

Rees, D. I., & Sabia, J. J. (2010). Exercise and adolescent mental health: New evidence from longitudinal data. *Journal of Mental Health Policy and Economics, 13*(1), 13–25.

Regier, D. A., Myers, J. K., Kramer, M., et al. (1984). The NIMH epidemiological catchment area program: Historical context, major objectives, and study population characteristics. *Archives of General Psychiatry, 41,* 934–941.

Rendi, M., Szabo, A., Szabo, T., et al. (2008). Acute psychological benefits of aerobic exercise: A field study into the effects of exercise characteristics. *Psychology Health and Medicine, 13*(2), 180–184.

Richards, K. C., Campania, C., & Muse-Burke, J. L. (2010). Self-care and well-being in mental health professionals: The mediating effects of self-awareness and mindfulness. *Journal of Mental Health Counseling, 32*(3), 247–253.

Richardson, C., Faulkner, G., McDevitt, J., et al. (2005). Integrating physical activity into mental health services for persons with serious mental illness. *Psychiatric Services, 56*(3), 324–331.

Rosimini, C. (2003). Benefits of swim training for children and adolescents with asthma. *Journal of the American Academy of Nurse Practitioners, 15,* 247–252.

Salmon, P. (2001). Effects of physical exercise on anxiety, depression, and sensitivity to stress: A unifying theory. *Clinical Psychology Review, 21,* 33–61.

Sanson-Fisher, R. W., Bonevski, B., Green, L. W., & D'Este, C. (2007). Limitations of the randomized controlled trial in evaluating population-based health interventions. *American Journal of Preventive Medicine, 33*(2), 155–161.

Satcher, D (1999) Department of Health and Human Services. *Mental Health: A Report of the Surgeon General.* Washington, D. C.USDHHS

Satcher, D. (2001) Department of Health and Human Services. Mental Health: Culture, Race & Ethnicity-A Supplement to Mental Health: A Report of the Surgeon General. Washington, D. C. USDHHS.

Schlicht, W. (1994). Does physical exercise reduce anxious emotions: A meta-analysis. *Anxiety, Stress, and Coping, 6,* 275–288.

Schmalz, D. L., Deane, G. D., Birch, L. L., & Davison, K. K. (2007). A longitudinal assessment of the links between physical activity and self-esteem in early adolescent non-Hispanic females. *Journal of Adolescent Health, 41*(6), 559–565.

Shephard, R. J. (2001). Importance of sport and exercise to quality of life and longevity. In D. L. Mostofsky & L. D. Zaichkowsky (Eds.), *Medical and psychological aspects of sport and exercise.* Morgantown, WV: Fitness Information Technology.

Shephard, R. J. (1981) *Physiology and biochemistry of exercise.* New York: Praeger Publisher

Sibley, B. A., & Etnier, J. L. (2003). The relationship between physical activity and cognition in children: A meta-analysis. *Pediatric Exercise Science, 15,* 243–256.

Singh, N. A., Clements, K. M. & Fiatarone-Singh, M. A. (2001) The efficacy of exercise as a long term antidepressant in elderly subjects: A randomized control trial. *Journal of Gerontology, 56,* (8) 497–504.

Slawson, D. (2005) Aerobic exercise effective for mild to moderate depression. *American Family Physician, 71,* 9, 1769–1770.

Smith, S. C., Blair, S. N., Bonow, R. O., et al., (2001). AHA/ACC guidelines for preventing heart attack and death in patients with atherosclerotic cardiovascular disease: 2001 update a statement for healthcare professionals from the American Heart Association and the American College of Cardiology. *Circulation, 104,* 1577–1579.

Sobel, D. (n.d.) Exercise improves sleep. *healthy.net: healthy people, healthy planet.* Retrieved October 17, 2010, from http://www.healthy.net/scr/article.aspx?Id=424

Sonstroem, R. J. (1984). Exercise and self-esteem. *Exercise and Sport Science Reviews, 12,* 23–55.

Sonstroem, R. J. (1978) Physical estimation and attraction scales: Rationale and research. *Medicine and Science in Sports, 10,* (4), 219–239.

Spence, J. C., McGannon, K. R., & Poon, P. (2005). The effect of exercise on global self-esteem: A quantitative review. *Journal of Sport and Exercise Psychology, 27,* 311–334.

Spence, J. C., Poon, P., & Dyck, P. (1997). The effects of physical activity participation on self-concept: A meta-analysis. *Journal of Sport and Exercise Psychology, 19,* S109.

Stein, C. J., Fisher, L., Berkey, C., & Colditz, G. A. (2007). Adolescent physical activity and perceived competence: Does change in activity level impact self-perception? *Journal of Adolescent Health, 40*(5), 462–477.

Steinberg, H., & Sykes, E. A. (1985). Introduction to symposium on endorphins and behavioral processes: A review of literature on endorphins and exercise. *Pharmacology Biochemistry and Behavior, 23,* 857–862.

Strine, T. W., Chapman, D. P., Balluz, L. S., Moriarty, D. G. & Mokdad, A. H. 2008) The association between life satisfactionand health-related quality of life, chronic illnessand health behaviors among U. S. community dwelling adults. *Journal of Community Health, 33,* 1, 40–50

Tang, S. W., Stancer, H. C., Takahashi, S., et al. (1981). Controlled exercise elevate plasma but, not urinary MHPG and VMA. *Psychiatric Research, 4,* 13–20.

Taylor, A. (2000). Physical activity, anxiety, and stress. In S. J. S. Biddle, K. R. Fox, & S. H. Boutcher (Eds.), *Physical activity and psychological well-being* (pp. 10–45). London: Routledge.

Tehard, B., Frieddenreich, C. M., Oppert, J. M., et al. (2006). Effects of physical activity on women at increased risk of breast cancer: Results from the E3N cohort study. *Cancer Epidemiology, Biomarkers, and Prevention, 15*(1), 57–64.

Tomporowski, P. D. (2006). Physical activity, cognition, and aging: A review of reviews. In L. W. Poon, W. Chodzko-Zajko, & P. D. Tomporowski (Eds.), *Active living, cognitive functioning, and aging* (pp. 15–32). Champaign, IL: Human Kinetics.

Tremblay, M. S., Inman, J. W., & Wilms, J. D. (2000). The relationship between physical activity, self-esteem, and academic achievement in 12-year old children. *Pediatric and Exercise Science, 12,* 312–323.

US Department of Health and Human Services (US DHHS). (1996). *Physical activity and health: A report from the surgeon general.* Atlanta, GA: National Center for Chronic Disease Prevention and Health Promotion.

US Department of Health and Human Services. (1999). *Mental health: A report of the Surgeon General.* Rockville, MD: Substance Abuse and Mental Health Services Administration, Center for Mental Health Services, National Institute of Health, National Institute of Mental Health.

US Department of Health and Human Services. (2008). *2008 physical activity guidelines for Americans.* Washington, DC: Office of Disease Prevention and Health Promotion, Centers for Disease Control and Prevention, US Department of Health and Human Services.

US Public Health Service, Office of the Surgeon General (US PHS). (1996). *Physical activity and health: A report of the surgeon general.* Atlanta, GA: US Department of Health and Human Services, Centers for Disease Control and Prevention, National Centers for Chronic Disease Prevention and Health Promotion.

Utter, J., Denny, S., Robinson, E., et al. (2006). Perceived access to community facilities, social motivation, and physical activity among New Zealand youth. *Journal of Adolescent Health, 39,* 770–773.

Wallace, J. P. (2003). Exercise in hypertension. *Sports Medicine, 33*(8), 585–598.

Walsh, R. (2011). Lifestyle and mental health. *American Psychologist, 66*(7), 579–592. doi: 10.1037/a0021769

Wand, T., & Murray, L. (2008). Let's get physical. *International Journal of Mental Health Nursing, 17*(5), 363–369.

Wang, P. S., Angermeyer, M., Borges, G., et al. (2007). Delay and failure in treatment seeking after first onset of mental disorders in the World Health Organization's World Mental Health Survey Initiative. *World Psychiatry, 6,* 177–185.

Wang, P. S., Berglun, P., Olfson, M., Pincus, H., Wells, M. D., & Kessler, R. C. (2005) Failure and delay in initial treatment contact after first onset of mental disorders in the national comorbidity survey replication. *Archives of General Psychiatry, 62,* 6, 603–613.

Warburton, D. E. R., Nocol, C. W., & Bredin, S. S. D. (2006). Health benefits of physical activity: The evidence. *Canadian Medical Association Journal, 174*(6), 801–809.

Weinberg, R. S. & Gould, D. (2011) Foundations of Sport and Exercise Psychology. Champaign, Ill.: Human Kinetics Press.

Whelton, S. P., Chin, A., Xin, X., & He, J. (2002) Effects of aerobic exercise on blood pressure: A meta-analysis of ramdomized, controlled trials. Annals of Internal Medicine, 136 (7), 493–503

White, J., Case, D. A., McWhirter, D., & Matison, A. M. (1990). Enhanced sexual behavior in exercising men. *Archives of Sexual Behavior, 19*(3), 193–209.

World Health Report 2001. Mental Health: New Understanding, New Hope.Geneva, Switzerland.

Wigfield, A. & Eccles, J. S. (2000) Expectancy-value theory of achievement motivation. Contemporary Educational Psychology, 25, (1), 68-81.

Williams, M. A., Haskell, W. L., Ades, P. A., et al. (2007). Resistance exercise in individuals with and without cardiovascular disease: 2007 update; A scientific statement from the American Heart Association Council on Clinical Cardiology and Council on Nutrition, Physical Activity, and Metabolism. *Circulation, 116,* 572–584.

Wimer, C., Bouffard, S. M., Caronongan, P., Dearing, E., et. al. (2006) What are kids getting into these days? Demographic differences in youth out-of-school time participation. Cambridge, MA: Harvard Family Research Project.

Windle, G., Hughes, D., Linck, P., et al. (2010). Is exercise effective in promoting well-being in older age? A systematic review. *Aging and Mental Health, 14*(6), 652–669.

World Federation of Mental Health. (2004). *The relationship between physical and mental health: Co-occurring disorders.* Available from http://www.wfmh.org

World Health Organization. (2005). *Promoting mental health: Concepts, emerging evidence, practice; A report of the WHO, Department of Mental Health and Substance Abuse in collaboration with the Victorian Health Promotion Foundation and the University of Melbourne.* Geneva: Author.

World Health Report. (2001). *Mental health: New understanding, new hope.* Geneva: World Health Organization.

Xu, Q., Anderson, D., & Courtney, M. (2010). A longitudinal study of the relationship between lifestyle and mental health among midlife and older women in Australia: Findings from the healthy aging of women study. *Healthcare for Women International, 31*(12), 1082–1096.

Zacker, R. J. (2004). Exercise: A key component of diabetes management. *Diabetes Spectrum, 17*(3), 142–144.

PART 4

Conclusion and Future Directions

CHAPTER

32 Prevention in Counseling Psychology: We Have Seen the Future, and the Future Is Us

Elizabeth M. Vera *and* Megan K. Polanin

Abstract

The chapters in the *Handbook of Prevention in Counseling Psychology* demonstrate an impressive range of important work being done in many areas of prevention and mental health promotion. Each chapter outlines important directions for future research and practice. In this concluding chapter, general issues related to the future of prevention in counseling psychology and psychology as a whole will be presented. Among these issues are the challenges and opportunities of integrating technology into prevention programs, the benefits of interdisciplinary collaboration and international perspectives, the importance of prevention as part of a social justice agenda, the need for counseling psychologists to engage in advocacy and outreach, and the relevancy of expanding definitions of program effectiveness.

Key Words: technology and prevention, international prevention, advocacy, outreach

As was stated in the introductory chapter of this handbook, counseling psychology has demonstrated a wavering commitment to prevention throughout its history. Yet, at this point in the evolution of our field, there are many reasons to believe that prevention and mental health promotion will finally become mainstays in the field of psychology. There also exist many reasons to believe that counseling psychologists will be among those leading the way forward. The chapters in the *Handbook of Prevention in Counseling Psychology* demonstrate the wide range of significant work being done in many areas of prevention and mental health promotion. Each chapter has outlined important directions for future research and practice. In this concluding chapter, general issues related to the future of prevention in counseling psychology and psychology as a whole will be presented. Among these issues are the opportunities and challenges of integrating technology in prevention programs, the benefits of interdisciplinary collaboration and international perspectives, the importance of prevention as part of a social justice agenda, the need for counseling psychologists to engage in advocacy and outreach, and the relevancy of expanding definitions of program effectiveness.

Technology

Many chapters in this handbook have discussed the implications of our changing world for the future of prevention research and practice in their areas of specialty. One theme that emerged in many of these discussions is the opportunity and challenge of integrating technology in prevention programs. The current generation of US children and adolescents has never lived without the Internet or mobile phones. In fact, recent studies suggest that this cohort of youths consumes up to 53 hours of media per week on average, which includes activities such as watching television, texting, instant messaging, and surfing the Internet (Kaiser Family Foundation, 2010). This figure has increased considerably from even 5 years ago, suggesting that technology usage is a vital part of the way in which future generations will access information and develop social relationships. While the popular expectation of this generation and future generations is to possess access to information "on demand," there exist both challenges and opportunities for the field of new technology being integrated into prevention research and practice.

One challenge of integrating technology is attempting to understand how it may impact the development and subsequent expression of prosocial and antisocial behaviors. The area of bullying and violence prevention represent one domain where this is a relevant challenge. As Espelage and Low, in this volume, discussed, a large number of studies have been conducted to identify the predictors of bullying and their implications for prevention of bullying behavior. However, the majority of this research has focused on in-person bullying and relational aggression. The anonymity and accessibility of online correspondence has resulted in a rapid increase of cyber-bullying, or electronic means of peer victimization (e.g., spreading rumors via Facebook). While research is less than a decade old and thus remains an emerging discipline, it is less clear whether formerly nonparticipating youths will be tempted to perpetrate and participate in cyber-bullying. For example, it may well be the case that the privacy afforded by the Internet has created opportunities for perpetration by youths who would not engage in in-person bullying. Thus, research that aims to identify factors that put children and adolescents "at risk" for perpetrating bullying must expand to include this newer group of potential participants. It is also clear that cyber-bullying surpasses in-person bullying in frequency (Smith et al., 2008), perhaps due to the fact that a perpetrator may be able to avoid identification in the case of the former.

In a recent study, Ybarra, Diener-West, and Leaf (2007) examined the link between online bullying and in-person bullying in a cross-national sample of 10- to 15-year-olds. Although some overlap existed, the majority of youths who were harassed online (64%) did not report simultaneously being bullied in person at school. Yet, similar to what has been found of youths who have been bullied in person, those individuals harassed online were significantly more likely to also report two or more detentions or suspensions as well as skipping school in the previous year. A particularly worrisome finding of this study was the fact that youths who reported being targeted by Internet harassment were eight times more likely than all other youth to concurrently report carrying a weapon to school in the past 30 days. This research has implications for bullying prevention as well as violence prevention.

In the same way that technology facilitated the potential for antisocial behavior, technology may engender simultaneously opportunities for prosocial behavior development. Despite the fact that most of the scholarship to date on the increase in technology consumption has emphasized its risks to children and adolescents, Gross (2009) found that online social contact had a positive impact on the mental health of socially rejected adolescents. In this study, compared with solitary game play, instant messaging with an unfamiliar peer via the Internet facilitated greater replenishment of self-esteem and perceived relational value among socially rejected adolescents and young adults. Online communication also resulted in greater reduction of negative affect among adolescents. The results of this study suggest that the mental health benefits of social relationships and connection need not be limited to developing in-person relationships with familiar peers. The implications for prevention programming are numerous; however, it may be that connecting adolescents with virtual friends will become an important type of intervention for preventionists involved in positive youth development efforts that focus on building social capital for participants.

Perhaps the most direct implication of the emergence of technology for the prevention field has to do with new opportunities for content delivery of prevention programming. Romano, and Daly, Buchanan, Dasch, Eichen, and Lenhart, in this volume, discussed the potential for technology to improve access to program content by decreasing the need for program participants to receive interventions in-person. This possibility offers some potentially exciting implications for improving the participation rates of populations that are historically difficult to access, such as geographically isolated families or busy, working parents. An interesting inquiry to consider is whether a comparable impact of a prevention program could be attained by participants accessing content that is prerecorded (e.g., podcasts) at a time that is convenient versus having to attend a group session in-person at times that are not convenient. While the advantages of such a methodology may seem obvious, there are important concerns that must also be examined.

For example, while the gap is being shortened, there is still a considerable technology gap between middle- and upper-income families and their lower-income counterparts (Kaiser Family Foundation,

2010). Currently, many families do not have at-home Internet access or live close enough to public centers (e.g., libraries) that provide such access. Overrelying on virtual delivery of prevention programming content could further marginalize lower-income families who are unable to access the Internet. In addition, it is unknown whether the lack of personal interaction that results from virtually delivering prevention programs has an impact on the desired outcomes of the program. For example, it may be that helping parents feel less isolated would be one goal (or by-product) of initiating a parenting psychoeducation group. However, if parents download the psychoeducational content instead of physically attending the group, they may be denied the opportunity to experience increased support from other parents in similar situations. Given what Priester and Jones presented in this volume about the value of including interaction in alcohol and other substance abuse prevention programs, it may be that delivering prevention programs virtually will only be effective for certain types of prevention efforts. At this time, it is unclear as to where we should draw this line.

Creating Internet-based or virtual prevention programs could have the benefit of standardizing interventions, which would improve program fidelity. In addition, these types of programs may also allow participants to revisit material more than once, in essence creating individualized "booster" sessions. However, it is also the case that preventionists will lose control of larger environmental influences by permitting participants to access material in less controlled environments. For example, participants who attempt to multitask while watching intervention materials may have less opportunity to deeply process the material and thus recall it at a later time. Participants may also not be adequately motivated to schedule time to view the program module and, given that the exposure is not occurring in a physical location (e.g., school setting) where they may be more of a captive audience, the retention rates of participants in multicomponent programs may be negatively affected.

Despite the fact that these methodological concerns have yet to be fully understood, there is some preliminary indication that delivering interventions virtually may provide benefits. Ybarra, Eaton, and Bickman (2005) examined the efficacy of Internet-based interventions in relieving symptomatology (e.g., depressive symptoms) related to a variety of mental health disorders. Although relatively new, many Internet-based mental health interventions reported promising early results. The study found that both therapist-led as well as self-directed online interventions indicated significant alleviation of disorder-related symptomatology. The number of studies addressing child disorders lags behind those of adults, however. Given the frequency with which children and adolescents access online content, it will be salient for researchers to determine whether the Internet is an effective means of intervening with this particular population.

While there are undoubtedly both benefits and risks of implementing new technology into prevention program delivery, it will be paramount for future prevention researchers to both determine the type of program content that lends itself best to virtual delivery methods and to empirically demonstrate the efficacy of this method compared to traditional methods (i.e., in- person programs). It will also be important through meta-analytic research to demonstrate which components of model programs are most critical to their effectiveness and then to determine whether these necessary components can be replicated with virtual methods. This represents an exciting new opportunity for research in the area of prevention.

Interdisciplinary Collaboration and International Perspectives

As was presented in the introductory chapter, the history of prevention in counseling psychology in many ways overlaps with the emergence of the field of public health and the development of the field of community psychology. At this point in time, it is undeniable that the future of prevention will be an interdisciplinary effort, even if in the past the various specialties involved in prevention have operated relatively independently. As Romano noted in his chapter in this volume, there is federal support and encouragement for such collaboration in the allocation of grant funds. Funding agencies such as the National Institute of Mental Health (NIMH), Substance Abuse and Mental Health Services Administration (SAMHSA), and the Graduate Psychology Education (GPE) program (through the US Department of Health and Human Services [HHS]) emphasize the importance of collaboration across scholarly disciplines, community agencies, and institutions.

In addition to strengthening the collaborations among disciplines that are committed to prevention research and practice within the United States, it is essential that future collaboration include the perspectives of our international colleagues who are doing important work in many overlapping areas.

In fact, one of the most significant opportunities within the prevention field involves strengthening our international collaboration efforts. Much of preventionists' expertise in the United States comes from research based on populations living within the continental 48 states. However, many of the problems that exist as the targets of our prevention efforts are global epidemics. Preventing HIV, lowering drug and alcohol abuse rates, eliminating interpersonal violence, reducing poverty rates, and fostering healthier lives for aging populations are among the common goals shared internationally. Unfortunately, there tends to be less access to and availability of research on prevention efforts with international populations, in that fewer such articles are likely to appear in many mainstream US prevention journals. Yet, we have much to learn from our colleagues around the world in regard to best practices in prevention. Within a more global research base are key data that illustrate the similarities and differences between populations around the world, thus enhancing our ability to affect positive change for a richly diverse population of individuals.

For example, when examining the body of international research on factors impeding successful HIV/AIDS prevention, several consistent themes tend to emerge including the interactive effects of poverty and economic exploitation, gender power dynamics, sexual oppression, and racism (Parker, Easton, & Klein, 2000). Research has also established a fairly universal link between stigma and willingness to be tested for HIV and other STDs in many parts of the world. Converging data such as these led researchers to conclude that there are similar structures and processes at work that place communities at risk for HIV/AIDS infection in Africa, Asia, Latin America, the Caribbean, and within certain communities in North America. Thus, programs that attempt to ameliorate these barriers to program implementation that have been successful in other parts of the world could serve as model programs for preventionists in the United States who work with communities who experience similar impediments.

Research conducted in Puerto Rico has meaningful implications for HIV prevention with women of Latin American descent in the continental 48 states and around the world. Abreu, Sala, Candelaria, and Norman (2010) investigated barriers to HIV prevention in a sample of low-income Puerto Rican women. When questioned about barriers to safe sex, the participants specifically mentioned a lack of negotiation skills, fear of sexual violence, partner refusal to wear condoms, and a lack of control over their partners' sexual behavior. Additionally, the participants recommended that prevention efforts focus on utilizing media such as running informational ads or movies during telenovela programming as an effective way of targeting women. The authors interpreted the findings as a function of women's disempowerment in Puerto Rico, yet this is an issue that impacts women around the world.

Another example of the potential applicability of international prevention practice lies in the area of violence prevention. Research on violence prevention in Latin America has found that community violence occurs with frequencies comparable to and sometimes greater than what is seen in the United States. After decades of attempting to identify best practices in violence prevention, Latin American preventionists conclude that environment-centered programs may yield a bigger return than person-centered attempts. Among the best practices emerging from research conducted in Latin American in "hot spots," where violence is an enormous problem, are policies that limit access to guns, improving educational and employment opportunities, increasing the presence and reliability of law enforcement, and reestablishing community norms (PAHO, 1996).

For example, an intervention in Cali, Columbia, involved community members residing in high violence neighborhoods, who describe their own decisions to reject violence and portray strategies for maintaining peace through "street radio" programs. Due to the rampant poverty that exists in this part of the world, radio was found to be the medium that would reach the most people. In addition to the stories that documented community members' civic involvement and commitment to end community violence, residents recorded other stories describing the rejection of punitive child discipline strategies while also advocating for alternative parenting strategies. This strategy was aimed at altering community norms around violence and changing outsiders' misperceptions that all residents of the community were either violence perpetrators or condoning of violence. As a result of the intervention, residents' perceptions of their community and the norms pertaining to violence were altered (Weaver & Maddaleno, 1999). While media such as radio may not be the medium of choice for residents of many communities in the United States, this prevention approach could be replicated in this country utilizing the most effective and far-reaching forms of media.

Yet another area in which international research efforts represent opportunities for collaboration is obesity prevention. In a study of factors related to obesity in Australian school children, the authors found that obesity was four times greater in ethnic groups other than mainstream Anglo children (e.g., Maori, Middle Eastern immigrant populations). In an effort to understand underlying factors related to obesity, the authors held focus groups and determined that, in particular, for boys who were obese and from either of the two ethnic minority groups, there was not a perception of obesity as a problem (O'Dea, 2008). For example, of the boys who were obese, only half considered their weight to be "too fat." The authors interpreted these findings as possible indications that, within these ethnic groups, "bigness" is associated with masculinity and strength. They also speculated that there may exist some non-gender-related explanations due to the fact that two thirds of the Middle Eastern girls who were obese considered their weight to be "about right." Given that in some cultures being overweight may indicate a family's prosperity, it is important to determine how to motivate individuals to attempt to lose weight in an effort to stave off serious health-related issues such as type 2 diabetes.

Being part of an international collaboration within the subspecialties of prevention is not only important to the United States' ability to share data about the predictors and best practices in preventing particular types of issues with specific populations, but it also has implications for how we approach prevention within our own increasingly diverse society. One example of an interdisciplinary, international collaboration that exists is the violence prevention project known as CeaseFire (http://ceasefirechicago.org). Ceasefire would be considered an indicated approach to violence prevention that blends elements of person-centered and environment-centered interventions.

The CeaseFire program's primary environment-centered strategy is to select members of the targeted communities to act as "violence interrupters." These individuals serve to mediate conflicts between gangs as neutral parities and, in doing so, attempt to interrupt the cycle of retaliatory violence that often occurs in the aftermath of a shooting. The person-centered strategies include outreach workers counseling targeted youth and connecting them to a range of mental health services. Similar to the Cali project described in this chapter, Ceasefire aims to target specific neighborhoods that are known as hubs of violent activity. The goals of the project are to decrease violent behavior and to change community norms surrounding violence.

In its evaluation in the United States, the US Department of Justice investigated the effectiveness of Ceasefire programs in seven cities. Six of the seven CeaseFire sites assessed showed decreases in the size and intensity of shooting "hot spots." The evaluation (see Skogan, Hartnett, Bump, & Dubois, 2008) also indicated that, in comparison to control groups, decreases in overall violence occurred in four of the areas where Ceasefire operated. Reciprocal killings in retaliation for earlier events decreased more in the program areas than in the comparison areas. Additionally, the average gang involvement in homicides decreased in three of the CeaseFire areas. In some cases, decreases in murder rates were as high as 73%. Thus, the Department of Justice report validated the CeaseFire model as an *evidence-based intervention* that reduces shooting and killings and ultimately creates safer communities.

What is most impressive about CeaseFire is that it was developed by a group of professionals from multiple disciplines who had worked internationally with the World Health Organization in preventing major public health problems, including violence, tuberculosis, and HIV, worldwide. Through their previous research and experience, they recognized the commonalities in disease transmission throughout the world and subsequently developed collaborative community partnerships in order to begin to address the prevention of violence in the United States. The international partnership that Ceasefire has developed now includes Iraq, London, South Africa, and Trinidad and Tobago. The program stands as a successful model of how exposure to international venues where public health problems such as violence are at epidemic levels can inform and be informed by efforts to combat these issues in the United States. Thus, the bidirectional flow of global information can be an important component of the design, implementation, and evaluation of prevention efforts.

Several of the chapters in this handbook addressed the needs of immigrating cultural groups with respect to prevention and mental health promotion efforts. Understanding what has worked in both person-centered and environment-centered efforts worldwide can inform future prevention design, implementation, and the development of policies. Furthermore, it can be enormously helpful in our quest to design prevention programs that are culturally relevant and aimed at combating social injustices in our part of the world.

Social Justice and Prevention

Many of the contributors to the handbook, and other scholars (e.g., Vera & Speight, 2003), discussed the importance of making prevention programming culturally relevant and addressing social injustices through our work. As has been argued throughout many of the chapters and articulated as a *Best Practice* in prevention design (Hage et al., 2007), culturally relevant prevention efforts are an integral part of a social justice agenda. At this point in time, there are many positive indications that the field of counseling psychology is committed to creating effective prevention efforts that are culturally relevant. Specific specialty areas within the prevention field have made greater strides than others, but in general, there are many examples of the efforts that have been made to tailor programs to meet the cultural realities of participants.

For example, in the area of sexual risk-taking, there endures convincing evidence to suggest that girls and boys possess different motivations for engaging in risky sexual behavior (Robinson, Holmbeck, & Paikoff, 2007). Specifically, boys endorse more esteem-enhancing and power-related reasons for engaging in sex versus being motivated by a fear of losing a relationship or being in love with one's partner. Given that such differences may exist between boys and girls, it follows that different strategies should be utilized in designing interventions to promote delayed sexual activity. Based on the results of studies such as Robinson et al. (2007), for example, preventionists would do well to develop programs that focus on the relationship-motivating reasons that influence girls to engage in unwanted sexual activity and on the esteem-building motivations that often lead boys to engage in such behavior. Differences such as these may also justify the need for prevention programming focused on sexual risk taking to be conducted in gender-specific groups.

In the realm of reducing conduct problems, practitioners have made efforts to infuse the cultural characteristics of participants into the curriculum content. For example, Coard and her colleagues (2007) utilized an empirically supported parenting intervention (e.g., Parenting the Strong-Willed Child [PSWC]) program (Forehand & Long, 2002) and adapted it for use with African American families. These researchers adapted the curriculum by infusing traditional African American values/rituals into the curriculum (e.g., African proverbs, use of prayer) and promoting positive racial socialization via aiding parents in preparing their children for discrimination as well as bolstering their self-esteem and positive racial identity. Outcome studies suggested that this program is effective in increasing positive behaviors in children of the participants compared to a control group. Thomas et al., in this volume, spoke to the benefits of building the esteem and promoting positive identities in children of color as a strategy for a variety of mental health promotion efforts.

While in some areas of prevention clear efforts have been made to create prevention programs that are culturally relevant, as illustrated by the aforementioned examples, there are other realms of prevention in which fewer strides have been made in identifying specific ways that prevention can become culturally tailored for specific populations. For example, with respect to the prevention of interpersonal violence, there are few studies that have examined which changes in prevention programs may be important when working with gay or lesbian couples to prevent interpersonal violence. Researchers have identified similarities and differences in battering patterns between heterosexual and homosexual couples (Miller, Bobner, & Zarski, 2000). Among the factors that may impact the expression of interpersonal violence and its prevention in gay or lesbian couples are: the physical strength differential in most heterosexual couples is less common in gay and lesbian partners; the role of batterer may alternate between partners; a leverage to a threat to out one's partner may be part of the abuse; and the exacerbation of social isolation experienced by gay and lesbian partner violence victims because of lack of societal recognition (Elliot, 1996). There are also many ways in which the dynamics related to interpersonal violence are similar in heterosexual versus homosexual couples (Miller et al., 2000). However, it is crucial for preventionists focused on ameliorating interpersonal violence in gay and lesbian couples to address the unique cultural concerns of these communities.

Obesity prevention research also necessitates accounting for cultural issues in the design of prevention programming. As Parham noted in this volume, not all youth have equal access to the type of physical recreation that is a critical component of obesity prevention. Mazzeo and her colleagues discussed in this volume the disparities that exist with regard to the emergence of weight problems across racial and social class lines. However, there is a need for more research that considers how cultural differences in body perception and satisfaction may vary across cultures (O'Dea, 2008), and whether being overweight may mean different things in unique cultural groups. It is also imperative to determine how the focus on consuming technology in this generation of children, across cultures, has implications for the attractiveness of exercise as recreation.

In summary, it is essential for future research to explore how to move forward in adapting prevention programs to reflect the cultural discrepancies between heterosexual couples and same-sex couples and the differential predictors of obesity across cultural groups, both of which will result in more efficacious prevention efforts. This raises the issue of whether standard, empirically supported prevention efforts may be culturally adapted based on such research or whether such potential differences necessitate the design of entirely new programs. Regardless, implementing prevention programs that are meaningful and relevant for participants involved should be a foremost focus of preventionists.

One of the related important future directions for the prevention field with regard to cultural relevance involves documenting the mechanisms through which cultural adaptation may generate more effective programming. For example, if a program is based on an existing empirically supported prevention approach and specific adaptations have been made (e.g., changes to curricular examples, using culturally similar facilitators), it is essential to identify whether such adaptation yields superior outcomes, and if so, which types of adaptation appear to be most directly responsible for any observed improvement in effectiveness. As Priester and Jones noted in this volume, the data are mixed in this area when it comes to substance abuse prevention. Such research enlightens those in the field of which types of modifications or adaptations are critical in delivering more culturally relevant programming. Research emphasizing similar goals is currently underway in the psychotherapy research arena.

Benish, Quintana, and Wampold (2011) utilized meta-analytic strategies to determine whether culturally adapted psychotherapy was relatively more effective than unadapted, bona fide psychotherapy approaches. This comparison is more significant than comparing a culturally adapted approach to a no-treatment control group, which is more prevalent in the majority of outcome research. The authors also aimed to determine which aspects of culturally adapted therapy may account for its superiority. The authors found that, in fact, culturally adapted psychotherapy was more effective than unadapted psychotherapy for ethnic minority clients ($d = .32$). Furthermore, they discovered that adapting the "illness myth" or the explanation of the illness accounted for its superiority. In other words, when psychotherapy is adapted in such a way that a culturally viable explanation of the client's symptoms are incorporated into the therapy, its effectiveness prevails over what could be accomplished by not incorporating this explanation.

The implications of this study for the prevention field are clear. First, it behooves researchers who are studying the effectiveness of culturally relevant prevention programs to determine whether such efforts are superior to existing evidence-based programs as opposed to solely relying on no-treatment control groups. In other words, rather than providing evidence that prevention programs are better than nothing, it is highly advantageous to document that culturally relevant programs exceed what we know already may work.

Second, it may be important to include participants' understanding of why a particular problem has emerged in the design of the intervention. For example, if a cultural belief about obesity involves its perception among participants as a sign of prosperity, then incorporating these beliefs into the curriculum may be a critical aspect of not only gaining the "buy-in" of the participants but also creating consistency between the philosophy of the prevention program and the illness myth of the participants. Benish et al. (2011) argued that participants are less invested in a scientific explanation of a particular set of symptoms and more interested in to what extent there exists congruence of the explanation with their cultural beliefs.

Third, in addition to demonstrating the potential superiority of cultural adaption in such prevention efforts, it is critical to determine why such efforts may be superior. Resnicow, Solar, Braithwaite, Ahluwalia, and Butler (2000), for example, have made the case that surface-structure modification of prevention programs (e.g., translating content into the primary language of the participants, using program staff that share the same cultural background as participants) are less effective than deep-structure modifications of programs. Deep-structure modifications may include utilizing significant and meaningful content and examples (i.e., cultural validity) for participants, relying on processes that reflect cultural rituals (e.g., engaging elders in leading discussions), or infusing cultural values (e.g., collectivism) into program design. While Rensicow et al.'s arguments are persuasive, it is important for future researchers to provide evidence of what particular aspects of cultural adaptation account for their successes. The Benish et al. (2011) study provided a superb illustration for how such evidence might be produced. However, given that their study was based on secondary data analysis, it is important for preventionists who are designing and evaluating culturally relevant prevention programs to provide the primary outcome data that may be used in future meta-analyses.

However, in order to obtain the kind of information that results in deep-structure modification of prevention efforts, participants must be actively involved in the design of programs. Lerner (1995), among others, has discussed the importance of true community partnerships in which prevention specialists collaborate with participants in creating programs that address problems prioritized by the community and which reflect norms, values, traditions, and interpretations of behavior that are culturally valid. Taking the time to gain familiarity with a particular community is a key prerequisite of successful prevention work in that many professionals are "outsiders" to the community members with whom they work (Reiss & Price, 1996). As a result, it may be important to spend time in the community and make contributions valued by the community before, during, and after interventions begin (Kenny & Gallagher, 2000; Lerner, 1995). Dryfoos (1990), Lerner (1995), Reiss and Price (1996), as well as others, suggested that the most effective, culturally relevant prevention programs include the target program participants in the planning, implementation, and evaluation of the program. If researchers and practitioners undertake this approach, the content of the program may not only become more relevant, but the very structure of the program may also look significantly different than a program designed for a culturally dissimilar population (Reese & Vera, 2007).

In addition to the differences in how programs may be comprised when they are designed based on intimate knowledge of a community, there is also a need to address the existing social conditions in the community that may be contributing to the emergence of a particular issue. As such, advocacy and outreach efforts become a critical component of culturally relevant, social justice–oriented prevention.

Advocacy and Outreach

Another related theme that has emerged in the chapters of the handbook concerns the importance of environment-centered prevention and the use of advocacy as prevention. Pieterse and his colleagues, in this volume, made a convincing argument that it is the best way for preventionists to ameliorate toxic social conditions that contribute to dysfunction in many areas. Advocacy involves prevention professionals working with and/or on behalf of a community faced with challenging, unjust institutional barriers and policies. Some activism-focused work involves direct efforts to reduce oppression and adverse social conditions (Chávez, et al., 2007; Kenny & Hage, 2009). One important strategy in social justice advocacy is the dissemination of research findings to policy makers such as politicians to increase awareness of systemic factors that foster injustice (Toporek, Lewis, & Crethar, 2009).

Direct attempts to alter social conditions and policies that foster disproportionate risk for particular communities have been identified as an appropriate focus of social justice–oriented prevention. In the Best Practice Guidelines on Prevention in this volume and in Hage et al. (2007), prevention specialists are encouraged "to engage in governmental, legislative and political advocacy activities that enhance the health and well-being of the broader population served" (p. 550). Not only have such efforts been critical as a best practice, but attempts to influence policy development have been successful in impacting larger systemic factors (Speight & Vera, 2008). Citing the work of Shore (1994) and Albee (1986), Hage et al. noted the historic social justice impact of legislative accomplishments such as the desegregation of schools and the reauthorization of the Individuals with Disabilities Act. While the outcomes of these efforts may be much more long-term in nature than is typical for most prevention programming (as was stated in the introductory chapter of the handbook), the effects of such change have the potential to improve well-being for generations to come.

Although advocating for such changes is absolutely political, it is important to note Prilleltensky's (2008) and Prilleltensky and Nelson's (this volume) analysis of the ways in which power and politics inevitably pervade research and practice in psychology. To utilize our research in order to influence policy, then, could be argued a responsible application of our efforts. Choi et al. (2005) argued that prevention science must inform policy because the consequences of social policy developed without valid data have the potential to be catastrophic. The authors offered recommendations for how scientists may best engage in the process of presenting their data to policy makers.

Despite this realized importance of advocacy in the development of sound policy, there is reason to believe that the field is underpreparing its students and trainees to partake in such activities. In their review of course syllabi from APA approved doctoral training programs, Pieterse, Evans, Risner-Butner, Collins, and Mason (2009) found that, for courses that offered training in social justice knowledge bases, only 13% of the courses addressed advocacy skills. One of the training implications of this research as well as a critical direction for the future is that training must infuse the skills that are necessary for becoming effective advocates. As was stated in the introductory chapter of this handbook, it has been argued by scholars such as Albee (1986, 2002) that large-scale societal factors (e.g., poverty, racism, sexism) are largely responsible for the emergence of mental illness. These forces result in an unequal distribution of resources that may lead to or exacerbate reactions of powerlessness and distress for the majority of people who face them. Thus, the overarching reason we need to train the future generation of preventionists to become effective advocates is to eliminate negative social conditions that result in personal dysfunction (Kessler & Albee, 1975; Albee, 1986).

In addition to advocacy skills, engaging in truly collaborative, community-based partnerships is key to delivering socially just prevention services. "Outreach scholarship" (Jensen, Hoagwood, & Trickett, 1999; Lerner & Overton, 2008) refers to collaborations between university researchers and community members that strive to advance knowledge of a community in order not only to implement prevention programs but also to ensure they are mutually beneficial and sustainable. The goal of such collaborations, then, is to design and implement programs that are meaningful to the community itself. Community-based participatory action research (PAR) is one type of outreach scholarship that gives voice to the community (Arthur & Lalande, 2009; Cohen & Wolfe, 2007). PAR involves an ongoing process of collaborative planning, action, observation, reflection, evaluation, and change among all stakeholders for a shared purpose (Stringer, 2004). Outreach scholarship and PAR are compatible with social justice–oriented prevention models. However, when the community is closely involved in all aspects of prevention, it is often the case that definitions of successful prevention must be revisited and sometimes negotiated.

Program Evaluation

The aforementioned discussion necessitates a conversation about what type of evidence we truly value in the field of prevention and how prevention programs that are both culturally relevant and social justice–oriented are best evaluated. Demonstrating a program's success is often essential to securing resources in order to support its expansion and continuation. For example, to secure funding for a culturally relevant, social justice–oriented approach to the prevention of sexually transmitted diseases such as HIV, researchers may need to demonstrate that their program reduces incidents of such diseases and does so more effectively than a traditional sex education curriculum housed within a public school. Such criteria make sense in times when resources are finite and funding priorities must be defined.

Therefore, one important issue for the future of the field of prevention is to revisit how program evaluation is conceptualized. Traditional program evaluation prioritizes the use of scientifically rigorous clinical trials, often involving random assignment of participants to a program, and narrowly attempts to address the question of "did it work?" (Jacobs & Goldberg, 2009). Unfortunately, traditional manners of evaluating programs have also deemphasized questions of participant satisfaction, social utility, and other justice-oriented types of outcomes. These outcomes may provide us valuable information about the interests of the participants or community members, our partners in this work. Fortunately, advances in the field of program evaluation may reduce some of the tension historically experienced between the seemingly opposing goals of protecting the interests of participants and defending the characteristics of good science.

Contemporary approaches to program evaluation are becoming much more flexible and pluralistic than traditional approaches (Jacobs & Goldberg, 2009). Rather than solely focusing on program outcomes, such as changes observed during and after the course of the intervention, more modern evaluation methods also value the program process or the ways in which programs are implemented, adapted, utilized, and retooled to respond to changes in the financial, political, or community arenas (Wight & Obasi, 2002). Jacobs and Goldberg (2009), Rosencrans et al. (2008), and Bledsoe and Graham (2005) all argue that attending to the processes of change within prevention programs ultimately yields improvements in design and implementation, as well as outcomes. Some of the following approaches to prevention program evaluation may represent philosophies for the task that are highly compatible with a social justice orientation.

Empowerment evaluation, according to Bledsoe and Graham (2005) and Fetterman (1996), is a form of participatory evaluation (Upshur & Barreto-Cortez, 1995), that incorporates the perspectives of all those with a vested interest in a prevention program (i.e., stakeholders), usually those who are most invested in program development and the distribution of services. In short, empowerment evaluation allows for increased involvement of program stakeholders so that they may identify, define, and explain the most effective ways to evaluate those needs that are most important to a program. This approach utilizes both qualitative and quantitative methodologies and seeks to highlight processes necessary for success.

Inclusive program evaluation is another type of evaluation meant not only to include stakeholders who have traditionally been recognized, such as funders, administrators, staff members, and participants, but also to seek representation of members of groups who have been traditionally excluded from or perhaps misrepresented in the evaluation process (Mertens, 2003). This inclusive approach encourages the development and use of qualitative measures, such as interviews, to provide rich data about the organizational and community context of a population (Bledsoe & Graham, 2005). Often, these types of data include discussions about race, ethnicity, immigrant status, and socioeconomic status that aid in elucidating how this diversity influences the types of experiences participants had in the program and the types of feedback generated. Thus, this approach is likely to be useful in explaining how programs may be differentially effective for participants based on cultural backgrounds and past experiences of marginalization.

While these more contemporary approaches to program evaluation may be more consistent with the philosophy of prevention scholars such as Lerner (1995), who argued that participants *must* have an active voice in the design, implementation, and evaluation of our prevention efforts if they are to be successful, tensions continue to arise when different priorities emerge for various stakeholders absorbed in the process. For example, the need for randomized, control-group program evaluation was stated as the sole criterion for prevention programs that would be both found in a best practice list (see Priester and Jones's discussion in this volume) and those that would be eligible for federal grants (Biglan, Mrazek, Carnine, & Flay, 2003). However, oftentimes randomization and control groups, even if they are delayed-treatment control groups, are highly objectionable to community participants of prevention programs, especially in communities with few resources and significant problems to address (Reese & Vera, 2007).

To be truly consistent with the principles of social justice–oriented, culturally relevant prevention, researchers might opt to forego the utilization of random assignment and control groups in program evaluation if it is deemed problematic for the program constituents and community members. However, such a decision may have significant scientific implications such as limiting the investigators' ability to speak confidently about the internal validity of their results should they find positive effects as well as securing funding for future work. Being culturally responsive and scientifically rigorous are not necessarily incompatible goals, but when such conflicts arise, prevention scientists are often faced with difficult and substantial dilemmas (Reese & Vera, 2007).

Practicing flexible, community-oriented approaches to program evaluation creates opportunities for social justice–oriented prevention scientists to consider traditional outcomes of prevention program evaluation (e.g., formative and summative outcome data). In addition, researchers may simultaneously gather data that is meaningful to the sustainability of a program, seek to understand the ways in which the culture of the participants may be best reflected in program content, and realize how perceptions based on cultural differences could affect the implementation of the program in the future (Bledsoe & Graham, 2005). In sum, a pluralistic approach to both program design and evaluation that utilizes methods reflecting processes consistent with social justice is the best way to alleviate the tension between consumer- and science-driven priorities.

Conclusion

The future of prevention in counseling psychology and the general field of psychology is laden with hope at this point in our evolution. The alignment of mental health prevention with a national agenda on wellness and health promotion bodes well for our future. It will be critical for currently active preventionists to continue to generate scholarship that may guide the design, implementation, and evaluation of prevention programs spanning a gamut of topical areas. It is also important for the field of counseling psychology to guide the larger field of psychology in adopting policies that prioritize prevention. Perhaps of most importance, however, is the need for counseling psychology programs to train the next generation of professionals to foster the passion, dispositions, and competencies necessary to take prevention to the next level. That next level will undoubtedly involve forging international, interdisciplinary coalitions that work to ameliorate a host of large-scale societal issues that plague our world. It will also include active engagement of psychologists in the development of policy as well as research that allows us the knowledge to effectively create programming that is culturally responsive and focused on fighting social injustices. This handbook represents a compendium of the contributions counseling psychologists are making to the prevention arena in research and practice. We look forward to future publications that will highlight the contributions of the next generation.

References

Abreu, S., Sala, A., Candelaria, E., & Norman, L. (2010). Understanding the barriers that reduce the effectiveness of HIV/AIDS prevention strategies for Puerto Rican women living in low-income households in Ponce, PR: A qualitative study. *Journal of Immigrant Minority Health*, 12, 83–92.

Albee, G. W. (1986). Toward a just society: Lessons from observations on the primary prevention of psychopathology. *The American Psychologist, 41*(8), 891–898.

Albee, G. W. (2002). Just say not to psychotropic drugs! *Journal of Clinical Psychology, 58*(6), 635–648.

Arthur, N., & Lalande, V. (2009). Diversity and social justice implications for outcome approaches to evaluation. *International Journal of Advanced Counseling, 31*, 1–16.

Benish, S., Quintana, S., & Wampold, B. (2011). Culturally adapted psychotherapy and the legitimacy of myth: A direct-comparison meta-analysis. *Journal of Counseling Psychology, 58*, 279–289.

Biglan, A., Mrazek, P. J., Carnine, D., & Flay, B. R. (2003). The integration of research and practice in the prevention of youth problem behaviors. *American Psychologist, 58*(6–7) 433–440.

Bledsoe, K., & Graham, J. (2005). The use of multiple evaluation approaches in program evaluation. *American Journal of Evaluation, 26*, 302–319.

Chávez, V., Minkler, M., Wallerstein, N., & Spencer, M.S. (2007). Community organizing for health and social justice. In L. Cohen, V. Chávez, & S. Chehimi (Eds.), *Prevention is primary: Strategies for community well-being* (pp. 95–120). San Francisco, CA: Jossey-Bass.

Choi, B., Pang, T., Lin, V., Puska, P., Sherman, G., Goddard, M.,... Clottey, C. (2005). Can scientists and policy makers work together? *Journal of Epidemiology and Community Health, 59*, 632–637.

Coard, S. I., Foy-Watson, S., Zimmer, C., & Wallace, A. (2007). Considering culturally relevant parenting practices in intervention development and adaptation: A randomized controlled trial of the Black Parenting Strengths and Strategies (BPSS) program. *The Counseling Psychologist, 35*, 797–820.

Cohen, L., & Wolfe, A. (2007). Working collaboratively to advance prevention. In L. Cohen, V. Chávez, & S. Chehimi (Eds.), *Prevention is primary: Strategies for community well-being* (pp. 141–160). San Francisco, CA: Jossey-Bass.

Dryfoos, J. (1990). *Adolescents at risk: Prevalence and prevention*. New York: Oxford University Press.

Elliot, P. (1996). Shattering illusions: Same sex domestic violence. *Gay and Lesbian Social Services, 4*, 1–8.

Fetterman, D. M. (1996). Empowerment evaluation: An introduction to theory and practice. In D. M. Fetterman, S. J. Kaftarian, & A. Wandersman (Eds.), *Empowerment evaluation: Knowledge and tools for self-assessment and accountability* (pp. 3–49). Thousand Oaks, CA: Sage.

Forehand, R. L., & Long, N. (2002). *Parenting the strong willed child: The clinically proven five-week program for parents of two- to six-year-olds*. Chicago: Contemporary Books.

Gross, E. (2009). Logging on, bouncing back: An experimental investigation of online communication following social exclusion. *Developmental Psychology, 45*, 1787–1793.

Hage, S. M., Romano, J., Kenny, M. E., Matthews, C. R., Schwartz, J. P., & Waldo, M. (2007). Best practice guidelines on prevention practice, research, training, and social advocacy for psychologists. *The Counseling Psychologist, 35*, 493–566.

Jacobs, F., & Goldberg, J. (2009). Evaluating contemporary social programs: Challenges and opportunities. In M. E. Kenny, A. M. Horne, P. Orpinas, & L. E. Reese (Eds.), *Realizing social justice: The challenge of preventive interventions* (pp. 97–122). Washington, DC: American Psychological Association.

Jensen, P., Hoagwood, K. & Trickett, E. (1999). Ivory towers or earthen trenches? Community collaborations to foster "real world" research. *Applied Developmental Science, 3*, 206–212.

Kaiser Family Foundation. (2010). *Generation M2: Media in the Lives of 8- to 18-Year-Olds. 15–18*. Retrieved on August 24, 2011, from: http://www.kff.org/entmedia/8010.cfm

Kenny, M., & Gallagher, L. (2000). Service learning as a vehicle in training psychologists for revised professional roles. In F. T. Sherman & W. R. Torbert (Eds.), *Transforming social inquiry, transforming social action* (pp. 189–206). Norwell, MA: Kluwer Academic.

Kenny, M. E., & Hage, S. M. (2009). The next frontier: Prevention as an instrument of social justice. *Journal of Primary Prevention, 30*, 1–10.

Kessler, M., & Albee, G. W. (1975). Primary prevention. *Annual Review of Psychology, 26*, 557–591.

Lerner, R. M. (1995). *America's youth in crisis: Challenges and options for programs and policies*. Thousand Oaks, CA: Sage.

Lerner, R. M., & Overton, W. F. (2008). Exemplifying the integrations of the relational developmental system. *Journal of Adolescent Research, 23*, 245–255.

Mertens, D. L. (2003). The inclusive view of evaluation: Visions for the new millennium. In S. I. Donaldson & M. Scriven (Eds.), *Evaluating social programs and problems: Visions for the new millennium* (pp. 91–108). Mahwah, NJ: Erlbaum.

Miller, A., Bobner, R., & Zarski, J. (2000). Sexual identity development: A base for work with same-sex couple partner abuse. *Contemporary Family Therapy, 22*, 189–200.

O'Dea, J. (2008). Gender, ethnicity, culture, and social class influences on childhood obesity among Australian schoolchildren: Implications for treatment, prevention, and community education. *Health and Social Care in the Community, 16,* 282–290.

Pan American Health Organization (PAHO). (1996). *Memoirs of the Interamerican conference on society, violence, and health.* Washington, DC: Author.

Parker, R., Easton, D., & Klein, C. (2000). Structural barriers and facilitators in HIV Prevention: A review of international research. *AIDS, 14,* 22–32.

Pieterse, A. L., Evans, S. A., Risner-Butner, A., Collins, N. M., & Mason, L. B. (2009). Multicultural competence and social justice training in counseling psychology and counselor education: A review and analysis of a sample of multicultural course syllabi, *The Counseling Psychologist, 37,* 93–115.

Prilleltensky, I. (2008). Migrant well-being is a multilevel, dynamic, and value dependent phenomenon. *American Journal of Community Psychology, 42*(3–4), 359–364.

Reese, L. E., & Vera, E. M. (2007). Culturally relevant prevention: The scientific and practical considerations of community-based programs. *The Counseling Psychologist, 35,* 763–778.

Reiss, D., & Price, R. H. (1996). National research agenda for prevention research: The National Institute of Mental Health Report. *American Psychologist, 51,* 1109–1115.

Resnicow, K., Solar, R., Braithwaite, R., Ahluwalia, J., & Butler, J. (2000). Cultural sensitivity in substance abuse prevention. *Journal of Community Psychology, 28,* 271–290.

Robinson, M., Holmbeck, G., & Paikoff, R. (2007). Self-esteem enhancing reasons for having sex and the sexual behaviors of African American adolescents. *Journal of Youth and Adolescence, 36*(4), 453–464.

Rosencrans, A., Gittlesohn, J., Ho, L., Harris, S., Naqushbandi, M., & Sharma, S. (2008). Process evaluation of a multi-institutional community-based program for diabetes prevention among First Nations. *Health Education Research, 23,* 272–286.

Shore, M. (1994, September). Narrowing prevention. *Readings: A Journal of Reviews and Commentary in Mental Health,* 13–17.

Skogan, W., Hartnett, S., Bump, N., & Dubois, J. (2008). Evaluation of CeaseFire-Chicago. Washington, DC: National Institute of Justice/JCJRS. Retrieved August 24, 2011, from http://www.ncjrs.gov/App/publications/abstract.aspx?ID=249182

Smith, P. K., Mahdavi, J., Carvalho, M., Fisher, S., Russell, S., & Tippett, N. (2008). Cyberbullying: Its nature and impact in secondary school pupils. *Journal of Child Psychology and Psychiatry, 49,* 376–385.

Speight, S. L., & Vera, E. M. (2008). Social justice and counseling psychology. In R. Lent & S. Brown (Eds.), *Handbook of counseling psychology* (pp. 54–67). Hoboken, NJ: Wiley.

Stringer, E. (2004). *Action research in education.* Upper Saddle River, NJ: Pearson.

Toporek, R. L., Lewis, J. A., & Crethar, H. C. (2009). Promoting systemic change through the ACA advocacy competencies. *Journal of Counseling and Development, 87,* 260–268.

Upshur, C., & Barreto-Cortez, E. (1995). What is participatory evaluation? What are its roots? *The Evaluation Exchange, 1,* 7–9.

Vera, E. M., & Speight, S. (2003). Multicultural competence, social justice, and counseling psychology: Expanding our roles. *The Counseling Psychologist, 31,* 253–272.

Weaver, K., & Maddaleno, M. (1999). Youth violence in Latin America: Current situation and violence prevention strategies. *Pan American Journal of Public Health, 5,* 338–344.

Wight, D., & Obasi, A. (2002). Unpacking the "black box:" The importance of process data to explain outcomes. In J. Stephenson, J. Imrie, & C. Bonell (Eds.), *Effective sexual health interventions: Issues in experimental evaluation* (pp. 151–166). Oxford, England: Oxford University Press.

Ybarra, M., Diener-West, M., & Leaf, P. (2007). Examining the overlap in internet harassment and school bullying: Implications for school intervention. *Journal of Adolescent Health, 41,* 42–50.

Ybarra, M., Eaton, W., & Bickman, L. (2005). Internet-based mental health interventions. *Mental Health Services Research, 7,* 75–87.

INDEX

D

E

F

G

S